^{THE}Java™ Class Libraries

Second Edition, Volume 2

The Java™ Series

Lisa Friendly, Series Editor

Tim Lindholm, Technical Editor

Please see our web site (http://www.awl.com /cseng/javaseries) for more information on these titles.

Ken Arnold and James Gosling, *The Java™ Programming Language, Second Edition*
ISBN 0-201-31006-6

Mary Campione and Kathy Walrath, *The Java™ Tutorial, Second Edition: Object-Oriented Programming for the Internet* (Book/CD)
ISBN 0-201-31007-4

Patrick Chan, *The Java™ Developers Almanac*
ISBN 0-201-37967-8

Patrick Chan and Rosanna Lee, *The Java™ Class Libraries, Second Edition, Volume 2: java.applet, java.awt, java.beans*
ISBN 0-201-31003-1

Patrick Chan, Rosanna Lee, and Doug Kramer, *The Java™ Class Libraries, Second Edition, Volume 1: java.io, java.lang, java.math, java.net, java.text, java.util*
ISBN 0-201-31002-3

James Gosling, Bill Joy, and Guy Steele, *The Java™ Language Specification*
ISBN 0-201-63451-1

James Gosling, Frank Yellin, and The Java Team, *The Java™ Application Programming Interface, Volume 1: Core Packages*
ISBN 0-201-63453-8

James Gosling, Frank Yellin, and The Java Team, *The Java™ Application Programming Interface, Volume 2: Window Toolkit and Applets*
ISBN 0-201-63459-7

Graham Hamilton, Rick Cattell, and Maydene Fisher, *JDBC™ Database Access with Java™: A Tutorial and Annotated Reference*
ISBN 0-201-30995-5

Jonni Kanerva, *The Java™ FAQ*
ISBN 0-201-63456-2

Doug Lea, *Concurrent Programming in Java™: Design Principles and Patterns*
ISBN 0-201-69581-2

Tim Lindholm and Frank Yellin, *The Java™ Virtual Machine Specification*
ISBN 0-201-63452-X

Henry Sowizral, Kevin Rushforth, and Michael Deering, *The Java™ 3D API Specification*
ISBN 0-201-32576-4

THE Java™ Class Libraries

Second Edition, Volume 2
java.applet, java.awt, java.beans

Patrick Chan
and
Rosanna Lee

ADDISON-WESLEY

An imprint of Addison Wesley Longman, Inc.

Reading, Massachusetts • Harlow, England • Menlo Park, California
Berkeley, California • Don Mills, Ontario • Sydney
Bonn • Amsterdam • Tokyo • Mexico City

The publisher offers discounts on this book when ordered in quantity for special sales.

For more information, please contact:

> Corporate & Professional Publishing Group
> Addison Wesley Longman
> One Jacob Way
> Reading, Massachusetts 01867

Library of Congress Cataloging-in-Publication Data

Chan, Patrick, 1961-
    The Java class libraries / Patrick Chan and
Rosanna Lee -- 2nd ed.
        p.   cm. -- (The Java series)
    Includes index.
    ISBN 0-201-31003-1
        1. Java (Computer program language)   I. Lee, Rosanna, 1960-
II. Title.   III. Series.
QA76.73.J38C47   1998
005.13'3--dc21   97-33423
                                                          CIP

ISBN   0-201-31003-1

3 4 5 6 7 8   CRW 01 00 99 98

3rd Printing September, 1998

To our parents

Agatha and Fai Chan
Patricia and Warren Lee

Contents

Package Overviews

Alphabetical Reference of Classes

Contents

Contents

List of Figures

List of Tables

Preface

How to Use This Book

This book is intended as a reference rather than a tutorial. Its format is similar to a dictionary's in that it is designed to optimize the time it takes for you to look up information on a class or class member. For a tutorial-style presentation of the class libraries, see *The Java™ Tutorial*, by Mary Campione and Kathy Walrath. *The Java™ Class Libraries* does not explain any part of the Java language. There are several books you can use to learn the language. These include *The Java™ Programming Language*, by Ken Arnold and James Gosling, and *The Java™ Language Specification*, by James Gosling, Bill Joy, and Guy Steele.

Following is an overview of this book.

Package Overviews

This part briefly describes each package and all of the classes in it. Also included are diagrams that show the inheritance hierarchy of the classes that appear in a package.

Alphabetical Reference of Classes

This part covers the alphabetical listing of the classes from the following packages:

```
java.applet
java.awt
java.awt.datatransfer
java.awt.event
java.awt.image
java.awt.peer
java.beans
```

Probably the most notable aspect about the structure of this book is the order in which the classes appear. Most Java books that contain an API alphabetically order the classes within a package and then alphabetically order the packages. The problem with this format is that it always takes two or more steps to locate a class. If you do not know which package contains the class you're looking for, you basically need to review each package looking for the class. If you do know which package, you first need to find the package and then find the class.

The classes in this book are ordered alphabetically without regard to package name. This makes looking up a class as straightforward as looking up a word in a dictionary.

Each class is described in its own chapter. Each chapter contains a picture of the class hierarchy, a class description, a class example, a member summary, and descriptions for every member in the class.

Class Hierarchy Diagrams

We include a class diagram for each class in the Java API. The class diagram shows all of the ancestors of the class, its siblings, its immediate descendents, and any interfaces that the class implements. In these diagrams, if a package name precedes a class or interface name, the class or interface is not in the same package as the current class.

In the diagrams, we visually distinguish the different kinds of Java entities, as follows:

1. The interface: A rounded rectangle
2. The class: A rectangle
3. The abstract class: A rectangle with an empty dot
4. The final class: A rectangle with a black dot
5. Classes with subclasses: A rectangle with a small black triangle on the lower right corner

Most of these elements are shown in Figure i. The class or interface being described in the current chapter is shaded grey. A solid line represents `extends`, while a dotted line represents `implements`.

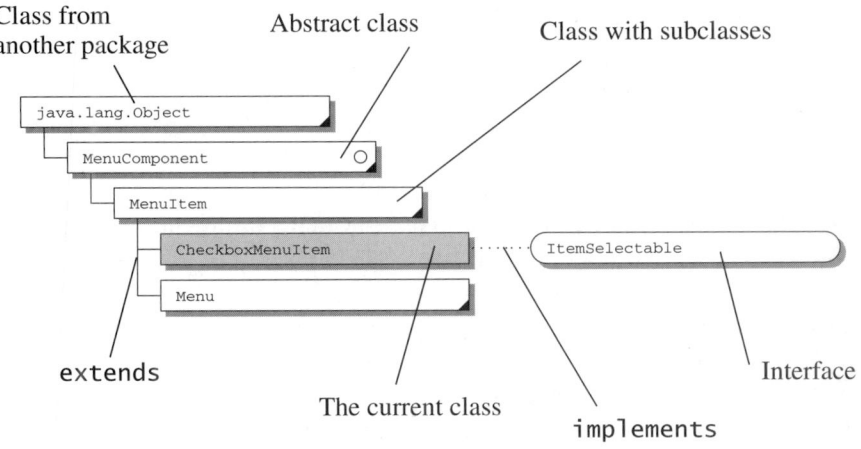

FIGURE i: Class Hierarchy Diagram

Class Descriptions

In the class descriptions, we describe all of the properties of the class. For example, the properties of the `Graphics` class include the current color, font, paint mode, origin, and clipping area. Describing in one place all of a class's available properties and how the properties behave makes learning all of the capabilities of a class much easier than if the property descriptions were scattered throughout the member descriptions.

Any terminology used in the member descriptions is introduced and described in the class descriptions. If you find that the member description lacks detail, go to the class description for more information.

Class Examples

Ideally, we would have included a unique example for every single member in the Java API. We simply did not have enough time. So we tried to make sure that every member appeared in at least one example.

We worked to make the examples as useful as possible so that they demonstrate the member as it would typically be used. For example, in the example for a button we not only show how a button is created; we also show how button events are handled. In some cases, we also try to demonstrate some other class in the Java API. For example, in the Graphics.draw-Oval() example, we demonstrate not only how to draw an oval; we also show how to use the BufferedReader class to read integers from standard input that are used to locate the oval. We feel that gently introducing other classes in the Java API is a good way to help you become aware of all available classes in the Java API, as long as the introduction does not confuse the example.

Member Summaries

The Member Summary section for each class is intended to help the reader quickly grasp the key points of the class. It groups the members of the class into categories that are specific to that class. For example, in the List class the Selection Methods category lists all methods having to do with selections. It is meant to be a quick summary of the class's members, so it does not contain any syntax information other than the name of the member.

Member Descriptions

The member descriptions appear in alphabetical order within a class chapter regardless of what kind of method or field they are. This was done to make locating a member proceed as fast as possible.

Overloaded methods are placed together in one member description because they share very similar functionality. The different overloaded forms are typically provided as a convenience for the programmer when specifying parameters. For instance, some overloads eliminate parameters by providing common defaults. To describe overloads with missing parameters, we use a phrase of the form "if the parameter p is not specified, it defaults to the value 3.14." Other overloads take different representations of a value. For example, one overload could take a particular parameter as an integer, while another could take the same parameter as a string containing an integer.

Each member description contains some or all of the following fields:

PURPOSE   A brief description of the purpose of this member

SYNTAX   The syntactic declaration of this member

DESCRIPTION	A full description of this member
PARAMETERS	The parameters accepted by this member, if any, listed in alphabetical order
RETURNS	The value and its range returned by this member, if any
EXCEPTIONS	The exceptions and errors thrown by this member, if any, listed in alphabetical order
SEE ALSO	Other related classes or members, if any, listed in alphabetical order
OVERRIDES	The method that this member overrides, if any
EXAMPLE	A code example that illustrates how this member is used. This is sometimes a reference to an example that illustrates the use of this method in another member example or class example.

Deprecation

A method or class is *deprecated* if its use is no longer recommended. A deprecated method appears in the Member Summary under the Deprecated Methods section. In the chapter body, the deprecated method is annotated by a "deprecated" tag in its method heading. For example, `Component.size()` is a deprecated method. It has the following method heading:

size() *DEPRECATED*

If not all of the overloaded forms of the method are deprecated, a "deprecated" tag appears beside the syntax of the deprecated forms. For example, one of the two forms of `BorderLayout.addLayoutComponent()` is deprecated. The second form shown below—the one with the "deprecated" tag—is deprecated.

SYNTAX	`public void addLayoutComponent(Component comp, Object location)`
DEPRECATED	`public void addLayoutComponent(String location, Component comp)`

The method description contains a deprecation section with instructions on how to replace the usage of the deprecated method, like this:

DEPRECATION	A description of how to replace the usage of this deprecated method

How to Access the Examples

All of the code examples in this book have been compiled and run on the FCS version of Java 1.1.2, either on Solaris or Windows NT or both. Most of the complete examples are available on-line. You can access them and other information about this book by using the URL

```
http://www.awl.com/cp/chan-lee.html
```

Conventions Used in This Book

`Lucida Sans Typewriter` is used for examples, syntax declarations, class names, method names, values, and field names. *Italic* is used when defining a new term and for emphasis.

Acknowledgments

We want to thank the many people who made this book possible.

We want to thank all of the wonderful readers of our first edition who sent us nice comments and suggestions. You gave us the strength to do this second edition.

Mike Hendrickson, the Acquisition Editor for this book, assisted us throughout the production of the book, from formatting the raw manuscript, to finding us experts to help with PostScript and formatting, to performing numerous coordination tasks. Thanks Mike!

Lisa Friendly, the series editor and a wonderful friend, was extremely helpful in providing all kinds of assistance in JavaSoft.

Sarah Weaver, Laura Michaels, Rosemary Simpson, Tracy Russ, Chris Norum, Jason Jones, and Yvo Riezebos all played a part in the production of this book and were wonderful to work with.

Tomas G. Rokicki provided invaluable expert advice (and code) so that we could generate all of the class diagrams automatically. Joseph Newcomer provided us with helpful hints for dealing with FrameMaker. And Ramin Sedehi rescued a week's worth of words after our laptop went south.

The following people provided many helpful comments and information: Calvin Austin, Tom Ball, Amy Fowler, Jim Graham, David Holmes, Doug Kramer, Tim Lindholm, Tim Prinzing, Georges Saab, and Kathy Walrath.

Roselyn and Norman Chin spent countless hours entertaining our children while we worked on the book.

Patrick Chan
Rosanna Lee
Palo Alto, California
August, 1997

java.applet

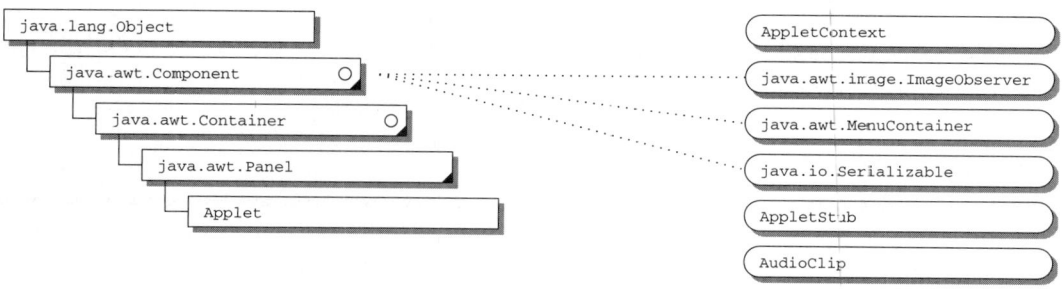

The applet framework involves two entities: the *applet* and the *applet context*. An applet is an embeddable window (see the `Panel` class) with a few extra methods that the applet context can use to initialize, start, and stop the applet.

The applet context is an application that is responsible for loading and running applets. For example, the applet context could be a Web browser or an applet development environment, as shown in Figure 1.

This package contains the classes necessary to create an applet and the classes an applet uses to communicate with its applet context.

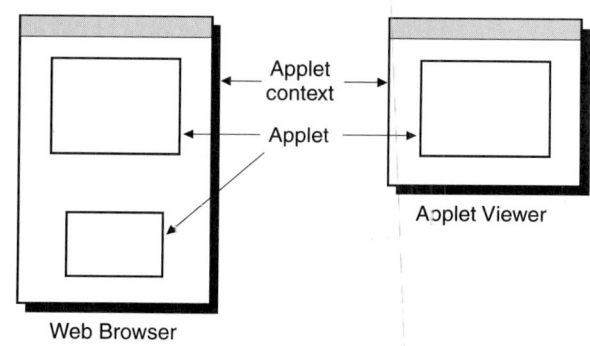

FIGURE 1: Relationship Between Applet Contexts and Applets.

Applet

Applet	Used for building an applet. All applets must be a subclass of this class.

A class becomes an applet by subclassing this class. It contains methods that the applet can override and methods for retrieving media via a URL.

java.applet

Audio

`AudioClip`	Used to play and stop sound clips.

This class contains methods for fetching and playing sound clips at a URL. A sound clip can be played once or in a continuous loop.

Applet Context

`AppletContext`	Used by an applet for communicating with the applet context.
`AppletStub`	Used in the implementation of the `AppletContext`. Not directly used.

These interfaces specify the methods that all applet contexts must provide to applets. For example, there are methods to display a status message in the applet context's status bar and methods for discovering other applets that the applet context may contain.

java.awt

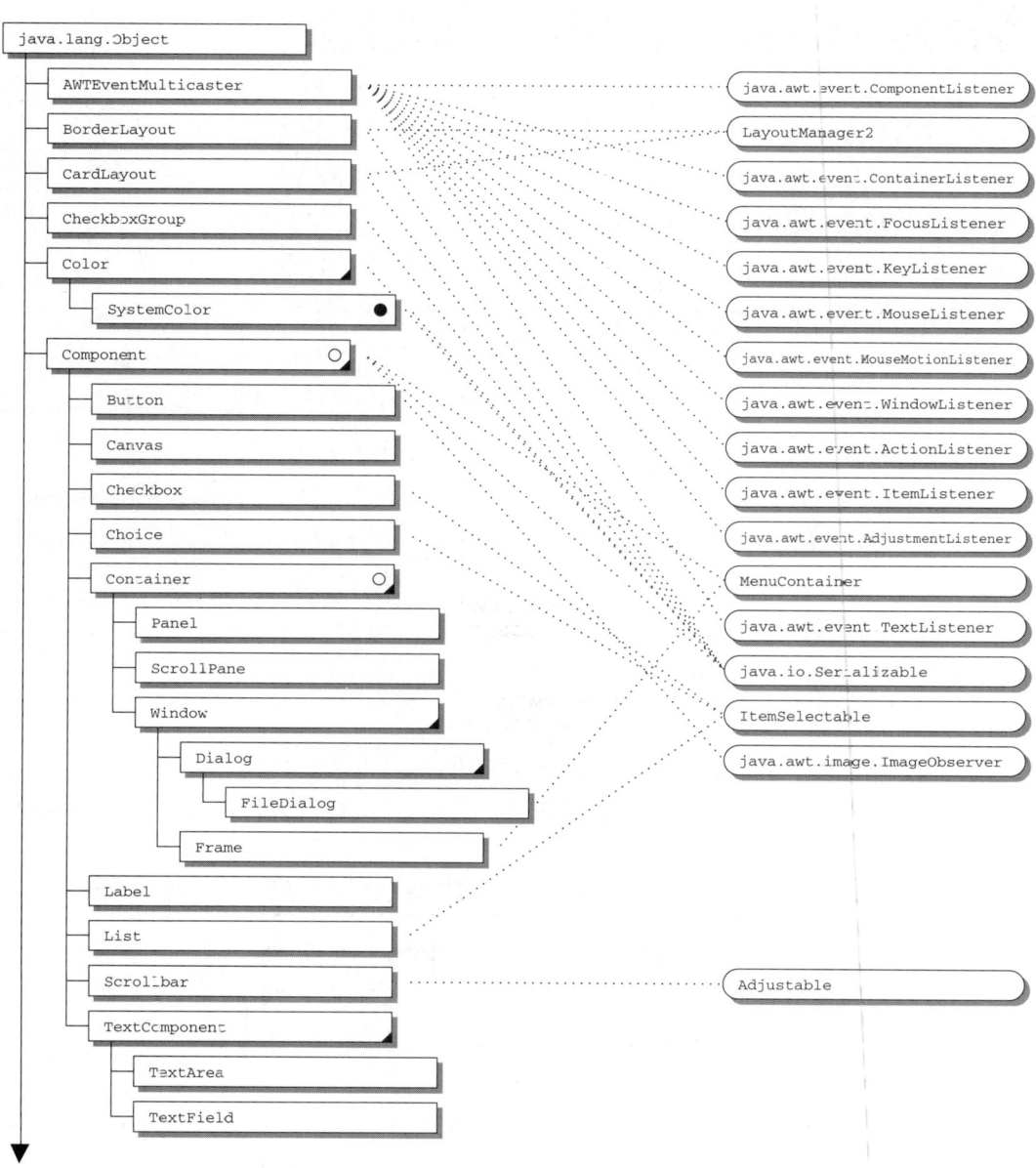

Continued

Continued from previous page

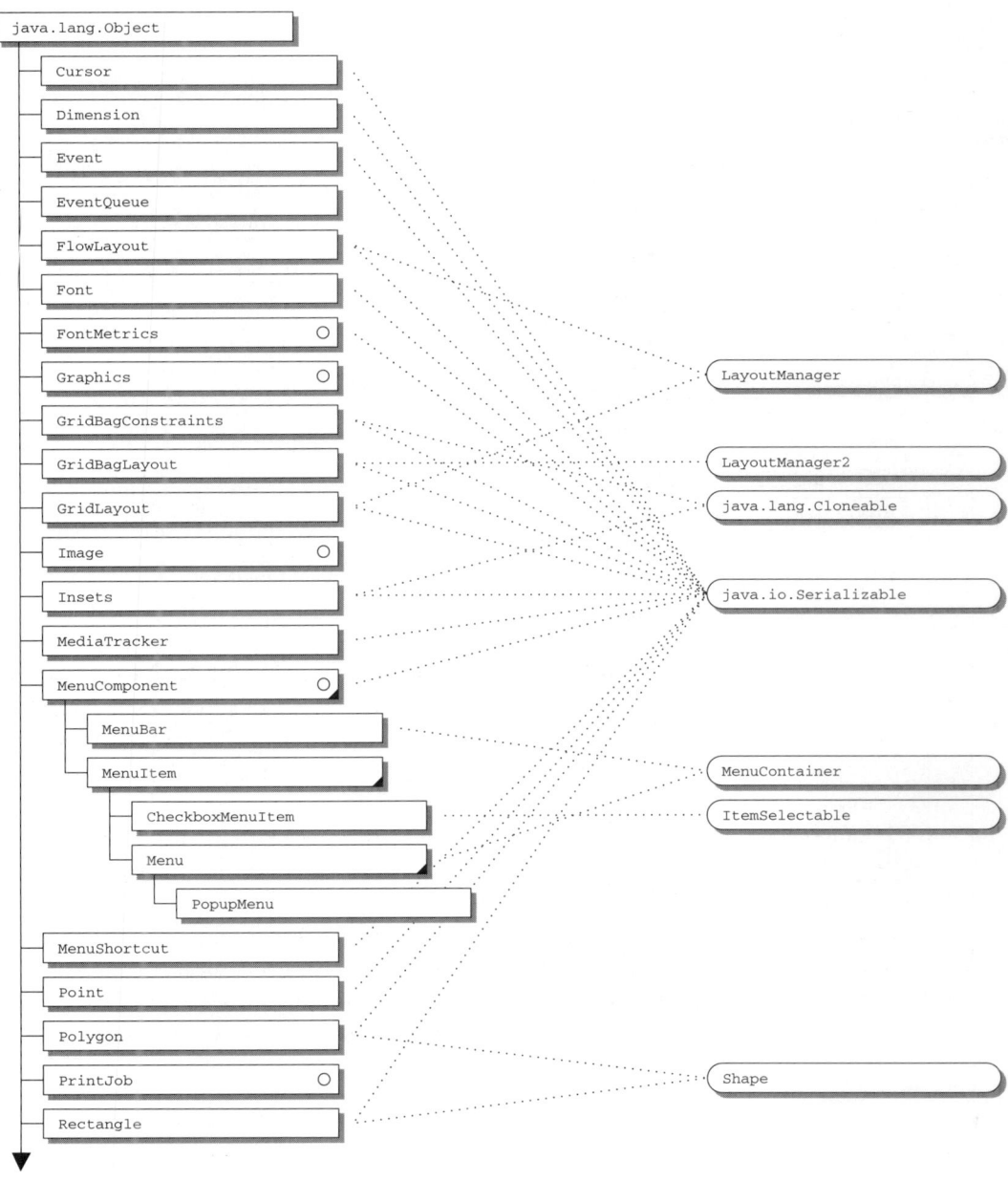

The Abstract Window Toolkit (AWT) package contains all of the classes for creating user interfaces and for painting graphics and images. A user interface object such as a button or a scrollbar is called, in AWT terminology, a *component*. The Component class is the root of all AWT components. See Component for a detailed description of properties that all AWT components share.

Some components *fire* events when a user interacts with the components. The AWTEvent class and its subclasses are used to represent the events that AWT components can fire. See AWTEvent for a description of the AWT event model.

A *container* is a component that can contain components and other containers. A container can also have a layout manager that controls the visual placement of components in the container. The AWT package contains several layout manager classes and an interface for building your own layout manager. See Container and LayoutManager for more information.

Graphics

`Graphics`	Used for painting basic shapes like lines and rectangles and for painting images.
`Color`	Represents a color; includes methods for converting between RGB and HSB values.
`Font`	Represents a font.
`FontMetrics`	Used for determining information about a font, such as height and character widths.
`Image`	Represents an image with methods for retrieving its dimensions.
`MediaTracker`	Used for preloading images.
`SystemColor`	Contains the colors used by the platform to paint native components.

This set of classes is used to draw shapes, text, and images on a drawing surface. Drawing surfaces can include the screen, an offscreen-image, and the printer. To draw on a drawing surface, you must first create a graphics context on the drawing surface (see Figure 2) and then use the graphics context to draw. Since drawing is always done through a graphics context, a drawing routine is easily written to be independent of the drawing surface.

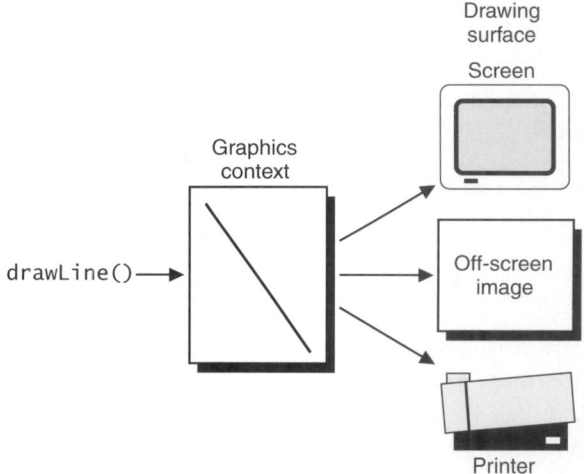

FIGURE 2: **Graphics Contexts and Drawing Surfaces.**

Printing

`PrintGraphics`	Used for painting to a printer.
`PrintJob`	Used for printing to the system's printer.

This group of classes is used for printing. An application must first acquire a print job object (see `Toolkit.getPrintJob()`) and then use that object to create a graphics context. The application can then use the graphics context to draw pages for printing.

Components

Adjustable	Interface implemented by a component that has an adjustable value.
Button	A component that generates an event when clicked.
Canvas	A component typically used to render graphics.
Checkbox	A component that maintains a `boolean` state.
CheckboxGroup	Used for implementing a set of radio buttons.
Choice	A component that implements a drop-down list.
Component	The superclass of components.
ItemSelectable	Interface implemented by a component that has items that can be selected (such as an item in a list).
Label	A component that displays a text string.
List	A component that displays a list of items.
Scrollbar	A component that implements a scrollbar.
TextArea	A component that provides editing for a multiline text string.
TextComponent	The superclass of text components.
TextField	A component that provides editing for a one-line text string.

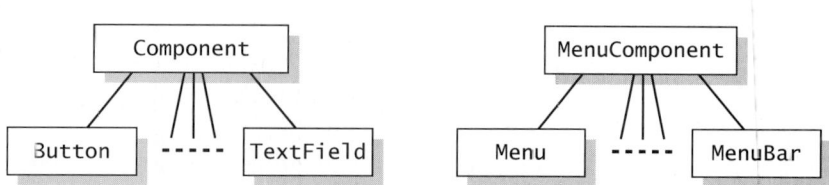

FIGURE 3:   Component and MenuComponent.

The classes in this group represent the components that the AWT provides for building user interfaces. Components interact with a program, which uses them via *events*. For example, when a user clicks a component with the mouse, that component fires a mouse down event. Events in the AWT are organized into a class hierarchy rooted at the abstract class AWTEvent. Each component fires a different set of events, so you must check with each component's class description to determine the type of events a component fires.

All of the classes in this group and in the following containers group are subclasses of Component, as shown in Figure 3. See the Component class to learn about the properties common to all components.

This group also contains two interfaces—Adjustable and ItemSelectable—which are implemented by some of the component subclasses.

Menu Components

CheckboxMenuItem	A menu item that maintains a `boolean` state.
Menu	A menu that contains menu items.
MenuBar	A menu bar that contains menus.
MenuComponent	The superclass of menu components.
MenuContainer	The superclass of menu containers.
MenuItem	A menu item can be inserted into a menu.
MenuShortcut	A sequence of key strokes that can be used to select a menu item.
PopupMenu	A menu that pops up near a component as a result of the user's making a popup menu gesture.

The classes in this group are used to build menus. Except for `MenuShortcut`, all of the classes in this group are subclasses of `MenuComponent`, as shown in Figure 3. See the `MenuComponent` class to learn about the properties common to all menu components.

Containers

Container	The superclass of containers.
Dialog	The superclass of dialog boxes.
FileDialog	A dialog box for selecting an existing file or naming a new file.
Frame	A top-level window that has a title, a menu bar, and borders.
Panel	A container that can be embedded in other containers.
ScrollPane	A container that contains a single component that can be viewed using scrollbars.
Window	A top-level window that does not have a title, a menu bar, or borders.

A container can contain components and other containers. A container can also have a layout manager that controls the visual placement of components in the container. Some containers are top-level windows that cannot be embedded in another container.

Cursor

Cursor	Used to represent a cursor.

This class contains definitions of default cursor types.

Layout

BorderLayout	A layout manager that places components along each edge and in the center.
CardLayout	A layout manager that displays one component at a time.
FlowLayout	A layout manager that places components left-to-right, top-to-bottom.
GridBagConstraints	Used to specify constraints in a GridBagLayout object.
GridBagLayout	A layout manager that places components in a grid that has flexible-sized cells.
GridLayout	A layout manager that places components in a rigid grid that has fixed-sized cells.
LayoutManager	The interface that a layout manager must implement.
LayoutManager2	The interface for supporting alignment-based layouts.

A layout manager is responsible for arranging the components in a container. For example, the GridLayout layout manager arranges components in a grid whose cells are exactly the same size. The AWT provides a number of useful layout managers. The most versatile but difficult to use is the GridBagLayout layout manager. If none of these layout managers are appropriate, you can build your own using the LayoutManager and LayoutManager2 interfaces.

Geometry

Dimension	Used to specify the size of a rectangle (width and height).
Insets	Used to specify the insets of a rectangle (top, left, bottom, and right).
Point	Used to specify a point using x- and y-coordinates.
Polygon	Used to hold an array of points.
Rectangle	Used to specify the location and size of a rectangle (x, y, width, and height).
Shape	Interface for shapes such as a rectangle.

The classes in this group are used to hold collections of values. For example, a Rectangle object holds four values that represent the locations of the edges of a rectangle. These classes are used throughout the AWT classes.

Events

AWTEvent	The superclass of the event class hierarchy.
AWTEventMulticaster	An event dispatcher for the AWT events.
Event *DEPRECATED*	Replaced by AWTEvent and its hierarchy of event subclasses.
EventQueue	A queue for posting and dispatching AWT events.

When a user interacts with a program using AWT components, the user's actions are translated into *events*. The Java 1.1 event model is a notification-based system. When a user clicks a component with the mouse, that component generates a mouse down event that is placed on the *system event queue*. When the event reaches the head of the queue, it is dispatched to the component.

Objects that fire events are called *event sources*. An object can listen for events from such event sources. These objects are called *event listeners*. For each type of event that is fired, the source maintains a list of event listeners for that event type. An event listener registers with the event source. When an event of the corresponding type is fired by the source, the listener is notified. See Figure 4.

The AWTEventMulticaster class is used to notify event listeners. The event is not forwarded to other components in the AWT component hierarchy, regardless of whether any listeners processed the event. See Figure 5(a).

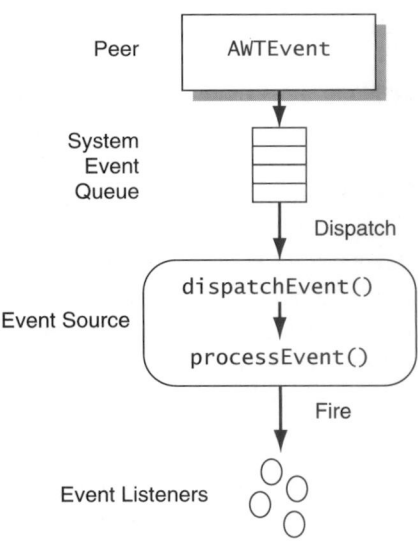

FIGURE 4: AWT Event Flow.

Events in the AWT are organized into a class hierarchy rooted at the abstract class AWTEvent. The AWT event hierarchy organizes the different types of events that AWT components can fire. A subclass of an event class provides more details on the nature of the event. For example, KeyEvent and MouseEvent are subclasses of the more general InputEvent. A KeyEvent contains not only general InputEvent information, for example, about the pressed modifier keys and the time of the input, but also information about the key that was pressed or released. For details of the AWT event model, see AWTEvent.

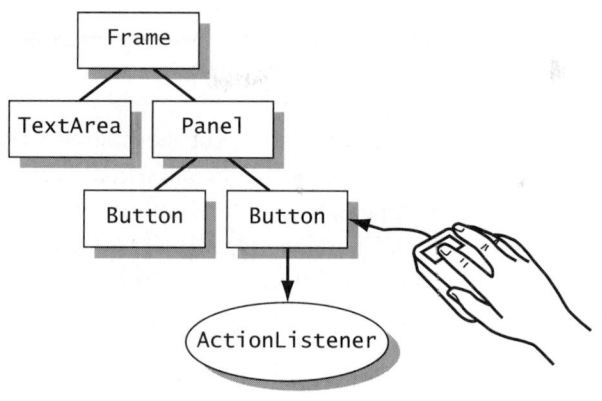

(a) New Java 1.1 Event Model

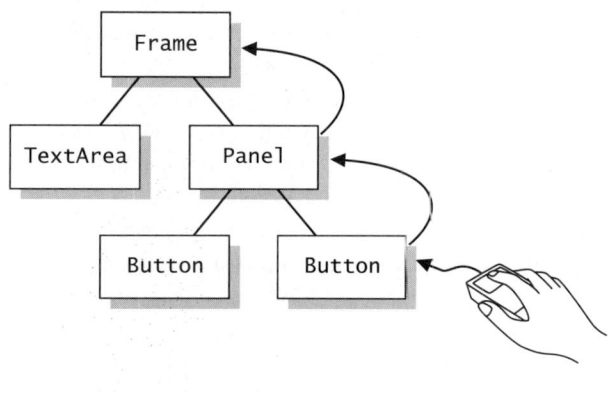

(b) Old Java 1.0 Event Model

FIGURE 5:   Event Flow in Component Hierarchy.

In Java 1.0, an event is represented by the now-deprecated Event class and automatically flows up the component's containment hierarchy until it is handled by one or more *event handlers*. Figure 5(b) shows a component hierarchy and an event flowing through that hierarchy. It shows a user event first being delivered to a button component and then passing through all of the component's ancestors. As the event flows up the hierarchy, any component receiving the event can handle the event and therefore stop the event from continuing upward. As noted previously, Java 1.1 events are not forwarded in this manner. This model is still available in Java 1.1 for compatibility. However, it should no longer be used.

Toolkit

`Toolkit`	Used to retrieve information about the screen.

This class contains methods that return information about the platform's screen, such as its dimension and resolution. It also contains methods that create native versions of Java components called *peers*. For example, when you create a `Button` component, the `Button` class uses the `Toolkit` class to create a button peer. These peer creation methods are not normally used directly, since each component class automatically calls the `Toolkit` methods to create and destroy its associated peers.

Errors and Exceptions

`AWTError`	Thrown if an unrecoverable condition arises. This error should not be caught.
`AWTException`	Thrown if an error occurs in an AWT operation. This exception must be caught or declared in a `throws` clause.
`IllegalComponentStateException`	Thrown when the program attempts to perform an operation on an AWT component while the component is not in an appropriate state to perform the operation.

These are the errors and exceptions declared in the AWT package.

java.awt.datatransfer

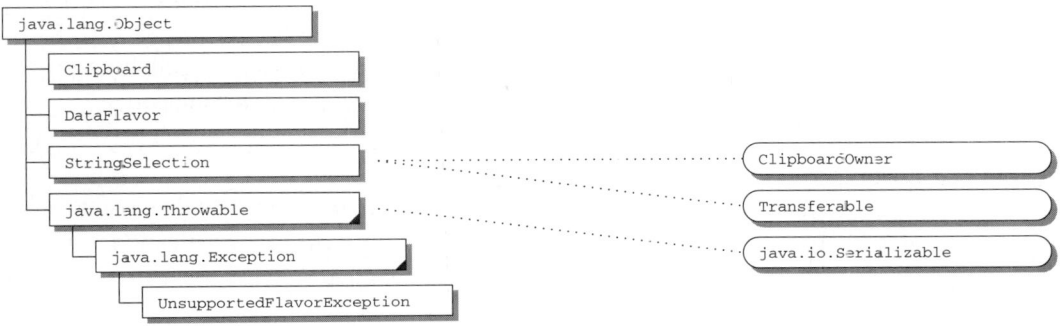

```
java.lang.Object
    Clipboard
    DataFlavor
    StringSelection ................................ ClipboardOwner
    java.lang.Throwable ........................... Transferable
        java.lang.Exception ...................... java.io.Serializable
            UnsupportedFlavorException
```

This package contains interfaces and classes for transferring data between and within applications.

Clipboard

Clipboard	Used for copy and paste operations between or within an application.
ClipboardOwner	Used by an object wishing to be notified that its data is no longer in the clipboard.

A *clipboard* is an object that temporarily holds data as it is being transferred between or within an application. It is typically used in copy and paste operations. Although it is possible to create a clipboard to use within an application, most applications will use the *system clipboard*. To retrieve a handle to the system clipboard, use `Toolkit.getSystemClipboard()`.

A clipboard does not hold data directly. Instead, the data must be encapsulated in a transferable object before it can be placed on the clipboard. See the `Transferable` interface for more details. *Note*: In Java 1.1.2, the system clipboard can hold only string selections (see `StringSelection`).

The *clipboard owner* of a clipboard is the object whose data is presently in the clipboard. By implementing the `ClipboardOwner` interface, it can be notified when its data is no longer in the clipboard.

Clipboard Data

DataFlavor	Used to retrieve the data in a transferable object.
StringSelection	A data flavor for retrieving the data in a transferable object as a string.
Transferable	The type of objects that can be placed on a clipboard.
UnsupportedFlavorException	Thrown if a transferable object does not support a requested flavor.

When an application wants to place data on a clipboard, it must first encapsulate the data in an object that implements the Transferable interface. Similarly, when an application retrieves the contents of a clipboard, it is given a transferable object that it must use to retrieve the encapsulated data.

To retrieve the actual data from the transferable object, an application must use a *data flavor*. The data flavor specifies exactly how the data should be delivered to the requestor. For example, if the clipboard contains a string, the requestor could ask for the data in the form of a String object or as an StringReader object.

java.awt.event

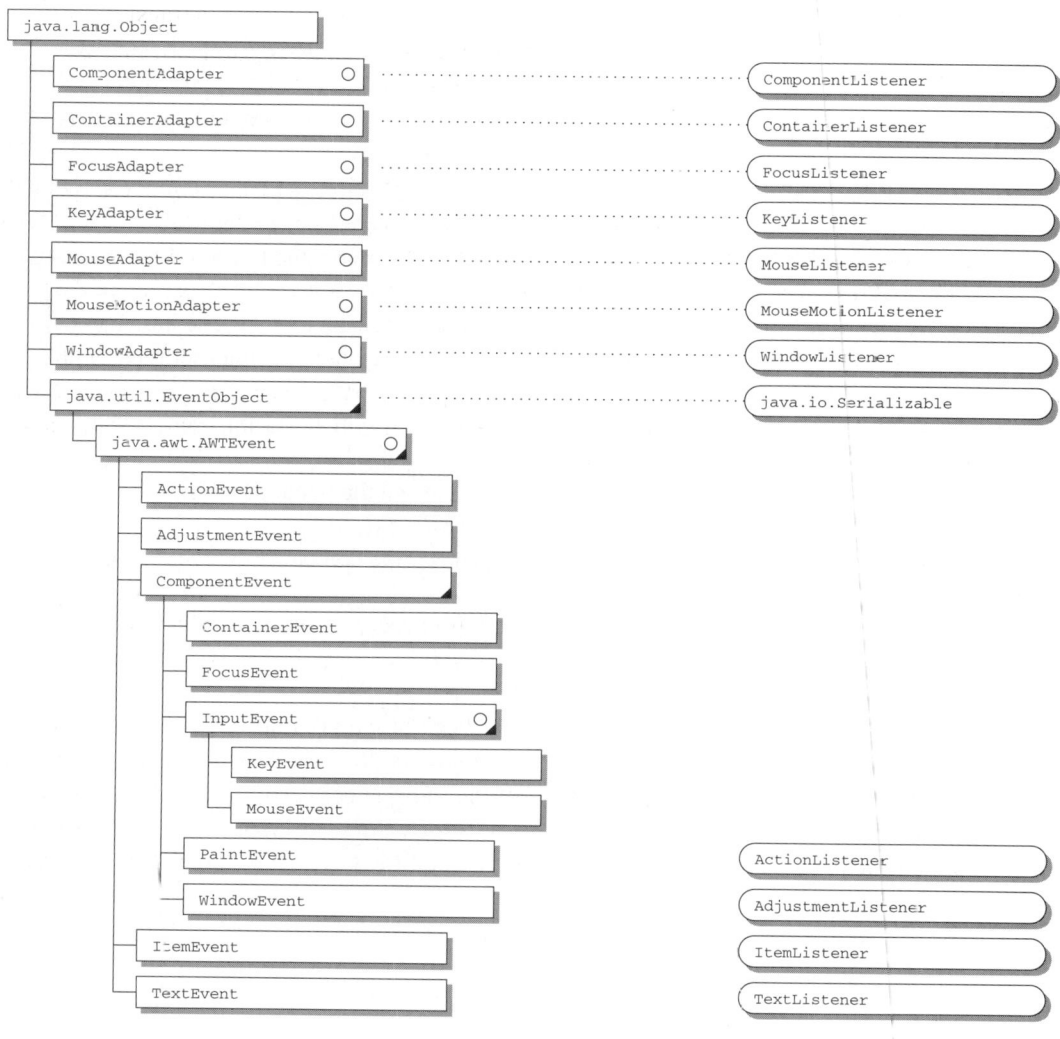

Components interact with a program that uses them through the use of *events*. For example, when a user clicks a component with the mouse, that component fires a mouse down event. Events in the AWT are organized into a class hierarchy rooted at the abstract class AWTEvent. This package contains interfaces and classes for dealing with different types of events fired by AWT components. See the AWTEvent class for details on the event model.

Event Class Hierarchy

ActionEvent	Fired by a component or menu component to indicate that an action has occurred.
AdjustmentEvent	Fired by an adjustable object to indicate that its adjustment value has changed.
ComponentEvent	Fired by a component whenever it is moved, resized, hidden, or made visible.
ContainerEvent	Fired by a container whenever a component is added or removed from it.
FocusEvent	Fired by a component whenever it gains or loses focus.
InputEvent	Fired by a component whenever the user uses the keyboard and/or mouse to interact with the component.
ItemEvent	Fired by an item-selectable object to indicate that its state has changed.
KeyEvent	Fired by a component that has the focus whenever the user types at the keyboard.
MouseEvent	Fired by a component that has the focus whenever the user uses the mouse.
PaintEvent	Used internally by the AWT to manage the updating of the component's display area.
TextEvent	Fired by a text component whenever the contents of the text component changes.
WindowEvent	Fired by a window whenever it is opened/closed, activated/deactivated, or iconified/deiconified.

The AWT event hierarchy organizes the different types of events that AWT components can fire. A subclass of an event class provides more details on the nature of the event. For example, KeyEvent and MouseEvent are subclasses of the more general InputEvent. A KeyEvent contains not only general InputEvent information, for example, about the pressed modifier keys and the time of the input, but also information about the key that was pressed or released.

Event Listeners

`ActionListener`	Interface implemented by objects wishing to receive action events.
`AdjustmentListener`	Interface implemented by objects wishing to receive adjustment events.
`ComponentListener`	Interface implemented by objects wishing to receive component events.
`ContainerListener`	Interface implemented by objects wishing to receive container events.
`FocusListener`	Interface implemented by objects wishing to receive focus events.
`ItemListener`	Interface implemented by objects wishing to receive item events.
`KeyListener`	Interface implemented by objects wishing to receive key events.
`MouseListener`	Interface implemented by objects wishing to receive mouse pressed/released, entered/exited, and clicked events.
`MouseMotionListener`	Interface implemented by objects wishing to receive mouse dragged or mouse moved events
`TextListener`	Interface implemented by objects wishing to receive text events.
`WindowListener`	Interface implemented by objects wishing to receive window events.

The Java event model is a notification-based system. Objects that fire events are called *event sources*. A single event source can fire one or more different types of events. For each type of event it fires, the source maintains a list of *event listeners* for that event type. An event listener registers with the event source using the registration methods provided. When an event of the corresponding type is fired by the source, the listener is notified.

Each subclass of AWTEvent has an associated interface called the *event listener interface*. For example, the ActionEvent class has an associated ActionListener interface. Each interface defines one or more *listener methods* that a listener of that event type must implement. For example, the ActionListener interface contains the single listener method actionPerformed(), which is invoked on the listener when an action event is fired by the object with which it has registered.

Event Listener Adapters

`ComponentAdapter`	A component listener in which all callback methods are empty implementations.
`ContainerAdapter`	A container listener in which all callback methods are empty.
`FocusAdapter`	A focus listener in which all callback methods are empty.
`KeyAdapter`	A key listener in which all callback methods are empty.
`MouseAdapter`	A mouse listener in which all callback methods are empty.
`MouseMotionAdapter`	A mouse motion listener in which all callback methods are empty.
`WindowAdapter`	A window listener in which all callback methods are empty.

For convenience, when an event listener interface has more than one listener method (`ComponentEvent`, `ContainerEvent`, `KeyEvent`, `MouseEvent`, `FocusEvent`, and `WindowEvent`), the AWT also defines *event adapter classes*. An event adapter class defines empty implementations for all of the methods in the corresponding event listener interface. This means a subclass of an event adapter needs to provide (override) only implementations of the methods it wants to handle. For example, if you want the listener to handle only the `KEY_PRESSED` subtype of `KeyEvent`, you would subclass from `KeyAdapter` and `override keyPressed()`. To achieve the same effect directly using the `KeyListener` interface, you would need to provide implementations for all three methods (`keyPressed()`, `keyReleased()`, and `keyTyped()`).

java.awt.image

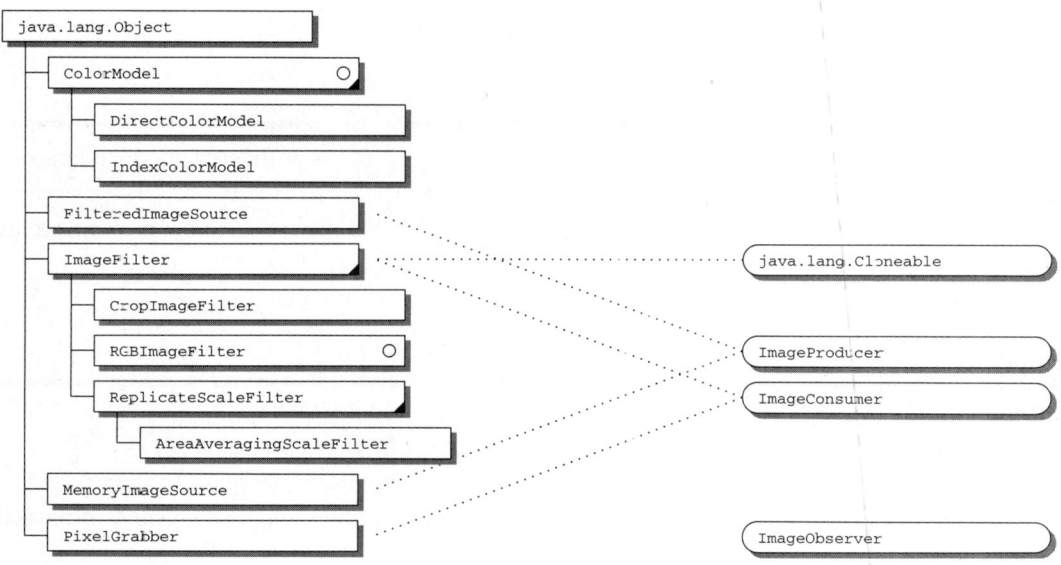

This package contains classes for creating and modifying images. Images are processed using a streaming framework that involves an image producer and an image consumer. This framework makes it possible to progressively render an image while it is being fetched or generated. Moreover, the framework allows an application to discard the storage used by an image and to regenerate it at any time.

In between the image producer and the consumer, you can insert one or more image filters that can modify the image data as it passes through the image filter. Figure 6 shows an image stream.

This package provides a number of image producers, consumers, and filters that you can configure for your image processing needs. If none of the provided classes suits your needs, you can construct your own image producers, consumers, and filters by using the supplied classes, which serve as excellent examples.

Another participant in the image streaming framework is the image observer. The image observer can receive notifications on the progress of an image as it is being

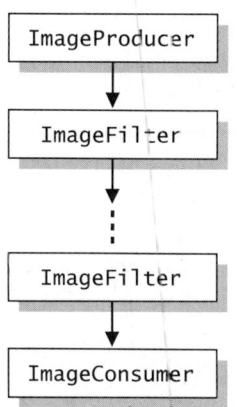

FIGURE 6: Image Producer, Consumers, and Filters.

loaded. A class can become an image observer by implementing the `ImageObserver` interface.

Also included in this package are classes that deal with an image's color model, which specifies how to translate the image's pixel value into colors.

Image Observer

`ImageObserver`	Used for obtaining the progress status of the loading of an image.

A class must implement this interface if it wants to receive the progress status of an image as the image is being loaded.

Image Producers

`ImageProducer`	The superclass of all image producers.
`MemoryImageSource`	Used for producing an image from an array of pixels.

The `ImageProducer` class is used to build image producers. One image producer is provided for producing an image from an array of pixels.

Image Consumers

`ImageConsumer`	The superclass of all image consumers.
`PixelGrabber`	Used for extracting the pixel values from an image.

The `ImageConsumer` class is used to build image consumers. One image consumer, `Pixel-Grabber`, is provided for extracting pixel values from an image.

Image Filters

`AreaAveragingScaleFilter`	Used to scale images using an area-averaging algorithm.
`ImageFilter`	The superclass of all image filters.
`CropImageFilter`	An image filter for creating a subimage from an image.
`FilteredImageSource`	Used for inserting an image filter into an image stream.
`ReplicateScaleFilter`	Used to scale images using a simple pixel replication algorithm.
`RGBImageFilter`	Used to create an image filter.

The `ImageFilter` class is used to build image consumers. Three image filter classes are available for various kinds of image filtering. Two classes for scaling images are also available.

Color Models

ColorModel	The superclass of all color models.
DirectColorModel	A color model whereby the colors are encoded in the pixel values.
IndexColorModel	A color model whereby pixel values are indexes into a color table.

A color model is associated with an image and specifies how to translate the image's pixel values into colors.

java.awt.peer

- ActiveEvent
- ButtonPeer
- CanvasPeer
- CheckboxMenuItemPeer
- CheckboxPeer
- ChoicePeer
- ComponentPeer
- ContainerPeer
- DialogPeer
- FileDialogPeer
- FontPeer
- FramePeer
- LabelPeer
- LightweightPeer
- ListPeer
- MenuBarPeer
- MenuComponentPeer
- MenuItemPeer
- MenuPeer
- PanelPeer
- PopupMenuPeer
- ScrollbarPeer
- ScrollPanePeer
- TextAreaPeer
- TextComponentPeer
- TextFieldPeer
- WindowPeer

An AWT component such as a button uses the platform's native implementation of a button. For example, on Solaris the AWT button uses the Motif button widget, while on Windows 95 the AWT button uses the button control. To make the AWT button component behave the same on all platforms, the button is assigned a *peer*, whose task is to take care of translating the behavior of the platform's native button to the behavior of the AWT button.

For the AWT subsystem to be able to use a set of peers with a platform and a vendor-dependent implementation, the peers must implement a set of common interfaces called the *peer interfaces*. These peer interfaces are all contained in this package as part of the Java package hierarchy. The *peer classes* that implement these interfaces, however, are *not* part of the Java package hierarchy. Rather, they are located in a package that has a platform- and vendor-dependent name, such as `sun.awt.win32`. The name of the package is contained in a system property (so that the AWT subsystem can find it). Figure 7 shows a component hierarchy and its corresponding peer hierarchy.

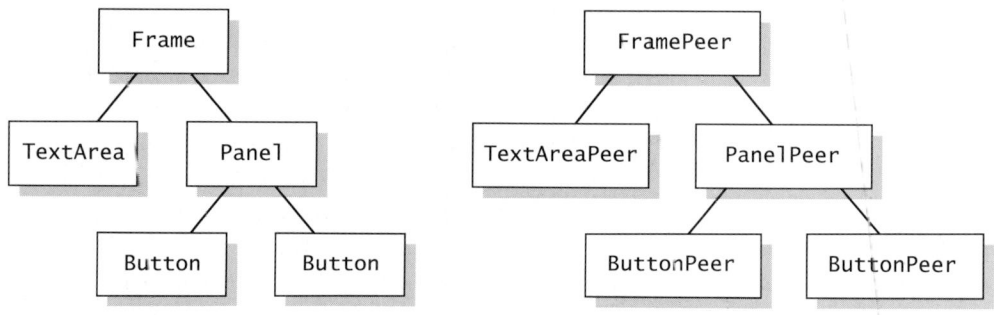

FIGURE 7: The Component Hierarchy and Its Corresponding Peer Class Hierarchy.

Component Peers

ButtonPeer	The peer interface for the Button component.
CanvasPeer	The peer interface for the Canvas component.
CheckboxMenuItemPeer	The peer interface for the CheckboxMenuItem component.
CheckboxPeer	The peer interface for the Checkbox component.
ChoicePeer	The peer interface for the Choice component.
ComponentPeer	The peer interface for the Component component.
ContainerPeer	The peer interface for the Container component.
DialogPeer	The peer interface for the Dialog component.
FileDialogPeer	The peer interface for the FileDialog component.
FramePeer	The peer interface for the Frame component.
LabelPeer	The peer interface for the Label component.
ListPeer	The peer interface for the List component.
MenuBarPeer	The peer interface for the MenuBar component.
MenuComponentPeer	The peer interface for the MenuComponent component.
MenuItemPeer	The peer interface for the MenuItem component.
MenuPeer	The peer interface for the Menu component.
PanelPeer	The peer interface for the Panel component.
PopupMenuPeer	The peer interface for the PopupMenu component.
ScrollbarPeer	The peer interface for the Scrollbar component.
ScrollPanePeer	The peer interface for the ScrollPane component.
TextAreaPeer	The peer interface for the TextArea component.
TextComponentPeer	The peer interface for the TextComponent component.
TextFieldPeer	The peer interface for the TextField component.
WindowPeer	The peer interface for the Window component.

Lightweight Component Peer

LightweightPeer	The peer interface for components that do not have a native peer.

A *lightweight component* is a component that does not have a corresponding native peer. Instead, it has a *lightweight peer*. A lightweight peer contains information used by the AWT system to make lightweight components behave like a native component. See Component for more information about lightweight components.

Font Peer

FontPeer	The peer interface for the Font class.

A font also has a *font peer* that uses the platform's native font resources. This is analogous to a windowing system component's having a component peer.

Event

ActiveEvent	The interface for an event that dispatches itself.

ActiveEvent is a special type of event that dispatches itself. (Normally, an event is dispatched to the event source that is typically an AWT component.) See AWTEvent for a description of events fired by AWT components.

java.beans

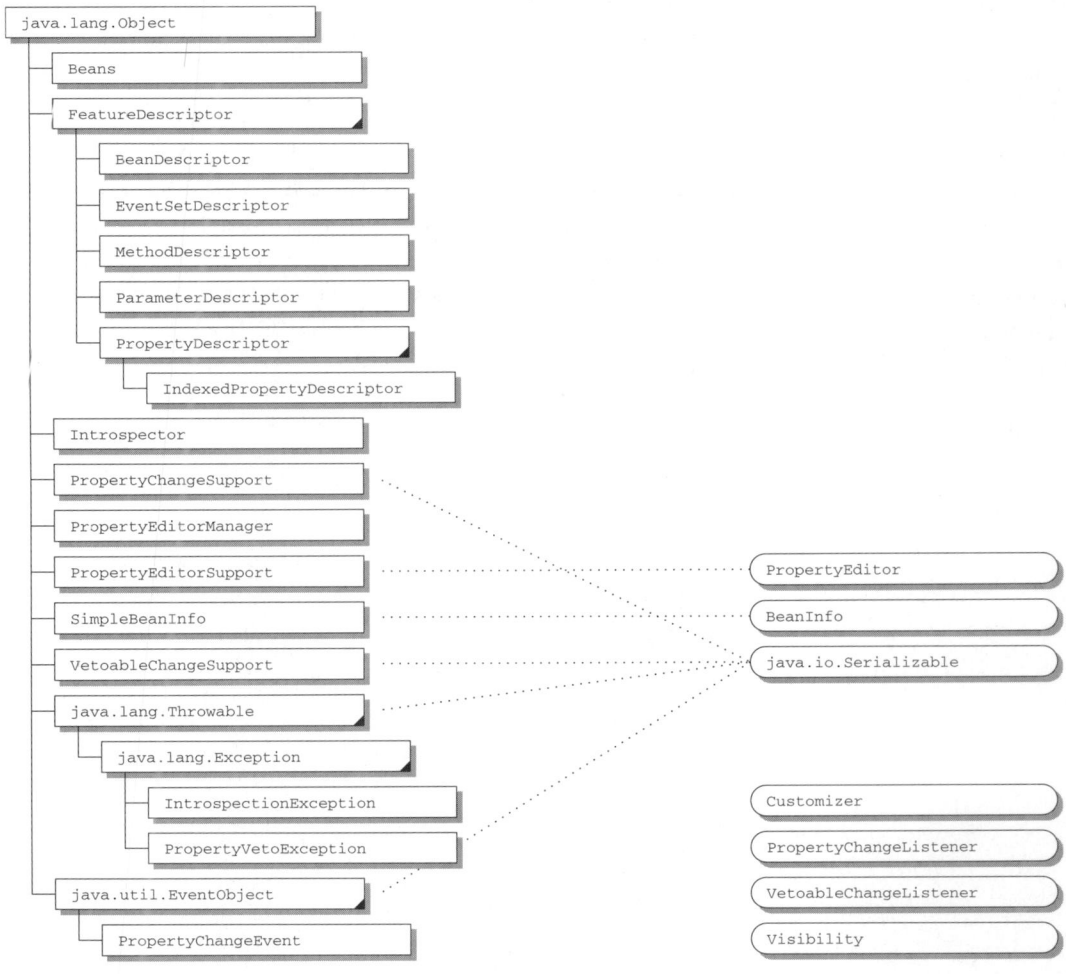

The `java.beans` package contains classes related to Java Beans development. A few of the classes are used by beans while they run in an application. For example, the event classes are used by beans that fire property and vetoable change events (see `PropertyChangeEvent`). However, most of the classes in this package are meant to be used by a bean editor (that is, a development environment for customizing and putting together beans to create an application). In particular, these classes help the bean editor create a user interface that the user can use to customize the bean. For example, a bean may contain a property of a special type that a bean editor may not know how to handle. By using the `PropertyEditor` interface, a bean developer can provide an editor for this special type.

To minimize the resources used by a bean, the classes used by bean editors are loaded only when the bean is being edited. They are not needed while the bean is running in an application and therefore not loaded. This information is kept in what's called a *bean-info* (see `BeanInfo`).

Feature Descriptors

`BeanDescriptor`	Contains global information about the bean.
`EventSetDescriptor`	Contains information about the events fired by the bean.
`FeatureDescriptor`	Common superclass of all feature descriptors.
`IndexedPropertyDescriptor`	Contains information about the bean's indexed properties.
`MethodDescriptor`	Contains information about the bean's public methods.
`ParameterDescriptor`	Contains information about the parameters in the bean's public methods.
`PropertyDescriptor`	Contains information about the bean's nonindexed properties.

A *feature descriptor* is an object used to hold information about some part (called a *feature*) of a bean. For example, the feature descriptor of a bean property specifies whether it is bound or constrained. A bean has six kinds of features: bean, event set, indexed property, method, parameter, and property. Each of these features is represented by its own feature descriptor class.

The parts of a feature descriptor are called *attributes*. All feature descriptors share a common set of attributes. These are contained in the class `FeatureDescriptor`. All feature descriptor classes extend from this class to inherit the common attributes.

There are two kinds of feature descriptors: *implicit* and *explicit*. Implicit feature descriptors are created through the process of introspection. Explicit feature descriptors are explicitly supplied

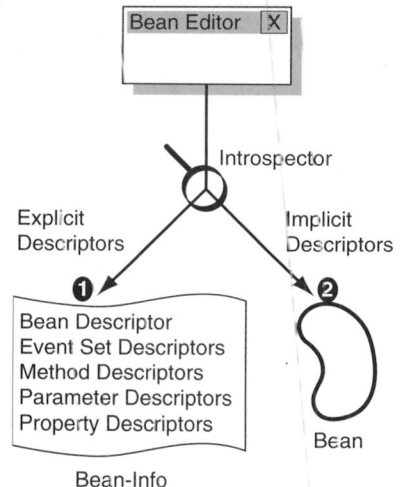

FIGURE 8: Implicit and Explicit Descriptors.

by the bean developer. See Figure 8. See the various feature descriptor class descriptions for details on the default attribute values for implicit feature descriptors. See the `BeanInfo` class for information on how to provide explicit feature descriptors.

The Bean-info

`BeanInfo`	Interface implemented by bean-info objects.
`SimpleBeanInfo`	A default bean-info that can be customized by subclassing.

When a bean editor loads a bean, it asks the introspector (see `Introspector`) to construct a set of feature descriptors (see `FeatureDescriptor`). These descriptors contain information used by a bean editor to create an interface for editing the bean. By default, the introspector uses a process called *introspection* to discover the feature descriptors for a bean. This process basically involves detecting signature patterns in the bean's public methods (see `Introspector` for more details).

However, some feature descriptors created by introspection may not have the desired values (since there are some things that the introspector cannot determine). In this case, the bean must provide explicit feature descriptors for the introspector. These explicit feature descriptors are packaged in an object called a *bean-info*. See Figure 8.

Introspection

`IntrospectionException`	Thrown if an error is encountered during introspection.
`Introspector`	Used to apply introspection on a bean.

Introspection is a process used by a bean editor to discover information about a bean. The bean editor uses this information to construct a user interface for customizing the bean. One type of information discovered through introspection is the bean's set of properties. The bean editor uses the set of properties (and their types) to create a *property sheet* that the user can use to customize the bean.

There are two places in which introspection looks for this information. The first is in the bean's *bean-info*, if one exists. The bean-info contains explicit information that a bean developer has associated with a bean. For example, the developer may have provided localized names for all of the bean's properties. See `BeanInfo` for more information about bean-infos.

The second place in which introspection looks for information is the bean's list of public methods. The bean specification defines conventions for methods that deal with properties and events. For example, if the methods

```
public String getFlavor()
public void setFlavor(String flavor)
```

are found, it is assumed that the bean has a string property called "flavor." See `PropertyDescriptor` and `EventSetDescriptor` for details about the method signature conventions.

The Property Change Event

PropertyChangeEvent	Fired when bound properties *are* modified and when constrained properties are *about to be* modified.
PropertyChangeListener	Interface that must be implemented by property change listeners.
PropertyChangeSupport	Contains convenient methods for beans that fire property change events.
PropertyVetoException	Thrown by a listener that is vetoing a vetoable change event.
VetoableChangeListener	Interface that must be implemented by vetoable change listeners.
VetoableChangeSupport	Contains convenient methods for beans that fire vetoable change events.

The beans package introduces an event called the *property change event*. The property change event behaves very much like all of the other events in the java.awt.event package. For example, this event is delivered only to objects that have been registered by a call to the bean's addPropertyChangeListener() method.

The property change event is fired when certain bean properties are modified. These properties are called *bound* properties. Another type of property, called a *constrained* property, causes a property change event to be fired *just before* the event is modified. Any vetoable change listener can *veto* (or cancel) the event, thereby preventing the property from being modified. A listener vetoes a vetoable change event by throwing PropertyVetoException.

Both the property and vetoable change events are instances of PropertyChangeEvent. They are distinguishable by the listeners because the events are delivered to the listeners via different callback methods. See PropertyChangeEvent for more information about the property and vetoable change events.

Property Editors

Customizer	A specialized user interface for editing bean properties.
PropertyEditor	A user interface for editing a bean property.
PropertyEditorManager	Used for locating property editors.
PropertyEditorSupport	A default implementation of a property editor.

A *property editor* is essentially a user interface for editing a bean property and hence is used only by a bean editor. Different property types require different property editors. For example, in the case of a string property, the string property editor might provide a text field for editing the string. In the case of a color, the color property editor might provide knobs for controlling each of the color's components.

A *customizer* is a user interface for editing all of a bean's properties as opposed to a property editor, which is a user interface for editing a single bean property. For example, if the bean has graphical properties, the customizer may provide a more productive way of editing the bean compared to ways offered by the bean editor's default property editors. Another use of a customizer is to provide a step-by-step way of customizing a bean. See Customizer for more details.

The Bean Environment

Beans	Contains methods for controlling and querying the bean environment.
Visibility	Used by beans that can run with or without a window system.

A bean environment is an environment that can load, instantiate, and execute beans. The Beans class contains methods that apply to a single bean environment. Any changes to the state of Beans are seen by all beans in that bean environment. For example, Beans has a design-time property that, when set to true, causes all of the beans in the bean environment to enter design mode.

The Visibility interface is implemented by beans that can be run in a server-based bean environment. The server may or may not have a display and hence a window system. If a bean implements Visibility, the bean environment will inform the bean whether a window system is available.

ActionEvent

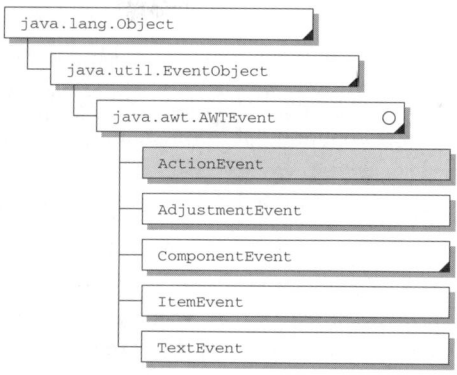

```
java.lang.Object

    java.util.EventObject

        java.awt.AWTEvent                    O

            ActionEvent

            AdjustmentEvent

            ComponentEvent

            ItemEvent

            TextEvent
```

Syntax

```
public class ActionEvent extends AWTEvent
```

Description

An action event is typically fired by a component to trigger some high-level activity in an application. For example, double-clicking a filename in a list component fires an action event that might cause the application to open a file. Action events are fired by the components `Button`, `List`, `MenuItem`, and `TextField`. For more general information about events, see `AWTEvent`.

Listening for Action Events

To listen for action events from an object, the listener must implement the `ActionListener` interface. After that, the listener must be registered with the object. It becomes registered by calling the object's `addActionListener()` method.

Action Command

When a component creates an action event, it can include a nonlocalized string, called the *action command*, that gives a little more detail about what caused the event. The content of the action command is very specific to the component that fired it. For example, the action command of a menu item is the menu item's label, whereas the action command of a list is the currently selected item. Table 1 shows all the AWT components that fire action events and what they include as the action command.

B
C
D
E
F
G
H
I
J
K
L
M
N
O
P
Q
R
S
T
U
V
W
X
Y
Z

Component	Action Command
Button	A string containing the button's label or its programmatically set action command.
List	A string containing the list's selected item.
MenuItem	A string containing the menu item's label.
TextField	A string containing the contents of the text field.

TABLE 1: AWT Components That Fire Action Events.

Modifiers

The key modifiers that were pressed at the time the action event was created are available in an action event. They can be retrieved using the getModifiers() method. See the InputEvent class description for more details.

Note: In Java 1.1.2, the modifier state for action events is not yet implemented.

Action Event Flow

Figure 9 shows how action events typically flow through the system. First, the event is fired by a component peer in response to some user gesture. This event is posted on the event queue (see Event-Queue). When the event makes its way to the front of the queue, it is given to the component via its dispatchEvent() method. The main purpose of this method is to discard the event if the action event type is not enabled or if there are no action event listeners. Otherwise, dispatchEvent() calls processEvent(), which in turn calls different methods depending on the event type. Since this is an action event, processActionEvent() is called. The main purpose of this method is to notify the action event listeners.

A component can override processAction-Event() to process action events before they are delivered to its listeners. The overridden method should call super.processActionEvent() to ensure that events are dispatched to the component's listeners.

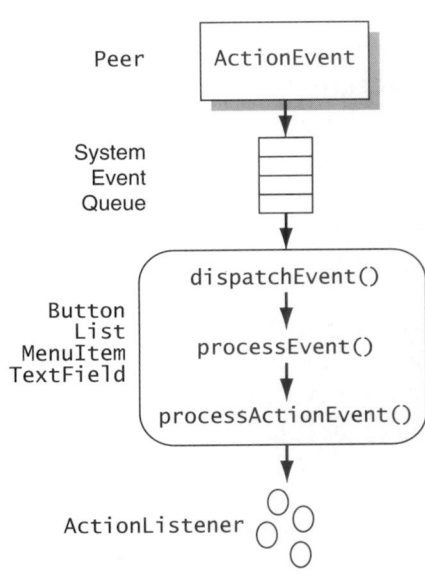

FIGURE 9:   Action Event Flow.

MEMBER SUMMARY	
Constructor	
ActionEvent()	Constructs an ActionEvent instance.
Property Methods	
getActionCommand()	Retrieves the action event's action command.
getModifiers()	Retrieves the state of the action event's modifier keys.
Action Event Ids	
ACTION_FIRST	Constant specifying the first id in the range of action event ids.
ACTION_LAST	Constant specifying the last id in the range of action event ids
ACTION_PERFORMED	Event id indicating that an action event occurred.
Modifier Masks	
ALT_MASK	Used to determine the state of the Alt key.
CTRL_MASK	Used to determine the state of the Control key.
META_MASK	Used to determine the state of the Meta key.
SHIFT_MASK	Used to determine the state of the Shift key.
Debugging Method	
paramString()	Generates a string representing the action event's state.

A
B
C
D
E
F
G
H
I
J
K
L
M
N
O
P
Q
R
S
T
U
V
W
X
Y
Z

See Also

```
ActionListener, java.awt.AWTEvent, java.awt.Button,
java.awt.Component.dispatchEvent(), java.awt.Component.processEvent(),
java.awt.List, java.awt.MenuItem, java.awt.TextField.
```

Example

This example shows all the components that can fire action events. When a component fires an action event, the frame prints it out. See Figure 10.

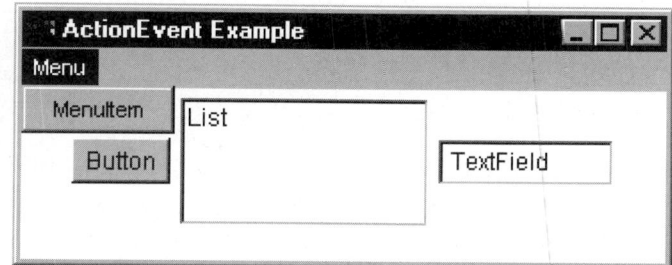

FIGURE 10:   Components That Fire Action Events.

```
import java.awt.*;
import java.awt.event.*;

public class Main extends Frame implements ActionListener {
    MenuItem menuitem = new MenuItem("MenuItem");
```

```
        Button button = new Button("Button");
        List list = new List();
        TextField textfield = new TextField("TextField");

        Main() {
            super("ActionEvent Example");

            list.addItem("List");

            // Create menubar and initialize.
            MenuBar mb = new MenuBar();
            Menu m = new Menu("Menu");
            m.add(menuitem);
            mb.add(m);
            setMenuBar(mb);

            // Listen for events
            menuitem.addActionListener(this);
            button.addActionListener(this);
            list.addActionListener(this);
            textfield.addActionListener(this);

            // Layout components
            setLayout(new FlowLayout());
            add(button);
            add(list);
            add(textfield);
            pack();
            show();
        }

        public void actionPerformed(ActionEvent evt) {
            System.out.println(evt);
        }

        public static void main(String args[]) {
            new Main();
        }
    }
```

ACTION_FIRST

PURPOSE	Constant specifying the first id in the range of action event ids.
SYNTAX	`public static final int ACTION_FIRST`
DESCRIPTION	All action event ids must be greater than or equal to `ACTION_FIRST` (value 1001).
SEE ALSO	`ACTION_LAST`.
EXAMPLE	See `java.awt.Component.processEvent()`.

A
B
C
D
E
F
G
H
I
J
K
L
M
N
O
P
Q
R
S
T
U
V
W
X
Y
Z

ACTION_LAST

PURPOSE	Constant specifying the last id in the range of action event ids.
SYNTAX	`public static final int ACTION_LAST`
DESCRIPTION	All action event ids must be less than or equal to `ACTION_LAST` (value `1001`).
SEE ALSO	`ACTION_FIRST`.
EXAMPLE	See `java.awt.Component.processEvent()`.

ACTION_PERFORMED

PURPOSE	Event id indicating that an action event occurred.
SYNTAX	`public static final int ACTION_PERFORMED`
DESCRIPTION	All action events fired by the components `Button`, `List`, `MenuItem`, and `TextField` have this id (value `1001`).
SEE ALSO	`ActionEvent()`.
EXAMPLE	See the `java.awt.Canvas` class example.

ActionEvent()

PURPOSE	Constructs an `ActionEvent` instance.

SYNTAX	`public ActionEvent(Object source, int id, String command)`
	`public ActionEvent(Object source, int id, String command, int`
	   `modifiers)`

DESCRIPTION	This constructor creates an action event with `source` as the object firing this event. If `modifiers` is not specified, `modifier` defaults to `0`. At present, there is only one action event id, so `id` must be set to `ACTION_PERFORMED`. The source object should implement the various methods that support action event listeners: `addActionListener()`, `removeActionListener()`, `processEvent()`, and `processActionEvent()`. For an example of a component implementing these methods, see the `Canvas` class example. After the action event is created, the source object can distribute the event to its listeners by calling `AWTEventMulticaster.actionPerformed()`. If the event is not created by `source`, the creator can deliver the event to the source component either by posting the event to the event queue (see `EventQueue.postEvent()`) or by calling the source component's `Component.dispatchEvent()` method directly.

PARAMETERS
command	The possibly `null` action command string.
id	Must be `ACTION_PERFORMED`.
modifiers	The state of the modifier keys.
source	The non-`null` object that is firing this action event.

SEE ALSO   `ACTION_PERFORMED`, `getActionCommand()`, `getModifiers()`, `java.awt.AWTEvent.getID()`, `java.util.EventObject.getSource()`.

EXAMPLE   See the `java.awt.Canvas` and `java.awt.Component` class examples.

ALT_MASK

PURPOSE   Modifier mask used to determine the state of the Alt key.

SYNTAX   `public static final int ALT_MASK`

DESCRIPTION   This mask (value 8) should be bitwise and'ed with the results of `getModifiers()` to determine the state of the Alt key at the time the action event was created. If the result is 0, the Alt key was not pressed; otherwise, the key was pressed.

Note: In Java 1.1.2, the modifier state for action events is not yet implemented.

SEE ALSO   `CTRL_MASK`, `getModifiers()`, `META_MASK`, `SHIFT_MASK`.

EXAMPLE   See also the `getModifiers()` example.

```
boolean isAltDown(ActionEvent evt) {
    return (evt.getModifiers() & ActionEvent.ALT_MASK) != 0;
}
```

CTRL_MASK

PURPOSE   Modifier mask used to determine the state of the Control key.

SYNTAX   `public static final int CTRL_MASK`

DESCRIPTION   This mask (value 2) should be bitwise and'ed with the results of `getModifiers()` to determine the state of the Control key at the time the action event was created. If the result is 0, the Control key was not pressed; otherwise, the key was pressed.

Note: In Java 1.1.2, the modifier state for action events is not yet implemented.

SEE ALSO   `ALT_MASK`, `getModifiers()`, `META_MASK`, `SHIFT_MASK`.

EXAMPLE   See also the `getModifiers()` example.

```
boolean isControlDown(ActionEvent evt) {
    return (evt.getModifiers() & ActionEvent.CTRL_MASK) != 0;
}
```

getActionCommand()

PURPOSE	Retrieves the action event's action command.
SYNTAX	`public String getActionCommand()`
DESCRIPTION	The action command is a nonlocalized string that gives a little more detail about the cause of the event. For example, the action command of a list component is the currently selected item. See the class description for more details about the action command.
RETURNS	The possibly `null` command action string.
EXAMPLE	See the class example.

getModifiers()

PURPOSE	Retrieves the state of the action event's modifier keys.
SYNTAX	`public int getModifiers()`
DESCRIPTION	Stored with an action event is the state of the modifier keys at the time an action event is fired. This method retrieves the state of all the modifier keys as a bit set where the state of each modifier key is represented by a particular bit in the bit set. To determine whether a modifier key was pressed, you must use the appropriate modifier mask with the bit set. See the various modifier masks for examples.
	Note: In Java 1.1.2, the modifier state for action events is not yet implemented.
RETURNS	A bit set containing the state of the modifier keys.
SEE ALSO	`ALT_MASK, CTRL_MASK, META_MASK, SHIFT_MASK`.
EXAMPLE	This example demonstrates how to get action events from a component that fires them and then determine the event's modifiers. The example creates a button and listens for action events from the button. In response to an action event, the specifics of the event are printed. See Figure 11.

FIGURE 11:
ActionEvent.getModifiers().

```
import java.awt.*;
import java.awt.event.*;

class Main extends Frame implements ActionListener {
    Main() {
        super("ActionEvent Example");
```

B
C
D
E
F
G
H
I
J
K
L
M
N
O
P
Q
R
S
T
U
V
W
X
Y
Z

```
        Button button = new Button("Button");

        // Listen for action events.
        button.addActionListener(this);

        add(button, BorderLayout.CENTER);
        pack();
        show();
    }

    // Note: modifiers for action events is not yet working in Java 1.1.1.
    public void actionPerformed(ActionEvent evt) {
        if ((evt.getModifiers() & ActionEvent.ALT_MASK) != 0) {
            System.out.print("alt ");
        } else if ((evt.getModifiers() & ActionEvent.CTRL_MASK) != 0) {
            System.out.print("ctrl ");
        } else if ((evt.getModifiers() & ActionEvent.META_MASK) != 0) {
            System.out.print("meta ");
        } else if ((evt.getModifiers() & ActionEvent.SHIFT_MASK) != 0) {
            System.out.print("shift ");
        }
        System.out.println(evt.getActionCommand());
    }

    public static void main(String args[]) {
        new Main();
    }
}
```

META_MASK

PURPOSE   Modifier mask used to determine the state of the Meta key.

SYNTAX   `public static final int META_MASK`

DESCRIPTION   This mask (value 4) should be bitwise and'ed with the results of `getModifiers()` to determine the state of the Meta key at the time the action event was created. If the result is 0, the Meta key was not pressed; otherwise, the key was pressed.

Note: In Java 1.1.2, the modifier state for action events is not yet implemented.

SEE ALSO   `ALT_MASK`, `CTRL_MASK`, `getModifiers()`, `SHIFT_MASK`.

EXAMPLE

```
    boolean isMetaDown(ActionEvent evt) {
        return (evt.getModifiers() & ActionEvent.META_MASK) != 0;
    }
```

paramString()

PURPOSE   Generates a string representing the action event's state.

SYNTAX   `public String paramString()`

DESCRIPTION The returned string contains the name of the action event and the action command. A subclass of this class should override this method and return a concatenation of its state with the results of `super.paramString()`. This method is called by the `AWTEvent.toString()` method and is typically used for debugging.

RETURNS   A non-`null` string representing the action event's state.

OVERRIDES   `java.awt.AWTEvent.paramString()`.

SEE ALSO   `java.awt.AWTEvent.toString()`, `java.lang.Object.toString()`.

EXAMPLE   See the `java.awt.AWTEvent` class example.

SHIFT_MASK

PURPOSE   Modifier mask used to determine the state of the Shift key.

SYNTAX   `public static final int SHIFT_MASK`

DESCRIPTION This mask (value 1) should be bitwise and'ed with the results of `getModifiers()` to determine the state of the Shift key at the time the action event was created. If the result is 0, the Shift key was not pressed; otherwise, the key was pressed.

Note: In Java 1.1.2, the modifier state for action events is not yet implemented.

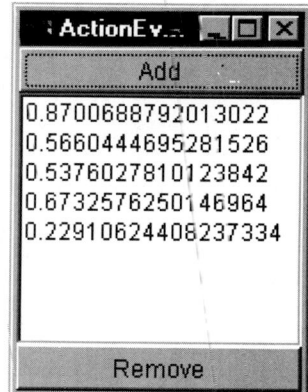

FIGURE 12:
ActionEvent.SHIFT_MASK.

SEE ALSO   `ALT_MASK`, `CTRL_MASK`, `getModifiers()`, `META_MASK`.

EXAMPLE   This example creates a list of random numbers in a list. Pressing the Add button adds more random numbers. Pressing Remove removes the selected number from the list. Pressing Shift-Remove removes all the numbers from the list. See Figure 12.

B
C
D
E
F
G
H
I
J
K
L
M
N
O
P
Q
R
S
T
U
V
W
X
Y
Z

```java
import java.awt.*;
import java.awt.event.*;

public class Main extends Frame implements ActionListener {
    Button addButton = new Button("Add");
    Button removeButton = new Button("Remove");
    List list = new List();

    Main() {
        super("ActionEvent.SHIFT_MASK Example");
        addItems();

        // Listen for events
        addButton.addActionListener(this);
        removeButton.addActionListener(this);

        // Layout components
        add(addButton, BorderLayout.NORTH);
        add(removeButton, BorderLayout.SOUTH);
        add(list, BorderLayout.CENTER);
        setSize(150, 200);
        show();
    }

    public void actionPerformed(ActionEvent evt) {
        if ("Add".equals(evt.getActionCommand())) {
            addItems();
        } else if ("Remove".equals(evt.getActionCommand())) {
            // If the shift key is enabled, remove all the items.
            if ((evt.getModifiers() & ActionEvent.SHIFT_MASK) != 0) {
                list.removeAll();
            } else if (list.getSelectedIndex() >= 0) {
                list.remove(list.getSelectedIndex());
            }
        }
    }

    // Generate some random items.
    void addItems() {
        for (int i=0; i<5; i++) {
            list.addItem(""+Math.random());
        }
    }

    public static void main(String args[]) {
        new Main();
    }
}
```

A
B
C
D
E
F
G
H
I
J
K
L
M
N
O
P
Q
R
S
T
U
V
W
X
Y
Z

ActionLishener

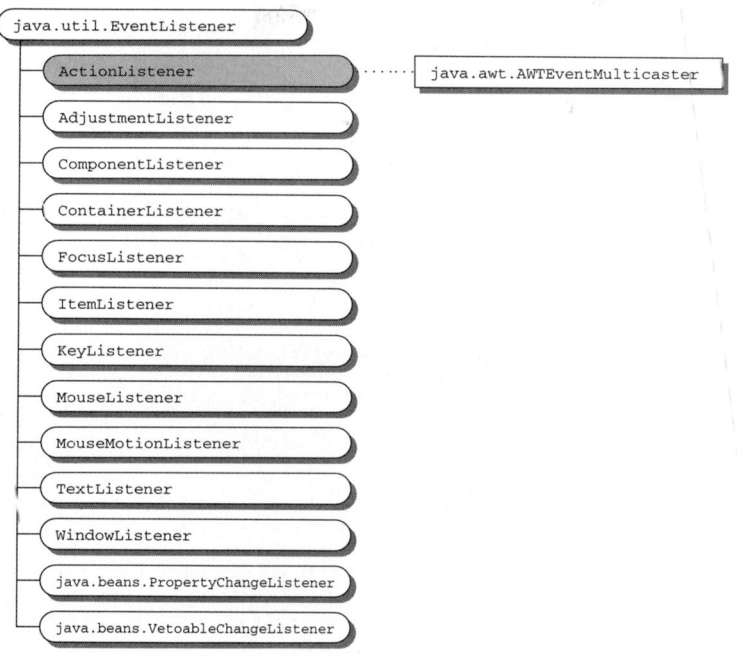

Syntax
```
public interface ActionListener extends EventListener
```

Description
When an object (listener) wishes to receive action events from an object that fires them (the source object), two things must be done:

1. The listener must implement this interface and the `actionPerformed()` method required by this interface.
2. The listener must be registered with the source object by making a call to the source object's `addActionListener()` method.

An action event is typically fired by a component to trigger some high-level activity in an application. For example, double-clicking a filename in a list component fires an action event that might cause the application to open a file. Action events are fired by the components `Button`, `List`, `MenuItem`, and `TextField`. See `ActionEvent` for more details.

A
B
C
D
E
F
G
H
I
J
K
L
M
N
O
P
Q
R
S
T
U
V
W
X
Y
Z

MEMBER SUMMARY

Action Event Callback Method

actionPerformed() Called when an object fires an action event.

See Also

ActionEvent, java.awt.AWTEventMulticaster, java.awt.Button,
java.awt.List, java.awt.MenuItem, java.awt.TextField,
java.util.EventListener.

Example

This example creates a grid of 256 buttons, one button for each 8-bit Latin-1 (ISO 8859-1) character. See Figure 13.

When you click a button, the program creates a Java Unicode character (\u00nn) and places it in the system clipboard. You can then paste the Java Unicode character into a text editor.

The button label shows the character if it is not an ISO control character. If the character is an ISO control character, the hex value of the character is displayed.

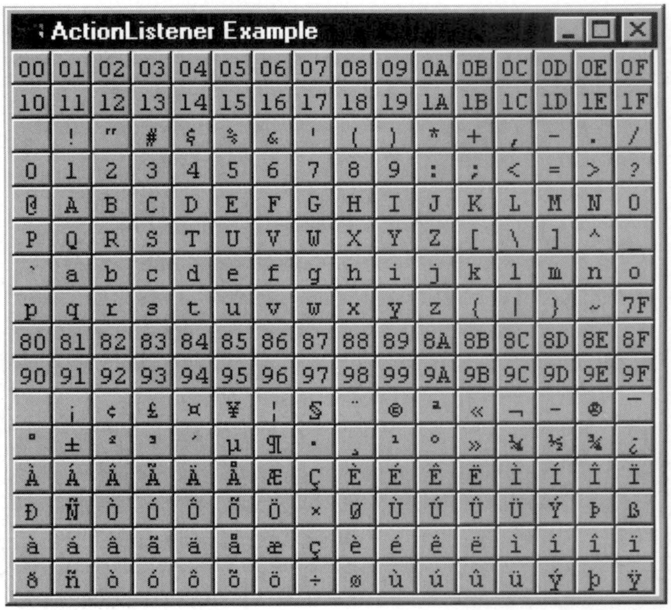

The button name is used to hold the single Latin-1 charac-

FIGURE 13: Latin-1 Character Selector.

ter. When an action event is fired, the handler fetches the button's single-character name and converts the character into a Java Unicode character.

```
import java.awt.*;
import java.awt.event.*;
import java.awt.datatransfer.*;

class Main extends Frame implements ActionListener {
    Main() {
        super("ActionListener Example");
        setFont(new Font("Monospaced", Font.PLAIN, 12));

        // Create the 256 buttons.
```

```
        Panel p = new Panel(new GridLayout(16, 0));
        for (int i=0; i<256; i++) {
            Button b = new Button("" + (char)i);

            // If control character, display hex value.
            if (Character.isISOControl((char)i)) {
                String s = "0" + Integer.toHexString(i).toUpperCase();

                b.setLabel(s.substring(s.length()-2));
            }

            b.setName(""+(char)i);

            // Listen for events.
            b.addActionListener(this);

            // Add to panel.
            p.add(b);
        }

        // Layout and show components.
        add(p, BorderLayout.CENTER);
        pack();
        show();
    }

    public void actionPerformed(ActionEvent evt) {
        // Fetch the character.
        char c = ((Component)evt.getSource()).getName().charAt(0);

        // Format the unicode string for 'c'.
        String result = "\\u00" + Integer.toHexString(c&0xff);

        // Place result in system clipboard.
        StringSelection contents = new StringSelection(result);
        getToolkit().getSystemClipboard().setContents(contents, null);
    }

    public static void main(String args[]) {
        new Main();
    }
}
```

actionPerformed()

PURPOSE   Called when an object fires an action event.

SYNTAX   `public void actionPerformed(ActionEvent evt)`

DESCRIPTION   This method is called when the source object fires an action event.

PARAMETERS

evt   The non-null action event.

EXAMPLE   See the class example.

ActiveEvent

ActiveEvent

Syntax

```
public interface ActiveEvent
```

Description

Normally, when an event reaches the head of the system's event queue (see EventQueue), the AWT system dispatches it to the event source that will fire the event. For example, when the user presses a key, a key event is created and placed on the system event queue. When the key event reaches the head of the queue, it is dispatched to the source component that will fire the key event by invoking the event source's dispatchEvent() method.

An *active event* is an event that is dispatched to itself. In particular, when the active event reaches the head of the event queue, the AWT system discovers that it is an active event (by noting that it implements the ActiveEvent interface). Instead of calling the event source's dispatchEvent() method, the system will call the active event's dispatch() method. In short, an active event's source is the active event itself.

Active events are used in situations in which it is necessary to serialize with other events. For example, an application would post an event into the system's event queue followed by an active event. When the active event reached the head of the queue, it would inform the poster. The poster would then know that the event preceding the active event had been dispatched.

At present, no AWT component generates active events.

MEMBER SUMMARY
Peer Method
dispatch()   Dispatches this active event.

See Also

java.awt.EventQueue, java.awt.Toolkit.getSystemEventQueue().

Example

This example demonstrates how to create an active event and add it to the system event queue. When dispatched, the active event simply displays a message in the frame. See Figure 14.

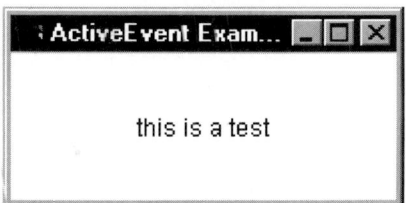

FIGURE 14: ActiveEvent.

```
import java.awt.peer.ActiveEvent;
import java.awt.*;

class Main extends Frame {
    public Main() {
        super("ActiveEvent Example");

        Label label = new Label("", Label.CENTER);
        add(label, BorderLayout.CENTER);
        setSize(200, 100);
        show();

        // Add active event to system event queue.
        EventQueue queue = getToolkit().getSystemEventQueue();
        queue.postEvent(new SampleActiveEvent("this is a test", label));
    }

    public static void main(String[] args) {
        new Main();
    }
}

class SampleActiveEvent extends AWTEvent implements ActiveEvent {
    static final int TESTEVENTMASK = AWTEvent.RESERVED_ID_MAX+100;
    Label label;
    String msg;

    SampleActiveEvent(String msg, Label l) {
        super(msg, TESTEVENTMASK);
        this.label = l;
        this.msg = msg;
    }

    public void dispatch() {
        label.setText(msg);
    }
}
```

A
B
C
D
E
F
G
H
I
J
K
L
M
N
O
P
Q
R
S
T
U
V
W
X
Y
Z

dispatch( )

PURPOSE	Dispatches this active event.
SYNTAX	`public void dispatch()`
DESCRIPTION	This method is implemented by the active event to perform the tasks associated with this event. This may include notifying listeners, updating state holders, and any event-specific tasks.
	This method is called by an event-dispatching thread when this event reaches the head of the event queue.
	`dispatch()` is similar to `Component.dispatchEvent()` and `MenuComponent.dispatchEvent()`, except that `dispatch()` dispatches itself, while these other two methods dispatch the given `AWTEvent` argument.
SEE ALSO	`java.awt.Component.dispatchEvent()`, `java.awt.EventQueue`, `java.awt.MenuComponent.dispatchEvent()`.

A
B
C
D
E
F
G
H
I
J
K
L
M
N
O
P
Q
R
S
T
U
V
W
X
Y
Z

Adjustable .... Scrollbar

Syntax
`public interface Adjustable`

Description
This interface is typically used by components that maintain an integer value, called the *adjustable value*, which can be interactively modified by the user. Such components include scrollbars, gauges, meters, and sliders. This interface is currently used by the `Scrollbar` and `ScrollPane` classes.

The Adjustable Value and Its Range
An adjustable object has an *adjustable value range*, which is defined by two integer values: the *minimum* and the *maximum*. The range can be any integer value, positive or negative. However, the maximum value must be greater than or equal to the minimum value. The range can be modified at any time.

Some adjustable objects are used to scroll around a large document. The adjustable object has a *visible* property that indicates how much of the document is visible. The adjustable object typically gives a visual indication of this value. For example, the visible value is the size of the scrollbar's scroll box. Adjustable objects such as gauges and sliders do not typically support the visible property. The visible property in these adjustable objects should be 0.

The adjustable object maintains the *adjustable value* and ensures that it stays within the adjustable range. The adjustable object typically has some visual indication of its adjustable value. For example, a scrollbar indicates its adjustable value by the position of its scroll box. When the user moves the scroll box, the adjustable value is automatically updated and an adjustment event is fired.

There are presently no specific rules that the adjustable value must obey with respect to the minimum, maximum, and visible values. You may implement whatever rules you like. If possible, however, you should implement the rules used by the AWT scrollbar (see `Scrollbar`), which at least establishes a precedent. Doing this will make it easier for others to understand your adjustable object. The AWT scrollbar implements the following rule:

`minimum <= adjustable value <= maximum-visible`

The `visible` value refers to the length of the proportional indicator (or scroll box). Its value must be positive. The minimum and maximum values can be negative.

A
B
C
D
E
F
G
H
I
J
K
L
M
N
O
P
Q
R
S
T
U
V
W
X
Y
Z

47

Block and Unit Increments

Most adjustable components provide a means to increase or decrease the value by a small or large amount. The small amount is called the *unit increment* and is typically associated with a line. The large amount is called the *block increment* and is typically associated with a page.

The adjustable value can be increased/decreased by a *block* or *unit* amount. These increments must be positive. A block is typically associated with a page and a unit with a line in a document. Therefore, if the user clicks the adjustable object to view the next page, a BLOCK_INCREMENT adjustment event is fired. Similarly, if the user clicks the adjustable object to view a previous line, a UNIT_DECREMENT adjustment event is fired.

The adjustable object's block *increment* specifies the amount to increase or decrease the adjustable's value when the user makes a block adjustment gesture. The same is true for the adjustable object's *unit increment*.

Events

Adjustment events are fired whenever the value maintained by an adjustable object is changed. See AdjustmentEvent for more details. See the AWTEvent class for general information on events and how to filter or handle an event.

MEMBER SUMMARY

Orientation Constants and Method

getOrientation()	Retrieves the adjustable's orientation.
HORIZONTAL	The orientation constant specifying a horizontal adjustable object.
VERTICAL	The orientation constant specifying a vertical adjustable object.

Property Methods

getMaximum()	Retrieves the adjustable's maximum value.
getMinimum()	Retrieves the adjustable's minimum value.
getValue()	Retrieves the adjustable's adjustable value.
getVisibleAmount()	Retrieves the adjustable's visible value.
setMaximum()	Sets the adjustable's maximum value.
setMinimum()	Sets the adjustable's minimum value.
setValue()	Sets the adjustable's adjustable value.
setVisibleAmount()	Sets the adjustable's visible value.

Value Adjustment Methods

getBlockIncrement()	Retrieves the adjustable's block increment.
getUnitIncrement()	Retrieves the adjustable's unit increment.
setBlockIncrement()	Sets the adjustable's block increment.
setUnitIncrement()	Sets the adjustable's unit increment.

> ### MEMBER SUMMARY
>
> **Listener Methods**
> addAdjustmentListener()   Adds a listener for receiving adjustment events.
> removeAdjustmentListener() Removes a listener from receiving adjustment events.

See Also

java.awt.event.AdjustmentEvent, java.awt.event.AdjustmentListener, Scrollbar, ScrollPane.

Example

This example creates a slider that implements the Adjustable interface. The slider maintains a value and displays an image. Each slider has a round knob whose position in the slider represents the slider's value. The slider fires an adjustment event each time the slider's value changes. See Figure 15.

FIGURE 15:   A Slider.

The slider's value can be modified in many ways, including the following:

- Dragging the knob changes the value continuously.
- Pressing the Left, Right, Up, or Down keys moves the knob up/left or down/right by a unit.
- Pressing the PageUp or PageDown keys moves the knob up/left or down/right by a block.
- Clicking above/left or below/right the knob moves the pointer by a block.

The example creates a frame with two sliders. The frame draws an oval of a particular color in its center. The color of the oval is controlled by the two sliders. The vertical slider controls the color's saturation; the horizontal slider controls the color's hue.

Both components, the frame and the slider, use double-buffering to eliminate flickering.

The visible property of an adjustable indicates the ratio of the visible area with respect to the size of the total area. Since the visible property does not apply to the slider, it is ignored.

One improvement that can be made to the slider in this example is a visual cue to indicate that the slider has the focus. With this improvement, you can tell which slider will be affected when you use the keyboard to move the slider.

```
import java.awt.*;
import java.awt.event.*;

class Main extends Frame implements AdjustmentListener {
    Slider ver = new Slider(Adjustable.VERTICAL);
    Slider hor = new Slider(Adjustable.HORIZONTAL);
```

```
        float[] hsb = {1.0f, 0.1f, 0.7f};

        // This off-screen image is used for double-buffering.
        Image bbuf;

        Main() {
            super("Adjustable Example");

            ver.setMaximum(1000);
            hor.setMaximum(1000);

            // Register listeners.
            ver.addAdjustmentListener(this);
            hor.addAdjustmentListener(this);

            // Set up the frame
            setLayout(new BorderLayout());
            add(ver, BorderLayout.EAST);
            add(hor, BorderLayout.SOUTH);
            setSize(200, 200);
            setVisible(true);
        }

        // Updates the color of the oval.
        public void adjustmentValueChanged(AdjustmentEvent evt) {
            Adjustable a = evt.getAdjustable();

            if (a.getOrientation() == Adjustable.VERTICAL) {
                hsb[1] = (float)a.getValue()/(float)a.getMaximum();
            } else {
                hsb[0] = (float)a.getValue()/(float)a.getMaximum();
            }
            repaint();
        }

        public void paint(Graphics g) {
            update(g);
        }

        public void update(Graphics g) {
            int w = getSize().width;
            int h = getSize().height;
            Insets insets = getInsets();

            // Create or enlarge the double-buffer if necessary.
            if (bbuf == null
                || bbuf.getWidth(this) < w
                || bbuf.getHeight(this) < h) {
                if (bbuf != null) {
                    bbuf.flush();
                }
                bbuf = createImage(w, h);
            }
            Graphics bbufG = bbuf.getGraphics();

            bbufG.setColor(getBackground());
            bbufG.fillRect(0, 0, w, h);

            // Draw oval.
            bbufG.setColor(new Color(Color.HSBtoRGB(hsb[0], hsb[1], hsb[2])));
```

A
B
C
D
E
F
G
H
I
J
K
L
M
N
O
P
Q
R
S
T
U
V
W
X
Y
Z

```
            bbufG.fillOval(insets.left, insets.top,
                w-insets.right-insets.left -ver.getSize().width,
                h-insets.bottom-insets.top -hor.getSize().height);

            // Paint double-buffer on screen.
            g.drawImage(bbuf, 0, 0, this);
            bbufG.dispose();
        }

        public static void main(String args[]) {
            new Main();
        }
    }

class Slider extends Canvas implements Adjustable {
        // The location of the ball.
        Point locPt = new Point(0, 0);

        // If non-null, the ball is being dragged and this field
        // holds the location of the cursor relative to the ball
        // when the mouse was pressed.
        Point downPt;

        // The image of the ball.
        Image image;

        // Dimensions of the ball.
        int ballW, ballH;

        // Off-screen image is used for double-buffering.
        Image bbuf;

        Slider(int o) {
            orient = o;
            image = Toolkit.getDefaultToolkit().getImage("ball.gif");

            // Wait for the image to be loaded so that we
            // can determine its size.
            MediaTracker tracker = new MediaTracker(this);
            tracker.addImage(image, 0);
            try {
                tracker.waitForAll();
            } catch (Exception e) {
                e.printStackTrace();
            }

            setSize(ballW = image.getWidth(this),
                ballH = image.getHeight(this));

            // Register listeners.
            addMouseListener(new MouseEventListener());
            addMouseMotionListener(new MouseMotionEventListener());
            addKeyListener(new KeyEventListener());
        }

        public void invalidate() {
            super.invalidate();

            // The bounds of the slider has changed so recompute
            // the ball location.
```

```
            setValues(value, min, max);
        }

        public void paint(Graphics g) {
            update(g);
        }

        public void update(Graphics g) {
            int w = getSize().width;
            int h = getSize().height;

            // Create or enlarge the double-buffer if necessary.
            if (bbuf == null
                    || bbuf.getWidth(this) < w
                    || bbuf.getHeight(this) < h) {
                if (bbuf != null) {
                    bbuf.flush();
                }
                bbuf = createImage(w, h);
            }
            Graphics bbufG = bbuf.getGraphics();

            // Clear the background.
            bbufG.setColor(getBackground());
            bbufG.fillRect(0, 0, w, h);

            // Draw the track.
            bbufG.setColor(Color.gray);
            if (orient == Adjustable.VERTICAL) {
                bbufG.fillRoundRect(w/2-1, ballH/2, 3, h - ballH, 5, 5);
            } else {
                bbufG.fillRoundRect(ballW/2, h/2-1, w - ballW, 3, 5, 5);
            }

            // Draw the ball.
            bbufG.drawImage(image, locPt.x, locPt.y, this);

            // Paint double-buffer on screen.
            g.drawImage(bbuf, 0, 0, this);
            bbufG.dispose();
        }

        // Returns -1 if above/left of ball;
        //          0 if on ball.
        //          1 if below/right of ball;
        int onBall(MouseEvent e) {
            int x = e.getX();
            int y = e.getY();

            if (orient == Adjustable.VERTICAL) {
                if (y < locPt.y) {
                    return -1;
                } else if (y > locPt.y+ballH) {
                    return 1;
                }
            } else {
                if (x < locPt.x) {
                    return -1;
                } else if (x > locPt.x+ballW) {
                    return 1;
```

A

B

C

D

E

F

G

H

I

J

K

L

M

N

O

P

Q

R

S

T

U

V

W

X

Y

Z

```
            }
        }
        return 0;
    }

    // Handle the events.
    class MouseEventListener extends MouseAdapter {
        public void mousePressed(MouseEvent evt) {
            switch (onBall(evt)) {
              case -1:
                inc(AdjustmentEvent.BLOCK_DECREMENT, -blockInc);
                break;
              case 0:
                // Enter dragging mode.
                (downPt = evt.getPoint()).translate(-locPt.x, -locPt.y);
                break;
              case 1:
                inc(AdjustmentEvent.BLOCK_INCREMENT, blockInc);
                break;
            }
            requestFocus();
        }

        public void mouseReleased(MouseEvent evt) {
            downPt = null;
        }

        public void mouseEntered(MouseEvent evt) {
            if (onBall(evt) == 0) {
                setCursor(Cursor.getPredefinedCursor(Cursor.HAND_CURSOR));
            }
        }

        public void mouseExited(MouseEvent evt) {
            setCursor(Cursor.getPredefinedCursor(Cursor.DEFAULT_CURSOR));
        }
    }

    class MouseMotionEventListener extends MouseMotionAdapter {
        public void mouseDragged(MouseEvent evt) {
            if (downPt != null) {
                if (orient == Adjustable.VERTICAL) {
                    setValues(evt.getY() * (max-min)
                        / (getSize().height-ballH) + min, min, max);
                } else {
                    setValues(evt.getX() * (max-min)
                        / (getSize().width-ballW) + min, min, max);
                }
                inc(AdjustmentEvent.TRACK, 0);
            }
        }
        public void mouseMoved(MouseEvent evt) {
            if (onBall(evt) == 0) {
                setCursor(Cursor.getPredefinedCursor(Cursor.HAND_CURSOR));
            }
        }
    }
    class KeyEventListener extends KeyAdapter {
        public void keyPressed(KeyEvent evt) {
            switch (evt.getKeyCode()) {
```

A
B
C
D
E
F
G
H
I
J
K
L
M
N
O
P
Q
R
S
T
U
V
W
X
Y
Z

53

```
                    case KeyEvent.VK_DOWN:
                    case KeyEvent.VK_RIGHT:
                      inc(AdjustmentEvent.UNIT_INCREMENT, unitInc);
                      break;
                    case KeyEvent.VK_PAGE_DOWN:
                      inc(AdjustmentEvent.BLOCK_INCREMENT, blockInc);
                      break;
                    case KeyEvent.VK_UP:
                    case KeyEvent.VK_LEFT:
                      inc(AdjustmentEvent.UNIT_DECREMENT, -unitInc);
                      break;
                    case KeyEvent.VK_PAGE_UP:
                      inc(AdjustmentEvent.BLOCK_DECREMENT, -blockInc);
                      break;
                }
            }
        }


        // ***** Adjustable Get Methods *****

        // The properties.
        int orient;
        int min = 0;
        int max = 100;
        int unitInc = 1;
        int blockInc = 10;
        int visible = 0;
        int value = 0;

        public int getOrientation() {
            return orient;
        }

        public int getValue() {
            return value;
        }

        public int getMinimum() {
            return min;
        }

        public int getMaximum() {
            return max;
        }

        public int getVisibleAmount() {
            return 0;
        }

        public int getUnitIncrement() {
            return unitInc;
        }

        public int getBlockIncrement() {
            return blockInc;
        }

        // ***** Adjustable Set Methods *****
```

```
void setValues(int va, int mn, int mx) {
    value = va;
    min = mn;
    max = mx;
    if (max <= min) {
        max = min + 1;
    }
    if (value < min) {
        value = min;
    }
    if (value > max) {
        value = max;
    }

    // Update the location of the ball.
    if (orient == Adjustable.VERTICAL) {
        locPt.y = (value-min) * (getSize().height-ballH)
            / (max-min);
    } else {
        locPt.x = (value-min) * (getSize().width-ballW)
            / (max-min);
    }

    // Generate an adjustment event.
    inc(AdjustmentEvent.TRACK, 0);
    repaint();
}

public void setValue(int v) {
    setValues(v, min, max);
}

public void setMinimum(int m) {
    setValues(value, m, max);
}

public void setMaximum(int m) {
    setValues(value, min, m);
}

public void setVisibleAmount(int v) {
}

public void setUnitIncrement(int u) {
    unitInc = u;
}

public void setBlockIncrement(int b) {
    blockInc = b;
}

// ***** Adjustable Event Methods *****

protected void processEvent(AWTEvent evt) {
    if (evt instanceof AdjustmentEvent) {
        processAdjustmentEvent((AdjustmentEvent)evt);
        return;
    }
    super.processEvent(evt);
}
```

A
B
C
D
E
F
G
H
I
J
K
L
M
N
O
P
Q
R
S
T
U
V
W
X
Y
Z

```
        // Deliver event to listeners.
        protected void processAdjustmentEvent(AdjustmentEvent evt) {
            if (adjustmentListener != null) {
                adjustmentListener.adjustmentValueChanged(evt);
            }
        }

        void inc(int type, int inc) {
            if (inc != 0) {
                setValues(value + inc, min, max);
            }
            if (adjustmentListener != null) {
                processEvent(new AdjustmentEvent(this,
                    AdjustmentEvent.ADJUSTMENT_VALUE_CHANGED, type, value));
            }
        }

        // ***** Adjustable Listener Methods *****

        transient AdjustmentListener adjustmentListener;

        public void addAdjustmentListener(AdjustmentListener l) {
            adjustmentListener = AWTEventMulticaster.add(adjustmentListener, l);
        }

        public void removeAdjustmentListener(AdjustmentListener l) {
            adjustmentListener = AWTEventMulticaster.remove(adjustmentListener, l);
        }

    }
```

addAdjustmentListener()

PURPOSE   Adds a listener for receiving adjustment events.

SYNTAX   `public void addAdjustmentListener(AdjustmentListener l)`

DESCRIPTION   Adjustment events are fired whenever the value maintained by an adjustable object is changed. See `AdjustmentEvent` for more details. After this method has been called, the adjustment listener l will receive adjustment events fired by this adjustable object.

PARAMETERS

l   The non-`null` listener to receive adjustment events.

SEE ALSO   `java.awt.event.AdjustmentEvent`,
`java.awt.event.AdjustmentListener`, `removeAdjustmentListener()`.

EXAMPLE   See the class example.

getBlockIncrement()

PURPOSE	Retrieves the adjustable's block increment.
SYNTAX	`public int getBlockIncrement()`
DESCRIPTION	The block increment determines the amount to increase or decrease the adjustable value when the user makes a block adjustment gesture. See the class description for more information on blocks.
RETURNS	The non-negative block increment.
SEE ALSO	`setBlockIncrement()`.
EXAMPLE	See the class example.

getMaximum()

PURPOSE	Retrieves the adjustable's maximum value.
SYNTAX	`public int getMaximum()`
DESCRIPTION	See the class description for details. The actual maximum that the adjustable value can attain is `getMaximum()-getVisibleAmount()`.
RETURNS	The adjustable's maximum value.
SEE ALSO	`getMinimum()`, `getValue()`, `getVisibleAmount()`, `setMaximum()`.
EXAMPLE	See the class example.

getMinimum()

PURPOSE	Retrieves the adjustable's minimum value.
SYNTAX	`public int getMinimum()`
DESCRIPTION	The adjustable's minimum value is the minimum value that the adjustable can attain. See the class description for details.
RETURNS	The adjustable's minimum value.
SEE ALSO	`getMaximum()`, `getValue()`, `getVisibleAmount()`, `setMinimum()`.
EXAMPLE	See the class example.

getOrientation()

PURPOSE	Retrieves the adjustable's orientation.

A
B
C
D
E
F
G
H
I
J
K
L
M
N
O
P
Q
R
S
T
U
V
W
X
Y
Z

SYNTAX	`public int getOrientation()`
RETURNS	The adjustable's orientation. This value can be either VERTICAL or HORIZONTAL.
SEE ALSO	`HORIZONTAL, VERTICAL.`
EXAMPLE	See the class example.

getUnitIncrement()

PURPOSE	Retrieves the adjustable's unit increment.
SYNTAX	`public int getUnitIncrement()`
DESCRIPTION	The unit increment determines the amount to increase or decrease the adjustable value when the user makes a unit adjustment gesture. See the class description for details.
RETURNS	The non-negative unit increment.
SEE ALSO	`getBlockIncrement(), setUnitIncrement().`

getValue()

PURPOSE	Retrieves the adjustable's adjustable value.
SYNTAX	`public int getValue()`
DESCRIPTION	See the class description for details.
RETURNS	The current value of the adjustable.
SEE ALSO	`getMaximum(), getMinimum(), getVisibleAmount().`
EXAMPLE	See the class example.

getVisibleAmount()

PURPOSE	Retrieves the adjustable's visible value.
SYNTAX	`public int getVisibleAmount()`
DESCRIPTION	The adjustable's visible value determines the size of its scroll box. See the class description for details.
RETURNS	The non-negative visible value.
SEE ALSO	`setVisibleAmount().`
EXAMPLE	See the class example.

HORIZONTAL

PURPOSE	The orientation constant specifying a horizontal adjustable object.
SYNTAX	`public static final int HORIZONTAL`
SEE ALSO	`getOrientation()`, `VERTICAL`.
EXAMPLE	See the class example.

removeAdjustmentListener()

PURPOSE	Removes a listener from receiving adjustment events.
SYNTAX	`public void removeAdjustmentListener(AdjustmentListener l)`
DESCRIPTION	Adjustment events are fired whenever the value maintained by an adjustable object is changed. See `AdjustmentEvent` for more details. After this method has been called, the adjustment listener l will no longer receive adjustment events fired by this adjustable object.
PARAMETERS	
l	The non-`null` adjustment listener.
SEE ALSO	`addAdjustmentListener`, `java.awt.event.AdjustmentEvent`, `java.awt.event.AdjustmentListener`.
EXAMPLE	See the usage of `removeActionListener()` in `MenuItem.disableEvents()`.

setBlockIncrement()

PURPOSE	Sets the adjustable's block increment.
SYNTAX	`public void setBlockIncrement(int b)`
DESCRIPTION	The block increment determines the amount to increase or decrease the adjustable value when the user makes a block adjustment gesture. See the class description for more information on blocks.
	Most implementations will silently modify the block increment to be at most the adjustable object's maximum value, although this is not strictly necessary.
PARAMETERS	
b	The non-negative block increment.
SEE ALSO	`getBlockIncrement()`, `setUnitIncrement()`.
EXAMPLE	See the class example.

A
B
C
D
E
F
G
H
I
J
K
L
M
N
O
P
Q
R
S
T
U
V
W
X
Y
Z

setMaximum()

PURPOSE	Sets the adjustable's maximum value.
SYNTAX	`public void setMaximum(int max)`
DESCRIPTION	If `max` is less than the adjustable's minimum value, the implementation should set the maximum value to be equal to the minimum value.
PARAMETERS	
`max`	The maximum value.
SEE ALSO	`getMaximum()`, `setMinimum()`.
EXAMPLE	See the class example.

setMinimum()

PURPOSE	Sets the adjustable's minimum value.
SYNTAX	`public void setMinimum(int min)`
DESCRIPTION	If `min` is greater than the adjustable's maximum value, the implementation should set the minimum value to be equal to the maximum value.
PARAMETERS	
`min`	The minimum value.
SEE ALSO	`getMinimum()`, `setMaximum()`.
EXAMPLE	See the class example.

setUnitIncrement()

PURPOSE	Sets the adjustable's unit increment.
SYNTAX	`public void setUnitIncrement(int u)`
DESCRIPTION	The unit increment determines the amount to increase or decrease the adjustable value when the user makes a unit adjustment gesture. See the class description for details.
	Most implementations will silently modify the unit increment to be at most the adjustable object's maximum value, although this is not strictly necessary.
PARAMETERS	
`u`	The non-negative unit increment.
SEE ALSO	`getUnitIncrement()`, `setBlockIncrement()`.
EXAMPLE	See the class example.

setValue()

PURPOSE	Sets the adjustable's adjustable value.
SYNTAX	`public void setValue(int v)`
DESCRIPTION	This method sets the adjustable's value. See the class description for details.
PARAMETERS	
v	The new value. It must be within the range defined by the minimum and maximum values for this adjustable.
SEE ALSO	`getMaximum()`, `getMinimum()`, `getValue()`, `getVisibleAmount()`.
EXAMPLE	See the class example.

setVisibleAmount()

PURPOSE	Sets the adjustable's visible value.
SYNTAX	`public void setVisibleAmount(int v)`
DESCRIPTION	The adjustable's visible value determines the size of its scroll box. See the class description for details.
PARAMETERS	
v	The non-negative visible value.
SEE ALSO	`getVisibleAmount()`.
EXAMPLE	See the class example.

VERTICAL

PURPOSE	The orientation constant specifying a vertical adjustable object.
SYNTAX	`public static final int VERTICAL`
SEE ALSO	`getOrientation()`, `HORIZONTAL`.
EXAMPLE	See the class example.

AdjustmentEvent

```
java.lang.Object
    java.util.EventObject
        java.awt.AWTEvent                    ○
            AdjustmentEvent
            ActionEvent
            ComponentEvent
            ItemEvent
            TextEvent
```

Syntax

`public class AdjustmentEvent extends AWTEvent`

Description

Adjustment events are fired by adjustable objects (see `Adjustable`). An adjustable object maintains an integer value and fires adjustment events whenever that value changes. Adjustable objects are typically used in sliders and for scrolling a document.

In the AWT, both the `Scrollbar` and `ScrollPane` components fire adjustment events (more accurately, the `ScrollPane` component has two adjustable objects that fire the adjustment events). For more general information about events, see `AWTEvent`.

Listening for Adjustment Events

To listen for adjustment events from an object, the listener must implement the `AdjustmentListener` interface. After that, the listener must be registered with the object. It becomes registered by calling the object's `addAdjustmentListener()` method. As with most events, an adjustment event is delivered to its listeners after the operation has taken place.

The Value Property

The value property of an adjustment event holds the new value of the adjustable object. This value will always be within a range that's associated with the adjustable object. See the `Adjustable` interface for more details.

Adjustment Types

The adjustment type describes how the adjustable's value was changed. The value can be increased/decreased by a *block* or *unit* amount. A block is typically associated with a page and a unit with a line in a document. Therefore, if the user clicks the adjustable object to view the next page, a BLOCK_INCREMENT adjustment event is fired. Similarly, if the user clicks the adjustable object to view a previous line, a UNIT_DECREMENT adjustment event is fired.

Finally, an adjustable object may allow the user to continuously adjust the value (e.g., to smoothly scroll through the document). In this case, the adjustable object fires TRACK adjustment events.

Adjustment Event Flow

Figure 16 shows how adjustment events typically flow through the system. First, the event is fired by a component peer in response to some user gesture. This event is posted on the event queue (see EventQueue). When the event makes its way to the front of the queue, it is given to the component via its dispatch-Event() method. The main purpose of this method is to discard the event if the adjustment event type is not enabled or if there are no adjustment event listeners. Otherwise, the dispatchEvent() method calls process-Event(), which in turn calls different methods depending on the event type. Since this is an adjustment event, processAdjustment-Event() is called. The main purpose of this method is to notify adjustment event listeners.

A component can override processAd-justmentEvent() to process adjustment

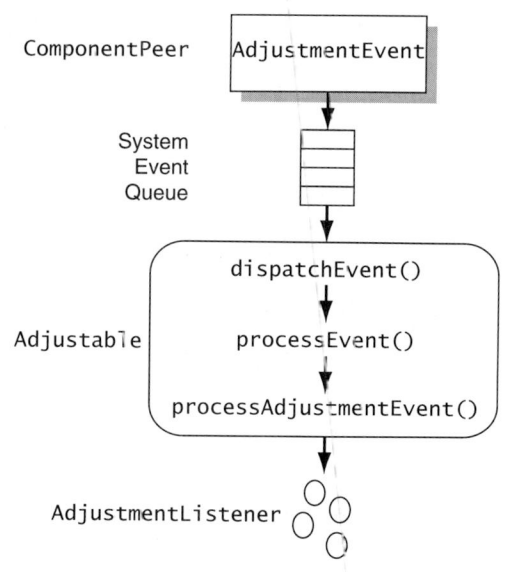

FIGURE 16: Adjustment Event Flow.

events before they are delivered to its listeners. The overridden method should call super.processAdjustmentEvent() to ensure that events are dispatched to the component's listeners

---

MEMBER SUMMARY	
Constructor	
AdjustmentEvent()	Constructs an AdjustmentEvent instance.
Property Methods	
getAdjustable()	Retrieves the adjustable object that fired this event.
getAdjustmentType()	Retrieves the adjustment event's adjustment type.
getValue()	Retrieves the adjustment event's value.
	Continued

A
B
C
D
E
F
G
H
I
J
K
L
M
N
O
P
Q
R
S
T
U
V
W
X
Y
Z

MEMBER SUMMARY

Adjustment Event Id Constants

ADJUSTMENT_FIRST	Constant specifying the first id in the range of adjustment event ids.
ADJUSTMENT_LAST	Constant specifying the last id in the range of adjustment event ids.
ADJUSTMENT_VALUE_CHANGED	Event id indicating that an adjustment event occurred.

Adjustment Types

BLOCK_DECREMENT	Adjustment type indicating a block decrement.
BLOCK_INCREMENT	Adjustment type indicating a block increment.
TRACK	Adjustment type indicating a tracking change.
UNIT_DECREMENT	Adjustment type indicating a unit decrement.
UNIT_INCREMENT	Adjustment type indicating a unit increment.

Debugging Method

paramString()	Generates a string representing the adjustment event's state.

See Also

AdjustmentListener, java.awt.Adjustable, java.awt.AWTEvent,
java.awt.Component.dispatchEvent(), java.awt.Component.processEvent(),
java.awt.Scrollbar, java.awt.ScrollPane.

Example

This example demonstrates how to get adjustment events from a component that fires them. The example creates a horizontal scrollbar and listens for adjustment events from the scrollbar. In response to an adjustment event, the specifics of the event are printed. See Figure 17.

For an example of how to create a component that fires adjustment events, see Adjustable.

FIGURE 17: AdjustmentEvent.

```java
import java.awt.*;
import java.awt.event.*;

class Main extends Frame implements AdjustmentListener {
    Main() {
        super("AdjustmentEvent Example");
        Scrollbar sb = new Scrollbar(Scrollbar.HORIZONTAL);

        // Listen for adjustment events.
        sb.addAdjustmentListener(this);

        add(sb, BorderLayout.CENTER);
        pack();
```

```
        show();
    }
    public void adjustmentValueChanged(AdjustmentEvent evt) {
        System.out.println("adjustable: "+evt.getAdjustable());
        switch (evt.getAdjustmentType()) {
          case AdjustmentEvent.BLOCK_DECREMENT:
            System.out.print("BLOCK_DECREMENT");
            break;
          case AdjustmentEvent.BLOCK_INCREMENT:
            System.out.print("BLOCK_INCREMENT");
            break;
          case AdjustmentEvent.TRACK:
            System.out.print("TRACK");
            break;
          case AdjustmentEvent.UNIT_DECREMENT:
            System.out.print("UNIT_DECREMENT");
            break;
          case AdjustmentEvent.UNIT_INCREMENT:
            System.out.print("UNIT_INCREMENT");
            break;
        }
        System.out.println("  ("+evt.getValue()+")");
    }

    public static void main(String args[]) {
        new Main();
    }
}
```

ADJUSTMENT_FIRST

PURPOSE	Constant specifying the first id in the range of adjustment event ids.
SYNTAX	`public static final int ADJUSTMENT_FIRST`
DESCRIPTION	All adjustment event ids must be greater than or equal to `ADJUSTMENT_FIRST` (value 601).
SEE ALSO	`ADJUSTMENT_LAST`.
EXAMPLE	See `java.awt.Component.processEvent()`.

ADJUSTMENT_LAST

PURPOSE	Constant specifying the last id in the range of adjustment event ids.
SYNTAX	`public static final int ADJUSTMENT_LAST`
DESCRIPTION	All adjustment event ids must be less than or equal to `ADJUSTMENT_LAST` (value 601).

A
B
C
D
E
F
G
H
I
J
K
L
M
N
O
P
Q
R
S
T
U
V
W
X
Y
Z

ADJUSTMENT_VALUE_CHANGED

SEE ALSO	ADJUSTMENT_FIRST.
EXAMPLE	See `java.awt.Component.processEvent()`.

ADJUSTMENT_VALUE_CHANGED

PURPOSE	Event id indicating that an adjustment event occurred.
SYNTAX	`public static final int ADJUSTMENT_VALUE_CHANGED`
DESCRIPTION	All scrollable objects in the AWT fire adjustment events with this id (value 601).
SEE ALSO	`AdjustmentEvent()`.
EXAMPLE	See the `java.awt.ScrollPane` class example.

AdjustmentEvent()

PURPOSE	Constructs an `AdjustmentEvent` instance.
SYNTAX	`public AdjustmentEvent(Adjustable source, int id, int adjType, int value)`
DESCRIPTION	This constructor constructs a new adjustment event instance with `source` as the object firing this event. `value` is the new value of the adjustable object `source`. At present, there is only one adjustable event id, so `id` must be set to ADJUSTMENT_VALUE_CHANGED.
	After the adjustment event is created, the source object can distribute the event to its listeners by calling `AWTEventMulticaster.adjustment-ValueChanged()`. If the event is not created by `source`, the creator can deliver the event to the source component either by posting the event to the event queue (see `EventQueue.postEvent()`) or by calling the source component's `Component.dispatchEvent()` method directly.

PARAMETERS

`adjType`	One of the adjustment types.
`id`	Must be ADJUSTMENT_VALUE_CHANGED.
`source`	The non-`null` adjustable object that is firing this adjustment event.
`value`	The new value that must be in the range `source.getMinimum()` and `source.getMaximum()`.

SEE ALSO	ADJUSTMENT_VALUE_CHANGED, BLOCK_INCREMENT, BLOCK_DECREMENT, `getAdjustable()`, `getValue()`, `java.awt.AWTEvent.getID()`, `java.util.EventObject.getSource()`, TRACK, UNIT_DECREMENT, UNIT_INCREMENT.
EXAMPLE	See the `java.awt.ScrollPane` class example.

BLOCK_DECREMENT

PURPOSE	Adjustment type indicating a block decrement.
SYNTAX	`public static final int BLOCK_DECREMENT`
DESCRIPTION	A block is typically associated with a page in a document. Therefore, if the user clicks the adjustable object to view the previous page, a BLOCK_DECREMENT (value 3) adjustment event is fired. The new value of the adjustable object can be retrieved with `getValue()`.
SEE ALSO	`BLOCK_INCREMENT, getAdjustmentType(), TRACK, UNIT_DECREMENT, UNIT_INCREMENT`.
EXAMPLE	See the class example.

BLOCK_INCREMENT

PURPOSE	Adjustment type indicating a block increment.
SYNTAX	`public static final int BLOCK_INCREMENT`
DESCRIPTION	A block is typically associated with a page in a document. Therefore, if the user clicks the adjustable object to view the next page, a BLOCK_INCREMENT (value 4) adjustment event is fired. The new value of the adjustable object can be retrieved with `getValue()`.
SEE ALSO	`BLOCK_DECREMENT, getAdjustmentType(), TRACK, UNIT_DECREMENT, UNIT_INCREMENT`.
EXAMPLE	See the class example.

getAdjustable()

PURPOSE	Retrieves the adjustable object that fired this event.
SYNTAX	`public Adjustable getAdjustable()`
DESCRIPTION	This method returns the adjustable object that fired the adjustment event. This is the same object returned by `EventObject.getSource()`.
RETURNS	A non-`null` adjustable object.
SEE ALSO	`java.util.EventObject.getSource()`.
EXAMPLE	See the class example.

A
B
C
D
E
F
G
H
I
J
K
L
M
N
O
P
Q
R
S
T
U
V
W
X
Y
Z

getAdjustmentType()

PURPOSE	Retrieves the adjustment event's adjustment type.
SYNTAX	`public int getAdjustmentType()`
DESCRIPTION	The adjustment type describes how the adjustable's value was changed. See the class description for more details.
RETURNS	One of the five adjustment types.
SEE ALSO	`BLOCK_DECREMENT, BLOCK_INCREMENT, TRACK, UNIT_DECREMENT, UNIT_INCREMENT.`
EXAMPLE	See the class example.

getValue()

PURPOSE	Retrieves the adjustment event's value.
SYNTAX	`public int getValue()`
DESCRIPTION	The value property of an adjustment event holds the new value of the adjustable object. This value will always be within a range that's associated with the adjustable object. See the `Adjustable` interface for more details.
RETURNS	The adjustment event's value.
EXAMPLE	See the class example.

paramString()

PURPOSE	Generates a string representing the adjustment event's state.
SYNTAX	`public String paramString()`
DESCRIPTION	The returned string contains the name of the adjustment type and the value. A subclass of this class should override this method and return a concatenation of its state with the results of `super.paramString()`. This method is called by the `AWTEvent.toString()` method and is typically used for debugging.
RETURNS	A non-`null` string representing the adjustment event's state.
OVERRIDES	`java.awt.AWTEvent.paramString().`
SEE ALSO	`java.awt.AWTEvent.toString(), java.lang.Object.toString().`
EXAMPLE	See the `java.awt.AWTEvent` class example.

B
C
D
E
F
G
H
I
J
K
L
M
N
O
P
Q
R
S
T
U
V
W
X
Y
Z

TRACK

PURPOSE	Adjustment type indicating a tracking change.
SYNTAX	`public static final int TRACK`
DESCRIPTION	An adjustable object may allow the user to continuously adjust the value (e.g., to smoothly scroll through the document). In this case, the adjustable object fires TRACK (value 5) adjustment events. The new value of the adjustable object can be retrieved with `getValue()`.
SEE ALSO	BLOCK_DECREMENT, BLOCK_INCREMENT, getAdjustmentType(), UNIT_DECREMENT, UNIT_INCREMENT.
EXAMPLE	See the class example.

UNIT_DECREMENT

PURPOSE	Adjustment type indicating a unit decrement.
SYNTAX	`public static final int UNIT_DECREMENT`
DESCRIPTION	A unit is typically associated with a line in a document. Therefore, if the user clicks the adjustable object to view the previous line, a UNIT_DECREMENT (value 2) adjustment event is fired. The new value of the adjustable object can be retrieved with `getValue()`.
SEE ALSO	BLOCK_DECREMENT, BLOCK_INCREMENT, getAdjustmentType(), TRACK, UNIT_INCREMENT.
EXAMPLE	See the class example.

UNIT_INCREMENT

PURPOSE	Adjustment type indicating a unit increment.
SYNTAX	`public static final int UNIT_INCREMENT`
DESCRIPTION	A unit is typically associated with a line in a document. Therefore, if the user clicks the adjustable object to view the next line, a UNIT_INCREMENT (value 1) adjustment event is fired. The new value of the adjustable object can be retrieved with `getValue()`.
SEE ALSO	BLOCK_DECREMENT, BLOCK_INCREMENT, getAdjustmentType(), TRACK, UNIT_DECREMENT.
EXAMPLE	See the class example.

A
B
C
D
E
F
G
H
I
J
K
L
M
N
O
P
Q
R
S
T
U
V
W
X
Y
Z

AdjustmentListener

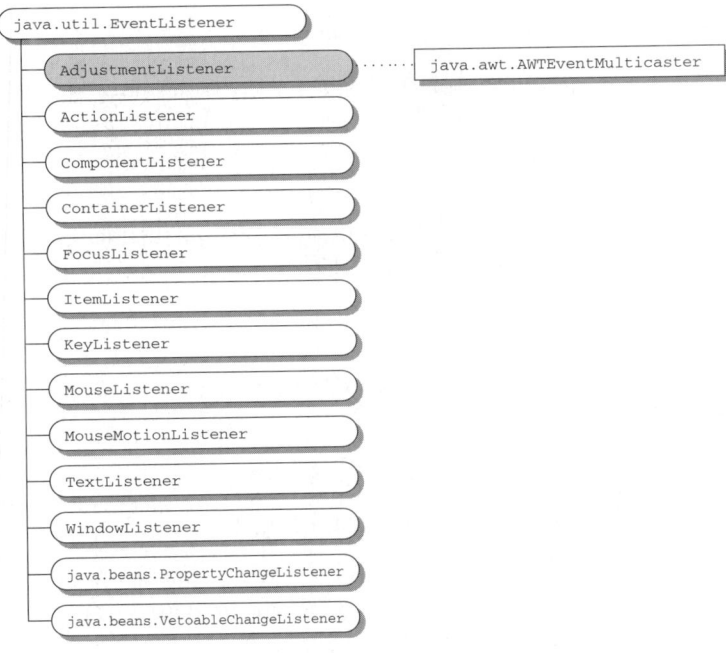

Syntax

`public interface AdjustmentListener extends EventListener`

Description

When an object (listener) wishes to receive adjustment events from an adjustable object (the source object), two things must be done:

1. The listener must implement this interface and the `adjustmentValueChanged()` method required by this interface.
2. The listener must be registered with the source object by making a call to the source object's `addAdjustmentListener()` method.

In the AWT, both the `Scrollbar` and `ScrollPane` components generate adjustment events (more accurately, the `ScrollPane` component has two adjustable objects that generate the adjustment events). See `AdjustmentEvent` for more information about adjustment events

---

MEMBER SUMMARY

Adjustment Event Callback Method
adjustmentValueChanged()   Called after the value of an adjustable object changes.

A
B
C
D
E
F
G
H
I
J
K
L
M
N
O
P
Q
R
S
T
U
V
W
X
Y
Z

See Also

AdjustmentEvent, java.awt.Adjustable, java.awt.AWTEvent,
java.awt.AWTEventMulticaster, java.awt.Scrollbar, java.awt.ScrollPane,
java.util.EventListener.

Example

This example implements a happy/ sad face meter. The scrollbar is used to adjust the happiness/sadness of the face. See Figure 18.

The class Face has a setSmile() method that takes a real number from 0 to 1. The higher the value, the happier the face. The lower the value, the sadder the face.

FIGURE 18: **AdjustmentListener.**

```java
import java.awt.*;
import java.awt.event.*;

public class Main extends
Frame implements AdjustmentListener {
    Scrollbar sb = new Scrollbar(
        Scrollbar.HORIZONTAL, 99, 1, 0, 100);
    Face face = new Face();

    Main() {
        super("AdjustmentListener Example");

        // Listen for events
        sb.addAdjustmentListener(this);

        // Layout components
        add(face, BorderLayout.CENTER);
        add(sb, BorderLayout.SOUTH);
        setSize(300, 300);
        show();
    }

    // Handle adjustment events.
    public void adjustmentValueChanged(AdjustmentEvent evt) {
        face.setSmile((evt.getValue()-50)/50.0);
    }
```

```
            public static void main(String args[]) {
                new Main();
            }
        }

        class Face extends Component {
            double smile = 1.0;

            public void paint(Graphics g) {
                int size = getSize().width;

                // Keep it square
                if (size > getSize().height) {
                    size = getSize().height;
                }

                // Paint yellow.
                g.setColor(Color.yellow);
                g.fillOval(0, 0, size-1, size-1);

                // Paint outline
                g.setColor(Color.black);
                g.drawOval(0, 0, size-1, size-1);
                g.drawOval(1, 1, size-2, size-2);

                // Paint eyes.
                int eyew = (int)(size * .18);
                int eyeh = Math.abs((int)(size * .36 * smile));
                g.fillOval(size/3-eyew/2, size/3-eyeh/2, eyew, eyeh);
                g.fillOval(size*2/3-eyew/2, size/3-eyeh/2, eyew, eyeh);

                // Paint mouth.
                int mouthw = size/3+eyew;
                int mouthh = Math.abs((int)(size * .4 * smile));
                int startAngle = smile < 0 ? 0 : 180;
                int mouthy = size*2/3-mouthh/2;

                // If frown, move rectangle lower.
                if (smile < 0) {
                    mouthy += mouthh/2;
                }
                g.drawArc((size-mouthw)/2, mouthy, mouthw, mouthh,
                    startAngle, 180);
                g.drawArc((size-mouthw)/2, mouthy+1, mouthw, mouthh,
                    startAngle, 180);
            }

            // -1.0 is a frown; 1.0 is a smile.
            public void setSmile(double smile) {
                this.smile = smile;
                repaint();
            }
        }
```

A
B
C
D
E
F
G
H
I
J
K
L
M
N
O
P
Q
R
S
T
U
V
W
X
Y
Z

adjustmentValueChanged()

PURPOSE   Called after the value of an adjustable object changes.

SYNTAX   `public void adjustmentValueChanged(AdjustmentEvent evt)`

DESCRIPTION   This method is called after the value in the source adjustable object changes.

PARAMETERS

   evt   The non-`null` adjustment event.

EXAMPLE   See the class example.

A
B
C
D
E
F
G
H
I
J
K
L
M
N
O
P
Q
R
S
T
U
V
W
X
Y
Z

```
java.lang.Object

    java.awt.Component        ○

        java.awt.Container        ○

            java.awt.Panel

                Applet
```

Syntax

```
public class Applet extends Panel
```

Description

Applets and Applet Contexts

An *applet* is basically a specialized panel (see `Panel`) that is embedded in a specialized component container called an *applet context*. An applet context can be a Web browser or other type of application that can display applets. It can contain more than one applet. An applet implements a number of methods that the applet context calls when it wants to initialize, start, stop, or destroy the applet. An applet also has access to a number of methods for retrieving resources such as images and audio clips based on URLs. Although these methods do not provide any more functionality that is available by other Java classes, they have been specially designed to be convenient to use by an applet. An applet can also access applet context information, such as the URL of the document containing the applet and, in some cases, control the applet context, such as to display a status message.

Handling Events and Painting

An applet is a subclass of `Panel`, so you handle events in an applet just as you do events in a component. See the `Component` and `AWTEvent` classes for more information on event handling. Similarly, an applet paints itself in exactly the same way that a component paints itself. That is, it overrides the `paint()` and `update()` methods. See the `Component` class for more information.

As a subclass of `Panel`, an applet can hold embedded components. The default layout manager of an applet is a flow layout (see `FlowLayout`).

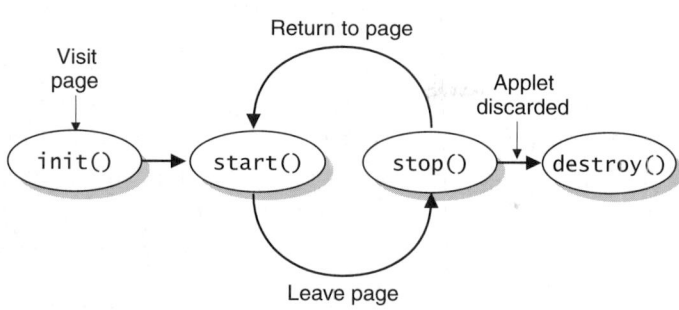

Visit page

Return to page

Applet discarded

Leave page

FIGURE 19: Applet Transitions.

States

An applet can be in an *active* or *inactive* state. When the applet is first loaded, it is in the inactive state. When the applet is first displayed on the screen, it becomes active. The applet then moves between the active and inactive states until it is destroyed by the applet context. Exactly what causes the applet to become active or inactive is up to the applet context. For example, the applet context might decide to make the applet inactive if the applet is scrolled out of view. Or it might make the applet inactive if the user views another document and leaves the document with the applet. Or it might make the applet inactive if the user clicks a special button. Figure 19 shows the transitions that an applet can go through.

Creating an Applet

An applet is created by declaring a class that extends from the Applet class. The applet then overrides one or more methods to implement the behavior. There are only six methods that can be overridden, any of which are optional: destroy(), init(), start(), stop(), get-AppletInfo(), and getParameterInfo(). The init() method is called just after the applet is loaded. The start() method is called just after the applet becomes active. The stop() method is called just after the applet becomes inactive. The destroy() method is called just before the applet context destroys the applet. The getAppletInfo() and getParameter-Info() methods return some textual information about the applet and are typically called by the applet context when the user wants to display the information.

Serialization of an Applet

An applet can be serialized and reconstituted from its serialized form to create another instance of the applet. After an applet context reconstitutes an applet, it invokes start() on it. Since the applet context calls start() directly, the applet's init(), start(), and stop() methods should have been called, in that order, before the applet was serialized, thus ensuring that the applet is in the stopped state when it gets reconstituted. See the description of the object attribute in Table 2 for details on serialized applets.

Code and Document Bases

An applet can fetch resources by way of a URL object. If it is desirable to fetch the applet using a relative URL, then there are two prefixes available to the applet: *code base* and *document base*. The code base is the URL prefix that contains the applet code. For example, suppose an applet were located at http://www.sun.com/applets/Main.class. The

A
B
C
D
E
F
G
H
I
J
K
L
M
N
O
P
Q
R
S
T
U
V
W
X
Y
Z

code base would be `http://www.sun.com/applets/`. The code base is typically used to fetch resources specific to the applet, such as icons and configuration information.

The document base is the URL prefix that contains the document that contains the applet. For example, suppose the document containing the applet were located at `http://www.sun.com/products/sparcstation/index.html`. The document base would be `http://www.sun.com/products/sparcstation/`. The document base is typically used to fetch resources specific to the document. For example, if some animation was designed for a particular HTML document, the animation images would typically be located somewhere relative to that document.

Archives

A single applet may consist of multiple class files and may make use of resources such as images and audio clips. A network connection is created to download each of these files and resources when the applet or applet context needs one of these files. To improve download time, you can package all of the class files and resources needed by the applet into one or more *archives*. An archive is downloaded using a single network connection. Subsequent requests for files and resources are satisfied by using the contents of the archives. If the files or resources are not in the archives, they are downloaded by creating new network connections.

Java Archive (JAR) specifies a platform-independent file format for archives. The Java archive tool, `jar`, available on Solaris and Windows platforms, allows you to create a JAR archive using multiple class and resource (such as image and sound) files.

See `http://java.sun.com/products/jdk/1.1/docs/guide/jar/` for details on JAR and the `jar` command.

Digests and Signed Applets

JAR allows you not only to package multiple files into a single archive for quicker downloads, but also to sign or provide a digest of individual files within the archive. This allows the applet context (either a browser or applet viewer) to verify the integrity of individual files and/or determine the identity of the supplier of the file.

A message digest algorithm accepts a sequence of bytes and produces a compact representation of it, called a *digest*. You cannot reproduce the original stream of bytes from the digest, but you can use the digest to verify whether a sequence of bytes has been modified (by recalculating the sequence's digest and comparing it with the original digest). Popular message digest algorithms supported by JAR include MD5 and SHA. A single file can have both MD5 and SHA digests.

Supplying a digest with a file allows the receiver of the file to verify its integrity. However, someone could have substituted both the file and its digest, thereby providing to the receiver information different from what was intended by its supplier. JAR also provides support for signing individual files within an archive. Signature specifications supported by JAR include RSA, DSA, and PGP. Using one of these algorithms, the sender can "sign" the file with a digital signature. The signed file contains information that can subsequently be used to verify the identity of the signer.

Parameters

An applet context can pass parameters to an applet. Parameters are simply string names associated with an arbitrary string value. The applet retrieves a parameter using the `getParameter()` method.

The Applet HTML Tag

Two HTML tags are used to embed an applet in an HTML document: `<applet>` and `<param>`. The two tags are typically used as follows:

```
<applet name=Main codebase=http://www.sun.com code=Main width=300 height=200>
<param name=name1 value="value1">
<param name=name2 value="value2">
<param name=name3 value="value3">

If you don't have a Java enabled browser ... get one.

<a href="http://www.sun.com"><IMG SRC="javacup.gif" height=60 width=60 alt="get
Java"></a>
</applet>
```

A Java-enabled browser recognizes the `<applet>` tag and interprets everything up to the `</applet>` tags. Between the `<applet>` and `</applet>` tags, it recognizes only `<param>` tags and ignores everything else. A non-Java-enabled browser ignores the `<applet>`, `</applet>`, and `<param>` tags and interprets everything else. In this way, you can set up an HTML document that serves up the Java applet in a Java-enabled browser and displays something else for a non-Java-enabled browser. Table 2 lists the attributes of the `<applet>` and `<param>` tags.

Mandatory Attributes of the `<applet>` Tag

code	Specifies the class name or class filename of the applet. The code tag specifies only the name of the class file and cannot contain any part of the path to the class file. The class file is in the directory specified by the `codebase` tag or in one of the archive files specified by the `archive` tag. Either the `code` attribute or the `object` attribute must be present. If both attributes are present, the `object` attribute is ignored.
height	Specifies the initial height in pixels of the applet's display area.

Continued

TABLE 2:   Attributes of the `<applet>` and `<param>` Tags.

object	Specifies the filename containing the serialized applet. The browser or applet viewer runs the applet by first deserializing it and then invoking the `start()` method. Note that the `init()` method will not be invoked on it, so before serializing the applet, you must first call `init()` on the applet and then call `start()` and `stop()` on it. Any attributes or parameters available to the original applet before it was serialized are not available to this applet. This applet has access only to the attributes and parameters available to this instance of the applet. The file is in the directory specified by the `codebase` tag or in one of the archive files specified by the `archive` tag. Either the `code` attribute or the `object` attribute must be present. If both attributes are present, the `object` attribute is ignored.
width	Specifies the initial width in pixels of the applet's display area.

Optional Attributes of the \<applet\> Tag

align	Specifies the alignment of the applet. Its possible values are left, right, top, texttop, middle, absmiddle, baseline, bottom, and absbottom.
alt	Specifies the text to display if the browser understands the `applet` tag but for some reason cannot run Java applets.
archive	Specifies a comma-separated list of archive files in JAR format. Each archive file contains classes and other files (such as images and audio files) used by the applet. The archive files are in the directory specified by the `codebase` attribute.
codebase	Specifies the applet's code base. This base can be either any absolute URL or a URL relative to the document containing the applet. This attribute is optional and defaults to "."(the same directory as the document). Applets that use the same `codebase` attribute share the same classloader.
hspace	Specifies the horizontal space on the left and right sides of the applet.
name	Specifies the name of the applet. An applet can name itself, thereby allowing other applets to retrieve a reference to it. This attribute is equivalent to specifying a parameter with the name "name". Therefore an applet can retrieve its name by calling `getParameter("name")`. This attribute is optional and defaults to `null`.
vspace	Specifies the vertical space on the top and bottom of the applet.

Attributes of the \<param\> Tag

name	Specifies the name of the parameter. The name must be different from the names of other parameters in the same pair of \<applet\> and \</applet\> tags. This attribute is mandatory. A special parameter called "name" is automatically supported by all applet contexts and is the name of the applet. There are two ways to name an applet: through the name attribute of the applet tag or by specifying a parameter called "name".
value	Specifies a string that is associated with the parameter name. This attribute is mandatory.

TABLE 2:   **Attributes of the \<applet\> and \<param\> Tags.**

MEMBER SUMMARY

Methods to Override

destroy()	Called by the applet context to destroy the applet.
init()	Called by the applet context just after the applet is loaded.
start()	Called by the applet context just after the applet is made active.
stop()	Called by the applet context just after the applet is made inactive.
getParameterInfo()	Retrieves information about parameters that the applet recognizes.
getAppletInfo()	Retrieves a string containing information about the applet.

State Method

isActive()	Retrieves the active state of the applet.

Audio and Image Methods

getAudioClip()	Retrieves an audio clip from a URL.
getImage()	Retrieves an image at a URL.
play()	Fetches and plays an audio clip.

Parameter Methods

getCodeBase()	Retrieves the applet's code base URL.
getDocumentBase()	Retrieves the applet's document base URL.
getParameter()	Retrieves the value of a parameter.

Applet Context Methods

getAppletContext()	Retrieves the applet context.
showStatus()	Displays a message in the applet context.

Locale Method

getLocale()	Retrieves this applet's locale.

Size Method

resize()	Resizes the bounds of the applet.

Stub Method

setStub()	Sets the applet's stub.

B
C
D
E
F
G
H
I
J
K
L
M
N
O
P
Q
R
S
T
U
V
W
X
Y
Z

Example

This example implements a game. The goal is to catch duke while he's jumping around. If you catch him, he plays a sound. You also can drag him around. If the applet is active, the game plays some background music using the loop() method so that it plays continuously until stopped. All the images and sounds are fetched relative to the document base. See Figure 20.

A button is created and embedded in the applet. If you click the button, `getApp-pletContext().showDocument()` is called to display the source code. Since the source code is typically located with the compiled applet code, `getCodeBase()` is used to locate the source code.

To eliminate flashing, the applet first paints the duke image into a second buffer and then displays the second buffer on the screen. To keep things simple, the applet paints the entire buffer every time Duke moves. It is much more efficient to paint only the parts of the image that have changed.

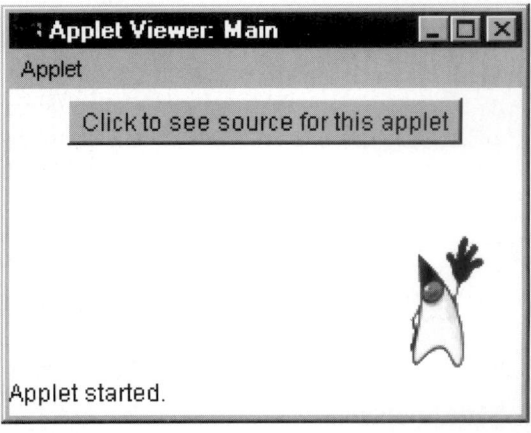

FIGURE 20:   Catch Duke Applet.

The following is the HTML source for the applet. It uses an archive file `main.jar` to store the class files, image files, and audio files.

```
<applet name="Applet Example" code=Main archive=main.jar width=200 height=100>
<param name=image value=duke.gif>
<param name=audio value=oww.au>
<param name=bg-audio value=bgmusic.au>
<param name=delay value=1000>
<param name=source value=Main.java>
</applet>
```

The following is the source for the applet:

```
import java.applet.*;
import java.awt.*;
import java.awt.event.*;
import java.net.*;

public class Main extends Applet implements Runnable, ActionListener {
    Image backBuffer;        // image for double-buffering.
    Graphics backBufferG;    // graphics context for double-buffer.

    AudioClip bgAudio;
    Image image;
    int imageX, imageY;      // current position of image.

    // Applet State Methods
    public void init() {
        backBuffer = createImage(400, 200);
        backBufferG = backBuffer.getGraphics();

        // load resources
        image = getImage(getDocumentBase(), getParameter("image"));
        bgAudio = getAudioClip(getDocumentBase(), getParameter("bg-audio"));

        Button b = new Button("Click to see source for this applet");
        b.addActionListener(this);
```

```
        add(b);
        addMouseListener(new MouseEventHandler());
        addMouseMotionListener(new MouseMotionEventHandler());

        resize(400, 200);
    }
    public void start() {
        startTickThread(true);
        bgAudio.loop();
    }
    public void stop() {
        startTickThread(false);
        bgAudio.stop();
    }

    public void destroy() {
        backBufferG.dispose(); // get rid of the double buffer.
        backBuffer.flush();
        image.flush();
    }

    // Paint Methods
    public void paint(Graphics g) {
        update(g);
    }

    public void update(Graphics g) {
        int w = getSize().width;
        int h = getSize().height;

        // Create the double-buffer if needed or enlarge.
        if (backBuffer == null
                || backBuffer.getWidth(this) < w
                || backBuffer.getHeight(this) < h) {
            backBuffer = createImage(w, h);
            backBufferG = backBuffer.getGraphics();
        }
        backBufferG.clearRect(0, 0, w, h);
        backBufferG.drawImage(image, imageX, imageY, this);
        g.drawImage(backBuffer, 0, 0, this);
    }

    // Event listeners

    public class MouseEventHandler extends MouseAdapter {
        public void mousePressed(MouseEvent evt) {
            int x = evt.getX(), y = evt.getY();
            if (x > imageX && x < imageX + image.getWidth(Main.this)
                && y > imageY && y < imageY + image.getHeight(Main.this)) {
                startTickThread(false);
                imageX = x-image.getWidth(Main.this)/2;
                imageY = y-image.getHeight(Main.this)/2;
                getAppletContext().showStatus("OWWW! Ya got me! Let go!");
                play(getDocumentBase(), getParameter("audio"));
                repaint();
            }
        }
        public void mouseReleased(MouseEvent evt) {
            if (tickThread == null) {
                startTickThread(true);
```

```
                                    getAppletContext().showStatus("Nah, Nah!");
                                }
                            }
                        }

                        class MouseMotionEventHandler extends MouseMotionAdapter {
                            public void mouseDragged(MouseEvent evt) {
                                int x = evt.getX(), y = evt.getY();
                                if (tickThread == null) {
                                    imageX = x-image.getWidth(Main.this)/2;
                                    imageY = y-image.getHeight(Main.this)/2;
                                    repaint();
                                }
                            }
                        }

                        // Called when the "See Source" button is pressed.
                        public void actionPerformed(ActionEvent evt) {
                            try {
                                getAppletContext().showDocument(new URL(getCodeBase(),
                                                        getParameter("source")));
                            } catch (MalformedURLException e) {
                                e.printStackTrace();
                            }
                        }

                        // Tick Thread Methods
                        Thread tickThread;
                        void startTickThread(boolean start) {
                            if (start) {
                                tickThread = new Thread(this);
                                tickThread.start();
                            } else {
                                tickThread = null;
                            }
                        }

                        public void run() {
                            int delay = Integer.parseInt(getParameter("delay"));
                            while (Thread.currentThread() == tickThread) {
                                try {
                                    imageX = (int)Math.floor(Math.random()*getSize().width);
                                    imageX = Math.min(imageX,
                                                    getSize().width-image.getWidth(this));
                                    imageY = (int)Math.floor(Math.random()*getSize().height);
                                    imageY = Math.min(imageY,
                                                    getSize().height-image.getHeight(this));
                                    repaint();
                                    Thread.sleep(delay);
                                } catch (InterruptedException e) {
                                }
                            }
                        }

                        public String getAppletInfo() {
                            return "Patrick Chan and Rosanna Lee (c) 1997";
                        }

                        String[][] parameterInfo = {
                            {"image", "document-based url", "image to move around"},
```

```
            {"audio", "document-based url", "sound to play when image is hit"},
            {"bg-audio", "document-based url", "background music"},
            {"audio", "code-based url", "sound to play when image is hit"},
            {"delay", "integer", "delay between moves in milliseconds"},
        };
        public String[][] getParameterInfo() {
            return parameterInfo;
        }
    }
```

A
B
C
D
E

destroy()

F

PURPOSE	Called by the applet context to destroy the applet.
SYNTAX	`public void destroy()`

G

DESCRIPTION   This method is called by the applet context when it decides to destroy the applet. This may occur if the applet context is low on space or when it exits. A subclass should override this method if it needs to dispose of any resources created by the applet. For example, if the applet creates a thread to do some background work, this method should be overridden so as to destroy the thread.

H

I

J

K

If an applet is active, the applet context will always call the stop() method before calling the destroy() method.

L

M

SEE ALSO   stop().

N

EXAMPLE   See the class example.

O

P

getAppletContext()

Q

R

PURPOSE	Retrieves the applet context.
SYNTAX	`public AppletContext getAppletContext()`

S

T

DESCRIPTION   See the class description for more information about the applet context.

U

RETURNS   The non-null reference to the applet context.

V

SEE ALSO   AppletContext.

W

EXAMPLE   See the class example.

X

Y

getAppletInfo()

Z

PURPOSE   Retrieves a string containing information about the applet.

SYNTAX	`public String getAppletInfo()`
DESCRIPTION	This method can be overridden by an applet to return information about itself. This returned string typically includes information about the author, version, and copyright.
RETURNS	A possibly `null` string containing information about the applet.
EXAMPLE	See the class example.

getAudioClip()

PURPOSE	Retrieves an audio clip from a URL.
SYNTAX	`public AudioClip getAudioClip(URL url)` `public AudioClip getAudioClip(URL url, String name)`
DESCRIPTION	This method retrieves an audio clip at the URL `url`. If `name` is specified, the audio clip is fetched from a new URL created by appending `name` to `url`.
PARAMETERS	
`name`	The non-`null` name to append to `url`.
`url`	The non-`null` URL at which to fetch the audio clip.
RETURNS	The audio clip at `url`. Returns `null` if the audio clip cannot be found.
SEE ALSO	`AudioClip`, `java.net.URL`.
EXAMPLE	See the class example.

getCodeBase()

PURPOSE	Retrieves the applet's code base URL.
SYNTAX	`public URL getCodeBase()`
DESCRIPTION	The code base is the URL prefix that contains the applet code. For example, suppose an applet were located at `http://www.sun.com/applets/Main.class`. The code base would be `http://www.sun.com/applets/`. The code base is typically used to fetch resources specific to the applet, such as icons and configuration information.
RETURNS	The non-`null` applet's code base URL.
SEE ALSO	`getDocumentBase()`, `java.net.URL`.
EXAMPLE	See the class example.

getDocumentBase()

PURPOSE   Retrieves the applet's document base URL.

SYNTAX   `public URL getDocumentBase()`

DESCRIPTION   The document base is the URL prefix of the document that contains the applet. For example, suppose the document containing the applet was located at `http://www.sun.com/products/sparcstation/index.html`. The document base would be `http://www.sun.com/products/sparcstation/`. The document base is typically used to fetch resources specific to the document. For example, if some animation was to be designed for a particular HTML document, the animation images would typically be located somewhere relative to that document.

SEE ALSO   `getCodeBase()`, `java.net.URL`.

EXAMPLE   See the class example.

getImage()

PURPOSE   Retrieves an image at a URL.

SYNTAX   `public Image getImage(URL url)`
                   `public Image getImage(URL url, String name)`

DESCRIPTION   This method retrieves an image at the URL `url`. If `name` is specified, the image is fetched from a new URL created by appending `name` to `url`. This method returns immediately and does not actually fetch the pixels of the image. The pixels are fetched at the time they are needed (see `Image`).

                   As long as the image is found, the return image reference will not be `null`. However, an error may occur while loading the image. To check for errors, use the `Component.checkImage()` method call.

PARAMETERS
name   The non-`null` name to append to `url`.
url   The non-`null` URL at which to fetch the image.

RETURNS   The image at `url`. Returns `null` if the image cannot be found.

SEE ALSO   `java.awt.Image`, `java.awt.Component.checkImage()`, `java.net.URL`.

EXAMPLE   See the class example.

getLocale()

PURPOSE   Retrieves this applet's locale.

A
B
C
D
E
F
G
H
I
J
K
L
M
N
O
P
Q
R
S
T
U
V
W
X
Y
Z

SYNTAX	`public Locale getLocale()`
RETURNS	This method returns this applet's locale or the locale of its closest ancestor with a locale. If this applet does not have its own locale and it does not have an ancestor from which to get the locale, the default locale (`Locale.getDefault()`) is returned.
RETURNS	The applet's non-`null` locale.
OVERRIDES	`java.awt.Component.getLocale()`.
SEE ALSO	`java.awt.Component.setLocale()`, `java.util.Locale.getDefault()`.
EXAMPLE	See `java.awt.Component.getName()`.

getParameter( )

PURPOSE	Retrieves the value of a parameter.
SYNTAX	`public String getParameter(String name)`
DESCRIPTION	See the class description about applet parameters and the `param` HTML tag.
PARAMETERS	
name	The non-`null` name of the parameter value to retrieve.
RETURNS	Returns the value of the parameter; otherwise, it returns `null` if the parameter does not exist.
EXAMPLE	See the class example.

getParameterInfo( )

PURPOSE	Retrieves information about parameters that the applet recognizes.
SYNTAX	`public String[][] getParameterInfo()`
DESCRIPTION	This method is called by the applet context when it needs to display information about the applet parameters. This method returns an array of string arrays containing the desired information. Each parameter is described using three strings: the name of the parameter, the type of the parameter value (which is an arbitrary string), and a short description of the parameter.
RETURNS	A possibly `null` array of string arrays containing information about the applet parameters.
EXAMPLE	The `getParameterInfo()` method in this example describes an applet that displays an image and a message under the image:

```
String[][] parameterInfo = {
    {"location", "x y",
        "the location to display the image"},
    {"image", "url",
        "the location of the image"},
    {"message",  "string",
        "the message to display under the image"},
};
public String[][] getParameterInfo() {
        return parameterInfo;
}
```

init()

PURPOSE   Called by the applet context just after the applet is loaded.

SYNTAX   `public void init()`

DESCRIPTION   A subclass should override this method if it needs to implement behavior that
               occurs before the applet becomes active for the first time. For example, if the
               applet needs a background thread to do some work regardless of the applet's
               state, then this method should be overridden to create the thread.

SEE ALSO   `destroy()`.

EXAMPLE   See the class example.

isActive()

PURPOSE   Retrieves the active state of the applet.

SYNTAX   `public boolean isActive()`

DESCRIPTION   An applet becomes active just before the `start()` method is called and
               becomes inactive just before the `stop()` method is called.

RETURNS   `true` if the applet is active; `false` otherwise.

SEE ALSO   `start()`.

EXAMPLE   This example implements an applet that fetches a list of images. See Figure 21.
               A fetcher thread is created when the applet is loaded. When the fetcher thread
               finishes fetching an image, it calls `repaint()` to update the display, but only if
               the applet is active. Otherwise, it avoids calling `repaint()` and continues
               fetching images.

               The list of images to fetch are supplied through the parameters. The applet
               looks for parameter names of the form image*N*, where *N* starts at 0. Once a
               parameter name doesn't exist, the applet stops looking and assumes that all of
               the images have been specified.

A
B
C
D
E
F
G
H
I
J
K
L
M
N
O
P
Q
R
S
T
U
V
W
X
Y
Z

A
B
C
D
E
F
G
H
I
J
K
L
M
N
O
P
Q
R
S
T
U
V
W
X
Y
Z

```java
import java.applet.*;
import java.awt.*;

public class Main extends Applet
    implements Runnable {
    String[] imagesToFetch;
    Image[] fetchedImages;
    int fetched;    // number of fetched images.
    Thread fetcherThread;

    // Applet State Methods
    public void init() {
        int i = 0;

        while (getParameter("image"+i) != null) {
            i++;
        }
        imagesToFetch = new String[i];
        fetchedImages = new Image[i];

        if (i > 0) {
            fetcherThread = new Thread(this);
            fetcherThread.start();
        }
        for (i=0; i<imagesToFetch.length; i++) {
            imagesToFetch[i] =
                getParameter("image"+i);
        }
        resize(200, imagesToFetch.length * 70);
    }

    public void destroy() {
        fetcherThread = null;
    }

    // Paint Methods
    public void paint(Graphics g) {
        int w = getSize().width;
        int h = getSize().height;
        FontMetrics fm = g.getFontMetrics();
        int y = 0;

        for (int i=0; i<imagesToFetch.length; i++) {
            if (i < fetched) {
                g.drawImage(fetchedImages[i], 0, y, 50, 50, this);
            }
            g.drawString(imagesToFetch[i], 60, y + fm.getAscent());
            y += 70;
        }
    }

    public void run() {
        while (Thread.currentThread() == fetcherThread
                && fetched < imagesToFetch.length) {
            try {
                fetchedImages[fetched]= getImage(
                    getDocumentBase(), imagesToFetch[fetched]);
                while (!prepareImage(fetchedImages[fetched], this)) {
                    Thread.sleep(2000);
```

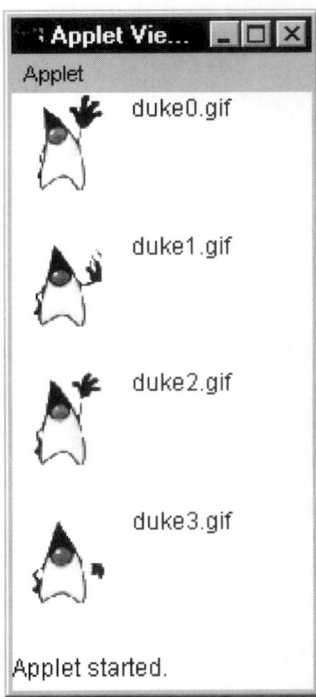

FIGURE 21:
Fetch Image Applet.

88

```
            }
            fetched++;
            if (isActive()) {
                repaint();
            }
        } catch (InterruptedException e) {
        }
    }
    }
}
```

play()

PURPOSE	Fetches and plays an audio clip.
SYNTAX	`public void play(URL url)`
	`public void play(URL url, String name)`
DESCRIPTION	This method fetches the audio clip from the URL `url` and immediately plays the audio clip. If `name` is specified, the image is fetched from a new URL created by appending `name` to `url`. This method is ignored if the audio clip could not be fetched from `url`.
PARAMETERS	
`name`	The non-`null` name to append to `url`.
`url`	The non-`null` URL from which to fetch the audio clip.
EXAMPLE	See the class example.

resize()

PURPOSE	Resizes the bounds of the applet.
SYNTAX	`public void resize(Dimension d)`
	`public void resize(int width, int height)`
DESCRIPTION	The bounds of the applet is the area in which it can paint. The `resize()` method makes a request to the applet context to resize the bounds of the applet. This request can be ignored by the applet context. The new bounds can be specified either as a width and height or as a dimension.
PARAMETERS	
`d`	The non-`null` dimension containing the new size in pixels.
`height`	The height of the new bounds in pixels.
`width`	The width of the new bounds in pixels.
OVERRIDES	`java.awt.Component.resize()`.

SEE ALSO	`java.awt.Dimension`.
EXAMPLE	See the class example.

setStub( )

PURPOSE	Sets the applet's stub.
SYNTAX	`public final void setStub(AppletStub stub)`
DESCRIPTION	The stub is used internally by the `Applet` class. It is called by the applet context just after the applet is loaded. The stub is part of the implementation of the applet context and is not used by the applet programmer.
PARAMETERS	
`stub`	The non-`null` stub.

showStatus( )

PURPOSE	Displays a message in the applet context.
SYNTAX	`public void showStatus(String msg)`
DESCRIPTION	This method can be ignored by the applet context. But typically the applet context displays `msg` in a status bar, which is often located at the bottom of its window.
PARAMETERS	
`msg`	The message to display. If `null`, the previous message is cleared.
EXAMPLE	See the class example.

start( )

PURPOSE	Called by the applet context just after the applet is made active.
SYNTAX	`public void start()`
DESCRIPTION	A subclass should override this method if it needs to implement behavior that occurs when the applet becomes active. For example, if the applet plays background music only when it is active, this method should be overridden to start the background music.
SEE ALSO	`stop()`.
EXAMPLE	See the class example.

stop()

PURPOSE   Called by the applet context just after the applet is made inactive.

SYNTAX   `public void stop()`

DESCRIPTION A subclass should override this method if it needs to implement behavior that occurs when the applet becomes inactive. For example, if the applet plays background music only when it is active, this method should be overridden to stop the background music.

If an applet is active, the applet context will always call this method before calling `destroy()`.

SEE ALSO   `destroy()`, `start()`.

EXAMPLE   See the class example.

A
B
C
D
E
F
G
H
I
J
K
L
M
N
O
P
Q
R
S
T
U
V
W
X
Y
Z

A
B
C
D
E
F
G
H
I
J
K
L
M
N
O
P
Q
R
S
T
U
V
W
X
Y
Z

AppletContext

Syntax
```
public interface AppletContext
```

Description
This interface corresponds to an applet's environment. It can be used by an applet to obtain information from the applet's environment, which is usually the browser or the applet viewer.

Figure 22 illustrates the relationship between applet contexts and applets.

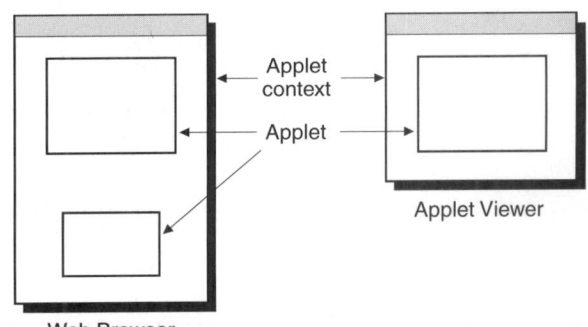

FIGURE 22: **Relationship Between Applet Contexts and Applets.**

MEMBER SUMMARY	
Audio and Image Methods	
getAudioClip()	Retrieves an audio clip at a URL.
getImage()	Retrieves an image at a URL.
Applet Methods	
getApplet()	Retrieves a reference to an applet.
getApplets()	Enumerates the accessible applets in this applet context.
Display Methods	
showDocument()	Causes the applet context to display another HTML document.
showStatus()	Displays a message in the applet context.

See Also
Applet.

Example
This example implements two kinds of applets that communicate with each other through the applet context. The master applet keeps track of a color, and the bullet applet paints an oval in the color maintained by the master. See Figures 23 and 24. The master applet has a choice

component containing several color names. Changing the selected color in the master causes all the bullet applets to redisplay their bullets in the selected color. The master applet notifies all the bullet applets by calling their repaint() method.

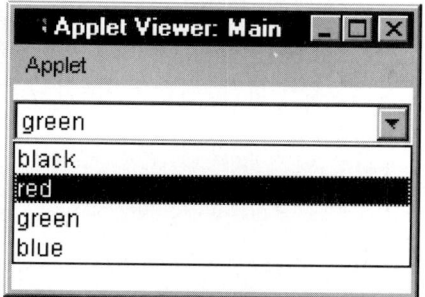

FIGURE 23:   Master Applet.

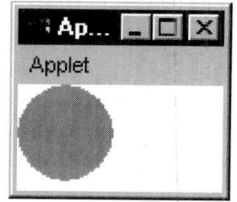

FIGURE 24:   Bullet Applet.

```java
import java.applet.*;
import java.awt.*;
import java.awt.event.*;
import java.util.*;

public class Main extends Applet implements ItemListener {
    Color color;

    public void init() {
        Choice c = new Choice();

        setLayout(new BorderLayout());
        c.addItem("black");
        c.addItem("red");
        c.addItem("green");
        c.addItem("blue");
        add(c, BorderLayout.CENTER);
        c.addItemListener(this);
    }

    public Color getColor() {
        return color;
    }

    public void itemStateChanged(ItemEvent evt) {
        Object arg = evt.getItem();
        if ("black".equals(arg)) {
            color = Color.black;
        } else if ("red".equals(arg)) {
            color = Color.red;
        } else if ("green".equals(arg)) {
            color = Color.green;
        } else if ("blue".equals(arg)) {
            color = Color.blue;
        }
        for (Enumeration e=getAppletContext().getApplets();
            e.hasMoreElements(); ) {
```

```
                    Applet a = (Applet)e.nextElement();
                    if (a != null && a != this) {
                        a.repaint();
                    }
                }
            }
        }
```

```
import java.applet.Applet;
import java.awt.*;

public class Bullet extends Applet {
    Color color = Color.black;

    public void paint(Graphics g) {
        Main applet = (Main)getAppletContext().getApplet("Master");
        g.setColor(applet.getColor());
        g.fillOval(0, 0, getSize().width-1, getSize().height-1);
    }
}
```

getApplet( )

PURPOSE   Retrieves a reference to an applet.

SYNTAX   `Applet getApplet(String appletName)`

DESCRIPTION   This method retrieves the applet with the name `appletName`. If there is more than one applet with the name `appletName`, one of them will be returned. You cannot predict which one will be returned.

PARAMETERS

  `appletName`   The name of the applet. See the `Applet` class for a description of how to name an applet.

RETURNS   A reference to the applet; otherwise, `null` if the applet does not exist.

SEE ALSO   `Applet`.

EXAMPLE   See the class example.

getApplets( )

PURPOSE   Enumerates the accessible applets in this applet context.

SYNTAX   `Enumeration getApplets()`

DESCRIPTION   This method returns an enumeration of the accessible applets in this applet context. The enumeration always includes the current applet.

Some applet references in the enumeration could be null. This can happen if applets are being added or destroyed in the applet context during the enumeration.

RETURNS A non-null enumeration of applet references. An applet reference in the enumeration can be null.

EXAMPLE This example creates three identical applets, each with a different name. The applets call getApplets() to get a list of all accessible applets. The applets then display the names of all the applets, highlighting their names in red. See Figure 25.

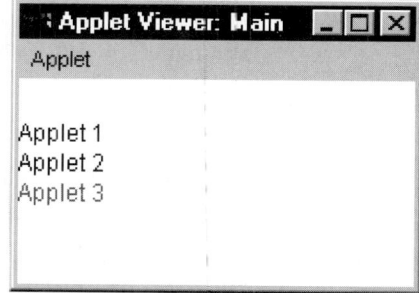

FIGURE 25:
AppletContext.getApplets().

```java
import java.applet.*;
import java.awt.*;
import java.util.*;

public class Main extends Applet {
    public void paint(Graphics g) {
        FontMetrics fm = g.getFontMetrics();
        int y = fm.getAscent() + 20;

        for (Enumeration e=getAppletContext().getApplets();
                e.hasMoreElements(); ) {
            Applet a = (Applet)e.nextElement();
            if (a == null) {
                continue;
            } else if (a == this) {
                g.setColor(Color.red);
            } else {
                g.setColor(Color.black);
            }
            if (a.getParameter("name") != null) {
                g.drawString(a.getParameter("name"), 0, y);
            } else {
                g.drawString("no name", 0, y);
            }
            y += fm.getHeight();
        }
    }
}
```

A
B
C
D
E
F
G
H
I
J
K
L
M
N
O
P
Q
R
S
T
U
V
W
X
Y
Z

getAudioClip( )

PURPOSE	Retrieves an audio clip at a URL.
SYNTAX	`AudioClip getAudioClip(URL url)`
DESCRIPTION	This method retrieves an audio clip at the URL `url`.
PARAMETERS	
`url`	The non-`null` URL from which to fetch the audio clip.
RETURNS	The audio clip at `url`. Returns `null` if the audio clip cannot be found.
SEE ALSO	`AudioClip`, `java.net.URL`.
EXAMPLE	See the `Applet` class example.

getImage( )

PURPOSE	Retrieves an image at a URL.
SYNTAX	`Image getImage(URL url)`
DESCRIPTION	This method retrieves an image at the URL `url`. It returns immediately and does not actually fetch the pixels of the image. The pixels are fetched at the time they are needed (see `Image`).
PARAMETERS	
`url`	The non-`null` URL from which to fetch the image.
RETURNS	The image at `url`. Returns `null` if the image cannot be found.
SEE ALSO	`java.awt.Image`, `java.net.URL`.
EXAMPLE	See the `Applet` class example.

showDocument( )

PURPOSE	Causes the applet context to display another HTML document.
SYNTAX	`public void showDocument(URL url)` `public void showDocument(URL url, String target)`
DESCRIPTION	This method shows a new document in a target window or frame. The frame is an HTML frame, not an AWT frame. If `target` is not specified, it defaults to `"_self"`. This method may be ignored by the applet context. Table 3 shows the list of valid target strings.

PARAMETERS

target   The name of the frame in which to display the document.

url   The non-null URL containing the document to display.

EXAMPLE   See the Applet class example.

_self	Show in current frame.
_parent	Show in parent frame.
_top	Show in topmost frame.
_blank	Show in new unnamed top-level window.
<other>	Show in new top-level window named <other>.

TABLE 3: `AppletContext.showDocument()` **Valid Target Strings.**

showStatus()

PURPOSE   Displays a message in the applet context.

SYNTAX   `public void showStatus(String msg)`

DESCRIPTION   This method can be ignored by the applet context. But typically the applet context displays msg in a status bar, which is often located at the bottom of its window.

PARAMETERS

msg   The message to display. If null, the previous message is cleared.

EXAMPLE   See the Applet class example.

A
B
C
D
E
F
G
H
I
J
K
L
M
N
O
P
Q
R
S
T
U
V
W
X
Y
Z

AppletStub

Syntax
```
public interface AppletStub
```

Description
This interface is essentially an internal interface used by the applet context. It is not normally used by applet programmers. It differs from the `AppletContext` interface mainly in that it supports methods that set and retrieve information specific for one particular applet. The applet context, on the other hand, maintains information for all the applets that it contains.

MEMBER SUMMARY	
Stub Methods	
appletResize()	Resizes the bounds of the applet.
getAppletContext()	Retrieves the applet context.
getCodeBase()	Retrieves the applet's code base URL.
getDocumentBase()	Retrieves the applet's document base URL.
getParameter()	Retrieves the value of a parameter.
isActive()	Retrieves the active state of the applet.

See Also
`AppletContext`.

Example
See the `Applet` class.

appletResize()

PURPOSE	Resizes the bounds of the applet.
SYNTAX	`void appletResize(int w, int h)`

DESCRIPTION   The bounds of the applet is the area in which it can paint. This request may be ignored. If the request is satisfied, the new bounds will have the width w and the height h.

PARAMETERS
h   The height of the new bounds in pixels.
w   The width of the new bounds in pixels.

EXAMPLE   See `Applet.resize()`.

getAppletContext( )

PURPOSE   Retrieves the applet context.

SYNTAX   `public AppletContext getAppletContext()`

DESCRIPTION   See the `Applet` class for more information about applet contexts.

RETURNS   The non-`null` reference to the applet context.

SEE ALSO   `AppletContext`.

EXAMPLE   See `Applet.getAppletContext()`.

getCodeBase( )

PURPOSE   Retrieves the applet's code base URL.

SYNTAX   `URL getCodeBase()`

DESCRIPTION   The code base is the URL prefix that contains the applet code. For example, suppose an applet were located at `http://www.sun.com/applets/Main.class`. The code base would be `http://www.sun.com/applets/`. The code base is typically used to fetch resources specific to the applet, such as icons and configuration information.

RETURNS   The non-`null` applet's code base URL.

SEE ALSO   `getDocumentBase()`, `java.net.URL`.

EXAMPLE   See `Applet.getCodeBase()`.

getDocumentBase( )

PURPOSE   Retrieves the applet's document base URL.

SYNTAX   `URL getDocumentBase()`

A
B
C
D
E
F
G
H
I
J
K
L
M
N
O
P
Q
R
S
T
U
V
W
X
Y
Z

DESCRIPTION	The document base is the URL prefix that contains the document that contains the applet. For example, suppose the document containing the applet was located at `http://www.sun.com/products/sparcstation/index.html`. The document base would be `http://www.sun.com/products/sparcsta-tion/`. The document base is typically used to fetch resources specific to the document. For example, if some animation was to be designed for a particular HTML document, the animation images would typically be located somewhere relative to that document.
SEE ALSO	`getCodeBase()`, `java.net.URL`.
EXAMPLE	See `Applet.getDocumentBase()`.

getParameter( )

PURPOSE	Retrieves the value of a parameter.
SYNTAX	`String getParameter(String name)`
DESCRIPTION	This method returns the value of the parameter identified by the name `name`.
PARAMETERS	
name	The non-`null` name of the parameter value to retrieve.
RETURNS	Returns the value of the parameter; otherwise, returns `null` if the parameter does not exist.
EXAMPLE	See `Applet.getParameter()`.

isActive( )

PURPOSE	Retrieves the active state of the applet.
SYNTAX	`boolean isActive()`
DESCRIPTION	An applet becomes active just before the `start()` method is called and becomes inactive just before the `stop()` method is called. See the `Applet` class for more information about applet states.
RETURNS	`true` if the applet is active; `false` otherwise.
SEE ALSO	`Applet.start()`.
EXAMPLE	See `Applet.isActive()`.

AreaAveragingScaleFilter

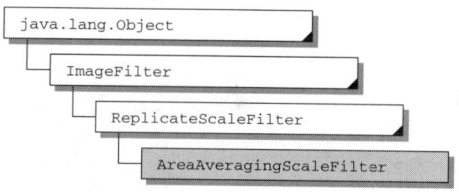

```
java.lang.Object
    ImageFilter
        ReplicateScaleFilter
            AreaAveragingScaleFilter
```

Syntax

```
public class AreaAveragingScaleFilter extends ReplicateScaleFilter
```

Description

The area averaging scale filter is an image filter that scales images, producing results that are superior to the simpler replicate scale filter (see ReplicateScaleFilter). In both filters, when an image is scaled larger, pixels are replicated to achieve "larger" pixels. However, the area averaging scale filter does an extra step of blending the new pixels with adjacent pixels. The result is an image with less "jaggies." The trade-off of using an area averaging scale filter is that it takes longer to scale the image. If the image is scaled for some animation effect, it may be better to use the simpler replicate scale filter since the higher quality scaled images may not be noticed.

This image filter is meant to be used in conjunction with a FilteredImageSource object, which assumes the responsibility for delivering an image to this image filter to scale. See ImageFilter for more information about the image filtering architecture.

For the scaling algorithm to work, the producer must deliver the pixels to the filter in top-down, left-to-right order (see ImageProducer). If the image producer cannot do this, the area averaging scale filter resorts to the simple pixel replication algorithm as implemented by the replicate scale filter.

MEMBER SUMMARY	
Constructor	
AreaAveragingScaleFilter()	Constructs an AreaAveragingScaleFilter instance.
Image Consumer Methods	
setHints()	Called by the image producer to specify how the pixels will be delivered to this image filter.
setPixels()	Called by the image producer to deliver pixels to this image filter.

A
B
C
D
E
F
G
H
I
J
K
L
M
N
O
P
Q
R
S
T
U
V
W
X
Y
Z

See Also

`ImageConsumer`.

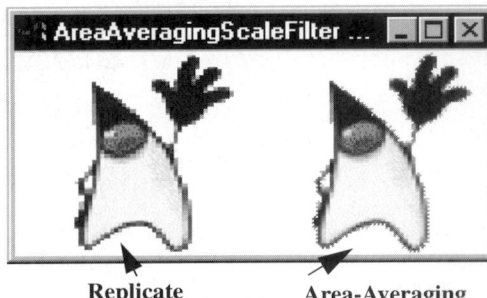

FIGURE 26:   Images loaded using `ReplicateScaleFilter` and `AreaAveragingScaleFilter`.

Example

This example allows you to compare the effects of `AreaAveragingScaleFilter` with the simpler `ReplicateScaleFilter`. The example creates a windows with two panes. The image on the left is scaled with `ReplicateScaleFilter`, and the image on the right is scaled with `AreaAveragingScaleFilter`. Figure 26 shows two examples of these windows.

```java
import java.awt.*;
import java.awt.image.*;
import java.net.*;

class Main extends Frame {
    Main(String filename) {
        super("AreaAveragingScaleFilter Example");
        Image image = null;

        if (filename != null) {
            // Retrieve the image.
            image = getToolkit().getImage(filename);

            // Ensure that the image is completely loaded since we
            // need the width and heigth information immediately.
            MediaTracker tracker = new MediaTracker(this);
            try {
                tracker.addImage(image, 0);
                tracker.waitForID(0);
            } catch (Exception e) {
                e.printStackTrace();
            }
        } else {
            // Type an X in the image.
            Font font = new Font("Serif", Font.BOLD, 72);
            FontMetrics fontM = getFontMetrics(font);
```

```
            addNotify();
            image = createImage(fontM.charWidth('X'), fontM.getHeight());
            Graphics g = image.getGraphics();
            g.setFont(new Font("Serif", Font.BOLD, 72));
            g.drawString("X", 0, fontM.getAscent());
            g.dispose();
        }

        // Layout components.
        setLayout(new GridLayout(1, 0));
        add(new ImageScaler(image, false));
        add(new ImageScaler(image, true));
        setSize(300, 300);
        show();
    }

    static public void main(String[] args) {
        if (args.length == 1) {
            new Main(args[0]);
        } else {
            new Main(null);
        }
    }
}

class ImageScaler extends Canvas {
    Image origImage;
    Image curImage;
    Dimension curSize = new Dimension(0, 0);
    boolean areaAvr;

    ImageScaler(Image image, boolean areaAvr) {
        origImage = image;
        this.areaAvr = areaAvr;
    }

    public void paint(Graphics g) {
        if (!curSize.equals(getSize())) {
            curSize = new Dimension(getSize());

            // The size has change so create a new scaled image.
            if (areaAvr) {
                curImage = createImage(
                    new FilteredImageSource(origImage.getSource(),
                    //new AreaAveragingScaleFilter(curSize.width,
                    //   curSize.height)));
                    new AreaAveragingScaleFilter(-2, curSize.height)));
            } else {
                curImage = createImage(
                    new FilteredImageSource(origImage.getSource(),
                    //new ReplicateScaleFilter(curSize.width, curSize.height)));
                    new ReplicateScaleFilter(-10, curSize.height)));
            }
        }
        g.drawImage(curImage, 0, 0, this);
    }
}
```

A
B
C
D
E
F
G
H
I
J
K
L
M
N
O
P
Q
R
S
T
U
V
W
X
Y
Z

A
B
C
D
E
F
G
H
I
J
K
L
M
N
O
P
Q
R
S
T
U
V
W
X
Y
Z

AreaAveragingScaleFilter()

PURPOSE	Constructs an `AreaAveragingScaleFilter` instance.
SYNTAX	`public AreaAveragingScaleFilter(int width, int height)`
DESCRIPTION	This constructor creates an area averaging scale filter that scales an image to `width` and `height`. This image filter is meant to be used in conjunction with a `FilteredImageSource` object, which assumes the responsibility for delivering an image to this image filter to scale.
	If `width` is negative, it defaults to the width of the incoming image. Likewise for `height`.
PARAMETERS	
`height`	The new height of the image in pixels. If < 0, it defaults to the height of the incoming image.
`width`	The new width of the image in pixels. If < 0, it defaults to the width of the incoming image.
SEE ALSO	`FilteredImageSource`.
EXAMPLE	See the class example.

setHints()

PURPOSE	Called by the image producer to specify how the pixels will be delivered to this image filter.
SYNTAX	`public void setHints(int hints)`
DESCRIPTION	Although this method is public, it is not meant to be called. This method is part of the image filtering process and is called by an image producer. For more information on image filters, see `ImageFilter`.
PARAMETERS	
`hints`	A bit vector specifying how the pixels will be delivered.
OVERRIDES	`ImageFilter.setHints()`.
SEE ALSO	`ImageConsumers.setHints()`.
EXAMPLE	See `ImageConsumer`.

setPixels()

PURPOSE	Called by the image producer to deliver pixels to this image filter.

SYNTAX	`public void setPixels(int x, int y, int w, int h, ColorModel`
	    `model, byte pixels[], int off, int scansize)`
	`public void setPixels(int x, int y, int w, int h, ColorModel`
	    `model, int pixels[], int off, int scansize)`

DESCRIPTION	Although this method is public, it is not meant to be called. This method is part of the image filtering process and is called by an image producer. For more information on image filters, see `ImageFilter`.

PARAMETERS

h	The height of the rectangle in which the pixels are destined.
model	The non-null color model used to translate the pixel values.
off	The index of the first pixel in the `pixel` array.
pixels	The non-null array of pixel values.
scansize	The width to use when extracting pixels from the `pixel` array.
w	The width of the rectangle in which the pixels are destined.
x	The x-coordinate of the rectangle in which the pixels are destined.
y	The y-coordinate of the rectangle in which the pixels are destined.

OVERRIDES	`ReplicateScaleFilter.setPixels()`.
SEE ALSO	`ImageConsumer.setPixels()`.
EXAMPLE	See `ImageConsumer`.

A
B
C
D
E
F
G
H
I
J
K
L
M
N
O
P
Q
R
S
T
U
V
W
X
Y
Z

AudioClip

AudioClip

Syntax
```
public interface AudioClip
```

Description
An *audio clip* is a sample of audio data. This class has minimal support for playing audio clips. You can start and stop playing an audio clip, and you can play an audio clip in a repeat loop.

MEMBER SUMMARY	
Play and Stop Methods	
loop()	Starts playing the audio clip in a loop.
play()	Starts playing the audio clip.
stop()	Stops playing the audio clip.

Example
See the Applet class example.

loop()

PURPOSE	Starts playing the audio clip in a loop.
SYNTAX	void loop()
DESCRIPTION	When this method is called, the audio clip is restarted at the beginning, regardless of whether the audio clip was already playing.
EXAMPLE	See the Applet class example.

play()

PURPOSE	Starts playing the audio clip.
SYNTAX	void play()

DESCRIPTION   The audio clip is played from the beginning, regardless of whether the audio clip was already playing. The audio clip is played once and does not repeat. In particular, if the audio clip was being played in a loop (see `loop()`), the `play()` method will terminate the loop and play the audio clip from the start one more time.

EXAMPLE   See the `Applet` class example.

stop()

PURPOSE   Stops playing the audio clip.

SYNTAX   `void stop()`

DESCRIPTION   If the audio clip is playing, either in a loop or not, it is immediately stopped.

EXAMPLE   See the `Applet` class example.

A
B
C
D
E
F
G
H
I
J
K
L
M
N
O
P
Q
R
S
T
U
V
W
X
Y
Z

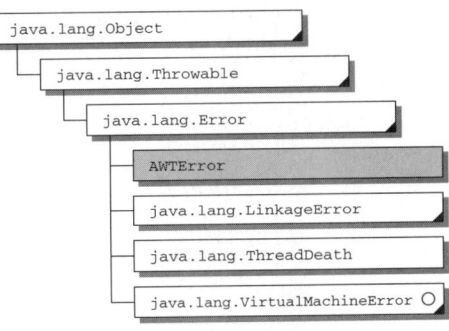

Syntax

`public class AWTError extends Error`

Description

This error is raised if the AWT encounters a fatal problem that renders the AWT usable.

MEMBER SUMMARY
Constructor
AWTError()   Constructs an AWTError instance.

See Also

ScrollPane.setLayout(), ScrollPane.setMaximum(), ScrollPane.setMinimum(), ScrollPane.setVisibleAmount(), Toolkit.getDefaultToolkit().

Example

The following example generates an AWTError when the program attempts to set a scroll pane's layout (the ScrollPane class disallows setting of its layout):

```
import java.awt.ScrollPane;
import java.awt.BorderLayout;

class Main {
    public static void main(String[] args) {
        System.out.println("AWTError example");

        ScrollPane sp = new ScrollPane();
        sp.setLayout(new BorderLayout());
    }
}
```

AWTError()

PURPOSE   Constructs an AWTError instance.

SYNTAX   public AWTError(String msg)

DESCRIPTION   This constructor creates a new instance of AWTError with a string msg that describes the details of this particular instance of the error.

PARAMETERS
msg   A string that gives details about this error.

A
B
C
D
E
F
G
H
I
J
K
L
M
N
O
P
Q
R
S
T
U
V
W
X
Y
Z

A
B
C
D
E
F
G
H
I
J
K
L
M
N
O
P
Q
R
S
T
U
V
W
X
Y
Z

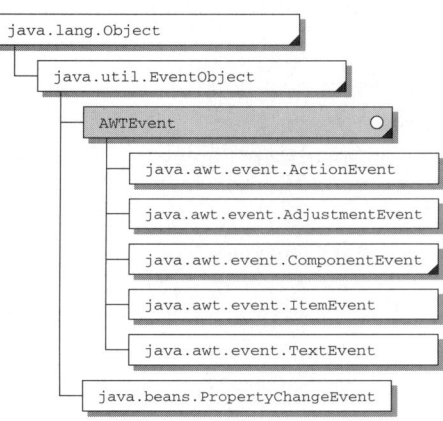

Syntax

```
public abstract class AWTEvent extends EventObject
```

Description

Components interact with a program that uses them through the use of *events*. For example, when a user clicks component with the mouse, that component fires a mouse-clicked event. Events in the AWT are organized into a class hierarchy rooted at the abstract class AWTEvent.

Event Types, Event Subtypes, and Event Class Hierarchy

The AWT event hierarchy organizes the different types of events that AWT components can fire. A subclass of an event class provides more details on the nature of the event. For example, KeyEvent and MouseEvent are subclasses of the more general InputEvent. A KeyEvent contains information about the key that was pressed or released in addition to general InputEvent information such as the pressed modifier keys and time of the input.

A single subclass such as KeyEvent can be used to represent different *event subtypes*. KeyEvent, for example, has three different event subtypes: KEY_PRESSED, KEY_RELEASED, and KEY_TYPED, each representing a specific kind of KeyEvent. Each event subtype is identified by an *event id*.

There are two categories of events: those that represent the low-level, basic manipulations that a user performs on AWT components and those that represent higher-level concepts. The low-level events include events such as input events via the keyboard or mouse, changing the focus of the component, showing and hiding components, adding and removing components from containers, and opening and closing windows. These events are subclasses of ComponentEvent.

The higher-level conceptual events, or *semantic* events, are events fired based on semantic interpretation of the user's actions. For example, when a user click a button, in addition to mouse events from the mouse press and release being fired, an *action event* indicating that the button has been pushed is also fired. Similarly, when a user selects a checkbox, in addition to mouse events being fired, an *item event* indicating that the state of the checkbox has changed is also fired. These semantic events allow the components and programs to deal with events at a higher level.

Event Sources, Event Listeners, and Event Adapters

The Java event model is a notification-based system. Objects that fire events are called *event sources*. A single event source can fire one or more different types of events. For each type of event that it fires, the event source maintains a list of *event listeners* for that event type. The event source contains methods for adding and removing event listeners for the different types of events that it fires. An event listener registers with the event source using the registration methods provided. When an event of the corresponding type is fired by the source, the listener is notified. In the case of events fired by AWT components, the AWTEventMulticaster class is used to notify event listeners. The order in which an event is delivered to its listeners is implementation-dependent and should not be depended upon. A listener that is registered first may or may not get the event first.

Each subclass of AWTEvent has an associated interface called the *event listener interface*. For example, the ActionEvent class has an associated ActionListener interface. Each interface specifies the methods that a listener of that event type must implement. For example, the ActionListener interface contains the single method actionPerformed(), which is invoked on the listener when an action event is fired by the object with which it has registered.

For convenience, the AWT event types with more than one subtype (AdjustmentEvent, ComponentEvent, ContainerEvent, KeyEvent, MouseEvent, FocusEvent, and Window-Event) also define *event adapter classes*. An event adapter class defines empty implementations for all of the methods in the corresponding event listener interface. This means a subclass of an event adapter needs only to provide (override) implementations of the methods in which it wants to handle. For example, if you want the listener to handle only the KEY_PRESSED subtype of KeyEvent, you would subclass from KeyAdapter and override keyPressed(). To achieve the same effect directly using the KeyListener interface, you would need to provide implementations for all three methods (keyPressed(), keyReleased(), and keyTyped()).

A
B
C
D
E
F
G
H
I
J
K
L
M
N
O
P
Q
R
S
T
U
V
W
X
Y
Z

A
B
C
D
E
F
G
H
I
J
K
L
M
N
O
P
Q
R
S
T
U
V
W
X
Y
Z

Event Flow

Figure 27 shows how events typically flow through the AWT. First, the event is generated by some component peer (either `Component` or `MenuComponent`) in response to some user gesture. This event is posted on the event queue (see `EventQueue`). When the event makes its way to the front of the queue, it is given to the component via its `dispatchEvent()` method. The main purpose of this method is to discard the event if the event type is not *enabled* (see the following *Enabling Events* discussion) or if the event source has no listeners registered for that event type. Otherwise, `dispatchEvent()` calls the event source's `processEvent()` method, which calls different methods depending on the event type. For example, if the incoming event is an `Action-Event`, the event source's `processAction-Event()` would be called. The main purpose of the `processSomeEvent()` methods is to notify the registered event listeners for `SomeEvent`.

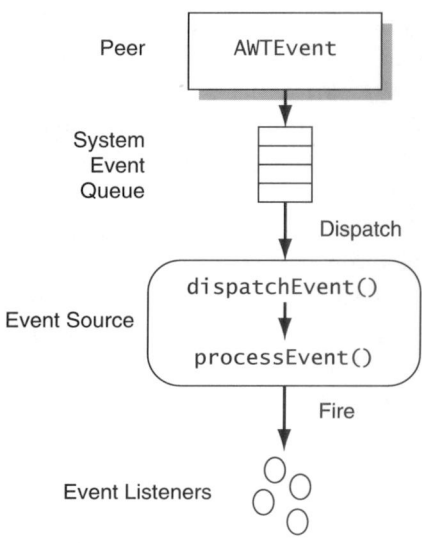

FIGURE 27:   AWT Event Flow.

With only one exception, when an event is dispatched to a component, that component fires the event to its listeners and no one else. The event is not passed up to the event source's parent regardless of whether the event source has any listeners. This is different from the Java 1.0 event model, where events automatically move up the parent hierarchy unless handled (see the deprecated `Event` class for details). The only exception is in the case of `ActionEvent` generated by `MenuItem`. If a menu item does not have any listeners, the action event is passed up to its parent menu. If the parent is not a menu component or if the parent does not have any registered action listeners, the action event is discarded. See `MenuItem` for details.

Event Notification

AWT components use the `AWTEventMulticaster` class to register, remove, and notify event listeners. Each time an event source updates its listener list, it is in effect using a new instance of an `AWTEventMulticaster` with the updated list. This updated multicaster is recorded with the event source.

Event listeners are notified synchronously in an implementation-dependent order determined by the multicaster. Once an event has started to proceed down the list of listeners, it will be delivered to all listeners in this list, even if a listener is removed from the event source. The next time an event is dispatched to the same event source, the removed listener will not be notified (because the event source is, in effect, using a new multicaster). Consequently, a listener should be prepared to receive a few more events even after it has been removed from the event source.

Consuming Events

Most events are delivered by the event source to its listeners *after* the operation has taken place. In other words, the event source's component peer has already performed the operation. For example, by the time an `ItemListener` receives notification of an `ItemEvent` from a checkbox, the checkbox's state has already been changed to its new state. Similarly, when a `COMPONENT_RESIZED` component event is delivered to a listener, the component peer has already been resized.

The exception is for `InputEvent` and its subclasses. An input event is first delivered to the event source and its listeners *before* is it processed by the event source's component peer. This allows the event source and its listeners to modify or *consume* (i.e., discard) the event before it is processed by the peer. An example of when this could be used is by a text field that accepts only numbers. Here, when the text field receives a key event that is not a number, it could emit a beep and then consume the event. The consumed key events would not appear in the text field. Note that *all* listeners are notified of the event, regardless of whether the event has been consumed. Consuming an event affects only whether the peer gets to process the event. When an input event is consumed, it cannot be "unconsumed."

Semantic events (`ActionEvent`, `ItemEvent`, `AdjustmentEvent`, and `TextEvent`) are consumed automatically because they are fired by the peer in response to some low-level events (such as mouse clicks). There is no need for the peer to do further processing related to the semantic events. Hence, they always appear "consumed."

Enabling Events and Event Masks

Enabling an event type for an event source means that events of that type will be delivered to the event source's `processEvent()` method.

An event type is automatically enabled for an event source when an event listener for that type is registered with the event source. For example, when you register an action listener with a button component, action events will be enabled for that instance of the button component. Each event type is enabled individually.

In addition, each event source maintains an *event mask* for keeping track of the event types that have been enabled. You can explicitly enable an event type for an event source by invoking the event source's `enableEvents()` method with the event type's mask. This technique is used by subclasses of `Component` to always deliver events of the specified type to its `processEvent()` method, regardless of whether the event source has any event listeners for that event type. The event source's `disableEvents()` is used to disable an event type for an event source. However, if the event source has event listeners for that event type, `processEvent()` will always be called. `disableEvents()` has only the effect of turning off the event type's mask; it does not preventing delivery of events to the event source's listeners.

Defining Your Own Event Types

You can define your own event type by subclassing `AWTEvent` or any of its subclasses. When you do this, you should define the new event type's event id to be greater than

A
B
C
D
E
F
G
H
I
J
K
L
M
N
O
P
Q
R
S
T
U
V
W
X
Y
Z

RESERVED_ID_MAX. The example for `Component.dispatchEvent()` defines a new subclass of `ActionEvent`, `SetFontEvent`, whose event id is RESERVED_ID_MAX+1.

Events Fired by Components

Events are inherited through the subclassing hierarchy. A component fires all the events fired by all of its superclasses. When you define new components by subclassing any of the AWT component classes, those new subclasses will fire all of the events fired by its superclass. You also can define these new subclasses to fire additional event types.

Note: In Java 1.1.2, components cannot fire predefined event types such as `ActionEvent` if its superclass does not already fire it. For example, if you define a subclass of `Canvas` to support `ActionEvent`, you cannot use the normal event dispatching mechanisms in the Component class (event queue or `dispatchEvent()`) to dispatch the action event. You can bypass the event-enabled checking by calling the overridden `processEvent()` directly. The workaround is to have the action event contain a different event id that is greater than RESERVED_MAX_ID.

Table 4 lists the AWT components and event types that they fire. See individual class descriptions of the components for details on the conditions under which the events are fired.

B
C
D
E
F
G
H
I
J
K
L
M
N
O
P
Q
R
S
T
U
V
W
X
Y
Z

	ActionEvent	AdjustmentEvent	ComponentEvent	ContainerEvent	FocusEvent	ItemEvent	KeyEvent	MouseEvent	TextEvent	WindowEvent
Button	X		X		X		X	X		
Canvas			X		X		X	X		
Checkbox			X		X	X	X	X		
CheckboxMenuItem	X[a]					X				
Choice			X		X	X	X	X		
Component			X		X		X	X		
Container			X	X	X		X	X		
Dialog			X	X	X		X	X		X
Frame			X	X	X		X	X		X
Label			X		X		X	X		
List	X		X		X	X	X	X		
MenuItem	X									
Panel			X	X	X		X	X		
Scrollbar		X	X		X		X	X		
ScrollPane			X	X	X		X	X		
TextArea			X		X		X	X	X	
TextComponent			X		X		X	X	X	
TextField	X		X		X		X	X	X	
Window			X	X	X		X	X		X

TABLE 4:   AWT Components and the Event Types They Fire.

  a. *Note:* In Java 1.1.2, CheckboxMenuItem does not fire ActionEvent, even though it is a subclass of MenuItem.

A
B
C
D
E
F
G
H
I
J
K
L
M
N
O
P
Q
R
S
T
U
V
W
X
Y
Z

MEMBER SUMMARY	
Constructor	
AWTEvent()	Constructs a new instance of AWTEvent.
Event Mask Constants	
ACTION_EVENT_MASK	Event mask for ActionEvent.
ADJUSTMENT_EVENT_MASK	Event mask for AdjustmentEvent.
COMPONENT_EVENT_MASK	Event mask for ComponentEvent.
CONTAINER_EVENT_MASK	Event mask for ContainerEvent.
FOCUS_EVENT_MASK	Event mask for FocusEvent.
ITEM_EVENT_MASK	Event mask for ItemEvent.
KEY_EVENT_MASK	Event mask for KeyEvent.
MOUSE_EVENT_MASK	Event mask for basic mouse events (subtypes of MouseEvent).
MOUSE_MOTION_EVENT_MASK	Event mask for mouse motion events (subtypes of MouseEvent).
TEXT_EVENT_MASK	Event mask for TextEvent.
WINDOW_EVENT_MASK	Event mask for WindowEvent.
Methods and Field for Consuming Events	
consume()	Consumes this event to prevent delivery to peer.
consumed	Indicates whether this event has been consumed.
isConsumed()	Determines whether this event has been consumed.
Event Type Members	
getID()	Retrieves the event id (event subtype) of this event.
id	Contains this event's event id.
RESERVED_ID_MAX	Lower limit for user-defined event ids.
Debugging Methods	
paramString()	Generates the string representation of this event.
toString()	Generates the string representation of this event.

See Also

Component.disableEvents(), Component.dispatchEvent(),
Component.enableEvents(), Component.processEvent(), EventQueue,
java.util.EventListener, java.util.EventObject,
Toolkit.getSystemEventQueue().

Example

This example illustrates how to define a new event type, ButtonClickEvent, that subclasses directly from AWTEvent.

The program implements a light-weight component, ImageButton, that behaves like an AWT Button. Instead of its having a label, however, it has an image as the face of the button. A sec-

FIGURE 28:   ImageButton Using ButtonClickEvent.

ond image is displayed while the button is held down. See Figure 28.

When the mouse is released from ImageButton, it creates a ButtonClickEvent and adds it to the system event queue. ButtonClickEvent is always "consumed" because it is a semantic event that need not be processed by the component's peer. ImageButton overrides processEvent() to add support for ButtonClickEvent. It also provides a method addButtonClickListener() for registering a listener for ButtonClickEvent. The program defines a corresponding listener interface ButtonClickListener for the new event.

See the AWTEventMulticaster class example for a similar example, which uses a new subclass of ActionEvent instead of directly subclassing from AWTEvent.

```
import java.awt.*;
import java.awt.image.*;
import java.awt.event.*;
import java.util.TooManyListenersException;

class Main extends Frame implements ButtonClickListener {
    Main(String upFile, String downFile) {
        super("AWTEvent Example");
        ImageButton b = new ImageButton(getToolkit().getImage(upFile),
                                        getToolkit().getImage(downFile),
                                        "Hello");
        add(b, BorderLayout.CENTER);

        try {
            b.addButtonClickListener(this);
        } catch (TooManyListenersException e) {
            e.printStackTrace();
            System.exit(-1);
        }

        setBackground(Color.lightGray);
        pack();
        show();
    }

    public void buttonClicked(ButtonClickEvent evt) {
        System.out.println(evt.toString());
        System.out.println(evt.getButtonRequest());
    }

    static public void main(String[] args) {
        if (args.length == 2) {
```

117

```
                    new Main(args[0], args[1]);
                } else {
                    System.err.println("usage: java Main <image1> <image2>");
                }
            }
        }

    // New subclass of AWTEvent
    class ButtonClickEvent extends AWTEvent {
        String request;
        // Event id must be greater than RESERVED_ID_MAX
        static final int BUTTON_CLICK_EVENT = AWTEvent.RESERVED_ID_MAX+100;

        ButtonClickEvent(Object source, String request) {
            super(source, BUTTON_CLICK_EVENT);
            this.request = request;
            consumed = true;   // semantic event need not go to peer
        }

        String getButtonRequest() {
            return request;
        }

        public String paramString() {
            return getButtonRequest() + super.paramString();
        }
    }

    // Interface of listener
    interface ButtonClickListener {
        public void buttonClicked(ButtonClickEvent evt);
    }

    // Component that fires ButtonClickEvent
    class ImageButton extends Component {
        Image upImage, downImage;
        transient ButtonClickListener listener;
        String cmd;
        boolean raised = true;
        int borderWidth = 5;

        ImageButton(Image upImage, Image downImage, String cmd) {
            this.upImage = upImage;
            this.downImage = downImage;
            this.cmd = cmd;

            // Load first image to get size of button.
            MediaTracker tracker = new MediaTracker(this);
            try {
                tracker.addImage(upImage, 0);
                tracker.waitForAll(0);
            } catch (InterruptedException e) {
                e.printStackTrace();
            }
            addMouseListener(new MouseEventHandler());
        }

        public Dimension getPreferredSize() {
            return new Dimension(upImage.getWidth(null)+2*borderWidth,
                                 upImage.getHeight(null)+2*borderWidth);
```

```
    }

    public boolean contains(int x, int y) {
        return (x < upImage.getWidth(null)+2*borderWidth &&
                y < upImage.getHeight(null)+2*borderWidth);
    }

    public void paint(Graphics g) {
        Image image = (raised ? upImage : downImage);
        g.drawImage(image, borderWidth, borderWidth, this);

        // Draw border around image
        int x = 0, y = 0;
        int w = image.getWidth(this)+2*borderWidth;
        int h = image.getHeight(this)+ 2*borderWidth;
        w -= 1;         // draw inside the rectangle.
        h -= 1;         // draw inside the rectangle.
        g.setColor(getBackground());
        for (int i=0; i<borderWidth; i++) {
            g.draw3DRect(x++, y++, w, h, raised);
            w -= 2;
            h -= 2;
        }
    }

    // Method for registering ButtonClickEvent listener
    public synchronized void addButtonClickListener(ButtonClickListener l)
        throws TooManyListenersException {
            if (listener != null) {
                throw new TooManyListenersException();
            }
            listener = l;
    }

    // Override processEvent() to handle new event type
    protected void processEvent(AWTEvent evt) {
        if (evt instanceof ButtonClickEvent) {
            processButtonClickEvent((ButtonClickEvent)evt);
            return;
        }
        super.processEvent(evt);
    }

    // Method for processing new event type
    protected void processButtonClickEvent(ButtonClickEvent evt) {
        if (listener != null) {
            listener.buttonClicked(evt);
        }
    }

    // Mouse handler for presses and releases inside this button
    // When mouse is released, fire ButtonClickEvent
    class MouseEventHandler extends MouseAdapter {
        public void mousePressed(MouseEvent evt) {
            raised = false;
            repaint();
        }
        public void mouseReleased(MouseEvent evt) {
            raised = true;
            repaint();
```

A
B
C
D
E
F
G
H
I
J
K
L
M
N
O
P
Q
R
S
T
U
V
W
X
Y
Z

```
                      ButtonClickEvent bd = new ButtonClickEvent(ImageButton.this, cmd);
                      Toolkit.getDefaultToolkit().getSystemEventQueue().postEvent(bd);
                  }
              }
          }
```

ACTION_EVENT_MASK

PURPOSE   Event mask for `ActionEvent`.

SYNTAX   `public final static long ACTION_EVENT_MASK`

DESCRIPTION   This constant is passed to `Component.enableEvents()` and `Compo-nent.disableEvents()` to enable and disable action events, respectively. See the class description for details on event masks. The value of this constant is `0x80`.

SEE ALSO   `Component.disableEvents()`, `Component.enableEvents()`, `java.awt.event.ActionEvent`.

EXAMPLE   See `MenuItem.disableEvents()`.

ADJUSTMENT_EVENT_MASK

PURPOSE   Event mask for `AdjustmentEvent`.

SYNTAX   `public final static long ADJUSTMENT_EVENT_MASK`

DESCRIPTION   This constant is passed to `Component.enableEvents()` and `Compo-nent.disableEvents()` to enable and disable adjustment events, respectively. See the class description for details on event masks. The value of this constant is `0x100`.

SEE ALSO   `Component.disableEvents()`, `Component.enableEvents()`, `java.awt.event.AdjustmentEvent`.

EXAMPLE   See the similar usage of `ACTION_EVENT_MASK` in `MenuItem.disable-Events()`.

AWTEvent()

PURPOSE   Constructs a new instance of `AWTEvent`.

SYNTAX   `public AWTEvent(Object source, int id)`
               `public AWTEvent(Event event)`

DESCRIPTION   The first form of this constructor creates an AWTEvent instance with event id id for the event source source. See the class description for details on event sources and event ids (event subtypes).

The second form of this constructor is for supporting Java 1.0 event model events (Event). The target and id fields from event are used to construct the new AWTEvent instance.

When an AWTEvent is created, its "consumed" state is false, except when id is one of the following:

```
ActionEvent.ACTION_PERFORMED,
AdjustmentEvent.ADJUSTMENT_VALUE_CHANGED,
ItemEvent.ITEM_STATE_CHANGED,
TextEvent.TEXT_VALUE_CHANGED.
```

For these event ids, the consumed state is true. See *Consuming Events* in the class description for details.

PARAMETERS

event   Java 1.0 event, whose target and id fields will be used for constructing the new AWTEvent.

id   The event id of the new event.

source   The event source that fired the new event.

EXCEPTIONS

IllegalArgumentException
                 If source is null.

SEE ALSO   consume(), getID(), isConsumed(),
                 java.util.EventObject.getSource().

EXAMPLE   See the class example (ButtonClickEvent's constructor calls the AWTEvent constructor).

COMPONENT_EVENT_MASK

PURPOSE   Event mask for ComponentEvent.

SYNTAX   public final static long COMPONENT_EVENT_MASK

DESCRIPTION   This constant is passed to Component.enableEvents() and Component.disableEvents() to enable and disable component events, respectively. See the class description for details on event masks. The value of this constant is 0x01.

SEE ALSO   Component.disableEvents(), Component.enableEvents(),
                 java.awt.event.ComponentEvent.

EXAMPLE   See the similar usage of ACTION_EVENT_MASK in MenuItem.disableEvents().

A
B
C
D
E
F
G
H
I
J
K
L
M
N
O
P
Q
R
S
T
U
V
W
X
Y
Z

121

consume()

PURPOSE   Consumes this event to prevent delivery to peer.

SYNTAX   `protected void consume()`

DESCRIPTION Only the following event subtypes can be consumed:
```
KeyEvent.KEY_PRESSED, KeyEvent.KEY_RELEASED,
MouseEvent.MOUSE_PRESSED, mouseEvent.MOUSE_RELEASED,
mouseEvent.MOUSE_MOVED, mouseEvent.MOUSE_DRAGGED,
mouseEvent.MOUSE_ENTERED, mouseEvent.MOUSE_EXITED.
```
Invoking `consume()` on events with any other event id does not do anything.

See class description for details on consuming events.

SEE ALSO   `consumed, isConsumed(), java.awt.event.InputEvent.`

EXAMPLE   See the `java.awt.event.InputEvent` class example.

consumed

PURPOSE   Field indicating whether this event has been consumed.

SYNTAX   `protected boolean consumed`

DESCRIPTION This field is set by the `consume()` method and used for determining the result of `isConsumed()`. See the class description for details on consuming events.

SEE ALSO   `consume(), isConsumed().`

EXAMPLE   See the class example.

CONTAINER_EVENT_MASK

PURPOSE   Event mask for `ContainerEvent`.

SYNTAX   `public final static long CONTAINER_EVENT_MASK`

DESCRIPTION This constant is passed to `Component.enableEvents()` and `Component.disableEvents()` to enable and disable container events, respectively. See the class description for details on event masks. The value of this constant is `0x02`.

SEE ALSO   `Component.disableEvents(), Component.enableEvents(),`
`java.awt.event.ComponentEvent.`

EXAMPLE   See the similar usage of `ACTION_EVENT_MASK` in `MenuItem.disableEvents()`.

FOCUS_EVENT_MASK

PURPOSE	Event mask for FocusEvent.
SYNTAX	`public final static long FOCUS_EVENT_MASK`
DESCRIPTION	This constant is passed to `Component.enableEvents()` and `Component.disableEvents()` to enable and disable focus events, respectively. See the class description for details on event masks. The value of this constant is `0x04`.
SEE ALSO	`Component.disableEvents()`, `Component.enableEvents()`, `java.awt.event.FocusEvent`.
EXAMPLE	See the similar usage of `ACTION_EVENT_MASK` in `MenuItem.disableEvents()`.

getID()

PURPOSE	Retrieves the event id (event subtype) of this event.
SYNTAX	`public int getID()`
DESCRIPTION	This method returns the event id with which this event was created. See the class description for details on event ids.
SEE ALSO	`AWTEvent()`, `id`, `RESERVED_ID_MAX`.
EXAMPLE	See the `java.awt.event.KeyEvent` class example.

id

PURPOSE	Field containing this event's event id.
SYNTAX	`protected int id`
DESCRIPTION	This field is set by the `AWTEvent` constructor and used for determining the result of `getID()`. See the class description for details on event ids. This field should not be used directly.
SEE ALSO	`AWTEvent()`, `getID()`.

isConsumed()

PURPOSE	Determines whether this event has been consumed.
SYNTAX	`protected boolean isConsumed()`

A
B
C
D
E
F
G
H
I
J
K
L
M
N
O
P
Q
R
S
T
U
V
W
X
Y
Z

DESCRIPTION   See *Consuming Events* in the class description for details.

RETURNS   true if this event has been consumed; false otherwise.

SEE ALSO   consume(), consumed.

ITEM_EVENT_MASK

PURPOSE   Event mask for ItemEvent.

SYNTAX   public final static long ITEM_EVENT_MASK

DESCRIPTION   This constant is passed to Component.enableEvents() and Component.disableEvents() to enable and disable item events, respectively. See the class description for details on event masks. The value of this constant is 0x200.

SEE ALSO   Component.disableEvents(), Component.enableEvents(), java.awt.event.ItemEvent.

EXAMPLE   See the ItemSelectable class example.

KEY_EVENT_MASK

PURPOSE   Event mask for KeyEvent.

SYNTAX   public final static long KEY_EVENT_MASK

DESCRIPTION   This constant is passed to Component.enableEvents() and Component.disableEvents() to enable and disable key events, respectively. See the class description for details on event masks. The value of this constant is 0x08.

SEE ALSO   Component.disableEvents(), Component.enableEvents(), java.awt.event.KeyEvent.

EXAMPLE   See the similar usage of ACTION_EVENT_MASK in MenuItem.disableEvents().

MOUSE_EVENT_MASK

PURPOSE   Event mask for basic mouse events (event subtypes of MouseEvent).

SYNTAX   public final static long MOUSE_EVENT_MASK

DESCRIPTION   This constant is passed to Component.enableEvents() and Component.disableEvents() to enable and disable basic mouse events, respectively. The basic mouse event subtypes are mouse pressed, mouse released, mouse clicked (when the mouse is pressed and released at the same coordinates), mouse entered, and mouse exited. See the class description for details on event masks. See the `MouseEvent` class for details on these mouse event subtypes. The value of this constant is `0x10`.

SEE ALSO   `Component.disableEvents()`, `Component.enableEvents()`,
`java.awt.event.MouseEvent`.

EXAMPLE   See the similar usage of `ACTION_EVENT_MASK` in `MenuItem.disable-`
`Events()`.

MOUSE_MOTION_EVENT_MASK

PURPOSE   Event mask for mouse motion events (event subtypes of `MouseEvent`).

SYNTAX   `public final static long MOUSE_MOTION_EVENT_MASK`

DESCRIPTION   This constant is passed to `Component.enableEvents()` and `Component.disableEvents()` to enable and disable mouse motion events, respectively. The mouse motion event subtypes are mouse moved and mouse dragged. See the class description for details on event masks. See the `MouseEvent` class for details on these mouse event subtypes. The value of this constant is `0x20`.

SEE ALSO   `Component.disableEvents()`, `Component.enableEvents()`,
`java.awt.event.MouseEvent`.

EXAMPLE   See the similar usage of `ACTION_EVENT_MASK` in `MenuItem.disable-`
`Events()`.

paramString()

PURPOSE   Generates the string representation of this event.

SYNTAX   `public String paramString()`

DESCRIPTION   The default implementation of this method returns the empty string "". Subclasses of AWTEvent should override this method to return the concatenation of its string representation with `super.paramString()`. This method is called by `toString()` and is typically used for debugging.

RETURNS   A non-`null` string representing the component event's state.

SEE ALSO   `toString()`, `java.lang.Object.toString()`.

EXAMPLE   See the class example.

B
C
D
E
F
G
H
I
J
K
L
M
N
O
P
Q
R
S
T
U
V
W
X
Y
Z

RESERVED_ID_MAX

PURPOSE	Lower limit for user-defined event ids.
SYNTAX	`public final static int RESERVED_ID_MAX`
DESCRIPTION	This constant defines the maximum value for reserved AWT event ids. Any user-defined events should use event ids greater than `RESERVED_ID_MAX`. Its value is 1999.
SEE ALSO	`AWTEvent()`, `getID()`.
EXAMPLE	See the class example.

TEXT_EVENT_MASK

PURPOSE	The event mask for selecting text events.
SYNTAX	`public final static long TEXT_EVENT_MASK`
DESCRIPTION	This constant is passed to `Component.enableEvents()` and `Component.disableEvents()` to enable and disable text events, respectively. See the class description for details on event masks. The value of this constant is `0x400`.
SEE ALSO	`Component.disableEvents()`, `Component.enableEvents()`, `java.awt.event.TextEvent`.
EXAMPLE	See the similar usage of `ACTION_EVENT_MASK` in `MenuItem.disableEvents()`.

toString()

PURPOSE	Generates the string representation of this event.
SYNTAX	`public String toString()`
DESCRIPTION	The string representation of this event consists of the event source's class name, the result of `paramString()`, and the event source's component name (`Component.getName()` or `MenuComponent.getName()`).
OVERRIDES	`java.util.EventObject.toString()`.
SEE ALSO	`Component.getName()`, `MenuComponent.getName()`, `java.lang.Class.getName()`, `java.util.EventObject.getSource()`.
EXAMPLE	See the class example.

WINDOW_EVENT_MASK

PURPOSE   Event mask for `WindowEvent`.

SYNTAX   `public final static long WINDOW_EVENT_MASK`

DESCRIPTION   This constant is passed to `Component.enableEvents()` and `Component.disableEvents()` to enable and disable window events, respectively. See the class description for details on event masks. The value of this constant is `0x40`.

SEE ALSO   `Component.disableEvents()`, `Component.enableEvents()`, `java.awt.event.WindowEvent`.

EXAMPLE   See the similar usage of `ACTION_EVENT_MASK` in `MenuItem.disableEvents()`.

A
B
C
D
E
F
G
H
I
J
K
L
M
N
O
P
Q
R
S
T
U
V
W
X
Y
Z

AWTEventMulticaster

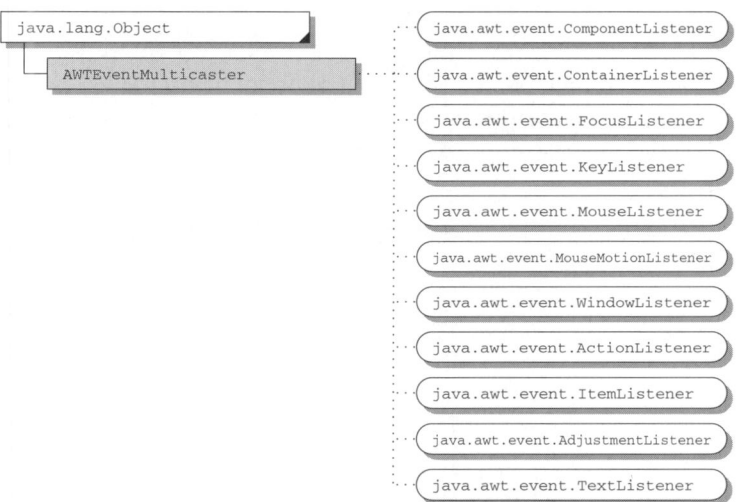

Syntax

```
public class AWTEventMulticaster implements ComponentListener,
    ContainerListener, FocusListener,KeyListener, MouseListener,
    MouseMotionListener, WindowListener, ActionListener,
    ItemListener, AdjustmentListener, TextListener
```

Description

The AWTEventMulticaster class implements a thread-safe event dispatcher for the AWT events defined in the java.awt.event package. Each multicaster consists of two event listeners, each of which can itself be a multicaster. When an event is dispatched to the top-level multicaster, it is propagated to the multicaster's two event listeners, which in turn propagate the event to their event listeners, and so on, thereby, creating a *multicast* effect.

The data structure maintained by each multicaster is immutable. So it is safe to use the methods in this class to add and remove listeners during the process of an event dispatch operation. "Updating" a multicaster basically generates a new instance of the multicaster with the updated list of listeners.

Event Notification in the AWT Event Model

When an event listener is registered with an AWT component (the *event source*), the component records the listener's reference using an AWTEventMulticaster. As other listeners are registered with or removed from the event source, the multicaster is updated and recorded with the event source.

B
C
D
E
F
G
H
I
J
K
L
M
N
O
P
Q
R
S
T
U
V
W
X
Y
Z

Event listeners are notified synchronously in the order in which they are found in the list maintained by the multicaster. Once an event has started down the list of listeners, it will be delivered to all listeners in this list, even those that have been removed from event source. The next time an event is dispatched to the same event source, the removed listener will not be notified (because the event source is, in effect, using a new multicaster).

See AWTEvent for details on event dispatching and the event model in general.

MEMBER SUMMARY	
Constructor	
AWTEventMulticaster()	Constructs an AWTEventMulticaster instance.
Action Event Method	
actionPerformed()	Invokes actionPerformed() on this multicaster's listeners.
Adjustment Event Method	
adjustmentValueChanged()	Invokes adjustmentValueChanged() on this multicaster's listeners.
Component Event Methods	
componentHidden()	Invokes componentHidden() on this multicaster's listeners.
componentMoved()	Invokes componentMoved() on this multicaster's listeners.
componentResized()	Invokes componentResized() on this multicaster's listeners.
componentShown()	Invokes componentShown() on this multicaster's listeners.
Container Event Methods	
componentAdded()	Invokes componentAdded() on this multicaster's listeners.
componentRemoved()	Invokes componentRemoved() on this multicaster's listeners.
Focus Event Methods	
focusGained()	Invokes focusGained() on this multicaster's listeners.
focusLost()	Invokes focusLost() on this multicaster's listeners.
Item Event Method	
itemStateChanged()	Invokes itemStateChanged() on this multicaster's listeners.
Key Event Methods	
keyPressed()	Invokes keyPressed() on this multicaster's listeners.
keyReleased()	Invokes keyReleased() on this multicaster's listeners.
keyTyped()	Invokes keyTyped() on this multicaster's listeners.

Continued

A
B
C
D
E
F
G
H
I
J
K
L
M
N
O
P
Q
R
S
T
U
V
W
X
Y
Z

A
B
C
D
E
F
G
H
I
J
K
L
M
N
O
P
Q
R
S
T
U
V
W
X
Y
Z

MEMBER SUMMARY	
Mouse Event Methods	
mouseEntered()	Invokes mouseEntered() on this multicaster's listeners.
mouseExited()	Invokes mouseExited() on this multicaster's listeners.
mousePressed()	Invokes mousePressed() on this multicaster's listeners.
mouseReleased()	Invokes mouseReleased() on this multicaster's listeners.
Mouse Motion Event Methods	
mouseDragged()	Invokes mouseDragged() on this multicaster's listeners.
mouseMoved()	Invokes mouseMoved() on this multicaster's listeners.
Text Event Method	
textValueChanged()	Invokes textValueChanged() on this multicaster's listeners.
Window Event Methods	
windowActivated()	Invokes windowActivated() on this multicaster's listeners.
windowClosed()	Invokes windowClosed() on this multicaster's listeners.
windowClosing()	Invokes windowClosing() on this multicaster's listeners.
windowDeactivated()	Invokes windowDeactivated() on this multicaster's listeners.
windowDeiconified()	Invokes windowDeiconified() on this multicaster's listeners.
windowIconified()	Invokes windowIconified() on this multicaster's listeners.
windowOpened()	Invokes windowOpened() on this multicaster's listeners.
Listener Fields and Methods	
a	Contains an event listener.
add()	Combines two listeners into a multicaster.
addInternal()	Combines two listeners into a multicaster.
b	Contains an event listener.
remove()	Removes a listener from a multicaster.
removeInternal()	Removes one listener from a multicaster.
Serialization Methods	
save()	Writes an event listener to an object stream.
saveInternal()	Writes this multicaster to an object stream.

See Also

java.awt.event.ActionListener, java.awt.event.AdjustmentListener,
java.awt.event.ComponentListener, java.awt.event.ContainerListener,
java.awt.event.FocusListener, java.awt.event.ItemListener,

java.awt.event.KeyListener, java.awt.event.MouseListener,
java.awt.event.MouseMotionListener, java.awt.event.TextListener,
java.awt.event.WindowListener, java.util.EventListener.

Example

This example illustrates how to use the AWTEventMulticaster to implement a lightweight component, ImageButton, that behaves like an AWT Button. However, instead of its having a label, it has an image as the face of the button. A second image is displayed while the button is held down. See Figure 29.

FIGURE 29: ImageButton Using ActionEvent.

ImageButton overrides getPreferredSize() to be the size of the image and its borders and overrides contains() to be within the bounds of the button.

See the AWTEvent class example for a similar example, which defines a new subclass of AWTEvent instead of using ActionEvent and ActionListener.

Note: mouseReleased() calls processEvent() to dispatch the event instead of calling Component.dispatchEvent() or using the system event queue. This is because in Java 1.1.2, components cannot fire a predefined event type such as ActionEvent if its superclass does not already fire it.

```
import java.awt.*;
import java.awt.image.*;
import java.awt.event.*;

class Main extends Frame implements ActionListener {
    Main(String upFile, String downFile) {
        super("AWTEventMulticaster Example");
        ImageButton b = new ImageButton(getToolkit().getImage(upFile),
                                        getToolkit().getImage(downFile),
                                        "Hello");
        add(b, BorderLayout.CENTER);
        b.addActionListener(this);
        setBackground(Color.lightGray);
        pack();
        show();
    }

    public void actionPerformed(ActionEvent evt) {
        System.out.println(evt.getActionCommand());
    }

    static public void main(String[] args) {
        if (args.length == 2) {
            new Main(args[0], args[1]);
        } else {
            System.err.println("usage: java Main <image1> <image2>");
        }
```

```
        }
    }

class ImageButton extends Component {
    Image upImage, downImage;
    transient ActionListener actionListener;
    String cmd;
    boolean raised = true;
    int borderWidth = 5;

    ImageButton(Image upImage, Image downImage, String cmd) {
        this.upImage = upImage;
        this.downImage = downImage;
        this.cmd = cmd;

        // Load first image to get size of button.
        MediaTracker tracker = new MediaTracker(this);
        try {
            tracker.addImage(upImage, 0);
            tracker.waitForAll(0);
        } catch (InterruptedException e) {
            e.printStackTrace();
        }
        addMouseListener(new MouseEventHandler());
    }

    public Dimension getPreferredSize() {
        return new Dimension(upImage.getWidth(null)+2*borderWidth,
                             upImage.getHeight(null)+2*borderWidth);
    }

    public boolean contains(int x, int y) {
        return (x < upImage.getWidth(null)+2*borderWidth &&
                y < upImage.getHeight(null)+2*borderWidth);
    }

    public void paint(Graphics g) {
        Image image = (raised ? upImage : downImage);
        g.drawImage(image, borderWidth, borderWidth, this);

        // Draw border around image
        int x = 0, y = 0;
        int w = image.getWidth(this)+2*borderWidth;
        int h = image.getHeight(this)+ 2*borderWidth;
        w -= 1;         // draw inside the rectangle.
        h -= 1;         // draw inside the rectangle.
        g.setColor(getBackground());
        for (int i=0; i<borderWidth; i++) {
            g.draw3DRect(x++, y++, w, h, raised);
            w -= 2;
            h -= 2;
        }
    }

    // Action listener management
    public synchronized void addActionListener(ActionListener l) {
        actionListener = AWTEventMulticaster.add(actionListener, l);
    }
    public void removeActionListener(ActionListener l) {
        actionListener = AWTEventMulticaster.remove(actionListener, l);
```

```
        }

        protected void processEvent(AWTEvent evt) {
            if (evt instanceof ActionEvent) {
                processActionEvent((ActionEvent)evt);
                return;
            }
            super.processEvent(evt);
        }

        protected void processActionEvent(ActionEvent evt) {
            if (actionListener != null) {
                actionListener.actionPerformed(evt);
            }
        }

        // Mouse handler for presses and releases inside this button
        class MouseEventHandler extends MouseAdapter {
            public void mousePressed(MouseEvent evt) {
                raised = false;
                repaint();
            }
            public void mouseReleased(MouseEvent evt) {
                raised = true;
                repaint();
                ActionEvent aevt = new ActionEvent(ImageButton.this,
                                            ActionEvent.ACTION_PERFORMED,
                                            cmd);
                processEvent(aevt);
            }
        }
    }
```

a

PURPOSE	Field containing an event listener.
SYNTAX	`protected final EventListener a`
DESCRIPTION	A multicaster consists of two event listeners, each of which can itself be a multicaster. This field contains one of this multicaster's two event listeners. It is set by the `AWTEventMulticaster` constructor. This field is typically not accessed directly.
SEE ALSO	`AWTEventMulticaster()`, `b`.

actionPerformed()

PURPOSE	Invokes `actionPerformed()` on this multicaster's listeners.

SYNTAX	`public void actionPerformed(ActionEvent evt)`
DESCRIPTION	This method is typically invoked inside a component's `processAction-Event()` method to dispatch the action event `evt` to this multicaster's listeners.
PARAMETERS	
`evt`	The non-`null` action event to pass on to the listeners.
SEE ALSO	`java.awt.event.ActionEvent`, `java.awt.event.ActionListener`.
EXAMPLE	See the class example.

add( )

PURPOSE	Combines two listeners into a multicaster.

SYNTAX	`public static ActionListener add(ActionListener a,`
	`    ActionListener b)`
	`public static AdjustmentListener add(AdjustmentListener a,`
	`    AdjustmentListener b)`
	`public static ComponentListener add(ComponentListener a,`
	`    ComponentListener b)`
	`public static ContainerListener add(ContainerListener a,`
	`    ContainerListener b)`
	`public static FocusListener add(FocusListener a, FocusListener b)`
	`public static KeyListener add(KeyListener a, KeyListener b)`
	`public static ItemListener add(ItemListener a, ItemListener b)`
	`public static MouseListener add(MouseListener a, MouseListener b)`
	`public static MouseMotionListener add(MouseMotionListener a,`
	`    MouseMotionListener b)`
	`public static TextListener add(TextListener a, TextListener b)`
	`public static WindowListener add(WindowListener a, WindowListener`
	`    b)`

DESCRIPTION	This method combines two listeners, a and b, into a multicaster and returns the resulting multicaster (multicast listener). If either a or b is `null`, the other non-`null` listener is returned unmodified. If both a and b are `null`, `null` is returned. Neither listeners a nor b are modified as a result of `add()`. Proper usage of `add()` requires that the result of `add()` be recorded and used subsequently as the new listener.
PARAMETERS	
`a`	An event listener to use. It can be `null`.
`b`	An event listener to use. It can be `null`.
RETURNS	The result of combining listeners a and b.

SEE ALSO   `addInternal()`, `AWTEventMulticaster()`, `remove()`.

EXAMPLE   See the definition of `ImageButton.addActionListener()` in the class example to see how to add an `ActionListener` to a multicaster. Addition of the other types of listeners works in exactly the same way as in this example.

addInternal()

PURPOSE   Combines two listeners into a multicaster.

SYNTAX   `protected static EventListener addInternal(EventListener a, EventListener b)`

DESCRIPTION   This method is the worker method used by `add()`. It is not typically used directly.

PARAMETERS

a   An event listener to use. It can be `null`.

b   An event listener to use. It can be `null`.

RETURNS   The result of combining listeners a and b.

SEE ALSO   `add()`, `AWTEventMulticaster()`, `removeInternal()`.

adjustmentValueChanged()

PURPOSE   Invokes `adjustmentValueChanged()` on this multicaster's listeners.

SYNTAX   `public void adjustmentValueChanged(AdjustmentEvent evt)`

DESCRIPTION   This method is typically invoked inside a component's `processAdjustmentEvent()` method to dispatch the adjustment event `evt` to this multicaster's listeners.

PARAMETERS

evt   The non-`null` adjustment event to pass on to listeners.

SEE ALSO   `java.awt.event.AdjustmentEvent`, `java.awt.event.AdjustmentListener`.

EXAMPLE   This example shows a typical definition of `processAdjustmentEvent()`:

```
transient AdjustmentListener adjustmentListener;

protected void processAdjustmentEvent(AdjustmentEvent evt) {
    if (adjustmentListener != null) {
        adjustmentListener.adjustmentValueChanged(evt);
    }
}
```

AWTEventMulticaster()

PURPOSE   Constructs a new instance of AWTEventMulticaster.

SYNTAX   `protected AWTEventMulticaster(EventListener a, EventListener b)`

DESCRIPTION   This constructor creates a new instance of AWTEventMulticaster using the two event listeners a and b. The constructor is typically not called directly. Instead, add() and remove() are called to create new instances of AWTEvent-Multicaster as needed.

PARAMETERS
a   An event listener to use. It cannot be null.
b   An event listener to use. It cannot be null.

SEE ALSO   add(), remove().

b

PURPOSE   Field containing an event listener.

SYNTAX   `protected final EventListener b`

DESCRIPTION   A multicaster consists of two event listeners, each of which can itself be a multicaster. This field contains one of this multicaster's two event listeners. It is set by the AWTEventMulticaster constructor. This field is typically not accessed directly.

SEE ALSO   AWTEventMulticaster(), b.

componentAdded()

PURPOSE   Invokes componentAdded() on this multicaster's listeners.

SYNTAX   `public void componentAdded(ContainerEvent evt)`

DESCRIPTION   This method is typically invoked inside a component's processContainer-Event() method to dispatch the container event evt to this multicaster's listeners.

PARAMETERS
evt   The non-null container event to pass on to the listeners.

SEE ALSO   java.awt.event.ContainerAdapter, java.awt.event.ContainerEvent, java.awt.event.Container.Listener.

EXAMPLE   This example shows a typical definition of processContainerEvent():

```
transient ContainerListener containerListener;

protected void processContainerEvent(ContainerEvent evt) {
    if (containerListener != null) {
        switch(evt.getID()) {
          case ContainerEvent.COMPONENT_ADDED:
            containerListener.componentAdded(evt);
            break;
          case ContainerEvent.COMPONENT_REMOVED:
            containerListener.componentRemoved(evt);
            break;
        }
    }
}
```

componentHidden()

PURPOSE   Invokes componentHidden() on this multicaster's listeners.

SYNTAX   public void componentHidden(ComponentEvent evt)

DESCRIPTION   This method is typically invoked inside a component's processCompo-
               nentEvent() method to dispatch the component event evt to this multi-
               caster's listeners.

PARAMETERS
    evt   The non-null component event to pass on to the listeners.

SEE ALSO   java.awt.event.ComponentAdapter, java.awt.event.ComponentEvent,
               java.awt.event.ComponentListener.

EXAMPLE   This example shows a typical definition of processComponentEvent():

```
transient ComponentListener componentListener;

protected void processComponentEvent(ComponentEvent evt) {
    if (componentListener != null) {
        switch(evt.getID()) {
          case ComponentEvent.COMPONENT_RESIZED:
            componentListener.componentResized(evt);
            break;
          case ComponentEvent.COMPONENT_MOVED:
            componentListener.componentMoved(evt);
            break;
          case ComponentEvent.COMPONENT_SHOWN:
            componentListener.componentShown(evt);
            break;
          case ComponentEvent.COMPONENT_HIDDEN:
            componentListener.componentHidden(evt);
            break;
        }
    }
}
```

A
B
C
D
E
F
G
H
I
J
K
L
M
N
O
P
Q
R
S
T
U
V
W
X
Y
Z

componentMoved()

PURPOSE   Invokes componentMoved() on this multicaster's listeners.

SYNTAX   public void componentMoved(ComponentEvent evt)

DESCRIPTION This method is typically invoked inside a component's processComponent-Event() method to dispatch the component event evt to this multicaster's listeners.

PARAMETERS

evt   The non-null component event to pass on to the listeners.

SEE ALSO   java.awt.event.ComponentAdapter, java.awt.event.ComponentEvent, java.awt.event.ComponentListener.

EXAMPLE   See componentHidden().

componentRemoved()

PURPOSE   Invokes componentRemoved() on this multicaster's listeners.

SYNTAX   public void componentRemoved(ContainerEvent evt)

DESCRIPTION This method is typically invoked inside a component's processContainer-Event() method to dispatch the container event evt to this multicaster's listeners.

PARAMETERS

evt   The non-null container event to pass on to the listeners.

SEE ALSO   java.awt.event.ContainerAdapter, java.awt.event.ContainerEvent, java.awt.event.ContainerListener.

EXAMPLE   See componentAdded().

componentResized()

PURPOSE   Invokes componentResized() on this multicaster's listeners.

SYNTAX   public void componentResized(ComponentEvent evt)

DESCRIPTION This method is typically invoked inside a component's processComponent-Event() method to dispatch the component event evt to this multicaster's listeners.

PARAMETERS

evt   The non-null component event to pass on to the listeners.

SEE ALSO `java.awt.event.ComponentAdapter`, `java.awt.event.ComponentEvent`, `java.awt.event.ComponentListener`.

EXAMPLE See `componentHidden()`.

componentShown()

PURPOSE Invokes `componentShown()` on this multicaster's listeners.

SYNTAX `public void componentShown(ComponentEvent evt)`

DESCRIPTION This method is typically invoked inside a component's `processComponent-Event()` method to dispatch the component event `evt` to this multicaster's listeners.

PARAMETERS

`evt` The non-`null` component event to pass on to the listeners.

SEE ALSO `java.awt.event.ComponentAdapter`, `java.awt.event.ComponentEvent`, `java.awt.event.ComponentListener`.

EXAMPLE See `componentHidden()`.

focusGained()

PURPOSE Invokes `focusGained()` on this multicaster's listeners.

SYNTAX `public void focusGained(FocusEvent evt)`

DESCRIPTION This method is typically invoked inside a component's `processFocus-Event()` method to dispatch the focus event `evt` to this multicaster's listeners.

PARAMETERS

`evt` The non-`null` focus event to pass on to the listeners.

SEE ALSO `java.awt.event.FocusAdapter`, `java.awt.event.FocustEvent`, `java.awt.event.FocusListener`.

EXAMPLE This example shows a typical definition of `processFocusEvent()`:

```
transient FocusListener focusListener;

protected void processFocusEvent(FocusEvent evt) {
    if (focusListener != null) {
        switch(evt.getID()) {
        case FocusEvent.FOCUS_GAINED:
            focusListener.focusGained(evt);
            break;
        case FocusEvent.FOCUS_LOST:
            focusListener.focusLost(evt);
            break;
```

A
B
C
D
E
F
G
H
I
J
K
L
M
N
O
P
Q
R
S
T
U
V
W
X
Y
Z

```
                }
            }
        }
```

focusLost()

PURPOSE	Invokes `focusLost()` on this multicaster's listeners.
SYNTAX	`public void focusLost(FocusEvent evt)`
DESCRIPTION	This method is typically invoked inside a component's `processFocusEvent()` method to dispatch the focus event `evt` to this multicaster's listeners.
PARAMETERS	
evt	The non-null focus event to pass on to the listeners.
SEE ALSO	`java.awt.event.FocusAdapter`, `java.awt.event.FocustEvent`, `java.awt.event.FocusListener`.
EXAMPLE	See `focusGained()`.

itemStateChanged()

PURPOSE	Invokes `itemStateChanged()` on this multicaster's listeners.
SYNTAX	`public void itemStateChanged(ItemEvent evt)`
DESCRIPTION	This method is typically invoked inside a component's `processItemEvent()` method to dispatch the item event `evt` to this multicaster's listeners.
PARAMETERS	
evt	The non-null item event to pass on to the listeners.
SEE ALSO	`java.awt.event.ItemEvent`, `java.awt.event.ItemListener`.
EXAMPLE	This example shows a typical definition of `processItemEvent()`:

```
    transient ItemListener itemListener;

    protected void processItemEvent(ItemEvent evt) {
        if (itemListener != null) {
            itemListener.itemStateChanged(evt);
        }
    }
```

B
C
D
E
F
G
H
I
J
K
L
M
N
O
P
Q
R
S
T
U
V
W
X
Y
Z

keyPressed()

PURPOSE   Invokes keyPressed() on this multicaster's listeners.

SYNTAX   `public void keyPressed(KeyEvent evt)`

DESCRIPTION This method is typically invoked inside a component's processKeyEvent() method to dispatch the key event evt to this multicaster's listeners.

PARAMETERS

evt   The non-null key event to pass on to the listeners.

SEE ALSO   java.awt.event.KeyAdapter, java.awt.event.KeyEvent, java.awt.event.KeyListener.

EXAMPLE   This example shows a typical definition of processKeyEvent():

```
transient KeyListener keyListener;

protected void processKeyEvent(KeyEvent evt) {
    if (keyListener != null) {
        switch(evt.getID()) {
            case KeyEvent.KEY_TYPED:
              keyListener.keyTyped(evt);
              break;
            case KeyEvent.KEY_PRESSED:
              keyListener.keyPressed(evt);
              break;
            case KeyEvent.KEY_RELEASED:
              keyListener.keyReleased(evt);
              break;
        }
    }
}
```

keyReleased()

PURPOSE   Invokes keyReleased() on this multicaster's listeners.

SYNTAX   `public void keyReleased(KeyEvent evt)`

DESCRIPTION This method is typically invoked inside a component's processKeyEvent() method to dispatch the key event evt to this multicaster's listeners.

PARAMETERS

evt   The non-null key event to pass on to the listeners.

SEE ALSO   java.awt.event.KeyAdapter, java.awt.event.KeyEvent, java.awt.event.KeyListener.

EXAMPLE   See keyPressed().

A
B
C
D
E
F
G
H
I
J
K
L
M
N
O
P
Q
R
S
T
U
V
W
X
Y
Z

keyTyped()

PURPOSE   Invokes keyTyped() on this multicaster's listeners.

SYNTAX   `public void keyTyped(KeyEvent evt)`

DESCRIPTION This method is typically invoked inside a component's `processKeyEvent()` method to dispatch the key event evt to this multicaster's listeners.

PARAMETERS

  evt   The non-`null` key event to pass on to the listeners.

SEE ALSO   `java.awt.event.KeyAdapter, java.awt.event.KeyEvent, java.awt.event.KeyListener.`

EXAMPLE   See keyPressed().

mouseClicked()

PURPOSE   Invokes mouseClicked() on this multicaster's listeners.

SYNTAX   `public void mouseClicked(MouseEvent evt)`

DESCRIPTION This method is typically invoked inside a component's `processMouseEvent()` method to dispatch the mouse event evt to this multicaster's listeners.

PARAMETERS

  evt   The non-`null` mouse event to pass on to the listeners.

SEE ALSO   `java.awt.event.MouseAdapter, java.awt.event.MouseEvent, java.awt.event.MouseListener.`

EXAMPLE   This example shows a typical definition of `processMouseEvent()`:

```
transient MouseListener mouseListener;

protected void processMouseEvent(MouseEvent evt) {
    if (mouseListener != null) {
        switch(evt.getID()) {
        case MouseEvent.MOUSE_PRESSED:
            mouseListener.mousePressed(evt);
            break;
        case MouseEvent.MOUSE_RELEASED:
            mouseListener.mouseReleased(evt);
            break;
        case MouseEvent.MOUSE_CLICKED:
            mouseListener.mouseClicked(evt);
            break;
        case MouseEvent.MOUSE_EXITED:
            mouseListener.mouseExited(evt);
            break;
        case MouseEvent.MOUSE_ENTERED:
            mouseListener.mouseEntered(evt);
```

```
            break;
        }
    }
}
```

mouseDragged()

PURPOSE   Invokes mouseDragged() on this multicaster's listeners.

SYNTAX   public void mouseDragged(MouseEvent evt)

DESCRIPTION   This method is typically invoked inside a component's processMouse-
                 MotionEvent() method to dispatch the mouse motion event evt to this multi-
                 caster's listeners.

PARAMETERS

evt   The non-null mouse event to pass on to the listeners.

SEE ALSO   java.awt.event.MouseMotionAdapter, java.awt.event.MouseEvent,
                 java.awt.event.MouseMotionListener.

EXAMPLE   This example shows a typical definition of processMouseMotionEvent():

```
    transient MouseMotionListener mouseMotionListener;

    protected void processMouseMotionEvent(MouseEvent evt) {
        if (mouseMotionListener != null) {
            switch(evt.getID()) {
            case MouseEvent.MOUSE_MOVED:
                mouseMotionListener.mouseMoved(evt);
                break;
            case MouseEvent.MOUSE_DRAGGED:
                mouseMotionListener.mouseDragged(evt);
                break;
            }
        }
    }
```

mouseEntered()

PURPOSE   Invokes mouseEntered() on this multicaster's listeners.

SYNTAX   public void mouseEntered(MouseEvent evt)

DESCRIPTION   This method is typically invoked inside a component's processMouse-
                 Event() method to dispatch the mouse event evt to this multicaster's listen-
                 ers.

PARAMETERS	
evt	The non-null mouse event to pass on to the listeners.
SEE ALSO	`java.awt.event.MouseAdapter`, `java.awt.event.MouseEvent`, `java.awt.event.MouseListener`.
EXAMPLE	See `mouseClicked()`.

mouseExited()

PURPOSE	Invokes `mouseExited()` on this multicaster's listeners.
SYNTAX	`public void mouseExited(MouseEvent evt)`
DESCRIPTION	This method is typically invoked inside a component's `processMouseEvent()` method to dispatch the mouse event `evt` to this multicaster's listeners.
PARAMETERS	
evt	The non-null mouse event to pass on to the listeners.
SEE ALSO	`java.awt.event.MouseAdapter`, `java.awt.event.MouseEvent`, `java.awt.event.MouseListener`.
EXAMPLE	See `mouseClicked()`.

mouseMoved()

PURPOSE	Invokes `mouseMoved()` on this multicaster's listeners.
SYNTAX	`public void mouseMoved(MouseEvent evt)`
DESCRIPTION	This method is typically invoked inside a component's `processMouseMotionEvent()` method to dispatch the mouse motion event `evt` to this multicaster's listeners.
PARAMETERS	
evt	The non-null mouse event to pass on to the listeners.
SEE ALSO	`java.awt.event.MouseMotionAdapter`, `java.awt.event.MouseEvent`, `java.awt.event.MouseMotionListener`.
EXAMPLE	See `mouseDragged()`.

mousePressed()

PURPOSE	Invokes `mousePressed()` on this multicaster's listeners.

SYNTAX	`public void mousePressed(MouseEvent evt)`
DESCRIPTION	This method is typically invoked inside a component's `processMouse-Event()` method to dispatch the mouse event evt to this multicaster's listeners.
PARAMETERS	
evt	The non-`null` mouse event to pass on to the listeners.
SEE ALSO	`java.awt.event.MouseAdapter`, `java.awt.event.MouseEvent`, `java.awt.event.MouseListener`.
EXAMPLE	See `mouseClicked()`.

mouseReleased()

PURPOSE	Invokes `mouseReleased()` on this multicaster's listeners.
SYNTAX	`public void mouseReleased(MouseEvent evt)`
DESCRIPTION	This method is typically invoked inside a component's `processMouse-Event()` method to dispatch the mouse event evt to this multicaster's listeners.
PARAMETERS	
evt	The non-`null` mouse event to pass on to the listeners.
SEE ALSO	`java.awt.event.MouseAdapter`, `java.awt.event.MouseEvent`, `java.awt.event.MouseListener`.
EXAMPLE	See `mouseClicked()`.

remove()

PURPOSE	Removes an event listener from this multicaster.
SYNTAX	`protected EventListener remove(EventListener target)`
	`public static ActionListener remove(ActionListener mc, ActionListener target)`
	`public static AdjustmentListener remove(AdjustmentListener mc, AdjustmentListener target)`
	`public static ComponentListener remove(ComponentListener mc, ComponentListener target)`
	`public static ContainerListener remove(ContainerListener mc, ContainerListener target)`
	`public static FocusListener remove(FocusListener mc, FocusListener target)`

A
B
C
D
E
F
G
H
I
J
K
L
M
N
O
P
Q
R
S
T
U
V
W
X
Y
Z

```
public static ItemListener remove(ItemListener mc, ItemListener
    target)
public static KeyListener remove(KeyListener mc, KeyListener
    target)
public static MouseListener remove(MouseListener mc, MouseListener
    target)
public static MouseMotionListener remove(MouseMotionListener mc,
    MouseMotionListener target)
public static TextListener remove(TextListener mc, TextListener
    target)
public static WindowListener remove(WindowListener mc,
    WindowListener target)
```

DESCRIPTION The first form of this method removes the event listener, `target`, from this multicaster. If `target` is not in the list of listeners managed by this multicaster, this multicaster is returned. If `target` is being managed by this multicaster, a new multicaster is created and returned using the rest of the listeners with `target` removed.

The rest of the forms of this method remove the event listener, `target`, from the multicaster `mc`. If `target` is not in the list of listeners managed by `mc`, it is ignored and `mc` is returned. Otherwise, a new multicaster of the same type as `mc` is created and returned using the rest of the listeners with `target` removed.

Neither `mc` nor `target` are modified as a result of `remove()`. Proper usage of `remove()` requires that the result of `remove()` be recorded and used subsequently as the new listener/multicaster.

PARAMETERS

`mc` The multicaster from which to remove `target`. It can be `null`.

`target` The non-`null` listener to be removed.

RETURNS A multicaster with `target` removed.

SEE ALSO `add()`, `removeInternal()`.

EXAMPLE See the definition of `ImageButton.removeActionListener()` in the class example for removing an `ActionListener` from a multicaster. The removal of the other types of listeners works in exactly the same way as in this example.

removeInternal()

PURPOSE Removes a listener from a multicaster.

SYNTAX
```
protected static EventListener removeInternal(EventListener mc,
    EventListener target)
```

DESCRIPTION	This method is the worker method used by remove(). It is typically not used directly.
PARAMETERS	
mc	The multicaster from which to remove target. It may be null.
target	The non-null listener to be removed.
RETURNS	A multicaster with target removed.
SEE ALSO	add(), remove().

save()

PURPOSE	Writes an event listener to an object stream.
SYNTAX	protected static void save(ObjectOutputStream out, String key, EventListener target) throws IOException
DESCRIPTION	This method writes the serialized forms of key and target to the object output stream out. Because a listener can implement multiple listener interfaces, key is a string (e.g., "actionL") that identifies the interface of interest. When the listener object is subsequently deserialized, key is used by the deserializing code to identify whether the interface is one of interest.
PARAMETERS	
key	A non-null string identifying the listener interface of the target of interest.
out	The non-null object output stream to which to write.
target	The listener to serialize. It can be null, in which case, nothing is written out.
SEE ALSO	java.io.IOException, java.io.ObjectOutputStream, java.io.Serializable, java.util.EventListener, saveInternal().
EXAMPLE	This code fragment illustrates how a serialization routine would typically use save().

```
final static String actionListenerK = "actionL";
transient ActionListener actionListener;

private void writeObject(ObjectOutputStream s)
    throws IOException {
    s.defaultWriteObject();

    AWTEventMulticaster.save(s, actionListenerK, actionListener);
    s.writeObject(null);
}
```

A
B
C
D
E
F
G
H
I
J
K
L
M
N
O
P
Q
R
S
T
U
V
W
X
Y
Z

saveInternal()

PURPOSE	Writes this multicaster to an object stream.
SYNTAX	`protected void saveInternal(ObjectOutputStream out, String key)` `    throws IOException`
DESCRIPTION	This method writes the serialized forms of `key` and this multicaster to the object output stream `out`. Because this multicaster can be used for multiple listener interfaces, `key` is a string (e.g., "actionL") that identifies the interface of interest. When this multicaster is subsequently deserialized, `key` is used by the deserializing code to identify whether the interface is one of interest. This method is a worker method used by `save()` and is not intended to be used directly.
PARAMETERS	`key` A non-`null` string identifying the listener interface of the target of interest. `out` The non-`null` object output stream to which to write.
SEE ALSO	`java.io.IOException`, `java.io.ObjectOutputStream`, `java.io.Serializable`, `java.util.EventListener`, `save()`.

textValueChanged()

PURPOSE	Invokes `textValueChanged()` on this multicaster's listeners.
SYNTAX	`public void textValueChanged(TextEvent evt)`
DESCRIPTION	This method is typically invoked inside a component's `processTextEvent()` method to dispatch the text event `evt` to this multicaster's listeners.
PARAMETERS	`evt` The non-`null` text event to pass on to the listeners.
SEE ALSO	`java.awt.event.TextEvent`, `java.awt.event.TextListener`.
EXAMPLE	This example shows a typical definition of `processTextEvent()`:

```
transient protected TextListener textListener;

protected void processTextEvent(TextEvent evt) {
    if (textListener != null) {
        textListener.textValueChanged(evt);
    }
}
```

windowActivated()

PURPOSE   Invokes `windowActivated()` on this multicaster's listeners.

SYNTAX   `public void windowActivated(WindowEvent evt)`

DESCRIPTION   This method is typically invoked inside a component's `processWindow-Event()` method to dispatch the window event `evt` to this multicaster's listeners.

PARAMETERS

evt   The non-`null` window event to pass on to the listeners.

SEE ALSO   `java.awt.event.WindowAdapter`, `java.awt.event.WindowEvent`, `java.awt.event.WindowListener`.

EXAMPLE   This example shows a typical definition of `processWindowEvent()`:

```
transient WindowListener windowListener;
protected void processWindowEvent(WindowEvent evt) {
    if (windowListener != null) {
        switch(evt.getID()) {
        case WindowEvent.WINDOW_OPENED:
          windowListener.windowOpened(evt);
          break;
        case WindowEvent.WINDOW_CLOSING:
          windowListener.windowClosing(evt);
          break;
        case WindowEvent.WINDOW_CLOSED:
          windowListener.windowClosed(evt);
          break;
        case WindowEvent.WINDOW_ICONIFIED:
          windowListener.windowIconified(evt);
          break;
        case WindowEvent.WINDOW_DEICONIFIED:
          windowListener.windowDeiconified(evt);
          break;
        case WindowEvent.WINDOW_ACTIVATED:
          windowListener.windowActivated(evt);
          break;
        case WindowEvent.WINDOW_DEACTIVATED:
          windowListener.windowDeactivated(evt);
          break;
        }
    }
}
```

windowClosed()

PURPOSE   Invokes `windowClosed()` on this multicaster's listeners.

SYNTAX   `public void windowClosed(WindowEvent evt)`

A
B
C
D
E
F
G
H
I
J
K
L
M
N
O
P
Q
R
S
T
U
V
W
X
Y
Z

DESCRIPTION	This method is typically invoked inside a component's `processWindow-Event()` method to dispatch the window event `evt` to this multicaster's listeners.
PARAMETERS	
`evt`	The non-`null` window event to pass on to the listeners.
SEE ALSO	`java.awt.event.WindowAdapter`, `java.awt.event.WindowEvent`, `java.awt.event.WindowListener`.
EXAMPLE	See `windowActivated()`.

windowClosing()

PURPOSE	Invokes `windowClosing()` on this multicaster's listeners.
SYNTAX	`public void windowClosing(WindowEvent evt)`
DESCRIPTION	This method is typically invoked inside a component's `processWindow-Event()` method to dispatch the window event `evt` to this multicaster's listeners.
PARAMETERS	
`evt`	The non-`null` window event to pass on to the listeners.
SEE ALSO	`java.awt.event.WindowAdapter`, `java.awt.event.WindowEvent`, `java.awt.event.WindowListener`.
EXAMPLE	See `windowActivated()`.

windowDeactivated()

PURPOSE	Invokes `windowDeactivated()` on this multicaster's listeners.
SYNTAX	`public void windowDeactivated(WindowEvent evt)`
DESCRIPTION	This method is typically invoked inside a component's `processWindow-Event()` method to dispatch the window event `evt` to this multicaster's listeners.
PARAMETERS	
`evt`	The non-`null` window event to pass on to the listeners.
SEE ALSO	`java.awt.event.WindowAdapter`, `java.awt.event.WindowEvent`, `java.awt.event.WindowListener`.
EXAMPLE	See `windowDeactivated()`.

A
B
C
D
E
F
G
H
I
J
K
L
M
N
O
P
Q
R
S
T
U
V
W
X
Y
Z

windowDeiconified()

PURPOSE	Invokes `windowDeiconified()` on this multicaster's listeners.
SYNTAX	`public void windowDeiconified(WindowEvent evt)`
DESCRIPTION	This method is typically invoked inside a component's `processWindow-Event()` method to dispatch the window event `evt` to this multicaster's listeners.
PARAMETERS	
evt	The non-`null` window event to pass on to the listeners.
SEE ALSO	`java.awt.event.WindowAdapter`, `java.awt.event.WindowEvent`, `java.awt.event.WindowListener`.
EXAMPLE	See `windowActivated()`.

windowIconified()

PURPOSE	Invokes `windowIconified()` on this multicaster's listeners.
SYNTAX	`public void windowIconified(WindowEvent evt)`
DESCRIPTION	This method is typically invoked inside a component's `processWindow-Event()` method to dispatch the window event `evt` to this multicaster's listeners.
PARAMETERS	
evt	The non-`null` window event to pass on to the listeners.
SEE ALSO	`java.awt.event.WindowAdapter`, `java.awt.event.WindowEvent`, `java.awt.event.WindowListener`.
EXAMPLE	See `windowActivated()`.

windowOpened()

PURPOSE	Invokes `windowOpened()` on this multicaster's listeners.
SYNTAX	`public void windowOpened(WindowEvent evt)`
DESCRIPTION	This method is typically invoked inside a component's `processWindow-Event()` method to dispatch the window event `evt` to this multicaster's listeners.
PARAMETERS	
evt	The non-`null` window event to pass on to the listeners.

A
B
C
D
E
F
G
H
I
J
K
L
M
N
O
P
Q
R
S
T
U
V
W
X
Y
Z

SEE ALSO   java.awt.event.WindowAdapter, java.awt.event.WindowEvent, java.awt.event.WindowListener.

EXAMPLE   See windowActivated().

B
C
D
E
F
G
H
I
J
K
L
M
N
O
P
Q
R
S
T
U
V
W
X
Y
Z

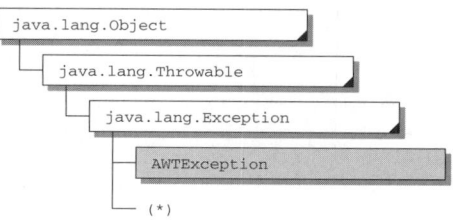

```
java.lang.Object
    java.lang.Throwable
        java.lang.Exception
            AWTException
            (*)
```

(*) 28 classes from other packages not shown; see java.lang.Exception for complete listing.

Syntax

```
public class AWTException extends Exception
```

Description

AWTException is an exception that is thrown when the program encounters an exception in the AWT. It currently is not thrown by any method in the Java runtime or its libraries.

MEMBER SUMMARY	
Constructor	
AWTException()	Constructs an AWTException instance.

AWTException()

PURPOSE	Constructs an AWTException instance.
SYNTAX	public AWTException(String msg)
DESCRIPTION	This constructor creates a new instance of AWTException. The string msg describes this particular instance of the exception.
PARAMETERS	
msg	A string that gives details about this exception.

```
java.lang.Object
    FeatureDescriptor
        BeanDescriptor
        EventSetDescriptor
        MethodDescriptor
        ParameterDescriptor
        PropertyDescriptor
```

A
B
C
D
E
F
G
H
I
J
K
L
M
N
O
P
Q
R
S
T
U
V
W
X
Y
Z

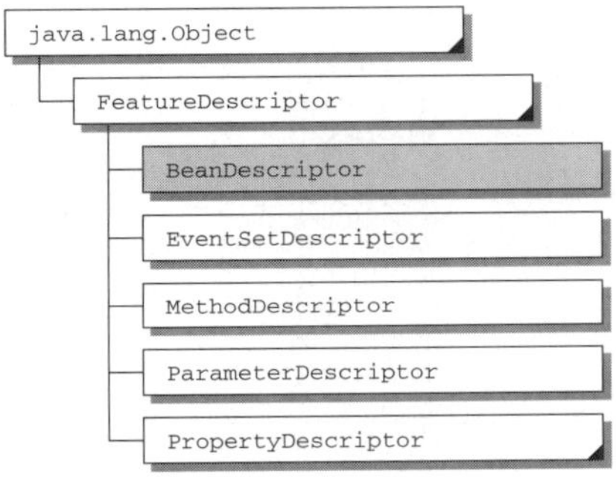

Syntax

`public class BeanDescriptor extends FeatureDescriptor`

Description

A *bean descriptor* contains global information about a bean, such its localized name and a localized description. The bean descriptor can be retrieved through the introspector by calling `Introspector.getBeanInfo().getBeanDescriptor()`.

For Bean Editors Only

The information contained in a bean descriptor is meant for programs such as bean editors (programs that help connect together beans into an application) and is not used by the bean itself. The bean descriptor, along with other descriptor types, essentially allows a bean editor to construct a meaningful user interface for editing the bean. When the bean is actually running in an application, the bean descriptor is never used.

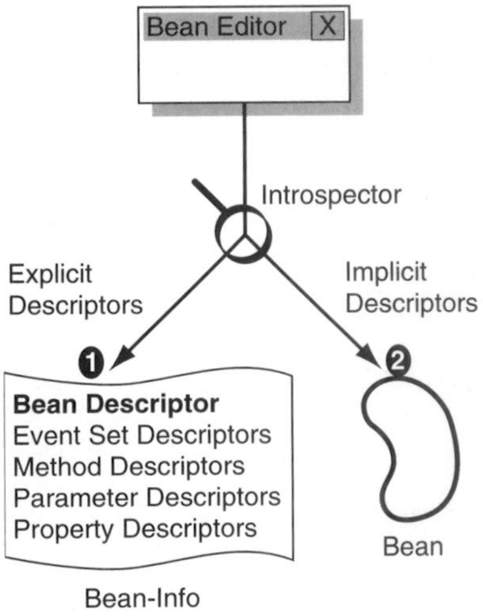

FIGURE 30: `BeanDescriptor`.

Implicit and Explicit Bean Descriptors

When retrieving the bean descriptor, the introspector first looks in the bean's *bean-info* (see `BeanInfo`) for a bean descriptor that the bean has explicitly supplied. This is called an *explicit* bean descriptor. If one is not found, the introspector creates an *implicit* bean descriptor with some default values. See Figure 30. Table 5 shows the attributes of a bean descriptor and what they contain. Also shown are the default values for an implicit bean descriptor.

Attribute	Contents	Implicit Default Value
Bean class	The bean's `Class` object	The bean's `Class` object
Customizer class	The bean's customizer `Class` object, if any.	`null`
Name	The bean's nonlocalized name.	The bean's class name without the package name.
Display name	The bean's localized name.	The bean's class name without the package name.
Short description	A localized description of the bean.	The bean's class name without the package name.
Expert	`true` if the bean is considered for use by experts only.	`false`
Hidden	`true` if the bean is meant to be used by a tool; `false` if it is meant to be use by a person.	`false`

TABLE 5:   **Bean Descriptor Attributes and Their Default Values.**

MEMBER SUMMARY	
Constructor	
`BeanDescriptor()`	Constructs a `BeanDescriptor` instance.
Attribute Methods	
`getBeanClass()`	Retrieves this bean descriptor's bean `Class` object.
`getCustomizerClass()`	Retrieves this bean descriptor's customizer Class object.

See Also

`BeanInfo.getBeanDescriptor()`, `Customizer`, `java.lang.Class`.

Example

This example demonstrates how to use the information in a bean descriptor. For an example of how to associate a bean descriptor with a bean, see the `BeanDescriptor` constructor example.

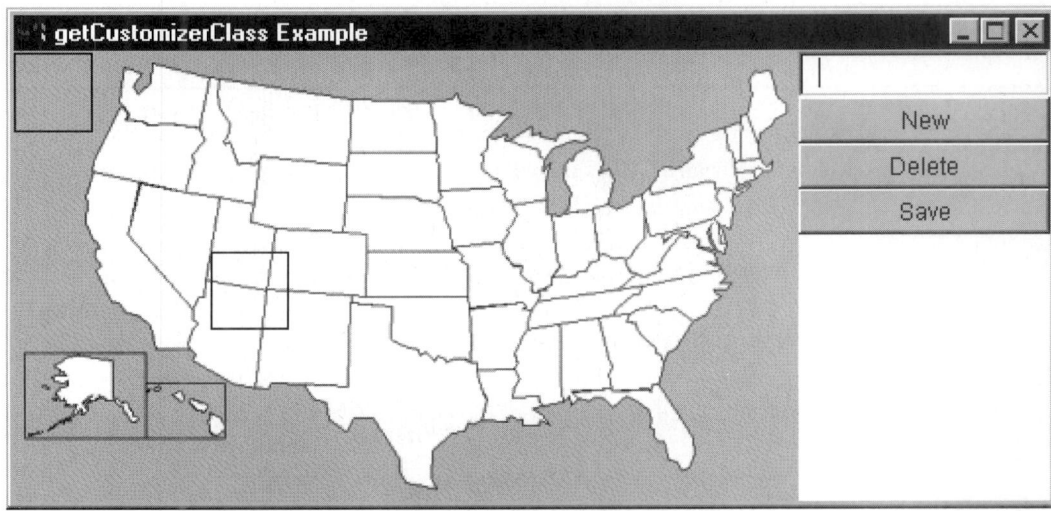

FIGURE 31:   A Bean Customizer.

When given the filename of a class file containing a bean with a customizer, this program creates an instance of the bean and its customizer. It then displays a frame containing a fully functional customizer. Figure 31 shows the frame when the program is run on the bean in the `Customizer` class example. You can run this example by executing the command (assuming you have the example files for this book):

Windows	`java Main ..\Customizer\Bean.class`
Unix	`java Main ../Customizer/Bean.class`

The program uses a simple class loader that can load the bean from a file. The simple class loader requires that the bean-info class file be in the same directory as the bean class file. One improvement that could be made to this program is to allow the user to serialize the bean after it has been modified with the customizer.

This example uses the `FileClassLoader` class. The source code for `FileClassLoader` is in the `Introspector` class example.

```
import java.awt.*;
import java.beans.*;

class Main {
    public static void main(String[] args) {
        if (args.length != 1) {
            System.err.println("Usage: java Main <name of bean class file>");
            System.exit(1);
        }

        try {
            // Get the bean class and customizer class.
```

```
            // (See the Introspector class example for FileClassLoader
            // source code.)
            Class beanClass = FileClassLoader.load(args[0]);
            BeanInfo beanInfo = Introspector.getBeanInfo(beanClass);
            BeanDescriptor beanDesc = beanInfo.getBeanDescriptor();
            Class customizerClass = (Class)beanDesc.getCustomizerClass();

            if (customizerClass != null) {
                try {
                    // Instantiate the bean and customizer.
                    Object bean = beanClass.newInstance();
                    Customizer customizer =
                        (Customizer) customizerClass.newInstance();

                    // Initialize the customizer.
                    customizer.setObject(bean);

                    // Create a frame for the customizer.
                    Frame frame = new Frame("BeanDescriptor Example");
                    frame.add((Component)customizer);
                    frame.pack();
                    frame.show();
                } catch (InstantiationException e) {
                    e.printStackTrace();
                } catch (IllegalAccessException e) {
                    e.printStackTrace();
                }
            }

    } catch (IntrospectionException e) {
        e.printStackTrace();
    }
  }
}
```

BeanDescriptor()

PURPOSE   Constructs a `BeanDescriptor` instance.

SYNTAX   `public BeanDescriptor(Class beanClass)`
                 `public BeanDescriptor(Class beanClass, Class customizerClass)`

DESCRIPTION   This constructor creates a bean descriptor for bean specified by `beanClass`. If
                 the bean has a customizer (see `Customizer`), the customizer's `Class` object
                 should be supplied as `customizerClass`.

                 If the bean does not have a customizer, it can set `customizerClass` to be
                 `null`. If `customizerClass` is not specified, it defaults to `null`.

                 A bean descriptor also has attributes that are inherited from `FeatureDe-`
                 `scriptor`. The default values for these attributes in a new constructed bean
                 descriptor is show in Table 5.

BeanDescriptor()

PARAMETERS

beanClass   The bean's non-null Class object.

customizerClass

The possibly null customizer's Class object.

SEE ALSO   BeanInfo.getBeanDescriptor(), Introspector.getBeanInfo().

EXAMPLE   This example implements a simple bean. It is a canvas component that paints the color red. The bean provides a bean-info that overrides all the default values. The example also demonstrates the use of resource bundles to help localize the display name and short description.

Figure 32 shows a picture of the Beanbox's toolbox with the example bean loaded. Notice that it displays the localized bean name.

A bean-info is necessary to associate the new bean descriptor information with the bean. The bean-info must be defined in a class with the bean's unqualified class name appended with "BeanInfo", which in this case, is BeanBeanInfo.

FIGURE 32:   A Simple Bean.

For an example of a bean descriptor where the customizer Class object is not null, see the Customizer class example.

Bean.java

```
import java.awt.*;

public class Bean extends Canvas {
    public Bean() {
        setSize(50, 50);
        setForeground(Color.red);
    }

    public void paint(Graphics g) {
        g.fillRect(0, 0, getSize().width, getSize().height);
    }
}
/*
    manifest.txt:
        Name: Bean.class
        Java-Bean: True
    jar command:
        jar cfm bean.jar manifest.txt *.class *.properties
*/
```

BeanBeanInfo.java

```java
import java.beans.*;
import java.util.*;

public class BeanBeanInfo extends SimpleBeanInfo {
    public BeanDescriptor getBeanDescriptor() {
        BeanDescriptor bd = new BeanDescriptor(Bean.class);

        bd.setName("Red Bean");
        bd.setExpert(true);
        bd.setHidden(true);

        // Pretend we're in the French locale.
        ResourceBundle bundle = ResourceBundle.getBundle("redbean",
            Locale.FRENCH);

        // Get the localized color name.
        String name = bundle.getString("red");

        // Modify the name by capitalizing it and then appending " Bean";
        name = Character.toUpperCase(name.charAt(0)) + name.substring(1)
            + " Bean";
        bd.setDisplayName(name);

        // Get the localized short description.
        bd.setShortDescription(bundle.getString("description"));
        return bd;
    }
}
```

redbean.properties.java

```
red=red
description=This bean is very red!
```

redbean_fr.properties.java

```
red=rouge
description=C'est bean est tres rouge!
```

getBeanClass()

PURPOSE	Retrieves this bean descriptor's bean Class object.
SYNTAX	public Class getBeanClass()
DESCRIPTION	This method is typically called by a bean editor when it needs to instantiate the bean. This method returns the bean Class object as supplied in the constructor.
RETURNS	The non-null Class object of the bean.
EXAMPLE	See the class example.

getCustomizerClass()

PURPOSE   Retrieves this bean descriptor's customizer `Class` object.

SYNTAX   `public Class getCustomizerClass()`

DESCRIPTION   This method is typically called by a bean editor when it needs to instantiate the bean's customizer. This method returns the customizer `Class` object as supplied in the constructor. If the bean does not have a customizer, this method returns `null`.

RETURNS   The possibly `null` `Class` object for the bean's customizer.

EXAMPLE   See the class example.

A
B
C
D
E
F
G
H
I
J
K
L
M
N
O
P
Q
R
S
T
U
V
W
X
Y
Z

BeanInfo $\cdots\cdots\cdots$ SimpleBeanInfo

Syntax
```
public interface BeanInfo
```

Description

When a bean editor loads a bean, it asks the introspec-tor (see `Introspector`) to construct a set of feature descriptors (see `FeatureDescriptor`) that contain information used by a bean editor to create an inter-face for editing the bean. By default, the introspector uses a process called *introspection* to discover the fea-ture descriptors for a bean. This process basically involves detecting signature patterns in the bean's pub-lic methods (see `Introspector` for more details).

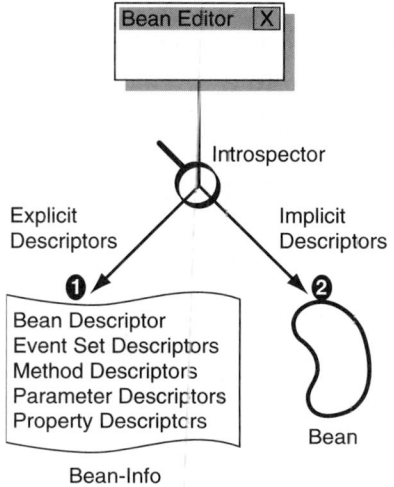

FIGURE 33: **Bean-info.**

However, some feature descriptors created by this process may not have the desired values, since there are some things that the introspector cannot deter-mine. In this case, the bean must provide explicit fea-ture descriptors for the introspector. For example, since the introspector cannot tell if a property is bound, it creates property descriptors whose bound attributes are set to `false`. If the property is indeed bound, the bean must supply an explicit property descriptor in which the bound attribute is set. These explicit feature descriptors are packaged in an object called a *bean-info*. See Figure 33.

There are four categories of feature descriptors in a bean-info, as follows:

1. Bean
2. Event set
3. Method
4. Property

When explicit feature descriptors are available in any of these categories, the introspector uses those feature descriptors and does not apply introspection to discover those feature descriptors. However, if a category does not contain any explicit feature descriptors (that is, it has the value `null`), the introspector applies introspection to discover those feature descriptors. For exam-ple, if a bean-info contains only a few explicit property descriptors, the introspector uses them and then applies introspection to discover the feature descriptors in the other three categories.

The `SimpleBeanInfo` class is a convenient class with which to build a bean-info. See `SimpleBeanInfo` for more details.

The Name of the Bean-info

A bean-info is an object defined by a class. The name of the bean-info class must be the name of the bean class name appended with `"BeanInfo"`. For example, if the bean class name is `"SpreadSheetCell"`, the bean-info class name must be `"SpreadSheetCellBeanInfo"`.

When the introspector looks for a bean's bean-info, it assembles the bean-info class name and then uses a class loader to locate the bean-info class file. In some cases, a bean-info class file is located in the same directory as the bean class file. However, you can give the introspector a path to search for a bean's bean-info.

Default Property and Event Set

One of bean's properties can be designated the *default property*, which means that it is the most commonly used property. Likewise, one of the bean's event sets can be designated the *default event set*.

A bean editor may use the default designation in different ways. For example, in the case in which some action causes a list of properties to be displayed, the bean editor can select the default property by default.

MEMBER SUMMARY

Descriptor Methods

`getBeanDescriptor()`	Retrieves the bean-info's bean descriptor.
`getEventSetDescriptors()`	Retrieves the bean-info's event set descriptors.
`getMethodDescriptors()`	Retrieves the bean-info's method descriptors.
`getPropertyDescriptors()`	Retrieves the bean-info's property descriptors.

Additional Info Method

`getAdditionalBeanInfo()`	Retrieves a set of additional bean-info objects.

Default Methods

`getDefaultEventIndex()`	Retrieves the index of the bean-info's default event set.
`getDefaultPropertyIndex()`	Retrieves the index of the bean-info's default property.

Icon Constants and Methods

`getIcon()`	Retrieves the bean-info's icon.
`ICON_COLOR_16x16`	Icon type for a 16-x-16 color image.
`ICON_COLOR_32x32`	Icon type for a 32-x-32 color image.
`ICON_MONO_16x16`	Icon type for a 16-x-16 monochrome image.
`ICON_MONO_32x32`	Icon type for a 32-x-32 monochrome image.

See Also

BeanDescriptor, EventSetDescriptor, IndexedPropertyDescriptor, Introspector, MethodDescriptor, PropertyDescriptor, SimpleBeanInfo.

Example

See the SimpleBeanInfo class example.

getAdditionalBeanInfo()

PURPOSE   Retrieves a set of additional bean-info objects.

SYNTAX   BeanInfo[] getAdditionalBeanInfo()

DESCRIPTION   A bean may provide additional bean-info objects in addition to its own. This gives a bean editor more information for editing the bean. In practice, the additional bean-info objects are typically of the bean's superclasses. For example, if a bean extends from Component, it may include the component's bean-info in the list of additional bean-info objects. In this way, the user will be able to edit not only the bean's features (properties, methods, and so on), but also the component's features.

                If additional bean-info objects are available, this method should return them in an array. If there are any conflicts between the bean-info objects in the returned array, the bean-info object with the highest index takes precedence (for example, one property descriptor says a property is bound, while the other says it is not). However, the descriptors in the bean's main bean-info information take precedence over the bean-info objects in the returned array.

RETURNS   A possibly null array of bean-info objects. The length of the array indicates the number of bean-info objects.

EXAMPLE   See the SimpleBeanInfo class example.

getBeanDescriptor()

PURPOSE   Retrieves the bean-info's bean descriptor.

SYNTAX   BeanDescriptor getBeanDescriptor()

DESCRIPTION   If an explicit bean descriptor is available, this method should return it. Otherwise, it should return null.

                This method is typically called by the introspector (see Introspector). When this method returns null, the introspector determines the bean descriptor through introspection.

A
B
C
D
E
F
G
H
I
J
K
L
M
N
O
P
Q
R
S
T
U
V
W
X
Y
Z

RETURNS	A possibly `null` bean descriptor.
SEE ALSO	`BeanDescriptor`.
EXAMPLE	See the `BeanDescriptor` class example.

getDefaultEventIndex()

PURPOSE	Retrieves the index of the bean-info's default event set.
SYNTAX	`int getDefaultEventIndex()`
DESCRIPTION	One of bean's event sets can be designated the *default event set. This* means that it is the most commonly used event set. If a default event set exists, this method should return the index of the event set descriptor for the default event set within the array returned by `getEventSetDescriptors()`.
	If `getEventSetDescriptors()` returns `null`, this method must return −1.
RETURNS	The index of the default event set in the `getEventSetDescriptors()` array, or −1 if no event set exists.
SEE ALSO	`getEventSetDescriptors()`, `EventSetDescriptor`.
EXAMPLE	See the `SimpleBeanInfo` class example.

getDefaultPropertyIndex()

PURPOSE	Retrieves the index of the bean-info's default property.
SYNTAX	`int getDefaultPropertyIndex()`
DESCRIPTION	One of bean's properties can be designated the *default property. This* means that it is the most commonly used property. If a default property exists, this method should return the index of the property descriptor for the default property within the array returned by `getPropertyDescriptors()`.
	If `getPropertyDescriptors()` returns `null`, this method must return −1.
RETURNS	The index of the default property in the `getPropertyDescriptors()` array, or −1 if no default property exists.
SEE ALSO	`getPropertyDescriptors()`, `PropertyDescriptor`.
EXAMPLE	See the `SimpleBeanInfo` class example.

getEventSetDescriptors()

PURPOSE	Retrieves the bean-info's event set descriptors.
SYNTAX	`EventSetDescriptor[] getEventSetDescriptors()`
DESCRIPTION	If the bean-info has any explicit event set descriptors, this method should return them in an array. Otherwise, it should return `null`.
	This method is typically called by the introspector (see `Introspector`). When this method returns `null`, the introspector determines the bean's event sets through introspection.
RETURNS	A possibly `null` array of event set descriptors. The length of the array indicates the number of event set descriptors.
SEE ALSO	`EventSetDescriptor`.
EXAMPLE	See the `EventSetDescriptor` class example.

getIcon()

PURPOSE	Retrieves the bean-info's icon.
SYNTAX	`Image getIcon(int iconKind)`
DESCRIPTION	This method should return an image that a bean editor can use to represent the bean. It should return `null` if no image is available. If the requested icon is a color image but is not available, the method may return a monochrome image in the requested size.
	The background pixels of the returned image should be transparent.
PARAMETERS	
`iconKind`	The desired icon type. Must be one of `ICON_COLOR_16x16`, `ICON_COLOR_32x32`, `ICON_MONO_16x16`, or `ICON_MONO_32x32`.
RETURNS	A possibly `null` image representing the bean's icon.
SEE ALSO	`java.awt.Image`.
EXAMPLE	See the class example.

getMethodDescriptors()

PURPOSE	Retrieves the bean-info's method descriptors.
SYNTAX	`MethodDescriptor[] getMethodDescriptors()`

A
B
C
D
E
F
G
H
I
J
K
L
M
N
O
P
Q
R
S
T
U
V
W
X
Y
Z

165

DESCRIPTION	If the bean-info has any explicit method descriptors, this method should return them in an array. Otherwise, it should return `null`.
	This method is typically called by the introspector (see `Introspector`). When this method returns `null`, the introspector determines the bean's methods through introspection.
RETURNS	A possibly `null` array of method descriptors. The length of the array indicates the number of method descriptors.
SEE ALSO	`MethodDescriptor`.
EXAMPLE	See the `MethodDescriptor` class example.

getPropertyDescriptors()

PURPOSE	Retrieves the bean-info's property descriptors.
SYNTAX	`PropertyDescriptor[] getPropertyDescriptors()`
DESCRIPTION	If the bean-info has any explicit property descriptors, this method should return them in an array. Otherwise, it should return `null`.
	Any indexed property descriptors should also be included in the returned array. The caller can determine which property descriptors are indexed property descriptors by using the `instanceof` operator.
	This method is typically called by the introspector (see `Introspector`). When this method returns `null`, the introspector determines the bean's properties through introspection.
RETURNS	A possibly `null` array of property descriptors. The length of the array indicates the number of property descriptors.
SEE ALSO	`PropertyDescriptor`.
EXAMPLE	See the `PropertyDescriptor` class example.

ICON_COLOR_16x16

PURPOSE	Icon type for a 16-x-16 color image.
SYNTAX	`final static int ICON_COLOR_16x16`
DESCRIPTION	This constant (value 1) is used by a bean editor in a call to `getIcon()` to fetch an icon image from the bean-info.
SEE ALSO	`getIcon()`.
EXAMPLE	See the `SimpleBeanInfo` class example.

ICON_COLOR_32x32

PURPOSE   Icon type for a 32-x-32 color image.

SYNTAX   `final static int ICON_COLOR_32x32`

DESCRIPTION This constant (value 2) is used by a bean editor in a call to `getIcon()` to fetch an icon image from the bean-info.

SEE ALSO   `getIcon()`.

EXAMPLE   See the `SimpleBeanInfo` class example.

ICON_MONO_16x16

PURPOSE   Icon type for a 16-x-16 monochrome image.

SYNTAX   `final static int ICON_MONO_16x16`

DESCRIPTION This constant (value 3) is used by a bean editor in a call to `getIcon()` to fetch an icon image from the bean-info.

SEE ALSO   `getIcon()`.

EXAMPLE   See the `SimpleBeanInfo` class example.

ICON_MONO_32x32

PURPOSE   Icon type for a 32-x-32 monochrome image.

SYNTAX   `final static int ICON_MONO_32x32`

DESCRIPTION This constant (value 4) is used by a bean editor in a call to `getIcon()` to fetch an icon image from the bean-info.

SEE ALSO   `getIcon()`.

EXAMPLE   See the `SimpleBeanInfo` class example.

A
B
C
D
E
F
G
H
I
J
K
L
M
N
O
P
Q
R
S
T
U
V
W
X
Y
Z

```
java.lang.Object
    Beans
```

Syntax

`public class Beans`

Description

The Beans class contains methods that apply to the bean environment. A *bean environment* is an environment that can load and instantiate beans. Any changes to the state of this class are seen by all beans in the bean environment.

GUI Available

The bean environment may or may not support a window system. If it does support a window system, the bean can create and show AWT components such as buttons and dialog boxes. An example of a bean environment that does not support a window system might be a server machine or a batch job.

Design Time

A bean environment may or may not be in design-time. When in design-time, the beans can be edited and configured by the user. When not in design-time, the beans cannot be edited, but the user can still interact with the beans.

Some bean environments can only instantiate beans. In such environments, the design-time flag is always `false`. Other bean environments, such a bean editor, allow the user to edit and configure its beans. In these environments, the state of the design-time flag can be controlled by the user.

MEMBER SUMMARY	
InstanceOf Methods	
getInstanceOf()	Casts the bean object into a superclass.
isInstanceOf()	Determines if a bean is a subclass of another class.
Instantiate Method	
instantiate()	Creates a new instance of a bean.
Design Time Methods	
isDesignTime()	Retrieves the environment's design-time flag.
setDesignTime()	Modifies the environment's design-time flag.

MEMBER SUMMARY

GUI Available Methods

isGuiAvailable()	Determines if the environment supports a window system.
setGuiAvailable()	Indicates whether the environment supports a window system.

See Also

Visibility.

Example

This example implements a bean that animates an image by shrinking and growing it. In design-time mode, the bean allows the user to change the location of the image by clicking anywhere on its bounds. In normal-use mode, the bean goes into its animation loop.

The main program instantiates the bean and initializes itself in design-time mode. It provides a checkbox for changing the state of the design-time mode. See Figure 34.

FIGURE 34: Design-time and Normal-use Modes.

```
import java.awt.*;
import java.awt.event.*;
import java.beans.*;

class Main extends Frame implements ItemListener {
    static Bean bean;
    Checkbox designTimeCb =
        new Checkbox("DesignTime", true);

    Main() {
        super("Beans Example");

        // Listen for action events.
        designTimeCb.addItemListener(this);

        // Layout components.
        add(bean, BorderLayout.CENTER);
        add(designTimeCb, BorderLayout.SOUTH);
        setSize(200, 200);
        show();

        // We are responsible for starting the bean.
        bean.start();
    }

    public void itemStateChanged(ItemEvent evt) {
        Beans.setDesignTime(designTimeCb.getState());
        ((Component)bean).repaint();
    }
```

A
B
C
D
E
F
G
H
I
J
K
L
M
N
O
P
Q
R
S
T
U
V
W
X
Y
Z

```
public static void main(String[] args) {
    // Initialize the environment in design-time mode.
    Beans.setDesignTime(true);

    try {
        // Create the bean.
        bean = (Bean)Beans.instantiate(Main.class.getClassLoader(), "Bean");

        new Main();
    } catch (Exception e) {
        e.printStackTrace();
        System.err.println("Failed to create bean.");
        System.exit(1);
    }
}
}
```

A
B
C
D
E
F
G
H
I
J
K
L
M
N
O
P
Q
R
S
T
U
V
W
X
Y
Z

Bean.java

```
import java.applet.*;
import java.awt.*;
import java.awt.event.*;
import java.beans.*;

public class Bean extends Applet implements Runnable {
    Image image;
    Thread thread;
    Point curLoc = new Point(0, 0);
    int scale = 1;

    // This method is automatically called by Beans.instantiate().
    public void init() {
        image = getImage(getDocumentBase(), "duke.gif");

        // Make sure the entire image is loaded so that we can safely
        // call getWidth() and getHeight() on it.
        MediaTracker tracker = new MediaTracker(this);
        try {
            tracker.addImage(image, 0);
            tracker.waitForAll(0);
        } catch (Exception e) {
            e.printStackTrace();
        }

        // Listen for mouse pressed events.
        addMouseListener(new MouseEventHandler());
    }

    public void start() {
        // Start the animation thread.
        (thread = new Thread(this)).start();
    }

    public void stop() {
        // Stop the animation thread.
        thread = null;
    }

    public void paint(Graphics g) {
```

```
    if (Beans.isDesignTime()) {
        g.drawImage(image, curLoc.x, curLoc.y, this);
    } else {
        g.drawImage(image, curLoc.x, curLoc.y,
            image.getWidth(null)/scale, image.getHeight(null)/scale, this);
    }
}

class MouseEventHandler extends MouseAdapter {
    public void mousePressed(MouseEvent evt) {
        // Ignore mouse events unless in design-time mode.
        if (Beans.isDesignTime()) {
            curLoc = evt.getPoint();
            repaint();
        }
    }
}

// Thread that constantly changes the scale value.
public void run() {
    int inc = 1;
    while (thread == Thread.currentThread()) {
        try {
            if (!Beans.isDesignTime()) {
                if (scale == 1) {
                    inc = 1;
                } else if (scale == 5) {
                    inc = -1;
                }
                scale += inc;
                repaint();
            }
            Thread.sleep(300);
        } catch (Exception e) {
        }
    }
}
}
```

getInstanceOf()

PURPOSE	Casts the bean object into a superclass.
SYNTAX	`public static Object getInstanceOf(Object bean, Class targetType)`
DESCRIPTION	This method casts a bean into an object of type `targetType`. If the `targetType Class` object is not a superclass of bean, then bean is returned.
PARAMETERS	
bean	A non-`null` bean.
targetType	A non-`null` `Class` object.
RETURNS	This method currently returns bean. It will be implemented in a future release.
SEE ALSO	`isInstanceOf()`.
EXAMPLE	See `PropertyDescriptor.getReadMethod()`.

instantiate()

A
B
C
D
E
F
G
H
I
J
K
L
M
N
O
P
Q
R
S
T
U
V
W
X
Y
Z

PURPOSE   Creates a new instance of a bean.

SYNTAX   `public static Object instantiate(ClassLoader cloader, String beanName) throws IOException, ClassNotFoundException`

DESCRIPTION   This method is used to load a bean from a serialized object or a class file. The string `beanName` must consist of dot-separated names such as `"candystore.jelly.Bean"`. This method first looks for a serialized object with `beanName`. It converts `beanName` into a resource pathname by replacing the dots with file separators and then appending the string `".ser"`. It then calls `cloader.getResource()` to see if it yields a serialized object.

If not, the bean is assumed to be a class file. The `beanName` is interpreted as a package-qualified class name and the `cloader` class loader is used to help locate the bean.

If `cloader` is `null`, the default system class loader is used instead.

If the bean is a subclass of `Applet`, it is given some special initialization. First, it is supplied with a default `AppletStub` and `AppletContext`. This means that `getDocumentBase()` and `getCodeBase()` returns valid values. If the bean was loaded from a class file rather than from a serialized object, the bean's `init()` method will be called. However, it is the caller's responsibility to call the bean's `start()` method. The `start()` method should be called after the bean has been added to a showing AWT container.

Note that applets created with this method run in a different environment than applets running inside browsers. In particular, bean applets cannot call `Applet.getParameter()`. A bean applet must provide another way of setting parameters. It is advisable to test your applet in both a bean editor and a browser.

PARAMETERS

`beanName`   The non-`null` bean class name.
`cloader`   A possibly `null` class loader.

RETURNS   A new instance of a bean loaded using `cloader`.

EXCEPTIONS

`ClassNotFoundException`
    If the bean class file could not be found.
`IOException` If an error occurred while trying to read the bean file or serialized object.

SEE ALSO   `java.applet.Applet, java.io.IOException, java.lang.ClassNotFoundException.`

EXAMPLE   See the `Visibility` class example.

isDesignTime()

PURPOSE	Retrieves the environment's design-time flag.
SYNTAX	`public static boolean isDesignTime()`
DESCRIPTION	When the bean environment is in design-time, the beans in the environment can be edited by a user. At present, when a bean editor changes the design-time flag, it repaints (see `Component.repaint()`) all the beans. Hence, a bean should check for changes in the environment's design-time mode in its `Component.update()` method.
RETURNS	`true` if the environment is in design-time; `false` otherwise.
SEE ALSO	`setDesignTime()`.
EXAMPLE	See the class example.

isGuiAvailable()

PURPOSE	Determines if the environment supports a window system.
SYNTAX	`public static boolean isGuiAvailable()`
DESCRIPTION	When a bean is loaded and instantiated in a bean environment, the environment may or may not support a window system. If it does support a window system, the bean can create and show AWT components such as buttons and dialog boxes. An example of a bean environment that does not support a window system might be a server machine or a batch job.
RETURNS	`true` if the environment supports a window system.
SEE ALSO	`setDesignTime()`, `Visibility`.

isInstanceOf()

PURPOSE	Determines if a bean is a subclass of another class.
SYNTAX	`public static boolean isInstanceOf(Object bean, Class targetType)`
DESCRIPTION	Essentially, this method returns `true` if `bean` is an instance of `targetType`. The `instanceof` operator cannot be used because the bean and `targetType` class object may have been loaded with different class loaders (`instanceof` would always return `false` in this case). If this method returns `true`, the bean can be cast to the target type by calling `getInstanceof()`.

A
B
C
D
E
F
G
H
I
J
K
L
M
N
O
P
Q
R
S
T
U
V
W
X
Y
Z

PARAMETERS	
`bean`	A non-null bean.
`targetType`	The class object of a type.
RETURNS	`true` if the bean is a subclass of `targetType`.
SEE ALSO	`getInstanceOf()`.
EXAMPLE	See `PropertyDescriptor.getReadMethod()`.

setDesignTime()

PURPOSE   Modifies the environment's design-time flag.

SYNTAX
```
public static void setDesignTime(boolean isDesignTime) throws
    SecurityException
```

DESCRIPTION   When the bean environment is in design-time, the beans in the environment can be edited by a user. To set the bean environment to be in design-time, `isDesignTime` should be `true`. To set the bean environment to be not in design-time, `isDesignTime` should be `false`.

At present, when a bean editor changes the design-time flag, it repaints (see `Component.repaint()`) all the beans. Hence, a bean should check for changes in the environment's design-time mode in its `Component.update()` method.

PARAMETERS
 `isDesignTime`
                `true` if the environment is in design-time.

EXCEPTIONS
 `SecurityException`
                If the method call is disallowed by the security manager.

SEE ALSO   `isDesignTime()`, `java.awt.Component`,
              `java.lang.SecurityException`, `java.lang.SecurityManager`.

EXAMPLE   See the class example.

setGuiAvailable()

PURPOSE   Indicates whether the environment supports a window system.

SYNTAX
```
public static void setGuiAvailable(boolean isGuiAvailable)
    throws SecurityException
```

DESCRIPTION   When a bean is loaded and instantiated in a bean environment, the environment may or may not support a window system. If it does support a window system, the bean can create and show AWT components such as buttons and dialog boxes. An example of a bean environment that does not support a window system might be a server machine or a batch job.

The `isGuiAvailable` parameter should be `true` if the bean environment supports a window system and `false` otherwise.

PARAMETERS
`isGuiAvailable`

> `true` if the environment supports a window system; `false` otherwise.

EXCEPTIONS
`SecurityException`

> If the method call is disallowed by the security manager.

SEE ALSO   `isGuiAvailable()`.

java.awt
BorderLayout

```
java.lang.Object
    BorderLayout                    LayoutManager2
                                    java.io.Serializable
```

Syntax
```
public class BorderLayout implements LayoutManager2, Serializable
```

Description

The border layout manager has exactly five locations at which it places its components. Figure 35 shows a container with a border layout manager and five buttons, one each occupying each of the five locations. The locations are north, south, east, west, and center, identified by the constants NORTH, SOUTH, EAST, WEST and CENTER, respectively (see Table 6). When a component is added to a container with a border layout manager, one of these five locations must be used..

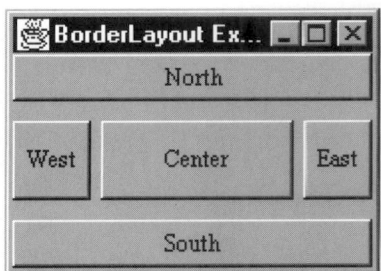

FIGURE 35:   The Five Border Layout Locations.

NORTH	Place the component at the northern border of the container and make it as wide as the container and as tall as the component's preferred height.
SOUTH	Place the component at the southern border of the container and make it as wide as the container and as tall as the component's preferred height.
WEST	Place the component at the western border of the container and make it as wide as the component's preferred width and as tall as the space between the bottom of the north and south components (if any) minus twice the vertical gap.
EAST	Place the component at the eastern border of the container and make it as wide as the component's preferred width and as tall as the space between the bottom of the north and south components (if any) minus twice the vertical gap.
CENTER	Place the component as wide as the space between the west and east components (if any) minus twice the horizontal gap and as high as the space between the north and south components (if any) minus twice the vertical gap.

TABLE 6:   BorderLayout Locations.

Not all five locations must be filled. If a location is not used, the space is distributed among the other locations. Figure 36 shows a north and west component, with the center component claiming all remaining space. An invisible component in a location is ignored during the layout, so the location is treated as if it is not occupied. Also notice that the border layout manager does not always fill up all available space.

For example, in Figure 37, although there is space between the north and south components, the border layout manager does not attempt to stretch the two components to fill up this space. Finally, the border layout manager places the components in a particular order. First, the north and south components are placed. Next, the west and east components are placed. Finally, the center component takes up all remaining space. Note that opposite-facing components are placed simultaneously. In other words, it is not the case that one component is placed first and the other takes up the remaining space. Figure 38 shows a container that is shorter than the combined widths of the west and east components. Notice that the two components overlap. You cannot control which one will appear on top.

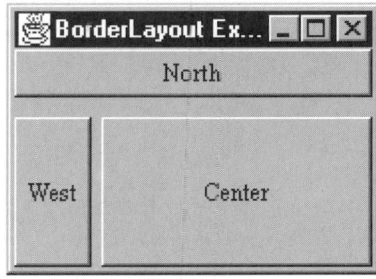

FIGURE 36: Buttons at Three Locations.

You must always identify the location of any components added to a container by using a border layout manager. You also should be careful to use the correct location. The border layout manager does not warn you if you use a location more than once. If this happens, the components simply won't be laid out correctly.

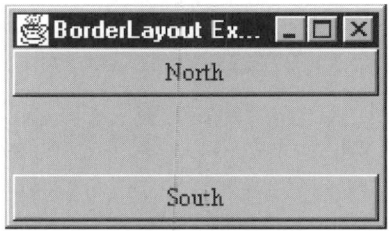

FIGURE 37: Buttons at Two Locations.

Gaps

The border layout manager allows you to separate the locations by gaps. The vertical gap specifies the space between the bottom of the north component, the top of the south component, and the components in between. The horizontal gap specifies the space between the west, center, and east components.

FIGURE 38: Overlapping Locations.

Note that if there are no components between the north and south components, the gap between them is two times the vertical gap. This is also true of the west and east components. This means that if you have a container with only two opposite-facing components and you pack the container to its minimum size, the gap may be larger than you want. If your gap size is even, you can simply set a gap that's half the size. If your gap size is odd, you'll have to subclass the border layout manager and implement your own gap rules.

177

A
B
C
D
E
F
G
H
I
J
K
L
M
N
O
P
Q
R
S
T
U
V
W
X
Y
Z

MEMBER SUMMARY

Constructor
BorderLayout()   Constructs a BorderLayout instance.

Location Constants
CENTER   Specifies the center location.
EAST   Specifies the east location.
NORTH   Specifies the north location.
SOUTH   Specifies the south location.
WEST   Specifies the west location.

Layout Manager Methods
addLayoutComponent()   Places a component at a location.
getLayoutAlignmentX()   Retrieves this layout manager's *x*-alignment.
getLayoutAlighmentY()   Retrieves this layout manager's *y*-alignment.
invalidateLayout()   Invalidates this layout manager's state.
layoutContainer()   Lays out the container's components based on the settings of
                          this layout manager.
maximumLayoutSize()   Calculates the maximum dimensions for laying out the compo-
                          nents.
minimumLayoutSize()   Calculates the minimum dimensions needed to lay out the com-
                          ponents.
preferredLayoutSize()   Calculates the preferred dimensions needed to lay out the com-
                          ponents.
removeLayoutComponent()   Removes a component from a location.

Gap Methods
getHgap()   Retrieves the horizontal gap between components.
getVgap()   Retrieves the vertical gap between components.
setHgap()   Sets the horizontal gap between components.
setVgap()   Sets the vertical gap between components.

Debugging Method
toString()   Generates a string representation of this layout manager's state.

See Also

LayoutManager, LayoutManager2, java.io.Serializable.

Example

This example demonstrates the typical way a border layout manager is used (see Figure 39). The center location is assigned a component that can stretch with the frame (in this case, just a blank canvas). The east location is assigned a scrollbar that controls the center component. The south position contains a window that displays status information. The north location contains buttons.

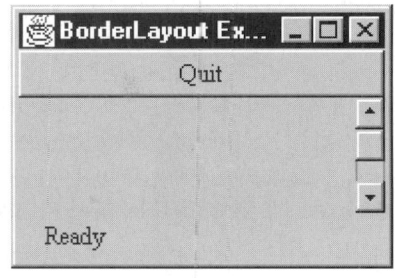

FIGURE 39: BorderLayout.

```
import java.awt.*;

class Main {
    public static void main(String[] args) {
        Frame f = new Frame("BorderLayout Example");

        f.setLayout(new BorderLayout());
        f.add(new Button("Quit"), BorderLayout.NORTH);
        f.add(new Canvas(), BorderLayout.CENTER);
        f.add(new Scrollbar(), BorderLayout.EAST);
        f.add(new Label("Ready"), BorderLayout.SOUTH);
        f.setSize(200, 200);
        f.pack();
        f.show();
    }
}
```

addLayoutComponent()

PURPOSE   Places a component at a location.

SYNTAX   `public void addLayoutComponent(Component comp, Object location)`
DEPRECATED   `public void addLayoutComponent(String location, Component comp)`

DESCRIPTION   This method places `comp` at the location `location`, which can be one of NORTH, SOUTH, WEST, EAST, CENTER, or `null`. `null` is equivalent to CENTER. The use of any other value for `location` results in an `IllegalArgumentException`.

PARAMETERS
comp   The non-`null` component that has just been added to the container. Table 6 details the resizing rules for each location in the border layout.

location   The location at which to place the component. It must be one of the border layout locations or `null`. `null` is equivalent to CENTER.

EXCEPTIONS
`IllegalArgumentException`
               If `location` is not one of the valid border layout locations.

BorderLayout( )

DEPRECATION	`addLayoutComponent()` now has a more generic form that can accept an arbitrary `Object` as a location instead of a `String`. Replaces the usage of the deprecated form:

     `addLayoutComponent("North", component);`

with

     `addLayoutComponent(component, BorderLayout.NORTH);`

SEE ALSO	`CENTER, EAST, LayoutManager2, NORTH, SOUTH, WEST.`
EXAMPLE	See the `LayoutManager` class example.

A
B
C
D
E
F
G
H
I
J
K
L
M
N
O
P
Q
R
S
T
U
V
W
X
Y
Z

BorderLayout( )

PURPOSE	Constructs a new `BorderLayout` instance.
SYNTAX	`public BorderLayout()` `public BorderLayout(int hgap, int vgap)`
DESCRIPTION	This constructor creates a new `BorderLayout` manager instance with the gaps `hgap` and `vgap`. If the gaps are not specified, they both default to 0. The gaps can be changed using `setHgap()` and `setVgap()`.
	The association between a location and a component is maintained in the border layout manager, so each container requires its own `BorderLayout` instance. That is, you cannot use the same `BorderLayout` instance in more than one container. Also, a container can be set to use a border layout only when the container has no components.
PARAMETERS	
hgap	A non-negative integer specifying the horizontal gap in pixels.
vgap	A non-negative integer specifying the vertical gap in pixels.
SEE ALSO	`setHgap(), setVgap().`
EXAMPLE	See the class example.

CENTER

PURPOSE	Constant specifying the center location.
SYNTAX	`public static final String CENTER`
DESCRIPTION	This constant specifies that the component is to be laid out as wide as the space between the west and east components (if any) minus twice the horizontal gap and as high as the space between the north and south components (if any) minus twice the vertical gap. Its value is "`Center`".

SEE ALSO   addLayoutComponent(), Container.add(), EAST, getHgap(), getVgap(), NORTH, SOUTH, WEST.

EXAMPLE   See the class example.

EAST

PURPOSE   Constant specifying the east location.

SYNTAX   `public static final String EAST`

DESCRIPTION   This constant specifies that the component is to be placed at the eastern border of the container, as wide as the component's preferred width and as tall as the space between the bottom of the north and south components (if any) minus twice the vertical gap. Its value is "East".

SEE ALSO   addLayoutComponent(), Container.add(), CENTER, getVgap(), NORTH, SOUTH, WEST.

EXAMPLE   See the class example.

getLayoutAlignmentX()

PURPOSE   Retrieves this layout manager's x-alignment.

SYNTAX   `public float getLayoutAlignmentX(Container cont)`

DESCRIPTION   This method returns `Component.CENTER_ALIGNMENT`. See `LayoutManager2` for more information about alignments.

PARAMETERS

cont   The non-`null` container using this layout manager instance.

RETURNS   This layout manager's x-alignment, which must be in the range `0.0f` to `1.0f`.

SEE ALSO   Component.getAlignmentX(), Container.getAlignmentX(), getLayoutAlignmentY(), LayoutManager2.

EXAMPLE   See the `LayoutManager2` class example.

getLayoutAlignmentY()

PURPOSE   Retrieves this layout manager's y-alignment.

SYNTAX   `public float getLayoutAlignmentY(Container cont)`

DESCRIPTION   This method returns `Component.CENTER_ALIGNMENT`. See `LayoutManager2` for more information about alignments.

PARAMETERS

cont   The non-null container using this layout manager instance.

RETURNS   This layout manager's *y*-alignment, which must be in the range 0.0f to 1.0f.

SEE ALSO   Component.getAlignmentY(), Container.getAlignmentY(), getLayoutAlignmentX(), LayoutManager2.

EXAMPLE   See the LayoutManager2 class example.

getHgap( )

PURPOSE   Retrieves the horizontal gap between components.

SYNTAX   public int getHgap()

DESCRIPTION   The horizontal gap specifies the space between the west, center, and east components. Note that if there are no components between the west and east components, the gap between them is two times the horizontal gap. See the class description for more details on the use of gaps in the layout. The horizontal gap is initialized by the BorderLayout constructor and changed using setHgap().

RETURNS   A non-negative integer specifying the horizontal gap in pixels.

SEE ALSO   getVgap(), setHgap().

EXAMPLE   This example creates a frame (with the default border layout) with vertical and horizontal gaps initialized to 0. Four buttons labeled V+, V-, H+, and H- control the vertical and horizontal gaps of the border layout. A status button in the center is used to display the current vertical and horizontal gaps in effect. See Figure 40.

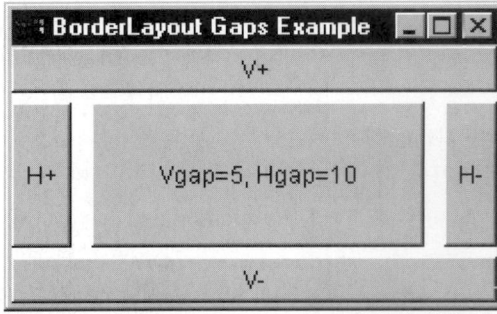

FIGURE 40: **BorderLayout's Horizontal and Vertical Gaps.**

```
import java.awt.*;
import java.awt.event.*;

class Main extends Frame implements ActionListener {
    Button status;
    BorderLayout layout;
    Main() {
        super("BorderLayout Gaps Example");

        // The default layout for Frame is BorderLayout
```

```
        layout = (BorderLayout)getLayout();

        Button b;
        add(b = new Button("V+"), BorderLayout.NORTH);
        b.addActionListener(this);
        add(b = new Button("H+"), BorderLayout.WEST);
        b.addActionListener(this);

        status = new Button("Vgap="+layout.getVgap() +
                            ", Hgap="+layout.getHgap());
        add(status, BorderLayout.CENTER);

        add(b = new Button("H-"), BorderLayout.EAST);
        b.addActionListener(this);
        add(b = new Button("V-"), BorderLayout.SOUTH);
        b.addActionListener(this);

        setSize(100, 200);
        show();
    }

    public void actionPerformed(ActionEvent evt) {
        String what = evt.getActionCommand();

        if ("H+".equals(what)) {
            layout.setHgap(layout.getHgap()+5);
        } else if ("H-".equals(what)) {
            layout.setHgap(Math.max(0, layout.getHgap()-5));
        } else if ("V+".equals(what)) {
            layout.setVgap(layout.getVgap()+5);
        } else if ("V-".equals(what)) {
            layout.setVgap(Math.max(0, layout.getVgap()-5));
        }
        // Update status button
        status.setLabel("Vgap="+layout.getVgap() +
                        ", Hgap="+layout.getHgap());
        invalidate();
        validate();
    }

    public static void main(String[] args) {
        new Main();
    }
}
```

A
B
C
D
E
F
G
H
I
J
K
L
M
N
O
P
Q
R
S
T
U
V
W
X
Y
Z

getVgap()

PURPOSE   Retrieves the vertical gap between components.

SYNTAX   `public int getVgap()`

DESCRIPTION   The vertical gap specifies the space between the north, center, and south components. Note that if there are no components between the north and south components, the gap between them is two times the vertical gap. See the class description for more details on the use of the gaps in the layout. The vertical

A
B
C
D
E
F
G
H
I
J
K
L
M
N
O
P
Q
R
S
T
U
V
W
X
Y
Z

gap is initialized by the `BorderLayout` constructor and changed using `setVgap()`.

RETURNS   A non-negative integer specifying the vertical gap in pixels.

SEE ALSO   `getHgap()`, `setVgap()`.

EXAMPLE   See `getHgap()`.

invalidateLayout( )

PURPOSE   Invalidates this layout manager's state.

SYNTAX   `public void invalidateLayout(Container cont)`

DESCRIPTION   This method is called by the layout manager's container to discard any cached information associated with this layout for the container `cont`. For `BorderLayout`, this method by default does not do anything.

PARAMETERS
cont   The non-`null` container using this layout instance.

SEE ALSO   `LayoutManager2`.

EXAMPLE   See the `LayoutManager2` class example.

layoutContainer( )

PURPOSE   Lays out the container's components based on the settings of the layout manager.

SYNTAX   `public void layoutContainer(Container container)`

DESCRIPTION   This method is called by `container` when the layout is invalidated and needs to be redone. It uses a component's preferred size when determining the dimensions of its location. The locations are also dependent on the current size of the container.

PARAMETERS
container   The non-`null` container using this layout instance.

EXAMPLE   See `LayoutManager`.

maximumLayoutSize( )

PURPOSE   Calculates the maximum dimensions for laying out the components.

SYNTAX	`public Dimension maximumLayoutSize(Container container)`
DESCRIPTION	For a border layout, the default maximum layout is the largest dimension available (`Integer.MAX_VALUE` by `Integer.MAX_VALUE`).
PARAMETERS	
cont	The non-`null` container using this layout instance.
RETURNS	A new non-`null` `Dimension` instance containing the maximum size of the border layout.
SEE ALSO	`Component.getMaximumSize()`, `Container`, `minimumLayoutSize()`, `LayoutManager2`, `preferredLayoutSize()`.
EXAMPLE	See the `LayoutManager2` class example.

minimumLayoutSize( )

PURPOSE	Calculates the minimum dimensions needed to lay out the components.
SYNTAX	`public Dimension minimumLayoutSize(Container container)`
DESCRIPTION	The minimum dimension is calculated by determining each visible component's minimum size and then laying out the components using just enough space so that they do not overlap. The minimum size also adds enough space for the gaps.
PARAMETERS	
container	The non-`null` container using this layout instance.
RETURNS	A new non-`null` `Dimension` instance containing the minimum size of the border layout.
SEE ALSO	`Component.getMinimumSize()`, `maximumLayoutSize()`, `preferredLayoutSize()`.
EXAMPLE	See `LayoutManager`.

NORTH

PURPOSE	Constant specifying the north location.
SYNTAX	`public static final String NORTH`
DESCRIPTION	This constant specifies that the component is to be placed at the northern border of the container, as wide as the container, and as tall as the component's preferred height twice the vertical gap. Its value is "`North`".

A
B
C
D
E
F
G
H
I
J
K
L
M
N
O
P
Q
R
S
T
U
V
W
X
Y
Z

SEE ALSO	addLayoutComponent(), Container.add(), CENTER, EAST, getHgap(), getVgap(), SOUTH, WEST.
EXAMPLE	See the class example.

preferredLayoutSize()

PURPOSE	Calculates the preferred dimensions needed to lay out the components.
SYNTAX	public Dimension preferredLayoutSize(Container container)
DESCRIPTION	The preferred dimension is calculated by determining each visible component's preferred size and then laying out the components using just enough space so that they don't overlap. The preferred size also adds enough space for the gaps.
PARAMETERS	
container	The non-null container using this layout instance.
RETURNS	A new non-null Dimension object containing the preferred size of the border layout.
SEE ALSO	Component.getPreferredSize(), maximumLayoutSize(), minimumLayoutSize().
EXAMPLE	See LayoutManager.

removeLayoutComponent()

PURPOSE	Removes a component from a location.
SYNTAX	public void removeLayoutComponent(Component comp)
DESCRIPTION	This method removes the component comp from the border layout manager's list of components. The border layout manager will no longer place comp. If comp does not have a name, the method call is ignored. This method is normally called by the container in response to the removal of any component from the container.
PARAMETERS	
comp	The non-null component about to be removed from the container.
EXAMPLE	See LayoutManager.

setHgap()

PURPOSE	Sets the horizontal gap between components.
SYNTAX	`public void setHgap(int hgap)`
DESCRIPTION	This method sets the horizontal gap of this layout to be `hgap`. See the class description for details on the use of gaps in border layout.
PARAMETERS	
hgap	A non-negative integer specifying the horizontal gap in pixels.
SEE ALSO	`getHgap()`, `setVgap()`.
EXAMPLE	See `getHgap()`.

setVgap()

PURPOSE	Sets the vertical gap between components.
SYNTAX	`public void setVgap(int vgap)`
DESCRIPTION	This method sets the vertical gap of this layout to be `vgap`. See the class description for details on the use of gaps in border layout.
PARAMETERS	
vgap	A non-negative integer specifying the vertical gap in pixels.
SEE ALSO	`getVgap()`, `setHgap()`.
EXAMPLE	See `getHgap()`.

SOUTH

PURPOSE	Constant specifying the south location.
SYNTAX	`public static final String SOUTH`
DESCRIPTION	This constant specifies that the component is to be placed at the southern border of the container, as wide as the container and as tall as the component's preferred height twice the vertical gap. Its value is "South".
SEE ALSO	`addLayoutComponent()`, `Container.add()`, `CENTER`, `EAST`, `getHgap()`, `getVgap()`, `NORTH`, `WEST`.
EXAMPLE	See the class example.

A
B
C
D
E
F
G
H
I
J
K
L
M
N
O
P
Q
R
S
T
U
V
W
X
Y
Z

toString( )

PURPOSE	Generates a string representation of this layout manager's state.
SYNTAX	`public String toString()`
DESCRIPTION	The string representation of a layout manager contains the layout manager's class name, the size of the two gaps, and which locations are occupied. This method returns this string representation. This method is typically used for debugging.
RETURNS	A non-`null` string representing the layout manager's state.
OVERRIDES	`java.lang.Object.toString()`.
EXAMPLE	See `java.lang.Object.toString()`.

WEST

PURPOSE	Constant specifying the west location.
SYNTAX	`public static final String WEST`
DESCRIPTION	This constant specifies that the component is to be placed at the western border of the container, as wide as the component's preferred width and as tall as the space between the bottom of the north and south components (if any) minus twice the vertical gap. Its value is "`West`".
SEE ALSO	`addLayoutComponent()`, `Container.add()`, `CENTER`, `EAST`, `getHgap()`, `getVgap()`, `NORTH`, `SOUTH`.
EXAMPLE	See the class example.

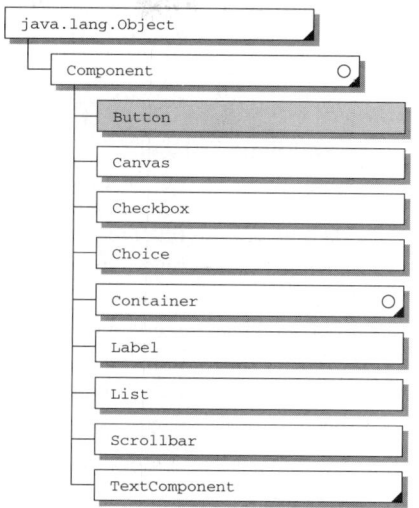

Syntax

`public class Button extends Component`

Description

A button is a component that has a label and that fires an event when pressed. A button is typically used when a command needs to be invoked. For example, a stopwatch application is shown in Figure 41 with three buttons to operate the stopwatch.

Events

An action event is fired when the mouse is pressed and released inside the button. See the Action-Event class for details. The action event contains an

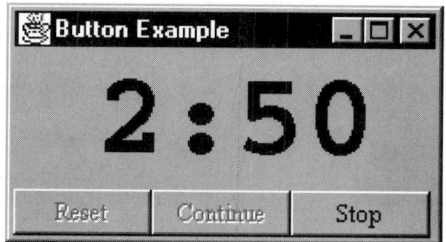

FIGURE 41: A Simple Stopwatch with Three Buttons.

action command that indicates the command issued by this button. By default, the action command is the label of the button unless it is set using setActionCommand().

In addition to the action event, a button fires all the events fired by the Component class. See the Component class for details. See the AWTEvent class for general information on events and how to filter or handle events.

See Also

AWTEvent, java.awt.event.ActionEvent, java.awt.event.ActionListener.

MEMBER SUMMARY	
Constructor	
Button()	Constructs a new Button instance.
Label Methods	
getLabel()	Retrieves this button's label.
setLabel()	Sets this button's label.
Event Methods	
addActionListener()	Adds a listener to receive action events from this button.
getActionCommand()	Retrieves the command name of action events fired by this button.
processActionEvent()	Processes an action event enabled for this button.
processEvent()	Processes an event enabled for this button.
removeActionListener()	Removes a listener from receiving action events from this button.
setActionCommand()	Sets the command names of the action events fired by this button.
Peer Method	
addNotify()	Creates this button's peer.
Debugging Method	
paramString()	Generates a string representing this button's state.

A
B
C
D
E
F
G
H
I
J
K
L
M
N
O
P
Q
R
S
T
U
V
W
X
Y
Z

Example

For a simple example using a button, see the Button() constructor. This is a more elaborate example of an application that uses buttons. The application is a (not very accurate) stopwatch with three buttons: Reset, Start, and Stop. Figure 41 shows a screen shot of the example. Depending on the mode of the stopwatch, certain buttons will be enabled or disabled to indicate which operations are currently appropriate. For example, if the stopwatch is stopped, the Stop button will be disabled.

A thread is created whenever the stopwatch is ticking and killed when no longer needed.

```
import java.awt.*;
import java.awt.event.*;

public class Main extends Frame implements Runnable {
    Label timeDisp = new Label(" 0:0 ", Label.CENTER);
    Thread timerThread;
    int time = 0;    // The time in seconds.
    Button btReset = new Button("Reset");
    Button btStart = new Button("Start");
```

```
Button btStop = new Button("Stop");

Main() {
    super("Button Example");
    // Use a grid layout manager for the 3 buttons.
    Panel p = new Panel(new GridLayout(1, 0));
    btReset.setEnabled(false);
    btStop.setEnabled(false);

    // Set listeners for each button
    btReset.addActionListener(new ResetListener());
    btStop.addActionListener(new StopListener());
    btStart.addActionListener(new StartListener());

    p.add(btReset);
    p.add(btStart);
    p.add(btStop);
    add(p, BorderLayout.SOUTH);

    // Make the time display very large.
    timeDisp.setFont(new Font("Courier", Font.BOLD, 60));
    add(timeDisp, BorderLayout.CENTER);
    pack();
    show();
}

// Returns only when the timerThread has terminated.
void stop() {
    Thread t = timerThread;
    if (t != null) {
        timerThread = null;
        try { t.join(); } catch (Exception e) {}
    }
}

public void run() {
    while (timerThread == Thread.currentThread()) {
        timeDisp.setText("" + time/10 + ":" + time%10 + "0");
        time++;
        try { Thread.sleep(100); } catch (Exception e) {};
    }
}

// Inner class definitions for listeners
class ResetListener implements ActionListener {
    public void actionPerformed(ActionEvent evt) {
        Main.this.stop();
        timeDisp.setText("0:0");
        time = 0;
        btReset.setEnabled(false);
        btStart.setEnabled(true);
        btStop.setEnabled(false);
        btStart.setLabel("Start");
    }
```

A
B
C
D
E
F
G
H
I
J
K
L
M
N
O
P
Q
R
S
T
U
V
W
X
Y
Z

```
            }

        class StopListener implements ActionListener {
            public void actionPerformed(ActionEvent evt) {
                Main.this.stop();
                btReset.setEnabled(true);
                btStart.setEnabled(true);
                btStop.setEnabled(false);
                btStart.setLabel("Continue");
            }
        }

        class StartListener implements ActionListener {
            public void actionPerformed(ActionEvent evt) {
                // Create and start the timer thread.
                timerThread = new Thread(Main.this);
                timerThread.start();
                btReset.setEnabled(false);
                btStart.setEnabled(false);
                btStop.setEnabled(true);
                btStart.setLabel("Continue");
            }
        }

        static public void main(String[] args) {
            new Main();
        }
    }
```

addActionListener()

PURPOSE	Adds a listener to receive action events fired by this button.
SYNTAX	`public synchronized void addActionListener(ActionListener` `    listener)`
DESCRIPTION	An action event is fired when the mouse is pressed and released inside this button. See `ActionEvent` for more details. After calling this method, the action listener `listener` will receive action events fired by this button. If `listener` is `null`, this method does not do anything.
PARAMETERS	
listener	The possibly `null` action listener to add.
SEE ALSO	`java.awt.event.ActionEvent`, `java.awt.event.ActionListener`, `removeActionListener()`.
EXAMPLE	See the class example, `Button()`, and `setLabel()`.

addNotify()

PURPOSE   Creates this button's peer.

SYNTAX   `public void addNotify()`

DESCRIPTION   This method creates the peer if it does not yet exist. The peer is created by a call to the `Toolkit.createButton()` method. The `addNotify()` method should never be called directly. It is normally called by the parent.

OVERRIDES   `Component.addNotify()`.

SEE ALSO   `Component, Toolkit`.

EXAMPLE   See `Component.setVisible()`.

Button()

PURPOSE   Constructs a new `Button` instance.

SYNTAX   `public Button()`
`public Button(String label)`

DESCRIPTION   These constructors create a new `Button` instance with the label `label`. If `label` is not specified, it defaults to "".

PARAMETERS
`label`   The non-`null` string specifying the button's label.

EXAMPLE   This is the simplest example of a complete program that uses a button. A button labeled "Button" is created and added to a frame. The frame's action event handler prints "Button pressed" whenever the button is pressed. See Figure 42.

FIGURE 42:   Simple Button.

```
import java.awt.*;
import java.awt.event.ActionListener;
import java.awt.event.ActionEvent;

public class Main extends Frame implements ActionListener {
    Button b = new Button("Button");

    Main() {
        super("Button Example");
        add(b, BorderLayout.CENTER);
        b.addActionListener(this);
        pack();
        show();
    }

    public void actionPerformed(ActionEvent evt) {
```

193

```
            System.out.println("Button pressed");
        }

        static public void main(String[] args) {
            new Main();
        }
    }
```

A

B

C

D

getActionCommand()

E PURPOSE   Retrieves the command name of action events fired by this button.

F SYNTAX   `public String getActionCommand()`

G DESCRIPTION   An action event is fired when the mouse is pressed and released inside this but-

H   ton. That action event contains an *action command* indicating the command issued by this button. By default, the action command is the label of the button.

I   The command action can be modified by using `setActionCommand()`.

J RETURNS   The command name of action events fired by this button. The button's label is

K   returned if no command name was set.

L SEE ALSO   `getLabel()`, `setActionCommand()`.

M EXAMPLE   This example creates a button and a text field. Pressing Return in the text field causes the button's action command to be set to the contents of the text field. Notice that this does not affect the button's label. Pressing the button will display the action command associated with the button. See Figure 43.

FIGURE 43: **Changing a Button's Action Command.**

```
import java.awt.*;
import java.awt.event.ActionListener;
import java.awt.event.ActionEvent;

class Main extends Frame implements ActionListener {
    Button bt = new Button("Button");
    TextField tf = new TextField(40);

    Main() {
        super("getActionCommand Example");
        add(bt, BorderLayout.NORTH);
        add(tf, BorderLayout.SOUTH);

        tf.setText(bt.getActionCommand());

        // Set listener for text field and button
        tf.addActionListener(this);
        bt.addActionListener(this);
```

```
        pack();
        show();
    }

    public void actionPerformed(ActionEvent evt) {
        Object src = evt.getSource();
        if (src instanceof TextField) {
            bt.setActionCommand(tf.getText());
        } else {
            System.out.println(evt.getActionCommand());
        }
    }

    static public void main(String[] args) {
        new Main();
    }
}
```

A
B
C
D
E
F
G
H
I
J
K
L
M
N
O
P
Q
R
S
T
U
V
W
X
Y
Z

getLabel()

PURPOSE	Retrieves this button's label.
SYNTAX	`public String getLabel()`
RETURNS	A non-`null` string containing this button's label.
SEE ALSO	`setLabel()`.
EXAMPLE	See `setLabel()`.

paramString()

PURPOSE	Generates a string representing this button's state.
SYNTAX	`protected String paramString()`
DESCRIPTION	The returned string includes this button's label. A subclass of this class should override this method and return a concatenation of its state with the results of `super.paramString()`. This method is called by the `toString()` method and is typically used for debugging.
RETURNS	A non-`null` string representing the button's state.
OVERRIDES	`Component.paramString()`.
SEE ALSO	`java.lang.Object.toString()`.
EXAMPLE	See `Component.paramString()`.

processActionEvent()

PURPOSE	Processes an action event enabled for this button.
SYNTAX	`protected void processActionEvent(ActionEvent evt)`

DESCRIPTION   An action event is fired when the mouse is pressed and released inside this button. See `ActionEvent` for more details. This method processes action events for this button by calling any registered `ActionListener`. This method is invoked only if action events have been enabled for this button. This can happen either when an action listener is added to this component or when action events are explicitly enabled via the use of `Component.enableEvents()`.

Typically, a program controls how action events for a button are processed. It does this by adding or removing action listeners. It overrides `process-ActionEvent()` only if it needs to do extra processing in addition to the processing performed by the registered listeners.

When a subclass does override `processActionEvent()`, it should call `super.processActionEvent()` to perform the processing intended by its base class (such as dispatching the listeners).

PARAMETERS
   evt   The event to be processed.

SEE ALSO   `java.awt.event.ActionEvent`, `java.awt.event.ActionListener`, `processEvent()`.

EXAMPLE   See `Component.dispatchEvent()`. The class `MainButton` overrides `processActionEvent()` to handle a new subclass of `ActionEvent` (`SetFontEvent`).

processEvent()

PURPOSE	Processes an event enabled for this button.
SYNTAX	`protected void processEvent(AWTEvent evt)`

DESCRIPTION   This method extends `Component.processEvent()` by adding support for `ActionEvent`. This method can be overridden to handle new types of events for this button. The subclass that overrides this should always invoke `super.processEvent()` to ensure proper processing is performed (such as dispatching listeners).

PARAMETERS
   evt   The event to be processed.

OVERRIDES   `Component.processEvent()`.

A
B
C
D
E
F
G
H
I
J
K
L
M
N
O
P
Q
R
S
T
U
V
W
X
Y
Z

SEE ALSO   AWTEvent, processActionEvent().

EXAMPLE   See the Component class example.

removeActionListener()

PURPOSE   Removes a listener from receiving action events from this button.

SYNTAX   public synchronized void removeActionListener(ActionListener
              listener)

DESCRIPTION   An action event is fired when the mouse is pressed and released inside this but-
              ton. See ActionEvent for more details. After calling this method, the action
              listener listener will no longer receive action events from this button. If
              listener is null, this method does not do anything.

PARAMETERS
listener   The possibly null action listener to remove.

SEE ALSO   addActionListener(), java.awt.event.ActionEvent,
              java.awt.event.ActionListener.

EXAMPLE   See MenuItem.disableEvents().

setActionCommand()

PURPOSE   Sets the command name of action events fired by this button.

SYNTAX   public void setActionCommand(String command)

DESCRIPTION   An action event is fired when the mouse is pressed and released inside this but-
              ton. That action event contains an *action command* indicating the command
              issued by this button. By default, the action command is the label of the button.
              This method sets the action command of this button to be command. If
              command is null, the action command of this button becomes the label of this
              button. In any case, this method does not affect the label of this button.

PARAMETERS
command   The command name of the action events fired by this button. It can be null.

SEE ALSO   getActionCommand(), getLabel(), setLabel().

EXAMPLE   See getActionCommand().

A
B
C
D
E
F
G
H
I
J
K
L
M
N
O
P
Q
R
S
T
U
V
W
X
Y
Z

setLabel( )

PURPOSE   Sets this button's label.

SYNTAX   `public void synchronized setLabel(String label)`

DESCRIPTION   This method sets this button's label to be `label`. If the action command of this button has not been explicitly set (via `setActionCommand()`) or if the action command has been set to `null`, the action command of this button becomes `label`.

As a result of the label's being set, the minimum and preferred sizes of the button may change, so resizing the button may be necessary. The example shows how to cause the button's parent to resize the button.

PARAMETERS

`label`   The non-`null` string specifying the button's new label.

SEE ALSO   `getActionCommand()`, `getLabel()`.

EXAMPLE   This example creates a button and a text field. Pressing Return in the text field causes the button label to be set to the contents of the text field. Changing the label does not automatically resize the button in the layout. This needs to be done explicitly. To do this, the button must first be invalidated and then its parent validated (this will resize the invalidated button). See Figure 43.

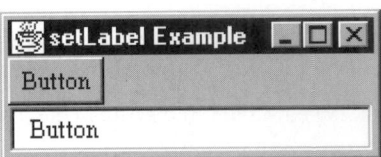

FIGURE 44: Changing a Button's Label.

A blank canvas is inserted in the center location of the border layout to force the button to be as small as possible.

```
import java.awt.*;
import java.awt.event.ActionListener;
import java.awt.event.ActionEvent;

class Main extends Frame implements ActionListener {
    Button bt = new Button("Button");
    TextField tf = new TextField(40);

    Main() {
        super("setLabel Example");
        add(new Canvas(), BorderLayout.CENTER);
        add(bt, BorderLayout.WEST);
        add(tf, BorderLayout.SOUTH);
        tf.setText(bt.getLabel());     // Initialize with current label
        tf.addActionListener(this);    // Set listener for updating label
        pack();
        show();
    }

    public void actionPerformed(ActionEvent evt) {
```

```
        bt.setLabel(tf.getText());

        // Invalidate this button because of size change
        bt.invalidate();

        // Validate parent to resize button
        bt.getParent().validate();
    }

    static public void main(String[] args) {
        new Main();
    }
}
```

A
B
C
D
E
F
G
H
I
J
K
L
M
N
O
P
Q
R
S
T
U
V
W
X
Y
Z

ButtonPeer

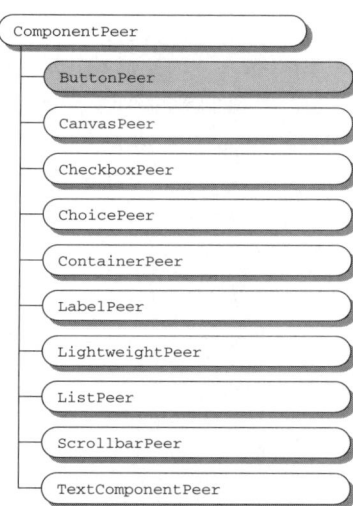

Syntax
`public interface ButtonPeer extends ComponentPeer`

Description
The button component (see the `Button` class) in the AWT uses the platform's native implementation of a button. To make the AWT button component behave the same on all platforms, the button is assigned a peer whose task is to translate the behavior of the platform's native button to the behavior of the AWT button.

AWT programmers normally do not directly use peer classes and interfaces. Instead they deal with AWT components in the `java.awt` package. These in turn automatically manage their peers. Only someone who is porting the AWT to another platform should be concerned with the peer classes and interfaces. Consequently, most peer documentation refers to `java.awt` counterparts.

See `Component` and `Toolkit` for additional information about component peers.

MEMBER SUMMARY

Peer Method
`setLabel()`	Sets the button's label.

See Also
java.awt.Button, java.awt.Component, java.awt.Toolkit.

setLabel()

PURPOSE	Sets the button's label.
SYNTAX	void setLabel(String label)
PARAMETERS	
label	The non-null string specifying the button peer's new label.
SEE ALSO	java.awt.Button.setLabel().

A
B
C
D
E
F
G
H
I
J
K
L
M
N
O
P
Q
R
S
T
U
V
W
X
Y
Z

Canvas

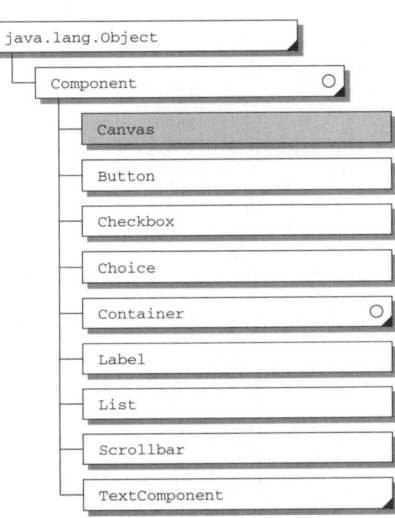

Syntax
`public class Canvas extends Component`

Description
A canvas component is a primitive component meant to be either subclassed into custom components or used for painting graphics. A canvas has no border or other bars.

Canvases and Lightweight Components
With the introduction of lightweight components (see `Component`), there is really no need for the canvas component. In fact, since a canvas has a native peer and a lightweight component does not, it is much more efficient to use a lightweight component. If you are presently using a canvas, you should consider changing it to a lightweight component.

In theory, changing your class from a canvas to a lightweight component simply involves changing the extends from `Canvas` to `Component`. However, there are a few problems with Java 1.1.2 that forces you to make a few more modifications before your class will work exactly the same. See the `Component` class description on lightweights for details.

Events
A canvas fires all of the events fired by the `Component` class. See the `Component` class for details. See the `AWTEvent` class for general information on events and how to filter or handle them.

MEMBER SUMMARY	
Peer Method	
addNotify()	Creates this canvas's peer.
Paint Override	
paint()	Paints this canvas.

Example

This example demonstrates how to build a custom button. The button displays a blinking colored circle rather than a text string. A thread is created to blink the button. The custom button also overrides the enabled and disabled methods in order to paint different images depending on the state of this property. The custom button also fires an action event when clicked.

This example creates three colored buttons to control the color of the main canvas. See Figure 45. After a color is chosen, the corresponding button becomes disabled.

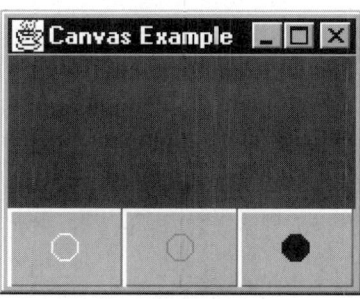

FIGURE 45: **Custom Button Using Canvas.**

```java
import java.awt.*;
import java.awt.event.*;

class Main extends Frame implements ActionListener {
    String[] colorNames = {"red", "green", "blue"};
    Color[] colorValues = {Color.red, Color.green, Color.blue};
    MainButton[] buttons = new MainButton[colorNames.length];
    Canvas cv = new Canvas();

    Main() {
        super("Canvas Example");
        Panel p = new Panel(new GridLayout(1, 0));
        for (int i=0; i<colorNames.length; i++) {
            p.add(buttons[i] = new MainButton(colorNames[i], colorValues[i]));
            buttons[i].addActionListener(this);
        }
        add(p, BorderLayout.SOUTH);
        cv.setSize(150, 150);
        add(cv, BorderLayout.CENTER);
        pack();
        show();
    }

    // When a MainButton is clicked, update color of main canvas
    public void actionPerformed(ActionEvent evt) {
        for (int i=0; i<colorNames.length; i++) {
            if (colorNames[i].equals(evt.getActionCommand())) {
                buttons[i].setEnabled(false);
                cv.setBackground(colorValues[i]);
```

```
                                cv.repaint();
                        } else {
                            buttons[i].setEnabled(true);
                        }
                    }
                }

                static public void main(String[] args) {
                    new Main();
                }
            }

            class MainButton extends Canvas implements Runnable {
                boolean on;
                boolean engaged;
                String label;
                Thread timerThread;
                ActionListener actionListener;

                MainButton(String label, Color color) {
                    this.label = label;
                    (timerThread = new Thread(this)).start();
                    setSize(40, 40);
                    setForeground(color);
                    setBackground(Color.gray);

                    addMouseListener(new MouseListener());
                }

                public void setEnabled(boolean on) {
                    super.setEnabled(on);
                    if (on) {
                        if (timerThread == null) {
                            (timerThread = new Thread(this)).start();
                        }
                    } else {
                        timerThread = null;
                    }
                    repaint();
                }

                public void addActionListener(ActionListener l) {
                    actionListener = AWTEventMulticaster.add(actionListener, l);
                }

                public void paint(Graphics g) {
                    update(g);
                }

                public void update(Graphics g) {
                    FontMetrics fm = g.getFontMetrics();
                    int w = getSize().width;
                    int h = getSize().height;
                    int ovalSize = Math.min(w/3, h/3);

                    g.clearRect(0, 0, w, h);
                    if (isEnabled()) {
                        if (engaged || on) {
                            g.fillOval((w-ovalSize)/2, (h-ovalSize)/2,
                                ovalSize, ovalSize);
```

```
        } else {
            g.drawOval((w-ovalSize)/2, (h-ovalSize)/2,
                ovalSize, ovalSize);
        }
    } else {
        g.setColor(Color.white);
        g.drawOval((w-ovalSize)/2, (h-ovalSize)/2, ovalSize, ovalSize);
    }
    g.setColor(getBackground());
    g.draw3DRect(0, 0, w-1, h-1, !engaged);
    g.draw3DRect(1, 1, w-2, h-2, !engaged);
}


// Mouse event listener
class MouseListener extends MouseAdapter {
    public void mousePressed(MouseEvent evt) {
        engaged = true;
        repaint();
    }

    public void mouseReleased(MouseEvent evt) {
        engaged = false;
        repaint();

        if (actionListener != null) {
        // Create action event for listener to process
            ActionEvent action =
                new ActionEvent(this, ActionEvent.ACTION_PERFORMED, label);
            actionListener.actionPerformed(action);
        }
    }
}

public void run() {
    while (timerThread == Thread.currentThread()) {
        on = !on;
        repaint();
        try { Thread.sleep(1000); } catch (Exception e) {};
    }
}
}
```

addNotify()

PURPOSE   Creates this canvas's peer.

SYNTAX   `public void addNotify()`

DESCRIPTION   This method creates the peer if it does not yet exist. The peer is created by call-
               ing the `Toolkit.createCanvas()` method. This method should never be
               called directly. It is normally called by the parent.

OVERRIDES   `Component.addNotify()`.

SEE ALSO   `Component, Toolkit`.

paint()

PURPOSE   Paints the canvas.

SYNTAX   `public void paint(Graphics graphics)`

DESCRIPTION   This method is called when part of the canvas that was previously occluded by some other window is now exposed. You can determine the bounds of the exposed area by using the `getClipBounds()` method on the graphics context. This method, by default, simply clears the exposed area with the canvas's background color. Override this method to implement your drawing routines. Note that the system does not automatically clear the exposed area.

Note: Canvases have been replaced by lightweight components. See the class description for details.

PARAMETERS

graphics   The non-`null` graphics context used to paint on the component.

OVERRIDES   `Component.paint()`.

EXAMPLE   This is the simplest example of a program that uses a canvas to draw a graphic. A subclass of canvas is defined and its `paint()` method over-ridden. The `paint()` method simply draws an oval. See Figure 46.

FIGURE 46:   **Painting on a Canvas.**

```
import java.awt.*;
class Main {
    static public void main(String[] args) {
        Frame f = new Frame("paint Example");
        f.add(new MainCanvas(), BorderLayout.CENTER);
        f.setSize(200, 100);
        f.show();
    }
}

class MainCanvas extends Canvas {
    public void paint(Graphics g) {
        g.drawOval(0, 0, getSize().width-1, getSize().height-1);
    }
}
```

A
B
C
D
E
F
G
H
I
J
K
L
M
N
O
P
Q
R
S
T
U
V
W
X
Y
Z

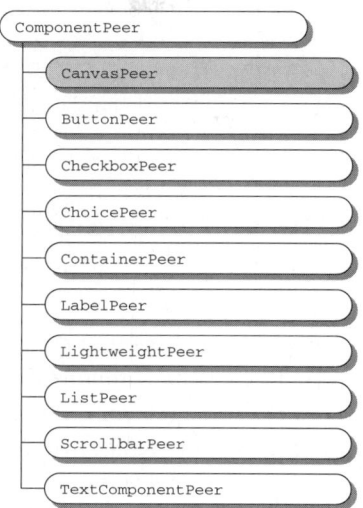

Syntax

```
public interface CanvasPeer extends ComponentPeer
```

Description

The canvas component (see the Canvas class) in the AWT uses the platform's native implementation of a canvas. So that the AWT canvas component behaves the same on all platforms, the canvas is assigned a *peer*, whose task is to translate the behavior of the platform's native canvas to the behavior of the AWT canvas.

AWT programmers normally do not directly use peer classes and interfaces. Instead, they deal with AWT components in the java.awt package. These in turn automatically manage their peers. Only someone who is porting the AWT to another platform should be concerned with the peer classes and interfaces. Consequently, most peer documentation refers to java.awt counterparts.

See Component and Toolkit for additional information about component peers.

See Also

java.awt.Canvas, java.awt.Component, java.awt.Toolkit.

java.awt
CardLayout

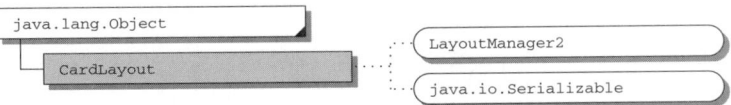

```
java.lang.Object

CardLayout

LayoutManager2

java.io.Serializable
```

Syntax
```
public class CardLayout implements LayoutManager2, Serializable
```

Description
The card layout manager shows only one component in the container at a time; all other components in the container are hidden. The visible component, called the *current component*, is resized to take up the entire visible area of the container (that is, the container's bounds less the space taken up by the container insets and card layout manager gaps).

Several methods allow you to change the current component. One of them is the show() method, which allows you to make any component current via its name. Unless you need to use the show() method, it is not necessary to name the components.

The card layout manager uses the visibility state of the components to keep track of the current component, so you should not directly change the visibility state of the components while they are under the control of a card layout manager.

Gaps
The card layout's gaps are really insets. The vertical gap specifies the space between the top and bottom edges of the container and the current component. The horizontal gap specifies the space between the left and right edges of the container and the current component.

MEMBER SUMMARY	
Constructor	
CardLayout()	Constructs a new CardLayout instance.
Show Methods	
first()	Makes the container's first component current.
last()	Makes the container's last component current.
next()	Makes the next component current.
previous()	Makes the previous component current.
show()	Makes a named component current.

MEMBER SUMMARY	
Layout Manager Methods	
addLayoutComponent()	Associates a name with a component.
getLayoutAlignmentX()	Retrieves this layout manager's *x*-alignment.
getLayoutAlighmentY()	Retrieves this layout manager's *y*-alignment.
invalidateLayout()	Invalidates this layout manager's state.
layoutContainer()	Lays out the container's components based on the settings of this layout manager.
maximumLayoutSize()	Calculates the maximum dimensions for laying out the components.
minimumLayoutSize()	Calculates the minimum dimensions needed to lay out the components.
preferredLayoutSize()	Calculates the preferred dimensions needed to lay out the components.
removeLayoutComponent()	Removes a component from this layout manager.
Gap Methods	
getHgap()	Retrieves this layout manager's horizontal gap.
getVgap()	Retrieves this layout manager's vertical gap.
setHgap()	Sets this layout manager's horizontal gap.
setVgap()	Sets this layout manager's vertical gap.
Debugging Method	
toString()	Generates the string representation of this layout manager's state.

See Also

java.io.Serializable, LayoutManager, LayoutManager2.

Example

This example creates a panel with a card layout manager (see Figure 47). A number of labels are added to the panel, each labeled with its position in the container. A row of buttons at the bottom controls the current component in the card layout.

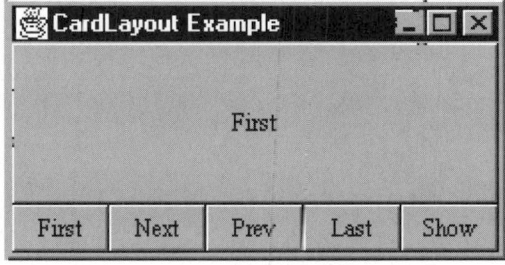

FIGURE 47: Button-controlled CardLayout.

```java
import java.awt.*;
import java.awt.event.ActionListener;
import java.awt.event.ActionEvent;

class Main extends Frame implements ActionListener {
    CardLayout cardLayout = new CardLayout();
    Panel cardCont = new Panel(cardLayout);
    Main() {
        super("CardLayout Example");

        cardCont.add(new Label("First", Label.CENTER), "First");
        cardCont.add(new Label("Second", Label.CENTER), "Second");
        cardCont.add(new Label("Third", Label.CENTER), "Third");
        cardCont.add(new Label("Show", Label.CENTER), "Show");
        cardCont.add(new Label("Last", Label.CENTER), "Last");
        add(cardCont, BorderLayout.CENTER);

        // Create control buttons
        Panel p = new Panel(new GridLayout(1, 0));
        Button button;
        p.add(button = new Button("First"));
        button.addActionListener(this);
        p.add(button = new Button("Next"));
        button.addActionListener(this);
        p.add(button = new Button("Prev"));
        button.addActionListener(this);
        p.add(button = new Button("Last"));
        button.addActionListener(this);
        p.add(button = new Button("Show"));
        button.addActionListener(this);

        // Add row of buttons to bottom
        add(p, BorderLayout.SOUTH);
        pack();
        show();
    }

    public void actionPerformed(ActionEvent evt) {
        String cmd = evt.getActionCommand();
        if ("First".equals(cmd)) {
            cardLayout.first(cardCont);
        } else if ("Prev".equals(cmd)) {
            cardLayout.previous(cardCont);
        } else if ("Next".equals(cmd)) {
            cardLayout.next(cardCont);
        } else if ("Last".equals(cmd)) {
            cardLayout.last(cardCont);
        } else if ("Show".equals(cmd)) {
            cardLayout.show(cardCont, cmd);
        }
    }

    public static void main(String args[]) {
        new Main();
    }
}
```

addLayoutComponent()

PURPOSE   Associates a name with a component.

SYNTAX   `public void addLayoutComponent(Component comp, Object compname)`
DEPRECATED   `public void addLayoutComponent(String compname, Component comp)`

DESCRIPTION   This method associates the name `compname` with the component `comp`. If
               another component in the same layout already has the same name, `compname`
               becomes associated with `comp` and the old association is lost. The component
               that was previously associated with `compname` can no longer be addressed by a
               name, but it can still be displayed using the `first()`, `last()`, `next()`, and
               `previous()` methods.

PARAMETERS
  comp   The non-`null` named component that has just been added to the container.
  compname   The non-`null` string name of the component to be added.

EXCEPTIONS
  `IllegalArgumentException`
               If `compname` is not an instance of `String`.

DEPRECATION   `addLayoutComponent()` now has a more generic form that can accept an
               arbitrary `Object` as a location instead of a `String`. Replace the usage of the
               deprecated form
                 `addLayoutComponent("top", component);`
               with
                 `addLayoutComponent(component, "top");`

EXAMPLE   See `LayoutManager`.

CardLayout()

PURPOSE   Constructs a new `CardLayout` instance.

SYNTAX   `public CardLayout()`
               `public CardLayout(int hgap, int vgap)`

DESCRIPTION   This constructor creates a new card layout manager instance with the gaps
               `hgap` and `vgap`. If the gaps are not specified, they both default to 0.

               The first component added to the container becomes the default current com-
               ponent. The component names are maintained in the card layout manager, so
               each container requires its own `CardLayout` instance. A container can be set
               to use a card layout only when the container has no components.

PARAMETERS
  hgap   A non-negative integer specifying the horizontal gap in pixels.

vgap	A non-negative integer specifying the vertical gap in pixels.
EXAMPLE	See the class example.

first( )

PURPOSE	Makes the container's first component current.
SYNTAX	`public void first(Container cont)`
DESCRIPTION	The current component in the container `cont` is hidden and `cont`'s first component is made current. The component need not have a name.
PARAMETERS	
cont	The non-`null` container using this layout instance.
SEE ALSO	`last()`, `next()`, `previous()`, `show()`.
EXAMPLE	See the class example.

getLayoutAlignmentX( )

PURPOSE	Retrieves this layout manager's *x*-alignment.
SYNTAX	`public float getLayoutAlignmentX(Container cont)`
DESCRIPTION	This method returns `Component.CENTER_ALIGNMENT`. See `LayoutManager2` for more information about alignments.
PARAMETERS	
cont	The non-`null` container using this layout manager instance.
RETURNS	This layout manager's *x*-alignment, which must be in the range `0.0f` to `1.0f`.
SEE ALSO	`Component.getAlignmentX()`, `Container.getAlignmentX()`, `getLayoutAlignmentY()`, `LayoutManager2`.
EXAMPLE	See the `LayoutManager2` class example.

getLayoutAlignmentY( )

PURPOSE	Retrieves this layout manager's *y*-alignment.
SYNTAX	`public float getLayoutAlignmentY(Container cont)`
DESCRIPTION	This method returns `Component.CENTER_ALIGNMENT`. See `LayoutManager2` for more information about alignments.

PARAMETERS

cont   The non-null container using this layout manager instance.

RETURNS   This layout manager's *y*-alignment, which must be in the range 0.0f to 1.0f.

SEE ALSO   Component.getAlignmentY(), Container.getAlignmentY(),
            getLayoutAlignmentX(), LayoutManager2.

EXAMPLE   See the LayoutManager2 class example.

getHgap()

PURPOSE   Retrieves this layout manager's horizontal gap.

SYNTAX   public int getHgap()

DESCRIPTION The horizontal gap specifies the space between the left and right edges of the
            container and the current component. The horizontal gap is initialized by the
            CardLayout constructor and updated using setHgap().

RETURNS   A non-negative integer specifying the horizontal gap in pixels.

SEE ALSO   getVgap(), setHgap().

EXAMPLE   This example
            is a variation
            on the class
            example. Four
            buttons label-
            ed V+, V-, H+,
            and H- control
            the vertical
            and horizontal
            gaps of the
            card layout. A
            status button

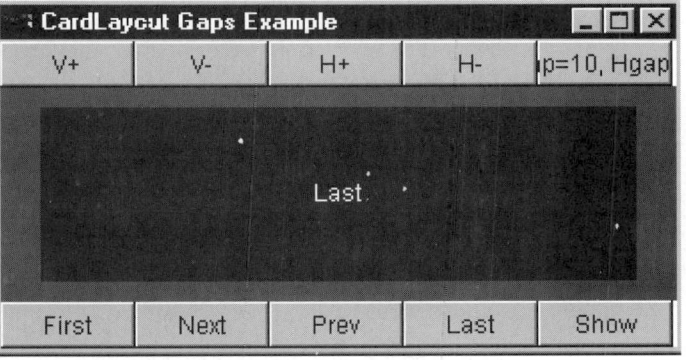

FIGURE 48: CardLayout's Horizontal and Vertical Gaps.

in the center is
used to display the current vertical and horizontal gaps in effect. The component inside the panel has a blue background, while the panel itself has a red
background. See Figure 48.

```
import java.awt.*;
import java.awt.event.ActionListener;
import java.awt.event.ActionEvent;

class Main extends Frame implements ActionListener {
    CardLayout cardLayout = new CardLayout();
    Panel cardCont = new Panel(cardLayout);
    Button status;
```

A
B
C
D
E
F
G
H
I
J
K
L
M
N
O
P
Q
R
S
T
U
V
W
X
Y
Z

```
Main() {
    super("CardLayout Gaps Example");

    cardCont.add(makeComponent("First"), "First");
    cardCont.add(makeComponent("Second"), "Second");
    cardCont.add(makeComponent("Third"), "Third");
    cardCont.add(makeComponent("Show"), "Show");
    cardCont.add(makeComponent("Last"), "Last");
    add(cardCont, BorderLayout.CENTER);
    cardCont.setBackground(Color.red);

    // Create card layout control buttons
    Panel p = new Panel(new GridLayout(1, 0));
    Button button;
    p.add(button = new Button("First"));
    button.addActionListener(this);
    p.add(button = new Button("Next"));
    button.addActionListener(this);
    p.add(button = new Button("Prev"));
    button.addActionListener(this);
    p.add(button = new Button("Last"));
    button.addActionListener(this);
    p.add(button = new Button("Show"));
    button.addActionListener(this);

    // Add row of buttons to bottom
    add(p, BorderLayout.SOUTH);

    // Create card layout control buttons
    p = new Panel(new GridLayout(1, 0));
    ActionListener gapHandler = new GapActionHandler();
    p.add(button = new Button("V+"));
    button.addActionListener(gapHandler);
    p.add(button = new Button("V-"));
    button.addActionListener(gapHandler);
    p.add(button = new Button("H+"));
    button.addActionListener(gapHandler);
    p.add(button = new Button("H-"));
    button.addActionListener(gapHandler);
    status = new Button("Vgap="+cardLayout.getVgap() +
                        ", Hgap="+cardLayout.getHgap());
    p.add(status);

    // Add gap control buttons to top
    add(p, BorderLayout.NORTH);

    pack();
    show();
}

public Component makeComponent(String label) {
    Label l = new Label(label, Label.CENTER);
    l.setBackground(Color.blue);
    l.setForeground(Color.white);
    return l;
}

public void actionPerformed(ActionEvent evt) {
    String cmd = evt.getActionCommand();
    if ("First".equals(cmd)) {
```

```
                cardLayout.first(cardCont);
        } else if ("Prev".equals(cmd)) {
                cardLayout.previous(cardCont);
        } else if ("Next".equals(cmd)) {
                cardLayout.next(cardCont);
        } else if ("Last".equals(cmd)) {
                cardLayout.last(cardCont);
        } else if ("Show".equals(cmd)) {
                cardLayout.show(cardCont, cmd);
        }
    }

    class GapActionHandler implements ActionListener {
        public void actionPerformed(ActionEvent evt) {
            String what = evt.getActionCommand();

            if ("H+".equals(what)) {
                cardLayout.setHgap(cardLayout.getHgap()+5);
            } else if ("H-".equals(what)) {
                cardLayout.setHgap(Math.max(0, cardLayout.getHgap()-5));
            } else if ("V+".equals(what)) {
                cardLayout.setVgap(cardLayout.getVgap()+5);
            } else if ("V-".equals(what)) {
                cardLayout.setVgap(Math.max(0, cardLayout.getVgap()-5));
            }
            // Update status button
            status.setLabel("Vgap="+cardLayout.getVgap() +
                            ", Hgap="+cardLayout.getHgap());
            cardCont.invalidate();
            cardCont.validate();
        }
    }

    public static void main(String args[]) {
        new Main();
    }
}
```

getVgap()

PURPOSE	Retrieves this layout manager's vertical gap.
SYNTAX	`public int getVgap()`
DESCRIPTION	The vertical gap specifies the space between the top and bottom edges of the container and the current component. The vertical gap is initialized by the CardLayout constructor and updated using setVgap().
RETURNS	A non-negative integer specifying the vertical gap in pixels.
SEE ALSO	getHgap(), setVgap().
EXAMPLE	See getHgap().

A
B

D
E
F
G
H
I
J
K
L
M
N
O
P
Q
R
S
T
U
V
W
X
Y
Z

215

invalidateLayout( )

PURPOSE Invalidates this layout manager's state.

SYNTAX `public void invalidateLayout(Container cont)`

DESCRIPTION This method is called by the layout manager's container to discard any cached information associated with this layout for the container `cont`. For `CardLayout`, this method by default does not do anything.

PARAMETERS
cont The non-`null` container using this layout instance.

SEE ALSO `LayoutManager2`.

EXAMPLE See the `LayoutManager2` class example.

last( )

PURPOSE Makes the container's last component current.

SYNTAX `public void last(Container cont)`

DESCRIPTION The current component in the container `cont` is hidden and `cont`'s last component is made current. The component need not have a name.

PARAMETERS
cont The non-`null` container using this layout instance.

SEE ALSO `first()`, `next()`, `previous()`, `show()`.

EXAMPLE See the class example.

layoutContainer( )

PURPOSE Lays out the container's components based on the settings of this layout manager.

SYNTAX `public void layoutContainer(Container cont)`

DESCRIPTION This method is called by the container when the layout is invalidated and needs to be redone. The current component in the container `cont` is resized to `cont`'s current dimensions, less the space used by the gaps and the container's insets.

PARAMETERS
cont The non-`null` container using this layout instance.

EXAMPLE See `LayoutManager`.

A
B

D
E
F
G

H
I

J

K

L
M

N

O

P

Q

R
S

T
U
V
W

X

Y
Z

maximumLayoutSize()

PURPOSE   Calculates the maximum dimensions for laying out the components.

SYNTAX   `public Dimension maximumLayoutSize(Container cont)`

DESCRIPTION   For a card layout, the maximum layout is by default the largest dimension available (`Integer.MAX_VALUE` by `Integer.MAX_VALUE`).

PARAMETERS
cont   The non-`null` container using this layout instance.

RETURNS   A new non-`null` `Dimension` instance containing the maximum size of the card layout.

SEE ALSO   `Component.getMaximumSize()`, `Container`, `minimumLayoutSize()`, `LayoutManager2`, `preferredLayoutSize()`.

EXAMPLE   See the `LayoutManager2` class example.

minimumLayoutSize()

PURPOSE   Calculates the minimum dimensions needed to lay out the components.

SYNTAX   `public Dimension minimumLayoutSize(Container cont)`

DESCRIPTION   The minimum dimension is calculated by determining the minimum size of each component in the container `cont`. The minimum dimension of the layout is the maximum of these minimum dimensions plus the added space for the gaps and `cont`'s insets.

PARAMETERS
cont   The non-`null` container using this layout instance.

RETURNS   A non-`null` `Dimension` object containing the minimum size of the card layout.

SEE ALSO   `Component.getMinimumSize()`, `maximumLayoutSize()`, `preferredLayoutSize()`.

EXAMPLE   See `LayoutManager`.

next()

PURPOSE   Makes the next component current.

SYNTAX   `public void next(Container cont)`

A
B
C
D
E
F
G
H
I
J
K
L
M
N
O
P
Q
R
S
T
U
V
W
X
Y
Z

DESCRIPTION   The current component in the container `cont` is hidden, and the component after the current component is made current. If the current component is already the last component, the method call is ignored. The component need not have a name.

PARAMETERS

   `cont`   The non-`null` container using this layout instance.

SEE ALSO   `first()`, `last()`, `previous()`, `show()`.

EXAMPLE   See the class example.

preferredLayoutSize()

PURPOSE   Calculates the preferred dimensions needed to lay out the components.

SYNTAX   `public Dimension preferredLayoutSize(Container cont)`

DESCRIPTION   The preferred dimension is calculated by determining the preferred size of each component in the container `cont`. The preferred dimension of the layout is the maximum of these preferred dimensions plus the added space for the gaps and `cont`'s insets.

PARAMETERS

   `cont`   The non-`null` container using this layout instance.

RETURNS   A non-`null` `Dimension` object containing the preferred size of the card layout.

SEE ALSO   `Component.getPreferredSize()`, `maximumLayoutSize()`, `minimumLayoutSize()`.

EXAMPLE   See `LayoutManager`.

previous()

PURPOSE   Makes the previous component current.

SYNTAX   `public void previous(Container cont)`

DESCRIPTION   The current component in the container `cont` is hidden, and the component before the current component is made current. If the current component is already the first component, the method call is ignored. The component need not have a name.

PARAMETERS

   `cont`   The non-`null` container using this layout instance.

SEE ALSO   `first()`, `last()`, `next()`, `show()`.

EXAMPLE   See the class example.

removeLayoutComponent()

PURPOSE   Removes a component from this layout manager.

SYNTAX   `public void removeLayoutComponent(Component comp)`

DESCRIPTION   This method removes the component `comp` from the layout.

PARAMETERS
comp   The non-`null` component about to be removed from the container.

EXAMPLE   See `LayoutManager`.

setHgap()

PURPOSE   Sets this layout manager's horizontal gap.

SYNTAX   `public void setHgap(int hgap)`

DESCRIPTION   See the class description for a discussion of a card layout manager's gaps. This method sets the horizontal gap of this layout to be `hgap`.

PARAMETERS
hgap   A non-negative integer specifying the horizontal gap in pixels.

SEE ALSO   `getHgap()`, `setVgap()`.

EXAMPLE   See `getHgap()`.

setVgap()

PURPOSE   Sets this layout manager's vertical gap.

SYNTAX   `public void setVgap(int vgap)`

DESCRIPTION   See the class description for discussion of a card layout manager's gaps. This method sets the vertical gap of this layout to be `vgap`.

PARAMETERS
vgap   A non-negative integer specifying the vertical gap in pixels.

SEE ALSO   `getVgap()`, `setHgap()`.

EXAMPLE   See `getHgap()`.

A
B

D
E
F
G
H
I
J
K
L
M
N
O
P
Q
R
S
T
U
V
W
X
Y
Z

A
B
C
D
E
F
G
H
I
J
K
L
M
N
O
P
Q
R
S
T
U
V
W
X
Y
Z

show( )

PURPOSE	Makes a named component current.
SYNTAX	`public void show(Container cont, String name)`
DESCRIPTION	This method makes the component named by name the current component in the container cont. name is the component's name as declared via the `addLayoutComponent()` method call. This call is ignored if name does not name a component in cont.
PARAMETERS	
cont	The non-null container containing the component.
name	The non-null string specifying the component's name.
EXAMPLE	See the class example.

toString( )

PURPOSE	Generates a string representation of this layout manager's state.
SYNTAX	`public String toString()`
DESCRIPTION	The string representation contains the layout manager's class name and the size of the two gaps. This method returns this string representation.

This method is typically used for debugging. |
RETURNS	A non-null string representing the layout manager's state.
OVERRIDES	`java.lang.Object.toString()`.
EXAMPLE	See `java.lang.Object.toString()`.

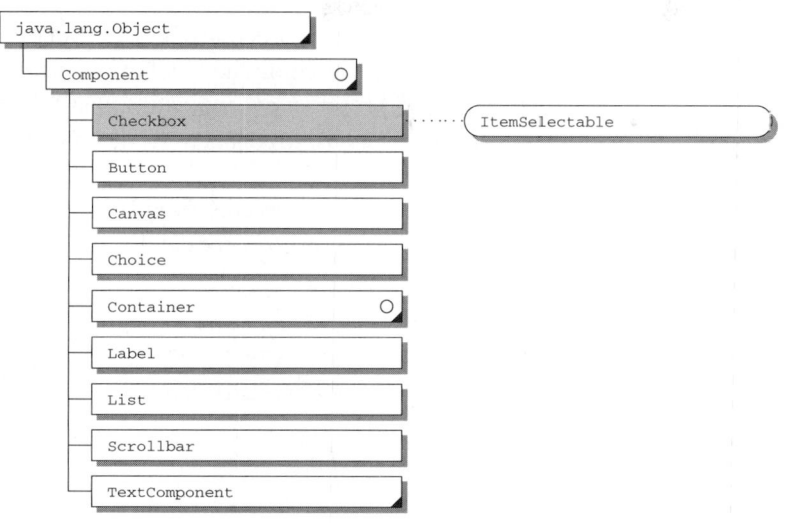

Syntax

`public class Checkbox extends Component implements ItemSelectable`

Description

The checkbox is a component that maintains and displays a check state that can be either *on* or *off*. The check state can be changed by either the user or the program. A checkbox is typically used to indicate a two-value choice in an application. For example, in a mail application you may or may not want an audible signal of new mail. A checkbox with the label "Play sound for new mail" would be a typical way to display the current preference and to allow the user to change it.

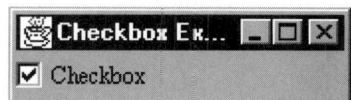

FIGURE 49:   Simple Checkbox.

Figure 49 shows a checkbox component with the label "Checkbox"; the checkbox is set to *on*.

Checkbox Groups

Two or more checkboxes can be grouped together so that at most one of the checkboxes in the group is set to *on*. That checkbox is the *current checkbox*. Figure 50 shows a checkbox group containing four checkboxes. See the `Checkbox-Group` class for more information about checkbox groups.

FIGURE 50:   CheckboxGroup.

Events

A checkbox fires an item event whenever it is clicked. See `ItemEvent` for details about item. The item of the item event is the label of the checkbox.

A grouped checkbox fires an item event whenever it is clicked. The event is fired only by the new current checkbox, with the item of the event being the label of the new current checkbox. The previous current checkbox does not fire an event indicating that it has been turned off. If the current checkbox is clicked, an event is fired because the modifiers may have changed.

In addition to item events, a checkbox fires all the events fired by the `Component` class. See the `Component` class for details. See the `AWTEvent` class for details on how to filter or handle events.

MEMBER SUMMARY	
Constructor	
`Checkbox()`	Constructs a new `Checkbox` instance.
Checkbox Group Methods	
`getCheckboxGroup()`	Retrieves the checkbox's checkbox group.
`setCheckboxGroup()`	Sets the checkbox's checkbox group to the specified group.
Property Methods	
`getLabel()`	Retrieves the checkbox's label.
`getState()`	Retrieves the check state of the checkbox.
`setLabel()`	Sets the checkbox's label.
`setState()`	Sets the checkbox's check state.
Selection Method	
`getSelectedObjects()`	Retrieves the checkbox label if this checkbox is selected.
Event Methods	
`addItemListener()`	Adds a listener to receive item events fired by this checkbox.
`processEvent()`	Processes an event enabled for this checkbox.
`processItemEvent()`	Processes an item event enabled for this checkbox.
`removeItemListener()`	Removes a listener from receiving item events fired by this checkbox.
Peer Method	
`addNotify()`	Creates the checkbox's peer.
Debugging Method	
`paramString()`	Generates a string representation of the checkbox's state.

Example

For a simple example using a checkbox, see the Check-
box() constructor. The example given here is more elaborate and features a program that displays a set of options
that can be applied to the purchase of a car. As more options
are enabled, the price of the car increases. See Figure 51.

FIGURE 51: Use of Checkbox for Multiple Options.

```java
import java.awt.*;
import java.awt.event.ItemListener;
import java.awt.event.ItemEvent;

class Main extends Frame implements ItemListener
{
    Checkbox cbAC =
        new Checkbox("Air Conditioning");
    Checkbox cbSR = new Checkbox("Sun Roof");
    Checkbox cbSW = new Checkbox("Steering Wheel");
    Checkbox cbTR = new Checkbox("Tires");
    Label status = new Label();

    Main() {
        super("Checkbox Example");
        Panel gridPanel = new Panel(new GridLayout(0, 1));
        gridPanel.add(cbAC);
        gridPanel.add(cbSR);
        gridPanel.add(cbSW);
        gridPanel.add(cbTR);
        add(gridPanel, BorderLayout.CENTER);

        // Set listener for each checkbox
        cbAC.addItemListener(this);
        cbSR.addItemListener(this);
        cbSW.addItemListener(this);
        cbTR.addItemListener(this);

        computeTotal();
        add(status, BorderLayout.SOUTH);
        pack();
        show();
    }

    public void itemStateChanged(ItemEvent evt) {
        computeTotal();
    }

    void computeTotal() {
        int total = 25000;
        if (cbAC.getState()) total += 510;
        if (cbSR.getState()) total += 2222;
        if (cbSW.getState()) total += 150;
        if (cbTR.getState()) total += 320;
        status.setText("Total Sticker Price: $" + total);
    }

    static public void main(String[] args) {
        new Main();
    }
}
```

A
B
C
D
E
F
G
H
I
J
K
L
M
N
O
P
Q
R
S
T
U
V
W
X
Y
Z

addItemListener()

PURPOSE	Adds a listener to receive item events fired by this checkbox.
SYNTAX	`public synchronized void addItemListener(ItemListener listener)`
DESCRIPTION	An item event is fired when this checkbox is checked. See `ItemEvent` and the class description for more details. After this method is called, the item listener `listener` will receive item events fired by this checkbox. If `listener` is `null`, this method does nothing.
PARAMETERS	
`listener`	The possibly `null` item listener to add.
SEE ALSO	`ItemSelectable, java.awt.event.ItemEvent,` `java.awt.event.ItemListener, removeItemListener().`
EXAMPLE	See the class example.

addNotify()

PURPOSE	Creates the checkbox's peer.
SYNTAX	`public void addNotify()`
DESCRIPTION	This method creates the peer if it does not exist. The peer is created by calling the `Toolkit.createCheckbox()` method.
	This method should never be called directly. It is normally called by the parent.
OVERRIDES	`Component.addNotify().`
SEE ALSO	`Component, Toolkit.`
EXAMPLE	See `Component.setVisible().`

Checkbox()

PURPOSE	Constructs a new `Checkbox` instance.
SYNTAX	`public Checkbox()`
	`public Checkbox(String label)`
	`public Checkbox(String label, boolean state)`
	`public Checkbox(String label, boolean state, CheckboxGroup group)`
	`public Checkbox(String label, CheckboxGroup group, boolean state)`
DESCRIPTION	This constructor creates a new visible `checkbox` component with the label `label`, checkbox group `group`, and initial check state `state`. A `null` label is the same as "". If the label is not specified, it defaults to `null`. If `state` is not

Sidebar: A B C D E F G H I J K L M N O P Q R S T U V W X Y Z

specified, it defaults to `false`. If group is `null`, the checkbox will not be included in any checkbox group. If group is not specified, it defaults to `null`.

PARAMETERS

group   The checkbox group in which to include the new checkbox. May be `null`.

label   A string specifying the label on the checkbox. May be `null`.

state   A `boolean` specifying the checkbox's initial check state.

EXAMPLE   This simple example creates a checkbox with the label "Checkbox" and prints the current state of the checkbox each time it is clicked. See Figure 52.

FIGURE 52: Simple Checkbox.

```
import java.awt.*;
import java.awt.event.ItemListener;
import java.awt.event.ItemEvent;

class Main extends Frame implements ItemListener {
    Checkbox cb = new Checkbox("Checkbox");

    Main() {
        super("Checkbox Example");
        add(cb, BorderLayout.NORTH);
        cb.addItemListener(this);
        pack();
        show();
    }

    public void itemStateChanged(ItemEvent evt) {
    Object obj = evt.getSource();
    if (obj instanceof Checkbox) {
        System.out.println("checkbox: " + ((Checkbox)obj).getState());
    }
    }

    static public void main(String[] args) {
        new Main();
    }
}
```

getCheckboxGroup( )

PURPOSE   Retrieves the checkbox's checkbox group.

SYNTAX   `public CheckboxGroup getCheckboxGroup()`

DESCRIPTION   If the return value is `null`, the checkbox is not a group checkbox.

RETURNS   The checkbox's checkbox group. The return value may be `null`. This means the checkbox is not in a checkbox group.

225

SEE ALSO   `setCheckboxGroup()`.

EXAMPLE   See `setCheckboxGroup()`.

getLabel( )

PURPOSE   Retrieves the checkbox's label.

SYNTAX   `public String getLabel()`

RETURNS   A string containing the checkbox's label. The result value may be `null`.

SEE ALSO   `setLabel()`.

EXAMPLE   See `setLabel()`.

getSelectedObjects( )

PURPOSE   Retrieves the checkbox's label if this checkbox is selected.

SYNTAX   `public Object[] getSelectedObjects()`

RETURNS   An array with one item containing the checkbox's label if the checkbox is selected; `null` otherwise.

SEE ALSO   `getLabel()`, `ItemSelectable`.

EXAMPLE   See the class example of `ItemSelectable`.

getState( )

PURPOSE   Retrieves the check state of the checkbox.

SYNTAX   `public boolean getState()`

RETURNS   `true` if the check state is set to *on*; `false` otherwise.

SEE ALSO   `setState()`.

EXAMPLE   This example creates a checkbox and a text area. If the checkbox is set to *off*, the text area behaves normally. If the checkbox is set to *on*, all characters typed in the text area are converted to uppercase. See Figure 53.

FIGURE 53: Using Checkbox to Control a TextArea.

```
import java.awt.*;
import java.awt.event.*;
class Main extends Frame {
    Checkbox cb = new Checkbox("Upper Case");
    TextArea ta = new TextArea(10, 40);

    Main() {
        super("getState Example");
        add(cb, BorderLayout.NORTH);
        add(ta, BorderLayout.CENTER);

        ta.addKeyListener(new KeyListener());

        pack();
        show();
    }

    // Define listener to deal with upper case mode
    class KeyListener extends KeyAdapter {
        public void keyPressed(KeyEvent evt) {
            char ch = evt.getKeyChar();

            if (cb.getState() && Character.isLowerCase(ch)) {
                evt.setKeyChar(Character.toUpperCase(ch));
            }
        }
    }

    static public void main(String[] args) {
        new Main();
    }
}
```

A
B
C
D
E
F
G
H
I
J
K
L
M
N
O
P
Q
R
S
T
U
V
W
X
Y
Z

paramString()

PURPOSE	Generates a string representation of the checkbox's state.
SYNTAX	`protected String paramString()`
DESCRIPTION	The returned string includes the checkbox's label and check state. A subclass of this class should override this method and return a concatenation of its state with the results of `super.paramString()`. This method is called by the `toString()` method and is typically used for debugging.
RETURNS	A non-`null` string representing the checkbox's state.
OVERRIDES	`Component.paramString()`.
SEE ALSO	`toString()`.
EXAMPLE	See `Component.paramString()`.

A
B
C
D
E
F
G
H
I
J
K
L
M
N
O
P
Q
R
S
T
U
V
W
X
Y
Z

processEvent()

PURPOSE   Processes an event enabled for this checkbox.

SYNTAX   `protected void processEvent(AWTEvent evt)`

DESCRIPTION   This method extends `Component.processEvent()` by adding support for `ItemEvent`.

When a subclass overrides `processEvent()`, it should call `super.process-Event()` to perform the processing intended by its base class (such as dispatching the listeners).

PARAMETERS

evt   The event to be processed.

OVERRIDES   `Component.processEvent()`.

SEE ALSO   `AWTEvent`, `processItemEvent()`.

EXAMPLE   See `ItemSelectable`'s class example.

processItemEvent()

PURPOSE   Processes an item event on this checkbox.

SYNTAX   `protected void processItemEvent(ItemEvent evt)`

DESCRIPTION   An item event is fired when this checkbox is clicked. See `ItemEvent` and the class description for more details. This method processes item events for this checkbox by calling any registered `ItemListener`. This method is invoked only if item events have been enabled for this checkbox. This can happen either when an item listener is added to this component or if item events are enabled explicitly via `Component.enableEvents()`.

Typically, a program controls how item events for a checkbox are processed. It does this by adding or removing item listeners. It overrides `processItem-Event()` only if it needs to do processing in addition to that performed by the registered listeners.

When a subclass does override `processItemEvent()`, it should call `super.processItemEvent()` to perform the processing intended by its base class (such as dispatching the listeners).

PARAMETERS

evt   The event to be processed.

SEE ALSO   `java.awt.event.ItemEvent`, `ItemSelectable`,
`java.awt.event.ItemListener`, `processEvent()`.

EXAMPLE   See `ItemSelectable`'s class example.

removeItemListener()

PURPOSE	Removes a listener from receiving item events from this checkbox.
SYNTAX	`public synchronized void removeItemListener(ItemListener listener)`
DESCRIPTION	An item event is fired when this checkbox is clicked. See `ItemEvent` in the class description for more details. After this method is called, the item listener `listener` will no longer receive item events from this checkbox. If `listener` is `null`, this method does nothing.
PARAMETERS	
listener	The possibly `null` item listener to remove.
SEE ALSO	`addItemListener()`, `ItemSelectable`, `java.awt.event.ItemEvent`, `java.awt.event.ItemListener`.
EXAMPLE	See the usage of `removeActionListener()` in `MenuItem.dispatch-Events()`.

setCheckboxGroup()

PURPOSE	Sets the checkbox's checkbox group.
SYNTAX	`public void setCheckboxGroup(CheckboxGroup group)`
DESCRIPTION	This method is used to change a checkbox's checkbox group. It is not used very often, as checkboxes do not typically change groups after they are created. The checkbox group of a checkbox is typically known at the time the checkbox is created, so it is supplied to the checkbox constructor method.
PARAMETERS	
group	The checkbox's new checkbox group. A value of `null` removes the checkbox from its current group.
SEE ALSO	`getCheckboxGroup()`.
EXAMPLE	This example creates two checkbox groups called "Left" and "Right." By using the choice component at the bottom, the user can make the checkbox at the top part be of either group or of no group. See Figure 54.

FIGURE 54: Dynamically Modifying CheckboxGroup Membership.

```
import java.awt.*;
import java.awt.event.ItemListener;
import java.awt.event.ItemEvent;
```

A
B
C
D
E
F
G
H
I
J
K
L
M
N
O
P
Q
R
S
T
U
V
W
X
Y
Z

229

setLabel( )

```
class Main extends Frame implements ItemListener {
    CheckboxGroup cgLeft = new CheckboxGroup();
    CheckboxGroup cgRight = new CheckboxGroup();
    Choice choice = new Choice();
    Checkbox cb = new Checkbox("Left", cgLeft, true);

    Main() {
        super("setCheckboxGroup Example");
        Panel p = new Panel(new GridLayout(0, 1));

        add(cb, BorderLayout.NORTH);

        p.add(new Checkbox("Left", cgLeft, false));
        p.add(new Checkbox("Left", cgLeft, false));
        add(p, BorderLayout.WEST);

        p = new Panel(new GridLayout(0, 1));
        p.add(new Checkbox("Right", cgRight, false));
        p.add(new Checkbox("Right", cgRight, false));
        add(p, BorderLayout.EAST);

        choice.addItem("None");
        choice.addItem("Left");
        choice.addItem("Right");
        choice.select("Left");
        choice.addItemListener(this);
        add(choice, BorderLayout.SOUTH);

        pack();
        show();
    }

    public void itemStateChanged(ItemEvent evt) {
        String what = (String)(evt.getItem());
        cb.setLabel((String)what);
        if ("None".equals(what)) {
            cb.setCheckboxGroup(null);
        } else if ("Left".equals(what)) {
            cb.setCheckboxGroup(cgLeft);
        } else if ("Right".equals(what)) {
            cb.setCheckboxGroup(cgRight);
        }
    }

    static public void main(String[] args) {
        new Main();
    }
}
```

A
B
C
D
E
F
G
H
I
J
K
L
M
N
O
P
Q
R
S
T
U
V
W
X
Y
Z

setLabel( )

PURPOSE   Sets the checkbox's label.

SYNTAX   `public synchronized void setLabel(String label)`

DESCRIPTION   Note that the minimum and preferred sizes of the checkbox may change, so it may be necessary to resize the checkbox. The example shows how to cause the checkbox's parent to resize the checkbox.

PARAMETERS

label   The non-null string specifying the checkbox's new label.

SEE ALSO   getLabel().

EXAMPLE   This example creates a checkbox and a text field. Pressing Return in the text field causes the checkbox label to be set to the contents of the text field. When the label changes, so does its minimum size. This example also shows how to cause the checkbox's parent to properly resize the checkbox.

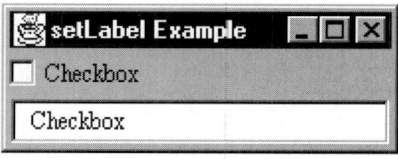

FIGURE 55:   **Changing Checkbox's Label.**

The canvas to the right of the checkbox is there to force the checkbox to be as narrow as possible. See Figure 55.

```java
import java.awt.*;
import java.awt.event.ActionListener;
import java.awt.event.ActionEvent;
class Main extends Frame implements ActionListener {
    Checkbox cb = new Checkbox("Checkbox");
    TextField tf = new TextField(40);

    Main() {
        super("setLabel Example");
        add(new Canvas(), BorderLayout.CENTER);
        add(cb, BorderLayout.WEST);
        add(tf, BorderLayout.SOUTH);
        tf.setText(cb.getLabel());        // Initialize with current label
        tf.addActionListener(this);       // Set listener for updating label
        pack();
        show();
    }

    public void actionPerformed(ActionEvent evt) {
        cb.setLabel(tf.getText());

    // Invalidate this checkbox because of size change
        cb.invalidate();

        // Validate parent to resize checkbox
        cb.getParent().validate();
    }

    static public void main(String[] args) {
        new Main();
    }
}
```

A
B
C
D
E
F
G
H
I
J
K
L
M
N
O
P
Q
R
S
T
U
V
W
X
Y
Z

setState()

PURPOSE   Sets the checkbox's check state.

SYNTAX   `public void setState(boolean state)`

DESCRIPTION   The method call is ignored when this is both a group checkbox and the current checkbox.

PARAMETERS
state   If `true`, the checkbox's check state is set to *on*; otherwise, it is set to *off*.

SEE ALSO   `getState()`.

EXAMPLE   This example creates a checkbox and a checkbox menu item and synchronizes their check states. If the checkbox is set to *on*, so is the checkbox menu item. See Figure 56.

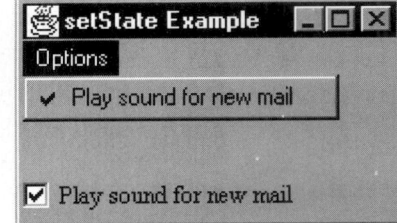

FIGURE 56:   Changing Checkbox's State.

```java
import java.awt.*;
import java.awt.event.ItemListener;
import java.awt.event.ItemEvent;
class Main extends Frame
    implements ItemListener {
    CheckboxMenuItem mi = new CheckboxMenuItem("Play sound for new mail");
    Checkbox cb = new Checkbox("Play sound for new mail");

    Main() {
        super("setState Example");
        MenuBar mb = new MenuBar();
        Menu m = new Menu("Options");

        m.add(mi);
        mb.add(m);
        setMenuBar(mb);
        add(cb, BorderLayout.SOUTH);
        // Set listeners for checkbox and checkbox menu item
        cb.addItemListener(this);
        mi.addItemListener(this);
        pack();
        show();
    }

    public void itemStateChanged(ItemEvent evt) {
        if (evt.getSource() == mi) {
            cb.setState(mi.getState());
        } else {
            mi.setState(cb.getState());
        }
        // playSoundForNewMail();
    }
    static public void main(String[] args) {
        new Main();
    }
}
```

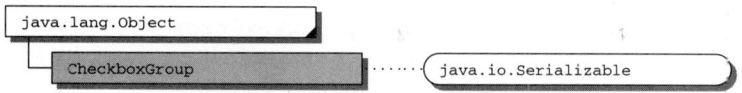

```
java.lang.Object

    CheckboxGroup · · · · · · · java.io.Serializable
```

Syntax

`public class CheckboxGroup implements Serializable`

Description

The checkbox group is used to group checkbox components; it is not an AWT component. In a checkbox group, at most one checkbox is in the *on* state. This checkbox is the *currently selected* checkbox. Selecting any of the other checkboxes in the group causes that checkbox to become the currently selected checkbox and all other checkboxes in the group to be automatically set to *off*. Figure 57 shows a checkbox group that contains four checkboxes; the "Send later" checkbox is set to *on*. See the `Checkbox` class for more information about checkboxes.

FIGURE 57: CheckboxGroup.

It is possible that none of the checkboxes in the group are set to *on*. This can happen in one of two ways:

1. If none of the checkboxes that are added to the group are set to *on*.
2. If the current checkbox in the group is removed from the group.

Checkbox Group versus Choice Component

The choice component is similar to the checkbox group in that it lets the user choose from a fixed set of items (see the `Choice` class). Following are two design guidelines to consider when deciding between the checkbox group and the choice component. As with all user interface "principles," these guidelines are intended to summarize the issues and not mandate your design.

1. The larger the number of items, the more appropriate the choice component becomes. You should probably use a choice component if you have five or more items.
2. If a group of one or more components is related to one particular item and is therefore enabled only if that item is selected, a checkbox group might be appropriate.

A
B
C
D
E
F
G
H
I
J
K
L
M
N
O
P
Q
R
S
T
U
V
W
X
Y
Z

MEMBER SUMMARY	
Constructor	
CheckboxGroup()	Constructs a new CheckboxGroup instance.
Selected Checkbox Methods	
getSelectedCheckbox()	Retrieves the currently selected checkbox.
setSelectedCheckbox()	Sets the currently selected checkbox.
Debugging Method	
toString()	Generates a string representation of the checkbox group's state.
Deprecated Methods	
getCurrent()	Replaced by getSelectedCheckbox().
setCurrent()	Replaced by setSelectedCheckbox().

A
B
D
E
F
G
H
I
J
K
L
M
N
O
P
Q
R
S
T
U
V
W
X
Y
Z

See Also

Checkbox, Choice, java.io.Serializable.

Example

This example creates a checkbox group and a collection of colored canvases. Clicking a checkbox causes its associated color canvas to be selected. Also, clicking a colored canvas causes its associated checkbox to be current. See Figure 58.

FIGURE 58: Use of CheckboxGroup for Exclusive Options.

```java
import java.awt.*;
import java.awt.event.*;

class Main extends Frame implements ItemListener {
    Color[] cbColor = {Color.red, Color.green, Color.blue};
    String[] cbName = {"Red", "Green", "Blue"};
    MainCanvas[] cbCanvas = new MainCanvas[3];
    CheckboxGroup cgroup = new CheckboxGroup();

    Main() {
        super("CheckboxGroup Example");
        Panel p = new Panel(new GridLayout(0, 1)),
            colorPanel = new Panel(new GridLayout(1, 0));

        for (int i=0; i<cbColor.length; i++) {
            Checkbox cb = new Checkbox(cbName[i], cgroup, i == 0);
            p.add(cb);
            cb.addItemListener(this);
            colorPanel.add(cbCanvas[i] = new MainCanvas(cbColor[i], cb));
```

```
                cbCanvas[i].setSize(70, 70);
            }
            add(p, BorderLayout.WEST);
            add(colorPanel, BorderLayout.CENTER);
            pack();
            show();
        }

        public void itemStateChanged(ItemEvent evt) {
            // Update canvases when checkbox pressed
            for (int i=0; i<cbCanvas.length; i++) {
                cbCanvas[i].repaint();
            }
        }

        static public void main(String[] args) {
            new Main();
        }
    }

    class MainCanvas extends Canvas {
        Checkbox cb;

        MainCanvas(Color color, Checkbox cb) {
            setBackground(color);
            this.cb = cb;
            addMouseListener(new MouseListener());
        }

        public void paint(Graphics g) {
            if (cb.getCheckboxGroup().getSelectedCheckbox() == cb) {
                Dimension d = getSize();
                g.setColor(Color.black);
                g.fillOval(d.width/3, d.height/3, d.width/3, d.height/3);
            }
        }

        class MouseListener extends MouseAdapter {
            public void mousePressed(MouseEvent evt) {
                // Update checkbox group
                cb.getCheckboxGroup().setSelectedCheckbox(cb);

                // Update all sibling canvases.
                for (int i=0; i<getParent().getComponentCount(); i++) {
                    getParent().getComponent(i).repaint();
                }
            }
        }
    }
}
```

A
B

D
E
F
G
H
I
J
K
L
M
N
O
P
Q
R
S
T
U
V
W
X
Y
Z

CheckboxGroup( )

PURPOSE   Constructs a new **CheckboxGroup** instance.

SYNTAX   `public CheckboxGroup()`

EXAMPLE   This example creates a checkbox group that has three buttons. When a checkbox is clicked, it prints out the new state of the checkbox. See Figure 59.

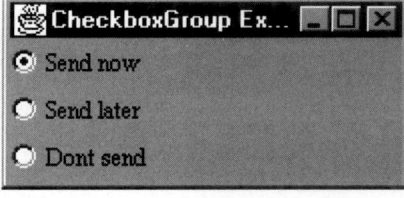

FIGURE 59:   **CheckboxGroup( )**.

```java
import java.awt.*;
import java.awt.event.ItemListener;
import java.awt.event.ItemEvent;

class Main extends Frame implements ItemListener {
    CheckboxGroup cg = new CheckboxGroup();

    Main() {
        super("CheckboxGroup Example");
        Panel p = new Panel(new GridLayout(0, 1));

        Checkbox cb;
        p.add(cb = new Checkbox("Send now", cg, true));
        cb.addItemListener(this);
        p.add(cb = new Checkbox("Send later", cg, false));
        cb.addItemListener(this);
        p.add(cb = new Checkbox("Dont send", cg, false));
        cb.addItemListener(this);

        add(p, BorderLayout.CENTER);
        pack();
        show();
    }

    public void itemStateChanged(ItemEvent evt) {
        String what = (String)(evt.getItemSelectable().
            getSelectedObjects()[0]);
        System.out.println(what);
    }

    static public void main(String[] args) {
        new Main();
    }
}
```

getCurrent( )   *DEPRECATED*

PURPOSE   Replaced by `getSelectedCheckbox()`.

SYNTAX   `public Checkbox getCurrent()`

DEPRECATION   Replace the usage of the deprecated method

```
    Checkbox cb = cbgroup.getCurrent();
with
    Checkbox cb = cbgroup.getSelectedCheckbox();
```

RETURNS   The currently selected checkbox in the group. The return value may be `null`.

getSelectedCheckbox()

PURPOSE   Retrieves the currently selected checkbox.

SYNTAX   `public Checkbox getSelectedCheckbox()`

DESCRIPTION   This method retrieves the currently selected checkbox. The check state of the currently selected checkbox will always be set to *on*. If the return value is `null`, then either there are no checkboxes in the group or none of the checkboxes are set to *on*.

RETURNS   The currently selected checkbox in the group. The return value may be `null`.

SEE ALSO   `setSelectedCheckbox()`.

EXAMPLE   See the class example.

setCurrent()   *DEPRECATED*

PURPOSE   Replaced by `setSelectedCheckbox()`.

SYNTAX   `public synchronized void setCurrent(Checkbox checkbox)`

PARAMETERS
checkbox   The checkbox to be selected. May be `null`.

DEPRECATION   Replace the usage of the deprecated method
```
    cbgroup.setCurrent(checkbox);
```
with
```
    cbgroup.setSelectedCheckbox(checkbox);
```

setSelectedCheckbox()

PURPOSE   Sets the selected checkbox.

SYNTAX   `public synchronized void setSelectedCheckbox(Checkbox checkbox)`

DESCRIPTION   This method sets `checkbox` to be the currently selected checkbox. If `checkbox` is `null`, none of the checkboxes in the group will be made current. The method is ignored if `checkbox` belongs to a different group.

A
B
D
E
F
G
H
I
J
K
L
M
N
O
P
Q
R
S
T
U
V
W
X
Y
Z

PARAMETERS

checkbox　　The checkbox to be selected. May be `null`.

SEE ALSO　　`getSelectedCheckbox()`.

EXAMPLE　　See the class example.

toString()

PURPOSE　　Generates a string representation of the checkbox group's state.

SYNTAX　　`public String toString()`

DESCRIPTION　　This method returns the string representation of this checkbox group's state (the checkbox that is currently selected). It is typically used for debugging.

RETURNS　　A non-`null` string representing the checkbox group's state.

OVERRIDES　　`java.lang.Object.toString()`.

EXAMPLE

```
CheckboxGroup gb = new CheckboxGroup();
Checkbox cb = new Checkbox("Read-only", gb, true);
System.out.println(gb);
```

CheckboxMenuItem

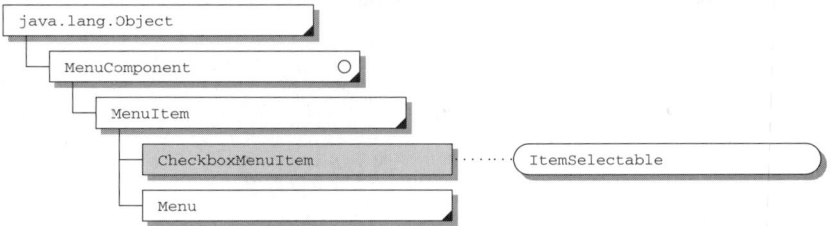

Syntax

```
public class CheckboxMenuItem extends MenuItem implements ItemSelectable
```

Description

A checkbox menu item adds an additional property to a `MenuItem` object: the *check state*. The checkbox menu item's check state is always in one of two states: *on* or *off*. It can be changed at any time by either the user or a program. A checkbox menu item is typically used to indicate a two-value choice in an application. For example, in a mail application you may or may not want an audible signal of new mail. A checkbox menu item with the label "Play sound for new mail" would be a typical way to display the current preference and to allow the user to change it.

Figure 60 shows a menu displaying two checkbox menu items. The one labeled "Play sound for new mail" is set to *on*, while the one labeled "Pop dialog for new mail" is set to *off*.

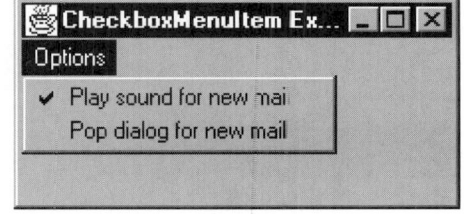

FIGURE 60: `CheckboxMenuItem`.

Events

The checkbox menu item fires an action event just like the menu item does (see `MenuItem` for details).[1] In addition, the checkbox menu item also fires an item event when the state of the checkbox changes. The item of the item event is the label of the checkbox menu item.

The checked state of the checkbox menu item is automatically set before the action or item event is fired. For example, if the checked state is currently `true` and the user selects the checkbox menu item, the checked state is set to `false` and then the event is fired.

---

1. In Java 1.1.2, a checkbox menu item does not fire action events even though it is a subclass of `MenuItem`. This is a bug.

See the `MenuItem` class for more details about the action event. See `ItemEvent` for more details about item events. See the `AWTEvent` class for general information on events and how to filter or handle them.

A
B

D
E
F
G
H
I
J
K
L
M
N
O
P
Q
R
S
T
U
V
W
X
Y
Z

MEMBER SUMMARY	
Constructor	
CheckboxMenuItem()	Constructs a new `CheckboxMenuItem` instance.
State Methods	
getState()	Retrieves the checked state of the checkbox menu item.
setState()	Sets the checkbox menu item's check state.
Selection Method	
getSelectedObjects()	Retrieves the checkbox menu item's label if this item is selected.
Event Methods	
addItemListener()	Adds a listener to receive item events fired by this checkbox menu item.
processItemEvent()	Processes an item event enabled for this checkbox menu item.
processEvent()	Processes an event enabled for this checkbox menu item.
removeItemListener()	Removes a listener from receiving item events fired by this checkbox menu item.
Peer Method	
addNotify()	Creates the checkbox menu item's peer.
Debugging Method	
paramString()	Generates a string representation of the checkbox menu's state.

See Also

AWTEvent, Checkbox, java.awt.event.ActionEvent,
java.awt.event.ActionListener, java.awt.event.ItemEvent,
java.awt.event.ItemListener, MenuItem.

Example

This example creates a menu with two checkbox menu items. The one labeled "Play sound for new mail" is enabled and the one labeled "Pop dialog for new mail" is disabled. See Figure 60 for a screen shot of the example. The menu is installed in a menu bar, which in turn is installed in a frame. This example also shows you how to handle item events fired by a checkbox menu item.

```
import java.awt.*;
import java.awt.event.ItemListener;
import java.awt.event.ItemEvent;

class Main extends Frame implements ItemListener {
    CheckboxMenuItem sound, popup;
    Main() {
        super("CheckboxMenuItem Example");
        MenuBar mb = new MenuBar();
        Menu m = new Menu("Options");

        m.add(sound = new CheckboxMenuItem("Play sound for new mail"));
        sound.addItemListener(this);
        m.add(popup = new CheckboxMenuItem("Pop dialog for new mail"));
        popup.addItemListener(this);
        mb.add(m);

        // Set the menu bar on the frame.
        setMenuBar(mb);
        setSize(100, 50);
        show();
    }

    public void itemStateChanged(ItemEvent evt) {
        Object src = evt.getSource();
        if (src == sound) {
            // playSound();
            System.out.println("Play sound");
        } else if (src == popup) {
            // popDialog();
            System.out.println("Pop dialog");
        }
    }

    static public void main(String[] args) {
        new Main();
    }
}
```

A
B
C
D
E
F
G
H
I
J
K
L
M
N
O
P
Q
R
S
T
U
V
W
X
Y
Z

addItemListener()

PURPOSE   Adds a listener to receive item events fired by this checkbox menu item.

SYNTAX   `public synchronized void addItemListener(ItemListener listener)`

DESCRIPTION   An item event is fired when this checkbox menu item is selected or deselected.
                See `ItemEvent` for more details. After this method is called, the item listener
                `listener` will receive item events fired by this checkbox menu item.

PARAMETERS
listener   The item listener to add.

SEE ALSO   `ItemSelectable`, `java.awt.event.ItemEvent`,
                `java.awt.event.ItemListener`, `removeItemListener()`.

EXAMPLE   See the class example.

A
B
C
D
E
F
G
H
I
J
K
L
M
N
O
P
Q
R
S
T
U
V
W
X
Y
Z

addNotify()

PURPOSE	Creates the checkbox menu item's peer.
SYNTAX	`public void addNotify()`
DESCRIPTION	This method creates the checkbox menu item's peer if it does not exist. The peer is created by calling the `Toolkit.createCheckboxMenuItem()` method.
	This method should never be called directly. It is normally called by the checkbox menu item's parent.
OVERRIDES	`MenuItem.addNotify()`.
SEE ALSO	`MenuItem`, `Toolkit`.
EXAMPLE	See the similar usage of `Component.addNotify()` in `Component.setVisible()`.

CheckboxMenuItem()

PURPOSE	Constructs a new `CheckBoxMenuItem` instance.

SYNTAX	`public CheckboxMenuItem()`
	`public CheckboxMenuItem(String label)`
	`public CheckboxMenuItem(String label, boolean state)`

DESCRIPTION	This constructor creates a new `CheckBoxMenuItem` instance with the label `label` and initial check state `state`. A `null` label is the same as `""`. If the label is not specified, it defaults to `null`. If `state` is not specified, it defaults to `false`.
PARAMETERS	
`label`	The non-`null` string specifying the checkbox menu item's label.
`state`	A `boolean` specifying the checkbox menu item's initial checked state.
SEE ALSO	`MenuItem`.
EXAMPLE	See the class example.

getSelectedObjects()

PURPOSE	Retrieves the checkbox menu item's label if this item is selected.
SYNTAX	`public Object[] getSelectedObjects()`
RETURNS	An array with one item containing the checkbox menu item's label if the item is selected; `null` otherwise.

A
B
C
D
E
F
G
H
I
J
K
L
M
N
O
P
Q
R
S
T
U
V
W
X
Y
Z

SEE ALSO   `ItemSelectable`.

EXAMPLE   See `ItemSelectable`'s class example.

getState()

PURPOSE   Retrieves the checked state of the checkbox menu item.

SYNTAX   `public boolean getState()`

RETURNS   `true` if the checkbox menu item is checked; `false` otherwise.

EXAMPLE   This method prints the checked state of all checkbox menu items in the menu bar.

```
void printMenuLabels(MenuBar menubar) {
    for (int i=0; i<menubar.getMenuCount(); i++) {
        Menu menu = menubar.getMenu(i);
        for (int j=0; j<menu.getItemCount(); j++) {
            if (menu.getItem(j) instanceof CheckboxMenuItem) {
                CheckboxMenuItem mi = (CheckboxMenuItem)menu.getItem(j);
                System.out.println(mi.getLabel() + ": "
                    + mi.getState());
            }
        }
    }
}
```

paramString()

PURPOSE   Generates a string representation of the checkbox menu item's state.

SYNTAX   `public String paramString()`

DESCRIPTION   The string includes the label and the enabled and checked states of the checkbox menu item component. This method is called by the `toString()` method and is typically used for debugging.

RETURNS   A non-`null` string representing the checkbox menu item's state.

OVERRIDES   `MenuItem.paramString()`.

SEE ALSO   `MenuComponent.toString()`, `java.lang.Object.toString()`.

processEvent()

PURPOSE   Processes an event enabled for this checkbox menu item.

SYNTAX   `protected void processEvent(AWTEvent evt)`

DESCRIPTION   This method extends `MenuItem.processEvent()` by adding support for `ItemEvent`.

When a subclass does override `processEvent()`, it should call `super.processEvent()` to perform the processing intended by its base class (such as dispatching the listeners).

PARAMETERS
evt   The event to be processed.

OVERRIDES   `MenuItem.processEvent()`.

SEE ALSO   `AWTEvent`, `processItemEvent()`.

EXAMPLE   See `Component`'s class example.

processItemEvent()

PURPOSE   Processes an item event enabled for this checkbox menu item.

SYNTAX   `protected void processItemEvent(ItemEvent evt)`

DESCRIPTION   An item event is fired when this checkbox menu item is selected or deselected. See `ItemEvent` for more details. This method processes item events for this checkbox menu item by calling any registered `ItemListener`. This method is invoked only if item events have been enabled for this checkbox menu item. This enabling happens automatically when an item listener is added to this component.

Typically, a program controls how item events for a checkbox menu item are processed by adding or removing item listeners. It overrides `processItem-Event()` only if it needs to do processing in addition to that performed by the registered listeners.

When a subclass does override `processItemEvent()`, it should call `super.processItemEvent()` to perform the processing intended by its base class (such as dispatching the listeners).

PARAMETERS
evt   The event to be processed.

SEE ALSO   `java.awt.event.ItemEvent`, `ItemSelectable`, `java.awt.event.ItemListener`, `processEvent()`.

EXAMPLE   See `ItemSelectable`'s class example.

removeItemListener()

PURPOSE	Removes a listener from receiving item events from this checkbox menu item.
SYNTAX	`public synchronized void removeItemListener(ItemListener` `    listener)`
DESCRIPTION	An item event is fired when this checkbox menu item is selected or deselected. See `ItemEvent` for more details. After this method is called, the item listener `listener` will no longer receive item events from this checkbox menu item.
PARAMETERS	
`listener`	The item listener to remove.
SEE ALSO	`addItemListener()`, `ItemSelectable`, `java.awt.event.ItemEvent`, `java.awt.event.ItemListener`.
EXAMPLE	See `removeActionListener()` in `MenuItem.disableEvents()`.

setState()

PURPOSE	Sets the checkbox menu item's check state.
SYNTAX	`public synchronized void setState(boolean state)`
DESCRIPTION	The method call is ignored if the check state does not change.

FIGURE 61: **Synchronizing a Checkbox with a CheckboxMenuItem.**

PARAMETERS	
`state`	If `true`, the checkbox's check state is set to *on*; otherwise, it is set to *off*.
SEE ALSO	`getState()`.
EXAMPLE	This example creates a checkbox and a checkbox menu item and synchronizes their check states. If the checkbox is set to *on*, so is the checkbox menu item. See Figure 61.

```
import java.awt.*;
import java.awt.event.ItemListener;
import java.awt.event.ItemEvent;
class Main extends Frame implements ItemListener {
    CheckboxMenuItem mi = new CheckboxMenuItem("Save All Files On Exit");
    Checkbox cb = new Checkbox("Save All Files On Exit");

    Main() {
        super("setState Example");
        MenuBar mb = new MenuBar();
        Menu m = new Menu("File");
```

245

```
            m.add(mi);
            m.add("Exit");
            mb.add(m);
            setMenuBar(mb);

            // Add the checkbox
            add(cb, BorderLayout.SOUTH);

            // Set listeners for checkbox and checkbox menu item
            cb.addItemListener(this);
            mi.addItemListener(this);

            pack();
            show();
        }

        public void itemStateChanged(ItemEvent evt) {
            if (evt.getSource() == mi) {
                cb.setState(mi.getState());
            } else {
                mi.setState(cb.getState());
            }
            // saveAllFiles();
        }

        static public void main(String[] args) {
            new Main();
        }
    }
```

CheckboxMenuItemPeer

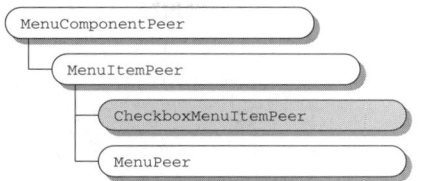

Syntax

```
public interface CheckboxMenuItemPeer extends MenuItemPeer
```

Description

The checkbox menu item component (see `CheckboxMenuItem` class) in the AWT uses the platform's native implementation of a checkbox menu item. So that the AWT checkbox menu item component behaves the same on all platforms, the checkbox menu item is assigned a *peer,* whose task is to translate the behavior of the platform's native checkbox menu item to the behavior of the AWT checkbox menu item.

AWT programmers normally do not directly use peer classes and interfaces. Instead, they deal with AWT components in the `java.awt` package. These in turn automatically manage their peers. Only someone who is porting the AWT to another platform should be concerned with the peer classes and interfaces. Consequently, most peer documentation refers to `java.awt` counterparts.

See `Component` and `Toolkit` for additional information about component peers.

MEMBER SUMMARY
Peer Method
`setState()`   Sets the checkbox menu item's check state.

See Also

`java.awt.CheckboxMenuItem`, `java.awt.Component`, `java.awt.Toolkit`.

setState()

PURPOSE	Sets the checkbox menu item's check state.
SYNTAX	`void setState(boolean state)`
PARAMETERS	
state	If `true`, the checkbox's check state is set to on; otherwise it is set to off.
SEE ALSO	`java.awt.CheckboxMenuItem.setState()`.

A
B

D
E
F
G
H
I
J
K
L
M
N
O
P
Q
R
S
T
U
V
W
X
Y
Z

CheckboxPeer

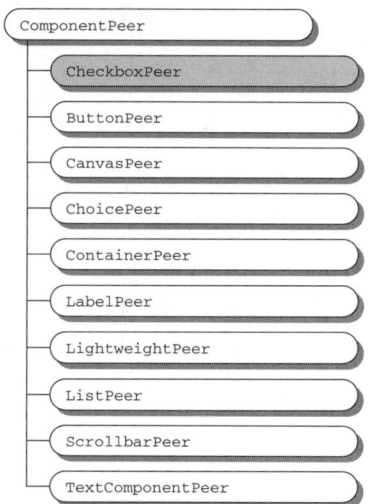

A
B
C
D
E
F
G
H
I
J
K
L
M
N
O
P
Q
R
S
T
U
V
W
X
Y
Z

Syntax

`public interface CheckboxPeer extends ComponentPeer`

Description

The checkbox component (see the Checkbox class) in the AWT uses the platform's native implementation of a checkbox. So that the AWT checkbox component behaves the same on all platforms, the checkbox is assigned a peer, whose task is to translate the behavior of the platform's native checkbox to the behavior of the AWT checkbox.

AWT programmers normally do not directly use peer classes and interfaces. Instead, they deal with AWT components in the java.awt. These in turn automatically manage their peers. Only someone who is porting the AWT to another platform should be concerned with the peer classes and interfaces. Consequently, most peer documentation refers to java.awt counterparts.

See Component and Toolkit for additional information about component peers.

MEMBER SUMMARY	
Peer Methods	
setCheckboxGroup()	Sets the checkbox peer's checkbox group.
setLabel()	Sets the checkbox peer's label.
setState()	Sets the checkbox peer's check state.

See Also

java.awt.Checkbox, java.awt.Component, java.awt.Toolkit.

setCheckboxGroup( )

PURPOSE Sets the checkbox peer's checkbox group.

SYNTAX   void setCheckboxGroup(CheckboxGroup g)

PARAMETERS

 g   The checkbox peer's new checkbox group. A value of null removes the checkbox peer from its current group.

SEE ALSO java.awt.Checkbox.setCheckboxGroup().

setLabel( )

PURPOSE Sets the checkbox peer's label.

SYNTAX   void setLabel(String label)

PARAMETERS

 label   The non-null string specifying the checkbox peer's new label.

SEE ALSO java.awt.Checkbox.setLabel().

setState( )

PURPOSE Sets the checkbox peer's check state.

SYNTAX   void setState(boolean state)

PARAMETERS

 state   If true, the checkbox peer's check state is set to on; otherwise it is set to off.

SEE ALSO java.awt.Checkbox.setState().

Choice

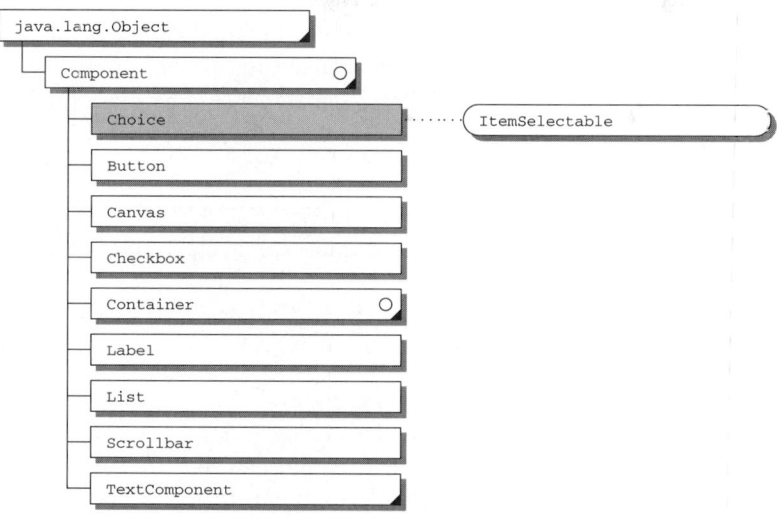

Syntax

```
public class Choice extends Component implements ItemSelectable
```

Description

A *choice* is a component that lets the user choose from a fixed set of string items. It is similar to a list, except that it occupies much less screen space in its normal state. In its normal state, the choice component displays the currently selected item. In its activated state, it displays the entire list of choices. Once a selection has been made, the choice component shrinks to a single line and displays the newly selected item.

The checkbox group is a component that resembles a choice component in that it lets the user choose from a fixed set of items (see the Checkbox class). Following are two design guidelines to consider when deciding between the choice component and the checkbox group. As with all user interface "principles," these guidelines are intended to summarize the issues, not to mandate your design.

1. The larger the number of items, the more appropriate the choice component becomes. You should probably use a choice component if you have five or more items.
2. If a group of one or more components is related to one particular item and is therefore enabled only if that item is selected, a checkbox group might be more appropriate.

The Selected Item

If there are any items in the choice, one is always selected. This is called the *selected item*. The selected item can be changed by either the program or the user.

Events

A choice fires an item event whenever the user selects an item. See ItemEvent for more details. The item of the item event is the label of choice's newly selected item. Even if the selected item is reselected, an item event is fired, since the modifier keys may have changed.

In addition to generating item events, a choice also fires all the events fired by the Component class. See the Component class for details. See the AWTEvent class for details on how to filter or handle events.

A
B
C
D
E
F
G
H
I
J
K
L
M
N
O
P
Q
R
S
T
U
V
W
X
Y
Z

MEMBER SUMMARY	
Constructor	
Choice()	Constructs a new Choice instance.
Item Methods	
add()	Adds an item to this choice.
addItem()	Adds an item to this choice.
getItem()	Retrieves an item from this choice.
getItemCount()	Retrieves the number of items in this choice.
insert()	Inserts an item into this choice.
remove()	Removes an item from this choice.
removeAll()	Removes all items from this choice.
Selection Methods	
getSelectedIndex()	Retrieves the index of this choice's currently selected item.
getSelectedItem()	Retrieves this choice's currently selected item.
getSelectedObjects()	Retrieves this choice's currently selected item.
select()	Selects an item in this choice.
Event Methods	
addItemListener()	Adds a listener to receive item events fired by this choice.
processEvent()	Processes an event enabled for this choice.
processItemEvent()	Processes an item event enabled for this choice.
removeItemListener()	Removes a listener from receiving item events fired by this choice.
Peer Method	
addNotify()	Creates the choice's peer.
Debugging Method	
paramString()	Generates a string representing the choice's state.
Deprecated Method	
countItems()	Replaced by getItemCount().

See Also

java.awt.event.ItemEvent, java.awt.event.ItemListener.

Example

For a simple example using the choice component, see the example for the Choice() constructor. This more elaborate example creates two
choice components for controlling the appearance
of a message that is displayed in the center (see
Figure 62). One choice controls the font name,
and the other controls the font style. You can use
the text field at the bottom to change the text of
the message. The message is painted in the middle of the frame container. Since frame containers
have insets, the paint() method needs to sub-

FIGURE 62: Using Choice to Control a
Component.

tract the insets from the frame's bounds. For containers without insets (such as Panel), this
calculation is not necessary.

```java
import java.awt.*;
import java.awt.event.*;

class Main extends Frame implements ItemListener, ActionListener {
    String[] styleNames = {"plain", "italic", "bold", "bold-italic"};
    int[] styleValues = {Font.PLAIN, Font.ITALIC, Font.BOLD,
                         Font.ITALIC|Font.BOLD};
    Choice chFont = new Choice();
    Choice chStyle = new Choice();
    TextField tf = new TextField("Hello");

    Main() {
        super("Choice Example");
        Panel p = new Panel();

        // Retrieve all the font names.
        for (int i=0; i<getToolkit().getFontList().length; i++) {
            chFont.addItem(getToolkit().getFontList()[i]);
        }
        // Initialize the font style choice.
        for (int i=0; i<styleNames.length; i++) {
            chStyle.addItem(styleNames[i]);
        }
        p.setLayout(new GridLayout(1, 0));
        p.add(chFont);
        p.add(chStyle);

        // Listen for events on choices
        chFont.addItemListener(this);
        chStyle.addItemListener(this);

        // Listen for events on text field
        tf.addActionListener(this);
```

```
            add(p, BorderLayout.NORTH);
            add(tf, BorderLayout.SOUTH);
            setSize(300, 150);
            setVisible(true);
        }

        public void paint(Graphics g) {
            Insets insets = getInsets();
            int w = getSize().width-insets.left-insets.right-2;
            int h = getSize().height-insets.top-insets.bottom-2;
            Font f = new Font(chFont.getSelectedItem(),
                styleValues[chStyle.getSelectedIndex()], 24);
            FontMetrics fm = g.getFontMetrics(f);
            String str = tf.getText();

            g.clearRect(0, 0, w, h);
            g.setFont(f);
            g.drawString(str, (w-fm.stringWidth(str))/2,
                (h-fm.getHeight())/2+fm.getAscent());
        }

        // Update action for choice components
        public void itemStateChanged(ItemEvent e) {
            repaint();
        }

        // Update action for text field
        public void actionPerformed(ActionEvent e) {
            repaint();
        }

        static public void main(String[] args) {
            new Main();
        }
    }
}
```

add( )

PURPOSE	Adds an item to this choice.
SYNTAX	`public synchronized void add(String item)`
DESCRIPTION	This method adds the item `item` to the end of this choice. If the item is the first one in the list, then the item is selected; otherwise, the selected item does not change. This method is the same as `addItem()`.
PARAMETERS	
`item`	The non-`null` item.
SEE ALSO	`addItem()`, `insert()`, `remove()`, `removeAll()`.
EXAMPLE	See `Choice()`.

addItem( )

PURPOSE	Adds an item to this choice.
SYNTAX	`public synchronized void addItem(String item)`
DESCRIPTION	This method adds the item `item` to the end of this choice. If the item is the first one in the list, then the item is selected; otherwise, the selected item does not change. This method is the same as `add()`.
PARAMETERS	
`item`	The non-`null` item.
SEE ALSO	`add()`, `insert()`, `remove()`, `removeAll()`.
EXAMPLE	See the class example.

addItemListener( )

PURPOSE	Adds a listener to receive item events fired by this choice.
SYNTAX	`public synchronized void addItemListener(ItemListener listener)`
DESCRIPTION	An item event is fired when an item in this choice is selected. See `ItemEvent` and the class description for more details. After this method is called, the item listener `listener` will receive item events fired by this choice. If `listener` is `null`, this method does not do anything.
PARAMETERS	
`listener`	The possibly `null` item listener to add.
SEE ALSO	`ItemSelectable`, `java.awt.event.ItemEvent`, `java.awt.event.ItemListener`, `removeItemListener()`.
EXAMPLE	See the class example, `Choice()`, and `select()`.

addNotify( )

PURPOSE	Creates the choice's peer.
SYNTAX	`public void addNotify()`
DESCRIPTION	This method creates the peer if it does not yet exist. The peer is created by calling the `Toolkit.createChoice()` method. This method should never be called directly. It is normally called by the parent.
OVERRIDES	`Component.addNotify()`.
SEE ALSO	`Component`, `Toolkit`.
EXAMPLE	See `Component.setVisible()`.

A
B

D
E
F
G
H
I
J
K
L
M
N
O
P
Q
R
S
T
U
V
W
X
Y
Z

Choice( )

PURPOSE   Constructs a new Choice instance.

SYNTAX   public Choice()

DESCRIPTION   This constructor constructs a new visible choice component.

EXAMPLE   This example creates a choice component with two items. The program simply prints out the current item whenever the current item in the choice changes. See Figure 63.

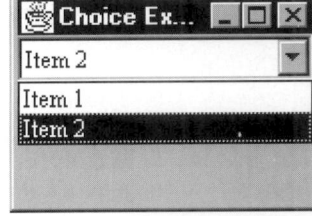

FIGURE 63: Simple Choice.

```java
import java.awt.*;
import java.awt.event.*;

class Main extends Frame implements ItemListener {
    Main() {
        super("Choice Example");
        Choice choice = new Choice();

        choice.add("Item 1");
        choice.add("Item 2");
        add(choice, BorderLayout.CENTER);

        // Add listener for choice
        choice.addItemListener(this);

        setSize(150, 75);
        setVisible(true);
    }

    public void itemStateChanged(ItemEvent evt) {
        // get choice's selection and display to stdout
        ItemSelectable s = evt.getItemSelectable();
        Object[] selected = s.getSelectedObjects();
        if (selected != null)
            System.out.println(selected[0]);
    }

    static public void main(String[] args) {
        new Main();
    }
}
```

countItems( )   *DEPRECATED*

PURPOSE   Replaced by getItemCount().

SYNTAX   public int countItems()

RETURNS   The number of items in this choice.

DEPRECATION   Replace usage of the deprecated method
```
int count = choice.countItems();
```
with
```
int count = choice.getItemCount();
```

getItem( )

PURPOSE   Retrieves an item from this choice.

SYNTAX   `public String getItem(int index)`

DESCRIPTION   This method retrieves the item at the index `index` from this choice.

PARAMETERS
index   The non-negative zero-based index of the item.

RETURNS   A non-`null` string containing the item's name.

SEE ALSO   `getItemCount()`, `getSelectedItem()`.

EXAMPLE   See `select()`.

getItemCount( )

PURPOSE   Retrieves the number of items in this choice.

SYNTAX   `public int getItemCount()`

RETURNS   The number of items in this choice.

SEE ALSO   `getItem()`.

EXAMPLE   See `select()`.

getSelectedIndex( )

PURPOSE   Retrieves the index of this choice's selected item.

SYNTAX   `public int getSelectedIndex()`

RETURNS   The zero-based index of the selected item; -1 if this choice has no items.

SEE ALSO   `getSelectedItem()`.

EXAMPLE   See the class example.

getSelectedItem( )

PURPOSE	Retrieves this choice's currently selected item.
SYNTAX	`public synchronized String getSelectedItem()`
RETURNS	The selected item; `null` if this choice has no items.
SEE ALSO	`getSelectedIndex()`.
EXAMPLE	See the class example.

getSelectedObjects( )

PURPOSE	Retrieves this choice's currently selected item.
SYNTAX	`public synchronized Object[] getSelectedObjects()`
RETURNS	An array with one item containing this choice's currently selected item; `null` if this choice has no items.
SEE ALSO	`getSelectedIndex()`, `getSelectedItem()`, `ItemSelectable`.
EXAMPLE	See `Choice()`.

insert( )

PURPOSE	Inserts an item into this choice.
SYNTAX	`public synchronized void insert(String item, int index)`
DESCRIPTION	This method inserts the item `item` at the index `index` of this choice. Existing items at an index greater than or equal to `index` are shifted up by one to accommodate the new item. If `index` is greater than or equal to the number of items in this choice, `item` is added to the end of this choice.
	If the item is the first one being added to the choice, then the item becomes selected. Otherwise, if the selected item was one of the items shifted, the first item in the choice becomes the selected item. If the selected item was not among those shifted, it remains the selected item.

PARAMETERS

`index`	The position at which to insert the new item.
`item`	The non-`null` item.

EXCEPTIONS

`IllegalArgumentException`
        If `index` is negative.

A
B

D
E
F
G
H
I
J
K
L
M
N
O
P
Q
R
S
T
U
V
W
X
Y
Z

SEE ALSO   `add()`, `addItem()`, `getItemCount()`, `remove()`, `removeAll()`.

EXAMPLE   See `remove()`.

paramString()

PURPOSE   Generates a string representing the choice's state.

SYNTAX   `protected String paramString()`

DESCRIPTION   This method returns the string representation of this choice's state; the returned string includes the selected item. A subclass of this class should override this method and return a concatenation of its state with the results of `super.paramString()`. This method is called by the `toString()` method and is typically used for debugging.

RETURNS   A non-`null` string representing the choice's state.

OVERRIDES   `Component.paramString()`.

SEE ALSO   `Component.toString()`, `java.lang.Object.toString()`.

EXAMPLE   See `Component.paramString()`.

processEvent()

PURPOSE   Processes an event enabled for this choice.

SYNTAX   `protected void processEvent(AWTEvent evt)`

DESCRIPTION   This method extends `Component.processEvent()` by adding support for `ItemEvent`.

When a subclass does override `processEvent()`, it should call `super.processvent()` to perform the processing intended by its base class (such as dispatching the listeners).

PARAMETERS
  evt   The event to be processed.

OVERRIDES   `Component.processEvent()`.

SEE ALSO   `AWTEvent`, `processItemEvent()`.

EXAMPLE   See `Component`'s class example.

A
B
D
E
F
G
H
I
J
K
L
M
N
O
P
Q
R
S
T
U
V
W
X
Y
Z

processItemEvent()

PURPOSE	Processes an item event enabled for this choice.
SYNTAX	`protected void processItemEvent(ItemEvent evt)`

DESCRIPTION

An item event is fired when an item in this choice is selected. See `ItemEvent` and class description for more details. This method processes item events for this choice by calling any registered `ItemListener`. This method is invoked only if item events have been enabled for this choice. This can happen either when an item listener is added to this choice or if item events are enabled explicitly via `Component.enableEvents()`.

Typically, a program controls how item events for a choice are processed. This is done by adding or removing item listeners. It overrides `processItem-Event()` only if it needs to do processing in addition to that performed by the registered listeners.

When a subclass does override `processItemEvent()`, it should call `super.processItemEvent()` to perform the processing intended by its base class (such as dispatching the listeners).

PARAMETERS

evt   The event to be processed.

SEE ALSO   `java.awt.event.ItemEvent, ItemSelectable,`
                    `java.awt.event.ItemListener, processEvent().`

EXAMPLE   See `ItemSelectable`'s class example.

remove()

PURPOSE	Removes an item from this choice.
SYNTAX	`public synchronized void remove(String item)` `public synchronized void remove(int index)`

DESCRIPTION

This method removes an item from this choice. The item can be identified either by its index `index` in the choice or by its name `item`. If several matches exist for `item`, the item with the smallest index is removed.

If the item being removed is the currently selected item, then the first item in the choice becomes the selected item. Otherwise, the currently selected item remains selected (and the selected index is updated accordingly).

PARAMETERS

index   The position from which to remove the item.
item   The non-`null` item to remove.

EXCEPTIONS

IllegalArgumentException

If index is negative or if item is not in this choice.

SEE ALSO   add(), addItem(), getItemCount(), insert(), removeAll().

EXAMPLE   This example creates a choice and a row of buttons that controls the insertion and removal of items from the choice. See Figure 64.

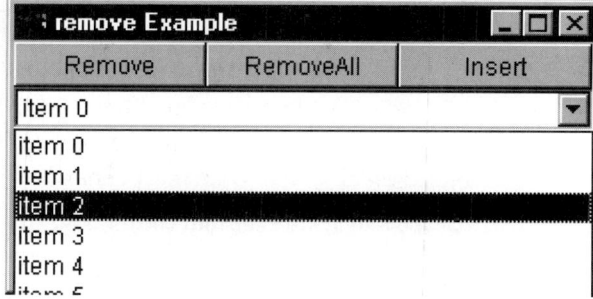

FIGURE 64:   Inserting and Removing Items from a Choice.

```java
import java.awt.*;
import java.awt.event.*;

class Main extends Frame
implements ActionListener {
    Choice choice = new Choice();
    Button removeBtn = new Button("Remove");
    Button removeAllBtn = new Button("RemoveAll");
    Button addBtn = new Button("Insert");
    int lastItemCount = 0;

    Main() {
        super("remove Example");

        // Initialize the choice with 10 items.
        for (int i=0; i<10; i++) {
            choice.addItem("item "+(lastItemCount++));
        }

        // Listen for events.
        removeBtn.addActionListener(this);
        addBtn.addActionListener(this);
        removeAllBtn.addActionListener(this);

        Panel p = new Panel(new GridLayout(1, 0));
        p.add(removeBtn);
        p.add(removeAllBtn);
        p.add(addBtn);

        add(choice, BorderLayout.CENTER);
        add(p, BorderLayout.NORTH);
        setSize(300, 150);
        show();
    }

    public void actionPerformed(ActionEvent e) {
        String cmd = e.getActionCommand();
        if (cmd.equals("RemoveAll")) {
            choice.removeAll();
```

A
B

D
E
F
G
H
I
J
K
L
M
N
O
P
Q
R
S
T
U
V
W
X
Y
Z

261

```
            } else {
                int target = choice.getSelectedIndex();
                if (cmd.equals("Remove")) {
                    if (target >= 0) {
                        choice.remove(target);
                    }
                    // else add
                } else {
                    if (target >= 0) {
                        choice.insert("item "+(lastItemCount++), target);
                        choice.select(target);
                    } else {
                        choice.add("item "+(lastItemCount++));
                    }
                }
            }
            removeBtn.setEnabled(choice.getItemCount() > 0);
            removeAllBtn.setEnabled(choice.getItemCount() > 0);
        }

        static public void main(String[] args) {
            new Main();
        }
    }
```

removeAll()

PURPOSE   Removes all items from this choice.

SYNTAX   `public synchronized void removeAll()`

SEE ALSO   `add()`, `addItem()`, `getItemCount()`, `insert()`, `remove()`.

EXAMPLE   See `remove()`.

removeItemListener()

PURPOSE   Removes an item listener from receiving item events from this choice.

SYNTAX   `public synchronized void removeItemListener(ItemListener`
               `    listener)`

DESCRIPTION   An item event is fired when an item in this choice is selected. See `ItemEvent`
               and the class description for more details. After this method is called, the item
               listener `listener` will no longer receive item events from this choice. If `lis-`
               `tener` is `null`, this method does nothing.

PARAMETERS
  `listener`   The possibly `null` item listener to remove.

SEE ALSO   `addItemListener()`, `ItemSelectable`, `java.awt.event.ItemEvent`,
               `java.awt.event.ItemListener`.

EXAMPLE   See `removeActionListener()` in `MenuItem.disableEvents()`.

select()

PURPOSE   Selects an item in this choice.

SYNTAX
```
public synchronized void select(int index)
public synchronized void select(String string)
```

DESCRIPTION   This method selects an item either by its name or by its index. If index is specified, the item at index index is selected. If string is specified, the item's name is string. If several matches exist, the item with the smallest index is selected. If string does not match any item(s), then the method call is ignored.

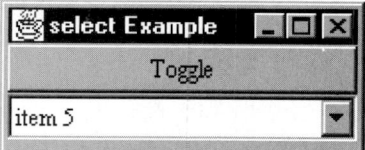

FIGURE 65:   **Toggle to Choice.**

PARAMETERS.

index   The non-negative zero-based index of the item.

string   The non-null item to select.

SEE ALSO   getSelectedIndex(), getSelectedItem().

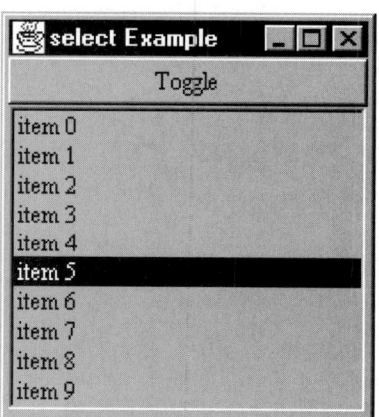

FIGURE 66:   **Toggle to List.**

EXAMPLE   This example creates a frame with a button and initially with a choice component (see Figure 65). Clicking the button causes the choice component to be replaced by a list component (see Figure 66). Clicking the button again causes the list to revert to a choice component (see Figure 65). The program uses select() to maintain the selected item between transformations.

```java
import java.awt.*;
import java.awt.event.*;

class Main extends Frame implements ActionListener, ItemListener {
    List list;
    Choice choice = new Choice();
    Button toggle = new Button("Toggle");

    Main() {
        super("select Example");

        for (int i=0; i<10; i++) {
            choice.addItem("item "+i);
        }
```

A
B

D
E
F
G
H
I
J
K
L
M
N
O
P
Q
R
S
T
U
V
W
X
Y
Z

```java
            // Set listeners
            choice.addItemListener(this);
            toggle.addActionListener(this);

            add(choice, BorderLayout.SOUTH);
            add(toggle, BorderLayout.NORTH);
            pack();
            show(true);
        }

        // When button is pushed
        public void actionPerformed(ActionEvent evt) {
            if (choice != null) {
                // Create a list and transfer items to the list.
                list = new List(choice.getItemCount(), false);
                for (int i=0; i<choice.getItemCount(); i++) {
                    list.addItem(choice.getItem(i));
                    if (i == choice.getSelectedIndex()) {
                        list.select(i);
                    }
                }
                // Add list
                list.addItemListener(this);
                add(list, BorderLayout.CENTER);

                // Remove choice
                remove(choice);
                choice = null;
            } else {
                // Create a choice and transfer items to the list.
                choice = new Choice();
                for (int i=0; i<list.getItemCount(); i++) {
                    choice.addItem(list.getItem(i));
                    if (i == list.getSelectedIndex()) {
                        choice.select(i);
                    }
                }
                // Add choice
                choice.addItemListener(this);
                add(choice, BorderLayout.SOUTH);

                // Remove list
                remove(list);
                list = null;
            }
            pack();
        }

        // When list or choice is updated
        public void itemStateChanged(ItemEvent evt) {
            repaint();
        }

        static public void main(String[] args) {
            new Main();
        }
    }
```

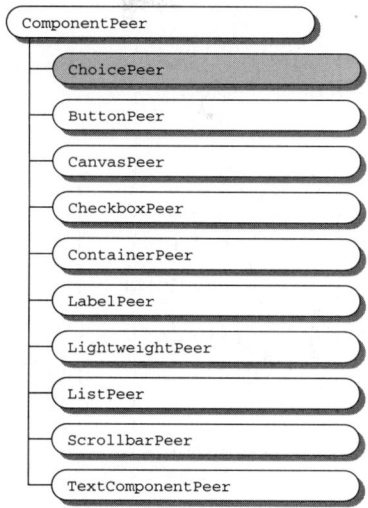

Syntax

```
public interface ChoicePeer extends ComponentPeer
```

Description

The choice component (see the Choice class) in the AWT uses the platform's native implementation of a choice component. So that the AWT choice component behaves the same on all platforms, the choice component is assigned a *peer*, whose task is to translate the behavior of the platform's native choice component to the behavior of the AWT choice component.

AWT programmers normally do not directly use peer classes and interfaces. Instead, they deal with AWT components in the java.awt package. These in turn automatically manage their peers. Only someone who is porting the AWT to another platform should be concerned with the peer classes and interfaces. Consequently, most peer documentation refers to its java.awt counterparts.

See Component and Toolkit for additional information about component peers.

MEMBER SUMMARY	
Peer Methods	
add()	Adds an item to the choice.
remove()	Removes an item from the choice.
select()	Selects an item in the choice.
Deprecated Method	
addItem()	Replaced by add().

See Also

java.awt.Choice, java.awt.Component, java.awt.Toolkit.

add()

PURPOSE	Adds an item to the choice.
SYNTAX	void add(String item, int index)
DESCRIPTION	This method adds the item item to the choice list at the index specified by index.
PARAMETERS	
index	The position in the choice list at which to place item.
item	The non-null item to be added.
SEE ALSO	java.awt.Choice.add().

addItem()   *DEPRECATED*

PURPOSE	Replaced by add().
SYNTAX	void addItem(String item, int index)
PARAMETERS	
index	The position in the choice list at which to place item.
item	The non-null item to be added.
DEPRECATION	Replace usage of this deprecated method, as in

```
    peer.addItem(item, index);
```
with
```
    peer.add(item, index);
```

remove( )

PURPOSE	Removes an item from the choice.
SYNTAX	`void remove(int index)`
DESCRIPTION	This method removes the item at the index specified by `index` from the choice.
PARAMETERS	
`index`	The item's position in the choice.
SEE ALSO	`java.awt.Choice.remove()`.

select( )

PURPOSE	Selects an item in the choice.
SYNTAX	`void select(int index)`
DESCRIPTION	This method selects the item at the index indicated by `index`.
PARAMETERS	
`index`	The non-negative zero-based index of the item.
SEE ALSO	`java.awt.Choice.select()`.

```
java.lang.Object

    Clipboard
```

Syntax

```
public class Clipboard
```

Description

A *clipboard* is an object that temporarily holds data as it is being transferred between or within an application. It is typically used in cut/copy/paste operations. An application can create as many clipboard objects as it wants, but these clipboard objects can be used only within that one application. That is, the clipboard cannot be shared between different applications. However, there is one special clipboard that is created and maintained by the AWT system that can be shared between applications. In fact, the system clipboard is shared by all applications running on the system, Java or otherwise. This clipboard is called the *system clipboard*. Most applications typically use the system clipboard rather than create and manage their own.

Note: In Java 1.1.2, the system clipboard can hold only string selections (see `StringSelection`)

A clipboard does not hold data directly. Instead, the data must be encapsulated in a transferable object before it can be placed on the clipboard. See the `Transferable` interface for more details.

At present, there is no facility for registering a clipboard so that other objects can use it. The creator of a clipboard must supply a reference to the clipboard to all objects wishing to exchange data via that clipboard. You can retrieve a handle to the system clipboard by calling `Toolkit.getSystemClipboard()`.

The Clipboard Name

The clipboard name is an arbitrary string associated with the clipboard object at the time the clipboard object is created. The name cannot be changed. At present, the name is not significant other than for debugging purposes.

The Clipboard Owner

A clipboard can have an owner. The owner is the last object to place contents on the clipboard. The owner of the clipboard is notified when some other object places contents on the clipboard.

An object need not take ownership of the clipboard when placing contents on the clipboard.

MEMBER SUMMARY

Constructor
Clipboard()   Constructs a Clipboard instance.

Content Methods
getContents()   Retrieves the contents of this clipboard.
setContents()   Places a transferable object in this clipboard.

Name Method
getName()   Retrieves the clipboard name of this clipboard.

Fields
contents   Contains the contents of this clipboard.
owner   Contains the current clipboard owner.

See Also
Transferable.

Example

This example is a program that can be used to view the contents of the system clipboard in a text area. The example can view only strings objects. If the clipboard is empty or contains something other than a string, the text area becomes red and displays an error message. See Figure 67.

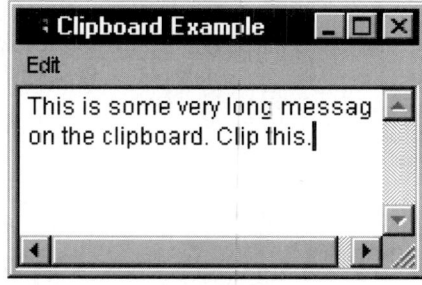

FIGURE 67:   Viewing Clipboard Contents.

```
import java.awt.*;
import java.io.*;
import java.awt.datatransfer.*;
import java.awt.event.*;

class Main extends Frame implements
ActionListener, ClipboardOwner {
    TextArea textArea = new TextArea();

    Main() {
        super("Clipboard Example");
        MenuBar mb = new MenuBar();
        Menu m = new Menu("Edit");

        // Add text area.
        setLayout(new BorderLayout());
        add("Center", textArea);

        // Prepare menu and menubar.
```

```
            m.add("Cut");
            m.add("Copy");
            m.add("Paste");
            mb.add(m);
            setMenuBar(mb);

            // Listen to events from the menu items.
            for (int i=0; i<m.getItemCount(); i++) {
                m.getItem(i).addActionListener(this);
            }

            setSize(300, 300);
            show();
        }

        public void actionPerformed(ActionEvent evt) {
            if ("Paste".equals(evt.getActionCommand())) {
                boolean error = true;
                Transferable t =
                    getToolkit().getSystemClipboard().getContents(this);

                try {
                    if (t != null
                            && t.isDataFlavorSupported(DataFlavor.stringFlavor)) {
                        textArea.setBackground(Color.white);
                        textArea.setForeground(Color.black);
                        textArea.replaceRange(
                            (String)t.getTransferData(DataFlavor.stringFlavor),
                            textArea.getSelectionStart(),
                            textArea.getSelectionEnd());
                        error = false;
                    }
                } catch (UnsupportedFlavorException e) {
                } catch (IOException e) {
                }
                // Display an error message.
                if (error) {
                    textArea.setBackground(Color.red);
                    textArea.setForeground(Color.white);
                    textArea.repaint();
                    textArea.setText("ERROR: \nEither the clipboard"
                        + " is empty or the contents is not a string.");
                }
            } else if ("Copy".equals(evt.getActionCommand())) {
                setContents();
            } else if ("Cut".equals(evt.getActionCommand())) {
                setContents();
                textArea.replaceRange("", textArea.getSelectionStart(),
                    textArea.getSelectionEnd());
            }
        }

        void setContents() {
            String s = textArea.getSelectedText();

            StringSelection contents = new StringSelection(s);
            getToolkit().getSystemClipboard().setContents(contents, this);
        }

        public void lostOwnership(Clipboard clipboard, Transferable contents) {
```

A
B
C
D
E
F
G
H
I
J
K
L
M
N
O
P
Q
R
S
T
U
V
W
X
Y
Z

```
        System.out.println("lost ownership");
    }
    public static void main(String args[]) {
        new Main();
    }
}
```

Clipboard()

PURPOSE   Constructs a Clipboard instance.

SYNTAX   `public Clipboard(String name)`

DESCRIPTION   This constructor creates a new clipboard object with the name name. The name is an arbitrary string associated with the clipboard object and cannot be changed. At present, the name is not significant other than for debugging purposes.

PARAMETERS
name   A possibly null string.

EXAMPLE   See the Transferable class example.

contents

PURPOSE   Field containing the current clipboard contents.

SYNTAX   `protected Transferable contents`

DESCRIPTION   This field may be null; this means the clipboard is empty. Note that it is possible for the clipboard to be empty and owned.

getContents()

PURPOSE   Retrieves the contents of this clipboard.

SYNTAX   `public synchronized Transferable getContents(Object requester)`

DESCRIPTION   This method does not return the actual data on the clipboard. Rather it returns a Transferable object, which can then be used to retrieve the actual data. See Transferable for details.

If the clipboard is empty, null is returned.

Note: In Java 1.1.2, this method returns null if the clipboard is holding an object that is not a string selection (see StringSelection). This may eventu-

A
B
C
D
E
F
G
H
I
J
K
L
M
N
O
P
Q
R
S
T
U
V
W
X
Y
Z

A
B
C
D
E
F
G
H
I
J
K
L
M
N
O
P
Q
R
S
T
U
V
W
X
Y
Z

ally change to return a non-`null` transferable object that returns a zero-length array when `getTransferDataFlavors()` is called on it.

PARAMETERS

requester This parameter is currently ignored.

RETURNS A possibly `null Transferable` object.

SEE ALSO `Transferable.getTransferDataFlavors()`.

EXAMPLE

Copy   Paste

FIGURE 68:   Big5 to Unicode Converter.

This example converts Big5-encoded characters to Unicode. The program reads the contents of the system clipboard and converts it into a Java string of Unicode characters that are suitable for inserting into a resource bundle (see `java.util.ResourceBundle`) or a Java program.

Figure 68 shows a browser displaying an on-line English-to-Chinese dictionary. The dictionary generates Big5-encoded characters, and the browser is set to display Big5-encoded characters. In the figure, two Chinese characters have been selected. When these characters are copied into the system clipboard, they can be pasted into the example program by clicking in the area above the text field. When this is done, the text field shows the Java Unicode string of the two Big5-encoded characters.

When Big5-encoded characters are copied from the system clipboard, they are retrieved as a string of bytes. In other words, each character in the resulting string is actually a byte value. These byte values are copied into a byte array and passed to a `sun.io.ByteToCharConverter` object for conversion. Although the `sun.io.ByteToCharConverter` class is not yet part of the core set of classes, it is part of the runtime and available for use. Just be aware that this class may be moved to another package at some point. See the *Internation-alization Specification* document at the java.sun.com Web site for information on supported converter classes. This document also describes how to install Big5 fonts on your system.

```java
import java.awt.*;
import java.io.*;
import java.awt.datatransfer.*;
import java.awt.event.*;

class Main extends Frame {
    TextField textField = new TextField();
    TextDisplay textDisplay = new TextDisplay(textField);

    Main() {
        super("getContents() Example");

        // Layout component.
        add(textDisplay, BorderLayout.CENTER);
        add(textField, BorderLayout.SOUTH);

        setSize(300, 100);
        show();
    }

    public static void main(String args[]) {
        new Main();
    }
}

class TextDisplay extends Canvas {
    String text = "";
    TextField textField;
    Font f = new Font("Monospaced", Font.BOLD, 24);

    TextDisplay(TextField textField) {
        this.textField = textField;
        setFont(new Font("Monospaced", Font.BOLD, 24));

        // Listen for events.
        addMouseListener(new MouseEventHandler());
    }

    public void paint(Graphics g) {
        FontMetrics fm = getFontMetrics(f);

        // Draw the character centered in the canvas area.
        g.setFont(f);
        g.drawString(text, (getSize().width-fm.stringWidth(text))/2,
            (getSize().height-fm.getHeight())/2+fm.getAscent());
    }

    class MouseEventHandler extends MouseAdapter {
        public void mousePressed(MouseEvent evt) {
            Transferable t =
                getToolkit().getSystemClipboard().getContents(this);

            try {
```

A
B
C
D
E
F
G
H
I
J
K
L
M
N
O
P
Q
R
S
T
U
V
W
X
Y
Z

```
                        if (t != null
                                && t.isDataFlavorSupported(DataFlavor.stringFlavor)) {
                            text =
                                (String)t.getTransferData(DataFlavor.stringFlavor);

                            // Generate the unicode string for 'text'.
                            String result = "";
                            byte big5[] = new byte[text.length()];
                            char unicode[] = new char[text.length()/2];

                            for (int i=0; i<text.length(); i++) {
                                big5[i] = (byte)text.charAt(i);
                            }

                            // Create the converter object.
                            sun.io.ByteToCharConverter toUnicodeConv
                                    = sun.io.ByteToCharConverter.getConverter("Big5");

                            // Convert the big5 array to unicode.
                            int len = toUnicodeConv.convert(big5, 0, big5.length,
                                unicode, 0, unicode.length);

                            // Display the Java unicode characters
                            // field in the text.
                            for (int i=0; i<len; i++) {
                                String s;

                                result += "\\u";
                                s = "0000" + Integer.toHexString(unicode[i]);
                                result += s.substring(s.length()-4);
                            }
                            text = new String(unicode);

                            // Set it in the text field.
                            textField.setText(result);

                            repaint();
                        }
                    } catch (UnsupportedFlavorException e) {
                        e.printStackTrace();
                    } catch (IOException e) {
                        e.printStackTrace();
                    }
                }
            }
        }
```

getName()

PURPOSE	Retrieves the clipboard name of this clipboard.
SYNTAX	`public String getName()`
DESCRIPTION	The name is an arbitrary string associated with the clipboard object. At present, the name has no significance other than for debugging purposes.
RETURNS	A possibly `null` string containing the clipboard's name.

owner

PURPOSE   Field containing the current clipboard owner.

SYNTAX   `protected ClipboardOwner owner`

DESCRIPTION   This field may be `null`. This means the clipboard does not have an owner. In this case, the clipboard may still have contents.

setContents()

PURPOSE   Places a transferable object in this clipboard.

SYNTAX   `public synchronized void setContents(Transferable contents, ClipboardOwner owner)`

DESCRIPTION   This method sets `contents` to be the new contents of the clipboard and registers `owner` as the new clipboard owner. If `contents` is `null`, the clipboard is cleared of all contents.

The `owner` parameter may be `null`. This indicates that the object placing contents on the clipboard does not want to be notified when the content changes.

If `owner` differs from the previous clipboard owner, the previous clipboard owner is notified that it has lost ownership of the clipboard (see `Clipboard-Owner.lostOwnership()`).

Note: In Java 1.1.2, the system clipboard can hold only string selections (see `StringSelection`). All other transferable objects are ignored.

PARAMETERS

`contents`   A possibly `null` transferable object to place on the clipboard.

`owner`   The possibly `null` owner of `contents`.

SEE ALSO   `StringSelection`.

EXAMPLE   See the class example.

A
B

D
E
F
G
H
I
J
K
L
M
N
O
P
Q
R
S
T
U
V
W
X
Y
Z

```
ClipboardOwner  ········  StringSelection
```

Syntax
```
public interface ClipboardOwner
```

Description
When an object sets some data in the clipboard, the object can be notified when the data is no longer in the clipboard. Such an object must implement the `ClipboardOwner` interface and then supply a reference to itself when calling `Clipboard.setContents()`. After doing so, the object becomes the *owner* of the clipboard. When the object loses ownership of the clipboard, its `lostOwnership()` method is called.

One use for this capability is to allow an object to dispose of resources used by the clipboard contents, since it is no longer being used.

MEMBER SUMMARY
Lost Ownership Callback Method
`lostOwnership()`　　　　　　Called when an object loses ownership of the clipboard.

See Also
`Clipboard.setContents()`.

Example
This example sets a string selection in the system clipboard and makes itself the clipboard owner. When the string selection is replaced by some other application, the program prints a message and terminates.

```
import java.awt.*;
import java.awt.datatransfer.*;

class Main implements ClipboardOwner {
    //ClipboardOwner Example
    Main() {
        // Retrieve handle to clipboard and contents
        Clipboard clipboard =
            Toolkit.getDefaultToolkit().getSystemClipboard();

        clipboard.setContents(new StringSelection("Hello"), this);
```

```
        }

        public void lostOwnership(Clipboard clipboard, Transferable contents) {
            System.out.println("lost ownership");
            System.exit(0);
        }

        public static void main(String[] args) {
            new Main();
        }
    }
```

lostOwnership()

PURPOSE   Called when an object loses ownership of the clipboard.

SYNTAX   `public void lostOwnership(Clipboard clipboard, Transferable`
               `    contents)`

DESCRIPTION   The `contents` parameter should be equal to (the same reference as) the transferable that this object placed on the clipboard using `Clipboard.set-Contents()`.

               This method is not called if the current owner of the clipboard changes the clipboard contents.

PARAMETERS
`clipboard`   The non-`null` handle to a clipboard.
`contents`   The non-`null` old contents of the clipboard.

EXAMPLE   See the class example.

Color

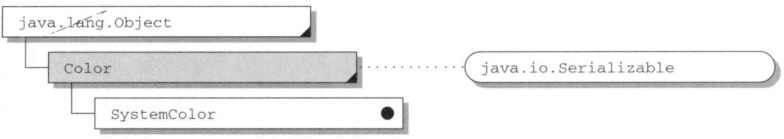

Syntax

```
public class Color implements java.io.Serializable
```

Description

A Color instance specifies a color that is used in graphics operations. Colors are also used when setting the background and foreground colors of components. The actual color displayed by the system may not exactly match the desired color because of limitations in the rendering device. In this case, the closest matching color is used.

A color can be specified using either the *RGB* (*red, green, blue*) or *HSB* (*hue, saturation, brightness*) color coding system. In the RGB system, the three color components are values in the range 0–255; the higher the value, the brighter the component. An RGB value of (0, 0, 0) is black and an RGB value of (255, 255, 255) is white. In the HSB system, the three color components are values between 0.0 and 1.0. An HSB value of (0.0, 0.0, 0.0) is black and an HSB value of (0.0, 0.0, 1.0) is white.

MEMBER SUMMARY

Constructor

Color() Constructs a new Color instance.

Predefined Color Constants

black	The color black (0, 0, 0).
blue	The color blue (0, 0, 255).
cyan	The color cyan (0, 255, 255).
darkGray	The color dark gray (64, 64, 64).
gray	The color gray (128, 128, 128).
green	The color green (0, 255, 0).
lightGray	The color light gray (192, 192, 192).
magenta	The color magenta (255, 0, 255).
orange	The color orange (255, 200, 0).
pink	The color pink (255, 175, 175).
red	The color red (255, 0, 0).
white	The color white (255, 255, 255).
yellow	The color yellow (255, 255, 0).

A
B

D
E
F
G
H
I
J
K
L
M
N
O
P
Q
R
S
T
U
V
W
X
Y
Z

MEMBER SUMMARY

Color Converters

`brighter()`	Calculates a brighter version of the color.
`darker()`	Calculates a darker version of the color.

Color Component Methods

`getBlue()`	Retrieves the blue component of the color.
`getGreen()`	Retrieves the green component of the color.
`getRed()`	Retrieves the red component of the color.
`getRGB()`	Retrieves the 24-bit RGB representation of the color.

HSB Methods

`getHSBColor()`	Creates a new `Color` instance from an HSB specification.
`HSBtoRGB()`	Converts an HSB color specification to a 24-bit RGB color specification.
`RGBtoHSB()`	Converts an RGB color specification to an HSB color specification.

Other Color Creation Methods

`decode()`	Creates a color using a numeric string that represent its RGB value.
`getColor()`	Creates a color whose RGB value is specified in a system property.

Debugging Method

`toString()`	Generates a string representation of the color.

General Methods

`equals()`	Determines if an object is equal to the color.
`hashCode()`	Calculates the hash code for the color.

A
B

D
E
F
G
H
I
J
K
L
M
N
O
P
Q
R
S
T
U
V
W
X
Y
Z

See Also

`SystemColor`.

Example

This example creates two sets of scrollbars that are used to pick a color (see Figure 69). One set is based on RGB values and the other on HSB values. Changing a scrollbar in one set modifies the scrollbars in the other. An uneditable text field is located at the bottom of the frame and shows the current color in both the RGB and HSB color coding systems.

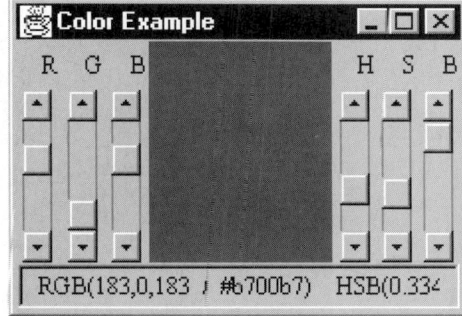

FIGURE 69: Pick a Color.

Since the HSB values are in the range 0.0–1.0 and scrollbars handle only integer values, you must multiply the HSB values by 1,000 to get an integer value. Hence, a scrollbar representing an HSB component uses the range 0–1000.

The scrollbar sets the value 0 at the top of the scrollbar. However, since it is more intuitive to have the value 0 appear at the bottom of the scrollbar, the direction of the scrollbar is "reversed." Reversing the direction of the scrollbar involves subtracting the value of the scrollbar from the maximum value. The sizes of the scrollbars are larger than the range of the RGB and HSB values in order to account for the scrollbars' "visible size" (see Scrollbar).

A gridbag layout (see GridBagLayout) is used to lay out a set of scrollbars. The first row is a row of labels and the second a row of scrollbars. The weight is given to the second row so that if the window is enlarged, then the scrollbars, rather than the labels, stretch.

```java
import java.awt.*;
import java.awt.event.*;

class Main extends Frame implements AdjustmentListener {
    int r = 255;
    int g = 255;
    int b = 255;
    Scrollbar sbRed = new Scrollbar(Scrollbar.VERTICAL, 0, 1, 1, 257);
    Scrollbar sbGreen = new Scrollbar(Scrollbar.VERTICAL, 0, 1, 1, 257);
    Scrollbar sbBlue = new Scrollbar(Scrollbar.VERTICAL, 0, 1, 1, 257);
    Scrollbar sbH = new Scrollbar(Scrollbar.VERTICAL, 0, 1, 1, 1002);
    Scrollbar sbS = new Scrollbar(Scrollbar.VERTICAL, 0, 1, 1, 1002);
    Scrollbar sbB = new Scrollbar(Scrollbar.VERTICAL, 0, 1, 1, 1002);
    TextField status = new TextField();
    float[] hsb;

    Main() {
        super("Color Example");
        sbRed.addAdjustmentListener(this);
        sbGreen.addAdjustmentListener(this);
        sbBlue.addAdjustmentListener(this);
        sbH.addAdjustmentListener(this);
        sbS.addAdjustmentListener(this);
        sbB.addAdjustmentListener(this);

        add(makeScrollbars("R", sbRed, "G", sbGreen, "B", sbBlue),
            BorderLayout.WEST);
        add(makeScrollbars("H", sbH, "S", sbS, "B", sbB), BorderLayout.EAST);
        status.setEditable(false);
        add(status, BorderLayout.SOUTH);
        setSize(300, 300);
        show();
        setBackground(adjustHSBScrollbars());
        adjustRGBScrollbars();
    }

    Panel makeScrollbars(String l1, Scrollbar sb1,
            String l2, Scrollbar sb2, String l3, Scrollbar sb3) {
        double[] rowWeights = {0.0, 1.0};
        GridBagLayout gbl = new GridBagLayout();
        Panel p = new Panel(gbl);

        gbl.rowWeights = rowWeights;
```

```
        p.setLayout(gbl);
        add(p, gbl, new Label(l1, Label.CENTER),
            0, 0, GridBagConstraints.NONE);
        add(p, gbl, sb1, 0, 1, GridBagConstraints.VERTICAL);
        add(p, gbl, new Label(l2, Label.CENTER),
            1, 0, GridBagConstraints.NONE);
        add(p, gbl, sb2, 1, 1, GridBagConstraints.VERTICAL);
        add(p, gbl, new Label(l3, Label.CENTER),
            2, 0, GridBagConstraints.NONE);
        add(p, gbl, sb3, 2, 1, GridBagConstraints.VERTICAL);
        return p;
    }

    void add(Panel p, GridBagLayout gbl, Component comp, int x, int y, int fill)
{
        GridBagConstraints gbc = new GridBagConstraints();
        gbc.gridx = x;
        gbc.gridy = y;
        gbc.fill = fill;
        gbl.setConstraints(comp, gbc);
        p.add(comp);
    }

    public void adjustmentValueChanged(AdjustmentEvent evt) {
        Color c = getBackground();
        Object src = evt.getSource();

        // Value from scrollbar is one greater than actual RGB or HSB value

        if (src == sbRed) {
            r = 255-(sbRed.getValue()-1);
            c = adjustHSBScrollbars();
        } else if (src == sbGreen) {
            g = 255-(sbGreen.getValue()-1);
            c = adjustHSBScrollbars();
        } else if (src == sbBlue) {
            b = 255-(sbBlue.getValue()-1);
            c = adjustHSBScrollbars();
        } else if (src == sbH) {
            hsb[0] = (1000-(sbH.getValue()-1)) / 1000.0f;
            c = adjustRGBScrollbars();
        } else if (src == sbS) {
            hsb[1] = (1000-(sbS.getValue()-1)) / 1000.0f;
            c = adjustRGBScrollbars();
        } else if (src == sbB) {
            hsb[2] = (1000-(sbB.getValue()-1)) / 1000.0f;
            c = adjustRGBScrollbars();
        }
        setBackground(c);
        repaint();
        status.setText("RGB("+r+","+g+","+b+"   /   "+
            "#"+Integer.toString(c.getRGB()&0xffffff, 16)+")"+
            "   HSB("+hsb[0]+","+hsb[1]+","+hsb[2]+")");
    }

    Color adjustHSBScrollbars() {
        hsb = Color.RGBtoHSB(r, g, b, null);
        // need to offset values by 1 to account for 'visible' part
        // of scrollbar
        sbH.setValue(1001-(int)(hsb[0] * 1000));
```

A
B
C
D
E
F
G
H
I
J
K
L
M
N
O
P
Q
R
S
T
U
V
W
X
Y
Z

```
                    sbS.setValue(1001-(int)(hsb[1] * 1000));
                    sbB.setValue(1001-(int)(hsb[2] * 1000));
                    return new Color(r, g, b);
                }

                Color adjustRGBScrollbars() {
                    Color c = Color.getHSBColor(hsb[0], hsb[1], hsb[2]);

                    // An alternate way of converting the HSB values to RGB:
                    // Color c = new Color(Color.HSBtoRGB(hsb[0], hsb[1], hsb[2]));

                    // need to offset values by 1 to account for 'visible' part
                    // of scrollbar
                    sbRed.setValue(256-(r = c.getRed()));
                    sbGreen.setValue(256-(g = c.getGreen()));
                    sbBlue.setValue(256-(b = c.getBlue()));
                    return c;
                }

                public static void main(String[] args) {
                    new Main();
                }
            }
```

black

PURPOSE   This constant field holds the color black (0, 0, 0).

SYNTAX   `public final static Color black`

EXAMPLE   This example paints dots at random positions on the screen using random colors taken from the predefined palette of colors. It also demonstrates the use of a thread to continually paint a dot every 16 ms. See Figure 70.

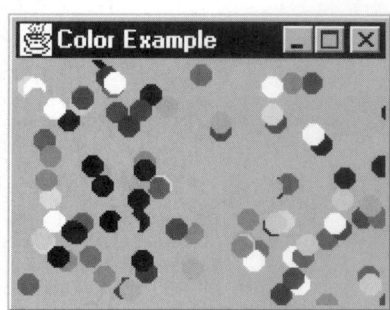

FIGURE 70: Predefined Colors.

```
import java.awt.*;
class Main extends Frame implements Runnable {
    Color[] colors = {Color.black, Color.blue, Color.cyan,
        Color.darkGray, Color.gray, Color.green, Color.lightGray,
        Color.magenta, Color.orange, Color.pink, Color.red,
        Color.white, Color.yellow};

    Main() {
        super("Color Example");
        setSize(200, 200);
        show();
        (new Thread(this)).start();
    }
```

A
B
C
D
E
F
G
H
I
J
K
L
M
N
O
P
Q
R
S
T
U
V
W
X
Y
Z

```
    int random(int r) {
        return (int)Math.floor(Math.random() * r);
    }

    public void update(Graphics g) {
        g.setColor(colors[random(colors.length)]);
        g.fillOval(random(getSize().width), random(getSize().height), 10, 10);
    }

    public void run() {
        while (true) {
            repaint();
            try {
                Thread.sleep(16);
            } catch (Exception e) {
            }
        }
    }

    public static void main(String[] args) {
        new Main();
    }
}
```

blue

PURPOSE	This constant field holds the color blue (0, 0, 255).
SYNTAX	`public final static Color blue`
EXAMPLE	See `black`.

brighter()

PURPOSE	Calculates a brighter version of the color.
SYNTAX	`public Color brighter()`
RETURNS	A new non-`null` color instance containing a brighter version of the color.
EXAMPLE	See `getColor()`.

Color()

PURPOSE	Constructs a new `Color` instance.

SYNTAX	`public Color(int red, int green, int blue)`
	`public Color(float redF, float greenF, float blueF)`
	`public Color(int rgb)`

DESCRIPTION   This constructor creates a new `Color` with the specified RGB values. The RGB values can be specified in three ways. The first is with three integers in the range 0–255. If an integer is larger than 255, in Java 1.1.x, an `IllegalArgumentException` is thrown; in Java 1.0.x, only the lower 8 bits are used.

The second way is with three `float`s in the range 0.0–1.0. These floating-point numbers are converted into integers in the range 0–255.

The third way is with a 24-bit integer. See `getRGB()` for information about how the values are encoded. If the integer is larger than 24 bits, only the lower 24 bits are used.

PARAMETERS

blue	The blue component of the color. This value must be in the range 0–255.
blueF	The blue component of the color. This value must be in the range 0.0–1.0.
green	The green component of the color. This value must be in the range 0–255.
greenF	The green component of the color. This value must be in the range 0.0–1.0.
red	The red component of the color. This value must be in the range 0–255.
redF	The red component of the color. This value must be in the range 0.0–1.0.
rgb	The RGB value encoded as 24 bits. See `getRGB()` for details about the encoding.

EXCEPTIONS

`IllegalArgumentException`
> If any of the values supplied to the constructor is invalid.

EXAMPLE   This simple example creates a frame and draws a yellow oval in the middle of the frame. See Figure 71.

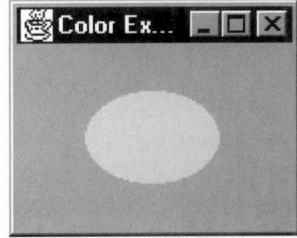

FIGURE 71: **A simple use of** `Color`.

```
import java.awt.*;
class Main extends Frame {
    Main() {
        super("Color Example");
        setSize(100, 100);
        show();
    }

    public void paint(Graphics g) {
        Insets insets = getInsets();
        int x = insets.left, y = insets.top;
        int w = getSize().width - insets.left - insets.right;
        int h = getSize().height - insets.top - insets.bottom;

        g.setColor(new Color(255, 255, 0));
        g.fillOval(x+w/4, y+h/4, w/2, h/2);
    }

    public static void main(String[] args) {
        new Main();
    }
}
```

cyan

PURPOSE   This constant field holds the color cyan (0, 255, 255).

SYNTAX   `public final static Color cyan`

EXAMPLE   See `black`.

darker( )

PURPOSE   Calculates a darker version of the color.

SYNTAX   `public Color darker()`

RETURNS   A new non-`null` `Color` instance containing a darker version of the color.

EXAMPLE   See `getColor()`.

darkGray

PURPOSE   This constant field holds the color dark gray (64, 64, 64).

SYNTAX   `public final static Color darkGray`

EXAMPLE   See `black`.

decode( )

PURPOSE   Creates a color using a numeric string representing its RGB value.

SYNTAX   `public static Color decode(String numstr) NumberFormatException`

DESCRIPTION This method creates a new instance of `Color` represented by the 24-bit RGB value decoded from the string `numstr`. `numstr` is first decoded into an integer, whose value is then treated as a 24-bit RGB value.

PARAMETERS
`numstr`   A string containing the numeric 24-bit RGB value of the color. It can be a decimal, hexadecimal, or octal number. See `Integer.decode()` for acceptable formats.

RETURNS   A new instance of `Color` represented by the RGB value specified by `numstr`.

EXCEPTIONS
`NumberFormatException`
          If `numstr` cannot be parsed into a valid integer.

A
B
C
D
E
F
G
H
I
J
K
L
M
N
O
P
Q
R
S
T
U
V
W
X
Y
Z

SEE ALSO   `getColor()`, `Integer.decode()`.

EXAMPLE   This example reads in a list of hexa-decimal numbers from a file and uses `decode()` to turn them into RGB values. The input file that produced the results in Figure 72 is shown after the code.

FIGURE 72:   **Decoding an RGB String.**

```java
import java.awt.*;
import java.io.*;
import java.util.Vector;

class Main extends Frame implements Runnable {
    int dotSize = 30;
    Vector vec = new Vector();

    Main(String filename) {
        super("decode Example");

        try {
            BufferedReader in =
                new BufferedReader(new InputStreamReader(
                    new FileInputStream(filename)));
            String str;
            while ((str = in.readLine()) != null) {
                vec.addElement(str);
            }
        } catch (IOException e) {
        }

        setSize(200, 200);
        show();
        (new Thread(this)).start();
    }

    public void update(Graphics g) {
        Insets insets = this.getInsets();
        int x = 0, y = 0, rowCount = 0;
        for (int i = 0; i<vec.size(); i++) {
            g.setColor(Color.decode((String)vec.elementAt(i)));
            g.fillOval(insets.left+x-x%dotSize, insets.top+y-y%dotSize,
                        dotSize, dotSize);
            x += dotSize;
            if (rowCount == 5) {
                y += dotSize;
                x = 0;
                rowCount = 0;
            } else {
                ++rowCount;
            }
        }
    }

    public void run() {
        while (true) {
            try {Thread.sleep(100);} catch (Exception e) {}
```

```
                repaint();
            }
        }

    public static void main(String[] args) {
        if (args.length != 1) {
            System.err.println("java Main <input_file>");
            System.exit(-1);
        }
        new Main(args[0]);
    }
}
```

input
```
#e286ff
#ff90ff
#73909a
#732c9a
#1f2c51
#c56c20
#ab31df
#b3021f
#23f39d
#123c90
```

A
B

D
E
F
G
H
I
J
K
L

equals( )

PURPOSE	Determines if an object is equal to the color.
SYNTAX	`public boolean equals(Object obj)`
DESCRIPTION	An object `obj` is equal to this color if `obj` is a `Color` instance and its red, green, and blue component values are identical to those of this color.
PARAMETERS	
`obj`	The object with which to compare. `obj` may be `null`.
RETURNS	`true` if object is equal to this color; `false` otherwise.
OVERRIDES	`java.lang.Object.equals()`.
EXAMPLE	See `getColor()`.

M
N
O
P
Q
R
S
T
U
V

getBlue( )

PURPOSE	Retrieves the blue component of the color.
SYNTAX	`public int getBlue()`
RETURNS	The blue component of the color that is a value in the range 0–255.
SEE ALSO	`Color()`.
EXAMPLE	See the class example.

W
X
Y
Z

A
B
C
D
E
F
G
H
I
J
K
L
M
N
O
P
Q
R
S
T
U
V
W
X
Y
Z

getColor( )

PURPOSE   Creates a color whose RGB value is specified in a system property.

SYNTAX

```
public static Color getColor(String propertyName)
public static Color getColor(String propertyName, int defaultInt)
public static Color getColor(String propertyName, Color
    defaultColor)
```

DESCRIPTION   These methods create a new instance of `Color` whose 24-bit RGB value is specified by the system property `propertyName`. If `propertyName` is not defined or the value is not an integer, then one of three things can be returned. First, if `defaultInt` is defined, then a new `Color` instance containing the 24-bit RGB `defaultInt` value is returned. Second, if `defaultColor` is specified, then it is returned. Third, if neither `defaultInt` nor `defaultColor` are specified, then `null` is returned.

PARAMETERS

     `defaultColor` The `Color` instance to use if the system property is not defined or the value is malformed.

     `defaultInt`   The 24-bit color value to use if the system property is not defined or the value is malformed.

     `propertyName` The non-`null` name of the system property.

RETURNS   A new non-`null` `Color` instance containing the color as specified by the value of the system property `propertyName`.

SEE ALSO   `decode()`, `getRGB()`, `java.lang.System.getProperty()`.

EXAMPLE   This example reads in some properties from a file that defines some text, the color of the text, and its background color. Figure 73(a) shows the contents of the properties file. Figure 73(b) shows the frame that displays the text. To see how the two methods `brighter()` and `darker()` work, click the window; the text brightens and the background color darkens.

```
# text
text.value=Java

# blue text
text.fg=#000088

# yellow background
text.bg=#eeee00
```

(a)

(b)

FIGURE 73:   **Using Foreground and Background Colors.**

```java
import java.awt.*;
import java.awt.event.*;
import java.io.*;
import java.util.*;

class Main extends Frame {
    Color fg, originalFg;
    Color bg, originalBg;
    String str;

    Main() {
        super("getColor Example");
        try {
            System.getProperties().load(
                new FileInputStream("properties.txt"));
            System.getProperties().list(System.out);
            fg = originalFg = Color.getColor("text.fg", 0x000000);
            bg = originalBg = Color.getColor("text.bg", Color.white);
            str = System.getProperties().getProperty("text.value");
        } catch (Exception e) {
            e.printStackTrace();
        }

        addMouseListener(new MouseListener());

        setSize(200, 100);
        show();
    }

    public void paint(Graphics g) {
        Insets insets = getInsets();
        int w = getSize().width-insets.left-insets.right;
        int h = getSize().height-insets.top-insets.bottom;
        Font f = new Font("Helvetica", Font.BOLD, 40);
        FontMetrics fm = g.getFontMetrics(f);

        g.setFont(f);
        g.setColor(bg);
        g.fillRect(insets.left, insets.top, w, h);
        g.setColor(fg);
        g.drawString(str, insets.left + (w-fm.stringWidth(str))/2,
                    insets.top + (h-fm.getHeight())/2+fm.getAscent());
    }

    // Mouse event listener
    class MouseListener extends MouseAdapter {
        public void mousePressed(MouseEvent evt) {
            // If darkening or brightening either color has no
            // effect, simply swap the colors.
            if (originalFg.brighter().equals(originalFg)
                    || originalBg.brighter().equals(originalBg)) {
                fg = originalBg;
                bg = originalFg;
            } else {
                fg = originalFg.brighter();
                bg = originalBg.darker();
            }
            repaint();
        }
```

A
B
C
D
E
F
G
H
I
J
K
L
M
N
O
P
Q
R
S
T
U
V
W
X
Y
Z

```
        public void mouseReleased(MouseEvent evt) {
            // Restore original colors
            fg = originalFg;
            bg = originalBg;
            repaint();
        }
    }

        public static void main(String[] args) {
            new Main();
        }
    }
```

A

B

D

E

F

getGreen()

PURPOSE	Retrieves the green component of the color.
SYNTAX	`public int getGreen()`
RETURNS	The green component of the color. It is a value in the range 0–255.
SEE ALSO	`Color()`.
EXAMPLE	See the class example.

G

H

I

J

K

L

M

getHSBColor()

N

PURPOSE	Creates a new `Color` instance from an HSB specification.
SYNTAX	`public static Color getHSBColor(float hue, float saturation, float brightness)`
DESCRIPTION	This method is equivalent to

O

P

Q

R

```
new Color(HSBtoRGB(hue, saturation, brightness));
```

S

PARAMETERS	
`brightness`	The brightness component of the color. This value must be in the range 0.0–1.0.
`hue`	The hue component of the color. This value must be in the range 0.0–1.0.
`saturation`	The saturation component of the color. This value must be in the range 0.0–1.0.
RETURNS	A new non-`null` `Color` instance based on the specified HSB values.
EXAMPLE	See the class example.

T

U

V

W

X

Y

Z

getRed()

PURPOSE	Retrieves the red component of the color.
SYNTAX	`public int getRed()`
RETURNS	The red component of the color. It is a value in the range 0–255.
SEE ALSO	`Color()`.
EXAMPLE	See the class example.

getRGB()

PURPOSE	Retrieves the 24-bit RGB representation of the color.
SYNTAX	`public int getRGB()`
DESCRIPTION	This method returns the RGB representation of the color. It always has the following format. Bits 24–31 always have the value `0xff`. Bits 16–23 contain the value of the red component. Bits 8–15 contain the value of the green component. Bits 0–7 contain the value of the blue component.
RETURNS	The 24-bit RGB representation of the color.
SEE ALSO	`Color()`.
EXAMPLE	See the class example.

gray

PURPOSE	This constant field holds the color gray (128, 128, 128).
SYNTAX	`public final static Color gray`
EXAMPLE	See `black`.

green

PURPOSE	This constant field holds the color green (0, 255, 0).
SYNTAX	`public final static Color green`
EXAMPLE	See `black`.

A
B
C
D
E
F
G
H
I
J
K
L
M
N
O
P
Q
R
S
T
U
V
W
X
Y
Z

hashCode()

PURPOSE	Calculates the hash code for the color.
SYNTAX	`public int hashCode()`
DESCRIPTION	This method calculates this color's hash code from its RGB value. If `equals(c1, c2)` is `true`, then `c1` and `c2` will have the same hash codes; otherwise, `c1` and `c2` will likely have different hash codes.
RETURNS	The color's hash code.
OVERRIDES	`Object.hashCode()`.
SEE ALSO	`equals()`.
EXAMPLE	See `Object.hashCode()`.

HSBtoRGB()

PURPOSE	Converts an HSB color specification to a 24-bit RGB color specification.
SYNTAX	`public static int HSBtoRGB(float hue, float saturation, float brightness)`
DESCRIPTION	The RGB color as a 24-bit integer. See `getRGB()` for details about the encoding.
PARAMETERS	
brightness	The brightness component of the color. This value must be in the range 0.0–1.0.
hue	The hue component of the color. This value must be in the range 0.0–1.0.
saturation	The saturation component of the color. This value must be in the range 0.0–1.0.
SEE ALSO	`ColorModel.getRGBdefault()`, `getRGB()`.
EXAMPLE	See the class example.

lightGray

PURPOSE	This constant field holds the color light gray (192, 192, 192).
SYNTAX	`public final static Color lightGray`
EXAMPLE	See `black`.

magenta

PURPOSE	This constant field holds the color magenta (255, 0, 255).
SYNTAX	`public final static Color magenta`
EXAMPLE	See `black`.

orange

PURPOSE	This constant field holds the color orange (255, 200, 0).
SYNTAX	`public final static Color orange`
EXAMPLE	See `black`.

pink

PURPOSE	This constant field holds the color pink (255, 175, 175).
SYNTAX	`public final static Color pink`
EXAMPLE	See `black`.

red

PURPOSE	This constant field holds the color red (255, 0, 0).
SYNTAX	`public final static Color red`
EXAMPLE	See `black`.

RGBtoHSB()

PURPOSE	Converts an RGB color specification to an HSB color specification.
SYNTAX	`public static float[] RGBtoHSB(int red, int green, int blue,` `    float[] hsbReturnValues)`
DESCRIPTION	If `hsbReturnValues` is not `null`, the HSB values are placed in the `hsbReturnValues` and `hsbReturnValues` itself is returned. If `hsbReturnValues` is `null`, a new array containing the HSB values is returned.
PARAMETERS	
`blue`	The blue component of the color. This value must be in the range 0–255.

green	The green component of the color. This value must be in the range 0–255.
hsbReturnValues	
	The array to be used to return the three HSB values—hue, saturation, and brightness—or null. If non-null, the array must have length of at least 3.
red	The red component of the color. This value must be in the range 0–255.
RETURNS	A non-null array containing three values in the range 0.0–1.0. The first element contains the hue; the second, saturation; and the third, brightness.
SEE ALSO	ColorModel.getRGBdefault(), getRGB(), Image.
EXAMPLE	See the class example.

toString( )

PURPOSE	Generates a string representation of the color.
SYNTAX	`public String toString()`
DESCRIPTION	This method returns the string representation of this color. It consists of its RGB values.
	This method is typically used for debugging.
RETURNS	A non-null string representing the color.
OVERRIDES	`java.lang.Object.toString()`.
EXAMPLE	See `java.lang.Object.toString()`.

white

PURPOSE	This constant field holds the color white (255, 255, 255).
SYNTAX	`public final static Color white`
EXAMPLE	See `black`.

yellow

PURPOSE	This constant field holds the color yellow (255, 255, 0).
SYNTAX	`public final static Color yellow`
EXAMPLE	See `black`.

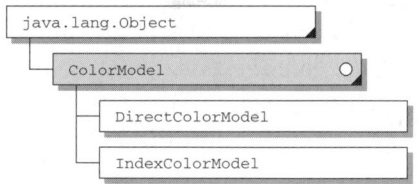

Syntax
```
public abstract class ColorModel
```

Description

An image is a collection of pixels. Each pixel has a location in the image and a value. The purpose of the ColorModel class is to convert these pixel values into colors. There are many ways to encode a color as a pixel value; the two main ones are described in the following sections. However, the important fact to remember is that a set of pixel values is meaningless unless it is associated with an instance of ColorModel to interpret the values.

The Index Color Model

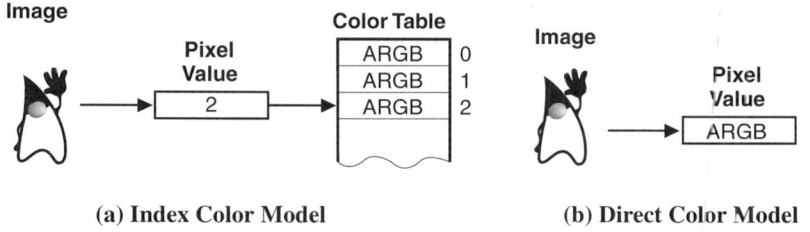

(a) Index Color Model   (b) Direct Color Model

FIGURE 74:   The Two Types of Color Models.

In the *index color model*, pixel values do not themselves contain any information from which you could extract a color. Rather, pixel values are used to index into a color table (see Figure 74a). The actual set of colors in the table are encapsulated in a ColorModel instance and can vary from instance to instance.

You can tell if a color model instance is using the index color model by determining if it is an instance of IndexColorModel. Using the IndexColorModel class, you can create an instance with your own set of colors. See the IndexColorModel class for additional methods.

The Direct Color Model

In the *direct color model*, the pixel values actually contain the color information. In this case, the color mode is to extract the color information from the pixel value (see Figure 74b). The typical encoding used in a direct color model is to divide the bits in a pixel value among the components of a color. For example, in one encoding you could allow 2 bits for red and green, 10 bits for blue, and 4 bits for alpha.

You can tell if a color model instance is using the direct color model by determining if it is an instance of `DirectColorModel`. The `DirectColorModel` class allows you to specify an encoding that divides the bits of a pixel value among the four color components. See the `DirectColorModel` class for additional methods.

The main advantage of the index color model over the direct color model is that an image using an index color model can be represented in much less space (three to four times smaller). The disadvantage is that the available colors that the image can use are limited to the ones in the color table.

The Default Color Model

The AWT package specifies what is called the *default color model,* which is used as a "standard" when converting between different color models. If a method is described to return pixel values in the default color model, it doesn't need to return an instance of any other color model. To interpret such pixels, you need only to retrieve the default color model using the `getRGB-default()` method in this class.

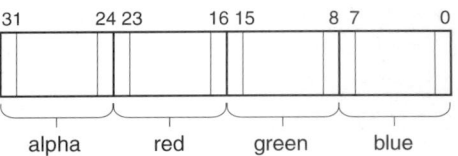

FIGURE 75: Pixel Value Format for the Default Color Model.

The format for pixel values in the default color model is an integer with 8 bits each of alpha, red, green, and blue color components ordered correspondingly from the most significant byte to the least significant byte. This is shown in Figure 75.

MEMBER SUMMARY

Constructor Method

`ColorModel()`	Constructs a new `ColorModel` instance.

Color Component Methods

`getAlpha()`	Retrieves the alpha component of a pixel value.
`getBlue()`	Retrieves the blue component of a pixel value.
`getGreen()`	Retrieves the green component of a pixel value.
`getRed()`	Retrieves the red component of a pixel value.
`getRGB()`	Converts a pixel value to a pixel value in the default color model.

A
B
C
D
E
F
G
H
I
J
K
L
M
N
O
P
Q
R
S
T
U
V
W
X
Y
Z

MEMBER SUMMARY

Pixel Size Members

`getPixelSize()`	Retrieves the bit size of pixel values in the color model.
`pixel_bits`	Holds the bit size of pixel values using this color model.

Default Color Model Method

`getRGBdefault()`	Retrieves the default color mode.

Example

This example retrieves the color model used by an AWT component (which is platform-dependent). If an index color model is used, all the colors in the color model's color table are displayed in a grid (see Figure 76). If a direct color model is used, 256 random colors are generated and displayed.

When the cursor is moved over a displayed color, the program displays the color components of the color in a label located at the top of the window.

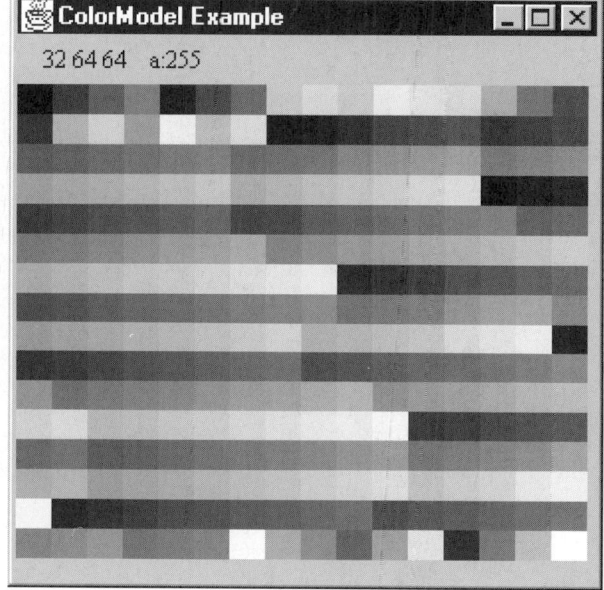

FIGURE 76: `ColorModel`.

```java
import java.awt.*;
import java.awt.image.*;
import java.awt.event.*;
import java.util.Random;

class Main extends Frame {
    ColorGrid cgrid;
    Label label = new Label();

    Main() {
        super("ColorModel Example");
        ColorModel colorModel = Toolkit.getDefaultToolkit().getColorModel();
        int bitsize = colorModel.getPixelSize();

        if (colorModel instanceof IndexColorModel) {
            // index color model
            cgrid = new ColorGrid(1 << bitsize);
            for (int i=0; i<1<<bitsize; i++) {
                cgrid.setColor(i, colorModel.getRGB(i));
            }
        } else {
            // direct color model
```

```
                    Random r = new Random();
                    cgrid = new ColorGrid(256);
                    for (int i=0; i<256; i++) {
                        cgrid.setColor(i, r.nextInt());
                    }
                }
                add(cgrid, BorderLayout.CENTER);
                add(label, BorderLayout.NORTH);

                // Add mouse motion listener for color grid
                cgrid.addMouseMotionListener(new MouseMotionEventHandler());

                setSize(300, 300);
                show();
            }

            class MouseMotionEventHandler extends MouseMotionAdapter {
                public void mouseMoved(MouseEvent evt) {
                    ColorModel cm = ColorModel.getRGBdefault();
                    int x = evt.getX(), y = evt.getY();
                    int rgb = cgrid.getRGB(x, y);

                    label.setText(cm.getRed(rgb) + " " + cm.getGreen(rgb)
                                + " " + cm.getBlue(rgb) + "     a:" + cm.getAlpha(rgb));
                }
            }

            public static void main(String[] args) {
                new Main();
            }
        }

    // This class displays a grid that is used for displaying colors.
    class ColorGrid extends Component {
        int rows, cols;
        int colors[];
        ColorGrid(int numColors) {
            colors = new int[numColors];
            cols = Math.min(16, numColors);
            rows = (numColors - 1) / cols + 1;
        }

        // Sets the color at the cell located at position 'i'.
        // 'rgb' is a color in the default RGB color model.
        void setColor(int i, int rgb) {
            colors[i] = rgb;
        }

        // Returns the pixel value at (x, y).  The pixel value is encoded
        // using the default color model.
        int getRGB(int x, int y) {
            int cellW = getSize().width / cols;
            int cellH = getSize().height / rows;

            x /= cellW;
            y /= cellH;

            // Return the last color if out of bounds.
            return colors[Math.min(colors.length-1, y * cols + x)];
        }
```

```java
public void paint(Graphics g) {
    int cellW = getSize().width / cols;
    int cellH = getSize().height / rows;

    for (int i=0; i<colors.length; i++) {
        int r = i / cols;
        int c = i % cols;

        g.setColor(new Color(colors[i]));
        g.fillRect(c * cellW, r * cellH, cellW, cellH);
    }
}
```

ColorModel()

PURPOSE   Constructs a new ColorModel instance.

SYNTAX   public ColorModel(int b)

DESCRIPTION   This constructor is used by subclasses of this class to specify that the bit size of pixel values of this color model instance is b bits wide. This class cannot be directly instantiated.

PARAMETERS

b   A non-negative number specifying the bit size of pixel values using this color model.

EXAMPLE   This class cannot be directly instantiated. See the ColorModel subclasses IndexColorModel and DirectColorModel for examples for constructing ColorModel instances.

getAlpha()

PURPOSE   Retrieves the alpha component of a pixel value.

SYNTAX   public abstract int getAlpha(int pixelValue)

DESCRIPTION   Subclasses must implement this method to return the alpha component of a color specified by the pixel value pixelValue. The return value must be in the range 0–255, where the value 0 means completely transparent and 255 means completely opaque.

PARAMETERS

pixelValue   The pixel value specifying a color in the color model.

RETURNS   The alpha transparency component in the range 0–255.

EXAMPLE   See the class example.

getBlue( )

PURPOSE	Retrieves the blue component of a pixel value.
SYNTAX	`public abstract int getBlue(int pixelValue)`
DESCRIPTION	Subclasses must implement this method to return the blue component of the color specified by the pixel value `pixelValue`. The return value must be in the range 0–255, where the value 0 means no blue and 255 means maximum blue.
PARAMETERS	`pixelValue` The pixel value specifying a color in the color model.
RETURNS	The blue color component in the range 0–255.
EXAMPLE	See the class example.

getGreen( )

PURPOSE	Retrieves the green component of a pixel value.
SYNTAX	`public abstract int getGreen(int pixelValue)`
DESCRIPTION	Subclasses must implement this method to return the green component of the color specified by the pixel value `pixelValue`. The return value must be in the range 0–255, where the value 0 means no green and 255 means maximum green.
PARAMETERS	`pixelValue` The pixel value specifying a color in the color model.
RETURNS	The green color component in the range 0–255.
EXAMPLE	See the class example.

getPixelSize( )

PURPOSE	Retrieves the bit size of pixel values in the color model.
SYNTAX	`public int getPixelSize()`
DESCRIPTION	The returned value is the same as the one supplied to the constructor.
RETURNS	The bit size of pixel values in the color model.
EXAMPLE	See the class example.

getRed()

PURPOSE   Retrieves the red component of a pixel value.

SYNTAX   `public abstract int getRed(int pixelValue)`

DESCRIPTION   Subclasses must implement this method to return the red component of the color specified by the pixel value `pixelValue`. The return value must be in the range 0–255, where the value 0 means no red and 255 means maximum red.

PARAMETERS
`pixelValue`   The pixel value specifying a color in the color model.

RETURNS   The red color component in the range 0–255.

EXAMPLE   See the class example.

getRGB()

PURPOSE   Converts a pixel value to a pixel value in the default color model.

SYNTAX   `public int getRGB(int pixelValue)`

DESCRIPTION   The pixel value `pixelValue` is converted to an equivalent pixel value that must be interpreted using the default color model. The color of the new pixel value may not necessarily be identical to the color of `pixelValue`. There may be some loss of color information.

PARAMETERS
`pixelValue`   The pixel value specifying a color in the color model.

RETURNS   A pixel value that specifies a color in the default color model.

SEE ALSO   `getRGBdefault()`.

EXAMPLE   See the class example.

getRGBdefault()

PURPOSE   Retrieves the default color model.

SYNTAX   `public static ColorModel getRGBdefault()`

DESCRIPTION   The color model instance returned by this method is used to translate pixel values encoded with the default color model into colors.

RETURNS   A non-`null` instance of the default color model.

EXAMPLE   See the class example.

A
B
C
D
E
F
G
H
I
J
K
L
M
N
O
P
Q
R
S
T
U
V
W
X
Y
Z

pixel_bits

PURPOSE	This field holds the bit size of pixel values using this color model.
SYNTAX	`protected int pixel_bits`
DESCRIPTION	This holds the value that was specified by the `ColorModel` constructor.
SEE ALSO	See `ColorModel()`.

A
B
C
D
E
F
G
H
I
J
K
L
M
N
O
P
Q
R
S
T
U
V
W
X
Y
Z

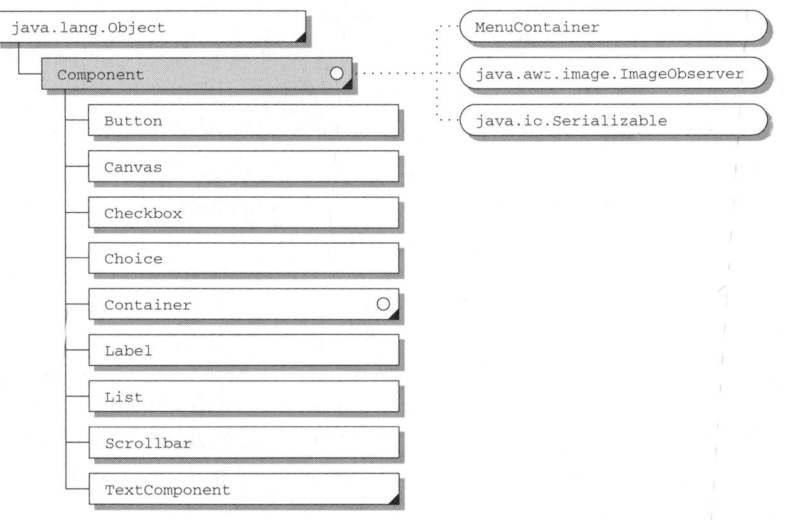

Syntax

```
public abstract class Component implements ImageObserver, MenuContainer,
    Serializable
```

Description

A *component* is a user interface object that can be displayed on the screen and can interact with the user. Such user interface objects include buttons, scrollbars, and text fields. The Component class is the superclass of all nonmenu-related components (the MenuComponent class is the superclass of all menu-related components).

The Component Hierarchy

Some components are containers that have all the properties of a component, plus the ability to contain other components (called *children*). A user interface is made of many components and containers. All components (and containers) must exist inside another container (called the *parent*); only the topmost container lacks a parent. This arrangement produces a hierarchy of components that affects how components are laid out and how events travel from one component to another. Figure 77 shows an exam-

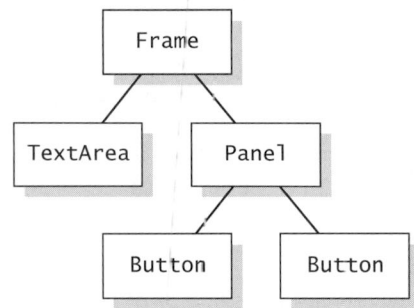

FIGURE 77: Component Hierarchy.

ple of a component hierarchy. More information about layout and events are described in this section.

The Bounds

The *bounds* of a component specify the absolute size of the component and its location within its parent. The bounds includes any decorations or borders that the component may have. The *x*- and *y*-coordinates of the bounds specify the coordinates of the component relative to the bounds of its parent.

All coordinates used by the classes in the AWT package, such as in mouse events or graphics painting, are relative to a component's bounds.

The Minimum, Maximum, and Preferred Sizes

Every component has a *minimum*, *maximum*, and *preferred* size. The minimum size and preferred size of a button, for example, is such that the button's label can be properly displayed in its current font. The maximum size of the button might be such that its width is "infinite" but its height is exactly the font height. For noncontainer components like buttons and scrollbars, the preferred and minimum sizes are usually the same and the maximum size is usually "infinite" in both dimensions.

The minimum, maximum, and preferred sizes of a component is strictly a hint to the layout manager. The layout manager can ignore these hints and resize the component to whatever size it chooses. In other words, these sizes are not enforced in any way.

It's important to note that the results of calling getMinimumSize(), getMaximum-Size(), and getPreferredSize() differ depending on whether the component's peer exists (see "Layout and the Valid State" later in this section). In general, the peers of the component hierarchy should be created before the calculation of the minimum, maximum, or preferred size of the component hierarchy.

The Alignment Property

The alignment property is a pair of floating-point values, one that specifies the *x*-alignment and one that specifies the *y*-alignment. Together the *x*- and *y*-alignment values specify an *alignment point* on the component. This alignment point affects how some layout managers place the components in a container. See the LayoutManager2 class description for more information about this property. More specifically, the alignment point on a component c is

$$(x\_alignment * c.width, y\_alignment * c.height)$$

Table 7 shows the alignment constants available in this class for the most common alignment values.

Constant Name	Numeric Value	Alignment Meaning
LEFT_ALIGNMENT	0.0	*x*-alignment point is at the left edge of the component.
RIGHT_ALIGNMENT	1.0	*x*-alignment point is at the right edge of the component.
CENTER_ALIGNMENT	0.5	*x*- or *y*-alignment point is at the center of the component.
TOP_ALIGNMENT	0.0	*y*-alignment point is at the top edge of the component.
BOTTOM_ALIGNMENT	1.0	*y*-alignment point is at the bottom edge of the component.

TABLE 7: Alignment Constants.

The Enabled Property

A component can be either enabled or disabled. When it is enabled, the user can interact with the component to cause it to fire events. When it is disabled, the component will not respond to user gestures and so will not fire events. Enabled and disabled components look different so that they can be visually distinguished.

Disabled components are also transparent to mouse events. Therefore, if the user clicks a disabled component, the mouse event will be dispatched to the first enabled component behind the disabled component or to the container.

The Focus

When the user presses a key on the keyboard, a key event is created and dispatched to the component with the *focus*. There can be only one component with the focus at any time, but any component can acquire the focus at any time by calling `requestFocus()`. A component will fire the focus gained/focus lost event (see FocusEvent) whenever it gains or loses the focus. Currently, there is no easy way for an object to determine which component in a hierarchy of components has the focus (the only way is for the object to walk the component hierarchy and register for focus events on each component.)

A component should give some kind of visual indication that it has the focus so that the user can easily identify the component that will be affected by keyboard activity.

Focus Traversal

The user can move the focus from one component to another by pressing the Tab or Shift-Tab keys. This action is called *focus traversal*. See the `Container` class for more information.

The Visible Property

A component can be made visible or invisible. Components are typically created visible by default. Only top-level components like frames and windows are created invisible by default.

The Name

A component has a locale-independent *name* that is primarily used by a program to identify the component. For example, when a program receives an event, it could retrieve the event's

A
B
C
D
E
F
G
H
I
J
K
L
M
N
O
P
Q
R
S
T
U
V
W
X
Y
Z

source and use its name to determine which component fired the event. The name is, by default, initialized to a unique identifier. For example, the `Button` class assigns a name of the form "button" concatenated with the value of a counter that it increments for each new instance of `Button` (e.g., "button0"). The program can overwrite this default by using `set-Name()` to set it to another locale-independent string.

The Locale

A component can have a locale associated with it. If a component does not have its locale set explicitly, it inherits the locale from its closest ancestor that does have a locale. If no locale is found, the locale defaults to `Locale.getDefault()`.

A component can use its locale setting to display localized resources (such as text, colors, and images). This fine-grained locale association allows a component or a hierarchy of components to maintain and manage their own locales. This enables a single applet or application to have components using different locales. It also enables different applets running within a single applet context like a Web browser to have different locales from each other and from the applet context itself.

Layout and the Valid State

Layout normally applies to components that are containers. A container has associated with it a layout manager that controls the placement of children within the container. See the `Container` class for more information about layout managers. However, all components maintain a valid state that is used by the layout manager. In particular, if a component is invalid, the component's `doLayout()` method will be called the next time the layout manager is invoked.

Peers

A component such as a button uses the platform's native implementation of a button. For example, on Solaris, the AWT button uses the Motif button widget, while on Windows 95, the AWT button uses the button control. So that the AWT button component behaves the same on all platforms, the button is assigned a *peer* that takes care of translating the behavior of the platform's native button to the behavior of the AWT button.

When a user interface with components and containers is constructed, the component hierarchy is created without any peers. Even without the peers, it is possible to initialize all the properties on the components. When the user interface is ready to be displayed on the screen, the peers for each component are finally created and properly initialized with the current state of the component. Once the peer exists, any modifications to the component's properties are forwarded directly to the peer. (With the peers in existence, the component may or may not maintain the state changes. However, when the peer is destroyed, any state that the peer maintained for the component must be transferred back to the component.)

The peers of a component hierarchy are created by calling the `addNotify()` method of the top-level container. Although all components have an `addNotify()` method, the method cannot be called directly. Only the `addNotify()` method of a subclass of `Window` can be called. When this happens, it sets off a chain reaction that results in a call to the `addNotify()`

method of every component in the hierarchy. The opposite sequence occurs when the removeNotify() method is called on the top-level container.

Figure 78 shows a component hierarchy and its corresponding peer hierarchy.

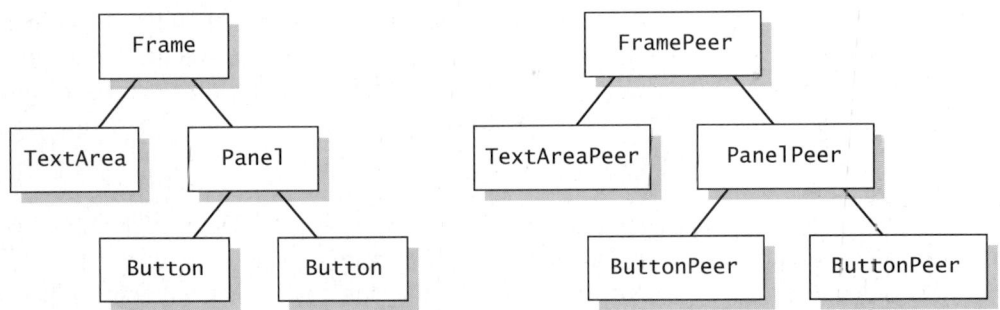

FIGURE 78:　A Component Hierarchy and Its Corresponding Peer Class Hierarchy.

Events

Components interact with a program that uses them through the use of *events*. For example, clicking a component with the mouse fires a mouse-clicked event. For a complete discussion on available events, event handlers, and event flow through a component hierarchy, see the AWTEvent class.

A component fires the following types of events: KeyEvent, MouseEvent, FocusEvent, and ComponentEvent. A KeyEvent is fired when a key is pressed or released inside the component. A basic MouseEvent is fired when the mouse enters or exits the component and when a mouse button is pressed or released while the mouse is inside the component. A mouse-motion MouseEvent is fired when the mouse is moved or dragged inside the component. A FocusEvent is fired when the component gains or loses keyboard focus. Finally, a ComponentEvent is fired whenever the component is moved, resized, hidden, or made visible. See the class descriptions of these events for details.

Popup Menus

A component can have one or more popup menus associated with it. These popup menus contain menu items that are specific to the component (or its component hierarchy) and are typically displayed in response to a special mousing gesture. The particular mousing gesture is platform-specific. For example, on Windows 95, clicking the right mouse button causes a popup menu to appear. When the user makes the special popup mousing gesture, the generated mouse event is flagged. The application can then decided whether to display a popup.

The Tree Lock

The *tree lock* is a lock that protects the AWT hierarchies. It is a global lock and is shared by all live components running in the system (or more precisely, from one class loader). It must be held whenever it is necessary to walk or modify the hierarchy. For example, the tree lock should be held while climbing the ancestor chain looking for a frame or while a container is laying out its children.

The tree lock is intended to prevent inconsistent states if two or more threads are simultaneously using the hierarchy. For example, suppose you retrieve a container's component count just before another thread removes the last child. As you walk the list of children, you will get unexpected results as you try to retrieve the last child. To prevent this, you need to acquire the tree lock before retrieving the component count and release it only after you have finished walking the list of children.

Painting

When a component wants to do some painting, such as display an image or draw a circle, it must override its `paint()` method and paint with the supplied graphics context. The `paint()` method is called by the AWT whenever it discovers that some part of the component has been damaged and needs repainting.

When a component wishes to change some part of the drawing—for example, if the component is a button and the user has just clicked it—the component should not create a graphics context and make the change. Instead, the component should request the AWT system to invoke its `paint()` method.

In the case of native components, calling `repaint()` actually results in a call to `update()` rather than to `paint()`. The difference between `paint()` and `update()` is that when `paint()` is called, you can assume that the background has been cleared to the component's background color. When `update()` is called, you assume that the background has not been damaged. The default implementation of `update()` is to clear the background and call `paint()`. If the component's painting is fairly simple, there is no need to override the `paint()` method. However, if the painting involves an continuous animation, you may notice an annoying effect called _flickering_, where the animation seems to flash the background on and off. The flickering effect is caused by the background's continuously being cleared and repainted. If this happens, you need to override the `update()` and implement a technique called _double-buffering_. See the `createImage()` example for an example of how to implement double-buffering.

Native and Lightweight Components

There are two kinds of components: _native_ and _lightweight_. A native component has a peer that uses a user interface object provided by the platform. `Button` and `List` are examples of native components. A lightweight component behaves like a native component, except that its peer does not use any system resources. Its advantage is more-efficient use of the platform's resources. You can freely mix lightweight and native components in a lightweight or native container. However, a lightweight component requires the use of one native component in order to function. In particular, one of its ancestors must be a native component. For example, an application needs to have only a single `Window` component, which is a native component. All the other components and containers in the window could be lightweights.

A
B

D
E
F
G
H
I
J
K
L
M
N
O
P
Q
R
S
T
U
V
W
X
Y
Z

At present, the AWT does not supply any lightweight components; many will be available in a future release. However, the lightweight support is fully implemented and you can (and are encouraged to) create your own lightweight components. To create a lightweight component, you must have your component extend from `Component`. To create a lightweight component that is a container, see `Container` for information about lightweight containers.

There are small differences between lightweight and native components. Here are some of them:

1. When a container contains lightweight and native components, the lightweights will always appear behind the native components, regardless of the z-ordering of the components. However, the relative z-ordering within each group (lightweight or native) is preserved. (See `Container` for more details on z-ordering.) So if a lightweight *L1* is in front of a lightweight *L2* with many native components in between, *L1* will appear in front of *L2* even though both *L1* and *L2* appear behind the native components. Mouse events are delivered to the native components before they are offered to the lightweight components, regardless of their z-orderings. When lightweight and native components are mixed in a container, it is highly recommended that a nonoverlapping layout manager be used to avoid confusion.

2. If you call `repaint()` on a lightweight, the AWT responds by calling its `paint()` method. In the case of a native component, the AWT will call its `update()` method. This means that the background for the lightweight is always cleared. Special steps must be taken to avoid flickering. It is not enough for the lightweight to implement double-buffering. See the `Container` class for more information.

3. The default implementation of `getPreferredSize()` for lightweight returns 1-×-1. The `getPreferredSize()` method for a native component returns its current size. The result of this difference is that when the components are laid out, they may not take on the sizes you expect. To have the lightweight behave exactly like a native component, the lightweight should override `getPreferredSize()` and return its current size.

4. When a graphics context is created on a lightweight component, either by the AWT system or by a call to `getGraphics()`, the graphics context is not initialized with values from the component. Instead, its background color, foreground color, and font are initialized with the values from its closest native container. What this means is that when the `paint()` method is called on a lightweight, the colors and fonts must be properly initialized.

A
B
C
D
E
F
G
H
I
J
K
L
M
N
O
P
Q
R
S
T
U
V
W
X
Y
Z

MEMBER SUMMARY

Constructor
`Component()`   Constructs a new instance of `Component`.

Continued

A
B
C
D
E
F
G
H
I
J
K
L
M
N
O
P
Q
R
S
T
U
V
W
X
Y
Z

MEMBER SUMMARY

Alignment Methods and Fields

BOTTOM_ALIGNMENT	Constant indicating alignment along a component's bottom edge.
CENTER_ALIGNMENT	Constant indicating alignment along a component's center.
getAlignmentX()	Retrieves this component's preferred alignment along the x-axis.
getAlignmentY()	Retrieves this component's preferred alignment along the y-axis.
LEFT_ALIGNMENT	Constant indicating alignment along a component's left edge.
RIGHT_ALIGNMENT	Constant indicating alignment along a component's right edge.
TOP_ALIGNMENT	Constant indicating alignment along a component's top edge.

Color Methods

getBackground()	Retrieves this component's background color.
getColorModel()	Retrieves this component's color model.
getForeground()	Retrieves this component's foreground color.
setBackground()	Sets this component's background color.
setForeground()	Sets this component's foreground color.

Cursor Methods

getCursor()	Retrieves this component's cursor image.
setCursor()	Sets this component's cursor image.

Enable Methods

isEnabled()	Determines if this component is enabled.
setEnabled()	Enables and disables this component.

Event Methods

dispatchEvent()	Dispatches an event to this component.
enableEvents()	Enables event types for this component.
disableEvents()	Disables event types for this component.
processComponentEvent()	Processes a component event enabled for this component.
processEvent()	Processes an event enabled for this component.
processFocusEvent()	Processes a focus event enabled for this component.
processKeyEvent()	Processes a key event enabled for this component.
processMouseEvent()	Processes a mouse event enabled for this component.
processMouseMotionEvent()	Processes a mouse motion event enabled for this component.

MEMBER SUMMARY

Event Listener Methods

addComponentListener()	Adds a listener to receive this component's component events.
addFocusListener()	Adds a listener to receive this component's focus events.
addKeyListener()	Adds a listener to receive this component's key events.
addMouseListener()	Adds a listener to receive this component's mouse events.
addMouseMotionListener()	Adds a listener to receive this component's mouse motion events.
removeComponentListener()	Removes a listener from receiving this component's component events.
removeFocusListener()	Removes a listener from receiving this component's focus events.
removeKeyListener()	Removes a listener from receiving this component's key events.
removeMouseListener()	Removes a listener from receiving this component's mouse events.
removeMouseMotionListener()	Removes a listener from receiving this component's mouse motion events.

Focus Methods

isFocusTraversable()	Determines if this component is focus traversable.
requestFocus()	Requests that the focus be given to this component.
transferFocus()	Moves the focus to the next focus traversable component.

Font Methods

getFont()	Retrieves this component's font.
getFontMetrics()	Retrieves the font metrics for a font for this component.
setFont()	Sets this component's font.

Graphics and Painting Methods

getGraphics()	Creates a graphics context for this component.
paint()	Called to repaint this component.
paintAll()	Called to repaint this component and its descendants.
repaint()	Requests that this component be repainted.
update()	Called to repaint this component without the background's having been cleared.

Image Methods

checkImage()	Retrieves the construction status of an image.
createImage()	Creates an off-screen image or an image from an image producer.
imageUpdate()	Called to deliver status information about the loading of an image.
prepareImage()	Triggers the loading of image data for an image.

Continued

A
B
C
D
E
F
G
H
I
J
K
L
M
N
O
P
Q
R
S
T
U
V
W
X
Y
Z

MEMBER SUMMARY

Localization Methods

getLocale()	Retrieves this component's locale.
setLocale()	Sets this component's locale.

Layout Methods

contains()	Determines if this component contains a specified point.
doLayout()	Invokes the layout manager on this component.
getBounds()	Retrieves this component's bounds.
getComponentAt()	Retrieves the component containing a specified point.
getLocation()	Retrieves this component's location relative to its parent.
getLocationOnScreen()	Retrieves this component's location on the screen.
getMaximumSize()	Calculates this component's maximum size dimensions.
getMinimumSize()	Calculates this component's minimum size dimensions.
getPreferredSize()	Calculates this component's preferred size dimensions.
getSize()	Retrieves this component's size.
invalidate()	Invalidates this component.
isValid()	Retrieves this component's valid state.
setBounds()	Moves and resizes this component.
setLocation()	Moves this component.
setSize()	Sets this component's size.
validate()	Validates this component.

Lock Method

getTreeLock()	Retrieves the lock object for the entire AWT component tree.

Name Methods

getName()	Retrieves this component's name.
setName()	Sets this component's name.

Parent Method

getParent()	Retrieves this component's parent.

Popup Menu Methods

add()	Adds a popup menu to this component.
remove()	Removes a popup menu from this component.

Print Methods

print()	Prints this component on a graphics context.
printAll()	Prints this component and its descendants on a graphics context.

Visibility Methods

isShowing()	Determines if this component is visible and is showing on the screen.
isVisible()	Determines whether this component is visible.
setVisible()	Makes this component visible or invisible.

A
B
C
D
E
F
G
H
I
J
K
L
M
N
O
P
Q
R
S
T
U
V
W
X
Y
Z

MEMBER SUMMARY	

Peer Methods

`addNotify()`	Creates this component's peer.
`getToolkit()`	Retrieves this component's toolkit.
`removeNotify()`	Destroys this component's peer.

Debugging Methods

`list()`	Prints out information about this component and its descendants.
`paramString()`	Generates a string representation of this component's state.
`toString()`	Generates a string representation of this component's state.

Deprecated Methods

`action()`	Use `ActionListener` interface instead.
`bounds()`	Replaced by `getBounds()`.
`deliverEvent()`	Replaced by `dispatchEvent()`.
`disable()`	Replaced by `setEnabled()`.
`enable()`	Replaced by `setEnabled()`.
`getPeer()`	Should not manipulate peers directly.
`gotFocus()`	Use the `FocusListener` interface instead.
`handleEvent()`	Replaced by `processEvent()`.
`hide()`	Replaced by `setVisible()`.
`inside()`	Replaced by `contains()`.
`keyDown()`	Use the `KeyListener` interface instead.
`keyUp()`	Use the `KeyListener` interface instead.
`layout()`	Replaced by `doLayout()`.
`locate()`	Replaced by `getComponentAt()`.
`location()`	Replaced by `getLocation()`.
`lostFocus()`	Use the `FocusListener` interface instead.
`minimumSize()`	Replaced by `getMinimumSize()`.
`mouseDown()`	Use the `MouseListener` interface instead.
`mouseDrag()`	Use the `MouseMotionListener` interface instead.
`mouseEnter()`	Use the `MouseListener` interface instead.
`mouseExit()`	Use the `MouseListener` interface instead.
`mouseMove()`	Use the `MouseMotionListener` interface instead.
`mouseUp()`	Use the `MouseListener` interface instead.
`move()`	Replaced by `setLocation()`.
`nextFocus()`	Replaced by `transferFocus()`.
`postEvent()`	Replaced by `dispatchEvent()`.
`preferredSize()`	Replaced by `getPreferredSize()`.
`reshape()`	Replaced by `setBounds()`.

Continued

A
B
C
D
E
F
G
H
I
J
K
L
M
N
O
P
Q
R
S
T
U
V
W
X
Y
Z

A
B
D
E
F
G
H
I
J
K
L
M
N
O
P
Q
R
S
T
U
V
W
X
Y
Z

MEMBER SUMMARY	
Deprecated Methods *(Continued)*	
resize()	Replaced by setSize().
show()	Replaced by setVisible().
size()	Replaced by getSize().

See Also

ComponentPeer, Container, java.awt.image.ImageObserver,
java.io.Serializable, MenuContainer, Toolkit.

Example

This example demonstrates most of the methods in this class by implementing a simple text field component using a lightweight component (see Figure 79). When the text field has the focus, a block cursor appears, indicating where the next character will go. If the text field is not full, the block cursor blinks. When the cursor is in the text field, the cursor is changed to a Cursor.TEXT_CURSOR. Pressing Return in the text field causes it to fire an action event filled with the current contents of the text field. The action event is dispatched using the overridden processEvent() method, which has support for processing ActionEvent.

The component's isFocusTraversable() method returns true, so it is a focus-traversable component.

FIGURE 79: **Simple Text Field Based on a Lightweight Component.**

```java
import java.awt.*;
import java.awt.event.*;

class Main extends Frame implements ActionListener {
    Main() {
        super("Component Example");
        SimpleTextField canvas = new SimpleTextField(30, 5);
        add(canvas, BorderLayout.CENTER);
        canvas.addActionListener(this);
        pack();
        show();
    }
    public void actionPerformed(ActionEvent evt) {
        System.out.println(evt);
    }
    static public void main(String[] args) {
```

```
            new Main();
        }
}

class SimpleTextField extends Component implements Runnable {
    int border;
    int length;
    Font font;
    FontMetrics fontM;
    char[] buffer;
    int bufferIx;

    boolean hasFocus;
    boolean cursorOn;

    SimpleTextField(int len, int bor) {
        super();
        border = bor;
        length = len;
        buffer = new char[len];
        font = getFont();
        if (font == null) {
            font = new Font("Dialog", Font.PLAIN, 20);
        }
        fontM = getFontMetrics(font);

        // Listen for key and mouse events.
        this.addMouseListener(new MouseEventHandler());
        this.addFocusListener(new FocusEventHandler());
        this.addKeyListener(new KeyEventHandler());

        // Set text cursor.
        setCursor(Cursor.getPredefinedCursor(Cursor.TEXT_CURSOR));

        // Start the thread that blinks the cursor.
        (new Thread(this)).start();
    }

    public Dimension getMinimumSize() {
        // The minimum height depends on the point size.
        int w = fontM.charWidth('m') * length;
        return new Dimension(w + 2*border, fontM.getHeight() + 2*border);
    }
    public Dimension getPreferredSize() {
        return getMinimumSize();
    }
    public Dimension getMaximumSize() {
        return new Dimension(Short.MAX_VALUE, getPreferredSize().height);
    }

    public boolean isFocusTraversable() {
        return true;
    }

    public void paint(Graphics g) {
        int y = (getSize().height-fontM.getHeight())/2;

        // Clear the background using the text background color.
        g.setColor(SystemColor.text);
        g.fillRect(0, 0, getSize().width, getSize().height);
```

A
B
C
D
E
F
G
H
I
J
K
L
M
N
O
P
Q
R
S
T
U
V
W
X
Y
Z

```
                        g.setFont(font);
                        g.setColor(SystemColor.textText);
                        g.drawChars(buffer, 0, bufferIx, border, y + fontM.getAscent());

                        // Draw blinking cursor.
                        int x = fontM.charsWidth(buffer, 0, bufferIx) + border;
                        int w = fontM.charWidth('c');
                        if (hasFocus) {
                            g.setColor(getForeground());
                            g.fillRect(x, y, w, fontM.getHeight());
                            if (cursorOn) {
                                if (bufferIx < buffer.length) {
                                    g.setColor(SystemColor.text);
                                    g.fillRect(x+2, y+2, w-4, fontM.getHeight()-4);
                                }
                            }
                        }
                    }

                    // Event handlers
                    class MouseEventHandler extends MouseAdapter {
                        public void mousePressed(MouseEvent evt) {
                            requestFocus();
                        }
                    }
                    class FocusEventHandler extends FocusAdapter {
                        public void focusGained(FocusEvent evt) {
                            hasFocus = true;
                            repaint();
                        }
                        public void focusLost(FocusEvent evt) {
                            hasFocus = false;
                            repaint();
                        }
                    }
                    class KeyEventHandler extends KeyAdapter {
                        public void keyPressed(KeyEvent evt) {
                            switch (evt.getKeyCode()) {
                              case KeyEvent.VK_DELETE:
                              case KeyEvent.VK_BACK_SPACE:
                                if (bufferIx > 0) {
                                    bufferIx--;
                                    repaint();
                                }
                                break;
                              case KeyEvent.VK_ENTER:
                                ActionEvent action =
                                    new ActionEvent(SimpleTextField.this,
                                                ActionEvent.ACTION_PERFORMED,
                                                String.valueOf(buffer, 0, bufferIx));
                                // Send contents of buffer to listeners
                                processEvent(action);
                                break;
                              default:
                                repaint();
                            }
                        }
                        public void keyTyped(KeyEvent evt) {
                            if (bufferIx < buffer.length
```

```
                    && !evt.isActionKey()
                    && !Character.isISOControl(evt.getKeyChar())) {
                buffer[bufferIx++] = evt.getKeyChar();
            }
        }
    }

    // Support for Action Listener.
    ActionListener actionListener;

    public void addActionListener(ActionListener l) {
        actionListener = AWTEventMulticaster.add(actionListener, l);
    }

    // Override processEvent() to deal with ActionEvent.
    protected void processEvent(AWTEvent evt) {
        if (evt instanceof ActionEvent) {
            processActionEvent((ActionEvent)evt);
        } else {
            super.processEvent(evt);
        }
    }

    // Supply method to process Action event.
    protected void processActionEvent(ActionEvent evt) {
        if (actionListener != null) {
            actionListener.actionPerformed(evt);
        }
    }

    public void run() {
        while (true) {
            try {
                // If component has focus, blink the cursor every 1/2 second.
                Thread.sleep(500);
                cursorOn = !cursorOn;
                if (hasFocus) {
                    repaint();
                }
            } catch (Exception e) {
                e.printStackTrace();
            }
        }
    }
}
```

action()   *DEPRECATED*

PURPOSE   Use the ActionListener interface instead.

SYNTAX   public boolean action(Event evt, Object arg)

PARAMETERS

arg   An object whose contents depend on the component that fired the event.

evt   The non-null event.

RETURNS   `false` if the event should be passed up to the component's parent; `true` otherwise.

DEPRECATION   Formerly, the component would override `action()` to handle action events.

```java
import java.awt.*;
class Old extends Frame {
    Button b = new Button("Button");
    Old() {
        super("Deprecated action() example");
        add(b, BorderLayout.CENTER);
        show();
        pack();
    }
    public boolean action(Event evt, Object what) {
        if (evt.target == b) {
            System.out.println("Button pressed");
            return true;
        }
        return false;
    }
    public static void main(String[] args) {
        new Old();
    }
}
```

Replace the usage of `action()` with the `ActionListener` interface. An action listener is first defined to implement the `actionPerformed()` method and then added as a listener for the component.

```java
import java.awt.*;
import java.awt.event.*;
class New extends Frame {
    Button b = new Button("Button");
    New() {
        super("New ActionEvent Example");
        add(b, BorderLayout.CENTER);
        b.addActionListener(new ActionEventHandler());
        pack();
        show();
    }
    class ActionEventHandler implements ActionListener {
        public void actionPerformed(ActionEvent evt) {
            System.out.println("Button pressed");
        }
    }
    public static void main(String[] args) {
        new New();
    }
}
```

SEE ALSO   `java.awt.event.ActionEvent`.

add()

PURPOSE	Adds a popup menu to this component.
SYNTAX	`public synchronized void add(PopupMenu popup)`
DESCRIPTION	A component can have a list of popup menus that can be dynamically displayed on the component. This method adds the popup menu `popup` to the end of the list of popup menus for this component.

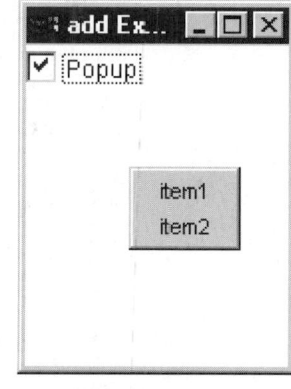

FIGURE 80: **Canvas with Popup Menu.**

PARAMETERS

popup   The non-null popup menu to add.

SEE ALSO   PopupMenu, remove().

EXAMPLE   This example creates a frame with a checkbox and a canvas. The checkbox controls whether the canvas has a popup menu. The canvas overrides `processMouseEvent()` to display the popup if the mouse event indicates a popup trigger. See Figure 80.

```java
import java.awt.*;
import java.awt.event.*;

class CanvasWithPopup extends Canvas {
    PopupMenu popup;

    CanvasWithPopup(PopupMenu popup) {
        enableEvents(AWTEvent.MOUSE_EVENT_MASK);
        this.popup = popup;
    }

    void addPopup() {
        add(popup);
    }

    void removePopup() {
        remove(popup);
    }

    protected void processMouseEvent(MouseEvent evt) {
        // Display popup only if it has not been removed
        if (popup.getParent() != null && evt.isPopupTrigger()) {
            popup.show(evt.getComponent(), evt.getX(), evt.getY());
        }
        super.processMouseEvent(evt);
    }
}

public class Main extends Frame implements ItemListener, ActionListener {
    Checkbox cb = new Checkbox("Popup", false);
    CanvasWithPopup canvas;
```

A
B
C
D
E
F
G
H
I
J
K
L
M
N
O
P
Q
R
S
T
U
V
W
X
Y
Z

```
Main() {
    super("add Example");
    add(cb, BorderLayout.NORTH);
    cb.addItemListener(this);

    PopupMenu popup = new PopupMenu("Button Control");
    popup.add("item1");
    popup.add("item2");
    popup.addActionListener(this);

    canvas = new CanvasWithPopup(popup);
    add(canvas, BorderLayout.CENTER);

    setSize(100, 200);
    show();
}

// Handler for checkbox
public void itemStateChanged(ItemEvent evt) {
    switch (evt.getStateChange()) {
    case ItemEvent.SELECTED:
        canvas.addPopup();
        break;
    case ItemEvent.DESELECTED:
        canvas.removePopup();
        break;
    }
}

// Handler for popup menu
public void actionPerformed(ActionEvent evt) {
    System.out.println(evt.getActionCommand());
}

static public void main(String[] args) {
    new Main();
}
}
```

addComponentListener()

PURPOSE	Adds a listener for receiving this component's component events.
SYNTAX	`public synchronized void addComponentListener(ComponentListener listener)`
DESCRIPTION	A component fires component events as it is resized, moved, or made visible or invisible. See ComponentEvent for more details. After this method is called, the component event listener `listener` will receive component events fired by this component. If `listener` is `null`, this method does nothing.
PARAMETERS	
listener	The possibly `null` component listener to add.

SEE ALSO   `java.awt.event.ComponentAdapter`, `java.awt.event.ComponentEvent`,
            `java.awt.event.ComponentListener`, `removeComponentListener()`.

EXAMPLE   See the `java.awt.event.ComponentEvent` class example.

addFocusListener()

PURPOSE   Adds a listener for receiving this component's focus events.

SYNTAX   `public synchronized void addFocusListener(FocusListener`
           `listener)`

DESCRIPTION   A component fires focus events as it gains or loses keyboard focus. See
           `FocusEvent` for more details. After this method is called, the focus listener
           `listener` will receive focus events fired by this component. If `listener` is
           `null`, this method does nothing.

PARAMETERS
`listener`   The possibly `null` focus listener to add.

SEE ALSO   `java.awt.event.FocusAdapter`, `java.awt.event.FocusEvent`,
            `java.awt.event.FocusListener`, `removeFocusListener()`.

EXAMPLE   See the class example.

addKeyListener()

PURPOSE   Adds a listener for receiving this component's key events.

SYNTAX   `public synchronized void addKeyListener(KeyListener listener)`

DESCRIPTION   Key events are fired when a key has been pressed, or released in a component.
           See `KeyEvent` for more details. After this method is called, the key listener
           `listener` will receive key events fired by this component. If `listener` is
           `null`, this method does nothing.

PARAMETERS
`listener`   The possibly `null` key listener to add.

SEE ALSO   `java.awt.event.KeyAdapter`, `java.awt.event.KeyEvent`,
            `java.awt.event.KeyListener`, `removeKeyListener()`.

EXAMPLE   See the class example.

addMouseListener()

PURPOSE   Adds a listener for receiving this component's mouse events.

A
B

D
E
F
G
H
I
J
K
L
M
N
O
P
Q
R
S
T
U
V
W
X
Y
Z

SYNTAX   `public synchronized void addMouseListener(MouseListener`
                       `listener)`

DESCRIPTION   Mouse events are fired when the mouse enters, exits, or when a mouse button has been pressed, or released on a component. See `MouseEvent` for more details. After this method is called, the mouse listener `listener` will receive mouse events fired by this component. If `listener` is `null`, this method does nothing.

PARAMETERS
`listener`   The possibly `null` mouse listener to add.

SEE ALSO   `addMouseMotionListener()`, `java.awt.event.MouseAdapter`, `java.awt.event.MouseEvent`, `java.awt.event.MouseListener`, `removeMouseListener()`.

EXAMPLE   See the class example.

addMouseMotionListener()

PURPOSE   Adds a listener for receiving this component's mouse motion events.

SYNTAX   `public synchronized void`
             `addMouseMotionListener(MouseMotionListener listener)`

DESCRIPTION   Mouse motion events are fired when the mouse is moved or dragged. See `MouseEvent` for more details. After this method is called, the mouse motion listener `listener` will receive mouse motion events fired by this component. If `listener` is `null`, this method does nothing.

PARAMETERS
`listener`   The possibly `null` mouse motion listener to add.

SEE ALSO   `addMouseListener()`, `java.awt.event.MouseMotionAdapter`, `java.awt.event.MouseEvent`, `java.awt.event.MouseMotionListener`, `removeMouseMotionListener()`.

EXAMPLE   See the `Container` class example.

addNotify()

PURPOSE   Creates this component's peer.

SYNTAX   `public void addNotify()`

DESCRIPTION   This method notifies this component that this component has been added to a container and to create a peer for this component if necessary. By default, this method invalidates this component and invokes `addNotify()` on any of its popup menus. This method must be overridden by a component subclass in order to actually create the peer.

This method can be called directly only if this component is a top-level window, such as a frame or dialog (see `Window.addNotify()`).

SEE ALSO   `invalidate()`, `removeNotify()`.

EXAMPLE   See `setVisible()`.

BOTTOM_ALIGNMENT

PURPOSE   Constant indicating alignment along a component's bottom edge.

SYNTAX   `public static final float BOTTOM_ALIGNMENT`

DESCRIPTION   This constant specifies that the *y*-coordinate of the component's alignment point be at the component's bottom edge. Its value is `1.0f`.

SEE ALSO   `CENTER_ALIGNMENT`, `getAlignmentY()`, `TOP_ALIGNMENT`.

EXAMPLE   See the `LayoutManager2` class example.

bounds( )   *DEPRECATED*

PURPOSE   Replaced by `getBounds()`.

SYNTAX   `public Rectangle bounds()`

RETURNS   A new non-`null` rectangle containing the bounds of this component.

DEPRECATION   Replace the usage of the deprecated method
```
Rectangle b = comp.bounds();
```
with
```
Rectangle b = comp.getBounds();
```

CENTER_ALIGNMENT

PURPOSE   Constant indicating alignment along a component's center.

SYNTAX   `public static final float CENTER`

DESCRIPTION   This constant specifies that the *y*-coordinate of the component's alignment point be at the component's center. Its value is `0.5f`.

SEE ALSO   `BOTTOM_ALIGNMENT`, `CENTER_ALIGNMENT`, `getAlignmentX()`, `getAlignmentY()`, `LEFT_ALIGNMENT`, `RIGHT_ALIGNMENT`, `TOP_ALIGNMENT`.

EXAMPLE   See the `LayoutManager2` class example.

A
B
C
D
E
F
G
H
I
J
K
L
M
N
O
P
Q
R
S
T
U
V
W
X
Y
Z

checkImage()

PURPOSE	Retrieves the construction status of an image.

SYNTAX	`public int checkImage(Image image, ImageObserver obs)`
	`public int checkImage(Image image, int width, int height,`
	    `ImageObserver obs)`

DESCRIPTION This method retrieves the status of an image that is being constructed. As far as this method is concerned, an image that has been scaled is treated as a completely different image. Therefore, when checking the status of an image, you must also indicate which scaled version of the image to check. Do this by setting the `width` and `height` parameters to the dimensions of the scaled image.

The image may not be in the process of being constructed; this method does not start the process. To start the image construction process, use `prepare-Image()`. If the image observer `obs` is not `null`, any status changes are delivered it.

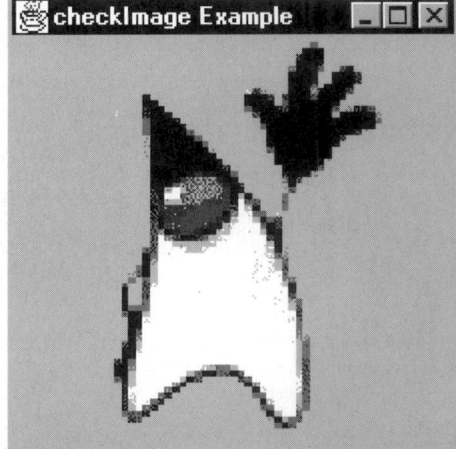

FIGURE 81: Checking the Status of a Scaled Image.

PARAMETERS

`height`	If >= 0, specifies the height of the scaled version of the image to check.
`image`	The non-`null` image to check.
`obs`	If non-`null`, specifies the image observer to be notified whenever the status changes.
`width`	If >= 0, specifies the width of the scaled version of the image to check.

RETURNS The combination of status bits as defined by the `ImageObserver` interface.

SEE ALSO `java.awt.image.ImageObserver`, `prepareImage()`.

EXAMPLE While an image is being loaded and displayed, a background thread is created to create a scaled version of the image. The thread uses the `checkImage()` to wait until the scaled image is complete. When the scaled image is complete, it is displayed on the screen. See Figure 81 for a screen shot of this example.

```
import java.awt.*;
import java.awt.image.*;

class Main extends Frame {
```

```
    Main(String filename) {
        super("checkImage Example");
        add(new ImageCanvas(getToolkit().getImage(filename)),
            BorderLayout.CENTER);
        setSize(300, 300);
        show();
    }

    static public void main(String[] args) {
        if (args.length == 1) {
            new Main(args[0]);
        } else {
            System.err.println("usage: java Main <image file>");
        }
    }
}

class ImageCanvas extends Component implements Runnable {
    int newWidth = 200, newHeight = 200;
    boolean drawScaled;
    Image image;

    ImageCanvas(Image image) {
        this.image = image;
        (new Thread(this)).start();
    }

    public void paint(Graphics g) {
        update(g);
    }
    public void update(Graphics g) {
        if (drawScaled) {
            g.clearRect(0, 0, getSize().width, getSize().height);
            g.drawImage(image, 0, 0, newWidth, newHeight, this);
        } else {
            g.drawImage(image, 0, 0, this);
        }
    }

    public void run() {
        prepareImage(image, newWidth, newHeight, null);
        while (true) {
            int status = checkImage(image, newWidth, newHeight, null);
            if ((status&ImageObserver.ERROR) != 0) {
                System.out.println("Error encountered while scaling image");
                System.exit(1);
            }
            if ((status&ImageObserver.ALLBITS) != 0) {
                drawScaled = true;
                repaint();
                break;
            }
            try {
                Thread.sleep(100);
            } catch (InterruptedException e) {
            }
        }
    }
}
```

A
B
C
D
E
F
G
H
I
J
K
L
M
N
O
P
Q
R
S
T
U
V
W
X
Y
Z

Component( )

PURPOSE   Constructs a new instance of `Component`.

SYNTAX   `protected Component()`

DESCRIPTION This constructor is used when implementing lightweight components. See the
class description for details on lightweight components.

EXAMPLE   See the class example's `SimpleTextField`, `checkImage()`'s `ImageCanvas`,
and `createImage()`'s `MainCanvas`.

contains( )

PURPOSE   Determines if a point is inside this component.

SYNTAX   `public boolean contains(int x, int y)`
`public boolean contains(Point pt)`

DESCRIPTION This method is used to determine whether the point `pt` is inside or outside of
this component. By default, this method returns `true` if `pt` is inside this component's bounds. If a component is a lightweight component with a nonrectangular shape, this component should override this method and return `true` only
if `pt` is inside the shape (heavy-weight components cannot have a nonrectangular shape).

The AWT system calls this method to determine whether the cursor has moved
in or out of this component. It needs this information to determine when to fire
a mouse enter or exit event (see `MouseEvent`).

PARAMETERS
 `pt`   The point to check.
 `x`   The *x*-coordinate relative to this component.
 `y`   The *y*-coordinate relative to this component.

RETURNS   `true` if the point is within this component's bounds; `false` otherwise.

SEE ALSO   `getComponentAt()`.

EXAMPLE   This example demonstrates
how to implement a nonrectangular lightweight component. The component is an
image button that fires action
events only when the user
clicks a nontransparent pixel.
To show which pixels are

FIGURE 82:   **Nonrectangular Lightweight
Component.**

nontransparent, the image button displays a hand cursor when the cursor is over a nontransparent pixel. See Figure 82.

The image button constructor takes an image and uses the pixel grabber class to extract the color map and pixels from the image. The color map is used to determine the transparent pixel value (if any).

The contains() method of the lightweight component uses the array of pixels and the transparent pixel value to determine if the coordinate is on a nontransparent pixel.

The image button also implements all the methods necessary to support action listeners.

```java
import java.awt.*;
import java.awt.image.*;
import java.awt.event.*;

class Main extends Frame implements ActionListener {
    Main(String filename) {
        super("Component.contains()");

        // Create image button and listen for events.
        ImageComponent c = new ImageComponent(filename);
        c.addActionListener(this);

        // Layout and show components.
        add(c, BorderLayout.CENTER);
        pack();
        show();
    }

    public void actionPerformed(ActionEvent evt) {
        System.out.println(evt);
    }

    public static void main(String[] args) {
        if (args.length != 1) {
            System.err.println("Usage: java Main <image-file>");
            System.exit(1);
        }
        new Main(args[0]);
    }
}

class ImageComponent extends Component {
    Dimension imageDim;
    Image image;
    int transparentPixel;
    byte[] pixels;

    ImageComponent(String filename) {
        // Retrieve the image from a file.
        image = getToolkit().getImage(filename);

        // Use -1 for the width and height to grab everything.
        PixelGrabber pg = new PixelGrabber(image, 0, 0, -1, -1, false);
```

```
                          // Get the pixels.
                          pg.startGrabbing();
                          try {
                              pg.grabPixels();
                          } catch (Exception e) {
                              e.printStackTrace();
                          }
                          imageDim = new Dimension(pg.getWidth(), pg.getHeight());

                          // If the color map is an index color map, get the
                          // pixels and the transparent pixel.
                          if (pg.getColorModel() instanceof IndexColorModel) {
                              pixels = (byte[])pg.getPixels();
                              transparentPixel =
                                  ((IndexColorModel)pg.getColorModel()).getTransparentPixel();
                          }

                          // Enable mouse events.
                          addMouseListener(new MouseEventHandler());

                          // Set the default cursor to be a hand cursor.
                          setCursor(Cursor.getPredefinedCursor(Cursor.HAND_CURSOR));
                      }

                      public boolean contains(int x, int y) {
                          // Return true on if the cursor is over non-transparent pixels.
                          if (x >= 0 && x < imageDim.width
                              && y >= 0 && y < imageDim.height) {
                              return pixels == null ||
                                  pixels[x+y*imageDim.width] != transparentPixel;
                          }
                          return false;
                      }

                      public Dimension getPreferredSize() {
                          return imageDim;
                      }

                      public void paint(Graphics g) {
                          g.setColor(Color.pink);
                          g.fillRect(0, 0, getSize().width, getSize().height);
                          g.drawImage(image, 0, 0, this);
                      }

                      class MouseEventHandler extends MouseAdapter {
                          public void mousePressed(MouseEvent evt) {
                              if (actionListener != null) {
                                  actionListener.actionPerformed(
                                      new ActionEvent(ImageComponent.this,
                                          ActionEvent.ACTION_PERFORMED, null));
                              }
                          }
                      }

                      // Action listener support methods.
                      transient ActionListener actionListener;
                      public synchronized void addActionListener(ActionListener l) {
                          actionListener = AWTEventMulticaster.add(actionListener, l);
                      }
```

Letters running down the left margin: A B C D E F G H I J K L M N O P Q R S T U V W X Y Z

```
        public synchronized void removeActionListener(ActionListener l) {
            actionListener = AWTEventMulticaster.remove(actionListener, l);
        }
    }
```

createImage()

PURPOSE   Creates an off-screen image or an image from an image producer.

SYNTAX   public Image createImage(int width, int height)
                public Image createImage(ImageProducer prod)

DESCRIPTION   There are two forms of createImage(). The first form uses a width and
                height to create an off-screen image on which you can paint. The off-screen
                image is often used to achieve smooth animation. The image is first con-
                structed in the off-screen image and then painted on the screen in its entirety.
                This technique is called *double-buffering*. The following example demon-
                strates the use of createImage() for double-buffering.

                The second form of createImage() takes an image producer prod and cre-
                ates an image based on the data supplied by the image producer. See the
                RGBImageFilter class for an example that uses this form of createImage().

PARAMETERS
    height   The height of the off-screen image in pixels.
    prod   The non-null image producer prod.
    width   The width of the off-screen image in pixels.

RETURNS   The image or null.

EXAMPLE   This example imple-
                ments a simple anima-
                tion of the word "Java"
                slowly rising in the cen-
                ter of a "brown bubbling
                liquid," as shown in Fig-
                ure 83. To eliminate
                flickering, the program
                calls createImage() to
                create an off-screen
                image and uses that

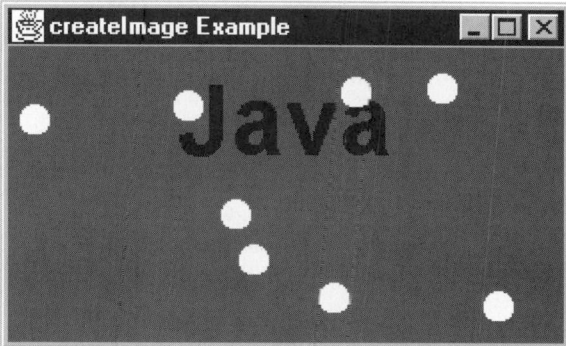

FIGURE 83: **Simple Animation Using Double-buffering.**

image to implement
double-buffering. Each
frame of the animation is first generated on the off-screen image and then
painted whole on the screen.

```java
import java.awt.*;
class Main {
    static public void main(String[] args) {
        Frame f = new Frame("createImage Example");
        f.add(new MainCanvas(), BorderLayout.CENTER);
        f.setSize(200, 100);
        f.show();
    }
}

class MainCanvas extends Component implements Runnable {
    Image backBuffer;
    Graphics backG;
    String str = "Java";
    int pointSize = 15;
    Point[] points = new Point[10];
    int[] pointRates = new int[points.length];
    Point stringPt = new Point(0, 0);

    MainCanvas() {
        for (int i=0; i<points.length; i++) {
            points[i] = new Point(0, 0);
            initPoint(i);
        }
        (new Thread(this)).start();
    }

    void initPoint(int i) {
        points[i].x = (int)(Math.floor(Math.random()*getSize().width));
        points[i].y = getSize().height;
        pointRates[i] = (int)(Math.floor(Math.random()*30)) + 5;
    }

    public void paint(Graphics g) {
        update(g);
    }

    public void update(Graphics g) {
        int w = getBounds().width;
        int h = getBounds().height;

        if (backBuffer == null
                || backBuffer.getWidth(null) != w
                || backBuffer.getHeight(null) != h) {
            backBuffer = createImage(w, h);
            if (backBuffer != null) {
                if (backG != null) {
                    backG.dispose();
                }
                backG = backBuffer.getGraphics();
                backG.setFont(new Font("Helvetica", Font.BOLD, 48));
                FontMetrics fm = backG.getFontMetrics();
                stringPt.x = (w-fm.stringWidth(str))/2;
            }
        }

        if (backBuffer != null) {
            backG.setColor(new Color(130, 80, 80));  // brown
```

A
B
C
D
E
F
G
H
I
J
K
L
M
N
O
P
Q
R
S
T
U
V
W
X
Y
Z

```
        backG.fillRect(0, 0, w, h);

        // Bubbles behind the string.
        backG.setColor(Color.white);
        for (int i=0; i<points.length/3; i++) {
            backG.fillOval(points[i].x, points[i].y, pointSize, pointSize);
        }

        // Paint the string
        backG.setColor(Color.black);
        backG.drawString(str, stringPt.x, stringPt.y % h + h);
        backG.drawString(str, stringPt.x, stringPt.y % h + 2*h);

        // Bubbles in front of the string.
        backG.setColor(Color.white);
        for (int i=points.length/3; i<points.length; i++) {
            backG.fillOval(points[i].x, points[i].y, pointSize, pointSize);
        }
        g.drawImage(backBuffer, 0, 0, null);
        }
    }

    public void run() {
        while (true) {
            for (int i=0; i<points.length; i++) {
                points[i].y -= pointRates[i];
                if (points[i].y < -pointSize) {
                    initPoint(i);
                }
            }
            stringPt.y--;
            repaint();
            try { Thread.sleep(80); } catch (Exception e) {};
        }
    }
}
```

deliverEvent()   *DEPRECATED*

PURPOSE	Replaced by dispatchEvent().
SYNTAX	public void deliverEvent(Event e)
PARAMETERS	
e	The non-null event.
DEPRECATION	Replace the usage of this deprecated method, as in
	deliverEvent(e);
	with
	dispatchEvent(awtEvent);
SEE ALSO	AWTEvent.

disable()   *DEPRECATED*

PURPOSE   Replaced by `setEnabled()`.

SYNTAX   `public void disable()`

DEPRECATION   Replace the usage of this deprecated method, as in
               `disable();`
               with
               `setEnabled(false);`

disableEvents()

PURPOSE   Disables event types for this component.

SYNTAX   `protected final void disableEvents(long eventTypes)`

DESCRIPTION   An event type is enabled when a listener for that type is added to this compo-
               nent or when `enableEvents()` is invoked explicitly on this component with
               the event type's mask. This method disables the event types specified by the
               mask `eventTypes`. It is used by subclasses of `Component` to undo the effects
               of `enableEvents()`. If a component has listeners corresponding to the event
               type, events will always be delivered to its `processEvent()` method, inde-
               pendent of the effects of `enableEvents()` or `disableEvents()`.

PARAMETERS
  `eventTypes` The event mask specifying the event types to disable. Event mask values are
               defined in `AWTEvent`.

SEE ALSO   `AWTEvent`, `dispatchEvent()`, `enableEvents()`, `processEvent()`.

EXAMPLE   `MenuItem.disableEvents()` serves the same purpose as `Component.dis-
               ableEvents()`, except that it is for `MenuItem` and its subclasses. See `Menu-
               Item.disableEvents()` for an example.

dispatchEvent()

PURPOSE   Dispatches an event to this component.

SYNTAX   `public final void dispatchEvent(AWTEvent evt)`

DESCRIPTION   This method dispatches the event `evt` to this component or one of its ances-
               tors. If `evt` is one of the event types that have been enabled for this compo-
               nent, it is processed using `processEvent()`. If the event is not consumed by
               this component and it is a key event, it is passed on to this component's parent
               and up the ancestor component tree until it is consumed.

PARAMETERS

evt   The non-null AWTEvent.

SEE ALSO   AWTEvent, enableEvents(), disableEvents(), processEvent().

EXAMPLE   This example creates a frame with two buttons. See Figure 84(a). Clicking the buttons changes the fonts of all the components in the frame. In particular, clicking the SmallFont button causes the components to assume a small font, while clicking the LargeFont button causes all the components to assume a large font. See Figure 84(b).

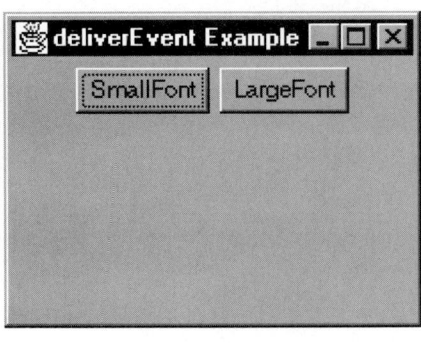
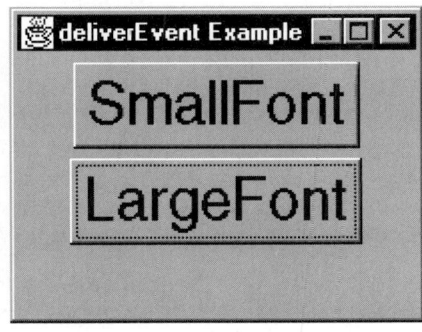

(a)   (b)

FIGURE 84: Component.dispatchEvent(): (a) Initial State and (b) after Changing Font Sizes.

Changing the size of the button label's font does not invalidate the button or its container automatically. Updating the button's size requires the button itself first to be invalidated (this automatically invalidates all of its ancestors, including its container). Calling doLayout() on the container then corrects the position and size of the button. An alternative to calling doLayout() is calling validate().

Changing the font of the container's components could have been achieved by simply calling their setFont() methods. However, for the purposes of this example, the same effect is achieved by delivering a special action event—SetFontEvent—to the components using dispatchEvent().

```
import java.awt.*;
import java.awt.event.*;

class Main extends Frame implements ActionListener {

    Main() {
        super("dispatchEvent Example");

        setLayout(new FlowLayout());
        Button b;
        add(b = new MainButton("SmallFont"));
        b.addActionListener(this);
        add(b = new MainButton("LargeFont"));
```

```
                b.addActionListener(this);

                setSize(200, 200);
                show();
        }

        public void actionPerformed(ActionEvent evt) {
            String arg = evt.getActionCommand();
            Font f = null;

            if ("SmallFont".equals(arg)) {
                f = new Font("Serif", Font.PLAIN, 12);
            } else if ("LargeFont".equals(arg)) {
                f = new Font("Serif", Font.PLAIN, 30);
            }
            if (f != null) {
                SetFontEvent fevt = new SetFontEvent(this, f);
                for (int i=0; i<getComponentCount(); i++) {
                    Component c = getComponent(i);
                    c.dispatchEvent(fevt);
                }
            }
            doLayout();
        }

        public static void main(String[] args) {
            new Main();
        }
    }

    // Define new event for setting font of button
    class SetFontEvent extends ActionEvent {
        Font font;
        public static final int SET_FONT_EVENT =  AWTEvent.RESERVED_ID_MAX + 1;
        public SetFontEvent(Object source, Font f) {
            super(source, SET_FONT_EVENT, null);
            font = f;
        }
        public Font getFont() {
            return font;
        }
    }

    class MainButton extends Button {
        MainButton(String label) {
            super(label);
        }

        // Override to handle special new event (SetFontEvent)
        protected void processActionEvent(ActionEvent evt) {
            if (evt instanceof SetFontEvent) {
                // Change font as requested
                setFont(((SetFontEvent)evt).getFont());
                invalidate();    // invalid button so it'll get resized
            } else {
                // Handle normal ActionEvent as before
                super.processActionEvent(evt);
            }
        }
    }
}
```

doLayout()

PURPOSE	Invokes the layout manager on this component.
SYNTAX	`public void doLayout()`
DESCRIPTION	If this component is a container, the container's layout manager is invoked (see `Container.doLayout()` for more details). Otherwise, by default this method does nothing.
SEE ALSO	`Container.doLayout()`.
EXAMPLE	See `dispatchEvent()`.

enable()   *DEPRECATED*

PURPOSE	Replaced by `setEnabled()`.
SYNTAX	`public void enable()` `public void enable(boolean cond)`
PARAMETERS	
cond	If `true`, this component is enabled; otherwise, this component is disabled.

DEPRECATION	Replace the usage of these deprecated methods, as in
	`  enable();`
	`  enable(false);`
	with
	`  setEnabled(true);`
	`  setEnabled(false);`

enableEvents()

PURPOSE	Enables event types for this component.
SYNTAX	`protected final void enableEvents(long eventTypes)`
DESCRIPTION	An event type is enabled when a listener for that type is added to this component. This method is used by subclasses of `Component` to always deliver events of the specified type to its `processEvent()` method, regardless of whether it has any listeners. This method enables the event types specified by the mask `eventTypes`.
PARAMETERS	
eventTypes	The event mask specifying the event types to enable. Event mask values are defined in `AWTEvent`.
SEE ALSO	`AWTEvent`, `disableEvents()`, `processEvent()`.
EXAMPLE	See `add()` and `processEvent()`.

A
B

D
E
F
G
H
I
J
K
L
M
N
O
P
Q
R
S
T
U
V
W
X
Y
Z

getAlignmentX()

PURPOSE	Retrieves this component's preferred alignment along the *x*-axis.
SYNTAX	`public float getAlignmentX()`
DESCRIPTION	This method returns the component's *x*-alignment value. This affects the way some layout managers place their components. See the class description for more information. The default implementation of this method returns `CENTER_ALIGNMENT`. For a different *x*-alignment value to be returned, this method must be overridden.
RETURNS	This component's *x*-alignment in the range `0.0f` to `1.0f`.
SEE ALSO	`CENTER_ALIGNMENT`, `getAlignmentY()`, `LEFT_ALIGNMENT`, `RIGHT_ALIGNMENT`.
EXAMPLE	See the `LayoutManager2` class example.

getAlignmentY()

PURPOSE	Retrieves this component's preferred alignment along the *y*-axis.
SYNTAX	`public float getAlignmentY()`
DESCRIPTION	This method returns the component's *y*-alignment value. This affects the way some layout managers place their components. See the class description for more information. The default implementation of this method returns `CENTER_ALIGNMENT`. For a different *y*-alignment value to be returned, this method must be overridden.
RETURNS	This component's *y*-alignment in the range `0.0f` to `1.0f`.
SEE ALSO	`BOTTOM_ALIGNMENT`, `CENTER_ALIGNMENT`, `getAlignmentX()`, `TOP_ALIGNMENT`.
EXAMPLE	See the `LayoutManager2` class example.

getBackground()

PURPOSE	Retrieves this component's background color.
SYNTAX	`public Color getBackground()`
DESCRIPTION	Some part of a component's visual appearance is painted using the background color. For example, a button is painted in the background color, while the label is painted in the foreground color.

A
B
C
D
E
F
G
H
I
J
K
L
M
N
O
P
Q
R
S
T
U
V
W
X
Y
Z

If this component does not have a background color set (for example, by call-ing `setBackground()` with a `null` color), it inherits its background color from the closest ancestor whose background color has been set. If no back-ground setting is found, `null` is returned.

RETURNS   The possibly `null` background color of this component.

SEE ALSO   `getForeground()`, `setBackground()`.

EXAMPLE   See the class example.

getBounds()

PURPOSE   Retrieves this component's bounds.

SYNTAX   `public Rectangle getBounds()`

DESCRIPTION   The bounds of a component specify the size of this component and its location within its parent. The width and height of the bounds specify the dimensions of this component without regard to any insets. The x- and y-coordinates of the bounds specify the location of this component relative to its parent.

RETURNS   A new non-`null` rectangle containing the bounds of this component.

SEE ALSO   `getLocation()`, `setSize()`.

EXAMPLE   See `createImage()`.

getColorModel()

PURPOSE   Retrieves this component's color model.

SYNTAX   `public ColorModel getColorModel()`

DESCRIPTION   If this component's peer exists, this method returns the peer's color model. Otherwise, it returns the default toolkit's color model (see `Toolkit.getDe-faultToolkit()`).

RETURNS   A non-`null` color model instance.

SEE ALSO   `ColorModel`, `Toolkit.getDefaultToolkit()`.

EXAMPLE   See the `ColorModel` class example.

getComponentAt()

PURPOSE   Retrieves the component containing a specified point.

A
B
C
D
E
F
G
H
I
J
K
L
M
N
O
P
Q
R
S
T
U
V
W
X
Y
Z

SYNTAX | `public Component getComponentAt(int x, int y)`
`public Component getComponentAt(Point pt)`

DESCRIPTION | This method is used to determine which, if any, component is at the pixel specified by the point `pt` or the coordinate `x`, `y`. The coordinates must be relative to the component's bounds. If this component is not a container, then this method uses `contains()` to determine whether this component contains the point. If this component is a container, see `Container.getComponentAt()` for details on the effects.

PARAMETERS
`pt` | The point to check.
`x` | The *x*-coordinate relative to this component's bounds.
`y` | The *y*-coordinate relative to this component's bounds.

RETURNS | The child component at the specified point. If no child component is at the point but the point is inside this component, returns this component itself. Returns `null` if the point is not in this component.

SEE ALSO | `contains()`.

EXAMPLE | See `Container.getComponentAt()`.

getCursor( )

PURPOSE | Retrieves this component's cursor image.

SYNTAX | `public Cursor getCursor()`

DESCRIPTION | This method retrieves the cursor image set for this component. If `setCursor()` has never been called on this component, this method returns the default cursor image.

RETURNS | The non-`null` cursor image for this component.

SEE ALSO | `Cursor, setCursor()`.

EXAMPLE | See the class example.

getFont( )

PURPOSE | Retrieves this component's font.

SYNTAX | `public Font getFont()`

DESCRIPTION | This method returns the font supplied in the most recent call to `setFont()` on this component. If `setFont()` has never been called on this component, this method returns the font of this component's parent. If this font also has never been set, the search continues up the parent chain until an ancestor component whose font has been set is encountered. If the search yields no such component, `null` is returned.

RETURNS   This component's font or the font of the closest ancestor whose font has been set. `null` is returned if no ancestor has a font set.

SEE ALSO   `setFont()`.

EXAMPLE   See the class `example`.

getFontMetrics()

PURPOSE   Retrieves the font metrics for a font for this component.

SYNTAX   `public FontMetrics getFontMetrics(Font fnt)`

DESCRIPTION   If this component's peer exists, this method asks the peer for the font metrics of the font `fnt`. Otherwise, this method returns the result of calling `Toolkit.getFontMetrics(fnt)`. The results of either action are typically the same.

PARAMETERS
 `fnt`   The non-`null` font.

RETURNS   The non-`null` font metrics for `fnt`.

SEE ALSO   `getFont()`.

EXAMPLE   See the class example.

getForeground()

PURPOSE   Retrieves this component's foreground color.

SYNTAX   `public Color getForeground()`

DESCRIPTION   Some part of a component's visual appearance is painted using the foreground color. For example, a button is painted in the background color, while the label is painted in the foreground color.

                 If this component does not have a foreground color set (for example, by calling `setForeground()` with a `null` color), this component inherits its foreground color from the closest ancestor whose foreground color has been set. If no foreground color has been set, `null` is returned.

RETURNS   The possibly `null` foreground color of this component.

SEE ALSO   `getBackground()`, `setForeground()`.

EXAMPLE   See the class example.

A
B
C
D
E
F
G
H
I
J
K
L
M
N
O
P
Q
R
S
T
U
V
W
X
Y
Z

339

getGraphics( )

PURPOSE	Creates a graphics context for this component.
SYNTAX	`public Graphics getGraphics()`
DESCRIPTION	This method returns a graphics context that uses this component as a drawing surface. The result is `null` if this component's peer does not exist.
	If this component is a native component, the background and foreground colors and the font of the returned graphics context are initialized using the values in this component. Otherwise, the background color is white, the foreground color is black, and the initial font is undetermined. The origin of the new graphics context is the northwest corner of this component's bounds.
RETURNS	A possibly `null` graphics context on this component.
SEE ALSO	`Graphics`, `paint()`.

getLocale( )

PURPOSE	Retrieves this component's locale.
SYNTAX	`public Locale getLocale()`
DESCRIPTION	If a locale has been set for this component, it is returned. Otherwise, the locale of the closest ancestor with a locale is returned. `Applet` and `Window`, which are subclasses of `Component`, return `Locale.getDefault()` if their locales have not been explicitly set. See the class description for more details.
RETURNS	A non-`null` locale.
EXCEPTIONS	
`IllegalComponentStateException`	
	If this component does not have its own locale and it does not have a parent.
SEE ALSO	`java.util.Locale`, `setLocale()`.
EXAMPLE	See `getName()`.

getLocation( )

PURPOSE	Retrieves this component's location relative to its parent.
SYNTAX	`public Point getLocation()`
DESCRIPTION	The location of this component is the top-left corner of this component's bounds. The location of this component is relative to its parent.

RETURNS   A new non-null point containing this component's location relative to its parent.

SEE ALSO   `setLocation()`.

EXAMPLE   See the `Container` class example.

getLocationOnScreen()

PURPOSE   Retrieves this component's location on the screen.

SYNTAX   `public Point getLocationOnScreen()`

DESCRIPTION   The location of this component on the screen is the top-left corner of this component's bounds relative to the screen's coordinate space. This component must be visible and showing on the screen in order for its location on the screen to be determined.

RETURNS   A new non-null point containing this component's location relative to the screen.

EXCEPTIONS

`IllegalComponentStateException`
     If this component is not showing on the screen.

SEE ALSO   `isShowing()`.

EXAMPLE   This example creates a number of components inside a frame. Clicking any of the components displays its absolute location on the screen. See Figure 85.

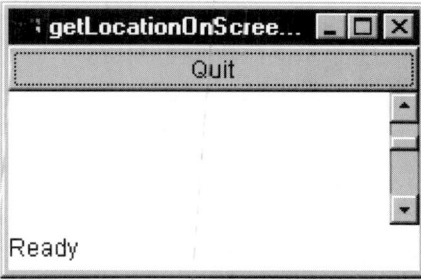

FIGURE 85: **Determining a Component's Location.**

```
import java.awt.*;
import java.awt.event.*;

class Main extends Frame {
    Main () {
        super("getLocationOnScreen example");
        Component c;
        MouseEventHandler ml = new MouseEventHandler();

        add(c = new Button("Quit"), BorderLayout.NORTH);
        c.addMouseListener(ml);
        add(c=new Canvas(), BorderLayout.CENTER);
        c.addMouseListener(ml);
        add(c=new Scrollbar(), BorderLayout.EAST);
        c.addMouseListener(ml);
```

A
B

D
E
F
G
H
I
J
K
L
M
N
O
P
Q
R
S
T
U
V
W
X
Y
Z

341

```
                add(c=new Label("Ready"), BorderLayout.SOUTH);
                c.addMouseListener(ml);

                setSize(200, 200);
                pack();
                show();
            }

            class MouseEventHandler extends MouseAdapter {
                public void mousePressed(MouseEvent evt) {
                    Component src = (Component)evt.getSource();
                    System.out.println(src.getLocationOnScreen());
                }
            }

            public static void main(String[] args) {
                new Main();
            }
        }
```

getMaximumSize( )

PURPOSE	Calculates this component's maximum size dimensions.
SYNTAX	`public Dimension getMaximumSize()`
DESCRIPTION	This method returns the maximum size that this component wants to be. By default, this method returns a width of `Short.MAX_VALUE` and a height `Short.MAX_VALUE`.
RETURNS	A new non-`null` dimension object containing this component's maximum size.
SEE ALSO	`Container.getMaximumSize()`, `getMinimumSize()`, `getPreferredSize()`, `getSize()`.

getMinimumSize( )

PURPOSE	Calculates this component's minimum size dimensions.
SYNTAX	`public Dimension getMinimumSize()`
DESCRIPTION	For native components, the result of this method depends on whether its peer exists. If the peer doesn't exist, this component's current size is returned. If the peer exists, the peer's minimum size is returned (this may also be this component's current size). For the most accurate result, this component's peer should be created before minimum size information is calculated (see `Window.addNotify()`).

For lightweight components, this method returns 1-×-1 by default. For the lightweight to behave exactly like a native component, the lightweight should override `getMinimumSize()` and return the current size.

RETURNS   A new non-`null` dimension object containing this component's minimum size. If this component is a container, see `Container.getPreferredSize()` for more information on how the preferred size is calculated.

SEE ALSO   `Container.getMinimumSize()`, `getMaximumSize()`, `getPreferredSize()`, `getSize()`.

EXAMPLE   See the class example.

getName()

PURPOSE   Retrieves this component's name.

SYNTAX   `public String getName()`

DESCRIPTION   The component's name is a nonlocalized string that can be used by a program to identify the component. For example, when a program receives an event, it could retrieve the event's source and use its name to determine which component fired the event.

RETURNS   A possibly `null` string containing this component's name.

SEE ALSO   `setName()`.

EXAMPLE   This example creates a checkbox group that has three localized labels. The locale of the component is set dynamically by `main()`. The `Main` component uses this locale to get the localized labels and uses `setName()` to record their nonlocalized names. The item listener for the `Main` component uses nonlocalized names for the checkboxes in order to determine which checkbox has been selected. See Figure 86.

FIGURE 86: Simple Component Localization.

```
import java.awt.*;
import java.awt.event.*;
import java.util.ResourceBundle;
import java.util.Locale;

public class Main extends Frame {
    Main() {
        super("getName Example");
    }

    void init(ItemListener l) {
        // Get localized labels for checkboxes
```

A
B
C
D
E
F
G
H
I
J
K
L
M
N
O
P
Q
R
S
T
U
V
W
X
Y
Z

```java
        ResourceBundle rb = ResourceBundle.getBundle("MyBundle", getLocale());
        String one = rb.getString("checkboxOne");
        String two = rb.getString("checkboxTwo");
        String three = rb.getString("checkboxThree");

        // Create checkboxes
        CheckboxGroup cg = new CheckboxGroup();
        Checkbox c1 = new Checkbox(one, cg, true);
        Checkbox c2 = new Checkbox(two, cg, false);
        Checkbox c3 = new Checkbox(three, cg, false);

        // Set internationalized identifiers for checkboxes
        c1.setName("one");
        c2.setName("two");
        c3.setName("three");

        // Add listener for checkboxes
        c1.addItemListener(l);
        c2.addItemListener(l);
        c3.addItemListener(l);

        // Add checkboxes to frame
        add(c1, BorderLayout.NORTH);
        add(c2, BorderLayout.CENTER);
        add(c3, BorderLayout.SOUTH);

        setSize(100, 100);
        show();
    }

    static public void main(String[] args) {
        Main m = new Main();

        // Set locale of component
        m.setLocale(Locale.FRANCE);
        m.init(new ItemEventHandler());
    }
}

class ItemEventHandler implements ItemListener {
    public void itemStateChanged(ItemEvent evt) {
        Component src = (Component)evt.getSource();
        String target = src.getName();
        int number = 0;

        if (target.equals("one")) {
            number = 1;
        } if (target.equals("two")) {
            number = 2;
        } if (target.equals("three")) {
            number = 3;
        }
        System.out.println("number=" + number);
    }
}
```

getParent()

PURPOSE	Retrieves this component's parent.
SYNTAX	`public Container getParent()`
DESCRIPTION	This method retrieves this component's parent. It returns `null` if this component does not have a parent. If this component hierarchy is part of a stand-alone application rather than an applet, the top-level window can be determined by following the parent chain until a component without a parent is found.
RETURNS	The parent of this component; `null` if this component does not have a parent.
EXAMPLE	See `Button.setLabel()`.

getPeer()   *DEPRECATED*

PURPOSE	Should not manipulate peers directly.
SYNTAX	`public ComponentPeer getPeer()`
RETURNS	This component's peer; `null` if this component does not have a peer.

getPreferredSize()

PURPOSE	Calculates this component's preferred size dimensions.
SYNTAX	`public Dimension getPreferredSize()`
DESCRIPTION	For native components, the result of this method depends on whether its peer exists. In particular, if the peer doesn't exist, this component's current size is returned. If the peer exists, the peer's preferred size is returned (this may also be this component's current size). For the most accurate result, this component's peer should be created before the preferred size information is calculated (see `Window.addNotify()`).
	For lightweight components, this method returns 1-×-1 by default. For the lightweight to behave exactly like a native component, the lightweight should override `getPreferredSize()` and return the current size.
	If this component is a container, see `Container.getPreferredSize()` for more information on how the preferred size is calculated.
RETURNS	A non-`null` dimension object containing this component's preferred size.
SEE ALSO	`Container.getPreferredSize()`, `getMaximumSize()`, `getMinimumSize()`, `getSize()`.
EXAMPLE	See the class example.

A
B

D
E
F
G
H
I
J
K
L
M
N
O
P
Q
R
S
T
U
V
W
X
Y
Z

345

getSize()

PURPOSE	Retrieves the size of this component.
SYNTAX	`public Dimension getSize()`
DESCRIPTION	The size of this component is derived from this component's bounds. In particular, `getSize().width == getBounds().width` and `getSize().height == getBounds().height`.
RETURNS	A non-`null` `Dimension` object containing the size of this component.
SEE ALSO	`setSize()`.
EXAMPLE	See the class example.

getToolkit()

PURPOSE	Retrieves this component's toolkit.
SYNTAX	`public Toolkit getToolkit()`
DESCRIPTION	A toolkit (see `Toolkit`) provides a portable interface on many system services that are related to the AWT. For example, with a toolkit instance you can create a print job or get information about the screen dimensions. This method retrieves this component's toolkit. If this component's peer exists, the peer returns this component's toolkit. Otherwise, this method searches up the component hierarchy looking for a component whose peer exists and uses the peer to return a non-`null` toolkit. If none is found, this method returns `Toolkit.getDefaultToolkit()`. Note that if a component is moved from one frame to another, the returned toolkit in the new frame differ from the original, since the frames may be on different screens.
RETURNS	A non-`null` reference to this component's toolkit.
SEE ALSO	`Toolkit`.
EXAMPLE	See `Toolkit.getImage()`.

getTreeLock()

PURPOSE	Retrieves the lock object for the entire AWT component tree.
SYNTAX	`public final Object getTreeLock()`

DESCRIPTION   The tree lock must be held whenever you need to walk or modify the hierarchy. This method retrieves the lock object for the entire AWT component tree. See the class description for more information.

RETURNS   The non-null lock object for the entire AWT component tree.

EXAMPLE   Here is a simple example that walks the ancestor chain looking for a frame. For a more elaborate example, see LayoutManager.

```
Frame getFrame(Component c) {
    synchronized (c.getTreeLock()) {
        Component p = c.getParent();

        while (p != null && !(p instanceof Frame)) {
            p = p.getParent();
        }
        return (Frame)p;
    }
}
```

gotFocus()   *DEPRECATED*

PURPOSE   Use the FocusListener interface instead.

SYNTAX   `public boolean gotFocus(Event evt, Object arg)`

PARAMETERS
  arg   An object whose contents depend on the component that fired the event.
  evt   The non-null event.

RETURNS   false if the event should be passed up to the component's parent; true otherwise.

DEPRECATION   Formerly, you would override the deprecated methods gotFocus() and lostFocus() in order to receive focus events.

```
import java.awt.*;
class Old extends Frame {
    TextField tf = new TextField(20);
    Old() {
        super("Deprecated Focus example");
        add(new TextField(), BorderLayout.NORTH);
        add(tf, BorderLayout.SOUTH);
        setSize(100, 100);
        pack();
        show();
    }
    public boolean gotFocus(Event evt, Object what) {
        if (evt.target == tf) {
            System.out.println("got focus");
            return true;
        }
        return false;
```

```
        }
    public boolean lostFocus(Event evt, Object what) {
        if (evt.target == tf) {
            System.out.println("lost focus");
            return true;
        }
        return false;
    }
    public static void main(String[] args) {
        new Old();
    }
}
```

Replace the usage of the deprecated methods `gotFocus()` and `lostFocus()` by defining a `FocusListener` and then adding it as a listener to the component of interest.

```
import java.awt.*;
import java.awt.event.*;
class New extends Frame {
    TextField tf = new TextField(20);
    New() {
        super("New FocusEvent example");
        add(new TextField(), BorderLayout.NORTH);
        add(tf, BorderLayout.SOUTH);
        setSize(100, 100);
        tf.addFocusListener(new FocusEventHandler());
        pack();
        show();
    }
    class FocusEventHandler implements FocusListener {
        public void focusGained(FocusEvent evt) {
            System.out.println("got focus");
        }
        public void focusLost(FocusEvent evt) {
            System.out.println("lost focus");
        }
    }
    public static void main(String[] args) {
        new New();
    }
}
```

SEE ALSO   `addFocusListener()`, `java.awt.event.FocusAdapter`,
`java.awt.event.FocusEvent`, `processFocusEvent()`,
`removeFocusListener()`.

handleEvent()   *DEPRECATED*

PURPOSE   Replaced by `processEvent()`.

SYNTAX   `public boolean handleEvent(Event evt)`

PARAMETERS
  evt   The non-null event.

RETURNS   `false` if the event should be passed up to this component's parent; `true` otherwise.

DEPRECATION   Formerly, the component would override `handleEvent()` to handle any event received by the component. Replace the usage of `handleEvent()` by `processEvent()` or by defining listeners for the various events of interest and adding them as listeners for the component.

SEE ALSO   `AWTEvent`.

hide()   *DEPRECATED*

PURPOSE   Replaced by `setVisible()`.

SYNTAX   `public void hide()`

DEPRECATION   Replace the usage of this deprecated method, as in

    `hide();`

with

    `setVisible(false);`

imageUpdate()

PURPOSE   Called to deliver status information about the loading of an image.

SYNTAX   `public boolean imageUpdate(Image img, int infoflags, int x, int y, int w, int h)`

DESCRIPTION   This method is called if this component requested some information about the image `img` and the information was not yet available. For example, if this component called `Image.getWidth()` and the width information was not yet available (that is, the method returned –1), the `imageUpdate()` method will be called as soon as the width becomes available.

See `ImageObserver.imageUpdate()` for more details.

PARAMETERS

`height`   Depends on the status bits enabled in `infoflags`.

`img`   The non-`null` image being updated.

`infoflags`   A set of status bits.

`width`   Depends on the status bits enabled in `infoflags`.

`x`   Depends on the status bits enabled in `infoflags`.

`y`   Depends on the status bits enabled in `infoflags`.

RETURNS   `true` if further calls to `imageUpdate()` are needed.

EXAMPLE   See the `java.awt.image.ImageObserver` example.

A
B
C
D
E
F
G
H
I
J
K
L
M
N
O
P
Q
R
S
T
U
V
W
X
Y
Z

A
B

D
E
F
G
H
I
J
K
L
M
N
O
P
Q
R
S
T
U
V
W
X
Y
Z

inside( )   *DEPRECATED*

PURPOSE	Replaced by `contains()`.
SYNTAX	`public boolean inside(int x, int y)`
PARAMETERS	
x	The *x*-coordinate relative to this component.
y	The *y*-coordinate relative to this component.
RETURNS	`true` if x and y are within this component's bounds.
DEPRECATION	Replace the usage of this deprecated method, as in

```
if (hitarea.inside(x,y)) {
    flag = true;
}
```
with
```
if (hitarea.contains(x,y)) {
    flag = true;
}
```

invalidate( )

PURPOSE	Invalidates this component.
SYNTAX	`public void invalidate()`
DESCRIPTION	This method invalidates this component and all of its ancestors. See the class description and the `validate()` method for more details about the valid state.
SEE ALSO	`isValid()`, `validate()`.
EXAMPLE	See `validate()`.

isEnabled( )

PURPOSE	Determines if this component is enabled.
SYNTAX	`public boolean isEnabled()`
DESCRIPTION	A component can be either enabled or disabled. See the class description for more information about a component's enabled state.
RETURNS	`true` if this component is enabled; `false` otherwise.
SEE ALSO	`setEnabled()`.
EXAMPLE	See the `Canvas` class example.

isFocusTraversable( )

PURPOSE   Determines if this method is focus-traversable.

SYNTAX   `public boolean isFocusTraversable()`

DESCRIPTION   A component is focus-traversable if it is enabled, it is visible, and its `isFocusTraversable()` method returns `true`. The focus can be moved around focus-traversable components when the user hits the Tab or Shift-Tab keys. Tab moves the focus forward, while Shift-Tab moves the focus backwards. The order of the traversal is exactly the order of the components in the container. For example, if the component at index 0 has the focus, then hitting the Tab key moves the focus to the component at index 1 (assuming it is focus-traversable).

A disabled component should return `false`.

Even if this method returns `false`, this component can still gain the focus by using `requestFocus()`.

By default, a native component is focus-traversable if its peer is focus-traversable. Lightweight components are, by default, not focus-traversable.

RETURNS   `true` if the focus of this component is traversable via the Tab or Shift-Tab keys.

SEE ALSO   `java.awt.event.FocusEvent`, `requestFocus()`, `transferFocus()`.

EXAMPLE   This example creates three focus- traversable components: two text fields and a FocusCanvas (Canvas, by default, is not focus-traversable). To make Canvas's focus traversable, you must override `isFocusTravers-able()` to return `true` and call `requestFocus()` when the mouse is clicked. FocusCanvas changes its background color to blue when it gains focus. Notice that the order of the focus traversal is the order of the components in the frame. See Figure 87.

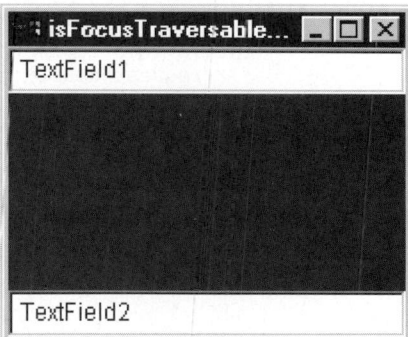

FIGURE 87:   **Focus Traversal.**

```
import java.awt.*;
import java.awt.event.*;

class Main extends Frame {
    Main () {
        super("isFocusTraversable example");
```

```
                    // Create components that are focus traversable by default.
                    add(new TextField("TextField1"), BorderLayout.NORTH);
                    add(new TextField("TextField2"), BorderLayout.SOUTH);

                    // Create focus traversable
                    add(new FocusCanvas(200, 100), BorderLayout.CENTER);

                    setSize(200, 200);
                    pack();
                    show();
                }

                public static void main(String[] args) {
                    new Main();
                }
            }

            class FocusCanvas extends Canvas {
                boolean hasFocus = false;
                FocusCanvas(int x, int y) {
                    super();
                    setSize(x, y);

                    // Listen for events.
                    addMouseListener(new MouseEventHandler());
                    addFocusListener(new FocusEventHandler());
                }

                // Implement focus traversable.
                public boolean isFocusTraversable() {
                    return true;
                }

                class MouseEventHandler extends MouseAdapter {
                    public void mousePressed(MouseEvent evt) {
                        requestFocus();
                    }
                }

                // Change background color to blue when focus is gained.
                class FocusEventHandler extends FocusAdapter {
                    public void focusGained(FocusEvent evt) {
                        hasFocus = true;
                        repaint();
                    }
                    public void focusLost(FocusEvent evt) {
                        hasFocus = false;
                        repaint();
                    }
                }

                public void paint(Graphics g) {
                    if (hasFocus) {
                        setBackground(Color.blue);
                    } else {
                        setBackground(Color.white);
                    }
                }
            }
```

A
B
C
D
E
F
G
H
I
J
K
L
M
N
O
P
Q
R
S
T
U
V
W
X
Y
Z

isShowing()

PURPOSE	Determines if this component is visible and showing on the screen.
SYNTAX	`public boolean isShowing()`
DESCRIPTION	This method is used to determine if this component is visible on the screen. A component can be "visible" even though it doesn't appear on the screen. However, if this component's visible state is `true` and this component has a peer, this component will appear on the screen.
RETURNS	`true` if this component is visible and has a peer.
SEE ALSO	`isVisible()`, `setVisible()`.

isValid()

PURPOSE	Retrieves this component's valid state.
SYNTAX	`public boolean isValid()`
DESCRIPTION	Each component maintains a valid state to indicate whether it needs to be re-laid out by the layout manager. See the class description and the `validate()` method for more details about the valid state.
RETURNS	`true` if this component is valid; `false` otherwise.
SEE ALSO	`invalidate()`, `validate()`.
EXAMPLE	See `validate()`.

isVisible()

PURPOSE	Retrieves this component's visible state.
SYNTAX	`public boolean isVisible()`
DESCRIPTION	By default, most components are created visible. Top-level windows such as frames are created invisible.
RETURNS	`true` if this component is visible; `false` otherwise.
SEE ALSO	`isShowing()`, `setVisible()`.
EXAMPLE	See `setVisible()`.

A
B
C
D
E
F
G
H
I
J
K
L
M
N
O
P
Q
R
S
T
U
V
W
X
Y
Z

keyDown()   *DEPRECATED*

PURPOSE   Use the KeyListener interface instead.

SYNTAX   `public boolean keyDown(Event evt, int key)`

PARAMETERS

  evt   The non-null event.

  key   The key that was pressed.

RETURNS   `false` if the event should be passed up to this component's parent; `true` otherwise.

DEPRECATION   Formerly, this component would override this method to handle events fired when the user presses a key.

```java
import java.awt.*;
class Old extends Frame {
    TextArea ta = new TextArea(10, 40);
    Old() {
        super("Deprecated key example");
        add(ta, BorderLayout.CENTER);
        pack();
        show();
    }
    public boolean keyDown(Event evt, int key) {
        if (evt.target == ta) {
            System.out.println("Pressed: " + (char)key);
            return true;
        }
        return false;
    }
    public boolean keyUp(Event evt, int key) {
        if (evt.target == ta) {
            System.out.println("Released: " + (char)key);
            return true;
        }
        return false;
    }
    static public void main(String[] args) {
        new Old();
    }
}
```

Replace the usage of the deprecated methods keyUp() and keyDown() by defining a KeyListener and adding it as a listener for this component.

```java
import java.awt.*;
import java.awt.event.*;
class New extends Frame {
    TextArea ta = new TextArea(10, 40);
    New() {
        super("New KeyEvent example");
        add(ta, BorderLayout.CENTER);
        ta.addKeyListener(new KeyEventHandler());
        pack();
```

```
            show();
        }
        class KeyEventHandler implements KeyListener {
            public void keyTyped(KeyEvent evt) {
                System.out.println("Typed: " + evt.getKeyChar());
            }
            public void keyPressed(KeyEvent evt) {
                System.out.println("Pressed: " + evt.getKeyChar());
            }
            public void keyReleased(KeyEvent evt) {
                System.out.println("Released: " + evt.getKeyChar());
            }
        }
        static public void main(String[] args) {
            new New();
        }
    }
```

SEE ALSO   addKeyListener(), AWTEvent, java.awt.event.KeyAdapter,
            java.awt.event.KeyEvent, processKeyEvent(), removeKeyListener().

keyUp()   *DEPRECATED*

PURPOSE   Use the KeyListener interface instead.

SYNTAX   public boolean keyUp(Event evt, int key)

PARAMETERS
  evt   The non-null event.
  key   The key that was released.

RETURNS   false if the event should be passed up to this component's parent; true other-
            wise.

DEPRECATION See keyDown() for an example of how to replace the usage of this deprecated
            method.

SEE ALSO   addKeyListener(), AWTEvent, java.awt.event.KeyAdapter,
            java.awt.event.KeyEvent, processKeyEvent(), removeKeyListener().

layout()   *DEPRECATED*

PURPOSE   Replaced by doLayout().

SYNTAX   public void layout()

DEPRECATION Replace the usage of this deprecated method, as in
              layout();
            with
              doLayout();

A
B
C
D
E
F
G
H
I
J
K
L
M
N
O
P
Q
R
S
T
U
V
W
X
Y
Z

LEFT_ALIGNMENT

PURPOSE	Constant indicating alignment along a component's left edge.
SYNTAX	`public static final float LEFT_ALIGNMENT`
DESCRIPTION	This constant specifies that the *x*-coordinate of the component's alignment point be at the component's left edge. Its value is `0.0f`.
SEE ALSO	`CENTER_ALIGNMENT`, `getAlignmentX()`, `RIGHT_ALIGNMENT`.
EXAMPLE	See the `LayoutManager2` class example.

list()

PURPOSE	Prints out information about this component.

SYNTAX	`public void list()`
	`public void list(PrintStream out)`
	`public void list(PrintStream out, int indent)`
	`public void list(PrintWriter outwriter)`
	`public void list(PrintWriter outwriter, int indent)`

DESCRIPTION	This method prints the results of calling `toString()` to the print stream `out` or print writer `outwriter`. If this component is a container, this method recursively prints the results of calling `toString()` on each of the container's descendants. The component hierarchy is traversed in depth-first order. Children that are further down the hierarchy are printed with more indents. The first line of output is printed with indent spaces. If neither `out` nor `outwriter` is specified, it defaults to `System.out`. If `indent` is not specified, it defaults to `0`.
PARAMETERS	
`indent`	The indentation of the first line of output.
`out`	The non-`null` output stream in which to print.
`outwriter`	The non-`null` output writer in which to print.
SEE ALSO	`java.io.PrintStream`, `java.io.PrintWriter`, `java.lang.System.out`, `toString()`.
EXAMPLE	See `Container.list()`.

locate()   *DEPRECATED*

PURPOSE	Replaced by `getComponentAt()`.

SYNTAX   `public Component locate(int x, int y)`

PARAMETERS

x   The *x*-coordinate relative to this component's bounds.

y   The *y*-coordinate relative to this component's bounds.

RETURNS   The subcomponent at x, y or this component itself if no component is at x, y but x, y is in this component. Returns `null` if x, y is not in this component.

DEPRECATION   Replace the usage of this deprecated method, as in

```
Component comp = locate(x, y);
```
with
```
Component comp = getComponentAt(x, y);
```

location()   *DEPRECATED*

PURPOSE   Replaced by `getLocation()`.

SYNTAX   `public Point location()`

RETURNS   A new non-`null` point containing this component's location relative to this component's parent.

DEPRECATION   Replace the usage of this deprecated method, as in

```
Point pt = location();
```
with
```
Point pt = getLocation();
```

lostFocus()   *DEPRECATED*

PURPOSE   Use the `FocusListener` interface instead.

SYNTAX   `public boolean lostFocus(Event evt, Object arg)`

PARAMETERS

arg   An object whose contents depend on the component that fired the event.

evt   The non-`null` event.

RETURNS   `false` if the event should be passed up to this component's parent; `true` otherwise.

DEPRECATION   See `gotFocus()` for an example of how to replace usage of `lostFocus()` using `FocusListener`.

SEE ALSO   `java.awt.event.FocusAdapter`, `java.awt.event.FocusEvent`, `processFocusEvent()`.

A
B

D
E
F
G
H
I
J
K
L
M
N
O
P
Q
R
S
T
U
V
W
X
Y
Z

minimumSize( )   *DEPRECATED*

PURPOSE   Replaced by `getMinimumSize()`.

SYNTAX   `public Dimension minimumSize()`

RETURNS   A new non-`null` dimension object containing this component's minimum size.

DEPRECATION   Replace the usage of this deprecated method, as in

```
Dimension min = minimumSize();
```
with
```
Dimension min = getMinimumSize();
```

mouseDown( )   *DEPRECATED*

PURPOSE   Use `MouseListener` interface instead.

SYNTAX   `public boolean mouseDown(Event evt, int x, int y)`

PARAMETERS

evt   The non-`null` event.

x   The *x*-coordinate of the cursor relative to this component's bounds at the time of the mouse event.

y   The *y*-coordinate of the cursor relative to this component's bounds at the time of the mouse event.

RETURNS   `false` if the event should be passed up to this component's parent; `true` otherwise.

DEPRECATION   Formerly, this component would override `mouseDown()`, `mouseUp()`, `mouseExit()`, and `mouseEnter()` to handle events fired when the user presses a mouse button.

```
import java.awt.*;
class Old extends Frame {
    Old () {
        super("Deprecated Mouse Events example");
        setSize(100, 50);
        show();
    }
    public boolean mouseEnter(Event evt, int x, int y) {
        System.out.println("Mouse Enter(" + x + "," + y + ")");
        return true;
    }
    public boolean mouseExit(Event evt, int x, int y) {
        System.out.println("Mouse Exit(" + x + "," + y + ")");
        return true;
    }
    public boolean mouseDown(Event evt, int x, int y) {
        System.out.println("Mouse Down(" + x + "," + y + ")");
        return true;
    }
```

```
    public boolean mouseUp(Event evt, int x, int y) {
        System.out.println("Mouse Up(" + x + "," + y + ")");
        return true;
    }
    public static void main(String[] args) {
        new Old();
    }
}
```

Replace the usage of these deprecated methods by defining a `MouseListener` and then adding it as a listener for the component's mouse events.

```
import java.awt.*;
import java.awt.event.*;
class New extends Frame {
    New() {
        super("New MouseEvent example");
        setSize(100, 50);
        this.addMouseListener(new MouseEventHandler());
        show();
    }
    class MouseEventHandler implements MouseListener {
        public void mouseEntered(MouseEvent evt) {
            System.out.println("Mouse Enter(" + evt.getX() + "," +
evt.getY() + ")");
        }
        public void mouseExited(MouseEvent evt) {
            System.out.println("Mouse Exit(" + evt.getX() + "," +
evt.getY() + ")");
        }
        public void mousePressed(MouseEvent evt) {
            System.out.println("Mouse Down(" + evt.getX() + "," +
evt.getY() + ")");
        }
        public void mouseReleased(MouseEvent evt) {
            System.out.println("Mouse Up(" + evt.getX() + "," +
evt.getY() + ")");
        }
        public void mouseClicked(MouseEvent evt) {
            System.out.println("Mouse Clicked(" + evt.getX() + "," +
evt.getY() + ")");
        }
    }
    public static void main(String[] args) {
        new New();
    }
}
```

SEE ALSO   `addMouseListener()`, `java.awt.event.MouseAdapter`, `java.awt.event.MouseEvent`, `processMouseEvent()`, `removeMouseListener()`.

mouseDrag()   *DEPRECATED*

PURPOSE   Use the `MouseMotionListener` interface instead.

A
B
C
D
E
F
G
H
I
J
K
L
M
N
O
P
Q
R
S
T
U
V
W
X
Y
Z

SYNTAX

```
public boolean mouseDrag(Event evt, int x, int y)
```

PARAMETERS

evt   The non-null event.

x   The *x*-coordinate of the cursor relative to this component's bounds at the time of the mouse event.

y   The *y*-coordinate of the cursor relative to this component's bounds at the time of the mouse event.

RETURNS   false if the event should be passed up to this component's parent; true otherwise.

DEPRECATION   Formerly, this component overrode mouseDrag() and mouseMove() to handle events fired when the user drags the mouse as a mouse button is held down.

```
import java.awt.*;
class Old extends Frame {
    Old () {
        super("Deprecated Mouse Motion Events example");
        setSize(100, 50);
        show();
    }
    public boolean mouseDrag(Event evt, int x, int y) {
        System.out.println("Mouse Drag(" + x + "," + y + ")");
        return true;
    }
    public boolean mouseMove(Event evt, int x, int y) {
        System.out.println("Mouse Move(" + x + "," + y + ")");
        return true;
    }
    public static void main(String[] args) {
        new Old();
    }
}
```

Replace the usage of these deprecated methods by defining a MouseMotion-Listener and adding it as a listener for this component's mouse motion events.

```
import java.awt.*;
import java.awt.event.*;
class New extends Frame {
    New() {
        super("New Mouse-related MouseEvent example");
        setSize(100, 50);
        this.addMouseMotionListener(new MouseMotionEventHandler());
        show();
    }
    class MouseMotionEventHandler implements MouseMotionListener {
        public void mouseDragged(MouseEvent evt) {
            System.out.println("Mouse Dragged(" + evt.getX() + "," +
evt.getY() + ")");
        }
        public void mouseMoved(MouseEvent evt) {
```

```
                    System.out.println("Mouse Moved(" + evt.getX() + "," +
        evt.getY() + ")");
                }
            }
            public static void main(String[] args) {
                new New();
            }
        }
```

SEE ALSO   `addMouseMotionListener()`, `java.awt.event.MouseMotionAdapter`,
`java.awt.event.MouseEvent`, `processMouseMotionEvent()`,
`removeMouseMotionListener()`.

mouseEnter()   *DEPRECATED*

PURPOSE   Use the `MouseListener` interface instead.

SYNTAX   `public boolean mouseEnter(Event evt, int x, int y)`

PARAMETERS

evt   The non-null event.

x   The *x*-coordinate of the cursor relative to this component's bounds at the time
of the mouse event.

y   The *y*-coordinate of the cursor relative to this component's bounds at the time
of the mouse event.

RETURNS   `false` if the event should be passed up to this component's parent, `true` otherwise.

DEPRECATION   See `mouseDown()` for an example of how to replace deprecated usage of this
method.

SEE ALSO   `addMouseListener()`, `java.awt.event.MouseAdapter`,
`java.awt.event.MouseEvent`, `processMouseEvent()`,
`removeMouseListener()`.

mouseExit()   *DEPRECATED*

PURPOSE   Use the `MouseListener` interface instead.

SYNTAX   `public boolean mouseExit(Event evt, int x, int y)`

PARAMETERS

evt   The non-null event.

x   The *x*-coordinate of the cursor relative to this component's bounds at the time
of the mouse event.

y   The *y*-coordinate of the cursor relative to this component's bounds at the time
of the mouse event.

mouseMove()

RETURNS	`false` if the event should be passed up to this component's parent; `true` otherwise.
DEPRECATION	See `mouseDown()` for an example of how to replace deprecated usage of this method.
SEE ALSO	`addMouseListener()`, `java.awt.event.MouseAdapter`, `java.awt.event.MouseEvent`, `processMouseEvent()`, `removeMouseListener()`.

A
B
C
D
E

mouseMove()   *DEPRECATED*

F

PURPOSE	Use the `MouseMotionListener` interface instead.
SYNTAX	`public boolean mouseMove(Event evt, int x, int y)`
PARAMETERS	
`evt`	The non-`null` event.
`x`	The *x*-coordinate of the cursor relative to this component's bounds at the time of the mouse event.
`y`	The *y*-coordinate of the cursor relative to this component's bounds at the time of the mouse event.
RETURNS	`false` if the event should be passed up to this component's parent; `true` otherwise.
DEPRECATION	See `mouseDrag()` for an example of how to replace deprecated usage of this method.
SEE ALSO	`addMouseMotionListener()`, `java.awt.event.MouseMotionAdapter`, `java.awt.event.MouseEvent`, `processMouseMotionEvent()`, `removeMouseMotionListener()`.

G
H
I
J
K
L
M
N
O
P
Q
R

mouseUp()   *DEPRECATED*

S
T

PURPOSE	Use the `MouseListener` interface instead.
SYNTAX	`public boolean mouseUp(Event evt, int x, int y)`
PARAMETERS	
`evt`	The non-`null` event.
`x`	The *x*-coordinate of the cursor relative to this component's bounds at the time of the mouse event.
`y`	The *y*-coordinate of the cursor relative to this component's bounds at the time of the mouse event.
RETURNS	`false` if the event should be passed up to this component's parent; `true` otherwise.

U
V
W
X
Y
Z

DEPRECATION   See mouseDown() for an example of how to replace deprecated usage of this method.

SEE ALSO   addMouseListener(), java.awt.event.MouseAdapter, java.awt.event.MouseEvent, processMouseEvent(), removeMouseListener().

move( )   *DEPRECATED*

PURPOSE   Replaced by setLocation().

SYNTAX   public void move(int x, int y)

PARAMETERS
x   The new *x*-coordinate.
y   The new *y*-coordinate.

DEPRECATION   Replace the usage of this deprecated method, as in
```
move(x, y);
```
with
```
setLocation(x, y);
```

nextFocus( )   *DEPRECATED*

PURPOSE   Replaced by transferFocus().

SYNTAX   public void nextFocus()

DEPRECATION   Replace the usage of this deprecated method, as in
```
nextFocus();
```
with
```
transferFocus();.
```

paint( )

PURPOSE   Called to repaint this component.

SYNTAX   public void paint(Graphics gc)

DESCRIPTION   This method should be overridden if this component wishes to paint. It will be called by the AWT system whenever it detects that some area has been damaged and needs to be repainted. The graphics context gc should be used to repaint the damaged area. This method is similar to update(), except that the system automatically clears the damaged area with this component's background color before calling paint(); the damaged area is not cleared when update() is called. See the class description on "Painting" for more information.

The damaged area is not necessarily the whole area of this component. To discover the damaged area, call gc.getClipBounds(). Note that when this component is made larger, the clipping area may only include the new area. If by enlarging this component some other part of the component changes and needs to be repainted, a call to repaint() must be made so that the area can be repainted.

If this is a native component, three properties of gc are initialized with values taken from the same three properties of this component. The properties are the background color, the foreground color, and the font.

PARAMETERS

gc   The non-null graphics context in which to paint this component.

SEE ALSO   getBackground(), repaint(), update().

EXAMPLE   See createImage().

paintAll()

PURPOSE   Called to repaint this component and its descendants.

SYNTAX   public void paintAll(Graphics gc)

DESCRIPTION   This method should be overridden if a component wishes to paint. This method will be called by the AWT system in response to a request to paint all visible descendants of this component. If this method is overridden, this component should paint itself on the graphics context gc and then, if this component is a container, invoke the paintAll() method on all of its children.

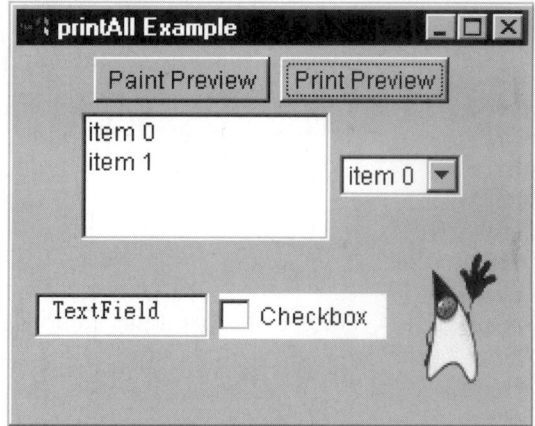

FIGURE 88: **Paint and Print Previewer's Control Panel.**

If not overridden, this method, by default, calls either paint() (if this component is a lightweight component) or its peer's paint() method (if this is a native component).

PARAMETERS

gc   The non-null graphics context in which to paint this component and its descendants.

SEE ALSO   paint().

EXAMPLE   This example demonstrates how to implement a paint or print previewer for a frame using paintAll() and printAll(). The example frame contains a number of miscellaneous components (see Figure 88). If the user clicks the button labeled Paint Preview, an off-screen image is created and all of the frame contents are painted to the image. The image is then displayed in a separate viewer. If Print Preview is pressed, the frame contents are printed to the off-screen image and then displayed in the viewer (Figure 89).

Note that the results are not necessarily identical to what's displayed on the screen. In particular, the borders around the frame and native components are not painted or printed. This will get better over time.

Note: In Java 1.1.2, Container.paintComponents() contains a bug, so the viewer created by the PrintPreview button will not show any native components.

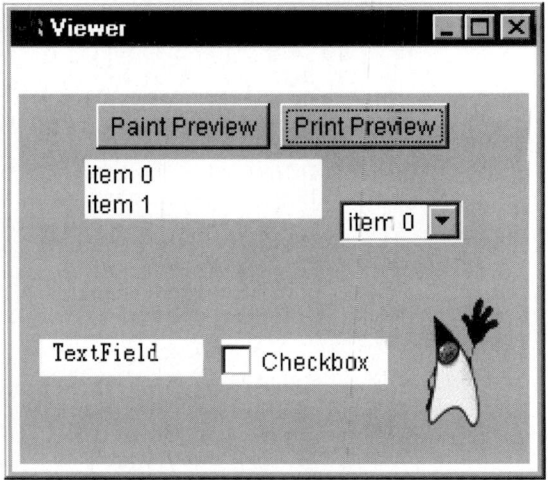

FIGURE 89: Paint and Print Previewer.

```
import java.awt.*;
import java.awt.event.*;

class Main extends Frame implements ActionListener {
    Main() {
        super("printAll Example");

        // Create the paint and print buttons and listen for events.
        Button b = new Button("Paint Preview");
        b.addActionListener(this);
        add(b);
        b = new Button("Print Preview");
        b.addActionListener(this);
        add(b);

        // Now create and add a bunch of miscellaneous components
        // in no particular order.
        List l = new List();
```

```
            l.addItem("item 0");
            l.addItem("item 1");
            add(l);
            Choice ch = new Choice();
            ch.addItem("item 0");
            ch.addItem("item 1");
            add(ch);
            add(new TextField("TextField"));
            Panel p = new Panel(new FlowLayout());
            p.add(new Checkbox("Checkbox"));
            // Add a lightweight component.
            p.add(new ImageComponent("duke.gif"));
            add(p);

            // Layout and show.
            setLayout(new FlowLayout());
            pack();
            show();
    }

    // Color just the inset area.
    public void paint(Graphics g) {
        Insets insets = getInsets();

        g.setColor(Color.lightGray);
        g.fillRect(insets.left, insets.top,
            getSize().width-insets.left-insets.right,
            getSize().height-insets.top-insets.bottom);

        // Don't forget to paint the lightweights.
        super.paint(g);
    }

    public void actionPerformed(ActionEvent evt) {
        // Create an off-screen image and a graphics context on it.
        Image image = createImage(getSize().width, getSize().height);
        Graphics g = image.getGraphics();

        // A workaround for a clipping bug in
        // Container.paintComponents() and Container.printComponents().
        g.setClip(0, 0, Short.MAX_VALUE, Short.MAX_VALUE);

        // Paint or print the components in the graphics context.
        if (evt.getActionCommand().equals("Paint Preview")) {
            paintAll(g);

            // The following is almost the same except that the frame's
            // paint() method is not be called.
            //paintComponents(g);

            // The following only invokes the paint() method of the frame
            // and any lightweight children.
            //paint(g);

            // Create the viewer to see the results.
            new Previewer(image, "Paint");
        } else if (evt.getActionCommand().equals("Print Preview")) {
            printAll(g);

            // The following is almost the same except that the frame's
```

```
                // print() method is not be called.
                //printComponents(g);

                // The following only invokes the print() method of the frame
                // and any lightweight children.
                //print(g);

                // Create the viewer to see the results.
                new Previewer(image, "Print");
            }
            g.dispose();

    }

    public static void main(String[] args) {
        new Main();
    }
}

class ImageComponent extends Component {
    Image image;
    ImageComponent(String filename) {
        image = getToolkit().getImage(filename);

        // Load the image with a media tracker because
        // we need the dimensions immediately.
        MediaTracker tracker = new MediaTracker(this);
        try {
            tracker.addImage(image, 0);
            tracker.waitForAll(0);
        } catch (Exception e) {
            e.printStackTrace();
        }
    }

    public Dimension getPreferredSize() {
        return new Dimension(image.getWidth(null), image.getHeight(null));
    }

    public void paint(Graphics g) {
        g.drawImage(image, 0, 0, this);
    }
}

class Previewer extends Frame {
    Image image;

    Previewer(Image image, String title) {
        super(title + " Viewer");
        int w = image.getWidth(null);
        int h = image.getHeight(null);

        this.image = image;

        // This call creates the frame's peers.
        // Without this call, getInsets() will return invalid values.
        addNotify();

        // When the frame's insets.
        Insets insets = getInsets();
```

A

B

```
            // Adjust the dimensions of the frame to account for the insets.
            w += insets.left + insets.right;
            h += insets.top + insets.bottom;

            // Size and show the viewer.
            setSize(w, h);
            show();
        }

        // Shows the image.
        public void paint(Graphics g) {
            Insets insets = getInsets();

            g.drawImage(image, insets.left, insets.top, this);
        }
    }
```

D

E

F

G

H

I

paramString( )

J

PURPOSE   Generates a string representation of this component's state.

K

SYNTAX   `protected String paramString()`

L

M

DESCRIPTION   The default string representation of a component consists of its name, *x*- and *y*-coordinates, width, height, and whether it is valid, hidden, or enabled.

N

O

A subclass of this class should override this method and return a concatenation of its state with the results of `super.paramString()`. This method is called by the `toString()` method and is typically used for debugging.

P

RETURNS   A non-`null` string representing this component's state.

Q

SEE ALSO   `toString()`.

R

S

EXAMPLE   This example shows how a subclass should override the `paramString()` method. The override appends three extra pieces of state to the superclass's state.

T

U

V

W

X

Y

```
    boolean myBool = false;
    int myInt = 59;
    String myStr = "Testing";
    protected String paramString() {
        String str = super.paramString();
        str += ",myBool=" + myBool;
        str += ",myInt=" + myInt;
        if (myStr != null) {
            str += ",myStr=" + myStr;
        }
        return str;
    }
```

Z

postEvent()   *DEPRECATED*

PURPOSE   Replaced by dispatchEvent().

SYNTAX   `public boolean postEvent(Event evt)`

PARAMETERS
evt   The non-null event.

RETURNS   `false` if the event should be passed up to this component's parent; `true` otherwise.

DEPRECATION   Replace the usage of this deprecated method, as in
```
postEvent(evt);
```
with
```
dispatchEvent(awtEvt);
```

SEE ALSO   AWTEvent.

preferredSize()   *DEPRECATED*

PURPOSE   Replaced by getPreferredSize().

SYNTAX   `public Dimension preferredSize()`

RETURNS   A non-null dimension object containing this component's preferred size.

DEPRECATION   Replace the usage of this deprecated method, as in
```
Dimension ps = preferredSize();
```
with
```
Dimension ps = getPreferredSize();
```

prepareImage()

PURPOSE   Triggers the loading of image data for an image.

SYNTAX   `public boolean prepareImage(Image img, ImageObserver obs)`
`public boolean prepareImage(Image img, int w, int h, ImageObserver obs)`

DESCRIPTION   This method starts the loading or production of image data associated with image `img` or a scaled version of `img`. If w and h are -1, no scaling of `img` is done. If w and h are non-negative, `img` is loaded and scaled so that its width is w and its height is h. The image observer `obs` will receive image update notifications as the image is being loaded or produced.

A
B
C
D
E
F
G
H
I
J
K
L
M
N
O
P
Q
R
S
T
U
V
W
X
Y
Z

This method is typically used to preload image data for an image or a scaled version of an image so that `Graphics.drawImage()` can operate as quickly as possible.

If w and h are not specified, they default to -1, that is, the image should not be scaled.

PARAMETERS

h	-1 or the scaled height of the returned image in pixels.
img	The non-null image to load.
obs	The non-null image observer.
w	-1 or the scaled width of the returned image in pixels.

RETURNS   `true` if all of the image data for `img` is available; `false` otherwise.

SEE ALSO   `java.awt.image.ImageObserver`.

EXAMPLE   See `checkImage()`.

print( )

PURPOSE   Prints this component on a graphics context.

SYNTAX   `public void print(Graphics gc)`

DESCRIPTION   By default, this method calls `paint(gc)`. If this component does not look the same when it is displayed on the screen and when it is printed, this method should be overridden to render the printed appearance of this component.

PARAMETERS

gc   The non-null graphics context on which to print.

SEE ALSO   `paint()`, `printAll()`, `PrintJob`.

EXAMPLE   See `paintAll()`.

printAll( )

PURPOSE   Prints this component and its descendants on a graphics context.

SYNTAX   `public void printAll(Graphics gc)`

DESCRIPTION   This method prints this component and its descendants on the graphics context gc. If a component is a container, this component is first validated and then it and all of its descendants are also printed on gc.

PARAMETERS

gc   The non-null graphics context on which to print.

SEE ALSO   `Container.printComponents()`, `print()`, `validate()`.

EXAMPLE   See `paintAll()`.

processComponentEvent( )

PURPOSE   Processes a component event enabled for this component.

SYNTAX   `protected void processComponentEvent(ComponentEvent evt)`

DESCRIPTION   Component events are fired when this component is resized, moved, or made visible or invisible. See `ComponentEvent` for more details. This method processes component events for this component by calling any registered `ComponentListener`. This method is invoked only if component events have been enabled for this component. This can happen either when a component listener is added to this component or when component events are explicitly enabled via the use of `enableEvents()`.

Typically, a component controls how its component events are processed. It does this by adding or removing component listeners. It overrides `process-ComponentEvent()` only if it needs to do processing in addition to that performed by the registered listeners.

When a component does override `processComponentEvent()`, it should call `super.processComponentEvent()` to perform the processing intended by its base class (such as dispatching the listeners).

PARAMETERS
evt   The non-`null` component event.

SEE ALSO   `addComponentListener()`, `enableEvents()`, `disableEvents()`, `java.awt.event.ComponentAdapter`, `java.awt.event.ComponentEvent`, `java.awt.event.ComponentListener`, `processEvent()`, `removeComponentListener()`.

EXAMPLE   See `AWTEventMulticaster.componentHidden()`.

processEvent( )

PURPOSE   Processes an event enabled for this component.

SYNTAX   `protected void processEvent(AWTEvent evt)`

DESCRIPTION   This method is called to deliver the event `evt` to this component. Depending on the class of `evt`, this method calls another method in this class. For example, if `evt` is an instance of `ComponentEvent`, this component's `processComponentEvent()` method is called with `evt`. The event types handled by default are ComponentEvent, FocusEvent, KeyEvent, and MouseEvent (a MouseEvent is handled either by processMouseEvent() or processMouse-MotionEvent()).

This method is invoked only if evt is an event type that has been enabled for this component. This can happen either when a listener of that type is added to this component or when the event type is explicitly enabled via the use of enableEvents().

Typically, a component controls how its events are processed by adding or removing the appropriate listeners. It overrides processEvent() only if it needs to handle other types of events in addition to the four basic types. If a component needs to perform special processing for one of the four basic types, it should override one of the type-specific methods, such as processComponentEvent().

When a component does override processEvent(), it should call super.processEvent() to perform the processing intended by its base class (such as dispatching the listeners for the five basic event types).

PARAMETERS

  evt   The non-null event.

SEE ALSO   addComponentListener(), addFocusListener(), addKeyListener(), addMouseListener(), addMouseMotionListener(), enableEvents(), disableEvents(), processComponentEvent(), processFocusEvent(), processKeyEvent(), processMouseEvent(), processMouseMotionEvent(), removeComponentListener(), removeFocusListener(), removeKeyListener(), removeMouseListener(), removeMouseMotionListener().

EXAMPLE   This example creates a subclass of List—MainList—that overrides processEvent() to print debugging information about the events received by the list. See Figure 90.

For other examples of processEvent(), see the class example and dispatch-Event().

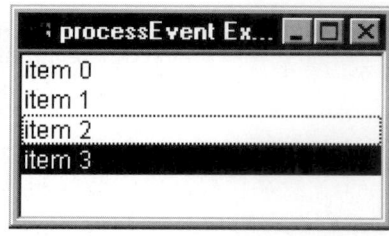

FIGURE 90: **Debugging Events Using processEvent().**

```
import java.awt.*;
import java.awt.event.*;

class Main extends Frame {
    public static void main(String args[]) {
        Frame f = new Frame("processEvent Example");
        MainList l = new MainList(4, true);

        for (int i=0; i<4; i++) {
            l.addItem("item "+i);
```

```
            }

            f.add(l, BorderLayout.CENTER);
            f.pack();
            f.show();
        }
    }

    class MainList extends List {
        public MainList(int rows, boolean multipleMode) {
            super(rows, multipleMode);

            enableEvents(-1);    // Enable all events.
        }

        protected void processEvent(AWTEvent evt) {
            int id = evt.getID();

            if (id >= ActionEvent.ACTION_FIRST && id <= ActionEvent.ACTION_LAST) {
                System.out.println("action event("+id+")");
            } else if (id >= AdjustmentEvent.ADJUSTMENT_FIRST
                    && id <= AdjustmentEvent.ADJUSTMENT_LAST) {
                System.out.println("adjustment event("+id+")");
            } else if (id >= ComponentEvent.COMPONENT_FIRST &&
                        id <= ComponentEvent.COMPONENT_LAST) {
                System.out.println("component event("+id+")");
            } else if (id >= ContainerEvent.CONTAINER_FIRST &&
                        id <= ContainerEvent.CONTAINER_LAST) {
                System.out.println("container event("+id+")");
            } else if (id >= WindowEvent.WINDOW_FIRST &&
                        id <= WindowEvent.WINDOW_LAST) {
                System.out.println("window event("+id+")");
            } else if (id >= FocusEvent.FOCUS_FIRST &&
                        id <= FocusEvent.FOCUS_LAST) {
                System.out.println("focus event("+id+")");
            } else if (id >= ItemEvent.ITEM_FIRST && id <= ItemEvent.ITEM_LAST) {
                System.out.println("item event"+id+")");
            } else if (id >= KeyEvent.KEY_FIRST && id <= KeyEvent.KEY_LAST) {
                System.out.println("key event"+id+")");
            } else if (id >= MouseEvent.MOUSE_FIRST &&
                        id <= MouseEvent.MOUSE_LAST) {
                System.out.println("mouse event"+id+")");
            } else if (id >= TextEvent.TEXT_FIRST && id <= TextEvent.TEXT_LAST) {
                System.out.println("text event"+id+")");
            }
            super.processEvent(evt);
        }
    }
}
```

processFocusEvent()

PURPOSE   Processes a focus event enabled for this component.

SYNTAX   `protected void processFocusEvent(FocusEvent evt)`

A B D E F G H I J K L M N O P Q R S T U V W X Y Z

DESCRIPTION   A component fires focus events when it gains or loses keyboard focus. See `FocusEvent` for more details. This method processes focus events for this component by delivering them to any registered listeners. This method is invoked only if focus events have been enabled for this component. This can happen either when a focus listener is added to this component or when focus events are explicitly enabled via the use of `enableEvents()`.

Typically, a component controls how its focus events are processed by adding or removing focus listeners. It overrides `processFocusEvent()` only if it needs to do processing in addition to that performed by the registered listeners.

When a component does override `processFocusEvent()`, it should call `super.processFocusEvent()` to perform the processing intended by its base class (such as dispatching the listeners).

PARAMETERS
  evt   The non-`null` focus event.

SEE ALSO   `addFocusListener()`, `enableEvents()`, `disableEvents()`, `java.awt.event.FocusAdapter`, `java.awt.event.FocusEvent`, `java.awt.event.FocusListener`, `processEvent()`, `removeFocusListener()`.

EXAMPLE   See `AWTEventMulticaster.focusGained()`.

processKeyEvent()

PURPOSE   Processes a key event enabled for this component.

SYNTAX   `protected void processKeyEvent(KeyEvent evt)`

DESCRIPTION   Key events are fired when a key has been pressed, or released in a component. See `KeyEvent` for more details. This method processes key events for this component by calling any registered `KeyListener`. This method is invoked only if key events have been enabled for this component. This can happen either when a key listener is added to this component or when key events are explicitly enabled via the use of `enableEvents()`.

Typically, a component controls how its key events are processed by adding or removing key listeners. It overrides `processKeyEvent()` only if it needs to do processing in addition to that performed by the registered listeners.

When a component does override `processKeyEvent()`, it should call `super.processKeyEvent()` to perform the processing intended by its base class (such as dispatching the listeners).

PARAMETERS
  evt   The non-`null` key event.

SEE ALSO	`addKeyListener()`, `enableEvents()`, `disableEvents()`, `java.awt.event.KeyAdapter`, `java.awt.event.KeyEvent`, `java.awt.event.KeyListener`, `processEvent()`, `removeKeyListener()`.
EXAMPLE	See `AWTEventMulticaster.keyPressed()`.

processMouseEvent( )

PURPOSE	Processes a mouse event enabled for this component.
SYNTAX	`protected void processMouseEvent(MouseEvent evt)`
DESCRIPTION	Mouse events are fired when the mouse enters or exits a component or when a mouse button has been pressed, or released on a component. See `MouseEvent` for more details. This method processes mouse events for this component by calling any registered `MouseListener`. This method is invoked only if mouse events have been enabled for this component. This can happen either when a mouse listener is added to this component or when mouse events are explicitly enabled via the use of `enableEvents()`.

Typically, a component controls how its mouse events are processed by adding or removing mouse listeners. It overrides `processMouseEvent()` only if it needs to do processing in addition to that performed by the registered listeners.

When a component does override `processMouseEvent()`, it should call `super.processMouseEvent()` to perform the processing intended by its base class (such as dispatching the listeners). |
PARAMETERS	
evt	The non-`null` mouse event.
SEE ALSO	`addMouseListener()`, `enableEvents()`, `disableEvents()`, `java.awt.event.MouseAdapter`, `java.awt.event.MouseEvent`, `java.awt.event.MouseListener`, `processEvent()`, `removeMouseListener()`.
EXAMPLE	See `add()`.

processMouseMotionEvent( )

PURPOSE	Processes a mouse motion event enabled for this component.
SYNTAX	`protected void processMouseMotionEvent(MouseEvent e)`
DESCRIPTION	Mouse motion events are fired when the mouse has been moved or dragged. See `MouseEvent` for more details. This method processes mouse motion events for this component by calling any registered `MouseMotionListener`.

A
B

D
E
F
G
H
I
J
K
L
M
N
O
P
Q
R
S
T
U
V
W
X
Y
Z

This method is invoked only if mouse motion events have been enabled for this component. This can happen either when a mouse motion listener is added to this component or when mouse motion events are explicitly enabled via the use of `enableEvents()`.

Typically, a component controls how its mouse motion events are processed by adding or removing mouse motion listeners. It overrides `processMouseMotionEvent()` only if it needs to do processing in addition to that performed by the registered listeners.

When a component does override `processMouseMotionEvent()`, it should call `super.processMouseMotionEvent()` to perform the processing intended by its base class (such as dispatching the listeners).

PARAMETERS
  `evt`   The non-`null` mouse motion event.

SEE ALSO   `addMouseMotionListener()`, `enableEvents()`, `disableEvents()`, `java.awt.event.MouseEvent`, `java.awt.event.MouseMotionAdapter`, `java.awt.event.MouseMotionListener`, `processEvent()`, `removeMouseMotionListener()`.

EXAMPLE   See `AWTEventMulticaster.mouseDragged()`.

remove()

PURPOSE   Removes a popup menu from this component.

SYNTAX   `public synchronized void remove(MenuComponent popup)`

DESCRIPTION   A component can have a list of popup menus that can be dynamically displayed on the component. This method removes the popup menu `popup` from the list of popup menus for this component. If `popup` is not on the list, this method does nothing.

PARAMETERS
  `popup`   The popup menu to remove.

SEE ALSO   `PopupMenu`, `add()`.

EXAMPLE   See `add()`.

removeComponentListener()

PURPOSE   Removes a listener from receiving this component's component events.

SYNTAX   `public synchronized void`
        `removeComponentListener(ComponentListener listener)`

A
B

D
E
F
G
H
I
J
K
L
M
N
O
P
Q
R
S
T
U
V
W
X
Y
Z

DESCRIPTION A component fires component events when it is resized, moved, or made visible or invisible. See ComponentEvent for more details. After this method is called, the component listener listener will no longer receive component events from this component. If listener is null, this method does nothing.

PARAMETERS
listener   The possibly null component listener to remove.

SEE ALSO   addComponentListener(), java.awt.event.ComponentAdapter, java.awt.event.ComponentEvent, java.awt.event.ComponentListener.

EXAMPLE   See removeActionListener() in MenuItem.disableEvents().

removeFocusListener( )

PURPOSE   Removes a listener from receiving this component's focus events.

SYNTAX   public synchronized void removeFocusListener(FocusListener listener)

DESCRIPTION   A component fires focus events when it gains or loses keyboard focus. See FocusEvent for more details. After this method is called, the focus listener listener will no longer receive focus events from this component. If listener is null, this method does nothing.

PARAMETERS
listener   The possibly null focus listener to remove.

SEE ALSO   addFocusListener(), java.awt.event.FocusAdapter, java.awt.event.FocusEvent, java.awt.event.FocusListener.

EXAMPLE   See removeActionListener() in MenuItem.disableEvents().

removeKeyListener( )

PURPOSE   Removes a listener from receiving this component's key events.

SYNTAX   public synchronized void removeKeyListener(KeyListener listener)

DESCRIPTION   Key events are fired when a key has been pressed, or released in a component. See KeyEvent for more details. After this method is called, the key listener listener will no longer receive key events from this component. If listener is null, this method does nothing.

PARAMETERS
listener   The possibly null key listener to remove.

A
B
C
D
E
F
G
H
I
J
K
L
M
N
O
P
Q
R
S
T
U
V
W
X
Y
Z

377

SEE ALSO	`addKeyListener()`, `java.awt.event.KeyAdapter`, `java.awt.event.KeyEvent`, `java.awt.event.KeyListener`.
EXAMPLE	See `removeActionListener()` in `MenuItem.disableEvents()`.

removeMouseListener( )

PURPOSE	Removes a listener from receiving this component's mouse events.
SYNTAX	`public synchronized void removeMouseListener(MouseListener listener)`
DESCRIPTION	Mouse events are fired when the mouse enters or exits a component or when a mouse button has been pressed, or released on a component. See `MouseEvent` for more details. After this method is called, the mouse listener `listener` will no longer receive mouse events from this component. If `listener` is `null`, this method does nothing.
PARAMETERS	
`listener`	The possibly `null` mouse listener to remove.
SEE ALSO	`addMouseListener()`, `java.awt.event.MouseAdapter`, `java.awt.event.MouseEvent`, `java.awt.event.MouseListener`.
EXAMPLE	See `removeActionListener()` in `MenuItem.disableEvents()`.

removeMouseMotionListener( )

PURPOSE	Removes a listener from receiving this component's mouse motion events.
SYNTAX	`public synchronized void addMouseMotionListener(MouseMotionListener listener)`
DESCRIPTION	Mouse motion events are fired when the mouse has been moved or dragged. See `MouseEvent` for more details. After this method is called, the mouse motion listener `listener` will no longer receive mouse motion events from this component. If `listener` is `null`, this method does nothing.
PARAMETERS	
`listener`	The possibly `null` mouse motion listener to add.
SEE ALSO	`addMouseMotionListener()`, `java.awt.event.MouseMotionAdapter`, `java.awt.event.MouseEvent`, `java.awt.event.MouseMotionListener`.
EXAMPLE	See `removeActionListener()` in `MenuItem.disableEvents()`.

removeNotify()

PURPOSE	Destroys this component's peer.
SYNTAX	`public void removeNotify()`
DESCRIPTION	The default implementation of this method invokes `removeNotify()` on any popup menus for this component. This method must be overridden by a component subclass in order to destroy the peer. This method can be called directly only if this component is a top-level window, such as a frame or dialog (see `Window.addNotify()`).
SEE ALSO	`addNotify()`, `getPeer()`.
EXAMPLE	See `setVisible()`.

repaint()

PURPOSE	Makes a request to repaint this component.

SYNTAX	`public void repaint()`
	`public void repaint(long ms)`
	`public void repaint(int x, int y, int width, int height)`
	`public void repaint(long ms, int x, int y, int width, int height)`

DESCRIPTION	This method makes a request to repaint the rectangular area of this component specified by `x`, `y`, `width`, and `height`. If `x`, `y`, `width`, and `height` are not specified, they default to the bounds of this component. The scheduled repaint will occur no later than `ms` milliseconds later. If `ms` is not specified, it defaults to `0`. The AWT system will repaint this component by calling the `update()` method.
PARAMETERS	
height	The height of the rectangular area to repaint.
ms	Maximum delay in milliseconds before the `update()` method is called.
width	The width of the rectangular area to repaint.
x	The *x*-coordinate of the rectangular area to repaint.
y	The *y*-coordinate of the rectangular area to repaint.
SEE ALSO	`update()`.
EXAMPLE	This example paints various four-leaved roses and cardoids. As a figure is painted, a path of the figure is left behind. A thread is used to update the location of the dot and then to invoke the repaint method to paint the dot every 50 ms. See Figure 91.

A
B
C
D
E
F
G
H
I
J
K
L
M
N
O
P
Q
R
S
T
U
V
W
X
Y
Z

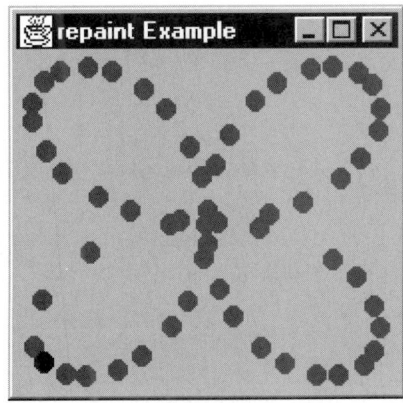 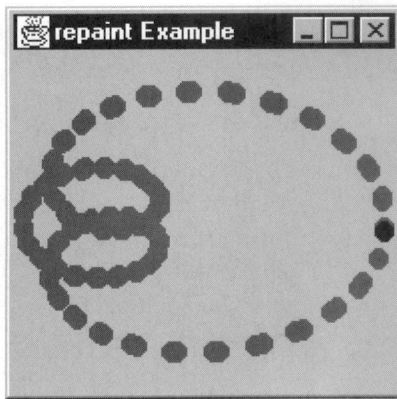

FIGURE 91: Cardoids.

```java
import java.awt.*;
import java.awt.event.*;

class Main extends Frame implements Runnable {
    int curX = -100, curY = -100;
    double newX, newY;
    double angle = 0.0;
    double maxX, maxY, minX, minY;
    int figure;
    boolean clearBg = true;

    Main() {
        super("repaint Example");
        setSize(200, 200);
        this.addMouseListener(new MouseEventHandler());
        show();
        (new Thread(this)).start();
    }
    public void update(Graphics g) {
        int dotSize = 10;
        Insets insets = getInsets();
        int x = insets.left, y = insets.top;
        int w = getSize().width-insets.left-insets.right-dotSize;
        int h = getSize().height-insets.top-insets.bottom-dotSize;

        if (clearBg) {
            g.clearRect(x, y, getSize().width, getSize().height);
            curX = curY = -100;
            clearBg = false;
        } else {
            g.setColor(Color.red);
            g.fillOval(x+curX, y+curY, dotSize, dotSize);
            g.setColor(Color.black);
            curX = (int)(newX*w);
            curY = (int)(newY*h);
            g.fillOval(x+curX, y+curY, dotSize, dotSize);
        }
    }
    class MouseEventHandler extends MouseAdapter {
```

```
            public void mousePressed(MouseEvent evt) {
                figure++;
                angle = 0;
                clearBg = true;
            }
        }
        double plot(double theta) {
            switch (figure % 5) {
            case 0:
                maxX = .8; maxY = .8; minX = -.8; minY = -.8;
                return Math.sin(2 * theta);
            case 1:
                maxX = 1; maxY = 1; minX = -1; minY = -1;
                return Math.cos(2 * theta);
            case 2:
                maxX = 2; maxY = 2; minX = -1.3; minY = -2;
                return Math.cos(theta/2) + 1;
            case 3:
                maxX = 3; maxY = 3; minX = -1.5; minY = -3;
                return 2 * Math.cos(theta/2) + 1;
            case 4:
                maxX = 4; maxY = 4; minX = -2; minY = -4;
                return 3 * Math.cos(theta/2) + 1;
            }
            return 0;
        }
        public void run() {
            while (true) {
                double r = plot(angle);
                newX = (r * Math.cos(angle)-minX)/(maxX-minX);
                newY = (r * Math.sin(angle)-minY)/(maxY-minY);
                repaint();
                try { Thread.sleep(50); } catch (Exception e) {};
                angle += .2;
            }
        }
        static public void main(String[] args) {
            new Main();
        }
    }
```

A
B
C
D
E
F
G
H
I
J
K
L
M
N
O
P
Q
R
S
T
U
V
W
X
Y
Z

requestFocus()

PURPOSE	Requests that the focus be given to this component.
SYNTAX	`public void requestFocus()`
DESCRIPTION	This method requests that the focus be given to this component. If the request is granted, a focus event (see `FocusEvent`) will be posted to this component. The conditions under which a component is granted or denied the focus is platform-dependent.
SEE ALSO	`isFocusTraversable()`, `java.awt.event.FocusEvent`, `processFocusEvent()`, `transferFocus()`.
EXAMPLE	See the class example, `isFocusTraversable()`.

A
B
C
D
E
F
G
H
I
J
K
L
M
N
O
P
Q
R
S
T
U
V
W
X
Y
Z

reshape( )   *DEPRECATED*

PURPOSE   Replaced by `setBounds()`.

SYNTAX   `public void reshape(int x, int y, int w, int h)`

PARAMETERS

h   The new height of this component in pixels.

w   The new width of this component in pixels.

x   The new *x*-coordinate of this component in pixels.

y   The new *y*-coordinate of this component in pixels.

DEPRECATION   Replace the usage of this deprecated method, as in
```
reshape(x, y, w, h);
```
with
```
setBounds(x, y, w, h);
```

resize( )   *DEPRECATED*

PURPOSE   Replaced by `setSize()`.

SYNTAX   `public void resize(int w, int h)`
               `public void resize(Dimension d)`

PARAMETERS

d   The non-`null` component dimension.

h   The new height of this component in pixels.

w   The new width of this component in pixels.

DEPRECATION   Replace the usage of this deprecated method, as in
```
resize(w, h);
resize(dimension);
```
with
```
setSize(w, h);
setSize(dimension);
```

RIGHT_ALIGNMENT

PURPOSE   Constant indicating alignment along a component's right edge.

SYNTAX   `public static final float RIGHT_ALIGNMENT`

DESCRIPTION   This constant specifies that the *x*-coordinate of the component's alignment point be at the component's right edge. Its value is `1.0f`.

SEE ALSO   `LEFT_ALIGNMENT`, `CENTER_ALIGNMENT`, `getAlignmentX()`.

EXAMPLE   See the `LayoutManager2` class example.

setBackground()

PURPOSE   Sets this component's background color.

SYNTAX   `public void setBackground(Color c)`

DESCRIPTION   This method sets this component's background color to c. The background color affects each component differently. For example, a button is painted in the background color, while its label is painted in the foreground color. See Figure 92.

If c is `null`, this component will inherit its background color from the closest ancestor whose background color has been set.

If this component is already displayed, the `repaint()` method must be called to force this component to redraw itself using the new background color.

PARAMETERS

c   The new background color, which can be `null`.

SEE ALSO   `getBackground()`, `setForeground()`.

EXAMPLE   This method creates a text area that has a black background and white foreground. The white foreground causes the text to be painted in white. Also, the text area is set with a very large font.

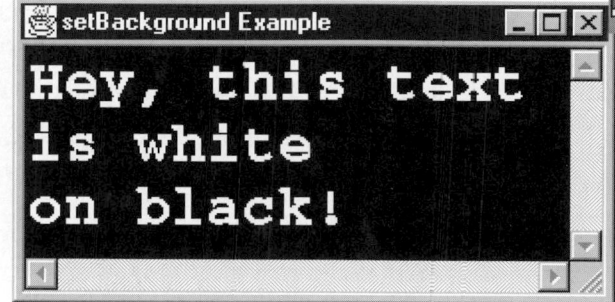

FIGURE 92:   **White on Black Text Area.**

```
import java.awt.*;
class Main extends Frame {
    Main() {
        super("setBackground Example");
        TextArea ta = new TextArea();

        ta.setBackground(Color.black);
        ta.setForeground(Color.white);
        ta.setFont(new Font("Monospaced", Font.BOLD, 30));
        add(ta, BorderLayout.CENTER);
        setSize(200, 200);
        show();
    }

    static public void main(String[] args) {
        new Main();
    }
}
```

A
B
C
D
E
F
G
H
I
J
K
L
M
N
O
P
Q
R
S
T
U
V
W
X
Y
Z

383

A
B
D
E
F
G
H
I
J
K
L
M
N
O
P
Q
R
S
T
U
V
W
X
Y
Z

setBounds()

PURPOSE	Moves and resizes this component.
SYNTAX	`public void setBounds(int x, int y, int w, int h)` `public void setBounds(Rectangle rect)`
DESCRIPTION	This first form of this method moves this component to position x, y and resizes it to have width w and height h. x and y are relative to this component's parent bounds. The second form of this method moves this component to the position specified by the new bounding rectangle `rect`. This method may be ignored if this component is embedded in an applet context. See the `Applet` class for more information about applet contexts.
PARAMETERS	
h	The new height of this component in pixels.
rect	The new bounding rectangle.
w	The new width of this component in pixels.
x	The new _x_-coordinate of this component in pixels.
y	The new _y_-coordinate of this component in pixels.
SEE ALSO	`getBounds()`, `setLocation()`, `setSize()`.
EXAMPLE	See the `Container` class example.

setCursor()

PURPOSE	Sets this component's cursor image.
SYNTAX	`public synchronized void setCursor(Cursor cursor)`
DESCRIPTION	This method sets the cursor image for this component to be `cursor`.
PARAMETERS	
cursor	The non-`null` cursor image.
SEE ALSO	`Cursor`, `getCursor()`.
EXAMPLE	See the class example.

setEnabled()

PURPOSE	Enables or disables this component.
SYNTAX	`public void setEnabled(boolean cond)`

DESCRIPTION   If cond is true, this method enables this component; otherwise, it disables this component. When enabled, this component is able to respond to user input. When disabled, this component not only will not respond to user input, but it also becomes transparent to user input. For example, if the user clicks a disabled component, the AWT system determines the top-most enabled component that contains the cursor position and posts an event for that component. See the class description for more information about a component's enabled state.

PARAMETERS
cond   If true, this component is enabled; otherwise, this component is disabled.

SEE ALSO   isEnabled().

EXAMPLE   See the Button class example.

setFont()

PURPOSE   Sets this component's font.

SYNTAX   public synchronized void setFont(Font f)

DESCRIPTION   If f is not null, this method sets this component's font so that if this component paints any strings, it will paint them in the font f. Moreover, any graphics context that is created on this component will be initialized to f.

If f is null, this component's font is cleared. This means that this component's font will be inherited from the closest ancestor whose font has been set.

PARAMETERS
f   The font. This parameter can be null.

SEE ALSO   getFont().

EXAMPLE   See the class example and dispatchEvent().

setForeground()

PURPOSE   Sets this component's foreground color.

SYNTAX   public void setForeground(Color c)

DESCRIPTION   This method sets this component's foreground color to c. The foreground color affects each component differently. For example, a button is painted in the background color, while its label is painted in the foreground color.

If c is null, this component will inherit its foreground color from the closest ancestor whose foreground color has been set.

A
B
C
D
E
F
G
H
I
J
K
L
M
N
O
P
Q
R
S
T
U
V
W
X
Y
Z

If this component is already displayed, `repaint()` must be called to force this component to redraw itself using the new foreground color.

PARAMETERS

c   The new foreground color, which can be `null`.

SEE ALSO   `getForeground()`, `setBackground()`.

EXAMPLE   See `setBackground()`.

setLocale()

PURPOSE   Sets this component's locale.

SYNTAX   `public void setLocale(Locale locale)`

DESCRIPTION   This method sets the locale of this component to `locale`. See the class description for more information on component locales. If locale is `null`, this component will use the locale of the closest ancestor that has been assigned a locale. If no ancestor has been assigned a locale, this component's locale will be `Locale.getDefault()`.

PARAMETERS

locale   The locale to use.

SEE ALSO   `java.util.Locale`, `getLocale()`.

EXAMPLE   See `getName()`.

setLocation()

PURPOSE   Moves this component.

SYNTAX   `public void setLocation(int x, int y)`
                   `public void setLocation(Point pt)`

DESCRIPTION   This method moves this component such that its top-left corner coincides with the point specified by `pt` or `x, y` in the bounds of this component's parent. Note that unlike with graphics and events, whose coordinates are relative to a component's inset area, move coordinates are relative to a component's bounds.

PARAMETERS

pt   The point of the new location.

x   The new *x*-coordinate.

y   The new *y*-coordinate.

SEE ALSO   `getBounds()`, `setBounds()`, `setSize()`.

EXAMPLE   See the `Container` class example.

setName()

PURPOSE	Sets this component's name.
SYNTAX	`public void setName(String name)`
DESCRIPTION	The component's name is a nonlocalized string that can be used by a program to identify the component. For example, when a program receives an event, it could retrieve the event's source and use its name to determine which component fired the event. This method sets the name of this component to name.
PARAMETERS	
name	This component's possibly `null` new name.
SEE ALSO	`getName()`.
EXAMPLE	See `getName()`.

setSize()

PURPOSE	Sets this component's size.
SYNTAX	`public void setSize(int w, int h)` `public void setSize(Dimension d)`
DESCRIPTION	This method resizes this component so that it has width w and height h. If dimension d is specified instead, this component will have width `d.width` and height `d.height`. The current location of this component is not altered.
	This method may be ignored if this component is embedded in an applet context. See the `Applet` class for more information about applet contexts.
PARAMETERS	
d	The non-`null` component dimension.
h	The new height of this component in pixels.
w	The new width of this component in pixels.
SEE ALSO	`getBounds()`, `setBounds()`, `getSize()`.
EXAMPLE	See the `Container` class example.

setVisible()

PURPOSE	Makes this component visible or invisible.
SYNTAX	`public void setVisible(boolean vis)`

A
B

D
E
F
G
H
I
J
K
L
M
N
O
P
Q
R
S
T
U
V
W
X
Y
Z

DESCRIPTION   If `vis` is `true`, this component is made visible, if not already visible. Otherwise, this component is made invisible, if not already invisible. Some layout managers completely ignore invisible components, so when this component is made visible, it appears at the wrong location and size. To update this component's bounds, this component's container should be invalidated and then validated immediately after this component is made visible.

PARAMETERS
 `vis`   If `true`, this component is made visible; otherwise, this component is hidden.

SEE ALSO   `isShowing()`, `isVisible()`.

EXAMPLE   This example creates two buttons. One has a blinking label, and the other shows or hides the blinking button. See Figure 93.

The blinking button overrides the `addNotify()` method to start the blinking thread that periodically sets and clears the button's label. The blinking button also overrides the `removeNotify()` method to remove the thread.

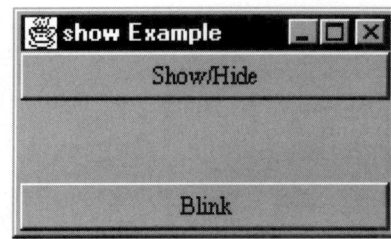

FIGURE 93: **Component Visibility.**

```
import java.awt.*;
import java.awt.event.*;

class Main extends Frame implements ActionListener {
    BlinkButton blink = new BlinkButton("Blink");
    Main() {
        super("setVisible Example");
        Button ctl = new Button("Show/Hide");
        ctl.addActionListener(this);
        add(ctl, BorderLayout.NORTH);
        add(blink, BorderLayout.SOUTH);
        pack();
        show();
    }

    public void actionPerformed(ActionEvent evt) {
        if (blink.isVisible()) {
            blink.setVisible(false);
        } else {
            blink.setVisible(true);
            invalidate();
            validate();
        }
    }

    static public void main(String[] args) {
        new Main();
    }
}
```

```
class BlinkButton extends Button implements Runnable {
    String label;
    Thread thread;

    BlinkButton(String label) {
        super(label);
        this.label = label;
    }

    public void addNotify() {
        super.addNotify();
        (thread = new Thread(this)).start();
    }

    public void removeNotify() {
    thread = null;
        super.removeNotify();
    }

    public void run() {
        boolean on = false;
        while (thread == Thread.currentThread()) {
        if (on) {
        setLabel(label);
        } else {
        setLabel("");
        }
        on = !on;
            try {
                Thread.sleep(1000);
            } catch (Exception e) {
            }
        }
    }
}
```

show()   *DEPRECATED*

PURPOSE	Replaced by `setVisible()`.
SYNTAX	`public void show()`
	`public void show(boolean vis)`
PARAMETERS	
vis	If `true`, this component is made visible; otherwise, this component is hidden.
DEPRECATION	Replace the usage of this deprecated method, as in

```
show();
show(false);
```

with

```
setVisible(true);
setVisible(false);
```

A
B

D
E
F
G
H
I
J
K
L
M
N
O
P
Q
R
S
T
U
V
W
X
Y
Z

size( ) *DEPRECATED*

PURPOSE	Replaced by `getSize()`.
SYNTAX	`public Dimension size()`
RETURNS	A non-`null` `Dimension` object containing the size of this component.

DEPRECATION	Replace the usage of this deprecated method, as in
	`Dimension sz = size();`
	with
	`Dimension sz = getSize();`

TOP_ALIGNMENT

PURPOSE	Constant indicating alignment along a component's top edge.
SYNTAX	`public static final float TOP_ALIGNMENT`
DESCRIPTION	This constant specifies that the *y*-coordinate of the component's alignment point be at the component's top edge. Its value is `0.0f`.
SEE ALSO	`BOTTOM_ALIGNMENT`, `CENTER_ALIGNMENT`, `getAlignmentY()`.
EXAMPLE	See the `LayoutManager2` class example.

toString( )

PURPOSE	Generates a string representation of this component's state.
SYNTAX	`public String toString()`
DESCRIPTION	The result string contains this component's class name and the results of calling `paramString()`. The Java compiler automatically generates code to call this method when it needs to translate this component instance to a string. This method is typically used for debugging.
RETURNS	A non-`null` string representing this component's state.
OVERRIDES	`java.lang.Object.toString()`.
SEE ALSO	`paramString()`.
EXAMPLE	See `java.lang.Object.toString()`.

transferFocus( )

PURPOSE   Moves the focus to the next focus-traversable component.

SYNTAX   `public void transferFocus()`

DESCRIPTION   This method transfers the focus to the next focus-traversable component in the container after this component. This component need not have the focus. See "Focus Traversal" in the class description for more information.

SEE ALSO   `isFocusTraversable()`, `java.awt.event.FocusEvent`, `processFocusEvent()`, `requestFocus()`.

EXAMPLE   See the class example.

update( )

PURPOSE   Called to repaint this component without the background's having been cleared.

SYNTAX   `public void update(Graphics gc)`

DESCRIPTION   This method is called by the AWT system in response to a call to `repaint()` by a native component. Like `paint()`, this method is intended to repaint some area of this component because that area has been damaged or has changed. Unlike with `paint()`, when this method is called, the background of this component has not been cleared by the caller. See "Painting" in the class description for more information.

This method is typically overridden to avoid the clearing of the background— the clearing of the background is critical to flicker-free animation. The clipping area of gc (see `getClipBounds()`) contains the area that needs to be updated, and gc should be used to update the area. Note that it is possible for two or more `repaint()` method calls to be batched into a single call to the `update()` method. When this happens, the resulting clipping area is enlarged to include all of the smaller areas that need to be updated.

If not overridden, this method clears the background and calls `paint()`.

Three properties of gc are initialized with values taken from the same three properties of this component. The properties are the background color, the foreground color, and the font.

PARAMETERS
gc   The non-`null` graphics context on which to paint this component.

SEE ALSO   `paint()`, `repaint()`.

EXAMPLE   This example demonstrates how to implement a simple scrolling image. The image is repeated horizontally as often as necessary to fill the screen. The image is loaded from a file and a thread is created to move the location of the image 1 pixel every 100 ms. See Figure 94.

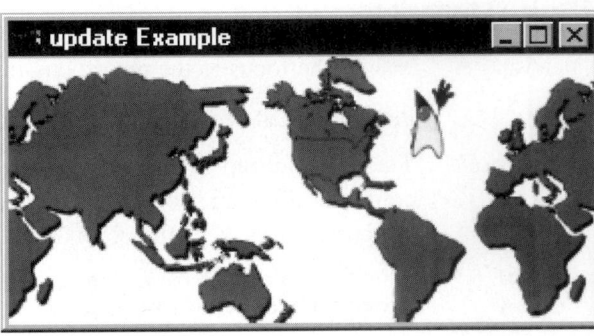

FIGURE 94:   Scrolling Image.

In the update() method, the first image is drawn, regardless of whether the dimension or pixel information is available. However, if the width of the image is not yet available, it does not paint the subsequent images.

```java
import java.awt.*;

class Main extends Frame implements Runnable {
    int x;         // Continuously moving x-location of the image.
    Image image;

    Main(String filename) {
        super("update Example");

        // Get the image.
        image = getToolkit().getImage(filename);

        (new Thread(this)).start();
        setSize(300, 160);
        show();
    }

    public void paint(Graphics g) {
        update(g);
    }

    public void update(Graphics g) {
        int w = image.getWidth(this);

        // Draw left-most image.
        g.drawImage(image, x, getInsets().top, this);

        if (w > 0) {
            // Draw additional images to fill the display.
            for (int i=1; i<=getSize().width/w+1; i++) {
                g.drawImage(image, x+i*w, getInsets().top, this);
            }
        }
    }

    public void run() {
```

```
        try {
            while (true) {
                int w = image.getWidth(this);

                if (w > 0) {
                    x = (x-1) % w;
                    repaint();
                }
                Thread.sleep(100);
            }
        } catch (Exception e) {
            e.printStackTrace();
        }
    }

    public static void main(String[] args) {
        if (args.length == 1) {
            new Main(args[0]);
        } else {
            System.err.println("Usage: java Main <image-file>");
        }
    }
}
```

validate()

PURPOSE   Validates this component.

SYNTAX   `public void validate()`

DESCRIPTION This method validates this component if it is invalid. Subclasses of `Component` override `validate()` to perform the validation. If this component is a container, it validates its child components and recomputes their layout. However, note that for efficiency, the `validate()` method is not invoked on valid children. So if the valid child contains an invalid child, the invalid child will not be validated. This situation rarely arises because, by default, calling `invalidate()` on a component also invalidates all of its ancestors. This method is normally used on components that are containers.

See the `Container` class for more information about layouts.

SEE ALSO   `Container.validate()`, `invalidate()`, `doLayout()`.

EXAMPLE   This example demonstrates that layouts are not automatically validated. In the program, when a button is clicked its font is increased by 1 point and the button is invalidated; the button label has become too big and needs to be validated. Clicking the Validate button invokes the `validate()` method on the frame, thereby validating the entire component hierarchy.

Figure 95(a) shows a button whose label has increased in size and is therefore invalid. Figure 95(b) shows the same button after the component hierarchy has been validated.

A
B

D
E
F
G
H
I
J
K
L
M
N
O
P
Q
R
S
T
U
V
W
X
Y
Z

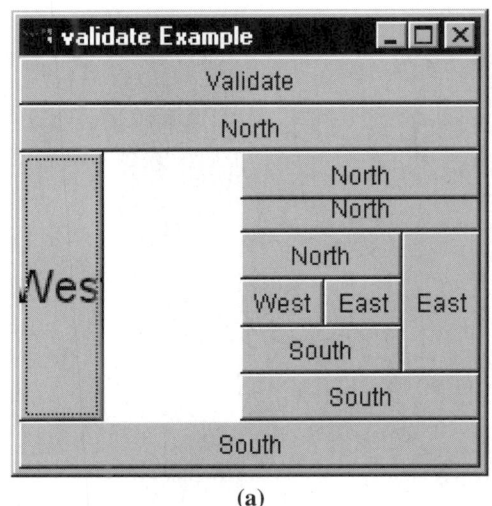
(a)

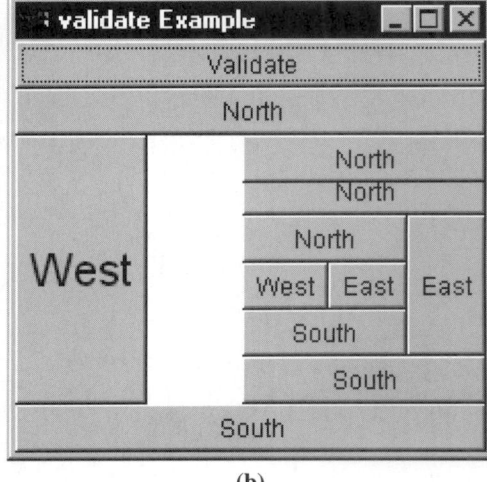
(b)

FIGURE 95: Validating Layouts.

```java
import java.awt.*;
import java.awt.event.*;

class Main extends Frame implements ActionListener {
    Button ctl = new Button("Validate");
    Main() {
        super("validate Example");

        ctl.addActionListener(this);
        add(ctl, BorderLayout.NORTH);
        add(makePanel(BorderLayout.EAST,
                makePanel(BorderLayout.SOUTH,
                  makePanel(BorderLayout.WEST,
                    makePanel(null, null)))),
            BorderLayout.CENTER);
        setSize(300, 300);
        show();
    }

    Panel makePanel(String name, Component c) {
        Panel p = new Panel(new BorderLayout());
        Button b;
        p.add(b = new Button("North"), BorderLayout.NORTH);
        b.addActionListener(this);
        p.add(b = new Button("South"), BorderLayout.SOUTH);
        b.addActionListener(this);
        p.add(b = new Button("West"), BorderLayout.WEST);
```

```
            b.addActionListener(this);
            p.add(b = new Button("East"), BorderLayout.EAST);
            b.addActionListener(this);
            if (name != null) {
                p.add(c, name);
            }
            return p;
        }

    public void actionPerformed(ActionEvent evt) {
        Object src = evt.getSource();
        if (src == ctl) {
            validate();
        } else {
            Font f = ((Component)src).getFont();

            f = new Font(f.getFamily(), f.getStyle(), f.getSize()+1);
            ((Component)src).setFont(f);
            ((Component)src).invalidate();
        }
    }

    static public void main(String[] args) {
        new Main();
    }
}
```

A

B

D

E

F

G

H

I

J

K

L

M

N

O

P

Q

R

S

T

U

V

W

X

Y

Z

ComponentAdapter

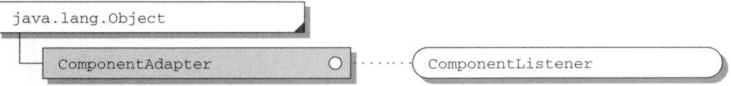

```
java.lang.Object
    ComponentAdapter    O ........ ( ComponentListener
```

Syntax

`public abstract class ComponentAdapter implements ComponentListener`

Description

The component adapter is a component listener in which all callback methods are empty implementations. The purpose of the component adapter is to make it more convenient for an object to listen for component events. In particular, by using the component adapter, you can implement only those callback methods in which you are interested. Without the component adapter, you are required to implement all callback methods, even if the method is empty.

To use a component adapter, you create a subclass of ComponentAdapter and override the desired callback methods. You then create an instance of the component adapter subclass and call the component's addComponentListener() method to register it for receiving component events. The component adapter subclass is typically an inner class.

MEMBER SUMMARY	
Component Event Callback Methods	
componentHidden()	Called after a component has been hidden.
componentMoved()	Called after a component has been moved.
componentResized()	Called after a component has been resized.
componentShown()	Called after a component has been made visible.

See Also

ComponentEvent, ComponentListener,
java.awt.Component.addComponentListener().

Example

This example shows how to implement a "slave" frame that follows its master frame wherever it goes. The slave frame always stays a fixed distance from the master frame, except if some part of the slave frame would appear outside the screen bounds. See Figure 96.

It defines an adapter that overrides the component-Moved() method to update the location of the frame.

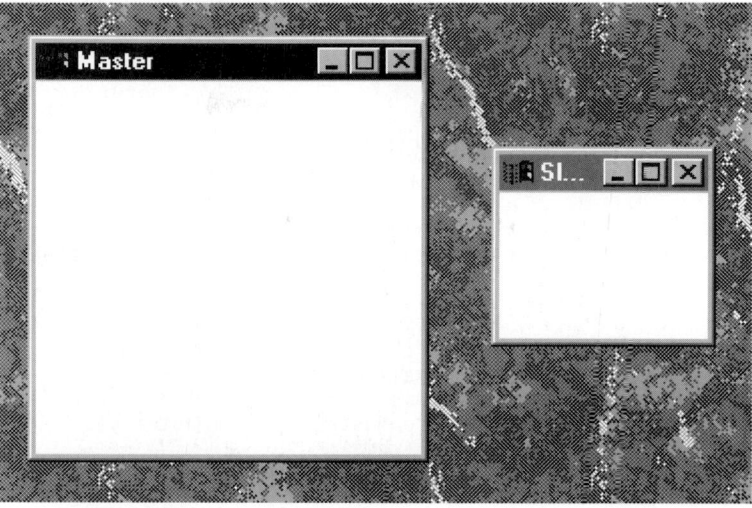

FIGURE 96:   Master/Slave Frames.

One use for this functionality is to have the slave frame be a palette of tools that can be used on objects in the master frame.

Note: This example does not work when the master frame is iconified. The location of the slave frame will be incorrect when the master frame is iconified and deiconified. This is because in the current implementation, the process of iconification fires spurious component events that have not been specified. Since there is no way to test whether a window is iconified, the master frame does not know to ignore the spurious component events. (Watching for WINDOW_ICONIFIED events does not help because these events may come before or after the spurious component events.)

```
import java.awt.*;
import java.awt.event.*;
import java.text.*;
import java.util.*;

class Main extends Frame {
    Main() {
        super("Master");
        setSize(200, 200);
        show();
    }

    public static void main(String[] args) {
        // Create master frame.
        Frame f = new Main();

        // Create slave frame.
        new SlaveFrame(f);
    }
}
```

A
B
C
D
E
F
G
H
I
J
K
L
M
N
O
P
Q
R
S
T
U
V
W
X
Y
Z

```
class SlaveFrame extends Frame {
    Frame master;
    Point fromMaster;

    SlaveFrame(Frame master) {
        super("Slave");
        this.master = master;

        // Listen for events.
        ComponentEventHandler ceh = new ComponentEventHandler();
        master.addComponentListener(ceh);
        addComponentListener(ceh);

        // Initialize the slave so that on the right side of the frame.
        fromMaster = master.getLocation();
        fromMaster.translate(master.getSize().width, 20);
        setLocation(fromMaster.x, fromMaster.y);
        updateLocation(this);

        setSize(100, 100);
        show();
    }

    void updateLocation(Component componentMoved) {
        Dimension screenSize = getToolkit().getScreenSize();

        if (componentMoved == master) {
            Point newloc = master.getLocation();

            // Determine the new location.
            newloc.translate(fromMaster.x, fromMaster.y);

            // Ensure that slave is within the screen bounds.
            newloc.x = Math.max(0,
                Math.min(newloc.x, screenSize.width-getSize().width));
            newloc.y = Math.max(0,
                Math.min(newloc.y, screenSize.height-getSize().height));

            // Move the slave to the new location.
            setLocation(newloc.x, newloc.y);

            // Correct the offset from master in case it changed.
            fromMaster = master.getLocation();
            fromMaster.translate(newloc.x, newloc.y);

            // Keep the slave above the master.
            toFront();
        } else {
            // Update the offset from master.
            fromMaster = getLocation();
            fromMaster.translate(
                -master.getLocation().x, -master.getLocation().y);
        }
    }

    class ComponentEventHandler extends ComponentAdapter {
        public void componentMoved(ComponentEvent evt) {
            // Master or slave moved.
            updateLocation((Component)evt.getSource());
```

A
B
C
D
E
F
G
H
I
J
K
L
M
N
O
P
Q
R
S
T
U
V
W
X
Y
Z

```
        }
      }
    }
```

componentHidden()

PURPOSE   Called after a component has been hidden.

SYNTAX   `public void componentHidden(ComponentEvent evt)`

DESCRIPTION   This method is called after the source component is made invisible by a call to `Component.setVisible(false)`. This method is not called if the component was made invisible because its parent became invisible.

This method by default has an empty implementation.

PARAMETERS
evt   The non-`null` component event.

EXAMPLE   See the `ComponentEvent` class example.

componentMoved()

PURPOSE   Called after a component has been moved.

SYNTAX   `public void componentMoved(ComponentEvent evt)`

DESCRIPTION   This method is called after the source component is moved. The source component can be moved either by the user or by calling `Component.setLocation()`. Moreover, this method is called regardless of the component's visible state. The source component's new location can be retrieved by calling `Component.getLocation()`.

This method, by default, has an empty implementation.

PARAMETERS
evt   The non-`null` component event.

EXAMPLE   See the `ComponentEvent` class example.

componentResized()

PURPOSE   Called after a component has been resized.

SYNTAX   `public void componentResized(ComponentEvent evt)`

A
B
C
D
E
F
G
H
I
J
K
L
M
N
O
P
Q
R
S
T
U
V
W
X
Y
Z

399

A
B
C
D
E
F
G
H
I
J
K
L
M
N
O
P
Q
R
S
T
U
V
W
X
Y
Z

DESCRIPTION   This method is called after the source component has been resized. A component can be resized either by the user or by calling `Component.setSize()`. Moreover, this method is called regardless of the component's visible state. The component's new size can be retrieved by calling `Component.get-Size()`.

This method, by default, has an empty implementation.

PARAMETERS
evt   The non-`null` component event.

EXAMPLE   See the `ComponentEvent` class example.

componentShown()

PURPOSE   Called after a component has been made visible.

SYNTAX   `public void componentShown(ComponentEvent evt)`

DESCRIPTION   In the simplest terms, this method is called whenever the source component appears on the screen or, more technically, is *shown*. A component is *showing* if it is visible, its peer exists, and its parent is *showing*. For more information about the showing property, see `Component.isShowing()`.

However, this method is not called in all cases. In particular, it will be called only if `Component.setVisible()` or `Window.show()` is called on the component. In other words, the method is not called if the component becomes shown because some ancestor became shown.

This method, by default, has an empty implementation.

PARAMETERS
evt   The non-`null` component event.

EXAMPLE   See the `ComponentEvent` class example.

ComponentEvent

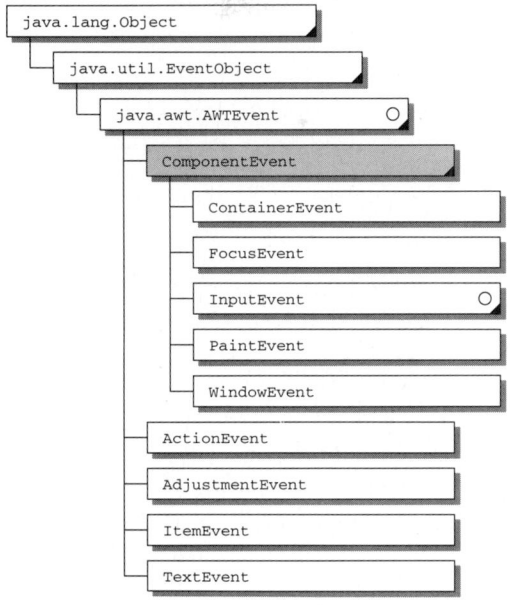

Syntax

public class ComponentEvent extends AWTEvent

Description

Component events are fired by a component (see Component) whenever the component is moved, resized, hidden, or made visible. For more general information about events, see AWTEvent.

Listening for Component Events

To listen for component events from an object, the listener must implement the ComponentListener interface. After that, the listener must be registered with the object. An object is registered by calling the object's addComponentListener() method.

An alternative, and possibly more convenient, way of receiving component events is to use a component adapter. See ComponentAdapter for more details.

As with most events, a component event is delivered to its listeners after the operation has taken place.

Component Event Flow

Figure 97 shows how component events typically flow through the system. First, the event is fired by some component peer in response to some user gesture. This event is posted on the event queue (see `Event-Queue`). When the event makes its way to the front of the queue, it is given to the component via its `dispatchEvent()` method. The main purpose of this method is to discard the event if the component event type is not enabled or if there are no component event listeners. Otherwise, `dispatchEvent()` calls `processEvent()`, which calls different methods depending on the event type. Since this is a component event, `processComponentEvent()` is called. The main purpose of this method is to notify the component event listeners.

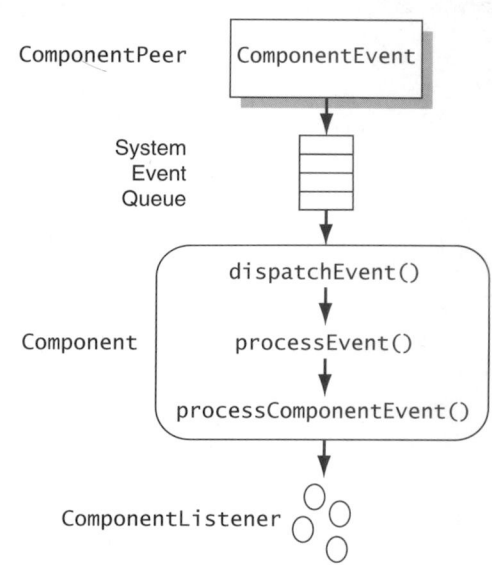

FIGURE 97: Component Event Flow.

A component can override `process-ComponentEvent()` to process component events before they are delivered to its listeners. The overridden method should call `super.processComponentEvent()` to ensure that events are dispatched to the component's listeners.

MEMBER SUMMARY	
Constructor	
ComponentEvent()	Constructs a ComponentEvent instance.
Component Method	
getComponent()	Retrieves the component that fired this event.
Component Event Constants	
COMPONENT_FIRST	Constant specifying the first id in the range of component event ids.
COMPONENT_HIDDEN	Event id indicating that a component was hidden.
COMPONENT_LAST	Constant specifying the last id in the range of component event ids.
COMPONENT_MOVED	Event id indicating that a component was moved.
COMPONENT_RESIZED	Event id indicating that a component was resized.
COMPONENT_SHOWN	Event id indicating that a component was made visible on the screen.
Debugging Method	
paramString()	Generates a string representing the component event's state.

See Also

ComponentAdapter, ComponentListener, java.awt.AWTEvent,
java.awt.Component, java.awt.Component.dispatchEvent(),
java.awt.Component.processComponentEvent(),
java.awt.Component.processEvent().

Example

This example demonstrates how to listen to and handle component events from a component. The example creates a frame that listens for component events on itself. In response to a component event, the specifics of the event are printed. Also printed is the new value that has changed (this shows that the values have been updated before the event is delivered to the listeners). See Figure 98.

FIGURE 98:   ComponentEvent.

```java
import java.awt.*;
import java.awt.event.*;

class Main extends Frame implements ComponentListener, ActionListener, Runnable
{
    Main() {
        super("ComponentEvent Example");
        Button b = new Button("Hide Me");

        add(b, BorderLayout.CENTER);

        // Listen for events.
        b.addActionListener(this);
        addComponentListener(this);

        setSize(100, 100);
        show();
    }

    public void componentResized(ComponentEvent evt) {
        System.out.print("COMPONENT_RESIZED: ");
        System.out.println("new bounds="+evt.getComponent().getBounds());
    }
    public void componentMoved(ComponentEvent evt) {
        System.out.print("COMPONENT_MOVED: ");
        System.out.println("new bounds="+evt.getComponent().getBounds());
    }
    public void componentShown(ComponentEvent evt) {
        System.out.print("COMPONENT_SHOWN: ");
        System.out.println("new visible state=" +
                    evt.getComponent().isVisible());
    }
    public void componentHidden(ComponentEvent evt) {
        System.out.print("COMPONENT_HIDDEN: ");
        System.out.println("new visible state=" +
                    evt.getComponent().isVisible());
    }
```

A
B
C
D
E
F
G
H
I
J
K
L
M
N
O
P
Q
R
S
T
U
V
W
X
Y
Z

```
        // Hide the frame and start the thread.
        public void actionPerformed(ActionEvent evt) {
            setVisible(false);
            (new Thread(this)).start();
        }

        // This thread waits for 2 seconds and then shows the frame.
        public void run() {
            try {
                Thread.sleep(2000);
            } catch (Exception e) {
            }
            // This causes a COMPONENT_MOVED event to be generated even though
            // the frame is not visible.
            setLocation(100, 100);
            setVisible(true);
        }

        public static void main(String args[]) {
            new Main();
        }
    }
```

A
B

D
E
F
G
H
I
J
K
L
M
N
O
P
Q
R
S
T
U
V
W
X
Y
Z

COMPONENT_FIRST

PURPOSE	Constant specifying the first id in the range of component event ids.
SYNTAX	`public static final int COMPONENT_FIRST`
DESCRIPTION	All component event ids must be greater than or equal to COMPONENT_FIRST (value 100).
SEE ALSO	COMPONENT_LAST.
EXAMPLE	See `java.awt.Component.processEvent()`.

COMPONENT_HIDDEN

PURPOSE	Event id indicating that a component was hidden.
SYNTAX	`public static final int COMPONENT_HIDDEN`
DESCRIPTION	An event with this id (value 103) is fired by a component after it is made invisible by a call to `Component.setVisible(false)`. A component does not fire this event if it was made invisible because its parent became invisible.
SEE ALSO	`java.awt.Component.setVisible()`.
EXAMPLE	See the class example.

COMPONENT_LAST

PURPOSE	Constant specifying the last id in the range of component event ids.
SYNTAX	`public static final int COMPONENT_LAST`
DESCRIPTION	All component event ids must be less than or equal to `COMPONENT_LAST` (value 103).
SEE ALSO	`COMPONENT_FIRST`.
EXAMPLE	See `java.awt.Component.processEvent()`.

COMPONENT_MOVED

PURPOSE	Event id indicating that a component was moved.
SYNTAX	`public static final int COMPONENT_MOVED`
DESCRIPTION	An event with this id (value 100) is fired by a component when it is moved. A component can be moved either by the user or by calling `Component.setLocation()`. Moreover, the event is fired regardless of the component's visible state. The component's new location can be retrieved by calling `Component.getLocation()`.
SEE ALSO	`java.awt.Component.getLocation()`, `java.awt.Component.setLocation()`.
EXAMPLE	See the class example.

COMPONENT_RESIZED

PURPOSE	Event id indicating that a component was resized.
SYNTAX	`public static final int COMPONENT_RESIZED`
DESCRIPTION	An event with this id (value 101) is fired by a component when it is resized. A component can be resized either by the user or by calling `Component.setSize()`. Moreover, the event is fired regardless of the component's visible state. The component's new size can be retrieved by calling `Component.getSize()`.
SEE ALSO	`java.awt.Component.getSize()`.
EXAMPLE	See the class example.

A
B
C
D
E
F
G
H
I
J
K
L
M
N
O
P
Q
R
S
T
U
V
W
X
Y
Z

405

COMPONENT_SHOWN

PURPOSE   Event id indicating that a component was made visible on the screen.

SYNTAX   `public static final int COMPONENT_SHOWN`

DESCRIPTION   In the simplest terms, a component fires an event of this id (value 102) whenever it appears on the screen or, more technically, is *shown*. A component is *showing* if it is visible, its peer exists, and its parent is *showing*. For more information about the showing property, see `Component.isShowing()`.

However, a component does not fire this event in all cases. In particular, it will fire the event only if `Component.setVisible()` or `Window.show()` is called on the component. In other words, a component does not fire this event if the component becomes shown because some ancestor became shown.

SEE ALSO   `java.awt.Component.isShowing()`, `java.awt.Component.setVisible()`, `java.awt.Window.show()`.

EXAMPLE   See the class example.

ComponentEvent()

PURPOSE   Constructs a `ComponentEvent` instance.

SYNTAX   `public ComponentEvent(Component source, int id)`

DESCRIPTION   This method creates a new component event instance with `source` as the component firing this event.

After the component event is created, the source object can distribute the event to its listeners by calling the component event-related methods in `AWTEventMulticaster`. If the event is not created by `source`, the creator can deliver the event to the source component either by posting the event to the event queue (see `EventQueue.postEvent()`) or by calling the source component's `Component.dispatchEvent()` method directly.

PARAMETERS

source   The non-`null` component that is firing this component event.

id   One of the component event ids.

SEE ALSO   `java.awt.AWTEvent.getID()`, `java.awt.AWTEventMulticaster`, `java.awt.EventQueue`, `java.util.EventObject.getSource()`.

getComponent()

PURPOSE   Retrieves the component that fired this event.

SYNTAX   `public Component getComponent()`

DESCRIPTION   This method returns the component that fired the component event. This is the same object returned by `EventObject.getSource()`.

RETURNS   The non-`null` component that fired this event.

SEE ALSO   `java.awt.Component`, `java.util.EventObject.getSource()`.

EXAMPLE   See the class example.

paramString()

PURPOSE   Generates a string representing the component event's state.

SYNTAX   `public String paramString()`

DESCRIPTION   The returned string contains the name of the component event and, if appropriate, the new bounds of the component. A subclass of this class should override this method and return a concatenation of its state with the results of `super.paramString()`. This method is called by the `AWTEvent.toString()` method and is typically used for debugging.

RETURNS   A non-`null` string representing the component event's state.

OVERRIDES   `java.awt.AWTEvent.paramString()`.

SEE ALSO   `java.awt.AWTEvent.toString()`, `java.lang.Object.toString()`.

EXAMPLE   See the `java.awt.AWTEvent` class example.

A
B
C
D
E
F
G
H
I
J
K
L
M
N
O
P
Q
R
S
T
U
V
W
X
Y
Z

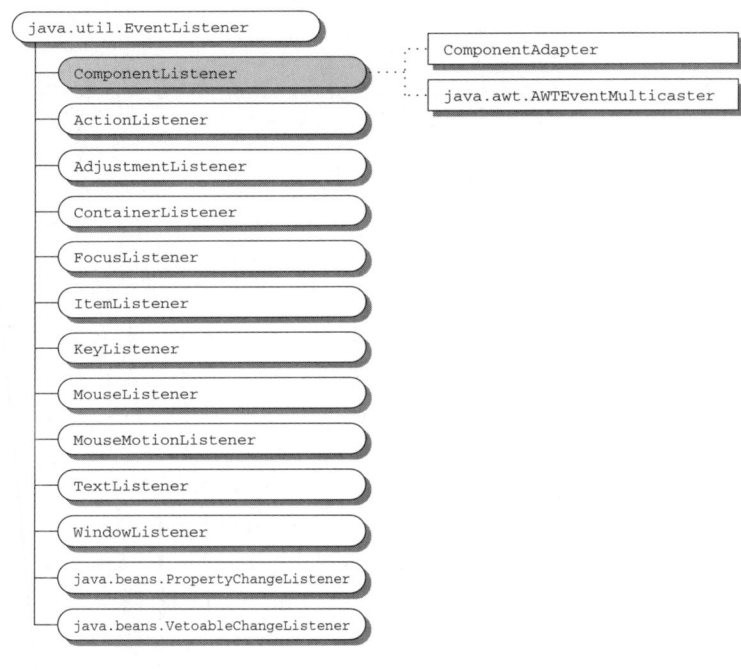

Syntax

```
public interface ComponentListener extends EventListener
```

Description

When an object (listener) wishes to receive component events from a component (the source component), two things must be done:

1. The listener must implement this interface and all the methods required by this interface.
2. The listener must be registered with the source component. It becomes registered by making a call to the source component's addComponentListener() method.

For more information about component events, see ComponentEvent.

MEMBER SUMMARY	
Component Event Callback Methods	
componentHidden()	Called after a component has been hidden.
componentMoved()	Called after a component has been moved.
componentResized()	Called after a component has been resized.
componentShown()	Called after a component has been made visible.

See Also

ComponentAdapter, ComponentEvent, java.awt.AWTEventMulticaster,
java.awt.Component.addComponentListener(), java.util.EventListener.

Example

See the ComponentEvent class example.

componentHidden()

PURPOSE	Called after a component has been hidden.
SYNTAX	public void componentHidden(ComponentEvent evt)
DESCRIPTION	This method is called after the source component is made invisible by a call to Component.setVisible(false). This method is not called if the component was made invisible because its parent became invisible.
PARAMETERS	
evt	The non-null component event.
EXAMPLE	See the ComponentEvent class example.

componentMoved()

PURPOSE	Called after a component has been moved.
SYNTAX	public void componentMoved(ComponentEvent evt)
DESCRIPTION	This method is called after the source component is moved. The source component can be moved either by the user or by calling Component.setLocation(). Moreover, this method is called regardless of the component's visible state. The source component's new location can be retrieved by calling Component.getLocation().

A
B

D
E
F
G
H
I
J
K
L
M
N
O
P
Q
R
S
T
U
V
W
X
Y
Z

This method defines the code that is to be executed when this listener receives `ComponentEvent.COMPONENT_MOVED` events. See `ComponentEvent.COMPO-NENT_MOVED` for details.

PARAMETERS

evt   The non-null component event.

EXAMPLE   See the `ComponentEvent` class example.

componentResized()

PURPOSE   Called after a component has been resized.

SYNTAX   `public void componentResized(ComponentEvent evt)`

DESCRIPTION This method is called after the source component has been resized. A component can be resized either by the user or by calling `Component.setSize()`. Moreover, this method is called regardless of the component's visible state. The component's new size can be retrieved by calling `Component.get-Size()`.

PARAMETERS

evt   The non-null component event.

EXAMPLE   See the `ComponentEvent` class example.

componentShown()

PURPOSE   Called after a component has been made visible.

SYNTAX   `public void componentShown(ComponentEvent evt)`

DESCRIPTION In the simplest terms, this method is called whenever the source component appears on the screen or, more technically, is *shown*. A component is *showing* if it is visible, its peer exists, and its parent is *showing*. For more information about the showing property, see `Component.isShowing()`.

However, this method is not called in all cases. In particular, it will be called only if `Component.setVisible()` or `Window.show()` is called on the component. In other words, the method is not called if the component becomes shown because some ancestor became shown.

PARAMETERS

evt   The non-null component event.

EXAMPLE   See the `ComponentEvent` class example.

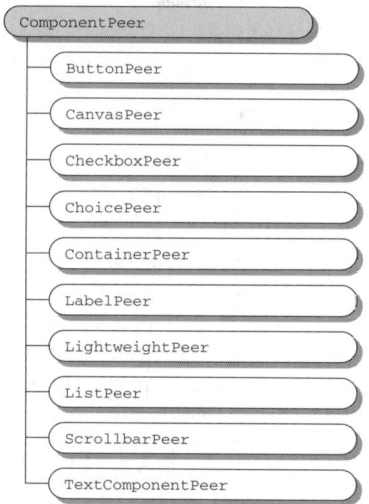

Syntax
```
public interface ComponentPeer
```

Description

A component such as a button uses the platform's native implementation of a button. For example, on Solaris, the AWT button uses the Motif button widget, while on Windows 95, the AWT button uses the button control. So that the AWT button component behaves the same on all platforms, the button is assigned a *peer* that takes care of translating the behavior of the platform's native button to the behavior of the AWT button.

Every component in the AWT has a peer associated with it. Just as the Component class is the superclass of all AWT components, the ComponentPeer class is the superclass of all peer classes.

AWT programmers normally do not directly use peer classes and interfaces. Instead, they deal with AWT components in the java.awt package. These in turn automatically manage their peers. Only someone who is porting the AWT to another platform should be concerned with the peer classes and interfaces. Consequently, most peer documentation refers to java.awt counterparts.

See Component and Toolkit for additional information about component peers.

A
B
C
D
E
F
G
H
I
J
K
L
M
N
O
P
Q
R
S
T
U
V
W
X
Y
Z

MEMBER SUMMARY

Peer Methods

`checkImage()`	Retrieves the construction status of an image.
`createImage()`	Creates an off-screen image or an image from an image producer.
`dispose()`	Destroys a component.
`getColorModel()`	Retrieves the component's color model.
`getFontMetrics()`	Retrieves the font metrics for a font.
`getGraphics()`	Creates a graphics context for the component.
`getLocationOnScreen()`	Retrieves the component's location on the screen.
`getMinimumSize()`	Calculates the component's minimum size dimensions.
`getPreferredSize()`	Calculates the component's preferred size dimensions.
`getToolkit()`	Retrieves the component's toolkit.
`handleEvent()`	Called when the component receives an event.
`isFocusTraversable()`	Determines whether this component's focus can be traversed using the Tab or Shift-Tab keys.
`paint()`	Called to repaint the component.
`prepareImage()`	Triggers the loading of image data for an image.
`print()`	Prints the component on a graphics context.
`repaint()`	Makes a request to repaint a component.
`requestFocus()`	Requests that the focus be given to the component.
`setBounds()`	Moves and resizes a component.
`setBackground()`	Sets the component's background color.
`setCursor()`	Sets the component's cursor image.
`setEnabled()`	Enables or disables a component.
`setFont()`	Sets the component's font.
`setForeground()`	Sets the component's foreground color.
`setVisible()`	Makes the component visible or invisible.

Deprecated Methods

`disable()`	Replaced by `setEnabled()`.
`enable()`	Replaced by `setEnabled()`.
`hide()`	Replaced by `setVisible()`.
`minimumSize()`	Replaced by `getMinimumSize()`.
`preferredSize()`	Replaced by `getPreferredSize()`.
`reshape()`	Replaced by `setBounds()`.
`show()`	Replaced by `setVisible()`.

See Also

`java.awt.Component`, `java.awt.Toolkit`.

checkImage( )

PURPOSE   Retrieves the construction status of an image.

SYNTAX
```
int checkImage(Image image, int width, int height,
    ImageObserver obs)
```

PARAMETERS
height   If >= 0, specifies the height of the scaled version of the image to check.
image   The non-null image to check.
obs   If non-null, specifies the image observer to be notified whenever the status changes.
width   If >= 0, specifies the width of the scaled version of the image to check.

RETURNS   The combination of status bits as defined by the `ImageObserver` interface.

SEE ALSO   `java.awt.Component.checkImage()`.

createImage( )

PURPOSE   Creates an off-screen image or an image from an image producer.

SYNTAX
```
Image createImage(int width, int height)
Image createImage(ImageProducer prod)
```

PARAMETERS
height   The height of the off-screen image in pixels.
prod   The non-null image producer.
width   The width of the off-screen image in pixels.

RETURNS   A new off-screen image.

SEE ALSO   `java.awt.Component.createImage()`.

disable( )   *DEPRECATED*

PURPOSE   Replaced by `setEnabled()`.

SYNTAX   `void disable()`

DEPRECATION   Replace the usage of this deprecated method, as in
```
peer.disable();
```
with
```
peer.setEnabled(false);.
```

A
B
C
D
E
F
G
H
I
J
K
L
M
N
O
P
Q
R
S
T
U
V
W
X
Y
Z

dispose( )

PURPOSE	Destroys this component.
SYNTAX	`void dispose()`
DESCRIPTION	This method releases any resources associated with this component.
SEE ALSO	`java.awt.Component.removeNotify()`.

enable( )   *DEPRECATED*

PURPOSE	Replaced by `setEnabled()`.
SYNTAX	`void enable()`

DEPRECATION	Replace the usage of this deprecated method, as in
	  `peer.enable();`
	with
	  `peer.setEnabled(true);`

getColorModel( )

PURPOSE	Retrieves the component's color model.
SYNTAX	`ColorModel getColorModel()`
RETURNS	A non-`null` color model instance.
SEE ALSO	`java.awt.Component.getColorModel()`.

getFontMetrics( )

PURPOSE	Retrieves the font metrics for a font.
SYNTAX	`FontMetrics getFontMetrics(Font font)`
PARAMETERS	
`font`	The non-`null` font.
RETURNS	The non-`null` font metrics for `font`.
SEE ALSO	`java.awt.Component.getFontMetrics()`.

getGraphics( )

PURPOSE	Creates a graphics context for the component.

A
B
C
D
E
F
G
H
I
J
K
L
M
N
O
P
Q
R
S
T
U
V
W
X
Y
Z

SYNTAX `Graphics getGraphics()`

RETURNS A graphics context for the component.

SEE ALSO `java.awt.Component.getGraphics()`.

A
B
C
D
E
F
G
H
I
J
K
L
M
N
O
P
Q
R
S
T
U
V
W
X
Y
Z

getLocationOnScreen()

PURPOSE Retrieves this component's location on the screen.

SYNTAX `Point getLocationOnScreen()`

RETURNS A new non-`null` point containing this component's location relative to the screen.

SEE ALSO `java.awt.Component.getLocationOnScreen()`.

getMinimumSize()

PURPOSE Calculates the component's minimum size dimensions.

SYNTAX `Dimension getMinimumSize()`

RETURNS A non-`null` dimension object containing the component's minimum size.

SEE ALSO `java.awt.Component.getMinimumSize()`.

getPreferredSize()

PURPOSE Calculates the component's preferred size dimensions.

SYNTAX `Dimension getPreferredSize()`

RETURNS A non-`null` dimension object containing the component's preferred size.

SEE ALSO `java.awt.Component.getPreferredSize()`.

getToolkit()

PURPOSE Retrieves the component's toolkit.

SYNTAX `Toolkit getToolkit()`

RETURNS A non-`null` reference to the component's toolkit.

SEE ALSO `java.awt.Component.getToolkit()`, `java.awt.Toolkit`.

handleEvent( )

PURPOSE	Called when the component receives an event.
SYNTAX	`boolean handleEvent(AWTEvent evt)`
PARAMETERS	
`evt`	The non-`null` AWT event.
RETURNS	`false` if the event should be passed up to the component's parent; `true` otherwise.
SEE ALSO	`java.awt.AWTEvent`, `java.awt.Component.processEvent()`.

hide( )   *DEPRECATED*

PURPOSE	Replaced by `setVisible()`.
SYNTAX	`void hide()`
DEPRECATION	Replace the usage of this deprecated method, as in

```
 peer.hide();
```
with
```
 peer.setVisible(false);
```

isFocusTraversable( )

PURPOSE	Determines whether this component's focus can be traversed using the Tab or Shift-Tab keys.
SYNTAX	`boolean isFocusTraversable()`
SEE ALSO	`java.awt.Component.isFocusTraversable()`.

minimumSize( )   *DEPRECATED*

PURPOSE	Replaced by `getMinimumSize()`.
SYNTAX	`Dimension minimumSize()`
RETURNS	A non-`null` dimension object containing the component's minimum size.
DEPRECATION	Replace the usage of this deprecated method, as in

```
 Dimension min = peer.minimumSize();
```
with
```
 Dimension min = peer.getMinimumSize();
```

A
B
C
D
E
F
G
H
I
J
K
L
M
N
O
P
Q
R
S
T
U
V
W
X
Y
Z

paint( )

PURPOSE	Called to repaint the component.
SYNTAX	`void paint(Graphics gc)`
PARAMETERS	
`gc`	The non-`null` graphics context in which to paint the component.
SEE ALSO	`java.awt.Component.paint()`.

preferredSize( )   *DEPRECATED*

PURPOSE	Replaced by `getPreferredSize()`.
SYNTAX	`Dimension preferredSize()`
RETURNS	A non-`null` dimension object containing the component's preferred size.
DEPRECATION	Replace the usage of this deprecated method, as in

```
    Dimension pref = peer.preferredSize();
with
    Dimension pref = peer.getPreferredSize();
```

prepareImage( )

PURPOSE	Triggers the loading of image data for an image.
SYNTAX	`boolean prepareImage(Image img, int w, int h, ImageObserver obs)`
PARAMETERS	
`h`	`-1` or the scaled height of the returned image.
`img`	The non-`null` image to load.
`obs`	The non-`null` image observer.
`w`	`-1` or the scaled width of the returned image.
RETURNS	`true` if all the image data for `img` is available; `false` otherwise.
SEE ALSO	`java.awt.Component.prepareImage()`.

print( )

PURPOSE	Prints the component on a graphics context.
SYNTAX	`void print(Graphics gc)`

PARAMETERS	
gc	The non-`null` graphics context on which to print.
SEE ALSO	`java.awt.Component.print()`.

repaint( )

PURPOSE	Makes a request to repaint a component.
SYNTAX	`void repaint(long ms, int x, int y, int w, int h)`

PARAMETERS	
h	The height of the rectangular area to repaint.
ms	Maximum delay in milliseconds before the `update()` method is called.
w	The width of the rectangular area to repaint.
x	The x-coordinate of the rectangular area to repaint.
y	The y-coordinate of the rectangular area to repaint.
SEE ALSO	`java.awt.Component.repaint()`.

requestFocus( )

PURPOSE	Requests that the focus be given to the component.
SYNTAX	`void requestFocus()`
SEE ALSO	`java.awt.Component.requestFocus()`.

reshape( )   *DEPRECATED*

PURPOSE	Replaced by `setBounds()`.
SYNTAX	`void reshape(int x, int y, int w, int h)`

PARAMETERS	
h	The new height of the component in pixels.
w	The new width of the component in pixels.
x	The new x-coordinate of the component in pixels.
y	The new y-coordinate of the component in pixels.
DEPRECATION	Replace the usage of this deprecated method, as in

```
 peer.reshape(x. y, w, h);
```
with
```
 peer.setBounds(x, y, w, h);.
```

setBackground()

PURPOSE	Sets the component's background color.
SYNTAX	`void setBackground(Color c)`
PARAMETERS	
c	The new background color, which can be `null`.
SEE ALSO	`java.awt.Component.setBackground()`.

setBounds()

PURPOSE	Moves and resizes a component.
SYNTAX	`void setBounds(int x, int y, int w, int h)`
PARAMETERS	
h	The new height of the component in pixels.
w	The new width of the component in pixels.
x	The new *x*-coordinate of the component in pixels.
y	The new *y*-coordinate of the component in pixels.
SEE ALSO	`java.awt.Component.setBounds()`.

setCursor()

PURPOSE	Sets the component's cursor image.
SYNTAX	`void setCursor(Cursor cursor)`
PARAMETERS	
cursor	The non-`null` cursor image.
SEE ALSO	`java.awt.Component.setCursor()`.

setEnabled()

PURPOSE	Enables or disables a component.
SYNTAX	`void setEnabled(boolean cond)`
PARAMETERS	
cond	If `true`, this component is enabled; otherwise, this component is disabled.
SEE ALSO	`java.awt.Component.setEnabled()`.

A
B
C
D
E
F
G
H
I
J
K
L
M
N
O
P
Q
R
S
T
U
V
W
X
Y
Z

A
B

D
E
F
G
H
I
J
K
L
M
N
O
P
Q
R
S
T
U
V
W
X
Y
Z

setFont()

PURPOSE   Sets the component's font.

SYNTAX   `void setFont(Font f)`

PARAMETERS

  f   The font. This parameter can be `null`.

SEE ALSO   `java.awt.Component.setFont()`.

setForeground()

PURPOSE   Sets the component's foreground color.

SYNTAX   `void setForeground(Color c)`

PARAMETERS

  c   The new foreground color, which can be `null`.

SEE ALSO   `java.awt.Component.setForeground()`.

setVisible()

PURPOSE   Makes the component visible.

SYNTAX   `void setVisible(boolean cond)`

PARAMETERS

  cond   If `true`, makes the component visible; if `false`, makes the component invisible.

SEE ALSO   `java.awt.Component.setVisible()`.

show()   *DEPRECATED*

PURPOSE   Replaced by `setVisible()`.

SYNTAX   `void show()`

DEPRECATION   Replace the usage of this deprecated method, as in
```
peer.show();
```
with
```
peer.setVisible(true);
```

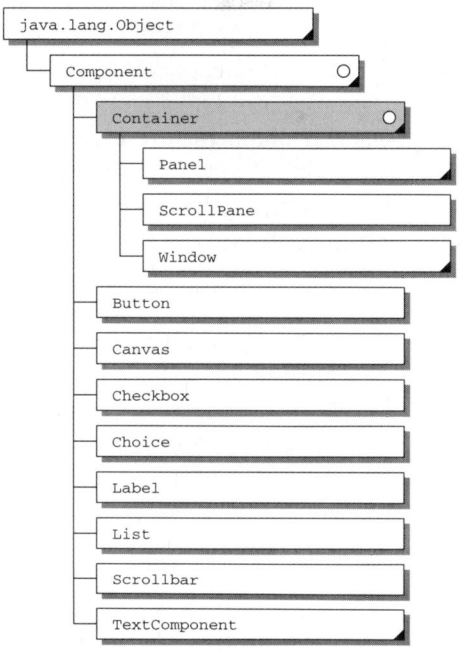

Syntax

```
public abstract class Container extends Component
```

Description

A *container* is a component that can contain other components. A container has a list of child components and a layout manager to lay out the children.

Layout Management

A container can have a layout manager associated with it to determine the size and placement of its components. A container maintains a *valid* state, which indicates whether the children of the container are properly laid out. Actions such as removing or adding a component to a container cause the container to become invalid. Only when the user causes the resizing of the container (by resizing the top-level window) is the layout manager automatically invoked by the system. In all other situations, such as after adding a new button, the layout manager must be invoked explicitly with a call to `validate()`.

When the layout manager is invoked on a container, it first checks whether the container is valid. If so, it does not lay out the container. If not, it lays out all the children and then invokes the layout manager of any invalid children. The layout process continues recursively until all reachable components are valid. Note that if a component is invalid but is embedded in a valid container, the layout process will not be applied to the invalid component.

Although the layout manager recursively traverses the component hierarchy, it does not recurse below valid components. Note that with this behavior, an invalid component will *not* be validated if it is in a valid container. To remedy this, you need either to invoke the layout manager directly on the invalid component or to invalidate the component's container.

Certain operations on the container automatically invalidate the container. However, in many cases the container needs to be explicitly invalidated. For example, if a component's size is changed (such as by changing its label), its container is not automatically marked invalid. See layout() and validate() for more details.

Insets

An *inset* is a distance from a rectangle's edge (see Insets). A container maintains four insets—left, top, right, bottom—that correspond to the edges of the container. The insets are applied to a container's bounds to yield another, typically smaller, area called the *inset area*, in which the container's components are constrained. Insets are most often present in containers that have borders, such as the frame (see Frame). They are primarily used by layout managers to ensure that the components are laid out to stay within the container's borders.

Disabled Containers

Disabling a container intercepts the delivery of all mouse and keyboard events made by the user to the container's child components. Disabling the container is not the same as disabling all components in the container. For example, most components look different when disabled. In a disabled container, the components will appear as though they were enabled.

The Alignment Property

The alignment property is a pair of floating-point values—one that specifies the *x*-alignment and one that specifies the *y*-alignment. Together the *x*- and *y*-alignment values specify an *alignment point* on the container. This alignment point affects how some layout managers place the components in a container. More specifically, the alignment point on a container c is

```
(x_alignment * c.width, y_alignment * c.height)
```

Unlike the alignment property for a component, the alignment property for a container depends on how its children are laid out. In particular, the layout manager is responsible for determining the container's alignment value. See LayoutManager2 for more details.

Events

A container event (see ContainerEvent) is fired when a component is added or removed from a container. In addition to container events, a container fires all of the events fired by the Component class. See the Component class for details. See the AWTEvent class for general information on events and how to filter or handle them.

Z-Ordering

The z-ordering of components in a container specifies the front-to-back ordering of overlapping components. For example, the first component in the z-order will appear above all other siblings; the last component in the z-order will appear behind all other siblings. It turns out that the z-order is exactly the order in which components appear in a container (see Figure 99). That is, the component at index position 0 will

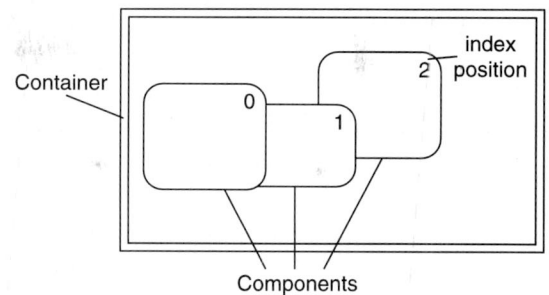

FIGURE 99: Z-Ordering.

appear in front of all of its siblings. By changing the position of the component in its container, you can control how it will overlap with respect to its siblings. For example, if you want to bring a component up front, you would remove it from its current position and insert it at index position 0.

Focus Traversal

Most platforms support a gesture for moving the focus from component to component. For example, on Windows you press the Tab key to move the focus forward and Shift-Tab to move the focus backwards. When the gesture is invoked, the AWT system must determine which component should receive the focus. A component that can receive the focus in this way must be *focus-traversable*. A component is focus-traversable if it is enabled, it is visible, and its `isFocusTraversable()` method returns `true`.

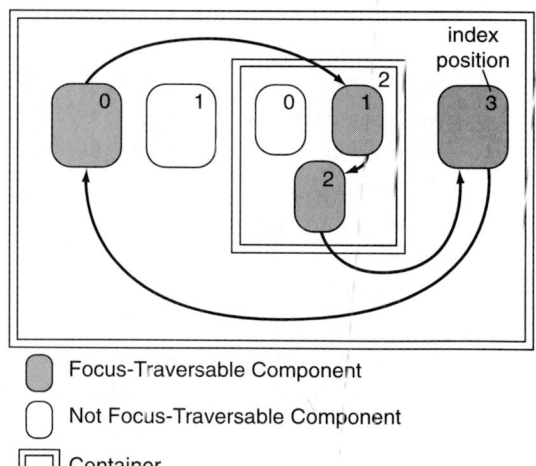

    ☐ Focus-Traversable Component

    ☐ Not Focus-Traversable Component

    ☐ Container

FIGURE 100: Focus Traversal.

The order of focus traversal is exactly the order of the components in a container. If a component has the focus and is at index position P, the AWT system will search for the next focus-traversable component starting at $P+1$ and continue forward either until one is found or that last component in the container is reached. In the latter case, the AWT system resumes the search at index position 0 and continues until one is found or the component at index position P is reached (in which case, no focus-traversable components were found). If one of the components is a container, the component the AWT system starts to search for focus-traversable components inside that container at the component at index position 0. See Figure 100.

A
B

D
E
F
G
H
I
J
K
L
M
N
O
P
Q
R
S
T
U
V
W
X
Y
Z

Native and Lightweight Containers

There are two kinds of containers: *native* and *lightweight*. A native container has a peer that uses a container supplied by the platform. `Panel` and `Frame` are examples of native containers. A lightweight container behaves just like a native container, except that its peer does not use any system resources. Its advantage is more efficient use of the platform's resources. You can freely mix lightweight and native components in a lightweight or native container. However, a lightweight container requires the use of one native container in order to function. Specifically, one of its ancestors must be a native container.

At present, the AWT does not supply any lightweight containers. However, the lightweight support is fully implemented and you can (and are encouraged to) create your own lightweight containers. To create a lightweight container, you must have your container extend from `Container`.

There are small differences between lightweight containers and native containers. Here are some of them:

1. When a lightweight container overrides `paint()`, `paint()` should do its painting and then call `super.paint()`. Calling `super.paint()` causes any lightweight children to be painted.

2. When a container contains lightweight and native components, the lightweight components will always appear behind the native components, regardless of the z-ordering of the components. However, the relative z-ordering within each group (lightweight or native) is preserved. So if a lightweight *L1* is in front of a lightweight *L2* with many native components in between, *L1* will appear in front of *L2* even though both *L1* and *L2* appear behind the native components. Mouse events are delivered to the native components before the lightweight components regardless of their z-orderings. When lightweight and native components are mixed in a container, it is highly recommended that a nonoverlapping layout manager is used to avoid confusion. See `Component` for information about lightweight components.

3. If you call `repaint()` on a lightweight container, the AWT responds by calling its `paint()` method. In the case of a native container, the AWT will call its `update()` method. This means that the background for the lightweight is always cleared. Special steps must be taken to avoid flickering; it is not enough for the lightweight to implement double-buffering.

4. When a graphics context is created on a lightweight container, either by the AWT system or by a call to `getGraphics()`, the graphics context is not initialized with values from the container. Instead, its background color, foreground color, and font are initialized with the values from its closest native container. This means that when the `paint()` method is called on a lightweight container, the colors and fonts must be properly initialized.

MEMBER SUMMARY

Constructor

Container()	Constructs a new instance of `Container`.

Alignment Methods

getAlignmentX()	Retrieves this container's preferred alignment along the *x*-axis.
getAlignmentY()	Retrieves this container's preferred alignment along the *y*-axis.

Component Methods

add()	Adds a component to this container.
addImpl()	Adds a component to this container.
getComponent()	Retrieves a component in this container.
getComponentAt()()	Locates the component at a point in this container.
getComponentCount()	Retrieves the number of components in this container.
getComponents()	Retrieves all the components in this container.
isAncestorOf()	Determines if this container is an ancestor of a component.
remove()	Removes a component from this container.
removeAll()	Removes all components from this container.

Event Methods

addContainerListener()	Adds a listener to receive this container's container events.
processEvent()	Processes an event enabled for this container.
processContainerEvent()	Processes a container event enabled for this container.
removeContainerListener()	Removes a listener from receiving this container's container events.

Layout Methods

doLayout()	Invokes the layout manager on this container.
getInsets()	Retrieves this container's insets.
getLayout()	Retrieves this container's layout manager.
getMaximumSize()	Calculates this container's maximum size dimensions.
getMinimumSize()	Calculates this container's minimum size dimensions.
getPreferredSize()	Calculates this container's preferred size dimensions.
invalidate()	Invalidates this container.
setLayout()	Sets the layout manager for this container.
validate()	Validates this container by laying out its components again.
validateTree()	Called by `validate()` to again layout the components in this container.

Rendering Methods

paint()	Paints this container on a graphics context.
paintComponents()	Paints this container's components on a graphics context.

Continued

A
B

D
E
F
G
H
I
J
K
L
M
N
O
P
Q
R
S
T
U
V
W
X
Y
Z

425

MEMBER SUMMARY	
Rendering Methods (*Continued*))	
`print()`	Prints this container on a graphics context.
`printComponents()`	Prints this container's components on a graphics context.
Peer Methods	
`addNotify()`	Creates the peers for this container and its descendants.
`removeNotify()`	Destroys the peer hierarchy of this container and its descendants.
Debugging Methods	
`list()`	Prints a listing of this container's component hierarchy.
`paramString()`	Generates a string representing the container's state.
Deprecated Methods	
`countComponents()`	Replaced by `getComponentCount()`.
`deliverEvent()`	Replaced by `Component.dispatchEvent()`.
`insets()`	Replaced by `getInsets()`.
`layout()`	Replaced by `doLayout()`.
`locate()`	Replaced by `getComponentAt()`.
`minimumSize()`	Replaced by `getMinimumSize()`.
`preferredSize()`	Replaced by `getPreferredSize()`.

A
B
C
D
E
F
G
H
I
J
K
L
M
N
O
P
Q
R
S
T
U
V
W
X
Y
Z

Example

This example program implements a rudimentary user interface builder. Using it, the user can create AWT components on the canvas and then move them about. The Add menu contains the names of various components that, when

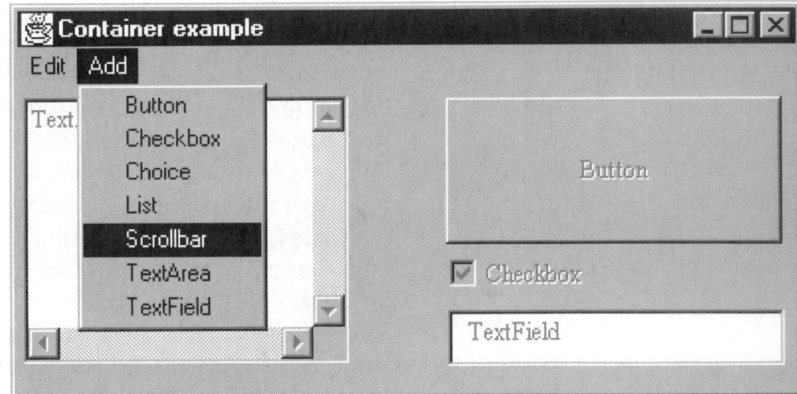

FIGURE 101:   Container.

selected, create the component on the canvas. See Figure 101. The components are created disabled so that they can respond to mouse events. Any mouse event directed at a disabled component is delivered to its parent. In this case, the program catches the mouse event and determines if it occurred over a component. If so, one of several actions can occur. If the left mouse button was pressed, the component can be dragged around. If the right mouse button was pressed, the component is resized. If both the Shift and Control keys were held down during the mouse click, the component is removed.

The Edit menu contains two commands: Remove All and Test. See Figure 102. Remove All removes all the components on the canvas. Test changes the enabled state of all the components on the canvas. When the program is in test mode, the components are enabled and so behave nor-

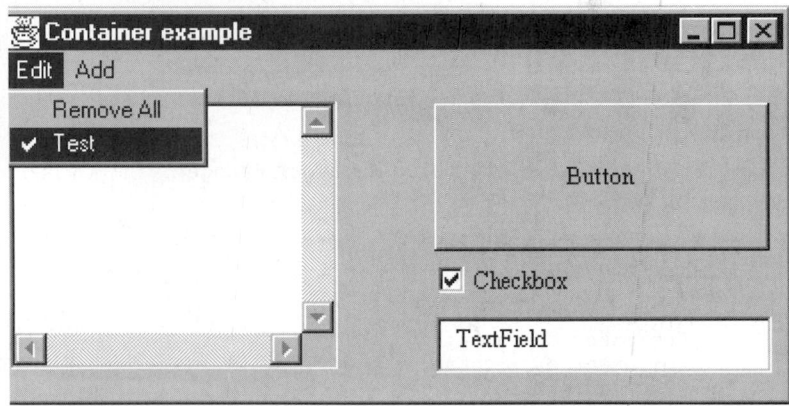

FIGURE 102: Container: Edit Menu.

mally; the components cannot be moved or resized. When the program is not in test mode, the components are disabled and can be moved and resized.

```java
import java.awt.*;
import java.awt.event.*;

class Main extends Frame {
    CheckboxMenuItem testCB = new CheckboxMenuItem("Test");

    Main() {
        super("Container Example");
        MenuBar mb = new MenuBar();
        ActionListener actionListener = new ActionEventHandler();
        MouseEventHandler mouseListener = new MouseEventHandler();

        // Initialize Edit Menu
        Menu m = new Menu("Edit");
        m.add("Remove All");
        testCB.addItemListener(new ItemEventHandler());
        m.add(testCB);
        mb.add(m);
        m.addActionListener(actionListener);

        // Initialize Add Menu
        m = new Menu("Add");
        m.add("Button");
        m.add("Checkbox");
        m.add("Choice");
        m.add("List");
        m.add("Scrollbar");
        m.add("TextArea");
        m.add("TextField");
        m.add("Lightweight");
```

```
            mb.add(m);

            // Set the menubar.
            setMenuBar(mb);

            // Listen for events.
            m.addActionListener(actionListener);
            addMouseListener(mouseListener);
            addMouseMotionListener(mouseListener);


            // Remove the default layout manager.
            setLayout(null);

            setSize(400, 200);
            show();
        }

    Component dragging;
    Component stretching;
    Point offset;

    class MouseEventHandler extends MouseAdapter
        implements MouseMotionListener {
        public void mousePressed(MouseEvent evt) {
            int x = evt.getX();
            int y = evt.getY();
            Component c = getComponentAt(x, y);

            if (c != null && c != Main.this) {
                if (evt.isShiftDown() && evt.isControlDown()) {
                    remove(c);
                } else if (evt.isAltDown()) {
                    stretching = c;

                    // Bring to front.
                    remove(c);
                    add(c, 0);
                } else {
                    offset = new Point(x-c.getLocation().x,
                                        y-c.getLocation().y);
                    dragging = c;

                    // Bring to front.
                    remove(c);
                    add(c, 0);
                }
            }
        }
        public void mouseReleased(MouseEvent evt) {
            stretching = dragging = null;
        }
        public void mouseDragged(MouseEvent evt) {
            int x = evt.getX();
            int y = evt.getY();
            if (dragging != null) {
                dragging.setLocation(x-offset.x, y-offset.y);
            } else if (stretching != null) {
                stretching.setSize(x-stretching.getBounds().x,
                                    y-stretching.getBounds().y);
```

```
                }
            }
        public void mouseMoved(MouseEvent evt) {
            }
    }

    int newX, newY;
    class ActionEventHandler implements ActionListener {
        public void actionPerformed(ActionEvent evt) {
            newX = Math.max(getInsets().left, newX);
            newY = Math.max(getInsets().top, newY);
            Component c = null;
            String arg = evt.getActionCommand();

            if ("Button".equals(arg)) {
                add(c = new Button("Button"));
            } else if ("Checkbox".equals(arg)) {
                add(c = new Checkbox("Checkbox"));
            } else if ("Choice".equals(arg)) {
                add(c = new Choice());
            } else if ("List".equals(arg)) {
                add(c = new List());
            } else if ("Scrollbar".equals(arg)) {
                add(c = new Scrollbar());
            } else if ("TextArea".equals(arg)) {
                add(c = new TextArea("TextArea", 3, 20));
            } else if ("TextField".equals(arg)) {
                add(c = new TextField("TextField"));
            } else if ("Lightweight".equals(arg)) {
                add(c = new Lightweight());
            } else if ("Remove All".equals(arg)) {
                removeAll();
                // The following is needed to clear the lightweights.
                repaint();
            }
            if (c != null) {
                Dimension d = c.getPreferredSize();

                c.setBounds(newX, newY, d.width, d.height);
                c.setEnabled(testCB.getState());
                newX += 20;
                newY += 20;
                if (newX > getSize().width*3/4) {
                    newX = 0;
                }
                if (newY > getSize().height*3/4) {
                    newY = 0;
                }
            }
        }
    }

    class ItemEventHandler implements ItemListener {
        public void itemStateChanged(ItemEvent evt) {
            Component[] all = getComponents();
            boolean newState = (evt.getStateChange() == ItemEvent.SELECTED);

            // Enable all the components.
            for (int i=0; i<all.length; i++) {
                all[i].setEnabled(newState);
```

A
B
C
D
E
F
G
H
I
J
K
L
M
N
O
P
Q
R
S
T
U
V
W
X
Y
Z

429

```
            }
          }
        }

        static public void main(String[] args) {
            new Main();
        }
    }

class Lightweight extends Component implements FocusListener {
    boolean hasFocus;
    Lightweight() {
        // Listen for focus events.
        addFocusListener(this);
        setSize(80, 80);
    }
    public void paint(Graphics g) {
        if (hasFocus) {
            g.setColor(Color.green);
        } else {
            g.setColor(Color.red);
        }
        g.fillOval(0, 0, getSize().width, getSize().height);
        g.setColor(Color.black);
        g.drawOval(0, 0, getSize().width-1, getSize().height-1);
    }

    public Dimension getPreferredSize() {
        return getSize();
    }

    public boolean isFocusTraversable() {
    return true;
    }

    public boolean contains(int x, int y) {
        int midX = getSize().width/2;
        int midY = getSize().height/2;

        // This formula doesn't really work for ovals.
        return (midX-x)*(midX-x) + (midY-y)*(midY-y) <= midX*midX;
    }

    public void focusGained(FocusEvent evt) {
    hasFocus = true;
        repaint();
    }
    public void focusLost(FocusEvent evt) {
    hasFocus = false;
        repaint();
    }
}
```

add( )

PURPOSE   Adds a component to this container.

SYNTAX   public Component add(Component comp)
               public void add(Component comp, Object constraints)
               public void add(Component comp, Object constraints, int pos)
               public Component add(Component comp, int pos)
               public Component add(String name, Component comp)

DESCRIPTION   This method adds the component comp to the container at position pos. If pos
               is 0, the new component will be the first component in the container. If pos is
               -1, the new component will be the last component in the container. If pos is
               not specified, it defaults to -1.

               If comp is already in another container, it is removed from its old container and
               added to this container. If this container has a peer, a peer is created for comp
               and added to the peer hierarchy of this container.

               The component's layout constraints, as specified by name or constraints,
               are used by the container's layout manager. After the component is added to
               the container, the container's layout manager is notified of the addition. The
               addition of a component always invalidates the layout. A container event is
               fired, and if container events have been enabled for this container, any con-
               tainer listeners for this container are notified.

               Use of the last form of this method (the one that accepts name) is not recom-
               mended. Its use should be replaced by use of the more generic forms that
               accept constraints in place of name.

PARAMETERS
  comp   The non-null component to be added to the container.
  constraints The object specifying layout constraints.
  name   The component name, which may be null.
  pos   The position at which to insert the component. 0 means the first position; -1
               means the last position.

RETURNS   The component being added (comp). (Note that the return type of two forms of
               this method are void and so return nothing.)

EXCEPTIONS
  IllegalArgumentException
               If pos is greater than the number of components in this container, or if comp is
               a window, or if comp is a container that contains this container.

SEE ALSO   addImpl(), addContainerListener(),
               java.awt.event.ContainerEvent,
               java.awt.event.ContainerListener, LayoutManager, LayoutManager2.

EXAMPLE   See the class example.

431

A
B
C
D
E
F
G
H
I
J
K
L
M
N
O
P
Q
R
S
T
U
V
W
X
Y
Z

addContainerListener()

PURPOSE   Adds a listener for receiving this container's container events.

SYNTAX   `public synchronized void addContainerListener(ContainerListener listener)`

DESCRIPTION   Container events are fired when a component is added or removed from a container. See `ContainerEvent` for more details. After this method is called, the container listener `listener` will receive container events fired by this container. If `listener` is `null`, this method does nothing.

PARAMETERS
`listener`   The possibly `null` container listener to add.

SEE ALSO   `java.awt.event.ContainerAdapter`, `java.awt.event.ContainerEvent`, `java.awt.event.ContainerListener`, `removeContainerListener()`.

EXAMPLE   See `java.awt.event.ContainerEvent`.

addImpl()

PURPOSE   Adds a component to this container.

SYNTAX   `protected void addImpl(Component comp, Object constraints, int pos)`

DESCRIPTION   This method is used by `add()` to add a component to this container. A subclass that wants to perform additional processing during an `add()` should override this method. The overriding method should call `super.addImpl()` to ensure that the component is added properly to the container.

PARAMETERS
`comp`   The non-`null` component to be added to the container.
`constraints`   The object specifying layout constraints.
`pos`   The position at which to insert the component. 0 means the first position; -1 means the last position.

EXCEPTIONS
`IllegalArgumentException`
               If `pos` is greater than the number of components in this container, or if `comp` is a window, or if `comp` is a container that contains this container.

SEE ALSO   `add()`, `addContainerListener()`, `java.awt.event.ContainerEvent`, `java.awt.event.ContainerListener`, `LayoutManager`, `LayoutManager2`.

EXAMPLE his example creates a frame that overrides `addImpl()` to print out debugging information. See Figure 103.

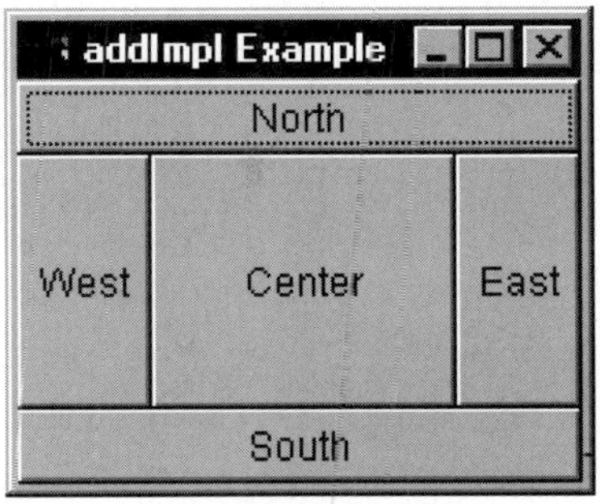

FIGURE 103: Container.addImpl()

```java
import java.awt.*;
import java.awt.event.*;

class Main extends Frame
    implements ActionListener {
    Main() {
        super("addImpl Example");
        Button b;

        // Add  buttons
        add(b = new Button("North"), BorderLayout.NORTH);
        b.addActionListener(this);
        add(b = new Button("South"), BorderLayout.SOUTH);
        b.addActionListener(this);
        add(b = new Button("Center"), BorderLayout.CENTER);
        b.addActionListener(this);
        add(b = new Button("West"), BorderLayout.WEST);
        b.addActionListener(this);
        add(b = new Button("East"), BorderLayout.EAST);
        b.addActionListener(this);

        setSize(300, 150);
        show();
    }

    protected void addImpl(Component comp, Object constraints, int index) {
        System.err.println("adding " + comp + " with constraints " + constraints
+ " at index " + index);
        super.addImpl(comp, constraints, index);
    }

    // Action handler for buttons
    public void actionPerformed(ActionEvent evt) {
        System.out.println(evt.getActionCommand());
    }

    static public void main(String[] args) {
        new Main();
    }
}
```

addNotify()

PURPOSE Creates the peers for this container and its components.

SYNTAX public void addNotify()

433

DESCRIPTION	This method creates the container's peer if it does not exist. Since `Container` is an abstract class, the actual peer created is based on a subclass of `Container`. This method also calls `addNotify()` on all the container's children.
OVERRIDES	`Component.addNotify()`.
SEE ALSO	`Component`, `Toolkit`.
EXAMPLE	See `Component.setVisible()`.

Container( )

PURPOSE	Constructs a new instance of `Container`.
SYNTAX	`protected Container()`
DESCRIPTION	This constructor is used when implementing a lightweight container. A lightweight container can contain lightweight or native components. The lightweight container must have an ancestor that is a native component. See the `Component` class description for details on lightweight and native components.
SEE ALSO	`Component`.
EXAMPLE	See class `ItemSelectable`. It creates a lightweight container `ButtonPanel` that contains AWT `Button` components.

countComponents( )   *DEPRECATED*

PURPOSE	Replaced by `getComponentCount()`.
SYNTAX	`public int countComponents()`
RETURNS	The number of components in the container.

DEPRECATION	Replace the usage of this deprecated method, as in
	  `int howmany = container.countComponents();`
	with
	  `int howmany = container.getComponentCount();`

deliverEvent( )   *DEPRECATED*

PURPOSE	Replaced by `Component.dispatchEvent()`.
SYNTAX	`public void deliverEvent(Event e)`
PARAMETERS	
e	The non-`null` event to be delivered.

OVERRIDES   Component.deliverEvent().

SEE ALSO   Component.handleEvent().

doLayout()

PURPOSE   Invokes the layout manager on this container.

SYNTAX   public void doLayout()

DESCRIPTION   This method invokes the layout manager to resize and position the container's components. Unlike validate(), this method ignores the valid state of the container. Moreover, validate() attempts to validate all of the descendants of the container, while doLayout() does not.

Programs typically should not call doLayout() directly; instead, they should call validate().

OVERRIDES   Component.doLayout().

SEE ALSO   getLayout(), setLayout(), validate().

EXAMPLE   See Component.dispatchEvent(). This example causes the components in the frame to change font size. doLayout() is called on the frame to resize all of its components and to again lay them out.

getAlignmentX()

PURPOSE   Retrieves this container's preferred alignment along the x-axis.

SYNTAX   public float getAlignmentX()

DESCRIPTION   This method returns the container's x-alignment value, which is used by some layout managers to help place container's components. Unlike the alignment property for a component, the alignment property for a container depends on how the container's children are laid out. In particular, the layout manager is responsible for determining the container's alignment value. See LayoutManager2 for more details.

If the layout manger for this container is not an instance of LayoutManager2, this method returns Component.CENTER_ALIGNMENT. For a different x-alignment value to be returned, this method must be overridden.

RETURNS   This component's x-alignment in the range 0.0f to 1.0f.

OVERRIDES   Component.getAlignmentX().

SEE ALSO   getAlignmentY(), LayoutManager2.getLayoutAlignmentX().

EXAMPLE   See the LayoutManager2 class example.

getAlignmentY()

PURPOSE	Retrieves this container's preferred alignment along the *y*-axis.
SYNTAX	`public float getAlignmentY()`

DESCRIPTION This method returns the container's *y*-alignment value, which is used by some layout managers to help place the container's components. Unlike the alignment property for a component, the alignment property for a container depends on how the container's children are laid out. In particular, the layout manager is responsible for determining the container's alignment value. See `LayoutManager2` for more details.

If the layout manger for this container is not an instance of `LayoutManager2`, this method returns `Component.CENTER_ALIGNMENT`. For a different *y*-alignment value to be returned, this method must be overridden.

RETURNS	This component's *y*-alignment in the range `0.0f` to `1.0f`.
OVERRIDES	`Component.getAlignmentY()`.
SEE ALSO	`getAlignmentX()`, `LayoutManager2.getLayoutAlignmentY()`.
EXAMPLE	See the `LayoutManager2` class example.

getComponent()

PURPOSE	Retrieves a component in this container.
SYNTAX	`public Component getComponent(int n)`

DESCRIPTION This method retrieves the component at index `n` in this container. The index is zero-based, so the index of the first component is 0.

PARAMETERS

n The zero-based index of the component in this container.

RETURNS The non-`null` component at index `n`.

EXCEPTIONS

ArrayIndexOutOfBoundsException
   If `n` does not refer to a component.

SEE ALSO	`getComponentCount()`, `getComponents()`.
EXAMPLE	See `Component.dispatchEvent()`.

getComponentAt( )

PURPOSE   Locates the component at a point in this container.

SYNTAX
```
public Component getComponentAt(int x, int y)
public Component getComponentAt(Point pt)
```

DESCRIPTION   This method is used to determine which, if any, component is at the pixel coordinate specified by `pt` or `x`, `y`. The coordinates must be relative to this container's bounds, not to its insets.

The returned component is a direct descendent of this container; that is, it does not recurse down the component hierarchy to find the actual component at the point. So, for example, if the container contains another container which in turn contains buttons, then `getComponentAt()` can return only the subcontainer, not any of the subcontainer's buttons.

PARAMETERS
pt   The point in this container.
x   The *x*-coordinate relative to this container's bounds.
y   The *y*-coordinate relative to this container's bounds.

RETURNS   The component at the specified point, or the container itself if no component is at the point but the point is in the container. Returns `null` if the point is not in the container.

OVERRIDES   `Component.getComponentAt()`.

EXAMPLE   See the class example.

getComponentCount( )

PURPOSE   Retrieves the number of components in this container.

SYNTAX   `public int getComponentCount()`

RETURNS   The number of components in this container.

EXAMPLE   See `Component.dispatchEvent()`.

getComponents( )

PURPOSE   Retrieves all of the components in this container.

SYNTAX   `public Component[] getComponents()`

DESCRIPTION   This method retrieves all of the components in this container. The length of the returned array indicates the number of children in the container.

A
B
C
D
E
F
G
H
I
J
K
L
M
N
O
P
Q
R
S
T
U
V
W
X
Y
Z

437

RETURNS	A non-null array of all the components in this container.
SEE ALSO	getComponent(), getComponentCount().
EXAMPLE	See the class example.

getInsets( )

PURPOSE	Retrieves this container's insets.
SYNTAX	public Insets getInsets()
DESCRIPTION	If this container's peer has not been created, the returned insets will be (0, 0, 0, 0).

A container can override this method to modify the container's default insets. The override should take into account the peer's insets (i.e., the override should call super.insets()). Therefore, if the override increases the default insets, the container should first retrieve the peer's insets and then add the extra insets.

A container's insets are primarily used by the layout manager. Other objects such as mouse events and graphics contexts are based on the container peer's insets and ignore the results of an overridden insets() method. In particular, the mouse coordinate (0, 0) is situated at

```
(bounds().x+peer.insets().left,
    bounds().y+peer.insets().top).
```

Also, when a graphics context is created on the container, (0, 0) of the graphics context is at the same location.

RETURNS	A non-null instance of the container's insets. This instance should not be modified because it is used by the container. To create a copy that can be modified, use clone().
SEE ALSO	Insets.
EXAMPLE	This example creates a frame that contains a panel with a grid layout manager. See Figure 104. The frame overrides the getInsets() method and increases the insets on all sides. This causes the grid layout panel to be positioned and resized within the new insets.

FIGURE 104:
Container.getInsets().

A
B
C
D
E
F
G
H
I
J
K
L
M
N
O
P
Q
R
S
T
U
V
W
X
Y
Z

The frame also paints a 3-D border around the grid layout panel. This is to demonstrate that the origin of mouse coordinates do not depend on the frame's `getInsets()` override and are still relative to the peer's insets.

```java
import java.awt.*;
import java.awt.event.*;

class Main extends Frame {
    int borderSize = 8;
    Main() {
        super("getInsets Example");

        // Listen for mouse events
        addMouseMotionListener(new MouseMotionEventHandler());

        Button b = new Button("Button");
        add(b, BorderLayout.CENTER);

        // Disable button to let mouse motion events pass through
        b.setEnabled(false);
        setSize(150, 200);
        show();
    }

    class MouseMotionEventHandler extends MouseMotionAdapter {
        public void mouseMoved(MouseEvent evt) {
            System.out.println(evt.getX() + "," + evt.getY());
        }
    }

    public Insets getInsets() {
        Insets insets = (Insets)(super.getInsets()).clone();

        insets.top += borderSize;
        insets.left += borderSize;
        insets.bottom += borderSize;
        insets.right += borderSize;
        return insets;
    }

    public void paint(Graphics g) {
        Insets insets = super.getInsets();
        int w = getSize().width-insets.left-insets.right;
        int h = getSize().height-insets.top-insets.bottom;

        g.setColor(new Color(200, 100, 100));
        for (int i=0; i<borderSize; i++) {
            g.draw3DRect(i+insets.left, i+insets.top,
                         w-2*i-1, h-2*i-1, i<borderSize/2);
        }
    }

    static public void main(String[] args) {
        new Main();
    }
}
```

A
B
C
D
E
F
G
H
I
J
K
L
M
N
O
P
Q
R
S
T
U
V
W
X
Y
Z

getLayout( )

PURPOSE	Retrieves this container's layout manager.
SYNTAX	`public LayoutManager getLayout()`
RETURNS	This container's layout manager. The return value may be `null`.
SEE ALSO	`doLayout()`, `setLayout()`.
EXAMPLE	See `setLayout()`.

getMaximumSize( )

PURPOSE	Calculates this container's maximum size dimensions.
SYNTAX	`public Dimension getMaximumSize()`
DESCRIPTION	By default, this method determines the maximum size of this container based on the layout's maximum size. In particular, if the layout manager is an instance of `LayoutManager2` and is not `null`, the result of calling the layout manager's `maximumLayoutSize()` method is returned. Otherwise, the dimension returned is that of `Component.getMaximumSize()`.

Note that if this method is overridden, the maximum size must include the container's insets. |
RETURNS	A new non-`null` dimension object containing this component's maximum size.
OVERRIDES	`Component.getMaximumSize()`.
SEE ALSO	`getMinimumSize()`, `getPreferredSize()`, `Component.getSize()`, `LayoutManager2.maximumLayoutSize()`.

getMinimumSize( )

PURPOSE	Calculates this container's minimum size dimensions.
SYNTAX	`public Dimension getMinimumSize()`
DESCRIPTION	By default, this method uses the container's layout manager to determine the container's minimum size. In particular, if the layout manager is not `null`, the result of calling the layout manager's `minimumLayoutSize()` method is returned.

Note that if this method is overridden, the minimum size must include the container's insets. For example, if the container must display a 10-×-10 pixel |

A
B
C
D
E
F
G
H
I
J
K
L
M
N
O
P
Q
R
S
T
U
V
W
X
Y
Z

image and has an inset border of 3 pixels on all edges, then the minimum size is 16-×-16.

RETURNS	A non-`null` dimension object containing the container's minimum size.
OVERRIDES	`Component.getMinimumSize()`.
SEE ALSO	`getMaximumSize()`, `getPreferredSize()`, `Component.getSize()`, `LayoutManager.minimumLayoutSize()`.
EXAMPLE	See the `LayoutManager` class example.

getPreferredSize( )

PURPOSE	Calculates this container's preferred size dimensions.
SYNTAX	`public Dimension getPreferredSize()`
DESCRIPTION	By default, this method uses the container's layout manager to determine this container's preferred size. In particular, if the layout manager is not `null`, the result of calling the layout manager's `preferredLayoutSize()` method is returned.
	Note that if this method is overridden, the preferred size must include the container's insets. For example, if the container must display a 10-×-10 pixel image and has an inset border of 3 pixels on all edges, then the preferred size is 16-×-16.
RETURNS	A non-`null` dimension object containing the container's preferred size.
OVERRIDES	`Component.getPreferredSize()`.
SEE ALSO	`getMaximumSize()`, `getMinimumSize()`, `Component.getSize()`, `LayoutManager.preferredLayoutSize()`.
EXAMPLE	See the `LayoutManager` class example.

insets( )   *DEPRECATED*

PURPOSE	Replaced by `getInsets()`.
SYNTAX	`public Insets insets()`
RETURNS	A new non-`null` instance of the container's insets.
DEPRECATION	Replace the usage of this deprecated method, as in

```
Insets ins = cont.insets();
```
with
```
Insets ins = cont.getInsets();
```

invalidate()

PURPOSE	Invalidates this container.
SYNTAX	`public void invalidate()`
DESCRIPTION	This method invalidates this container and all of its ancestors. See "Layout Management" earlier in the class description discussion and the `validate()` method for more details about the valid state.
OVERRIDES	`Component.invalidate()`.
SEE ALSO	`LayoutManager2.invalidateLayout2()`, `validate()`.
EXAMPLE	See `Component.setVisible()`.

isAncestorOf()

PURPOSE	Determines if this container is an ancestor of a component.
SYNTAX	`public boolean isAncestorOf(Component comp)`
DESCRIPTION	This method determines whether the component `comp` is in the hierarchy of components rooted at this container.
PARAMETERS	
`comp`	The component to check.
RETURNS	`true` if this container is an ancestor of `comp`; `false` otherwise.
SEE ALSO	`Component.getParent()`.

EXAMPLE

This example creates two columns (panels) of buttons (see Figure 105) and keeps count of how many times buttons on each column are clicked using a shared action listener. The listener checks whether the button clicked is contained in the hierarchy of the left panel. The same effect could have been achieved using separate action listeners, one for each panel.

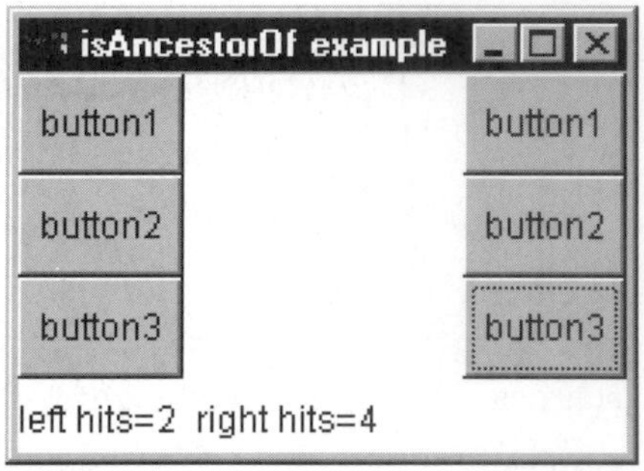

FIGURE 105: `Container.isAncestorOf()`.

```
import java.awt.*;
import java.awt.event.*;

class Main extends Frame implements ActionListener {
    int leftHits = 0, rightHits = 0;
```

```
    Label scoreBoard = new Label("left hits=0  right hits=0");
    Panel left;
    Main() {
        super("isAncestorOf example");
        // create left buttons
        left = new Panel(new GridLayout(0, 1));
        Button b;
        left.add(b = new Button("button1"));
        b.addActionListener(this);
        left.add(b = new Button("button2"));
        b.addActionListener(this);
        left.add(b = new Button("button3"));
        b.addActionListener(this);

        // create right buttons
        Panel right = new Panel(new GridLayout(0, 1));
        right.add(b = new Button("button1"));
        b.addActionListener(this);
        right.add(b = new Button("button2"));
        b.addActionListener(this);
        right.add(b = new Button("button3"));
        b.addActionListener(this);

        add(right, BorderLayout.EAST);
        add(left, BorderLayout.WEST);
        add(scoreBoard, BorderLayout.SOUTH);

        setSize(300, 150);
        show();
    }

    // Action handler for buttons
    public void actionPerformed(ActionEvent evt) {
        if (left.isAncestorOf((Component)evt.getSource())) {
            ++leftHits;
        } else {
            ++rightHits;
        }
        scoreBoard.setText("left hits=" + leftHits + "  right hits=" + right-
Hits);
    }

    static public void main(String[] args) {
        new Main();
    }
}
```

A
B
C
D
E
F
G
H
I
J
K
L
M
N
O
P
Q
R
S
T
U
V
W
X
Y
Z

layout()

DEPRECATED

PURPOSE	Replaced by doLayout().
SYNTAX	public void layout()
DEPRECATION	Replace the usage of this deprecated method, as in

```
container.layout();
```

with

```
                    container.doLayout();
```

OVERRIDES   Component.layout().

list()

PURPOSE   Prints a listing of this container's component hierarchy.

SYNTAX
```
public void list(PrintStream out, int indent)
public void list(PrintWriter outwriter, int indent)
```

DESCRIPTION   This method recursively prints the
                 results of calling `toString()` on
                 each of the container's descendants.
                 The component hierarchy is tra-
                 versed in depth-first order. Children
                 that are deeper down the hierarchy
                 are printed with more indents. The
                 first line of output is printed with
                 `indent` spaces.

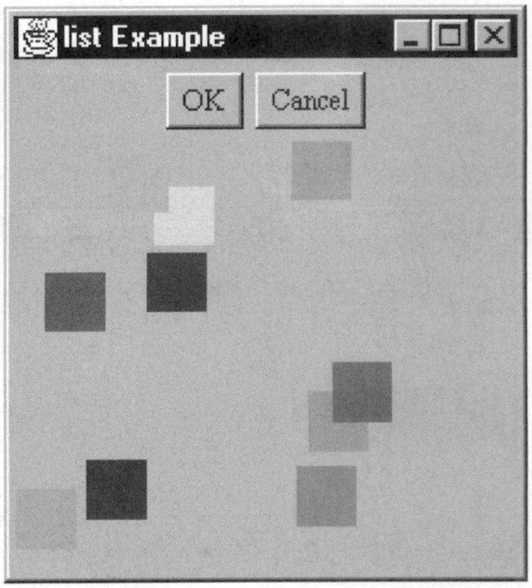

FIGURE 106: Container.list().

PARAMETERS

indent   The indentation of the first line of
                 output.

out   The non-`null` output stream in
                 which to print.

outwriter   The non-`null` output writer to
                 which to print.

OVERRIDES   Component.list().

SEE ALSO   Object.toString().

EXAMPLE   This example creates a frame with many nested containers. See Figure 106.
                 Pressing F1 prints the frame's entire component hierarchy.

```java
import java.awt.*;
import java.awt.event.*;
class Main extends Frame {
    Main() {
        super("list Example");
        Panel p = new Panel(new BorderLayout());

        Panel card = new Panel(new CardLayout());
        add(card, BorderLayout.NORTH);

        p = new Panel(new FlowLayout());
        p.add(new Button("OK"));
        p.add(new Button("Cancel"));
        card.add(p, "1");
```

```
            p = new Panel(new GridLayout(1, 0));
            p.add(new Box());
            card.add(p, "2");

            p = new Panel();
            p.setLayout(null);
            for (int i=0; i<10; i++) {
                p.add(new Box());
            }
            p.add(new Button("Button"));
            add(p, BorderLayout.CENTER);

            setSize(350, 350);
            this.addKeyListener(new KeyEventHandler());
            show();
        }

        class KeyEventHandler extends KeyAdapter {
            public void keyPressed(KeyEvent evt) {
                if (evt.getKeyCode() == KeyEvent.VK_F1) {
                    list(System.out);
                }
            }
        }

        static public void main(String[] args) {
            new Main();
        }
    }

class Box extends Component {
    Color c = new Color(random(256), random(256), random(256));

    Box() {
        setBounds(random(150), random(150), 25, 25);
    }

    int random(int r) {
        return (int)(Math.floor(Math.random()*r));
    }

    public void paint(Graphics g) {
        g.setColor(c);
        g.fillRect(0, 0, getSize().width, getSize().height);
        g.setColor(Color.black);
    }

    protected String paramString() {
        String str = super.paramString();

        return str + ",color=" + c;
    }
}
```

OUTPUT

```
Main[0,0,218x241,layout=java.awt.BorderLayout,resizable,title=list Example]
  java.awt.Panel[4,23,210x34,layout=java.awt.CardLayout]
    java.awt.Panel[4,23,210x34,layout=java.awt.FlowLayout]
```

```
        java.awt.Button[63,5,32x24,label=OK]
        java.awt.Button[100,5,46x24,label=Cancel]
     java.awt.Panel[0,0,0x0,hidden,layout=java.awt.GridLayout]
       Box[4,23,0x0,color=java.awt.Color[r=245,g=49,b=99]]
  java.awt.Panel[4,57,210x180]
    Box[115,0,25x25,color=java.awt.Color[r=147,g=183,b=170]]
    Box[55,47,25x25,color=java.awt.Color[r=68,g=42,b=86]]
    Box[39,5,25x25,color=java.awt.Color[r=174,g=169,b=240]]
    Box[132,93,25x25,color=java.awt.Color[r=70,g=101,b=217]]
    Box[58,19,25x25,color=java.awt.Color[r=182,g=236,b=107]]
    Box[122,105,25x25,color=java.awt.Color[r=255,g=140,b=121]]
    Box[13,55,25x25,color=java.awt.Color[r=97,g=88,b=233]]
    Box[30,133,25x25,color=java.awt.Color[r=152,g=18,b=87]]
    Box[1,145,25x25,color=java.awt.Color[r=187,g=176,b=42]]
    Box[117,136,25x25,color=java.awt.Color[r=147,g=134,b=177]]
    java.awt.Button[0,0,0x0,label=Button]
```

locate()   *DEPRECATED*

PURPOSE	Replaced by getComponentAt().
SYNTAX	public Component locate(int x, int y)
PARAMETERS	
x	The *x*-coordinate relative to the container's bounds.
y	The *y*-coordinate relative to the container's bounds.
RETURNS	The component at x, y, or the container itself if no component is at x, y but x, y is in the container. Returns null if x, y is not in the container.

DEPRECATION Replace the usage of this deprecated method, as in
```
Component target = container.locate(x, y);
```
with
```
Component target = container.getComponentAt(x, y);
```

OVERRIDES   Component.locate().

minimumSize()   *DEPRECATED*

PURPOSE	Replaced by getMinimumSize().
SYNTAX	public Dimension minimumSize()
RETURNS	A non-null dimension object containing the container's minimum size.

DEPRECATION Replace the usage of this deprecated method, as in
```
Dimension dim = container.minimumSize();
```
with
```
Dimension dim = container.getMinimumSize();
```

OVERRIDES   Component.minimumSize().

paint()

PURPOSE   Called to repaint this container.

SYNTAX   `public void paint(Graphics gc)`

DESCRIPTION   This method is called whenever some part of this container needs to be repainted. The graphics context `gc` should be used to repaint the damaged area. The system automatically clears the damaged area with this container's background color before calling this method.

This method, if not overridden, looks for any lightweight children that intersect `gc`'s clipping area. If any are found, their `paint()` methods are called.

The damaged area is not necessarily the whole area of this container. To discover the damaged area, call `gc.getClipBounds()`. Note that when this container is made larger, the clipping area may include only the new area. If as a result of enlarging this component some other part of the container changes and needs to be repainted, a call to `repaint()` must be made so that the area can be repainted.

If this is a native container, three properties of `gc` are initialized with values taken from the same three properties of this component. The properties are the background color, the foreground color, and the font.

If this method is overridden, it should call `super.paint()` after painting itself to ensure its lightweight descendants are painted properly.

PARAMETERS

gc   The non-`null` graphics context on which to paint this component.

OVERRIDES   `Component.paint()`.

SEE ALSO   `Component.repaint()`, `Component.update()`, `paintComponents()`.

EXAMPLE   This example demonstrates how a native container can implement double-buffering to eliminate the flickering of its lightweight descendants. The example defines a button that blinks when you rollover the button. It places the buttons so that they overlap each other. See Figure 107.

Without the double-buffering, all the buttons would flicker as the current button blinked. The double-buffer is created in the frame's `paint()` method. If the dimensions of the frame increases, a new buffer is created.

FIGURE 107: `Container.paint()`.

A
B

D
E
F
G
H
I
J
K
L
M
N
O
P
Q
R
S
T
U
V
W
X
Y
Z

```java
import java.awt.*;
import java.awt.event.*;

class Main extends Frame {
    Main() {
        super("Container.paint Example");

        // The method causes getInsets() to return correct results.
        addNotify();

        // Get the frame's insets.
        Insets insets = getInsets();

        // Add a few buttons.
        for (int i=0; i<4; i++) {
            FakeButton fb = new FakeButton("Push Me");
            add(fb, 0);
            fb.setBounds(insets.left+i*20, insets.top+i*20, 100, 100);
        }

        // Show the frame.
        setLayout(null);
        setSize(300, 300);
        show();
    }

    public void paint(Graphics g) {
        update(g);
    }

    Image bbuf;
    Graphics bbufG;
    public void update(Graphics g) {
        FontMetrics fm = g.getFontMetrics();
        int w = getSize().width;
        int h = getSize().height;

        // Create or enlarge the double-buffer if necessary.
        if (bbuf == null
                || bbuf.getWidth(null) < w
                || bbuf.getHeight(null) < h) {
            bbuf = createImage(w, h);
            bbufG = bbuf.getGraphics();
        }

        // Needed to workaround a bug in Java 1.1.2.
        bbufG.setClip(0, 0, w, h);

        // Paint all of the lightweight's children.
        super.paint(bbufG);

        // Show the double-buffer.
        g.drawImage(bbuf, 0, 0, this);
    }

    public static void main(String[] args) {
        new Main();
    }
}
```

```
class FakeButton extends Component implements Runnable {
    String label;
    boolean blink = false;
    boolean blinkOn;

    FakeButton(String l) {
        label = l;

        // Listen for mouse clicks.
        addMouseListener(new MouseEventHandler());

        // Start the blinking thread.
        (new Thread(this)).start();
    }

    public void paint(Graphics g) {
        FontMetrics fm = g.getFontMetrics();
        int w = getSize().width;
        int h = getSize().height;

        g.setColor(Color.black);
        g.fillRect(0, 0, w, h);

        // Paint component text.
        if (blink && blinkOn) {
            g.setColor(Color.red);
        } else {
            g.setColor(Color.white);
        }

        // Paint label and outline.
        g.drawString(label, (w-fm.stringWidth(label))/2,
            (h-fm.getHeight())/2 + fm.getAscent());
        g.drawRect(0, 0, w-1, h-1);
    }

    class MouseEventHandler extends MouseAdapter {
        public void mouseEntered(MouseEvent evt) {
            // Start blinking.
            blink = true;
            repaint();
        }
        public void mouseExited(MouseEvent evt) {
            // Stop blinking.
            blink = false;
            repaint();
        }
    }

    public void run() {
        while (true) {
            try {
                blinkOn = !blinkOn;
                if (blink) {
                    repaint();
                }
                Thread.sleep(250);
            } catch (Exception e) {
            }
        }
    }
```

A
B

D
E
F
G
H
I
J
K
L
M
N
O
P
Q
R
S
T
U
V
W
X
Y
Z

449

```
        }
    }
```

paintComponents( )

PURPOSE	Paints the container's components on a graphics context.
SYNTAX	`public void paintComponents(Graphics gc)`

This method is called by the AWT system in response to a request to paint this container's components and all of their descendants. It can either paint directly on `gc` or call each of the component's `paintAll()` methods. The main difference between this method and `paintAll()` is that this method does not cause this container `paint()` method to be invoked.

The default implementation of this method calls `Component.paintAll()` on all of this container's components.

Note: In Java 1.1.2, this method does not work.

PARAMETERS	
gc	The non-`null` graphics context on which to paint the container's children.
SEE ALSO	`Component.paint()`, `Component.paintAll()`, `paint()`.
EXAMPLE	See `Component.paintAll()`.

paramString( )

PURPOSE	Generates a string representing the container's state.
SYNTAX	`protected String paramString()`
DESCRIPTION	The returned string includes the container's layout manager. A subclass of this class should override this method and return a concatenation of its state with the results of `super.paramString()`. This method is called by the `toString()` method and is typically used for debugging.
RETURNS	A non-`null` string representing the container's state.
OVERRIDES	`Component.paramString()`.
SEE ALSO	`Component.toString()`, `java.lang.Object.toString()`.
EXAMPLE	See `Component.paramString()`.

preferredSize( )　　　　　　　　　　　　　　　　　　　　*DEPRECATED*

PURPOSE	Replaced by `getPreferredSize()`.
SYNTAX	`public Dimension preferredSize()`
RETURNS	A non-`null` dimension object containing the container's preferred size.
OVERRIDES	`Component.preferredSize()`.
DEPRECATION	Replace the usage of this deprecated method, as in

```
  Dimension dim = container.preferredSize();
```
with
```
  Dimension dim = container.getPreferredSize();
```

print( )

PURPOSE	Prints this container's components on a graphics context.
SYNTAX	`public void print(Graphics gc)`
DESCRIPTION	This method prints this container onto the graphics context `gc`. This method, if not overridden, looks for any lightweight children that intersect `gc`'s clipping area. If any are found, their `print()` methods are called.
	If this method is overridden, it should call `super.paint()` after painting itself to ensure its lightweight descendants are painted properly.
PARAMETERS	
gc	The non-`null` graphics context on which to print.
OVERRIDES	`Component.print()`.
SEE ALSO	`paint()`, `printComponents()`.
EXAMPLE	See the `PrintJob` class example.

printComponents( )

PURPOSE	Prints this container's components on a graphics context.
SYNTAX	`public void printComponents(Graphics gc)`
	This method is called by the AWT system in response to a request to print this container's components and all of their descendants. This method can either print directly on `gc` or call each of the component's `printAll()` methods. The main difference between this method and `printAll()` is that this method does not cause this container's `print()` method to be invoked.

The default implementation of this method calls `Component.printAll()` on all of this container's components.

PARAMETERS

gc   The non-null graphics context on which to print the container's components.

SEE ALSO   `Component.print()`, `Component.printAll()`.

EXAMPLE   See `Component.paintAll()`.

processContainerEvent( )

PURPOSE   Processes a container event enabled for this container.

SYNTAX   `protected void processContainerEvent(ContainerEvent evt)`

DESCRIPTION Container events are fired when a component is added or removed from a container. See `ContainerEvent` for more details. This method processes container events for this container by calling any registered `ContainerListener`. This method is invoked only if container events have been enabled for this container. This can happen either when a container listener is added to this container or when container events are explicitly enabled via the use of `Component.enableEvents()`.

Typically, a container controls how its container events are processed by adding or removing container listeners. It overrides `processContainerEvent()` only if it needs to do processing in addition to that performed by the registered listeners.

When a container does override `processContainerEvent()`, it should call `super.processContainerEvent()` to perform the processing intended by its base class (such as dispatching the listeners).

PARAMETERS

evt   The non-null container event.

SEE ALSO   `addContainerListener()`, `Component.enableEvents()`, `Component.disableEvents()`, `java.awt.event.ContainerAdapter`, `java.awt.event.ContainerEvent`, `java.awt.event.ContainerListener`, `processEvent()`, `removeContainerListener()`.

EXAMPLE   See `AWTEventMulticaster.componentAdded()`.

processEvent( )

PURPOSE   Processes an event enabled for this container.

SYNTAX   `protected void processEvent(AWTEvent evt)`

DESCRIPTION   This method extends `Component.processEvent()` by adding support for `ContainerEvent`.

When a container does override `processEvent()`, it should call `super.processEvent()` to perform the processing intended by its base class (such as dispatching the listeners).

PARAMETERS

evt   The non-`null` event.

OVERRIDES   `Component.processEvent()`.

SEE ALSO   `addContainerListener()`, `Component.enableEvents()`, `Component.disableEvents()`, `java.awt.event.ContainerEvent`, `java.awt.event.ContainerListener`, `processMouseEvent()`, `processContainerEvent()`, `removeContainerListener()`.

EXAMPLE   See Component's class example.

remove()

PURPOSE   Removes a component from the container.

SYNTAX   `public void remove(Component comp)`
              `public void remove(int pos)`

DESCRIPTION   When a component is removed, its peer is first destroyed and then removed from the container's list of components. Also, the layout manager is notified of the removal by way of the `LayoutManager.removeLayoutComponent()` method. The container and all of its ancestors are also invalidated. A container event is fired, and if container events have been enabled for this container, any container listeners for this container are notified.

PARAMETERS

comp   The non-`null` component to be removed.
pos   The zero-based index of the component to remove.

SEE ALSO   `add()`, `java.awt.event.ContainerEvent`, `LayoutManager.removeLayoutComponent()`, `removeAll()`.

EXAMPLE   See the class example.

removeAll()

PURPOSE   Removes all of the components in this container.

SYNTAX   `public void removeAll()`

A
B

D
E
F
G
H
I
J
K
L
M
N
O
P
Q
R
S
T
U
V
W
X
Y
Z

DESCRIPTION   This method removes all of the components in the container. It is equivalent to calling `remove()` on each component. The layout manager is notified of the removal of each by way of the `LayoutManager.removeLayoutComponent()` method. The container and all of its ancestors are also invalidated.

SEE ALSO   `add()`, `LayoutManager.removeLayoutComponent()`, `remove()`.

EXAMPLE   See the class example.

removeContainerListener( )

PURPOSE   Removes a listener from receiving this component's container events.

SYNTAX   `public void removeContainerListener(ContainerListener listener)`

DESCRIPTION   Container events are fired when a component is added or removed from a container. See `ContainerEvent` for more details. After this method is called, the container listener `listener` will no longer receive container events from this container. If `listener` is `null`, this method does nothing.

PARAMETERS
listener   The possibly `null` container listener to remove.

SEE ALSO   `addContainerListener()`, `java.awt.event.ContainerAdapter`, `java.awt.event.ContainerEvent`, `java.awt.event.ContainerListener`.

EXAMPLE   See `removeActionListener()` in `MenuItem.dispatchEvents()`.

removeNotify( )

PURPOSE   Destroys the peer hierarchy of this container and all of its children.

SYNTAX   `public void removeNotify()`

DESCRIPTION   This method destroys the peer hierarchy of this container and all of its children, if any. This method should never be called directly. It is normally called by the component's container.

OVERRIDES   `Component.removeNotify()`.

SEE ALSO   `Component`, `Toolkit`.

setLayout( )

PURPOSE   Sets the layout manager for this container.

SYNTAX   `public void setLayout(LayoutManager mgr)`

DESCRIPTION   This method sets mgr to be this container's layout manager. mgr can be null. This means the components in the container will not be moved or resized.

PARAMETERS

mgr   The layout manager to set for the container.

SEE ALSO   getLayout(), layout().

EXAMPLE   This example creates a row of buttons and a panel with a card layout manager. See Figure 108. Clicking a button causes the card layout panel to display the component identified by the button. For example, clicking the TextArea button displays a TextArea component.

FIGURE 108: Container.setLayout()

```java
import java.awt.*;
import java.awt.event.*;

class Main extends Frame implements ActionListener {
    Panel flow = new Panel();
    Panel card = new Panel();

    Main() {
        super("setLayout Example");

        flow.setLayout(new FlowLayout());
        card.setLayout(new CardLayout());

        addComp("Button", new Button("Button"));
        addComp("TextArea", new TextArea("TextArea"));
        addComp("List", new List());

        add(flow, BorderLayout.NORTH);
        add(card, BorderLayout.CENTER);

        setSize(200, 200);
        show();
    }

    void addComp(String label, Component c) {
        Button b = new Button(label);
        card.add(c, label);
        flow.add(b);
        b.addActionListener(this);
    }

    public void actionPerformed(ActionEvent evt) {
        String arg = evt.getActionCommand();
        CardLayout l = (CardLayout)card.getLayout();
        l.show(card, arg);
    }
```

A
B
C
D
E
F
G
H
I
J
K
L
M
N
O
P
Q
R
S
T
U
V
W
X
Y
Z

455

```
        static public void main(String[] args) {
            new Main();
        }
    }
```

validate()

PURPOSE   Validates this container by again laying out its components.

SYNTAX   `public void validate()`

DESCRIPTION If the container is invalid, this method validates it by calling the `doLayout()` method; otherwise, the method call is ignored. After the container is validated, this method calls `validate()` on each of the container's components. However, note that for efficiency, the `validate()` method is not invoked on valid children. So if the valid child contains an invalid child, the invalid child will not be validated.

OVERRIDES   `Component.validate()`.

SEE ALSO   `doLayout()`, `invalidate()`, `LayoutManager`, `validateTree()`.

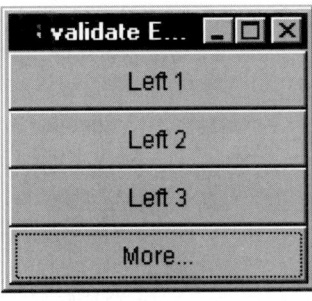 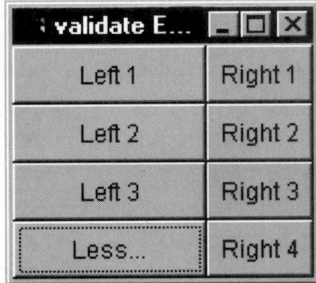

FIGURE 109: `Container.validate()`.

EXAMPLE   This example demonstrates how to dynamically show and hide a set of components in a dialog box. When a component is shown or hidden in a container, the container is automatically invalidated. However, you must explicitly validate the container to update the layout. See Figure 109.

```
import java.awt.*;
import java.awt.event.*;

class Main extends Frame implements ActionListener {
    Panel extraButtons = new Panel(new GridLayout(0, 1));
    Main() {
        super("validate Example");
        Panel p = new Panel(new GridLayout(0, 1));

        p.add(new Button("Left 1"));
```

```
        p.add(new Button("Left 2"));
        p.add(new Button("Left 3"));
        Button b;
        p.add(b = new Button("More..."));
        b.addActionListener(this);
        add(p, BorderLayout.CENTER);

        extraButtons.add(new Button("Right 1"));
        extraButtons.add(new Button("Right 2"));
        extraButtons.add(new Button("Right 3"));
        extraButtons.add(new Button("Right 4"));
        extraButtons.setVisible(false);
        add(extraButtons, BorderLayout.EAST);

        setSize(200, 200);
        show();
    }

    public void actionPerformed(ActionEvent evt) {
        String arg = evt.getActionCommand();
        Button button = (Button)evt.getSource();
        if ("More...".equals(arg)) {
            button.setLabel("Less...");
            extraButtons.setVisible(true);
            //invalidate();    - not necessary
            validate();
        } else if ("Less...".equals(arg)) {
            button.setLabel("More...");
            extraButtons.setVisible(false);
            //invalidate();    - not necessary
            validate();
        }
    }

    public static void main(String[] args) {
        new Main();
    }
}
```

A
B
C
D
E
F
G
H
I
J
K
L
M
N
O
P
Q
R
S
T
U
V
W
X
Y
Z

validateTree()

PURPOSE   Called by validate() to again lay out the components in this container.

SYNTAX   protected void validateTree()

DESCRIPTION   This method is used by validate() to recursively lay out again this container's components and their descendants. Any locking necessary should be performed by the caller of validateTree() before invoking validateTree(). A method that needs to perform special processing when validating components in a tree should override this method (instead of validate()).

SEE ALSO   doLayout(), invalidate(), LayoutManager, validate().

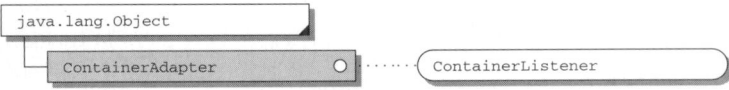

Syntax

public abstract class ContainerAdapter implements ContainerListener

Description

The container adapter is a container listener in which all callback methods are empty implementations. The purpose of the container adapter is to make it more convenient for an object to listen for container events. In particular, by using the container adapter, you need to implement only those callback methods in which you are interested. Without the container adapter, you must implement all callback methods, even if the method is empty.

To use a container adapter, you create a subclass of ContainerAdapter and override the desired callback methods. You then create an instance of the container adapter subclass and call the container's addContainerListener() method with it. The container adapter subclass is typically an inner class.

MEMBER SUMMARY	
Container Event Callback Methods	
componentAdded()	Called after a component has been added to a container.
componentRemoved()	Called after a component has been removed from a container.

See Also

ContainerEvent, ContainerListener, java.awt.AWTEventMulticaster,
java.awt.Container.addContainerListener(), java.util.EventListener.

Example

See the ContainerEvent class example for a simple usage of a container adapter.

componentAdded()

PURPOSE   Called after a component has been added to a container.

SYNTAX   `public void componentAdded(ContainerEvent evt)`

DESCRIPTION   This method is called after a component has been added to the source container. The added component can be retrieved by calling `evt.getChild()`.

                This method, by default, has an empty implementation.

PARAMETERS

  `evt`   The non-`null` container event.

EXAMPLE   See the `ContainerEvent` class example.

componentRemoved()

PURPOSE   Called after a component has been removed from a container.

SYNTAX   `public void componentRemoved(ContainerEvent evt)`

DESCRIPTION   This method is called after a component has been removed from the source container. The removed component can be retrieved by calling `evt.getChild()`.

                This method, by default, has an empty implementation.

PARAMETERS

  `evt`   The non-`null` container event.

EXAMPLE   See the `ContainerEvent` class example.

A
B
C
D
E
F
G
H
I
J
K
L
M
N
O
P
Q
R
S
T
U
V
W
X
Y
Z

ContainerEvent

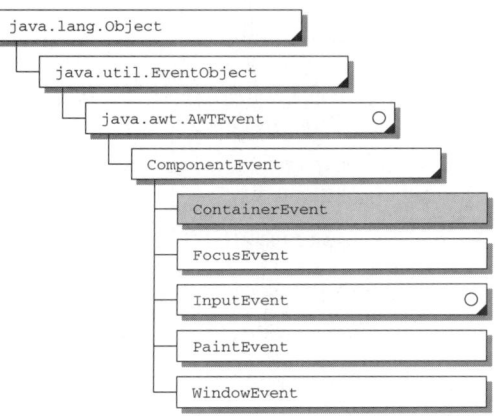

```
java.lang.Object
    java.util.EventObject
        java.awt.AWTEvent          ○
            ComponentEvent
                ContainerEvent
                FocusEvent
                InputEvent          ○
                PaintEvent
                WindowEvent
```

Syntax

```
public class ContainerEvent extends ComponentEvent
```

Description

Container events are fired by a container (see `Container`) whenever a component is added or removed from the container. For more general information about events, see `AWTEvent`.

Listening for Container Events

To listen for container events from a container, the listener must implement the `ComponentListener` interface. After that, the listener must be registered with the object. It becomes registered by calling the object's `addContainerListener()` method.

An alternative, and possibly more convenient, way of receiving container events is to use a container adapter. See `ContainerAdapter` for more details.

Like most events, a container event is delivered to its listeners after the operation has taken place.

Container Event Flow

Figure 110 shows how container events typically flow through the system. First, the event is fired by some container peer in response to some user gesture. This event is posted on the event queue (see `EventQueue`). When the event makes its way to the front of the queue, it is given to the component via its `dispatchEvent()` method. The main purpose of this method is to discard the event if the container event type is not enabled or if there are no container event listeners. Otherwise, `dispatchEvent()` calls `processEvent()`, which in turn calls different methods depending on the event type. Since this is a container event, `processContainerEvent()` is called. The main purpose of this method is to notify the container event listeners.

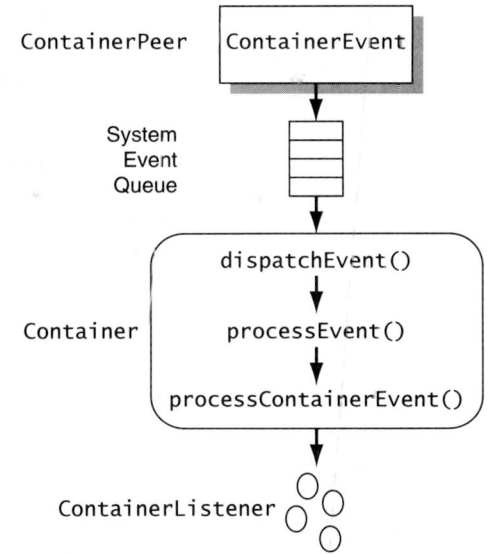

FIGURE 110: Container Event Flow.

A component can override `processContainerEvent()` to process container events before they are delivered to its listeners. The overridden method should call `super.processContainerEvent()` to ensure that events are dispatched to the container's listeners.

MEMBER SUMMARY	
Constructor	
ContainerEvent()	Constructs a ContainerEvent instance.
Property Methods	
getChild()	Retrieves the component that was added or removed.
getContainer()	Retrieves the event's source component.
Component Event Constants	
COMPONENT_ADDED	Indicates that a component has been added.
COMPONENT_REMOVED	Indicates that a component has been removed.
CONTAINER_FIRST	Constant specifying the first id in the range of container event ids.
CONTAINER_LAST	Constant specifying the last id in the range of container event ids.
Debugging Method	
paramString()	Generates a string representing the container event's state.

See Also

ContainerAdapter, ContainerListener, java.awt.AWTEvent.

Example

This example demonstrates how to listen to and handle container events. The example creates a frame with a button (called "New Button") that adds new buttons to the frame. The new buttons (called "Remove Me"), when clicked, remove themselves from the frame. See Figure 111.

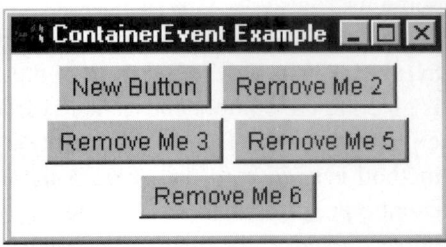

FIGURE 111:   ContainerEvent

The frame listens for container events on itself, and whenever a button is added or removed, the frame gets a container event. In response to the event, the specifics of the event are printed. Also printed is the child that was added or removed and the new number of children in the container.

```
import java.awt.*;
import java.awt.event.*;

class Main extends Frame implements ContainerListener, ActionListener {
    Main() {
        super("ContainerEvent Example");
        Button b = new Button("New Button");

        // Listen for events.
        b.addActionListener(this);
        addContainerListener(this);

        // Layout component
        setLayout(new FlowLayout());
        add(b);

        setSize(100, 100);
        show();
    }

    // Container event handler methods
    public void componentAdded(ContainerEvent evt) {
        System.out.println("COMPONENT_ADDED: "+evt.getChild());
        System.out.println("  There are now "
            +evt.getContainer().getComponentCount()+" children.");
    }
    public void componentRemoved(ContainerEvent evt) {
        System.out.println("COMPONENT_REMOVED: "+evt.getChild());
        System.out.println("  There are now "
            +evt.getContainer().getComponentCount()+" children.");
    }

    // This increasing number is used in naming the new buttons.
    int count;
```

```
    // Action event handler method
    public void actionPerformed(ActionEvent evt) {
        if (evt.getActionCommand().equals("New Button")) {
            // Add a button.
            Button b = new Button("Remove Me "+(count++));

            // Listen for events.
            b.addActionListener(this);
            add(b);
            validate(); // relayout container
        } else if (evt.getActionCommand().startsWith("Remove Me ")) {
            // Remove a button.
            remove((Component)evt.getSource());
            validate(); // relayout container
        }
    }

    public static void main(String args[]) {
        new Main();
    }
}
```

A
B
C
D
E
F
G
H
I
J
K
L
M
N
O
P
Q
R
S
T
U
V
W
X
Y
Z

COMPONENT_ADDED

PURPOSE   Event id indicating that a component has been added.

SYNTAX   `public static final int COMPONENT_ADDED`

DESCRIPTION   An event with this id (value 300) is fired by a container after a component has been added to it. The added component can be retrieved by calling `get-Child()`.

SEE ALSO   `getChild()`, `java.awt.Container.add()`.

EXAMPLE   See the class example.

COMPONENT_REMOVED

PURPOSE   Event id indicating that a component has been removed.

SYNTAX   `public static final int COMPONENT_REMOVED`

DESCRIPTION   An event with this id (value 301) is fired by a container after a component has been removed from it. The removed component can be retrieved by calling `getChild()`.

SEE ALSO   `getChild()`, `java.awt.Container.remove()`.

EXAMPLE   See the class example.

463

CONTAINER_FIRST

PURPOSE	Constant specifying the first id in the range of container event ids.
SYNTAX	`public static final int CONTAINER_FIRST`
DESCRIPTION	All component event ids must be greater than or equal to `CONTAINER_FIRST` (value 300).
SEE ALSO	`CONTAINER_LAST`.
EXAMPLE	See `java.awt.Component.processEvent()`.

CONTAINER_LAST

PURPOSE	Constant specifying the last id in the range of container event ids.
SYNTAX	`public static final int CONTAINER_LAST`
DESCRIPTION	All container event ids must be less than or equal to `CONTAINER_LAST` (value 301).
SEE ALSO	`CONTAINER_FIRST`.
EXAMPLE	See `java.awt.Component.processEvent()`.

ContainerEvent()

PURPOSE	Constructs a `ContainerEvent` instance.
SYNTAX	`public ContainerEvent(Component source, int id, Component child)`
DESCRIPTION	This constructor creates a new container event instance with `source` as the container firing this event.
	After the container event is created, the source container can distribute the event to its listeners by calling the container event-related methods in `AWTEventMulticaster`. If the event is not created by `source`, the creator can deliver the event to the source container either by posting the event to the event queue (see `EventQueue.postEvent()`) or by calling the source container's `Component.dispatchEvent()` method directly.

PARAMETERS

`child`	The non-null component being added or removed.
`id`	One of the container event ids.
`source`	The non-null container that is firing this container event.

`getChild(), java.awt.AWTEvent.getID(),`
`java.awt.AWTEventMulticaster, java.awt.EventQueue,`
`java.util.EventObject.getSource().`

A
B
C
getChild()
D
PURPOSE	Retrieves the component that was added or removed.
SYNTAX	`public Component getChild()`
RETURNS	The non-`null` component that was added or removed from the container.
EXAMPLE	See the class example.

D
E
F
G
getContainer()
H
PURPOSE	Retrieves the event's source component.
SYNTAX	`public Container getContainer()`
DESCRIPTION	This method returns the component that fired the container event.
RETURNS	The non-`null` container that fired this event.
EXAMPLE	See the class example.

I
J
K
L
M
N
O
paramString()
P
PURPOSE	Generates a string representing the container event's state.
SYNTAX	`public String paramString()`
DESCRIPTION	The returned string contains the name of the container event and the name of the child that was added or removed. A subclass of this class should override this method and return a concatenation of its state with the results of `super.paramString()`. This method is called by the `AWTEvent.toString()` method and is typically used for debugging.
RETURNS	A non-`null` string representing the container event's state.
OVERRIDES	`java.awt.AWTEvent.paramString()`.
SEE ALSO	`java.awt.AWTEvent.toString(), java.lang.Object.toString().`
EXAMPLE	See the `java.awt.AWTEvent` class example.

Q
R
S
T
U
V
W
X
Y
Z

ContainerListener

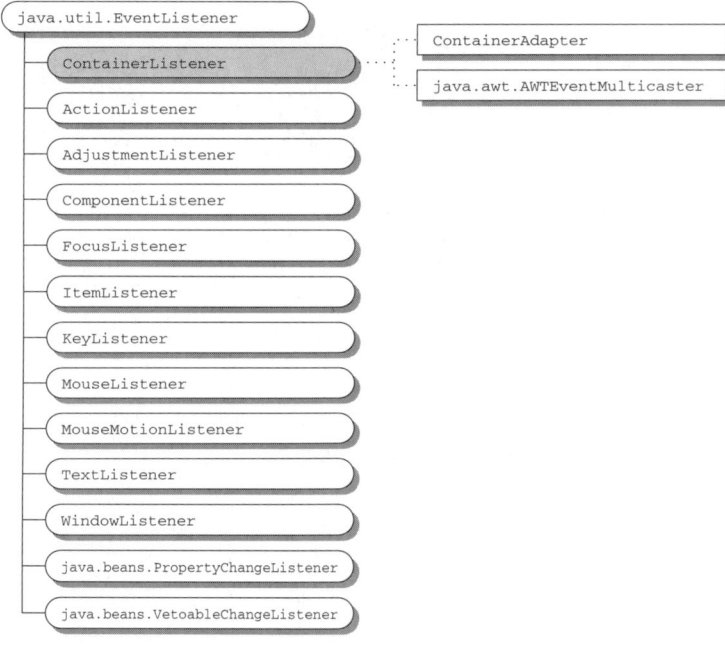

Syntax

```
public interface ContainerListener extends EventListener
```

Description

When an object (listener) wishes to receive container events from a container (the source container), two things must be done:

1. The listener must implement this interface and all the methods required by this interface.
2. The listener must be registered with the source container. It becomes registered by making a call to the source container's addContainerListener() method.

For information about container events, see ContainerEvent.

MEMBER SUMMARY	
Container Event Callback Methods	
componentAdded()	Called when a component has been added to a container.
componentRemoved()	Called when a component has been removed from a container.

See Also

ContainerAdapter, ContainerEvent, java.awt.AWTEventMulticaster,
java.awt.Container.addContainerListener(), java.util.EventListener.

Example

See the ContainerEvent class example.

componentAdded()

PURPOSE	Called when a component has been added to a container.
SYNTAX	public void componentAdded(ContainerEvent evt)
DESCRIPTION	This method is called after a component has been added to the source container. The added component can be retrieved by calling evt.getChild().
PARAMETERS	
evt	The non-null container event.
EXAMPLE	See the ContainerEvent class example.

componentRemoved()

PURPOSE	Called when a component has been removed from a container.
SYNTAX	public void componentRemoved(ContainerEvent evt)
DESCRIPTION	This method is called after a component has been removed from the source container. The removed component can be retrieved by calling evt.getChild().
PARAMETERS	
evt	The non-null container event.
EXAMPLE	See the ContainerEvent class example.

A
B
C
D
E
F
G
H
I
J
K
L
M
N
O
P
Q
R
S
T
U
V
W
X
Y
Z

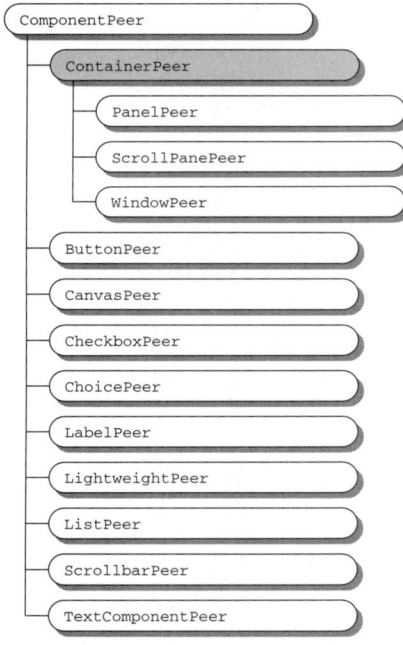

Syntax

```
public interface ContainerPeer extends ComponentPeer
```

Description

The container component (see the `Container` class) in the AWT uses the platform's native implementation of a container. So that the AWT container behaves the same on all platforms, the container is assigned a *peer*, whose task is to translate the behavior of the platform's native container to the behavior of the AWT container.

AWT programmers normally do not directly use peer classes and interfaces. Instead, they deal with AWT components in the `java.awt` package. These in turn automatically manage their peers. Only someone who is porting the AWT to another platform should be concerned with the peer classes and interfaces. Consequently, most peer documentation refers to `java.awt` counterparts.

See `Component` and `Toolkit` for additional information about component peers.

MEMBER SUMMARY	
Peer Methods	
beginValidate()	Signifies the start of validation of components in the container.
endValidate()	Signifies the end of validation of components in the container.
getInsets()	Retrieves the container's insets.
Deprecated Method	
insets()	Replaced by getInsets().

See Also

java.awt.Component, java.awt.Container, java.awt.Toolkit.

beginValidate( )

PURPOSE	Signifies the start of validation of components in the container.
SYNTAX	void beginValidate()
SEE ALSO	java.awt.Container.validate().

endValidate( )

PURPOSE	Signifies the end of validation of components in the container.
SYNTAX	void endValidate()
SEE ALSO	java.awt.Container.validate().

getInsets( )

PURPOSE	Retrieves the container's insets.
SYNTAX	Insets getInsets()
RETURNS	A new non-null instance of the container's insets.
SEE ALSO	java.awt.Container.getInsets(), java.awt.Insets.

insets( )   *DEPRECATED*

PURPOSE   Replaced by `getInsets()`.

SYNTAX   `Insets insets()`

RETURNS   A new non-`null` instance of the container's insets.

DEPRECATION Replace the usage of this deprecated method, as in
```
Insets insets = peer.insets();
```
with
```
Insets insets = peer.getInsets();
```

CropImageFilter

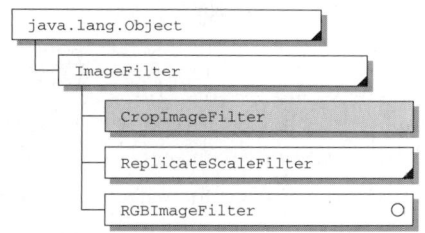

```
java.lang.Object

    ImageFilter

        CropImageFilter

        ReplicateScaleFilter

        RGBImageFilter          ○
```

Syntax
```
public class CropImageFilter extends ImageFilter
```

Description
This class extends the basic `ImageFilter` class to extract a given rectangular region of an existing `Image` and to provide a source for a new image that contains just the extracted region. It is meant to be used in conjunction with a `FilteredImageSource` object to produce cropped versions of existing images.

Here is how the crop image filter is typically used:

```
Image copySubImage(Image image, Rectangle r) {
    CropImageFilter filter = new CropImageFilter(r.x, r.y, r.width, r.height);
    return getToolkit().createImage(new FilteredImageSource(image.getSource(),
filter));
}
```

MEMBER SUMMARY	
Constructor Method	
CropImageFilter()	Constructs a new `CropImageFilter` instance.
Image Consumer Methods	
setDimensions()	Called by the image producer to deliver the dimensions of the source image.
setPixels()	Called by the image producer to deliver pixels to the image consumer.
setProperties()	Called by the image producer to deliver the properties for the source image.

See Also

`FilteredImageSource, ImageFilter, java.awt.Toolkit.createImage().`

Example

This example implements a small application for copying areas in an image (see Figure 112). The application reads in an image and allows you to select rectangular areas in the image. To make a selection, you click and hold the left mouse button and drag downward and to the right. The pixels in the selected area are painted in XOR mode (see `Graphics.setXOR-Mode()`).

FIGURE 112: `CropImageFilter.`

To make a copy of the selected area, press the 'c' key. The copy is created using the `CropImageFilter` image filter. You can then move the copy around the image just by moving the cursor around. To paint the copy on the image, click the mouse. To delete either the selected area or the copy, press any key.

When moving the copy around the image, you will notice a lot of flickering. You can eliminate the flickering by using the double-buffering techniques demonstrated in the `Component.createImage()` example.

```java
import java.awt.*;
import java.awt.image.*;
import java.awt.event.*;

class Main extends Frame {
    Main(String filename) {
        super("CropImage Example");
        try {
            Image fileImage = getToolkit().getImage(filename);

            // Use a media tracker object to wait until all the pixels
            // have been retrieved.
            MediaTracker tracker = new MediaTracker(this);
            tracker.addImage(fileImage, 0);
            tracker.waitForID(0);

            // Now copy the retrieved image to an offscreen image.
            addNotify();    // otherwise the following code will fail.
            Image image = createImage(fileImage.getWidth(this),
                                      fileImage.getHeight(this));
            Graphics g = image.getGraphics();
            g.drawImage(fileImage, 0, 0, this);
            g.dispose();

            add(new ImageCanvas(image), BorderLayout.CENTER);
        } catch (Exception e) {
            e.printStackTrace();
        }
        setSize(300, 300);
        show();
    }
```

```
        static public void main(String[] args) {
            if (args.length == 1) {
                new Main(args[0]);
            } else {
                System.err.println("usage: java Main <image file>");
            }
        }
    }

class ImageCanvas extends Canvas {
    Image image;
    Rectangle selected = new Rectangle();
    Image cropImage;
    Rectangle cropImageRect = new Rectangle();

    ImageCanvas(Image image) {
        this.image = image;

        // Add listeners for mouse and key events
        addMouseListener(new MouseEventHandler());
        addMouseMotionListener(new MouseMotionEventHandler());
        addKeyListener(new KeyEventHandler());
    }

    public void update(Graphics g) {
        paint(g);
    }

    public void paint(Graphics g) {
    g.setClip(0, 0, image.getWidth(null), image.getHeight(null));
        g.drawImage(image, 0, 0, this);
        if (cropImage != null) {
            g.drawImage(cropImage, cropImageRect.x, cropImageRect.y, this);
        } else if (!selected.isEmpty()) {
            g.setXORMode(getBackground());
            g.fillRect(selected.x, selected.y,
                        selected.width, selected.height);
            g.setPaintMode();
        }
    }

    // Convenience method.
    void repaintRect(Rectangle r) {
        repaint(r.x, r.y, r.width, r.height);
    }

    // Event handlers
    class MouseEventHandler extends MouseAdapter {
        public void mousePressed(MouseEvent evt) {
            if (cropImage != null) {
                // Add cropImage to main image.
                Graphics g = image.getGraphics();
                g.drawImage(cropImage, cropImageRect.x, cropImageRect.y,
                            ImageCanvas.this);
                g.dispose();
                cropImage = null;
            }
            repaintRect(selected);
            selected.setLocation(evt.getX(), evt.getY());
```

```
                    repaintRect(selected);
                }

                public void mouseReleased(MouseEvent evt) {
                    repaintRect(selected);
                    selected.width = Math.max(0, evt.getX() - selected.x);
                    selected.height = Math.max(0, evt.getY() - selected.y);
                    repaintRect(selected);
                }
            }

            class MouseMotionEventHandler extends MouseMotionAdapter {
                public void mouseDragged(MouseEvent evt) {
                    repaintRect(selected);
                    selected.width = Math.max(0, evt.getX() - selected.x);
                    selected.height = Math.max(0, evt.getY() - selected.y);
                    repaintRect(selected);
                }

                public void mouseMoved(MouseEvent evt) {
                    if (cropImage != null) {
                        // Move the cropped image around.
                        repaintRect(cropImageRect);
                        cropImageRect.setLocation(evt.getX(), evt.getY());
                        repaintRect(cropImageRect);
                    }
                }
            }

            class KeyEventHandler extends KeyAdapter {
                public void keyPressed(KeyEvent evt) {
                    char key = evt.getKeyChar();
                    if (key == 'c') {
                        if (!selected.isEmpty()) {
                            // Create crop image using a CropImageFilter.
                            CropImageFilter imgf =
                                new CropImageFilter(selected.x, selected.y,
                                                selected.width, selected.height);
                            ImageProducer ip = image.getSource();
                            ip = new FilteredImageSource(ip, imgf);
                            cropImage = getToolkit().createImage(ip);
                            cropImageRect = new Rectangle(selected.x, selected.y,
                                                        selected.width,
                                                        selected.height);
                        }
                    } else if (cropImage != null) {
                        repaintRect(cropImageRect);
                        cropImage = null;
                    }
                    // Delete the selection.
                    repaintRect(selected);
                    selected.width = selected.height = 0;
                }
            }
        }
    }
```

CropImageFilter()

PURPOSE	Constructs a new CropImageFilter instance.
SYNTAX	public CropImageFilter(int x, int y, int width, int height)
DESCRIPTION	The new crop image filter extracts the pixels in the rectangular region specified by x, y, width, and height of the source image. It will translate the locations of the extracted pixels to the image consumer such that the top-left pixel will have the coordinate (0, 0).
PARAMETERS	
height	The height of the rectangle in pixels.
width	The width of the rectangle in pixels.
x	The *x*-coordinate of the left edge of the rectangle in pixels.
y	The *y*-coordinate of the top of the rectangle in pixels.
EXAMPLE	See the class example.

setDimensions()

PURPOSE	Called by the image producer to deliver the dimensions of the source image.
SYNTAX	public void setDimensions(int width, int height)
DESCRIPTION	The CropImageFilter class implements this method as part of the Image-Consumer interface. This method should not be used.
PARAMETERS	
height	The height of the image in pixels.
width	The width of the image in pixels.
OVERRIDES	ImageFilter.setDimensions().
SEE ALSO	ImageConsumer.setDimensions().

setPixels()

PURPOSE	Called by the image producer to deliver pixels to the image consumer.
SYNTAX	public void setPixels(int x, int y, int w, int h, ColorModel model, byte[] pixels, int offset, int scansize) public void setPixels(int x, int y, int w, int h, ColorModel model, int[] pixels, int offset, int scansize)
DESCRIPTION	The CropImageFilter class implements this method as part of the Image-Consumer interface. This method should not be used.

PARAMETERS

h	The height of the rectangle in which the pixels are destined.
model	The non-null color model used to translate the pixel values.
offset	The index of the first pixel in the pixel array.
pixels	The non-null array of pixel values.
scansize	The width to use when extracting pixels from `pixels`.
w	The width of the rectangle in which the pixels are destined.
x	The x-coordinate of the rectangle in which the pixels are destined.
y	The y-coordinate of the rectangle in which the pixels are destined.

OVERRIDES   `ImageFilter.setPixels()`.

SEE ALSO   `ImageConsumer.setPixels()`.

setProperties( )

PURPOSE   Called by the image producer to deliver the properties for the source image.

SYNTAX   `public void setProperties(Hashtable props)`

DESCRIPTION   The `CropImageFilter` class implements this method as part of the `Image-Consumer` interface. The method should not be used.

PARAMETERS

props	A non-null hashtable of properties.

OVERRIDES   `ImageFilter.setProperties()`.

SEE ALSO   `ImageConsumer.setProperties()`.

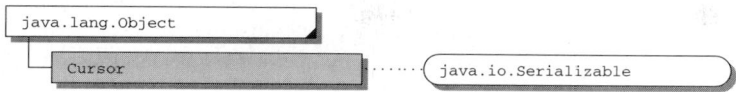

Syntax

`public class Cursor extends Serializable`

Description

A component normally has a default cursor—typically an arrow—when the cursor is moved within the component. This cursor can be changed at any time. Since each component can set its own cursor, the cursor can also change as it is moved from one component to another. The `Cursor` class is used to represent a cursor.

The exact cursor shapes available are platform-dependent. On some platforms, the cursor shapes are also system-configurable. Table 8 shows the cursor shapes for the Windows platform using a default set of system-configured cursors.

CROSSHAIR_CURSOR	N_RESIZE_CURSOR	SW_RESIZE_CURSOR
DEFAULT_CURSOR	NE_RESIZE_CURSOR	TEXT_CURSOR
E_RESIZE_CURSOR	NW_RESIZE_CURSOR	W_RESIZE_CURSOR
HAND_CURSOR	S_RESIZE_CURSOR	WAIT_CURSOR
MOVE_CURSOR	SE_RESIZE_CURSOR	

TABLE 8:   Cursor Shapes for the Windows Platform.

A
B
C
D
E
F
G
H
I
J
K
L
M
N
O
P
Q
R
S
T
U
V
W
X
Y
Z

MEMBER SUMMARY	
Constructor	
Cursor()	Constructs a new Cursor instance.
Cursor Types	
CROSSHAIR_CURSOR	The cursor type specifying a crosshair cursor.
DEFAULT_CURSOR	The cursor type specifying the default cursor.
E_RESIZE_CURSOR	The cursor type specifying a type of resizing cursor.
HAND_CURSOR	The cursor type specifying a hand cursor.
MOVE_CURSOR	The cursor type specifying a moving cursor.
N_RESIZE_CURSOR	The cursor type specifying a type of resizing cursor.
NE_RESIZE_CURSOR	The cursor type specifying a type of resizing cursor.
NW_RESIZE_CURSOR	The cursor type specifying a type of resizing cursor.
S_RESIZE_CURSOR	The cursor type specifying a type of resizing cursor.
SE_RESIZE_CURSOR	The cursor type specifying a type of resizing cursor.
SW_RESIZE_CURSOR	The cursor type specifying a type of resizing cursor.
TEXT_CURSOR	The cursor type specifying a caret cursor.
W_RESIZE_CURSOR	The cursor type specifying a type of resizing cursor.
WAIT_CURSOR	The cursor type specifying an hourglass cursor.
Methods for Retrieving Cursors	
getDefaultCursor()	Retrieves the system default cursor.
getPredefinedCursor()	Retrieves the cursor of a predefined cursor type.
Cursor Type Method	
getType()	Retrieves the cursor type of this cursor.

See Also

Component.getCursor(), Component.setCursor(), java.io.Serializable.

Example

This example creates a list containing the names of all available cursor types. Selecting a cursor name from the list sets that cursor. The program also creates a background thread that simply waits 10 sec, sets the cursor to the default cursor, waits 2 sec, and then restores the cursor to its set value. See Figure 113.

```
import java.awt.*;
import java.awt.event.*;

class Main extends Frame implements Runnable,
ItemListener {
    List l = new List();
    String[] cursors = {
        "DEFAULT_CURSOR",
        "CROSSHAIR_CURSOR",
        "TEXT_CURSOR",
        "WAIT_CURSOR",
        "SW_RESIZE_CURSOR",
        "SE_RESIZE_CURSOR",
        "NW_RESIZE_CURSOR",
        "NE_RESIZE_CURSOR",
        "N_RESIZE_CURSOR",
        "S_RESIZE_CURSOR",
        "W_RESIZE_CURSOR",
        "E_RESIZE_CURSOR",
        "HAND_CURSOR",
        "MOVE_CURSOR",};

    Main() {
        super("setCursor Example");
        for (int i=0; i<cursors.length; i++) {
            l.addItem(cursors[i]);
        }
        add(l, BorderLayout.CENTER);

        // Add item listener to list
        l.addItemListener(this);

        (new Thread(this)).start();
        pack();
        show();
    }

    public void itemStateChanged(ItemEvent evt) {
        setCursor(Cursor.getPredefinedCursor(l.getSelectedIndex()));
    }

    public void run() {
        while (true) {
            try {
                Cursor cursor = getCursor();

                setCursor(Cursor.getDefaultCursor());
                Thread.sleep(2000);
                setCursor(cursor);
                Thread.sleep(10000);
            } catch (Exception e) {
            }
        }
    }

    static public void main(String[] args) {
        new Main();
    }
}
```

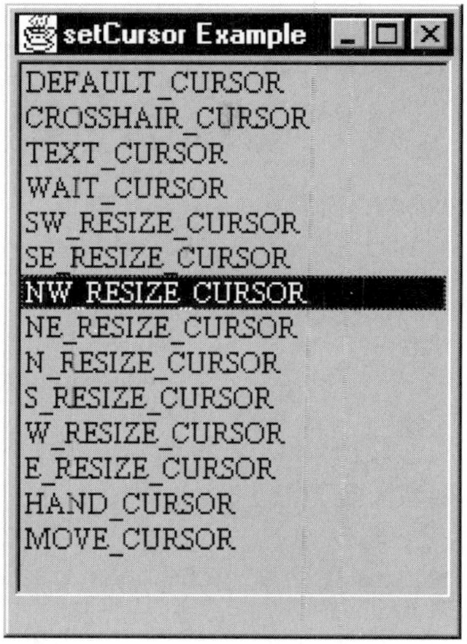

FIGURE 113: Cursor.

A

B

D

E

F

G

H

I

J

K

L

M

N

O

P

Q

R

S

T

U

V

W

X

Y

Z

479

Cursor( )

PURPOSE	Constructs a new instance of `Cursor`.
SYNTAX	`public Cursor(int cursorType)`
DESCRIPTION	This method creates a new instance of `Cursor` for the cursor type `cursorType`. It typically should not be called directly. You should use `getPredefinedCursor()` instead.

PARAMETERS

cursorType   The cursor type. Must be one of the cursor types defined in the `Cursor` class.

EXCEPTIONS

IllegalArgumentException

If `cursorType` is not one of the cursor types defined in the `Cursor` class.

SEE ALSO	`getPredefinedCursor()`.
EXAMPLE	See the class example for a usage of `getPredefinedCursor()`.

CROSSHAIR_CURSOR

PURPOSE	The cursor type specifying a crosshair cursor.
SYNTAX	`public static final int CROSSHAIR_CURSOR`
DESCRIPTION	This cursor type is typically displayed when drawing graphics. Its value is 1.
EXAMPLE	See the class example.

DEFAULT_CURSOR

PURPOSE	The cursor type specifying the default pointer cursor.
SYNTAX	`public static final int DEFAULT_CURSOR`
DESCRIPTION	This cursor type should be displayed when the cursor is not over a special kind of window or if the application is not in any mode. A cursor of this type is returned by `getDefaultCursor()`. Its value is 0.
SEE ALSO	`getDefaultCursor()`.
EXAMPLE	See the class example.

E_RESIZE_CURSOR

PURPOSE	The cursor type specifying a type of resizing cursor.
SYNTAX	`public static final int E_RESIZE_CURSOR`
DESCRIPTION	This cursor type is typically displayed while the user is resizing the eastern border of an object. Its value is 11.
EXAMPLE	See the class example.

getDefaultCursor()

PURPOSE	Retrieves the system's default cursor.
SYNTAX	`public static Cursor  getDefaultCursor()`
DESCRIPTION	This method creates a new instance of `Cursor` for the cursor type `type`. This constructor typically should not be called directly. You should use `getPredefinedCursor()` instead.
PARAMETERS	
`type`	The cursor type. Must be one of the cursor types defined in the `Cursor` class.
EXCEPTIONS	
`IllegalArgumentException`	
	If `type` is not one of the cursor types defined in the `Cursor` class.
SEE ALSO	`getPredefinedCursor().`
EXAMPLE	See the class example.

getPredefinedCursor()

PURPOSE	Retrieves the cursor of a predefined cursor type.
SYNTAX	`public static Cursor  getPredefinedCursor(int cursorType)`
PARAMETERS	
`cursorType`	The cursor type. Must be one of the cursor types defined in the `Cursor` class.
EXCEPTIONS	
`IllegalArgumentException`	
	If `cursorType` is not one of the cursor types defined in the `Cursor` class.
SEE ALSO	`getDefaultCursor().`
EXAMPLE	See the class example.

A
B

D
E
F
G
H
I
J
K
L
M
N
O
P
Q
R
S
T
U
V
W
X
Y
Z

481

getType()

PURPOSE   Retrieves this cursor's cursor type.

SYNTAX   `public int getType()`

RETURNS   This cursor's cursor type. One of DEFAULT_CURSOR, CROSSHAIR_CURSOR, TEXT_CURSOR, WAIT_CURSOR, SW_RESIZE_CURSOR, SE_RESIZE_CURSOR, NW_RESIZE_CURSOR, NE_RESIZE_CURSOR, N_RESIZE_CURSOR, S_RESIZE_CURSOR, W_RESIZE_CURSOR, E_RESIZE_CURSOR, HAND_CURSOR, or MOVE_CURSOR.

SEE ALSO   `Cursor()`, `getPredefinedCursor()`.

EXAMPLE   This example creates a thread that alternately sets the frame's cursor between the crosshair cursor and the wait cursor. When the crosshair cursor is displayed, clicking the mouse draws a black circle. When the wait cursor is displayed, mouse clicks are ignored.

```java
import java.awt.*;
import java.awt.event.*;

class Main extends Frame implements Runnable {
    int curX, curY;

    Main() {
        super("getType Example");
        setSize(200, 200);

        this.addMouseListener(new MouseEventListener());
        show();
        (new Thread(this)).start();
    }

    public void update(Graphics g) {
        g.fillOval(curX, curY, 20, 20);
    }

    public int myCursorType() {
        return getCursor().getType();
    }

    class MouseEventListener extends MouseAdapter {
        public void mousePressed(MouseEvent evt) {
            if (myCursorType() != Cursor.WAIT_CURSOR) {
                curX = evt.getX();
                curY = evt.getY();
                repaint();
            }
        }
    }

    public void run() {
        while (true) {
            try {
                if (myCursorType() == Cursor.WAIT_CURSOR) {
```

```
                setCursor(Cursor.getPredefinedCursor(Cur-
    sor.CROSSHAIR_CURSOR));
                } else {
                    setCursor(Cursor.getPredefinedCursor(Cursor.WAIT_CURSOR));
                }
                Thread.sleep(3000);
            } catch (InterruptedException e) {};
        }
    }

    static public void main(String[] args) {
        new Main();
    }
}
```

A
B
C
D
E
F
G
H
I
J
K
L
M
N
O
P
Q
R
S
T
U
V
W
X
Y
Z

HAND_CURSOR

PURPOSE	The cursor type specifying a hand cursor.
SYNTAX	`public static final int HAND_CURSOR`
DESCRIPTION	This cursor type is typically displayed if the cursor is over an object that can be dragged. Its value is 12.
EXAMPLE	See the class example.

MOVE_CURSOR

PURPOSE	The cursor type specifying a moving cursor.
SYNTAX	`public static final int MOVE_CURSOR`
DESCRIPTION	This cursor type is typically displayed while the user is moving an object. Its value is 13.
EXAMPLE	See the class example.

N_RESIZE_CURSOR

PURPOSE	The cursor type specifying a type of resizing cursor.
SYNTAX	`public static final int N_RESIZE_CURSOR`
DESCRIPTION	This cursor type is typically displayed while the user is resizing the north border of an object. Its value is 8.
EXAMPLE	See the class example.

NE_RESIZE_CURSOR

PURPOSE   The cursor type specifying a type of resizing cursor.

SYNTAX   `public static final int NE_RESIZE_CURSOR`

DESCRIPTION This cursor type is typically displayed while the user is resizing the northeastern border of an object. Its value is 7.

EXAMPLE   See the class example.

NW_RESIZE_CURSOR

PURPOSE   The cursor type specifying a type of resizing cursor.

SYNTAX   `public static final int NW_RESIZE_CURSOR`

DESCRIPTION This cursor type is typically displayed while the user is resizing the northwestern border of an object. Its value is 6.

EXAMPLE   See the class example.

S_RESIZE_CURSOR

PURPOSE   The cursor type specifying a type of resizing cursor.

SYNTAX   `public static final int S_RESIZE_CURSOR`

DESCRIPTION This cursor type is typically displayed while the user is resizing the southern border of an object. Its value is 9.

EXAMPLE   See the class example.

SE_RESIZE_CURSOR

PURPOSE   The cursor type specifying a type of resizing cursor.

SYNTAX   `public static final int SE_RESIZE_CURSOR`

DESCRIPTION This cursor type is typically displayed while the user is resizing the southeastern border of an object. Its value is 5.

EXAMPLE   See the class example.

SW_RESIZE_CURSOR

PURPOSE	The cursor type specifying a type of resizing cursor.
SYNTAX	`public static final int SW_RESIZE_CURSOR`
DESCRIPTION	This cursor type is typically displayed while the user is resizing the south-western border of an object. Its value is 4.
EXAMPLE	See the class example.

TEXT_CURSOR

PURPOSE	The cursor type specifying a caret cursor.
SYNTAX	`public static final int TEXT_CURSOR`
DESCRIPTION	This cursor type is typically displayed while the cursor is over an object and text on the object can be selected. Its value is 2.
EXAMPLE	See the class example.

W_RESIZE_CURSOR

PURPOSE	The cursor type specifying a type of resizing cursor.
SYNTAX	`public static final int W_RESIZE_CURSOR`
DESCRIPTION	This cursor type is typically displayed while the user is resizing the western border of an object. Its value is `10`.
EXAMPLE	See the class example.

WAIT_CURSOR

PURPOSE	The cursor type specifying an hourglass cursor.
SYNTAX	`public static final int WAIT_CURSOR`
DESCRIPTION	This cursor type is typically displayed while the application is busy and cannot respond to user input. Its value is 3.
EXAMPLE	See the class example.

A
B

D
E
F
G
H
I
J
K
L
M
N
O
P
Q
R
S
T
U
V
W
X
Y
Z

485

java.beans
Customizer

Customizer

Syntax

```
public interface Customizer
```

Description

A *customizer* is a specialized user interface for editing the properties of a bean.

When editing a bean, the bean editor presents to the user one property editor for each editable bean property. The set of property editors is called a *property sheet*. The bean editor provides default property editors for typical types such as strings and integers (see `PropertyEditor`). If a bean property is of a type that cannot be edited by any of the bean's default property editors, the bean must supply a custom property editor (see `PropertyEditor`). However, in some cases, a property sheet is not the best way to edit a bean. For example, in an animation bean, it is very awkward to set the animation rate, frame sequence, motion path, and so on, through a property sheet. In such cases, a bean can have a customizer that is a specialized user interface for editing the bean. A bean editor can display either the property sheet or the customizer or both.

A customizer must be a component (see `Component`) because the bean editor will add the customizer to its own container in order to display the customizer. Also, the customizer must have a public null constructor.

BeanInfo

To specify a customizer for a bean, you must provide a bean-info (see `BeanInfo`) for the bean and associate the customizer class with the bean class. See `BeanDescriptor` for more details.

Property Change Events

When a bean editor creates a customizer, the bean editor registers itself as a listener to the customizer for property change events. The customizer must fire a property change event whenever it changes any of the bean's properties. This allows the bean editor to updates its copy of the bean's properties. The events should include the name of the property that changes, as well as the property's old and new values.

MEMBER SUMMARY

Bean Method

setObject()   Called by the bean editor to set the customizer's bean.

Event Listener Methods

addPropertyChangeListener()   Adds a listener for receiving property change events.
removePropertyChangeListener()   Stops a listener from receiving property change
                                      events.

See Also

java.awt.Container, PropertyEditor.

Example

This is a somewhat elaborate example of a customizer. The bean is an image map that is an application that can display a background image with "hot" areas. The hot areas display a message when you roll the cursor over them (see Figure 114).

The image map bean comes complete with a built-in image map editor (Figure 115) that allows you to set areas on the image map such that when the user rolls into an area, a message is displayed. You can change the location of an area by selecting it and dragging it around. You can change the size of an area by selecting it and the dragging the handle at the lower-right corner. You can change the message displayed by an area by selecting the area, typing the new text in the text field, and then pressing Return. You can create a new area by clicking the New button. You can delete an area by selecting the area and then clicking the Delete button. The customizer does not immediately update the bean's property value with each modification. You need to manually update the bean's property value by clicking the Save button.

This example uses PropertyChangeSupport to implement the property change listener methods.

The mapping functionality is separated into its own class called Map. The Map class is used by both the bean and the customizer. A map object has a design-time switch that allows it to be easily switched between edit mode or normal-use mode. While in the bean, the map object is in normal-use mode; while in the customizer, it is in edit mode. While in edit mode, the map object also reads the Beans.isDesignTime() flag. If the flag yields false, the map object switches into normal-use mode. This means that you can switch the map object in the customizer between edit and normal-use modes by changing the bean editor's design-time state.

Note: In the Beanbox in BDK 1.0apr97, the customizer dialog box is modal, so you cannot actually change the design-time state while the customizer is displayed.

Note: When you start up the customizer for this bean, notice that the window is too narrow. This is due to a bug in the Beanbox in BDK 1.0apr97. The Beanbox is retrieving the sizes of the customizer before the peers have been created.

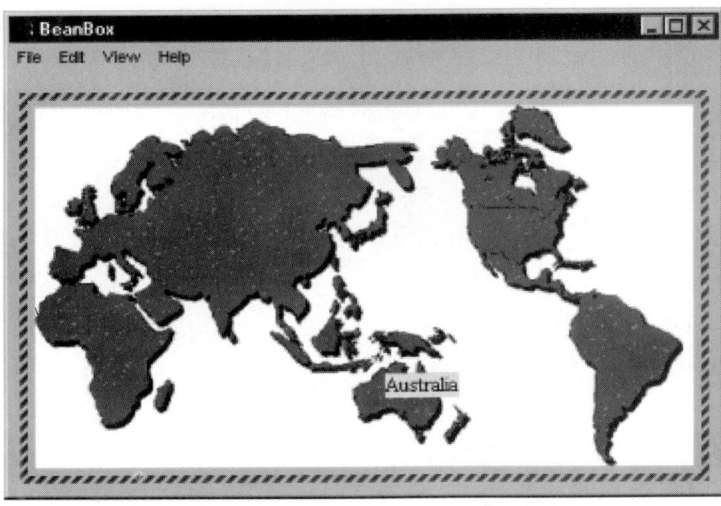

FIGURE 114:   **Image Map Bean.**

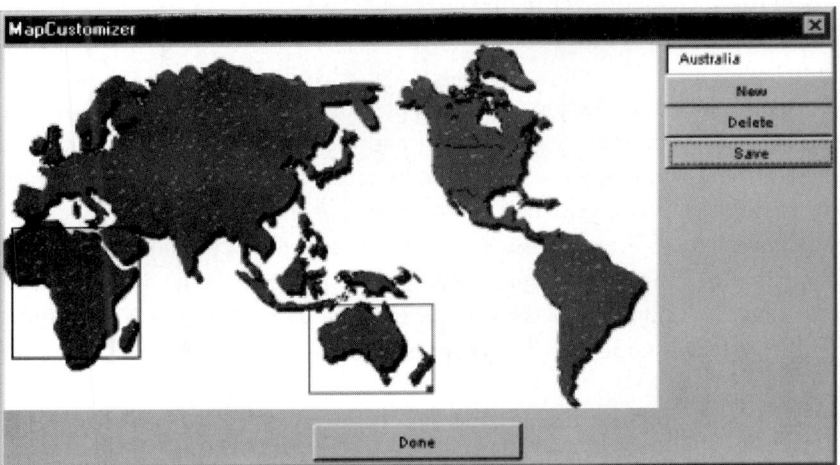

FIGURE 115:   **Image Map Bean Customizer.**

Note: If you run the Beanbox in BDK 1.0apr97 in the same directory as the class files, the Beanbox will not be able to create the customizer. The Beanbox must be run from some other directory because there is a problem with the Beanbox's class loaders.

Bean.java

```
import java.awt.*;
import java.awt.event.*;
import java.awt.image.*;
import java.beans.*;
import java.net.*;
```

```
public class Bean extends Panel {
    Map map = new Map();

    // Constructor
    public Bean() {
        // Initialize the bean with some data for testing purposes.
        Area[] as = {
            new Area(new Rectangle(0, 0, 40, 40), "Area1"),
            new Area(new Rectangle(100, 100, 40, 40), "Area2")};

        map.setAreas(as);
        map.setImage(loadImage("world.gif"));

        add(map, BorderLayout.CENTER);
    }

    // The image accessor methods.
    public Image getImage() {
        return map.image;
    }

    public void setImage(Image newImage) {
        Image oldImage = map.image;

        map.setImage(newImage);
        pceListeners.firePropertyChange("image", oldImage, newImage);
    }

    // The area accessor methods.
    public Area[] getAreas() {
        return map.areas;
    }

    public void setAreas(Area[] newAreas) {
        Area[] oldAreas = map.areas;

        map.setAreas(newAreas);
        pceListeners.firePropertyChange("areas", oldAreas, newAreas);
    }

    // Create the listener list.
    PropertyChangeSupport pceListeners =
        new PropertyChangeSupport(this);

    // The listener list wrapper methods.
    public synchronized void addPropertyChangeListener(
                        PropertyChangeListener l) {
        pceListeners.addPropertyChangeListener(l);
    }

    public synchronized void removePropertyChangeListener(
                        PropertyChangeListener l) {
        pceListeners.removePropertyChangeListener(l);
    }

    // This method will load an image relative to the location of the
    // bean class file.  A bean should always use a method like this one
    // to load resources that are located relative to itself.  Otherwise the
    // resource will be looked for relative to the location of the bean
```

A
B

D
E
F
G
H
I
J
K
L
M
N
O
P
Q
R
S
T
U
V
W
X
Y
Z

```
        // container's current working directory.
        public Image loadImage(String imageName) {
            try {
                URL url = getClass().getResource(imageName);
                return getToolkit().createImage((ImageProducer)url.getContent());
            } catch (Exception e) {
                return null;
            }
        }
    }
    /*
        manifest.txt file:
            Name: Bean.class
            Java-Bean: True
        jar command:
            jar cfm bean.jar manifest.txt *.class
    */
```

BeanBeanInfo.java

```
    import java.beans.*;

    public class BeanBeanInfo extends SimpleBeanInfo {
        public BeanDescriptor getBeanDescriptor() {
            return new BeanDescriptor(Bean.class, MapCustomizer.class);
        }
        public java.awt.Image getIcon(int iconKind) {
            switch (iconKind) {
              case ICON_COLOR_16x16:
                return loadImage("world-color-16x16.gif");
              case ICON_COLOR_32x32:
                return loadImage("world-color-32x32.gif");
              case ICON_MONO_16x16:
                return loadImage("world-mono-16x16.gif");
              case ICON_MONO_32x32:
                return loadImage("world-mono-32x32.gif");
              default:
                return null;
            }
        }
    }
```

Area.java

```
    import java.awt.*;
    import java.io.*;
    import java.util.*;

    public class Area implements Serializable {
        Rectangle bounds;
        String label;

        Area(Rectangle bounds, String label) {
            this.bounds = bounds;
            this.label = label;
        }

        // Utility function for converting an array to a vector
        static Vector toVector(Area[] areas) {
```

```
        Vector v = new Vector();

        for (int i=0; i<areas.length; i++) {
            v.addElement(areas[i]);
        }
        return v;
    }

    // Utility function for converting a vector to an array.
    static Area[] fromVector(Vector v) {
        Area[] result = new Area[v.size()];

        for (int i=0; i<v.size(); i++) {
            result[i] = (Area)v.elementAt(i);
        }
        return result;
    }

}
```

Map.java

```
import java.awt.*;
import java.awt.event.*;
import java.beans.*;

public class Map extends Canvas implements ItemSelectable {
    // These fields are used by clients of this class.
    public transient Image image;
    public Area[] areas;
    int curArea = -1;

    // Offscreen image used for double-buffering.
    transient Image bbuf;

    // If true, the map is in a customizer and so the map can be edited.
    boolean inCustomizer = false;

    // If true, the user is dragging an area.
    boolean dragging;

    // If true, the user is stretching an area.
    boolean stretching;

    // Location of cursor when the user pressed the mouse.
    // When dragging, it is relative to the origin of the area rather than
    // to the component.
    // When stretching, it holds distance to the se corner of the area;
    // both coordinates are always positive.
    Point downPt;

    public Map() {
        // Listen for mouse and mouse motion events.
        addMouseMotionListener(new MouseMotionEventHandler());
        addMouseListener(new MouseEventHandler());
    }

    // Change the background image.
    public void setImage(Image newImage) {
        MediaTracker tracker = new MediaTracker(this);
        image = newImage;
```

A
B
C
D
E
F
G
H
I
J
K
L
M
N
O
P
Q
R
S
T
U
V
W
X
Y
Z

```
                    try {
                        tracker.addImage(image, 0);
                        tracker.waitForAll();
                    } catch (Exception e) {
                        e.printStackTrace();
                    }
A
                    setSize(image.getWidth(null), image.getHeight(null));
                    repaint();
B
                }

C               public void setAreas(Area[] newAreas) {
                    areas = newAreas;
D                   curArea = -1;
                    repaint();
E               }


F
                // This method is need to implement ItemSelectable.
G               public Object[] getSelectedObjects() {
                    if (curArea >= 0) {
H                       Object[] result = {areas[curArea]};

I                       return result;
                    }
J                   return null;
                }
K
                // Paint methods.
L               public void paint(Graphics g) {
                    update(g);
M               }

N               public void update(Graphics g) {
                    // Copy the value in case it gets changed by the event handler methods.
O                   int ca = curArea;

P                   if (!inCustomizer || !Beans.isDesignTime()) {
                        g.drawImage(image, 0, 0, this);
Q                       return;
                    }
R
                    // Create the offscreen image if necessary.
S                   if (bbuf == null) {
                        bbuf = createImage(image.getWidth(null), image.getHeight(null));
T                   }
                    Graphics bbufG = bbuf.getGraphics();
U
                    // Draw the background image.
V                   bbufG.drawImage(image, 0, 0, this);

W                   // Paint all the area rectangles.
                    for (int i=0; i<areas.length; i++) {
X                       if (i == ca) {
                            bbufG.setColor(Color.red);
Y                           // Paint the handle.
                            bbufG.fillRect(handleRect.x, handleRect.y,
Z                               handleRect.width-1, handleRect.height-1);
                        } else {
                            bbufG.setColor(Color.black);
                        }
```

```
        bbufG.drawRect(areas[i].bounds.x, areas[i].bounds.y,
            areas[i].bounds.width-1, areas[i].bounds.height-1);
    }

    bbufG.dispose();
    g.drawImage(bbuf, 0, 0, this);
}

class MouseMotionEventHandler extends MouseMotionAdapter {
    public void mouseMoved(MouseEvent evt) {
        if (inCustomizer && Beans.isDesignTime()) {
            return;
        }
        int x = evt.getX();
        int y = evt.getY();

        for (int i=0; i<areas.length; i++) {
            if (areas[i].bounds.contains(x, y)) {
                showTip(areas[i].label, x, y);
                return;
            }
        }
        showTip(null, 0, 0);
    }
    public void mouseDragged(MouseEvent evt) {
        if (dragging) {
            areas[curArea].bounds.x = evt.getX()-downPt.x;
            areas[curArea].bounds.y = evt.getY()-downPt.y;

            // Keep the area within the imagemap.
            areas[curArea].bounds.x = Math.max(0, Math.min(
                areas[curArea].bounds.x, image.getWidth(null)
                -areas[curArea].bounds.width));
            areas[curArea].bounds.y = Math.max(0, Math.min(
                areas[curArea].bounds.y, image.getHeight(null)
                -areas[curArea].bounds.height));
            updateHandle();
            repaint();
        } else if (stretching) {
            // Keep the box within the image.
            int x = Math.min(evt.getX(), image.getWidth(null)-1);
            int y = Math.min(evt.getY(), image.getHeight(null)-1);

            areas[curArea].bounds.width = x+downPt.x
                -areas[curArea].bounds.x;
            areas[curArea].bounds.height = y+downPt.y
                -areas[curArea].bounds.y;

            // Don't make the area too small.
            areas[curArea].bounds.width = Math.max(20,
                areas[curArea].bounds.width);
            areas[curArea].bounds.height = Math.max(20,
                areas[curArea].bounds.height);

            updateHandle();
            repaint();
        }
    }
}
```

A
B
C
D
E
F
G
H
I
J
K
L
M
N
O
P
Q
R
S
T
U
V
W
X
Y
Z

A
B
C
D
E
F
G
H
I
J
K
L
M
N
O
P
Q
R
S
T
U
V
W
X
Y
Z

```java
        void updateHandle() {
            if (curArea >= 0) {
                handleRect = new Rectangle(areas[curArea].bounds);

                handleRect.x = handleRect.x+handleRect.width-5;
                handleRect.y = handleRect.y+handleRect.height-5;
                handleRect.width = 5;
                handleRect.height = 5;
            }
        }

        Rectangle handleRect;
        class MouseEventHandler extends MouseAdapter {
            public void mousePressed(MouseEvent evt) {
                int x = evt.getX();
                int y = evt.getY();

                for (int i=0; i<areas.length; i++) {
                    if (areas[i].bounds.contains(x, y)) {
                        curArea = i;

                        // Check if on handle
                        updateHandle();
                        if (handleRect.contains(x, y)) {
                            stretching = true;
                            // The down point is relative to the se corner.
                            downPt = new Point(areas[i].bounds.x+
                                    areas[i].bounds.width-x,
                                 areas[i].bounds.y+areas[i].bounds.height-y);
                        } else {
                            dragging = true;
                            // The down point is relative to the nw corner.
                            downPt = new Point(x-areas[i].bounds.x,
                                y-areas[i].bounds.y);
                        }
                        processItemEvent(new ItemEvent(Map.this,
                            ItemEvent.ITEM_STATE_CHANGED, new Integer(i),
                            ItemEvent.SELECTED));
                        repaint();
                        break;
                    }
                }
            }
            public void mouseReleased(MouseEvent evt) {
                dragging = false;
                stretching = false;
            }
        }

        public Dimension getPreferredSize() {
            return new Dimension(image.getWidth(null), image.getHeight(null));
        }

        // Tip methods
        TipWindow tip;
        public void showTip(String tipLabel, int x, int y) {
            if (tip == null) {
                // Find the parent.
                Component c = getParent();
                while (!(c instanceof Frame)) {
```

```
                c = c.getParent();
            }
            tip = new TipWindow((Frame)c);
        }
        tip.setLabel(tipLabel);
        if (tipLabel != null) {
            if (!tip.isShowing()) {
                Point pt = getLocationOnScreen();

                tip.setLocation(pt.x+x, pt.y+y);
                tip.show();
            }
        } else {
            tip.hide();
        }
    }

    // Item listener support methods.
    transient ItemListener itemListener;
    public synchronized void addItemListener(ItemListener l) {
        itemListener = AWTEventMulticaster.add(itemListener, l);
    }
    public synchronized void removeItemListener(ItemListener l) {
        itemListener = AWTEventMulticaster.remove(itemListener, l);
    }
    protected void processItemEvent(ItemEvent evt) {
        if (itemListener != null) {
            itemListener.itemStateChanged(evt);
        }
    }
}
```

MapCustomizer.java

```
import java.awt.*;
import java.awt.event.*;
import java.beans.*;
import java.util.*;

public class MapCustomizer extends Panel
        implements ActionListener, ItemListener, Customizer {
    Bean bean;

    // Components
    Button newBtn = new Button("New");
    Button deleteBtn = new Button("Delete");
    TextField labelTf = new TextField(15);
    Button saveBtn = new Button("Save");

    // Offscreen image for double-buffering.
    transient Image bbuf;

    Map map;

    public MapCustomizer() {
        map = new Map();
        map.inCustomizer = true;

        // Layout buttons.
        Panel p = new Panel(new GridLayout(0, 1));
```

A
B
C
D
E
F
G
H
I
J
K
L
M
N
O
P
Q
R
S
T
U
V
W
X
Y
Z

```
            p.add(labelTf);
            p.add(newBtn);
            p.add(deleteBtn);
            p.add(saveBtn);
            Panel q = new Panel(new BorderLayout());
            q.add(p, BorderLayout.NORTH);

            // Layout map and buttons.
            setLayout(new BorderLayout());
            add(q, BorderLayout.EAST);
            add(map, BorderLayout.CENTER);

            // Listen for events.
            map.addItemListener(this);
            labelTf.addActionListener(this);
            newBtn.addActionListener(this);
            deleteBtn.addActionListener(this);
            saveBtn.addActionListener(this);
        }

        public void setObject(Object b) {
            bean = (Bean)b;
            map.setAreas(bean.getAreas());
            map.setImage(bean.getImage());
        }

        // Action event handler.
        public void actionPerformed(ActionEvent evt) {
            if (evt.getSource() == newBtn) {
                // Add a new entry.
                Vector v = Area.toVector(map.areas);
                Area a = new Area(new Rectangle(0, 0, 30, 30), "Unknown");
                v.addElement(a);
                map.setAreas(Area.fromVector(v));
            } else if (evt.getSource() == deleteBtn) {
                if (map.curArea >= 0) {
                    // Delete the current entry.
                    Vector v = Area.toVector(map.areas);
                    v.removeElementAt(map.curArea);
                    map.setAreas(Area.fromVector(v));
                }
            } else if (evt.getSource() == saveBtn) {
                Area[] oldAreas = bean.getAreas();
                bean.setAreas(map.areas);
                pceListeners.firePropertyChange("areas", oldAreas, map.areas);
            } else if (evt.getSource() == labelTf) {
                map.areas[map.curArea].label = labelTf.getText();
            }
            repaint();
        }

        // Item event handler.
        public void itemStateChanged(ItemEvent evt) {
            labelTf.setText(map.areas[((Integer)evt.getItem()).intValue()].label);
        }

        // Create the listener list.
        PropertyChangeSupport pceListeners =
            new PropertyChangeSupport(this);
```

```
        // The listener list wrapper methods.
        public synchronized void addPropertyChangeListener(
                                  PropertyChangeListener l) {
            pceListeners.addPropertyChangeListener(l);
        }

        public synchronized void removePropertyChangeListener(
                                  PropertyChangeListener l) {
            pceListeners.removePropertyChangeListener(l);
        }
    }
```

TipWindow.java
```
    import java.awt.*;

    public class TipWindow extends Window {
        String label;
        Font f = new Font("Serif", Font.PLAIN, 14);
        FontMetrics fm;

        public TipWindow(Frame frame) {
            super(frame);

            setFont(f);
            fm = getFontMetrics(f);
        }

        public void setLabel(String label) {
            this.label = label;
            if (label != null) {
                setSize(fm.stringWidth(label), fm.getHeight());
            }
        }

        public void paint(Graphics g) {
            g.setColor(Color.yellow);
            g.fillRect(0, 0, getSize().width, getSize().height);

            g.setColor(Color.black);
            if (label != null) {
                g.drawString(label, (getSize().width - fm.stringWidth(label))/2,
                    (getSize().height - fm.getHeight())/2 + fm.getAscent());
            }
        }

        public Dimension getPreferredSize() {
            return new Dimension(20, 20);
        }
    }
```

A

B

D

E

F

G

H

I

J

K

L

M

N

O

P

Q

R

S

T

U

V

W

X

Y

Z

addPropertyChangeListener()

PURPOSE   Adds a listener for receiving property change events.

SYNTAX   `void addPropertyChangeListener(PropertyChangeListener listener)`

DESCRIPTION   This method should add `listener` to the listener list. It is typically called by the bean editor just after it creates the customizer.

After this method is called, the property editor should fire a property change event to the listeners of any changes that the customizer makes to the bean. The property name of the event should contain the name of the property that changed. The old and new values of the event should contain the previous and new property values, respectively.

This method is typically called by a bean editor so that the editor can be notified when the user changes the property of a bean. The bean editor uses these notifications to update its display of any bean properties.

PARAMETERS
`listener`   A non-`null` property change event listener.

SEE ALSO   `removePropertyChangeListener()`.

EXAMPLE   See the class example.

removePropertyChangeListener()

PURPOSE   Stops a listener from receiving property change events.

SYNTAX   `void removePropertyChangeListener(PropertyChangeListener listener)`

DESCRIPTION   This method should remove `listener` from the listener list. If `listener` is not in the listener list, the method call should be ignored. This method is typically called by the bean editor just after it creates the customizer.

The implementation of this method does not have to stop the delivery of events immediately. That is, after this method is called, the listener may receive a few more property change events. See `PropertyChangeListener` for more details.

PARAMETERS
`listener`   A non-`null` property change event listener.

SEE ALSO   `addPropertyChangeListener()`.

EXAMPLE   See the class example.

A
B
C
D
E
F
G
H
I
J
K
L
M
N
O
P
Q
R
S
T
U
V
W
X
Y
Z

setObject()

PURPOSE   Called by the bean editor to set the customizer's bean.

SYNTAX   void setObject(Object bean)

DESCRIPTION   Just after a bean editor creates a customizer, the bean editor calls this method once to give the customizer a reference to the bean. The bean editor calls this method before it adds the customizer to a container. Essentially, this means that this method cannot do any work that involves component sizes. See Component.getPreferredSize() for more details.

PARAMETERS
  bean   The non-null bean to be customized.

EXAMPLE   See the class example.

A
B

D
E
F
G
H
I
J
K
L
M
N
O
P
Q
R
S
T
U
V
W
X
Y
Z

```
java.lang.Object
    DataFlavor
```

Syntax
```
public class DataFlavor
```

Description

When an application retrieves data from a clipboard, it is given a transferable object (see `Transferable`), which holds the actual data. To retrieve the actual data from the transferable object, an application must use a *data flavor*. A data flavor specifies two things: a data type (image, text, a bean, and so on) and a delivery method (a byte stream, an `Image` object, an array of pixels, and so on). For example, if an application wishes to retrieve an image as an array of pixels from the transferable object, it must construct (or use) a data flavor containing this information and then present it to the transferable object. The transferable object can either reject the request (because it either does not have an image or cannot deliver it as an array of pixels) or deliver the data.

When an application places some data on the clipboard, it must also include with the data all of the data flavors that are supported. All of this information is kept in a transferable object.

Note: This class is still under development. It currently supports string data flavors but not much else. Many of the methods have not been thoroughly designed and implemented. The class and method descriptions should improve greatly in the near future as other data types are allowed on the system clipboard and as drag-and-drop becomes available.

Using Data Flavors

There are two ways to use data flavors when trying to extract data from a transferable object. The first is to ask the transferable object for all of the data flavors that it will recognize. The application can then go through each data flavor and use one that it likes.

The second way is to create a data flavor with the right specifications and then present it to the transferable object. The transferable object could grant or reject the request. In practice, this is the simpler of the two ways. An application typically deals only in a fixed set of data flavors, and it can just try each one in a particular order until one or none works.

The MIME Content Type

When an application retrieves the contents of a clipboard, it must interrogate the transferable object to determine if it contains data of a type with which it can deal. For example, a text editor would ignore the contents if it were anything but text, while a paint program would ignore all but images.

The data type of a transferable object is specified using MIME types. The MIME type is a nonlocalized string that serves as a standard way of naming data types. For example, the MIME type "`image/jpeg`" refers to a JPEG image and "`text/plain; charset=us-ascii`" refers to an ASCII string. If an application expects a JPEG image, it needs to create a data flavor using the JPEG MIME type ("`image/jpeg`") and use that to interrogate the transferable object.

The MIME type specification is described in RFC 1341, which can be viewed on the Internet at `http://ds.internic.net/rfc/rfc1341.txt`.

The Representation Class

Although the MIME type can determine *what* the transferable object contains, it does not say *how* the data is to be delivered to the application. For example, a JPEG image could be delivered as an `Image` object, a byte stream, or an array of pixels. This delivery information must also be specified when interrogating a transferable object. This information is called the *representation class*.

The representation class describes how the data in a transferable object is delivered to an application. If the data is desired in the form of a `java.awt.Image` object, then the representation class is the `java.awt.Image` `Class` object (see later in this discussion for more information). If the data is desired in the form of a byte stream, then the representation class is the `java.io.ByteArrayInputStream` `Class` object.

In summary, a data flavor has two components: the MIME content type, which describes *what* data type is desired, and the representation class, which describes *how* the data type is to be delivered.

Human-presentable Name

A data flavor contains a localizable, human-presentable name that is meant to help a user identify a data flavor. The value of this name has no effect on how the data is transferred.

Class Objects

Every object has associated with it a `Class` object that contains information about the object's class, such as its superclass. These `Class` objects are used as the representation class in a data flavor. A `Class` object can be retrieved in one of three ways:

1. By calling the object's `getClass()` method
2. By calling `Class.forName()` with the object's fully-qualified class name
3. By appending ".class" to the class name.

For example:

```
Integer i = new Integer(42);

// Method 1
Class the_IntegerClassDescriptor1 = i.getClass();

// Method 2
Class the_IntegerClassDescriptor2 = Class.forName("java.lang.Integer");
```

A
B
C
D
E
F
G
H
I
J
K
L
M
N
O
P
Q
R
S
T
U
V
W
X
Y
Z

```
//Method 3
Class = Integer.class;
```

String Data Flavors

The `DataFlavor` class contains two standard data flavors. These data flavors are for strings and are used by the `StringSelection` class. Table 9 shows each data flavor and its MIME type and representation class.

Data Flavor	Representation Class	MIME Type
stringFlavor	java.lang.String.class	application/x-java-serialized-object; class=java.lang.String
plainTextFlavor	java.io.StringReader.class	text/plain; charset=unicode

TABLE 9:   Data Flavors and Their MIME Types and Representation Classes.

Note: In Java 1.1.2, the representation class for a plain text data flavor is actually `null`. Also, the MIME type for the string data flavor is `"application/x-java-serialized-object"`. *These are bugs.*

MEMBER SUMMARY	
Constructor	
DataFlavor()	Construct a `DataFlavor` instance.
MIME Methods	
getMimeType()	Retrieves this data flavor's MIME type.
isMimeTypeEqual()	Determines if two MIME types are equal.
normalizeMimeType()	Called to normalize a MIME type.
normalizeMimeTypeParameter()	Called to normalize a parameter in a MIME type.
Representation Class Method	
getRepresentationClass()	Retrieves this data flavor's representation class.
Human-presentable Name Methods	
getHumanPresentableName()	Retrieves this data flavor's human-presentable name.
setHumanPresentableName()	Sets this data flavor's human-presentable name.
Predefined Flavors	
plainTextFlavor	A standard data flavor for a string.
stringFlavor	A standard data flavor for a string.
Data Flavor Equality Method	
equals()	Determines if two data flavors are equal.

Example

See `Transferable`.

DataFlavor()

PURPOSE   Construct a `DataFlavor` instance.

SYNTAX   `public DataFlavor(String mimeType, String humanPresentableName)`
`public DataFlavor(Class representationClass, String`
      `humanPresentableName)`

DESCRIPTION   A data flavor can be constructed with either a MIME type or a representation class. There is no way to specify both; it is necessary to subclass `DataFlavor` in order to specify both properties.

If a MIME type is used to construct a data flavor, the representation class is set to `java.io.InputStream`. If the MIME type is "`application/x-java-serialized-object; class=`<*name of representation class*>", the representation class is set to `Class.forName`(<*name of representation class*>).

If `representationClass` is specified, the MIME type for the data flavor is set to "`application/x-java-serialized-object; class=`<*name of representation class*>". For example, if the representation class is `java.lang.String.class`, then the MIME type would be "`application/x-java-serialized-object; class=java.lang.String`".

Note: The semantics described here are not entirely implemented in Java 1.1.2. In particular, when the MIME type is "`application/x-java-serialized-object; class=`<*name of representation class*>", the representation class is not set to `Class.forName`(<*name of representation class*>) Instead, it is set to `java.io.InputStream.class`. Also, note that when the data flavor is constructed with a representation class, the inclusion of the class parameter in the MIME type has not been implemented; if you try this, you'll discover that the class parameter is missing.

The `humanPresentableName` parameter is a localizable string that is meant to help a user identify the data flavor. This name is not used by the data transfer mechanism.

Note: In Java 1.1.2, `getMimeType()` returns `mimeType` (or the derived MIME type). In a future release, the MIME type stored in the data flavor may possibly be the normalized version of the one supplied to the constructor.

A
B
C
D
E
F
G
H
I
J
K
L
M
N
O
P
Q
R
S
T
U
V
W
X
Y
Z

PARAMETERS

  mimeType   A non-null string containing a MIME type.

  representationClass

               A non-null Class object.

  humanPresentableName

               A non-null localizable string.

SEE ALSO   java.io.InputStream, java.lang.Class, normalizeMimeType().

EXAMPLE   See Transferable.

equals()

PURPOSE   Determines if two data flavors are equal.

SYNTAX   public boolean equals(DataFlavor dataFlavor)

DESCRIPTION   Two data flavors df1 and df2 are equal if isMimeTypeEqual(df1, df2) is true and

               df1.getRepresentationClass() == df2.getRepresentationClass().

PARAMETERS

  dataFlavor   A non-null data flavor.

RETURNS   true if dataFlavor is equal to this data flavor; false otherwise.

OVERRIDES   java.lang.Object.equals().

SEE ALSO   getRepresentationClass(), isMimeTypeEqual().

EXAMPLE   See Transferable.

getHumanPresentableName()

PURPOSE   Retrieves this data flavor's human-presentable (localizable) name.

SYNTAX   public String getHumanPresentableName()

DESCRIPTION   This method returns a human-presentable (localizable) name that is meant to help a user identify a data flavor. The value of this name has no effect on how the data is transferred.

RETURNS   A possibly null string containing the data flavor's human-presentable (localizable) name.

EXAMPLE   See StringSelection.getTransferDataFlavors().

getMimeType()

PURPOSE   Retrieves the data flavor's MIME type.

SYNTAX   `public String getMimeType()`

DESCRIPTION   The data flavor's MIME type specifies a particular data type such as a JPEG image or a unicode string. See the class description for information about a data flavor's MIME type.

The MIME type is determined when the data flavor is created. It cannot be changed.

Note: In Java 1.1.2, the returned MIME type is identical to the one supplied in the constructor. The returned MIME type may in a future release be the normalized version of the one supplied to the constructor.

RETURNS   A non-`null` string containing the data flavor's MIME type.

SEE ALSO   `DataFlavor()`, `normalizeMimeType()`.

EXAMPLE   See `StringSelection.getTransferDataFlavors()`.

getRepresentationClass()

PURPOSE   Retrieves the data flavor's representation class.

SYNTAX   `public Class getRepresentationClass()`

DESCRIPTION   The data flavor's representation class specifies how a transferable object should deliver its encapsulated data such as a byte stream or an array of bytes. See the class description for more information about the data flavor's representation class.

RETURNS   A non-`null` `Class` object.

EXAMPLE   See `StringSelection.getTransferDataFlavors()`.

isMimeTypeEqual()

PURPOSE   Determines if two MIME types are equal.

SYNTAX   `public boolean isMimeTypeEqual(String mimeType)`
               `public final boolean isMimeTypeEqual(DataFlavor flavor)`

DESCRIPTION   This method normalizes `mimeType` (using `normalizeMimeType()`) and compares it with the normalized version MIME type of this data flavor. If the two strings are equal, this method returns `true`. Otherwise, `false` is returned.

A
B
C
D
E
F
G
H
I
J
K
L
M
N
O
P
Q
R
S
T
U
V
W
X
Y
Z

The second form of this method (where `flavor` is specified) is equivalent to calling `isMimeTypeEqual(dataFlavor.getMimeType())`.

Note: In Java 1.1.2, this method simply does a string comparison between `mimeType` and this data flavor's MIME type. The implementation will be completed in a future release.

PARAMETERS

`flavor`   A non-`null` data flavor.

`mimeType`   A non-`null` string containing a MIME type.

SEE ALSO   `getMimeType()`.

normalizeMimeType()

PURPOSE   Called to normalize a MIME type.

SYNTAX   `protected String normalizeMimeType(String mimeType)`

DESCRIPTION This method is called to normalize a MIME type so that it can be compared with another MIME type. This method also takes each parameter in the MIME type and normalizes them by calling `nomalizeMimeTypeParameter()`.

A subclass of a data flavor should call `super.normalizeMimeType()` before applying its own normalizing procedure.

Note: In Java 1.1.2, this method simply returns `mimeType`. A normalizing algorithm will be implemented in a future version.

PARAMETERS

`mimeType`   A non-`null` string containing a MIME type.

normalizeMimeTypeParameter()

PURPOSE   Called to normalize a parameter in a MIME type.

SYNTAX   `protected String normalizeMimeTypeParameter(String`
`                parameterName, String parameterValue)`

DESCRIPTION This method is called by `normalizeMimeType()` as it normalizes a MIME type. The `normalizeMimeType()` method takes each parameter in the MIME type and normalizes it by calling this method.

A subclass of a data flavor should call `super.normalizeMimeTypeParameter()` before applying its own normalizing procedure.

Note: In Java 1.1.2, this method simply returns
`parameterType + "=" + parameterValue`

A normalizing algorithm will be implemented in a future version.

PARAMETERS

`parameterName`

A non-`null` string containing the name of a MIME type parameter.

`parameterValue`

A non-`null` string containing a MIME type parameter value.

plainTextFlavor

PURPOSE   A standard data flavor for a string.

SYNTAX   `public static DataFlavor plainTextFlavor`

DESCRIPTION   When string data is being transferred via a clipboard, an application should use either this plain text data flavor or the string data flavor (see `stringFlavor`). This data flavor is used by the `StringSelection` class.

The MIME type for this data flavor is `"text/plain; charset=unicode"`. The representation class for this data flavor is `java.io.StringReader`.

Note: In Java 1.1.2, the representation class for a plain text data flavor is actually `null`. *This is a bug.*

EXAMPLE   See `StringSelection.getTransferData()`.

setHumanPresentableName()

PURPOSE   Sets this data flavor's human-presentable name.

SYNTAX   `public void setHumanPresentableName(String humanPresentableName)`

DESCRIPTION   A data flavor's human-presentable name is a localizable string that is meant to help a user identify a data flavor. The value of this name has no effect on how the data is transferred.

PARAMETERS

`humanPresentableName`

A possibly `null` string containing the data flavor's human presentable name.

EXAMPLE   See `Transferable`.

stringFlavor

PURPOSE A standard data flavor for a string.

SYNTAX `public static DataFlavor stringFlavor`

DESCRIPTION When string data is being transferred via a clipboard, an application should use either this string data flavor or the plain text data flavor (see `plainTextFlavor`). This data flavor is used by the `StringSelection` class.

The MIME type for this data flavor is `"application/x-java-serialized-object; class=java.lang.String"`. The representation class for this data flavor is `java.lang.String`.

Note: In Java 1.1.2, the actual MIME type for this data flavor is `"application/x-java-serialized-object"`.

EXAMPLE See `StringSelection.getTransferData()`.

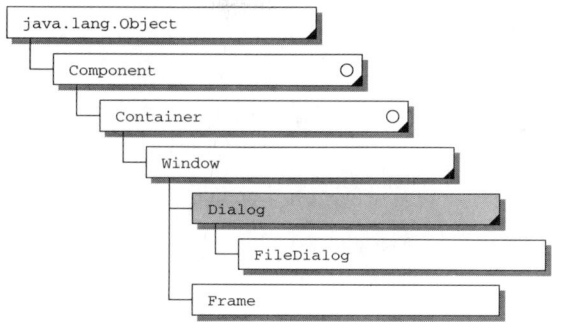

Syntax

```
public class Dialog extends Window
```

Description

A dialog component is a top-level window with a title bar and a border. A dialog can be modal. It resembles a frame, but it has fewer properties. It does not have, for example, an icon image or a cursor.

The Modal Property

A *modal* dialog, when visible, prevents the user from interacting with any other AWT window. A *modeless* dialog does not have this affect; it behaves more like a frame. The modal property can be changed at any time.

The Title Property

The title bar is a strip across the top of the dialog that displays a short description of the dialog. The title can be changed at any time.

The Resizable Property

A resizable dialog allows the user to change the size of the dialog. The resizable property can be changed at any time. The precise manner in which the user resizes the dialog is platform-dependent.

Events

The dialog fires the same events as a window does. See the Window class for more details.

A
B
C
D
E
F
G
H
I
J
K
L
M
N
O
P
Q
R
S
T
U
V
W
X
Y
Z

MEMBER SUMMARY

Constructor
Dialog()   Constructs a new Dialog instance.

Property Methods
getTitle()   Retrieves this dialog's title.
isModal()   Retrieves this dialog's modal state.
isResizable()   Retrieves this dialog's resizable state.
setModal()   Sets this dialog's modal property.
setResizable()   Sets this dialog's resizable property.
setTitle()   Sets this dialog's title.

Visibility Method
show()   Makes this dialog visible and in front of all other windows.

Peer Method
addNotify()   Creates this dialog's peer hierarchy.

Debugging Method
paramString()   Generates a string representation of the dialog's state.

Example

This example demonstrates how to center a dialog with respect to its parent frame. The dialog is always positioned so that its bounds is within the screen bounds (Figure 116). It is defined to show a one-line message. Also, it is modal and can be closed by clicking either OK or the close icon on the window title. The dialog is set up such that it shows itself in the constructor.

A frame with a single button is used to create the message dialog. The message that is displayed in the message dialog is the current time in the default locale.

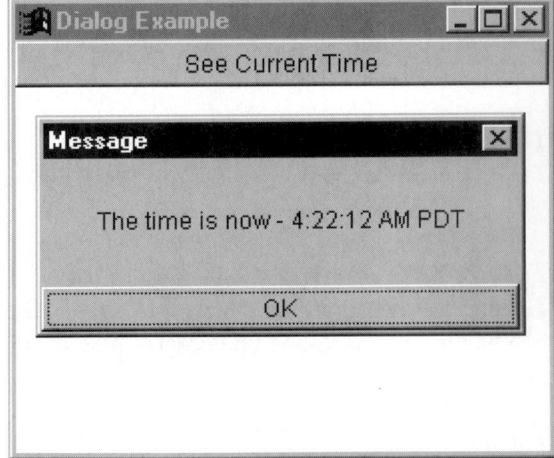

FIGURE 116:   Centering a Dialog.

```
import java.awt.*;
import java.awt.event.*;
import java.text.*;
import java.util.*;

class Main extends Frame implements ActionListener {
```

```
        Button b = new Button("See Current Time");

        Main() {
            super("Dialog Example");

            // Listener for events.
            b.addActionListener(this);

            // Layout components.
            add(b, BorderLayout.NORTH);
            pack();
            show();
        }

        public void actionPerformed(ActionEvent evt) {
            // Get the current time in the default locale.
            String time = DateFormat.getTimeInstance(
                DateFormat.LONG).format(new Date());

            // Create the message dialog.
            new MessageDialog(this, "The time is now - "+time);
        }

        public static void main(String[] args) {
            new Main();
        }
}
class MessageDialog extends Dialog implements ActionListener {
        MessageDialog(Frame f, String msg) {
            super(f, "Message", true);

            // Create the components.
            Button b = new Button("OK");
            Label l = new Label(msg, Label.CENTER) {
                // This adds some space around the text.
                public Dimension getPreferredSize() {
                    Dimension d = super.getPreferredSize();
                    return new Dimension(d.width+40, d.height+40);
                }
            };

            // Listen for events.
            b.addActionListener(this);
            addWindowListener(new WindowEventHandler());

            // Layout components.
            add(l, BorderLayout.NORTH);
            add(b, BorderLayout.SOUTH);

            pack();
            Dimension myDim = getSize();
            Dimension frameDim = f.getSize();
            Dimension screenSize = getToolkit().getScreenSize();
            Point loc = f.getLocation();

            // Center the dialog w.r.t. the frame.
            loc.translate((frameDim.width-myDim.width)/2,
                (frameDim.height-myDim.height)/2);
```

A
B
C
D
E
F
G
H
I
J
K
L
M
N
O
P
Q
R
S
T
U
V
W
X
Y
Z

```
            // Ensure that slave is withing screen bounds.
            loc.x = Math.max(0, Math.min(loc.x, screenSize.width-getSize().width));
            loc.y = Math.max(0,
                Math.min(loc.y, screenSize.width-getSize().height));

            setLocation(loc.x, loc.y);
            show();
        }

        public void actionPerformed(ActionEvent evt) {
            dispose();
        }

        class WindowEventHandler extends WindowAdapter {
            public void windowClosing(WindowEvent evt) {
                dispose();
            }
        }
    }
```

addNotify( )

PURPOSE   Creates this dialog's peer hierarchy.

SYNTAX   `public void addNotify()`

DESCRIPTION This method creates the dialog's peer hierarchy, if necessary. The hierarchy is created by calling the `Toolkit.createDialog()` method. This method should be called before the dialog's minimum or preferred size is calculated. The methods `Window.pack()` and `Window.show()` automatically call `addNotify()`.

OVERRIDES   `Component.addNotify()`.

SEE ALSO   `Component, Component.getMinimumSize(),`
            `Component.getPreferredSize(), Toolkit, Window.pack(),`
            `Window.show().`

EXAMPLE   See `Component.setVisible()`.

Dialog( )

PURPOSE   Constructs a new `Dialog` instance.

SYNTAX   `public Dialog(Frame parent)`
            `public Dialog(Frame parent, boolean modal)`
            `public Dialog(Frame parent, String title, boolean modal)`

DESCRIPTION This constructor creates a new invisible `Dialog` instance. If `title` is null, the dialog's title is blank. If `title` is not specified, the dialog's title defaults to null. If modal is true, the dialog is modal; otherwise, the dialog is modeless. If modal is not specified, the dialog is modeless. Both the dialog's modal property and title can be changed at any time.

The default layout manager for the dialog is BorderLayout.

PARAMETERS

modal   If true, dialog is modal; otherwise, dialog is modeless.

parent   The non-null parent of the dialog.

title   The string specifying the dialog's title. Can be null.

EXCEPTIONS

IllegalArgumentException

        If parent is null.

SEE ALSO   Component.setVisible(), setModal(), setResizable(), setTitle().

EXAMPLE   This example creates a frame that has two buttons. One creates a modal dialog; the other creates a modeless dialog. Figure 117 shows the dialog creator as well as the newly created modal and modeless dialogs.

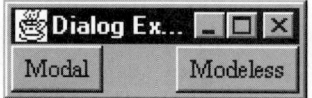 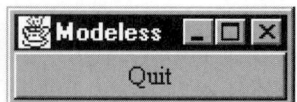 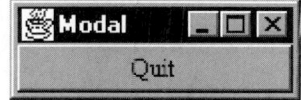

FIGURE 117: **Dialog Creator, Modeless, and Modal Dialogs.**

This example also shows how to create the dialog at a particular position on the screen. This is done by calling the setLocation() method before calling the show() method on the dialog.

```java
import java.awt.*;
import java.awt.event.*;

class Main extends Frame implements ActionListener {
    Main() {
        super("Dialog Example");
        Button b;
        add(b = new Button("Modal"), BorderLayout.WEST);
        b.addActionListener(this);
        add(b = new Button("Modeless"), BorderLayout.EAST);
        b.addActionListener(this);
        pack();
        show();
    }

    public void actionPerformed(ActionEvent evt) {
        String what = evt.getActionCommand();
        if ("Modal".equals(what)) {
            new MainDialog(this, true);
        } else if ("Modeless".equals(what)) {
            new MainDialog(this, false);
```

A
B
C
D
E
F
G
H
I
J
K
L
M
N
O
P
Q
R
S
T
U
V
W
X
Y
Z

513

```
                }
            }

        static public void main(String[] args) {
            new Main();
        }
    }
    class MainDialog extends Dialog implements ActionListener {
        // These two integers hold the location of the last window.
        // New windows are created at an offset to the previous one.
        static int offsetX, offsetY;

        MainDialog(Frame frame, boolean modal) {
            super(frame, modal);
            setTitle(isModal() ? "Modal" : "Modeless");
            Button b;
            add(b = new Button("Quit"), BorderLayout.CENTER);
            b.addActionListener(this);
            offsetX += 20;
            offsetY += 20;
            setLocation(offsetX, offsetY);
            pack();
            show();
        }

        public void actionPerformed(ActionEvent evt) {
            dispose();
        }
    }
```

A
B
C
D
E
F
G
H
I
J
K
L
M
N
O
P
Q
R
S
T
U
V
W
X
Y
Z

getTitle()

PURPOSE   Retrieves the dialog's title.

SYNTAX   `public String getTitle()`

RETURNS   A string containing the dialog's title. The result value may be `null`.

EXAMPLE   See `setTitle()`.

isModal()

PURPOSE   Retrieves this dialog's modal state.

SYNTAX   `public boolean isModal()`

DESCRIPTION   A visible modal dialog prevents the user from interacting with any other AWT window. A modeless dialog does not have this affect; it behaves more like a frame.

RETURNS   `true` if the dialog is modal; `false` if the dialog is modeless.

SEE ALSO   setModal().

EXAMPLE   See Dialog().

isResizable()

PURPOSE   Retrieves this dialog's resizable state.

SYNTAX   `public boolean isResizable()`

RETURNS   `true` if this dialog is currently resizable; `false` otherwise.

EXAMPLE   See setResizable().

paramString()

PURPOSE   Generates a string representation of this dialog's state.

SYNTAX   `protected String paramString()`

DESCRIPTION   The string representation of a dialog consists of its container string representa-
               tion and its title and whether it is modal.

               If you subclass `Dialog`, you should override this method to add your addi-
               tional state to the dialog's state by concatenating the new information with the
               results of `super.paramString()`. This method is called by the `toString()`
               method and is typically used for debugging.

RETURNS   A non-`null` string representing the dialog's state.

OVERRIDES   Container.paramString().

SEE ALSO   Component.toString(). java.lang.Object.toString().

EXAMPLE   This example shows how to override the `paramString()` method. The over-
               ride appends an extra piece of state (`myData`) to the returned string. Figure 118
               shows the output of the example.

```
Main[0,0,0x0,invalid,hidden,layout=java.awt.BorderLayout,mode-
less,title=paramString Example,myData=Testing]
```

FIGURE 118: Dialog.paramString() Output.

```java
import java.awt.*;

class Main extends Dialog {
    String myData = "Testing";
```

```
Main() {
    super(new Frame(), "paramString Example", false);
}

protected String paramString() {
    String str = super.paramString();
    if (myData != null) {
        str += ",myData=" + myData;
    }
    return str;
}

static public void main(String[] args) {
    Main m = new Main();
    System.out.println(m);
}
}
```

A
B
C
D
E
F
G
H
I
J
K
L
M
N
O
P
Q
R
S
T
U
V
W
X
Y
Z

setModal()

PURPOSE   Sets this dialog's modal property.

SYNTAX   `public void setModal(boolean modal)`

DESCRIPTION   This method sets the dialog's modal property as specified by `modal`.

PARAMETERS

`modal`   If `true`, dialog becomes modal; if `false`, dialog becomes modeless.

SEE ALSO   `isModal()`.

setResizable()

PURPOSE   Sets this dialog's resizable property.

SYNTAX   `public synchronized void setResizable(boolean resizable)`

DESCRIPTION   This method sets this dialog box to be resizable or nonresizable. If `resizable` is `true`, resizing is enabled; otherwise, it is disabled.

PARAMETERS

`resizable`   If `true`, the dialog becomes resizable; otherwise, the dialog becomes nonresizable.

EXAMPLE   This example creates a dialog with a checkbox indicating whether the dialog can be resized. Clicking the checkbox changes the resizable property of the dialog. See Figure 119.

FIGURE 119: `Dialog.setResizable()`.

516

```
import java.awt.*;
import java.awt.event.*;

class Main extends Dialog implements ItemListener {
    Main() {
        super(new Frame(), "setResizable Example", false);
        Checkbox cb = new Checkbox("Resizable", null, isResizable());
        cb.addItemListener(this);
        add(cb, BorderLayout.NORTH);
        pack();
        show();
    }

    public void itemStateChanged(ItemEvent evt) {
        setResizable(evt.getStateChange() == ItemEvent.SELECTED);
    }

    static public void main(String[] args) {
        new Main();
    }
}
```

setTitle()

PURPOSE   Sets this dialog's title.

SYNTAX   `public synchronized void setTitle(String title)`

DESCRIPTION   This method sets the dialog's title to be the string `title`.

PARAMETERS
`title`   The string specifying the dialog's new title. A value of `null` clears the title.

SEE ALSO   `getTitle()`.

EXAMPLE   This example creates a text field in a dialog. The text field is initialized with the current title of the frame. Pressing Return while in the text field sets the frame's title to the text in the text field. See Figure 120.

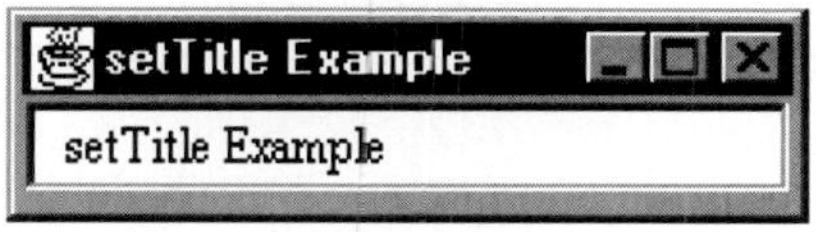

FIGURE 120: Dialog.setTitle().

```
import java.awt.*;
import java.awt.event.*;

class Main extends Dialog implements ActionListener {
    TextField t;

    Main() {
        super(new Frame(), "setTitle Example", false);
        // Initialize the text field with the current title.
        t = new TextField(getTitle(), 50);
```

```
        t.addActionListener(this);
            add( t, BorderLayout.NORTH);
            pack();
            show();
        }

        public void actionPerformed(ActionEvent evt) {
        setTitle((String)evt.getActionCommand());
        }

        static public void main(String[] args) {
            new Main();
        }
    }
```

A
B
C
D
E
F
G

show()

H
I
J
K
L
M
N
O
P
Q
R
S
T
U
V
W
X
Y
Z

PURPOSE   Makes this dialog visible and in front of all other windows.

SYNTAX   `public void show()`

DESCRIPTION   This method calls the `addNotify()` method, validates the dialog's layout, and then makes the dialog visible. If the dialog is already visible, it is brought to the front. If the dialog is modal, `show()` will block until the dialog is no longer visible (via `setVisible(false)` or `dispose()`).

OVERRIDES   `Window.show()`.

SEE ALSO   `Component.setVisible()`.

EXAMPLE   See `setResizable()`, `setTitle()`.

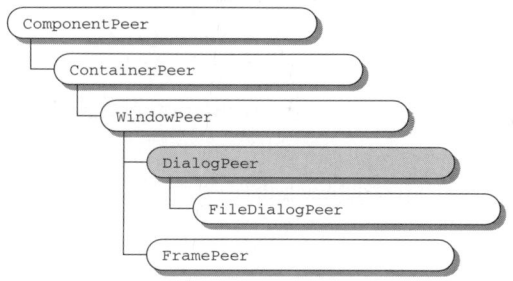

Syntax

```
public interface DialogPeer extends WindowPeer
```

Description

The dialog component (see the `Dialog` class) in the AWT uses the platform's native implementation of a dialog box. So that the AWT dialog box behaves the same on all platforms, the dialog box is assigned a *peer*, whose task is to translate the behavior of the platform's native dialog box to the behavior of the AWT dialog box.

AWT programmers normally do not directly use peer classes and interfaces. Instead, they deal with AWT components in the `java.awt` package. These in turn automatically manage their peers. Only someone who is porting the AWT to another platform should be concerned with the peer classes and interfaces. Consequently, most peer documentation refers to `java.awt` counterparts.

See `Component` and `Toolkit` for additional information about component peers.

MEMBER SUMMARY	
Peer Methods	
`setResizable()`	Sets the resizable property.
`setTitle()`	Sets the dialog's title.

See Also

`java.awt.Component`, `java.awt.Dialog`, `java.awt.Toolkit`.

A
B
C
D
E
F
G
H
I
J
K
L
M
N
O
P
Q
R
S
T
U
V
W
X
Y
Z

setResizable( )

PURPOSE	Sets the resizable property.
SYNTAX	`void setResizable(boolean resizeable)`
PARAMETERS	
`resizable`	If `true`, the dialog becomes resizable; otherwise, the dialog becomes nonresizable.
SEE ALSO	`java.awt.Dialog.setResizable()`.

setTitle( )

PURPOSE	Sets the dialog's title.
SYNTAX	`void setTitle(String title)`
PARAMETERS	
`title`	The string specifying the dialog's new title. A value of `null` clears the title.
SEE ALSO	`java.awt.Dialog.setTitle()`.

Dimension

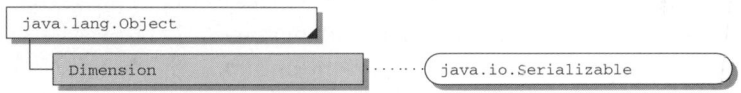

```
java.lang.Object
        Dimension ..............java.io.Serializable
```

Syntax
```
public class Dimension implements Serializable
```

Description
A dimension is used to represent a size. It holds two values: a width and height. In general, when returning a dimension instance in a method call, you should either have a copy returned, if you need to retain the instance, or have the instance discarded after it is returned. If you have a dimension instance passed in a method call and wish to continue using the instance, note whether the method will retain the instance or copy the values.

MEMBER SUMMARY	
Constructor	
Dimension()	Constructs a new Dimension instance.
Size Methods	
getSize()	Retrieves a copy of this dimension.
setSize()	Changes the value of this dimension.
Fields	
height	Holds the dimension's height.
width	Holds the dimension's width.
Object Override Methods	
equals()	Determines whether an object is equal to this dimension.
toString()	Generates a string representation of this dimension's values.

See Also
Component.getSize(), Component.setSize(), java.io.Serializable.

Example

This example implements a `Circle` class, which is an object that has an origin and radius. This `Circle` class implements the `getSize()` method, which returns the circle's dimension. The example creates a circle object and paints it in a frame. See Figure 121.

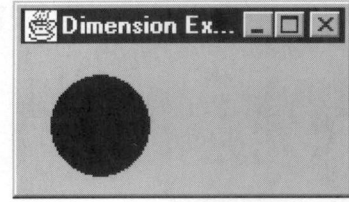

FIGURE 121: Dimension.

A
B
C
D
E
F
G
H
I
J
K
L
M
N
O
P
Q
R
S
T
U
V
W
X
Y
Z

```java
import java.awt.*;

class Main extends Frame {
    Circle c = new Circle(new Point(60, 60), 25);

    Main() {
        super("Dimension Example");
        setSize(100, 100);
        show();
    }

    public void paint(Graphics g) {
        c.draw(g);
    }

    public static void main(String[] args) {
        new Main();
    }
}

class Circle {
    Point origin;
    int radius;

    Circle(Point origin, int radius) {
        this.origin = origin;
        this.radius = radius;
    }

    public Dimension getSize() {
        return new Dimension(2 * radius, 2 * radius);
    }

    public void draw(Graphics g) {
        g.fillOval(origin.x-radius, origin.y-radius,
                getSize().width, getSize().height);
    }
}
```

Dimension( )

PURPOSE   Constructs a new `Dimension` instance.

SYNTAX   `public Dimension()`
             `public Dimension(Dimension dimension)`

522

`public Dimension(int width, int height)`

DESCRIPTION   This constructor creates a new `Dimension` instance that has the specified initial values. If `dimension` is specified, the initial values for the new dimension are taken from `dimension`. If neither `dimension` nor `width` and `height` are specified, the default is 0.

PARAMETERS

`dimension`   The non-`null` dimension containing the initial values.
`height`   The dimension's height.
`width`   The dimension's width.

EXAMPLE   See the class example.

equals()

PURPOSE   Determines whether an object is equal to this dimension.

SYNTAX   `public boolean equals(Object obj)`

DESCRIPTION   An object `obj` is equal to this dimension if `obj` is an instance of `Dimension` and has the same width and height as this dimension.

PARAMETERS

`obj`   The object to compare.

RETURNS   `true` if obj is equal; `false` otherwise.

OVERRIDES   `java.lang.Component.equals()`.

EXAMPLE   See `getSize()`.

getSize()

PURPOSE   Retrieves a copy of this dimension.

SYNTAX   `public Dimension getSize()`

RETURNS   A new instance of `Dimension` that is a copy of this dimension.

SEE ALSO   `height`, `setSize()`, `width`.

EXAMPLE   This example is a variation on the class example. It allows the user to dynamically change the size of the circle. See Figure 122.

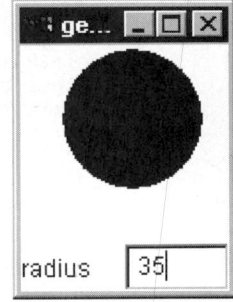

FIGURE 122:
`Dimension.getSize()`.

```
import java.awt.*;
import java.awt.event.*;

class Main extends Frame implements ActionListener {
    Circle c = new Circle(new Point(60, 60), 25);
    TextField textfield;

    Main() {
        super("getSize Example");

        Panel p = new Panel(new GridLayout(1, 0));
        p.add(new Label("radius"));
        p.add(textfield=new TextField("25"));
        textfield.addActionListener(this);

        add(p, BorderLayout.SOUTH);
        setSize(100, 150);
        show();
    }

    public void paint(Graphics g) {
        c.draw(g);
    }

    public void actionPerformed(ActionEvent evt) {
        Dimension orig = c.getSize();
        Dimension sz = orig.getSize(); // make copy
        int radius = Integer.parseInt(evt.getActionCommand());
        sz.setSize(radius*2, radius*2);
        if (sz.equals(orig)) {
            System.out.println("Radius unchanged");
        } else {
            c.setSize(sz);
        }
        repaint();
    }

    public static void main(String[] args) {
        new Main();
    }
}

class Circle {
    Point origin;
    int radius;

    Circle(Point origin, int radius) {
        this.origin = origin;
        this.radius = radius;
    }

    public Dimension getSize() {
        return new Dimension(2 * radius, 2 * radius);
    }

    public void setSize(Dimension d) {
        radius = d.width/2;
    }

    public void draw(Graphics g) {
```

A
B
C
D
E
F
G
H
I
J
K
L
M
N
O
P
Q
R
S
T
U
V
W
X
Y
Z

```
        g.fillOval(origin.x-radius, origin.y-radius,
                getSize().width, getSize().height);
    }
}
```

height

PURPOSE	This field holds this dimension's height.
SYNTAX	`public int height`
SEE ALSO	`getSize()`, `setSize()`, `width`.
EXAMPLE	See the class example.

setSize()

PURPOSE	Changes the value of this dimension.
SYNTAX	`public void setSize(Dimension dim)` `public void setSize(int width, int height)`
DESCRIPTION	This method changes the value of this dimension. If the dimension `dim` is supplied, the `width` and `height` of this dimension are set to `dim.width` and `dim.height`, respectively. If `width` and `height` are supplied, they are used as the new width and height values for this dimension.
PARAMETERS	
`dim`	The dimension to use.
`height`	The height to use.
`width`	The width to use.
SEE ALSO	`getSize()`, `height`, `width`.
EXAMPLE	See `getSize()`.

toString()

PURPOSE	Generates a string representation of this dimension.
SYNTAX	`public String toString()`
DESCRIPTION	This method generates this dimension's string representation, which consists of its width and height. This method is typically used for debugging.

A
B
C
D
E
F
G
H
I
J
K
L
M
N
O
P
Q
R
S
T
U
V
W
X
Y
Z

RETURNS	A non-`null` string representing this dimension's state.
OVERRIDES	`java.lang.Object.toString()`.
EXAMPLE	See `java.lang.Object.toString()`.

width

PURPOSE	This field holds this dimension's width.
SYNTAX	`public int width`
SEE ALSO	`getSize()`, `height`, `setSize()`.
EXAMPLE	See the class example.

DirectColorModel

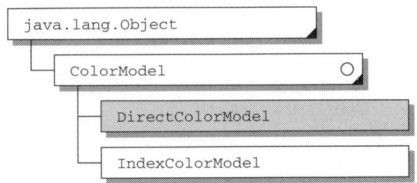

Syntax
`public class DirectColorModel extends ColorModel`

Description

A pixel value in an image can be encoded in either a *direct color model* or an *indexed color model*. In the direct color model encoding, pixel values actually contain the color information; the color model is used to extract the color infor-

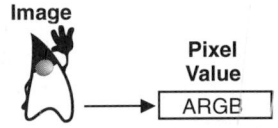

FIGURE 123: **Direct Color Model Pixel Values.**

mation from the pixel value (see Figure 123). The typical encoding used in a direct color model is to divide the bits in a pixel value among the colors of this dimension's components. For example, in one encoding you could allow 2 bits each for red and green, 10 bits for blue, and 4 bits for alpha.

See the `ColorModel` class for more information about color models. See `IndexColorModel` for more information about indexed color models.

MEMBER SUMMARY

Constructor

`DirectColorModel()`	Constructs a `DirectColorModel` from the given masks.

Color Component Retrieval Methods

`getAlpha()`	Retrieves the alpha component of a pixel value.
`getBlue()`	Retrieves the blue component of a pixel value.
`getGreen()`	Retrieves the green component of a pixel value.
`getRed()`	Retrieves the red component of a pixel value.
`getRGB()`	Converts a pixel value to a pixel value in the default color model.

Color Component Mask Retrieval Methods

`getAlphaMask()`	Retrieves the bit mask for the alpha transparency component.
`getBlueMask()`	Retrieves the bit mask for the blue color component.
`getGreenMask()`	Retrieves the bit mask for the green color component.
`getRedMask()`	Retrieves the bit mask for the red color component.

Example

This example creates a low-resolution color filter that reduces the number of bits of a color. See Figure 124. A frame is created that displays an image plus a text field for entering the number of bits per color component. When you change the value in the text field, the image is passed through the filter and then redisplayed. For example, if you enter the value 1 in the text field, each of the four color components— red, green, blue, and alpha—of every pixel value in the image will be reduced to 1 bit.

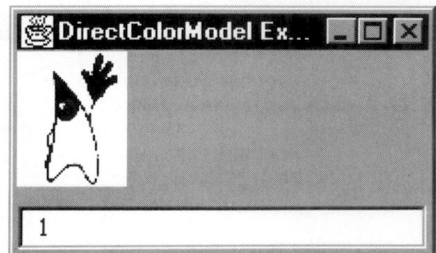

FIGURE 124: DirectColorModel.

The filter is derived from RGBImageFilter. This makes it convenient for modifying image colors by flowing all pixel values through a single method called filterRGB() (see RGBImageFilter for details). Whenever the bit size for the color components is changed, a new direct color model is created to represent the new encoding. As pixels flow through the filter, the colors of the pixel values are reduced and the filter's direct color model is substituted for the image producer's color model.

```java
import java.awt.*;
import java.awt.image.*;
import java.awt.event.*;
import java.net.*;
import java.util.*;

class Main extends Frame implements ActionListener {
    TextField textField = new TextField();
    ImageCanvas icv;

    Main(String filename) {
        super("DirectColorModel Example");
        try {
            // Retrieve the image.
            Image image = getToolkit().getImage(filename);

            add(icv = new ImageCanvas(image), BorderLayout.CENTER);
            add(textField, BorderLayout.SOUTH);
        } catch (Exception e) {
            e.printStackTrace();
        }

        // Add listener for text field
        textField.addActionListener(this);
        setSize(50, 100);
        show();
    }

    public void actionPerformed(ActionEvent evt) {
        icv.setColorBits(Integer.parseInt(textField.getText()));
    }

    static public void main(String[] args) {
        if (args.length == 1) {
```

```
                new Main(args[0]);
            } else {
                System.err.println("usage: java Main <image file>");
            }
        }
    }

class ImageCanvas extends Component {
    Image newImage;
    Image image;
    LowResFilter imgf = new LowResFilter();

    ImageCanvas(Image image) {
        this.image = image;
        processImage();
    }

    void setColorBits(int bits) {
        imgf.setColorBits(bits);
        processImage();
    }

    public void paint(Graphics g) {
        update(g);
    }

    public void update(Graphics g) {
        g.drawImage(newImage, 0, 0, this);
    }

    void processImage() {
        ImageProducer ip = image.getSource();

        ip = new FilteredImageSource(ip, imgf);
        newImage = getToolkit().createImage(ip);
        repaint();
    }
}

class LowResFilter extends RGBImageFilter {
    int bits;    // bits for each color.
    DirectColorModel lowResColorModel =
        (DirectColorModel)ColorModel.getRGBdefault();

    void setColorBits(int bits) {
        int mask = 0;
        this.bits = bits;

        for (int i=0; i<bits; i++) {
            mask |= (mask<<1) + 1;
        }
        lowResColorModel = new DirectColorModel(bits * 3,
            mask<<(2 * bits), mask<<bits, mask);
        System.out.println(
            Integer.toString(lowResColorModel.getAlphaMask(), 16));
        System.out.println(
            Integer.toString(lowResColorModel.getRedMask(), 16));
        System.out.println(
            Integer.toString(lowResColorModel.getGreenMask(), 16));
        System.out.println(
```

A
B
C
D
E
F
G
H
I
J
K
L
M
N
O
P
Q
R
S
T
U
V
W
X
Y
Z

```
                    Integer.toString(lowResColorModel.getBlueMask(), 16));
        }

        public void setColorModel(ColorModel model) {
            consumer.setColorModel(lowResColorModel);
        }

        public int filterRGB(int x, int y, int rgb) {
            int res = 1 << bits;
            int a = ColorModel.getRGBdefault().getAlpha(rgb);
            int r = ColorModel.getRGBdefault().getRed(rgb);
            int g = ColorModel.getRGBdefault().getGreen(rgb);
            int b = ColorModel.getRGBdefault().getBlue(rgb);

            return ((a * res / 256) << 3*bits)
                | ((r * res / 256) << 2*bits)
                | ((g * res / 256) << bits)
                | ((b * res / 256)));
        }

        public void filterRGBPixels(int x, int y, int w, int h,
                                int pixels[], int off, int scansize) {
            int index = off;
            for (int cy = 0; cy < h; cy++) {
                for (int cx = 0; cx < w; cx++) {
                    pixels[index] = filterRGB(x + cx, y + cy, pixels[index]);
                    index++;
                }
                index += scansize - w;
            }
            consumer.setPixels(x, y, w, h, lowResColorModel, pixels, off, scansize);
        }
    }
```

DirectColorModel()

PURPOSE Constructs a DirectColorModel instance.

SYNTAX public DirectColorModel(int bits, int rmask, int gmask, int
bmask)
public DirectColorModel(int bits, int rmask, int gmask, int bmask,
int amask)

DESCRIPTION These constructors construct a new DirectColorModel object based on the
specified masks. A mask for a color component specifies which bit positions in
the pixel values are occupied by the color component. For example, the value 3
specifies the bit positions 0 and 1 (small endian). The bit positions in a mask
must be contiguous, and the masks must not overlap. The sum of all of the
masks must be no more than the number of bits specified by bits.

PARAMETERS

amask The mask for the alpha color component.

`bits`	The total number of bits used by the pixel values.
`bmask`	The mask for the blue color component.
`gmask`	The mask for the green color component.
`rmask`	The mask for the red color component.

EXAMPLE   See the class example.

getAlpha()

PURPOSE   Retrieves the alpha component of a pixel value.

SYNTAX   `final public int getAlpha(int pixelValue)`

DESCRIPTION   This method retrieves the alpha component of the pixel value `pixelValue`. The return value must be in the range 0–255, where the value 0 means completely transparent and the value 255 means completely opaque.

PARAMETERS
`pixelValue`   The pixel value specifying a color in the color model.

RETURNS   The alpha transparency component in the range 0–255.

EXAMPLE   See the class example.

getAlphaMask()

PURPOSE   Retrieves the bit mask for the alpha transparency component.

SYNTAX   `final public int getAlphaMask()`

DESCRIPTION   The return value is identical to the one supplied to the constructor.

RETURNS   The mask for the alpha component.

EXAMPLE   See the class example.

getBlue()

PURPOSE   Retrieves the blue component of a pixel value.

SYNTAX   `final public int getBlue(int pixelValue)`

DESCRIPTION   This method retrieves the blue component of the pixel value `pixelValue`. The return value must be in the range 0–255, where the value 0 means no blue and the value 255 means maximum blue.

A
B
C
D
E
F
G
H
I
J
K
L
M
N
O
P
Q
R
S
T
U
V
W
X
Y
Z

PARAMETERS

  `pixelValue`   The pixel value specifying a color in the color model.

RETURNS   The blue color component in the range 0–255.

EXAMPLE   See the class example.

getBlueMask()

PURPOSE   Retrieves the bit mask for the blue color component.

SYNTAX   `final public int getBlueMask()`

DESCRIPTION   The return value is identical to the one supplied to the constructor.

RETURNS   The mask for the blue component.

EXAMPLE   See the class example.

getGreen()

PURPOSE   Retrieves the green component of a pixel value.

SYNTAX   `final public int getGreen(int pixelValue)`

DESCRIPTION   This method retrieves the green component of the pixel value `pixelValue`. The return value must be in the range 0–255, where the value 0 means no green and the value 255 means maximum green.

PARAMETERS

  `pixelValue`   The pixel value specifying a color in the color model.

RETURNS   The green color component in the range 0–255.

EXAMPLE   See the class example.

getGreenMask()

PURPOSE   Retrieves the bit mask for the green color component.

SYNTAX   `final public int getGreenMask()`

DESCRIPTION   The return value is identical to the one supplied to the constructor.

RETURNS   The mask for the green component.

EXAMPLE   See the class example.

getRed()

PURPOSE   Retrieves the red component of a pixel value.

SYNTAX   `final public int getRed(int pixelValue)`

DESCRIPTION   This method retrieves the red component of the pixel value `pixelValue`. The return value must be in the range 0–255, where the value 0 means no red and the value 255 means maximum red.

PARAMETERS
`pixelValue`   The pixel value specifying a color in the color model.

RETURNS   The red color component in the range 0–255.

EXAMPLE   See the class example.

getRedMask()

PURPOSE   Retrieves the mask that specifies which bits in the pixel value contain the red color component.

SYNTAX   `final public int getRedMask()`

DESCRIPTION   The return value is identical to the one supplied to the constructor.

RETURNS   The mask for the red component.

EXAMPLE   See the class example.

getRGB()

PURPOSE   Converts a pixel value to a pixel value in the default color model.

SYNTAX   `final public int getRGB(int pixelValue)`

DESCRIPTION   The pixel value `pixelValue` is converted to an equivalent pixel value that must be interpreted using the default color model. The color of the new pixel value might not be identical to the color of `pixelValue`, so there may be some loss of color information.

PARAMETERS
`pixelValue`   The pixel value specifying a color in the direct color model.

RETURNS   A pixel value that specifies a color in the default color model.

OVERRIDES   `ColorModel.getRGB()`.

SEE ALSO   `ColorModel.getRGBdefault()`.

EXAMPLE   See the `ColorModel` class example.

A
B
C
D
E
F
G
H
I
J
K
L
M
N
O
P
Q
R
S
T
U
V
W
X
Y
Z

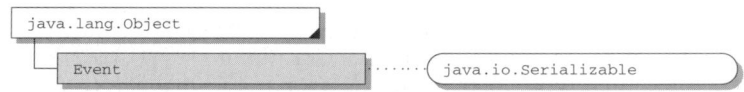

Note: Use of the Event class is deprecated. Use AWTEvent and its hierarchy of event sub-classes instead.

Syntax
```
public class Event
```

Description

In Java 1.0, events that flow between the AWT components are represented by objects of the Event class. When an event such as a mouse click or a keyboard press occurs, a new platform-independent Event object is created to hold data about the event. All events use the Event class and so have the same fields, but not all fields are used for all events. The event type determines which fields are to be used.

In Java 1.1, event types are organized into a class hierarchy rooted at AWTEvent. For example, there is a MouseEvent for describing mouse-related events and a KeyEvent for describing keyboard input related events. Each of these classes might have event subtypes. For example, a focus event has two event subtypes: gaining the focus and losing the focus. Each AWTEvent subclass contains methods for retrieving properties specific to its event type.

In Java 1.1, the old event model is still supported, but the usage of it is deprecated. You should migrate your program to use the new event model, which is described in detail in AWTEvent.

Firing Events

Events can be fired by a component as the user interacts with the component. In Java 1.0, not all components fire events such as mouse and keyboard events. Instead, the component may hide all mouse and keyboard events and fire only a single action event. In Java 1.1, all AWT components can fire mouse and keyboard events, as well as focus and component events. To determine what additional events a component fires, check the component's class description.

Events can also be fired other than in response to user interaction. For example, you may want a component to become enabled when some asynchronous activity completes. The thread doing the asynchronous activity could either disable the component directly or send it a special event to perform that task itself. The latter method would be more appropriate if disabling the component also involved other activities known only to the component.

In Java 1.0, special events can be created either by subclassing `Event` or by creating an action event and filling in the `arg` and `target` fields. The event handler can then identify the special event by testing the `arg` and/or `target` fields using the `instanceof` operator. In Java 1.1, special events can be created by subclassing the appropriate subclass of `AWTEvent` (see *See Also* later in this discussion) and defining additional properties for the new event. You can get a feel for how to do this by examining the existing subclasses of `AWTEvent`.

Event Flow

In Java 1.0, events flow up the component hierarchy. For example, a button that fires an action event can either handle the event itself or not. If it doesn't, the AWT framework automatically forwards the event onto the button's parent. The parent can either handle the event or not. If it doesn't, the AWT framework again forwards the event, this time to the next parent. If no one handles the event, the event is simply discarded. See Figure 125(a).

In Java 1.1, the event flow does not flow up the component hierarchy. In the new event model, *event listeners* are registered with a component for receiving events fired by the component. There are different types of event listeners registered for the corresponding types of events. When the component fires an event, event listeners of that event type are notified to handle the event. The event does not flow up the component hierarchy unless one of the event listeners explicitly redispatches the event to the component's parent. If there are no event listeners for the event type registered with the component that fired the event, the event is simply discarded. See Figure 125(b).

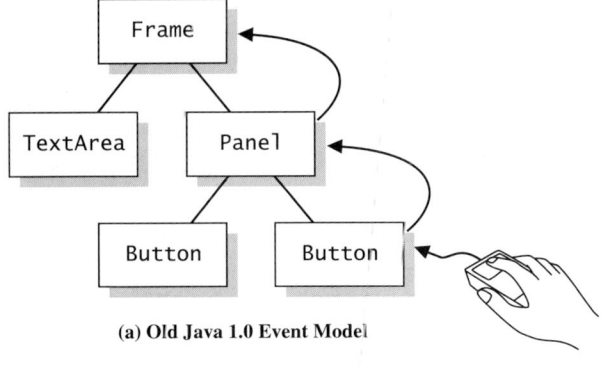

(a) Old Java 1.0 Event Model

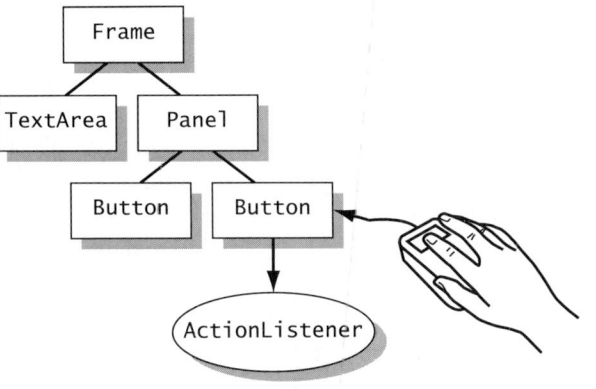

(b) New Java 1.1 Event Model

FIGURE 125:   Event Flow in Component Hierarchy.

Event Handlers

In Java 1.0, events are handled by overriding a component's handleEvent() method. In Java 1.1, events are handled by event listeners registered with the event's source. Typically, a component controls how its different types of events are processed by adding or removing event listeners of the corresponding type. If the component requires special processing to be performed prior to the dispatching of the event to its listeners, it overrides Component.processEvent().

Mouse Events

In Java 1.0, the AWT assumes that the mouse has only one button. This means that on a mouse with more than one button, pressing any of the buttons fires the same event type. A specific bit set in the event's modifiers field indicates which button was pressed. In particular, if the ALT_MASK bit is set, the middle mouse button was pressed; if the META_MASK bit is set, the right mouse button was pressed. On platforms with mice that have fewer than three buttons, the extra buttons can be simulated by holding down the appropriate modifier key (Shift, Control, or Alt) while pressing the mouse button.

This design does not allow you to determine, for example, on a platform with a three-button mouse, whether the right button was pressed or whether the left button was pressed while the META_MASK was held down.

In Java 1.1, the mouse event's modifiers contain different bit masks for the mouse button keys and the Alt, Meta, and Control keys. This means that you can always determine which mouse button was pushed, as well as the modifier key (if any) held while pressing the mouse button. See MouseEvent for details.

Cursor Coordinates

In Java 1.0, the coordinates of the cursor are captured in the x and y fields for mouse-related events. As an event travels up the component hierarchy, the cursor coordinates are automatically translated to be relative to the bounds of the component currently holding the event. This means the cursor coordinates are always relative to the bounds of the component that handles the event, not to the bounds of the component that fires the event. For example, if an event was fired by a button in a panel and the event was handled by the panel, the cursor coordinates in x and y would be relative to the bounds of the panel, not to the bounds of the button.

Another important fact about cursor coordinates in an event is that if the component handling the event is a container with nonzero insets, the cursor coordinates are relative to the container's inset area rather than to the container's bounds; see the Container class for more details.

In Java 1.1, the coordinates of the cursor are captured in the MouseEvent instance and are obtained using its getX() and getY() methods. These coordinates are not translated relative to the listeners handling the event because a listener need not even be a component. The coordinates in a mouse event are always relative to the bounds of the source component that fired the event.

Compatibility of Event Models

The Java 1.1 AWT can handle both components that use the Java 1.1 event model and components that use the Java 1.0 event model. However, mixing components that use both models in a single application or applet or mixing Java 1.1 and Java 1.0 events within a single component is not recommended.

When an event is fired, the AWT must determine whether to use the Java 1.1 model or the Java 1.0 model to process it. An event is classified as a Java 1.1 event if the event's source has *any* registered listeners (regardless of event type) or if `Component.enableEvents()` has been called on it (regardless of event type). Otherwise, the event will be treated as a Java 1.0 event and processed using the target component's `handleEvent()` method as described previously.

Because the event flows of the two event models are different, a Java 1.0 event will be propagated up its component hierarchy, while a Java 1.1 event will not be propagated further than the event's source. This is true independent of the model used by the object's containers in its component hierarchy. In other words, a Java 1.1 event will never propagate up its source's container hierarchy, even if the source's parent is using the Java 1.0 event model, while a Java 1.0 event will always be propagate up its component hierarchy.

MEMBER SUMMARY	
Constructor	
Event()	Use constructors for one of AWTEvent's subclasses instead.
Event Types	
ACTION_EVENT	Replaced by ActionEvent.ACTION_PERFORMED.
GOT_FOCUS	Replaced by FocusEvent.FOCUS_GAINED.
KEY_ACTION	Replaced by KeyEvent.KEY_PRESSED.
KEY_ACTION_RELEASE	Replaced by KeyEvent.KEY_RELEASED.
KEY_PRESS	Replaced by KeyEvent.KEY_PRESSED.
KEY_RELEASE	Replaced by KeyEvent.KEY_RELEASED.
LIST_DESELECT	Replaced by ItemEvent.ITEM_STATE_CHANGED.
LIST_SELECT	Replaced by ItemEvent.ITEM_STATE_CHANGED.
LOAD_FILE	Not used.
LOST_FOCUS	Replaced by FocusEvent.FOCUS_LOST.
MOUSE_DOWN	Replaced by MouseEvent.MOUSE_PRESSED.
MOUSE_DRAG	Replaced by MouseEvent.MOUSE_DRAGGED.
MOUSE_ENTER	Replaced by MouseEvent.MOUSE_ENTERED.
MOUSE_EXIT	Replaced by MouseEvent.MOUSE_EXITED.
MOUSE_MOVE	Replaced by MouseEvent.MOUSE_MOVED.
MOUSE_UP	Replaced by MouseEvent.MOUSE_RELEASED.
SAVE_FILE	Not used.
SCROLL_ABSOLUTE	Replaced by AdjustmentEvent.TRACK.
SCROLL_LINE_DOWN	Replaced by AdjustmentEvent.UNIT_INCREMENT.
SCROLL_LINE_UP	Replaced by AdjustmentEvent.UNIT_DECREMENT.
SCROLL_PAGE_DOWN	Replaced by AdjustmentEvent.BLOCK_INCREMENT.
SCROLL_PAGE_UP	Replaced by AdjustmentEvent.BLOCK_DECREMENT.
WINDOW_DEICONIFY	Replaced by WindowEvent.WINDOW_DEICONIFIED.
WINDOW_DESTROY	Replaced by WindowEvent.WINDOW_CLOSING.
WINDOW_EXPOSE	Replaced by WindowEvent.WINDOW_ACTIVATED.
WINDOW_ICONIFY	Replaced by WindowEvent.WINDOW_ICONIFIED.
WINDOW_MOVED	Replaced by ComponentEvent.MOVED.
Event Fields	
arg	Replaced by event-specific property.
clickCount	Replaced by MouseEvent.getClickCount().
evt	Replaced by EventQueue.
id	Replaced by AWTEvent.getID().
key	Replaced by KeyEvent.getKeyCode().
modifiers	Replaced by InputEvent.getModifiers().
target	Replaced by EventObject.getSource().
when	Replaced by InputEvent.getWhen().
x	Replaced by MouseEvent.getX().
y	Replaced by MouseEvent.getY().

MEMBER SUMMARY

Keyboard Modifier Masks

ALT_MASK	Replaced by InputEvent.ALT_MASK.
CTRL_MASK	Replaced by InputEvent.CTRL_MASK.
META_MASK	Replaced by InputEvent.META_MASK.
SHIFT_MASK	Replaced by InputEvent.SHIFT_MASK.

Keyboard Modifier Methods

controlDown()	Replaced by InputEvent.isControlDown().
metaDown()	Replaced by InputEvent.isMetaDown().
shiftDown()	Replaced by InputEvent.isShiftDown().

Non-ASCII Key Constants

DOWN	Replaced by KeyEvent.VK_DOWN.
END	Replaced by KeyEvent.VK_END.
F1	Replaced by KeyEvent.VK_F1.
F10	Replaced by KeyEvent.VK_F10.
F11	Replaced by KeyEvent.VK_F11.
F12	Replaced by KeyEvent.VK_F12.
F2	Replaced by KeyEvent.VK_F2.
F3	Replaced by KeyEvent.VK_F3.
F4	Replaced by KeyEvent.VK_F4.
F5	Replaced by KeyEvent.VK_F5.
F6	Replaced by KeyEvent.VK_F6.
F7	Replaced by KeyEvent.VK_F7.
F8	Replaced by KeyEvent.VK_F8.
F9	Replaced by KeyEvent.VK_F9.
HOME	Replaced by KeyEvent.VK_HOME.
LEFT	Replaced by KeyEvent.VK_LEFT.
PGDN	Replaced by KeyEvent.VK_PAGE_DOWN.
PGUP	Replaced by KeyEvent.VK_PAGE_UP.
RIGHT	Replaced by KeyEvent.VK_RIGHT.
UP	Replaced by KeyEvent.VK_UP.

Translate Method

translate()	Replaced by MouseEvent.translatePoint().

Debugging Methods

paramString()	Replaced by AWTEvent.paramString().
toString()	Replaced by AWTEvent.toString().

A
B
C
D

F
G
H
I
J
K
L
M
N
O
P
Q
R
S
T
U
V
W
X
Y
Z

See Also

AWTEvent, AWTEventMulticaster, Component.dispatchEvent(),
Component.processEvent(), java.awt.event.ActionEvent,
java.awt.event.ActionListener, java.awt.event.AdjustmentEvent,
java.awt.event.AdjustmentListener, java.awt.event.ComponentEvent,
java.awt.event.ComponentListener, java.awt.event.ContainerEvent,
java.awt.event.ContainerListener, java.awt.event.FocusEvent,
java.awt.event.FocusListener, java.awt.event.InputEvent,
java.awt.event.ItemEvent, java.awt.event.ItemListener,
java.awt.event.KeyEvent, java.awt.event.KeyEventListener,
java.awt.event.MouseEvent, java.awt.event.MouseListener,
java.awt.event.MouseMotionListener, java.awt.event.TextEvent,
java.awt.event.TextListener, java.awt.event.WindowEvent,
java.awt.event.WindowListener.

Example

As mentioned previously in this section, the events that are fired by the AWT components in Java 1.0 are not consistent. To cope with this, you can use the following example to experiment with each component to determine exactly what events it fires and in what situations. The program handles every event that is fired by any of the components and prints the details of the event to standard output.

An example written using the Java 1.1 event model providing the same functionality is shown as well.

See Figure 126 for a screen shot of this example.

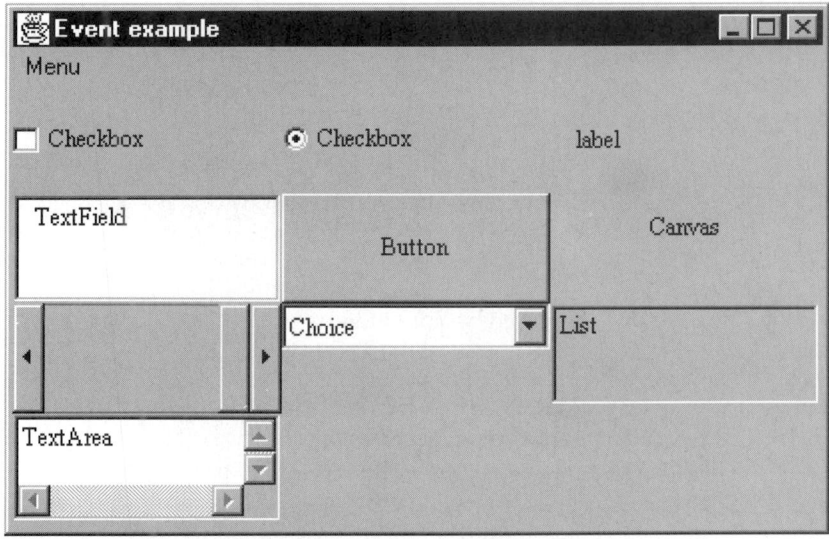

FIGURE 126:   A Container of All AWT Components.

Java 1.0

```java
import java.awt.*;
class Main extends Frame {
    Main() {
        super("Event example");

        // Menu bar with a menu and menu item.
        MenuBar mb = new MenuBar();
        Menu m = new Menu("Menu");
        m.add("MenuItem");
        m.add(new CheckboxMenuItem("CheckboxMenuItem"));
        mb.add(m);
        setMenuBar(mb);

        setLayout(new GridLayout(0, 3));

        // checkbox, grouped checkbox, label, text field, scrollbar, button
        add(new Checkbox("Checkbox"));
        add(new Checkbox("Checkbox", new CheckboxGroup(), true));
        add(new Label("label"));
        add(new TextField("TextField"));
        add(new Button("Button"));
        add(new MyCanvas());

        // scrollbar
        Scrollbar sb = new Scrollbar(Scrollbar.HORIZONTAL);
        sb.setValues(50, 50, 0, 100);
        add(sb);

        // choice
        Choice choice = new Choice();
        choice.addItem("Choice");
        choice.addItem("a choice item");
        add(choice);

        // list
        List list = new List();
        list.addItem("List");
        list.addItem("a list item");
        add(list);

        // text area
        TextArea textArea = new TextArea("TextArea");
        textArea.resize(100, 50);
        add(textArea);

        pack();
        show();
    }

    public boolean handleEvent(Event evt) {
        if (evt.target instanceof Button) {
            System.out.print("Button");
        } else if (evt.target instanceof Choice) {
            System.out.print("Choice");
        } else if (evt.target instanceof Checkbox) {
            System.out.print("Checkbox");
        } else if (evt.target instanceof CheckboxGroup) {
            System.out.print("CheckboxGroup");
        } else if (evt.target instanceof Label) {
```

A
B
C
D
E
F
G
H
I
J
K
L
M
N
O
P
Q
R
S
T
U
V
W
X
Y
Z

```
                        System.out.print("Label");
            } else if (evt.target instanceof TextField) {
                System.out.print("TextField");
            } else if (evt.target instanceof Scrollbar) {
                System.out.print("Scrollbar");
            } else if (evt.target instanceof Canvas) {
                System.out.print("Canvas");
            } else if (evt.target instanceof List) {
                System.out.print("List");
            } else if (evt.target instanceof TextField) {
                System.out.print("TextField");
            } else if (evt.target instanceof TextArea) {
                System.out.print("TextArea");
            } else if (evt.target instanceof MenuItem) {
                System.out.print("MenuItem");
            } else if (evt.target instanceof Container) {
                System.out.print("Container");
            }
    System.out.print(" ");

    switch (evt.id) {
        case Event.ACTION_EVENT:
            System.out.print("ACTION_EVENT"); break;
        case Event.GOT_FOCUS:
            System.out.print("GOT_FOCUS"); break;
        case Event.KEY_ACTION:
            System.out.print("KEY_ACTION"); break;
        case Event.KEY_ACTION_RELEASE:
            System.out.print("KEY_ACTION_RELEASE"); break;
        case Event.KEY_PRESS:
            System.out.print("KEY_PRESS"); break;
        case Event.KEY_RELEASE:
            System.out.print("KEY_RELEASE"); break;
        case Event.LIST_DESELECT:
            System.out.print("LIST_DESELECT"); break;
        case Event.LIST_SELECT:
            System.out.print("LIST_SELECT"); break;
        case Event.LOAD_FILE:
            System.out.print("LOAD_FILE"); break;
        case Event.LOST_FOCUS:
            System.out.print("LOST_FOCUS"); break;
        case Event.MOUSE_DOWN:
            System.out.print("MOUSE_DOWN"); break;
        case Event.MOUSE_DRAG:
            System.out.print("MOUSE_DRAG"); break;
        case Event.MOUSE_ENTER:
            System.out.print("MOUSE_ENTER"); break;
        case Event.MOUSE_EXIT:
            System.out.print("MOUSE_EXIT"); break;
        case Event.MOUSE_MOVE:
            System.out.print("MOUSE_MOVE"); break;
        case Event.MOUSE_UP:
            System.out.print("MOUSE_UP"); break;
        case Event.SAVE_FILE:
            System.out.print("SAVE_FILE"); break;
        case Event.SCROLL_ABSOLUTE:
            System.out.print("SCROLL_ABSOLUTE"); break;
        case Event.SCROLL_LINE_DOWN:
            System.out.print("SCROLL_LINE_DOWN"); break;
        case Event.SCROLL_LINE_UP:
```

A
B
C
D
E
F
G
H
I
J
K
L
M
N
O
P
Q
R
S
T
U
V
W
X
Y
Z

```
                    System.out.print("SCROLL_LINE_UP"); break;
            case Event.SCROLL_PAGE_DOWN:
                System.out.print("SCROLL_PAGE_DOWN"); break;
            case Event.SCROLL_PAGE_UP:
                System.out.print("SCROLL_PAGE_UP"); break;
            case Event.WINDOW_DEICONIFY:
                System.out.print("WINDOW_DEICONIFY"); break;
            case Event.WINDOW_DESTROY:
                System.out.print("WINDOW_DESTROY"); break;
            case Event.WINDOW_EXPOSE:
                System.out.print("WINDOW_EXPOSE"); break;
            case Event.WINDOW_ICONIFY:
                System.out.print("WINDOW_ICONIFY"); break;
            case Event.WINDOW_MOVED:
                System.out.print("WINDOW_MOVED"); break;
        }
        System.out.print(" ("+evt.x+" "+evt.y+") w("+evt.when+")");
        System.out.print(" k("+(char)evt.key+") m("+evt.modifiers+")");
        System.out.print(" c("+evt.clickCount+") a("+evt.arg+")");
        System.out.println();
        return false;
    }

    static public void main(String[] args) {
        new Main();
    }
}

class MyCanvas extends Canvas {
    public void paint(Graphics g) {
        FontMetrics fm = g.getFontMetrics();
        g.drawString("Canvas",
            (size().width-fm.stringWidth("Canvas"))/2,
        (size().height-fm.getAscent())/2);
    }
}
```

Output

```
    Canvas KEY_RELEASE (540 183) w(827558080120) k(_) m(0) c(0) a(null)
    Canvas LOST_FOCUS (540 183) w(0) k(_) m(0) c(0) a(null)
    Canvas MOUSE_ENTER (347 454) w(827558089680) k(_) m(0) c(0) a(null)
    Canvas MOUSE_MOVE (347 454) w(827558089680) k(_) m(0) c(0) a(null)
    Canvas GOT_FOCUS (302 452) w(0) k(_) m(0) c(0) a(null)
    Canvas MOUSE_MOVE (343 465) w(827558090010) k(_) m(0) c(0) a(null)
    Canvas MOUSE_DOWN (343 464) w(827558090010) k(_) m(0) c(1) a(null)
    Canvas MOUSE_DRAG (331 480) w(827558092040) k(_) m(0) c(0) a(null)
    Canvas MOUSE_UP (331 480) w(827558092040) k(_) m(0) c(0) a(null)
    Canvas MOUSE_MOVE (331 480) w(827558092040) k(_) m(0) c(0) a(null)
    Canvas MOUSE_MOVE (309 477) w(827558092150) k(_) m(0) c(0) a(null)
    Canvas MOUSE_EXIT (251 467) w(827558092260) k(_) m(0) c(0) a(null)
    Canvas LOST_FOCUS (302 452) w(0) k(_) m(0) c(0) a(null)
    Button ACTION_EVENT (153 93) w(0) k(_) m(0) c(0) a(Button)
    TextField KEY_PRESS (4 93) w(827558094240) k(k) m(0) c(0) a(null)
    TextField KEY_RELEASE (4 93) w(827558094340) k(k) m(0) c(0) a(null)
    TextField KEY_PRESS (4 93) w(827558094450) k(l) m(0) c(0) a(null)
    Checkbox ACTION_EVENT (4 42) w(0) k(_) m(0) c(0) a(true)
    Checkbox ACTION_EVENT (4 42) w(0) k(_) m(0) c(0) a(false)
    Scrollbar SCROLL_PAGE_UP (4 144) w(0) k(_) m(0) c(0) a(40)
    Scrollbar SCROLL_ABSOLUTE (4 144) w(0) k(_) m(0) c(0) a(20)
    Scrollbar SCROLL_LINE_UP (4 144) w(0) k(_) m(0) c(0) a(17)
```

A
B
C
D
E
F
G
H
I
J
K
L
M
N
O
P
Q
R
S
T
U
V
W
X
Y
Z

```
            Scrollbar SCROLL_ABSOLUTE (4 144) w(0) k(_) m(0) c(0) a(22)
            Scrollbar SCROLL_LINE_DOWN (4 144) w(0) k(_) m(0) c(0) a(23)
            List LIST_SELECT (302 144) w(0) k(_) m(0) c(0) a(0)
            List ACTION_EVENT (302 144) w(0) k(_) m(0) c(0) a(List)
            TextArea KEY_PRESS (4 195) w(827558105110) k(k) m(0) c(0) a(null)
            TextArea KEY_RELEASE (4 195) w(827558105490) k(j) m(0) c(0) a(null)
            Container MOUSE_MOVE (799 10) w(827558114500) k(_) m(0) c(0) a(null)
            Container MOUSE_MOVE (799 2) w(827558114670) k(_) m(0) c(0) a(null)
            Container WINDOW_DESTROY (0 0) w(0) k(_) m(0) c(0) a(null)
```

Java 1.1

```java
            import java.awt.*;
            import java.awt.event.*;

            class Main11 extends Frame {
                Main11() {
                    super("Event example using Java 1.1");

                    // Create listeners for all components
                    MouseListener ml = new MouseEventHandler();
                    MouseMotionListener mml = new MouseMotionEventHandler();
                    FocusListener fl = new FocusEventHandler();
                    ComponentListener cpl = new ComponentEventHandler();
                    KeyListener kl = new KeyEventHandler();

                    ContainerListener ctl = new ContainerEventHandler();
                    WindowListener wl = new WindowEventHandler();

                    // Handles Action, Text, Item and Adjustement events
                    SemanticEventHandler sl = new SemanticEventHandler();

                    // Add listeners for frame, this will catch
                    // events as components are added
                    addMouseListener(ml);
                    addMouseMotionListener(mml);
                    addFocusListener(fl);
                    addComponentListener(cpl);
                    addKeyListener(kl);
                    addContainerListener(ctl);
                    addWindowListener(wl);

                    // Menu bar with a menu and menu item.
                    MenuBar mb = new MenuBar();
                    Menu m = new Menu("Menu");
                    CheckboxMenuItem cbm = new CheckboxMenuItem("CheckboxMenuItem");
                    m.add("MenuItem");
                    m.add(cbm);
                    mb.add(m);
                    setMenuBar(mb);

                    setLayout(new GridLayout(0, 3));

                    // checkbox, grouped checkbox, label, text field, scrollbar, button

                    Checkbox cb1, cb2;
                    Label label;
                    TextField textField;
```

```
Button button;
MyCanvas canvas;

add(cb1 = new Checkbox("Checkbox"));
add(cb2 = new Checkbox("Checkbox", new CheckboxGroup(), true));
add(label = new Label("label"));
add(textField = new TextField("TextField"));
add(button = new Button("Button"));
add(canvas = new MyCanvas());

// scrollbar
Scrollbar sb = new Scrollbar(Scrollbar.HORIZONTAL);
sb.setValues(50, 50, 0, 100);
add(sb);

// choice
Choice choice = new Choice();
choice.addItem("Choice");
choice.addItem("a choice item");
add(choice);

// list
List list = new List();
list.addItem("List");
list.addItem("a list item");
add(list);

// text area
TextArea textArea = new TextArea("TextArea");
textArea.setSize(100, 50);
add(textArea);


// Add listeners to components

// Checkboxes
cb1.addMouseListener(ml);
cb1.addMouseMotionListener(mml);
cb1.addFocusListener(fl);
cb1.addComponentListener(cpl);
cb1.addKeyListener(kl);
cb1.addItemListener(sl);

cb2.addMouseListener(ml);
cb2.addMouseMotionListener(mml);
cb2.addFocusListener(fl);
cb2.addComponentListener(cpl);
cb2.addKeyListener(kl);
cb2.addItemListener(sl);

// Choice
choice.addMouseListener(ml);
choice.addMouseMotionListener(mml);
choice.addFocusListener(fl);
choice.addComponentListener(cpl);
choice.addKeyListener(kl);
choice.addItemListener(sl);

// Label
label.addMouseListener(ml);
```

A

B

C

D

F

G

H

I

J

K

L

M

N

O

P

Q

R

S

T

U

V

W

X

Y

Z

```
            label.addMouseMotionListener(mml);
            label.addFocusListener(fl);
            label.addComponentListener(cpl);
            label.addKeyListener(kl);

            // Button
            button.addMouseListener(ml);
            button.addMouseMotionListener(mml);
            button.addFocusListener(fl);
            button.addComponentListener(cpl);
            button.addKeyListener(kl);
            button.addActionListener(sl);

            // Scrollbar
            sb.addMouseListener(ml);
            sb.addMouseMotionListener(mml);
            sb.addFocusListener(fl);
            sb.addComponentListener(cpl);
            sb.addKeyListener(kl);
            sb.addAdjustmentListener(sl);

            // List
            list.addMouseListener(ml);
            list.addMouseMotionListener(mml);
            list.addFocusListener(fl);
            list.addComponentListener(cpl);
            list.addKeyListener(kl);
            list.addItemListener(sl);
            list.addActionListener(sl);

            // Text Field
            textField.addMouseListener(ml);
            textField.addMouseMotionListener(mml);
            textField.addFocusListener(fl);
            textField.addComponentListener(cpl);
            textField.addKeyListener(kl);
            textField.addActionListener(sl);
            textField.addTextListener(sl);

            // Text Area
            textArea.addMouseListener(ml);
            textArea.addMouseMotionListener(mml);
            textArea.addFocusListener(fl);
            textArea.addComponentListener(cpl);
            textArea.addKeyListener(kl);
            textArea.addTextListener(sl);

            // canvas
            canvas.addMouseListener(ml);
            canvas.addMouseMotionListener(mml);
            canvas.addFocusListener(fl);
            canvas.addComponentListener(cpl);
            canvas.addKeyListener(kl);

            // Checkbox Menu
            cbm.addItemListener(sl);
            cbm.addActionListener(sl);

            // Menu
            m.addActionListener(sl);
```

A
B
C
D

F
G
H
I
J
K
L
M
N
O
P
Q
R
S
T
U
V
W
X
Y
Z

```
        pack();
        show();
    }

    class MouseEventHandler implements MouseListener {
        void printEvent(MouseEvent evt) {
            System.out.print(" ("+evt.getX()+" "+evt.getY()+") w(");
            System.out.println(evt.getWhen()+")");
            System.out.print("m("+evt.getModifiers()+")"+" c(");
            System.out.println(evt.getClickCount()+")");
        }

        public void mouseClicked(MouseEvent evt) {
            System.out.print(" ("+evt.getX()+" "+evt.getY()+") w(");
            System.out.print("MOUSE_CLICKED");
            printEvent(evt);
        }

        public void mousePressed(MouseEvent evt) {
            System.out.print(" ("+evt.getX()+" "+evt.getY()+") w(");
            System.out.print("MOUSE_DOWN");
            printEvent(evt);
        }

        public void mouseReleased(MouseEvent evt) {
            System.out.print(" ("+evt.getX()+" "+evt.getY()+") w(");
            System.out.print("MOUSE_UP");
            printEvent(evt);
        }

        public void mouseEntered(MouseEvent evt) {
            System.out.print(" ("+evt.getX()+" "+evt.getY()+") w(");
            System.out.print("MOUSE_ENTER");
            printEvent(evt);
        }
        public void mouseExited(MouseEvent evt) {
            System.out.print(" ("+evt.getX()+" "+evt.getY()+") w(");
            System.out.print("MOUSE_EXIT");
            printEvent(evt);
        }
    }

    class MouseMotionEventHandler implements MouseMotionListener {
        void printEvent(MouseEvent evt) {
            System.out.print(" ("+evt.getX()+" "+evt.getY()+") w(");
            System.out.println(evt.getWhen()+")");
            System.out.print("m("+evt.getModifiers()+")"+" c(");
            System.out.println(evt.getClickCount()+")");
        }
        public void mouseDragged(MouseEvent evt) {
            System.out.print(evt.getSource().getClass() + " ");
            System.out.print("MOUSE_DRAG");
            printEvent(evt);
        }
        public void mouseMoved(MouseEvent evt) {
            System.out.print(evt.getSource().getClass() + " ");
            System.out.print("MOUSE_MOVE");
            printEvent(evt);
        }
    }
```

A
B
C
D
E
F
G
H
I
J
K
L
M
N
O
P
Q
R
S
T
U
V
W
X
Y
Z

```
        }

        // Implements methods for Action, Text, Item, Adjustment
        class SemanticEventHandler implements ActionListener, ItemListener,
            TextListener, AdjustmentListener {
            public void actionPerformed(ActionEvent evt) {
                System.out.print(evt.getSource().getClass() + " ");
                System.out.print("ACTION_EVENT");
                System.out.println(" cmd(" + evt.getActionCommand() + ")");
            }

            public void itemStateChanged(ItemEvent evt) {
                System.out.print(evt.getSource().getClass() + " ");
                switch (evt.getStateChange()) {
                case ItemEvent.SELECTED:
                    System.out.print("ITEM_SELECT");
                    break;

                case ItemEvent.DESELECTED:
                    System.out.print("ITEM_DESELECT");
                }
                System.out.println(" item( " + evt.getItem() + ")");
            }

            public void adjustmentValueChanged(AdjustmentEvent evt) {
                System.out.print(evt.getSource().getClass() + " ");
                switch (evt.getID()) {
                case AdjustmentEvent.TRACK:
                    System.out.print("SCROLL_ABSOLUTE");
                    break;
                case AdjustmentEvent.UNIT_INCREMENT:
                    System.out.print("SCROLL_LINE_DOWN");
                    break;
                case AdjustmentEvent.UNIT_DECREMENT:
                    System.out.print("SCROLL_LINE_UP");
                    break;
                case AdjustmentEvent.BLOCK_DECREMENT:
                    System.out.print("SCROLL_PAGE_DOWN");
                    break;
                case AdjustmentEvent.BLOCK_INCREMENT:
                    System.out.print("SCROLL_PAGE_UP");
                    break;
                }
                System.out.print(" value (" + evt.getValue() + ")");
                System.out.println(" adjustable (" + evt.getAdjustable() + ")");
            }

            public void textValueChanged(TextEvent evt) {
                System.out.print(evt.getSource().getClass() + " ");
                System.out.println("TEXT_VALUE_CHANGED");
            }
        }

        class WindowEventHandler implements WindowListener {
            public void windowDeiconified(WindowEvent evt) {
                System.out.print(evt.getSource().getClass() + " ");
                System.out.print("WINDOW_DEICONIFY");
                System.out.println(" window (" + evt.getWindow() + ")");
            }
            public void windowClosing(WindowEvent evt) {
```

```
            System.out.print(evt.getSource().getClass() + " ");
            System.out.print("WINDOW_DESTROY");
            System.out.println(" window (" + evt.getWindow() + ")");
        }
        public void windowClosed(WindowEvent evt) {
            System.out.print(evt.getSource().getClass() + " ");
            System.out.print("WINDOW_CLOSED");
            System.out.println(" window (" + evt.getWindow() + ")");
        }
        public void windowActivated(WindowEvent evt) {
            System.out.print(evt.getSource().getClass() + " ");
            System.out.print("WINDOW_EXPOSE");
            System.out.println(" window (" + evt.getWindow() + ")");
        }
        public void windowDeactivated(WindowEvent evt) {
            System.out.print(evt.getSource().getClass() + " ");
            System.out.print("WINDOW_DEACTIVATED");
            System.out.println(" window (" + evt.getWindow() + ")");
        }
        public void windowIconified(WindowEvent evt) {
            System.out.print(evt.getSource().getClass() + " ");
            System.out.print("WINDOW_ICONIFY");
            System.out.println(" window (" + evt.getWindow() + ")");
        }
        public void windowOpened(WindowEvent evt) {
            System.out.print(evt.getSource().getClass() + " ");
            System.out.print("WINDOW_OPENED");
            System.out.println(" window (" + evt.getWindow() + ")");
        }
    }

    class ComponentEventHandler implements ComponentListener {
        public void componentMoved(ComponentEvent evt) {
            System.out.print(evt.getSource().getClass() + " ");
            System.out.print("COMPONENT_MOVED");
            System.out.println(" component(" + evt.getComponent() + ")");
        }
        public void componentResized(ComponentEvent evt) {
            System.out.print(evt.getSource().getClass() + " ");
            System.out.print("COMPONENT_RESIZED");
            System.out.println(" component(" + evt.getComponent() + ")");
        }
        public void componentShown(ComponentEvent evt) {
            System.out.print(evt.getSource().getClass() + " ");
            System.out.print("COMPONENT_SHOWN");
            System.out.println(" component(" + evt.getComponent() + ")");
        }
        public void componentHidden(ComponentEvent evt) {
            System.out.print(evt.getSource().getClass() + " ");
            System.out.print("COMPONENT_HIDDEN");
            System.out.println(" component(" + evt.getComponent() + ")");
        }
    }

    class ContainerEventHandler implements ContainerListener {
        public void componentAdded(ContainerEvent evt) {
            System.out.print(evt.getSource().getClass() + " ");
            System.out.print("CONTAINER_ADDED");
            System.out.println(" container("+evt.getContainer()+") child(" +
                            evt.getChild() +")");
```

```
            }
            public void componentRemoved(ContainerEvent evt) {
                System.out.print(evt.getSource().getClass() + " ");
                System.out.print("CONTAINER_REMOVED");
                System.out.println(" container("+evt.getContainer()+") child(" +
                                    evt.getChild() +")");
            }
        }

        class FocusEventHandler implements FocusListener {
            public void focusGained(FocusEvent evt) {
                System.out.print(evt.getSource().getClass() + " ");
                System.out.print("FOCUS_GAINED");
                System.out.println(evt.isTemporary() ? " temporary." : ".");
            }
            public void focusLost(FocusEvent evt) {
                System.out.print(evt.getSource().getClass() + " ");
                System.out.print("FOCUS_LOST");
                System.out.println(evt.isTemporary() ? " temporary." : ".");
            }
        }

        class KeyEventHandler implements KeyListener {
            public void keyPressed(KeyEvent evt) {
                System.out.print(evt.getSource().getClass() + " ");
                if (evt.isActionKey()) {
                    System.out.print("KEY_ACTION");
                } else {
                    System.out.print("KEY_PRESS");
                }
                System.out.print(" k("+(char)evt.getKeyCode()+") m(");
                System.out.println(
                    KeyEvent.getKeyModifiersText(evt.getModifiers())+")");
            }

            public void keyReleased(KeyEvent evt) {
                System.out.print(evt.getSource().getClass() + " ");
                if (evt.isActionKey()) {
                    System.out.print("KEY_ACTION_RELEASE");
                } else {
                    System.out.print("KEY_RELEASE");
                }
                System.out.print(" k("+(char)evt.getKeyCode()+") m(");
                System.out.println(
                    KeyEvent.getKeyModifiersText(evt.getModifiers())+")");
            }

            public void keyTyped(KeyEvent evt) {
                System.out.print(evt.getSource().getClass() + " ");
                System.out.print("KEY_TYPED");
                System.out.print(" k("+(char)evt.getKeyCode()+") m(");
                System.out.println(
                    KeyEvent.getKeyModifiersText(evt.getModifiers())+")");
            }
        }

        static public void main(String[] args) {
            new Main11();
        }
    }
```

A
B
C
D
E
F
G
H
I
J
K
L
M
N
O
P
Q
R
S
T
U
V
W
X
Y
Z

550

```
class MyCanvas extends Canvas {
    public void paint(Graphics g) {
        FontMetrics fm = g.getFontMetrics();
        g.drawString("Canvas",
            (getSize().width-fm.stringWidth("Canvas"))/2,
            (getSize().height-fm.getAscent())/2);
    }
}
```

A
B
C
D
E
F
G
H
I
J
K
L
M
N
O
P
Q
R
S
T
U
V
W
X
Y
Z

ACTION_EVENT
DEPRECATED

PURPOSE   Replaced by `ActionEvent.ACTION_PERFORMED`.

SYNTAX   `public static final int ACTION_EVENT`

DEPRECATION   Replace the usage of this deprecated constant, as in

```
Event evt;
switch(evt.id) {
case Event.ACTION_EVENT:
    ...
```

either by using `ActionListener.actionPerformed()` or by using event subtypes as follows:

```
AWTEvent evt;
if (evt instanceof ActionEvent) {
    if (evt.getID() == ActionEvent.ACTION_PERFORMED) {
        ...
```

ALT_MASK
DEPRECATED

PURPOSE   Replaced by `InputEvent.ALT_MASK`.

SYNTAX   `public static final int ALT_MASK`

DEPRECATION   Replace the usage of this deprecated constant, as in

```
public static boolean isAltDown(Event evt) {
    return (evt.modifiers & Event.ALT_MASK) != 0;
}
```

with

```
public static boolean isAltDown(InputEvent evt) {
    return (evt.getModifiers() & InputEvent.ALT_MASK);
}
```

arg
DEPRECATED

PURPOSE   Replaced by event-specific fields and methods.

SYNTAX   `public Object arg`

DEPRECATION   Instead of using the `arg` field to represent an argument to be passed along with the event, the Java 1.1 event model has a more flexible way of passing arguments with an event. Each event subclass defines the properties relevant for an event type to be passed along with that event. For example, an action event has an *action command* associated with it that takes the place of the `arg` field for events of type ACTION_EVENT. See individual event subclasses for details.

Replace usage of this deprecated field, as in

```
Event evt;
if (evt.target instanceof Button) {
    String cmd = (String)evt.arg;
    ...
```

with

```
AWTEvent evt;
if (evt.getSource() instanceof Button) {
    String cmd = ((ActionEvent)evt).getActionCommand();
    ...
```

clickCount   *DEPRECATED*

PURPOSE   Replaced by MouseEvent.getClickCount().

SYNTAX   `public int clickCount`

DEPRECATION   Replace the usage of this deprecated field, as in

```
Event evt;
if (evt.clickCount > 1) ...
```

with

```
MouseEvent evt;
if (evt.getClickCount() > 1) ...
```

controlDown()   *DEPRECATED*

PURPOSE   Replaced by InputEvent.isControlDown().

SYNTAX   `public boolean controlDown()`

DESCRIPTION   In Java 1.1, MouseEvent and KeyEvent are subclasses of InputEvent. Replace the usage of this deprecated method, as in

```
Event evt;
if (evt.controlDown()) ...
```

with

```
MouseEvent evt; // or KeyEvent
if (evt.isControlDown()) ...
```

CTRL_MASK   *DEPRECATED*

PURPOSE   Replaced by `InputEvent.CTRL_MASK`.

SYNTAX   `public static final int CTRL_MASK`

DEPRECATION   Replace the usage of this deprecated method, as in

```
public static boolean isControlDown(Event evt) {
    return (evt.modifiers & Event.CTRL_MASK) != 0;
}
```

with

```
public static boolean isControlDown(InputEvent evt) {
    return (evt.getModifiers() & InputEvent.CTRL_MASK) != 0;
}
```

DOWN   *DEPRECATED*

PURPOSE   Replaced by `KeyEvent.VK_DOWN`.

SYNTAX   `public static final int DOWN`

DEPRECATION   Replace the usage of this deprecated constant, as in

```
Event evt;
if (evt.key == Event.DOWN) ...
```

with

```
KeyEvent evt;
if (evt.getKeyCode() == KeyEvent.VK_DOWN) ...
```

END   *DEPRECATED*

PURPOSE   Replaced by `KeyEvent.VK_END`.

SYNTAX   `public static final int END`

DEPRECATION   Replace the usage of this deprecated constant, as in

```
Event evt;
if (evt.key == Event.END) ...
```

with

```
KeyEvent evt;
if (evt.getKeyCode() == KeyEvent.VK_END) ...
```

Event( )   *DEPRECATED*

PURPOSE   Use the constructor for one of `AWTEvent`'s subclasses instead.

SYNTAX   `public Event(Object target, long when, int id, int x, int y, int`
               `    key, int modifiers, Object arg)`

A
B
C
D
E
F
G
H
I
J
K
L
M
N
O
P
Q
R
S
T
U
V
W
X
Y
Z

```
public Event(Object target, long when, int id, int x, int y, int
    key, int modifiers)
public Event(Object target, int id, Object arg)
```

PARAMETERS

`arg`	The object to be associated with this event.
`id`	The event type.
`key`	The key that fired the event. Used by keyboard-related event types.
`modifiers`	The state of the modifier keys at the time of the event.
`target`	The non-null component that fired the event.
`when`	The event's time stamp at the time of the event.
`x`	The *x*-coordinate of the cursor at the time of the event.
`y`	The *y*-coordinate of the cursor at the time of the event.

DEPRECATION `Event` has been replaced by a class hierarchy of event subclasses rooted at `AWTEvent`. See the individual event subclasses for details on their constructors. For example, instead of creating an `ACTION_EVENT` event for a button as follows:

```
Event evt = new Event(button,Event.ACTION_EVENT,button.getLabel());
```

use the subclass's constructor:

```
ActionEvent evt = new ActionEvent(button,
    ActionEvent.ACTION_PERFORMED, button.getActionCommand());
```

evt   *DEPRECATED*

PURPOSE Replaced by `EventQueue`.

SYNTAX `public Event evt`

DEPRECATION In Java 1.0, this field is used when the event needs to be inserted into a linked list. In Java 1.1, events are chained together using `EventQueue`. See the `postEvent()`, `getNextEvent()`, and `peekEvent()` in the `EventQueue` class for details.

Replace the usage of this deprecated field, as in

```
Event list;
void queueEvent(Event event) {
    event.evt = list;
    list = event;
}
```

with

```
EventQueue queue;
AWTEvent evt;
queue.postEvent(evt);
```

F1 *DEPRECATED*

PURPOSE Replaced by `KeyEvent.VK_F1`.

SYNTAX `public static final int F1`

DEPRECATION Replace the usage of this deprecated constant, as in
```
Event evt;
if (evt.key == Event.F1) ...
```
with
```
KeyEvent evt;
if (evt.getKeyCode() == KeyEvent.VK_F1) ...
```

F10 *DEPRECATED*

PURPOSE Replaced by `KeyEvent.VK_F10`.

SYNTAX `public static final int F10`

DEPRECATION Replace the usage of this deprecated constant, as in
```
Event evt;
if (evt.key == Event.F10) ...
```
with
```
KeyEvent evt;
if (evt.getKeyCode() == KeyEvent.VK_F10) ...
```

F11 *DEPRECATED*

PURPOSE Replaced by `KeyEvent.VK_F11`.

SYNTAX `public static final int F11`

DEPRECATION Replace the usage of this deprecated constant, as in
```
Event evt;
if (evt.key == Event.F11) ...
```
with
```
KeyEvent evt;
if (evt.getKeyCode() == KeyEvent.VK_F11) ...
```

F12 *DEPRECATED*

PURPOSE Replaced by `KeyEvent.VK_F12`.

SYNTAX `public static final int F12`

DEPRECATION Replace the usage of this deprecated constant, as in
```
Event evt;
if (evt.key == Event.F12) ...
```

A
B
C
D
E
F
G
H
I
J
K
L
M
N
O
P
Q
R
S
T
U
V
W
X
Y
Z

```
with
    KeyEvent evt;
    if (evt.getKeyCode() == KeyEvent.VK_F12) ...
```

F2   *DEPRECATED*

PURPOSE   Replaced by KeyEvent.VK_F2.

SYNTAX   `public static final int F2`

DEPRECATION   Replace the usage of this deprecated constant, as in
```
Event evt;
if (evt.key == Event.F2) ...
```
with
```
KeyEvent evt;
if (evt.getKeyCode() == KeyEvent.VK_F2) ...
```

F3   *DEPRECATED*

PURPOSE   Replaced by KeyEvent.VK_F3.

SYNTAX   `public static final int F3`

DEPRECATION   Replace the usage of this deprecated constant, as in
```
Event evt;
if (evt.key == Event.F3) ...
```
with
```
KeyEvent evt;
if (evt.getKeyCode() == KeyEvent.VK_F3) ...
```

F4   *DEPRECATED*

PURPOSE   Replaced by KeyEvent.VK_F4.

SYNTAX   `public static final int F4`

DEPRECATION   Replace the usage of this deprecated constant, as in
```
Event evt;
if (evt.key == Event.F4) ...
```
with
```
KeyEvent evt;
if (evt.getKeyCode() == KeyEvent.VK_F4) ...
```

F5   *DEPRECATED*

PURPOSE   Replaced by KeyEvent.VK_F5.

SYNTAX   `public static final int F5`

DEPRECATION   Replace the usage of this deprecated constant, as in
```
Event evt;
if (evt.key == Event.F5) ...
```
with
```
KeyEvent evt;
if (evt.getKeyCode() == KeyEvent.VK_F5) ...
```

F6   *DEPRECATED*

PURPOSE   Replaced by `KeyEvent.VK_F6`.

SYNTAX   `public static final int F6`

DEPRECATION   Replace the usage of this deprecated constant, as in
```
Event evt;
if (evt.key == Event.F6) ...
```
with
```
KeyEvent evt;
if (evt.getKeyCode() == KeyEvent.VK_F6) ...
```

F7   *DEPRECATED*

PURPOSE   Replaced by `KeyEvent.VK_F7`.

SYNTAX   `public static final int F7`

DEPRECATION   Replace the usage of this deprecated constant, as in
```
Event evt;
if (evt.key == Event.F7) ...
```
with
```
KeyEvent evt;
if (evt.getKeyCode() == KeyEvent.VK_F7) ...
```

F8   *DEPRECATED*

PURPOSE   Replaced by `KeyEvent.VK_F8`.

SYNTAX   `public static final int F8`

DEPRECATION   Replace the usage of this deprecated constant, as in
```
Event evt;
if (evt.key == Event.F8) ...
```
with
```
KeyEvent evt;
if (evt.getKeyCode() == KeyEvent.VK_F8) ...
```

A
B
C
D
E
F
G
H
I
J
K
L
M
N
O
P
Q
R
S
T
U
V
W
X
Y
Z

A
B
C
D

F
G
H
I
J
K
L
M
N
O
P
Q
R
S
T
U
V
W
X
Y
Z

F9 *DEPRECATED*

PURPOSE	Replaced by KeyEvent.VK_F9.
SYNTAX	`public static final int F9`
DEPRECATION	Replace the usage of this deprecated constant, as in

```
Event evt;
if (evt.key == Event.F9) ...
```
with
```
KeyEvent evt;
if (evt.getKeyCode() == KeyEvent.VK_F9) ...
```

GOT_FOCUS *DEPRECATED*

PURPOSE	Replaced by FocusEvent.FOCUS_GAINED.
SYNTAX	`public static final int GOT_FOCUS`
DEPRECATION	Replace the usage of this deprecated constant, as in

```
Event evt;
switch(evt.id) {
case Event.GOT_FOCUS:
    ...
case Event.LOST_FOCUS:
    ...
```

by using a `FocusListener.focusGained()` or by using event subtypes as follows:

```
AWTEvent evt;
if (evt instanceof FocusEvent) {
    switch (evt.getID()) {
    case FocusEvent.FOCUS_GAINED:
    ...
    case FocusEvent.FOCUS_LOST:
    ...
```

HOME *DEPRECATED*

PURPOSE	Replaced by KeyEvent.VK_HOME.
SYNTAX	`public static final int HOME`
DEPRECATION	Replace the usage of this deprecated constant, as in

```
Event evt;
if (evt.key == Event.HOME) ...
```
with
```
KeyEvent evt;
if (evt.getKeyCode() == KeyEvent.VK_HOME) ...
```

id *DEPRECATED*

PURPOSE   Replaced by `AWTEvent.getID()`.

SYNTAX   `public int id`

DEPRECATION   Replace the usage of this deprecated field, as in

```
Event evt;
switch (evt.id) {
   ...
```

with the usage of the appropriate event subclass, or `AWTEvent.getID()`, as follows:

```
AWTEvent evt;
switch (evt.getID()) {
   ...
```

key *DEPRECATED*

PURPOSE   Replaced by `KeyEvent.getKeyCode()`.

SYNTAX   `public int key`

DEPRECATION   Replace the usage of this deprecated field, as in

```
Event evt;
switch (evt.key) {
case 'a':
case 'b':
   ...
```

with

```
KeyEvent evt;
switch (evt.getKeyCode()) {
case KeyEvent.VK_A:
case KeyEvent.VK_B:
   ...
```

KEY_ACTION *DEPRECATED*

PURPOSE   Replaced by `KeyEvent.KEY_PRESSED`.

SYNTAX   `public static final int KEY_ACTION`

DEPRECATION   In the Java 1.1 event model, all key presses fire a `KEY_PRESSED` event, regardless of whether the key is an action key. You use `isActionKey()` on the key event to determine whether the key pressed was an action key.

Replace the usage of this deprecated constant, as in

```
Event evt;
switch (evt.id) {
case Event.KEY_ACTION: ...
case Event.KEY_ACTION_RELEASE: ...
```

A
B
C
D
E
F
G
H
I
J
K
L
M
N
O
P
Q
R
S
T
U
V
W
X
Y
Z

by using KeyListener.keyPressed() with KeyEvent.isActionKey() or by using event subtypes as follows:

```
KeyEvent evt;
switch (evt.getID()) {
case KEY_PRESSED:
    if (evt.isActionKey()) ...
case KEY_RELEASED:
    if (evt.isActionKey()) ...
```

KEY_ACTION_RELEASE   *DEPRECATED*

PURPOSE   Replaced by KeyEvent.KEY_RELEASED.

SYNTAX   public static final int KEY_ACTION_RELEASE

DEPRECATION   In the Java 1.1 event model, all key releases fire a KEY_RELEASED event, regardless of whether the key is an action key. Use isActionKey() on the key event to determine whether the key released was an action key.

Replace the usage of this deprecated constant by using KeyListener.keyReleased() with KeyEvent.isActionKey() or by using event subtypes, as shown in KEY_ACTION.

KEY_PRESS   *DEPRECATED*

PURPOSE   Replaced by KeyEvent.KEY_PRESSED.

SYNTAX   public static final int KEY_PRESS

DEPRECATION   In the Java 1.1 event model, all key presses fire a KEY_PRESSED event, regardless of whether the key is an action key. You use isActionKey() on the key event to determine whether the key pressed was an action key.

Replace the usage of this deprecated constant, as in

```
Event evt;
switch (evt.id) {
case Event.KEY_PRESS: ...
case Event.KEY_RELEASE: ...
```

by using KeyListener.keyPressed() with KeyEvent.isActionKey() or by using event subtypes as follows:

```
KeyEvent evt;
switch (evt.getID()) {
case KEY_PRESSED:
    if (!evt.isActionKey()) ...
case KEY_RELEASED:
    if (!evt.isActionKey()) ...
```

KEY_RELEASE   *DEPRECATED*

PURPOSE   Replaced by `KeyEvent.KEY_RELEASED`.

SYNTAX   `public static final int KEY_ACTION_RELEASE`

DEPRECATION   In the Java 1.1 event model, all key releases fire a `KEY_RELEASED` event, regardless of whether the key is an action key. You use `isActionKey()` on the key event to determine whether the key released was an action key.

Replace the usage of this deprecated constant by using `KeyListener.keyReleased()` with `KeyEvent.isActionKey()` or by using event subtypes, as shown in `KEY_PRESS`.

LEFT   *DEPRECATED*

PURPOSE   Replaced by `KeyEvent.VK_LEFT`.

SYNTAX   `public static final int LEFT`

DEPRECATION   Replace the usage of this deprecated constant, as in

```
Event evt;
if (evt.key == Event.LEFT) ...
```

with

```
KeyEvent evt;
if (evt.getKeyCode() == KeyEvent.VK_LEFT) ...
```

LIST_DESELECT   *DEPRECATED*

PURPOSE   Replaced by `ItemEvent.DESELECT`.

SYNTAX   `public static final int LIST_DESELECT`

DEPRECATION   The Java 1.1 event model contains a generic event subclass `ItemEvent` for representing selection/deselection of items in a component. `Checkbox`, `CheckboxMenuItem`, `Choice`, and `List` are AWT classes that fire `ItemEvent`.

Replace the usage of this deprecated constant, as in

```
Event evt;
switch (evt.id) {
case Event.LIST_DESELECT: ...
case Event.LIST_SELECT: ...
```

by using `ItemListener.itemStateChanged()` and using `ItemEvent.getStateChange()` as follows:

```
public void itemStateChanged(ItemEvent evt) {
    switch (evt.getStateChange()) {
    case ItemEvent.SELECT: ...
    case ItemEvent.DESELECT: ...
}
```

561

LIST_SELECT

DEPRECATED

PURPOSE   Replaced by `ItemEvent.DESELECT`.

SYNTAX   `public static final int LIST_SELECT`

DEPRECATION   See `LIST_DESELECT`.

LOAD_FILE

DEPRECATED

PURPOSE   Not used.

SYNTAX   `public static final int LOAD_FILE`

DESCRIPTION   This constant was not used in Java 1.0. There is no corresponding constant for it in Java 1.1.

LOST_FOCUS

DEPRECATED

PURPOSE   Replaced by `FocusEvent.FOCUS_LOST`.

SYNTAX   `public static final int LOST_FOCUS`

DEPRECATION   See `GOT_FOCUS`.

META_MASK

DEPRECATED

PURPOSE   Replaced by `InputEvent.META_MASK`.

SYNTAX   `public static final int META_MASK`

DEPRECATION   Replace the usage of this deprecated constant, as in
```
public static boolean isMetaDown(Event evt) {
    return (evt.modifiers & Event.META_MASK) != 0;
}
```
with
```
public static boolean isMetaDown(InputEvent evt) {
    return (evt.getModifiers() & InputEvent.META_MASK);
}
```

metaDown()

DEPRECATED

PURPOSE   Replaced by `InputEvent.isMetaDown()`.

SYNTAX   `public boolean metaDown()`

DESCRIPTION   In Java 1.1, `MouseEvent` and `KeyEvent` are subclasses of `InputEvent`. Replace the usage of this deprecated method, as in

```
Event evt;
if (evt.metaDown()) ...
```

with

```
MouseEvent evt; // or KeyEvent
if (evt.isMetaDown()) ...
```

modifiers   *DEPRECATED*

PURPOSE   Replaced by `InputEvent.getModifiers()`.

SYNTAX   `public int modifiers`

DESCRIPTION   In Java 1.1, `MouseEvent` and `KeyEvent` are subclasses of `InputEvent`. Replace the usage of this deprecated field, as in

```
Event evt;
if ((evt.modifiers & Event.META_MASK) != 0) ...
```

with

```
MouseEvent evt; // or KeyEvent
if ((evt.getModifiers() & InputEvent.META_MASK) ...
```

MOUSE_DOWN   *DEPRECATED*

PURPOSE   Replaced by `MouseEvent.MOUSE_PRESSED`.

SYNTAX   `public static final int MOUSE_DOWN`

DEPRECATION   Replace the usage of this deprecated constant, as in

```
Event evt;
switch(evt.id) {
case Event.MOUSE_DOWN:
    ...
case Event.MOUSE_UP:
    ...
case Event.MOUSE_ENTER:
    ...
case Event.MOUSE_EXIT:
    ...
```

by using `MouseListener.mousePressed()` or by using event subtypes as follows:

```
AWTEvent evt;
if (evt instanceof MouseEvent) {
    switch (evt.getID()) {
    case MouseEvent.MOUSE_PRESSED:
    ...
    case MouseEvent.MOUSE_RELEASED:
    ...
    case MouseEvent.MOUSE_ENTERED:
    ...
    case MouseEvent.MOUSE_EXITED:
    ...
```

A
B
C
D
E
F
G
H
I
J
K
L
M
N
O
P
Q
R
S
T
U
V
W
X
Y
Z

A
B
C
D
E
F
G
H
I
J
K
L
M
N
O
P
Q
R
S
T
U
V
W
X
Y
Z

MOUSE_DRAG

DEPRECATED

PURPOSE Replaced by `MouseEvent.MOUSE_DRAGGED`.

SYNTAX `public static final int MOUSE_DRAG`

DEPRECATION Replace the usage of this deprecated constant, as in

```
Event evt;
switch(evt.id) {
case Event.MOUSE_DRAG:
    ...
case Event.MOUSE_MOVE:
    ...
```

by using `MouseMotionListener.mouseDragged()` or by using event subtypes as follows:

```
AWTEvent evt;
if (evt instanceof MouseEvent) {
    switch (evt.getID()) {
    case MouseEvent.MOUSE_DRAGGED:
    ...
    case MouseEvent.MOUSE_MOVED:
    ...
```

MOUSE_ENTER

DEPRECATED

PURPOSE Replaced by `MouseEvent.MOUSE_ENTERED`.

SYNTAX `public static final int MOUSE_ENTER`

DEPRECATION Replace the usage of this deprecated constant by using a `MouseListener.mouseEntered()` or by using event subtypes, as shown in `MOUSE_DOWN`.

MOUSE_EXIT

DEPRECATED

PURPOSE Replaced by `MouseEvent.MOUSE_EXITED`.

SYNTAX `public static final int MOUSE_EXIT`

DEPRECATION Replace the usage of this deprecated constant by using a `MouseListener.mouseExited()` or by using event subtypes, as shown in `MOUSE_DOWN`.

MOUSE_MOVE

DEPRECATED

PURPOSE Replaced by `MouseEvent.MOUSE_MOVED`.

SYNTAX `public static final int MOUSE_MOVE`

DEPRECATION   Replace the usage of this deprecated constant by using a `MouseLis-tener.mouseMoved()` or by using event subtypes, as shown in `MOUSE_DRAG`.

MOUSE_UP
DEPRECATED

PURPOSE   Replaced by `MouseEvent.MOUSE_RELEASED`.

SYNTAX   `public static final int MOUSE_UP`

DEPRECATION   Replace the usage of this deprecated constant by using a `MouseLis-tener.mouseReleased()` or by using event subtypes, as shown in `MOUSE_DOWN`.

paramString()
DEPRECATED

PURPOSE   Replaced by `AWTEvent.paramString()`.

SYNTAX   `protected String paramString()`

DEPRECATION   The `Event` class is deprecated. Use `AWTEvent` instead.

PGDN
DEPRECATED

PURPOSE   Replaced by `KEYEvent.VK_PAGE_DOWN`.

SYNTAX   `public static final int PGDN`

DEPRECATION   Replace the usage of this deprecated constant, as in

```
Event evt;
if (evt.key == Event.PGDN) ...
```

with

```
KeyEvent evt;
if (evt.getKeyCode() == KeyEvent.VK_PAGE_DOWN) ...
```

PGUP
DEPRECATED

PURPOSE   Replaced by `KeyEvent.VK_PAGE_UP`.

SYNTAX   `public static final int PGUP`

DEPRECATION   Replace the usage of this deprecated constant, as in

```
Event evt;
if (evt.key == Event.PGUP) ...
```

with

```
KeyEvent evt;
if (evt.getKeyCode() == KeyEvent.VK_PAGE_UP) ...
```

A
B
C
D
E
F
G
H
I
J
K
L
M
N
O
P
Q
R
S
T
U
V
W
X
Y
Z

RIGHT

DEPRECATED

PURPOSE Replaced by KeyEvent.VK_RIGHT.

SYNTAX `public static final int RIGHT`

DEPRECATION Replace the usage of this deprecated constant, as in

```
Event evt;
if (evt.key == Event.RIGHT) ...
```
with
```
KeyEvent evt;
if (evt.getKeyCode() == KeyEvent.VK_RIGHT) ...
```

SAVE_FILE

DEPRECATED

PURPOSE Not used.

SYNTAX `public static final int SAVE_FILE`

DESCRIPTION This constant was not used in Java 1.0. There is no corresponding constant for it in Java 1.1.

SCROLL_ABSOLUTE

DEPRECATED

PURPOSE Replaced by AdjustmentEvent.TRACK.

SYNTAX `public static final int SCROLL_ABSOLUTE`

DEPRECATION Replace the usage of this deprecated constant, as in

```
Event evt;
switch(evt.id) {
case Event.SCROLL_ABSOLUTE:
    ...
case Event.SCROLL_LINE_DOWN:
    ...
case Event.SCROLL_LINE_UP:
    ...
case Event.SCROLL_PAGE_DOWN:
    ...
case Evebt,SCROLL_PAGE_UP:
    ...
```

by using AdjustmentListener.adjustmentValueChanged() and adjustment types as follows:
```
public void adjustmentValueChanged(AdjustmentEvent evt) {
    switch (evt.getAdjustmentType) {
    case AdjustmentEvent.TRACK:
        ...
    case AdjustmentEvent.UNIT_INCREMENT:
        ...
    case AdjustmentEvent.UNIT_DECREMENT:
        ...
```

A
B
C
D
E
F
G
H
I
J
K
L
M
N
O
P
Q
R
S
T
U
V
W
X
Y
Z

```
        case AdjustmentEvent.BLOCK_INCREMENT:
        ...
        case AdjustmentEvent.BLOCK_DECREMENT:
        ...
}
```

SCROLL_LINE_DOWN   *DEPRECATED*

PURPOSE   Replaced by AdjustmentEvent.UNIT_INCREMENT.

SYNTAX   public static final int SCROLL_LINE_DOWN

DEPRECATION   See SCROLL_ABSOLUTE.

SCROLL_LINE_UP   *DEPRECATED*

PURPOSE   Replaced by AdjustmentEvent.UNIT_DECREMENT.

SYNTAX   public static final int SCROLL_LINE_UP

DEPRECATION   See SCROLL_ABSOLUTE.

SCROLL_PAGE_DOWN   *DEPRECATED*

PURPOSE   Replaced by AdjustmentEvent.BLOCK_DECREMENT.

SYNTAX   public static final int SCROLL_PAGE_DOWN

DEPRECATION   See SCROLL_ABSOLUTE.

SCROLL_PAGE_UP   *DEPRECATED*

PURPOSE   Replaced by AdjustmentEvent.BLOCK_DECREMENT.

SYNTAX   public static final int SCROLL_PAGE_UP

DEPRECATION   See SCROLL_ABSOLUTE.

SHIFT_MASK   *DEPRECATED*

PURPOSE   Replaced by InputEvent.SHIFT_MASK.

SYNTAX   public static final int SHIFT_MASK

DEPRECATION   Replace the usage of this deprecated method, as in
```
public static boolean isShiftDown(Event evt) {
```

A
B
C
D
E
F
G
H
I
J
K
L
M
N
O
P
Q
R
S
T
U
V
W
X
Y
Z

```
            return (evt.modifiers & Event.SHIFT_MASK) != 0;
        }
    with
        public static boolean isShiftDown(InputEvent evt) {
            return (evt.getModifiers() & InputEvent.SHIRT_MASK) != 0;
        }
```

shiftDown( ) *DEPRECATED*

PURPOSE Replaced by InputEvent.isShiftDown().

SYNTAX `public boolean shiftDown()`

DESCRIPTION In Java 1.1, MouseEvent and KeyEvent are subclasses of InputEvent.
Replace the usage of this deprecated method, as in

```
Event evt;
if (evt.shiftDown()) ...
```
with
```
MouseEvent evt; // or KeyEvent
if (evt.isShiftDown()) ...
```

target *DEPRECATED*

PURPOSE Replaced by AWTEvent.getSource().

SYNTAX `public Object target`

DEPRECATION Replace the usage of this deprecated field, as in

```
Event evt;
if (evt.target instanceof Button) ...
```
with
```
AWTEvent evt;
if (evt.getSource() instanceof Button) ...
```

toString( ) *DEPRECATED*

PURPOSE Replaced by AWTEvent.toString().

SYNTAX `public String toString()`

DEPRECATION The usage of the Event class is deprecated. Use AWTEvent instead.

translate( ) *DEPRECATED*

PURPOSE Replaced by MouseEvent.translatePoint().

SYNTAX `public void translate(int x, int y)`

PARAMETERS

x   The value to add to the event's *x*-coordinate.

y   The value to add to the event's *y*-coordinate.

DEPRECATION   In Java 1.0, the AWT adjusts the event's coordinates so that they are relative to the component that is receiving the event. In Java 1.1, the coordinates are not translated automatically and are, by default, relative to the bounds of the component that fired the event. See the `MouseMotionListener` class example for the usage of `MouseEvent.translatePoint()`.

Replace the usage of this deprecated method, as in

```
Event evt;
Component comp;
evt.translate(comp.getBounds().x, comp.getBounds().y);
```

with

```
MouseEvent evt;
Component comp;
evt.translatePoint(comp.getBounds().x, comp.getBounds().y);
```

UP   *DEPRECATED*

PURPOSE   Replaced by `KeyEvent.VK_UP`.

SYNTAX   `public static final int UP`

DEPRECATION   Replace the usage of this deprecated constant, as in

```
Event evt;
if (evt.key == Event.UP) ...
```

with

```
KeyEvent evt;
if (evt.getKeyCode() == KeyEvent.VK_UP) ...
```

when   *DEPRECATED*

PURPOSE   Replaced by `InputEvent.getWhen()`.

SYNTAX   `public long when`

DEPRECATION   Replace the usage of this deprecated field, as in

```
Event evt;
System.out.println("time: " + evt.when);
```

with

```
KeyEvent evt; // or MouseEvent
System.out.println("time: " + evt.getWhen());
```

A
B
C
D
E
F
G
H
I
J
K
L
M
N
O
P
Q
R
S
T
U
V
W
X
Y
Z

WINDOW_DEICONIFY   *DEPRECATED*

PURPOSE   Replaced by `WindowEvent.WINDOW_DEICONIFIED`.

SYNTAX   `public static final int WINDOW_DEICONIFY`

DEPRECATION Replace the usage of this deprecated constant, as in

```
Event evt;
switch(evt.id) {
case Event.WINDOW_DEICONIFY:
    ...
case Event.WINDOW_ICONIFY:
    ...
case Event.WINDOW_DESTROY:
    ...
case Event.WINDOW_EXPOSE:
    ...
```

by using `WindowListener.windowDeiconified()` or by using event subtypes as follows:

```
AWTEvent evt;
if (evt instanceof MouseEvent) {
    switch (evt.getID()) {
    case WindowEvent.WINDOW_DEICONIFIED:
        ...
    case WindowEvent.WINDOW_ICONIFIED:
        ...
    case WindowEvent.WINDOW_CLOSING:
        ...
    case WindowEvent.WINDOW_ACTIVATED:
        ...
```

WINDOW_DESTROY   *DEPRECATED*

PURPOSE   Replaced by `WindowEvent.WINDOW_CLOSING`.

SYNTAX   `public static final int WINDOW_DESTROY`

DEPRECATION Replace the usage of this deprecated constant by using a `Window.window-Closing()` or by using event subtypes, as shown in `WINDOW_DEICONIFY`.

WINDOW_EXPOSE   *DEPRECATED*

PURPOSE   Replaced by `WindowEvent.WINDOW_ACTIVATED`.

SYNTAX   `public static final int WINDOW_EXPOSE`

DEPRECATION Replace the usage of this deprecated constant by using a `Window.windowActivated()` or by using event subtypes, as shown in `WINDOW_DEICONIFY`.

WINDOW_ICONIFY   *DEPRECATED*

PURPOSE   Replaced by `WindowEvent.WINDOW_ICONIFIED`.

SYNTAX   `public static final int WINDOW_ICONIFY`

DEPRECATION   Replace the usage of this deprecated constant by using a `Window.window-Iconified()` or by using event subtypes, as shown in `WINDOW_DEICONIFY`.

WINDOW_MOVED   *DEPRECATED*

PURPOSE   Replaced by `ComponentEvent.COMPONENT_MOVED`.

SYNTAX   `public static final int WINDOW_MOVED`

DEPRECATION   In Java 1.1, any component can fire "move" events, not just windows. Replace the usage of this deprecated constant, as in

```
Event evt;
switch(evt.id) {
case Event.WINDOW_MOVED:
    ...
```

by using `ComponentListener.componentMoved()` or by using event subtypes as follows:

```
AWTEvent evt;
if (evt instanceof ComponentEvent) {
    switch (evt.getID()) {
    case ComponentEvent.COMPONENT_MOVED:
        ...
```

X   *DEPRECATED*

PURPOSE   Replaced by `MouseEvent.getX()`.

SYNTAX   `public int x`

DEPRECATION   In Java 1.0, the AWT adjusts the event's coordinates so that they are relative to the component that is receiving the event. In Java 1.1, the coordinates are, by default, relative to the bounds of the component that fired the event. This difference means that other calculations might be required when the usage of this deprecated field is replaced, as in

```
Event evt;
int x = evt.x + offset;
```

with

```
MouseEvent evt;
int x = evt.getX() + offset;
```

A
B
C
D

F
G
H
I
J
K
L
M
N
O
P
Q
R
S
T
U
V
W
X
Y
Z

y   *DEPRECATED*

PURPOSE   Replaced by `MouseEvent.getY()`.

SYNTAX   `public int y`

DEPRECATION   In Java 1.0, the AWT adjusts the event's coordinates so that they are relative to the component that is receiving the event. In Java 1.1, the coordinates are, by default, relative to the bounds of the component that fired the event. This difference means other calculations might be required when the usage of this deprecated field is replaced, as in

```
Event evt;
int y = evt.y + offset;
```

with

```
MouseEvent evt;
int y = evt.getY() + offset;
```

A
B
C
D
E
F
G
H
I
J
K
L
M
N
O
P
Q
R
S
T
U
V
W
X
Y
Z

EventQueue

```
java.lang.Object
    EventQueue
```

Syntax

```
public class EventQueue
```

Description

When an event source fires an event, that source may not be the one that created the event; the event may have been created by some other object. In particular, for components that have peers, the event is actually created by the peer and then delivered to the component. When the event source is not the creator of the event, the event should be delivered to the event source via an *event queue*. The event queue is a first-in/first-out queue. When an event is added (*posted*) to the event queue, it is delivered to the event source only when the event reaches the front of the queue.

Each queue has a separate *event-dispatching thread* that sequentially removes a queue item from the head of the queue and dispatches it to its event source. If the event source is a `Component` or `MenuComponent`, its `dispatchEvent()` method is invoked to dispatch the event. Otherwise, if the event is an `ActiveEvent`, the event's `dispatch()` method is called (see `ActiveEvent`). After the event-dispatching thread has completed dispatching the event to its event source and any registered listeners, it removes the next event from the event queue and performs the same process on it. If there are no more events on the event queue, the event-dispatching thread blocks until one is available.

The event queue enables two features not possible with direct delivery of events (i.e., by calling `dispatchEvent()` directly):

1. It allows for asynchronous delivery of events. As soon as the peer posts the event, it is free to do other things. If the peer delivered the event directly to the event source, it would be blocked while the event source and all of its listeners completed the processing of the event.
2. It serializes the events. For example, if you click button *A* and then button *B*, button *A* will get the click event before button *B*.

System Event Queue

The AWT system uses a single *system event queue* for posting events (see `Toolkit.getSystemEventQueue()`). The system event queue can include not only events generated by the AWT, but also system events that are added programmatically, if allowed by the security manager that is installed.

MEMBER SUMMARY	
Constructor	
`EventQueue()`	Constructs a new instance of `EventQueue`.
Event Queue Methods	
`getNextEvent()`	Removes the next event from this queue and returns it.
`peekEvent()`	Retrieves an event from this queue without removing it.
`postEvent()`	Adds an event to the end of this queue.

See Also

`AWTEvent`, `Component.dispatchEvent()`, `java.awt.peer.ActiveEvent`,
`java.lang.SecurityManager.checkAwtEventQueueAccess()`,
`MenuComponent.dispatchEvent()`, `Toolkit.getSystemEventQueue()`.

EventQueue()

PURPOSE	Constructs a new instance of `EventQueue`.
SYNTAX	`public EventQueue()`
DESCRIPTION	This method creates a new event queue and creates a new event-dispatching thread responsible for dispatching events that are added to the new event queue.

getNextEvent()

PURPOSE	Removes the next event from this queue and returns it.
SYNTAX	`public synchronized AWTEvent getNextEvent() throws` `    InterruptedException`
DESCRIPTION	If the event queue is empty, this method blocks until an event is available. This method is usually invoked only by the event-dispatching thread.
RETURNS	The next event from this queue.
EXCEPTIONS	
`InterruptedException`	
	If another thread has interrupted this thread.
SEE ALSO	`peekEvent()`, `postEvent()`.

peekEvent()

PURPOSE	Retrieves an event from this queue without removing it.
SYNTAX	`public synchronized AWTEvent peekEvent()` `public synchronized AWTEvent peekEvent(int id)`
DESCRIPTION	If an event id `id` is specified, this method searches from the beginning of the queue to find the first occurrence of an event that has event id `id`. If no such event is found, this method returns `null`. If `id` has not been specified, the first event in the queue is returned. If the queue is empty, `null` is returned.
PARAMETERS	
id	The event id of the event to retrieve.
RETURNS	The first event that has event id `id`, or the first event if `id` has not been specified. `null` if the queue is empty or `id` is not found.
SEE ALSO	`getNextEvent()`.

postEvent()

PURPOSE	Adds an event to the end of this queue.
SYNTAX	`public synchronized void postEvent(AWTEvent evt)`
DESCRIPTION	This event will eventually be dispatched by the event-dispatching thread associated with this event queue when it reaches the front of the queue.
PARAMETERS	
evt	The event to add.
SEE ALSO	`getNextEvent()`.
EXAMPLE	See the `AWTEvent` class example.

A
B
C
D
E
F
G
H
I
J
K
L
M
N
O
P
Q
R
S
T
U
V
W
X
Y
Z

java.beans
EventSetDescriptor

```
java.lang.Object
    FeatureDescriptor
        EventSetDescriptor
        BeanDescriptor
        MethodDescriptor
        ParameterDescriptor
        PropertyDescriptor
```

Syntax

`public class EventSetDescriptor extends FeatureDescriptor`

Description

For each event that a bean can fire, there is an associated *event set*. The event set refers to the supporting methods and interfaces of that event and basically consists of three things:

1. The *listener methods,* a group of callback methods that are associated with an event. In particular, when an object fires the event, one of the listener methods will be called. All the listener methods must take a single parameter: the `Class` object of the event itself.
2. The *listener interface,* an interface (or possibly a class) that defines all of the listener methods. A listener that wants to listen for the event must implement the listener interface.
3. The two *listener support methods,* which are provided by the bean and are used by listeners to register for the event. The listener support methods take a single parameter: an object of the same type as the listener interface.

For example, the event set of the focus event (see `FocusEvent`) comprises the following:

1. Two listener methods: `focusGained()` and `focusLost()`
2. A listener interface: `FocusListener`
3. Two listener support methods: `addFocusListener()` and `removeFocusListener()`

An *event set descriptor* contains information about an event set. The event set descriptor also contains other attributes about the event set, such as its localized name and whether it is a unicast event. There is one event set descriptor for each event that a bean can fire. The list of event set descriptors can be retrieved through the introspector by calling `Introspector.get-BeanInfo().getEventSetDescriptors()`.

For Bean Editors Only

The information contained in an event set descriptor is meant for programs such as bean editors (programs that help connect together beans into an application) and is not used by the bean itself. These and other descriptors essentially help a bean editor to construct a meaningful user interface for editing the bean. When the bean is actually running in an application, the event set descriptors are not used.

Implicit and Explicit Event Set Descriptors

The introspector first looks for *explicit* event set descriptors in the bean's bean-info, if present (see `BeanInfo`). If explicit event set descriptors are not found, the introspector creates *implicit* event set descriptors with some default values for each event set attribute. See Figure 127. Table 10 shows the attributes of event set descriptors and what they contain. Also shown are the default values for implicit event set descriptors.

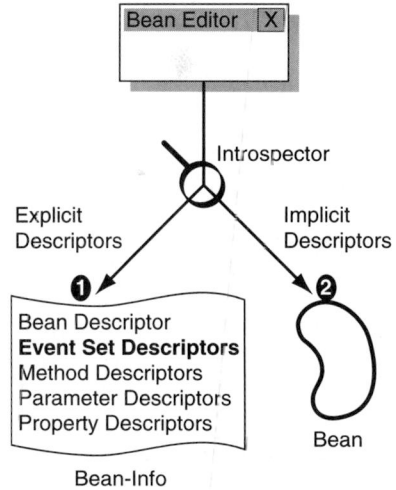

FIGURE 127: Event Set Descriptor.

Attribute	Contents	Implicit Default Value
Source	The `Class` object that fires the event.	The `Class` object that fires the event.
Listener type	The `Class` object of the listener interface.	The `Class` object of the listener interface.
Add listener method	The `Method` object of the add listener support method.	The `Method` object of the add listener support method.
Remove listener method	The `Method` object of the remove listener support method.	The `Method` object of the remove listener support method.
Listener methods	The `Method` objects for the collection of callback methods.	The `Method` objects for the collection of callback methods.
In default set	`true` if the event set is in the default set.	`true`.
Unicast	`true` if the event set is unicast.	`false`.[a]
		Continued

TABLE 10: Event Set Descriptor Attributes.

577

Attribute	Contents	Implicit Default Value
Name	The event set's nonlocalized name.	The event set's nonlocalized name.
Display name	The event set's localized name	The event set's localized name.
Short description	A localized description of the event set.	The event set's nonlocalized name.
Expert	`true` if the event set is considered for use by experts only.	`false`.
Hidden	`true` if the event set is meant to be used by a tool; `false` if it is meant to be use by a person.	`false`.

TABLE 10:   Event Set Descriptor Attributes.

a. If the introspector discovers that an event set's add listener method throws `TooManyListenersException`, unicast is set to `true`.

Conventions Regarding the Listener Support Method Signature

The bean specification defines conventions for the signature of a listener support method. These conventions serve two purposes:

1. They make the bean's API easier for a programmer to read. That is, it's easy to see which methods are listener support methods and which are not.
2. They make it possible for the introspector to discover a bean's event sets and create implicit event set descriptors. In other words, the introspector looks at the entire list of a bean's public methods. When a method is found that matches the listener support method signature convention, the introspector assumes that it must be a listener support method.

The names of the listener support methods are based on the name of the listener interface. For example, if the name of the listener interface (without the package name) is *EventName*Listener, then the add listener method signature convention.

```
public void addEventNameListener(EventNameListener l)
```

where *EventName*Listener must be a subclass of `java.util.EventListener` and `l` is any arbitrary parameter name. The remove listener method signature convention is

```
public void removeEventNameListener(EventNameListener l)
```

For example, if the listener interface name is `FocusListener`, the listener support methods would be

```
public void addFocusListener(FocusListener listener)
public void removeFocusListener(FocusListener listener)
```

Unicast Event Sets

Most event sets are *multicast*. This means that an object firing a multicast event will support many listeners. However, some events are *unicast*, that is, an object firing a unicast event will support only one listener. An event set is unicast if its add listener method throws `java.util.TooManyListenersException`. For example, if the event name is `"jump"`, the signature of the add listener method will be

```
public void addJumpListener(JumpListener listener)
    throws TooManyListenersException
```

MEMBER SUMMARY	
Constructor	
`EventSetDescriptor()`	Constructs an `EventSetDescriptor` instance.
Listener Methods	
`getAddListenerMethod()`	Retrieves the event set's add listener support method.
`getListenerMethodDescriptors()`	Retrieves the method descriptors for the event set's listener methods.
`getListenerMethods()`	Retrieves the event set's listener methods.
`getListenerType()`	Retrieves the event set's listener interface.
`getRemoveListenerMethod()`	Retrieves the event set's remove listener support method.
Default Set Methods	
`isInDefaultEventSet()`	Retrieves the state of the event set's "default set" attribute.
`setInDefaultEventSet()`	Sets the event set's "default set" attribute.
Unicast Methods	
`isUnicast()`	Determines if the event set is unicast.
`setUnicast()`	Specifies whether the event set is unicast.

See Also

`BeanInfo.getEventSetDescriptors()`, `java.awt.AWTEvent`, `java.lang.Class`, `java.util.EventObject`, `java.util.TooManyListenersException`.

Example

This example demonstrates how to use the four different event set descriptor constructors. See Figure 128. A new `"jump"` event is defined to demonstrate all of the pieces needed to define an event. An event first needs a class to represent the event, which, in general, should be a subclass of `EventObject` (see `java.util.EventObject`). An event also needs a listener interface that defines all of the callback methods that can be invoked when the event is fired. The jump event has only a single callback method: `beanJumped()`. (The listener interface could be a class, but making it an interface allows any object to listen for the event.)

The other three constructors are demonstrated using events that are already defined in the `java.awt.event` package.

A bean-info is necessary to hold the four event set descriptors. It must be defined in a class with the bean's name appended with "Bean-Info"—in this case, `BeanBean-Info`.

Note: The Beanbox in BDK 1.0apr97 requires that the listener interface be in a named package. When it is in an unnamed package, the Beanbox will not hook up the bean listener to the bean.

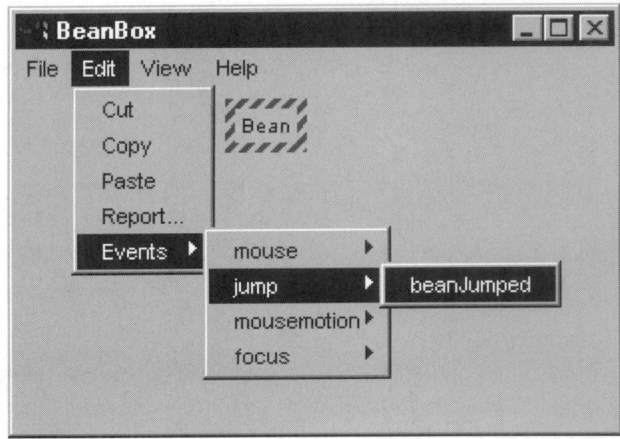

FIGURE 128:   Using Event Set Descriptors.

classexample/Bean.java

```java
package classexample;

import java.awt.event.*;
import java.beans.*;

public class Bean {
    // Jump events.
    public void addJumpListener(JumpListener listener)
        throws java.util.TooManyListenersException {}
    public void removeJumpListener(JumpListener listener) {}

    // Focus events.
    public void addFocusListener(FocusListener listener) {}
    public void removeFocusListener(FocusListener listener) {}

    // MouseMotion events.
    public void addMouseMotionListener(ActionListener listener) {}
    public void removeMouseMotionListener(ActionListener listener) {}

    // Mouse events.
    public void addMouseListener(ActionListener listener) {}
    public void removeMouseListener(ActionListener listener) {}

    public static void main(String[] args) {
        try {
            BeanInfo beanInfo = Introspector.getBeanInfo(Bean.class);
            EventSetDescriptor[] eds = beanInfo.getEventSetDescriptors();
        } catch (IntrospectionException e) {
            e.printStackTrace();
```

```
            }
        }
    }
```

classexample/BeanBeanInfo.java
```
    package classexample;

    import java.beans.*;
    import java.lang.reflect.*;

    public class BeanBeanInfo extends SimpleBeanInfo {
        public EventSetDescriptor[] getEventSetDescriptors() {
            try {
                EventSetDescriptor[] esd = new EventSetDescriptor[4];

                // First form of the constructor.
                esd[0] = new EventSetDescriptor(Bean.class,
                        "jump",
                        JumpListener.class,
                        "beanJumped");
                esd[0].setUnicast(true);
                esd[0].setInDefaultEventSet(true);

                // Second form of the constructor.
                String[] listenerNames1 = {"focusGained", "focusLost"};
                esd[1] = new EventSetDescriptor(Bean.class,
                        "focus",
                        java.awt.event.FocusListener.class,
                        listenerNames1,
                        "addFocusListener", "removeFocusListener");

                // Third form of the constructor.
                Method[] listeners2 = {
                    getMethod(java.awt.event.MouseMotionListener.class,
                        "mouseMoved", 1),
                    getMethod(java.awt.event.MouseMotionListener.class,
                        "mouseDragged", 1),    };
                esd[2] = new EventSetDescriptor(
                        "mousemotion",
                        java.awt.event.MouseMotionListener.class,
                        listeners2,
                        getMethod(Bean.class, "addMouseMotionListener", 1),
                        getMethod(Bean.class, "removeMouseMotionListener", 1));

                // Fourth form of the constructor.
                MethodDescriptor[] listeners3 = {
                    getMethodDesc(java.awt.event.MouseListener.class,
                        "mouseClicked", 1),
                    getMethodDesc(java.awt.event.MouseListener.class,
                        "mousePressed", 1),
                    getMethodDesc(java.awt.event.MouseListener.class,
                        "mouseReleased", 1),
                    getMethodDesc(java.awt.event.MouseListener.class,
                        "mouseEntered", 1),
                    getMethodDesc(java.awt.event.MouseListener.class,
                        "mouseExited", 1),    };
                esd[3] = new EventSetDescriptor(
                        "mouse",
                        java.awt.event.MouseListener.class,
                        listeners3,
```

A
B
C
D
E
F
G
H
I
J
K
L
M
N
O
P
Q
R
S
T
U
V
W
X
Y
Z

581

```
                            getMethod(Bean.class, "addMouseListener", 1),
                            getMethod(Bean.class, "removeMouseListener", 1));

                return esd;
            } catch (IntrospectionException e) {
                e.printStackTrace();
            }
            return null;
        }

        Method getMethod(Class cls, String methodName, int argCount)
                throws IntrospectionException {
            Method methods[] = cls.getMethods();

            for (int i = 0; i < methods.length; i++) {
                Method method = methods[i];

                if (method.getName().equals(methodName)
                        && method.getParameterTypes().length == argCount) {
                    return method;
                }
            }
            throw new IntrospectionException("No method \"" + methodName
                + "\" with " + argCount + " argument");
        }

        MethodDescriptor getMethodDesc(Class cls, String methodName, int argCount)
                throws IntrospectionException {
            return new MethodDescriptor(getMethod(cls, methodName, argCount));
        }
    }
```

classexample/JumpEvent.java

```
    package classexample;

    import java.util.*;

    public class JumpEvent extends EventObject {
        public JumpEvent(Object source) {
            super(source);
        }
    }
```

classexample/JumpListener.java

```
    package classexample;

    public interface JumpListener {
        // This method is called whenever the bean "jumps".
        public void beanJumped(JumpEvent evt);
    }
```

EventSetDescriptor()

PURPOSE   Constructs an EventSetDescriptor instance.

SYNTAX

```
public EventSetDescriptor(Class sourceClass, String
    eventSetName, Class listenerType, String listenerMethodName)
    throws IntrospectionException
public EventSetDescriptor(Class sourceClass, String eventSetName,
    Class listenerType, String listenerMethodNames[], String
    addListenerMethodName, String removeListenerMethodName) throws
    IntrospectionException
public EventSetDescriptor(String eventSetName, Class
    listenerType, Method listenerMethods[], Method
    addListenerMethod, Method removeListenerMethod) throws
    IntrospectionException
public EventSetDescriptor(String eventSetName, Class
    listenerType, MethodDescriptor listenerMethodDescriptors[],
    Method addListenerMethod, Method removeListenerMethod) throws
    IntrospectionException
```

DESCRIPTION

Event set descriptors are either implicitly created by the introspector or explicitly created by a bean. See the class description for more information.

When an event set descriptor is created, five attributes are initialized:

- The event set name
- The listener type
- The listener methods
- The add listener method
- The remove listener method

All other attributes are given default values that can be changed by methods in this class and in the FeatureDescriptor class. The default values for an event set descriptor are shown in Table 10.

eventSetName is arbitrary and is not used during introspection. It is mainly used for presentation purposes.

The class name of listenerType must end with "Listener." If the listener support methods are not supplied, they are determined using the name of listenerType. For example, if listenerType is java.awt.event.FocusListener.class, the listener support methods are

```
public void addFocusListener(FocusListener listener)
public void removeFocusListener(FocusListener listener)
```

The listener support methods must take a single parameter and not return any values. The parameter must be an object of the same type as the listener interface. For example, the listener support methods of the action event are

```
public void addActionListener(ActionListener listener)
public void removeActionListener(ActionListener listener)
```

When either listenerMethodNames or listenerMethods is specified (instead of listenerMethodDescriptors), a method descriptor is implicitly

A
B
C
D

F
G
H
I
J
K
L
M
N
O
P
Q
R
S
T
U
V
W
X
Y
Z

created for each of the listener support methods. See `MethodDescriptor` for more information on the default values for the method descriptor attributes.

When only one listener method exists (e.g., `actionPerformed()` in `Action-Event`), the constructor that takes the `listenerMethodName` parameter can be used. If this constructor is used, the listener support methods are automatically determined as described previously.

However, in most cases, there is more than one listener method, so one of `listenerMethodNames`, `listenerMethods`, or `listenerMethodDescriptors` must be specified. If the listener methods or the listener support methods are specified as strings, the `Class` object of the bean (`sourceClass`) must also be specified so that the string names can be converted into `Method` objects.

The listener methods must take a single parameter and not return any values. The parameter must be the event. For example, the action event (see `Action-Event`) has only one listener method. It has the following signature:

```
public void actionPerformed(ActionEvent evt)
```

PARAMETERS

addListenerMethod
:   The non-`null` `Method` object of the add listener support method.

addListenerMethodName
:   The non-`null` name of the add listener support method.

eventSetName
:   The nonlocalized name of the event.

listenerMethodDescriptors
:   A non-`null` array of method descriptors for the listener methods.

listenerMethodName
:   The non-`null` name of the listener method. Used only if the listener interface defines one listener method.

listenerMethodNames
:   A non-`null` array of listener method names.

listenerMethods
:   A non-`null` array of `Method` objects for the listener methods.

listenerType
:   The non-`null` `Class` object of the listener interface.

removeListenerMethod
:   The non-`null` `Method` object of the remove listener support method.

removeListenerMethodName
:   The non-`null` name of the remove listener support method.

sourceClass
:   The non-`null` `Class` object of the bean that fires the event.

EXCEPTIONS

IntrospectionException

If the signature of any method is not compatible with the signature conventions described in the class description.

SEE ALSO   `java.lang.reflect.Method.`

EXAMPLE   See the class example.

getAddListenerMethod()

PURPOSE   Retrieves the event set's add listener support method.

SYNTAX   `public Method getAddListenerMethod()`

DESCRIPTION   If an object fires an event, it must provide an add listener method so that other objects can listen for those events. The add listener method must be invoked with a single parameter: the listener object. The listener object must implement or extend from the event set's listener type (see `getListenerType()`), otherwise `IllegalArgumentException` is thrown.

RETURNS   The non-`null` `Method` object of the add listener method.

EXCEPTIONS

`IllegalArgumentException`
    The listener does not implement or extend from the event set's listener type.

SEE ALSO   `java.lang.reflect.Method, getListenerType(),`
`getRemoveListenerMethod().`

EXAMPLE   This example demonstrates how to invoke a bean's listener support methods. It loads a bean from a class file and then examines all of its event set descriptors, looking for one that fires action events. When it finds one, it instantiates the bean and displays it in a frame. The frame registers itself with the bean, listening for action events. When the frame is closed, it invokes the remove listener method on the bean to unregister itself for action events.

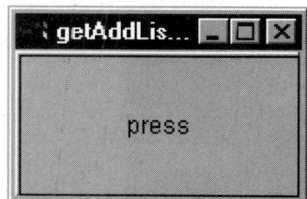

FIGURE 129:
Invoking a Bean's Listener Support Methods.

Figure 129 shows the example program executed on the `OurButton` example bean in BDK 1.0apr97.

```
import java.awt.*;
import java.awt.event.*;
import java.beans.*;
import java.io.*;
import java.lang.reflect.*;
import java.util.*;
```

A
B
C
D

F
G
H
I
J
K
L
M
N
O
P
Q
R
S
T
U
V
W
X
Y
Z

```
class Main extends Frame {
    public static void main(String[] args) {
        if (args.length != 1) {
            System.err.println(
                "Usage: java Main <name of component bean class file>");
            System.exit(1);
        }

        try {
            // Load the bean class.
            // (See the Introspector class example for FileClassLoader source.)
            Class beanClass = FileClassLoader.load(args[0]);
            BeanInfo beanInfo = Introspector.getBeanInfo(beanClass);

            // Get the event set descriptors, looking for one that fires
            // action events.
            EventSetDescriptor eds[] = beanInfo.getEventSetDescriptors();
            for (int i=0; i<eds.length; i++) {
                if (eds[i].getListenerType() ==
                        java.awt.event.ActionListener.class) {
                    // Instantiate the bean.
                    Object bean = beanClass.newInstance();

                    // Put the bean in a frame.
                    new TestFrame((Component)bean, eds[i]);
                    break;
                }
            }
        } catch (InstantiationException e) {
            e.printStackTrace();
        } catch (IllegalAccessException e) {
            e.printStackTrace();
        } catch (IntrospectionException e) {
            e.printStackTrace();
        }
    }
}

class TestFrame extends Frame implements ActionListener {
    Component bean;
    EventSetDescriptor esd;

    TestFrame(Component bean, EventSetDescriptor esd) {
        super("getAddListenerMethod Example");
        Method adder = esd.getAddListenerMethod();
        this.bean = bean;
        this.esd = esd;

        // Register with the bean for action events.
        Object[] adderArgs = {this};
        try {
            adder.invoke(bean, adderArgs);
        } catch (InvocationTargetException e) {
            e.printStackTrace();
        } catch (IllegalAccessException e) {
            e.printStackTrace();
        }

        // Watch for window closing events.
        addWindowListener(new WindowEventHandler());
```

A
B
C
D
E
F
G
H
I
J
K
L
M
N
O
P
Q
R
S
T
U
V
W
X
Y
Z

```
        // Layout and show bean.
        add((Component)bean, BorderLayout.CENTER);
        setSize(100, 100);
        show();
    }

    // Window events.

    class WindowEventHandler extends WindowAdapter {
        public void windowClosing(WindowEvent evt) {
            // Get remove listener method.
            Method remover = esd.getRemoveListenerMethod();

            // Remove frame from listening for action events.
            Object[] removerArgs = {TestFrame.this};
            try {
                remover.invoke(bean, removerArgs);
            } catch (InvocationTargetException e) {
                e.printStackTrace();
            } catch (IllegalAccessException e) {
                e.printStackTrace();
            }

            // Destroy the frame.
            dispose();
        }
    }

    // Action events.
    public void actionPerformed(ActionEvent evt) {
        System.out.println(evt);
    }
}
```

getListenerMethodDescriptors()

PURPOSE   Retrieves the method descriptors for the event set's listener methods.

SYNTAX   public MethodDescriptor[] getListenerMethodDescriptors()

DESCRIPTION   The listener methods are a group of callback methods that are associated with
               an event. In particular, when a bean fires the event, one of the listener methods
               will be called. For example, the focus event (see FocusEvent) has two listener
               methods: focusGained() and focusLost(). When a bean component loses
               the focus, the focusLost() listener method is called.

               The number of elements returned by this method should be identical to the
               number of elements returned by getListenerMethods().

RETURNS   A non-null array of MethodDescriptor objects, one for each listener
               method.

SEE ALSO   java.lang.reflect.Method, getListenerMethods().

EXAMPLE   See the MethodDescriptor class example.

A
B
C
D
E
F
G
H
I
J
K
L
M
N
O
P
Q
R
S
T
U
V
W
X
Y
Z

getListenerMethods()

PURPOSE	Retrieves the event set's listener methods.
SYNTAX	`public Method[] getListenerMethods()`
DESCRIPTION	The listener methods are a group of callback methods that are associated with an event. In particular, when a bean fires the event, one of the listener methods will be called. For example, the focus event (see `FocusEvent`) has two listener methods: `focusGained()` and `focusLost()`. When a bean component loses the focus, the `focusLost()` listener method is called.
	The number of elements returned by this method should be identical to the number of elements returned by `getListenerMethodDescriptors()`.
RETURNS	A non-`null` array of `Method` objects, one for each listener method.
SEE ALSO	`java.awt.event.FocusEvent, java.awt.event.FocusListener, java.lang.reflect.Method, getListenerMethodDescriptors()`.
EXAMPLE	See the `Introspector` class example.

getListenerType()

PURPOSE	Retrieves the event set's listener interface.
SYNTAX	`public Class getListenerType()`
DESCRIPTION	The listener interface defines all the callback methods that can be invoked when the source object fires an event. For example, in the case of the focus event (see `FocusEvent`), this method returns `FocusListener.class`.
	The event set's two listener support methods must take a single parameter of the same type as returned by this method. For example, if the listener interface is `FocusListener`, the two listener support methods have the signatures

```
public void addFocusListener(FocusListener listener)
public void removeFocusListener(FocusListener listener)
```

	When the listener support methods are not explicitly specified, the listener interface is used to determine them through introspection. See the class description for more information.
RETURNS	The non-`null` listener interface `Class` object.
SEE ALSO	`getAddListenerMethod(), getListenerMethods(), getRemoveListenerMethod(),java.awt.event.FocusEvent, java.awt.event.FocusListener`.
EXAMPLE	See `getAddListenerMethod()`.

getRemoveListenerMethod()

PURPOSE   Retrieves the event set's remove listener support method.

SYNTAX   `public Method getRemoveListenerMethod()`

DESCRIPTION   A listener that is registered with an event source can be unregistered by invoking the remove listener method. The remove listener method must be invoked with a single parameter: the listener object. The listener object must implement or extend from the event set's listener type (see `getListenerType()`): otherwise, `IllegalArgumentException` is thrown.

RETURNS   The non-`null` `Method` object of the remove listener method.

EXCEPTIONS

`IllegalArgumentException`
                If the listener object and its parents do not implement the event set's listener type.

SEE ALSO   `java.lang.reflect.Method`, `getAddListenerMethod()`, `getListenerType()`.

EXAMPLE   See `getAddListenerMethod()`.

isInDefaultEventSet()

PURPOSE   Retrieves the state of the event set's "default set" attribute.

SYNTAX   `public boolean isInDefaultEventSet()`

DESCRIPTION   *Note*: We can't elaborate on the "default set" attribute because it's not yet defined in the JavaBeans specification.

RETURNS   `true` if the event set is in the "default set"; `false` otherwise.

SEE ALSO   `setInDefaultEventSet()`.

isUnicast()

PURPOSE   Determines if the event set is unicast.

SYNTAX   `public boolean isUnicast()`

DESCRIPTION   An object firing a unicast event will support only one listener for that event. See the class description for more details of unicast events.

A
B
C
D
E
F
G
H
I
J
K
L
M
N
O
P
Q
R
S
T
U
V
W
X
Y
Z

The introspector can discover implicitly that an event set is unicast if its add listener method throws `TooManyListenersException`. You can also explicitly specify that an event set is unicast by using `setUnicast()`.

RETURNS   `true` if the event set is unicast; `false` if the event set is multicast.

SEE ALSO   `java.util.TooManyListenersException`, `setUnicast()`.

EXAMPLE   See the `Introspector` class example.

setInDefaultEventSet()

PURPOSE   Sets the event set's "default set" attribute.

SYNTAX   `public void setInDefaultEventSet(boolean inDefaultEventSet)`

DESCRIPTION   *Note*: We can't elaborate on the "default set" attribute because it's not yet defined in the JavaBeans™ specification.

PARAMETERS
  `inDefaultEventSet`
          `true` if the event set should be in the "default set."

SEE ALSO   `isInDefaultEventSet()`.

setUnicast()

PURPOSE   Specifies whether the event set is unicast.

SYNTAX   `public void setUnicast(boolean unicast)`

DESCRIPTION   An object firing a unicast event will support only one listener for that event. See the class description for more details of unicast events.

The introspector can discover implicitly that an event set is unicast if its add listener method throws `TooManyListenersException`. You can also explicitly specify that an event set is unicast by using this method.

PARAMETERS
  `unicast`   `true` if this event set is unicast; `false` if this event set is multicast.

SEE ALSO   `isUnicast()`.

EXAMPLE   See the class example.

FeatureDescriptor

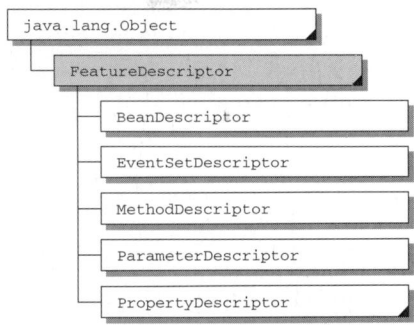

Syntax

```
public class FeatureDescriptor
```

Description

A *feature descriptor* is an object used to hold information about some part—a *feature*—of a bean. For example, the feature descriptor of a bean property specifies whether it is bound or constrained, while the feature descriptor of a bean method specifies whether the method should be used only by experts. Table 11 shows all of the bean parts that are features.

Feature	FeatureDescriptor Subclass
Bean	`BeanDescriptor`
Event set	`EventSetDescriptor`
Property	`PropertyDescriptor`
Indexed property	`IndexedPropertyDescriptor`
Method	`MethodDescriptor`
Method parameter	`ParameterDescriptor`

TABLE 11: **Features and Their Feature Descriptor Classes.**

Attributes

The parts of a feature descriptor are called *attributes*. For example, the feature descriptor for a bean property includes attribute information on the property's accessor methods, while the feature descriptor for a bean event set includes attribute information on whether the event is multicast. Since each bean feature contains attributes that are specific to the feature, each feature is represented by different classes, where each class contains those special attributes needed by the feature. Table 11 shows the associated bean descriptor classes for each of the bean features.

Although there is a class for each bean feature, all bean feature descriptors share a set of common attributes. This common set is contained in the class `FeatureDescriptor`. All other feature descriptors extend from this class and add their own special attributes. Table 12 shows all of the attributes in the `FeatureDescriptor` class.

Attribute	Contents	Default Value
Name	The feature's nonlocalized name.	`null`
Display name	The feature's localized name.	`null`
Short description	A localized description of the feature.	`null`
Expert	`true` if the feature is considered for use by experts only.	`false`
Hidden	`true` if the feature is meant to be used by a tool; `false` if it is meant to be use by a person.	`false`

TABLE 12:   Feature Descriptor Attributes and Their Default Values.

In general, a bean does not typically define new bean features. But in the event that it does, the bean should not use `FeatureDescriptor` to describe the new bean feature. Instead, the bean should define a new subclass of `FeatureDescriptor` and use the subclass, even if the subclass does not add any extra attributes. For example, `ParameterDescriptor` is a feature descriptor that does not add any extra attributes. This allows a bean editor to distinguish between different types of feature descriptors.

Extension Attributes
A feature descriptor supports the ability to specify extra attributes called *extension attributes*. An extension attribute has a name, which is a string, and a value, which is any non-null object. Extension attributes are used when a bean editor may treat a bean differently if it detects a particular extension attribute. For example, a bean editor may refuse to edit a bean unless it contains a "serial-number" attribute with an appropriate value.

For Bean Editors Only
The information contained in a feature descriptor is meant for programs such as bean editors (programs that help connect together beans into an application) and is not used by the bean itself. These and other descriptors essentially help a bean editor to construct a meaningful user interface for editing the bean. When the bean is actually running in an application, the feature descriptors are never used.

MEMBER SUMMARY	
Constructor	
`FeatureDescriptor()`	Constructs a `FeatureDescriptor` instance.
Get Attribute Methods	
`getDisplayName()`	Retrieves the feature's display name.
`getName()`	Retrieves the feature's name.
`getShortDescription()`	Retrieves a short description of the feature.
`isExpert()`	Retrieves the feature's expert attribute.
`isHidden()`	Retrieves the feature's hidden attribute.
Set Attribute Methods	
`setDisplayName()`	Sets the feature's display name.
`setExpert()`	Retrieves the feature's expert attribute.
`setHidden()`	Sets the feature's hidden attribute.
`setName()`	Sets the feature's name.
`setShortDescription()`	Sets a short description of the feature.
Attribute Extension Methods	
`attributeNames()`	Retrieves the feature descriptor's extension attribute names.
`getValue()`	Retrieves the value of an extension attribute.
`setValue()`	Defines an extension attribute.

See Also

`BeanDescriptor, EventSetDescriptor, IndexedPropertyDescriptor, MethodDescriptor, ParameterDescriptor, PropertyDescriptor.`

Example

This example demonstrates how to add extension attributes to a feature descriptor. The example implements a bean-info that returns a bean descriptor with two extension attributes: author and created. The author attribute is a simple string and the created attribute is a calendar object.

The main program invokes the introspector to retrieve the bean descriptor and print its contents into a text area. See Figure 130.

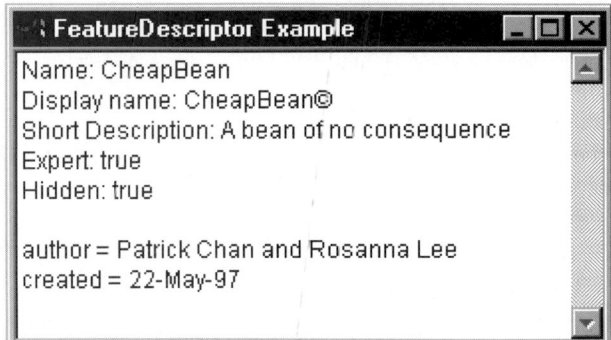

FIGURE 130:   Adding Extension Attributes to `FeatureDescriptor`.

The empty bean class is needed in order for the introspector to find the bean-info.

Main.java

```java
import java.awt.*;
import java.awt.event.*;
import java.beans.*;
import java.util.*;
import java.text.*;

class Main extends Frame {
    Main(BeanDescriptor beanDesc) {
        super("FeatureDescriptor Example");
        TextArea ta = new TextArea("", 10, 40,
            TextArea.SCROLLBARS_VERTICAL_ONLY);

        // Make the text area readonly.
        ta.setEditable(false);

        // Print the attributes that are in FeatureDescriptor
        ta.append("Name: " + beanDesc.getName() + "\n");
        ta.append("Display name: " + beanDesc.getDisplayName() + "\n");
        ta.append("Short Description: " +
            beanDesc.getShortDescription() + "\n");
        ta.append("Expert: " + beanDesc.isExpert() + "\n");
        ta.append("Hidden: " + beanDesc.isHidden() + "\n\n");

        // Print all the extension attributes.
        Enumeration enum = beanDesc.attributeNames();
        for (Enumeration e=enum; e.hasMoreElements(); ) {
            String name = (String)e.nextElement();
            Object value = beanDesc.getValue(name);

            // Look for Calendar objects.
            if (value instanceof Calendar) {
                value = DateFormat.getDateInstance().format(
                    ((Calendar)value).getTime());
            }
            ta.append(name + " = " + value + "\n");
        }

        // Layout and show.
        add(ta, BorderLayout.CENTER);
        setSize(200, 100);
        show();
    }

    public static void main(String[] args) {
        try {
            // Retrieve the bean-info and then the bean descriptor.
            BeanInfo beanInfo = Introspector.getBeanInfo(Bean.class);
            BeanDescriptor beanDesc = beanInfo.getBeanDescriptor();

            // Display the bean descriptor information.
            new Main(beanDesc);
        } catch (IntrospectionException e) {
            e.printStackTrace();
        }
    }
}
```

A
B
C
D
E
F
G
H
I
J
K
L
M
N
O
P
Q
R
S
T
U
V
W
X
Y
Z

BeanBeanInfo.java
```
import java.beans.*;
import java.util.*;

public class BeanBeanInfo extends SimpleBeanInfo {
    public BeanDescriptor getBeanDescriptor() {
        BeanDescriptor bd = new BeanDescriptor(Bean.class);

        // Initialize FeatureDescriptor attributes.
        bd.setName("CheapBean");
        bd.setDisplayName("CheapBean\u00a9");    // Copyright symbol
        bd.setExpert(true);
        bd.setHidden(true);
        bd.setShortDescription("A bean of no consequence");

        // Add an "author" attribute.
        bd.setValue("author", "Patrick Chan and Rosanna Lee");

        // Add a "created" attribute.
        Calendar calendar = Calendar.getInstance();
        calendar.set(1997, 4, 22, 10, 49);
        bd.setValue("created", calendar);
        bd.setValue("created", null);

        return bd;
    }
}
```

Bean.java
```
public class Bean {
    // An empty bean.
}
```

attributeNames()

PURPOSE	Retrieves the feature descriptor's extension attribute names.
SYNTAX	`public Enumeration attributeNames()`
DESCRIPTION	This method retrieves all of the feature descriptor's extension attribute names, if any.
RETURNS	A non-`null` enumeration containing the attribute names.
SEE ALSO	`getValue()`, `java.util.Enumeration`, `setValue()`.
EXAMPLE	See the class example.

A B C D E F G H I J K L M N O P Q R S T U V W X Y Z

FeatureDescriptor()

PURPOSE	Constructs a `FeatureDescriptor` instance.
SYNTAX	`public FeatureDescriptor()`
DESCRIPTION	In general, a bean does not typically define new bean features. But if it does, the bean should not use `FeatureDescriptor` to describe the new bean feature. Instead, the bean should define a new subclass of `FeatureDescriptor` and use that instead, even if the subclass does not have any extra attributes. For example, `ParameterDescriptor` is a feature descriptor that does not add any extra attributes. This allows a bean editor to distinguish between different types of feature descriptors.
	The default values for a feature descriptor are shown in Table 12.
EXAMPLE	See the class example.

getDisplayName()

PURPOSE	Retrieves the feature's display name.
SYNTAX	`public String getDisplayName()`
DESCRIPTION	The feature's display name is a localized string that a bean editor displays to identify the feature. For example, a bean could have a property called "color" but whose display name is "colour."
	If the display name has not been explicitly set or if it is set to `null` by `setDisplayName()`, this method returns `getName()`.
RETURNS	A possibly `null` localized string containing the feature's display name.
SEE ALSO	`getName()`, `setDisplayName()`.
EXAMPLE	See the class example.

getName()

PURPOSE	Retrieves the feature's name.
SYNTAX	`public String getName()`
DESCRIPTION	The feature's name is a nonlocalized string used by a program when referring to the feature.
RETURNS	A possibly `null` string containing the feature's name.
SEE ALSO	`getDisplayName()`, `setName()`.

A
B
C
D
E
F
G
H
I
J
K
L
M
N
O
P
Q
R
S
T
U
V
W
X
Y
Z

getShortDescription()

PURPOSE	Retrieves a short description of the feature.
SYNTAX	`public String getShortDescription()`

DESCRIPTION   The feature's short description contains a string that a bean editor can present to users to provide a little more detail about the feature. The string should be around 40 characters or fewer.

If the short description has not been explicitly set or if it is set to `null` by `setShortDescription()`, this method returns `getDisplayName()`.

RETURNS   A possibly `null` localized string containing a short description of the feature.

SEE ALSO   `getDisplayName()`, `setShortDescription()`.

EXAMPLE   See the class example.

getValue()

PURPOSE   Retrieves the value of an extension attribute.

SYNTAX   `public Object getValue(String attributeName)`

PARAMETERS

`attributeName`
> The non-`null` nonlocalized attribute name.

RETURNS   The attribute's non-`null` value; `null` if the attribute is not defined.

SEE ALSO   `attributeNames()`, `setValue()`.

EXAMPLE   See the class example for a longer example.

```
void printSerialNumber(BeanDescriptor beanDesc) {
    Object value = beanDesc.getValue("serial-number");

    if (value == null) {
        System.out.prinltn("The extension attribute is not defined");
    } else {
        System.out.prinltn(value);
    }
}
```

A
B
C
D
E

G
H
I
J
K
L
M
N
O
P
Q
R
S
T
U
V
W
X
Y
Z

isExpert()

PURPOSE	Retrieves the feature's expert attribute.
SYNTAX	`public boolean isExpert()`
DESCRIPTION	If this method returns `true`, the feature is meant to be used by experts only. A bean editor could use this information to hide expert-only features and display those features only if the user asks to see them.
RETURNS	`true` if the feature is intended for use by experts only; `false` otherwise.
SEE ALSO	`setExpert()`.
EXAMPLE	See the class example.

isHidden()

PURPOSE	Retrieves the feature's hidden attribute.
SYNTAX	`public boolean isHidden()`
DESCRIPTION	If this method returns `true`, the feature should not be modified by users. Hidden features are maintained by programs. A bean editor could use this information to hide the feature from the user.
RETURNS	`true` if the feature is meant to be used by a tool; `false` if it is meant to be used by a person.
SEE ALSO	`setHidden()`.
EXAMPLE	See the class example.

setDisplayName()

PURPOSE	Sets the feature's display name.
SYNTAX	`public void setDisplayName(String displayName)`
DESCRIPTION	The feature's display name is a localized string that a bean editor displays to identify the feature. For example, a bean could have a property called "color" but whose display name is "colour."
PARAMETERS	`displayName` A possibly-`null` localized string containing the feature's display name.
SEE ALSO	`getDisplayName()`.
EXAMPLE	See the class example.

setExpert()

PURPOSE	Retrieves the feature's expert attribute.
SYNTAX	`public void setExpert(boolean expert)`
DESCRIPTION	This attribute lets you designate a feature to be for experts only. A bean editor could use this information to hide expert-only features and display those feature only if the user asks to see them.
PARAMETERS	
expert	`true` if the feature is intended for use by experts only; `false` otherwise.
SEE ALSO	`isExpert()`.
EXAMPLE	See the class example.

setHidden()

PURPOSE	Sets the feature's hidden attribute.
SYNTAX	`public void setHidden(boolean hidden)`
DESCRIPTION	This attribute lets you to designate a feature to be for program use only. Hidden features should not be modified by users. A bean editor could use this information to hide the feature from the user.
PARAMETERS	
hidden	`true` if the feature is meant to be used by a tool; `false` otherwise.
SEE ALSO	`isHidden()`.
EXAMPLE	See the class example.

setName()

PURPOSE	Sets the feature's name.
SYNTAX	`public void setName(String name)`
DESCRIPTION	The feature's name is a nonlocalized string that is used by a program when referring to the feature.
PARAMETERS	
name	A possibly-null localized string containing the feature's display name.
SEE ALSO	`getName()`.
EXAMPLE	See the class example.

A
B
C
D
E

G
H
I
J
K
L
M
N
O
P
Q
R
S
T
U
V
W
X
Y
Z

A
B
C
D
E
F
G
H
I
J
K
L
M
N
O
P
Q
R
S
T
U
V
W
X
Y
Z

setShortDescription()

PURPOSE	Sets a short description of the feature.
SYNTAX	`public void setShortDescription(String text)`
DESCRIPTION	The feature's short description contains a string that a bean editor can present to users to provide a little more detail about the feature. The string should be around 40 characters or fewer.
PARAMETERS	
`text`	A non-`null` localized string containing a short description of the feature.
SEE ALSO	`getShortDescription()`.
EXAMPLE	See the class example.

setValue()

PURPOSE	Defines an extension attribute.
SYNTAX	`public void setValue(String attributeName, Object value)`
DESCRIPTION	Defines an attribute that has a non-`null` value. If the attribute is already defined, the old value of the attribute is replaced with `value`.
PARAMETERS	
`attributeName`	
	The non-`null` nonlocalized attribute name.
`value`	A non-`null` value.
SEE ALSO	`attributeNames()`, `getValue()`.
EXAMPLE	See the class example.

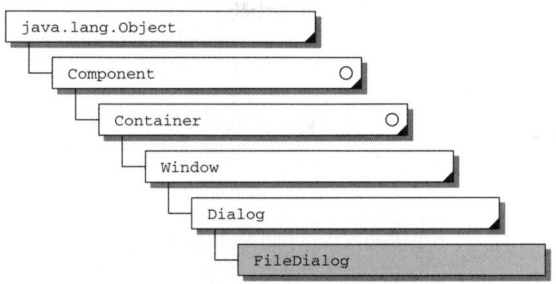

```
java.lang.Object
    Component          ○
        Container          ○
            Window
                Dialog
                    FileDialog
```

Syntax
`public class FileDialog extends Dialog`

Description
The `FileDialog` component displays a dialog for selecting a file in the file system. The file dialog can be used to either load or save a file. It is a modal dialog and blocks the calling thread until the user has chosen a file.

The Mode Property
There are two file dialog modes: *load* and *save*. A *load file dialog* is used to select an existing file in the file system. A *save file dialog* is used either to select an existing file or to select an existing directory and then to allow the user to name a new file. The mode is set at the time a file dialog instance is created and can be changed at any time.

The Directory and File Property
The *directory property* of a file dialog indicates the directory that the file dialog is currently displaying. The *file property* indicates either the file that is currently selected in the file dialog or the text in the filename entry text field.

These properties can be set before the file dialog is displayed and queried after the dialog is closed.

The Filter Property
The *filter property* controls which files are displayed in the file dialog. The filter is a class that implements the `FilenameFilter` interface that defines the `accept()` method. The `accept()` method is passed a directory and a filename. It returns `true` if the file should be displayed and `false` otherwise.

See Also
`FilenameFilter`.

A
B
C
D
E
G
H
I
J
K
L
M
N
O
P
Q
R
S
T
U
V
W
X
Y
Z

MEMBER SUMMARY	
Constructor	
FileDialog()	Constructs a new FileDialog instance.
File Dialog Types	
LOAD	The file dialog mode that specifies a load file dialog.
SAVE	The file dialog mode that specifies a save file dialog.
Property Methods	
getDirectory()	Retrieves this file dialog's directory property.
getFile()	Retrieves this file dialog's file property.
getFilenameFilter()	Retrieves this filename filter object.
getMode()	Retrieves this file dialog's mode.
setDirectory()	Sets this file dialog's directory property.
setFile()	Sets this file dialog's file property.
setFilenameFilter()	Sets this file dialog's filename filter.
setMode()	Sets this file dialog's mode.
Peer Method	
addNotify()	Creates the file dialog's peer hierarchy.
Debugging Method	
paramString()	Generates a string representing the file dialog's state.

Example

This example creates a frame with two buttons
(Figure 131). One button creates a load file dialog
(Figure 132), while the other creates a save file
dialog (Figure 133). In addition, the frame contains three text fields—directory, file, and filter—
for showing and changing the current values of
the file dialog's properties. Just before the file is
displayed, the directory and file properties are initialized to the values in the respective text fields.
After a file has been selected and the file dialog is
closed, the two text fields are updated with the
values in the dialog.

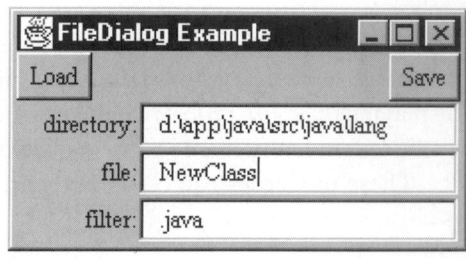

FIGURE 131: **FileDialog: Control Panel.**

The file filter is implemented by the accept() method. It returns true if the file dialog
mode is LOAD and the filename suffix matches the contents of the filter text field. If the file dialog mode is SAVE, accept() always returns true.

Note: In Java 1.1.2, filename filtering does not work. Nor does setting the directory and the filename. The file dialog always displays the entire contents of the current working directory.

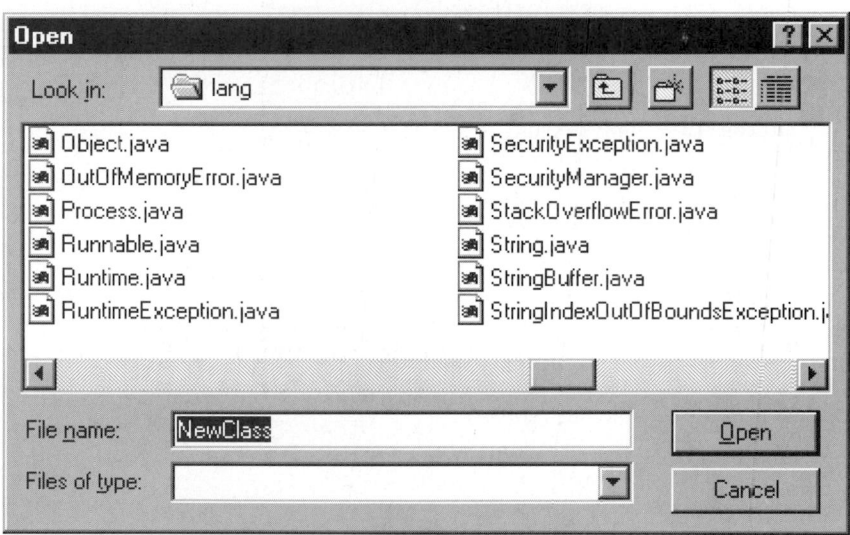

FIGURE 132: **A Load File Dialog.**

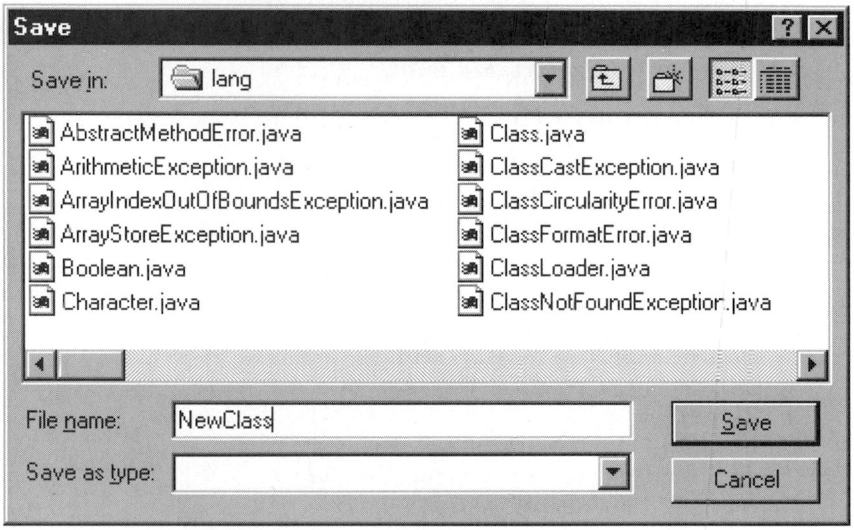

FIGURE 133: **A Save File Dialog.**

```
import java.awt.*;
import java.awt.event.*;
import java.io.*;

class Main extends Frame implements FilenameFilter, ActionListener {
    FileDialog fd;
    TextField tfDirectory = new TextField();
    TextField tfFile = new TextField();
    TextField tfFilter = new TextField();

    Main() {
        super("FileDialog Example");
        Button lb = new Button("Load");
        lb.addActionListener(this);
        Button sb = new Button("Save");
        sb.addActionListener(this);
        add(lb, BorderLayout.WEST);
        add(sb, BorderLayout.EAST);

        Panel p = new Panel(new GridBagLayout());
        addRow(p, new Label("directory:", Label.RIGHT), tfDirectory);
        addRow(p, new Label("file:", Label.RIGHT), tfFile);
        addRow(p, new Label("filter:", Label.RIGHT), tfFilter);

        add(p, BorderLayout.SOUTH);
        pack();
        show();
    }

    // Adds a row in a gridbag layout where the c2 is stretchy
    // and c1 is not.
    void addRow(Container cont, Component c1, Component c2) {
        GridBagLayout gbl = (GridBagLayout)cont.getLayout();
        GridBagConstraints c = new GridBagConstraints();
        Component comp;

        c.fill = GridBagConstraints.BOTH;
        cont.add(c1);
        gbl.setConstraints(c1, c);

        c.gridwidth = GridBagConstraints.REMAINDER;
        c.weightx = 1.0;
        cont.add(c2);
        gbl.setConstraints(c2, c);
    }

    public boolean accept(File dir, String name) {
        if (fd.getMode() == FileDialog.LOAD) {
            return name.lastIndexOf(tfFilter.getText()) > 0;
        }
        return true;
    }

    public void actionPerformed(ActionEvent evt) {
        String what = evt.getActionCommand();
        boolean load = "Load".equals(what);

        if ("Load".equals(what)) {
            fd = new FileDialog(this, null, FileDialog.LOAD);
```

```
    } else if ("Save".equals(what)) {
        fd = new FileDialog(this, null, FileDialog.SAVE);
    } else {
        return;
    }

    fd.setDirectory(tfDirectory.getText());
    fd.setFile(tfFile.getText());
    fd.setFilenameFilter(Main.this);

    fd.show();

    // Update text fields with input from dialogs
    tfDirectory.setText(fd.getDirectory());
    tfFile.setText(fd.getFile());
}

static public void main(String[] args) {
    new Main();
}

}
```

addNotify()

PURPOSE	Creates this file dialog's peer hierarchy.
SYNTAX	`public void addNotify()`
DESCRIPTION	This method creates this file dialog's peer hierarchy, if necessary. The file dialog's peer is created by calling the `Toolkit.createFileDialog()` method.
OVERRIDES	`Dialog.addNotify()`.
SEE ALSO	`Component`, `Toolkit`.
EXAMPLE	See `Component.setVisible()`.

FileDialog()

PURPOSE	Constructs a new `FileDialog` instance.

SYNTAX	`public FileDialog(Frame parent)`
	`public FileDialog(Frame parent, String title)`
	`public FileDialog(Frame parent, String title, int mode)`

DESCRIPTION	This constructor creates a new invisible `FileDialog` instance with the parent `parent`, title `title`, and file dialog mode `mode`. If `mode` is not specified, it defaults to LOAD. The title can be `null` or not specified, in which case it defaults to "Open" for a load file dialog and "Save" for a save file dialog.

By default, all of the properties of the file dialog—directory, file, and filter—are set to `null`.

PARAMETERS

`mode`	An integer specifying the file dialog mode.
`parent`	The file dialog's non-`null` parent.
`title`	The string specifying the title of the file dialog. If `null`, it defaults to either "Open" or "Save", depending on the mode.

EXCEPTIONS

`IllegalArgumentException`
             If `parent` is null.

SEE ALSO   `LOAD`, `SAVE`.

EXAMPLE   See the class example.

getDirectory()

PURPOSE   Retrieves the file dialog's directory property.

SYNTAX   `public String getDirectory()`

DESCRIPTION   This method should not be called while the dialog is visible.

RETURNS   The non-`null` directory of the file dialog.

SEE ALSO   `setDirectory()`.

EXAMPLE   See the class example.

getFile()

PURPOSE   Retrieves the file dialog's file property.

SYNTAX   `public String getFile()`

DESCRIPTION   This method should not be called while the dialog is visible.

RETURNS   The file property. A return value of `null` indicates that no file was selected.

SEE ALSO   `setFile()`.

EXAMPLE   See the class example.

getFilenameFilter()

PURPOSE	Retrieves the filename filter object.
SYNTAX	`public FilenameFilter getFilenameFilter()`
RETURNS	The object that is implementing the filename filter. May be `null`.
SEE ALSO	`FilenameFilter`, `setFilenameFilter()`.
EXAMPLE	See the class example.

getMode()

PURPOSE	Retrieves this file dialog's mode.
SYNTAX	`public int getMode()`
RETURNS	An integer indicating the file dialog's mode, which can be either LOAD or SAVE.
SEE ALSO	`LOAD, SAVE, setMode()`.
EXAMPLE	See the class example.

LOAD

PURPOSE	The file dialog mode that specifies a load file dialog.
SYNTAX	`public static final int LOAD`
DESCRIPTION	This integer constant is used to specify a load file dialog when a file dialog is created.
EXAMPLE	See the class example.

paramString()

PURPOSE	Generates a string representing this file dialog's state.
SYNTAX	`protected String paramString()`
DESCRIPTION	This method returns a string representing the file dialog, including the selected item. A subclass of this class should override this method and return a concatenation of its state with the results of `super.paramString()`. This method is called by the `Component.toString()` method and is typically used for debugging.
RETURNS	A non-`null` string representing the file dialog's state.

A B C D E F G H I J K L M N O P Q R S T U V W X Y Z

OVERRIDES	`Dialog.paramString()`.
SEE ALSO	`Component.toString()`, `java.lang.Object.toString()`.
EXAMPLE	See `Component.paramString()`.

SAVE

PURPOSE	The file dialog mode that specifies a save file dialog.
SYNTAX	`public static final int SAVE`
DESCRIPTION	This integer constant is used to specify a save file dialog when a file dialog is created.
EXAMPLE	See the class example.

setDirectory()

PURPOSE	Sets this file dialog's directory property.
SYNTAX	`public synchronized void setDirectory(String dir)`
DESCRIPTION	If `dir` is `null` or specifies an invalid directory, no exception is raised. The behavior of the file dialog in this case depends on the platform, but typically some default directory is displayed.
	This method should be called *before* the file dialog is made visible. It should not be called when the file dialog is visible.
PARAMETERS	
`dir`	The string specifying the directory to display in the file dialog. May be `null`.
SEE ALSO	`getDirectory()`.
EXAMPLE	See the class example.

setFile()

PURPOSE	Sets this file dialog's file property.
SYNTAX	`public synchronized void setFile(String file)`
DESCRIPTION	When the file dialog is displayed, its filename text field contains the string `file`. If the file dialog's current directory has a file with the name `file`, that file will be selected. If `file` is `null`, the filename defaults to "".

This method should be called *before* the file dialog is made visible. It should not be called when the file dialog is visible.

PARAMETERS

file   The string specifying the initial value of the filename text field in the file dialog. May be `null`.

SEE ALSO   `getFile()`.

EXAMPLE   See the class example.

setFilenameFilter( )

PURPOSE   Sets the file dialog's filename filter.

SYNTAX   `public synchronized void setFilenameFilter(FilenameFilter filter)`

DESCRIPTION   This method installs `filter` as the file dialog's filename filter. The file dialog will display only files whose names are accepted by the filename filter. If `filter` is `null`, the file dialog displays all files.

PARAMETERS

filter   The possibly `null` filename filter for the file dialog.

SEE ALSO   `FilenameFilter`, `getFilenameFilter()`.

EXAMPLE   See the class example.

setMode( )

PURPOSE   Sets this file dialog's mode.

SYNTAX   `public void setMode(int mode)`

PARAMETERS

mode   An integer indicating the file dialog's mode, which must be either `LOAD` or `SAVE`.

EXCEPTIONS

`IllegalArgumentException`
      If `mode` is neither `LOAD` nor `SAVE`.

SEE ALSO   `getMode()`, `LOAD`, `SAVE`.

EXAMPLE   The class example could have been written to use `setMode()` instead of creating a new instance of `FileDialog` each time the Load button or Save button is clicked. This example is a simplified version of the class example that uses

A
B
C
D
E
F
G
H
I
J
K
L
M
N
O
P
Q
R
S
T
U
V
W
X
Y
Z

only a single instance of `FileDialog`. The Load and Save buttons control the mode of the file dialog and display the file dialog. Because file dialog windows are modal, you must exit the file dialog before making another button selection.

```java
import java.awt.*;
import java.awt.event.*;

class Main extends Frame implements ActionListener {
    FileDialog fd;
    Main() {
        super("setMode example");

        Panel p = new Panel(new GridLayout(1, 0));
        Button b;
        b = new Button("Load");
        p.add(b);
        b.addActionListener(this);

        b = new Button("Save");
        p.add(b);
        b.addActionListener(this);

        add(p, BorderLayout.SOUTH);

        pack();
        show();

        // Create file dialog
        fd = new FileDialog(this);
    }

    public void actionPerformed(ActionEvent evt) {
        String cmd = evt.getActionCommand();
        if (cmd.equals("Load")) {
            fd.setMode(FileDialog.LOAD);
            fd.show();
        } else {
            fd.setMode(FileDialog.SAVE);
            fd.show();
        }
    }

    static public void main(String[] args) {
        new Main();
    }
}
```

FileDialogPeer

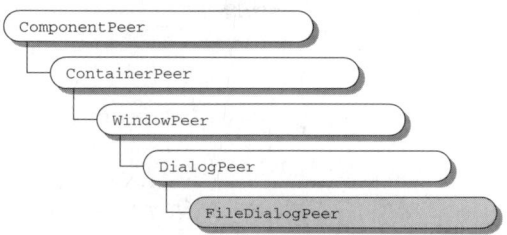

Syntax
```
public interface FileDialogPeer extends DialogPeer
```

Description

The file dialog component (see the FileDialog class) in the AWT uses the platform's native implementation of a file dialog box. So that the AWT file dialog box behaves the same on all platforms, the file dialog box is assigned a *peer,* whose task is to translate the behavior of the platform's native file dialog box to the behavior of the AWT file dialog box.

AWT programmers normally do not directly use peer classes and interfaces. Instead, they deal with AWT components in the java.awt package. These in turn automatically manage their peers. Only someone who is porting the AWT to another platform should be concerned with the peer classes and interfaces. Consequently, most peer documentation refers to java.awt counterparts.

See Component and Toolkit for additional information about component peers.

MEMBER SUMMARY	
Peer Methods	
setDirectory()	Sets the file dialog's directory property.
setFile()	Sets the file dialog's file property.
setFilenameFilter()	Sets the file dialog's filename filter.

See Also
java.awt.Component, java.awt.FileDialog, java.awt.Toolkit.

A
B
C
D
E
F
G
H
I
J
K
L
M
N
O
P
Q
R
S
T
U
V
W
X
Y
Z

setDirectory()

PURPOSE	Sets the file dialog's directory property.
SYNTAX	`void setDirectory(String dir)`
PARAMETERS	
`dir`	The string specifying the directory to display in the file dialog.
SEE ALSO	`java.awt.FileDialog.setDirectory()`.

setFile()

PURPOSE	Sets the file dialog's file property.
SYNTAX	`void setFile(String file)`
PARAMETERS	
`file`	The string specifying the initial value of the filename text field in the file dialog.
SEE ALSO	`java.awt.FileDialog.setFile()`.

setFilenameFilter()

PURPOSE	Sets the file dialog's filename filter.
SYNTAX	`void setFilenameFilter(FilenameFilter filter)`
PARAMETERS	
`filter`	The possibly `null` filename filter for the file dialog.
SEE ALSO	`java.awt.FileDialog.setFilenameFilter()`.

FilteredImageSource

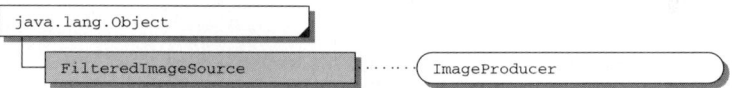

```
java.lang.Object
    FilteredImageSource ...... ImageProducer
```

Syntax
```
public class FilteredImageSource implements ImageProducer
```

Description
This class is used to build a stream of image filters. This class takes an image producer and an image filter (see `ImageFilter`) and creates a new image producer. This new image producer can be combined with yet another image filter to create yet another image producer. Image consumers that get pixels from the new image producer will get pixels that have been modified by the associated image filter.

MEMBER SUMMARY	
Constructor	
FilteredImageSource()	Constructs a new FilteredImageSource object.
Image Producer Methods	
addConsumer()	Registers an image consumer with this image producer.
isConsumer()	Determines if an image consumer is registered with this image producer.
removeConsumer()	Removes a registered image consumer from this image producer.
requestTopDownLeftRightResend()	Request by an image consumer to retransmit pixels in top-down, left-to-right order.
startProduction()	Adds an image consumer to the list of consumers interested in pixels.

See Also
`ImageConsumer`, `ImageFilter`, `ImageProducer`.

Example

This example creates a filter stream with two image filters. See Figure 134. The first image filter closest to the source image is a crop filter that extracts a portion of the source image. In this example, the bottom quarter of the image is removed. The next filter down the pixel stream is an RGB filter that swaps the red and blue components of all of the colors in the image.

FIGURE 134: FilteredImageSource.

```java
import java.awt.*;
import java.awt.image.*;
import java.awt.event.*;
import java.net.*;
import java.util.*;

class Main extends Frame {
    Main(String filename) {
        super("FilteredImageSource Example");
        try {
            Image image = getToolkit().getImage(filename);

            // Use a media tracker object to wait until all the pixels
            // have been retrieved.
            MediaTracker tracker = new MediaTracker(this);
            tracker.addImage(image, 0);
            tracker.waitForID(0);

            add(new ImageCanvas(image), BorderLayout.CENTER);
        } catch (Exception e) {
            e.printStackTrace();
        }
        setSize(50, 100);
        show();
    }

    static public void main(String[] args) {
        if (args.length == 1) {
            new Main(args[0]);
        } else {
            System.err.println("usage: java Main <image file>");
        }
    }
}

class ImageCanvas extends Component {
    Image newImage;

    ImageCanvas(Image image) {
        ImageProducer ip = image.getSource();

        ip = new FilteredImageSource(ip, new CropImageFilter(0, 0,
                        image.getWidth(this), image.getHeight(this)*3/4));
        ip = new FilteredImageSource(ip, new RedBlueSwapFilter());
        newImage = getToolkit().createImage(ip);
    }
```

```
        public void paint(Graphics g) {
            g.drawImage(newImage, 0, 0, this);
        }
    }

    class RedBlueSwapFilter extends RGBImageFilter {
        public RedBlueSwapFilter() {
            canFilterIndexColorModel = true;
        }

        public int filterRGB(int x, int y, int rgb) {
            return ((rgb & 0xff00ff00)
                    | ((rgb & 0xff0000) >> 16)
                    | ((rgb & 0xff) << 16));
        }
    }
```

addConsumer()

PURPOSE   Registers an image consumer with this image producer.

SYNTAX   `public synchronized void addConsumer(ImageConsumer ic)`

DESCRIPTION   See `ImageProducer.addConsumer()` for details on how an image consumer should use this method.

PARAMETERS
ic   The non-null image consumer to register.

SEE ALSO   `ImageConsumer`.

EXAMPLE   See `ImageProducer.addConsumer()`.

FilteredImageSource()

PURPOSE   Constructs a new `FilteredImageSource` object.

SYNTAX   `public FilteredImageSource(ImageProducer ip, ImageFilter filter)`

DESCRIPTION   This constructor constructs a new filtered image source that combines an image producer with an image filter. The new filtered image source becomes a new image producer, which takes pixels from `ip`, converts them using `filter`, and then passes them on to its registered image consumers.

PARAMETERS
filter   The non-null image filter.
ip   The non-null image producer.

SEE ALSO   `ImageFilter, ImageProducer`.

EXAMPLE   See the class example.

615

isConsumer( )

PURPOSE	Determines if an image consumer is registered with this image producer.
SYNTAX	`public synchronized boolean isConsumer(ImageConsumer ic)`
DESCRIPTION	See `ImageProducer.isConsumer()` for details on how an image consumer should use this method.
PARAMETERS	
`ic`	The possibly `null` image consumer to check if registered.
RETURNS	`true` if `ic` has been registered; `false` otherwise.
SEE ALSO	`ImageConsumer`.
EXAMPLE	See `ImageProducer.isConsumer()`.

removeConsumer( )

PURPOSE	Removes a registered image consumer from this image producer.
SYNTAX	`public synchronized void removeConsumer(ImageConsumer ic)`
DESCRIPTION	See `ImageProducer.removeConsumer()` for details on how an image consumer should use this method.
PARAMETERS	
`ic`	The non-`null` image consumer to be removed.
EXAMPLE	See `ImageProducer.removeConsumer()`.

requestTopDownLeftRightResend( )

PURPOSE	Request by an image consumer to retransmit pixels in top-down, left-to-right order.
SYNTAX	`public void requestTopDownLeftRightResend(ImageConsumer ic)`
DESCRIPTION	See `ImageProducer.requestTopDownLeftRightResend()` for details on how an image consumer should use this method.
PARAMETERS	
`ic`	The non-`null` image consumer requesting the retransmission.
SEE ALSO	`ImageConsumer`.
EXAMPLE	See `ImageProducer.requestTopDownLeftRightResend()`.

startProduction()

PURPOSE   Adds an image consumer to the list of consumers interested in pixels.

SYNTAX   `public void startProduction(ImageConsumer ic)`

DESCRIPTION   See `ImageProducer.startProduction()` for details on how an image consumer should use this method.

PARAMETERS
ic   The non-`null` image consumer ready to receive pixels.

SEE ALSO   `ImageConsumer`.

EXAMPLE   See `ImageProducer.startProduction()`.

A
B
C
D
E
F
G
H
I
J
K
L
M
N
O
P
Q
R
S
T
U
V
W
X
Y
Z

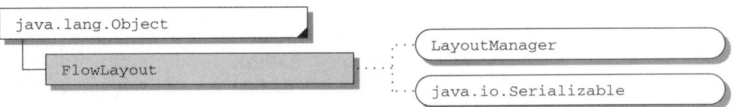

java.lang.Object

FlowLayout

LayoutManager

java.io.Serializable

Syntax

```
public class FlowLayout implements LayoutManager, Serializable
```

Description

The flow layout manager places components in rows in left-to-right, top-to-bottom order. When a component cannot be placed on a row without being clipped, a new row is created. The components are centered vertically on each row.

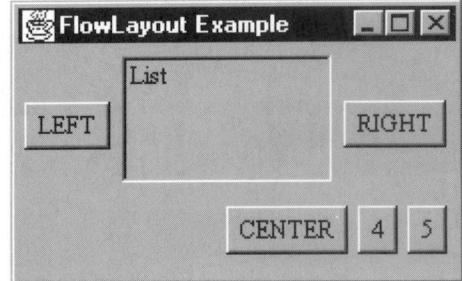

FIGURE 135: FlowLayout.

Component Alignment

A flow layout has an alignment property that determines how each row distributes empty space. The alignment can be one of three values: LEFT, CENTER, or RIGHT. A flow layout with left alignment moves the empty space to the right of the row, thereby moving all of the components left. A flow layout with right alignment moves the empty space to the left. A flow layout with center alignment divides the empty space and distributes it at the left and right ends of the rows, thereby centering all the components.

Gaps

The flow layout manager allows you to separate the components with gaps. The vertical gap specifies the space between rows, while the horizontal gap specifies the space between components.

The vertical and horizontal gaps are also applied around the edges of the container. If you do not want this space, you can eliminate it only by subclassing the container and overriding its insets() method. The override should retrieve the peer's required insets (if a peer exists), subtract the vgap and hgap from the peer's insets, and return the result. Doing this might make the insets negative, but it will eliminate the gaps around the edges.

MEMBER SUMMARY

Constructor

FlowLayout()	Creates new FlowLayout instance.

Alignment Methods and Constants

CENTER	Alignment constant specifying center alignment.
getAlignment()	Retrieves the alignment of components using this layout.
LEFT	Alignment constant specifying left alignment.
RIGHT	Alignment constant specifying right alignment.
setAlignment()	Sets the alignment of components using this layout.

Layout Manager Methods

addLayoutComponent()	A no-op.
layoutContainer()	Lays out the container's components according to the settings of the layout manager.
minimumLayoutSize()	Calculates the minimum dimensions needed to lay out the components.
preferredLayoutSize()	Calculates the preferred dimensions needed to lay out the components.
removeLayoutComponent()	A no-op.

Gap Methods

getHgap()	Retrieves the horizontal gap between components.
getVgap()	Retrieves the vertical gap between components.
setHgap()	Sets the horizontal gap between components.
setVgap()	Sets the vertical gap between components.

Debugging Method

toString()	Generates a string representation of the layout manager's state.

See Also

BorderLayout, CardLayout, GridLayout, GridBagLayout, java.io.Serializable.

Example

This example creates a frame with a flow layout manager (see Figure 135). Three buttons labeled LEFT, CENTER, and RIGHT control the alignment of the flow layout. A list component is added to the container to introduce a different height in the row to show that the components in a row are centered vertically.

```
import java.awt.*;
import java.awt.event.*;
```

```
class Main extends Frame implements ActionListener {
    FlowLayout layout = new FlowLayout(FlowLayout.RIGHT);
    Main() {
        super("FlowLayout Example");
        List list = new List();

        setLayout(layout);
        Button b;
        add(b = new Button("LEFT"));
        b.addActionListener(this);
        list.addItem("List");
        add(list);
        add(b = new Button("RIGHT"));
        b.addActionListener(this);
        add(b = new Button("CENTER"));
        b.addActionListener(this);

        add(new Button("4"));
        add(new Button("5"));

        setSize(100, 200);
        show();
    }

    public void actionPerformed(ActionEvent evt) {
        String what = evt.getActionCommand();

        if ("LEFT".equals(what)) {
            layout.setAlignment(FlowLayout.LEFT);
        } else if ("CENTER".equals(what)) {
            layout.setAlignment(FlowLayout.CENTER);
        } else if ("RIGHT".equals(what)) {
            layout.setAlignment(FlowLayout.RIGHT);
        }

    String label;
        switch(layout.getAlignment()) {
        case FlowLayout.LEFT:
            label = "left";
            break;
        case FlowLayout.CENTER:
            label = "center";
            break;
        case FlowLayout.RIGHT:
            label = "right";
            break;
        default:
            label = "example"; // impossible
        }
        setTitle(label);

        invalidate();
        validate();
    }

    public static void main(String[] args) {
        new Main();
    }
}
```

addLayoutComponent()

PURPOSE   A no-op.

SYNTAX   `public void addLayoutComponent(String name, Component comp)`

DESCRIPTION   This method is called by the container when a component is added along with a name. However, component names are ignored by the flow layout manager, so this method does nothing. This method needs to be defined in order to satisfy the `LayoutManager` interface.

PARAMETERS

comp   The non-`null` named component that has just been added to the container. Ignored.

name   The name of the component. Ignored.

CENTER

PURPOSE   Alignment constant specifying center alignment.

SYNTAX   `public static final int CENTER`

DESCRIPTION   The center alignment causes all of the components in a row to be packed together and centered.

EXAMPLE   See the class example.

FlowLayout()

PURPOSE   Constructs a new `FlowLayout` instance.

SYNTAX   `public FlowLayout()`
             `public FlowLayout(int align)`
             `public FlowLayout(int align, int hgap, int vgap)`

DESCRIPTION   This constructor constructs a new flow layout manager instance with the alignment `align` and the gaps `hgap` and `vgap`. If the alignment is not specified, it defaults to CENTER. If the gaps are not defined, they both default to 5.

An instance of the flow layout manager can be shared by more than one container. Also, the flow layout manager can be set on a container at any time, regardless of the number of the components already in the container.

PARAMETERS

align   The alignment, which must be one of LEFT, CENTER, or RIGHT.

hgap   A non-negative integer specifying the horizontal gap in pixels.

A
B
C
D
E
F
G
H
I
J
K
L
M
N
O
P
Q
R
S
T
U
V
W
X
Y
Z

621

vgap	A non-negative integer specifying the vertical gap in pixels.
SEE ALSO	setAlignment(), setHgap(), setVgap().
EXAMPLE	See the class example.

getAlignment()

PURPOSE	Retrieves the alignment of components using this layout.
SYNTAX	public int getAlignment()
DESCRIPTION	See the class description for details on alignment of components using a flow layout.
RETURNS	The alignment of components using this layout; one of LEFT, RIGHT, or CENTER.
SEE ALSO	setAlignment().
EXAMPLE	See class example.

getHgap()

PURPOSE	Retrieves the horizontal gap between components.
SYNTAX	public int getHgap()
DESCRIPTION	The horizontal gap is initialized by the FlowLayout constructor and changed using setHgap(). See the class description for details on horizontal gaps.
RETURNS	A non-negative integer specifying the horizontal gap in pixels.
SEE ALSO	getVgap(), setHgap().
EXAMPLE	This example creates a frame with a flow layout manager (see Figure 136). Four buttons labeled V+, V-, H+, and H- control the vertical and horizontal gaps of the flow layout. Two other buttons are used to display the current vertical and horizontal gaps in effect.

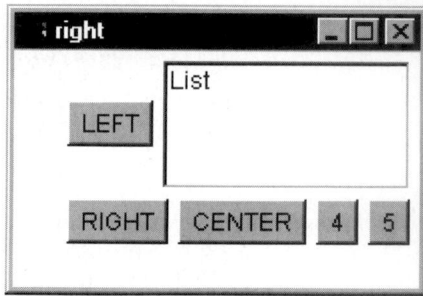

FIGURE 136:   Vertical and horizontal gaps in a FlowLayout.

```
import java.awt.*;
import java.awt.event.*;

class Main extends Frame implements ActionListener {
```

```
FlowLayout layout = new FlowLayout(FlowLayout.CENTER);
Button vgapbtn, hgapbtn;
Main() {
    super("FlowLayout Gaps Example");
    List list = new List();

    setLayout(layout);
    Button b;
    add(b = new Button("V+"));
    b.addActionListener(this);
    list.addItem("List");
    add(list);
    add(b = new Button("H+"));
    b.addActionListener(this);

    vgapbtn = new Button("Vgap="+layout.getVgap());
    add(vgapbtn);
    add(b = new Button("V-"));
    b.addActionListener(this);

    hgapbtn = new Button("Hgap="+layout.getHgap());
    add(hgapbtn);
    add(b = new Button("H-"));
    b.addActionListener(this);

    setSize(100, 200);
    show();
}

public void actionPerformed(ActionEvent evt) {
    String what = evt.getActionCommand();

    if ("H+".equals(what)) {
        layout.setHgap(layout.getHgap()+5);
    } else if ("H-".equals(what)) {
        layout.setHgap(Math.max(0, layout.getHgap()-5));
    } else if ("V+".equals(what)) {
        layout.setVgap(layout.getVgap()+5);
    } else if ("V-".equals(what)) {
        layout.setVgap(Math.max(0, layout.getVgap()-5));
    }

    vgapbtn.setLabel("Vgap="+layout.getVgap());
    hgapbtn.setLabel("Hgap="+layout.getHgap());

    invalidate();
    validate();
}

public static void main(String[] args) {
    new Main();
}
}
```

A
B
C
D
E
F
G
H
I
J
K
L
M
N
O
P
Q
R
S
T
U
V
W
X
Y
Z

A
B
C
D
E

G
H
I
J
K
L
M
N
O
P
Q
R
S
T
U
V
W
X
Y
Z

getVgap()

PURPOSE	Retrieves the vertical gap between components.
SYNTAX	`public int getVgap()`
DESCRIPTION	The vertical gap is initialized by the `FLowLayout` constructor and changed using `setVgap()`. See the class description for details on vertical gaps in a flow layout.
RETURNS	A non-negative integer specifying the vertical gap in pixels.
SEE ALSO	`getHgap()`, `setVgap()`.
EXAMPLE	See `getHgap()`.

layoutContainer()

PURPOSE	Lays out the container's components according to the settings of the layout manager.
SYNTAX	`public void layoutContainer(Container cont)`
DESCRIPTION	This method is called by the container `cont` when the layout is invalidated and needs to be redone. In placing the components, the flow layout manager sets the width of the rows to be the current width of the container and resizes the components based on their preferred sizes.
PARAMETERS	
cont	The non-`null` container using this layout instance.
SEE ALSO	`Container`.
EXAMPLE	See `LayoutManager.layoutContainer()`.

LEFT

PURPOSE	Alignment constant specifying left alignment.
SYNTAX	`public static final int LEFT`
DESCRIPTION	The left alignment causes all of the components in a row to be packed together and moved against the left edge of the container.
EXAMPLE	See the class example.

minimumLayoutSize()

PURPOSE   Calculates the minimum dimensions needed to lay out the components.

SYNTAX   `public Dimension minimumLayoutSize(Container cont)`

DESCRIPTION   This method calculates the minimum dimensions needed to lay out the components in the container `cont`. The minimum dimension of a flow layout is based on a layout of a single row. More precisely, the minimum dimension is calculated by determining each visible component's minimum size. The height of the result is determined by the maximum height of these minimum sizes plus 2 times the vertical gap plus any insets required by the container. The width of the result is the combined width of all of the minimum widths plus (number-of-components + 1) times the horizontal gap plus any insets required by the container.

PARAMETERS
cont   The non-null container using this layout instance.

RETURNS   A non-null `Dimension` object containing the minimum size of the flow layout.

SEE ALSO   `Component.getMinimumSize()`, `preferredLayoutSize()`.

preferredLayoutSize()

PURPOSE   Calculates the preferred dimensions needed to lay out the components.

SYNTAX   `public Dimension preferredLayoutSize(Container cont)`

DESCRIPTION   This method calculates the preferred dimensions needed to lay out the components in the container `cont`. The preferred dimension of a flow layout is based on a layout of a single row. More precisely, the preferred dimension is calculated by determining each visible component's preferred size. The height of the result is determined by the maximum height of these preferred sizes plus 2 times the vertical gap plus any insets required by the container. The width of the result is the combined width of all of the preferred widths plus (number-of-components + 1) times the horizontal gap plus any insets required by the container.

PARAMETERS
cont   The non-null container using this layout instance.

RETURNS   A non-null `Dimension` object containing the preferred size of the flow layout.

SEE ALSO   `Component.getPreferredSize()`, `minimumLayoutSize()`.

A
B
C
D
E

G
H
I
J
K
L
M
N
O
P
Q
R
S
T
U
V
W
X
Y
Z

A
B
C
D
E
F
G
H
I
J
K
L
M
N
O
P
Q
R
S
T
U
V
W
X
Y
Z

removeLayoutComponent( )

PURPOSE   This method is a no-op.

SYNTAX   `public void removeLayoutComponent(Component comp)`

DESCRIPTION   This method is called by the container `comp` whenever a component is removed from `comp`. Since the flow layout manager ignores component names, this method does nothing. It needs to be defined in order to satisfy the `LayoutManager` interface.

PARAMETERS
`comp`   The component about to be removed from the container. Ignored.

RIGHT

PURPOSE   Alignment constant specifying right alignment.

SYNTAX   `public static final int RIGHT`

DESCRIPTION   The right alignment causes all of the components in a row to be packed together and moved against the right edge of the container.

EXAMPLE   See the class example.

setAlignment( )

PURPOSE   Sets the alignment of components in this flow layout.

SYNTAX   `public void setHgap(int hgap)`

DESCRIPTION   This method sets the alignment of components in this layout to be `align`. See the class description regarding alignment in flow layouts.

PARAMETERS
`align`   One of `LEFT`, `RIGHT`, or `CENTER`.

SEE ALSO   `getAlignment()`.

EXAMPLE   See the class example.

setHgap( )

PURPOSE   Sets the horizontal gap between components.

SYNTAX   `public void setHgap(int hgap)`

DESCRIPTION	This method sets the horizontal gap of this layout to be `hgap`. See the class description for details on the use of gaps in flow layout.
PARAMETERS	
`hgap`	A non-negative integer specifying the horizontal gap in pixels.
SEE ALSO	`getHgap()`, `setVgap()`.
EXAMPLE	See `getHgap()`.

setVgap()

PURPOSE	Sets the vertical gap between components.
SYNTAX	`public void setVgap(int vgap)`
DESCRIPTION	This method sets the vertical gap of this layout to be `vgap`. See the class description for details on the use of gaps in flow layout.
PARAMETERS	
`vgap`	A non-negative integer specifying the vertical gap in pixels.
SEE ALSO	`getVgap()`, `setHgap()`.
EXAMPLE	See `getHgap()`.

toString()

PURPOSE	Generates a string representation of the layout manager's state.
SYNTAX	`public String toString()`
DESCRIPTION	This method generates the string representation of this layout manager's state. The string contains the layout manager's class name, the size of the two gaps, and the alignment.
	This method is typically used for debugging.
RETURNS	A non-`null` string representing the layout manager's state.
OVERRIDES	`java.lang.Object.toString()`.
EXAMPLE	See `java.lang.Object.toString()`.

A
B
C
D
E

G
H
I
J
K
L
M
N
O
P
Q
R
S
T
U
V
W
X
Y
Z

627

FocusAdapter

```
java.lang.Object
                                              Shape
        Rectangle
                                    java.io.Serializable
```

Syntax

`public abstract class FocusAdapter implements FocusListener`

Description

The focus adapter is a focus listener where all callback methods are empty implementations. The purpose of the focus adapter is to make it more convenient for an object to listen for focus events. In particular, by using the focus adapter, you can implement only those callback methods in which you are interested. Without the focus adapter, you are required to implement all callback methods, even if the method is empty.

To use a focus adapter, you create a subclass of `FocusAdapter` and override the desired callback methods. You then create an instance of the focus adapter subclass and call the component's `addFocusListener()` method with it. The focus adapter subclass is typically an inner class.

MEMBER SUMMARY	
Focus Event Callback Methods	
`focusGained()`	Called when this component gains the focus.
`focusLost()`	Called when this component loses the focus.

See Also

`FocusEvent`, `FocusListener`, `java.awt.AWTEventMulticaster`, `java.awt.Component.addFocusListener()`.

Example

This example demonstrates how to use a focus adapter to listen for focus events. The example creates a text area and a focus adapter. It registers the focus adapter with the text area. When the adapter receives a focus event, it prints the specifics of the event. See Figure 137.

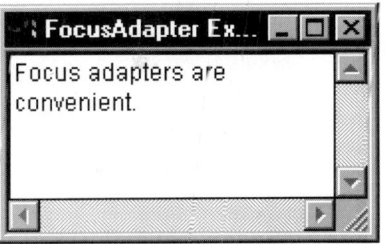

FIGURE 137: FocusAdapter.

```java
import java.awt.*;
import java.awt.event.*;

class Main extends Frame {
    Main() {
        super("FocusAdapter Example");
        TextArea ta = new TextArea();

        // Listen for focus events.
        ta.addFocusListener(new FocusEventHandler());

        add(ta, BorderLayout.CENTER);
        pack();
        show();
    }

    class FocusEventHandler extends FocusAdapter {
        public void focusGained(FocusEvent evt) {
            System.out.println("FOCUS_GAINED: "
                +(evt.isTemporary() ? "temporary" : "permanent"));
        }

        public void focusLost(FocusEvent evt) {
            System.out.println("FOCUS_LOST: "
                +(evt.isTemporary() ? "temporary" : "permanent"));
        }
    }

    public static void main(String args[]) {
        new Main();
    }
}
```

A
B
C
D
E
F
G
H
I
J
K
L
M
N
O
P
Q
R
S
T
U
V
W
X
Y
Z

focusGained()

PURPOSE	Called when this component gains the focus.
SYNTAX	`public void focusGained(FocusEvent evt)`
DESCRIPTION	This method is called after the source component has gained the focus. This method, by default, has an empty implementation.
PARAMETERS	
evt	The non-null focus event.
EXAMPLE	See the `FocusEvent` class example.

focusLost()

PURPOSE	Called when this component loses the focus.
SYNTAX	`public void focusLost(FocusEvent evt)`
DESCRIPTION	This method is called after source component loses the focus. This method, by default, has an empty implementation.
PARAMETERS	
evt	The non-null focus event.
EXAMPLE	See the `FocusEvent` class example.

A
B
C
D
E
F
G
H
I
J
K
L
M
N
O
P
Q
R
S
T
U
V
W
X
Y
Z

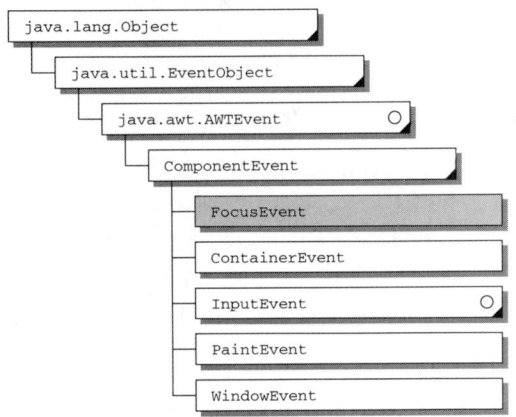

Syntax

`public class FocusEvent extends ComponentEvent`

Description

The *focus* or *keyboard focus* is a property of a component and determines where keyboard events are delivered. At most one component in the entire system can have the focus.

A component gains the focus in one of three ways:

1. The component can call `Component.requestFocus()`.
2. The user can interact with the component.
3. The user can hit the Tab or Shift-Tab key to move the focus from component to component.

See `Component` for more information about the focus.

All components can fire focus events. A component that loses the focus fires a `FOCUS_LOST` event. A component that gains the focus fires a `FOCUS_GAIN` event. A component that fires a `FOCUS_GAIN` event will subsequently fire a `FOCUS_LOST` event. Since there can be only one component with the focus at any time, the component with the focus will fire a `FOCUS_LOST` event before the component receiving the focus will fire a `FOCUS_GAIN` event.

Listening for Focus Events

To listen for focus events from an component, the listener must implement the `FocusListener` interface. After that, the listener must be registered with the component. It becomes registered by calling the component's `addFocusListener()` method.

An alternative, and possibly more convenient, way of receiving focus events is to use a focus adapter. See `FocusAdapter` for more details.

As with most events, focus events are delivered to its listeners after the operation has taken place.

Focus Levels

A FOCUS_LOST focus event can have one of two *focus level*: *temporary* or *permanent*. In general, if a component fires a temporary FOCUS_LOST event, it is because some operation temporarily took away the focus and it will restore the focus when it completes. The exact operations for which temporary FOCUS_LOST events are fired vary by platform. However, the usual situation are when component *A* loses the focus to component *B* in another top-level window. In this case, when the focus is restored to *A*'s window, component *A* will gain the focus. In fact, if the users clicks a different component in component *A*'s window, component *A* will gain the focus (and fire a FOCUS_GAIN event) and immediately lose it (and fire a FOCUS_LOST event) to the other component.

In short, when a component fires a FOCUS_LOST event, it is guaranteed to fire a FOCUS_GAIN event before any other component in the same window.

The main purpose of the temporary FOCUS_LOST event is to allow a component to visually indicate (for example, in Windows 95, by a dotted surround) that if the focus was to be restored to its containing window, that component would receive the focus.

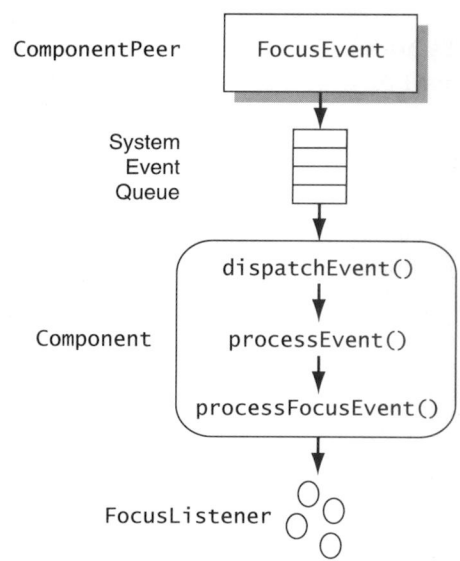

In general, a component fires a permanent FOCUS_LOST event when it loses the focus to some other component in the same window. The exact ways in which this can happen depend on the platform. Typical ways are when another component calls Component.requestFocus() or when the user moves the focus by pressing the Tab or Shift-Tab key.

All FOCUS_GAIN events are permanent.

Focus Event Flow

Figure 138 shows how focus events typically flow through the system. First, the event is fired by a component peer in response to some user gesture.

FIGURE 138:   Focus Event Flow.

This event is posted on the event queue (see EventQueue). When the event makes its way to the front of the queue, it is given to the component via its dispatchEvent() method. The main purpose of this method is to discard the event if the focus event type is not enabled or if there are no focus event listeners. Otherwise, dispatchEvent() calls processEvent(), which in turn calls different methods depending on the event type. Since this is a focus event, processFocusEvent() is called. The main purpose of this method is to notify the focus event listeners.

A component can override `processFocusEvent()` to process focus events before they are delivered to its listeners. The overridden method should call `super.processFocusEvent()` to ensure that events are dispatched to the component's listeners.

MEMBER SUMMARY	
Constructor	
`FocusEvent()`	Constructs a `FocusEvent` instance.
Focus Level Method	
`isTemporary()`	Retrieves the focus event's focus level.
Item Event Constants	
`FOCUS_FIRST`	Constant specifying the first id in the range of focus event ids.
`FOCUS_GAINED`	Event id indicating that the component has gained the focus.
`FOCUS_LAST`	Constant specifying the first id in the range of focus event ids.
`FOCUS_LOST`	Event id indicating that the component has lost the focus.
Debugging Method	
`paramString()`	Generates a string representing the focus event's state.

See Also

FocusAdapter, FocusListener, java.awt.AWTEvent, java.awt.Component.

Example

This example demonstrates how to get focus events from a component that fires them. The example creates a text area and listens for focus events from the text area. In response to a focus event, the specifics of the event are printed. See Figure 139.

This example could have been implemented using a focus adapter. To see how this is done, see the `Focus-Adapter` class example.

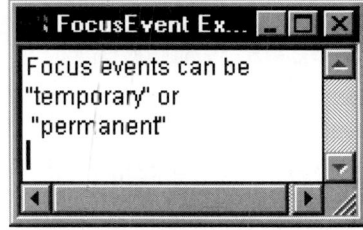

FIGURE 139:   FocusEvent.

```java
import java.awt.*;
import java.awt.event.*;

class Main extends Frame implements FocusListener {
    Main() {
        super("FocusEvent Example");
        TextArea ta = new TextArea();

        // Listen for focus events.
        ta.addFocusListener(this);
```

```
                add(ta, BorderLayout.CENTER);
                pack();
                show();
            }

        public void focusGained(FocusEvent evt) {
            System.out.println("FOCUS_GAINED: "
                +(evt.isTemporary() ? "temporary" : "permanent"));
        }
        public void focusLost(FocusEvent evt) {
            System.out.println("FOCUS_LOST: "
                +(evt.isTemporary() ? "temporary" : "permanent"));
        }

        public static void main(String args[]) {
            new Main();
        }
    }
```

A
B
C
D
E

G
H
I
J
K
L
M
N
O
P
Q
R
S
T
U
V
W
X
Y
Z

FOCUS_FIRST

PURPOSE   Constant specifying the first id in the range of focus event ids.

SYNTAX   `public static final int FOCUS_FIRST`

DESCRIPTION All action event ids must be greater than or equal to FOCUS_FIRST (value 1004).

SEE ALSO   FOCUS_LAST.

EXAMPLE   See `java.awt.Component.processEvent()`.

FOCUS_GAINED

PURPOSE   Event id indicating that the component has gained the focus.

SYNTAX   `public static final int FOCUS_GAINED`

DESCRIPTION A focus event with this event id (value 1004) indicates that the event's source has gained the focus.

SEE ALSO   FocusEvent().

EXAMPLE   See the class example.

FOCUS_LAST

PURPOSE   Constant specifying the last id in the range of focus event ids.

SYNTAX	`public static final int FOCUS_LAST`
DESCRIPTION	All action event ids must be less than or equal to FOCUS_LAST (value `1005`).
SEE ALSO	FOCUS_FIRST.
EXAMPLE	See `java.awt.Component.processEvent()`.

FOCUS_LOST

PURPOSE	Event id indicating that the component has lost the focus.
SYNTAX	`public static final int FOCUS_LOST`
DESCRIPTION	A focus event with this event id (value `1005`) indicates that the event's source has lost the focus.
SEE ALSO	FocusEvent().
EXAMPLE	See the class example.

FocusEvent()

PURPOSE	Constructs a FocusEvent instance.
SYNTAX	`public FocusEvent(Component source, int id)` `public FocusEvent(Component source, int id, boolean temporary)`
DESCRIPTION	This constructor creates a new focus event with `source` as the component firing this event. If `temporary` is not specified, it defaults to `false`. See the class description for more information about temporary focus events.
	After the focus event is created, the source object can distribute the event to its listeners by calling the focus event-related methods in `AWTEventMulticaster`. If the event is not created by `source`, the creator can deliver the event to the source component either by posting the event to the event queue (see `EventQueue.postEvent()`) or by calling the source component's `Component.dispatchEvent()` method directly.
PARAMETERS	
source	The non-`null` object that is firing this focus event.
id	One of the focus event ids.
temporary	`true` if the focus event is to be temporary; `false` otherwise.
SEE ALSO	`isTemporary()`, `java.awt.AWTEvent.getID()`, `java.util.EventObject.getSource()`.

A
B
C
D
E
F
G
H
I
J
K
L
M
N
O
P
Q
R
S
T
U
V
W
X
Y
Z

A
B
C
D
E
F
G
H
I
J
K
L
M
N
O
P
Q
R
S
T
U
V
W
X
Y
Z

isTemporary()

PURPOSE	Retrieves the focus event's focus level.
SYNTAX	`public boolean isTemporary()`
DESCRIPTION	See the class description for more details about focus levels.
RETURNS	`true` if the event's focus level is temporary; `false` otherwise.
EXAMPLE	See the class example.

paramString()

PURPOSE	Generates a string representing the focus event's state.
SYNTAX	`public String paramString()`
DESCRIPTION	The returned string contains the name of the focus event and whether the event is temporary or permanent. A subclass of this class should override this method and return a concatenation of its state with the results of `super.paramString()`. This method is called by the `AWTEvent.toString()` method and is typically used for debugging.
RETURNS	A non-`null` string representing the focus event's state.
OVERRIDES	`java.awt.AWTEvent.paramString()`.
SEE ALSO	`java.awt.AWTEvent.toString()`, `java.lang.Object.toString()`.
EXAMPLE	See the `java.awt.AWTEvent` class example.

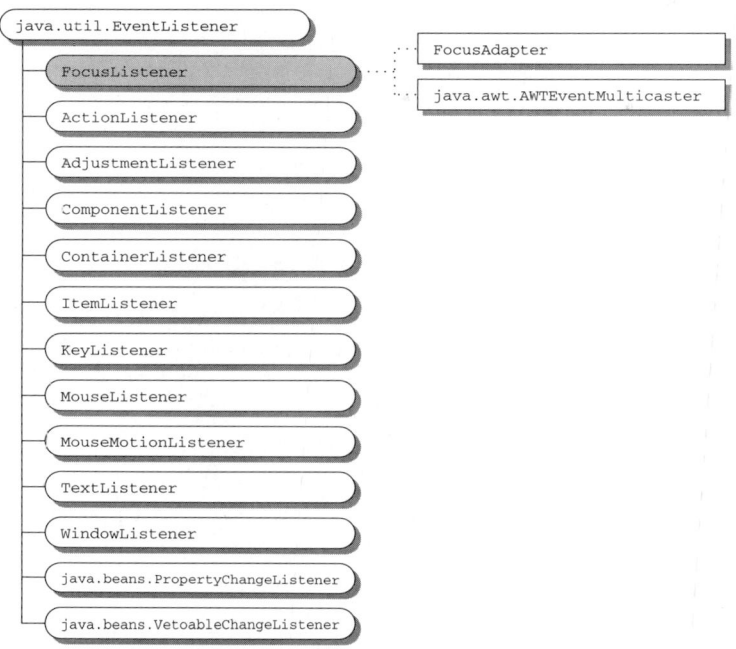

java.util.EventListener
- FocusListener
- ActionListener
- AdjustmentListener
- ComponentListener
- ContainerListener
- ItemListener
- KeyListener
- MouseListener
- MouseMotionListener
- TextListener
- WindowListener
- java.beans.PropertyChangeListener
- java.beans.VetoableChangeListener

FocusAdapter
java.awt.AWTEventMulticaster

Syntax
```
public interface FocusListener extends EventListener
```

Description
When an object (listener) wishes to receive focus events from a component that fires them (the source component), two things must be done:

1. The listener must implement this interface and all of the methods required by this interface.
2. The listener must be registered with the source component by making a call to the source component's addFocusListener() method.

For more information about component events, see FocusEvent.

MEMBER SUMMARY	
Focus Event Callback Methods	
focusGained()	Called after the source component gains the focus.
focusLost()	Called after the source component loses the focus.

See Also

`FocusAdapter, FocusEvent, java.awt.AWTEventMulticaster,`
`java.util.EventListener.`

Example

See the `FocusEvent` class example.

focusGained()

PURPOSE	Called after the source component gains the focus.
SYNTAX	`public void focusGained(FocusEvent evt)`
DESCRIPTION	This method is called after the source component has gained the focus.
PARAMETERS	
evt	The non-null focus event.
EXAMPLE	See the `FocusEvent` class example.

focusLost()

PURPOSE	Called after the source component loses the focus.
SYNTAX	`public void focusLost(FocusEvent evt)`
DESCRIPTION	This method is called after source component loses the focus.
PARAMETERS	
evt	The non-null focus event.
EXAMPLE	See the `FocusEvent` class example.

A
B
C
D
E
F
G
H
I
J
K
L
M
N
O
P
Q
R
S
T
U
V
W
X
Y
Z

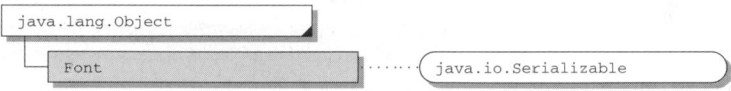

```
java.lang.Object

    Font ..........( java.io.Serializable )
```

Syntax

`public class Font implements Serializable`

Description

A *font* determines how text looks when it is painted. In particular, a font is used when painting text on a `Graphics` context and as a property of AWT components. A font has three properties that contribute to the appearance of the text: the *logical name*, the *style*, and the *point size*. The properties of a font are specified at the time the font is created; they cannot be changed later.

At present, the AWT system supports only a very small set of fonts and does not allow your program to access the fonts on your system. This restriction ensures that the fonts used by a program will look the same on all platforms. However, this restriction will be relaxed in a future release.

The Default Font

The font of an AWT component can be changed at any time. If an AWT component has a font whose value is `null`, the component will inherit its font from the closest ancestor whose font is not `null`.

Logical Font Name

The logical font name determines the shape of the font characters. For example, the logical name `SansSerif` specifies a font that has variable-width characters, while `Monospaced` specifies a font that has fixed-width characters. These logical font names are mapped into real font names on your system. For example, on Windows, `SansSerif` is mapped to `Arial`.

The method `Toolkit.getFontList()` returns a list of valid logical font names. Currently, the supported logical font names are `Serif`, `SansSerif`, `Monospaced`, `Dialog`, and `DialogInput`. The use of the logical names `TimesRoman`, `Helvetica`, `Courier`, and `ZapfDingbats` is deprecated but still supported. Figure 140 shows a window that displays text in each of these logical font names. The `Font` class provides methods and variables to retrieve the properties of a font.

Font Style

A font's style determines the weight (thickness) and slant of the font. The font style is really a combination of *style bits*. The plain style bit specifies a normal weight font with no slant. The bold style bit specifies a heavyweight font. The italic style bit specifies a font with slanted characters. The bold style bit can be combined with the italic style bit. Figure 140 shows text in various font styles.

Font Point Size

A font's point size determines the size of the font. One point is approximately 1/72 of an inch. Although the AWT system tries to map the logical font names to scalable fonts, the process isn't guaranteed to succeed. So some requested point sizes may end up being mapped to a different point size. To ensure your painting code will work on all platforms, you should always retrieve and use a font's metrics when painting text in the font (see `FontMetrics`).

Font Family

The font family is a platform-specific font name. The platform-independent logical name is automatically translated to the font family at the time the `Font` object is created. The font name-to-font family translation map is specified via system properties; it cannot be specified when the `Font` object is created.

Font System Resources

The `Font` object is only a specification for a font. The actual font system resource that the platform uses to render text in a specified font is created only when needed. These system resources are automatically managed and in fact cannot be accessed via any AWT methods. You should not worry too much about trying to minimize the creation of these `Font` objects.

FIGURE 140:   Font.

MEMBER SUMMARY

Constructor
Font()	Constructs a new Font instance.

Property Methods and Fields
getName()	Retrieves this font's logical name.
getSize()	Retrieves this font's point size.
getStyle()	Retrieves this font's style.
isBold()	Determines if this font is bold.
isItalic()	Determines if this font is italic.
isPlain()	Determines if this font is plain.
name	Contains this font's logical name.
size	Contains this font's point size.
style	Contains this font's style.

Style Bits
BOLD	This style bit is used in creating a bold style font.
ITALIC	This style bit is used in creating an italic style font.
PLAIN	This style bit is used in creating a plain style font.

Font Methods
decode()	Creates a font based on its font specification.
getFamily()	Retrieves the platform-specific family name of this font.
getFont()	Creates a font based on the value of a system property.

Peer Method
getPeer()	Retrieves this font's peer.

General Methods
equals()	Compares this object with another object for equality.
hashCode()	Computes this font's hash code.
toString()	Generates the string representation of the font.

See Also

FontMetrics, java.io.Serializable.

Example

This example creates a frame and displays in it all available fonts in all four possible font styles (see Figure 140).

```
import java.awt.*;
class Main extends Frame {
    int[] styles = {
```

```
                    Font.PLAIN, Font.ITALIC, Font.BOLD, Font.BOLD|Font.ITALIC};
            String[] styleNames = {
                "plain", "italic", "bold", "bold-italic", "plain-bold-italic"};

            Main() {
                super("Font Example");

                setSize(300, 400);
                show();
            }

            public void paint(Graphics g) {
                int y = 5;

                String[] fontNames = Toolkit.getDefaultToolkit().getFontList();
                for (int i=0; i<fontNames.length; i++) {
                    for (int j=0; j<styles.length; j++) {
                        Font f = new Font(fontNames[i], styles[j], 13);
                        FontMetrics fm = g.getFontMetrics(f);

                        y += fm.getAscent();
                        g.setFont(f);
                        g.drawString(fontNames[i]+" "+styleNames[j]
                            +" ("+f.getFamily()+")", 5, y);
                        y += fm.getLeading();
                    }
                    y += 13;
                }
            }

            static public void main(String[] args) {
                new Main();
            }
        }
```

BOLD

PURPOSE   This style bit is used in creating a bold style font.

SYNTAX   `public static final int BOLD`

DESCRIPTION   This style bit can be or'd with the ITALIC style bit to specify a bold-italic style font.

SEE ALSO   `ITALIC, PLAIN, getStyle(), isBold().`

EXAMPLE   These statements create a bold and bold-italic style font.

```
    Font f1 = new Font("Dialog", Font.BOLD, 12);
    Font f2 = new Font("Dialog", Font.BOLD|Font.ITALIC, 12);
```

decode()

PURPOSE	Creates a font based on the font specification.
SYNTAX	`public static Font decode(String fontSpec)`
DESCRIPTION	This method creates and returns a `Font` object as specified by the font specification `fontSpec`. `fontSpec` is a string with the following form:

```
<logical font name>-<style>-<point size>
```

Each of the three font properties are separated by a short dash (-). The logical font name must be one of the valid logical font names (see the class description). The style can be one of `plain`, `italic`, `bold`, or `bolditalic`. The point size can be any positive integer. Table 13 shows some examples of font specifications and their equivalent constructor statements.

Font Specification	Equivalent Constructor Statement
`Monospaced-bold-14`	`new Font("Monospaced", Font.BOLD, 14)`
`Monospaced-plain`	`new Font("Monospaced", Font.PLAIN, 12)`
`Serif--18`	`new Font("Serif", Font.PLAIN, 18)`
`SansSerif`	`new Font("SansSerif", Font.PLAIN, 12)`
`Dialog-bolditalic-16`	`new Font("Dialog", Font.BOLD|Font.ITALIC, 16)`

TABLE 13:   **Examples of Font Properties.**

The logical font name is required, but the style and point size are optional. If the style is not specified or is blank or invalid, `plain` is assumed. If the point size is not specified, 12 is assumed.

If the system property `propName` is not defined and `defaultFont` is specified, `defaultFont` is returned. Also, if there is some error in the font specification, `defaultFont` is returned. However, if both the system property and `defaultFont` are not specified, `null` is returned.

PARAMETERS	
fontSpec	A non-`null` string specifying the font.
RETURNS	A `Font` object or `null`.
SEE ALSO	`Font()`, `getFont()`.
EXAMPLE	This example creates a bold 14-point monospaced font.

```
Font f = Font.decode("Monospaced-bold-14");
```

equals( )

PURPOSE	Compares this object with another object for equality.
SYNTAX	`public boolean equals(Object object)`
DESCRIPTION	Two font objects are equal only if their logical names, styles, and point sizes are equal. This method returns `true` if the two fonts are equal. If they are not equal or if `object` is `null` or is not of class `Font`, this method returns `false`.
PARAMETERS	
`object`	The object with which to compare.
RETURNS	`true` if the objects are equal; `false` otherwise.
OVERRIDES	`java.lang.Object.equals()`.
EXAMPLE	This method displays a string. The specified font is selected into the graphics context only if it differs from the currently selected font.

```
Font curFont;
void paintString(Graphics g, Font f, String s) {
    if (!curFont.equals(f)) {
        g.setFont(f);
        curFont = f;
    }
    g.drawString(s, x ,y);
}
```

Font( )

PURPOSE	Constructs a new `Font` instance.
SYNTAX	`public Font(String name, int style, int size)`
DESCRIPTION	This method constructs a new font (and its peer) with the specified logical name, style, and point size. The logical name of the font must be one of `Dialog`, `DialogInput`, `Monospaced`, `Serif`, `SansSerif`, or `Symbol`. If name is not one of these, a default font is chosen. The actual font chosen is platform-dependent. The new `Font` instance can be used in more than one AWT object. For example, you could set the font in a number of button instances.
PARAMETERS	
`name`	The font's logical name.
`size`	The font's point size.
`style`	The font's style.
DEPRECATION	The following logical font names have been deprecated. `Courier` is replaced by `Monospaced`. `TimesRoman` is replaced by `Serif`. `Helvetica` is replaced by

SansSerif. ZapfDingbats is replaced by use of Unicode characters starting at \u2700.

SEE ALSO   Toolkit.getFontList().

EXAMPLE   This code fragment creates a 36-point bold Serif font and sets it to two buttons.

```
Font f = new Font("Serif", Font.BOLD, 36);
Button b1 = new Button("OK");
Button b2 = new Button("Cancel");

b1.setFont(f);
b2.setFont(f);
```

getFamily( )

PURPOSE   Retrieves the font's family name.

SYNTAX   public String getFamily()

DESCRIPTION   The font family is the platform-specific font name that's assigned to the font's logical name. The font family name is determined at the time the font is created and cannot be changed.

RETURNS   The font's family name as a non-null string.

EXAMPLE   This example prints out the family name for each available logical font name.

```
import java.awt.*;
class Main extends Frame {
    static public void main(String[] args) {
        String[] fontNames = Toolkit.getDefaultToolkit().getFontList();

        for (int i=0; i<fontNames.length; i++) {
            Font f = new Font(fontNames[i], Font.PLAIN, 12);
            System.out.println(fontNames[i] + " -> " + f.getFamily());
        }
    }
}
```
Output
```
Dialog -> Dialog
SansSerif -> SansSerif
Serif -> Serif
Monospaced -> Monospaced
```

A
B
C
D
E
F
G
H
I
J
K
L
M
N
O
P
Q
R
S
T
U
V
W
X
Y
Z

```
Helvetica -> Helvetica
TimesRoman -> TimesRoman
Courier -> Courier
DialogInput -> DialogInput
ZapfDingbats -> ZapfDingbats
```

A
B
C
D
E
F
G
H
I
J
K
L
M
N
O
P
Q
R
S
T
U
V
W
X
Y
Z

getFont( )

PURPOSE   Creates a font based on the value of a system property.

SYNTAX   `public static Font getFont(String propName)`
                  `public static Font getFont(String propName, Font defaultFont)`

DESCRIPTION   The two forms of this method create and return a Font object associated with the system property name propName. The font specification in the system property value has the form described in decode().

If the system property propName is not defined and defaultFont is specified, defaultFont is returned. Also, if there is some error in the font specification, defaultFont is returned. However, if both the system property and default-Font are not specified, null is returned.

PARAMETERS

defaultFont   The font that is returned if the system property propName is not defined.

propName   A non-null string specifying the system property name.

RETURNS   A Font object or null.

SEE ALSO   decode(), java.lang.System.getProperty().

EXAMPLE   This example searches for a system property called "myapp.button.font" and creates a font based on the value of this property. If the property is not found, it returns a 12-point monospaced font.

```
    Font f = Font.getFont("myapp.button.font",
                    new Font("Monospaced", Font.PLAIN, 12));
```

getName( )

PURPOSE   Retrieves the font's logical name.

SYNTAX   `public String getName()`

DESCRIPTION   The font's logical name is specified during the creation of the Font object and cannot be changed.

RETURNS   The font's logical name as a non-null string.

SEE ALSO   Font, name.

EXAMPLE   This example method returns `true` if the logical names for `f1` and `f2` are the same.

```
boolean compareFontNames(Font f1, Font f2) {
    return f1.getName().equals(f2.getName());
}
```

getPeer()

PURPOSE   Retrieves this font's peer.

SYNTAX   `public FontPeer getPeer()`

DESCRIPTION   The font's peer is an internal object created and used by the underlying font machinery. This method should not be used and may be deprecated in the future.

RETURNS   The possibly `null` font's peer.

SEE ALSO   `FontPeer`.

getSize()

PURPOSE   Retrieves this font's point size.

SYNTAX   `public int getSize()`

DESCRIPTION   The font's point size is specified during the creation of the `Font` object and cannot be changed.

RETURNS   The font's point size.

SEE ALSO   `Font`.

EXAMPLE   This example increases the point size of a font by 1 pt.

```
Font increasePointSize(Font f) {
    return new Font(f.getName(), f.getStyle(), f.getSize()+1);
}
```

getStyle()

PURPOSE   Retrieves this font's style.

SYNTAX   `public int getStyle()`

DESCRIPTION   The font style is a collection of font style bits. To test whether a style bit is included in the font style, use the bitwise "and" operator (see the example).

A
B
C
D
E
F
G
H
I
J
K
L
M
N
O
P
Q
R
S
T
U
V
W
X
Y
Z

The plain style differs from the other style bits in that it is really the absence of all style bits; hence, it has the value 0. So to test if the font style is plain, test it against the value 0 (see the example).

This method is typically used when saving the font style or using it to create another font with the same style. When determining which style bits are included in the font style, it is better to use the methods isBold(), isItalic(), and isPlain().

RETURNS The font's style.

SEE ALSO isBold(), isItalic(), isPlain().

EXAMPLE This example retrieves the default font of a frame and prints its styles.

```
import java.awt.*;
class Main {
    static public void main(String[] args) {
        Frame f = new Frame();
        f.pack();  // otherwise the default font is null.
        int s = f.getFont().getStyle();

        System.out.println("plain: " + (s == 0));
        System.out.println("bold: " + ((s&Font.BOLD) != 0));
        System.out.println("italic: " + ((s&Font.ITALIC) != 0));
    }
}
```

OUTPUT
```
plain: true
bold: false
italic: false
```

hashCode()

PURPOSE Computes the hash code for the font.

SYNTAX `public int hashCode()`

DESCRIPTION The font's hash code is an integer that's calculated from the font's properties. Two Font objects with the same properties will have the same hash code. However, two Font objects that do not have the same properties might also have the same hash code, although the hash code algorithm minimizes this possibility. The hash code is typically used as the key in a hash table.

Note, it is not really necessary to cache Font objects, since they are reasonably small. The actual system font resources contain all of the necessary information for the system to paint text and so can be much larger. These are automatically maintained by the AWT system and cannot be accessed.

RETURNS The font's hash code.

OVERRIDES	`java.lang.Object.hashCode()`.
SEE ALSO	`java.util.Hashtable`.
EXAMPLE	See `java.lang.Object.equals()`.

A
B
C
D
E
F
G
H
I
J
K
L
M
N
O
P
Q
R
S
T
U
V
W
X
Y
Z

isBold()

PURPOSE	Determines if this font's style includes the bold style bit.
SYNTAX	`public boolean isBold()`
RETURNS	`true` if this font's style includes the BOLD style bit.
SEE ALSO	`BOLD, Font()`.
EXAMPLE	These statements remove a font's bold style, if present.

```
if (f.isBold()) {
    f = new Font(f.getName(), f.getStyle()&~Font.BOLD, f.getSize());
}
```

isItalic()

PURPOSE	Determines if this font's style includes the italic style bit.
SYNTAX	`public boolean isItalic()`
RETURNS	`true` if this font's style includes the ITALIC style bit.
SEE ALSO	`ITALIC, Font()`.
EXAMPLE	These statements remove a font's italic style, if present.

```
if (f.isItalic()) {
    f = new Font(f.getName(), f.getStyle()&~Font.ITALIC, f.getSize());
}
```

isPlain()

PURPOSE	Determines if this font's style is plain.
SYNTAX	`public boolean isPlain()`
RETURNS	`true` if this font's style does not include any style bits besides PLAIN.
SEE ALSO	`BOLD, Font(), ITALIC, PLAIN`.

EXAMPLE   These statements force a font to be a plain style.

```
if (!f.isPlain()) {
    f = new Font(f.getName(), Font.PLAIN, f.getSize());
}
```

A
B

ITALIC

C
D

PURPOSE   Used in creating an italic style font.

SYNTAX   `public static final int ITALIC`

E
F

DESCRIPTION   This constant can be or'd with the BOLD style bit to specify a bold-italic style font.

G

SEE ALSO   `BOLD, getStyle(), isBold(), PLAIN.`

H

EXAMPLE   These statements create an italic and a bold-italic font.

I
J

```
Font f1 = new Font("Monospaced", Font.ITALIC, 12);
Font f2 = new Font("Monospaced", Font.BOLD|Font.ITALIC, 12);
```

K

L

name

M
N

PURPOSE   Contains this font's logical name.

SYNTAX   `protected String name`

O
P

DESCRIPTION   This field is accessible only by subclasses of Font. It is meant to be read-only and should not be changed.

Q

SEE ALSO   `getName().`

R

S

PLAIN

T
U

PURPOSE   This style bit is used in creating a plain font.

V

SYNTAX   `public static final int PLAIN`

DESCRIPTION   The PLAIN style bit isn't really a style bit. It's actually the absence of all other style bits, which means it has the value 0. However, it's convenient to use when creating a plain style font.

W
X

SEE ALSO   `BOLD, getStyle(), isPlain(), ITALIC.`

Y

EXAMPLE   This statement creates a plain font.

Z

```
Font f = new Font("Monospaced", Font.PLAIN, 12);
```

size

PURPOSE	Contains this font's point size.
SYNTAX	`protected int size`
DESCRIPTION	The value in this field is identical to the one returned via `getSize()`. This field is accessible only by subclasses of `Font`. It is meant to be read-only and should not be changed.
SEE ALSO	`getSize()`.

style

PURPOSE	Contains this font's style.
SYNTAX	`protected int style`
DESCRIPTION	The value in this field is identical to the one returned via `getStyle()`. This field is accessible only by subclasses of `Font`. It is meant to be read-only and should not be changed.
SEE ALSO	`getStyle()`.

toString()

PURPOSE	Generates the string representation of this font.
SYNTAX	`public String toString()`
RETURNS	A non-`null` string representing the properties of this font (style, font family, size, and name). This method is used for debugging output.
OVERRIDES	`java.lang.Object.toString()`.
EXAMPLE	These statements print a string representation of a font.

```
Font f = new Font("Monospaced", Font.BOLD|Font.ITALIC, 12);
System.out.println(f.toString());
System.out.println(f);
```

A
B
C
D
E
F
G
H
I
J
K
L
M
N
O
P
Q
R
S
T
U
V
W
X
Y
Z

A
B
C
D
E
F
G
H
I
J
K
L
M
N
O
P
Q
R
S
T
U
V
W
X
Y
Z

FontPeer

Syntax
`public interface FontPeer`

Description
The `Font` class in the AWT is only a specification for a font. The actual font uses the platform's native font system resource, which is represented by a font peer.

AWT programmers normally do not directly use font peers. Instead, they deal with AWT fonts using the `Font` class. These in turn automatically use and manage their peers. Only someone who is porting the AWT to another platform should be concerned with the font peer.

See Also
`java.awt.Font, java.awt.Toolkit.getFontPeer().`

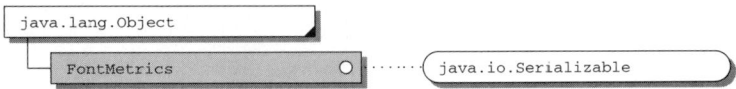

```
java.lang.Object
    FontMetrics ·······O······( java.io.Serializable )
```

Syntax

`public abstract class FontMetrics implements Serializable`

Description

A `FontMetrics` instance for a particular font contains information about the visual attributes of the font, such as its height and character widths.

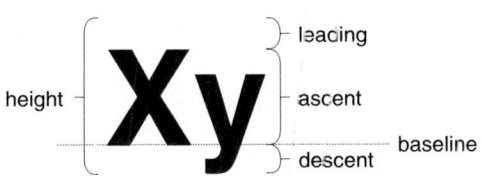

Figure 141 shows the attributes of a font. The values of these attributes are available through its font metrics.

Baseline

The baseline is an imaginary horizontal line that cuts through the characters in the font. The bottom of the character 'X', for example, is aligned on the font's baseline. Characters with descenders, such as the letter 'y,' are aligned such that only the descender extends below the baseline. When you are painting text of different font sizes, the text should be painted so that their baselines connect.

Ascent

The ascent of a font is the distance from the top of the font to the baseline. The ascent is typically used to determine the location of the font's baseline. The font's ascent is not the same as the maximum ascent of all the characters in the font. Some characters may extend beyond the font's ascent. The maximum ascent of all characters is called the *font's maximum ascent* and is available in a font metrics.

Descent

The descent of a font is the distance from the bottom of the font to the baseline. The font's descent is not the same as the maximum descent of all the characters in the font. Some characters may extend below the descent depth. The maximum descent of all characters is called the *font's maximum descent* and is available in a font metrics.

Leading

The leading is the spacing between rows of painted text. If the text were painted without the leading, the rows would touch each other. When the ascent does not match the maximum ascent or the descent does not match the maximum descent, parts of the character may appear in the leading space.

Height

The height of a font is the sum of the font's ascent, descent, and leading. When painting rows of text, you should make the distance between baselines be the font's height. The font's maximum height is the sum of its maximum ascent, maximum descent, and leading.

MEMBER SUMMARY

Constructor

FontMetrics	Constructs a new FontMetrics instance.

Size Methods

bytesWidth()	Determines the width of an array of bytes.
charsWidth()	Determines the width of an array of characters.
charWidth()	Retrieves the width of a character in the font.
getWidths()	Retrieves the width of the first 256 characters in the font.
stringWidth()	Determines the pixel width of a string.

Font Metric Attribute Methods

getAscent()	Retrieves the font's ascent.
getDescent()	Retrieves the font's descent.
getHeight()	Retrieves the font's height.
getLeading()	Retrieves the font's leading.
getMaxAdvance()	Retrieves the width of the widest character in the font.
getMaxAscent()	Retrieves the font's maximum ascent.
getMaxDescent()	Retrieves the font's maximum descent.

Font Fields and Methods

font	The font from which the font metrics were created.
getFont()	Retrieves the font used to create the font metrics.

Debugging Method

toString()	Generates a string representation of the font metrics.

Deprecated Method

getMaxDecent()	Replaced by getMaxDescent().

See Also
Font, java.io.Serializable.

A
B
C
D
E
F
G
H
I
J
K
L
M
N
O
P
Q
R
S
T
U
V
W
X
Y
Z

Example

This somewhat elaborate example demonstrates how to display text in multiple font styles and sizes. The text is input from a file, and formatting codes are embedded in the text. The text is painted in a default font, and the formatting codes can change one attribute of the font at a time—its name, style, or size. Figure 142 shows a screen shot of the example. Figure 143 shows the input file used to generate the screen shot.

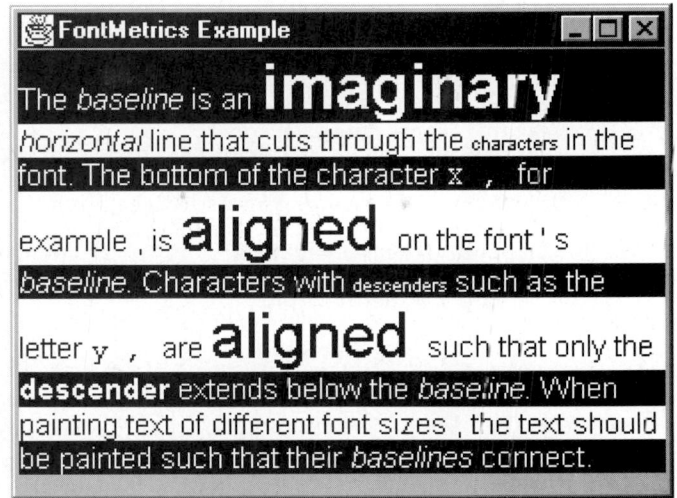

FIGURE 142: `FontMetrics`.

Input Format

A formatting code begins with the left angle character <. If the text that follows the < is a number, the current font size is changed to that number. If the code is <b, the font style is changed to bold. If the code is <i, the font style is changed to italics. If the code is <p, the font style is changed to plain. Otherwise, the font's name becomes the text following the < character.

To make it clearer to see the rectangles in which each line of text is painted, the background of each line alternates between black and white.

Implementation Notes: The leading for text is displayed above that line, except for the first line, which does not have any leading. The leading used is the maximum leading for all of the fonts that appear on that line. For simplicity's sake, the text is parsed into words and formatting codes; all the words and formatting codes are kept in a `Vector` object.

```
<15 <SansSerif The <i baseline <p <15 is an <32 <b
imaginary <15 <i horizontal <p line that cuts through
the <9 characters <15 in the font.
The bottom of the character <Monospaced X,
<SansSerif for example, is <32 aligned <15 on the font''s
<i baseline. <p <15  Characters with <9 descenders <15 such as
the letter <Monospaced y, <SansSerif are <32 aligned
<15 such that only the <b descender <p extends below
the <i baseline. <p <15  When painting text of different
font sizes, the text should be painted such that their
<i baselines <p <15 connect.
```

FIGURE 143: `FontMetrics` **Example Input File.**

A
B
C
D
E
F
G
H
I
J
K
L
M
N
O
P
Q
R
S
T
U
V
W
X
Y
Z

```
import java.awt.*;
import java.io.*;
import java.util.*;

class Main extends Frame {
    Vector tokens = new Vector();
    Font defaultFont = new Font("Serif", Font.PLAIN, 12);

    Main(String filename) throws IOException {
        super("FontMetrics Example");
        StreamTokenizer st =
            new StreamTokenizer(new FileReader(filename));
        Font f = defaultFont;;

        int t = st.nextToken();
        do {
            switch (t) {
            case '<':
                t = st.nextToken();
                switch (t) {
                case StreamTokenizer.TT_NUMBER:
                    f = new Font(f.getName(), f.getStyle(), (int)st.nval);
                    break;
                case StreamTokenizer.TT_WORD:
                    switch (st.sval.charAt(0)) {
                    case 'b':
                        f = new Font(f.getName(), Font.BOLD, f.getSize());
                        break;
                    case 'i':
                        f = new Font(f.getName(), Font.ITALIC, f.getSize());
                        break;
                    case 'p':
                        f = new Font(f.getName(), Font.PLAIN, f.getSize());
                        break;
                    default:
                        f = new Font(st.sval, f.getStyle(), f.getSize());
                        break;
                    }
                }
                tokens.addElement(f);
                break;
            case StreamTokenizer.TT_WORD:
                tokens.addElement(st.sval);
                break;
            case StreamTokenizer.TT_NUMBER:
                tokens.addElement(String.valueOf((int)st.nval));
                break;
            case StreamTokenizer.TT_EOL:
                break;
            default:
                tokens.addElement(String.valueOf((char)t));
                break;
            }
            t = st.nextToken();
        } while (t != StreamTokenizer.TT_EOF);
        setSize(300, 300);
        show();
    }

    int line = 0;
```

Labels in left margin from top to bottom: A B C D E F G H I J K L M N O P Q R S T U V W X Y Z

```
void paintLine(Graphics g, Font f, int start, int end,
            int y, int ht, int ac) {

    // adjust for insets
    int x = 0 + getInsets().left;
    y += getInsets().top;

    FontMetrics fm = g.getFontMetrics(f);

    if (line++ % 2 == 0) {
        g.setColor(Color.black);
        g.fillRect(0, y, getSize().width, ht);
        g.setColor(Color.white);
    } else {
        g.setColor(Color.white);
        g.fillRect(0, y, getSize().width, ht);
        g.setColor(Color.black);
    }
    g.setFont(f);
    for (int i=start; i<end; i++) {
        Object tk = tokens.elementAt(i);
        if (tk instanceof Font) {
            g.setFont(f = (Font)tk);
            fm = g.getFontMetrics();
        } else {
            g.drawString((String)tk, x, y + ac);
            x += fm.stringWidth((String)tk) + fm.charWidth(' ');
        }
    }
}

public void paint(Graphics g) {
    Insets insets = getInsets();
    int w = getSize().width-insets.left-insets.right;
    Font f = defaultFont;
    Font startFont = f;
    FontMetrics fm = g.getFontMetrics(f);

    g.clearRect(0, 0, w, getSize().height);
    g.setFont(f);

    int start = 0, x = 0, y = 0;
    int ht = fm.getMaxAscent() + fm.getLeading();
    int base = fm.getMaxAscent();
    line = 0;
    for (int i=0; i<tokens.size(); i++) {
        Object token = tokens.elementAt(i);
        if (token instanceof Font) {
            f = (Font)token;
            g.setFont(f);
            fm = g.getFontMetrics(f);
        } else {
            x += fm.stringWidth((String)token);
            if (x > w) {
                paintLine(g, startFont, start, i, y, ht, base);
                startFont = f;
                start = i--;
                y += ht;
                x = ht = base = 0;
            } else {
```

657

```
                       if (y == 0) {
                           ht = Math.max(ht, fm.getMaxAscent() + fm.getDescent());
                           base = Math.max(base, fm.getMaxAscent());
                       } else {
                           ht = Math.max(ht, fm.getHeight());
                           base = Math.max(base, fm.getAscent()+fm.getLeading());
                       }
                       x += fm.charWidth(' ');
                   }
               }
           }
           paintLine(g, startFont, start, tokens.size(), y, ht, base);
       }

    static public void main(String[] args) {
        try {
            new Main(args[0]);
        } catch (IOException e) {
            System.err.println("usage: java Main <input_file>");
        }
    }
}
```

bytesWidth()

PURPOSE	Determines the width of an array of bytes.
SYNTAX	`public int bytesWidth(byte[] data, int offset, int count)`
DESCRIPTION	This method determines the width of `count` number of bytes in the byte array `data` starting at the index `offset` when displayed using this font metrics. The bytes represent 8-bit characters. The bytes are converted to 16-bit `chars` and then supplied to `charsWidth()`.
PARAMETERS	
count	The number of bytes to consider. `count + offset` must be less than the length of `data`.
data	The non-`null` array of bytes.
offset	The index of the first byte to consider in `data`; `offset` must be less than the length of `data`.
RETURNS	The pixel width of the bytes in `data` that are displayed.
SEE ALSO	`charsWidth()`, `stringWidth()`.
EXAMPLE	See `getMaxAdvance()`.

charsWidth()

PURPOSE   Determines the width of an array of characters.

SYNTAX   `public int charsWidth(char[] data, int offset, int count)`

DESCRIPTION   This method determines the width of `count` number of characters in the character array `data` starting at the index `offset`.

PARAMETERS
count   The number of characters to consider. `count + offset` must be less than the length of `data`.
data   The non-`null` array of characters.
offset   The index of the first byte to consider in `data`; `offset` must be less than the length of `data`.

RETURNS   The pixel width of the characters in `data` when displayed.

SEE ALSO   `bytesWidth()`, `stringWidth()`.

EXAMPLE   See `getMaxAdvance()`.

charWidth()

PURPOSE   Retrieves the width of a character in the font.

SYNTAX   `public int charWidth(char ch)`
               `public int charWidth(int i)`

DESCRIPTION   This method retrieves the width of the character `ch` in the font of this font metric. If an integer `i` is specified, it is equivalent to `charWidth((char)i)`.

PARAMETERS
ch   The character whose width is to be retrieved.
i   The character whose width is to be retrieved. `i` is first converted to a `char`.

RETURNS   The pixel width of the character when displayed.

SEE ALSO   `stringWidth()`.

EXAMPLE   See the class example.

font

PURPOSE   The font from which the font metrics were created.

SYNTAX   `protected Font font`

SEE ALSO   `getFont()`.

FontMetrics()

PURPOSE   Constructs a new FontMetrics instance.

SYNTAX   protected FontMetrics(Font font)

DESCRIPTION   This constructor creates a new FontMetrics instance using the font font.

PARAMETERS

font   The non-null font.

EXAMPLE   This example demonstrates the most common use of the FontMetrics class—painting lines of text. The example prints two lines of output. Notice that when using Graphics.drawString(), you need to add the font's ascent to the *y*-coordinate. See Figure 144.

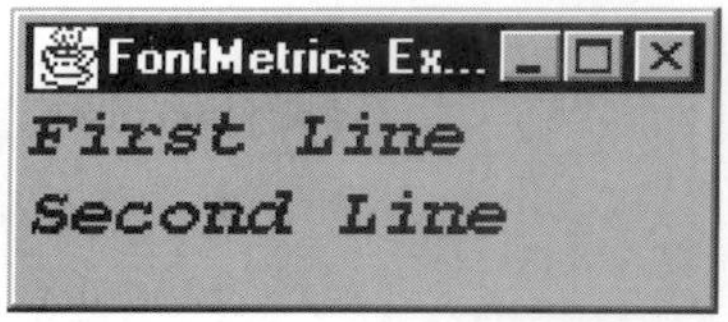

FIGURE 144: FontMetrics().

```
import java.awt.*;

class Main extends Frame {
    Main() {
        super("FontMetrics Example");
        setSize(150, 75);
        show();
    }

    public void paint(Graphics g) {
        Font f = new Font("Monospaced", Font.ITALIC+Font.BOLD, 18);
        FontMetrics fm = g.getFontMetrics(f);
        int y = getInsets().top;
        int x = getInsets().left;

        g.setColor(Color.blue);
        g.setFont(f);
        g.drawString("First Line", x, y + fm.getAscent());
        y += fm.getHeight();
        g.drawString("Second Line", x, y + fm.getAscent());
    }

    public static void main(String[] args) {
        new Main();
    }
}
```

getAscent( )

PURPOSE	Retrieves the font's ascent.
SYNTAX	`public int getAscent()`
RETURNS	The font's ascent in pixels.
SEE ALSO	`getMaxAscent()`.
EXAMPLE	See the class example.

getDescent( )

PURPOSE	Retrieves the font's descent.
SYNTAX	`public int getDescent()`
RETURNS	The font's descent in pixels.
SEE ALSO	`getMaxDescent()`.
EXAMPLE	See the class example.

getFont( )

PURPOSE	Retrieves the font used to create the font metrics.
SYNTAX	`public Font getFont()`
RETURNS	The non-`null` font used to create the font metrics.
EXAMPLE	See the `getMaxAdvance()`.

getHeight( )

PURPOSE	Retrieves the font's height.
SYNTAX	`public int getHeight()`
DESCRIPTION	This method retrieves the font's height, which is the sum of the values `getLeading()` + `getAscent()` + `getDescent()`.
	The font's height is used to determine the pixel distance between the baselines of adjacent lines of text.
RETURNS	The font's height in pixels.
EXAMPLE	See the class example.

A
B
C
D
E
F
G
H
I
J
K
L
M
N
O
P
Q
R
S
T
U
V
W
X
Y
Z

getLeading()

PURPOSE	Retrieves the font's leading.
SYNTAX	`public int getLeading()`
DESCRIPTION	This method returns the font's leading, which is the line spacing between adjacent lines of text.
RETURNS	The font's leading in pixels.
EXAMPLE	See the class example.

getMaxAdvance()

PURPOSE	Retrieves the width of the widest character in the font.
SYNTAX	`public int getMaxAdvance()`
RETURNS	The maximum width of the widest character in the font in pixels; –1 if the value is not available.
EXAMPLE	This example takes an array of characters and displays each character in a box. See Figure 145. All the boxes are of equal size. The maximum ascent, descent, and advance values are used to ensure that the characters do not extend outside the boxes. The font's leading size is used to separate the boxes and pad the interior of the boxes. Pressing the + key increases the size of the font; pressing the - key decreases the size of the font.

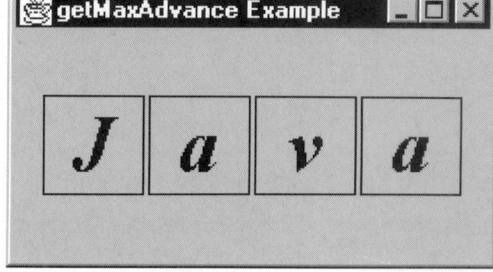

FIGURE 145: `FontMetrics.getMaxAdvance()`.

```
import java.awt.*;
import java.awt.event.*;

class Main extends Frame {
    int fontPointSize = 40;
    char[] message = {'J', 'a', 'v', 'a'};

    Main() {
        super("getMaxAdvance Example");

        addKeyListener(new KeyEventHandler());

        setSize(300, 150);
```

```
        show();
    }

    public void paint(Graphics g) {
        Insets insets = this.getInsets();
        int w = getSize().width-insets.left-insets.right;
        int h = getSize().height-insets.top-insets.bottom;
        int x = insets.left;
        int y = insets.top;
        FontMetrics fm = g.getFontMetrics(
            new Font("Serif", Font.BOLD+Font.ITALIC, fontPointSize));

        // Determine size of one box.  Add some padding (use the leading
        // value) around the inside of each box.
        Dimension dim = new Dimension(fm.getMaxAdvance()+2*fm.getLeading(),
            fm.getMaxAscent() + fm.getMaxDescent() + 2*fm.getLeading());

        // Determine bounding rectangle for all boxes; include some spacing
        // between the boxes.
        Rectangle r = new Rectangle(0, 0,
            message.length * dim.width + (message.length-1) * fm.getLeading(),
            dim.height);

        //Now center the rectangle.
        r.setLocation(x+(w-r.width)/2, y+(h-r.height)/2);

        g.clearRect(x, y, w, h);
        g.setFont(fm.getFont());
        for (int i=0; i<message.length; i++) {
            int cW = fm.charsWidth(message, i, 1);
            int cH = fm.getMaxAscent() + fm.getMaxDescent() + fm.getLeading();

            g.drawChars(message, i, 1, r.x + (dim.width-cW)/2,
                r.y + (dim.height-cH)/2 + fm.getMaxAscent());
            g.drawRect(r.x, r.y, dim.width-1, r.height-1);
            r.x += dim.width + fm.getLeading();
        }
    }

    class KeyEventHandler extends KeyAdapter {
        public void keyPressed(KeyEvent evt) {
            char key = evt.getKeyChar();
            if (key == '+') {
                fontPointSize++;
            } else if (key == '-') {
                fontPointSize--;
            }
            repaint();
        }
    }

    static public void main(String[] args) {
        new Main();
    }
}
```

A
B
C
D
E

G
H
I
J
K
L
M
N
O
P
Q
R
S
T
U
V
W
X
Y
Z

A
B
C
D
E

G
H
I
J
K
L
M
N
O
P
Q
R
S
T
U
V
W
X
Y
Z

getMaxAscent( )

PURPOSE	Retrieves the font's maximum ascent.
SYNTAX	`public int getMaxAscent()`
RETURNS	The font's maximum ascent in pixels.
SEE ALSO	`getAscent()`.
EXAMPLE	See `getMaxAdvance()`.

getMaxDecent( )   *DEPRECATED*

PURPOSE	Replaced by `getMaxDescent()`.
SYNTAX	`public int getMaxDecent()`
DEPRECATION	Replace the usage of this deprecated method, as in

```
   int md = fm.getMaxDecent();
```
with
```
   int md = fm.getMaxDescent();
```

getMaxDescent( )

PURPOSE	Retrieves the font's maximum descent.
SYNTAX	`public int getMaxDescent()`
RETURNS	The font's maximum descent.
SEE ALSO	`getDescent()`.
EXAMPLE	See `getMaxAdvance()`.

getWidths( )

PURPOSE	Retrieves the width of the first 256 characters in the font.
SYNTAX	`public int[] getWidths()`
RETURNS	A 256-element array containing the widths of the first 256 characters in the font.
EXAMPLE	This example displays text in columns, in top-to-bottom and left-to-right order. See Figure 146. The string can contain the newline character, which starts a new column. The descent of the font is used to determine the spacing between columns.

```
import java.awt.*;
import java.io.*;
import java.util.*;

class Main extends Frame {
    StringReader is = new StringReader(
        "Hello\nWorld!\nHow are\nyou\ntoday?");
    int[] charWidths;

    Main() {
        super("getWidths Example");
        setFont(new Font("SansSerif", Font.PLAIN,
            20));
        setSize(300, 200);
        show();
    }

    public void paint(Graphics g) {
        int x = getInsets().left,
            y = getInsets().top;
        int ch;
        char[] chs = new char[1];
        FontMetrics fm = g.getFontMetrics();

        if (charWidths == null) {
            charWidths = fm.getWidths();
        }

        try {
            is.reset();
            while ((ch = is.read()) != -1) {
                if (ch == '\n') {
                    x += fm.getMaxAdvance() + fm.getDescent();
                    y = getInsets().top;
                    continue;
                }
                chs[0] = (char)ch;
                g.drawChars(chs, 0, 1,
                        x + (fm.getMaxAdvance()-charWidths[ch])/2,
                        y + fm.getAscent());
                y += fm.getHeight();
            }
        } catch (IOException e) {
            System.err.println(e);
        }
    }

    static public void main(String[] args) {
        new Main();
    }
}
```

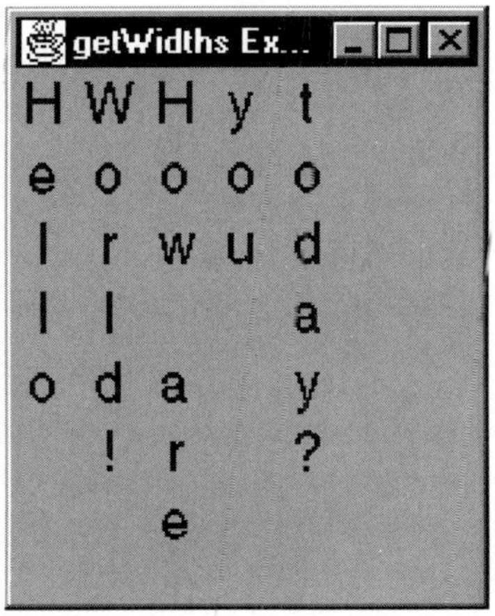

FIGURE 146: Font Widths.

stringWidth( )

PURPOSE	Determines the pixel width of a string.
SYNTAX	`public int stringWidth(String string)`
DESCRIPTION	This method determines the pixel width of a string. The result is equivalent to using `charWidth()` to add together the widths of the individual characters.
RETURNS	The width of the string in pixels.
PARAMETERS	
`string`	The non-null string whose width is to be determined.
SEE ALSO	`bytesWidth()`, `charsWidth()`.
EXAMPLE	See the class example.

toString( )

PURPOSE	Generates a string representation of this font metrics.
SYNTAX	`public String toString()`
DESCRIPTION	This method returns the string representation of this font metric. The result string contains the values for all of the font metrics's attributes. This method is typically used for debugging.
RETURNS	A non-null string representing the font metrics's state.
OVERRIDES	`java.lang.Object.toString()`.
EXAMPLE	See `java.lang.Object.toString()`.

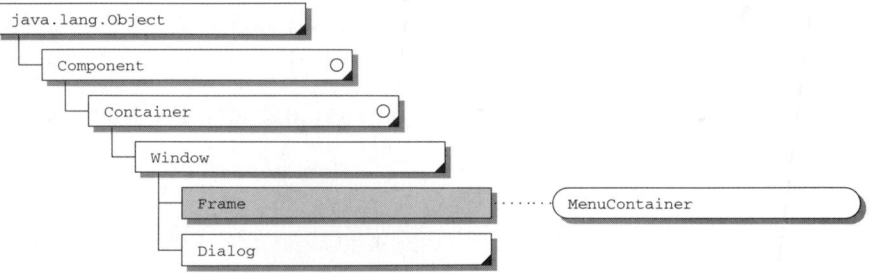

Syntax

```
public class Frame extends Window implements MenuContainer
```

Description

A *frame* is a window with additional properties: a title bar, a menu bar, a border, a cursor, and an icon image.

The Title Property

The *title bar* is a strip across the top of the frame that displays a short description of the frame, called the title. The title can be changed at any time.

The Resizable Property

A *resizable* frame can be resized by the user. The resizable property can be changed at any time. The precise steps to resize the frame are platform-dependent.

The Cursor Property

The frame normally displays the *default cursor*—typically an arrow—when the cursor is moved anywhere in the frame. This cursor shape can be changed at any time using `Component.setCursor()`. The exact cursor shapes available are platform-dependent.

The IconImage Property

A frame can be assigned an *icon image*. The icon image is a way to graphically represent the frame. It is up to the platform windowing system as to how the icon image is used. For example, most platforms will display the frame's icon when the frame is iconified.

Coordinates and Sizes

A frame has a nonempty inset because of the title bar, menu bar, and border. The frame has an interior area in which you can paint and place components. The insets of a frame can change because of the menu bar. For example, if the window is made small enough so that the menu bar requires additional lines in order to display the menu labels, `getInsets().top` will increase.

The origin of the frame is at the top-left corner of the frame. The *x*- and *y*-coordinates in the frame's bounds indicate the location of the frame on the screen.

Events
The frame fires the same events as a window. See the `Window` and `WindowEvent` classes for more details.

A
B
C
D
E
F
G
H
I
J
K
L
M
N
O
P
Q
R
S
T
U
V
W
X
Y
Z

MEMBER SUMMARY	
Constructor	
`Frame()`	Constructs a new `Frame` instance.
The Property Methods	
`getIconImage()`	Retrieves this frame's icon image.
`getTitle()`	Retrieves this frame's title.
`isResizable()`	Retrieves this frame's resizable state.
`setIconImage()`	Sets the image to display when this frame is iconified.
`setResizable()`	Sets this frame's resizable property.
`setTitle()`	Sets this frame's title.
Menu Bar and Popup Menu Methods	
`getMenuBar()`	Retrieves this frame's menu bar.
`remove()`	Removes this frame's menu bar or popup menu.
`setMenuBar()`	Sets this frame's menu bar.
Peer Methods	
`addNotify()`	Creates this frame's peer hierarchy.
`dispose()`	Destroys this frame's peer hierarchy.
Debugging Method	
`paramString()`	Generates a string representing this frame's state.
Deprecated Constants and Methods	
`CROSSHAIR_CURSOR`	Replaced by `Cursor.CROSSHAIR_CURSOR`.
`DEFAULT_CURSOR`	Replaced by `Cursor.DEFAULT_CURSOR`.
`E_RESIZE_CURSOR`	Replaced by `Cursor.E_RESIZE_CURSOR`.
`getCursorType()`	Replaced by `Component.getCursor().getType()`.
`HAND_CURSOR`	Replaced by `Cursor.HAND_CURSOR`.
`MOVE_CURSOR`	Replaced by `Cursor.MOVE_CURSOR`.
`N_RESIZE_CURSOR`	Replaced by `Cursor.N_RESIZE_CURSOR`.
`NE_RESIZE_CURSOR`	Replaced by `Cursor.NE_RESIZE_CURSOR`.
`NW_RESIZE_CURSOR`	Replaced by `Cursor.NW_RESIZE_CURSOR`.
`S_RESIZE_CURSOR`	Replaced by `Cursor.S_RESIZE_CURSOR`.

MEMBER SUMMARY	
SE_RESIZE_CURSOR	Replaced by Cursor.SE_RESIZE_CURSOR.
setCursor()	Replaced by Component.setCursor().
SW_RESIZE_CURSOR	Replaced by Cursor.SW_RESIZE_CURSOR.
TEXT_CURSOR	Replaced by Cursor.TEXT_CURSOR.
W_RESIZE_CURSOR	Replaced by Cursor.W_RESIZE_CURSOR.
WAIT_CURSOR	Replaced by Cursor.WAIT_CURSOR.

Example

This example creates a frame whose interior is exactly 150 pixels high and 150 pixels wide. Clicking anywhere in the interior causes a new frame to appear. Its northwest corner will be at the exact position you clicked (see Figure 147).

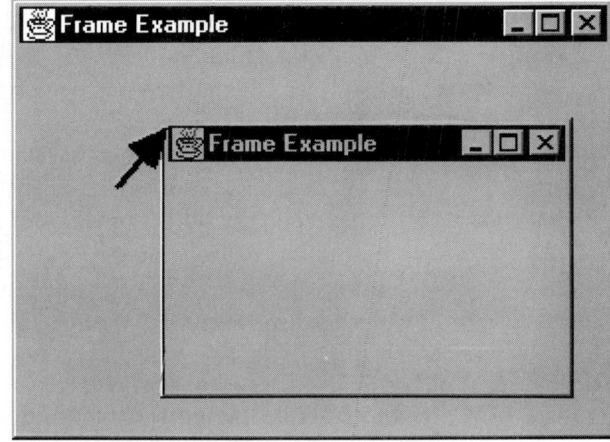

FIGURE 147: Frame.

```java
import java.awt.*;
import java.awt.event.*;

class Main extends Frame {
    // The contructor creates a frame with a window size that gives
    // the desired interior size.
    Main() {
        super("Frame Example");
        // Calling addNotify() creates the peers; otherwise insets()
        // does not return the right values.
        addNotify();

        Insets insets = getInsets();
        setSize(insets.left + insets.right + 150,
                insets.top + insets.bottom + 150);

        // Add listener
        this.addMouseListener(new MouseEventHandler());

    }

    class MouseEventHandler extends MouseAdapter {
        public void mousePressed(MouseEvent evt) {
            // x, y are in interior coordinates
            // must be translated to screen coordinates.
            Rectangle bounds = getBounds();
            int x = evt.getX() + bounds.x;
```

```
                int y = evt.getY() + bounds.y;

                // Set location of new frame
                Main m = new Main();
                m.setLocation(x, y);
                m.show();
            }
        }

        static public void main(String[] args) {
            (new Main()).show();
        }
    }
```

A
B
C
D
E
F
G
H
I
J
K
L
M
N
O
P
Q
R
S
T
U
V
W
X
Y
Z

addNotify()

PURPOSE	Creates this frame's peer hierarchy.
SYNTAX	`public synchronized void addNotify()`
DESCRIPTION	This method creates this frame's peer hierarchy, if necessary. The frame's peer is created by calling the `Toolkit.createFrame()` method. This method should be called before the frame's minimum or preferred size is calculated. The methods `pack()` and `show()` automatically call `addNotify()`.
OVERRIDES	`Window.addNotify()`.
SEE ALSO	`Component`, `Component.minimumSize()`, `Component.preferredSize()`, `Toolkit`, `Window.pack()`, `Window.show()`.
EXAMPLE	See the class example.

CROSSHAIR_CURSOR   *DEPRECATED*

PURPOSE	Replaced by `Cursor.CROSSHAIR_CURSOR`.
SYNTAX	`public static final int CROSSHAIR_CURSOR`

DEFAULT_CURSOR   *DEPRECATED*

PURPOSE	Replaced by `Cursor.DEFAULT_CURSOR`.
SYNTAX	`public static final int DEFAULT_CURSOR`

dispose( )

PURPOSE Destroys the frame's peer hierarchy.

SYNTAX `public synchronized void dispose()`

DESCRIPTION This method destroys the frame's peer hierarchy, if it exists, thereby freeing any resources used by the peers. The state of the frame hierarchy is left intact and can be reused. The peer hierarchy can be restored by calling `addNotify()`.

OVERRIDES `Window.dispose()`.

EXAMPLE This example creates two buttons. One creates a frame, and the other disposes of it. See Figure 148. Upon initialization, the dispose button is disabled. When a frame is created, the create button is disabled and the dispose button is enabled. The original frame also handles the `WindowEvent.WINDOW_CLOSING` event and disposes of itself.

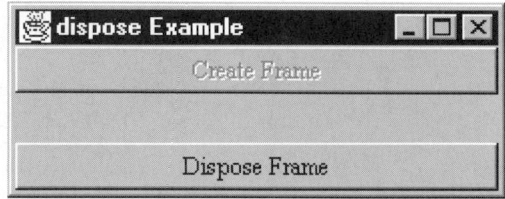
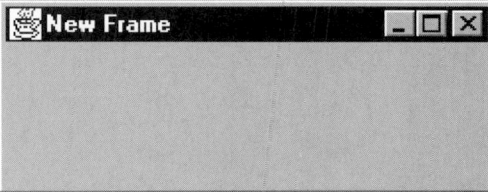

FIGURE 148: `Frame.dispose()`**: Initial Frame and Newly Created Frame.**

```
import java.awt.*;
import java.awt.event.*;

class Main extends Frame implements ActionListener {
    Button btnCreate = new Button("Create Frame");
    Button btnDispose = new Button("Dispose Frame");
    Frame f;

    Main() {
        super("dispose Example");

        btnDispose.setEnabled(false);
        add(btnCreate, BorderLayout.NORTH);
        add(btnDispose, BorderLayout.SOUTH);

        // Add Listeners
        btnDispose.addActionListener(this);
        btnCreate.addActionListener(this);
        this.addWindowListener(new WindowEventHandler());

        setSize(100, 100);
        show();
    }
```

```
public void actionPerformed(ActionEvent evt) {
    if (evt.getSource() == btnCreate) {
        btnCreate.setEnabled(false);
        btnDispose.setEnabled(true);
        f = new Frame("New Frame");
        f.setBounds(100, 100, 100, 100);
        f.show();
    } else if (evt.getSource() == btnDispose) {
        btnCreate.setEnabled(true);
        btnDispose.setEnabled(false);
        f.dispose();
    }
}

class WindowEventHandler extends WindowAdapter {
    public void windowClosing(WindowEvent evt) {
        dispose();
    }
}

static public void main(String[] args) {
    new Main();
}
}
```

E_RESIZE_CURSOR   *DEPRECATED*

PURPOSE   Replaced by `Cursor.E_RESIZE_CURSOR`.

SYNTAX   `public static final int E_RESIZE_CURSOR`

Frame()

PURPOSE   Constructs a new `Frame` instance.

SYNTAX   `public Frame()`
                 `public Frame(String title)`

DESCRIPTION The two forms of this constructor create a new invisible `Frame` instance with the title `title`. If `title` is not specified, it defaults to "Untitled." The icon image property is initially `null`. The cursor is initially `Cursor.DEFAULT_CURSOR`. The frame is initially resizable. The new frame has a border layout manager (see `BorderLayout`).

PARAMETERS

`title`   The string specifying the frame's title.

EXAMPLE   This example creates two frames: one with a title and one without. The second frame is created at a different location.

```
import java.awt.*;

class Main {
    static public void main(String[] args) {
        Frame f1 = new Frame("Frame Example");
        Frame f2 = new Frame();

        f1.setSize(200, 100);
        f1.show();
        f2.setBounds(100, 100, 200, 100);
        f2.show();
    }
}
```

A
B
C
D
E

G
H
I
J
K
L
M
N
O
P
Q
R
S
T
U
V
W
X
Y
Z

getCursorType( )   *DEPRECATED*

PURPOSE   Replaced by Component.getCursor().getType().

SYNTAX   public int getCursorType()

RETURNS   The frame's cursor type.

DEPRECATION   Replace the usage of this deprecated method, as in
                int cursorType = frame.getCursorType();
              with
                int cursorType = frame.getCursor().getType().

getIconImage( )

PURPOSE   Retrieves the frame's icon image.

SYNTAX   public Image getIconImage()

RETURNS   The frame's icon image. The return value can be null. This means the icon image has not yet been changed.

SEE ALSO   setIconImage().

EXAMPLE   See setIconImage().

getMenuBar( )

PURPOSE   Retrieves the frame's menu bar.

SYNTAX   public MenuBar getMenuBar()

RETURNS   The frame's menu bar. The return value is `null` if the frame does not have a menu bar.

EXAMPLE   See `MenuBar.add()`.

getTitle()

PURPOSE   Retrieves the frame's title.

SYNTAX   `public String getTitle()`

RETURNS   A string containing the frame's title. The result value may be `null`.

SEE ALSO   `setTitle()`.

EXAMPLE   See `setTitle()`.

HAND_CURSOR   *DEPRECATED*

PURPOSE   Replaced by `Cursor.HAND_CURSOR`.

SYNTAX   `public static final int HAND_CURSOR`

isResizable()

PURPOSE   Retrieves the frame's resizable state.

SYNTAX   `public boolean isResizable()`

RETURNS   `true` if the frame is currently resizable; `false` otherwise.

EXAMPLE   See `setResizable()`.

MOVE_CURSOR   *DEPRECATED*

PURPOSE   Replaced by `Cursor.MOVE_CURSOR`.

SYNTAX   `public static final int MOVE_CURSOR`

N_RESIZE_CURSOR   *DEPRECATED*

PURPOSE   Replaced by `Cursor.N_RESIZE_CURSOR`.

SYNTAX   `public static final int N_RESIZE_CURSOR`

NE_RESIZE_CURSOR   *DEPRECATED*

PURPOSE   Replaced by `Cursor.NE_RESIZE_CURSOR`.

SYNTAX   `public static final int NE_RESIZE_CURSOR`

NW_RESIZE_CURSOR   *DEPRECATED*

PURPOSE   Replaced by `Cursor.NW_RESIZE_CURSOR`.

SYNTAX   `public static final int NW_RESIZE_CURSOR`

paramString()

PURPOSE   Generates a string representing the frame's state.

SYNTAX   `protected String paramString()`

DESCRIPTION   The string representation of a frame consists of its container string representation, its title, and whether the frame is resizable.

 A subclass of this class should override this method and return a concatenation of its state with the results of `super.paramString()`. This method is called by the `toString()` method and is typically used for debugging.

RETURNS   A non-`null` string representing the frame's state.

OVERRIDES   `Container.paramString()`.

SEE ALSO   `Component.toString()`, `java.lang.Object.toString()`.

EXAMPLE   This example shows how to override the `paramString()` method. The subclass appends an extra piece of state (`myData`) to the result.

```
import java.awt.*;

class Main extends Frame {
    String myData = "Testing";

    Main() {
        super("paramString Example");
    }

    protected String paramString() {
    String str = super.paramString();
    if (myData != null) {
        str += ",myData=" + myData;
    }
    return str;
    }

    static public void main(String[] args) {
```

A
B
C
D
E
F
G
H
I
J
K
L
M
N
O
P
Q
R
S
T
U
V
W
X
Y
Z

```
                    Main m = new Main();
                    System.out.println(m);
            }
    }
```

remove()

PURPOSE   Removes the frame's menu bar or popup menu.

SYNTAX   `public synchronized void remove(MenuComponent comp)`

DESCRIPTION   This method removes the menu component `comp` from the frame. If `comp` is a
               `MenuBar` instance that is installed as this frame's menu bar, this frame's menu
               bar is removed.

               If `comp` is a `PopupMenu` instance that is installed for this frame, it is removed.
               If `comp` is not installed in the frame, this method call is ignored.

PARAMETERS
  comp   The non-`null` menu component (`MenuBar` or `PopupMenu`) to remove from the
               frame.

OVERRIDES   `Component.remove()`.

EXAMPLE   This example creates a frame with a
               menu bar and a checkbox component. If
               the checkbox state is `true`, then the menu
               bar is visible; otherwise, the menu bar is
               removed. See Figure 149. See `Compo-`
               `nent.add()` for an example of popup
               menu removal.

**FIGURE 149:   Removing a Frame's
Menu Bar.**

```
import java.awt.*;
import java.awt.event.*;

class Main extends Frame implements ItemListener {
    MenuBar mb = new MenuBar();
    Checkbox cb = new Checkbox("Display Menu Bar");

    Main() {
        super("remove Example");
        Menu m = new Menu("Menu");

        m.add("MenuItem");
        mb.add(m);

        add(cb, BorderLayout.SOUTH);
        cb.addItemListener(this);

        pack();
```

```
            show();
        }

        public void itemStateChanged(ItemEvent evt) {
            if (evt.getSource() == cb) {
                if (cb.getState()) {
                    setMenuBar(mb);
                } else {
                    remove(mb);
                }
            }
        }

        static public void main(String[] args) {
            new Main();
        }
    }
```

S_RESIZE_CURSOR   *DEPRECATED*

PURPOSE   Replaced by Cursor.S_RESIZE_CURSOR.

SYNTAX   public static final int S_RESIZE_CURSOR

SE_RESIZE_CURSOR   *DEPRECATED*

PURPOSE   Replaced by Cursor.SE_RESIZE_CURSOR.

SYNTAX   public static final int SE_RESIZE_CURSOR

SW_RESIZE_CURSOR   *DEPRECATED*

PURPOSE   Replaced by Cursor.SW_RESIZE_CURSOR.

SYNTAX   public static final int SW_RESIZE_CURSOR

setCursor()   *DEPRECATED*

PURPOSE   Replaced by Componente.setCursor().

SYNTAX   public void setCursor(int cursorType)

PARAMETERS
 cursorType   An integer specifying one of the valid cursor types.

EXCEPTIONS
 IllegalArgumentException
                If cursorType is not a valid cursor type.

<table>
<tr><td>DEPRECATION</td><td>Replace the usage of this deprecated method, as in</td></tr>
</table>

DEPRECATION

Replace the usage of this deprecated method, as in

```
setCursor(Frame.MOVE_CURSOR);
```

with

```
setCursor(Cursor.getPredefinedCursor(Cursor.MOVE_CURSOR));
```

SEE ALSO   Cursor.

setIconImage()

PURPOSE   Sets the image to display when this frame is iconified.

SYNTAX   `public synchronized void setIconImage(Image image)`

DESCRIPTION   This method sets `image` to be the image displayed when this frame is iconified. *Note*: Not all platforms support the concept of iconifying a window.

PARAMETERS

image   The non-`null` icon image.

SEE ALSO   `getIconImage()`.

EXAMPLE   This example sets the frame's icon image from a file. Pushing the button toggles the display of the icon image in the frame. Iconify the frame to see the icon image being used for the frame's icon. See Figure 150.

FIGURE 150: Changing Frame's Icon Image.

```
import java.awt.*;
import java.awt.event.*;

class Main extends Frame implements ActionListener {
    boolean showIconImage = false;

    Main(String filename) {
        super("setIconImage Example");
        try {
            Image image = getToolkit().getImage(filename);
            setIconImage(image);
        } catch (Exception e) {
            e.printStackTrace();
        }

        Button b;
        add(b = new Button("Icon Image"), BorderLayout.SOUTH);
        b.addActionListener(this);

        setSize(50, 150);
        show();
    }

    public void actionPerformed(ActionEvent evt) {
```

```
            showIconImage = !showIconImage;
            repaint();
        }

    public void paint(Graphics g) {
        if (showIconImage) {
            Insets insets = getInsets();
            g.drawImage(getIconImage(), insets.left, insets.top, this);
        }
    }

    static public void main(String[] args) {
        if (args.length == 1) {
            new Main(args[0]);
        } else {
            System.err.println("usage: java Main <image file>");
        }
    }
}
```

setMenuBar()

PURPOSE   Sets this frame's menu bar.

SYNTAX   `public synchronized void setMenuBar(MenuBar menubar)`

DESCRIPTION   This method sets the frame's menu bar to be menubar. If the frame already has a menu bar, the current menu bar is first removed. The frame becomes the menu bar's parent.

PARAMETERS
 menubar   The non-null menu bar to set.

EXAMPLE   This example creates two menu bars and two buttons. Clicking one button installs one of the menu bars; clicking the other installs the other menu bar. See Figure 151.

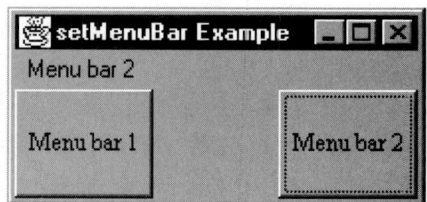

FIGURE 151:   **Changing a Frame's Menu Bar.**

```
import java.awt.*;
import java.awt.event.*;

class Main extends Frame implements ActionListener {
    MenuBar mb1 = new MenuBar();
    MenuBar mb2 = new MenuBar();

    Main(String title) {
        super(title);
        Menu menu;

        menu = new Menu("Menu bar 1");
```

679

```
                menu.add("One");
                mb1.add(menu);
                setMenuBar(mb1);

                menu = new Menu("Menu bar 2");
                menu.add("Two");
                mb2.add(menu);

                Button b;
                add(b = new Button("Menu bar 1"), BorderLayout.WEST);
                b.addActionListener(this);
                add(b = new Button("Menu bar 2"), BorderLayout.EAST);
                b.addActionListener(this);

                pack();
                show();
        }

        public void actionPerformed(ActionEvent evt) {
            String what = evt.getActionCommand();
            if ("Menu bar 1".equals(what)) {
                setMenuBar(mb1);
            } else if("Menu bar 2".equals(what)) {
                setMenuBar(mb2);
            }
        }

        static public void main(String[] args) {
            Main m = new Main("setMenuBar Example");
        }
    }
```

setResizable( )

PURPOSE   Sets the resizable property.

SYNTAX   `public synchronized void setResizable(boolean resizable)`

DESCRIPTION   This method sets this frame to be resizable or nonresizable. If `resizable` is `true`, the frame becomes resizable; otherwise, it becomes nonresizable.

PARAMETERS

resizable   If `true`, the frame becomes resizable; otherwise, the frame becomes nonresizable.

EXAMPLE   This example creates a frame with a checkbox indicating whether the frame should be resizable. Clicking the checkbox changes the resizable property of the frame. See Figure 152.

FIGURE 152:   **Resizable Frame.**

```
import java.awt.*;
import java.awt.event.*;

class Main extends Frame implements ItemListener {
    Checkbox cb;
    Main() {
        super("setResizable Example");
        cb = new Checkbox("Resizable", null, isResizable());
        add(cb, BorderLayout.NORTH);
        cb.addItemListener(this);
        pack();
        show();
    }

    public void itemStateChanged(ItemEvent evt) {
        setResizable(cb.getState());
    }

    static public void main(String[] args) {
        new Main();
    }
}
```

setTitle()

PURPOSE   Sets this frame's title.

SYNTAX   `public synchronized void setTitle(String title)`

DESCRIPTION   This method sets this frame's title to be the string `title`.

PARAMETERS
`title`   The string specifying the frame's new title. A value of `null` clears the title.

SEE ALSO   `getTitle()`.

EXAMPLE   This example creates a text field in a frame, initialized with the frame's current title. Pressing Return while in the text field sets the frame's title to the text in the text field. See Figure 153.

FIGURE 153:   **Changing a Frame's Title.**

```
import java.awt.*;
import java.awt.event.*;

class Main extends Frame implements ActionListener {
    TextField t = new TextField(50);

    Main() {
        super("setTitle Example");
        t.setText(getTitle());    // Initialize with current title.
```

```
        add(t, BorderLayout.NORTH);
        t.addActionListener(this);
        pack();
        show();
    }

    public void actionPerformed(ActionEvent evt) {
        setTitle(evt.getActionCommand());
    }

    static public void main(String[] args) {
        new Main();
    }
}
```

TEXT_CURSOR   *DEPRECATED*

PURPOSE   Replaced by Cursor.TEXT_CURSOR.

SYNTAX   `public static final int TEXT_CURSOR`

W_RESIZE_CURSOR   *DEPRECATED*

PURPOSE   Replaced by Cursor.W_RESIZE_CURSOR.

SYNTAX   `public static final int W_RESIZE_CURSOR`

WAIT_CURSOR   *DEPRECATED*

PURPOSE   Replaced by Cursor.WAIT_CURSOR.

SYNTAX   `public static final int WAIT_CURSOR`

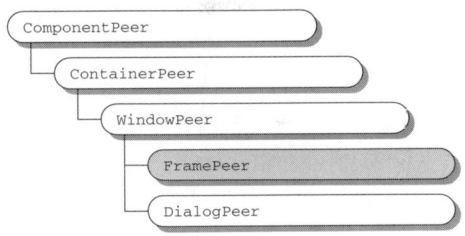

Syntax

```
public interface FramePeer extends WindowPeer
```

Description

The frame component (see the Frame class) in the AWT uses the platform's native implementation of a frame. So that the AWT frame behaves the same on all platforms, the frame is assigned a *peer*, whose task is to translate the behavior of the platform's native frame to the behavior of the AWT frame.

AWT programmers normally do not directly use peer classes and interfaces. Instead, they deal with AWT components in the java.awt package. These in turn automatically manage their peers. Only someone who is porting the AWT to another platform should be concerned with the peer classes and interfaces. Consequently, most peer documentation refers to java.awt counterparts.

See Component and Toolkit for additional information about component peers.

MEMBER SUMMARY	
Peer Methods	
setIconImage()	Sets the image to display when this frame is iconified.
setMenuBar()	Sets this frame's menu bar.
setResizable()	Sets this frame's resizable property.
setTitle()	Sets this frame's title.

See Also

java.awt.Component, java.awt.Frame, java.awt.Toolkit,
java.awt.Toolkit.createFrame().

setIconImage()

PURPOSE	Sets the image to display when this frame is iconified.
SYNTAX	`void setIconImage(Image image)`
PARAMETERS	
image	The icon image to be displayed.
SEE ALSO	`java.awt.Frame.setIconImage()`.

setMenuBar()

PURPOSE	Sets this frame's menu bar.
SYNTAX	`void setMenuBar(MenuBar menubar)`
PARAMETERS	
menubar	The non-null menu bar to set.
SEE ALSO	`java.awt.Frame.setMenuBar()`.

setResizable()

PURPOSE	Sets this frame's resizable property.
SYNTAX	`void setResizable(boolean resizable)`
PARAMETERS	
resizable	If `true`, the frame becomes resizable; otherwise, the frame becomes nonresizable.
SEE ALSO	`java.awt.Frame.setResizable()`.

setTitle()

PURPOSE	Sets this frame's title.
SYNTAX	`void setTitle(String title)`
PARAMETERS	
title	The string specifying the frame's new title. A value of `null` clears the title.
SEE ALSO	`java.awt.Frame.setTitle()`.

A
B
C
D
E
F
G
H
I
J
K
L
M
N
O
P
Q
R
S
T
U
V
W
X
Y
Z

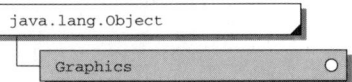

Syntax

`public abstract class Graphics`

Description

The *graphics context* is an object used to paint on a *drawing surface*. The drawing surface is a rendering device such as a screen or a printer. The drawing surface can also be an off-screen image (see Figure 154). A drawing surface has three properties that may affect a graphics context: a background color, a foreground color, and a font. These three properties are sometimes used to initialize a new graphics context created from a drawing surface.

When you are painting to the screen, the AWT system supplies you with a graphics context via the `Component.paint()` and `Compo-`

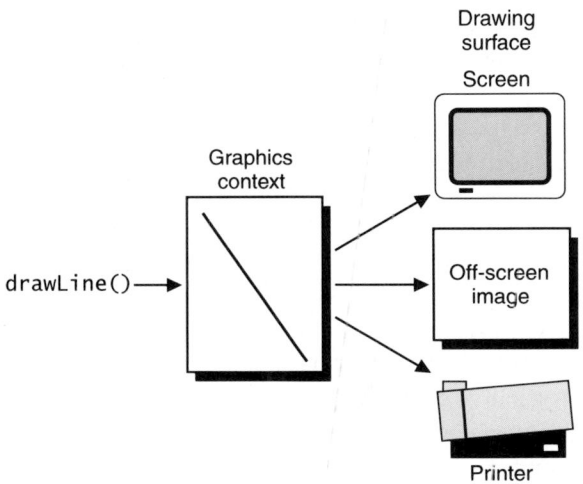

FIGURE 154:   Graphics Context Drawing Surfaces.

`nent.update()` methods. See the `Component` class for details. When painting to the printer, you must obtain a graphics context with a call to `PrintJob.getGraphics()`. See `PrintJob` for more details. When painting to an off-screen image, you create a graphics context on the image that you can paint to any time you wish. However, if you want to paint any part of the off-screen image to the screen, you need to do it indirectly through the `Compo-nent.repaint()` method. See the `Component` class for details.

A drawing surface can have more than one graphics context, and multiple contexts can be used simultaneously. Also, a graphics context can be cloned and each context can have a different property set. Having more than one graphics context, each with different property sets, can be useful in some situations when you need to constantly switch property values while painting a complex image.

In general, a graphics context should be disposed of as soon as it is no longer needed. This is because a graphics context is usually associated with a system resource. Such system resources are typically large but limited.

The Origin and Coordinates

The *x*-coordinates of a graphics context moves from left to right; the left edge has coordinate 0. The *y*-coordinates of a graphics context moves from top to bottom; the top edge has coordinate 0.

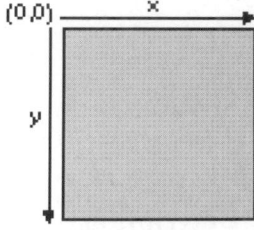

The graphics context has an origin, which is initially at the coordinates (0, 0) (see Figure 155). The coordinates supplied by the graphics operations are relative to the origin. The origin can be moved at any time. For example, if the origin is at (10, 10) and a circle is painted at (5, 5), the circle will appear on the drawing surface at (15, 15).

FIGURE 155:   Graphics Coordinates.

The Background and Foreground Colors

A graphics context has both a *background* and *foreground* color. If the drawing surface is a native component, the colors are inherited from the component. Changes to the component's color do not affect the colors in the graphics context. Otherwise, the background color is white and the foreground color is black.

When a graphics context is created, its background color is assigned and cannot be changed or queried. The only method that uses the background color is `clearRect()`. The foreground color is used by all of the other painting operations and can be changed at any time.

The Font

The graphics context has a font that is used when you are painting text. If the drawing surface is a native component, the initial font of the graphics context is copied from the current font of the component. Changes to the drawing surface's current font do not affect the font in the graphics context. The graphics context's font can be changed at any time. See `setFont()` for an example that uses fonts.

Paint Modes

A graphics context can be in one of two paint modes: *normal* or *xor*. In normal paint mode, the background colors have no effect on the paint operation. That is, if you paint a black circle, it will appear as a black circle no matter on what color background it was painted.

Xor paint mode is more complicated. In the simplest terms, if you paint the same object twice while you are in xor mode, the object disappears. Also, when you paint the object for the first time, it won't appear in the correct color. The color that appears is based on both the foreground and background colors; the exact color chosen is platform-dependent.

In xor paint mode, one special color called the xor color will not affect the foreground color. That is, if you paint on an xor color colored background, the foreground color will come out as expected. However, the previous rule of painting the same object twice still applies.

One final effect of xor paint mode: If the foreground color is the same as the xor color, the painting operation is ignored.

Xor mode is typically used in dragging operations. During the drag, the outline of the object is painted in xor mode. After the object is moved, the old outline is erased simply by painting the outline in the same place. This optimization is much more efficient than having to repaint the background to erase the old outline of the object.

See `setXORMode()` for an example that uses xor paint mode.

The Clipping Area

The *clipping area* is used to constrain the results of the painting operations so that they affect only a specific area. In particular, painting operations are effective only inside the clipping area; any painting done outside the clipping area is ignored. For example, to implement a rectangle with scrolling text, you would set a clipping area around that rectangle so that the scrolling text would not affect the surrounding area when you draw the string. As of Java 1.1.2, the clipping area is restricted to a rectangle. In future releases, the clipping area will be able to be any shape.

Image Painting

The `drawImage()` method is used to paint images in a graphics context. There are many variants of the method that lets you scale, flip, and crop the image.

Initial Values

For some drawing surfaces, when a graphics context is created from the drawing surface, three properties of the graphics context are initialized with the current settings of the drawing surface. In particular, if the drawing surface is a native component, the background and foreground color and font of the graphics context are initialized from the same three properties of the component. This is not true if the drawing surface is a lightweight component or a printed page.

MEMBER SUMMARY	
Constructors and Destructors	
create()	Constructs a new Graphics object that has the same properties as this graphics context.
dispose()	Releases this graphics context's system resources.
finalize()	Releases this graphics context's system resources.
Graphics()	Constructs a new Graphics object.
Color Methods	
getColor()	Retrieves this graphics context's foreground color.
setColor()	Sets this graphics context's foreground color.
Paint Mode Methods	
setPaintMode()	Sets this graphics context to normal paint mode.
setXORMode()	Sets this graphics context to xor paint mode.
	Continued

A
B
C
D
E
F
G
H
I
J
K
L
M
N
O
P
Q
R
S
T
U
V
W
X
Y
Z

A
B
C
D
E
F

H
I
J
K
L
M
N
O
P
Q
R
S
T
U
V
W
X
Y
Z

MEMBER SUMMARY	

Clipping Methods

clipRect()	Shrinks this graphics context's clipping area.
getClip()	Retrieves this graphics context's clipping area.
getClipBounds()	Retrieves the clipping area's bounds of this graphics context.
setClip()	Sets the clipping area of this graphics context.

Painting Methods

clearRect()	Paints a rectangle with the background color on this graphics context.
copyArea()	Copies an area of the drawing surface to another area of this drawing surface.
draw3DRect()	Paints a 3D outline around a rectangle on this graphics context.
drawArc()	Paints an elliptical arc inside a rectangle on this graphics context.
drawLine()	Paints a line on this graphics context.
drawOval()	Paints an oval outline inside a rectangle on this graphics context.
drawPolyline()	Paints an open polygon outline on this graphics context.
drawPolygon()	Paints a closed polygon outline on this graphics context.
drawRect()	Paints an outline around a rectangle on this graphics context.
drawRoundRect()	Paints an outline of a rectangle with rounded corners on this graphics context.
fill3DRect()	Paints a rectangle that has a 3D outline on this graphics context.
fillArc()	Paints a filled elliptical arc inside a rectangle on this graphics context.
fillOval()	Paints an oval area on this graphics context.
fillPolygon()	Paints a closed polygon on this graphics context.
fillRect()	Paints a rectangular area on this graphics context.
fillRoundRect()	Paints a rectangle with rounded corners on this graphics context.

Font and String Methods

drawBytes()	Paints an array of bytes as characters on this graphics context.
drawChars()	Paints an array of characters on this graphics context.
drawString()	Paints a string on this graphics context.
getFont()	Retrieves this graphics context's font.
getFontMetrics()	Retrieves the font metrics for a font.
setFont()	Sets this graphics context's font.

Image Method

drawImage()	Paints an image on this graphics context.

Translate Method

translate()	Moves this graphics context's origin.

Debugging Method

toString()	Generates a string representation of this graphics context's state.

Deprecated Method

getClipRect()	Replaced by getClipBounds().

Example

This example paints three colored figures. It demonstrates the simplest example of painting on the screen. See Figure 156.

FIGURE 156: **Simple Graphics.**

```
import java.awt.*;

class Main extends Frame {
    Main() {
        super("Graphics Example");
        setSize(200, 100);
        show();
    }

    public void paint(Graphics g) {
        Insets insets = getInsets();
        int x = insets.left;
        int y = insets.top;

        Polygon polygon = new Polygon();
        polygon.addPoint(x+125, y);
        polygon.addPoint(x+100, y+50);
        polygon.addPoint(x+150, y+50);

        g.setColor(Color.red);
        g.fillOval(x, y, 50, 50);
        g.setColor(Color.green);
        g.fillRect(x+50, y, 50, 50);
        g.setColor(Color.blue);
        g.fillPolygon(polygon);
    }

    static public void main(String[] args) {
        new Main();
    }
}
```

clearRect()

PURPOSE	Paints a rectangle with the background color on this graphics context.
SYNTAX	`public abstract void clearRect(int x, int y, int width, int height)`
DESCRIPTION	This method paints the area defined by x, y, width, and height with this graphics context's background color. If either width or height is less than or equal to 0, the method call is ignored.
PARAMETERS	
height	The height of the rectangular area in pixels.

689

width	The width of the rectangular area in pixels.
x	The *x*-coordinate in pixels.
y	The *y*-coordinate in pixels.

SEE ALSO   drawRect(), fillRect().

EXAMPLE   This example paints successively smaller and smaller rectangles, alternating between the background and foreground colors. See Figure 157.

FIGURE 157:   **Shrinking Rectangles.**

```java
import java.awt.*;

class Main extends Frame {
    Main() {
        super("clearRect Example");
        setBackground(Color.black);
        setSize(200, 200);
        show();
    }

    public void paint(Graphics g) {
        Insets insets = this.getInsets();
        int x = insets.left, y = insets.top;
        int w = getSize().width-insets.left-insets.right;
        int h = getSize().height-insets.top-insets.bottom;

        g.setColor(Color.red);
        while (w > 0 && h > 0) {
            g.clearRect(x++, y++, w, h);
            g.fillRect(x++, y++, w-2, h-2);
            w -= 4;
            h -= 4;
        }
    }

    static public void main(String[] args) {
        new Main();
    }
}
```

clipRect( )

PURPOSE   Shrinks this graphics context's clipping area.

SYNTAX   `public abstract void clipRect(int x, int y, int width, int height)`

DESCRIPTION   The intersection of this graphics context clipping area and the rectangle specified by x, y, width, and height becomes the new clipping area.

PARAMETERS

height	The height of the rectangle in pixels.
width	The width of the rectangle in pixels.
x	The *x*-coordinate in pixels.
y	The *y*-coordinate in pixels.

SEE ALSO   getClip(), getClipBounds(), setClip().

EXAMPLE   See create().

copyArea()

PURPOSE   Copies an area of the drawing surface to another area of the drawing surface.

SYNTAX
```
public abstract void copyArea(int x, int y, int width, int
    height, int deltax, int deltay)
```

DESCRIPTION   This method copies the pixels on the screen in the rectangular area defined by x, y, width, and height to the area defined by x+deltax, y+deltay, width, and height.

If some window is partially occluding the scrolled area, the paint() method will be called to repaint the damaged area. Optimally, the clipping area of the graphics context supplied by the paint() method will be exactly as large as needed. However, on some platforms this may not be the case.

PARAMETERS

deltax	The horizontal distance from the source in pixels.
deltay	The vertical distance from the source in pixels.
height	The height of the source in pixels.
width	The width of the source in pixels.
x	The *x*-coordinate of the source in pixels.
y	The *y*-coordinate of the source in pixels.

EXAMPLE   This example creates a canvas that paints a scrolling histogram. See Figure 158. The histogram is scrolled 1 pixel to the right, and a new line of data is added on the left. The copyArea() method is straightforward, unless some window is partially occluding the area being scrolled. In this case, the paint() method is called to paint the "damaged" areas. A blue rectangle is painted to indicate a complete paint, while a

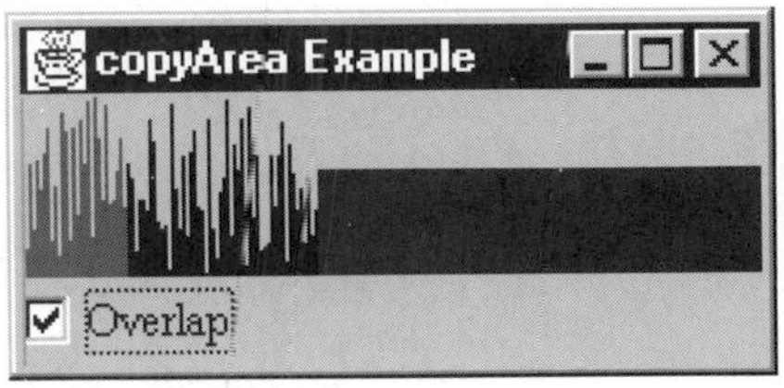

FIGURE 158: Scrolling Histogram.

red rectangle is painted to indicate a partial paint. A paint call is partial if the dimensions of `getClipBounds()` are smaller than `size()`.

So that you can invoke a partial paint, a checkbox component allows you to show or hide a 1-pixel-wide window that will overlap the scrolling histogram.

The scrolling histogram is embedded in another panel to guarantee that the overlapping window will overlap the scrolling histogram. If the overlapping window is a sibling of the scrolling histogram, there is no way to control whether the overlapping window will appear above or below the scrolling histogram.

```java
import java.awt.*;
import java.awt.event.*;

class Main extends Frame implements ItemListener {
    Panel panel = new Panel();

    MainCanvas cv = new MainCanvas();
    Canvas overlap = new Canvas();
    Checkbox cb = new Checkbox("Overlap", null, false);

    Main() {
        super("copyArea Example");
        panel.setLayout(new BorderLayout());
        panel.add(cv, BorderLayout.CENTER);

        add(overlap);
        add(panel);
        add(cb);
        cb.addItemListener(this);

        overlap.setBackground(Color.green);
        overlap.setVisible(false);
        setSize(400, 100);
        show();
    }

    // In order to get the overlapping window to overlap another,
    // we need to implement our own specific layout.
    public synchronized void doLayout() {
        Insets insets = this.getInsets();
        Dimension d = cb.getPreferredSize();
        int w = getSize().width - insets.left-insets.right;
        int h = getSize().height - insets.top-insets.bottom;

        panel.setBounds(insets.left, insets.top, w, h-d.height);
        cb.setBounds(insets.left, getSize().height-insets.bottom-d.height,
            w, d.height);
        overlap.setBounds(insets.left, insets.top, 1, h);
    }

    public void itemStateChanged(ItemEvent evt) {
    overlap.setVisible(cb.getState());
    }

    static public void main(String[] args) {
```

```
        new Main();
    }
}

class MainCanvas extends Canvas implements Runnable {
    MainCanvas() {
        (new Thread(this)).start();
    }

    //  Returns an integer in the range [0..r-1].
    int random(int r) {
        return (int)(Math.floor(Math.random()*r));
    }

    public void update(Graphics g) {
        int w = getSize().width;
        int h = getSize().height;

        // shift right by 1 pixel.
        g.copyArea(0, 0, w-1, h, 1, 0);
        g.clearRect(0, 0, 1, h);
        g.drawLine(0, random(h), 0, h);
    }

    public void paint(Graphics g) {
        int w = getSize().width;
        int h = getSize().height;
        Rectangle r = g.getClipBounds();

        if (r == null || (r.width == w && r.height == h)) {
            g.setColor(Color.blue); // full repaint
        } else {
            g.setColor(Color.red); // partial repaint
        }
        g.fillRect(0, random(h), w, h);
    }

    public void run() {
        while (true) {
            try {Thread.sleep(100);} catch (Exception e) {};
            repaint();
        }
    }
}
```

create()

PURPOSE	Constructs a new Graphics object that has the same properties as this graphics context.
SYNTAX	public Graphics create()
	public Graphics create(int x, int y, int width, int height)

DESCRIPTION   If `x`, `y`, `width`, and `height` are specified, the new graphics context will be translated by `x` and `y` and a rectangular clipping area set. More precisely, the second overload is similar to

```
Graphics g2 = g.create();
g2.translate(x, y);
g2.clipRect(0, 0, width, height);
```

The main difference is that the clipping area in the created graphics context cannot grow. In the previous code, it is possible to grow the clipping area with a call to `setClip()`.

PARAMETERS

`height`	The pixel height of the area.
`width`	The pixel width of the area.
`x`	The *x*-coordinate.
`y`	The *y*-coordinate.

RETURNS   A non-`null` graphics context.

SEE ALSO   `translate()`.

FIGURE 159: `Graphics.create()`.

EXAMPLE   This example requires three different nonoverlapping clipping rectangles on the drawing surface. See Figure 159. Two copies of the supplied graphics context are created, and a clipping rectangle is set on the copies. Finally, the original graphics context is clipped, since no more clipping rectangles need to be set.

```java
import java.awt.*;

class Main extends Frame {
    Main() {
        super("create Example");
        setSize(200, 200);
        show();
    }

    void paintFigure(Graphics g, int w, int h) {
        g.clipRect(5, 5, w-10, h-10);
        g.fillOval(0, 0, w, h);
    }
    public void paint(Graphics g) {
        Insets insets = this.getInsets();
        int x = insets.left, y = insets.top;
        int w = getSize().width-insets.left-insets.right;
        int h = getSize().height-insets.top-insets.bottom;

        Graphics g2 = g.create(x, y, w/3, h);
        g2.setColor(Color.red);
        paintFigure(g2, w/3, h);
        g2.dispose();

        g2 = g.create(x+w/3, y, w/3, h);
        g2.setColor(Color.green);
```

```
        paintFigure(g2, w/3, h);
        g2.dispose();

        // Safe to use original one.
        g.translate(x + w*2/3, y);
        g.setColor(Color.blue);
        paintFigure(g, w/3, h);
    }

    static public void main(String[] args) {
        new Main();
    }
}
```

dispose()

PURPOSE	Releases this graphics context's system resources.
SYNTAX	`public abstract void dispose()`
DESCRIPTION	This method releases any system resources that this graphics context has been using. Any further method calls on this object after it has been disposed of are ignored.
	Calling this method is not strictly necessary because the garbage collector will eventually call this graphics context's `finalize()` method, which in turn will call `dispose()`. However, when graphics contexts are created at a fast rate, the overall system performance may be helped by explicitly disposing of this graphics context.
SEE ALSO	`finalize()`.
EXAMPLE	See `create()`.

draw3DRect()

PURPOSE	Paints a 3D outline around a rectangle on this graphics context.
SYNTAX	`public void draw3DRect(int x, int y, int width, int height,` `    boolean raised)`
DESCRIPTION	This method paints a 1-pixel-thick outline *around* the rectangle defined by x, y, width, and height. The left and top edges of the outline are within the specified rectangle, but the right and bottom edges are just outside the defined rectangle. Hence, this method actually draws width+1 horizontal lines and height+1 vertical lines. Note that this method will paint a single pixel if width and height are both 0. Use draw3DRect(x, y, width-1, height-1)

A
B
C
D
E
F
G
H
I
J
K
L
M
N
O
P
Q
R
S
T
U
V
W
X
Y
Z

to paint the 3D outline inside the specified rectangle. If either `width` or `height` is less than 0, the method call is ignored.

If `raised` is `true`, the 3D effect is done by lightening the left and top edges and darkening the right and bottom edges. If `raised` is `false`, the left and top edges are darker and the right and bottom edges are lighter. The lighter and darker color shades are generated by the `Color.brighter()` and `Color.darker()` methods, respectively.

This method uses the foreground color to calculate the lighter and darker colors for the 3D rectangle. A common mistake is to forget to set the foreground color before calling this method. Generally, the foreground color should be set to the background color so that the 3D colors are based on the background. However, depending on the background color, the calculated 3D colors are not always very good. So you may have to experiment with different colors to achieve a better 3D effect.

PARAMETERS

height	The height of the rectangular area in pixels.
raised	Specifies whether the area should be raised or lowered.
width	The width of the rectangular area in pixels.
x	The *x*-coordinate in pixels.
y	The *y*-coordinate in pixels.

FIGURE 160: `Graphics.draw3DRect()` **Raised Border.**

SEE ALSO   `Color.brighter()`, `Color.darker()`, `fill3DRect()`.

EXAMPLE   This example paints a 3D border just within the frame's paintable area. The 3D border is thicker than 1 pixel. Clicking toggles the 3D border between a raised border and a lowered border. Figure 160 shows a raised border. Figure 161 shows a lowered border.

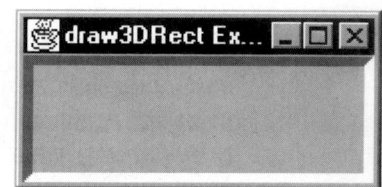

FIGURE 161: `Graphics.draw3DRect()`: **Lowered Border.**

```
import java.awt.*;
import java.awt.event.*;

class Main extends Frame {
    int borderWidth = 5;
    boolean raised = true;

    Main() {
        super("draw3DRect Example");
```

```
        setSize(200, 200);

        addMouseListener(new MouseEventHandler());
        show();
    }

    public void paint(Graphics g) {
        Insets insets = this.getInsets();
        int x = insets.left, y = insets.top;
        int w = getSize().width-insets.left-insets.right;
        int h = getSize().height-insets.top-insets.bottom;

        w -= 1;         // draw inside the rectangle.
        h -= 1;         // draw inside the rectangle.
        g.setColor(getBackground());
        for (int i=0; i<borderWidth; i++) {
            g.draw3DRect(x++, y++, w, h, raised);
            w -= 2;
            h -= 2;
        }
        g.fillRect(x, y, w+1, h+1);
    }

    class MouseEventHandler extends MouseAdapter {
        public void mousePressed(MouseEvent evt) {
            raised = !raised;
            repaint();
        }
    }

    static public void main(String[] args) {
        new Main();
    }
}
```

A
B
C
D
E
F
G
H
I
J
K
L
M
N
O
P
Q
R
S
T
U
V
W
X
Y
Z

drawArc()

PURPOSE   Paints an elliptical arc inside a rectangle on this graphics context.

SYNTAX   `public abstract void drawArc(int x, int y, int width, int height,`
               `int startAngle, int arcAngle)`

DESCRIPTION   This method paints a 1-pixel-thick elliptical arc in the foreground color within
               the rectangle defined by x, y, width, and height. If either width or height is
               less than 0, the method call is ignored.

               Logically, you form the arc first by using the drawOval() method to paint an
               oval inside the rectangle. Next, define a horizontal line that originates from the
               oval's center and extends to the containing rectangle's right edge. Then anchor
               the line at the oval's center and rotate the line startAngle degrees from its
               starting position. If startAngle is positive, rotate counterclockwise; if start-
               Angle is negative, rotate clockwise. The intersection of this line and the oval's

outline is the starting point for the arc. Finally, continue rotating the line arcAngle degrees. Again, if arcAngle is positive, rotate counterclockwise; otherwise, rotate clockwise. All the points that intersect this line and the oval's outline during the rotation are included in the arc.

PARAMETERS

arcAngle   The angle in degrees (360 degrees in a circle) that specifies the end of the arc. arcAngle is relative to startAngle.

height   The height of the rectangular area in pixels.

startAngle   The angle in degrees (360 degrees in a circle) that specifies the start of the arc; a value of 0 is at the 3 o'clock position.

width   The width of the rectangular area in pixels.

x   The *x*-coordinate in pixels.

y   The *y*-coordinate in pixels.

SEE ALSO   fillArc().

EXAMPLE   This example draws a 270-degree arc starting at 0 degrees. Four labels are used to show the start angle positions. See Figure 162.

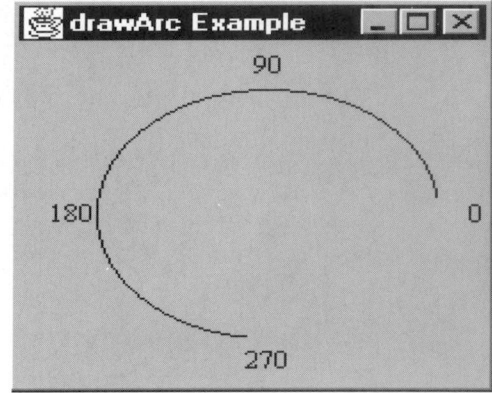

FIGURE 162: Graphics.drawArc().

```
import java.awt.*;

class Main extends Frame {
    Main() {
        super("drawArc Example");
        add(new MainCanvas(), Border-
Layout.CENTER);
        add(new Label("90", Label.CENTER), BorderLayout.NORTH);
        add(new Label("270", Label.CENTER), BorderLayout.SOUTH);
        add(new Label("0"), BorderLayout.EAST);
        add(new Label("180"), BorderLayout.WEST);
        setSize(200, 200);
        show();
    }

    static public void main(String[] args) {
        new Main();
    }
}

class MainCanvas extends Canvas {
    public void paint(Graphics g) {
        g.drawArc(0, 0, getSize().width, getSize().height, 0, 270);
    }
}
```

drawBytes( )

PURPOSE	Paints an array of bytes as characters on this graphics context.
SYNTAX	`public void drawBytes(byte[] buf, int offset, int count, int x,` `int y)`
DESCRIPTION	This method is equivalent to `drawString(new String(buf, 0, offset, count));` See the `drawString()` method for details.

PARAMETERS

`buf`	The non-`null` array of bytes to paint.
`count`	The number of characters in `buf` to paint.
`offset`	The starting index of the first character in `buf` to paint.
`x`	The x-coordinate of the baseline in pixels.
`y`	The y-coordinate of the baseline in pixels.

SEE ALSO	`drawChars()`, `drawString()`, `FontMetrics`.
EXAMPLE	See `drawString()`.

drawChars( )

PURPOSE	Paints an array of characters on this graphics context.
SYNTAX	`public void drawChars(char[] buf, int offset, int count, int x,` `int y)`
DESCRIPTION	This method is equivalent to `drawString(new String(buf, offset, count));` See the `drawString()` method for details.

PARAMETERS

`buf`	The non-`null` array of characters to paint.
`count`	The number of characters in `buf` to paint.
`offset`	The index of the first character in `buf` to paint.
`x`	The x-coordinate of the baseline in pixels.
`y`	The y-coordinate of the baseline in pixels.

SEE ALSO	`drawBytes()`, `drawString()`, `FontMetrics`.
EXAMPLE	See `drawString()`.

A
B
C
D
E
F
G
H
I
J
K
L
M
N
O
P
Q
R
S
T
U
V
W
X
Y
Z

699

drawImage( )

PURPOSE	Paints an image on this graphics context.

SYNTAX

```
public abstract boolean drawImage(Image image, int dx1, int dy1,
    ImageObserver observer)
public abstract boolean drawImage(Image image, int dx1, int dy1,
    Color bgColor, ImageObserver observer)
public abstract boolean drawImage(Image image, int dx1, int dy1,
    int width, int height, ImageObserver observer)
public abstract boolean drawImage (Image image, int dx1, int dy1,
    int width, int height, Color bgColor, ImageObserver observer)
public abstract boolean drawImage(Image image, int dx1, int dy1,
    int dx2, int dy2, int sx1, sy1, int sx2, int sy2, ImageObserver
    observer)
public abstract boolean drawImage(Image image, int dx1, int dy1,
    int dx2, int dy2, int sx1, sy1, int sx2, int sy2, Color
    bgColor, ImageObserver observer)
```

DESCRIPTION   The first four forms of this method paint the image image such that its north-west corner is at pixel location (dx1, dy1). If width and height are specified, the image is scaled so that its width is width and its height is height. A negative width or height indicates that *proportional values* are to be used. This means that, for example, if width is negative, then a width should be chosen so that the image maintains its correct portions when the height is supplied. If both width and height are negative, the width and height of the original image are used.

The last two forms of this method paint the subimage specified by the source coordinates (sx1, sy1, sx2, sy2) of image image to the rectangle specified by the destination coordinates (dx1, dy1, dx2, dy2). The source subimage is scaled and mapped to the destination rectangle such that (sx1, sy1) maps to (dx1, dy1) and (sx2, sy2) maps to (dx2, dy2). By specifying appropriate values for the coordinates, you can flip the image horizontally or vertically.

If observer is non-null, it will receive updates as the image is loaded. See the ImageObserver class for more information.

PARAMETERS

bgColor	The color to use for transparent pixels in the image. If null or unspecified, no color is used.
dx1	The *x*-coordinate of the northwest corner of the destination rectangle in pixels.
dx2	The *x*-coordinate of the southeast corner of the destination rectangle in pixels.
dy1	The *y*-coordinate of the northwest corner of the destination rectangle in pixels.
dy2	The *y*-coordinate of the southeast corner of the destination rectangle in pixels.
height	The height of the scaled image in pixels.
image	The image to paint.

observer	The image update observer. This value may be null.
sx1	The *x*-coordinate of the northwest corner of the source rectangle in pixels.
sx2	The *x*-coordinate of the southeast corner of the source rectangle in pixels.
sy1	The *y*-coordinate of the northwest corner of the source rectangle in pixels.
sy2	The *y*-coordinate of the southeast corner of the source rechanneling pixels.
width	The width of the scaled image in pixels.

RETURNS   true if the image is completely loaded or scaled and was painted successfully; false otherwise.

SEE ALSO   Image, ImageObserver.

EXAMPLE   This example renders an image five different ways using drawImage(): original size, shrunken to one-fourth the size, enlarged to twice the size, flipped horizontally, and flipped vertically. See Figure 163.

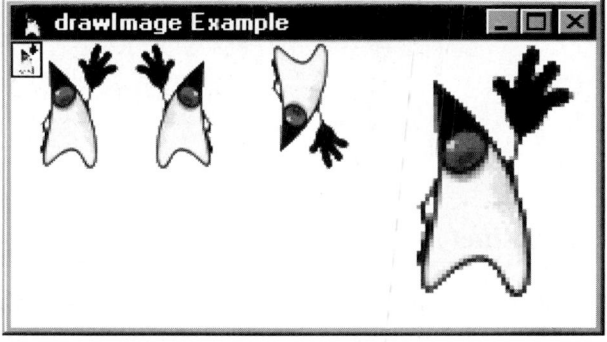

FIGURE 163:   Graphics.drawImage().

```
import java.awt.*;
class Main extends Frame {
    Image image;

    Main(String filename) {
        super("drawImage Example");
        try {
            image = getToolkit().getImage(filename);
            setIconImage(image);
        } catch (Exception e) {
            e.printStackTrace();
        }

        setSize(400, 200);
        show();
    }

    public void paint(Graphics g) {
        Insets insets = getInsets();
        int x = insets.left, y = insets.top;
        int w = image.getWidth(this);
        int h = image.getHeight(this);

        // original
        g.drawImage(image, x, y, this);

        // shrinken
        g.drawRect(x, y, w/4+1, h/4+1);
```

701

```
            g.drawImage(image, x+1, y+1, w/4, h/4, this);

            // horizontally flipped
            g.drawImage(image, x+w, y, x+2*w, y+h, w, 0, 0, h, this);

            // vertically flipped
            g.drawImage(image, x+2*w, y, x+3*w, y+h, 0, h, w, 0, this);

            // enlarged; use -1 to indicate proportional height
            g.drawImage(image, x+3*w, y, 2*w, -1, this);
        }

    static public void main(String[] args) {
        if (args.length == 1) {
            new Main(args[0]);
        } else {
            System.err.println("usage: java Main <image file>");
        }
    }
}
y
```

drawLine()

PURPOSE	Paints a line on this graphics context.
SYNTAX	`public abstract void drawLine(int x1, int y1, int x2, int y2)`
DESCRIPTION	This method paints a 1-pixel-thick line between the coordinates (x1, y1) and (x2, y2) in the foreground color. The pixel at (x2, y2) is included in the line. The `drawLine()` object always draws at least 1 pixel.
PARAMETERS	
x1	The first point's x-coordinate in pixels.
y1	The first point's y-coordinate in pixels.
x2	The second point's x-coordinate in pixels.
y2	The second point's y-coordinate in pixels.
SEE ALSO	`drawPolyline()`.
EXAMPLE	This example paints a series of connected lines. See Figure 164. Each time the mouse is clicked or dragged, a new line is added to the line list. This example also demonstrates how to use the `update()` method to avoid redrawing all of the lines and thus avoid flicker.

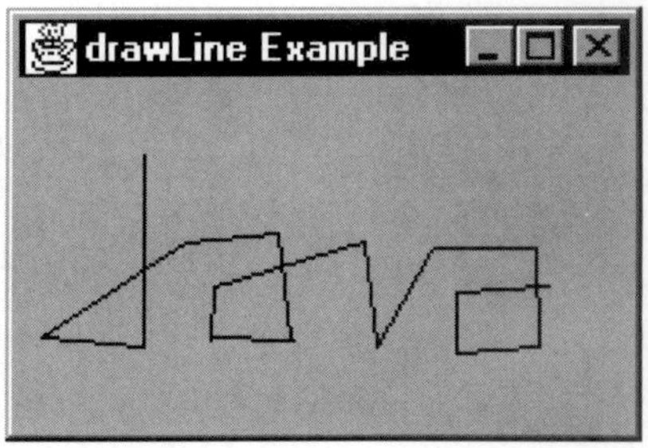

FIGURE 164: `Graphics.drawLine()`.

```
import java.awt.*;
import java.awt.event.*;
import java.util.*;
```

```java
class Main extends Frame {
    Vector points = new Vector();
    int lastDrawnPoint = 0;

    Main() {
        super("drawLine Example");
        setSize(200, 200);
        addMouseListener(new MouseEventHandler());
        addMouseMotionListener(new MouseMotionEventHandler());

        show();
    }

    public void paint(Graphics g) {
        Point curPt = null;
        for (int i=0; i<points.size(); i++) {
            Point pt = (Point)points.elementAt(i);

            if (curPt != null) {
                g.drawLine(curPt.x, curPt.y, pt.x, pt.y);
            }
            curPt = pt;
        }
        lastDrawnPoint = points.size();
    }

    public void update(Graphics g) {
        Point curPt = null;
        lastDrawnPoint = Math.max(0, lastDrawnPoint-1);
        for (int i=lastDrawnPoint; i<points.size(); i++) {
            Point pt = (Point)points.elementAt(i);

            if (curPt != null) {
                g.drawLine(curPt.x, curPt.y, pt.x, pt.y);
            }
            curPt = pt;
        }
        lastDrawnPoint = points.size();
    }

    class MouseEventHandler extends MouseAdapter {
        public void mousePressed(MouseEvent evt) {
            points.addElement(evt.getPoint());
            repaint();
        }
    }

    class MouseMotionEventHandler extends MouseMotionAdapter {
        public void mouseDragged(MouseEvent evt) {
            points.addElement(evt.getPoint());
            repaint();
        }
    }

    static public void main(String[] args) {
        new Main();
    }
}
```

A
B
C
D
E
F
G
H
I
J
K
L
M
N
O
P
Q
R
S
T
U
V
W
X
Y
Z

drawOval()

PURPOSE   Paints an oval outline inside a rectangle on this graphics context.

SYNTAX   ```
public abstract void drawOval(int x, int y, int width, int
    height)
```

DESCRIPTION    This method paints a 1-pixel-thick oval outline in the foreground color within the rectangle defined by x, y, width, and height. If either width or height is less than 0, the method call is ignored.

PARAMETERS
 height        The height of the rectangular area in pixels.
 width         The width of the rectangular area in pixels.
 x             The *x*-coordinate in pixels.
 y             The *y*-coordinate in pixels.

SEE ALSO       fillOval().

EXAMPLE        This example creates a frame and reads numbers from standard input. See Figure 165. Each line from standard input contains a coordinate. When two coordinates are retrieved, they form a point and a circle is painted around the point.

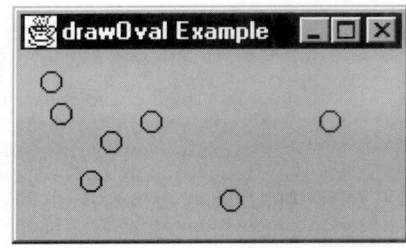

**FIGURE 165:** `Graphics.drawOval()`.

```
import java.awt.*;
import java.util.*;
import java.io.*;
class Main extends Frame {
    Vector points = new Vector();

    Main() {
        super("drawOval Example");
        setSize(200, 200);
        show();
    }

    void addPoint(Point p) {
        points.addElement(p);
        repaint();
    }

    public void paint(Graphics g) {
        Insets insets = getInsets();
        int x = insets.left, y = insets.top;

        for (int i=0; i<points.size(); i++) {
            Point p = (Point)points.elementAt(i);
            g.drawOval(x+p.x-5, y+p.y-5, 10, 10);
        }
    }
```
```

```
static public void main(String[] args) {
    Main m = new Main();
    BufferedReader dis =
        new BufferedReader(new InputStreamReader(System.in));

    while (true) {
        try {
            m.addPoint(new Point(
                Integer.parseInt(dis.readLine()),
                Integer.parseInt(dis.readLine())));
        } catch (Exception e) {
            e.printStackTrace();
            System.exit(1);
        }
    }
}
```

A
B
C
D
E
F
G
H
I
J
K
L
M
N
O
P
Q
R
S
T
U
V
W
X
Y
Z

drawPolygon()

PURPOSE   Paints a closed polygon outline on this graphics context.

SYNTAX   `public void drawPolygon(Polygon polygon)`
                `public abstract void drawPolygon(int[] xPoints, int[] yPoints, int`
                `    nPoints)`

DESCRIPTION   A *polygon* is a collection of lines connecting a series of points. The polygon is
                closed, meaning a line is automatically drawn between the first and last points
                if the two are different. This method paints a 1-pixel-thick polygon in the fore-
                ground color using the specified set of points.

                The points are either specified by the polygon `polygon` or by two arrays
                `xPoints` and `yPoints`. In the latter form, `xPoints[i]` and `yPoints[i]`
                together specify a point in the polygon. The series of points from index 0 to
                `nPoints-1` specifies the ordered list of points in the polygon.

PARAMETERS
`nPoints`   The number of points in `xPoints` and `yPoints`.
`polygon`   The non-`null` polygon to paint.
`xPoints`   The non-`null` array of *x*-coordinates (in pixels) in the polygon.
`yPoints`   The non-`null` array of *y*-coordinates (in pixels) in the polygon.

SEE ALSO   `drawPolyline()`, `fillPolygon()`, `Polygon`.

EXAMPLE   This example paints a polygon. When the
             mouse is clicked or dragged, a new point
             is added to the polygon. See Figure 166.

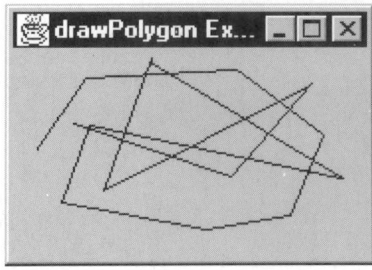

```
import java.awt.*;
import java.awt.event.*;

class Main extends Frame {
    Polygon polygon = new Polygon();
```

FIGURE 166:
Graphics.drawPolygon().

```
    Main() {
        super("drawPolygon Example");

        addMouseListener(new MouseEventHandler());
        addMouseMotionListener(new MouseMotionEventHandler());

        setSize(200, 200);
        show();
    }

    public void paint(Graphics g) {
        g.drawPolygon(polygon);
    }

    // The default update method clears the screen which causes
    // flicker.  This override avoids this.
    public void update(Graphics g) {
        paint(g);
    }

    class MouseEventHandler extends MouseAdapter {
        public void mousePressed(MouseEvent evt) {
            polygon.addPoint(evt.getX(), evt.getY());
            repaint();
        }
    }

    class MouseMotionEventHandler extends MouseMotionAdapter {
        public void mouseDragged(MouseEvent evt) {
            polygon.addPoint(evt.getX(), evt.getY());
            repaint();
        }
    }

    static public void main(String[] args) {
        new Main();
    }
}
```

A
B
C
D
E
F
G
H
I
J
K
L
M
N
O
P
Q
R
S
T
U
V
W
X
Y
Z

drawPolyline()

PURPOSE   Paints a nonclosed polygon outline on this graphics context.

SYNTAX   `public abstract void drawPolyline(int[] xPoints, int[] yPoints, int nPoints)`

DESCRIPTION A nonclosed polygon is a collection of lines connecting a series of points in which a line is not automatically drawn between the first and last points if the two points differ. This method paints a 1-pixel-thick nonclosed polygon in the foreground color using the specified set of points.

The points are specified by two arrays `xPoints` and `yPoints`. `xPoints[i]` and `yPoints[i]` together specify a point in the polygon. The series of points from index 0 to `nPoints-1` specifies the ordered list of points in the polygon.

PARAMETERS

nPoints   The number of points in `xPoints` and `yPoints`.

xPoints   The non-`null` array of *x*-coordinates (in pixels) in the polygon.

yPoints   The non-`null` array of *y*-coordinates (in pixels) in the polygon.

SEE ALSO   `drawLine()`, `drawPolygon`, `fillPolygon()`, `Polygon`.

EXAMPLE   This example paints a polyline. When the mouse is clicked or dragged, a new point is added to the polyline (until `100` points have been added). See Figure 167.

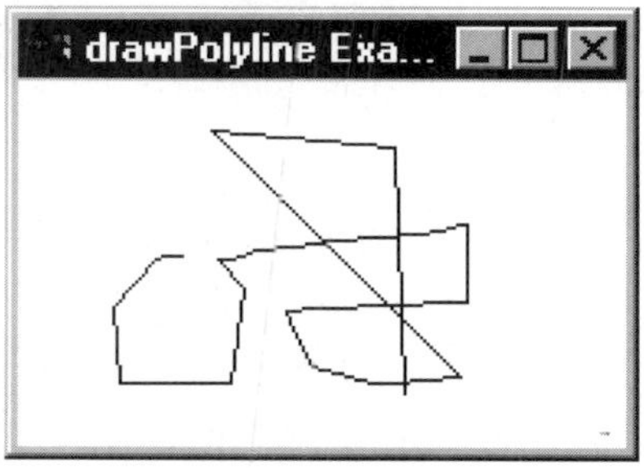

FIGURE 167:
Graphics.drawPolyline().

```
import java.awt.*;
import java.awt.event.*;

class Main extends Frame {
    int[] xPoints = new int[100];
    int[] yPoints = new int[100];
    int nPoints = 0;

    Main() {
        super("drawPolyline Example");

        addMouseListener(new MouseEventHandler());
        addMouseMotionListener(new MouseMotionEventHandler());

        setSize(200, 200);
        show();
    }

    public void paint(Graphics g) {
        g.drawPolyline(xPoints, yPoints, nPoints);
    }

    // The default update method clears the screen which causes
    // flicker.  This override avoids this.
    public void update(Graphics g) {
```

```
            paint(g);
        }

        class MouseEventHandler extends MouseAdapter {
            public void mousePressed(MouseEvent evt) {
                if (nPoints < 100) {
                    xPoints[nPoints] = evt.getX();
                    yPoints[nPoints] = evt.getY();
                    ++nPoints;
                }
                repaint();
            }
        }

        class MouseMotionEventHandler extends MouseMotionAdapter {
            public void mouseDragged(MouseEvent evt) {
                if (nPoints < 100) {
                    xPoints[nPoints] = evt.getX();
                    yPoints[nPoints] = evt.getY();
                    ++nPoints;
                }
                repaint();
            }
        }

        static public void main(String[] args) {
            new Main();
        }
    }
```

A
B
C
D
E
F
G
H
I
J
K
L
M
N
O

drawRect( )

P | PURPOSE | Paints an outline around a rectangle on this graphics context.

Q | SYNTAX | `public void drawRect(int x, int y, int width, int height)`

R | DESCRIPTION | This method paints a 1-pixel-thick outline *around* the rectangle defined by x,
S | | y, width, and height. The left and top edges of the outline are within the
 | | specified rectangle, but the right and bottom edges are just outside the defined
T | | rectangle. Hence, this method actually draws width+1 horizontal lines and
U | | height+1 vertical lines. Note that it will paint a single pixel if width and
 | | height are both 0. Use drawRect(x, y, width-1, height-1) to paint the
V | | outline inside the specified rectangle. If either width or height is less than 0,
W | | the method call is ignored.

X | PARAMETERS |
 | height | The height of the rectangular area in pixels.
Y | width | The width of the rectangular area in pixels.
 | x | The *x*-coordinate in pixels.
Z | y | The y-coordinate in pixels.

SEE ALSO   clearRect(), fillRect().

EXAMPLE   This example demonstrates how to implement an "outline rectangle," which is typically used for selecting objects in a user interface or for defining the size and location of new objects. See Figure 168. In this example, you create a rectangle by clicking and dragging an outline of a rectangle until you are satisfied with the size of the rectangle. When you release the mouse, a permanent rectangle is drawn on the display. The outline rectangle is painted using xor paint mode, you need not repaint the entire background each time the outline rectangle changes size. See setXORMode() for more details.

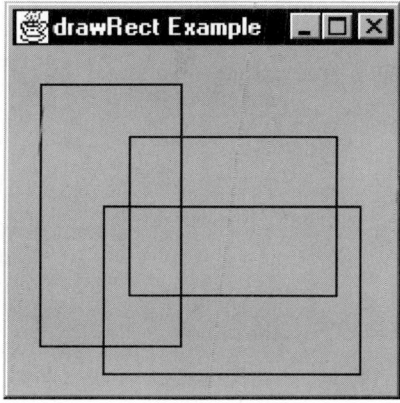

FIGURE 168: `Graphics.drawRect()`.

```java
import java.awt.*;
import java.awt.event.*;
import java.util.*;

class Main extends Frame {
    Main() {
        super("drawRect Example");
        add(new MainCanvas(), BorderLayout.CENTER);

        setSize(200, 200);
        show();
    }
    static public void main(String[] args) {
        new Main();
    }
}

class MainCanvas extends Canvas {
    Vector rects = new Vector();
    int startX, startY;
    Rectangle oldRect, newRect;

    MainCanvas() {
        addMouseListener(new MouseEventHandler());
        addMouseMotionListener(new MouseMotionEventHandler());
    }

    public void paint(Graphics g) {
        update(g);
    }

    public void update(Graphics g) {
        // First erase old rect.
        if (oldRect != null) {
```

A
B
C
D
E
F
G
H
I
J
K
L
M
N
O
P
Q
R
S
T
U
V
W
X
Y
Z

```
            g.setXORMode(Color.white);
            g.drawRect(oldRect.x, oldRect.y, oldRect.width, oldRect.height);
            g.setPaintMode();
        }
        // Now paint rectangles.
        for (int i=0; i<rects.size(); i++) {
            Rectangle r = (Rectangle)rects.elementAt(i);
            g.drawRect(r.x, r.y, r.width, r.height);
        }
        if (newRect != null) {
            g.setXORMode(Color.white);
            g.drawRect(newRect.x, newRect.y, newRect.width, newRect.height);
            g.setPaintMode();
        }
        oldRect = newRect;
        newRect = null;
    }

    class MouseEventHandler extends MouseAdapter {
        public void mousePressed(MouseEvent evt) {
            int x = evt.getX(), y = evt.getY();
            startX = x;
            startY = y;
            newRect = new Rectangle(x, y, 1, 1);
            repaint();
        }
        public void mouseReleased(MouseEvent evt) {
            int x = evt.getX(), y = evt.getY();
            rects.addElement(new Rectangle(startX, startY,
                                           x-startX, y-startY));
            newRect = null;
            repaint();
        }
    }

    class MouseMotionEventHandler extends MouseMotionAdapter {
        public void mouseDragged(MouseEvent evt) {
            int x = evt.getX(), y = evt.getY();
            newRect = new Rectangle(startX, startY, x-startX, y-startY);
            repaint();
        }
    }
}
```

drawRoundRect()

PURPOSE   Paints an outline of a rectangle with rounded corners on this graphics context.

SYNTAX   `public abstract void drawRoundRect(int x, int y, int width, int height, int arcWidth, int arcHeight)`

DESCRIPTION   This method paints a 1-pixel-thick rounded-rectangular outline in the foreground color within the rectangle defined by x, y, width, and height. If either width or height is less than 0, the method call is ignored.

arcWidth and arcHeight specify the shape and size of the arc to use for each corner. Logically, the arcs are formed by defining a rectangle of width arc-Width and height arcHeight and calling drawOval( ) using this rectangle. The rectangle is then sliced into four equal-sized quadrants. Each quadrant yields an arc for one of the rectangle's corners. If either arcWidth or arcHeight is 0, the painted rectangle will not have rounded corners. If either arcWidth or arcHeight is less than 0, both arcWidth and arcHeight are set to 0.

PARAMETERS

arcHeight	The height, in pixels, of the ellipse used to generate the rounded corners.
arcWidth	The width, in pixels, of the ellipse used to generate the rounded corners.
height	The height of the rectangular area in pixels.
width	The width of the rectangular area in pixels.
x	The *x*-coordinate in pixels.
y	The *y*-coordinate in pixels.

SEE ALSO   fillRoundRect( ).

EXAMPLE   This example implements a button with rounded corners. If the button is clicked, the outline and text change color. See Figure 169.

FIGURE 169:
Graphics.drawRoundRect( ).

```
import java.awt.*;
import java.awt.event.*;

class Main extends Frame {
    Main() {
        super("drawRoundRect Example");
        add(new MainCanvas(), BorderLayout.CENTER);
        setSize(150, 80);
        show();
    }

    static public void main(String[] args) {
        new Main();
    }
}

class MainCanvas extends Canvas {
    String label = "Round Button";
    boolean down;

    MainCanvas () {
        addMouseListener(new MouseEventHandler());
    }

    class MouseEventHandler extends MouseAdapter {
        public void mousePressed(MouseEvent evt) {
            down = true;
            repaint();
        }
```

711

```
                public void mouseReleased(MouseEvent evt) {
                    down = false;
                    repaint();
                }
            }

        public void paint(Graphics g) {
            int w = getSize().width;
            int h = getSize().height;
            FontMetrics fm = g.getFontMetrics();

            if (down) {
                g.setColor(Color.red);
            } else {
                g.setColor(Color.black);
            }
            g.drawRoundRect(0, 0, w-1, h-1, 20, 20);
            g.drawString(label, (w-fm.stringWidth(label))/2,
                (h-fm.getHeight())/2+fm.getAscent());
        }
    }
```

drawString()

PURPOSE   Paints a string on this graphics context.

SYNTAX   `public abstract void drawString(String string, int x, int y)`

DESCRIPTION   This method paints the string at position x, y using the current font and fore-ground color. Only the characters of the string are painted; the background of the characters is not. The color of the characters is determined by this graphics context's foreground color.

The position x, y specifies the baseline of the string (not the northwest corner of the string, as do most other methods). To paint the string such that the north-west corner of the string is at a point p, add the font ascent to p.y. For example:

```
Font fm = getFontMetrics();
// get metrics of current font
drawString(string, p.x, p.y+fm.getAscent();
```

PARAMETERS

  string   The non-null string to be painted.

  x   The *x*-coordinate of the baseline in pixels.

  y   The *y*-coordinate of the baseline in pixels.

SEE ALSO   `Font.getAscent()`, `drawBytes()`, `drawChars()`.

EXAMPLE

This example defines a canvas that paints a line of text on top of a colored background. It also creates a choice component to let you adjust the size of the font. See Figure 170.

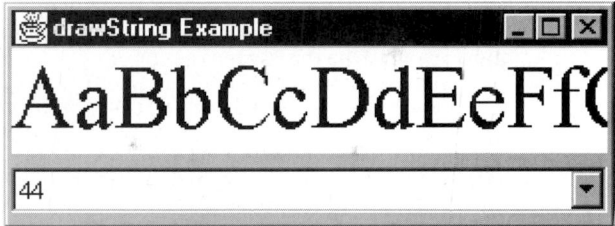

FIGURE 170: `Graphics.drawString()`.

A
B
C
D
E
F
G
H
I
J
K
L
M
N
O
P
Q
R
S
T
U
V
W
X
Y
Z

```java
import java.awt.*;
import java.awt.event.*;

class Main extends Frame implements ItemListener {
    MainCanvas cv = new MainCanvas();
    Choice choice = new Choice();

    Main() {
        super("drawString Example");

        for (int i=4; i<60; i += 4) {
            choice.addItem(""+i);
        }
        choice.select(0);
        choice.addItemListener(this);
        cv.setFontSize(4);
        cv.setSize(300, 100);
        add(cv, BorderLayout.CENTER);
        add(choice, BorderLayout.SOUTH);
        pack();
        show();
    }

    public void itemStateChanged(ItemEvent evt) {
        String what = (String)(evt.getItem());
        cv.setFontSize(Integer.parseInt(what));
    }

    static public void main(String[] args) {
        new Main();
    }
}

class MainCanvas extends Canvas {
    void setFontSize(int size) {
        Font f = getFont();

        if (f == null) {
            f = new Font("Serif", Font.PLAIN, size);
        } else {
            f = new Font(getFont().getName(), getFont().getStyle(), size);
        }
        setFont(f);
        repaint();
```

```
            }

    public void paint(Graphics g) {
        String s = "AaBbCcDdEeFfGgHhIiJjKkLlMmNnOoPpQqRrSsTtUuVvWwXxYyZz";
        FontMetrics fontM = g.getFontMetrics();

        g.setColor(Color.white);
        g.fillRect(0, 0, fontM.stringWidth(s), fontM.getHeight());
        g.setColor(Color.black);
        g.drawString(s, 0, fontM.getAscent());
    }
}
```

fill3DRect()

PURPOSE Paints a rectangle that has a 3D outline on this graphics context.

SYNTAX
```
public void fill3DRect(int x, int y, int width, int height,
    boolean raised)
```

DESCRIPTION This method paints a rectangle defined by x, y, width, and height and a 3D outline *around* this rectangle. The left and top edges of the outline are within the specified rectangle, but the right and bottom edges are just outside the defined rectangle. Hence, this method actually draws width+1 horizontal lines and height+1 vertical lines. Note that it will paint a single pixel if width and height are both 0. Use fill3DRect(x, y, width-1, height-1) to paint the 3D outline inside the specified rectangle. If either width or height is less than 0, the method call is ignored.

If raised is true, the 3D effect is done by lightening the left and top edges and darkening the right and bottom edges. If raised is false, the left and top edges are darker and the right and bottom edges are lighter. The lighter and darker color shades are generated by the Color.brigher() and Color.darker() methods, respectively.

PARAMETERS
height The height of the rectangular area in pixels.
raised Specifies whether the 3D effect should appear raised or lowered.
width The width of the rectangular area in pixels.
x The *x*-coordinate in pixels.
y The *y*-coordinate in pixels.

SEE ALSO Color.brighter(), Color.darker(), draw3DRect().

EXAMPLE   This example paints a 3D border just within
               the frame's paintable area. See Figure 171.
               The 3D border is thicker than 1 pixel. Click-
               ing toggles the 3D border between a raised
               border and a lowered border.

FIGURE 171:
Graphics.fill3DRect().

```java
import java.awt.*;
import java.awt.event.*;

class Main extends Frame {
    boolean raised = true;

    Main() {
        super("fill3DRect Example");

        addMouseListener(new MouseEventHandler());

        setSize(200, 200);
        show();
    }

    public void paint(Graphics g) {
        Insets insets = this.getInsets();
        int x = insets.left, y = insets.top;
        int w = getSize().width-insets.left-insets.right;
        int h = getSize().height-insets.top-insets.bottom;

        w -= 1;    // draw inside the rectangle.
        h -= 1;    // draw inside the rectangle.
        g.setColor(getBackground());
        g.fill3DRect(x++, y++, w, h, raised);
    }

    class MouseEventHandler extends MouseAdapter {
        public void mousePressed(MouseEvent evt) {
            raised = !raised;
            repaint();
        }
    }

    static public void main(String[] args) {
        new Main();
    }
}
```

fillArc()

PURPOSE   Paints a filled elliptical arc inside a rectangle on this graphics context.

SYNTAX   ```java
public abstract void fillArc(int x, int y, int width, int height,
        int startAngle, int arcAngle)
```

715
```

A
B
C
D
E
F
G
H
I
J
K
L
M
N
O
P
Q
R
S
T
U
V
W
X
Y
Z

DESCRIPTION   This method paints a filled elliptical arc in the foreground color within the rectangle defined by x, y, width, and height. If either width or height is less than 0, the method call is ignored.

Logically, you form the arc first by using the drawOval() method to paint an oval inside the rectangle. Next, define a horizontal line that originates from the oval's center and extends to the containing rectangle's right edge. Then anchor the line at the oval's center and rotate the line startAngle degrees from its starting position. If startAngle is positive, rotate counterclockwise; if startAngle is negative, rotate clockwise. The intersection of this line and the oval's outline is the starting point for the arc.

Next, continue rotating the line arcAngle degrees. Again, if arcAngle is positive, rotate counterclockwise; otherwise, rotate clockwise. All of the points that intersect this line and the oval's outline during the rotation are included in the arc.

PARAMETERS

arcAngle   The angle in degrees (360 degrees in a circle) that specifies the end of the arc. arcAngle is relative to startAngle.

height   The height of the rectangular area in pixels.

startAngle   The angle in degrees (360 degrees in a circle) that specifies the start of the arc.

width   The width of the rectangular area in pixels.

x   The *x*-coordinate in pixels.

y   The *y*-coordinate in pixels.

SEE ALSO   drawArc().

EXAMPLE   This example draws a 270-degree arc starting at 0 degrees. Four labels are used to show the startAngle positions. See Figure 172.

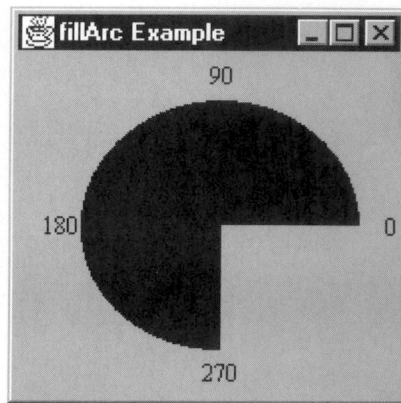

FIGURE 172: Graphics.fillArc().

```
import java.awt.*;

class Main extends Frame {
    Main() {
        super("fillArc Example");
        add(new MainCanvas(), BorderLayout.CENTER);
        add(new Label("90", Label.CENTER), BorderLayout.NORTH);
        add(new Label("270", Label.CENTER), BorderLayout.SOUTH);
        add(new Label("0"), BorderLayout.EAST);
        add(new Label("180"), BorderLayout.WEST);
        setSize(200, 200);
        show();
    }
```

```
        static public void main(String[] args) {
            new Main();
        }
    }

    class MainCanvas extends Component {
        public void paint(Graphics g) {
            g.fillArc(0, 0, getSize().width, getSize().height, 0, 270);
        }
    }
```

fillOval()

PURPOSE	Paints an oval area on this graphics context.
SYNTAX	`public abstract void fillOval(int x, int y, int width, int height)`
DESCRIPTION	This method paints an oval area on this graphics context. The oval area is defined to be the largest oval that fits into the rectangle defined by `x`, `y`, `width`, and `height`. It is filled with the foreground color. If either `width` or `height` is less than or equal to 0, the method call is ignored.

PARAMETERS

`height`	The height of the rectangular area in pixels.
`width`	The width of the rectangular area in pixels.
`x`	The *x*-coordinate in pixels.
`y`	The *y*-coordinate in pixels.
SEE ALSO	`drawOval()`.

EXAMPLE   This example creates and initializes an off-screen image with a circle-shaped pattern. See Figure 173. The image is then used to "texture" the frame's paintable area. For demonstration purposes, the image is scaled to half its size when painted.

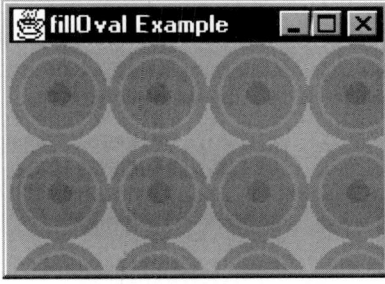

FIGURE 173: Graphics.fillOval().

```
import java.awt.*;

class Main extends Frame {
    Main() {
        super("fillOval Example");
        setSize(400, 200);
        show();
    }

    public void paint(Graphics g) {
```

A
B
C
D
E
F
G
H
I
J
K
L
M
N
O
P
Q
R
S
T
U
V
W
X
Y
Z

```
                    int iSize = 50;
                    Insets insets = this.getInsets();
                    int startx = insets.left, starty = insets.top;
                    int w = getSize().width-insets.left-insets.right;
                    int h = getSize().height-insets.top-insets.bottom;
                    Image image = createImage(iSize);

                    for (int y=0; y<h; y += iSize) {
                        for (int x=0; x<w; x += iSize) {
                            g.drawImage(image, startx+x, starty+y, iSize, iSize, null);
                        }
                    }
                }

            Image createImage(int size) {
                    Image im = createImage(size, size);
                    Graphics g = im.getGraphics();
                    Rectangle r = new Rectangle(size, size);

                    g.setColor(getBackground());
                    g.fillRect(0, 0, size, size);
                    while (!r.isEmpty()) {
                        int c = r.x * 2 * 63 / size;
                        g.setColor(new Color(255-c, 150, c+150));
                        g.fillOval(r.x, r.y, r.width, r.height);
                        r.grow(-1, -1);
                    }
                    return im;
                }

            static public void main(String[] args) {
                    new Main();
                }
            }
```

fillPolygon()

PURPOSE   Paints a closed polygon on this graphics context.

SYNTAX   `public void fillPolygon(Polygon p)`
               `public abstract void fillPolygon(int[] xPoints, int[] yPoints, int`
               `    nPoints)`

DESCRIPTION   A *polygon* is a collection of lines connecting a series of points. The polygon is
               closed. This means a line is automatically drawn between the first and last
               points. This method paints a polygon in the foreground color using the speci-
               fied set of points. The points are either specified by the polygon polygon or
               by two arrays xPoints and yPoints. In the latter form, xPoint[i] and
               yPoints[i] together specify a point in the polygon. The series of points from
               index 0 to nPoints-1 specify the ordered list of points in the polygon.

If the number of points is fewer than 3, the method call is ignored. If parts of the polygon overlap, the even-odd fill rule (otherwise known as an alternating rule) is applied.

PARAMETERS

nPoints   The number of points in xPoints and yPoints.

polygon   The non-null polygon to paint.

xPoints   The non-null array of *x*-coordinates (in pixels) in the polygon.

yPoints   The non-null array of *y*-coordinates (in pixels) in the polygon.

SEE ALSO   drawPolygon(), Polygon.

EXAMPLE   This example paints a filled polygon. See Figure 174. When the mouse is clicked or dragged, a new point is added to the polygon. Double-clicking clears the polygon.

FIGURE 174:
Graphics.fillPolygon().

```
import java.awt.*;
import java.awt.event.*;

class Main extends Frame {
    Polygon polygon = new Polygon();

    Main() {
        super("fillPolygon Example");

        addMouseListener(new MouseEventHandler());

        setSize(200, 200);
        show();
    }

    public void paint(Graphics g) {
        g.fillPolygon(polygon);
    }

    class MouseEventHandler extends MouseAdapter {
        public void mousePressed(MouseEvent evt) {
            Insets insets = getInsets();
            int x = insets.left, y = insets.top;

            if (evt.getClickCount() > 1) {    // double-click
                polygon = new Polygon();
            }
            polygon.addPoint(x + evt.getX(), y + evt.getY());
            repaint();
        }
    }

    static public void main(String[] args) {
        new Main();
    }
}
```

719

fillRect( )

PURPOSE	Paints a rectangular area on this graphics context.
SYNTAX	`public abstract void fillRect(int x, int y, int width, int height)`
DESCRIPTION	This method paints the area defined by x, y, width, and height with the foreground color. If either width or height is less than or equal to 0, the method call is ignored.

PARAMETERS

height	The height of the rectangular area in pixels.
width	The width of the rectangular area in pixels.
x	The *x*-coordinate in pixels.
y	The *y*-coordinate in pixels.

SEE ALSO `clearRect()`, `drawRect()`.

EXAMPLE This example creates a frame with two choices and a drawing area. See Figure 175. The choices specify the color and shape of a figure. Clicking anywhere in the drawing area draws the specified figure at the mouse coordinates. `fillRect()` is used to draw the rectangle and squares.

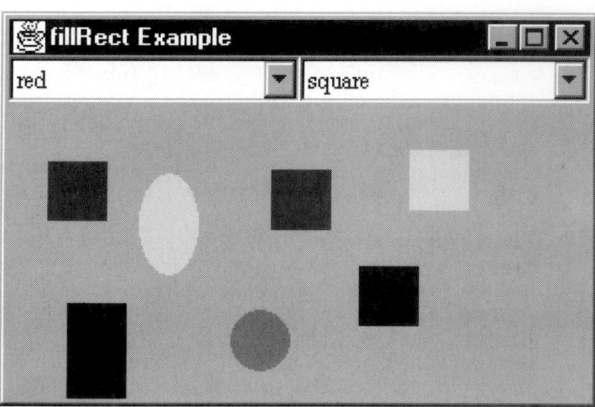

FIGURE 175: `Graphics.fillRect()`.

```java
import java.awt.*;
import java.awt.event.*;

class Main extends Frame {
    String[] figureNames = {"circle", "oval", "square", "rectangle"};
    String[] colorNames = {"red", "green", "blue", "yellow"};
    Color[] colorValues = {Color.red, Color.green,
                           Color.blue, Color.yellow};
    Choice chFigure = new Choice();
    Choice chColor = new Choice();
    int curX, curY;

    Main() {
        super("fillRect Example");
        Panel p = new Panel(new GridLayout(1, 0));
```

```
        for (int i=0; i<figureNames.length; i++) {
            chFigure.addItem(figureNames[i]);
        }
        for (int i=0; i<colorNames.length; i++) {
            chColor.addItem(colorNames[i]);
        }
        p.add(chColor);
        p.add(chFigure);
        add(p, BorderLayout.NORTH);

        addMouseListener(new MouseEventListener());

        setSize(300, 300);
        show();
    }

    public void update(Graphics g) {
        g.setColor(colorValues[chColor.getSelectedIndex()]);
        switch (chFigure.getSelectedIndex()) {
        case 0: // circle
            g.fillOval(curX, curY, 30, 30);
            break;
        case 1: // oval
            g.fillOval(curX, curY, 30, 50);
            break;
        case 2: // square
            g.fillRect(curX, curY, 30, 30);
            break;
        case 3: // rectangle
            g.fillRect(curX, curY, 30, 50);
            break;
        }
    }

    class MouseEventListener extends MouseAdapter {
        public void mousePressed(MouseEvent evt) {
            curX = evt.getX();
            curY = evt.getY();
            repaint();
        }
    }

    static public void main(String[] args) {
        new Main();
    }
}
```

A
B
C
D
E
F
G
H
I
J
K
L
M
N
O
P
Q
R
S
T
U
V
W
X
Y
Z

fillRoundRect()

PURPOSE   Paints a rectangle with rounded corners on this graphics context.

SYNTAX   ```
            public abstract void fillRoundRect(int x, int y, int width, int
                height, int arcWidth, int arcHeight)
            ```
            ```

A
B
C
D
E
F
G
H
I
J
K
L
M
N
O
P
Q
R
S
T
U
V
W
X
Y
Z

DESCRIPTION   This method paints a rounded rectangle in the foreground color within the rect-angle defined by x, y, width, and height. If either width or height is less than 0, the method call is ignored.

arcWidth and arcHeight specify the shape and size of the arc to use for each corner. Logically, you form the arc by defining a rectangle of width arcWidth and height arcHeight and calling drawOval() using this rectangle. Then slice the rectangle into four equal-sized quadrants. Each quadrant yields an arc for one of the rectangle's corners. If either arcWidth or arcHeight is 0, the painted rectangle will not have rounded corners. If either arcWidth or arcHeight is less than 0, both are set to 0.

PARAMETERS
arcHeight   The height, in pixels, of the ellipse used to generate the rounded corners.
arcWidth   The width, in pixels, of the ellipse used to generate the rounded corners.
height   The height of the rectangular area in pixels.
width   The width of the rectangular area in pixels.
x   The *x*-coordinate in pixels.
y   The *y*-coordinate in pixels.

SEE ALSO   drawRoundRect().

EXAMPLE   This example implements a simple framework for measuring the cost of operations in the Graphics class. See Figure 176. You select the graphics oper-ation to time by using the choice compo-nent at the bottom of the window. Clicking the main display area starts a timer thread and calls the repaint() method. This method causes the paint() method to be called. paint() enters a tight loop, executing the selected operation. The timer thread waits for 5 sec and then signals the

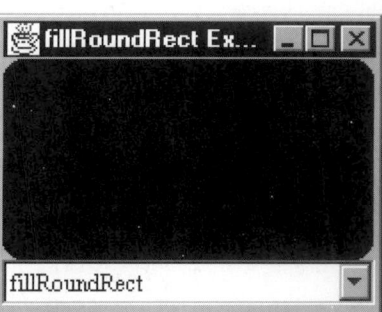

FIGURE 176:
Graphics.fillRoundRect().

paint() method to exit its tight loop. The results are then printed to standard output.

```
import java.awt.*;
import java.awt.event.*;

class Main extends Frame implements ItemListener {
    MainCanvas cv = new MainCanvas();
    Choice c = new Choice();
    Main() {
        super("fillRoundRect Example");
        add(cv, BorderLayout.CENTER);
```

```
        c.addItem("create/dispose");
        c.addItem("drawRect");
        c.addItem("drawRoundRect");
        c.addItem("fillRect");
        c.addItem("fillRoundRect");

        add(c, BorderLayout.SOUTH);
        c.addItemListener(this);

        setSize(200, 200);
        show();
    }

    public void itemStateChanged(ItemEvent evt) {
        cv.operation = c.getSelectedIndex();
    }

    static public void main(String[] args) {
        new Main();
    }
}

class MainCanvas extends Component implements Runnable {
    int operation;
    Thread timerThread;

    MainCanvas() {
        addMouseListener(new MouseEventHandler());
    }

    public void paint(Graphics g) {
        int w = getSize().width-1;
        int h = getSize().height-1;
        if (timerThread != null) {
            int count = 0;
            long startTime = System.currentTimeMillis();

            switch (operation) {
              case 0:
                while (timerThread != null) {
                    Graphics g2 = g.create();
                    g2.dispose();
                    count++;
                }
              case 1:
                while (timerThread != null) {
                    g.drawRect(0, 0, w, h);
                    count++;
                }
              case 2:
                while (timerThread != null) {
                    g.drawRoundRect(0, 0, w, h, 20, 20);
                    count++;
                }
              case 3:
                while (timerThread != null) {
                    g.fillRect(0, 0, w, h);
                    count++;
                }
```

```
                        case 4:
                          while (timerThread != null) {
                              g.fillRoundRect(0, 0, w, h, 20, 20);
                              count++;
                          }
                        }
                        System.out.print((double)count*1000.0
                            / (double)(System.currentTimeMillis()-startTime));
                        System.out.println(" paints/second");
                    }
                }

                public void run() {
                    try {
                        Thread.sleep(5000);
                    } catch (InterruptedException e) {
                    }
                    timerThread = null;
                }

                class MouseEventHandler extends MouseAdapter {
                    public void mousePressed(MouseEvent evt) {
                        if (timerThread == null) {
                            timerThread = new Thread(MainCanvas.this);
                            timerThread.start();
                            repaint();
                        }
                    }
                }
            }
        }
```

finalize()

PURPOSE	Releases this graphics context's system resources.
SYNTAX	`public void finalize()`
DESCRIPTION	This method simply calls the `dispose()` method. After this call, this graphics context can no longer be used. This method is normally called by the garbage collector after this graphics context has been reclaimed.
OVERRIDES	`java.lang.Object.finalize()`.
SEE ALSO	`dispose()`.
EXAMPLE	See `java.lang.Object.finalize()`.

getClip()

PURPOSE	Retrieves this graphics context's clipping area.
SYNTAX	`public abstract Shape getClip()`

| DESCRIPTION | The clipping area defines a set of pixels that can be affected by painting operations; any painting done outside the clipping area is ignored. As of Java 1.1.2, the clipping area is restricted to a rectangle. In future releases, the clipping area will be able to be any shape. |

RETURNS   A possibly `null` `Shape` object containing the clipping area.

SEE ALSO   `clipRect()`, `getClipBounds()`, `setClip()`, `Shape`.

EXAMPLE   See the `Window` class example.

A
B
C
D
E
F
G
H
I
J
K
L
M
N
O
P
Q
R
S
T
U
V
W
X
Y
Z

getClipBounds( )

PURPOSE   Retrieves the clipping area's bounds of this graphics context.

SYNTAX   `public abstract Rectangle getClipBounds()`

DESCRIPTION This method returns a rectangle that will contain the clipping area. The return result may be `null`, in which case the clipping area includes the entire visible area of the drawing surface.

RETURNS   A new, possibly `null` `Rectangle` object containing the bounds of the clipping area.

SEE ALSO   `clipRect()`, `getClip()`, `setClip()`.

EXAMPLE   See the `Window` class example.

getClipRect( )   *DEPRECATED*

PURPOSE   Replaced by `getClipBounds()`.

SYNTAX   `public abstract Rectangle getClipRect()`

RETURNS   A new `Rectangle` object containing the clipping area. The return value may be `null`.

DEPRECATION Replace the usage of this deprecated method, as in
```
Rectangle rect = graphics.getClipRect();
```
with
```
Rectangle rect = graphics.getClipBounds();
```

getColor( )

PURPOSE   Retrieves this graphics context's foreground color.

SYNTAX   `public abstract Color getColor()`

RETURNS   The non-null foreground color.

SEE ALSO   `Color, setColor()`.

EXAMPLE   This example uses `getColor()` to get the current foreground color of the graphics context and draws some dots of a different color than the current color. See Figure 177.

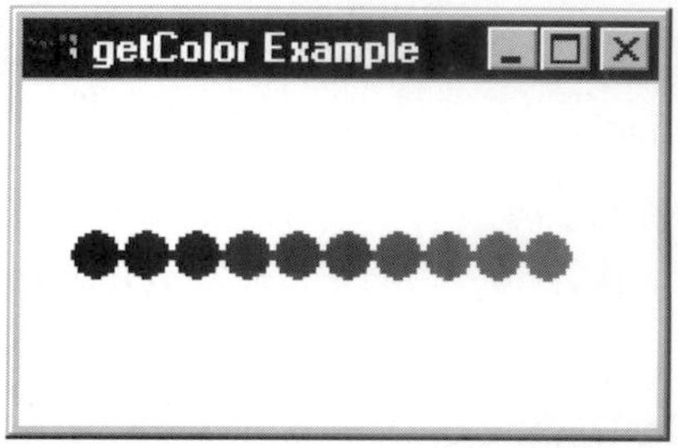

FIGURE 177: `Graphics.getColor()`.

```java
import java.awt.*;

class Main extends Frame {
    int dotSize = 15;

    Main() {
        super("getColor Example");
        setSize(150, 150);
        show();
    }

    public void paint(Graphics g) {
        Insets insets = this.getInsets();
        int w = getSize().width-insets.left-insets.right;
        int h = getSize().height-insets.top-insets.bottom;

        Color orig = g.getColor();
        int red = orig.getRed(), blue = orig.getBlue(), green = orig.getGreen();
        int y = 50, x = dotSize;
        for (int i=0; i<10; i++) {
            g.setColor(new Color(red+=10, green+=10, blue+=10));
            g.fillOval(insets.left+x-x%dotSize, insets.top+y-y%dotSize,
                        dotSize, dotSize);
            x += dotSize;
        }
    }

    static public void main(String[] args) {
        new Main();
    }
}
```

getFont( )

PURPOSE   Retrieves this graphics context's font.

SYNTAX   `public abstract Font getFont()`

RETURNS   The current non-null font.

SEE ALSO   `Font, setFont()`.

EXAMPLE

This example displays the attributes of the frame's default font. See Figure 178.

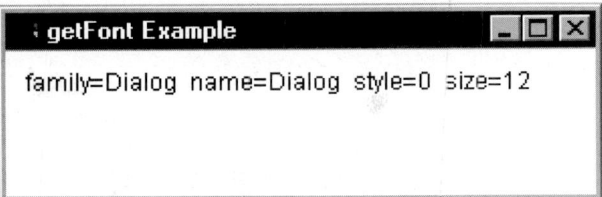

FIGURE 178: Graphics.getFont().

```
import java.awt.*;

class Main extends Frame {
    Main() {
        super("getFont Example");
        setSize(300, 100);
        show();
    }

    public void paint(Graphics g) {
        Insets insets = getInsets();
        Font f = g.getFont();
        FontMetrics fm = g.getFontMetrics(f);

        g.drawString("family="+f.getFamily()+"  name="+f.getName()
            +"  style="+f.getStyle()+"  size="+f.getSize(),
            insets.left+10, insets.top+20);
    }

    public static void main(String[] args) {
        new Main();
    }
}
```

getFontMetrics()

PURPOSE   Retrieves the font metrics for a font.

SYNTAX
```
public FontMetrics getFontMetrics()
public abstract FontMetrics getFontMetrics(Font font)
```

DESCRIPTION   The two forms of this method retrieve the font metrics for the font font. If font is not specified, it defaults to this graphics context's current font.

PARAMETERS
font   The non-null font.

RETURNS   The non-null font metrics for font.

SEE ALSO   Font, FontMetrics, getFont().

EXAMPLE   See the FontMetrics class example.

A
B
C
D
E
F

H
I
J
K
L
M
N
O
P
Q
R
S
T
U
V
W
X
Y
Z

Graphics( )

PURPOSE   Constructs a new graphics context.

SYNTAX   `protected Graphics()`

DESCRIPTION   The background and foreground color and font are inherited from the drawing
              surface. The initial paint mode is normal.

              A graphics context cannot be directly created from this constructor (note that
              the constructor is protected). The graphics context is supplied by classes that
              provide a drawing surface; for example, `Component.getGraphics()` and
              `Image.getGraphics()`.

SEE ALSO   `create()`.

EXAMPLE   See `Component.getGraphics()`, `Image.getGraphics()`.

setClip( )

PURPOSE   Sets this graphics context's clipping area.

SYNTAX   `public abstract void setClip(int x, int y, int width, int height)`
              `public abstract void setClip(Shape clipShape)`

DESCRIPTION   This method sets the new clipping area
              to be the rectangle defined by `x`, `y`,
              `width`, and `height` or the shape `clip-`
              `Shape`. See the class description for
              details on the clipping area.

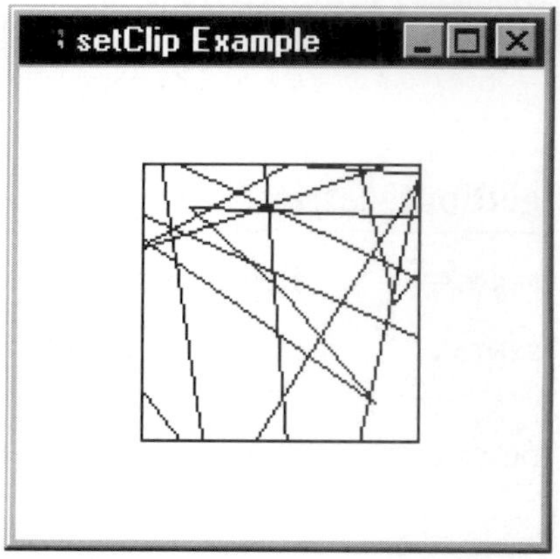

PARAMETERS

clipShape   The `Shape` object to use for the clip-
              ping area. Only instances of `Rectan-`
              `gle` are currently supported.

height   The height of the rectangle in pixels.
width   The width of the rectangle in pixels.
x   The *x*-coordinate in pixels.
y   The *y*-coordinate in pixels.

FIGURE 179:   Rotating Polygon.

SEE ALSO   `getClip()`, `getClipBounds()`,
              `setClip()`.

EXAMPLE   This example creates a random polygon and continuously rotates it. You can
              observe part of the rotating polygon by dragging a viewport around the screen.
              The viewport is implement by means of a clipping area. Just before the poly-
              gon is painted on the graphics context, a clipping area is set to the exact size of

the viewport. This causes only the part of the polygon inside the viewport to be
seen. See Figure 179.

```java
import java.awt.*;
import java.awt.event.*;

class Main extends Frame {
    // Returns a random number in the range [0 .. r)
    static int random(int r) {
        return (int)Math.floor(Math.random()*r);
    }

    public static void main(String[] args) {
        Frame f = new Frame("setClip Example");
        Polygon polygon = new Polygon();

        // Create some random points.  The points are no
        // more than 100 pixels from the origin.
        for (int i=0; i<25; i++) {
            polygon.addPoint(random(200)-100, random(200)-100);
        }

        // Layout and show components.
        f.add(new PolygonRotator(polygon), BorderLayout.CENTER);
        f.setSize(200, 200);
        f.show();
    }
}

class PolygonRotator extends Canvas implements Runnable {
    Polygon origPoly;
    Polygon curPoly;
    Rectangle view = new Rectangle(0, 0, 100, 100);

    PolygonRotator(Polygon polygon) {
        origPoly = polygon;

        // Listen for mouse events.
        addMouseListener(new MouseEventHandler());
        addMouseMotionListener(new MouseMotionEventHandler());

        // Start the rotating thread.
        (new Thread(this)).start();
    }

    public void paint(Graphics g) {
        // Draw an outline around the view.
        g.drawRect(view.x-1, view.y-1, view.width+1, view.height+1);

        // Set the clipping area.
        g.setClip(view.x, view.y, view.width, view.height);

        // The following would have worked just as well.
        // g.clipRect(view.x, view.y, view.width, view.height);

        // Now paint the polygon.
        if (curPoly != null) {
            // Place the polygon at the center of the canvas.
            g.translate(size().width/2, size().height/2);
```

```
                g.drawPolygon(curPoly);
            }
        }

        // Returns a rotated copy of p at the angle a.
        Polygon rotate(Polygon p, double a) {
            Polygon q = new Polygon();
            q.xpoints = new int[p.npoints];
            q.ypoints = new int[p.npoints];
            q.npoints = p.npoints;

            for (int i=0; i<p.npoints; i++) {
                q.xpoints[i] =
                    (int)(p.xpoints[i]*Math.cos(a)-p.ypoints[i]*Math.sin(a));
                q.ypoints[i] =
                    (int)(p.xpoints[i]*Math.sin(a)+p.ypoints[i]*Math.cos(a));
            }
            return q;
        }

        // If non-null, location of the down click.
        Point mouseDown;
        class MouseEventHandler extends MouseAdapter {
            public void mousePressed(MouseEvent evt) {
                if (view.inside(evt.getX(), evt.getY())) {
                    // Record the down click on if inside view.
                    mouseDown = evt.getPoint();
                    mouseDown.translate(-view.x, -view.y);
                }
            }
            public void mouseReleased(MouseEvent evt) {
                mouseDown = null;
            }
        }

        class MouseMotionEventHandler extends MouseMotionAdapter {
            public void mouseDragged(MouseEvent evt) {
                if (mouseDown != null) {
                    // Move the view.
                    view.move(evt.getX()-mouseDown.x, evt.getY()-mouseDown.y);
                    repaint();
                }
            }
        }

        public void run() {
            double angle = 0.0;

            try {
                while (true) {
                    // Create a rotated version of the original polygon.
                    curPoly = rotate(origPoly, angle);

                    // Change the angle at .1 radian every tick.
                    angle += .1;
                    repaint();
                    Thread.sleep(100);
                }
            } catch (Exception e) {
                e.printStackTrace();
```

```
        }
      }
    }
```

setColor()

PURPOSE   Sets this graphics context's foreground color.

SYNTAX   `public abstract void setColor(Color color)`

DESCRIPTION   This method sets this graphics context's foreground color to `color`.

PARAMETERS
color   The non-`null` new foreground `color`.

SEE ALSO   `Color`, `getColor()`.

EXAMPLE   This example is a set of random colored dots.
              A thread is created to continually change the
              colors of the dots. See Figure 180.

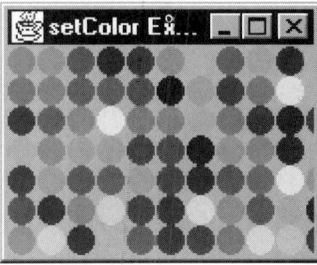

FIGURE 180:
Graphics.setColor().

```
import java.awt.*;

class Main extends Frame implements Runnable {
    int dotSize = 15;

    Main() {
        super("setColor Example");
        setSize(150, 150);
        show();
        (new Thread(this)).start();
    }

    // Returns an integer in the range [0..r-1].
    int random(int r) {
        return (int)(Math.floor(Math.random()*r));
    }

    public void update(Graphics g) {
        Insets insets = this.getInsets();
        int w = getSize().width-insets.left-insets.right;
        int h = getSize().height-insets.top-insets.bottom;

        for (int i=0; i<10; i++) {
            int x = random(w), y = random(h);
            g.setColor(new Color(random(256), random(256), random(256)));
            g.fillOval(insets.left+x-x%dotSize, insets.top+y-y%dotSize,
                        dotSize, dotSize);
        }
    }

    public void run() {
        while (true) {
            try {Thread.sleep(100);} catch (Exception e) {}
            repaint();
```

```
            }
        }

        static public void main(String[] args) {
            new Main();
        }
    }
```

setFont()

PURPOSE   Sets this graphics context's font.

SYNTAX   `public abstract void setFont(Font font)`

DESCRIPTION   This method sets this graphics context's font to `font`. The font affects only the string drawing operations.

PARAMETERS
font   The non-`null` font.

SEE ALSO   `drawBytes()`, `drawChars()`, `drawString()`, `Font`, `getFont()`.

EXAMPLE   This example paints some text at different point sizes. The text is white painted on a black background. See Figure 181.

FIGURE 181: Graphics.setFont().

```
import java.awt.*;

class Main extends Frame {
    Main() {
        super("setFont Example");
        setBackground(Color.black);
        setForeground(Color.white);
        setSize(200, 200);
        show();
    }

    public void paint(Graphics g) {
    Insets insets = getInsets();
        int x = insets.left, y = insets.top;
        for (int i=8; i<8*10; i+= 8) {
            Font f = new Font("Serif", Font.PLAIN, i);
            FontMetrics fm = g.getFontMetrics(f);

            g.setFont(f);
            g.drawString(f.getName()+" at "+i+" points.",
                x, y+fm.getAscent());
            y += fm.getHeight();
        }
    }

    static public void main(String[] args) {
```

```
        new Main();
    }
}
```

setPaintMode()

PURPOSE   Sets this graphics context to normal paint mode.

SYNTAX   `public abstract void setPaintMode()`

DESCRIPTION This method sets this graphics context to normal paint mode. See the class description for details about paint modes.

SEE ALSO   `setXORMode()`.

EXAMPLE   See `setXORMode()`.

setXORMode()

PURPOSE   Sets this graphics context to xor paint mode.

SYNTAX   `public abstract void setXORMode(Color xorColor)`

DESCRIPTION This method sets this graphics context to xor paint mode using the xor color `xorColor`. See the class description for details of how xor paint mode uses the current foreground color and `xor-Color`. Pixels of colors other than those two colors will be changed in an unpredictable, but reversible, manner. If you draw the same figure twice, all pixels will be restored to their original values.

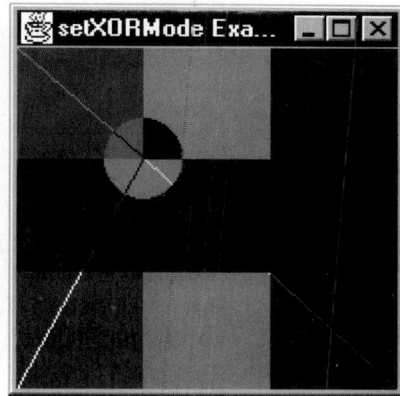

FIGURE 182: `Graphics.setXORMode()`.

PARAMETERS
  xorColor The non-`null` xor color.

SEE ALSO   `setPaintMode()`.

EXAMPLE   This example creates a four-band colored background and paints a black circle on the background in xor paint mode. See Figure 182. The circle can be moved around the background so that you can see the xor mode paint effect. Black is xor'd with green so that when the circle is on green, it appears black and when it is on black, it appears green. When the black circle is on some other color, it simply appears in some color other than black. Four lines in different colors are also painted to see the xor mode paint effect. Notice that the green line does not show up at all.

```java
import java.awt.*;
import java.awt.event.*;

class Main extends Frame {
    int curX, curY, newX, newY;

    Main() {
        super("setXORMode Example");
        setSize(200, 200);

        addMouseMotionListener(new MouseMotionEventHandler());
        show();
    }

    class MouseMotionEventHandler extends MouseMotionAdapter {
        public void mouseMoved(MouseEvent evt) {
            newX = evt.getX();
            newY = evt.getY();
            repaint();
        }
    }

    void drawLines(Graphics g, int x, int y, int w, int h) {
        g.setXORMode(Color.green);
        g.setColor(Color.red);
        g.drawLine(0, 0, x, y);
        g.setColor(Color.green);
        g.drawLine(w, 0, x, y);
        g.setColor(Color.blue);
        g.drawLine(0, h, x, y);
        g.setColor(Color.yellow);
        g.drawLine(w, h, x, y);
        g.setColor(Color.black);
        g.fillOval(x-20, y-20, 40, 40);
    }

    public void update(Graphics g) {
        Insets insets = this.getInsets();
        int w = getSize().width-insets.left-insets.right;
        int h = getSize().height-insets.top-insets.bottom;

        // Erase old image.
        drawLines(g, curX, curY, w, h);
        // Paint new one.
        drawLines(g, newX, newY, w, h);
        curX = newX;
        curY = newY;
    }

    public void paint(Graphics g) {
        Insets insets = this.getInsets();
        int startx = insets.left, starty = insets.top;
        int w = getSize().width-insets.left-insets.right;
        int h = getSize().height-insets.top-insets.bottom;

        g.setPaintMode();
```

```
        g.setColor(Color.red);
        g.fillRect(startx, starty, w/3, h);
        g.setColor(Color.green);
        g.fillRect(startx+w/3, starty, w/3, h);
        g.setColor(Color.blue);
        g.fillRect(startx+w*2/3, starty, w/3, h);
        g.setColor(Color.black);
        g.fillRect(startx, starty+h/3, w, h/3);
        drawLines(g, newX=curX=w/2, newY=curY=h/2, w, h);
    }

    static public void main(String[] args) {
        new Main();
    }
}
```

A
B
C
D
E
F
G
H

toString()

PURPOSE	Generates the string representation of this graphics context's state.
SYNTAX	`public String toString()`
DESCRIPTION	This method generates the string representation of this graphics context. The string contains this graphics context's class name and the results of calling `paramString()`.
	This method is typically used for debugging.
RETURNS	A non-`null` string representing this graphics context's state.
OVERRIDES	`java.lang.Object.toString()`.
SEE ALSO	`Component.paramString()`.
EXAMPLE	See `java.lang.Object.toString()`.

I
J
K
L
M
N
O
P
Q
R
S
T

translate()

PURPOSE	Moves this graphics context's origin.
SYNTAX	`public abstract void translate(int x, int y)`
DESCRIPTION	This method moves this graphics context's origin to x, y relative to the current origin. The coordinates of all subsequent graphics operations are interpreted relative to the new origin.
	Note that the new origin is located relative to the current one. So if you call `translate(5, 5)`, `translate(0, 0)` will not restore the origin to its original location. To do that, you need to call `translate(-5, -5)`.

U
V
W
X
Y
Z

PARAMETERS

x   The *x*-coordinate in pixels.

y   The *y*-coordinate in pixels.

EXAMPLE   This example creates a component that paints a histogram and a scroll bar to scroll the histogram. See Figure 183. The histogram is always twice as high as the available display area. The histogram is always painted in its entirety, and the scroll bar shifts the origin using the `translate()` method. You can select one of the histogram bars by clicking it. The example also demonstrates how to translate a position that is in mouse coordinates into graphics context coordinates.

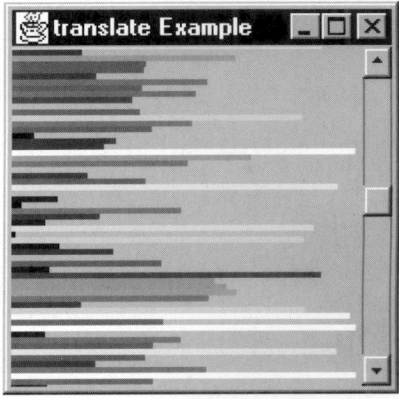

FIGURE 183:   `Graphics.translate()`.

```java
import java.awt.*;
import java.awt.event.*;

class Main extends Frame implements AdjustmentListener {
    MainCanvas cv = new MainCanvas();
    Scrollbar sb = new Scrollbar(Scrollbar.VERTICAL, 0, 40, 0, 100);

    Main() {
        super("translate Example");
        add(cv, BorderLayout.CENTER);
        add(sb, BorderLayout.EAST);

        sb.addAdjustmentListener(this);
        setSize(200, 200);
        show();
    }

    public void adjustmentValueChanged(AdjustmentEvent evt) {
    System.out.println(sb.getValue());
        cv.setOrigin(0, -cv.getSize().height * sb.getValue() / 100);
    }

    static public void main(String[] args) {
        new Main();
    }
}

class MainCanvas extends Component {
    int thick;
    double[] values = new double[100];
    int curX, curY;
    int originX, originY;

    MainCanvas() {
        for (int i=0; i<values.length; i++) {
```

A
B
C
D
E
F

H
I
J
K
L
M
N
O
P
Q
R
S
T
U
V
W
X
Y
Z

```
            values[i] = Math.random();
        }
        addMouseListener(new MouseEventHandler());
    }

    void setOrigin(int x, int y) {
        originX = x;
        originY = y;
        repaint();
    }

    public void paint(Graphics g) {
        int w = getSize().width;
        thick = getSize().height*2/values.length;

        g.translate(originX, originY);
        for (int i=0; i<values.length; i++) {
            int c = (int)(Math.floor(255 * values[i]));
            if (curY >= i * thick && curY < (i+1) * thick) {
                g.setColor(Color.red);
            } else {
                g.setColor(new Color(c, c, c));
            }
            g.fillRect(0, i * thick, (int)(w * values[i]), thick);
        }
    }

    class MouseEventHandler extends MouseAdapter {
        public void mousePressed(MouseEvent evt) {
            curX = evt.getX() - originX;
            curY = evt.getY() - originY;
            repaint();
        }
    }
}
```

A
B
C
D
E
F
G
H
I
J
K
L
M
N
O
P
Q
R
S
T
U
V
W
X
Y
Z

java.awt
GridBagConstraints

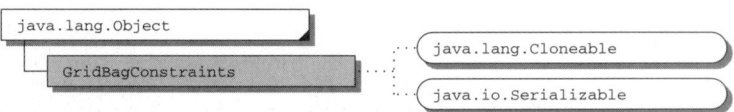

Syntax

`public class GridBagConstraints implements Cloneable, Serializable`

Description

A *gridbag* is a collection of components laid out using the gridbag layout manager (see `GridBagLayout`). Each component in the gridbag has a set of constraints that determines its size and position in the gridbag. These constraints are defined with a `GridBagConstraints` instance and are associated with a component. There are seven gridbag constraints.

Fill

The *fill* constraint determines whether to stretch a component to fill the component's display area. There are four fill types. See `fill` later in this section for an example that uses these fill types.

Anchor

If a component is not stretched to completely fill its display area, the *anchor* constraint specifies the component's position in its display area. There are nine anchor types. See `anchor` later in this section for an example that uses these anchor types.

Size

A component can span more than one column or row. The *size* constraint specifies the number of columns or rows that the component occupies.

Internal Padding

The *internal padding* constraint is used to adjust the width and height of a component after `Component.minimumSize()` or `Component.preferredSize()` is called. Separate values control the width and height. See `ipadx` later in this section for an example that uses internal padding.

Insets

The *insets* constraint for a component is applied to a component's display area. An inset has four values to control the inset at the four edges. A positive inset at an edge reduces the display area at that edge. See `insets` later in this section for an example that uses insets.

Position

A component can be positioned at a particular cell location in the gridbag. Cells in the gridbag are addressed by *x*- and *y*-coordinates.

Weights

Each component in the gridbag has a non-negative gridbag weight constraint. Together, the component weights define a weight for each column and row in the gridbag. The calculation for doing this is discussed later in this section.

The column and row weights determine how columns and rows stretch and shrink when the container is made larger or smaller and how extra space is distributed among the columns and rows. The extra space is determined by subtracting the container size from the preferred size for the gridbag. The preferred size of the gridbag is calculated by laying out all of the components in the gridbag using their preferred sizes. Here is how the extra space is distributed. First, no space is given to any row or column that has zero weight. The amount that a column (or row) gets depends on its weight in relation to the total weight for all of the columns (or rows) of the gridbag. For example, if the weight of a column c is 1 and the total weight is 10 (including c's weight), column c gets one-tenth of the total extra space.

If the total weight for all of the columns (or rows) is 0, then the extra space is distributed around the gridbag. For example, if the total weight of all of the columns is 0, the gridbag will be horizontally centered in its container.

It is important to note that if two components C and D both have weight 1, they will not necessarily be the same size. Only if C's and D's preferred sizes are identical will they be the same size. This is because only the extra space (after C's and D's preferred sizes are subtracted from the total available space) is distributed to C and D. For example, if C's preferred size is 10, D's preferred size is 20, and the extra space is 40 pixels, then C will be 30 pixels wide and D will be 40 pixels wide.

The following steps describe how column and row weights are derived from component weights:

1. Consider all of the components in a column whose grid widths are 1. The weight for that column is the maximal weight for those components.

2. Now consider all of the components whose grid widths are greater than 1. Consider them in the order that they were inserted into the container. Suppose component C spans columns $c_i.c_j$ and that the combined weight of these columns is w. If C's weight is less than w, nothing happens. If C's weight is greater than w, the extra weight is distributed among the columns. The distribution is based on the relative weight of the columns, so if one column has a weight of 1 while another has a weight of 5, the first column gets one-sixth of the extra weight. After the extra weight has been distributed, any remaining weight is given to the last column of the span. A zero weight column never gets any extra weight unless the column is the last column of the span and all of the columns in the span have zero weights. These rules also apply to each row.

If the container's dimensions are smaller than the gridbag's preferred size, the gridbag layout manager either attempts to shrink some rows or columns smaller than their preferred sizes or simply clips the components so that they appear off the container's visible area. You cannot control how the gridbag layout manager decides to fit a gridbag layout into an area smaller than the preferred size.

MEMBER SUMMARY	
Constructor	
GridBagConstraints()	Constructs a new GridBagConstraints instance.
Size Type Constant Fields	
RELATIVE	Specifies that subsequent cells in the row or column be occupied, except for the last cell.
REMAINDER	Specifies that subsequent cells in the row or column be occupied.
Fill Type Constant Fields	
BOTH	Specifies a fill in both directions.
NONE	Specifies no fill (the default).
HORIZONTAL	Specifies a horizontal-only fill.
VERTICAL	Specifies a vertical-only fill.
Anchor Type Constant Fields	
CENTER	Specifies center positioning.
EAST	Specifies east positioning.
NORTH	Specifies north positioning.
NORTHEAST	Specifies northeast positioning.
NORTHWEST	Specifies northwest positioning.
SOUTH	Specifies south positioning.
SOUTHEAST	Specifies southeast positioning.
SOUTHWEST	Specifies southwest positioning.
WEST	Specifies west positioning.
Fields	
anchor	Holds the component's anchor constraint.
fill	Holds the component's fill constraint.
gridheight	Holds the component's height in cells.
gridwidth	Holds the component's width in cells.
gridx	Holds the *x*-coordinate cell location for the component.
gridy	Holds the *y*-coordinate cell location for the component.
insets	Holds the insets constraints for the component.
ipadx	Holds the internal padding for the component's width.
ipady	Holds the internal padding for the component's height.
weightx	Holds the component's column weight.
weighty	Holds the component's row weight.

MEMBER SUMMARY

Copy Method
clone()   Creates a copy of the gridbag constraints.

See Also

java.io.Serializable.

Example

See GridBagLayout.

---

anchor

PURPOSE   Holds the component's anchor constraint.

SYNTAX   public int anchor

DESCRIPTION   There are nine anchor types, one for
each edge and each corner of a display
area and one for the center of the display area: CENTER, EAST, NORTH,
NORTHEAST, NORTHWEST, SOUTH,
SOUTHEAST, SOUTHWEST, and WEST.

EXAMPLE   This example creates a 3-×-3 gridbag
with nine buttons. See Figure 184. Each
button represents an anchor type. All
but the center button have a fill constraint of BOTH. Clicking a button modifies the center button's anchor
constraint.

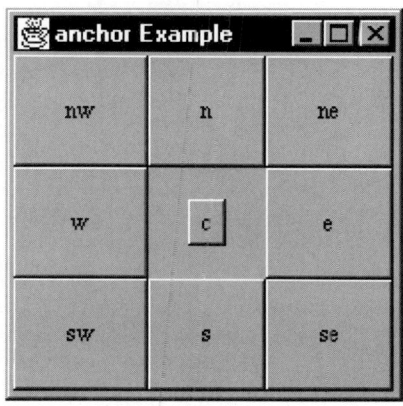

FIGURE 184:   Gridbag Anchor Types.

```
import java.awt.*;
import java.awt.event.*;

public class Main extends Frame implements ActionListener {
    Component centerButton;
    GridBagLayout gbl = new GridBagLayout();

    Main() {
        super("anchor Example");
        GridBagConstraints c = new GridBagConstraints();

        setLayout(gbl);
```

```
                      c.fill = GridBagConstraints.BOTH;
                      c.weightx = 1;
                      c.weighty = 1;

                      makeButton(this, "nw", c, 0, 0);
A                     makeButton(this, "n", c, 1, 0);
                      makeButton(this, "ne", c, 2, 0);
B                     makeButton(this, "w", c, 0, 1);
                      makeButton(this, "e", c, 2, 1);
C                     makeButton(this, "sw", c, 0, 2);
                      makeButton(this, "s", c, 1, 2);
D                     makeButton(this, "se", c, 2, 2);

E                     //  Make center button.
                      c.fill = GridBagConstraints.NONE;
F                     centerButton = makeButton(this, "c", c, 1, 1);

G                     setSize(200, 200);
                      show();
                  }

H
                  Component makeButton(Container cont, String label,
I                         GridBagConstraints c, int x, int y) {
                      GridBagLayout gbl = (GridBagLayout)cont.getLayout();
J                     Button b = new Button(label);

K                     cont.add(b);
                      c.gridx = x;
L                     c.gridy = y;
                      gbl.setConstraints(b, c);
M                     b.addActionListener(this);
                      return b;
N                  }

O                 public void actionPerformed(ActionEvent evt) {
                      String arg = evt.getActionCommand();
P                     GridBagConstraints c = gbl.getConstraints(centerButton);

Q                     if ("n".equals(arg)) {
                          c.anchor = GridBagConstraints.NORTH;
R                     } else if ("s".equals(arg)) {
                          c.anchor = GridBagConstraints.SOUTH;
S                     } else if ("e".equals(arg)) {
                          c.anchor = GridBagConstraints.EAST;
T                     } else if ("w".equals(arg)) {
                          c.anchor = GridBagConstraints.WEST;
U                     } else if ("nw".equals(arg)) {
                          c.anchor = GridBagConstraints.NORTHWEST;
V                     } else if ("ne".equals(arg)) {
                          c.anchor = GridBagConstraints.NORTHEAST;
W                     } else if ("sw".equals(arg)) {
                          c.anchor = GridBagConstraints.SOUTHWEST;
X                     } else if ("se".equals(arg)) {
                          c.anchor = GridBagConstraints.SOUTHEAST;
Y                     } else if ("c".equals(arg)) {
                          c.anchor = GridBagConstraints.CENTER;
Z                     }
                      gbl.setConstraints(centerButton, c);
                      invalidate();
                      validate();
```

```
        }

    static public void main(String[] args) {
        new Main();
    }
}
```

BOTH

PURPOSE	Fill type that specifies a fill in both directions.
SYNTAX	`public static final int BOTH`
DESCRIPTION	This constant field specifies that the component is to be stretched both horizontally and vertically to fill its display area. This constant is used in the `fill` field.
SEE ALSO	`fill`.
EXAMPLE	See `fill`.

CENTER

PURPOSE	Anchor type that specifies center positioning.
SYNTAX	`public static final int CENTER`
DESCRIPTION	This constant field specifies that the center of the component is to be anchored to the center of its display area. This constant is used in the `anchor` field.
SEE ALSO	`anchor`.
EXAMPLE	See `anchor`.

clone()

PURPOSE	Creates a copy of the gridbag constraints.
SYNTAX	`public Object clone()`
DESCRIPTION	This method makes a copy of the gridbag constraints. The new gridbag constraints have a complete copy of all of the values, including a new copy of the insets object. Changing any value in the new gridbag constraints will not affect this instance.
RETURNS	A copy of these gridbag constraints.

OVERRIDES

OVERRIDES   `java.lang.Object.clone()`.

EXAMPLE
```
GridBagConstraints c = new GridBagConstraints();
GridBagConstraints cCopy = (GridBagConstraints)c.clone();
```

EAST

PURPOSE   Anchor type that specifies east positioning.

SYNTAX   `public static final int EAST`

DESCRIPTION   This constant field specifies that the east corner of the component is to be anchored to the east corner of the component's display area and centered vertically. This constant is used in the `anchor` field.

SEE ALSO   `anchor`.

EXAMPLE   See `anchor`.

fill

PURPOSE   This field holds the fill constraint for a component.

SYNTAX   `public int fill`

DESCRIPTION   The fill type specifies how the component is stretched within its display area.

SEE ALSO   `NONE`, `VERTICAL`, `HORIZONTAL`, `BOTH`.

EXAMPLE   This example creates a 2-×-2 gridbag that has four labels. Each label has a different fill constraint. See Figure 185.

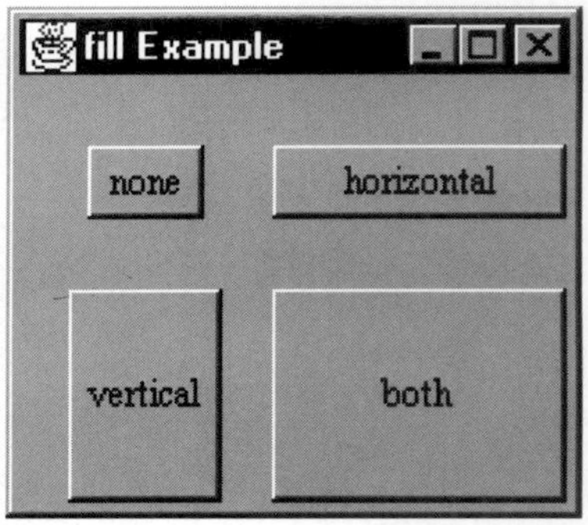

FIGURE 185:
GridBagConstraints.fill.

```
import java.awt.*;

public class Main {
    static void makeLabel(Container cont, String label,
            GridBagConstraints c, int fill) {
        GridBagLayout gbl = (GridBagLayout)cont.getLayout();
        Label b = new Label(label, Label.CENTER);
        b.setBackground(Color.blue);
        b.setForeground(Color.white);
        cont.add(b);
        c.fill = fill;
        gbl.setConstraints(b, c);
    }
```

```
static public void main(String[] args) {
    GridBagLayout gbl = new GridBagLayout();
    GridBagConstraints c = new GridBagConstraints();
    Frame f = new Frame("fill Example");

    f.setLayout(gbl);
    c.weightx = 1;
    c.weighty = 1;
    makeLabel(f, "none", c, GridBagConstraints.NONE);
    c.gridwidth = GridBagConstraints.REMAINDER;
    makeLabel(f, "horizontal", c, GridBagConstraints.HORIZONTAL);
    c.gridwidth = 1;    // Restore default value.
    makeLabel(f, "vertical", c, GridBagConstraints.VERTICAL);
    makeLabel(f, "both", c, GridBagConstraints.BOTH);
    f.setSize(200, 200);
    f.show();
}
}
```

GridBagConstraints( )

PURPOSE   Constructs a new `GridBagConstraints` instance.

SYNTAX   `public GridBagConstraints ()`

DESCRIPTION   This constructor creates a new `GridBagConstraints` instance using the defaults given in Table 14.

anchor	CENTER
fill	NONE
gridx	RELATIVE
gridy	RELATIVE
gridwidth	1
gridheight	1
ipadx	0
ipady	0
insets	new Insets(0, 0, 0, 0)
weightx	0
weighty	0

TABLE 14: **GridBagConstraints Defaults.**

EXAMPLE   See the class example.

A
B
C
D
E
F
G
H
I
J
K
L
M
N
O
P
Q
R
S
T
U
V
W
X
Y
Z

gridheight

PURPOSE	This field holds the component's height in cells.
SYNTAX	`public int gridheight`
DESCRIPTION	The component's height is measured in cells and must be non-negative. For example, a grid height of 2 means the component will be 2 cells high. If the grid height is REMAINDER, the component will occupy all of the cells below it. A grid height of 0 is the same as REMAINDER. If the grid height is RELATIVE, the component will occupy all of the cells below it, except for the last cell. Also, the grid height of the component that follows must be REMAINDER.
SEE ALSO	`gridwidth`, `RELATIVE`, `REMAINDER`.
EXAMPLE	See `gridwidth`.

gridwidth

PURPOSE	This field holds the component's width in cells.
SYNTAX	`public int gridwidth`
DESCRIPTION	The component's width is measured in cells and must be non-negative. For example, a grid width of 2 means the component will be 2 cells wide.

If the grid width is REMAINDER, the component will occupy all of the cells below it. A grid width of 0 is the same as REMAINDER.

If the grid width is RELATIVE, the component will occupy all of the cells below it, except for the last cell. Also, the grid width of the component that follows must be REMAINDER.

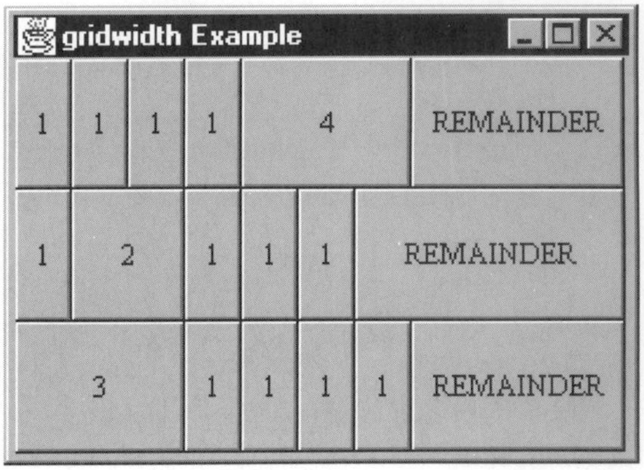

FIGURE 186:
`GridBagConstraints`'s Width and Height.

SEE ALSO	`RELATIVE`, `REMAINDER`.
EXAMPLE	This example creates a 6-×-3 gridbag with 18 buttons. See Figure 186. The button at the end of each row has the grid width constraint of REMAINDER. This means it will consume all remaining cells in that row. Each of the non-REMAINDER buttons, when

pushed, will increase its grid width by 1 (up to 4). Using this program, you can experiment with the effects of nonuniform grid widths in a gridbag.

```java
import java.awt.*;
import java.awt.event.*;

public class Main extends Frame implements ActionListener {
    GridBagLayout gbl = new GridBagLayout();

    Main() {
        super("gridwidth Example");
        setLayout(gbl);
        for (int i=0; i<18; i++) {
            if (i % 6 == 5) {
                makeButton("REMAINDER", GridBagConstraints.REMAINDER);
            } else {
                makeButton("1", 1);
            }
        }
        setSize(300, 300);
        show();
    }

    void makeButton(String label, int w) {
        GridBagConstraints c = new GridBagConstraints();
        Button b = new Button(label);

        c.gridwidth = w;
        c.gridheight = 1;
        c.fill = GridBagConstraints.BOTH;
        c.weightx = 1;
        c.weighty = 1;
        gbl.setConstraints(b, c);
        add(b);
        b.addActionListener(this);
    }

    public void actionPerformed(ActionEvent evt) {
        Button b = (Button)evt.getSource();
        GridBagConstraints gbc = gbl.getConstraints(b);

        if (gbc.gridwidth != GridBagConstraints.REMAINDER) {
            if (++gbc.gridwidth > 4) {
                gbc.gridwidth = 1;
            }
            gbl.setConstraints(b, gbc);
            b.setLabel("" + gbc.gridwidth);
            invalidate();
            validate();
        }
    }

    static public void main(String[] args) {
        new Main();
    }
}
```

gridx

A
B
C
D
E
F
G
H
I
J
K
L
M
N
O
P
Q
R
S
T
U
V
W
X
Y
Z

PURPOSE   This field holds the *x*-coordinate cell location for a component.

SYNTAX   `public int gridx`

DESCRIPTION   The cell locations are zero-based. This means the location of the cell at the gridbag's northwest corner is (0, 0).

SEE ALSO   `gridy`.

EXAMPLE   This example creates a 3-×-3 gridbag with eight buttons and one empty cell. See Figure 187. Pressing a button adjacent to the empty cell moves that button into the empty cell.

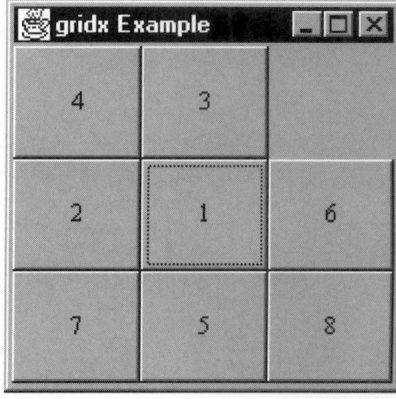

FIGURE 187: `GridBagConstraints` **Coordinates.**

```
import java.awt.*;
import java.awt.event.*;

public class Main extends Frame implements ActionListener {
    GridBagLayout gbl = new GridBagLayout();
    Point free = new Point(2, 2);

    Main() {
        super("gridx Example");
        Component c = null;

        setLayout(gbl);
        for (int i=0; i<3; i++) {
            for (int j=0; j<3; j++) {
                c = makeButton(String.valueOf((char)('1'+i+3*j)), i, j);
            }
        }
        remove(c);        // remove the last button
        setSize(200, 200);
        show();
    }

    // Returns the new button.
    Component makeButton(String label, int x, int y) {
        GridBagConstraints c = new GridBagConstraints();
        Button b = new Button(label);

        c.gridx = x;
        c.gridy = y;
        c.fill = GridBagConstraints.BOTH;
        c.weightx = 1;
        c.weighty = 1;
        gbl.setConstraints(b, c);
        add(b);
        b.addActionListener(this);
        return b;
    }
```

```
    public void actionPerformed(ActionEvent evt) {
        Button button = (Button)evt.getSource();
        GridBagConstraints gbc = gbl.getConstraints(button);
        Point p = new Point(gbc.gridx, gbc.gridy);

        if ((p.x == free.x && Math.abs(p.y-free.y) == 1)
                || (p.y == free.y && Math.abs(p.x-free.x) == 1)) {
            gbc.gridx = free.x;
            gbc.gridy = free.y;
            gbl.setConstraints(button, gbc);
            free = p;
            invalidate();
            validate();
        }
    }

    static public void main(String[] args) {
        new Main();
    }
}
```

gridy

PURPOSE   This field holds the *y*-coordinate cell location for a component.

SYNTAX   `public int gridy`

DESCRIPTION   The cell locations are zero-based. This means the location of the cell at the gridbag's northwest corner is (0, 0).

SEE ALSO   `gridx`.

EXAMPLE   See `gridx`.

HORIZONTAL

PURPOSE   Fill type that specifies a horizontal-only fill.

SYNTAX   `public static final int HORIZONTAL`

DESCRIPTION   This constant field specifies that the component is to be stretched horizontally to fill its display area. The component's height is not changed. This constant is used in the `fill` field.

SEE ALSO   `fill`.

EXAMPLE   See `fill`.

A
B
C
D
E
F
G
H
I
J
K
L
M
N
O
P
Q
R
S
T
U
V
W
X
Y
Z

insets

PURPOSE This field holds the insets constraints for the component.

SYNTAX `public Insets insets`

DESCRIPTION The insets constraint affects the dimensions of the component's display area. Although rare, an inset can be negative. This allows a component to extend outside its display area.

SEE ALSO Insets.

EXAMPLE This example creates a 4-×-4 gridbag with nine buttons. See Figure 188. There are two buttons along each edge of the gridbag that, when pressed, modify the center button's inset for that edge. The label of the center button shows the current values of the insets.

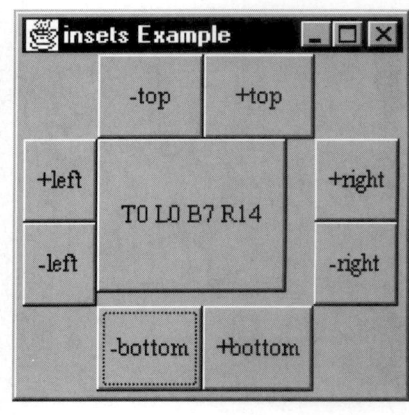

FIGURE 188:
GridbagConstraints's Insets.

```
import java.awt.*;
import java.awt.event.*;

public class Main extends Frame implements ActionListener {
    Button centerButton;
    GridBagLayout gbl = new GridBagLayout();

    Main() {
        super("insets Example");
        GridBagConstraints c = new GridBagConstraints();

        setLayout(gbl);
        c.fill = GridBagConstraints.BOTH;
        c.weightx = 1;
        c.weighty = 1;

        makeButton(this, "-top", c, 1, 0);
        makeButton(this, "+top", c, 2, 0);
        makeButton(this, "+left", c, 0, 1);
        makeButton(this, "-left", c, 0, 2);
        makeButton(this, "-bottom", c, 1, 3);
        makeButton(this, "+bottom", c, 2, 3);
        makeButton(this, "+right", c, 3, 1);
        makeButton(this, "-right", c, 3, 2);

        // Make center button.
        c.gridwidth = c.gridheight = 2;
        c.fill = GridBagConstraints.BOTH;
        centerButton = makeButton(this, "T0 L0 B0 R0", c, 1, 1);

        setSize(200, 200);
        show();
    }
```

```
    // Returns the new button.
    Button makeButton(Container cont, String label,
            GridBagConstraints c, int x, int y) {
        GridBagLayout gbl = (GridBagLayout)cont.getLayout();
        Button b = new Button(label);

        cont.add(b);
        c.gridx = x;
        c.gridy = y;
        gbl.setConstraints(b, c);
        b.addActionListener(this);
        return b;
    }

    public void actionPerformed(ActionEvent evt) {
        GridBagConstraints c = gbl.getConstraints(centerButton);
        String s = evt.getActionCommand();
        int sign = s.charAt(0) == '+' ? 1 : -1;

        s = s.substring(1);
        if ("top".equals(s)) {
            c.insets.top += sign;
        } else if ("left".equals(s)) {
            c.insets.left += sign;
        } else if ("bottom".equals(s)) {
            c.insets.bottom += sign;
        } else if ("right".equals(s)) {
            c.insets.right += sign;
        }
        gbl.setConstraints(centerButton, c);
        centerButton.setLabel("T"+c.insets.top+" L"+c.insets.left
                            +" B"+c.insets.bottom+" R"+c.insets.right);
        invalidate();
        validate();
    }

    static public void main(String[] args) {
        new Main();
    }
}
```

A
B
C
D
E
F
G
H
I
J
K
L
M
N
O
P
Q
R
S
T
U
V
W
X
Y
Z

ipadx

PURPOSE	This field holds the internal padding for the component's width
SYNTAX	`public int ipadx`
DESCRIPTION	This field increases the minimum or preferred width of a component by `ipadx` pixels.
SEE ALSO	`ipady`.

751

EXAMPLE   This example creates a three-cell gridbag with three buttons. See Figure 189. One button has negative padding, one has no padding, and the last has positive padding.

```
import java.awt.*;

public class Main {
    static public void main(String[] args) {
        GridBagConstraints c =
            new GridBagConstraints();
        Frame f = new Frame("ipadx Example");

        f.setLayout(new GridBagLayout());
        c.gridwidth =
            GridBagConstraints.REMAINDER;
        c.ipadx = -6;
        makeButton(f, "- pad", c);
        c.ipadx = 0;
        makeButton(f, "0 pad", c);
        c.ipadx = 6;
        makeButton(f, "+ pad", c);
        f.setSize(200, 200);
        f.show();
    }

    static void makeButton(Container cont, String label,
                           GridBagConstraints c) {
        GridBagLayout gbl = (GridBagLayout)cont.getLayout();
        Button b = new Button(label);

        cont.add(b);
        gbl.setConstraints(b, c);
    }
}
```

FIGURE 189:
GridBagConstraints's
Internal Padding.

ipady

PURPOSE   This field holds the internal padding for a component's height.

SYNTAX   `public int ipady`

DESCRIPTION   This field increases the minimum or preferred height of a component by `ipady` pixels.

SEE ALSO   `ipadx`.

EXAMPLE   See `ipadx`.

NONE

PURPOSE   Fill type that specifies no fill (the default).

SYNTAX   `public static final int NONE`

DESCRIPTION   This constant field specifies that the component cannot be stretched in any direction. This constant is used in the `fill` field.

SEE ALSO   `fill`.

EXAMPLE   See `fill`.

NORTH

PURPOSE   Anchor type that specifies north positioning.

SYNTAX   `public static final int NORTH`

DESCRIPTION   This constant field specifies that the north corner of the component is to be anchored to the north corner of the component's display area and centered horizontally. This constant is used in the `anchor` field.

SEE ALSO   `anchor`.

EXAMPLE   See `anchor`.

NORTHEAST

PURPOSE   Anchor type that specifies northeast positioning.

SYNTAX   `public static final int NORTHEAST`

DESCRIPTION   This constant field specifies that the northeast corner of the component is to be anchored to the northeast corner of the component's display area. This constant is used in the `anchor` field.

SEE ALSO   `anchor`.

EXAMPLE   See `anchor`.

NORTHWEST

PURPOSE   Anchor type that specifies northwest positioning.

SYNTAX   `public static final int NORTHWEST`

A
B
C
D
E
F
G
H
I
J
K
L
M
N
O
P
Q
R
S
T
U
V
W
X
Y
Z

DESCRIPTION	This constant field specifies that the northwest corner of the component is to be anchored to the northwest corner of the component's display area. This constant is used in the anchor field.
SEE ALSO	anchor.
EXAMPLE	See anchor.

RELATIVE

PURPOSE	Size type that specifies that subsequent cells in the row or column are to be occupied except for the last cell.
SYNTAX	`public static final int RELATIVE`
DESCRIPTION	If a component's grid width (or grid height) is RELATIVE, the component will occupy all of the cells to the right of (or below) it, except for the last cell. Also, the grid width (or grid height) of the component that follows must be REMAINDER.
SEE ALSO	gridheight, gridwidth, REMAINDER.
EXAMPLE	See REMAINDER.

REMAINDER

PURPOSE	Size type that specifies that subsequent cells in the row or column are to be occupied.
SYNTAX	`public static final int REMAINDER`
DESCRIPTION	If a component's grid width (or grid height) is REMAINDER, the component will occupy all of the cells to the right of (or below) it. A grid height of 0 is the same as REMAINDER. The component that follows will start a new row (or column).
SEE ALSO	gridheight, gridwidth, RELATIVE.
EXAMPLE	This example creates a gridbag with three rows. See Figure 190. All of the cells in the first row are occupied by a component. In the second row, the button labeled REMAINDER consumes all but the first cell. In the third row, the button labeled RELATIVE consumes all but the first and last cells.

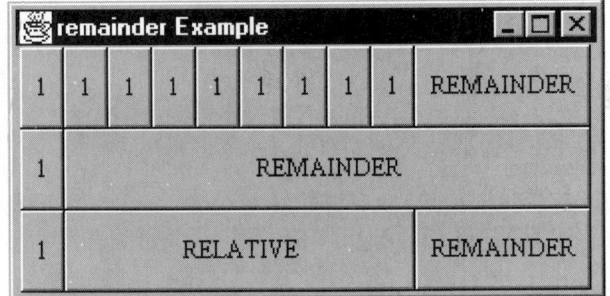

FIGURE 190: `GridBagConstraints.REMAINDER`.

```java
import java.awt.*;

public class Main extends Frame {
    GridBagLayout gbl = new GridBagLayout();

    Main() {
        super("remainder Example");
        setLayout(gbl);
        for (int i=0; i<9; i++) makeButton("1", 1);
        makeButton("REMAINDER", GridBagConstraints.REMAINDER);

        makeButton("1", 1);
        makeButton("REMAINDER", GridBagConstraints.REMAINDER);

        makeButton("1", 1);
        makeButton("RELATIVE", GridBagConstraints.RELATIVE);
        makeButton("REMAINDER", GridBagConstraints.REMAINDER);

        setSize(300, 150);
        show();
    }

    void makeButton(String label, int w) {
        GridBagConstraints c = new GridBagConstraints();
        Button b = new Button(label);

        c.gridwidth = w;
        c.gridheight = 1;
        c.fill = GridBagConstraints.BOTH;
        c.weightx = 1;
        c.weighty = 1;
        gbl.setConstraints(b, c);
        add(b);
    }

    static public void main(String[] args) {
        new Main();
    }
}
```

SOUTH

PURPOSE	Anchor type that specifies south positioning.
SYNTAX	`public static final int SOUTH`
DESCRIPTION	This constant field specifies that the south corner of the component is to be anchored to the south corner of the component's display area and centered horizontally. This constant is used in the `anchor` field.
SEE ALSO	`anchor`.
EXAMPLE	See `anchor`.

SOUTHEAST

PURPOSE	Anchor type that specifies southeast positioning.
SYNTAX	`public static final int SOUTHEAST`
DESCRIPTION	This constant field specifies that the southeast corner of the component is to be anchored to the southeast corner of the component's display area. This constant is used in the `anchor` field.
SEE ALSO	`anchor`.
EXAMPLE	See `anchor`.

SOUTHWEST

PURPOSE	Anchor type that specifies southwest positioning.
SYNTAX	`public static final int SOUTHWEST`
DESCRIPTION	This constant field specifies that the southwest corner of the component is to be anchored to the southwest corner of the component's display area. This constant is used in the `anchor` field.
SEE ALSO	`anchor`.
EXAMPLE	See `anchor`.

A
B
C
D
E
F
G
H
I
J
K
L
M
N
O
P
Q
R
S
T
U
V
W
X
Y
Z

VERTICAL

PURPOSE	Fill type that specifies a vertical-only fill.
SYNTAX	`public static final int VERTICAL`
DESCRIPTION	This constant field specifies that the component is to be stretched vertically to fill its display area. The component's width is not changed. This constant is used in the `fill` field.
SEE ALSO	`fill`.
EXAMPLE	See `fill`.

weightx

PURPOSE	This field holds the component's column weight.
SYNTAX	`public double weightx`
DESCRIPTION	See the class description for details on gridbag weights. This value must be non-negative.
EXAMPLE	This example creates a row of five buttons, each with a different weight. See Figure 191. Pressing a button increases its weight by 1. When the weight reaches 4, it is set back to 0.

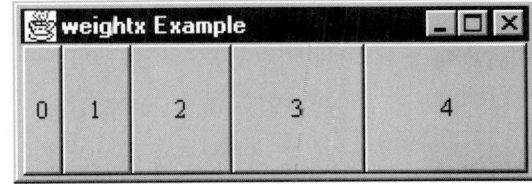

FIGURE 191: `GridBagConstraints`'s **Weights.**

```
import java.awt.*;
import java.awt.event.*;

public class Main extends Frame implements ActionListener {
    GridBagLayout gbl = new GridBagLayout();

    Main() {
        super("weightx Example");
        setLayout(gbl);
        for (int i=0; i<5; i++) {
            makeButton(i);
        }
        setSize(300, 150);
        show();
    }

    void makeButton(int w) {
        GridBagConstraints c = new GridBagConstraints();
        Button b = new Button("" + w);

        c.weightx = w;
```

A
B
C
D
E
F
G
H
I
J
K
L
M
N
O
P
Q
R
S
T
U
V
W
X
Y
Z

```
                        c.weighty = 1;
                        c.fill = GridBagConstraints.BOTH;
                        gbl.setConstraints(b, c);
                        b.addActionListener(this);
                        add(b);
                    }

                public void actionPerformed(ActionEvent evt) {
                        Button b = (Button)evt.getSource();
                        GridBagConstraints gbc = gbl.getConstraints(b);

                        if (++gbc.weightx > 4) {
                            gbc.weightx = 0;
                        }
                        gbl.setConstraints(b, gbc);
                        b.setLabel("" + gbc.weightx);
                        invalidate();
                        validate();
                    }

                static public void main(String[] args) {
                        new Main();
                    }
                }
```

weighty

PURPOSE	This field holds the component's row weight.
SYNTAX	`public double weighty`
DESCRIPTION	See the class description for details on gridbag weights. This value must be non-negative.
EXAMPLE	See `weightx`.

WEST

PURPOSE	Anchor type that specifies west positioning.
SYNTAX	`public static final int WEST`
DESCRIPTION	This constant field specifies that the west edge of the component is to be anchored to the west edge of the component's display area and centered vertically. This constant is used in the `anchor` field.
SEE ALSO	`anchor`.
EXAMPLE	See `anchor`.

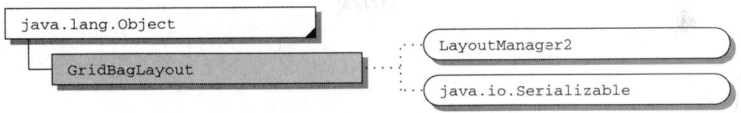

Syntax

`public class GridBagLayout implements LayoutManager2, Serializable`

Description

A *gridbag* is a container with a gridbag layout manager. The gridbag layout manager implements a 2D grid of cells in which all cells in a column have the same width and all cells in a row have the same height. Multiplying the number of columns by the number of rows in the gridbag yields the total number of cells in the gridbag. Unlike with the grid layout manager (see `GridLayout`), the columns in a gridbag can have different widths; similarly for rows.

A cell in a gridbag is addressed by the *x*- and *y*-coordinates. The coordinates are 0-based, so the first cell is at location (0, 0). A gridbag is initially created with no cells. Cells are automatically created as components are added. For example, if the first component was added to location (10, 10), the grid would automatically create 11-×-11 cells. See `getLayoutDimensions()` on how to obtain the gridbag's current dimensions.

A component can be located anywhere within the grid of cells (see Figure 192). A component can occupy one or more contiguous cells, which themselves must form a smaller but rectangular grid of cells. Not all cells must be occupied. (The gridbag allows more than one component to overlap a cell. However, this is considered a programming error.) The cell or cells that a component occupies is called the *component's display area*.

A component's location in the gridbag is specified with what are called gridbag constraints. Every component in the gridbag has associated with it gridbag constraints. The gridbag layout manager uses all the component gridbag constraints to do the layout. See the `GridBagConstraints` class for details about available gridbag constraints and their effects on the component.

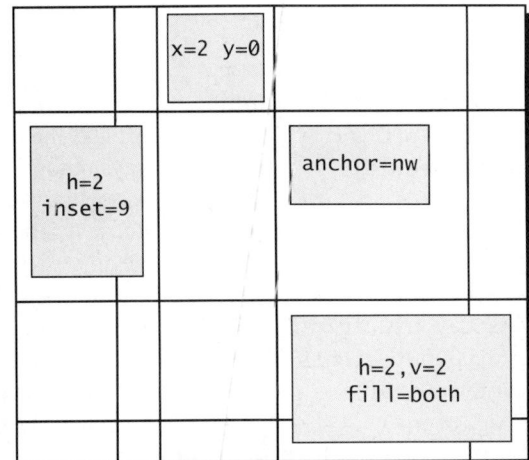

FIGURE 192: Cells in a `GridbagLayout`.

759

A
B
C
D
E
F
G
H
I
J
K
L
M
N
O
P
Q
R
S
T
U
V
W
X
Y
Z

MEMBER SUMMARY

Constructor

GridBagLayout()	Constructs a new GridBagLayout instance.

Constant Fields

MAXGRIDSIZE	Specifies the maximum number of cells in the gridbag.
MINSIZE	Layout constant specifying that calculations should use a component's minimum size.
PREFERREDSIZE	Layout constant specifying that calculations should use a component's preferred size.

Layout Fields

columnWeights	Holds the overrides to the column weights.
columnWidths	Holds the overrides to the column minimum widths.
comptable	This hash table maintains the association between a component and its gridbag constraints.
layoutInfo	Holds the gridbag's layout information.
rowHeights	Holds the overrides to the row minimum heights.
rowWeights	Holds the overrides to the row weights.

Constraints Methods and Field

defaultConstraints	This field holds a gridbag constraints instance containing the default values.
getConstraints()	Retrieves the gridbag constraints for a component.
lookupConstraints()	Retrieves the constraints for a component.
setConstraints()	Sets the gridbag constraints for a component.

GridBag Layout Methods

AdjustForGravity()	Adjusts the position of a component within its display area.
ArrangeGrid()	Lays out the container's components using the components' constraints.
getLayoutDimensions()	Retrieves the dimensions of each row and column in the gridbag.
GetLayoutInfo()	Calculates the layout for a gridbag container.
getLayoutOrigin()	Retrieves the gridbag's location within its container.
getLayoutWeights()	Retrieves the gridbag's row and column weights.
GetMinSize()	Retrieves the minimum dimension of the gridbag.
location()	Retrieves the cell location using a pixel location.

Layout Manager Methods

addLayoutComponent()	Adds a component to this layout.
getLayoutAlignmentX()	Retrieves the gridbag's x-alignment.
getLayoutAlighmentY()	Retrieves the gridbag's y-alignment.
invalidateLayout()	Invalidates the gridbag's state.

MEMBER SUMMARY	
layoutContainer()	Lays out the container's components using the components' constraints.
maximumLayoutSize()	Calculates the maximum dimensions for laying out the components.
minimumLayoutSize()	Calculates the minimum dimensions needed to lay out the components.
preferredLayoutSize()	Calculates the preferred dimensions needed to lay out the components.
removeLayoutComponent()	A no-op.
Debugging Method	
toString()	Generates a string representation of the gridbag's state.

See Also

GridBagConstraints, java.io.Serializable, LayoutManager2.

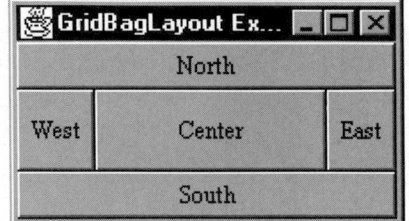

FIGURE 193: GridBagLayout Simulating BorderLayout.

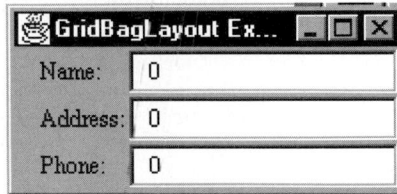

FIGURE 194: GridBagLayout Implementing a Form.

Example

This example creates three sample layouts. The first is a simulation of the BorderLayout layout manager (Figure 193). The second is a popular use of the gridbag layout: implementing a form-like layout (Figure 194). The third simply demonstrates the kinds of layouts that are possible (Figure 195).

```
import java.awt.*;

public class Main {
    static void makeCrazyLayout() {
        Frame f = new
```

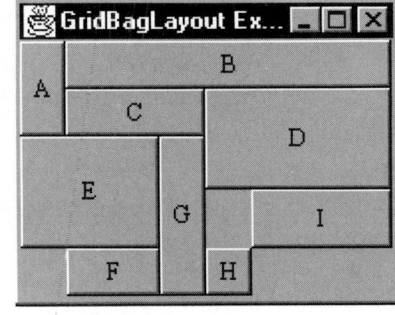

FIGURE 195: GridBagLayout.

```
                    Frame("GridBagLayout Example 1");

            f.setLayout(new GridBagLayout());
            makeButton(f, "A", 0, 0, 1, 2, 0.0,
                0.0);
            makeButton(f, "B", 1, 0, 4, 1, 2.0,
                0.0);
            makeButton(f, "C", 1, 1, 2, 1, 0.0,
                0.0);
            makeButton(f, "D", 3, 1, 2, 2, 0.0,
                2.0);
            makeButton(f, "E", 0, 2, 2, 2, 0.0, 0.0);
            makeButton(f, "F", 1, 4, 1, 1, 0.5, 0.0);
            makeButton(f, "G", 2, 2, 1, 3, 0.0, 0.0);
            makeButton(f, "H", 3, 4, 1, 1, 0.0, 0.0);
            makeButton(f, "I", 4, 3, 1, 1, 1.0, 0.5);
            f.pack();
            f.show();
        }

        static void makeBorderLayout() {
            Frame f = new Frame("GridBagLayout Example 2");

            f.setLayout(new GridBagLayout());
            makeButton(f, "North", 0, 0, 3, 1, 0.0, 0.0);
            makeButton(f, "South", 0, 2, 3, 1, 0.0, 0.0);
            makeButton(f, "West", 0, 1, 1, 1, 0.0, 1.0);
            makeButton(f, "East", 2, 1, 1, 1, 0.0, 1.0);
            makeButton(f, "Center", 1, 1, 1, 1, 1.0, 1.0);
            f.pack();
            f.show();
        }

        static void makeTableLayout() {
            Frame f = new Frame("GridBagLayout Example 3");

            f.setLayout(new GridBagLayout());
            makeButton(f, new Label("Name:"), 0, 0, 1, 1, 0.0, 0.0);
            makeButton(f, new Label("Address:"), 0, 1, 1, 1, 0.0, 0.0);
            makeButton(f, new Label("Phone:"), 0, 2, 1, 1, 0.0, 0.0);
            makeButton(f, new TextField("0", 5), 1, 0, 1, 1, 1.0, 0.0);
            makeButton(f, new TextField("0", 5), 1, 1, 1, 1, 1.0, 0.0);
            makeButton(f, new TextField("0", 5), 1, 2, 1, 1, 1.0, 0.0);
            f.pack();
            f.show();
        }

        static void makeButton(Container cont, Object arg,
                int x, int y, int w, int h, double weightx, double weighty) {
            GridBagLayout gbl = (GridBagLayout)cont.getLayout();
            GridBagConstraints c = new GridBagConstraints();
            Component comp;

            c.fill = GridBagConstraints.BOTH;
            c.gridx = x;
            c.gridy = y;
            c.gridwidth = w;
            c.gridheight = h;
            c.weightx = weightx;
            c.weighty = weighty;
```

A
B
C
D
E
F
G
H
I
J
K
L
M
N
O
P
Q
R
S
T
U
V
W
X
Y
Z

```
        if (arg instanceof String) {
            comp = new Button((String)arg);
        } else {
            comp = (Component)arg;
        }
        cont.add(comp);
        gbl.setConstraints(comp, c);
    }

    static public void main(String[] args) {
        makeCrazyLayout();
        makeBorderLayout();
        makeTableLayout();
    }
}
```

addLayoutComponent( )

PURPOSE   Adds a component to this layout.

SYNTAX   public void addLayoutComponent(String name, Component comp)
              public void addLayoutComponent(Component comp, Object constraints)

DESCRIPTION   This method is called by a container when the component comp is added to it.
              The first form of this method accepts a string name to be associated with comp.
              However, component names are ignored by the gridbag layout manager, so this
              method does nothing. It needs to be defined in order to satisfy the LayoutMan-
              ager interface.

              This second form of this method accepts a constraints argument that specifies
              how the component is to be laid out.

PARAMETERS
  comp   The non-null named component that has just been added to the container.
  constraints The constraint to use for this component. Must be an instance of GridBagCon-
              straints.
  name   The name of the component. Ignored.

EXCEPTIONS
  IllegalArgumentException
              If constraints is not an instance of GridBagConstraints.

SEE ALSO   LayoutManager2, setConstraints().

EXAMPLE   See LayoutManager.

763

AdjustForGravity( )

PURPOSE   Adjusts the position of a component within its display area.

SYNTAX   `protected void AdjustForGravity(GridBagConstraints constraints,`
               `    Rectangle displayArea)`

DESCRIPTION   The gridbag constraints `constraints` are used to adjust the component's
               bounds within its display area, which is represented by `displayArea`. In par-
               ticular, the insets, fill, size, and anchor gridbag constraints are used to deter-
               mine the component's bounds. After this method call, `displayArea` will
               contain the component's new bounds.

PARAMETERS
  `constraints` The non-`null` component gridbag constraints.
  `displayArea` A non-`null` rectangle representing a component's display area.

ArrangeGrid( )

PURPOSE   Lays out the container's components using the components' constraints.

SYNTAX   `protected void ArrangeGrid(Container container)`

DESCRIPTION   This method is equivalent to `layoutContainer()`.

PARAMETERS
  `container`   The non-`null` container using this layout instance.

EXAMPLE   See `layoutContainer()`.

columnWeights

PURPOSE   This field holds the overrides to the column weights.

SYNTAX   `public double[] columnWeights`

DESCRIPTION   If this field is non-`null`, the values in the field are applied to the gridbag after
               all of the column weights have been calculated. If `columnWeights[i]` is
               greater than the weight for column i, then column i is assigned the weight
               in `columnWeights[i]`. If `columnWeights` has more elements than the num-
               ber of columns, the excess elements in `columnWeights` are ignored. In partic-
               ular, they do not cause more columns to be created.

EXAMPLE   This example creates a 3-×-3 gridbag with nine buttons. The gridbag is set with some row/column weight and size overrides. See Figure 196.

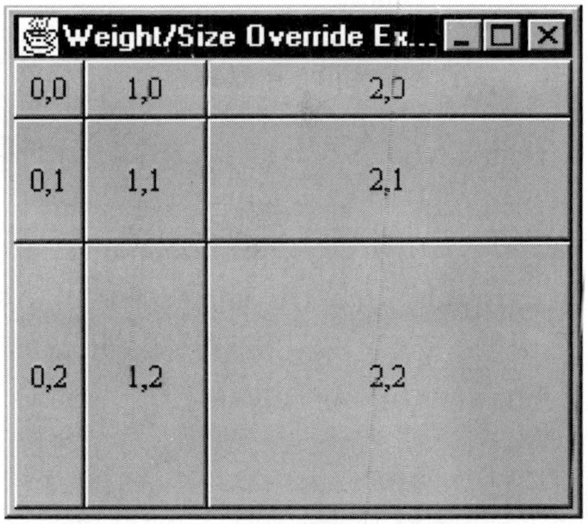

FIGURE 196:   GridBagLayout Weights/Sizes.

```java
import java.awt.*;

public class Main extends Frame {
    GridBagLayout gbl =
        new GridBagLayout();

    Main() {
        super(
          "Weight/Size Override Example");
        GridBagConstraints c =
            new GridBagConstraints();
        double rowWeights[] = {0, 0, 1.0};
        double colWeights[] = {0, 0, 1.0};
        int rowHeights[] = {20, 50};
        int colWidths[] = {20, 50};

        gbl.rowWeights = rowWeights;
        gbl.columnWeights = colWeights;
        gbl.rowHeights = rowHeights;
        gbl.columnWidths = colWidths;
        setLayout(gbl);

        c.fill = GridBagConstraints.BOTH;
        for (int i=0; i<3; i++) {
            for (int j=0; j<3; j++) {
                Button b = new Button(""+i+","+j);
                c.gridx = i;
                c.gridy = j;
                add(b);
                gbl.setConstraints(b, c);
            }
        }
        setSize(250, 150);
        show();
    }

    static public void main(String[] args) {
        new Main();
    }
}
```

columnWidths

PURPOSE	This field holds the overrides to the column minimum widths.
SYNTAX	`public int[] columnWidths`
DESCRIPTION	If this field is non-`null`, the values in the field are applied to the gridbag after all of the minimum column widths have been calculated. If `columnWidths` has more elements than the number of columns, columns are added to the gridbag to match the number of elements in `columnWidths`.
EXAMPLE	See `columnWeights`.

comptable

PURPOSE	This hash table maintains the association between a component and its gridbag constraints.
SYNTAX	`protected Hashtable comptable`
DESCRIPTION	The keys in `comptable` are the components, and the values are the instances of `GridBagConstraints`.

defaultConstraints

PURPOSE	This field holds a gridbag constraints instance containing the default values.
SYNTAX	`protected GridBagConstraints defaultConstraints`
DESCRIPTION	If a component is found not to have a gridbag constraints instance associated with it, the component is assigned a copy of `defaultConstraints`.

getConstraints()

PURPOSE	Retrieves the gridbag constraints for a component.
SYNTAX	`public GridBagConstraints getConstraints(Component comp)`
DESCRIPTION	This method retrieves a clone of gridbag constraints for the component `comp`.
PARAMETERS	
comp	The non-`null` component to be queried.
RETURNS	A non-`null` copy of the component's gridbag constraints.
EXAMPLE	See `getLayoutWeights()`.

getLayoutAlignmentX()

PURPOSE   Retrieves the gridbag's *x*-alignment.

SYNTAX   `public float getLayoutAlignmentX(Container cont)`

DESCRIPTION   This method returns `Component.CENTER_ALIGNMENT`. See `LayoutManager2` for more information about alignments.

PARAMETERS
cont   The non-`null` container using this gridbag.

RETURNS   This gridbag's *x*-alignment, which must be in the range `0.0f` to `1.0f`.

SEE ALSO   `Component.getAlignmentX()`, `Container.getAlignmentX()`, `getLayoutAlignmentY()`, `LayoutManager2`.

EXAMPLE   See the `LayoutManager2` class example.

getLayoutAlignmentY()

PURPOSE   Retrieves the gridbag's *y*-alignment.

SYNTAX   `public float getLayoutAlignmentY(Container cont)`

DESCRIPTION   This method returns `Component.CENTER_ALIGNMENT`. See `LayoutManager2` for more information about alignments.

PARAMETERS
cont   The non-`null` container using this gridbag.

RETURNS   This gridbag's *y*-alignment, which must be in the range `0.0f` to `1.0f`.

SEE ALSO   `Component.getAlignmentY()`, `Container.getAlignmentY()`, `getLayoutAlignmentX()`, `LayoutManager2`.

EXAMPLE   See the `LayoutManager2` class example.

getLayoutDimensions()

PURPOSE   Retrieves the dimensions of each row and column in the gridbag.

SYNTAX   `public int[][] getLayoutDimensions ()`

DESCRIPTION   If w = `getLayoutDimensions()`, then `w[0].length` contains the number of columns and `w[0][0]...w[0][w[0].length-1]` are the column widths. `w[1].length` contains the number of rows and `w[1][0]...w[1][w[1].length-1]` are the row heights. The resulting information is based on the most recent validation. So if the container is invalid or a

A
B
C
D
E
F
G
H
I
J
K
L
M
N
O
P
Q
R
S
T
U
V
W
X
Y
Z

constraint has been modified, the gridbag should be validated before this method is called.

RETURNS   A non-null 2D array containing the row and column weights.

EXAMPLE   See getLayoutWeights().

GetLayoutInfo()

PURPOSE   Calculates the layout for a gridbag container.

SYNTAX   protected GridBagLayoutInfo GetLayoutInfo(Container container, int sizeflag)

DESCRIPTION If sizeflag is MINSIZE, then the layout is based on the component's minimum size. If sizeflag is PREFERREDSIZE, then the layout is based on the component's preferred size.

PARAMETERS
container   The non-null container to query.
sizeflag   Can be either MINSIZE or PREFERREDSIZE.

RETURNS   A non-null GridBagLayoutInfo instance containing the layout information.

getLayoutOrigin()

PURPOSE   Retrieves the gridbag's location within its container.

SYNTAX   public Point getLayoutOrigin()

DESCRIPTION The gridbag's origin is the position of the gridbag's northwest corner in relation to its container. The resulting information is based on the most recent validation. So if the container is invalid or a constraint has been modified, the gridbag should be validated before this method is called.

RETURNS   A new non-null Point instance containing the gridbag's origin.

EXAMPLE   This example creates a gridbag with two checkboxes whose default weights are 0. This means that the extra space is distributed around the gridbag rather than to some

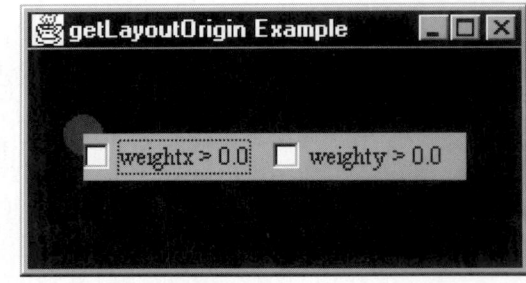

FIGURE 197: GridBagLayout.getLayoutOrigin().

gridbag column or row. See Figure 197. A red dot is painted centered at the gridbag's origin within the container. Clicking a checkbox, and thereby changing its weight, changes the gridbag size as well as its origin.

```java
import java.awt.*;
import java.awt.event.*;

public class Main extends Frame implements ItemListener {
    GridBagLayout gbl = new GridBagLayout();
    Main() {
        super("getLayoutOrigin Example");
        GridBagConstraints c = new GridBagConstraints();
        Checkbox cb;

        c.fill = GridBagConstraints.BOTH;
        setLayout(gbl);
        add(cb = new Checkbox("weightx = 0.0"));
        gbl.setConstraints(cb, c);
        cb.addItemListener(this);
        add(cb = new Checkbox("weighty = 0.0"));
        gbl.setConstraints(cb, c);
        cb.addItemListener(this);

        setSize(300, 100);
        show();
    }

    public void paint(Graphics g) {
        Insets insets = this.getInsets();
        int x = insets.left, y = insets.top;
        int dotSize = 20;
        Point p = gbl.getLayoutOrigin();

        g.setColor(Color.black);
        g.fillRect(x, y, getSize().width-x-insets.right,
                   getSize().height-y-insets.bottom);
        g.setColor(Color.red);
        g.fillOval(p.x-dotSize/2, p.y-dotSize/2, dotSize, dotSize);
    }

    public void itemStateChanged(ItemEvent evt) {
        Checkbox cb = (Checkbox)evt.getSource();
        GridBagConstraints c = gbl.getConstraints(cb);
        String label = cb.getLabel().substring(0, 7);
        int val = cb.getState() ? 1 : 0;

        if (label.equals("weightx")) {
            c.weightx = val;
        } else {
            c.weighty = val;
        }
        cb.setLabel(label + " = " + val + ".0");
        gbl.setConstraints(cb, c);
        invalidate();
        validate();
        repaint();
    }

    static public void main(String[] args) {
```

A
B
C
D
E
F
G
H
I
J
K
L
M
N
O
P
Q
R
S
T
U
V
W
X
Y
Z

769

```
                new Main();
        }
    }
```

A
B

getLayoutWeights( )

C

D

E

F

G

H

I

J

K

L

M

N

O

P

Q

R

S

T

U

V

W

X

Y

Z

PURPOSE   Retrieves the gridbag's row and column weights.

SYNTAX   `public double[][] getLayoutWeights()`

DESCRIPTION   If `w = getLayoutWeights()`, then `w[0].length` contains the number of
              columns and `w[0][0]...w[0][w[0].length-1]` are the column weights.
              `w[1].length` contains the number of rows and
              `w[1][0]...w[1][w[1].length-1]` are the row weights. The resulting infor-
              mation is based on the most recent validation. So if the container is invalid or a
              constraint has been modified, the gridbag should be validated before this
              method is called.

RETURNS   A non-`null` 2D array containing the row and column weights.

EXAMPLE   This example creates a gridbag that
              has four buttons. See Figure 198.
              Pressing a button changes either its
              `weightx` or `weighty` gridbag con-
              straints. The gridbag is then laid
              out again. After the constraints are
              changed, all the new row and col-
              umn weights and dimensions are
              printed to `System.out`.

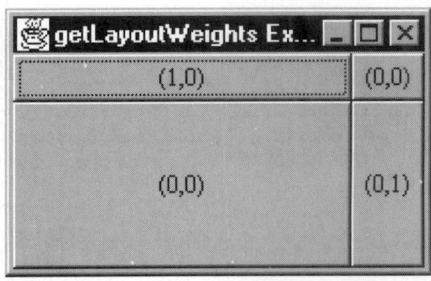

FIGURE 198:
`GridBagLayout.getLayoutWeights()`.

```
import java.awt.*;
import java.awt.event.*;

public class Main extends Frame implements ActionListener {
    GridBagLayout gbl = new GridBagLayout();

    Main() {
        super("getLayoutWeights Example");
        setLayout(gbl);
        printLayoutData(gbl);

        makeButton(0, 0);
        makeButton(0, 1);
        makeButton(1, 0);
        makeButton(1, 1);
        setSize(200, 200);
        show();
    }
```

```
void printLayoutData(GridBagLayout gbl) {
    System.out.println("====================================");
    // print layout weights
    System.out.println("Layout Weights");
    System.out.println("--------------");
    double[][]weights = gbl.getLayoutWeights();
    System.out.print("    "+weights[0].length+" columns: ");
    for (int i=0; i<weights[0].length; i++)  {
        System.out.print(weights[0][i]+" ");
    }
    System.out.println();
    System.out.print("    "+weights[1].length+" rows: ");
    for (int i=0; i<weights[1].length; i++) {
        System.out.print(weights[1][i]+" ");
    }

    // print layout dimensions
    System.out.println();
    System.out.println("Layout Dimensions");
    System.out.println("-----------------");
    int[][]dims = gbl.getLayoutDimensions();
    System.out.print("    "+dims[0].length+" columns: ");
    for (int i=0; i<dims[0].length; i++) {
        System.out.print(dims[0][i]+" ");
    }
    System.out.println();
    System.out.print("    "+dims[1].length+" rows: ");
    for (int i=0; i<dims[1].length; i++) {
        System.out.print(dims[1][i]+" ");
    }
    System.out.println();
}

void makeButton(int x, int y) {
    GridBagConstraints c = new GridBagConstraints();
    Button b = new Button("(0,0)");

    add(b);
    c.fill = GridBagConstraints.BOTH;
    c.gridx = x;
    c.gridy = y;
    gbl.setConstraints(b, c);
    b.addActionListener(this);
}

public void actionPerformed(ActionEvent evt) {
    Button b = (Button)evt.getSource();
    GridBagConstraints c = gbl.getConstraints(b);

    if (c.weightx == 0 && c.weighty == 0) {
        c.weighty = 1;
    } else if (c.weightx == 0 && c.weighty == 1) {
        c.weightx = 1;
    } else if (c.weightx == 1 && c.weighty == 1) {
        c.weighty = 0;
    } else {
        c.weightx = 0;
    }
    b.setLabel("("+c.weightx+","+c.weighty+")");
```

A
B
C
D
E
F
G
H
I
J
K
L
M
N
O
P
Q
R
S
T
U
V
W
X
Y
Z

```
            gbl.setConstraints(b, c);
            invalidate();
            validate();
            printLayoutData(gbl);
        }

        static public void main(String[] args) {
            new Main();
        }
    }
```

A
B
C
D
E
F
G
H
I
J
K
L
M
N
O
P
Q
R
S
T
U
V
W
X
Y
Z

GetMinSize()

PURPOSE	Retrieves the minimum dimension of the gridbag.
SYNTAX	`protected Dimension GetMinSize(Container container,` `    GridBagLayoutInfo info)`
DESCRIPTION	The minimum dimension of the gridbag is based on the layout information in `info`. Also, the insets of the container `container` are included in the result.
PARAMETERS	
`container`	The non-`null` gridbag's container.
`info`	The non-`null` layout information.
RETURNS	A new non-`null` `Dimension` instance containing the minimum dimensions of the gridbag.

GridBagLayout()

PURPOSE	Constructs a new `GridBagLayout` instance.
SYNTAX	`public GridBagLayout()`
DESCRIPTION	By default, the gridbag has no cells.
EXAMPLE	See the class example.

invalidateLayout()

PURPOSE	Invalidates the gridbag's state.
SYNTAX	`public void invalidateLayout(Container cont)`

DESCRIPTION	This method is called by the layout manager's container to discard any cached information associated with this gridbag for the container `cont`. For `GridBag-Layout`, this method, by default, does nothing.
PARAMETERS	
`cont`	The non-`null` container using this gridbag.
SEE ALSO	`LayoutManager2`.
EXAMPLE	See the `LayoutManager2` class example.

layoutContainer( )

PURPOSE	Lays out the container's components using the components' constraints.
SYNTAX	`public void layoutContainer(Container container)`
DESCRIPTION	This method is called by `container` when the layout is invalidated and needs to be redone. The gridbag layout manager uses the component's preferred size when calculating the layout.
PARAMETERS	
`container`	The non-`null` container using this layout instance.
EXAMPLE	See `LayoutManager`.

layoutInfo

PURPOSE	This field holds the gridbag's layout information.
SYNTAX	`protected GridBagLayoutInfo layoutInfo`
DESCRIPTION	The data in this field is based on the most recent validation of the gridbag. A value of `null` means either there are no components in the gridbag or the gridbag has not yet been validated.
EXAMPLE	See `GetLayoutInfo()`.

location( )

PURPOSE	Retrieves the cell location using a pixel location.
SYNTAX	`public Point location(int x, int y)`
DESCRIPTION	This method retrieves the cell location at pixel location (x, y). The cell locations are 0-based, so the top-left cell is at (0, 0). The cell at the bottom-right

A
B
C
D
E
F
G
H
I
J
K
L
M
N
O
P
Q
R
S
T
U
V
W
X
Y
Z

corner is at (number of column−1, number of rows−1). If x is to the left of the gridbag, it is set to 0; similarly for y. If x is to the right of the gridbag, it is set to the number of columns; similarly for y.

This calculation uses the data from the gridbag's most recent validation. Therefore, if the container is invalid or a constraint has been modified, the gridbag should be validated before calling this method.

PARAMETERS

x   The *x*-coordinate relative to the gridbag container's inset area.
y   The *y*-coordinate relative to the gridbag container's inset area.

RETURNS   A new non-`null` `Point` instance containing the coordinates of the cell.

EXAMPLE   This example creates a frame that has four custom canvases. See Figure 199. The canvas displays its cell position and forwards mouse motion events to its parent, which is the panel containing the canvases. The panel receives those events and uses them to locate a cell in the gridbag. The cell location is displayed at the bottom of the frame.

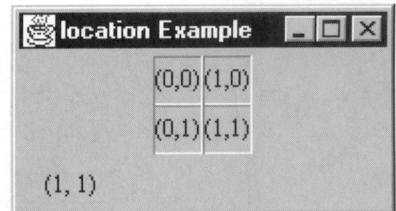

FIGURE 199:   `GridBagLayout.location( )`.

```
import java.awt.*;
import java.awt.event.*;

public class Main extends Frame {
    GridBagLayout gbl = new GridBagLayout();
    Label l = new Label("");

    Main() {
        super("location Example");
        Panel p = new Panel(gbl);
        for (int i=0; i<2; i++) {
            for (int j=0; j<2; j++) {
                makeCanvas(p, "("+i+","+j+")", i, j);
            }
        }

        setBackground(Color.lightGray);

        add(p, BorderLayout.CENTER);
        add(l, BorderLayout.SOUTH);

        p.addMouseMotionListener(new MouseMotionEventHandler());
        pack();
        show();
    }
```

```
    class MouseMotionEventHandler extends MouseMotionAdapter {
        public void mouseMoved(MouseEvent evt) {
            int x = evt.getX(), y = evt.getY();
            Point p = gbl.location(x, y);

            l.setText("("+p.x+", "+p.y+")");
        }
    }

    void makeCanvas(Container cont, String label, int x, int y) {
        GridBagConstraints c = new GridBagConstraints();
        MainCanvas cv = new MainCanvas(label);

        cont.add(cv);
        cv.setSize(30, 30);
        c.gridx = x;
        c.gridy = y;
        gbl.setConstraints(cv, c);
    }

    static public void main(String[] args) {
        new Main();
    }
}

class MainCanvas extends Canvas {
    String label;

    MainCanvas(String label) {
        this.label = label;
        addMouseMotionListener(new MouseMotionEventHandler());
    }

    public void paint(Graphics g) {
        int w = getSize().width;
        int h = getSize().height;
        FontMetrics fm = g.getFontMetrics();

        g.drawString(label, (w-fm.stringWidth(label))/2,
            (h-fm.getHeight())/2+fm.getAscent());
        g.setColor(getBackground());
        g.draw3DRect(0, 0, w-1, h-1, false);
    }

    class MouseMotionEventHandler extends MouseMotionAdapter {
        public void mouseMoved(MouseEvent evt) {
            evt.translatePoint(getLocation().x, getLocation().y);

            getParent().dispatchEvent(evt);
        }
    }
}
```

A
B
C
D
E
F
G
H
I
J
K
L
M
N
O
P
Q
R
S
T
U
V
W
X
Y
Z

lookupConstraints( )

PURPOSE	Retrieves the constraints for a component.
SYNTAX	`protected GridBagConstraints lookupConstraints(Component comp)`
DESCRIPTION	This method retrieves the constraints for the component `comp`. The return value is not a copy; it is the actual constraints instance used by the layout mechanism.
PARAMETERS	
`comp`	The non-`null` component to be queried.
RETURNS	The non-`null` constraints for the component.
SEE ALSO	`getConstraints()`.

MAXGRIDSIZE

PURPOSE	This constant specifies the maximum number of cells in the gridbag.
SYNTAX	`protected static final int MAXGRIDSIZE`
DESCRIPTION	Its value is 512.

maximumLayoutSize( )

PURPOSE	Calculates the maximum dimensions for laying out the components.
SYNTAX	`public Dimension maximumLayoutSize(Container cont)`
DESCRIPTION	For gridbag layout, the maximum layout is, by default, the largest dimension available (`Integer.MAX_VALUE` by `Integer.MAX_VALUE`).
PARAMETERS	
`cont`	The non-`null` container using this layout instance.
RETURNS	A new non-`null` `Dimension` instance containing the maximum size of the gridbag layout.
SEE ALSO	`Component.getMaximumSize()`, `Container`, `minimumLayoutSize()`, `LayoutManager2`, `preferredLayoutSize()`.
EXAMPLE	See the `LayoutManager2` class example.

A
B
C
D
E
F
G
H
I
J
K
L
M
N
O
P
Q
R
S
T
U
V
W
X
Y
Z

minimumLayoutSize()

PURPOSE	Calculates the minimum dimensions needed to lay out the components.
SYNTAX	`public Dimension minimumLayoutSize(Container container)`
DESCRIPTION	This method lays out the gridbag using the components' minimum sizes and returns the dimensions of the resulting gridbag.
PARAMETERS	
`container`	The non-null container using this layout instance.
RETURNS	A new non-null `Dimension` instance containing the minimum size of the gridbag.
SEE ALSO	`Component.minimumSize()`.
EXAMPLE	See `LayoutManager`.

MINSIZE

PURPOSE	Layout constant specifying that calculations should use a component's minimum size.
SYNTAX	`protected static final int MINSIZE`
DESCRIPTION	This constant is used in various layout methods. When a component's dimensions are needed, this constant specifies that the dimensions should be retrieved using `Component.getMinimumSize()` rather than `Component.getPreferredSize()`.
SEE ALSO	`PREFERREDSIZE`.
EXAMPLE	See `GetLayoutInfo()`.

preferredLayoutSize()

PURPOSE	Calculates the preferred dimensions needed to lay out the components.
SYNTAX	`public Dimension preferredLayoutSize(Container container)`
DESCRIPTION	This method lays out the gridbag using the components' preferred sizes and returns the dimensions of the resulting gridbag.
PARAMETERS	
`container`	The non-null container using this layout instance.
RETURNS	A new non-null `Dimension` instance containing the preferred size of the gridbag.

SEE ALSO	`Component.preferredSize()`.
EXAMPLE	See `LayoutManager`.

PREFERREDSIZE

PURPOSE	Layout constant specifying that calculations should use a component's preferred size.
SYNTAX	`protected static final int PREFERREDSIZE`
DESCRIPTION	This constant is used in various layout methods. When a component's dimensions are needed, this constant specifies that the dimensions should be retrieved using `Component.preferredSize()` rather than `Component.minimumSize()`.
SEE ALSO	`MINSIZE`.
EXAMPLE	See `GetLayoutInfo()`.

removeLayoutComponent()

PURPOSE	This method is a no-op.
SYNTAX	`public void removeLayoutComponent(Component comp)`
DESCRIPTION	This method is called by the layout manager's container whenever a component is removed from the container.
	This method does nothing. It needs to be defined in order to satisfy the `LayoutManager` interface.
PARAMETERS	
`comp`	The non-`null` component about to be removed from the container. Ignored.
EXAMPLE	See `LayoutManager`.

rowHeights

PURPOSE	This field holds the overrides to the row minimum heights.
SYNTAX	`public int rowHeights[]`
DESCRIPTION	If this field is non-`null`, the values in the field are applied to the gridbag after all the minimum row heights have been calculated. If `rowHeights` has more

elements than the number of rows, rows are added to the gridbag to match the number of elements in `rowHeights`.

EXAMPLE   See `rowWeights`.

rowWeights

PURPOSE   This field holds the overrides to the row weights.

SYNTAX   `public double[] rowWeights`

DESCRIPTION   If this field is non-`null`, the values in the field are applied to the gridbag after all of the row weights have been calculated. If `rowWeights[i]` is greater than the weight for row `i`, then row `i` is assigned the weight in `rowWeights[i]`. If `rowWeights` has more elements than the number of rows, the excess elements in `rowWeights` are ignored; they do not cause more rows to be created.

EXAMPLE   See `columnWeights`.

setConstraints()

PURPOSE   Sets the gridbag constraints for a component.

SYNTAX   `public void setConstraints(Component comp, GridBagConstraints constraints)`

DESCRIPTION   This method associates the gridbag constraints `constraints` to the component `comp`. The caller is free to modify `constraints`, since this method creates and uses a clone of `constraints`.

PARAMETERS

`comp`   The non-`null` component to associate with `constraints`.

`constraints` The non-`null` gridbag constraints to associate with `comp`. The values in `constraints` are copied.

SEE ALSO   `GridBagConstraints.clone()`.

EXAMPLE   See the class example.

A
B
C
D
E
F
G
H
I
J
K
L
M
N
O
P
Q
R
S
T
U
V
W
X
Y
Z

toString( )

A
B
C
D
E
F
G
H
I
J
K
L
M
N
O
P
Q
R
S
T
U
V
W
X
Y
Z

PURPOSE	Generates the string representation of the gridbag's state.
SYNTAX	`public String toString()`
DESCRIPTION	This method generates the string representation of this gridbag. The result string contains the gridbag's class name.
	This method is typically used for debugging.
RETURNS	A non-`null` string containing the gridbag's class name.
OVERRIDES	`Object.toString()`.
EXAMPLE	See `Object.toString()`.

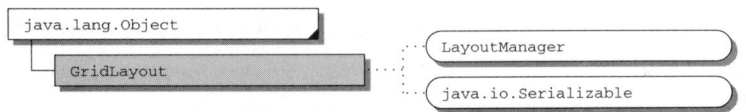

Syntax
public class GridLayout implements LayoutManager, Serializable

Description

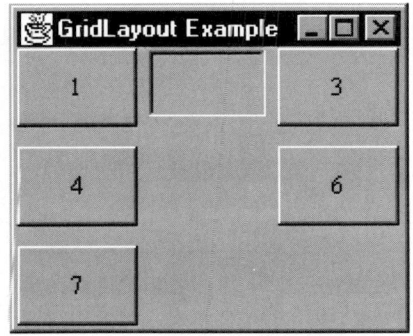

The grid layout manager places components in a grid of rows and columns. The components are laid out in left-to-right, top-to-bottom order. Figure 200 shows a container with a grid layout manager set to display a grid of three rows and three columns. The cells in the grid are exactly the same size and are as large as possible such that all cells are completely visible. Any remaining space is distributed to the right and bottom of the container. Every component is allocated a cell, regardless of whether the component is visible. An invisible component simply shows as an empty cell.

FIGURE 200: GridLayout.

The grid layout manager does not use the names of the components, so any name that is supplied with the addLayoutComponent() method call is ignored.

Rows and Columns
When creating a grid layout manager, you specify the number of rows and columns of the grid. The number of rows and columns can be changed at any time. Either of the dimensions can be set to "any" (value 0), meaning the number of rows (or columns) in that dimension depends on the other dimension. For example, if the number of rows is "any" and the number of columns is 2, then the number of rows will be (number-of-components+1)/2. An exception is thrown if both dimensions are set to "any." If both the rows and column is not "any," then the number of specified columns is treated as if it were "any."

Gaps
The grid layout manager allows you to separate the cells by gaps. The vertical gap specifies the space between rows, while the horizontal gap specifies the space between columns. The gaps can be changed at any time.

See Also
java.io.Serializable.

MEMBER SUMMARY	
Constructor	
GridLayout()	Constructs a grid layout with the specified rows and columns.
Layout Manager Methods	
addLayoutComponent()	Adds a component to this layout.
layoutContainer()	Lays out the container's components according to the settings of the layout manager.
minimumLayoutSize()	Calculates the minimum dimensions needed to layout the components.
preferredLayoutSize()	Calculates the preferred dimensions needed to layout the components.
removeLayoutComponent()	Removes a component from the layout.
Gap Methods	
getHgap()	Retrieves the horizontal gap between components.
getVgap()	Retrieves the vertical gap between components.
setHgap()	Sets the horizontal gap between components.
setVgap()	Sets the vertical gap between components.
Grid Methods	
getColumns()	Retrieves the number of columns in this grid layout.
getRows()	Retrieves the number of rows in this grid layout.
setColumns()	Sets the number of columns in this grid layout.
setRows()	Sets the number of rows in this grid layout.
Debugging Method	
toString()	Generates a string representation of the grid layout's values.

Example

This example creates a 3-×-3 grid layout with 5 pixels between columns and 10 pixels between rows (see Figure 200). Notice that button "5" is not visible, but it still occupies a cell.

```
import java.awt.*;

class Main {
    static public void main(String[] args) {
        Frame f = new Frame("GridLayout Example");
        Button b;
        f.setLayout(new GridLayout(3, 4, 5, 10));
        f.add(new Button("1"));
        f.add(new List());
        f.add(new Button("3"));
        f.add(new Button("4"));
        f.add(b = new Button("5"));
        f.add(new Button("6"));
```

```
        f.add(new Button("7"));
        f.pack();
        f.show();
        b.setVisible(false);
    }
}
```

A
B
C

addLayoutComponent()

D
E
F

PURPOSE   Adds a component to the layout.

SYNTAX   `public void addLayoutComponent(String name, Component comp)`

DESCRIPTION   This method is called by the container when a component is added with a
                name. However, component names are ignored by the grid layout manager, so
                this method does nothing. This method needs to be defined in order to satisfy
                the `LayoutManager` interface.

H
I
J

PARAMETERS
  comp   The named component that has just been added to the container. Ignored.
  name   The name of the component. Ignored.

K

EXAMPLE   See `LayoutManager`.

L

M

N

getColumns()

O
P

PURPOSE   Retrieves the number of columns in this grid layout.

SYNTAX   `public int getColumns()`

Q

DESCRIPTION   The number of columns in this layout is initialized by the `GridLayout` con-
                structor and changed using `setColumns()`. See the class description for
                details on rows and columns.

R
S

RETURNS   A non-negative integer specifying the number of columns. 0 means any num-
                ber of columns.

T
U

SEE ALSO   `getRows()`, `setColumns()`.

V

EXAMPLE   See `setColumns()`.

W

X

Y

Z

getHgap()

PURPOSE   Retrieves the horizontal gap between components.

SYNTAX   `public int getHgap()`

A

B

DESCRIPTION   The horizontal gap is initialized by the `GridLayout` constructor and changed using `setHgap()`. See the class description for details on horizontal gaps.

C

RETURNS   A non-negative integer specifying the horizontal gap in pixels.

D

SEE ALSO   `getVgap()`, `setHgap()`.

E

EXAMPLE   This example cre-
F
               ates a frame that
G
               has a 3-×-3 grid
H
               layout manager
               with vertical and
I
               horizontal gaps
               initialized to 0.
J
               Four buttons
K
               labeled V+, V-,
L
               H+, and H- con-
               trol the vertical
M
               and horizontal

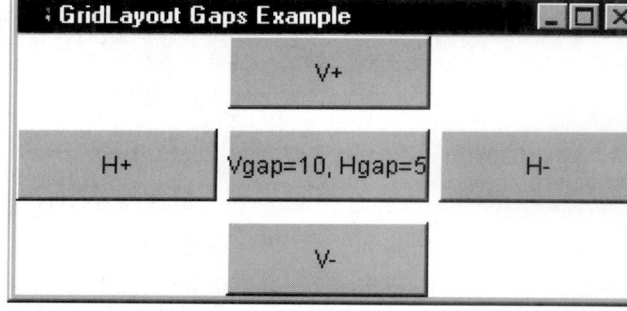

FIGURE 201:   **Horizontal and Vertical Gaps in a `GridLayout`.**

N
               gaps of the grid layout. A status button in the center is used to display the cur-
               rent vertical and horizontal gaps in effect. See Figure 201.

O

P

```
import java.awt.*;
import java.awt.event.*;

class Main extends Frame implements ActionListener {
    GridLayout layout = new GridLayout(3, 3);
    Button status;
    Main() {
        super("GridLayout Gaps Example");
        setLayout(layout);

        Button b;
        add(b = new Button());         // 1
        b.setVisible(false);
        add(b = new Button("V+"));     // 2
        b.addActionListener(this);
        add(b = new Button());         // 3
        b.setVisible(false);
        add(b = new Button("H+"));     // 4
        b.addActionListener(this);

        status = new Button("Vgap="+layout.getVgap() +
                            ", Hgap="+layout.getHgap());
        add(status);

        add(b = new Button("H-"));  // 6
```

Q

R

S

T

U

V

W

X

Y

Z

```
            b.addActionListener(this);
            add(b = new Button());          // 7
            b.setVisible(false);
            add(b = new Button("V-"));      // 8
            b.addActionListener(this);

            setSize(100, 200);
            show();
        }

    public void actionPerformed(ActionEvent evt) {
        String what = evt.getActionCommand();

        if ("H+".equals(what)) {
            layout.setHgap(layout.getHgap()+5);
        } else if ("H-".equals(what)) {
            layout.setHgap(Math.max(0, layout.getHgap()-5));
        } else if ("V+".equals(what)) {
            layout.setVgap(layout.getVgap()+5);
        } else if ("V-".equals(what)) {
            layout.setVgap(Math.max(0, layout.getVgap()-5));
        }
        // Update status button
        status.setLabel("Vgap="+layout.getVgap() +
                        ", Hgap="+layout.getHgap());
        invalidate();
        validate();
    }

    public static void main(String[] args) {
        new Main();
    }
}
```

getRows()

PURPOSE	Retrieves the number of rows in this grid layout.
SYNTAX	`public int getRows()`
DESCRIPTION	The number of rows in this layout is initialized by the `GridLayout` constructor and changed using `setRows()`. See the class description for details on rows and columns.
RETURNS	A non-negative integer specifying the number of rows. 0 means any number of rows.
SEE ALSO	`getColumns()`, `setRows()`.
EXAMPLE	See `setColumns()`.

A
B
C
D
E
F
G
H
I
J
K
L
M
N
O
P
Q
R
S
T
U
V
W
X
Y
Z

getVgap()

PURPOSE	Retrieves the vertical gap between components.
SYNTAX	`public int getVgap()`
DESCRIPTION	The vertical gap is initialized by the `GridLayout` constructor and changed using `setVgap()`. See the class description for details on vertical gaps.
RETURNS	A non-negative integer specifying the vertical gap in pixels.
SEE ALSO	`getHgap()`, `setVgap()`.
EXAMPLE	See `getHgap()`.

GridLayout()

PURPOSE	Constructs a new `GridLayout` instance.

SYNTAX	`public GridLayout()`
	`public GridLayout(int rows, int cols)`
	`public GridLayout(int rows, int cols, int hgap, int vgap)`

DESCRIPTION	The first form of this constructor creates a new grid layout manager instance with 1 row and 0 columns. The second and third forms of this constructor create a new grid layout manager instance with the specified rows and columns. If `rows` is greater than 0, the value of `cols` is set but ignored and is treated like 0, that is, any number of columns (see the class description for more details). `rows` and `cols` cannot both be 0. If `hgap` and `vgap` are not specified, they default to 0.
	An instance of the grid layout manager can be shared by more than one container. Also, the grid layout manager can be set on a container at any time, regardless of the number of the components already in the container.

PARAMETERS

`cols`	A non-negative integer specifying the number of columns in the grid; 0 means "any number" of columns.
`hgap`	A non-negative integer specifying the space between columns in pixels.
`rows`	A non-negative integer specifying the number of rows in the grid; 0 means "any number."
`vgap`	A non-negative integer specifying the space between rows in pixels.

EXCEPTIONS

`IllegalArgumentException`	
	If `rows` and `cols` are both 0.
EXAMPLE	See the class example.

layoutContainer( )

PURPOSE	Lays out the container's components according to the settings of the layout manager.
SYNTAX	`public void layoutContainer(Container cont)`
DESCRIPTION	This method is called by the container when the layout is invalidated and needs to be redone.
	The number of cells is determined by the number of specified rows and columns and the number of components in the container. The cell height is the largest integer such that rows * cellHeight + (rows−1) * (the vertical gap) does not exceed the current height of the container; likewise for the cell width. Neither the minimum nor preferred sizes of the components are used in the calculations. All of the components are resized to the cell size and then placed in order from left-to-right and top-to-bottom. Any remaining space is distributed to the right and bottom of the container.
PARAMETERS	
cont	The non-null container using this layout instance.
SEE ALSO	`Container.`
EXAMPLE	See `LayoutManager`.

minimumLayoutSize( )

PURPOSE	Calculates the minimum dimensions needed to lay out the components.
SYNTAX	`public Dimension minimumLayoutSize(Container cont)`
DESCRIPTION	The minimum dimension is calculated by determining each component's minimum size. The maximum of these minimum dimensions determines the size of a cell. The minimum dimensions of the entire layout is based on this cell size and all of the gaps between them.
PARAMETERS	
cont	The non-null container using this layout instance.
RETURNS	A non-null Dimension object containing the minimum size of the grid layout.
SEE ALSO	`Component.minimumSize().`
EXAMPLE	See `LayoutManager`.

A
B
C
D
E
F
G
H
I
J
K
L
M
N
O
P
Q
R
S
T
U
V
W
X
Y
Z

A
B
C
D
E
F
G
H
I
J
K
L
M
N
O
P
Q
R
S
T
U
V
W
X
Y
Z

preferredLayoutSize()

PURPOSE	Calculates the preferred dimensions needed to lay out the components.
SYNTAX	`public Dimension preferredLayoutSize(Container cont)`
DESCRIPTION	The preferred dimension is calculated by determining each component's preferred size. The maximum of these preferred dimensions determines the size of a cell. The preferred dimensions of the entire layout is based on this cell size and all of the gaps between them.
PARAMETERS	
`cont`	The non-`null` container using this layout instance.
RETURNS	A non-`null` `Dimension` object containing the preferred size of the grid layout.
SEE ALSO	`Component.preferredSize()`.
EXAMPLE	See `LayoutManager`.

removeLayoutComponent()

PURPOSE	Removes a component from the layout.
SYNTAX	`public void removeLayoutComponent(Component comp)`
DESCRIPTION	This method is called by the layout manager's container whenever a component is removed from the container. Since the grid layout does not use named components, this method does nothing. It needs to be defined in order to satisfy the `LayoutManager` interface.
PARAMETERS	
`comp`	The component about to be removed from the container. Ignored.
EXAMPLE	See `LayoutManager`.

setColumns()

PURPOSE	Sets the number of columns in this grid layout.
SYNTAX	`public void setColumns(int columns)`
DESCRIPTION	This method sets the number columns in this layout to be `columns`. When the components are laid out, if the number of rows is nonzero, the number of columns is ignored. See the class description for details.

PARAMETERS

columns   A non-negative integer specifying the number of columns. 0 means any number of columns. The number of rows and the number of columns cannot both be 0 at the same time.

EXCEPTIONS

IllegalArgumentException

If columns is 0 when the layout's number of rows is already 0.

SEE ALSO   getColumns(), setRows().

EXAMPLE   This example creates a frame with a 2-x-3 grid layout manager. Ten buttons are added to the grid to illustrate how the components are laid out. Four control buttons labeled row+, row-, column+, and

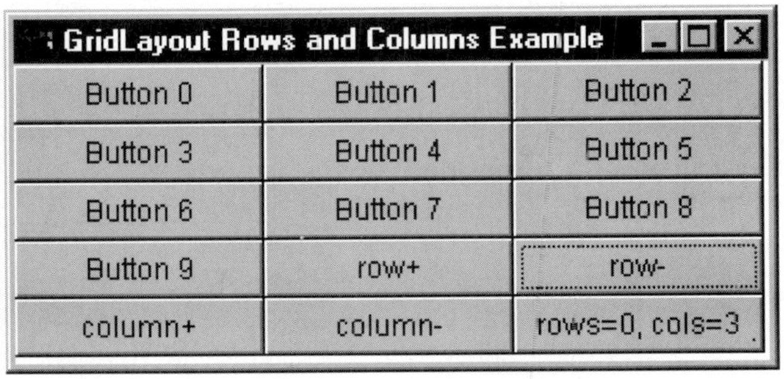

FIGURE 202:   Rows and Columns in a GridLayout.

column- are added to change the number of rows and columns in the grid layout. A status button (last button in the layout) is used to display the current rows and columns specified. See Figure 202.

The fifteen buttons are initially laid out in two rows (the number of columns is ignored because rows is nonzero). As you manipulate the number of rows and columns, notice that the number of columns is effective only when the number of rows is set to 0.

```
import java.awt.*;
import java.awt.event.*;

class Main extends Frame implements ActionListener {
    GridLayout layout = new GridLayout(2, 3);
    Button status;
    Main() {
        super("GridLayout Rows and Columns Example");
        setLayout(layout);

        // Create 10 buttons for layout
        for (int i=0; i <10; i++) {
            add( new Button("Button " + i));
        }

        // Add control buttons
        Button b;
        add(b = new Button("row+"));  // 1
```

```
                b.addActionListener(this);
                add(b = new Button("row-"));   // 2
                b.addActionListener(this);
                add(b = new Button("column+"));   // 3
                b.addActionListener(this);
                add(b = new Button("column-"));   // 4
                b.addActionListener(this);
                status = new Button("rows="+layout.getRows() +
                                    ", cols="+layout.getColumns());
                add(status);


                setSize(100, 200);
                show();
            }

        public void actionPerformed(ActionEvent evt) {
                String what = evt.getActionCommand();

                if ("row+".equals(what)) {
                    layout.setRows(layout.getRows()+1);
                } else if ("row-".equals(what)) {
                    int min = (layout.getColumns() != 0) ? 0 : 1;
                    layout.setRows(Math.max(min, layout.getRows()-1));
                } else if ("column+".equals(what)) {
                    layout.setColumns(layout.getColumns()+1);
                } else if ("column-".equals(what)) {
                    int min = (layout.getRows() != 0) ? 0 : 1;
                    layout.setColumns(Math.max(0, layout.getColumns()-1));
                }
                // Update status button
                status.setLabel("rows="+layout.getRows() +
                                ", cols="+layout.getColumns());
                invalidate();
                validate();
            }

        public static void main(String[] args) {
                new Main();
            }
        }
    }
```

setHgap()

PURPOSE	Sets the horizontal gap between components.
SYNTAX	`public void setHgap(int hgap)`
DESCRIPTION	This method sets the horizontal gap of this layout to be `hgap`. See the class description for details.
PARAMETERS	
`hgap`	A non-negative integer specifying the horizontal gap in pixels.
SEE ALSO	`getHgap()`, `setVgap()`.
EXAMPLE	See `getHgap()`.

setRows()

PURPOSE	Sets the number of rows in this grid layout.
SYNTAX	`public void setRows(int rows)`
DESCRIPTION	This method sets the number rows in this layout to be `rows`. When the components are laid out, if the number of rows is nonzero, the number of columns is ignored. See the class description for details.
PARAMETERS	
rows	A non-negative integer specifying the number of rows. 0 means any number of rows. The number of rows and the number of columns cannot both be 0 at the same time.
EXCEPTIONS	
`IllegalArgumentException`	If `rows` is 0 when the layout's number of columns is already 0.
SEE ALSO	`getRows()`, `setColumns()`.
EXAMPLE	See `setColumns()`.

setVgap()

PURPOSE	Sets the vertical gap between components.
SYNTAX	`public void setVgap(int vgap)`
DESCRIPTION	This method sets the vertical gap of this layout to be `vgap`. See the class description for details.
PARAMETERS	
vgap	A non-negative integer specifying the vertical gap in pixels.
SEE ALSO	`getVgap()`, `setHgap()`.
EXAMPLE	See `getHgap()`.

A
B
C
D
E
F
G
H
I
J
K
L
M
N
O
P
Q
R
S
T
U
V
W
X
Y
Z

toString( )

PURPOSE	Generates a string representation of the layout manager's state.
SYNTAX	`public String toString()`
DESCRIPTION	This method generates the string that contains the layout manager's class name, the size of the two gaps, and the number of rows and columns.
	This method is typically used for debugging.
RETURNS	A non-`null` string representing the layout manager's state.
OVERRIDES	`java.lang.Object.toString()`.
EXAMPLE	See `java.lang.Object.toString()`.

A
B
C
D
E
F
G
H
I
J
K
L
M
N
O
P
Q
R
S
T
U
V
W
X
Y
Z

IllegalComponentStateException

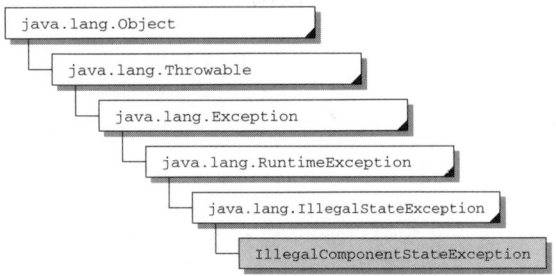

Syntax

class IllegalComponentStateException extends IllegalStateException

Description

IllegalComponentStateException is thrown when the program attempts to perform an operation on an AWT component while the component is not in an appropriate state to perform the operation.

IllegalComponentStateException should not be caught or declared in the throws clause of a method.

MEMBER SUMMARY
Constructor
IllegalComponentStateException()   Constructs an IllegalComponentStateException instance.

See Also

Component.getLocale(), Component.getLocationOnScreen(),
java.lang.IllegalStateException, TextComponent.setCaretPosition().

Example

The following code will throw an IllegalComponentStateException when it executes getLocationOnScreen() on the frame because the frame has not been made visible yet.

```
import java.awt.*;

class Main {
    static public void main(String[] args) {
```

IllegalComponentStateException()

```
            Frame f1 = new Frame("Frame Example");

            f1.setSize(200, 100);
            System.out.println("location on screen: " + f1.getLocationOnScreen());
        }
    }
```

A

B

C

IllegalComponentStateException()

D

E

PURPOSE   Constructs an IllegalComponentStateException instance.

F

SYNTAX   public IllegalComponentStateException()
              public IllegalComponentStateException(String msg)

G

H

DESCRIPTION   This constructor creates a new instance of IllegalComponentStateExcep-
              tion. An optional string msg can be supplied that describes this particular
              instance of the exception.

I

PARAMETERS

J

msg   A possibly null string that gives details about this exception.

K

L

M

N

O

P

Q

R

S

T

U

V

W

X

Y

Z

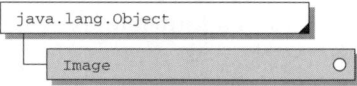

Syntax

`public abstract class Image`

Description

An *image* is a repository of pixel values. Images are typically created by way of an image stream that involves an *image producer*—the object that supplies pixel values—and an *image consumer*—the object that takes the pixel values and places them in an image object. See Figure 203. In this architecture, an image can be created without having all of the pixels in it. Typically methods that return images actually return an image object immediately and then fill in the pixels later. The image object can then be painted regardless of whether all of the pixels are available. If it is necessary to determine if all of the pixels are loaded, use `Component.checkImage()`. An object can register for updates as new pixels become available (see the "Image Observer" section later in this item) or it can wait until all of the pixels are loaded (see `MediaTracker`).

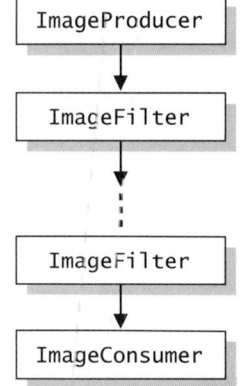

FIGURE 203: Image Producer, Consumers, and Filter.

If an error occurs during the delivery of the pixels, none of the methods that operate on the image (e.g., `Graphics.drawImage()`) will fail, although the image will not appear correctly on the screen. The program must explicitly check for errors to determine if an error occurred (see `Component.checkImage()`).

One or more image filters can be inserted between an image producer and the image consumer to modify the pixel values as they pass through the filters. See the `ImageFilter` class for more details.

It is not possible to directly retrieve the pixels in an image. It must be done indirectly by retrieving the image's producer (using `getSource()`) and then reading the pixels as the producer delivers them. The `PixelGrabber` class makes this process more convenient. See the `PixelGrabber` class for more details.

Image Observer

An *image observer* is an object that is interested in some information about an image that is not yet available. Two methods in this interface take an image observer as a parameter—`getWidth()` and `getHeight()`. If an image's dimensions are not yet available, these methods return -1. If an image observer is registered (that is, the image observer is not `null`), the image observer will immediately be notified via the `ImageObserver.imageUp-date()` method as soon as the dimension information is available. See `ImageObserver` class for more details.

All components are image observers. This means that whenever you paint an image that hasn't been completely loaded and register the component as an image observer, the component will be automatically notified whenever the image gets new pixels. This makes it extremely easy to render images progressively.

Multiframe Images

Not only can the pixels of an image not all be present, but also the set of pixels in an image can change with time. This can happen if the image is a *multiframe* image. An example of a multiframe image is an animated GIF. An image observer will be notified whenever the frame of an image changes. If the image observer is a component painting an animated GIF, the notification will cause the component to repaint itself.

Produced and Off-screen Images

There are two kinds of images: *produced* and *off-screen*. Produced images are generated via an image producer. Off-screen images are created with the method `Component.createImage()`. The main difference between the two is that graphics contexts can be created only for an off-screen image. If it is necessary to paint on a produced image, you must first copy the produced image to an off-screen image.

Image Properties

An *image property* is an arbitrary value that an image producer associates with an image. For example, an image producer that decodes GIF images might make the comments embedded in the image available as a property. Another example is image filters that set the "filters" property so that the final image consumer can determine how the image has been filtered. There is no predefined set of image properties that an image might have. So you need to consult the image producer's documentation to discover what image properties it might set. Note that any image filters used in creating an image may also add their own image properties to the image as the image flows through the filter.

By convention, the property name "comment" is used to store an optional comment that can be presented to the user as a description of the image, its source, or its author.

MEMBER SUMMARY	
Property Field and Method	
getProperty()	Retrieves an image property.
UndefinedProperty	This object is returned by getProperty() if the property is not defined.
Dimensions Methods	
getHeight()	Retrieves the height of this image.
getWidth()	Retrieves the width of this image.
Painting Method	
getGraphics()	Retrieves a graphics context for this image.
Scaling Method and Constants	
getScaledInstance()	Generates a scaled version of this image.
SCALE_AREA_AVERAGING	Use AreaAveragingScaleFilter as the scaling algorithm.
SCALE_DEFAULT	Use a default image scaling algorithm.
SCALE_FAST	Use an image scaling algorithm that emphasizes speed over smoothness.
SCALE_REPLICATE	Use ReplicateScaleFilter as the scaling algorithm.
SCALE_SMOOTH	Use a scaling algorithm that emphasizes image smoothness over speed.
Image Producer Method	
getSource()	Retrieves the image's producer.
Clean-up Method	
flush()	Destroys all resources used by this image.

See Also

java.awt.image.AreaAveragingScaleFilter, java.awt.image.ImageConsumer,
java.awt.image.ImageFilter, java.awt.image.ImageObserver,
java.awt.image.ReplicateScaleFilter.

Example

This example implements a thumbnail image viewer. You can run this program by supplying it with the name of a graphics file or the name of a directory. If the former, the image in the file is displayed; if the latter, all of the images (.gif and .jpg) in the directory are displayed. See Figure 204.

The images are displayed in an area consisting of 125-×-125 cells. If an image is larger than

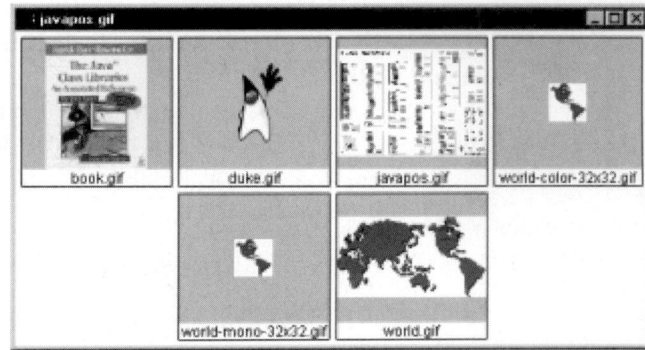

FIGURE 204:   Thumbnail Image Viewer.

this area, it is scaled down to fit; its aspect ratio is retained. If you click a thumbnail, the thumbnail creates a window that's large enough to hold the image in its entirety.

This program can be enhanced to show an expanded image within the same frame rather than another window's being created to hold it.

```java
import java.awt.*;
import java.awt.event.*;
import java.io.*;

class Main extends Frame {
    int cellSize = 125;

    Main(File dir) {
        String[] filenames;

        if (dir.isDirectory()) {
            // If directory, get files.
            filenames = dir.list();
        } else {
            // Otherwise, only show one image.
            filenames = new String[1];
            filenames[0] = dir.getName();

            // Set dir to be the directory rather than the file.
            dir = new File(dir.getParent());
        }

        for (int i=0; i<filenames.length; i++) {
            if (filenames[i].toLowerCase().endsWith(".gif")
                || filenames[i].toLowerCase().endsWith(".jpg")) {

                // Create and add the thumbnail component.
                // Also need to translate the relative filename to an
                // absolute filename in order to fetch the image.
                Component c = new Thumbnail(
                    getToolkit().getImage(dir.getAbsolutePath()
                        + File.separator + filenames[i]), filenames[i]);
                add(c);
```

```
                    c.setSize(cellSize, cellSize);
                }
            }

            // Listen for events and layout.
            addWindowListener(new WindowEventHandler());
            setLayout(new FlowLayout());
            pack();
            show();
        }

    public Dimension getPreferredSize() {
        Insets insets = getInsets();
        int count = getComponentCount();
        int hgap = ((FlowLayout)getLayout()).getHgap();
        int vgap = ((FlowLayout)getLayout()).getVgap();

        // Maximum of 4 columns.
        int cols = Math.max(1, Math.min(count, 4));

        // The following code exactly determines the size
        // necessary to show all the thumbnails.
        Dimension d = new Dimension(
            cols*(cellSize+hgap) + hgap,
            ((count-1)/cols+1)*(cellSize+vgap) + vgap);

        // Don't forge the frame's insets.
        d.width += insets.left+insets.right;
        d.height += insets.top+insets.bottom;

        // Make sure it's not larger than the screen.
        Dimension screenDim = getToolkit().getScreenSize();
        d.width = Math.min(d.width, screenDim.width);
        d.height = Math.min(d.height, screenDim.height);
        return d;
    }

    class WindowEventHandler extends WindowAdapter {
        public void windowClosing(WindowEvent evt) {
            // Destroy the window.
            dispose();
        }
    }

    public static void main(String[] args) {
        File dir;

        if (args.length == 1) {
            dir = new File(args[0]);
        } else {
            dir = new File(".");
        }
        new Main(dir);
    }
}

class Thumbnail extends Canvas {
    Image image;
    String name;
```

```
            Thumbnail(Image image, String name) {
                this.image = image;
                this.name = name;

                // Start loading the image.
                prepareImage(image, this);

                // Listen for mouse events.
                addMouseListener(new MouseEventHandler());
            }

            public void paint(Graphics g) {
                update(g);
            }
            public void update(Graphics g) {
                FontMetrics fm = g.getFontMetrics();
                int w = getSize().width;
                int h = getSize().height - fm.getHeight();
                int iw = image.getWidth(this);
                int ih = image.getHeight(this);

                if (iw > 0 && ih > 0) {
                    // Scale down if necessary.
                    if (iw > h) {
                        ih = ih * w / iw;
                        iw = w;
                    }
                    if (ih > h && ih > 0) {
                        iw = iw * h / ih;
                        ih = h;
                    }

                    // Clear background.
                    g.setColor(Color.lightGray);
                    g.fillRect(0, 0, w, h);

                    // Center the image.
                    g.drawImage(image, (w-iw)/2, (h-ih)/2, iw, ih, this);
                }
                // Draw the name.
                h = getSize().height;
                g.setColor(Color.black);
                g.clearRect(0, h, w, fm.getHeight());
                g.drawString(name,
                    (w-fm.stringWidth(name))/2, h-fm.getHeight()+fm.getAscent());
                g.drawRect(0, 0, w-1, h-1);
            }

            class MouseEventHandler extends MouseAdapter {
                public void mousePressed(MouseEvent evt) {
                    new ImageViewer(image, name);
                }
                public void mouseEntered(MouseEvent evt) {
                    // Set the frame's title.
                    findFrame().setTitle(name);
                }
                public void mouseExited(MouseEvent evt) {
                    // Clear the frame's title.
                    findFrame().setTitle(null);
                }
```

A
B
C
D
E
F
G
H
J
K
L
M
N
O
P
Q
R
S
T
U
V
W
X
Y
Z

```
        // Returns this component's frame.
        public Frame findFrame() {
            Component c = getParent();
            while (c != null && !(c instanceof Frame)) {
                c = c.getParent();
            }
            return (Frame)c;
        }
    }
}

class ImageViewer extends Frame {
    Image image;
    ImageViewer(Image image, String name) {
        super(name);
        this.image = image;

        // Listen for events and show frame.
        addWindowListener(new WindowEventHandler());
        pack();
        show();
    }

    // Determine the size of the frame that will show the image.
    public Dimension getPreferredSize() {
        Insets insets = getInsets();

        return new Dimension(image.getWidth(null) + insets.left + insets.right,
            image.getHeight(null) + insets.top + insets.bottom);
    }

    public void paint(Graphics g) {
        g.drawImage(image, getInsets().left, getInsets().top, this);
    }

    class WindowEventHandler extends WindowAdapter {
        public void windowClosing(WindowEvent evt) {
            // Destroy the window.
            dispose();
        }
    }
}
```

A
B
C
D
E
F
G
H
I
J
K
L
M
N
O
P
Q
R
S
T
U
V
W
X
Y
Z

flush()

PURPOSE	Destroys all resources used by this image.
SYNTAX	`public abstract void flush()`
DESCRIPTION	This method is used to explicitly free any resources that may be used by the image. This includes any cached information and any system resources used to store the image. All of the image data is automatically regenerated if the image is used again.

Explicitly calling flush() is not necessary, since the resources are disposed when the image object is reclaimed by the garbage collector. However, in some cases it may be desirable to free up some memory quickly if it is certain the image will not be used again or is unlikely to be used for a while.

getGraphics()

PURPOSE   Retrieves a graphics context for this image.

SYNTAX   public abstract Graphics getGraphics()

DESCRIPTION   This method succeeds only for off-screen images (see Component.createImage()). Attempting to call getGraphics() for an image that is not an off-screen image results in a ClassCastException being thrown.

RETURNS   A non-null Graphics object that can be used to paint on the image.

SEE ALSO   Component.createImage(), Graphics.

EXAMPLE   This example allows you to draw over an image read from the file system. See Figure 205. Since you cannot draw on a produced image, the program first copies the produced image to an off-screen image and then makes all drawing operations to the off-screen image.

```
import java.awt.*;
import java.awt.image.*;
import java.awt.event.*;

class Main extends Frame {
    Main(String filename) {
        super("getGraphics Example");
        // Retrieve the image.
        add(new ImageCanvas(
            getToolkit().getImage(filename)),
            BorderLayout.CENTER);
        setSize(200, 200);
        show();
    }

    static public void main(String[] args) {
        if (args.length == 1) {
            new Main(args[0]);
        } else {
            System.err.println("usage: java Main <image file>");
        }
    }
}

class ImageCanvas extends Component {
    Image image;
    Image backBuffer;
    Graphics backBufferG;
```

FIGURE 205:   Drawing Over an Image.

```
    ImageCanvas(Image image) {
        this.image = image;
        prepareImage(image, this);
        addMouseMotionListener(new MouseMotionHandler());
    }

    public void paint(Graphics g) {
        update(g);
    }

    public void update(Graphics g) {
        if (backBuffer == null) {
            if (g.drawImage(image, 0, 0, this) && backBuffer == null) {
                int w = image.getWidth(this);
                int h = image.getHeight(this);

                backBuffer = createImage(w, h);
                backBufferG = backBuffer.getGraphics();
                backBufferG.setColor(getBackground());
                backBufferG.fillRect(0, 0, w, h);
                backBufferG.drawImage(image, 0, 0, this);
            }
            return;
        }
        g.drawImage(backBuffer, 0, 0, this);
    }

    class MouseMotionHandler extends MouseMotionAdapter {
        public void mouseDragged(MouseEvent evt) {
            backBufferG.setColor(Color.red);
            backBufferG.fillOval(evt.getX(), evt.getY(), 5, 5);
            repaint();
        }
    }
}
```

getHeight()

PURPOSE	Retrieves the height of the image.
SYNTAX	`public abstract int getHeight(ImageObserver observer)`
DESCRIPTION	The height of the image may not yet be available. In this case, -1 is returned and if `observer` is non-null, `observer` will be notified when the height becomes available.
PARAMETERS	
observer	The image observer to register for image updates; if `null`, no updates are desired.
RETURNS	The height of the image or -1 if the height is not yet available.
SEE ALSO	`getWidth()`, `ImageObserver`.
EXAMPLE	See the class example and `getScaledInstance()`.

getProperty()

PURPOSE	Retrieves an image property.
SYNTAX	`public abstract Object getProperty(String name, ImageObserver observer)`

DESCRIPTION This method retrieves the image property called `name`. The image properties that are available depend on the image producer. If `name` refers to an image property that is not defined by an image producer, the `UndefinedProperty` object is returned. If `name` refers to an image property whose value is not yet available, `null` is returned.

If the `name` image property is not yet available and `observer` is not `null`, `observer` will be notified when the property does become available.

PARAMETERS

name The non-`null` image property name.

observer The possibly `null` image observer.

RETURNS The value of the property called `name`. `UndefinedProperty` is returned if the property is not defined. `null` is returned if the value of the property is not yet available.

SEE ALSO `ImageObserver.imageUpdate()`, `UndefinedProperty`.

EXAMPLE This code fragment displays any comments associated with an image.

```
Image image;
...
if (image.getProperty("comment", this) != Image.UndefinedProperty) {
    System.out.println(image.getProperty("comment", this);
}
```

getScaledInstance()

PURPOSE	Generates a scaled version of this image.
SYNTAX	`public Image getScaledInstance(int width, int height, int hints)`

DESCRIPTION This method generates and returns a scaled version of this image. The dimensions of the new image are specified by `width` and `height`. If `width` or `height` is negative, that dimension is derived from the other. In particular, the derived number is such that the aspect ratio of the original unscaled image is retained. For example, if the original image is 10 wide and 20 high and `width` is –1 while `height` is 60, `width` will be set to 30. All of the pixels in the new image may not be completely loaded.

If hints includes either SCALE_SMOOTH or SCALE_AREA_AVERAGING, AreaAveragingScaleFilter is used; otherwise, ReplicateScaleFilter is used. See the class descriptions of these filter classes for more details.

PARAMETERS

height   The possibly negative height of the scaled version.

hints   A mask or'd from one or more of SCALE_AREA_AVERAGING, SCALE_DEFAULT, SCALE_FAST, SCALE_REPLICATE, or SCALE_SMOOTH.

width   The possibly negative width of the scaled version.

RETURNS   A scaled version of this image.

SEE ALSO   java.awt.image.AreaAveragingScaleFilter, java.awt.image.ReplicateScaleFilter.

EXAMPLE   This example reads in an image and then displays the image along with a scaled-up version of the image. See Figure 206. To scale the image, it uses getScaledInstance() to get a scaled version of the image.

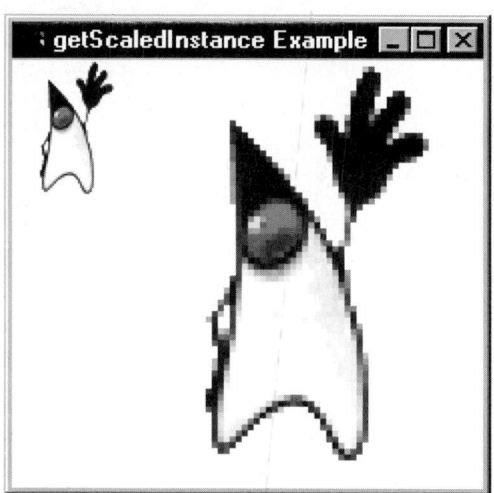

FIGURE 206: Scaling an Image.

```
import java.awt.*;
import java.awt.image.*;

class Main extends Frame {
    Main(String filename) {
        super("getScaledInstance Example");
        // Retrieve the image.
        add(new ImageCanvas(getToolkit().getImage(filename)),
            BorderLayout.CENTER);
        setSize(300, 300);
        show();
    }

    static public void main(String[] args) {
        if (args.length == 1) {
            new Main(args[0]);
        } else {
            System.err.println("usage: java Main <image file>");
        }
    }
}

class ImageCanvas extends Component {
```

```
                int scale = 3;
                Image image;
                Image scaledImage;

                ImageCanvas(Image image) {
                    this.image = image;
                    prepareImage(image, this);
                }

                public void paint(Graphics g) {
                    update(g);
                }

                public void update(Graphics g) {
                    int w = image.getWidth(this);
                    int h = image.getHeight(this);

                    if (w >= 0 || h >= 0) {
                        if (g.drawImage(image, 0, 0, this) && scaledImage == null) {
                            // The original image has completed loading
                            // Get its dimensions and get scaled version
                            scaledImage = image.getScaledInstance(w*scale, h*scale,
                                Image.SCALE_SMOOTH);
                        }
                    }
                    if (scaledImage != null) {
                        g.drawImage(scaledImage, w, 0, this);
                    }
                }
            }
```

getSource( )

PURPOSE Retrieves the image's producer.

SYNTAX   `public abstract ImageProducer getSource()`

DESCRIPTION The image producer is used to regenerate the image's pixels and is typically used in conjunction with image filters.

SEE ALSO `ImageFilter, ImageProducer`.

EXAMPLE This example reads in an image and scrambles it by swapping the left and right sides of the image. See Figure 207. A subimage of the original image is created with the help of the `CropImageFilter` class. The image producer of the original image is retrieved and used to create an image stream that passes through the crop image filter. An off-screen image holds the new scrambled image.

FIGURE 207:
`Image.getSource()`.

```
import java.awt.*;
import java.awt.image.*;

class Main extends Frame {
    Main(String filename) {
        super("getSource Example");
        add(new ImageCanvas(getToolkit().getImage(filename)),
            BorderLayout.CENTER);
        setSize(100, 100);
        show();
    }

    static public void main(String[] args) {
        if (args.length == 1) {
            new Main(args[0]);
        } else {
            System.err.println("usage: java Main <image file>");
        }
    }
}

class ImageCanvas extends Component {
    Image oldImage;
    Image image;

    ImageCanvas(Image image) {
        oldImage = image;
        waitForImage(image);
    }

    void waitForImage(Image image) {
        try {
            // Use a media tracker object to wait until all the pixels
            // have been retrieved.
            MediaTracker tracker = new MediaTracker(this);
            tracker.addImage(image, 0);
            tracker.waitForID(0);
        } catch (Exception e) {
            e.printStackTrace();
        }
    }

    Image getSubImage(Image image, Rectangle r) {
        // Create crop image using a CropImageFilter.
        CropImageFilter imgf = new CropImageFilter(
            r.x, r.y, r.width, r.height);
        ImageProducer ip = image.getSource();

        ip = new FilteredImageSource(ip, imgf);
        Image result = getToolkit().createImage(ip);
        waitForImage(result);
        return result;
    }

    public void paint(Graphics g) {
        int w = oldImage.getWidth(this);
        int h = oldImage.getHeight(this);
        if (image == null) {

            image = createImage(w, h);
```

A
B
C
D
E
F
G
H

J
K
L
M
N
O
P
Q
R
S
T
U
V
W
X
Y
Z

```
                    Graphics g2 = image.getGraphics();
                    g2.drawImage(getSubImage(oldImage, new Rectangle(0, 0, w/2, h)),
                        w/2, 0, this);
                    g2.drawImage(getSubImage(oldImage, new Rectangle(w/2, 0, w/2, h)),
                        0, 0, this);
                    g2.dispose();
                }
            g.drawImage(image, (getSize().width-w)/2, (getSize().height-h)/2,
        this);
            }
        }
```

getWidth( )

PURPOSE	Retrieves the width of the image.
SYNTAX	`public abstract int getWidth(ImageObserver observer)`
DESCRIPTION	This method retrieves the width of the image. If the width is not available, -1 is returned. If `observer` is non-`null`, `observer` will be notified when the width becomes available.
PARAMETERS	
`observer`	The image observer to register for image updates; if `null`, no updates are desired.
RETURNS	The width of the image; -1 if the width is not yet available.
SEE ALSO	`getHeight()`, `ImageObserver`.
EXAMPLE	See the class example and `getScaledInstance()`.

SCALE_AREA_AVERAGING

PURPOSE	Use `AreaAveragingScaleFilter` as the scaling algorithm.
SYNTAX	`public static final int SCALE_AREA_AVERAGING`
DESCRIPTION	This constant is used as a parameter to `getScaledInstance()`. The image object is free to substitute a different filter that performs the same algorithm as `AreaAveragingScaleFilter`. See `AreaAveragingScaleFilter` for details of the algorithm. The value of this constant is 16.
SEE ALSO	`getScaledInstance()`, `java.awt.image.AreaAveragingScaleFilter`.
EXAMPLE	See a similar usage of SCALE_SMOOTH in `getScaledInstance()`.

SCALE_DEFAULT

PURPOSE   Use the default scaling algorithm.

SYNTAX   `public static final int SCALE_DEFAULT`

DESCRIPTION   This constant is used as a parameter to `getScaledInstance()`. The default scaling algorithm uses `ReplicateScaleFilter`. The value of this constant is 1.

SEE ALSO   `getScaledInstance()`, `java.awt.image.ReplicateScaleFilter`.

EXAMPLE   See a similar usage of SCALE_SMOOTH in `getScaledInstance()`.

SCALE_FAST

PURPOSE   Use the scaling algorithm that emphasizes speed over smoothness.

SYNTAX   `public static final int SCALE_FAST`

DESCRIPTION   This constant is used as a parameter to `getScaledInstance()`. The value of this constant is 2.

SEE ALSO   `getScaledInstance()`.

EXAMPLE   See a similar usage of SCALE_SMOOTH in `getScaledInstance()`.

SCALE_REPLICATE

PURPOSE   Use `ReplicateScaleFilter` as the scaling algorithm.

SYNTAX   `public static final int SCALE_REPLICATE`

DESCRIPTION   This constant is used as a parameter to `getScaledInstance()`. The image object is free to substitute a different filter that performs the same algorithm as `ReplicateScaleFilter`. See `ReplicateScaleFilter` for the details of the algorithm. The value of this constant is 8.

SEE ALSO   `getScaledInstance()`, `java.awt.image.ReplicateScaleFilter`.

EXAMPLE   See a similar usage of SCALE_SMOOTH in `getScaledInstance()`.

SCALE_SMOOTH

PURPOSE   Use the scaling algorithm that emphasizes smoothness over speed.

SYNTAX   `public static final int SCALE_SMOOTH`

DESCRIPTION   This constant is used as a parameter to `getScaledInstance()`. When SCALE_SMOOTH is specified as a parameter to `getScaledInstance()`, it uses the `AreaAveragingScaleFilter`. See `AreaAveragingScaleFilter` for the details of the algorithm. The value of this constant is 4.

SEE ALSO   `getScaledInstance()`, `java.awt.image.AreaAveragingScaleFilter`.

EXAMPLE   See `getScaledInstance()`.

UndefinedProperty

PURPOSE   This object is returned by `getProperty()` if the property is not defined.

SYNTAX   `public static final Object UndefinedProperty`

SEE ALSO   `getProperty()`.

EXAMPLE   See `getProperty()`.

A
B
C
D
E
F
G
H

J
K
L
M
N
O
P
Q
R
S
T
U
V
W
X
Y
Z

```
ImageConsumer          ImageFilter

                       PixelGrabber
```

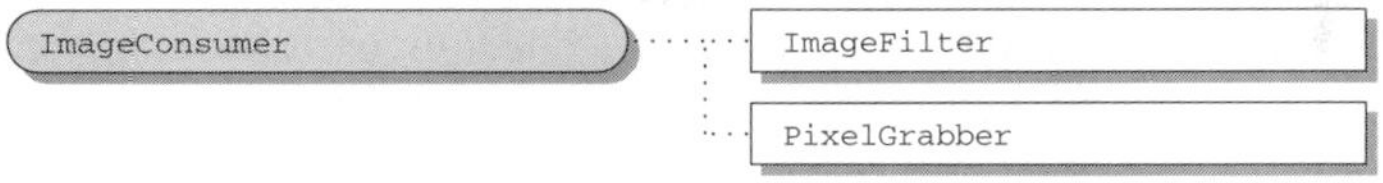

Syntax

`public interface ImageConsumer`

Description

Images are painted on a surface using a streaming architecture that involves an *image producer*, which is responsible for supplying a stream of pixel data, and an *image consumer*, which is responsible for displaying that stream. See Figure 208. This architecture allows the progressive rendering of images as the pixels are delivered from a remote source.

The `ImageConsumer` interface defines all of the methods that are necessary for a class to receive pixels from an image producer. See the `ImageProducer` interface for details on how to register an image consumer to receive pixels from an image producer.

```
ImageProducer

ImageFilter

ImageFilter

ImageConsumer
```

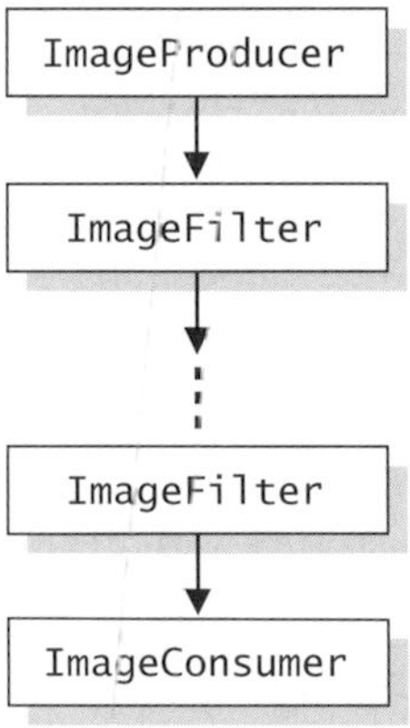

FIGURE 208: Image Producer, Consumers, and Filter.

Hints

A *hint* is a bit of information about pixel delivery that the image producer gives to the image consumer prior to delivering the pixels. Using these hints, the image consumer might be able to implement some optimizations that would speed up the processing time.

Multiframe Images

The image can contain multiple frames, as in the case of a video source. This is the default, in the absence of the `SINGLEFRAME` hint from the image producer.

MEMBER SUMMARY	
Image Completion Status Bits	
IMAGEABORTED	Specifies that the image production was aborted.
IMAGEERROR	Specifies an error occurred.
SINGLEFRAMEDONE	Specifies that one frame of a multiframe image is complete.
STATICIMAGEDONE	Specifies that the image is complete.

Continued

MEMBER SUMMARY

Pixel Delivery Hints

COMPLETESCANLINES	Specifies that pixels will be delivered in complete scanlines.
RANDOMPIXELORDER	Specifies that pixels will be delivered in an arbitrary order.
SINGLEFRAME	Specifies that the image contains only one frame.
SINGLEPASS	Specifies that pixels will be delivered in a single pass.
TOPDOWNLEFTRIGHT	Specifies that pixels will be delivered in left-right, top-down order.

Methods Called by the Image Producer

imageComplete()	Called to deliver completion status to the image consumer.
setColorModel()	Called to deliver the color model for the source image.
setDimensions()	Called to deliver the dimensions of the source image.
setHints()	Called to specify how the pixels will be delivered.
setPixels()	Called to deliver pixels to the image consumer.
setProperties()	Called to deliver the properties for the source image.

See Also

ColorModel, ImageFilter, ImageObserver, ImageProducer, java.awt.Image.

Example

This example implements the ImageInfoGrabber class. This class is used to retrieve all of the attributes of an image—width, height, color model, hints, properties, and pixels. The pixels that are retrieved using ImageInfoGrabber are the original pixels.

Note: Much of the functionality provided by the ImageInfoGrabber class is now available in the Java 1.1.2 version of PixelGrabber. The main difference is that PixelGrabber does not make the hints and properties of the image available.

The example also reads an image and prints the available information about the image. If the image's color model is an index color model (see ColorModel), then the colors in the image's color model are displayed, including the number of times each color is referenced in the image.

```java
import java.awt.*;
import java.awt.image.*;
import java.util.*;

class Main {
    Image image;

    Main(String filename) {
        ImageInfoGrabber iig = new ImageInfoGrabber();

        image = Toolkit.getDefaultToolkit().getImage(filename);
```

```
        if (!iig.grabInfo(image.getSource())) {
            System.err.println("Error fetching image " + filename);
            System.exit(1);
        }
        System.out.println("size = " + iig.width + "x" + iig.height);
        System.out.print("hints = ");
        if ((iig.hints & ImageConsumer.COMPLETESCANLINES) != 0)
            System.out.print("COMPLETESCANLINES ");
        if ((iig.hints & ImageConsumer.RANDOMPIXELORDER) != 0)
            System.out.print("RANDOMPIXELORDER ");
        if ((iig.hints & ImageConsumer.SINGLEPASS) != 0)
            System.out.print("SINGLEPASS ");
        if ((iig.hints & ImageConsumer.TOPDOWNLEFTRIGHT) != 0)
            System.out.print("TOPDOWNLEFTRIGHT ");
        System.out.println();

        System.out.println(iig.properties.size() + " properties");

        // Only deal with index color model images
        if (iig.colorModel instanceof IndexColorModel) {
            IndexColorModel cm = (IndexColorModel)iig.colorModel;
            int[] pixelValueCount = new int[1<<cm.getPixelSize()];
            System.out.println("transparent pixel = "
                + cm.getTransparentPixel());

            // Count number of times pixel values are used.
            for (int i=0; i<iig.bytePixels.length; i++) {
                pixelValueCount[iig.bytePixels[i]&0xff]++;
            }

            // Print colors in color model and their reference count.
            for (int i=0; i<pixelValueCount.length; i++) {
                System.out.println(i
                    + ": " + (cm.getRed(i)&0xff)
                    + " " + (cm.getGreen(i)&0xff)
                    + " " + (cm.getBlue(i)&0xff)
                    + "/" + (cm.getAlpha(i)&0xff)
                    + "   count:" + pixelValueCount[i]);
            }
        }
        System.exit(0);
    }

    static public void main(String[] args) {
        if (args.length != 1) {
            System.err.println("usage: java Main <image file>");
            System.exit(1);
        }
        new Main(args[0]);
    }
}

class ImageInfoGrabber implements ImageConsumer {
    // These are the public fields which the client can
    // use to retrieve the image info.
    public int width;
    public int height;
    public int hints;
    public Hashtable properties;
    public ColorModel colorModel;
```

A
B
C
D
E
F
G
H
I
J
K
L
M
N
O
P
Q
R
S
T
U
V
W
X
Y
Z

813

```
        public Vector additionalColorModels = new Vector();

        // One of the following fields is null and the other is not.
        public int[] intPixels;
        public byte[] bytePixels;

        // Private fields
        private int status;
        private ImageProducer producer;

        // Returns true if the image was fetched successfully; false otherwise.
        public synchronized boolean grabInfo(ImageProducer ip) {
            status = 0;
            (producer = ip).startProduction(this);
            try {
                while (status == 0) {
                    wait();
                }
            } catch (InterruptedException e) {
                return false;
            }
            return status > 0;
        }

        public void setDimensions(int w, int h) {
            width = w;
            height = h;
        }

        public void setHints(int h) {
            hints = h;
        }

        public void setProperties(Hashtable props) {
            properties = props;
        }

        public void setColorModel(ColorModel cm) {
            colorModel = cm;
        }

        public void setPixels(int srcX, int srcY, int srcW, int srcH,
                            ColorModel cm, byte pixels[], int srcOff, int srcScan)
        {
            if (cm != colorModel) {
                if (!additionalColorModels.contains(cm)) {
                    additionalColorModels.addElement(cm);
                }
            }
            if (bytePixels == null) {
                bytePixels = new byte[width * height];
            }
            for (int x=srcX; x<srcX + srcW; x++) {
                for (int y=srcY; y<srcY + srcH; y++) {
                    bytePixels[y * width + x] =
                        pixels[(y-srcY) * srcScan + (x-srcX) + srcOff];
                }
            }
        }
```

A
B
C
D
E
F
G
H
I
J
K
L
M
N
O
P
Q
R
S
T
U
V
W
X
Y
Z

```
    public void setPixels(int srcX, int srcY, int srcW, int srcH,
                   ColorModel cm, int pixels[], int srcOff, int srcScan) {
        if (cm != colorModel) {
            if (!additionalColorModels.contains(cm)) {
                additionalColorModels.addElement(cm);
            }
        }
        if (intPixels == null) {
            intPixels = new int[width * height];
        }
        for (int x=srcX; x<srcX + srcW; x++) {
            for (int y=srcY; y<srcY + srcH; y++) {
                intPixels[y * width + x] =
                    pixels[(y-srcY) * srcScan + (x-srcX) + srcOff];
            }
        }
    }

    public synchronized void imageComplete(int s) {
        switch (s) {
        case STATICIMAGEDONE:
        case SINGLEFRAMEDONE:
            status = 1;
            break;
        default:
        case IMAGEERROR:
        case IMAGEABORTED:
            status = -1;
            break;
        }
        producer.removeConsumer(this);
        notifyAll();
    }
}
```

Output

```
size = 55x68
hints = COMPLETESCANLINES SINGLEPASS TOPDOWNLEFTRIGHT
0 properties
transparent pixel = 58
0:  216 216 224/255    count:0
1:  152 144 136/255    count:1
2:  160 40 68/255    count:2
3:  128 32 48/255    count:2
4:  200 208 208/255    count:0
5:  184 40 84/255    count:0
6:  192 184 184/255    count:0
7:  40 32 40/255    count:3
8:  96 88 80/255    count:2
9:  216 32 56/255    count:1

    (lines deleted)

250:  240 232 216/255    count:2
251:  208 64 180/255    count:2
252:  248 248 240/255    count:223
253:  248 240 248/255    count:0
254:  240 248 248/255    count:0
255:  248 248 248/255    count:17
```

A

B

C

D

E

F

G

H

J

K

L

M

N

O

P

Q

R

S

T

U

V

W

X

Y

Z

COMPLETESCANLINES

PURPOSE	Hint specifying that pixels will be delivered in complete scanlines.
SYNTAX	`int COMPLETESCANLINES`
DESCRIPTION	This hint specifies that pixels delivered via `setPixels()` will be delivered in complete scanlines. More than one scanline may possibly be delivered in a `setPixels()` call. This constant is delivered as a hint using the `setHints()` method.
SEE ALSO	`setHints()`.
EXAMPLE	See the class example.

IMAGEABORTED

PURPOSE	Status bit specifying that the image production was aborted.
SYNTAX	`int IMAGEABORTED`
DESCRIPTION	This status bit is used in the `imageComplete()` method call to indicate that the image production process was aborted.
SEE ALSO	`imageComplete()`.
EXAMPLE	See the class example.

imageComplete()

PURPOSE	Called by the image producer to deliver the completion status to the image consumer.
SYNTAX	`void imageComplete(int status)`
DESCRIPTION	The `imageComplete()` method is called when the image producer has finished delivering all of the pixels that the source image contains or when a single frame of a multiframe sequence has been completed or when an error in loading or producing the image has occurred. The status bits in `status` indicate which of these preceding cases occurred. (See `ImageConsumer` for details.)
	Unless the image consumer is interested in subsequent frames, it should call `ImageProducer.removeConsumer()` to remove itself from the producer's list of registered consumers.
PARAMETERS	
`status`	A combination of the status bits as defined in the `ImageConsumer` class.

SEE ALSO   `ImageProducer.removeConsumer()`.

EXAMPLE   See the class example.

IMAGEERROR

PURPOSE   Status bit specifying that an error occurred.

SYNTAX   `int IMAGEERROR`

DESCRIPTION   This status bit is used in the `imageComplete()` method call to indicate that an error occurred while the image was being produced.

SEE ALSO   `imageComplete()`.

EXAMPLE   See the class example.

RANDOMPIXELORDER

PURPOSE   Hint specifying that pixels will be delivered in an arbitrary order.

SYNTAX   `int RANDOMPIXELORDER`

DESCRIPTION   This hint is set via the `setHints()` method and specifies that pixels in `setPixels()` calls will be delivered in an arbitrary order. This informs the consumer not to use any optimizations that depend on the order of pixel delivery. If neither the RANDOMPIXELORDER nor TOPDOWNLEFTRIGHT hints are specified, then RANDOMPIXELORDER is assumed.

An example of an image that has the RANDOMPIXELORDER hint is an interlaced GIF image.

SEE ALSO   `setHints()`, TOPDOWNLEFTRIGHT.

EXAMPLE   See the class example.

setColorModel()

PURPOSE   Called by the image producer to deliver the color model for the source image.

SYNTAX   `void setColorModel(ColorModel model)`

DESCRIPTION   This method is called by the image producer to inform the image consumer that `model` will be used by the majority of pixels in subsequent `setPixels()` calls. Note that each set of pixels delivered using `setPixels()` contains its own color model, so no assumption should be made that this model will be the only one used in delivering pixel values. An example of when the color model

A
B
C
D
E
F
G
H
I
J
K
L
M
N
O
P
Q
R
S
T
U
V
W
X
Y
Z

set by `setColorModel()` might differ from the model used in `setPixels()` calls is an image filter that changes colors by modifying the color model rather than the pixel values.

PARAMETERS		
	`model`	A non-`null` color model.
SEE ALSO		`ColorModel`.
EXAMPLE		See the class example.

setDimensions( )

PURPOSE	Called by the image producer to deliver the dimensions of the source image.
SYNTAX	`void setDimensions(int width, int height)`
DESCRIPTION	This method is called by an image producer to inform the image consumer that the image is `width` pixels wide and `height` pixels high. This method must be called before `setPixels()` so that the image consumer can preallocate any necessary storage beforehand.

PARAMETERS		
	`height`	The height of the image in pixels.
	`width`	The width of the image in pixels.
EXAMPLE		See the class example.

setHints( )

PURPOSE	Called by the image producer to specify how the pixels will be delivered.
SYNTAX	`void setHints(int hintFlags)`
DESCRIPTION	By default, the image producer can deliver pixels in any order it chooses, and the image consumer must be able to handle them. However, in some cases an image producer may produce pixels in a particular order that an image consumer can take advantage of. For example, the image consumer may process the pixels more quickly if it knows that pixels will be delivered in top-down fashion. See the `ImageConsumer` interface for the possible set of hints and what they mean.

PARAMETERS		
	`hintFlags`	A set of bits that specify how pixels will be delivered.
SEE ALSO		COMPLETESCANLINES, RANDOMPIXELORDER, SINGLEPASS, SINGLEFRAME, TOPDOWNLEFTRIGHT.
EXAMPLE		See the class example.

A
B
C
D
E
F
G
H
J
K
L
M
N
O
P
Q
R
S
T
U
V
W
X
Y
Z

setPixels( )

PURPOSE   Called by the image producer to deliver pixels to the image consumer.

SYNTAX

```
void setPixels(int x, int y, int w, int h, ColorModel model,
    byte[] pixels, int offset, int scansize);
void setPixels(int x, int y, int w, int h, ColorModel model, int[]
    pixels, int offset, int scansize);
```

DESCRIPTION   The image producer delivers the pixels of the image to the image consumer in one or more calls to the `setPixels()` method. The parameters x, y, w, and h specify the destination location of the pixels. In particular, the pixel x, y (the top-left corner pixel of the destination rectangle) is stored in the `pixels` array at [x + y * scansize + offset].

The pixel data is located in the `pixels` array. If the pixel values are 8 bits, the first form of the `setPixels()` method is called; otherwise, the second form is called. Only one of the two forms will be called.

The specified color model `model` should be used to convert the pixel values into colors and alpha components. The color model is not necessarily the same as the one supplied by the `setColorModel()` method call.

PARAMETERS
h	The height of the rectangle in which the pixels are destined.
model	The non-null color model used to translate the pixel values.
offset	The index of the first pixel in the pixel array.
pixels	The non-null array of pixel values.
scansize	The width to use when extracting pixels from `pixels`.
w	The width of the rectangle in which the pixels are destined.
x	The x-coordinate of the rectangle in which the pixels are destined.
y	The y-coordinate of the rectangle in which the pixels are destined.

SEE ALSO   `ColorModel`.

EXAMPLE   See the class example.

setProperties( )

PURPOSE   Called by the image producer to deliver the properties for the source image.

SYNTAX   `void setProperties(Hashtable props)`

DESCRIPTION   An image property is an arbitrary value that an image producer associates with an image. For example, an image producer that decodes GIF images might make the comments embedded in the image available as a property. Another example is an image filter that sets the "filters" property so that the final image consumer can determine how the image has been filtered.

Different image producers will set different image properties. See the documentation of a particular image producer to determine the property names and types that that producer will set.

PARAMETERS

props　　　　　A non-null hashtable of properties.

EXAMPLE　　　　See the class example.

SINGLEFRAME

PURPOSE　　　　Hint specifying that the image contains only one frame.

SYNTAX　　　　`int SINGLEFRAME`

DESCRIPTION　　This hint is set via the `setHints()` method and specifies that the image contains only one frame. When all of the pixels in the image have been delivered, the `imageComplete()` method is called with the status `STATICIMAGEDONE`.

If the `SINGLEFRAME` hint is not specified, the image consists of many frames. An example of an image type that does not have the `SINGLEFRAME` hint is an MPEG image. In this case, after all of the pixels of a frame have been delivered the `imageComplete()` method will be called with the status `SINGLEFRAMEDONE`.

SEE ALSO　　　`imageComplete()`, `setHints()`, `STATICIMAGEDONE`.

EXAMPLE　　　　See the class example.

SINGLEFRAMEDONE

PURPOSE　　　　Status bit specifying that one frame of a multiframe image is complete.

SYNTAX　　　　`int SINGLEFRAMEDONE`

DESCRIPTION　　This status bit is used in the `imageComplete()` method call to indicate that one frame of the image is complete but that there are more frames to be delivered.

SEE ALSO　　　`imageComplete()`.

EXAMPLE　　　　See the class example.

SINGLEPASS

PURPOSE   Hint specifying that pixels will be delivered in a single pass.

SYNTAX   int SINGLEPASS

DESCRIPTION   This hint is set via the `setHints()` method and specifies that pixels in `setPixels()` calls will be delivered in a single pass. That is, each pixel will appear in only one call to any of the `setPixels()` methods. An example of an image format that does not have this hint is a progressive JPEG image that defines pixels in multiple passes, each more refined than the previous.

SEE ALSO   `setHints()`.

EXAMPLE   See the class example.

STATICIMAGEDONE

PURPOSE   Status bit specifying that the image is complete.

SYNTAX   int STATICIMAGEDONE

DESCRIPTION   This status bit is used in the `imageComplete()` method call to indicate that the image is complete and that there are no more pixels or frames to be delivered.

SEE ALSO   `imageComplete()`.

EXAMPLE   See the class example.

TOPDOWNLEFTRIGHT

PURPOSE   Hint specifying that pixels will be delivered in left-right, top-down order.

SYNTAX   int TOPDOWNLEFTRIGHT

DESCRIPTION   This hint is set via the `setHints()` method and specifies that pixels in `setPixels()` method calls will be delivered left-to-right and then top-to-bottom. That is, each row of pixels is filled left-to-right and when the row is complete, the next row of pixels is filled left-to-right. If the hint COMPLETESCANLINES is not also specified and not all of the pixels in a scanline are delivered in a call to `setPixels()`, then the delivered pixels can be only a single pixel high. If TOPDOWNLEFTRIGHT is not specified, the RANDOMPIXELORDER hint is assumed, that is, pixels can be delivered in any order.

An example of an image that would have the TOPDOWNLEFTRIGHT hint is a noninterlaced GIF image. An interlaced GIF image would not have this hint.

SEE ALSO   RANDOMPIXELORDER, `setHints()`.

EXAMPLE   See the class example.

A
B
C
D
E
F
G
H

J
K
L
M
N
O
P
Q
R
S
T
U
V
W
X
Y
Z

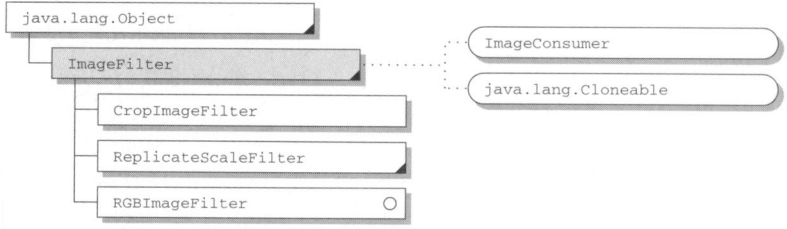

A
B
C
D
E
F
G
H
I
J
K
L
M
N
O
P
Q
R
S
T
U
V
W
X
Y
Z

Syntax

`public class ImageFilter implements ImageConsumer, Cloneable`

Description

Images are painted on a surface using a streaming architecture that involves an *image producer*, which is responsible for supplying a stream of pixel data, and an *image consumer*, which is responsible for displaying that stream. See Figure 209. This architecture allows the progressive rendering of images as the pixels are delivered from a remote source.

In this architecture, one or more *image filters* can be inserted between the image producer and the image consumer. An image filter is used to transform an image. For example, the crop image filter (see `CropImageFilter`) is used to extract a smaller image from an image, while the RGB image filter (see `RGBImageFilter`) is used to change the colors in an image.

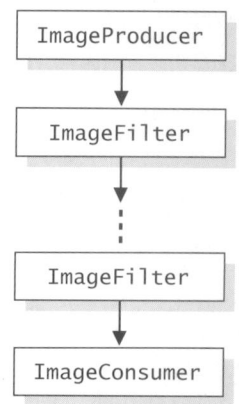

FIGURE 209: Image Producer, Consumers, and Filter.

You can build your own image filter by implementing the `ImageConsumer` interface. Alternatively, you can subclass the `ImageFilter` class, which provides default implementations for all the methods in the `ImageConsumer` interface. After subclassing the image filter, you can override only the necessary `ImageConsumer` methods. The other methods will provide the default behavior.

An instance of the `ImageFilter` class itself can be constructed and used in a pixel stream. However, it will have no effect on the pixels that pass through.

MEMBER SUMMARY

Creation Methods

clone()	Constructs a clone of this image filter.
getFilterInstance()	Creates a new ImageFilter instance.

Subclass Overrides Called by the Image Producer

imageComplete()	Called to deliver the completion status to the image consumer.
setColorModel()	Called to set the color model for the source image.
setDimensions()	Called to set the dimension of the source image.
setHints()	Called to specify how the pixels will be delivered.
setPixels()	Called to deliver pixels.
setProperties()	Called to set the properties for the source image.

Pixel Retransmit Method

resendTopDownLeftRight()	Retransmits the pixels in top-down, left-right order.

Consumer Field

consumer	Contains the image consumer of the pixel data.

See Also

ImageConsumer, ImageObserver, ImageProducer, java.awt.Image.

Example

This example implements a type of image filter that flips the image horizontally or vertically. See Figure 210.

Note: Flipping images is very easy to do using Graphics.drawImage(). However, this example is still useful for demonstrating how to implement an image filter.

FIGURE 210: ImageFilter.

The image is displayed in the ImageCanvas class. If you click the canvas, it flips the image either horizontally or vertically. The overridden setDimensions() method records the width and height of the image. These are used in moving the pixels to the new location as they pass through the filter. The setHints() override sets the ImageConsumer.RANDOMPIXELORDER bit and clears the ImageConsumer.TOP-DOWNLEFTRIGHT because as the pixels pass through the image filter, they are translated in an order different from what the filter's producer intended.

In the setPixels() override, notice that a temporary buffer must be allocated to store the displaced pixels. In other words, the image filter subclass cannot modify the pixel array supplied by setPixels().

In the setProperties() override, the flip filter adds the flipH and flipV properties using the current flip values. If there is more than one flip filter in the pixel stream, the final values of the flipH and flipV properties will reflect the resulting transformation. That is, if there are two filters that flip the image vertically, they will cancel out each other and the resulting flipV property value will be false.

```java
import java.awt.*;
import java.awt.image.*;
import java.awt.event.*;
import java.util.*;

class Main extends Frame {
    Main(String filename) {
        super("ImageFilter Example");
        add(new ImageCanvas(getToolkit().getImage(filename)),
            BorderLayout.CENTER);
        setSize(50, 100);
        show();
    }

    static public void main(String[] args) {
        if (args.length == 1) {
            new Main(args[0]);
        } else {
            System.err.println("usage: java Main <image file>");
        }
    }
}

class ImageCanvas extends Component {
    Image flipImage;
    Image image;
    boolean flipH = true, flipV = true;
    FlipFilter imgf = new FlipFilter();

    ImageCanvas(Image image) {
        this.image = image;
        processImage();

        // Add mouse listener
        addMouseListener(new MouseEventHandler());
    }

    public void paint(Graphics g) {
        g.drawImage(flipImage, 0, 0, this);
    }

    void processImage() {
        ImageProducer ip = image.getSource();

        imgf.setFlip(flipH, flipV);
        ip = new FilteredImageSource(ip, imgf);
        flipImage = getToolkit().createImage(ip);
        repaint();
    }

    class MouseEventHandler extends MouseAdapter {
        public void mousePressed(MouseEvent evt) {
```

A
B
C
D
E
F
G
H
I
J
K
L
M
N
O
P
Q
R
S
T
U
V
W
X
Y
Z

```
            if (flipH & flipV) {
                flipH = flipV = false;
            } else if (flipV) {
                flipH = true;
                flipV = false;
            } else {
                flipV = true;
            }
            processImage();
        }
    }
}

class FlipFilter extends ImageFilter {
    int width, height;
    boolean flipH, flipV;

    public void setFlip(boolean flipH, boolean flipV) {
        this.flipH = flipH;
        this.flipV = flipV;
    }

    public void setDimensions(int w, int h) {
        super.setDimensions(width = w, height = h);
    }

    public void setProperties(Hashtable props) {
        boolean h = false;
        boolean v = false;
        Object bh = props.get("flipH");
        Object bv = props.get("flipV");

        if (bh != null) {
            h = ((Boolean)bh).booleanValue();
        }
        if (bv != null) {
            v = ((Boolean)bv).booleanValue();
        }
        h ^= flipH;
        v ^= flipV;
        props.put("flipH", new Boolean(h));
        props.put("flipV", new Boolean(v));
        consumer.setProperties(props);
    }

    public void setHints(int h) {
        h |= ImageConsumer.RANDOMPIXELORDER;
        h &= ~ImageConsumer.TOPDOWNLEFTRIGHT;
        super.setHints(h);
    }

    public void setColorModel(ColorModel model) {
        super.setColorModel(model);
    }

    public void setPixels(int srcX, int srcY, int srcW, int srcH,
            ColorModel model, byte pixels[], int srcOff, int srcScan) {
        int s = srcOff;
        byte[] tempBuff = new byte[srcW * srcH];
```

A
B
C
D
E
F
G
H
I
J
K
L
M
N
O
P
Q
R
S
T
U
V
W
X
Y
Z

```
                for (int y=0; y<srcH; y++) {
                    for (int x=0; x<srcW; x++) {
                        int d = 0;
                        if (flipV) {
                            d += (srcH-y-1)*srcW;
                        } else {
                            d += y*srcW;
                        }
                        if (flipH) {
                            d += (srcW-x-1);
                        } else {
                            d += x;
                        }
                        tempBuff[d] = pixels[s];
                        s++;
                    }
                }

                if (flipH) {
                    srcX = width - (srcX+srcW);
                }
                if (flipV) {
                    srcY = height - (srcY+srcH);
                }
                super.setPixels(srcX, srcY, srcW, srcH, model, tempBuff, 0, srcScan);
            }

            public void setPixels(int srcX, int srcY, int srcW, int srcH,
                ColorModel model, int pixels[], int srcOff, int srcScan) {
                int s = srcOff;
                int[] tempBuff = new int[srcW * srcH];

                for (int y=0; y<srcH; y++) {
                    for (int x=0; x<srcW; x++) {
                        int d = 0;
                        if (flipV) {
                            d += (srcH-y-1)*srcW;
                        } else {
                            d += y*srcW;
                        }
                        if (flipH) {
                            d += (srcW-x-1);
                        } else {
                            d += x;
                        }
                        tempBuff[d] = pixels[s];
                        s++;
                    }
                }
                if (flipH) {
                    srcX = width - (srcX+srcW);
                }
                if (flipV) {
                    srcY = height - (srcY+srcH);
                }
                super.setPixels(srcX, srcY, srcW, srcH, model, tempBuff, 0, srcScan);
            }

            public synchronized void imageComplete(int status) {
                super.imageComplete(status);
```

A
B
C
D
E
F
G
H
I
J
K
L
M
N
O
P
Q
R
S
T
U
V
W
X
Y
Z

```
        }
    }
```

clone( )

PURPOSE	Constructs a clone of this image filter.
SYNTAX	`public Object clone()`
DESCRIPTION	The default implementation calls `Object.clone()`, which creates a new instance of this image filter that has a shallow copy of the variables. If the image filter refers to other objects or arrays that are modified during the filtering, this method must be overridden in order to clone these objects or arrays.
RETURNS	A copy of this image filter.
OVERRIDES	`java.lang.Object.clone()`.
EXAMPLE	See `java.lang.Object.clone()`.

consumer

PURPOSE	Contains the image consumer of the pixel data.
SYNTAX	`protected ImageConsumer consumer`
DESCRIPTION	The image filter delivers pixel data to the image consumer referred to by this field. This field is initialized by a `getFilterInstance()` method call, typically by the `FilteredImageSource` class during the construction of a pixel stream.
SEE ALSO	`getFilterInstance()`, `ImageConsumer`.

getFilterInstance( )

PURPOSE	Creates an instance of this filter.
SYNTAX	`public ImageFilter getFilterInstance(ImageConsumer ic)`
DESCRIPTION	This method returns a unique instance of this image filter that will deliver pixels to the image consumer `ic`. It is typically used by `FilteredImageSource` during the construction of an image stream. By default, it calls `clone()` and returns the result.
PARAMETERS	
`ic`	The non-`null` image consumer of the new image filter instance.
RETURNS	A non-`null` instance of this image filter.

imageComplete( )

PURPOSE   Called by the image producer to deliver the completion status to the image consumer.

SYNTAX   `public void imageComplete(int status)`

DESCRIPTION   By default, this method calls the consumer's `imageComplete()` method by using `status`. See `ImageConsumer.imageComplete()` for details on how to override this method and how to interpret `status`. An image filter need not remove itself from the image producer's registered list of consumers, since the image consumer at the end of the stream will remove it.

PARAMETERS
`status`   A combination of the status bits as defined in the `ImageConsumer` class.

SEE ALSO   `ImageConsumer`, `imageComplete()`.

resendTopDownLeftRight( )

PURPOSE   Retransmits the pixels in top-down, left-right order.

SYNTAX   `public void resendTopDownLeftRight(ImageProducer ip)`

DESCRIPTION   This method is called by the image consumer of this filter if the image consumer wants the pixels to be retransmitted in top-down, left-right order. `ip` should be the image producer that is sending pixels to this filter.

The image filter can respond to this request in one of three ways:
- If the filter does not move around the pixels, it can forward the request to the image producer by calling `requestTopDownLeftRightResend()`, using itself as the image consumer. This is the default behavior.
- If the filter has the pixels and can retransmit them in the right order, it should override this method and do so. See the `ImageProducer.requestTopDownLeftRightResend()` method for details on how it should deliver the pixels to the image consumer.
- The filter can ignore this call, and no retransmission will occur.

PARAMETERS
`ip`   The non-`null` image producer that supplies this image filter with pixels.

SEE ALSO   `ImageProducer.requestTopDownLeftRightResend()`.

setColorModel( )

PURPOSE   Called by the image producer to set the color model for the source image.

SYNTAX   `public void setColorModel(ColorModel model)`

DESCRIPTION   This method should be overridden to process `setColorModel()` calls from the image producer. The default implementation simply passes `model` to the image consumer.

PARAMETERS

   `model`   The non-`null` color model of the source image.

SEE ALSO   `ImageConsumer.setColorModel()`.

EXAMPLE   See the class example.

setDimensions( )

PURPOSE   Called by the image producer to set the dimension of the source image.

SYNTAX   `public void setDimensions(int width, int height)`

DESCRIPTION   This method should be overridden to intercept `setDimensions()` calls from the image producer. The default implementation simply passes the dimensions `width` and `height` to the image consumer.

PARAMETERS

   `height`   The height of the source image in pixels.
   `width`   The width of the source image in pixels.

SEE ALSO   `ImageConsumer.setDimensions()`.

EXAMPLE   See the class example.

setHints( )

PURPOSE   Called by the image producer to specify how the pixels will be delivered.

SYNTAX   `public void setHints(int hintFlags)`

DESCRIPTION   By default, the image filter simply passes the hints `hintFlags` to the image consumer. However, if the image filter moves pixels around, it must override this method and adjust the hints appropriately before sending them to the image consumer. See the `ImageConsumer` interface for the possible set of hints and what they mean.

PARAMETERS

   `hintFlags`   A set of bits that specify how pixels will be delivered.

SEE ALSO   `ImageConsumer.setHints()`.

EXAMPLE   See the class example.

A
B
C
D
E
F
G
H

J
K
L
M
N
O
P
Q
R
S
T
U
V
W
X
Y
Z

setPixels( )

PURPOSE	Called by the image producer to deliver pixels.

SYNTAX	`public void setPixels(int x, int y, int w, int h, ColorModel`
	    `model, byte[] pixels, int offset, int scansize)`
	`public void setPixels(int x, int y, int w, int h, ColorModel`
	    `model, int[] pixels, int offset, int scansize)`

DESCRIPTION	By default, the image filter simply passes off the pixels, unchanged, to the image consumer. If the image filter needs to modify the pixels, it must override both `setPixels()` methods. See `ImageConsumer.setPixels()` for details on how the parameters are used.

PARAMETERS

h	The height of the rectangle in which the pixels are destined.
model	The non-`null` color model used to translate the pixel values.
offset	The index of the first pixel in the pixel array `pixels`.
pixels	The non-`null` array of pixel values.
scansize	The width to use when extracting pixels from the pixel array `pixels`.
w	The width of the rectangle in which the pixels are destined.
x	The *x*-coordinate of the rectangle in which the pixels are destined.
y	The *y*-coordinate of the rectangle in which the pixels are destined.

SEE ALSO	`ImageConsumer.setPixels()`.
EXAMPLE	See the class example.

setProperties( )

PURPOSE	Called by the image producer to set the properties for the source image.
SYNTAX	`public void setProperties(Hashtable props)`
DESCRIPTION	By default, the image filter passes on the properties after adding its name to the "filters" property. The filter should override this method if it wants to add or query a property.

PARAMETERS

props	The non-`null` properties of the source image.

SEE ALSO	`ImageConsumer.setProperties()`.
EXAMPLE	See the class example.

ImageObserver ·········· java.awt.Component

Syntax

```
public interface ImageObserver
```

Description

An object that implements the `ImageObserver` interface can register itself for progress information as an image is loaded. For example, an AWT canvas might want to progressively display the image as it is being loaded. Methods such as `Image.drawImage()` and `Image.getWidth()` accept image observers and automatically register them with the image producer.

When an image observer is registered, it receives all progress information via the `image-Update()` method call. However, only progress information that the image observer asks for is delivered to the `imageUpdate()` method. For example, if the image observer were to call `Image.getWidth()` and the `Image.getWidth()` width information was not yet available (that is, `-1 was` returned), `imageUpdate()` would be called as soon as the width became available. Otherwise if `Image.getWidth()` was not called or if `Image.getWidth()` returned the width, the `imageUpdate()` method would not be called.

MEMBER SUMMARY	
Image Update Method	
`imageUpdate()`	Called by an image consumer to deliver status information about the loading of an image.
Image Update Status Bits	
`ABORT`	Indicates that the image loading process was aborted.
`ALLBITS`	Indicates that the entire image has been successfully loaded.
`ERROR`	Indicates that an error was encountered while the image was being loaded.
`FRAMEBITS`	Indicates that a frame of a multiframe image has been successfully loaded.
`HEIGHT`	Indicates that the height of the image is now available.
`PROPERTIES`	Indicates that the image properties are now available.
`SOMEBITS`	Indicates that additional pixels are now available.
`WIDTH`	Indicates that the width of the image is now available.

See Also

ImageConsumer, ImageFilter, ImageProducer, java.awt.Image.

Example

This example creates an image observer that can be wrapped around another image observer in order to "spy" on the calls to the imageUpdate() method. The information is printed on standard output. See Figure 211.

FIGURE 211: ImageObserver.

```java
import java.awt.*;
import java.awt.image.*;
import java.net.*;
import java.util.*;

class Main extends Frame {
    Main(String filename) {
        super("ImageObserver Example");
        try {
            // Retrieve the image.
            Image image = getToolkit().getImage(filename);

            add("Center", new ImageCanvas(image));
        } catch (Exception e) {
            e.printStackTrace();
        }
        setSize(50, 100);
        show();
    }

    static public void main(String[] args) {
        if (args.length == 1) {
            new Main(args[0]);
        } else {
            System.err.println("usage: java Main <image file>");
        }
    }
}

class ImageCanvas extends Component {
    Image image;
    ImageObserverSpy spy = new ImageObserverSpy(this);

    ImageCanvas(Image image) {
        this.image = image;
        image.getWidth(spy);
        image.getHeight(spy);
        image.getProperty("test", spy);
    }

    public void paint(Graphics g) {
        g.drawImage(image, 0, 0, spy);
    }
}
```

A
B
C
D
E
F
G
H
J
K
L
M
N
O
P
Q
R
S
T
U
V
W
X
Y
Z

```
class ImageObserverSpy implements ImageObserver {
    ImageObserver obs;

    ImageObserverSpy(ImageObserver obs) {
        this.obs = obs;
    }

    public boolean imageUpdate(Image img, int infoflags,
        int x, int y, int width, int height) {
        System.out.print("x="+x+" ");
        System.out.print("y="+y+" ");
        System.out.print("width="+width+" ");
        System.out.print("height="+height+" ");
        System.out.print("  infoflags=");
        if ((infoflags & ABORT) != 0) System.out.print("ABORT ");
        if ((infoflags & ALLBITS) != 0) System.out.print("ALLBITS ");
        if ((infoflags & ERROR) != 0) System.out.print("ERROR ");
        if ((infoflags & FRAMEBITS) != 0) System.out.print("FRAMEBITS ");
        if ((infoflags & HEIGHT) != 0) System.out.print("HEIGHT ");
        if ((infoflags & PROPERTIES) != 0) System.out.print("PROPERTIES ");
        if ((infoflags & SOMEBITS) != 0) System.out.print("SOMEBITS ");
        if ((infoflags & WIDTH)!= 0) System.out.print("WIDTH ");
        System.out.println();
        return obs.imageUpdate(img, infoflags, x, y, width, height);
    }
}
```

Output

```
x=0 y=0 width=55 height=68   infoflags=HEIGHT WIDTH
x=0 y=0 width=0 height=0   infoflags=PROPERTIES
x=0 y=0 width=55 height=1   infoflags=SOMEBITS
x=0 y=1 width=55 height=1   infoflags=SOMEBITS
x=0 y=2 width=55 height=1   infoflags=SOMEBITS
x=0 y=3 width=55 height=1   infoflags=SOMEBITS
x=0 y=4 width=55 height=1   infoflags=SOMEBITS

        <many similar lines deleted>

x=0 y=59 width=55 height=1   infoflags=SOMEBITS
x=0 y=60 width=55 height=1   infoflags=SOMEBITS
x=0 y=61 width=55 height=1   infoflags=SOMEBITS
x=0 y=62 width=55 height=1   infoflags=SOMEBITS
x=0 y=63 width=55 height=1   infoflags=SOMEBITS
x=0 y=64 width=55 height=1   infoflags=SOMEBITS
x=0 y=65 width=55 height=1   infoflags=SOMEBITS
x=0 y=66 width=55 height=1   infoflags=SOMEBITS
x=0 y=67 width=55 height=1   infoflags=SOMEBITS
x=0 y=0 width=55 height=68   infoflags=ALLBITS
```

A
B
C
D
E
F
G
H
I
J
K
L
M
N
O
P
Q
R
S
T
U
V
W
X
Y
Z

A
B
C
D
E
F
G
H

J
K
L
M
N
O
P
Q
R
S
T
U
V
W
X
Y
Z

ABORT

PURPOSE   Indicates that the image loading process was aborted.

SYNTAX   `public static final int ABORT`

DESCRIPTION   If the `ABORT` status bit is present in the status flags passed to the `imageUpdate()` method, no further status will be delivered via the `imageUpdate()` method. Unless the `ERROR` status bit is also present, the loading of the image can be restarted.

In the absence of any other status bits, the `x`, `y`, `width`, and `height` parameters passed to the `imageUpdate()` method should be ignored.

SEE ALSO   `ERROR`, `imageUpdate()`.

EXAMPLE   See the class example.

ALLBITS

PURPOSE   Indicates that the entire image has been successfully loaded.

SYNTAX   `public static final int ALLBITS`

DESCRIPTION   If the `ALLBITS` status bit is present in the status flags passed to the `imageUpdate()` method, no further status will be delivered via the `imageUpdate()` method. If the image has only one frame, the `ALLBITS` status bit is used (see the `ImageConsumer` interface for more information about multiframe images). If the image is multiframe, the `FRAMEBITS` status bit is used instead.

This status bit is delivered only if `Image.drawImage()` was called and returned `false`. In the absence of any other status bits, the `x`, `y`, `width`, and `height` parameters passed to the `imageUpdate()` method should be ignored.

SEE ALSO   `java.awt.Image.drawImage()`, `imageUpdate()`.

EXAMPLE   See the class example.

ERROR

PURPOSE   Indicates that an error was encountered while the image was being loaded.

SYNTAX   `public static final int ERROR`

DESCRIPTION   If the `ERROR` status bit is present in the status flags passed to the `imageUpdate()` method, no further status will be delivered via the `imageUpdate()` method. As a convenience, the `ABORT` flag is also set in the status flags whenever the ERROR flag is set. So if there is no need to distinguish between ABORT and ERROR, it is safe to test only for the ABORT flag.

SEE ALSO   imageUpdate().

EXAMPLE   See the class example.

FRAMEBITS

PURPOSE   Indicates that a frame of a multiframe image has been successfully loaded.

SYNTAX   `public static final int FRAMEBITS`

DESCRIPTION   If the image consists of only one frame, then the ALLBITS status bit is used instead to indicate that the image is complete.

This status bit is delivered only if Image.drawImage() was called and returned `false`. In the absence of any other status bits, the x, y, width, and height parameters passed to the imageUpdate() method should be ignored.

SEE ALSO   `java.awt.Image.drawImage()`, `imageUpdate()`.

EXAMPLE   See the class example.

HEIGHT

PURPOSE   Indicates that the height of the image is now available.

SYNTAX   `public static final int HEIGHT`

DESCRIPTION   If the HEIGHT status bit is present in the status flags passed to the imageUpdate() method, the height parameter contains the height of the image. This height can be retrieved also by using the Image.getHeight() method.

This status bit is delivered only if Image.getHeight() was called and returned -1.

SEE ALSO   `java.awt.Image.getHeight()`, `imageUpdate()`.

EXAMPLE   See the class example.

imageUpdate( )

PURPOSE
Called by an image consumer to deliver status information about the loading of an image.

SYNTAX
```
public boolean imageUpdate(Image img, int infoflags, int x, int
    y, int width, int height)
```

DESCRIPTION
This method is called when the image observer asks for a particular piece of information and the information is not yet available. For example, if the image observer called `Image.getWidth()` and the width information was not yet available (that is, `Image.getWidth()` returned -1), the `imageUpdate()` method would be called as soon as the width became available.

`infoflags` contains a combination of status bits that indicate the type of status information being provided. For example, the WIDTH status bit indicates that the width of the image is now available. `infoflags` may contain more than one status bit. To test for the presence of a bit, use the bitwise 'and' operator; for example:

```
if ((infoflags & WIDTH) != 0) {
    System.out.println("width information is now available");
}
```

The values that are supplied in x, y, `width`, and `height` depend on status bits present in `infoflags`. For example, if `infoflags` contains WIDTH, only the `width` parameter contains any information. See the other status bits in this interface for details on how the parameters should be interpreted.

PARAMETERS
`height`	This value depends on the status bits enabled in `infoflags`.
`img`	The non-`null` image being updated.
`infoflags`	A set of status bits.
`width`	This value depends on the status bits enabled in `infoflags`.
`x`	This value depends on the status bits enabled in `infoflags`.
`y`	This value depends on the status bits enabled in `infoflags`.

RETURNS
`true` if further calls to the `imageUpdate()` are needed.

EXAMPLE
See the class example.

PROPERTIES

PURPOSE	Indicates that the image properties are now available.
SYNTAX	`public static final int PROPERTIES`
DESCRIPTION	This status bit indicates that the properties of the image are now available. In the absence of any other status bits, the x, y, `width`, and `height` parameters passed to the `imageUpdate()` method should be ignored.
SEE ALSO	`java.awt.Image.getProperty()`, `imageUpdate()`.
EXAMPLE	See the class example.

SOMEBITS

PURPOSE	Indicates that additional pixels are now available.
SYNTAX	`public static final int SOMEBITS`
DESCRIPTION	The x, y, `width`, and `height` parameters to the `imageUpdate()` method indicate which pixels of the image are available.
SEE ALSO	`imageUpdate()`.
EXAMPLE	See the class example.

WIDTH

PURPOSE	Indicates that the width of the image is now available.
SYNTAX	`public static final int WIDTH`
DESCRIPTION	If the `WIDTH` status bit is present in the status flags passed to the `imageUpdate()` method, the `width` parameter contains the width of the image. This width can be retrieved also by using the `Image.getWidth()` method.
	This status bit is delivered only if `Image.getWidth()` was called and returned −1.
SEE ALSO	`java.awt.Image.getWidth()`, `imageUpdate()`.
EXAMPLE	See the class example.

A
B
C
D
E
F
G
H
I
J
K
L
M
N
O
P
Q
R
S
T
U
V
W
X
Y
Z

ImageProducer

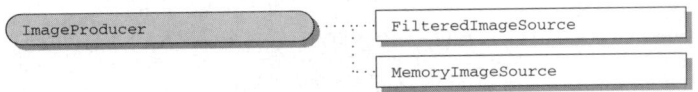

Syntax
```
public interface ImageProducer
```

Description

Images are painted on a surface using a streaming architecture that involves an *image producer*, which is responsible for supplying a stream of pixel data, and an *image consumer*, which is responsible for displaying that stream. See Figure 212. This architecture allows the progressive rendering of images as the pixels are delivered from a remote source.

The ImageProducer interface defines all of the methods that are necessary for a class to generate pixels as an image producer. See the ImageConsumer interface for details on what an image consumer expects from an image producer.

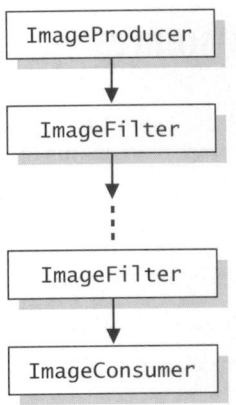

FIGURE 212: Image Producer, Consumers, and Filter.

MEMBER SUMMARY	
Image Consumer Registration Methods	
addConsumer()	Registers an image consumer with this image producer.
isConsumer()	Determines if an image consumer is registered with this image producer.
removeConsumer()	Removes a registered image consumer from this image producer.
Pixel Delivery Methods	
requestTopDownLeftRightResend()	Requests that pixel data be retransmitted in left-right, top-down order.
startProduction()	Triggers the delivery of image data.

See Also

`ImageConsumer, ImageFilter, ImageObserver, java.awt.Image.`

Example

This example demonstrates how one might build a new kind of image decoder. See Figure 213. The image producer reads information from a file and then interprets the data to build an image. The format and sample image file follow the example code. The image producer decodes the image file at the first request for the pixel data. Once the image is decoded, the image producer delivers the pixel data in an

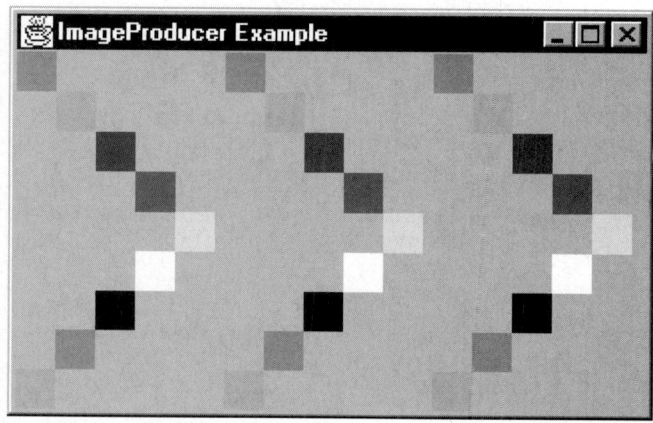

FIGURE 213: `ImageProducer`.

incremental fashion so that the image can be rendered incrementally. After all of the pixels are delivered to an image consumer, that consumer is automatically removed from the list of consumers.

An image consumer that makes a request for pixels while the image producer is producing pixels is added to the list of consumers and is given the pixel data as soon as possible. The example creates three images using the image producer to test the code that supports multiple consumers.

In response to the `requestTopDownLeftRightResend()` method, all of the pixel data is sent in a single call to `setPixels()`.

```
import java.awt.*;
import java.awt.image.*;
import java.awt.event.*;
import java.io.*;
import java.util.*;

class Main extends Frame {
    BlockImageDecoder ip;

    Main(String filename) {
        super("ImageProducer Example");
        Panel p = new Panel();

        try {
            ip = new BlockImageDecoder(new FileInputStream(filename));
        } catch (IOException e) {
            e.printStackTrace();
            System.exit(1);
        }
        p.setLayout(new GridLayout(1, 0));
```

```
                    p.add(new ImageCanvas(ip));
                    p.add(new ImageCanvas(ip));
                    p.add(new ImageCanvas(ip));
                    add(p, BorderLayout.CENTER);

                    setSize(325, 220);
                    show();
                }

                public static void main(String[] args) {
                    if (args.length == 1) {
                        new Main(args[0]);
                    } else {
                        System.err.println("usage: java Main <input file>");
                    }
                }
            }

            class ImageCanvas extends Component {
                ImageProducer ip;
                Image image;

                ImageCanvas(ImageProducer ip) {
                    this.ip = ip;
                    image = createImage(ip);
                    addMouseListener(new MouseEventHandler());
                }

                public void paint(Graphics g) {
                    g.drawImage(image, 0, 0, this);
                }

                class MouseEventHandler extends MouseAdapter {
                    public void mousePressed(MouseEvent evt) {
                        image = createImage(ip);
                        repaint();
                    }
                }
            }

            class BlockImageDecoder implements ImageProducer {
                StreamTokenizer st;
                ColorModel model;
                Vector consumers = new Vector();
                Hashtable properties = new Hashtable();
                byte[] pixels;
                int width = -1, height = -1;
                Rectangle[] rects;
                byte[] rectColors;

                BlockImageDecoder(InputStream is) {
                    Reader r = new BufferedReader(new InputStreamReader(is));
                    st = new StreamTokenizer(r);
                }

                public synchronized void addConsumer(ImageConsumer ic) {
                    if (rects != null) {
                        produce(ic);
                    } else if (!consumers.contains(ic)) {
```

A
B
C
D
E
F
G
H

J
K
L
M
N
O
P
Q
R
S
T
U
V
W
X
Y
Z

```
            consumers.addElement(ic);
        }
    }

    public synchronized boolean isConsumer(ImageConsumer ic) {
        return consumers.contains(ic);
    }

    public synchronized void removeConsumer(ImageConsumer ic) {
        consumers.removeElement(ic);
    }

    private int getInt() throws IOException {
        if (st.nextToken() != StreamTokenizer.TT_NUMBER) {
            throw (new IOException("format error"));
        }
        return (int)st.nval;
    }

    // Convert the contents of the input file to image data.
    private synchronized void processImage() {
        try {
            // Read width and height
            width = getInt();
            height = getInt();

            // Read colors
            int numColors = getInt();
            byte cmap[] = new byte[numColors * 3];
            for (int i=0; i<cmap.length; i++) {
                cmap[i] = (byte)getInt();
            }

            // Create color model.
            int n = numColors-1;
            int nbits = 0;
            while (n > 0) {
                n >>>= 1;
                nbits++;
            }
            model = new IndexColorModel(nbits, numColors, cmap, 0, false, 0);

            // Read rectangles and their colors
            rects = new Rectangle[getInt()];
            rectColors = new byte[rects.length];

            for (int i=0; i<rects.length; i++) {
                rects[i] = new Rectangle(getInt(), getInt(),
                                        getInt(), getInt());
                rectColors[i] = (byte)getInt();
            }
        } catch (Exception e) {
            e.printStackTrace();
        }
    }

    public void startProduction(ImageConsumer ic) {
        if (ic != null) {
            addConsumer(ic);
            if (rects == null) {
```

A
B
C
D
E
F
G
H

J
K
L
M
N
O
P
Q
R
S
T
U
V
W
X
Y
Z

```
                                processImage();
                            }
                            for (int i=consumers.size()-1; i>=0; i--) {
                                ic = (ImageConsumer)consumers.elementAt(i);
                                produce(ic);
                                consumers.removeElement(ic);
                            }
                        }
                    }

                    private void produce(ImageConsumer ic) {
                        if (width < 0) {
                            ic.imageComplete(ImageConsumer.IMAGEERROR);
                            return;
                        }
                        ic.setDimensions(width, height);
                        ic.setProperties(properties);
                        ic.setColorModel(model);
                        ic.setHints(ImageConsumer.SINGLEPASS |
                                    ImageConsumer.SINGLEFRAME);
                        pixels = new byte[width * height];
                        ic.setPixels(0, 0, width, height, model, pixels, 0, width);
                        for (int i=0; i<rects.length; i++) {
                            Rectangle r = rects[i];

                            for (int y=r.y; y<r.y+r.height; y++) {
                                for (int x=r.x; x<r.x+r.width; x++) {
                                    pixels[y*width+x] = rectColors[i];
                                }
                            }
                            ic.setPixels(r.x, r.y, r.width, r.height, model,
                                        pixels, r.x+r.y*width, width);
                        }
                        ic.imageComplete(ImageConsumer.STATICIMAGEDONE);
                    }

                    public void requestTopDownLeftRightResend(ImageConsumer ic) {
                        if (pixels != null) {
                            ic.setDimensions(width, height);
                            ic.setProperties(properties);
                            ic.setColorModel(model);
                            ic.setHints(ImageConsumer.SINGLEPASS |
                                        ImageConsumer.TOPDOWNLEFTRIGHT |
                                        ImageConsumer.SINGLEFRAME);
                            ic.setPixels(0, 0, width, height, model, pixels, 0, width);
                        }
                    }
                }
```

Input File
```
100 180          // image size
8                // number of colors
0 0 255          // color 0 transparent
0 255 0          // color 1
0 255 255        // color 2
255 0 0          // color 3
255 0 255        // color 4
255 255 0        // color 5
255 255 255      // color 6
```

```
0 0 0              // color 7
9                  // number of rectangles
0 0 20 20 1        // rectangle 0
20 20 20 20 2      // rectangle 1
40 40 20 20 3      // rectangle 2
60 60 20 20 4      // rectangle 3
80 80 20 20 5      // rectangle 4
60 100 20 20 6     // rectangle 5
40 120 20 20 7     // rectangle 6
20 140 20 20 1     // rectangle 7
0 160 20 20 2      // rectangle 0
```

addConsumer( )

PURPOSE   Registers an image consumer with this image producer.

SYNTAX   `public void addConsumer(ImageConsumer ic)`

DESCRIPTION   This method registers the image consumer `ic` with this image producer. The image producer may or may not start delivering the image data to the image consumer immediately. The delivery of the image data can be triggered by a call to the `startProduction()` method.

PARAMETERS
  `ic`   The non-`null` image consumer to register.

SEE ALSO   `startProduction()`.

EXAMPLE   See the class example.

isConsumer( )

PURPOSE   Determines if an image consumer is registered with this image producer.

SYNTAX   `public boolean isConsumer(ImageConsumer ic)`

PARAMETERS
  `ic`   The possibly `null` image consumer to check if registered.

RETURNS   `true` if `ic` has been registered; `false` otherwise.

EXAMPLE   See the class example.

removeConsumer( )

PURPOSE   Removes a registered image consumer from this image producer.

SYNTAX   `public void removeConsumer(ImageConsumer ic)`

A
B
C
D
E
F
G
H
J
K
L
M
N
O
P
Q
R
S
T
U
V
W
X
Y
Z

<table>
<tr><td>DESCRIPTION</td><td>This method removes the given <code>ImageConsumer</code> object from the image producer's registered list of image consumers. The image producer will stop sending pixel data to <code>ic</code> as soon as it is feasible. This method call is ignored if <code>ic</code> has not been registered with this image producer.</td></tr>
<tr><td>PARAMETERS</td><td></td></tr>
<tr><td><code>ic</code></td><td>The non-<code>null</code> image consumer to be removed.</td></tr>
<tr><td>EXAMPLE</td><td>See the class example.</td></tr>
</table>

requestTopDownLeftRightResend( )

PURPOSE	Requests that pixel data be retransmitted in left-right, top-down order.
SYNTAX	`public void requestTopDownLeftRightResend(ImageConsumer ic)`
DESCRIPTION	This method is used by an image consumer to request that the pixels be retransmitted in top-down, left-right order. Some algorithms can produce higher-quality output more efficiently if the pixels are received in this order.
	In response to this request and if the image producer can retransmit the data in the requested order, the producer should call `setHints()` again, this time including the `TOPDOWNLEFTRIGHT` hint.
	The image producer can ignore this call if it cannot retransmit the data in the requested order.
PARAMETERS	
`ic`	The non-`null` image consumer requesting the retransmission.
SEE ALSO	`ImageConsumer.imageComplete()`, `ImageConsumer.setHints()`, `ImageConsumer.setPixels()`.
EXAMPLE	See the class example.

startProduction( )

PURPOSE	Triggers the delivery of image data.
SYNTAX	`public void startProduction(ImageConsumer ic)`
DESCRIPTION	This method registers the image consumer `ic`, if not already registered, and starts the delivery of image data to the list of registered consumers.
PARAMETERS	
`ic`	The non-`null` image consumer awaiting image data.
SEE ALSO	`addConsumer()`.
EXAMPLE	See the class example.

IndexColorModel

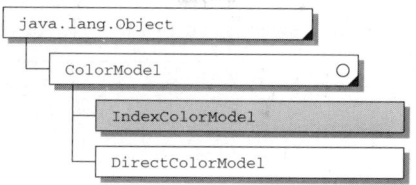

Syntax

`public class IndexColorModel extends ColorModel`

Description

An *index color model* maintains a particular palette of colors. Pixel values using the index color model are simply indexes into the palette of colors (see Figure 214). The number of colors in the palette is called the *color map size*. For more information about color models, see the `ColorModel` class.

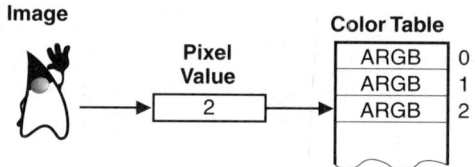

FIGURE 214: Index Color Model Pixel Values.

MEMBER SUMMARY

Constructor

`IndexColorModel()`	Constructs an `IndexColorModel` instance.

Component Access Methods

`getAlpha()`	Retrieves the alpha component of a pixel value.
`getAlphas()`	Retrieves the alpha component of all of the colors in this index color model.
`getBlue()`	Retrieves the blue component of a pixel value.
`getBlues()`	Retrieves the blue component of all of the colors in this index color model.
`getGreen()`	Retrieves the green component of a pixel value.
`getGreens()`	Retrieves the green component of all of the colors in this index color model.
`getRed()`	Retrieves the red component of a pixel value.
`getRGB()`	Converts a pixel value to a pixel value in the default color model.
`getTransparentPixel()`	Retrieves the index of the transparent pixel in this index color model.

Continued

MEMBER SUMMARY

Color Map Size Method
getMapSize()   Retrieves the color map size of this index color model.

Example

This example implements an image filter that can adjust the alpha component of the colors in an index color model. See Figure 215. The program creates a frame with an image canvas and a text field. The image canvas displays the image after it passes through the image filter. In the text field, you can type in a number in the range 0.0 to 1.0. The alpha components in an index color model are multiplied by this value, thereby increasing the transparency of the colors. A value of 0.0 forces all the colors to be transparent.

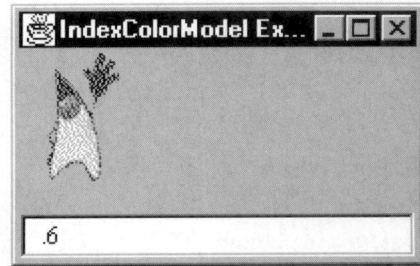

FIGURE 215:   IndexColorModel.

The setColorModel() method checks to see if the color model is an index color model. If it is, a copy of the color model is made that combines the old colors with the new alpha value. The new color model is forwarded to the image consumer. The setPixels() method substitutes the new color model and then forwards the pixels to the image consumer. (For brevity's sake, the setPixels() method does not properly handle the case in which the color model is not the same as the one supplied to setColorModel().)

```
import java.awt.*;
import java.awt.image.*;
import java.awt.event.*;
import java.net.*;
import java.util.*;

class Main extends Frame implements ActionListener {
    TextField textField = new TextField();
    ImageCanvas icv;

    Main(String filename) {
        super("IndexColorModel Example");
        try {
            // Retrieve the image.
            URL url = new URL("file:///" + System.getProperty("user.dir")
                + "/" + filename);
            Image urlImage = getToolkit().getImage(url);

            add(icv = new ImageCanvas(urlImage), BorderLayout.CENTER);
            add(textField, BorderLayout.SOUTH);
        } catch (Exception e) {
            e.printStackTrace();
```

```
        }

        // Add listener for text field
        textField.addActionListener(this);

        setSize(50, 100);
        show();
    }

    public void actionPerformed(ActionEvent evt) {
        icv.setAlphaFactor(Double.valueOf(textField.getText()).doubleValue());
    }

    static public void main(String[] args) {
        if (args.length == 1) {
            new Main(args[0]);
        } else {
            System.err.println("usage: java Main <image file>");
        }
    }
}

class ImageCanvas extends Component {
    Image newImage;
    Image image;
    AlphaFilter imgf = new AlphaFilter();

    ImageCanvas(Image image) {
        this.image = image;
        processImage();
    }

    void setAlphaFactor(double afactor) {
        imgf.setAlphaFactor(afactor);
        processImage();
    }

    public void paint(Graphics g) {
        g.drawImage(newImage, 0, 0, this);
    }

    void processImage() {
        ImageProducer ip = image.getSource();

        ip = new FilteredImageSource(ip, imgf);
        newImage = getToolkit().createImage(ip);
        repaint();
    }
}

class AlphaFilter extends ImageFilter {
    double afactor;
    ColorModel transColorModel;

    void setAlphaFactor(double afactor) {
        this.afactor = afactor;
    }

    public void setColorModel(ColorModel model) {
        if (model instanceof IndexColorModel) {
```

A
B
C
D
E
F
G
H

J
K
L
M
N
O
P
Q
R
S
T
U
V
W
X
Y
Z

```
                     IndexColorModel icm = (IndexColorModel)model;
                     byte[] reds = new byte[icm.getMapSize()];
                     byte[] greens = new byte[icm.getMapSize()];
                     byte[] blues = new byte[icm.getMapSize()];
                     byte[] alphas = new byte[icm.getMapSize()];
                     byte[] cmap = new byte[icm.getMapSize() * 4];

                     icm.getReds(reds);
                     icm.getGreens(greens);
                     icm.getBlues(blues);
                     icm.getAlphas(alphas);

                     int j = 0;
                     for (int i=0; i<icm.getMapSize(); i++) {
                         cmap[j++] = reds[i];
                         cmap[j++] = greens[i];
                         cmap[j++] = blues[i];
                         cmap[j++] = (byte)((alphas[i]&0xff)*afactor);
                     }
                     transColorModel = new IndexColorModel(icm.getPixelSize(),
                         icm.getMapSize(), cmap, 0, true, icm.getTransparentPixel());
                 } else {
                     transColorModel = model;
                 }
                 consumer.setColorModel(transColorModel);
             }

             public void setPixels(int x, int y, int w, int h,
                 ColorModel model, byte pixels[], int off, int scansize) {
                 consumer.setPixels(x, y, w, h, transColorModel, pixels, off, scansize);
             }

             public void setPixels(int x, int y, int w, int h,
                 ColorModel model, int pixels[], int off, int scansize) {
                 consumer.setPixels(x, y, w, h, transColorModel, pixels, off, scansize);
             }
         }
```

getAlpha( )

PURPOSE	Retrieves the alpha component of a pixel value.
SYNTAX	`final public int getAlpha(int pixelValue)`
DESCRIPTION	This method retrieves the alpha component of the pixel value `pixelValue`. The return value must be in the range 0–255, where 0 means completely transparent and 255 means completely opaque.
PARAMETERS	
`pixelValue`	The pixel value specifying a color in the color model.
RETURNS	The alpha transparency component in the range 0–255.
EXAMPLE	See the class example.

getAlphas()

PURPOSE   Retrieves the alpha component of all of the colors in this index color model.

SYNTAX   `final public void getAlphas(byte[] a)`

DESCRIPTION   This method retrieves the alpha component of all of the colors in this index color model and places the values in a. The number of values placed in a is determined by the color map size (see `getMapSize()`). a can be larger than the color map size; the unused array elements are not modified.

PARAMETERS
  a   A non-`null` array that is at least as large as the color map size.

SEE ALSO   `getMapSize()`.

EXAMPLE   See the class example.

getBlue()

PURPOSE   Retrieves the blue component of a pixel value.

SYNTAX   `final public int getBlue(int pixelValue)`

DESCRIPTION   This method retrieves the blue component of the pixel value `pixelValue`. The return value must be in the range 0–255, where 0 means no blue and 255 means maximum blue.

PARAMETERS
  `pixelValue`   The pixel value specifying a color in the color model.

RETURNS   The blue color component in the range 0–255.

EXAMPLE   See the class example.

getBlues()

PURPOSE   Retrieves the blue component of all of the colors in this index color model.

SYNTAX   `final public void getBlues(byte[] b)`

DESCRIPTION   This method retrieves the blue color component of all of the colors in this index color model and places the values in b. The number of values placed in b is determined by the color map size (see `getMapSize()`). b can be larger than the color map size; the unused array elements are not modified.

PARAMETERS
  b   A non-`null` array that is at least as large as the color map size.

A
B
C
D
E
F
G
H

J
K
L
M
N
O
P
Q
R
S
T
U
V
W
X
Y
Z

SEE ALSO	getMapSize().
EXAMPLE	See the class example.

getGreen( )

PURPOSE	Retrieves the green component of a pixel value.
SYNTAX	`final public int getGreen(int pixelValue)`
DESCRIPTION	This method retrieves the green component of the pixel value `pixelValue`. The return value must be in the range 0–255, where 0 means no green and 255 means maximum green.
PARAMETERS	
`pixelValue`	The pixel value specifying a color in the color model.
RETURNS	The green color component in the range 0–255.
EXAMPLE	See the class example.

getGreens( )

PURPOSE	Retrieves the green component of all of the colors in this index color model.
SYNTAX	`final public void getGreens(byte[] g)`
DESCRIPTION	This method retrieves the green color component of all of the colors in this index color model and places the values in g. The number of values placed in g is determined by the color map size (see `getMapSize()`). g can be larger than the color map size; the unused array elements are not modified.
PARAMETERS	
`g`	A non-`null` array that is at least as large as the color map size.
SEE ALSO	getMapSize().
EXAMPLE	See the class example.

getMapSize( )

PURPOSE	Retrieves the color map size of this index color model.
SYNTAX	`final public int getMapSize()`
RETURNS	The color map size.
EXAMPLE	See the class example.

getRed()

PURPOSE   Retrieves the red component of a pixel value.

SYNTAX   `final public int getRed(int pixelValue)`

DESCRIPTION   This method retrieves the red component of the pixel value `pixelValue`. The return value must be in the range 0–255, where 0 means no red and 255 means maximum red.

PARAMETERS
`pixelValue`   The pixel value specifying a color in the color model.

RETURNS   The red color component in the range from 0–255.

EXAMPLE   See the class example.

getReds()

PURPOSE   Retrieves the red component of all of the colors in this index color model.

SYNTAX   `final public void getReds(byte[] r)`

DESCRIPTION   This method retrieves the red color component of all of the colors in this index color model and places the values in `r`. The number of values placed in `r` is determined by the color map size (see `getMapSize()`). `r` can be larger than the color map size; the unused array elements are not modified.

PARAMETERS
`r`   A non-`null` array that is at least as large as the color map size.

SEE ALSO   `getMapSize()`.

EXAMPLE   See the class example.

getRGB()

PURPOSE   Converts a pixel value to a pixel value in the default color model.

SYNTAX   `final public int getRGB(int pixelValue)`

DESCRIPTION   The pixel value `pixelValue` is converted to an equivalent pixel value that must be interpreted using the default color model. The color of the new pixel value might not be identical to the color of `pixelValue`; there may be some loss of color information.

PARAMETERS
`pixelValue`   The pixel value specifying a color in the index color model.

RETURNS	A pixel value that specifies a color in the default color model.
OVERRIDES	`ColorModel.getRGB()`.
SEE ALSO	`ColorModel.getRGBdefault()`.
EXAMPLE	See the `ColorModel` class example.

getTransparentPixel( )

PURPOSE	Retrieves the index of the transparent pixel in this index color model.
SYNTAX	`final public int getTransparentPixel()`
RETURNS	The index of the transparent pixel. A return value of –1 indicates that there is no transparent pixel in the color model.
EXAMPLE	See the class example.

IndexColorModel( )

PURPOSE	Constructs an `IndexColorModel` instance.

SYNTAX	`public IndexColorModel(int nbits, int size, byte[] reds, byte[] greens, byte[] blues)`
	`public IndexColorModel(int nbits, int size, byte[] reds, byte[] greens, byte[] blues, int trans)`
	`public IndexColorModel(int nbits, int size, byte[] reds, byte[] greens, byte[] blues, byte[] alphas)`
	`public IndexColorModel(int nbits, int size, byte[] cmap, int start, boolean hasAlpha)`
	`public IndexColorModel(int nbits, int size, byte[] cmap, int start, boolean hasAlpha, int trans)`

DESCRIPTION	The forms of this constructor construct an `IndexColorModel` from a list of `size` colors. `nbits` specifies the number of bits needed to represent `size` colors. The number of colors can be smaller than the maximum value that `nbits` bits can represent.
	The list of colors can be specified in one of two ways: as four arrays or as a single array. In the case of four arrays, `reds` contains all of the reds, `greens` contains all of the greens, `blues` contains all of the blues, and `alphas` contains all of the alpha transparency values. The arrays must have at least `size` elements. `reds[i]`, `greens[i]`, `blues[i]`, and `alphas[i]` would hold the components for the `i`th color.
	If `alphas` is not specified, then all of the colors, except for the transparent color, are considered opaque (i.e., the value 255).

If `trans` is specified, it specifies which color should be treated as transparent, regardless of its alpha value. If `trans` is not specified or is −1, none of the colors will be treated as transparent.

In the case of specifying the colors with a single array `cmap`, the colors are encoded so that `cmap[i*4+start]` contains the red component for color i, `cmap[i*4+1+start]` contains the green component for color i, `cmap[i*4+2+start]` contains the blue component for color i, and `cmap[i*4+3+start]` contains the alpha component for color i. However, if `hasAlpha` is `false`, `cmap` is packed as follows:

- `cmap[i*3+start]` contains the red component for color i.
- `cmap[i*3+1+start]` contains the green component for color i.
- `cmap[i*3+2+start]` contains the blue component for color i.

PARAMETERS

`alphas`	The non-null array containing the alpha component of all of the colors.
`blues`	The non-null array containing the blue component of all of the colors.
`cmap`	The non-null array of packed color components.
`greens`	The non-null array containing the green component of all of the colors.
`hasAlpha`	If `true`, `cmap` contains alpha values; otherwise, `cmap` does not contain alpha values.
`nbits`	The number of bits required to hold all of the components of a color.
`reds`	The non-null array containing the red component of all of the colors.
`size`	The color map size.
`start`	The starting offset of the first color component in `cmap`.
`trans`	The index of the fully transparent color.

EXAMPLE   See the class example.

Syntax

`public class IndexedPropertyDescriptor extends PropertyDescriptor`

Description

An *indexed property* is a special kind of bean property whose type is an integer-indexed array of values. An example of an indexed property could be a list of recipient e-mail addresses in a "mail message bean." In this case, the indexed property's *array type* is an array of `String` and the indexed property's *element type* is a `String`. The indexed property's array type is always an indexed array of the property's element type. (Note that the element type can itself be an array.)

An indexed property is the same as any other bean property except for two differences:

1. The property type is an array.
2. In addition to the read and write accessor methods (the *nonindexed* accessor methods), which read and write an array, an indexed property provides two *indexed* accessor methods. These methods read and write elements in the array. Indexed accessor methods take an extra parameter—the integer index of the desired array element. For example, if you want to retrieve the fifth element of the indexed property, you would use the indexed read accessor method rather than the nonindexed read method (which would give you the whole array).

An *indexed property descriptor* contains information about an indexed property, such as its localized name and whether it is bound. There is one indexed property descriptor for each indexed property. A bean's indexed property descriptors can be retrieved through the introspector by calling `Introspector.getBeanInfo().getPropertyDescriptors()`. Since indexed property descriptors are subclasses of property descriptors (see `PropertyDescriptor`), you must use the `instanceof` operator to discover which property descriptors are actually indexed property descriptors.

For Bean Editors Only

The information contained in an indexed property descriptor is meant for programs such as bean editors (programs that help connect together beans into an application) and is not used by the bean itself. These and other descriptors essentially help a bean editor to construct a meaningful user interface for editing the bean. When the bean is actually running in an application, the indexed property descriptors are never used.

Implicit and Explicit Indexed Property Descriptors

The introspector first looks for *explicit* indexed property descriptors in the bean's bean-info, if present (see BeanInfo). If explicit indexed property descriptors are not found, the introspector creates *implicit* indexed property descriptors with some default values for each indexed property attribute. Table 15 shows the attributes of an indexed property descriptor and what they contain. Also shown are the default values for implicit indexed property descriptors.

Attribute	Contents	Implicit Default Value
Bound	true if the property is bound.	false.[a]
Constrained	true if the property is constrained.	false.[b]
Property type	The Class object of the property's array type.	The Class object of the property's array type.
Indexed property type	The Class object of the property's element type.	The Class object of the property's element type.
Read method	The Method object of the property's read accessor method.	The Method object of the property's read accessor method.
Write method	The Method object of the property's write accessor method.	The Method object of the property's write accessor method.
Indexed read method	The Method object of the property's indexed read accessor method.	The Method object of the property's indexed read accessor method.
Indexed write method	The Method object of the property's indexed write accessor method.	The Method object of the property's indexed write accessor method.
Property editor class	The Class object of the property's property editor.	null.
Name	The property's nonlocalized name.	The property's nonlocalized name.
Display name	The property's localized name.	The property's nonlocalized name.

Continued

TABLE 15: Indexed Property Descriptor Attributes.

Attribute	Contents	Implicit Default Value
Short description	A localized description of the property.	The property's nonlocalized name.
Expert	`true` if the property is considered for use by experts only.	`false`.
Hidden	`true` if the property is meant to be used by a tool; `false` if meant to be used by a person.	`false`.

TABLE 15:   Indexed Property Descriptor Attributes.

a. If the introspector discovers that the bean fires the property change event (see `PropertyChangeEvent`), then the bound attribute for all bean properties (indexed and nonindexed) will be `true`.

b. If the introspector discovers that the property's indexed or nonindexed write accessor methods throws `PropertyVetoException` (see `PropertyVetoException`), then the constrained attribute for the property will be `true`.

Accessor Method Signature Conventions

The bean specification defines conventions for the signature of property accessor methods. These conventions serve two purposes:

1. They make the bean's API easier for a programmer to read. That is, it's easy to see which methods are accessor methods and which are not.
2. They make it possible for the introspector to discover a bean's properties and create implicit property descriptors. In other words, the introspector looks at the entire list of a bean's public methods. When a method is found that matches the accessor method signature convention, the introspector assumes that it must be an accessor method. From the signature of the accessor method, it can deduce the name and type of the property.

For the conventions for the nonindexed accessor method signature, see `PropertyDescriptor`. The following describes the method signature conventions for an indexed property's indexed accessor methods.

If the name of an indexed property is *PropertyName* and its element type is *PropertyType*, the convention of an indexed read accessor method signature is

```
public PropertyType getCapPropertyName(int index)
```

where *CapPropertyName* is the property name with the first character capitalized and `index` is the 0-based index of the desired array element. The convention of a write accessor method signature is

```
public void setCapPropertyName(int index, PropertyType value)
```

If *PropertyType* is boolean, then the read method can be replaced or complemented by a read accessor with the signature

```
public boolean isCapPropertyName(int index)
```

For example, if the property name is "roasted" and the property type is boolean, then the set of accessor methods are

```
public boolean isRoasted(int index)
public boolean getRoasted(int index)
public void setRoasted(int index, boolean r)
```

When the read method is not explicitly specified and both "is" and "get" methods are available, the "is" read method is used. If only a read accessor method is found, the property is assumed to be read-only. If only a write accessor method is found, the property is assumed to be write-only.

MEMBER SUMMARY	
Constructor	
IndexedPropertyDescriptor()	Constructs an IndexedPropertyDescriptor instance.
Property Type Method	
getIndexedPropertyType()	Retrieves the property's element type.
Indexed Property Accessor Methods	
getIndexedReadMethod()	Retrieves the property's indexed read accessor method.
getIndexedWriteMethod()	Retrieves the property's indexed write accessor method.

See Also

PropertyDescriptor.

Example

This example implements a bean that has a string indexed property called "names." A property editor called NamesEditor is created to support the editing of this property. This property also requires the use of a custom editor called NamesCustomEditor.

The custom editor displays the list of names. It allows the user to change the list by adding or removing items. The custom editor does not update the property editor's value immediately. Instead, it keeps the changes to itself until the user hits the Save button, at which point it will update the property editor's value (which will then update the bean property; see Property-Editor for more details). See Figure 216.

A
B
C
D
E
F
G
H
I
J
K
L
M
N
O
P
Q
R
S
T
U
V
W
X
Y
Z

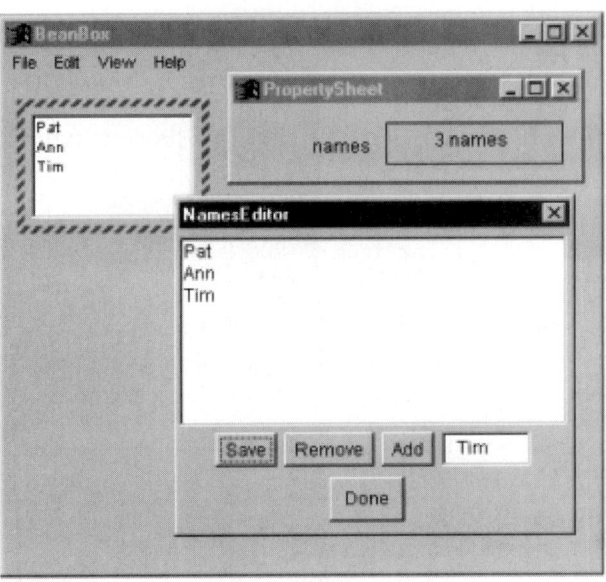

FIGURE 216:   Indexed Property Editor.

A bean-info is necessary to associate NamesEditor with the bean's "names" property. The bean-info must be defined in a class with the bean's name appended with "BeanInfo," which in this case, is BeanBeanInfo.

Bean.java
```java
import java.awt.*;
import java.beans.*;

public class Bean extends Panel {
    String[] names = {"Joe", "Pat", "Tim", "Ann", "Sue"};

    // Use a list to display the current names.
    List l = new List(5);

    public Bean() {
        // Initialize the list.
        for (int i=0; i<names.length; i++) {
            l.add(names[i]);
        }
        add(l);
    }
    // This method must not return null, otherwise the bean editor
    // may not create a property editor for this property.
    public String[] getNames() {
        return names;
    }
    public String getNames(int index) {
        return names[index];
    }
    public void setNames(String[] names) {
        this.names = names;
```

```
        // Update the list.
        l.removeAll();
        for (int i=0; i<names.length; i++) {
            l.add(names[i]);
        }
    }
    public void setNames(int index, String name) {
        names[index] = name;
        setNames(names);
    }
}
/*
    manifest.txt:
        Name: Bean.class
        Java-Bean: True
    jar command:
        jar cfm bean.jar manifest.txt Bean*.class Ip*.class
*/
```

BeanBeanInfo.java

```java
import java.beans.*;

public class BeanBeanInfo extends SimpleBeanInfo {
    public PropertyDescriptor[] getPropertyDescriptors() {
        PropertyDescriptor pd[] = new PropertyDescriptor[1];

        try {
            pd[0] = new IndexedPropertyDescriptor("names", Bean.class);
            pd[0].setPropertyEditorClass(NamesEditor.class);
            return pd;
        } catch (Exception e) {
            e.printStackTrace();
            return null;
        }
    }
}
```

NamesEditor.java:

```java
import java.awt.*;
import java.beans.*;
import java.util.*;

public class NamesEditor extends PropertyEditorSupport {
    // Paint area methods.
    public boolean isPaintable() {
        return true;
    }
    public void paintValue(Graphics g, Rectangle box) {
        String[] names = (String[])getValue();
        FontMetrics fm = g.getFontMetrics();
        String message  = "" + names.length + " names";

        // There's a bug in the bean box where box width and height
        // are too big by 4 pixels.
        box.width -= 4;
        box.height -= 4;
```

```
        g.setColor(Color.black);
        g.drawString(message, (box.width-fm.stringWidth(message))/2,
            (box.height-fm.getHeight())/2 + fm.getAscent());
        g.drawRect(box.x, box.y, box.width-1, box.height-1);
    }

    // Custom editor methods.
    public boolean supportsCustomEditor() {
        return true;
    }
    public java.awt.Component getCustomEditor() {
        return new NamesCustomEditor(this, (String[])getValue());
    }
  }
}
```

NamesCustomEditor.java

```
    import java.awt.*;
    import java.awt.event.*;
    import java.beans.*;

    public class NamesCustomEditor extends Panel implements ActionListener {
        PropertyEditor pe;
        List list = new List(10);
        TextField textField = new TextField(5);

        public NamesCustomEditor(PropertyEditor pe, String[] names) {
            Button saveBtn = new Button("Save");
            Button removeBtn = new Button("Remove");
            Button addBtn = new Button("Add");

            this.pe = pe;

            // Initialize list.
            for (int i=0; i<names.length; i++) {
                list.add(names[i]);
            }

            // Layout the components.
            setLayout(new BorderLayout());
            list.setSize(250, 150);
            add(list, BorderLayout.CENTER);
            Panel p = new Panel();
            p.add(saveBtn);
            p.add(removeBtn);
            p.add(addBtn);
            p.add(textField);
            add(p, BorderLayout.SOUTH);

            // Listen for events
            textField.addActionListener(this);
            saveBtn.addActionListener(this);
            removeBtn.addActionListener(this);
            addBtn.addActionListener(this);
        }

        public void actionPerformed(ActionEvent evt) {
            if (evt.getActionCommand().equals("Remove")) {
                int sel = list.getSelectedIndex();
```

A
B
C
D
E
F
G
H
J
K
L
M
N
O
P
Q
R
S
T
U
V
W
X
Y
Z

```
            if (sel >= 0) {
                list.remove(sel);
            }
        } else if (evt.getActionCommand().equals("Save")) {
            // Save the changes.
            String[] names = new String[list.getItemCount()];
            for (int i=0; i<names.length; i++) {
                names[i] = list.getItem(i);
            }
            pe.setValue(names);
        } else if (evt.getActionCommand().equals("Add")
                || evt.getSource() == textField) {
            list.add(textField.getText());
        }
    }
}
```

getIndexedPropertyType()

PURPOSE   Retrieves the property's element type.

SYNTAX   `public Class getIndexedPropertyType()`

DESCRIPTION The indexed property's element type is represented by a `Class` object of that type. For example, if the type is a `String` or an `int`, then this method returns `java.lang.String.class` or `int.class`, respectively.

The property's type is determined in the constructor. See the `IndexedPropertyDescriptor()` constructor for more details on how this is done.

If the property has nonindexed accessor methods, the indexed property's array type can be retrieved by calling `PropertyDescriptor.getProperty-Type()`.

RETURNS   The non-`null` `Class` object of the indexed property's type.

SEE ALSO   `PropertyDescriptor.getPropertyType()`.

EXAMPLE   See `getIndexedReadMethod()`.

getIndexedReadMethod()

PURPOSE   Retrieves the property's indexed read accessor method.

SYNTAX   `public Method getIndexedReadMethod()`

DESCRIPTION The property's indexed read accessor method is used to read one element from the indexed property's array of values. It is typically called by the bean editor as the user edits the property value through a property editor (see `Property-Editor`). The indexed read accessor method takes the index as its argument and returns an object of the same type as that returned by `getIndexed-PropertyType()`.

The property's indexed read accessor method is determined by the constructor. The method may have been specified in a bean-info or discovered through introspection. See the constructor for more details.

If the property does not have a public indexed read accessor method, this method returns `null`.

RETURNS The possibly-`null` indexed read accessor method.

SEE ALSO `java.lang.reflect.Method`, `getIndexedPropertyType()`, `getIndexedWriteMethod()`, `PropertyDescriptor`.

EXAMPLE This example demonstrates how to invoke the accessor methods on a property. The program loads a bean and its bean-info, if present, and then instantiates the bean. It then looks for string-based indexed properties. When if finds one, it does all of the following:

- Uses the read accessor method to retrieve the array.
- Sorts the array.
- Uses the write accessor method to write the sorted array.
- Uses the indexed read accessor method to retrieve each array element.
- Uses the indexed write accessor method to write the sorted elements backwards.

This example uses the `FileClassLoader` class to load the bean from a file. The source code for `FileClassLoader` is in the `Introspector` class example.

Main.java

```
import java.awt.*;
import java.beans.*;
import java.io.*;
import java.lang.reflect.*;
import java.util.*;
import java.net.*;

class Main {
    public static void main(String[] args) {
        if (args.length != 1) {
            System.err.println("Usage: java Main <name of bean class file>");
            System.exit(1);
        }

        try {
            // Load the bean and get the bean-info.
            // (See the Introspector class example for FileClassLoader
            // source code.)
            Class beanClass = FileClassLoader.load(args[0]);
            BeanInfo beanInfo = Introspector.getBeanInfo(beanClass);
```

```
// Instantiate the bean.
Object bean = beanClass.newInstance();

// Now print the indexed properties and their values.
PropertyDescriptor pds[] = beanInfo.getPropertyDescriptors();
for (int i=0; i<pds.length; i++) {
    if (pds[i] instanceof IndexedPropertyDescriptor) {
        IndexedPropertyDescriptor ipd =
            (IndexedPropertyDescriptor)pds[i];
        int arrayLength = 0;

        // Get the accessor method objects.
        Method reader = ipd.getReadMethod();
        Method indexedReader = ipd.getIndexedReadMethod();
        Method writer = ipd.getWriteMethod();
        Method indexedWriter = ipd.getIndexedWriteMethod();

        // If any of the accessor methods are missing,
        // just skip the property.
        if (reader == null || indexedReader == null
            || writer == null || indexedWriter == null
            || ipd.getIndexedPropertyType() != String.class) {
            /*
                An alternative test is:
                    ipd.getPropertyType() != String[].class
            */
            continue;
        }

        // Print the name of the property
        System.out.println(ipd.getName());

    // 1) Read and print the array.
        // Invoke the read accessor method and print the
        // contents of the array.
        Object[] readerArgs = {};
        Object array = reader.invoke(bean, readerArgs);
        arrayLength = Array.getLength(array);

        System.out.print("  non-indexed reader: ");
        for (int j=0; j<arrayLength; j++) {
            Object element = Array.get(array, j);

            System.out.print(element.toString() + " ");
        }
        System.out.println();

    // 2) Sort the array.
        array = sort((String[])array);

    // 3) Write the array.
        // Invoke the write accessor method on the sorted array.
        Object[] writerArgs = {array};
        writer.invoke(bean, writerArgs);

    // 4) Read and print the array elements.
        // Invoke the indexed read accessor method and print the
        // contents of the array.
        System.out.print("      indexed reader: ");
```

```
                            for (int j=0; j<arrayLength; j++) {
                                Object[] indexedReaderArgs = {new Integer(j)};
                                Object element =
                                    indexedReader.invoke(bean, indexedReaderArgs);

                                System.out.print(element.toString() + " ");
                            }
                            System.out.println();

                            // 5) Write the array elements backwards
                            // Invoke the indexed write accessor method and print the
                            // contents of the array.
                            array = (String[])((String[])array).clone();
                            for (int j=0; j<arrayLength; j++) {
                                Object[] indexedWriterArgs =
                                    {new Integer(arrayLength-j-1),
                                        Array.get(array, j)};

                                indexedWriter.invoke(bean, indexedWriterArgs);
                            }

                            // 6) Read and print the array again.
                            array = reader.invoke(bean, readerArgs);
                            arrayLength = Array.getLength(array);

                            System.out.print("  non-indexed reader: ");
                            for (int j=0; j<arrayLength; j++) {
                                Object element = Array.get(array, j);

                                System.out.print(element.toString() + " ");
                            }
                            System.out.println();
                        }
                    }
                } catch (IntrospectionException e) {
                    e.printStackTrace();
                } catch (IllegalAccessException e) {
                    e.printStackTrace();
                } catch (InvocationTargetException e) {
                    e.printStackTrace();
                } catch (InstantiationException e) {
                    e.printStackTrace();
                }
                System.exit(0);
            }

            // Prints s and pads the string with Math.max(1, width-s.length()) spaces.
            static void print(String s, int width) {
                System.out.print(s);
                for (int i=0; i<Math.max(1, (width-s.length())); i++) {
                    System.out.print(" ");
                }
            }

            // Returns a sorted copy of the string array.
            // Uses a simple bubble sort algorithm.
            static String[] sort(String[] a) {
                a = (String[])a.clone();

                for (int i=a.length-1; i>=0; i--) {
```

```
        for (int j=0; j<i; j++) {
            if (a[j].compareTo(a[j+1]) > 0) {
                String s = a[j];
                a[j] = a[j+1];
                a[j+1] = s;
            }
        }
    }
    return a;
  }
}
```

Output   Here is the output of the program when it is run on the bean developed in the class example.

```
names non-indexed reader: Joe Pat Tim Ann Sue
indexed reader: Ann Joe Pat Sue Tim
non-indexed reader: Tim Sue Pat Joe Ann
```

getIndexedWriteMethod()

PURPOSE   Retrieves the property's indexed write accessor method.

SYNTAX   `public Method getIndexedWriteMethod()`

DESCRIPTION   The indexed write accessor method is used to modify one element of the indexed property's array of values. It is typically called by the bean editor as the user edits the property value through a property editor (see `Property-Editor`). The indexed write accessor method takes two arguments and does not return any value. The first argument is an integer index, and the second argument the actual value. The value must be of the same type as returned by `getIndexedPropertyType()`.

The property's indexed write accessor method is determined by the constructor. The method may have been specified in a bean-info or discovered through introspection. See the constructor for more details.

If the property does not have a public indexed write accessor method, this method returns `null`.

RETURNS   The possibly `null` write accessor method.

SEE ALSO   `java.lang.reflect.Method`, `getIndexedPropertyType()`, `getIndexedReadMethod()`, `PropertyDescriptor`.

EXAMPLE   See `getIndexedReadMethod()`.

IndexedPropertyDescriptor()

PURPOSE   Constructs an `IndexedPropertyDescriptor` instance.

SYNTAX
```
public IndexedPropertyDescriptor(String propertyName, Class
    beanClass) throws IntrospectionException
public IndexedPropertyDescriptor(String propertyName, Class
    beanClass, String readerName, String writerName, String
    indexedReaderName, String indexedWriterName) throws
    IntrospectionException
public IndexedPropertyDescriptor(String propertyName, Method
    reader, Method writer, Method indexedReader, Method
    indexedWriter) throws IntrospectionException
```

DESCRIPTION   Indexed property descriptors are either implicitly created by the introspector or are explicitly created by a bean. See the class description for more information.

When an indexed property descriptor is created, eight attributes are initialized:
- Property name
- `Class` object of the bean
- Read accessor method
- Write accessor method
- Indexed read accessor method
- Indexed write accessor method
- Indexed property array type
- Indexed property element type

All other attributes are given default values that can be changed by methods in this class—the `PropertyDescriptor` class—and in the `FeatureDescriptor` class. The default values for an indexed property descriptor are shown in Table 15.

The indexed property element type is not specified. Rather, it is determined using reflection to examine the indexed read and write methods. Basically, the type returned by the indexed read method becomes the indexed property type.

See the `PropertyDescriptor()` constructor for information regarding the `readerName`, `writerName`, `reader`, and `writer` parameters,

If `indexedReader` and `indexedWriter` are specified, a check is made to ensure that the methods have the appropriate signatures. The signatures are discussed in the class description.

If `indexedReaderName` and `indexedWriterName` are specified, reflection is used to look for methods with these names. (Although they don't have to use the "is/get/set" naming conventions, it is still highly recommended that they do.) The method can be in either the bean or in one of its ancestors. Once these methods are found, they are subject to the signature compatibility check as discussed in the class description.

If the accessor methods are not specified, they are discovered using reflection and the following rules:

- The first letter of the property name is capitalized. For example, "roasted" becomes "Roasted." "Roasted" is referred to as the capitalized property name *CapPropertyName*.
- Reflection is used to look for a method named set*CapPropertyName* that has the appropriate signature. The method can be in either the bean class or one of its ancestors. If one is found, this becomes the indexed write method and the second parameter becomes the property element type; otherwise, `IntrospectionException` is thrown.
- If the property type is `boolean`, reflection is used to look for a method named is*CapPropertyName* that has the appropriate signature. The method can be in either the bean class or one of its ancestors. If one is found, this becomes the indexed read method.
- Otherwise, reflection is used to look for a method named get*CapPropertyName* that has the appropriate signature. The method can be in either the bean class or in one of its ancestors. If one is found, this becomes the indexed read method; otherwise, `IntrospectionException` is thrown.

PARAMETERS

`beanClass`	The bean's `Class` object.
`reader`	The possibly `null` `Method` object of the property's read accessor method.
`readerName`	The possibly `null` name of the property's read accessor method.
`indexedReader`	The method used for reading an indexed property value.
`indexedReaderName`	
	The name of the method used for reading
`indexedWriter`	The method used for writing an indexed property value.
`indexedWriterName`	
	The name of the method used for writing.
`propertyName`	The non-`null` nonlocalized name of the property.
`writer`	The possibly `null` `Method` object of the property's write accessor method.
`writerName`	The possibly `null` name of the property's write accessor method.

EXCEPTIONS

`IntrospectionException`

If the signatures of the read and write methods are incompatible. For example, the type returned by `reader` does not match that accepted by `writer`.

SEE ALSO   `java.lang.reflect.Method`, `java.lang.Class`.

EXAMPLE   This example simply demonstrates how to use the three different forms of the constructor. The bean has three indexed `float` properties: `property1`, `property2`, and `property3`. The bean-info class, `BeanBeanInfo`, creates three property descriptors, one for each of the three properties, using the three different constructors.

Bean.java

```java
public class Bean {
    int property1;
    int property2;
    int property3;

    public int getProperty1() {
        return property1;
    }
    public void setProperty1(int v) {
        property1 = v;
    }

    public int getProperty2() {
        return property2;
    }
    public void setProperty2(int v) {
        property2 = v;
    }

    public int getProperty3() {
        return property3;
    }
    public void setProperty3(int v) {
        property3 = v;
    }
}
/*
    manifest.txt:
        Name: Bean.class
        Java-Bean: True
    jar command:
        jar cfm bean.jar manifest.txt *.class
*/
```

BeanBeanInfo.java

```java
import java.beans.*;
import java.lang.reflect.*;

public class BeanBeanInfo extends SimpleBeanInfo {
    public PropertyDescriptor[] getPropertyDescriptors() {
        IndexedPropertyDescriptor pd[] = new IndexedPropertyDescriptor[3];

        try {
            // The getter and setter methods are derived from the property name.
            pd[0] = new IndexedPropertyDescriptor("property1", Bean.class);

            // The names of the getter and setter methods are supplied.
            pd[1] = new IndexedPropertyDescriptor("property2", Bean.class,
                "getProperty2", "setProperty2", "getProperty2", "setProperty2");

            // The Method objects of the getter and setter methods are supplied.

            // The getter method must not take any parameters.
            Class[] getArgs = {};
            Method getter = Bean.class.getMethod("getProperty3", getArgs);

            // The indexedGetter method takes one integer parameter.
            Class[] igetArgs = {Integer.TYPE};
```

```
Method indexedGetter =
    Bean.class.getMethod("getProperty3", igetArgs);

// The setter must take one parameter and it must have the
// same type as returned by the getter method.
Class[] setArgs = {getter.getReturnType()};
Method setter = Bean.class.getMethod("setProperty3", setArgs);

// The indexedSetter must take two parameters - an integer and
// an object of the same type as returned by the
// indexed getter method.
Class[] isetArgs = {Integer.TYPE, indexedGetter.getReturnType()};
Method indexedSetter =
    Bean.class.getMethod("setProperty3", isetArgs);

pd[2] = new IndexedPropertyDescriptor("property3", getter, setter,
            indexedGetter, indexedSetter);

    return pd;
} catch (NoSuchMethodException e) {
    e.printStackTrace();
} catch (IntrospectionException e) {
    e.printStackTrace();
}
    return null;
    }
}
```

Output
```
Class: Bean
Name: Bean
Display name: Bean
Short Description: Bean
Expert: false
Hidden: false

h:hidden, e:expert, i:indexed, *:default, c:constrained, b:bound
```

PROPERTIES
```
---------------------------------------------------------------------
Attr Name              Type                    Accessor methods
---------------------------------------------------------------------
i     property3        [F                      getProperty3/setProperty3
                       float                   getProperty3/setProperty3
i     property2        [F                      getProperty2/setProperty2
                       float                   getProperty2/setProperty2
ib    property1        [F                      getProperty1/setProperty1
                       float                   getProperty1/setProperty1
```

EVENT SETS
```
---------------------------------------------------------------------
Attr Name              Registration methods
        Callback methods
---------------------------------------------------------------------
```

METHODS
```
---------------------------------------------------------------------
Attr Signature
---------------------------------------------------------------------
```

A
B
C
D
E
F
G
H

J
K
L
M
N
O
P
Q
R
S
T
U
V
W
X
Y
Z

```
public float[] Bean.getProperty3()
public float[] Bean.getProperty2()
public float[] Bean.getProperty1()
public float Bean.getProperty3(int)
public float Bean.getProperty2(int)
public float Bean.getProperty1(int)
public final void java.lang.Object.wait(long,int)
     throws java.lang.InterruptedException
public final native void java.lang.Object.notifyAll()
public void Bean.setProperty2(float[])
public final void java.lang.Object.wait()
     throws java.lang.InterruptedException
public java.lang.String java.lang.Object.toString()
public final native void java.lang.Object.notify()
public void Bean.setProperty3(float[])
public void Bean.setProperty1(float[])
public native int java.lang.Object.hashCode()
public final native java.lang.Class java.lang.Object.getClass()
public final native void java.lang.Object.wait(long)
     throws java.lang.InterruptedException
public boolean java.lang.Object.equals(java.lang.Object)
public void Bean.setProperty3(int,float)
public void Bean.setProperty2(int,float)
public void Bean.setProperty1(int,float)
```

A
B
C
D
E
F
G
H
I
J
K
L
M
N
O
P
Q
R
S
T
U
V
W
X
Y
Z

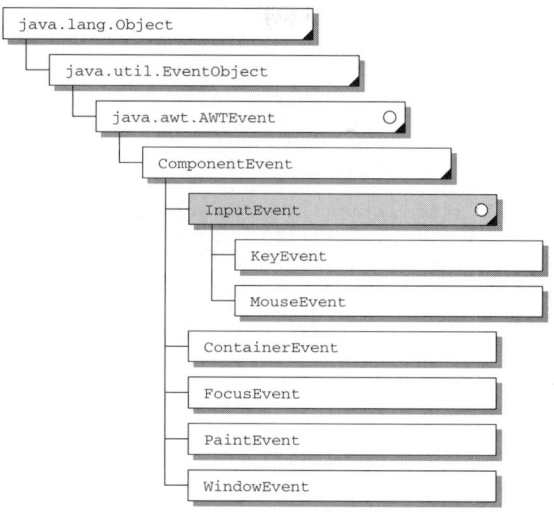

Syntax

```
public abstract class InputEvent extends ComponentEvent
```

Description

Input events are typically fired by a component while the user uses the keyboard and mouse to interact with the component (see KeyEvent and MouseEvent). Input events contain a time-stamp of when the input event occurred and the set of modifier keys pressed at the time the input event was fired. For more general information about events, see AWTEvent.

Listening for Input Events

To listen for either key or mouse input events, see KeyEvent and MouseEvent.

Consuming Input Events

The delivery flow of input events differs from other events. Events such as component events are fired by a component after the operation is completed. For example, when a COMPONENT_RESIZED component event is delivered to a listener, the component has already been resized. Input events are delivered to the component and its listeners before it is processed by the component peer. This allows the component and its listeners to modify or *consume* (i.e., discard) the event before it is processed by the peer. An example of where this could be used is by a text field that accepts only numbers. Here, when the text field receives a key event that is not a number, it could emit a beep and then consume the event. The consumed key events would not appear in the text field. Note that *all* listeners are notified of the event, regardless of whether the event has been consumed. Consuming an event affects only whether the peer gets to process the event.

When an input event is consumed, it cannot be "unconsumed."

Modifier Keys

An input event contains the state of the modifier keys at the time the input event was fired. The modifier key state is represented by a bit vector, where each bit position represents the state of one modifier key. The state of particular modifier key can be retrieved by using the mask for that modifier key (for example, SHIFT_MASK).

If the input event is a mouse event, the identity of the mouse button is encoded in the modifier key state. See the MouseEvent class description for more details.

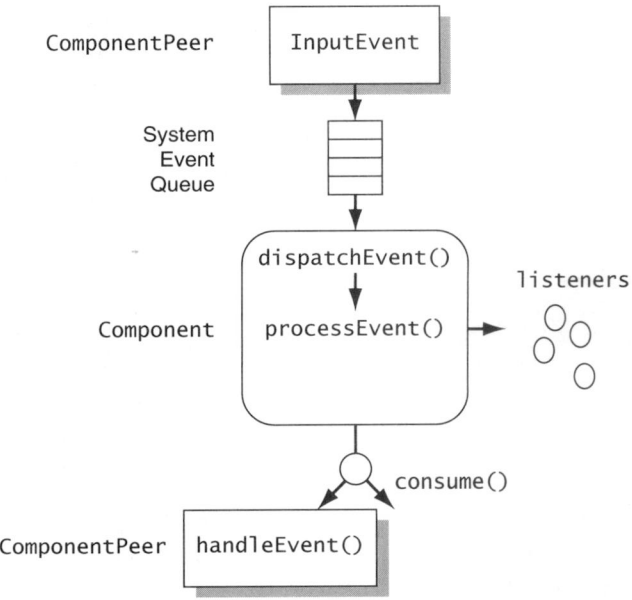

FIGURE 217:   Input Event Flow.

Timestamp

An input event has a timestamp that indicates when the input event was created. The timestamp is in UTC format. See Date for more details.

Input Event Flow

As discussed in the previous "Consuming Input Events" section, input events differ from non-input events in that the event is not processed by a component peer until after it has been processed by the component and all of its listeners. See Figure 217. See the "Event Flow" sections for KeyEvent and MouseEvent for more details about input event flow.

Simulating Input Events

Input events are normally created by the AWT system when the user interacts with a component. However, it is possible for any object to create input events in the same way. For example, a program designed to test a dialog box can create various key and mouse events and deliver them to the dialog box. The dialog box will treat the key and mouse events exactly as if it came from the user via the AWT system.

A simulated input event can be delivered to a component in one of two ways. Either by posting the event to the event queue (see EventQueue) or by calling the component's dispatchEvent() method directly.

MEMBER SUMMARY	
Consume Methods	
consume()	Consumes this input event.
isConsumed()	Retrieves the consumed state of the event.
Time Method	
getWhen()	Retrieves the input event's timestamp.
Modifier Masks	
ALT_MASK	Used to determine the state of the Alt key.
BUTTON1_MASK	Used to determine whether button1 was pressed.
BUTTON2_MASK	Used to determine whether button2 was pressed.
BUTTON3_MASK	Used to determine whether button3 was pressed
CTRL_MASK	Used to determine the state of the Control key.
META_MASK	Used to determine the state of the Meta key.
SHIFT_MASK	Used to determine the state of the Shift key.
Modifier Methods	
getModifiers()	Retrieves the state of the input event's modifier keys.
isAltDown()	Determines the state of the Alt key for this event.
isControlDown()	Determines the state of the Control key for this event.
isMetaDown()	Determines the state of the Meta key for this event.
isShiftDown()	Determines the state of the Shift key for this event.

See Also

java.util.Date, KeyEvent, MouseEvent.

Example

This example demonstrates how input events can be consumed. A text field is created that accepts only five digits. Nondigit characters are consumed and so never appear in the text field. Also, if a digit character is received and the text field is full, the key event is consumed.

Notice that nonprintable nondigit ASCII characters are not consumed so that keys such as KeyEvent.LEFT and KeyEvent.BACK_SPACE can continue to work. See Figure 218.

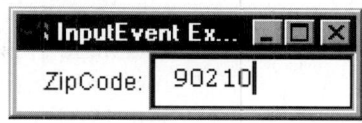

FIGURE 218:   Zip Code.

```
import java.awt.*;
```

```
import java.awt.event.*;

class Main extends Frame {
    Main() {
        super("InputEvent Example");
        TextField tf = new TextField(5);

        // Listen for text events.
        tf.addKeyListener(new KeyEventHandler());
        tf.setFont(new Font("Serif", Font.PLAIN, 14));

        add(new Label("ZipCode: ", Label.RIGHT), BorderLayout.WEST);
        add(tf, BorderLayout.CENTER);
        pack();
        show();
    }

    class KeyEventHandler extends KeyAdapter {
        public void keyPressed(KeyEvent evt) {
            char c = evt.getKeyChar();

            if (c >= 0x20 && c <= 0x7F && !Character.isDigit(c)) {
                // Only non-digit printable characters are consumed.
                evt.consume();
            } else if (Character.isDigit(c)
                    && ((TextComponent)evt.getComponent()).getText().length()
                        >= 5) {
                // Text field must not have more than 5 digits.
                evt.consume();
            }
        }
    }

    public static void main(String args[]) {
        new Main();
    }
}
```

ALT_MASK

PURPOSE   Modifier mask used to determine the state of the Alt key.

SYNTAX   `public static final int ALT_MASK`

DESCRIPTION This mask (value 8) should be bitwise and'd with the results of `getModifiers()` to determine the state of the Alt key at the time the input event was created. If the result is 0, the Alt key was not pressed; otherwise, the key was pressed.

Note that for mouse events, when the Alt key is pressed, the event is assumed to be button2 mouse event.

SEE ALSO   `CTRL_MASK`, `getModifiers()`, `isAltDown()`, `META_MASK`, `SHIFT_MASK`.

EXAMPLE

```
boolean isAltDown(InputEvent evt) {
    return (evt.getModifiers() & InputEvent.ALT_MASK) != 0;
}
```

BUTTON1_MASK

PURPOSE   Modifier mask used to determine whether button1 was pressed.

SYNTAX   `public static final int BUTTON1_MASK`

DESCRIPTION This mask (value 16) should be bitwise and'd with the results of `getModifi-ers()` to determine whether button1 on the mouse was pressed. There are a number of complications to be handled when determining which mouse button was pressed; see the `MouseEvent` class description for details.

SEE ALSO   `BUTTON2_MASK`, `BUTTON3_MASK`, `getModifiers()`.

EXAMPLE   For another example, see the `MouseEvent` class example.

```
boolean isButton1Down(InputEvent evt) {
    return (evt.getModifiers() & InputEvent.BUTTON1_MASK) != 0;
}
```

BUTTON2_MASK

PURPOSE   Modifier mask used to determine whether button2 was pressed.

SYNTAX   `public static final int BUTTON2_MASK`

DESCRIPTION This mask (value 8) should be bitwise and'd with the results of `getModifi-ers()` to determine whether the button2 on the mouse was pressed. There are a number of complications to be handled when determining which mouse button was pressed; see the `MouseEvent` class description for details.

SEE ALSO   `BUTTON1_MASK`, `BUTTON3_MASK`, `getModifiers()`.

EXAMPLE   For another example, see the `MouseEvent` class example.

```
boolean isButton2Down(InputEvent evt) {
    return (evt.getModifiers() & InputEvent.BUTTON2_MASK) != 0;
}
```

BUTTON3_MASK

PURPOSE   Modifier mask used to determine whether button3 was pressed.

SYNTAX   `public static final int BUTTON3_MASK`

DESCRIPTION This mask (value 4) should be bitwise and'd with the results of `getModifiers()` to determine whether the button3 on the mouse was pressed. There are a number of complications to be handled when determining which mouse button was pressed; see the `MouseEvent` class description for details.

SEE ALSO `BUTTON1_MASK`, `BUTTON2_MASK`, `getModifiers()`.

EXAMPLE For another example, see the `MouseEvent` class example.

```
boolean isButton3Down(InputEvent evt) {
    return (evt.getModifiers() & InputEvent.BUTTON3_MASK) != 0;
}
```

consume()

PURPOSE Consumes this input event.

SYNTAX `public void consume()`

DESCRIPTION Calling this method on this event prevents it from being processed by the peer of the component that fired the event. Once consumed, an event cannot be "unconsumed." See the class description for more information about consuming events.

OVERRIDES `java.awt.consume()`.

SEE ALSO `isConsumed()`.

EXAMPLE See the class example.

CTRL_MASK

PURPOSE Modifier mask used to determine the state of the Control key.

SYNTAX `public static final int CTRL_MASK`

DESCRIPTION This mask (value 2) should be bitwise and'd with the results of `getModifiers()` to determine the state of the Control key at the time the input event was created. If the result is 0, the Control key was not pressed; otherwise, the key was pressed.

SEE ALSO `ALT_MASK`, `getModifiers()`, `isControlDown()`, `META_MASK`, `SHIFT_MASK`.

EXAMPLE
```
boolean isCtrlDown(InputEvent evt) {
    return (evt.getModifiers() & InputEvent.CTRL_MASK) != 0;
}
```

getModifiers()

PURPOSE	Retrieves the state of the input event's modifier keys.
SYNTAX	`public int getModifiers()`
DESCRIPTION	Stored with an input event is the state of the modifier keys at the time an input event is fired. This method retrieves the state of all of the modifier keys as a bit vector, where the state of each modifier key is represented by a particular bit in the bit vector. To determine whether a modifier key was pressed, you must use the appropriate modifier mask with the bit vector. See the various modifier masks for examples.
RETURNS	A bit vector containing the state of the modifier keys.
SEE ALSO	`ALT_MASK, BUTTON1_MASK, BUTTON2_MASK, BUTTON3_MASK, CTRL_MASK, META_MASK, SHIFT_MASK.`
EXAMPLE	See the class example.

getWhen()

PURPOSE	Retrieves the input event's timestamp.
SYNTAX	`public long getWhen()`
DESCRIPTION	The timestamp is a time in UTC format (see `Date`) that indicates when the input event was created.
RETURNS	The time when the event was created.
SEE ALSO	`java.util.Date.`
EXAMPLE	This example simply displays the event's timestamp as a date. The frame overrides `processEvent()` to catch all input events. It calls `enableEvents()` to enable mouse and keyboard events; otherwise, the AWT system will not deliver the events to the frame. See Figure 219.

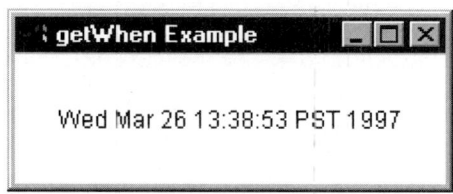

FIGURE 219: `InputEvent.getWhen().`

```
import java.awt.*;
import java.awt.event.*;
import java.util.*;

class Main extends Frame {
    Main() {
        super("getWhen Example");
        setSize(100, 100);
```

A
B
C
D
E
F
G
H

J
K
L
M
N
O
P
Q
R
S
T
U
V
W
X
Y
Z

A
B
C
D
E
F
G
H

J
K
L
M
N
O
P
Q
R
S
T
U
V
W
X
Y
Z

```
            show();

            // Enable mouse and keyboard events so processEvent() will be called.
            enableEvents(AWTEvent.MOUSE_EVENT_MASK|
                AWTEvent.MOUSE_MOTION_EVENT_MASK|AWTEvent.KEY_EVENT_MASK);
        }

        String date = "";
        protected void processEvent(AWTEvent evt) {
            if (evt instanceof InputEvent) {
                InputEvent ie = (InputEvent)evt;
                date = "" + (new Date(ie.getWhen()));
                repaint();
            }
            super.processEvent(evt);
        }

        public void paint(Graphics g) {
            Insets in = getInsets();
            FontMetrics fm = g.getFontMetrics();

            g.drawString(date, (getSize().width-fm.stringWidth(date))/2,
                in.top+(getSize().height-in.top-in.bottom-
                fm.getHeight())/2+fm.getAscent());
        }

        public static void main(String args[]) {
            new Main();
        }
    }
```

isAltDown()

PURPOSE	Determines the state of the Alt key for this event.
SYNTAX	`public boolean isAltDown()`
DESCRIPTION	See the class description for more information about modifier keys and mouse buttons.
RETURNS	`true` if the Alt key is down for this event; `false` otherwise.
SEE ALSO	`ALT_MASK`, `isControlDown()`, `isMetaDown()`, `isShiftDown()`.
EXAMPLE	See the KeyEvent or MouseEvent class example.

isConsumed()

PURPOSE	Retrieves the consumed state of the event.
SYNTAX	`public boolean isConsumed()`

DESCRIPTION	Unlike with other events, input events are delivered to a component and its listeners before they are processed by the peer. Any listener can prevent an input event from being processed by the peer by consuming the event. See the class description for more information about consuming events.
RETURNS	`true` if the event has been consumed; `false` otherwise.
OVERRIDES	`java.awt.AWTEvent.isConsumed()`.
SEE ALSO	`consume()`.
EXAMPLE	See `java.awt.AWTEvent.isConsumed()`.

isControlDown()

PURPOSE	Determines the state of the Control key for this event.
SYNTAX	`public boolean isControlDown()`
DESCRIPTION	See the class description for more information about modifier keys and mouse buttons.
RETURNS	`true` if the Control key is down for this event; `false` otherwise.
SEE ALSO	`CTRL_MASK`, `isAltDown()`, `isMetaDown()`, `isShiftDown()`.
EXAMPLE	See the `KeyEvent` or `MouseEvent` class example.

isMetaDown()

PURPOSE	Determines the state of the Meta key for this event.
SYNTAX	`public boolean isMetaDown()`
DESCRIPTION	See the class description for more information about modifier keys and mouse buttons.
RETURNS	`true` if the Meta key is down for this event; `false` otherwise.
SEE ALSO	`isAltDown()`, `isControlDown()`, `isShiftDown()`, `META_MASK`.
EXAMPLE	See the `KeyEvent` or `MouseEvent` class example.

isShiftDown()

PURPOSE	Determines the state of the Shift key for this event.
SYNTAX	`public boolean isShiftDown()`

A
B
C
D
E
F
G
H
I
J
K
L
M
N
O
P
Q
R
S
T
U
V
W
X
Y
Z

DESCRIPTION	See the class description for more information about modifier keys and mouse buttons.
RETURNS	`true` if the Shift key is down for this event; `false` otherwise.
SEE ALSO	`isAltDown()`, `isControlDown()`, `isMetaDown()`, `SHIFT_MASK`.
EXAMPLE	See the `KeyEvent` or `MouseEvent` class example.

META_MASK

PURPOSE	Modifier mask used to determine the state of the Meta key.
SYNTAX	`public static final int META_MASK`
DESCRIPTION	This mask (value 4) should be bitwise and'd with the results of `getModifiers()` to determine the state of the Meta key at the time the input event was created. If the result is 0, the Meta key was not pressed; otherwise, the key was pressed.
	Note that for mouse events, when the Meta key is pressed, the event is assumed to be button3 mouse event.
SEE ALSO	`ALT_MASK`, `CTRL_MASK`, `getModifiers()`, `isMetaDown()`, `SHIFT_MASK`.
EXAMPLE	

```
boolean isMetaDown(InputEvent evt) {
    return (evt.getModifiers() & InputEvent.META_MASK) != 0;
}
```

SHIFT_MASK

PURPOSE	Modifier mask used to determine the state of the Shift key.
SYNTAX	`public static final int SHIFT_MASK`
DESCRIPTION	`getModifiers()` to determine the state of the Shift key at the time the input event was created. If the result is 0, the Shift key was not pressed; otherwise, the key was pressed.
SEE ALSO	`ALT_MASK`, `CTRL_MASK`, `getModifiers()`, `isShiftDown()`, `META_MASK`.
EXAMPLE	

```
boolean isShiftDown(InputEvent evt) {
    return (evt.getModifiers() & InputEvent.SHIFT_MASK) != 0;
}
```

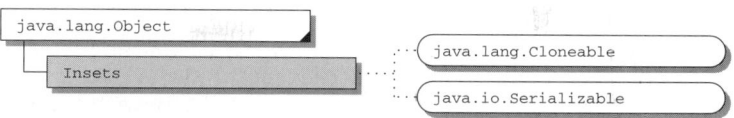

Syntax

```
public class Insets implements Cloneable, Serializable
```

Description

An inset has four inset values, each defining the amount to adjust the sides of a rectangle. The four values are left, right, top, and bottom. The left value is added to the left edge of a rectangle to yield a new location for the edge. The other values and other edges are handled similarly.

Insets are typically used by layout managers in calculating the component positions. For example, a container returns an inset, which is applied to the container's bounds to yield its paintable area.

In general, when returning an insets instance in a method call, either return a copy, if you need to retain the instance, or discard the instance after returning it. If you have an insets instance passed in a method call and wish to continue using the instance, note whether the method will retain the instance or copy the values.

MEMBER SUMMARY	
Constructor	
Insets()	Constructs a new Insets instance.
Fields	
bottom	Contains this inset's bottom value.
left	Contains this inset's left value.
right	Contains this inset's right value.
top	Contains this inset's top value.
Object Override Methods	
clone()	Creates a copy of the inset.
equals()	Determines whether an object is equal to this inset.
toString()	Generates the string representation of this inset.

A
B
C
D
E
F
G
H

J
K
L
M
N
O
P
Q
R
S
T
U
V
W
X
Y
Z

See Also

`Container.getInsets()`, `java.io.Serializable`, `java.lang.Cloneable`.

Example

This example creates a frame that displays a black rectangle inside the frame's paintable area. See Figure 220.

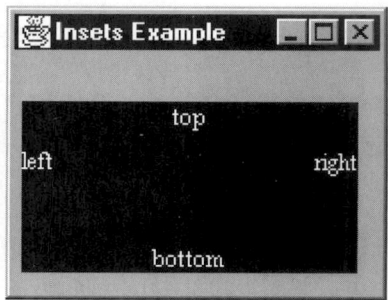

FIGURE 220:   The Four Insets.

The size and position of the rectangle depends on the values of an insets object. The values of the object can be increased by pressing the L (left), R (right), T (top), and/or B (bottom) keys. If the Shift key is held down while one of the keys is pressed, the affected inset is decreased. Each edge of the rectangle is labeled with a string that names the inset at that edge.

There are actually two insets involved in this example: `rectInsets` and `frameInsets`. `rectInsets` determines the size and position of the rectangle inside the container. However, since a frame is a container with an inset `frameInsets` (see `Container.getInsets()`), the frame's inset also needs to be taken into account. In this case, `frameInsets` is used to determine the size of the frame's paintable area. Once this is done, `rectInsets` is then applied to `frameInsets`, thereby yielding the area in which the rectangle is painted. This calculation would not be necessary if the rectangle were painted inside an "inset-less" container, such as a canvas or a panel.

```java
import java.awt.*;
import java.awt.event.*;

class Main extends Frame {
    Insets rectInsets = new Insets(0, 0, 0, 0);

    Main() {
        super("Insets Example");
        setSize(150, 150);
        addKeyListener(new KeyEventHandler());
        show();
    }

    public void paint(Graphics g) {
        Insets frameInsets = getInsets();
        int x = frameInsets.left, y = frameInsets.top;

        int w = getSize().width - frameInsets.right-frameInsets.left;
        int h = getSize().height - frameInsets.bottom-frameInsets.top;
        FontMetrics fm = g.getFontMetrics();

        g.fillRect(x+rectInsets.left, y+rectInsets.top,
            w - rectInsets.right - rectInsets.left,
            h - rectInsets.bottom - rectInsets.top);
        g.setColor(Color.white);
        // top
        g.drawString("top", x + rectInsets.left
```

```
                + (w-rectInsets.left-rectInsets.right-fm.stringWidth("top"))/2,
            y + rectInsets.top+fm.getAscent());
        // left
        g.drawString("left", x+ rectInsets.left,
                y+rectInsets.top +
                    (h-rectInsets.top-rectInsets.bottom-fm.getHeight())/2);
        // bottom
        g.drawString("bottom", x+rectInsets.left
                + (w-rectInsets.left-rectInsets.right-
                    fm.stringWidth("bottom"))/2,
            y+h-rectInsets.bottom-fm.getDescent());
        // right
        g.drawString("right", x+w-rectInsets.right-fm.stringWidth("right"),
                y+rectInsets.top +
                    (h-rectInsets.top-rectInsets.bottom-fm.getHeight())/2);
    }

    class KeyEventHandler extends KeyAdapter {
        public void keyTyped(KeyEvent evt) {
            char key = evt.getKeyChar();
            key = Character.toLowerCase(key);
            switch (key) {
            case 't':
                if (evt.isShiftDown()) {
                    if (rectInsets.top > 0) {
                        rectInsets.top--;
                    }
                } else {
                    rectInsets.top++;
                }
                break;
            case 'b':
                if (evt.isShiftDown()) {
                    if (rectInsets.bottom > 0) {
                        rectInsets.bottom--;
                    }
                } else {
                    rectInsets.bottom++;
                }
                break;
            case 'l':
                if (evt.isShiftDown()) {
                    if (rectInsets.left > 0) {
                        rectInsets.left--;
                    }
                } else {
                    rectInsets.left++;
                }
                break;
            case 'r':
                if (evt.isShiftDown()) {
                    if (rectInsets.right > 0) {
                        rectInsets.right--;
                    }
                } else {
                    rectInsets.right++;
                }
            }
            repaint();
        }
    }
}
```

A
B
C
D
E
F
G
H
I
J
K
L
M
N
O
P
Q
R
S
T
U
V
W
X
Y
Z

```
        public static void main(String[] args) {
            new Main();
        }
    }
```

bottom

PURPOSE	Contains the inset's bottom value.
SYNTAX	`public int bottom`
EXAMPLE	See the class example.

clone( )

PURPOSE	Creates a copy of the inset.
SYNTAX	`public Object clone()`
DESCRIPTION	Creates an insets instance with the same values as this inset.
RETURNS	A non-`null` copy of the inset.
OVERRIDES	`java.lang.Object.clone()`.
EXAMPLE	See `java.lang.Object.clone()`.

equals( )

PURPOSE	Determines whether an object is equal to this insets.
SYNTAX	`public boolean equals(Object obj)`
DESCRIPTION	This method determines whether `obj` is equal to this insets. It is equal if it is an instance of **Insets** and has the same left, right, top bottom values as this insets's values.
PARAMETERS	
obj	The object to check.
RETURNS	`true` if `obj` is equal to this insets; `false` otherwise.
OVERRIDES	`java.lang.Object.equals()`.
EXAMPLE	

```
    Insets first = comp.getInsets();
    Insets second = comp2.getInsets();
    if (first.equals(second))
        System.out.println("The insets are the same");
```

Insets( )

PURPOSE	Constructs a new Insets instance.
SYNTAX	`public Insets(int top, int left, int bottom, int right)`
DESCRIPTION	This constructor creates a new Insets instance that has the specified insets.
PARAMETERS	
bottom	The bottom inset.
left	The left inset.
right	The right inset.
top	The top inset.
EXAMPLE	See the class example.

left

PURPOSE	Contains the inset's left value.
SYNTAX	`public int left`
EXAMPLE	See the class example.

right

PURPOSE	Contains the inset's right value.
SYNTAX	`public int right`
EXAMPLE	See the class example.

top

PURPOSE	Contains the inset's top value.
SYNTAX	`public int top`
EXAMPLE	See the class example.

A
B
C
D
E
F
G
H
I
J
K
L
M
N
O
P
Q
R
S
T
U
V
W
X
Y
Z

toString()

PURPOSE	Generates the string representation of this inset.
SYNTAX	`public String toString()`
DESCRIPTION	This method generates the string representation of this inset. The representation consists of the inset's values. This method is typically used for debugging.
RETURNS	A non-`null` string representing the inset state.
OVERRIDES	`java.lang.Object.toString()`.
EXAMPLE	See `java.lang.Object.toString()`.

A
B
C
D
E
F
G
H
I
J
K
L
M
N
O
P
Q
R
S
T
U
V
W
X
Y
Z

IntrospectionException

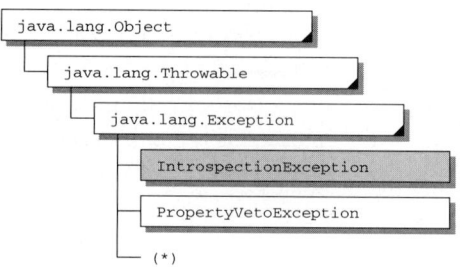

```
java.lang.Object

    java.lang.Throwable

        java.lang.Exception

            IntrospectionException

            PropertyVetoException

        (*)
```

(*) 27 classes from other packages not shown; see java.lang.Exception for complete listing.

Syntax

```
public class IntrospectionException extends Exception
```

Description

Introspection is the process of discovering a bean's properties, events, and methods by examining the bean's public methods. The discovery process is based on looking for special patterns in the signatures of each pattern. For example, suppose a bean has two methods with the following signatures.

```
public float getPrice()
public void setPrice(float price)
```

By introspection, we can deduce that the bean has a `float` property called "price." For more information about the introspection process and signature patterns, see `Introspector`.

IntrospectionException is rarely thrown when introspection is applied on an arbitrary bean. This is because introspection looks for signature patterns and reports only those it finds. IntrospectionException is most often encountered when the bean provides a bean-info (see `BeanInfo`). Whenever methods are specified in the bean-info, a check is made to see if the methods are compatible with each other. For example, if the bean-info claims that

```
public String getPrice()
public void setPrice(float price)
```

are the accessor methods for the "price" property, the introspection process will check the signatures, discover that they are not compatible, and then throw `IntrospectionException`.

MEMBER SUMMARY

Constructor
IntrospectionException()   Constructs an IntrospectionException instance.

See Also

Introspector.

Example

The following example causes an IntrospectionException to be thrown. The example
bean implements a pair of accessor methods for the "bad" property. The type returned by the
read accessor method does not match the type passed to the write accessor method.

A property descriptor (see PropertyDescriptor) specified in a bean-info (see Bean-
Info) is necessary to force the introspector to consider the two methods as accessor methods.
If the property descriptor was not there, the introspector would notice the incompatibility of
the two methods and simply ignore them, assuming that they were not accessor methods.

Bean.java

```java
import java.beans.*;

public class Bean {
    public String getBad() {
        return null;
    }
    public void setBad(int bad) {
    }

    public static void main(String[] args) {
        try {
            BeanInfo bi = Introspector.getBeanInfo(Bean.class);
        } catch (IntrospectionException e) {
            e.printStackTrace();
        }
    }
}
```

BeanBeanInfo.java

```java
import java.beans.*;

public class BeanBeanInfo extends SimpleBeanInfo {
    public PropertyDescriptor[] getPropertyDescriptors() {
    PropertyDescriptor pd[] = new PropertyDescriptor[1];

    try {
        pd[0] = new PropertyDescriptor("bad", Bean.class,
                "getBad", "setBad");
        return pd;
    } catch (Exception e) {
            e.printStackTrace(System.out);
```

```
        return null;
    }
  }
}
```

Output   Here is the output produced by running the example:

```
java.beans.IntrospectionException: type mismatch between read and write methods
    at java.beans.PropertyDescriptor.findPropertyType(PropertyDescriptor.java:252)
    at java.beans.PropertyDescriptor.<init>(PropertyDescriptor.java:86)
    at BeanBeanInfo.getPropertyDescriptors(BeanBeanInfo.java:8)
    at java.beans.Introspector.getTargetPropertyInfo(Introspector.java:254)
    at java.beans.Introspector.getBeanInfo(Introspector.java:202)
    at java.beans.Introspector.getBeanInfo(Introspector.java:83)
    at Bean.main(Bean.java:12)
```

IntrospectionException()

PURPOSE   Constructs an IntrospectionException instance.

SYNTAX   `public IntrospectionException(String msg)`

PARAMETERS
  msg   A possibly null string describing the reason for the exception.

EXAMPLE   See the MethodDescriptor class example.

java.beans
Introspector

`java.lang.Object`

`Introspector`

Syntax

`public class Introspector`

Description

The *introspector* constructs a complete set of feature descriptors (see `FeatureDescriptor`) for a bean. Some feature descriptors may be *explicit*, which means they were extracted from a bean-info object (see `BeanInfo`), and some may be *implicit*, which means they were deduced by the introspector. See Figure 221. The process by which the introspector deduces implicit feature descriptors is called *introspection* and is described in the next section.

When asked to return the feature descriptors for a bean, the introspector first tries to locate a bean-info for the bean (this process is described later in this item). If it finds one, it looks in the bean-info for explicit feature descriptors.

There are four categories of explicit feature descriptors in a bean-info:

1. Bean
2. Event set
3. Method
4. Property

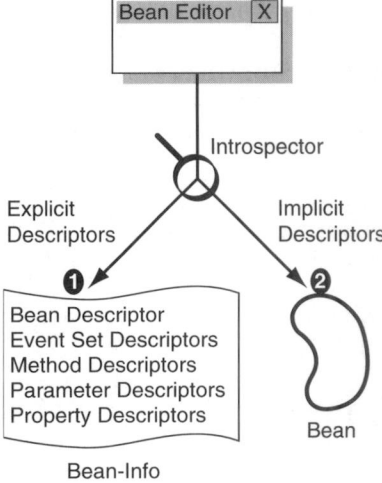

FIGURE 221:   Introspector.

When explicit feature descriptors are available in any of these categories, the introspector uses those feature descriptors and does not apply introspection to discover those feature descriptors. However, if a category does not contain any explicit feature descriptors (it has the value `null`), the introspector applies introspection to discover those feature descriptors. For example, if a bean-info contains only a few explicit property descriptors, the introspector uses them and then applies introspection to discover the feature descriptors in the other three categories.

Introspection

Introspection is the process of discovering feature descriptors by examining the signatures of the bean's public methods. This also includes all of the public methods in the bean's superclasses. For example, if there are no explicit property descriptors available (from a bean-info), the introspector creates a list of all of the public methods in the bean and then searches that list for signatures that match a particular pattern. Suppose the introspector finds a method with the following signature:

```
public void setFlavor(String flavor)
```

It will assume that the bean has a property called "flavor" and that this method is the write accessor method for the property.

Following are the patterns that are used to detect different types of features:

get/set Pattern

```
public PropertyType getPropertyName()
public void setPropertyName(PropertyType v)
```

The presence of these signatures indicates the bean has a property called *propertyName* of class *PropertyType*. If either of these signatures is detected, the introspector creates a property descriptor (see PropertyDescriptor) for a property called *propertyName*, which is the *decapitalized* version of *PropertyName* (see decapitalize()). The detected method(s) become the accessor methods for that property.

For example, the presence of either of the following methods indicates that the bean has a "flavor" property of class String:

```
public String getFlavor()
public void setFlavor(String flavor)
```

is/get/set Pattern

```
boolean public boolean isPropertyName()
public boolean getPropertyName()
public void setPropertyName(boolean v)
```

If any of these signatures is detected, the introspector creates a property descriptor (see PropertyDescriptor) for a property called *propertyName*, which is the decapitalized version of *PropertyName* (see decapitalize()). The detected method(s) become the accessor methods for that property. If both "is" and "get" methods are detected, the "is" method becomes the accessor method.

For example, the presence of either of the following methods indicates that the bean has a boolean "roasted" property:

```
public boolean isRoasted()
public boolean getRoasted()
public void setRoasted(boolean roasted)
```

A
B
C
D
E
F
G
H
I
J
K
L
M
N
O
P
Q
R
S
T
U
V
W
X
Y
Z

Indexed Property Pattern

```
public PropertyType[] getPropertyName()
public PropertyType getPropertyName(int i)
public void setPropertyName(PropertyType[] v)
public void setPropertyName(int i, PropertyType v)
```

If any of these signatures are detected, the introspector creates an indexed property descriptor (see `IndexedPropertyDescriptor`) for a property called *propertyName*, which is the decapitalized version of *PropertyName* (see `decapitalize()`). The detected method(s) become the accessor methods for the property.

For example, the presence of any of the following methods indicates that the bean has a property named "flavors" consisting of an array of `String` objects:

```
public String[] getFlavors()
public String getFlavors(int i)
public void setFlavors(int i, String flavor)
public void setFlavors(String[] flavors)
```

Public Method Pattern

The introspector creates method descriptors (see `MethodDescriptor`) for all of the bean's public methods. This includes all of the public methods in the bean's superclasses as well.

Multicast Event Set Pattern

```
public void addEventNameListener(EventNameListener l)
public void removeEventNameListener(EventNameListener l)
```

If both of these signatures are detected, the introspector creates an event set descriptor (see `EventSetDescriptor`) for an event set called *eventName*, which is the decapitalized version of *EventName* (see `decapitalize()`). The detected methods become the listener support methods for the event set. *EventName*`Listener` must be a subclass of `java.util.EventListener`.

For example, the presence of the following methods indicates that the bean fires `action` multicast event sets that will be processed by `ActionListeners`:

```
public void addActionListener(ActionListener listener)
public void removeActionListener(ActionListener listener)
```

Unicast Event Set Pattern

```
public void addEventNameListener(EventNameListener l)
    throws TooManyListenersException
public void removeEventNameListener(EventNameListener l)
```

If both of these signatures are detected, the event is considered to be a unicast event. An event set descriptor is created exactly like a multicast event, except that the unicast attribute is set to `true`.

For example, the presence of the following methods indicates that the bean fires `action` unicast event sets that will be handled by `ActionListeners`:

```
public void addActionListener(ActionListener listener)
    throws TooManyListenersException
public void removeActionListener(ActionListener listener)
```

The Search Path

The *search path* is an array of package names. The introspector uses this list to find a bean-info for a bean (described below). The introspector's default search path `"sun.beans.infos"`.

Locating the Bean-info

When locating the bean-info for a bean, the introspector first appends `"BeanInfo"` to the package-qualified class name of the bean. It then tries to instantiate a class with that name. For example, if the bean name is `java.util.Calendar`, it tries to instantiate a class named `java.util.CalendarBeanInfo`. If no class with that name is found, it removes the package name from the class name. For example, `java.util.CalendarBeanInfo` becomes `CalendarBeanInfo`. It then prefixes each of the package names in the search path with the class name (separated by ".") and then tries to instantiate that class. For example, if the search path contained `sun.first` and `sun.second`, the introspector tries to instantiate `sun.first.CalendarBeanInfo`. If that fails, it tries `sun.second.CalendarBeanInfo`.

MEMBER SUMMARY

Descriptor Method
`getBeanInfo()`   Retrieves the bean-info of a bean.

Search Path Methods
`getBeanInfoSearchPath()`   Retrieves the introspector's search path.
`setBeanInfoSearchPath()`   Sets the introspector's search path.

Decapitalize Method
`decapitalize()`   Decapitalizes a string.

See Also

BeanInfo, java.util.TooManyListenersException.

Example

This example runs the introspector on any class file containing a bean. The program implements a simple class loader that can load class files from the file system. The first parameter is the filename of the bean class file. Subsequent parameters are appended to the introspector's search path.

This version of the introspector searches for the bean's bean-info class file in the same directory that contains the bean class file. If that file is not found, it uses the search path to locate a bean-info class file.

```java
import java.beans.*;
import java.lang.reflect.*;
import java.util.*;

class Main {
    public static void main(String[] args) {
        if (args.length < 1) {
            System.err.println("Usage: java Main <name of bean class file>");
            System.exit(1);
        }

        // The other args are to be appended to the search path.
        String[] oldPath = Introspector.getBeanInfoSearchPath();
        String[] newPath = new String[oldPath.length + args.length - 1];
        for (int i=0; i<oldPath.length; i++) {
            newPath[i] = oldPath[i];
        }
        for (int i=0; i<args.length-1; i++) {
            newPath[i+oldPath.length] = args[i+1];
        }
        Introspector.setBeanInfoSearchPath(newPath);

        try {
            // Get the bean.
            Class bc = FileClassLoader.load(args[0]);

            printBeanInfo(bc);
        } catch (IntrospectionException e) {
            e.printStackTrace();
        }
    }

    public static void printBeanInfo(Class c) throws IntrospectionException {
        BeanInfo bi = Introspector.getBeanInfo(c);
        BeanDescriptor bd = bi.getBeanDescriptor();

        System.out.println("Class: " + bd.getBeanClass().getName());
        System.out.println("Name: " + bd.getName());
        System.out.println("Display name: " + bd.getDisplayName());
        System.out.println("Short Description: " + bd.getShortDescription());
        System.out.println("Expert: " + bd.isExpert());
        System.out.println("Hidden: " + bd.isHidden());
        if (bd.getCustomizerClass() != null) {
            System.out.println("Customizer: " +
                bd.getCustomizerClass().getName());
        }
        System.out.println();

        // Print legend
        System.out.println(
            "h:hidden, e:expert, i:indexed, *:default, c:constrained, b:bound");
        System.out.println("u:unicast, d:default set\n");
```

```
        // ** Print the property descriptors.
        printRepeat(" ", 30);
        System.out.println("PROPERTIES");
        printRepeat("-", 72);
        System.out.println();
        print("Attr", 5);
        print("Name", 20);
        print("Type", 25);
        print("Accessor methods", 25);
        System.out.println();
        printRepeat("-", 72);
        System.out.println();

        // Now print each descriptor.
        PropertyDescriptor pds[] = bi.getPropertyDescriptors();
        for (int i=0; i<pds.length; i++) {
            printProperty(pds[i], i == bi.getDefaultPropertyIndex());
        }
        System.out.println();

    // ** Print the event set descriptors.
        printRepeat(" ", 30);
        System.out.println("EVENT SETS");
        printRepeat("-", 72);
        System.out.println();
        print("Attr", 5);
        print("Name", 20);
        System.out.println("Registration methods");
        System.out.println("          Callback methods");
        printRepeat("-", 72);
        System.out.println();

        // Now print each event set descriptor.
        EventSetDescriptor esds[] = bi.getEventSetDescriptors();
        for (int i=0; i<esds.length; i++) {
            printEventSet(esds[i], i == bi.getDefaultEventIndex());
        }
        System.out.println();

    // ** Print the method descriptors.
        printRepeat(" ", 30);
        System.out.println("METHODS");
        printRepeat("-", 72);
        System.out.println();
        print("Attr", 5);
        System.out.println("Signature");
        printRepeat("-", 72);
        System.out.println();

        // Now print each method descriptor.
        MethodDescriptor methods[] = bi.getMethodDescriptors();
        for (int i=0; i<methods.length; i++) {
            printMethods(methods[i]);
        }
    }

    static void printProperty(PropertyDescriptor pd, boolean cef) {
        printAttributes(pd, def);
        print(pd.getName(), 20);
```

A
B
C
D
E
F
G
H

J
K
L
M
N
O
P
Q
R
S
T
U
V
W
X
Y
Z

```
                    printName(pd.getPropertyType(), 25);

                    // Print accessor methods.
                    printName(pd.getReadMethod(), -1);
                    System.out.print("/");
                    printName(pd.getWriteMethod(), -1);
                    System.out.println();

                    if (pd instanceof IndexedPropertyDescriptor) {
                        IndexedPropertyDescriptor ipd = (IndexedPropertyDescriptor)pd;

                        printAttributes(ipd, def, true);
                        print("", 20);
                        printName(ipd.getIndexedPropertyType(), 25);
                        printName(ipd.getIndexedReadMethod(), -1);
                        System.out.print("/");
                        printName(ipd.getIndexedWriteMethod(), -1);
                        System.out.println();
                    }
                }

                static void printEventSet(EventSetDescriptor esd, boolean def) {
                    printAttributes(esd, def);
                    printName(esd, 20);

                    // Print listener methods.
                    printName(esd.getAddListenerMethod(), -1);
                    System.out.print("/");
                    printName(esd.getRemoveListenerMethod(), -1);
                    System.out.println();

                    // Print callback methods.
                    Method ems[] = esd.getListenerMethods();
                    for (int j=0; j<ems.length; j++) {
                        System.out.print("        ");
                        printName(ems[j], -1);
                        System.out.println();
                    }
                }

                static void printMethods(MethodDescriptor md) {
                    printAttributes(md, false);
                    System.out.println(md.getMethod().toString());

                    if (md.getShortDescription() != null
                            && !md.getShortDescription().equals(md.getName())) {
                        System.out.println(".....\"" + md.getShortDescription() + "\"");
                    }

                    ParameterDescriptor[] pds = md.getParameterDescriptors();
                    if (pds != null) {
                        for (int i=0; i<pds.length; i++) {
                            System.out.print(".....");
                            printAttributes(pds[i], false);
                            print(pds[i].getName(), 10);
                            System.out.println();
                            if (pds[i].getShortDescription() != null) {
                                System.out.println(".....       \"" +
                                    pds[i].getShortDescription()+"\"");
                            }
                        }
```

```
            }
        }
    }

    // Prints s and pads the string with Math.max(1, width-s.length()) spaces.
    static void print(String s, int width) {
        System.out.print(s);
        for (int i=0; i<Math.max(1, (width-s.length())); i++) {
            System.out.print(" ");
        }
    }

    // Prints s 'count' times.
    static void printRepeat(String s, int count) {
        for (int i=0; i<count; i++) {
            System.out.print(s);
        }
    }

    // Prints the object's name.  If null, prints "?".
    // Also if width >= 0, pads the string with
    // Math.max(1, width-s.length()) spaces.
    static void printName(Object o, int width) {
        String result;

        if (o == null) {
            result = "?";
        } else if (o instanceof Class) {
            result = ((Class)o).getName();
        } else if (o instanceof Method) {
            result = ((Method)o).getName();
        } else if (o instanceof FeatureDescriptor) {
            result = ((FeatureDescriptor)o).getName();
        } else {
            throw (new RuntimeException());
        }
        if (width >= 0) {
            print(result, width);
        } else {
            System.out.print(result);
        }
    }

    static void printAttributes(FeatureDescriptor fd, boolean def) {
        printAttributes(fd, def, false);
    }
    static void printAttributes(FeatureDescriptor fd, boolean def,
                                boolean indexed) {
        String result = "";

        if (def) {
            result += "*";
        }
        if (fd.isHidden()) {
            result += "h";
        }
        if (fd.isExpert()) {
            result += "e";
        }
        if (indexed) {
```

```
                        result += "i";
                    }
                if (fd instanceof PropertyDescriptor) {
                    PropertyDescriptor pd = (PropertyDescriptor)fd;

                    if (pd.isConstrained()) {
                        result += "c";
                    }
                    if (pd.isBound()) {
                        result += "b";
                    }
                }
                if (fd instanceof EventSetDescriptor) {
                    EventSetDescriptor esd = (EventSetDescriptor)fd;

                    if (esd.isUnicast()) {
                        result += "u";
                    }
                    if (esd.isInDefaultEventSet()) {
                        result += "d";
                    }
                }
                print(result, 5);
            }
        }
}
```

Output   When the example program is run on the `OurButton` sample bean in the BDK
                 1.0apr97, the following output is produced:

```
Class: sunw.demo.buttons.OurButton
Name: OurButton
Display name: OurButton
Short Description: OurButton
Expert: false
Hidden: false

h:hidden, e:expert, i:indexed, *:default, c:constrained, b:bound
u:unicast, d:default set
                            PROPERTIES
---------------------------------------------------------------------
Attr Name              Type                    Accessor methods
---------------------------------------------------------------------
e    enabled           boolean                 isEnabled/setEnabled
b    preferredSize     java.awt.Dimension      getPreferredSize/?
b    foreground        java.awt.Color          getForeground/setForeground
b    label             java.lang.String        getLabel/setLabel
h    visible           boolean                 isVisible/setVisible
b    background        java.awt.Color          getBackground/setBackground
b    fontSize          int                     getFontSize/setFontSize
b    font              java.awt.Font           getFont/setFont
     name              java.lang.String        getName/setName
b    largeFont         boolean                 isLargeFont/setLargeFont
b    debug             boolean                 getDebug/setDebug
b    minimumSize       java.awt.Dimension      getMinimumSize/?
                            EVENT SETS
---------------------------------------------------------------------
Attr Name              Registration methods
         Callback methods
---------------------------------------------------------------------
d    mouse             addMouseListener/removeMouseListener
         mouseClicked
```

```
                mousePressed
                mouseReleased
                mouseEntered
                mouseExited
    d    key                    addKeyListener/removeKeyListener
                keyTyped
                keyPressed
                keyReleased
    d    component              addComponentListener/removeComponentListener
                componentResized
                componentMoved
                componentShown
                componentHidden
    d    action                 addActionListener/removeActionListener
                actionPerformed
    d    propertyChange         addPropertyChangeListener/removePropertyChangeListener
                propertyChange
    d    focus                  addFocusListener/removeFocusListener
                focusGained
                focusLost
    d    mouseMotion            addMouseMotionListener/removeMouseMotionListener
                mouseDragged
                mouseMoved

                        METHODS
    ------------------------------------------------------------------
    Attr Signature
    ------------------------------------------------------------------
        public boolean java.awt.Component.isVisible()
        public synchronized void
            java.awt.Component.addMouseListener(java.awt.event.MouseListener)
        public void java.awt.Component.enable()
        public void java.awt.Component.move(int,int)
        public java.awt.Dimension java.awt.Component.getSize()
        public void java.awt.Component.addNotify()

    <<< Two pages of output have been truncated. >>>
```

decapitalize()

PURPOSE   Decapitalizes a string.

SYNTAX   `public static String decapitalize(String name)`

DESCRIPTION   The decapitalization rule is that the first letter of name is decapitalized using `Character.toLowerCase()`. However, if name is at least two characters long and both the first and second characters are capitalized, this method simply returns name.

For example, if name is "Flavor," "flavor" is returned. If name is "J," "j" is returned. If name is "URL," "URL" is returned.

This method is used heavily by the introspector while it is creating implicit feature descriptors. It is used to derive property and event set names from the name of a method. For example, if a method name is `setFlavor`, the property name is "flavor."

A
B
C
D
E
F
G
H
I
J
K
L
M
N
O
P
Q
R
S
T
U
V
W
X
Y
Z

A
B
C
D
E
F
G
H
J
K
L
M
N
O
P
Q
R
S
T
U
V
W
X
Y
Z

PARAMETERS

  name   The non-`null` string to be decapitalized.

RETURNS   A non-`null` string containing the decapitalized version of `name`.

EXAMPLE   This example simply invokes `decapitalize()` on all of the program's arguments.

```
import java.beans.*;

class Main {
    public static void main(String[] args) {
        for (int i=0; i<args.length; i++) {
            System.out.println(args[i] + " -> "
                + Introspector.decapitalize(args[i]));
        }
    }
}
```

getBeanInfo()

PURPOSE   Retrieves the bean-info of a bean.

SYNTAX   `public static BeanInfo getBeanInfo(Class beanClass) throws`
    `IntrospectionException`
`public static BeanInfo getBeanInfo(Class beanClass, Class`
    `stopClass) throws IntrospectionException`

DESCRIPTION   This method constructs a bean-info from the bean's `Class` object. Some feature descriptors in the returned bean-info object may be explicit, which means
they were extracted from a bean-info object supplied by the bean (see `Bean-`
`Info`). Some may be implicit, which means they were deduced by the introspector using introspection. See the class description for more details on
locating and using a bean-info and on the process of introspection.

The descriptor arrays that are returned from this bean-info are never `null`. If
the descriptor array is empty, it merely has zero length. This differs from
directly accessing the bean-info object supplied by the bean, in which case the
descriptor array can be `null`.

By default, when the introspector introspects, it uses all of the bean's public
methods, including the public methods in the bean's superclasses. However, it
is possible to exclude some superclasses using `stopClass`. If `stopClass` is
specified, the introspector includes all of the public methods up to and including those in `stopClass` but not any of `stopClass`'s superclasses. `stopClass`
must specify a superclass of `beanClass` and must not be the same as `bean-`
`Class`.

PARAMETERS

beanClass	The Class object for a bean.
stopClass	The possibly null Class object of one of the bean's superclasses.

RETURNS   A non-null bean-info for beanClass.

EXCEPTIONS

IntrospectionException

> If an exception occurs during introspection or if stopClass is not a superclass of beanClass.

EXAMPLE   See the class example.

getBeanInfoSearchPath()

PURPOSE   Retrieves the introspector's search path.

SYNTAX   `public static String[] getBeanInfoSearchPath()`

DESCRIPTION   This method returns the introspector's search path, which is used to find the bean-info for a bean. See the class description for details on how the search path is used.

> The search path initially contains a single element: `"sun.beans.infos"`.

RETURNS   A possibly null array of package names.

SEE ALSO   `setBeanInfoSearchPath()`.

EXAMPLE   See the class example.

setBeanInfoSearchPath()

PURPOSE   Sets the introspector's search path.

SYNTAX   `public static void setBeanInfoSearchPath(String path[])`

DESCRIPTION   This method sets the introspector's search path, which is used to find a bean-info for a bean. See the class description for details on how the search path is used.

> When setting a new search path, include the elements of the current search path in the new search path. The current search path can be retrieved by calling `getBeanInfoSearchPath()`.

PARAMETERS

path	A possibly null array of package names.

SEE ALSO   `getBeanInfoSearchPath()`.

EXAMPLE   See the class example.

A
B
C
D
E
F
G
H

J
K
L
M
N
O
P
Q
R
S
T
U
V
W
X
Y
Z

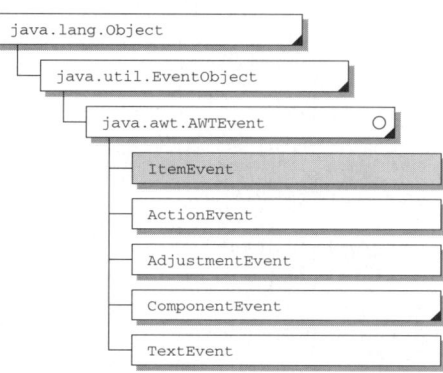

Syntax

```
public class ItemEvent extends AWTEvent
```

Description

An item event is fired by an item-selectable object (see `ItemSelectable`) when the selection state (selected or deselected) of an item changes. An item event that contains the affected item and its current selection state. The components that fire item events are `Checkbox`, `Checkbox-MenuItem`, `Choice`, and `List`.

Note that an item-selectable object may fire an item event even if the selection state of the item did not change (for example, by reselecting an already selected item). Also, an item-selectable object does not always fire an item event if an item is deselected (for example, when a change is made in a checkbox group or a choice). However, an item event is always fired for an item that is newly selected. For more general information about events, see `AWTEvent`.

Listening for Item Events

To listen for item events from an item-selectable object, the listener must implement the `Item-Listener` interface. After that, the listener must be registered with the object. It becomes registered by calling the object's `addItemListener()` method.

As with most events, an item event is delivered to its listeners after the operation has taken place.

The Item Property

The item property of an item event contains a representation of the item whose selection state has changed. The representation varies with the type of item-selectable object that fired the event. In particular, the item property from a checkbox, choice, or checkbox menu item component is the item label string. The item property from a list is an `Integer` object containing the index of the item.

The State Change Property

The state change property of an item event indicates whether the item was selected or deselected.

Item Event Flow

Figure 222 shows how item events typically flow through the system. First, the event is fired by a component peer in response to some user gesture. This event is posted on the event queue (see `EventQueue`). When the event makes its way to the front of the queue, it is given to the component via its `dispatchEvent()` method. The main purpose of this method is to discard the event if the item event type is not enabled or if there are no item event listeners. Otherwise, `dispatchEvent()` calls `processEvent()`, which in turn calls different methods depending on the event type. Since this is an item event,

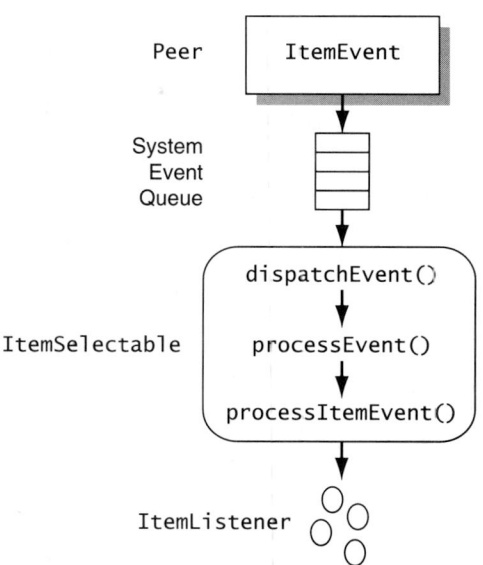

FIGURE 222: Item Event Flow.

`processItemEvent()` is called. The main purpose of this method is to notify the item event listeners.

A component can override `processItemEvent()` to process item events before they are delivered to its listeners. The overridden method should call `super.processItemEvent()` to ensure that events are dispatched to the component's listeners.

MEMBER SUMMARY	
Constructor	
ItemEvent()	Constructs an `ItemEvent` instance.
Property Methods	
getItem()	Retrieves the item whose selection state has changed.
getItemSelectable()	Retrieves the item-selectable object that fired this event.
getStateChange()	Retrieves the new selected state of the item.
Item Event Id Constants	
ITEM_FIRST	Constant specifying the first id in the range of item event ids.
ITEM_LAST	Constant specifying the last id in the range of item event ids.
ITEM_STATE_CHANGED	Event id indicating that an item event occurred.

Continued

MEMBER SUMMARY	
Selection State Change Types	
DESELECTED	Item state change type indicating that an item has been deselected.
SELECTED	Item state change type indicating that an item has been selected.
Debugging Method	
paramString()	Generates a string representing the item event's state.

See Also

ItemListener, java.awt.AWTEvent, java.awt.Checkbox,
java.awt.CheckboxMenuItem, java.awt.Choice, java.awt.ItemSelectable,
java.awt.List.

Example

This example demonstrates how to get item events from a component that fires them. The example creates a menu with some checkbox menu items and listens for item events from the menu items. In response to an item event, the specifics of the event are printed. See Figure 223.

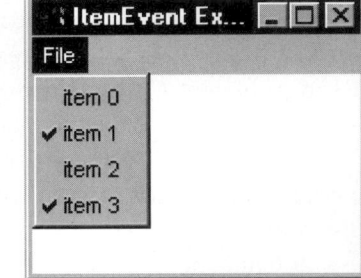

FIGURE 223: ItemEvent.

```
import java.awt.*;
import java.awt.event.*;

class Main extends Frame implements ItemListener
{
    Main() {
        super("ItemEvent Example");
        MenuBar mb = new MenuBar();
        Menu m = new Menu("File");

        mb.add(m);
        for (int i=0; i<4; i++) {
            CheckboxMenuItem c = new CheckboxMenuItem("item "+i);

            // Listen for item events.
            c.addItemListener(this);
            m.add(c);
        }

        setMenuBar(mb);
        show();
    }

    public void itemStateChanged(ItemEvent e) {
        System.out.println("item selectable: "+e.getItemSelectable());
        System.out.println("item: "+e.getItem());
        System.out.print("state change: ");
```

```
        switch (e.getStateChange()) {
          case ItemEvent.SELECTED:
            System.out.println("SELECTED");
            break;
          case ItemEvent.DESELECTED:
            System.out.println("DESELECTED");
            break;
        }
      }

    public static void main(String args[]) {
        new Main();
    }
  }
}
```

DESELECTED

PURPOSE   Item state change type indicating that an item has been deselected.

SYNTAX   `public static final int DESELECTED`

DESCRIPTION   When an item event is fired, the new selection state of the affected item can be retrieved by `getStateChange()`. A return value of DESELECTED (value 2) from `getStateChange()` indicates the item has been deselected.

SEE ALSO   `getStateChange()`, `SELECTED`.

EXAMPLE   See the class example.

getItem()

PURPOSE   Retrieves the item whose selection state has changed.

SYNTAX   `public Object getItem()`

DESCRIPTION   The item property of an item event contains a representation of the item whose selection state has changed. The representation varies with the type of item-selectable object that fired the event. In particular, the item property from a checkbox, choice, or checkbox menu item component is the item label string. The item property from a list is an `Integer` object containing the index of the item.

RETURNS   A non-`null` representation of the item that changed.

SEE ALSO   `CheckboxMenuItem`, `Choice`, `java.lang.Integer`, `List`.

EXAMPLE   See the class example.

A
B
C
D
E
F
G
H

J
K
L
M
N
O
P
Q
R
S
T
U
V
W
X
Y
Z

getItemSelectable()

PURPOSE	Retrieves the item-selectable object that fired this event.
SYNTAX	`public ItemSelectable getItemSelectable()`
DESCRIPTION	This method returns the item-selectable object that fired the item event. This is the same object returned by `EventObject.getSource()`.
RETURNS	A non-`null` item-selectable object.
SEE ALSO	`java.util.EventObject.getSource()`.
EXAMPLE	See the class example.

getStateChange()

PURPOSE	Retrieves the new selected state of the item.
SYNTAX	`public int getStateChange()`
DESCRIPTION	The state change property of an item event indicates whether the item was selected or deselected. This method retrieves the new selected state of the item.
RETURNS	Either `SELECTED` or `DESELECTED`.
SEE ALSO	`SELECTED, DESELECTED`.
EXAMPLE	See the class example.

ITEM_FIRST

PURPOSE	Constant specifying the first id in the range of item event ids.
SYNTAX	`public static final int ITEM_FIRST`
DESCRIPTION	All item event ids must be greater than or equal to `ITEM_FIRST` (value 701).
SEE ALSO	`ITEM_LAST`.
EXAMPLE	See `java.awt.Component.processEvent()`.

ITEM_LAST

PURPOSE	Constant specifying the last id in the range of item event ids.
SYNTAX	`public static final int ITEM_LAST`
DESCRIPTION	All item event ids must be less than or equal to `ITEM_LAST` (value 701).

A
B
C
D
E
F
G
H
I
J
K
L
M
N
O
P
Q
R
S
T
U
V
W
X
Y
Z

EXAMPLE   See `java.awt.Component.processEvent()`.

ITEM_STATE_CHANGED

PURPOSE   Event id indicating that an item event occurred.

SYNTAX   `public static final int ITEM_STATE_CHANGED`

DESCRIPTION   An item event with this event id (value 701) is fired when an item in an item-selectable object becomes selected. Item events are also sometimes fired if an item becomes deselected. The item that changed can be retrieved by a call to `getItem()`.

SEE ALSO   `ItemEvent()`.

EXAMPLE   See the `MenuContainer` class example.

ItemEvent()

PURPOSE   Constructs an `ItemEvent` instance.

SYNTAX   `public ItemEvent(ItemSelectable source, int id, Object item, int newState)`

DESCRIPTION   This constructor constructs an item event that has `source` as the item-selectable object firing the event. At present, there is only one item event type, so `id` must be set to `ITEM_STATE_CHANGED`. `newState` specifies whether the item was selected or deselected.

After the item event is created, the source object can distribute it to its listeners by calling `AWTEventMulticaster.itemStateChanged()`. If the event is not created by `source`, the creator can deliver the event to the source component either by posting the event to the event queue (see `EventQueue.postEvent()`) or by calling the source component's `Component.dispatchEvent()` method directly.

PARAMETERS

`id`   Must be `ITEM_STATE_CHANGED`.

`item`   The non-`null` item whose state has changed.

`source`   The non-`null` item-selectable object that is firing this item event.

`newState`   Either `SELECTED` or `DESELECTED`.

SEE ALSO   `DESELECTED`, `getItem()`, `getItemSelectable()`, `ITEM_STATE_CHANGED`, `java.awt.AWTEvent.getID()`, `java.awt.util.EventObject.getSource()`, `SELECTED`.

EXAMPLE   See the `java.awt.MenuContainer` class example.

A
B
C
D
E
F
G
H

J
K
L
M
N
O
P
Q
R
S
T
U
V
W
X
Y
Z

paramString()

PURPOSE	Generates a string representing the item event's state.
SYNTAX	`public String paramString()`
DESCRIPTION	The returned string contains the name of the item event, the name of the item, and an indication of the whether the item was selected or deselected. A subclass of this class should override this method and return a concatenation of its state with the results of `super.paramString()`. This method is called by the `AWTEvent.toString()` method and is typically used for debugging.
RETURNS	A non-`null` string representing the item event's state.
OVERRIDES	`java.awt.AWTEvent.paramString()`.
SEE ALSO	`java.awt.AWTEvent.paramString()`, `java.lang.Object.toString()`.
EXAMPLE	See the `java.awt.AWTEvent` class example.

SELECTED

PURPOSE	Item state change type indicating that an item has been selected.
SYNTAX	`public static final int SELECTED`
DESCRIPTION	When an item event is fired, the new selection state of the affected item can be retrieved by `getStateChange()`. A return value of SELECTED (value 1) by `getStateChange()` indicates the item has been selected.
SEE ALSO	`getStateChange()`, `DESELECTED`.
EXAMPLE	See the class example.

ItemListener

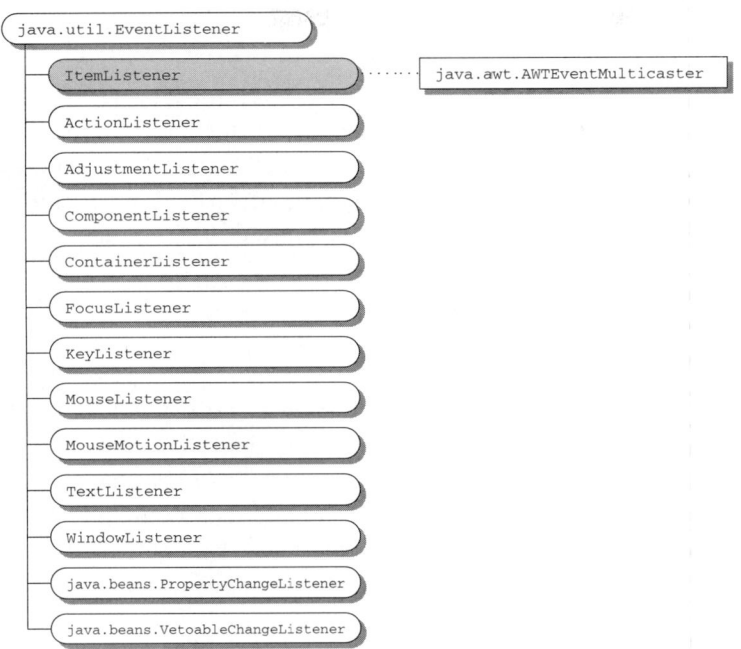

```
java.util.EventListener
    ItemListener .......... java.awt.AWTEventMulticaster
    ActionListener
    AdjustmentListener
    ComponentListener
    ContainerListener
    FocusListener
    KeyListener
    MouseListener
    MouseMotionListener
    TextListener
    WindowListener
    java.beans.PropertyChangeListener
    java.beans.VetoableChangeListener
```

Syntax
```
public interface ItemListener extends EventListener
```

Description

An item event is fired by an item-selectable object (see `ItemSelectable`). Item-selectable objects have a set of {items} that can be selected and deselected. When the selection state of an item changes, the item-selectable object fires an item event that contains the affected item and its current selection state. Item events are fired by the components `Checkbox`, `Checkbox-MenuItem`, `Choice`, `ItemSelectable`, and `List`. See `ItemEvent` for more details.

When an object (listener) wishes to receive item events from an item-selectable object (the source object), two things must be done:

1. The listener must implement the `ItemListener` interface and the `itemStateChanged()` method required by this interface.
2. The listener must be registered with the source item-selectable object by making a call to the object's `addItemListener()` method.

For more information about item events, see `ItemEvent`.

MEMBER SUMMARY
Item Event Callback Method
itemStateChanged()   Called when an item event occurs.

See Also

ItemEvent, java.awt.AWTEventMulticaster,
java.awt.CheckboxMenuItem, java.awt.Checkbox,
java.awt.Choice, java.awt.ItemSelectable,
java.awt.List, java.util.EventListener.

Example

This example implements a list that can display images and fire item
events. The list shows the currently selected image, and when the
selected image changes, it fires an item event. The image list fires first
an item event for the item that has been deselected and then an item
event for the newly selected item. See Figure 224.

The image list implements the ItemSelectable interface so that
it can fire item events.

FIGURE 224:
Image List.

```java
import java.awt.*;
import java.awt.event.*;
import java.util.*;

public class Main extends Frame
    implements ItemListener {
    ImageList list = new ImageList();

    Main(String[] filenames) {
        super("ItemListener Example");

        // Add images.
        for (int i=0; i<filenames.length; i++) {
            list.add(getToolkit().getImage(filenames[i]));
        }

        // Layout component and listen for item events.
        add(list, BorderLayout.CENTER);
        list.addItemListener(this);

        pack();
        show();
    }

    public void itemStateChanged(ItemEvent evt) {
        // Simply print out the event.
        System.out.println(evt);
    }
```

```
    public static void main(String args[]) {
        if (args.length < 1) {
            System.err.println(
                "Usage: java Main <imagefile 1> <imagefile 2>...");
            System.exit(1);
        }

        new Main(args);
    }
}

class ImageList extends Component implements ItemSelectable {
    // Number of pixels to surround each image.
    int margin = 3;

    // Currently selected image; -1 means no image selected.
    int curImage = -1;

    // Used to hold the images.
    Vector images = new Vector();

    ImageList() {
        addMouseListener(new MouseEventHandler());
    }

    // Adds an image to the image list.
    void add(Image image) {
        MediaTracker tracker = new MediaTracker(this);

        // We need to get the dimensions of the image.
        try {
            tracker.addImage(image, 0);
            tracker.waitForAll();
        } catch (Exception e) {
            e.printStackTrace();
        }
        images.addElement(image);
    }

    public Object[] getSelectedObjects() {
        if (curImage >= 0) {
            Object[] result = {images.elementAt(curImage)};

            return result;
        }
        return null;
    }

    // Paint the items.
    public void paint(Graphics g) {
        int y = margin;

        for (int i=0; i<images.size(); i++) {
            Image image = (Image)images.elementAt(i);
            int x = (getSize().width - image.getWidth(null))/2;

            g.drawImage(image, x, y, this);
            if (i == curImage) {
                // Draw an outline around selected image.
                g.setColor(Color.red);
```

A
B
C
D
E
F
G
H

J
K
L
M
N
O
P
Q
R
S
T
U
V
W
X
Y
Z

```
                    for (int j=1; j<=margin; j++) {
                        g.drawRect(x-j, y-j,
                            image.getWidth(null)+2*j-1,
                            image.getHeight(null)+2*j-1);
                    }
                }
                y += image.getHeight(null) + 2*margin;
            }
        }

        // Computes the preferred size of the whole image list.
        public Dimension getPreferredSize() {
            int width = 0;
            int height = 0;

            for (int i=0; i<images.size(); i++) {
                Image image = (Image)images.elementAt(i);

                width = Math.max(width, image.getWidth(null));
                height += image.getHeight(null);
            }

            // Add space for margins.
            width += 2*margin;
            height += 2*margin*(images.size());

            return new Dimension(width, height);
        }

        class MouseEventHandler extends MouseAdapter {
            public void mousePressed(MouseEvent evt) {
                int y = margin;

                // Find which image under the mouse coordinates.
                for (int i=0; i<images.size(); i++) {
                    Image image = (Image)images.elementAt(i);
                    int x = (getSize().width - image.getWidth(null))/2;

                    // Is the mouse coordinates on this image?
                    if (evt.getX() > x && evt.getX() < x+image.getWidth(null)
                      && evt.getY() > y && evt.getY() < y+image.getHeight(null)) {
                        // Fire an item event to deselect previous item.
                        if (curImage >= 0) {
                            processItemEvent(
                                new ItemEvent(ImageList.this,
                                    ItemEvent.ITEM_STATE_CHANGED,
                                    new Integer(curImage),
                                    ItemEvent.DESELECTED));
                        }

                        // Now fire an item event to select new item.
                        curImage = i;
                        processItemEvent(
                            new ItemEvent(ImageList.this,
                                ItemEvent.ITEM_STATE_CHANGED,
                                new Integer(curImage),
                                ItemEvent.SELECTED));

                        repaint();
                        break;
```

```
            }
            y += image.getHeight(null) + 2*margin;
        }
    }
}

// Methods to support item event listeners.
transient ItemListener itemListener;
public synchronized void addItemListener(ItemListener l) {
    itemListener = AWTEventMulticaster.add(itemListener, l);
}
public synchronized void removeItemListener(ItemListener l) {
    itemListener = AWTEventMulticaster.remove(itemListener, l);
}
protected void processItemEvent(ItemEvent e) {
    if (itemListener != null) {
        itemListener.itemStateChanged(e);
    }
}
}
```

itemStateChanged()

PURPOSE　　　Called when an item event occurs.

SYNTAX　　　`void itemStateChanged(ItemEvent evt)`

DESCRIPTION　This method is called after an item in an item-selectable object becomes selected. This method is sometimes called if an item becomes deselected. The item that changed can be retrieved by calling `evt.getItem()`. The new selected state of the item can be retrieve by calling `evt.getStateChange()`.

PARAMETERS

evt　　　　　The non-`null` item event.

EXAMPLE　　See the class example.

ItemSelectable

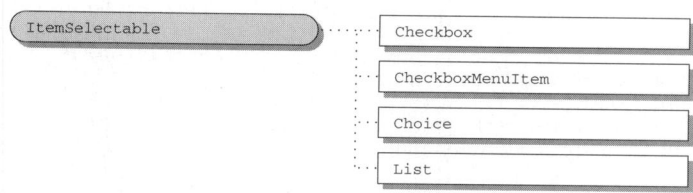

A
B
C
D
E
F
G
H
I
J
K
L
M
N
O
P
Q
R
S
T
U
V
W
X
Y
Z

Syntax

```
public interface ItemSelectable
```

Description

The `ItemSelectable` interface is implemented by components that support the selection of zero or more items in single or multiple selection mode. The AWT components that implement `ItemSelectable` are `Checkbox`, `CheckboxMenuItem`, `Choice`, and `List`.

Events

A component that implements `ItemSelectable` fires an item event whenever the state of the selection changes. For example, a checkbox fires an item event when it is clicked; a choice fires an item event when its selection changes. See `ItemEvent` and the class descriptions of the individual components that implement `ItemSelectable` for details.

See the `AWTEvent` class for details on how to filter or handle events.

MEMBER SUMMARY

Fields
`getSelectedObjects()`　　Retrieves this component's currently selected items.

Event Methods
`addItemListener()`　　Adds a listener to receive item events fired by this component.
`removeItemListener()`　　Removes a listener from receiving item events fired by this component.

See Also

`Checkbox`, `CheckboxMenuItem`, `Choice`, `List`.

Example

This example creates a panel of buttons, only one of which may be selected at any time. When a button is selected, the panel fires two item events, one to indicate which button was selected and one to indicate which one was deselected. See Figure 225.

FIGURE 225: ItemSelectable.

```java
import java.awt.*;
import java.awt.event.*;
import java.util.Vector;

class Main extends Frame implements ItemListener {
    Main() {
        super("ItemSelectable Example");
        ButtonPanel bp = new ButtonPanel();

        bp.add(new Button("first"));
        bp.add(new Button("second"));
        bp.add(new Button("third"));
        bp.add(new Button("fourth"));
        bp.add(new Button("fifth"));

        add(bp, BorderLayout.SOUTH);
        bp.addItemListener(this);

        pack();
        show();
    }

    public void itemStateChanged(ItemEvent evt) {
        ItemSelectable src = (ItemSelectable)evt.getSource();
        Object[] selected = src.getSelectedObjects();

        System.out.println("item event: " + evt);
        for (int i = 0; i <selected.length; i++) {
            System.out.println("selected: " + selected[i]);
        }
    }

    public static void main(String[] args) {
        new Main();
    }
}

class ButtonPanel extends Container implements ItemSelectable, ActionListener {
    transient ItemListener itemListener;
    int selected = -1;
    Vector vec = new Vector();

    ButtonPanel () {
        super();

        setLayout(new GridLayout(1, -1));
        enableEvents(AWTEvent.ITEM_EVENT_MASK);
```

```
        }

        void add(Button b) {
            super.add(b);

            b.addActionListener(this);
            vec.addElement(b);
            if (selected == -1) {
                selected = 0;
                b.setEnabled(false);
            } else {
                b.setEnabled(true);
            }
        }

        public void actionPerformed(ActionEvent evt) {
            Object src = evt.getSource();
            int where = vec.indexOf(src);

            if (where >= 0) {
                Button oldb = (Button)vec.elementAt(selected);
                oldb.setEnabled(true);
                Button newb = (Button)vec.elementAt(where);
                newb.setEnabled(false);
                selected = where;

                ItemEvent oldEvt =
                    new ItemEvent(this, ItemEvent.ITEM_STATE_CHANGED,
                                    oldb, ItemEvent.DESELECTED);
                // dispatch item event for old button
                processEvent(oldEvt);

                ItemEvent newEvt =
                    new ItemEvent(this, ItemEvent.ITEM_STATE_CHANGED,
                                    newb, ItemEvent.SELECTED);
                // dispatch item event for new button
                processEvent(newEvt);
            }
        }

        public Object[] getSelectedObjects() {
            if (selected >= 0) {
                Object[]  answer = new Object[1];
                answer[0] = vec.elementAt(selected);
                return answer;
            } else {
                return new Object[0];
            }
        }
        public synchronized void addItemListener(ItemListener l) {
            itemListener = AWTEventMulticaster.add(itemListener, l);
        }
        public void removeItemListener(ItemListener l) {
            itemListener = AWTEventMulticaster.remove(itemListener, l);
        }

        protected void processEvent(AWTEvent e) {
            if (e instanceof ItemEvent) {
                processItemEvent((ItemEvent)e);
                return;
```

```
        }
        super.processEvent(e);
    }

    protected void processItemEvent(ItemEvent e) {
        if (itemListener != null) {
            itemListener.itemStateChanged(e);
        }
    }
}
```

addItemListener( )

PURPOSE	Adds a listener to receive item events fired by this component.
SYNTAX	`public void addItemListener(ItemListener listener)`
DESCRIPTION	See `ItemEvent` for more details on item events. After this method is called, the item listener `listener` will receive item events fired by this component. If `listener` is `null`, this method does nothing.
PARAMETERS	
`listener`	The possibly `null` item listener to add.
SEE ALSO	`java.awt.event.ItemEvent`, `java.awt.event.ItemListener`, `removeItemListener()`.
EXAMPLE	See the class example.

getSelectedObjects( )

PURPOSE	Retrieves this component's currently selected items.
SYNTAX	`public synchronized Object[] getSelectedObjects()`
RETURNS	An array of strings containing this component's currently selected items. The return array is never `null` but may have length 0, which indicates that no items were selected.
EXAMPLE	See the class example.

A
B
C
D
E
F
G
H
I
J
K
L
M
N
O
P
Q
R
S
T
U
V
W
X
Y
Z

removeItemListener( )

PURPOSE   Removes an item listener from receiving item events fired by this component.

SYNTAX   `public void removeItemListener(ItemListener listener)`

DESCRIPTION   See `ItemEvent` for more details on item events. After this method is called, the item listener `listener` will no longer receive item events fired by this component. If `listener` is `null`, this method does nothing.

PARAMETERS
  `listener`   The possibly `null` item listener to remove.

SEE ALSO   `addItemListener()`, `java.awt.event.ItemEvent`, `java.awt.event.ItemListener`.

EXAMPLE   See `removeActionListener()` in `MenuItem.disableEvents()`.

```
java.lang.Object
      KeyAdapter                O ........( KeyListener )
```

Syntax
```
public abstract class KeyAdapter implements KeyListener
```

Description

The *key adapter* is a key listener in which all callback methods are empty implementations. The key adapter makes it more convenient for an object to listen for key events. In particular, by using the key adapter, you can implement only those callback methods in which you are interested. Without the key adapter, you are required to implement all callback methods, even if the method is empty.

To use a key adapter, you create a subclass of `KeyAdapter` and override the desired callback methods. You then create an instance of the key adapter subclass and call the component's `addKeyListener()` method with it. The key adapter subclass is typically an inner class.

MEMBER SUMMARY	
Key Event Callback Methods	
keyPressed()	Called when a key on the keyboard is pressed.
keyReleased()	Called when a key on the keyboard is released.
keyTyped()	Called when a pressed key or key-combination fires a key character.

See Also

`java.awt.Component.addKeyListener()`, `KeyEvent`, `KeyListener`.

Example

This example implements a "typing tutor." After you click the Start button, letters start dropping from the top. Your goal is to eliminate the letters before one hits the bottom. You eliminate a letter by typing the appropriate key. The number of eliminated letters is shown at the bottom of the display. See Figure 226.

The `TypingTutor` class uses a thread that is responsible for creating letters and moving them toward the bottom. A letter is created with a probability. That probability increases each time a letter is eliminated.

The typing tutor also handles focus and mouse events. When it receives a focus lost event, it stops the letters from moving. When it receives a mouse clicked event, it resumes moving the dropping letters. The typing tutor uses an off-screen image (bbuf) to implement double-buffering in order to eliminate flickering. The off-screen image is first cleared, and then all of the characters are painted at their current locations. The completed off-screen image is then painted on the screen

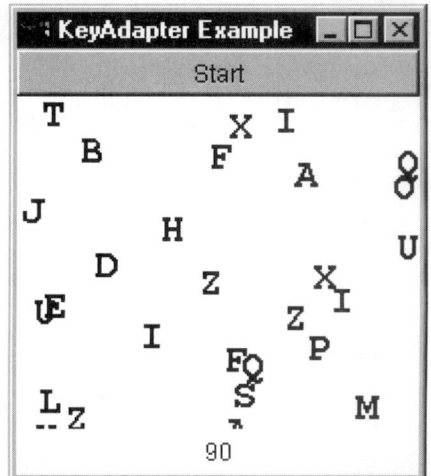

FIGURE 226:   Typing Tutor.

```java
import java.awt.*;
import java.awt.event.*;

public class Main extends Frame implements ActionListener {
    Label statusBar = new Label("", Label.CENTER);
    TypingTutor TypingTutor = new TypingTutor(statusBar);
    Button startButton = new Button("Start");

    Main() {
        super("KeyAdapter Example");

        // Listen for events
        startButton.addActionListener(this);

        // Layout components
        add(startButton, BorderLayout.NORTH);
        add(statusBar, BorderLayout.SOUTH);
        add(TypingTutor, BorderLayout.CENTER);
        pack();
        show();
    }

    public void actionPerformed(ActionEvent evt) {
        TypingTutor.requestFocus();
        TypingTutor.start();
    }

    public static void main(String args[]) {
        new Main();
    }
}

class TypingTutor extends Canvas implements Runnable {
    int width = 200;
    int height = 300;
    Label statusBar;
    int score;
```

```java
    // Reference to the timer thread.
    Thread timer;

    // Unless true, the start() method is ignored.
    boolean done = true;

    // Locations and value of letters.
    Point[] letterPts;
    char[] letters;

    // Double buffer variables
    Image bbuf;
    Graphics bbufG;

    // Font variables
    Font f = new Font("Monospaced", Font.BOLD, 20);
    FontMetrics fm;

    TypingTutor(Label statusBar) {
        this.statusBar = statusBar;
        addKeyListener(new KeyEventHandler());
        addFocusListener(new FocusEventHandler());
        addMouseListener(new MouseEventHandler());
    }

    // This method should be called only when the component
    // is visible.
    synchronized void start() {
        // Initialize font metrics if necessary.
        if (fm == null) {
            fm = getFontMetrics(f);
        }
        // Create the double buffer if necessary.
        if (bbuf == null) {
            bbuf = createImage(width, height);
            bbufG = bbuf.getGraphics();
        }

        // Set variables
        newLetterProbability = .05;
        letterPts = new Point[200];
        letters = new char[200];
        score = 0;
        statusBar.setText(""+score);

        done = false;
        (timer = new Thread(this)).start();
    }

    public void paint(Graphics g) {
        update(g);
    }

    public void update(Graphics g) {
        if (letterPts == null) {
            return;
        }
        // Clear the background.
        bbufG.setColor(Color.yellow);
```

A
B
C
D
E
F
G
H
I
J
K
L
M
N
O
P
Q
R
S
T
U
V
W
X
Y
Z

A
B
C
D
E
F
G
H
I
J
K
L
M
N
O
P
Q
R
S
T
U
V
W
X
Y
Z

```
        bbufG.fillRect(0, 0, width, height);
        bbufG.setColor(Color.black);
        bbufG.drawRect(0, 0, width-1, height-1);
        bbufG.setFont(f);

        // Paint all the letters.
        for (int i=0; i<letters.length; i++) {
            if (letterPts[i] != null) {
                bbufG.drawChars(letters, i, 1,
                    letterPts[i].x, letterPts[i].y);
            }
        }

        // Draw the off-screen image to the display.
        g.drawImage(bbuf, 0, 0, this);
    }

    public Dimension getPreferredSize() {
        return new Dimension(width, height);
    }

    // Key events.
    class KeyEventHandler extends KeyAdapter {
        public void keyTyped(KeyEvent evt) {
            int hiY = 0;
            int ltr = -1;

            // Find the lowest copy of that letter.
            for (int i=0; i<letters.length; i++) {
                if (letterPts[i] != null
                    && letters[i] == Character.toUpperCase(evt.getKeyChar())) {
                    if (letterPts[i].y > hiY) {
                        hiY = letterPts[i].y;
                        ltr = i;
                    }
                }
            }

            // If the letter is found, erase it.
            if (ltr >= 0) {
                letterPts[ltr] = null;
                score++;
                statusBar.setText(""+score);

                // Increase the probability of creating new letters
                newLetterProbability += .005;
                repaint();
            }
        }
    }

    // Focus events.
    class FocusEventHandler extends FocusAdapter {
        public void focusLost(FocusEvent evt) {
            timer = null;
        }
    }

    // Mouse events.
    class MouseEventHandler extends MouseAdapter {
```

```
        public void mousePressed(MouseEvent evt) {
            requestFocus();
            (timer = new Thread(TypingTutor.this)).start();
        }
    }

    // The duration of each tick.
    int delay = 120;

    // The probability of a new letter being created at each tick.
    double newLetterProbability;

    public void run() {
        int count = 0;
        try {
            while (!done && timer == Thread.currentThread()) {
                for (int i=0; i<letters.length; i++) {
                    if (letterPts[i] != null) {
                        letterPts[i].y += 3;

                        // Check if the letter is at the bottom
                        if (letterPts[i].y >= height) {
                            // If so, clear all letters
                            for (int j=0; j<letters.length; j++) {
                                letterPts[j] = null;
                                done = true;
                            }
                        }
                    }
                }
                if (Math.random() < newLetterProbability) {
                    // Find a slot
                    for (int i=0; i<letters.length; i++) {
                        if (letterPts[i] == null) {
                            // Create a starting position for the letter.
                            letterPts[i] = new Point(
                                (int)Math.floor(Math.random()*width), 0);
                            letterPts[i].x = Math.min(letterPts[i].x,
                                width-fm.charWidth('X'));

                            // Pick a letter
                            letters[i] = (char)('A'
                                + Math.floor(Math.random()*26));
                            break;
                        }
                    }
                }
                repaint();
                Thread.sleep(delay);
            }
        } catch (Exception e) {
            e.printStackTrace();
        }
    }
}
```

A
B
C
D
E
F
G
H
I
J
K
L
M
N
O
P
Q
R
S
T
U
V
W
X
Y
Z

A
B
C
D
E
F
G
H
I
J
K
L
M
N
O
P
Q
R
S
T
U
V
W
X
Y
Z

keyPressed()

PURPOSE   Called when a key on the keyboard is pressed.

SYNTAX   `public void keyPressed(KeyEvent evt)`

DESCRIPTION   This method is called if the source component has the focus and a key is pressed on the keyboard. The identity of the key that was pressed can be retrieved by calling `evt.getKeyCode()`. If the system supports autorepeat, this method is called each time the key is repeated. See the `KeyEvent.KEY_PRESSED` for more details about key pressed events.

                This method, by default, has an empty implementation.

PARAMETERS
  evt   The non-`null` key event.

EXAMPLE   See the `KeyEvent` class example.

keyReleased()

PURPOSE   Called when a key on the keyboard is released.

SYNTAX   `public void keyReleased(KeyEvent evt)`

DESCRIPTION   This method is called when a key is released. The identity of the key that was released can be retrieved by calling `evt.getKeyCode()`. See `KeyEvent.KEY_RELEASED` for details about key released events.

                This method, by default, has an empty implementation.

PARAMETERS
  evt   The non-`null` key event.

EXAMPLE   See the `KeyEvent` class example.

keyTyped()

PURPOSE   Called when a pressed key or key combination fires a key character.

SYNTAX   `public void keyTyped(KeyEvent evt)`

DESCRIPTION   This method is called when a pressed key or key combination produces a key character. If the platform supports autorepeat, this method is called each time the key character is repeated. See `KeyEvent.KEY_TYPED` for details about key typed events.

                This method, by default, has an empty implementation.

PARAMETERS

evt   The non-null key event.

EXAMPLE   See the class example.

A
B
C
D
E
F
G
H
I
J
K
L
M
N
O
P
Q
R
S
T
U
V
W
X
Y
Z

A

B

C

D

E

F

G

H

I

J

K

L

M

N

O

P

Q

R

S

T

U

V

W

X

Y

Z

```
java.lang.Object

    java.util.EventObject

        java.awt.AWTEvent              ○

            ComponentEvent

                InputEvent                    ○

                    KeyEvent

                    MouseEvent
```

Syntax
`public class KeyEvent extends InputEvent`

Description
Key events are fired by the component that has the focus (see Component) whenever the user types at the keyboard. For example, when the user presses the A key, a KEY_PRESSED event is fired by the component that has the focus. To listen for key events from a component, you need to call the component's addKeyListener() method. For more general information about events, see AWTEvent.

The key event type has three event subtypes, shown in Table 16. See the field descriptions for detailed information on these event subtypes.

Key Event Subtype ID	Fired When ...
KEY_PRESSED	A key on the keyboard is pressed.
KEY_RELEASED	A key on the keyboard is released.
KEY_TYPED	A key character on the keyboard is pressed.

TABLE 16: Key Event Subtypes.

Listening for Key Events
To listen for key events from a component, the listener must implement the KeyListener interface. After that, the listener must be registered with the component. It becomes registered by calling the component's addKeyListener() method.

An alternative, and possibly more convenient, way of receiving key events is to use a key adapter. See KeyAdapter for more details.

Unlike most events, key events are delivered to its listeners before the operation has taken place. This gives the listeners an opportunity to consume the event (see `InputEvent.consume()`).

Key Codes

Every key on the keyboard is assigned a unique value called a *key code*. When a key is pressed on the keyboard, it fires a key event containing the key's key code. The same key code is emitted by a key regardless of the state of the modifier keys. All keys on the keyboard (including the modifier keys) fire a `KEY_PRESSED` event when pressed and a `KEY_RELEASED` event when released. If the platform supports autorepeating keys, a `KEY_PRESSED` event is fired each time the key is repeated.

The AWT system defines a set of common key codes that can be fired by most keyboards. However, some keyboards may not be able to fire all of the key codes. Likewise, some keyboards may have keys that don't correspond to any of the standard AWT key codes. Such a key is called an *unknown key code*. An unknown key code will still fire a key event when pressed; the key code value in the event will simply not be one from the standard set.

It is important to use the symbolic name for a key code (e.g., `VK_HOME`) rather than the key code value itself. This is because in a future release of the Java, some key code values may possibly change.

The value `VK_UNDEFINED` is used to represent an undefined key code.

Key Characters

A *key character* is a valid Unicode character that is fired by a key or key combination on the keyboard. Whereas a key always fires the same key code, that key may fire different key characters depending on the state of the modifier keys. For example, the A key fires the key character "a" (value 97) when the Shift key is not pressed and "A" (value 65) when the Shift key is pressed.

The value `CHAR_UNDEFINED` is used to represent an undefined key character.

Action Keys

In Java 1.0.2, certain keys were designated as *action* keys. These were, in general, keys that did not fire Unicode characters (e.g., the Home key). These action keys, when pressed and released, were delivered to an application as the events `Event.KEY_ACTION` and `Event.KEY_ACTION_RELEASE`.

For the most part, these old-event-style action events are now delivered to an application as `KEY_PRESSED` and `KEY_RELEASED` events. The key character property of these events is always `CHAR_UNDEFINED`.

Table 17 shows the key codes that action keys can fire (this list may change in the future). Unless your application is interested in exactly the keys in this table, the action key designations will not be particularly useful to you. Some keys, such as the Help key, naturally belong in the action key group, but they are not there.

A
B
C
D
E
F
G
H
I
J

L
M
N
O
P
Q
R
S
T
U
V
W
X
Y
Z

VK_HOME	VK_END	VK_PAGE_UP
VK_PAGE_DOWN	VK_UP	VK_DOWN
VK_LEFT	VK_RIGHT	VK_F1
VK_F2	VK_F3	VK_F4
VK_F5	VK_F6	VK_F7
VK_F8	VK_F9	VK_F10
VK_F11	VK_F12	VK_PRINTSCREEN
VK_SCROLL_LOCK	VK_CAPS_LOCK	VK_NUM_LOCK
VK_PAUSE	VK_INSERT	

TABLE 17: Action Key Key Codes.

Key Event Flow

Figure 227 shows how key events typically flow through the system. First, the event is fired by a component peer in response to the user's pressing a key on the keyboard. This event is posted on the event queue (see `EventQueue`). When the event makes its way to the front of the queue, it is given to the component via its `dispatchEvent()` method. The main purpose of this method is to forward the event directly back to the component peer if the key event type is not enabled or if there are no key listeners. Otherwise, the `dispatchEvent()` method calls `processEvent()`, which in turn calls different methods depending on the event type.

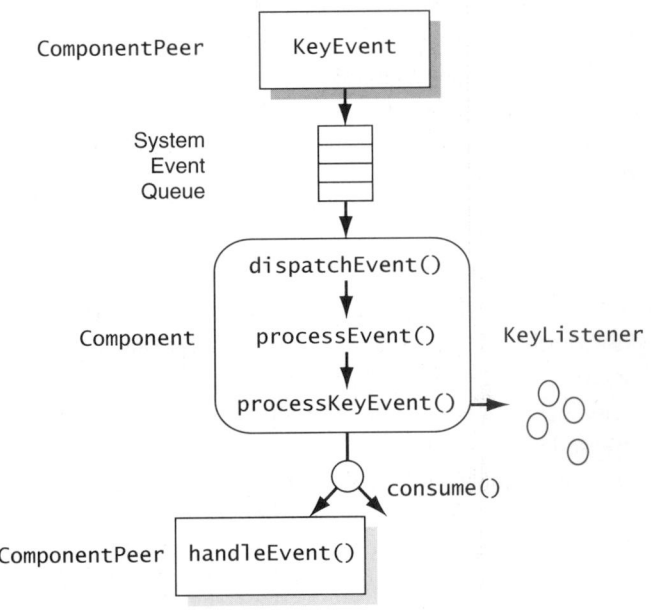

FIGURE 227: Key Event Flow.

Since this is a key event, `processKeyEvent()` is called. The main purpose of this method is to notify the key event listeners. Finally, if the event has not been consumed (see `InputEvent`), it is forwarded back to the originating component peer.

A component can override `processKeyEvent()` to process key events before they are delivered to its listeners. The overridden method should call `super.processKeyEvent()` to ensure that events are dispatched to the component's listeners.

Simulating Key Events

Key events are normally created by the AWT system when the user interacts with the keyboard. However, it is possible for any object to create key events in the same way. For example, a program designed to test a text field can create various key events and deliver them to the text field. The text field will treat the key events exactly as if they came from the AWT system.

A simulated key event can be delivered to a component in one of two ways—either by posting the event to the event queue (as in Figure 227) or by calling the component's `dispatchEvent()` method directly. See the `KEY_TYPED` field description for an example of simulating key events.

MEMBER SUMMARY	
Constructor	
KeyEvent()	Constructs a KeyEvent instance.
Property Methods	
getKeyChar()	Retrieves the key event's key character.
getKeyCode()	Retrieves the key event's key code.
isActionKey()	Determines if this key event was fired by an action key.
setKeyChar()	Modifies the key event's key character.
setKeyCode()	Modifies the key event's key code.
setModifiers()	Modifies the key event's set of modifier keys.
Key Event Id Constants	
KEY_FIRST	Constant specifying the first id in the range of key event ids.
KEY_LAST	Constant specifying the last id in the range of key event ids.
KEY_PRESSED	Event id indicating that a key on the keyboard was pressed.
KEY_RELEASED	Event id indicating that a key on the keyboard was released.
KEY_TYPED	Event id indicating that a pressed key or key combination fired a key character.
Key Codes	
CHAR_UNDEFINED	Constant specifying an undefined key character (0).
VK_0	The 0 key (48).
VK_1	The 1 key (49).
VK_2	The 2 key (50).
VK_3	The 3 key (51).
VK_4	The 4 key (52).
VK_5	The 5 key (53).
VK_6	The 6 key (54).
VK_7	The 7 key (55).
VK_8	The 8 key (56).

Continued

MEMBER SUMMARY	

Key Codes *(Continued)*

VK_9	The 9 key (57).
VK_A	The A key (65).
VK_ACCEPT	Asian keyboard-specific key (30).
VK_ADD	The numpad + key (107).
VK_ALT	The Alt key (18).
VK_B	The B key (66).
VK_BACK_QUOTE	The ' key (192).
VK_BACK_SLASH	The \ key (92).
VK_BACK_SPACE	The backspace key (8).
VK_C	The C key (67).
VK_CANCEL	The Cancel (Control-C) key (3).
VK_CAPS_LOCK	The Caps Lock action key (20).
VK_CLEAR	The Clear (Control-L) key (12).
VK_CLOSE_BRACKET	The] key (93).
VK_COMMA	The , key (44).
VK_CONTROL	The Control key (17).
VK_CONVERT	Asian keyboard-specific key (28).
VK_D	The D key (68).
VK_DECIMAL	The numpad . key (110).
VK_DELETE	The Delete key (127).
VK_DIVIDE	The numpad / key (111).
VK_DOWN	The Down action key (40).
VK_E	The E key (69).
VK_END	The End action key (35).
VK_ENTER	The Enter key (10).
VK_ESCAPE	The Esc (escape) key (27).
VK_F	The F key (70).
VK_F1	The F1 action key (112).
VK_F10	The F10 action key (121).
VK_F11	The F11 action key (122).
VK_F12	The F12 action key (123).
VK_F2	The F2 action key (113).
VK_F3	The F3 action key (114).
VK_F4	The F4 action key (115).
VK_F5	The F5 action key (116).
VK_F6	The F6action key (117).
VK_F7	The F7 action key (118).
VK_F8	The F8 action key (119).
VK_F9	The F9 action key (120).
VK_FINAL	Asian keyboard-specific key (24).
VK_G	The G key (71).

A
B
C
D
E
F
G
H
I
J
K
L
M
N
O
P
Q
R
S
T
U
V
W
X
Y
Z

MEMBER SUMMARY

VK_H	The H key (72).
VK_HELP	The Help key (156).
VK_HOME	The Home action key (36).
VK_I	The I key (73).
VK_INSERT	The Insert action key (155).
VK_J	The J key (74).
VK_K	The K key (75).
VK_KANA	Asian keyboard-specific key (21).
VK_KANJI	Asian keyboard-specific key (25).
VK_L	The L key (76).
VK_LEFT	The left action key (37).
VK_M	The M key (77).
VK_META	The Meta key (157).
VK_MODECHANGE	Asian keyboard-specific key (31).
VK_MULTIPLY	The numpad * key (106).
VK_N	The N key (78).
VK_NONCONVERT	Asian keyboard-specific key (29).
VK_NUM_LOCK	The Num Lock action key (144).
VK_NUMPAD0	The numpad-0 key (96).
VK_NUMPAD1	The numpad-1 key (97).
VK_NUMPAD2	The numpad-2 key (98).
VK_NUMPAD3	The numpad-3 key (99).
VK_NUMPAD4	The numpad-4 key (100).
VK_NUMPAD5	The numpad-5 key (101).
VK_NUMPAD6	The numpad-6 key (102).
VK_NUMPAD7	The numpad-7 key (103).
VK_NUMPAD8	The numpad-8 key (104).
VK_NUMPAD9	The numpad-9 key (105).
VK_O	The O key (79).
VK_OPEN_BRACKET	The [key (91).
VK_P	The P key (80).
VK_PAGE_DOWN	The PageDown action key (34).
VK_PAGE_UP	The PageUp action key (33).
VK_PAUSE	The Pause action key (19).
VK_PERIOD	The . key (46).
VK_PRINTSCREEN	The Print Screen action key (154).
VK_Q	The Q key (81).
VK_QUOTE	The ' key (222).
VK_R	The R key (82).
VK_RIGHT	The Right action key (39).
VK_S	The S key (83).

Continued

A
B
C
D
E
F
G
H
I
J
K
L
M
N
O
P
Q
R
S
T
U
V
W
X
Y
Z

A
B
C
D
E
F
G
H
I
J
K
L
M
N
O
P
Q
R
S
T
U
V
W
X
Y
Z

MEMBER SUMMARY	
Key Codes *(Continued)*	
VK_SCROLL_LOCK	The Scroll Lock action key (145).
VK_SEMICOLON	The ; key (59).
VK_SEPARATER	The numpad , key (108).
VK_SHIFT	The Shift key (16).
VK_SLASH	The / key (47).
VK_SPACE	The Space key (32).
VK_SUBTRACT	The numpad – (minus) key (109).
VK_T	The T key (84).
VK_TAB	The Tab key (9).
VK_U	The U key (85).
VK_UNDEFINED	Constant specifying an undefined key code (0).
VK_UP	The Up action key (38).
VK_V	The V key (86).
VK_W	The W key (87).
VK_X	The X key (88).
VK_Y	The Y key (89).
VK_Z	The Z key (90).
Debugging Method	
getKeyModifiersText()	Returns a printable representation of the key modifier state.
getKeyText()	Returns a printable name for a key code.
paramString()	Generates a string representing the key event's state.

See Also

```
KeyAdapter, KeyListener, java.awt.AWTEvent,
java.awt.Component.addKeyListener().
```

Example

This example demonstrates how to get key events from a component. It creates a text field and listens for key events from it. In response to a key event, the specifics of the event are printed. See Figure 228.

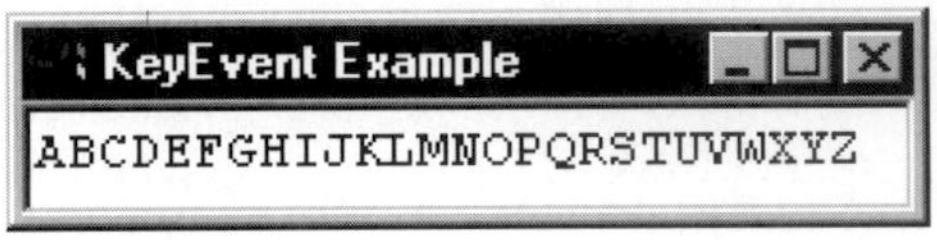

FIGURE 228: KeyEvent.

```
import java.awt.*;
import java.awt.event.*;

class Main extends Frame {
    Main() {
        super("KeyEvent Example");
        TextField tf = new TextField();
```

```
        // Listen for text events.
        tf.addKeyListener(new KeyEventHandler());
        tf.setFont(new Font("Courier", Font.PLAIN, 14));

        add(tf, BorderLayout.CENTER);
        pack();
        show();
    }

    class KeyEventHandler extends KeyAdapter {
        public void keyPressed(KeyEvent evt) {
            printKey(evt);
        }
        public void keyReleased(KeyEvent evt) {
            printKey(evt);
        }
        public void keyTyped(KeyEvent evt) {
            printKey(evt);
        }

        void printKey(KeyEvent evt) {
            switch (evt.getID()) {
              case KeyEvent.KEY_TYPED:
                System.out.print("KEY_TYPED");
                break;
              case KeyEvent.KEY_PRESSED:
                System.out.print("KEY_PRESSED");
                break;
              case KeyEvent.KEY_RELEASED:
                System.out.print("KEY_RELEASED");
                break;
            }
            System.out.print(": char="+evt.getKeyChar()
                +"("+(int)evt.getKeyChar()+")");
            System.out.print(" code="+evt.getKeyCode());
            if (evt.isActionKey()) {
                System.out.print(" actionkey");
            }
            System.out.println();
        }
    }

    public static void main(String args[]) {
        new Main();
    }
}
```

CHAR_UNDEFINED

PURPOSE   Constant specifying an undefined key character.

SYNTAX   `public static final char CHAR_UNDEFINED`

DESCRIPTION When the key code in a KEY_PRESSED or KEY_RELEASED event does not represent a key character (e.g., VK_HOME), the event's key character property is set to CHAR_UNDEFINED.

SEE ALSO KEY_PRESSED, KEY_RELEASED.

EXAMPLE This example watches all key transitions. When a key character is seen, it displays it. It erases the display as soon as the user releases the key character. See Figure 229.

FIGURE 229: Key character watcher.

```java
import java.awt.*;
import java.awt.event.*;

class Main extends Frame {
    char curKeyChar;

    Main() {
        super("CHAR_UNDEFINED Example");

        // Listen for text events.
        addKeyListener(new KeyEventHandler());

        setSize(200, 100);
        setFont(new Font("Monospaced", Font.BOLD, 36));
        show();
    }

    public void paint(Graphics g) {
        Insets in = getInsets();
        FontMetrics fm = g.getFontMetrics();
        String s = "" + curKeyChar;

        if (curKeyChar != KeyEvent.CHAR_UNDEFINED) {
            g.drawString(s, (getSize().width-fm.stringWidth(s))/2,
                in.top+(getSize().height-in.top-in.bottom-
                fm.getHeight())/2+fm.getAscent());
        }
    }

    class KeyEventHandler extends KeyAdapter {
        public void keyPressed(KeyEvent evt) {
            if (curKeyChar != evt.getKeyChar()) {
                curKeyChar = evt.getKeyChar();
                repaint();
            }
        }
        public void keyReleased(KeyEvent evt) {
            curKeyChar = KeyEvent.CHAR_UNDEFINED;
            repaint();
        }
    }

    public static void main(String args[]) {
```

```
        new Main();
    }
}
```

getKeyChar()

PURPOSE   Retrieves the key event's key character.

SYNTAX   `public char getKeyChar()`

DESCRIPTION   For all `KEY_TYPED` events, calling this method yields a key character, never `CHAR_UNDEFINED`. For `KEY_PRESSED` and `KEY_RELEASED` events, this method may return `CHAR_UNDEFINED`. See the class description for more information on key characters.

RETURNS   The event's key character or `CHAR_UNDEFINED`.

SEE ALSO   `CHAR_UNDEFINED`, `KEY_PRESSED`, `KEY_RELEASED`, `KEY_TYPED`.

EXAMPLE   This example implements a simple word game. The program chooses a word at random, and the user must guess the word. The number of characters in the word is displayed as a sequence of underlines, one underline per character. When the user types a character in the word, the characters appear on the screen. Wrongly guessed characters appear below the underlines in red. See Figure 230.

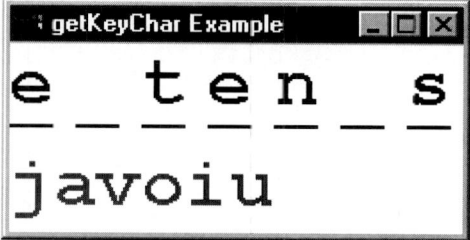

FIGURE 230:   Simple word game.

For each letter, the program listens for a `KEY_TYPED` event, retrieves the key character, makes it lowercase, and then checks to see if it's a correct letter.

```java
import java.awt.*;
import java.awt.event.*;

class Main extends Frame {
    String[] words = {"java", "class", "interface", "extends", "implements"};

    // Current mystery word.  Index into 'words'.
    int curWord;

    // Holds current set of correctly guessed letters.
    char[] letters;

    // Holds current set of incorrectly guessed letters.
    String wrongLetters;
```

```
// win is true if all letters have been guessed.
boolean win;

Main() {
    super("getKeyChar Example");

    // Listen for text events.
    addKeyListener(new KeyEventHandler());

    newGame();
    setSize(300, 150);
    setFont(new Font("Monospaced", Font.BOLD, 36));
    show();
}

void newGame() {
    curWord = (int)Math.floor(Math.random()*words.length);
    letters = new char[words[curWord].length()];
    wrongLetters = "";
    win = false;
}

public void paint(Graphics g) {
    Insets in = getInsets();
    FontMetrics fm = g.getFontMetrics();
    int chw = fm.stringWidth("M");

    for (int i=0; i<letters.length; i++) {
        if (letters[i] > 0) {
            g.drawChars(letters, i, 1, in.left+i*(chw+chw/2),
                        in.top+fm.getAscent());
        }
        g.fillRect(in.left+i*(chw+chw/2), in.top+fm.getHeight(), chw, 2);
    }

    if (win) {
        g.setColor(Color.blue);
        g.drawString("You Won!", in.left, in.top+fm.getHeight() * 2);
    } else {
        g.setColor(Color.red);
        g.drawString(wrongLetters, in.left, in.top+fm.getHeight() * 2);
    }
}

class KeyEventHandler extends KeyAdapter {
    public void keyTyped(KeyEvent evt) {
        char ch = evt.getKeyChar();

        if (win) {
            newGame();
        }

        // If not a letter, return.
        ch = Character.toLowerCase(ch);
        if (!Character.isLetter(ch)) {
            getToolkit().beep();
            return;
        }

        // Has the letter been guessed?
```

A
B
C
D
E
F
G
H
I
J
K
L
M
N
O
P
Q
R
S
T
U
V
W
X
Y
Z

```
                for (int i=0; i<letters.length; i++) {
                    if (ch == letters[i]) {
                        getToolkit().beep();
                        return;
                    }
                }

                // Is the letter already in the wrong letter list?
                if (wrongLetters.indexOf(ch) >= 0) {
                    getToolkit().beep();
                    return;
                }

                // Is the letter correct?
                if (words[curWord].indexOf(ch) >= 0) {
                    for (int i=0; i<letters.length; i++) {
                        if (words[curWord].charAt(i) == ch) {
                            letters[i] = ch;
                        }
                    }

                    boolean foundBlank = false;
                    for (int i=0; i<letters.length; i++) {
                        if (letters[i] == 0) {
                            foundBlank = true;
                        }
                    }
                    if (!foundBlank) {
                        win = true;
                    }
                } else {
                    wrongLetters += ch;
                }
                repaint();
            }
        }

        public static void main(String args[]) {
            new Main();
        }
    }
```

getKeyCode()

PURPOSE   Retrieves the key event's key code.

SYNTAX   `public int getKeyCode()`

DESCRIPTION For all KEY_TYPED events, calling this method yields VK_UNDEFINED. For all
            KEY_PRESSED and KEY_RELEASED events, calling this method never yields
            VK_UNDEFINED. See the class description for more information on key codes.

RETURNS   The event's key code or VK_UNDEFINED.

SEE ALSO   CHAR_UNDEFINED, KEY_PRESSED, KEY_RELEASED, KEY_TYPED.

EXAMPLE   See the class example.

A
B
C
D
E
F
G
H
I
J
K
L
M
N
O
P
Q
R
S
T
U
V
W
X
Y
Z

getKeyModifiersText()

PURPOSE	Returns a printable representation of the key modifier state.
SYNTAX	`public static String getKeyModifiersText(int mods)`
DESCRIPTION	This method examines `mods` for the state of four modifier keys: Alt, Control, Meta, and Shift. It then returns a string showing which modifier keys are pressed. The name of the modifier key that appears in the string is determined by calling `Toolkit.getProperty()`. Table 18 shows the property name of the modifier key code to use when retrieving the modifier key's printable name.

Modifier Key Code	Property Name	Default Printable Name
VK_ALT	AWT.alt	Alt
VK_CONTROL	AWT.control	Ctrl
VK_META	AWT.meta	Meta
VK_SHIFT	AWT.shift	Shift

TABLE 18: Modifier Key Property and Printable Names.

A key code's printable name is retrieved through a properties file so that the names can be localized. See `Toolkit.getProperty()` for more information on the format of property file entries and where the property file is located.

This method is typically used for debugging purposes.

PARAMETERS	
mods	A bit vector indicating the state of all modifier keys. See `InputEvent` for more details on modifier keys.
SEE ALSO	`InputEvent.ALT_MASK`, `InputEvent.CTRL_MASK`, `InputEvent.META_MASK`, `InputEvent.SHIFT_MASK`, `java.awt.Toolkit.getProperty()`.
EXAMPLE	See `getKeyText()`.

getKeyText()

PURPOSE	Returns a printable name for a key code.
SYNTAX	`public static String getKeyText(int keyCode)`

DESCRIPTION   This method returns a printable name for a key code. If the value of the key code is a printable ASCII character, the character is converted to a string and then returned. If the value is not a printable ASCII character (e.g., VK_HOME), this method calls `Toolkit.getProperty()` to retrieve the key code's printable name. Table 19 shows the key code's property name to use when retrieving the key code's printable name. If the property name does not exist in the properties file, the default name is used instead.

Retrieving a key code's printable name through a properties file allows the names to be localized. See `Toolkit.getProperty()` for more information on the format of property file entries and where the property file is located.

This method is typically used for debugging purposes.

Key Code	Property Name	Default Printable Name
unknown key code	AWT.unknown	Unknown keyCode
VK_ACCEPT	AWT.accept	Accept
VK_ADD	AWT.add	NumPad +
VK_ALT	AWT.alt	Alt
VK_BACK_QUOTE	AWT.backQuote	Back Quote
VK_BACK_SPACE	AWT.backSpace	Backspace
VK_CAPS_LOCK	AWT.capsLock	Caps Lock
VK_CLEAR	AWT.clear	Clear
VK_CONTROL	AWT.control	Ctrl
VK_CONVERT	AWT.convert	Convert
VK_DECIMAL	AWT.decimal	NumPad .
VK_DELETE	AWT.delete	Delete
VK_DIVIDE	AWT.divide	NumPad /
VK_DOWN	AWT.down	Down
VK_END	AWT.end	End
VK_ENTER	AWT.enter	Enter
VK_ESCAPE	AWT.escape	Escape
VK_F10	AWT.f10	F10
VK_F11	AWT.f11	F11
VK_F12	AWT.f12	F12
VK_F1	AWT.f1	F1

Continued

TABLE 19:   Key Code Properties and Printable Names.

A
B
C
D
E
F
G
H
I
J
K
L
M
N
O
P
Q
R
S
T
U
V
W
X
Y
Z

A
B
C
D
E
F
G
H
I
J
K
L
M
N
O
P
Q
R
S
T
U
V
W
X
Y
Z

Key Code	Property Name	Default Printable Name
VK_F2	AWT.f2	F2
VK_F3	AWT.f3	F3
VK_F4	AWT.f4	F4
VK_F5	AWT.f5	F5
VK_F6	AWT.f6	F6
VK_F7	AWT.f7	F7
VK_F8	AWT.f8	F8
VK_F9	AWT.f9	F9
VK_FINAL	AWT.final	Final
VK_HELP	AWT.help	Help
VK_HOME	AWT.home	Home
VK_INSERT	AWT.insert	Insert
VK_KANA	AWT.kana	Kana
VK_KANJI	AWT.kanji	Kanji
VK_LEFT	AWT.left	Left
VK_META	AWT.meta	Meta
VK_MODECHANGE	AWT.modechange	Mode Change
VK_MULTIPLY	AWT.multiply	NumPad *
VK_NONCONVERT	AWT.noconvert	No Convert
VK_NUMPAD0 – VK_NUMPAD1	AWT.numpad	NumPad
VK_NUM_LOCK	AWT.numLock	Num Lock
VK_PAUSE	AWT.pause	Pause
VK_PAGE_DOWN	AWT.pgdn	Page Down
VK_PAGE_UP	AWT.pgup	Page Up
VK_PRINTSCREEN	AWT.printScreen	Print Screen
VK_QUOTE	AWT.quote	Quote
VK_RIGHT	AWT.right	Right
VK_SCROLL_LOCK	AWT.scrollLock	Scroll Lock
VK_SEPARATER	AWT.separater	NumPad ,
VK_SHIFT	AWT.shift	Shift
VK_SPACE	AWT.space	Space
VK_SUBTRACT	AWT.subtract	NumPad -
VK_TAB	AWT.tab	Tab
VK_UP	AWT.up	Up

TABLE 19:   Key Code Properties and Printable Names.

RETURNS   A non-null string describing the key code.

SEE ALSO   java.awt.Toolkit.getProperty().

EXAMPLE   This example handles key pressed events and displays the results of calling
getKeyText() on the key event's key code. See Figure 231.

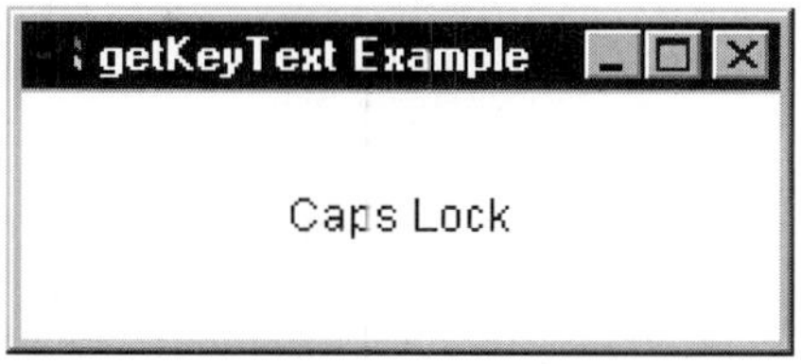

```java
import java.awt.*;
import java.awt.event.*;

class Main extends Frame {
    String curKeyCode = "";
    String curModifiers = "";

    Main() {
        super("getKeyText Example");

        // Listen for text events.
        addKeyListener(
            new KeyEventHandler());

        setSize(200, 100);
        show();
    }

    public void paint(Graphics g) {
        Insets in = getInsets();
        FontMetrics fm = g.getFontMetrics();
        String s = curModifiers + " " + curKeyCode;

        g.drawString(s, (getSize().width-fm.stringWidth(s))/2,
            in.top+(getSize().height-in.top-in.bottom-
                fm.getHeight())/2+fm.getAscent());
    }

    class KeyEventHandler extends KeyAdapter {
        public void keyPressed(KeyEvent evt) {
            curKeyCode = KeyEvent.getKeyText(evt.getKeyCode());
            curModifiers = KeyEvent.getKeyModifiersText(evt.getModifiers());
            repaint();
        }
    }

    public static void main(String args[]) {
        new Main();
    }
}
```

FIGURE 231:   KeyEvent.getKeyText().

isActionKey()

PURPOSE   Determines if this key event was fired by an action key.

SYNTAX   public boolean isActionKey()

DESCRIPTION	Action keys are a subset of keys that don't fire key characters. The action key group appears mainly for backward compatibility with Java 1.0.2. In Java 1.1.2, there are more keys that could be considered action keys (e.g., Help), but they are not considered action keys. So unless your application is interested in exactly those keys considered action keys, you may not find this method useful.
	See the class description for more information on action keys, including a list of action keys.
RETURNS	`true` if the key event was fired by an action key; `false` otherwise.
EXAMPLE	See the class example.

KEY_FIRST

PURPOSE	Constant specifying the first id in the range of key event ids.
SYNTAX	`public static final int KEY_FIRST`
DESCRIPTION	All key event ids must be greater than or equal to KEY_FIRST (value `400`).
SEE ALSO	`KEY_LAST`.
EXAMPLE	See `java.awt.Component.processEvent()`.

KEY_LAST

PURPOSE	Constant specifying the last id in the range of key event ids.
SYNTAX	`public static final int KEY_LAST`
DESCRIPTION	All key event ids must be less than or equal to KEY_LAST (value `402`).
SEE ALSO	`KEY_FIRST`.
EXAMPLE	See `java.awt.Component.processEvent()`.

KEY_PRESSED

PURPOSE	Event id indicating that a key on the keyboard was pressed.
SYNTAX	`public static final int KEY_PRESSED`
DESCRIPTION	A key event with this id (value `401`) is fired when a key is pressed on the keyboard. The event's key code property contains the identity of the key that was pressed. If the system supports autorepeat, a KEY_PRESSED event is fired each

time the key is repeated, so there can be more than one KEY_PRESSED event for each KEY_RELEASED event. See the class description for more information about key characters and key codes.

The event's key character property contains the key character. However, if the key does not fire a key character (e.g., the Home key), the key character property has the value CHAR_UNDEFINED.

The event's key modifiers are captured at the time the key was pressed.

The Caps Lock and Num Lock keys are treated differently from the rest. With these two keys, an event is fired only when the state of these keys change. For example, when the Caps Lock key is physically pressed and released, a KEY_PRESSED event is fired (to signify that the Caps Lock key is enabled). When the Caps Lock is physically pressed and released again, a KEY_RELEASED event is fired (to signify that the Caps Lock key is disabled). *Note*: In Java 1.1.2, this behavior has not yet been implemented.

SEE ALSO   KEY_RELEASED, KEY_TYPED.

EXAMPLE   See the class example.

KEY_RELEASED

PURPOSE   Event id indicating that a key on the keyboard was released.

SYNTAX   `public static final int KEY_RELEASED`

DESCRIPTION   A key event with this id (value 402) is fired when a key is released. The event's key code property contains the identity of the key that was released. See the class description for more information about key characters and key codes.

The event's key character property contains the key character. However, if the key does not fire a key character (e.g., the Home key), the key character property has the value CHAR_UNDEFINED.

The event's key modifiers are captured at the time the key was released.

SEE ALSO   KEY_PRESSED.

EXAMPLE   See the class example.

KEY_TYPED

PURPOSE   Event id indicating that a pressed key or key combination fired a key character.

SYNTAX   `public static final int KEY_TYPED`

DESCRIPTION　　A key event with this id (value 400) is fired when a pressed key or key combination fires a key character. If the platform supports autorepeat, a KEY_TYPED event is fired each time the key character is repeated. See the class description for more information about key characters and key codes.

KEY_TYPED events are delivered after KEY_PRESSED events but before KEY_RELEASED events. The event's key character is never CHAR_UNDEFINED, and its key code property is always VK_UNDEFINED. The event's key modifiers are captured at the time the key character was pressed.

SEE ALSO　　CHAR_UNDEFINED, KEY_PRESSED, KEY_RELEASED, VK_UNDEFINED.

EXAMPLE　　This example demonstrates how key events can be simulated to a text area. It implements a version of text area that can automatically insert some text when a function key is pressed. For example, if you press F1, the word "class" is inserted into the text area. Also, if the Shift key is pressed at the same time, the word "class" becomes "CLASS." See Figure 232.

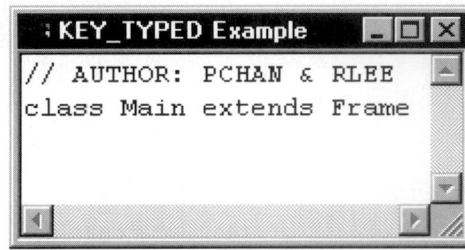

FIGURE 232:　KeyEvent.KEY_TYPED.

The text area overrides the processKeyEvent() method and watches for key press events. When an event does occur, it is converted to a series of key typed events and the original event is consumed.

Note: As of Java 1.1.2, this example may not work on platforms other than Win32.

```java
import java.awt.*;
import java.awt.event.*;

class Main extends Frame {
    Main() {
        super("KEY_TYPED Example");

        add(new MyTextArea(), BorderLayout.CENTER);
        pack();
        show();
    }

    public static void main(String args[]) {
        new Main();
    }
}

class MyTextArea extends TextArea {
    Object[] macros = {
        new Integer(KeyEvent.VK_F1), "class ",
        new Integer(KeyEvent.VK_F2), "interface ",
```

```
                new Integer(KeyEvent.VK_F3), "extends ",
                new Integer(KeyEvent.VK_F4), "implements ",
                new Integer(KeyEvent.VK_F5), "// author: pchan & rlee ",};

        MyTextArea() {
            enableEvents(AWTEvent.KEY_EVENT_MASK);
            setFont(new Font("Courier", Font.PLAIN, 14));
        }

        public void processKeyEvent(KeyEvent evt) {
            if (evt.getID() == KeyEvent.KEY_PRESSED) {
                for (int i=0; i<macros.length; i+=2) {
                    Integer ri = (Integer)macros[i];

                    if (ri.intValue() == evt.getKeyCode()) {
                        synthesizeKeyEvent((String)macros[i+1],
                            evt.isShiftDown());
                        evt.consume();
                        break;
                    }
                }
            }
            super.processKeyEvent(evt);
        }

        void synthesizeKeyEvent(String s, boolean uppercase) {
            for (int j=0; j<s.length(); j++) {
                char ch = s.charAt(j);

                if (uppercase) {
                    ch = Character.toUpperCase(ch);
                }

                KeyEvent ke = new KeyEvent(MyTextArea.this,
                    KeyEvent.KEY_TYPED,
                    System.currentTimeMillis(), 0,
                    KeyEvent.VK_UNDEFINED, ch);

                getToolkit().getSystemEventQueue().postEvent(ke);
            }
        }
    }
}
```

A
B
C
D
E
F
G
H
I
J
K
L
M
N
O
P
Q
R
S
T
U
V
W
X
Y
Z

KeyEvent()

PURPOSE   Constructs a KeyEvent instance.

SYNTAX   `public KeyEvent(Component source, int id, long when, int`
              `modifiers,int keyCode, char keyChar)`

DEPRECATED `public KeyEvent(Component source, int id, long when, int`
              `modifiers,int keyCode)`

DESCRIPTION	This constructor creates a key event with `source` as the component firing this event. See the class description for more information on key codes, key characters, timestamps, and modifier keys.

After the key event is created, the source object can distribute the event to its listeners by calling the key event-related methods in `AWTEventMulticaster`. If the event is not created by `source`, the creator can deliver the event to the source component either by posting the event to the event queue (see `Event-Queue.postEvent()`) or by calling the source component's `Component.dispatchEvent()` method directly.

PARAMETERS

`source`	The non-`null` component that is firing this key event.
`id`	One of the key event ids.
`when`	The timestamp for this event. See `System.currentTimeMillis()`.
`modifiers`	The current state of the modifier keys.
`keyCode`	A key code.
`keyChar`	A key character.

EXCEPTIONS

`IllegalArgumentException`
  If `id` is `KEY_TYPED` and either `keyChar` is `CHAR_UNDEFINED` or `keyCode` is not `VK_UNDEFINED`.

DEPRECATION   The usage of the second form of this constructor is deprecated. Since `keyChar` is not supplied, it casts `keyCode` to a `char`. Use only the first form of this constructor when creating `KeyEvent` instances.

SEE ALSO   `getKeyChar()`, `getKeyCode()`, `InputEvent.getModifiers()`, `InputEvent.getWhen()`, `java.awt.AWTEvent.getID()`, `java.awt.Component.dispatchEvent()`, `java.lang.System.currentTimeMillis()`, `java.util.EventObject.getSource()`.

EXAMPLE

This example implements a virtual keypad. Each key is a lightweight component set in a frame that has a grid layout. The virtual keys are highlighted when the cursor passes over them. When the user presses a mouse button while the cursor is over a virtual key, it fires a KEY_TYPED key event containing the key character displayed in the virtual key's label. See Figure 233.

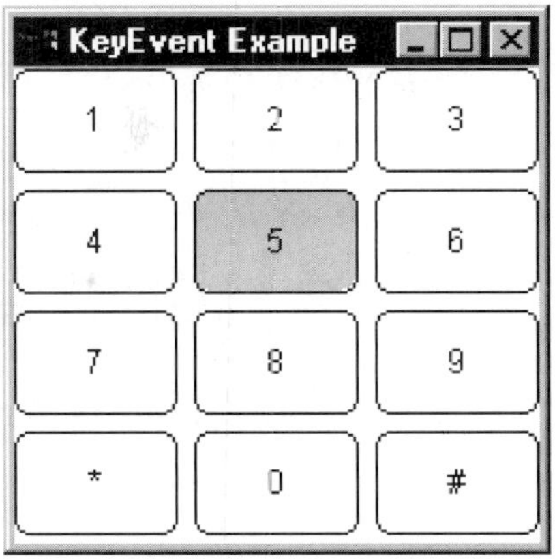

FIGURE 233: A virtual keypad.

```java
import java.awt.*;
import java.awt.event.*;
import java.util.*;

class Main extends Frame {
    String keys = "123456789*0#";

    Main() {
        super("KeyEvent Example");

        setLayout(new GridLayout(4, 3, 6, 6));

        for (int i=0; i<keys.length(); i++) {
            KeyButton kb = new KeyButton(keys.charAt(i));

            kb.addKeyListener(new KeyEventHandler());
            kb.setBackground(Color.pink);
            kb.setForeground(Color.black);
            add(kb);
        }

        setSize(200, 200);
        show();
    }

    class KeyEventHandler extends KeyAdapter {
        public void keyTyped(KeyEvent evt) {
            System.out.println(evt);
        }
    }

    public static void main(String[] args) {
        new Main();
    }
}

class KeyButton extends Component {
    KeyListener keyListener;
    boolean highlighted;
    char key;

    KeyButton(char k) {
        this.key = k;
        addMouseListener(new MouseEventHandler());
```

A
B
C
D
E
F
G
H
I
J

L
M
N
O
P
Q
R
S
T
U
V
W
X
Y
Z

```
        }

        public void paint(Graphics g) {
            int w = getSize().width;
            int h = getSize().height;
            String s = ""+key;
            FontMetrics fm = g.getFontMetrics();

            if (highlighted) {
                g.setColor(getBackground());
                g.fillRoundRect(0, 0, w-1, h-1, 10, 10);
            }
            g.setColor(getForeground());
            g.drawRoundRect(0, 0, w-1, h-1, 10, 10);
            g.drawString(s, (w-fm.stringWidth(s))/2,
                            (h-fm.getHeight())/2+fm.getAscent());
        }

        class MouseEventHandler extends MouseAdapter {
            public void mousePressed(MouseEvent evt) {
                if (keyListener != null) {
                    keyListener.keyTyped(
                        new KeyEvent(KeyButton.this, KeyEvent.KEY_TYPED,
                            System.currentTimeMillis(),
                            0, KeyEvent.VK_UNDEFINED, key));
                }
            }
            public void mouseEntered(MouseEvent evt) {
                highlighted = true;
                repaint();
            }
            public void mouseExited(MouseEvent evt) {
                highlighted = false;
                repaint();
            }
        }

        // Listener support methods
        public synchronized void addKeyListener(KeyListener l) {
            keyListener = AWTEventMulticaster.add(keyListener, l);
        }

        public synchronized void removeKeyListener(KeyListener l) {
            keyListener = AWTEventMulticaster.remove(keyListener, l);
        }
    }
```

paramString()

PURPOSE   Generates a string representing the key event's state.

SYNTAX   `public String paramString()`

DESCRIPTION   The returned string contains the name of the key event, the key code, the key character, and the key modifiers. A subclass of this class should override this method and return a concatenation of its state with the results of super.paramString(). This method is called by the AWTEvent.toString() method and is typically used for debugging.

RETURNS   A non-null string representing the key event's state.

OVERRIDES   java.awt.AWTEvent.paramString().

SEE ALSO   java.awt.AWTEvent.toString(), java.lang.Object.toString().

EXAMPLE   See the java.awt.AWTEvent class example.

setKeyChar()

PURPOSE   Modifies the key event's key character.

SYNTAX   public void setKeyChar(char keyChar)

DESCRIPTION   This method modifies the key character in the key event. Since key events are input events, the peer for the source component (the one that fired the event) will interpret the modified event.

                 If the event is modified by a listener, all subsequent listeners will see the modified event.

PARAMETERS
  keyChar   The new key character.

SEE ALSO   getKeyChar(), setKeyCode().

EXAMPLE   See setModifiers().

setKeyCode()

PURPOSE   Modifies the key event's key code.

SYNTAX   public void setKeyCode(int keyCode)

DESCRIPTION   This method modifies the key code in the key event. Since key events are input events, the peer for the source component (the one that fired the event) will interpret the modified event.

                 If the event is modified by a listener, all subsequent listeners will see the modified event.

PARAMETERS
  keyCode   The new key code.

SEE ALSO   getKeyCode(), setKeyChar().

EXAMPLE   See setModifiers().

A
B
C
D
E
F
G
H
I
J
K
L
M
N
O
P
Q
R
S
T
U
V
W
X
Y
Z

setModifiers()

PURPOSE   Modifies the key event's set of modifier keys.

SYNTAX   `public void setModifiers(int mods)`

DESCRIPTION   This method modifies the set of modifier keys in the key event. Since key events are input events, the peer for the source component (the one that fired the event) will interpret the modified event.

If the event is modified by a listener, all subsequent listeners will see the modified event.

PARAMETERS
mods   A bit set containing the new state of the modifier keys. See `InputEvent` on how to interpret this bit set.

SEE ALSO   `InputEvent.ALT_MASK`, `InputEvent.CTRL_MASK`, `InputEvent.getModifiers()`, `InputEvent.META_MASK`, `InputEvent.SHIFT_MASK`.

EXAMPLE   This example modifies KEY_TYPED events enroute to a text area. The four modifier keys are represented by four checkboxes. When a checkbox is set, the program modifies the key character to simulate the modifier key that the checkbox represents. For example, when the Shift checkbox is enabled, all key characters are converted to uppercase. See Figure 234.

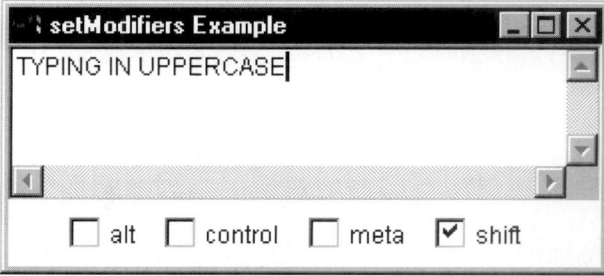

FIGURE 234: `KeyEvent.setModifiers()`.

```
import java.awt.*;
import java.awt.event.*;

class Main extends Frame {
    Checkbox altCb = new Checkbox("alt");
    Checkbox controlCb = new Checkbox("control");
    Checkbox metaCb = new Checkbox("meta");
    Checkbox shiftCb = new Checkbox("shift");

    Main() {
        super("setModifiers Example");
        TextArea ta = new TextArea();

        add(ta, BorderLayout.CENTER);
        ta.addKeyListener(new KeyEventHandler());
```

```
            Panel p = new Panel(new FlowLayout());
            p.add(altCb);
            p.add(controlCb);
            p.add(metaCb);
            p.add(shiftCb);
            add(p, BorderLayout.SOUTH);

            setSize(300, 200);
            show();
        }

        class KeyEventHandler extends KeyAdapter {
            public void keyTyped(KeyEvent evt) {
                int mods = evt.getModifiers();
                char ch = evt.getKeyChar();

                if (altCb.getState()) {
                    mods |= InputEvent.ALT_MASK;
                }
                if (controlCb.getState()) {
                    mods |= InputEvent.CTRL_MASK;
                    ch = (char)(Character.toUpperCase(ch) - 64);
                    evt.setKeyChar((char)Math.max(0, ch));
                }
                if (metaCb.getState()) {
                    mods |= InputEvent.META_MASK;
                }
                if (shiftCb.getState()) {
                    mods |= InputEvent.SHIFT_MASK;
                    evt.setKeyChar(Character.toUpperCase(ch));
                }
                evt.setModifiers(mods);
            }
        }

        public static void main(String[] args) {
            new Main();
        }
    }
```

A
B
C
D
E
F
G
H
I
J

L
M
N
O
P
Q
R
S

VK_UNDEFINED

T

PURPOSE	Constant specifying an undefined key code.
SYNTAX	`public static final int VK_UNDEFINED`
DESCRIPTION	When the key code in a key event does not represent a key code, the event's key code property is set to VK_UNDEFINED. The key code in all KEY_TYPED events is VK_UNDEFINED.
SEE ALSO	KEY_TYPED.
EXAMPLE	See KeyEvent().

U
V
W
X
Y
Z

KeyListener

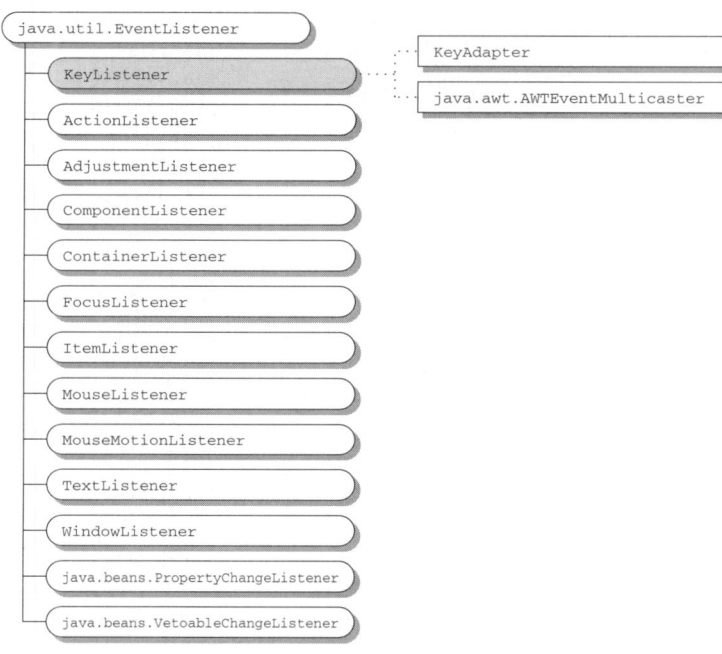

java.util.EventListener

KeyListener
ActionListener
AdjustmentListener
ComponentListener
ContainerListener
FocusListener
ItemListener
MouseListener
MouseMotionListener
TextListener
WindowListener
java.beans.PropertyChangeListener
java.beans.VetoableChangeListener

KeyAdapter
java.awt.AWTEventMulticaster

Syntax

`public interface KeyListener extends EventListener`

Description

When an object (listener) wishes to receive key events from a component (the source component), two things must be done:

1. The listener must implement the `KeyListener` interface and all of the methods it requires.
2. The listener must be registered with the source component. It becomes registered by calling the source component's `addKeyListener()` method.

For more information about key events, see `KeyEvent`.

MEMBER SUMMARY	
Key Event Callback Methods	
keyPressed()	Called when a key on the keyboard is pressed.
keyReleased()	Called when a key on the keyboard is released.
keyTyped()	Called when a pressed key or key combination generates a key character.

See Also

java.awt.Component.addKeyListener(), java.util.EventListener, KeyAdapter, KeyEvent.

Example

See the KeyEvent class example.

keyPressed()

PURPOSE   Called when a key on the keyboard is pressed.

SYNTAX   public void keyPressed(KeyEvent evt)

DESCRIPTION   This method is called if the source component has the focus and a key is pressed on the keyboard. The identity of the key that was pressed can be retrieved by calling evt.getKeyCode(). If the system supports autorepeat, this method is called each time the key is repeated. See the KeyEvent.KEY_PRESSED for more details about key pressed events.

PARAMETERS

evt   The non-null key event.

EXAMPLE   See the KeyEvent class example.

keyReleased()

PURPOSE   Called when a key on the keyboard is released.

SYNTAX   public void keyReleased(KeyEvent evt)

DESCRIPTION   This method is called when a key is released. The identity of the key that was released can be retrieved by calling evt.getKeyCode(). See KeyEvent.KEY_RELEASED for details about key released events.

PARAMETERS

evt   The non-null key event.

EXAMPLE   See the KeyEvent class example.

keyTyped()

PURPOSE   Called when a pressed key or key combination generates a key character.

SYNTAX   `public void keyTyped(KeyEvent evt)`

DESCRIPTION   This method is called when a pressed key or key combination produces a key character. If the platform supports autorepeat, this method is called each time the key character is repeated. See KeyEvent.KEY_TYPED for details about key typed events.

PARAMETERS

evt   The non-null key event.

EXAMPLE   See the KeyEvent class example.

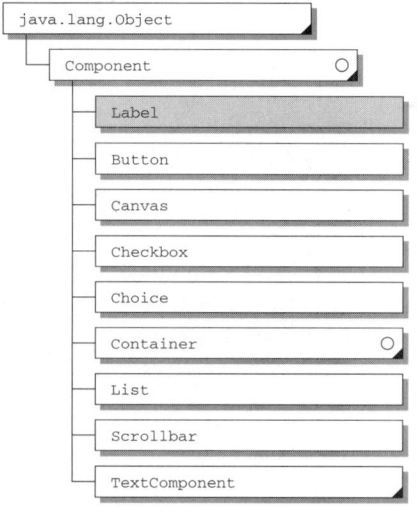

Syntax

```
public class Label extends Component
```

Description

A *label* is a component that displays a single line of text. The text can be modified by the program at any time but can never be modified by the user. A label is typically used in conjunction with other components that do not have labels, such as text fields and lists.

FIGURE 235: `Label`.

Label Alignment

A label has an alignment mode that controls the placement of the label's text in relation to the label's bounds. The text is always vertically centered but can be horizontally aligned to the left, center, or right.

Events

The label fires the same events as a component. See the `Component` class for more details.

A
B
C
D
E
F
G
H
I
J
K
M
N
O
P
Q
R
S
T
U
V
W
X
Y
Z

MEMBER SUMMARY	
Constructor	
Label()	Constructs a new Label instance.
Alignment Mode Constants	
CENTER	Specifies center alignment.
LEFT	Specifies left alignment.
RIGHT	Specifies right alignment.
Property Methods	
getAlignment()	Retrieves the label's alignment.
getText()	Retrieves the label's text.
setAlignment()	Sets the label's alignment.
setText()	Sets the label's text.
Peer Method	
addNotify()	Creates the label's peer.
Debugging Method	
paramString()	Generates a string representing the label's state.

Example

This example creates a label to serve as a status bar. The status bar displays mouse motion event information while the cursor is inside the frame's paintable area (see Figure 235).

```
import java.awt.*;
import java.awt.event.*;

public class Main extends Frame {
    Label statusBar = new Label();

    Main() {
        super("Label Example");
        add(statusBar, BorderLayout.SOUTH);
        addMouseMotionListener(new MouseMotionEventHandler());

        setSize(200, 200);
        show();
    }

    class MouseMotionEventHandler extends MouseMotionAdapter {
        private void updateStatus(MouseEvent evt) {
            String status = "("+evt.getX()+","+evt.getY()+") ";

            if (evt.isControlDown()) status += "C";
            if (evt.isShiftDown()) status += "S";
            if (evt.isMetaDown()) status += "M";
            if (evt.isAltDown()) status += "A";
```

```
            statusBar.setText(status);
        }
        public void mouseMoved(MouseEvent evt) {
            updateStatus(evt);
        }
        public void mouseDragged(MouseEvent evt) {
            updateStatus(evt);
        }
    }

    static public void main(String[] args) {
        new Main();
    }
}
```

addNotify()

PURPOSE   Creates the label's peer.

SYNTAX   `public void addNotify()`

DESCRIPTION   This method creates the label's peer if it does not exist. The peer is created by calling the `Toolkit.createLabel()` method. This method should never be called directly. It is normally called by the parent.

OVERRIDES   `Component.addNotify()`.

SEE ALSO   `Component, Toolkit`.

CENTER

PURPOSE   The alignment mode specifying center alignment.

SYNTAX   `public static final int CENTER`

DESCRIPTION   In center-alignment mode, the text is displayed in the center of the label.

EXAMPLE   See `setAlignment()`.

getAlignment()

PURPOSE   Retrieves the label's alignment.

SYNTAX   `public int getAlignment()`

RETURNS   The label's alignment. The return value is one of LEFT, CENTER, or RIGHT.

SEE ALSO   `setAlignment()`.

EXAMPLE   See `setAlignment()`.

A
B
C
D
E
F
G
H
I
J
K

M
N
O
P
Q
R
S
T
U
V
W
X
Y
Z

getText()
_____

PURPOSE	Retrieves the label's text.
SYNTAX	`public String getText()`
RETURNS	A non-`null` string containing the label's text.
SEE ALSO	`setText()`.
EXAMPLE	See `setText()`.

Label()
_____

PURPOSE	Constructs a new `Label` instance.

SYNTAX	`public Label()`
	`public Label(String text)`
	`public Label(String text, int alignment)`

DESCRIPTION	The three forms of this constructor create a new `Label` instance with the string text and the alignment `alignment`. If `label` is `null` or not specified, it defaults to "" (an empty string). If `alignment` is not specified, it defaults to LEFT.
PARAMETERS	
alignment	The label's alignment. It must be one of LEFT, CENTER, or RIGHT.
text	The string containing the label's text.
EXAMPLE	See the class example.

LEFT
_____

PURPOSE	The alignment mode specifying left alignment.
SYNTAX	`public static final int LEFT`
DESCRIPTION	In left-alignment mode, the left edge of the text is pinned to the left edge of the label.
EXAMPLE	See `setAlignment()`.

paramString()
_____

PURPOSE	Generates a string representing the label's state.
SYNTAX	`protected String paramString()`

DESCRIPTION   The returned string includes the label's alignment and text. A subclass of this class should override this method and return a concatenation of its state with the results of `super.paramString()`. This method is called by the `toString()` method and is typically used for debugging.

RETURNS   A non-`null` string representing the label's state.

OVERRIDES   `Component.paramString()`.

SEE ALSO   `Object.toString()`.

EXAMPLE   See `Component.paramString()`.

RIGHT

PURPOSE   The alignment mode specifying right alignment.

SYNTAX   `public static final int RIGHT`

DESCRIPTION   In right-alignment mode, the right edge text is pinned to the right edge of the label.

EXAMPLE   See `setAlignment()`.

setAlignment()

PURPOSE   Sets the label's alignment.

SYNTAX   `public synchronized void setAlignment(int alignment)`

DESCRIPTION   This method sets the label's alignment to be `alignment`.

PARAMETERS
`alignment`   The label's new alignment. It must be one of LEFT, CENTER, or RIGHT.

EXCEPTIONS
`IllegalArgumentException`
   If alignment is not one of the values LEFT, CENTER, or RIGHT.

SEE ALSO   `getAlignment()`.

EXAMPLE   This example creates a label and a checkbox group. Use the checkbox group to change the label's alignment. See Figure 236.

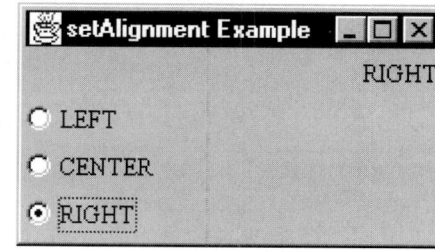

FIGURE 236: `Label.setAlignment()`.

A
B
C
D
E
F
G
H
I
J
K
L
M
N
O
P
Q
R
S
T
U
V
W
X
Y
Z

setText( )

```java
import java.awt.*;
import java.awt.event.*;

class Main extends Frame
    implements ItemListener {
    String[] alignLabels =
        {"LEFT", "CENTER", "RIGHT"};
    int[] alignValues =
        {Label.LEFT, Label.CENTER, Label.RIGHT};
    Label l = new Label("CENTER", Label.CENTER);

    Main() {
        super("setAlignment Example");
        CheckboxGroup cg = new CheckboxGroup();
        Panel p = new Panel(new GridLayout(3, 0));

        for (int i=0; i<alignLabels.length; i++) {
            Checkbox cb = new Checkbox(alignLabels[i], cg,
                l.getAlignment() == alignValues[i]);
            cb.addItemListener(this);
            p.add(cb);
        }
        add(p, BorderLayout.SOUTH);
        add(l, BorderLayout.CENTER);

        pack();
        show();
    }

    public void itemStateChanged(ItemEvent evt) {
        String target = (String)evt.getItem();
        for (int i=0; i<alignLabels.length; i++) {
            if (alignLabels[i].equals(target)) {
                l.setAlignment(alignValues[i]);
                l.setText(alignLabels[i]);
                return;
            }
        }
    }

    static public void main(String[] args) {
        new Main();
    }
}
```

setText( )

PURPOSE   Sets the label's text.

SYNTAX   `public synchronized void setText(String label)`

DESCRIPTION   This method sets the label's text to be the string `label`. If `label` is `null`, it is treated like an empty string "".

Note that the minimum and preferred sizes of the label may change, so it may be necessary to resize the label. The example shows how to cause the label's parent to resize the label.

PARAMETERS

`label`   The string specifying the label's new text. The value may be `null`.

SEE ALSO   `getText()`.

EXAMPLE   This example creates a label and a text field. Pressing Return while in the text field causes the label's text to be set to the contents of the text field. When the text changes, so does its minimum size. This example also shows how to cause the label's parent to properly resize the label. See Figure 237.

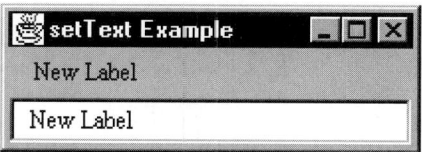

FIGURE 237: `Label.setText()`.

```java
import java.awt.*;
import java.awt.event.*;

class Main extends Frame implements ActionListener {
    Label l = new Label("Label");
    TextField tf = new TextField(40);

    Main() {
        super("setText Example");
        add(new Canvas(), BorderLayout.CENTER);
        add(l, BorderLayout.WEST);
        add(tf, BorderLayout.SOUTH);
        tf.setText(l.getText());    // init with current text
        tf.addActionListener(this);

        pack();
        show();
    }

    public void actionPerformed(ActionEvent evt) {
        l.setText(tf.getText());

        // the size has changed so get parent to validate itself.
        l.invalidate();
        l.getParent().validate();
    }

    static public void main(String[] args) {
        new Main();
    }
}
```

java.awt.peer
LabelPeer

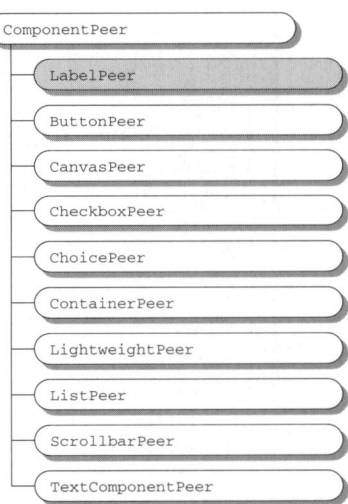

Syntax

```
public interface LabelPeer extends ComponentPeer
```

Description

The label component (see the Label class) in the AWT uses the platform's native implementation of a label. So that the AWT label behaves the same on all platforms, the label is assigned a *peer*, whose task is to translate the behavior of the platform's native label to the behavior of the AWT label.

AWT programmers normally do not directly use peer classes and interfaces. Instead, they deal with AWT components in the java.awt package. These in turn automatically manage their peers. Only someone who is porting the AWT to another platform should be concerned with the peer classes and interfaces. Consequently, most peer documentation refers to java.awt counterparts.

See Component and Toolkit for additional information about component peers.

MEMBER SUMMARY	
Peer Methods	
setAlignment()	Sets the label's alignment.
setText()	Sets the label's text.

See Also

java.awt.Component, java.awt.Label, java.awt.Toolkit.

setAlignment()

PURPOSE	Sets the label's alignment.
SYNTAX	void setAlignment(int alignment)
PARAMETERS	
alignment	The label's new alignment.
SEE ALSO	java.awt.Label.setAlignment().

setText()

PURPOSE	Sets the label's text.
SYNTAX	void setText(String label)
PARAMETERS	
label	The string specifying the label's new text. The value may be null.
SEE ALSO	java.awt.Label.setText().

A
B
C
D
E
F
G
H
I
J
K

M
N
O
P
Q
R
S
T
U
V
W
X
Y
Z

Syntax
`public interface LayoutManager`

Description

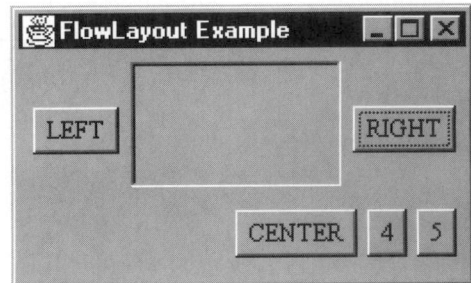

FIGURE 238: `FlowLayout`.

A layout manager is responsible for laying out components in a container. For example, the `FlowLayout` layout manager places the components in a left-right, top-down fashion. Figure 238 shows an example of a container with the `Flow-Layout` layout manager.

Typically, a newly created container has a default layout manager. For example, the default layout manager for the `Panel` container is `FlowLayout`. The layout manager for a container can be changed by calling `Container.setLayout()`, but deciding when it is safe to call this method is left to the layout manager. In general, any layout manager that maintains some state, such as the gridbag and border layout managers, can be safely set only when the container contains no components.

Container Validity

A container's layout manager is invoked only if the container is invalid. A container automatically becomes invalid if the container is resized or if a child component has been added, removed, or moved within the container. The system automatically calls the container's layout method if the user resizes the top-level window. However, if a container must be laid out again (perhaps because some layout parameter has changed), `Component.invalidate()` must be called on the container first, followed by `Component.validate()`.

Insets

When implementing the methods that return dimensions, you must always take into account the container's insets. That is, the components must be laid out within the area defined by the container's insets. See the `Container` class for a description of insets.

MEMBER SUMMARY	
Layout Manager Methods	
addLayoutComponent()	Adds a component to the layout.
layoutContainer()	Lays out the container in the specified panel.
removeLayoutComponent()	Removes the specified component from the layout.
Dimension Methods	
minimumLayoutSize()	Calculates the minimum size dimensions for the specified component.
preferredLayoutSize()	Calculates the preferred size dimensions for the specified component.

See Also

BorderLayout, CardLayout, FlowLayout, GridBagLayout, GridLayout, LayoutManager2.

Example

This example implements a layout manager that displays components in a horizontal or vertical list. See Figure 239. The name of the component specifies how the component should be stretched in the list. If the name is "*", the component will be stretched in both directions. If the name is "v", the component will be stretched only in the horizontal direction. If the name is "h", the component will be stretched only in the vertical direction. If the name is null or some other string, the component will not be stretched.

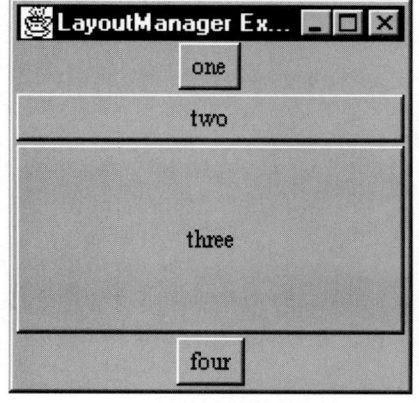

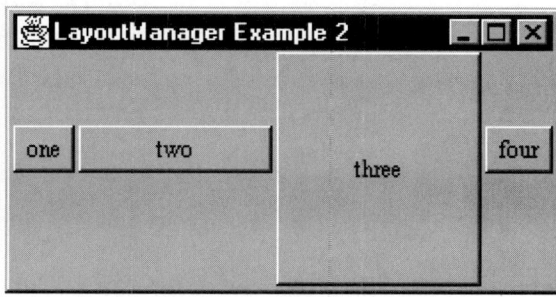

(a) Vertical List   (b) Horizontal List

FIGURE 239:   Vertical and Horizontal List Layouts.

```
import java.awt.*;
import java.util.*;

class Main extends Frame {
    Main(boolean vertical, String title) {
        super(title);
        setLayout(new FlexLayout(vertical, 2));
        add(new Button("one"));
        add("h", new Button("two"));
        add("*", new Button("three"));
        add(new Button("four"));

        setSize(100, 200);
        show();
    }
    public static void main(String args[]) {
        new Main(true, "LayoutManager Example 1");
        new Main(false, "LayoutManager Example 2");
    }
}

class FlexLayout implements LayoutManager {
    int gap;
    boolean ver;
    Hashtable comps = new Hashtable();

    public FlexLayout(boolean v, int gap) {
        ver = v;
        this.gap = gap;
    }

    public void addLayoutComponent(String name, Component comp) {
        comps.put(comp, name);
    }

    public void removeLayoutComponent(Component comp) {
        comps.remove(comp);
    }

    public Dimension layoutSize(Container parent, boolean minimum) {
        Insets insets = parent.getInsets();
        int w = 0, h = 0, n;

        // Grab tree lock to make sure components are not removed while
        // getting their sizes
        synchronized (parent.getTreeLock()) {
            n = parent.getComponentCount();

            for (int i=0; i<n; i++) {
                Component c = parent.getComponent(i);
                Dimension d = minimum ? c.getMinimumSize() :
                    c.getPreferredSize();

                if (ver) {
                    w = Math.max(w, d.width);
                    h += d.height;
                } else {
                    w += d.width;
                    h = Math.max(h, d.height);
                }
            }
```

A B C D E F G H I J K L M N O P Q R S T U V W X Y Z

```
        }
    }
    if (n > 0) {
        if (ver) {
            h += (n-1)*gap;
        } else {
            w += (n-1)*gap;
        }
    }
    return new Dimension(insets.left + insets.right + w,
                        insets.top + insets.bottom + h);
}

public Dimension minimumLayoutSize(Container parent) {
    return layoutSize(parent, true);
}

public Dimension preferredLayoutSize(Container parent) {
    return layoutSize(parent, false);
}

public boolean isFlexible(Component c, boolean v) {
    String name = (String)comps.get(c);
    if (name == null) {
        return false;
    } else if (name.equals("*")) {
        return true;
    } else if (v) {
        return name.equals("v");
    }
    return name.equals("h");
}

public void layoutContainer(Container parent) {
    Insets insets = parent.getInsets();
    Dimension dim = layoutSize(parent, false);

    // Grab tree lock to make sure components are not removed while
    // laying them out.
    synchronized (parent.getTreeLock()) {

        int n = parent.getComponentCount();
        int flexCnt = 0;
        int extra = 0;
        int add = 0;

        for (int i=0; i<n; i++) {
            if (isFlexible(parent.getComponent(i), ver)) {
                flexCnt++;
            }
        }
        if (flexCnt > 0) {
            if (ver) {
                extra = parent.getSize().height-dim.height;
            } else {
                extra = parent.getSize().width-dim.width;
            }
        }
        add = extra/flexCnt;
```

A
B
C
D
E
F
G
H
I
J
K
L
M
N
O
P
Q
R
S
T
U
V
W
X
Y
Z

```
                    if (ver) {
                        int y = insets.top;
                        for (int i=0; i<n; i++) {
                            int x = insets.left;
                            Component c = parent.getComponent(i);
                            String name = (String)comps.get(c);
                            Dimension d = c.getPreferredSize();

                            if (isFlexible(c, ver)) {
                                d.height += add;
                                extra -= add;
                                if (extra < 0) {     // adjust for round off error
                                    d.height += extra;
                                }
                            }
                            if (isFlexible(c, !ver)) {
                                d.width = parent.getSize().width -
                                    insets.left - insets.right;
                            } else {
                                x = (parent.getSize().width - d.width)/2;
                            }
                            c.setBounds(x, y, d.width, d.height);
                            y += d.height + gap;
                        }
                    } else {
                        int x = insets.left;
                        for (int i=0; i<n; i++) {
                            int y = insets.top;
                            Component c = parent.getComponent(i);
                            String name = (String)comps.get(c);
                            Dimension d = c.getPreferredSize();

                            if (isFlexible(c, ver)) {
                                d.width += add;
                                extra -= add;
                                if (extra < 0) {     // adjust for round off error
                                    d.width += extra;
                                }
                            }
                            if (isFlexible(c, !ver)) {
                                d.height = parent.getSize().height -
                                    insets.top - insets.bottom;
                            } else {
                                y = (parent.getSize().height - d.height)/2;
                            }
                            c.setBounds(x, y, d.width, d.height);
                            x += d.width + gap;
                        }
                    }
                }

        public String toString() {
            return getClass().getName() + "[ver=" + ver + ",gap=" + gap + "]";
        }
    }
```

addLayoutComponent()

PURPOSE   Adds a component to the layout manager's list of components.

SYNTAX   void addLayoutComponent(String name, Component comp)

DESCRIPTION   When a component is added to a container along with an accompanying name (i.e., the `Container.add(String, Component)` method is called), the container not only adds the component to its list of components but also calls this method with the component and its name. The container does not call this method if the component is added without a name (`null` is a valid name). The container does not use the component name at all. Nor does it remember the name. So this method must maintain the name-component association if necessary.

The name is, more accurately, layout information that the layout manager uses to place the component. The name does not have to be unique. Nor does it have to be non-`null`—it's up to the layout manager to decide what is a valid name. For example, in the `BorderLayout` layout manager, the name determines at which edge the component should be placed. Using the name "North" causes the component to be placed against the top edge of the container. `BorderLayout` expects the names of the components to be chosen from a fixed set of names and to be unique; the results are undefined if this rule is violated.

By the time this method is called, `comp` is already added to the container and a peer is created if necessary.

Note that the `Container` class does not include an `add()` method in which both the name and a position can be specified. To work around this deficiency, you can first insert the component without an accompanying name and then call `addLayoutComponent()` directly to assign a name to the component.

PARAMETERS
comp   The non-`null` named component that has just been added to the container.
name   A possibly `null` string specifying the name of the component.

SEE ALSO   `Container.add()`, `LayoutManager2.addLayoutComponent()`.

EXAMPLE   See the class example.

layoutContainer()

PURPOSE   Lays out the components in a container.

SYNTAX   void layoutContainer(Container cont)

DESCRIPTION   This method is called by the container's parent to lay out the components in `cont`. The size of `cont` can be retrieved by calling `cont.getSize()`, which

A
B
C
D
E
F
G
H
I
J
K
L
M
N
O
P
Q
R
S
T
U
V
W
X
Y
Z

will include the container's insets. The components should be laid out using `Component.setBounds()` and placed inside the area defined by the insets. When the dimensions of a component are retrieved, the component's preferred size should be used.

PARAMETERS

   `cont`   The non-null container using this layout instance.

EXAMPLE   See the class example.

minimumLayoutSize()

PURPOSE   Calculates the layout's minimum size dimensions.

SYNTAX   `Dimension minimumLayoutSize(Container cont)`

DESCRIPTION   This method calculates the minimum size dimensions for the container `cont`. The minimum sizes of the components are used in the calculations. The result includes the container's insets.

PARAMETERS

   `cont`   The non-null container using this layout instance.

RETURNS   The non-null dimension containing the container's preferred size.

SEE ALSO   `Component.getMinimumSize()`, `LayoutManager2.maximumLayoutSize()`, `preferredLayoutSize()`.

EXAMPLE   See the class example.

preferredLayoutSize()

PURPOSE   Calculates the layout's preferred size dimensions.

SYNTAX   `Dimension preferredLayoutSize(Container cont)`

DESCRIPTION   This method calculates the preferred size dimensions for the container `cont`. The preferred sizes of the components are used in the calculations. The result includes the container's insets.

PARAMETERS

   `cont`   The non-null container using this layout instance.

RETURNS   The non-null dimension containing the container's preferred size.

SEE ALSO   `Component.getPreferredSize()`, `LayoutManager2.maximumLayoutSize()`, `minimumLayoutSize()`.

EXAMPLE   See the class example.

removeLayoutComponent( )

PURPOSE	Removes a component from the layout manager's list of components.
SYNTAX	`void removeLayoutComponent(Component comp)`
DESCRIPTION	This method is called by a container whenever a component is removed from the container, regardless of whether the component was named. At the time this method is called, `comp` is not yet removed from the container.
PARAMETERS	
comp	The non-`null` component about to be removed from the container.
EXAMPLE	See the class example.

A
B
C
D
E
F
G
H
I
J
K

M
N
O
P
Q
R
S
T
U
V
W
X
Y
Z

Syntax

`public interface LayoutManager2 extends LayoutManager`

Description

This interface is an extension of `LayoutManager` that adds a few new methods to support alignment-based layout. These methods really belong in `LayoutManager`; they were not added so as to maintain compatibility with `LayoutManager` in Java 1.0. If they were included, all layout managers would fail to load in the Java 1.1 runtime because they would lack implementations for them. New layout managers should implement `LayoutManager2` rather than `LayoutManager`.

The Alignment Point on Components

A component has an alignment property that specifies an *alignment point* on the component. By default, the alignment point is the component's center. It is a value that affects how some layout managers do their layout. How a layout manager uses the alignment property differs by manager. For example, one type of layout manager could draw lines between the alignment points. Another could overlap all of its children so that their alignment points are coincident. Some may completely ignore the alignment property.

The alignment property is a pair of floating-point values—one that specifies the *x*-alignment and one that specifies the *y*-alignment. Together, the values specify the alignment point. In particular, the alignment point on a component c is

$$(x\_alignment * c.width, y\_alignment * c.height)$$

The alignment values lie in the range 0.0 to 1.0. For example, an alignment value of (0.0, 0.0) specifies the top-left corner of the component, while an alignment value of (0.5, 0.5) specifies the center of the component. Notice that the alignment point cannot be outside the bounds of the component.

Note: In Java 1.1.2, none of the AWT layout managers use a component's alignment property yet.

The Alignment Point on Containers

The alignment point for a container is determined by its layout manager. A layout manager may return a constant alignment point value, which is usually (0.5, 0.5). Or it first may need to lay out its children before it can determine the alignment point value. For instance, the layout manager in the class example places all of the components so that their y-alignment coordinates are colinear. This line determines the y-alignment value of the layout manager and of the container. The layout manager cannot determine the location of this line until it has laid out all of the components and adjusted its height so that all of the components are fully visible.

Setting Alignments

There are no methods for setting the alignment property. For a component to change the default alignments, it must override the "get alignment" methods and return the desired results. This means that you cannot change a component's alignment; the component must do it itself. If the ability to change the component's alignment is necessary, the component needs to provide its own "set alignment" methods.

MEMBER SUMMARY

Layout Manager Methods
addLayoutComponent()	Adds a component to the layout manager's list of components.
invalidateLayout()	Invalidates the layout manager.

Alignment Methods
getLayoutAlignmentX()	Calculates the layout manager's x-alignment value.
getLayoutAlignmentY()	Calculates the layout manager's y-alignment value.

Dimension Method
maximumLayoutSize()	Calculates the layout's maximum size dimensions.

See Also

Component, Container, LayoutManager.

Example

This example implements a special component that simply paints the word "java." The component can paint the word in different point sizes. By clicking the component with the left mouse button (button 1), you can increase the point size of the font; clicking with the right mouse button (button 3) decreases the point size. The size of the component is exactly the dimensions needed to display the string in the current point size (plus a half of a space character on the left and right side of the string).

The component also has an alignment value that is based on the string in its current point size. In particular, the x-alignment is always 0.5, but its y-alignment is such that it matches the font's baseline (see FontMetrics). For example, if the baseline is two-thirds from the top, the *y*-alignment would be 0.67. To help you see the baseline, the component draws a line on its baseline.

This example also implements a layout manager that lays out its children horizontally, like the flow layout manager does. However, it uses the component's *y*-alignment property to align the components vertically so that the *y*-coordinates of their alignment points are colinear. See Figure 240. The preferred width of the layout manager is the total width of the components. The preferred height is the height necessary for all of the components to be visible after their *y*-alignment points have been lined up.

The layout manager's *y*-alignment value is determined by the location of the baseline after the component's

FIGURE 240:   Baseline-aligned Components.

y-alignment points have been lined up. If the fonts used in all of the components are the same (as in this example), then the *y*-alignment of the layout manager is essentially the same as that of the component with the largest point size. This means that if you nest containers using this layout manager, all of the components will line up, no matter what containers they are in. This example demonstrates this by nesting a container of components.

To see different types of alignments, you can change a component's alignment by clicking it when the Shift key is held down. This changes the alignment from

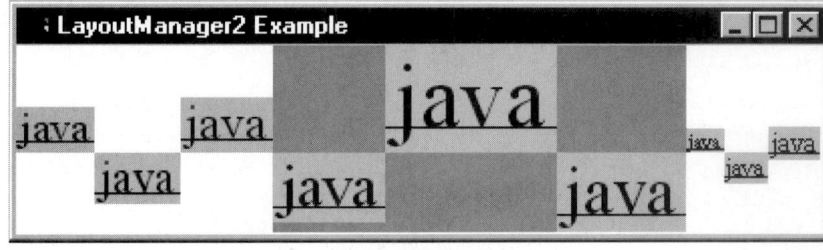

FIGURE 241:   Top- and Bottom-aligned Components.

baseline, to center, to top, and then to bottom. Figure 241 shows the components alternating between top and bottom alignment.

Finally, the component is made focus-traversable (see `Component.isFocusTraversable()`) (for no particular reason except for demonstrative purposes). Pressing the Tab or Shift-Tab keys moves the focus from one component to the next. Notice that when the focus reaches the container, the focus is given to a component inside the container.

```
import java.awt.*;
import java.awt.event.*;

class Main extends Frame {
    Main() {
        super("LayoutManager2 Example");
        setLayout(new TextFlowLayout());
```

```
        // Add a few of our special labels.
        for (int i=0; i<3; i++) {
            add(new LabelComponent("java", 20+2*i));
        }

        // Now add a container with a few of our special labels.
        Panel p = new Panel(new TextFlowLayout());
        p.setBackground(Color.green);
        for (int i=0; i<3; i++) {
            p.add(new LabelComponent("java", 30+2*i));
        }
        add(p);

        // Add a few more special labels.
        for (int i=0; i<3; i++) {
            add(new LabelComponent("java", 10+2*i));
        }

        pack();
        show();
    }

    public static void main(String[] args) {
        new Main();
    }
}

class TextFlowLayout implements LayoutManager2 {
    // If < 0, the layout is invalid.
    int maxAscent = -1;
    int maxDescent = 0;

    // type=0->minimum, type=1->preferred, type=2->maximum.
    public Dimension layoutSize(Container cont, int type) {
        Insets insets = cont.getInsets();
        int w = 0;

        // Grab tree lock to make sure components are not removed while
        // getting their sizes
        synchronized (cont.getTreeLock()) {
            Dimension d = new Dimension(0, 0);
            maxAscent = 0;
            maxDescent = 0;

            for (int i=0; i<cont.getComponentCount(); i++) {
                Component c = cont.getComponent(i);

                switch (type) {
                  case 0:
                    d = c.getMinimumSize();
                    break;
                  case 1:
                    d = c.getPreferredSize();
                    break;
                  case 2:
                    d = c.getMaximumSize();
                    break;
                }
```

A
B
C
D
E
F
G
H
I
J
K
L
M
N
O
P
Q
R
S
T
U
V
W
X
Y
Z

```
                                int a = (int)(c.getAlignmentY()*d.height);
                                maxAscent = Math.max(maxAscent, a);
                                maxDescent = Math.max(maxDescent, d.height-a);
                                w += d.width;
                            }
                        }
                        return new Dimension(insets.left + insets.right + w,
                            insets.top + insets.bottom + maxAscent+maxDescent);
                    }

                    public Dimension minimumLayoutSize(Container cont) {
                        return layoutSize(cont, 0);
                    }
                    public Dimension preferredLayoutSize(Container cont) {
                        return layoutSize(cont, 1);
                    }
                    public Dimension maximumLayoutSize(Container cont) {
                        return layoutSize(cont, 2);
                    }

                    public void layoutContainer(Container cont) {
                        Insets insets = cont.getInsets();
                        if (maxAscent < 0) {
                            layoutSize(cont, 1);
                        }

                        // Grab tree lock to make sure components are not removed while
                        // laying them out.
                        synchronized (cont.getTreeLock()) {
                            int x = insets.left;

                            for (int i=0; i<cont.getComponentCount(); i++) {
                                Component c = cont.getComponent(i);
                                Dimension d = c.getPreferredSize();

                                c.setBounds(x,
                                    insets.top + (int)(maxAscent-d.height*c.getAlignmentY()),
                                    d.width, d.height);
                                x += d.width;
                            }
                        }
                    }

                    public float getLayoutAlignmentX(Container cont) {
                        return 0.5f;
                    }
                    public float getLayoutAlignmentY(Container cont) {
                        if (maxAscent < 0) {
                            layoutSize(cont, 1);
                        }
                        if (maxAscent > 0) {
                            return (float)maxAscent / (float)(maxAscent+maxDescent);
                        }
                        return 0.5f;
                    }
                    public void invalidateLayout(Container cont) {
                        maxAscent = -1;
                    }

                    // These methods are not used.
```

```
        public void addLayoutComponent(String name, Component comp) {
        }
        public void addLayoutComponent(Component comp, Object constraints) {
        }
        public void removeLayoutComponent(Component comp) {
        }
}

class LabelComponent extends Canvas {
    String label;
    Font font;
    FontMetrics fontM;
    boolean hasFocus = false;
    int curAlignment = 0;
    float[] alignments = {-1.0f, //   baseline alignment
        Component.CENTER_ALIGNMENT,
        Component.TOP_ALIGNMENT,
        Component.BOTTOM_ALIGNMENT};

    LabelComponent(String label, int size) {
        this.label = label;
        font = new Font("Serif", Font.PLAIN, size);
        fontM = getFontMetrics(font);

        // Listen for mouse events.
        addMouseListener(new MouseEventHandler());
        addFocusListener(new FocusEventHandler());
    }

    public float getAlignmentY() {
        if (alignments[curAlignment] == -1.0f) {
            return (float)fontM.getAscent() / (float)fontM.getHeight();
        } else {
            return alignments[curAlignment];
        }
    }

    public Dimension getPreferredSize() {
        int space = fontM.charWidth(' ');
        return new Dimension(space + fontM.stringWidth(label),
            fontM.getHeight());
    }

    public void paint(Graphics g) {
        if (hasFocus) {
            g.setColor(Color.pink);
        } else {
            g.setColor(Color.lightGray);
        }
        g.fillRect(0, 0, getSize().width, getSize().height);
        g.setColor(Color.black);

        // The following isn't necessary in a native component.
        g.setFont(font);
        FontMetrics fontM = g.getFontMetrics();

        g.drawString(label, fontM.charWidth(' ')/2, fontM.getAscent());

        // Draw baseline.
        g.drawLine(0, fontM.getAscent(), getSize().width, fontM.getAscent());
```

```
            }

            public boolean isFocusTraversable() {
                return true;
            }

            class MouseEventHandler extends MouseAdapter {
                public void mousePressed(MouseEvent evt) {
                    int inc = 0;

                    if (evt.isShiftDown()) {
                        // Change the alignment.
                        curAlignment = (curAlignment + 1) % alignments.length;
                    } else if ((evt.getModifiers() & InputEvent.BUTTON3_MASK) != 0) {
                        // Decrease the font size.
                        if (font.getSize() > 6) {
                            inc = -1;
                        }
                    } else {
                        // Increase the font size.
                        inc = 1;
                    }

                    font = new Font(font.getFamily(), font.getStyle(),
                        font.getSize() + inc);
                    fontM = getFontMetrics(font);

                    // Invalidate current component and validate the entire frame.
                    invalidate();

                    // Find the top-level window.
                    Component c = getParent();
                    while (c != null) {
                        if (c instanceof Window) {
                            break;
                        }
                        c = c.getParent();
                    }

                    // Validate the whole tree.
                    if (c != null) {
                        c.validate();
                    }
                    requestFocus();
                    repaint();
                }
            }
            class FocusEventHandler extends FocusAdapter {
                public void focusGained(FocusEvent evt) {
                    hasFocus = true;
                    repaint();
                }
                public void focusLost(FocusEvent evt) {
                    hasFocus = false;
                    repaint();
                }
            }
        }
    }
```

A
B
C
D
E
F
G
H
I
J
K
M
N
O
P
Q
R
S
T
U
V
W
X
Y
Z

addLayoutComponent()

PURPOSE Adds a component to the layout manager's list of components.

SYNTAX `void addLayoutComponent(Component comp, Object constraints)`

DESCRIPTION When a component is added to a container along with an accompanying constraint object (in other words, the `Container.add(Component, Object)` method is called), the container not only adds the component to its list of components but also calls this method with the component and its constraints. The container does not use or remember the constraint object at all, so this method must maintain the component-constraint association if necessary.

The constraint is, more accurately, layout information that the layout manager uses to place the component. There is no special constraint class from which all constraints are derived. Instead, the constraint is an object that is specific to the layout manager. For example, the gridbag layout manager (see `GridBag-Layout`) understands only constraints that are gridbag constraint objects (see `GridBagConstraints`).

By the time this method is called, comp is already added to the container and a peer is created if necessary.

The layout manager does not need to invalidate its layout, since the container will have called `invalidateLayout()`.

PARAMETERS

comp The non-`null` component that has just been added to the container.

constraints A possibly `null` constraint object that is specific to this layout manager.

SEE ALSO `Container.add()`, `LayoutManager.addLayoutComponent()`.

EXAMPLE See the class example.

getLayoutAlignmentX()

PURPOSE Calculates the layout manager's x-alignment value.

SYNTAX `public float getLayoutAlignmentX(Container cont)`

DESCRIPTION The returned alignment value may be a constant, or it may depend on how the components are laid out. The returned value becomes the container's x-alignment value. See the class description for more information.

PARAMETERS

cont The non-`null` container using this layout instance.

RETURNS A `float` in the range `0.0` to `1.0`.

A
B
C
D
E
F
G
H
I
J
K

M
N
O
P
Q
R
S
T
U
V
W
X
Y
Z

SEE ALSO	`Component.getAlignmentX()`, `Container.getAlignmentX()`, `getLayoutAlignmentY()`.
EXAMPLE	See the class example.

getLayoutAlignmentY()

PURPOSE	Calculates the layout manager's *y*-alignment value.
SYNTAX	`public float getLayoutAlignmentY(Container cont)`
DESCRIPTION	The returned alignment value may be a constant, or it may depend on how the components are laid out. The returned value becomes the container's *y*-alignment value. See the class description for more information.
PARAMETERS	
`cont`	The non-`null` container using this layout instance.
RETURNS	A `float` in the range `0.0` to `1.0`.
SEE ALSO	`Component.getAlignmentY()`, `Container.getAlignmentY()`, `getLayoutAlignmentX()`.
EXAMPLE	See the class example.

invalidateLayout()

PURPOSE	Invalidates the layout manager.
SYNTAX	`public void invalidateLayout(Container cont)`
DESCRIPTION	This method is called whenever the container `cont` is invalidated. This method would be useful if the layout manager kept some state about the layout of the components. It might do this for performance reasons. This method would inform the layout manager that this state should no longer be used. Therefore it should recompute the layout or size the next time the `layoutContainer()` method or the layout size methods are called.
PARAMETERS	
`cont`	The non-`null` container using this layout instance.
SEE ALSO	`LayoutManager.layoutContainer()`.
EXAMPLE	See the class example.

maximumLayoutSize()

PURPOSE   Calculates the layout's maximum size dimensions.

SYNTAX   `public Dimension maximumLayoutSize(Container cont)`

DESCRIPTION   This method calculates the maximum size dimensions for the container `cont`. The maximum sizes of the components are used in the calculations. The result includes the container's insets.

PARAMETERS
cont   The non-`null` container using this layout instance.

RETURNS   The non-null dimension containing the container's maximum size.

SEE ALSO   `Component.getMaximumSize()`, `Container`, `LayoutManager.minimumLayoutSize()`, `LayoutManager.preferredLayoutSize()`.

EXAMPLE   See the `Component` class example.

A
B
C
D
E
F
G
H
I
J
K
L
M
N
O
P
Q
R
S
T
U
V
W
X
Y
Z

Syntax

```
public interface LightweightPeer extends ComponentPeer
```

Description

So that an AWT component behaves the same on all platforms, the component is assigned a *peer,* whose task is to translate the behavior of the platform's native component to the behavior of the AWT component. A *lightweight component* is a component that does not have a native peer. It is rendered to a representation in the native windowing system using the native peer of its first ancestor that has a native peer. A lightweight component is assigned a *lightweight peer*, instead of a native peer, to accept and propagate methods on the component to its native ancestor.

AWT programmers normally do not directly use peer classes and interfaces. Instead, they deal with AWT components in the `java.awt` package. These in turn automatically manage their peers. Only someone who is porting the AWT to another platform or building new lightweight toolkits should be concerned with the peer classes and interfaces. Consequently, most peer documentation refers to `java.awt` counterparts.

See `Component` and `Toolkit` for additional information about component peers.

See Also

`java.awt.Component`, `java.awt.Toolkit`.

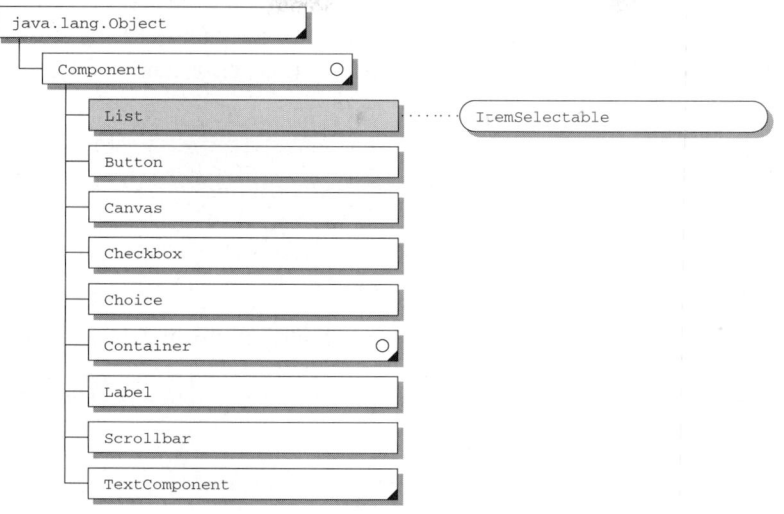

Syntax

`public class List extends Component implements ItemSelectable`

Description

The *list component* is a scrollable vertical list of string items. The user can select an item from the list. See Figure 242.

FIGURE 242: `List`.

Selection Modes and Selected Items

The list component can be in either single- or multiple-selection mode. When it is in single-selection mode, only one item can be selected at a time. When it is in multiple-selection mode, more than one item can be selected at one time. The gesture by which a selected item is deselected depends on the platform. For example, on Windows 95 a selected item is deselected by a click on the selected item.

The `List` class provides methods to modify and retrieve the set of selected items.

Events

A list fires an item event whenever the user selects or deselects one of its item. The item of the item event is the newly selected/deselected item. Even if the selected item is reselected, an item event is fired, since the modifier keys may have changed. In single-selection mode, the previously selected item does not fire an event indicating that it has been deselected. See `ItemEvent` for more details on item events.

A list fires an action event whenever the user double-clicks an item. The action command of the action event is the item that was double-clicked. See `ActionEvent` for more details on action events.

A list also fires all of the events fired by the `Component` class. See the `Component` class for details. See the `AWTEvent` class for details on how to filter or handle events.

MEMBER SUMMARY	
Constructor	
List()	Constructs a new `List` instance.
Visibility Methods	
getVisibleIndex()	Retrieves the index of the item that was last made visible.
makeVisible()	Scrolls this list so that an item is visible.
Item Methods	
add()	Adds an item to this list.
addItem()	Adds an item to this list.
delItem()	Deletes an item from this list.
getItem()	Retrieves an item from this list.
getItemCount()	Retrieves the number of items in this list.
getItems()	Retrieves the items in this list.
getRows()	Retrieves the number of rows in this list.
remove()	Removes an item from this list.
removeAll()	Removes all items from this list.
replaceItem()	Replaces an item in this list.
Selection Methods	
deselect()	Deselects an item in this list.
getSelectedIndex()	Retrieves the index of the selected item.
getSelectedIndexes()	Retrieves the indexes of the selected item.
getSelectedItem()	Retrieves this list's selected item.
getSelectedItems()	Retrieves this list's selected items.
getSelectedObjects()	Retrieves this list's currently selected items.
isIndexSelected()	Determines whether the item at an index is selected.
isMultipleMode()	Retrieves this list's selection mode.
select()	Selects an item in this list.
setMultipleMode()	Sets this list's selection mode.
Event Methods	
addActionListener()	Adds a listener to receive action events fired by this list.
addItemListener()	Adds a listener to receive item events fired by this list.
processEvent()	Processes an event enabled for this list.
processActionEvent()	Processes an action event enabled for this list.

MEMBER SUMMARY	
processItemEvent()	Processes an item event enabled for this list.
removeActionListener()	Removes a listener from receiving action events fired by this list.
removeItemListener()	Removes a listener from receiving item events fired by this list.
Layout Methods	
getMinimumSize()	Calculates the minimum dimensions of this list.
getPreferredSize()	Calculates the preferred dimensions needed for this list.
Peer Methods	
addNotify()	Creates this list's peer.
removeNotify()	Destroys this list's peer.
Debugging Method	
paramString()	Generates a string representing this list's state.
Deprecated Methods	
allowsMultipleSelections()	Replaced by isMultipleMode().
clear()	Replaced by removeAll().
countItems	Replaced by getItemCount().
delItems()	Replaced by multiple invocations of remove().
isSelected()	Replaced by isIndexSelected().
minimumSize()	Replaced by getMinimumSize().
preferredSize()	Replaced by getPreferredSize().
setMultipleSelections()	Replaced by setMultipleMode().

See Also

java.awt.event.ActionEvent, java.awt.event.ActionListener,
java.awt.event.ItemEvent, java.awt.event.ItemListener.

Example

For a simple example using the list component, see the example for the List() constructor. The more elaborate example presented here creates two lists and several buttons for moving items from one list to the other. See Figure 243. One or more items on either list can be selected and then moved to the other list. Making a selection on one list automatically clears all of the selections on the other list. Double-clicking an item adds an asterisk to the item's name (this was done just to demonstrate the use of replaceItem()).

A
B
C
D
E
F
G
H
I
J
K
M
N
O
P
Q
R
S
T
U
V
W
X
Y
Z

The > button moves the selected items in the left list to the right list; the < button does the opposite. The >> button moves all of the items in the left list to the right list; the << button does the opposite. The ! button deselects the selected items and selects unselected items. This operation is applied to the list that has at least one selection. If neither list has any selections, this operation is ignored.

The example uses a grid bag layout manager (see GridBagLayout) to lay out the lists and buttons. The center column is not given any weight, so the first and last columns stretch with the window.

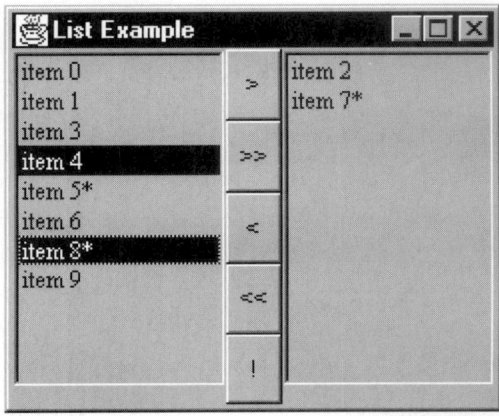

FIGURE 243: **Moving Items between Lists.**

```java
import java.awt.*;
import java.awt.event.*;

class Main extends Frame implements ActionListener, ItemListener {
    final static int ITEMS = 10;
    List ltList = new List(ITEMS, true);
    List rtList = new List(0, true);

    Main() {
        super("List Example");
        GridBagLayout gbl = new GridBagLayout();

        setLayout(gbl);
        add(ltList, 0, 0, 1, 5, 1.0, 1.0);
        add(rtList, 2, 0, 1, 5, 1.0, 1.0);
        // Add action and item listeners to list
        ltList.addActionListener(this);
        ltList.addItemListener(this);
        rtList.addActionListener(this);
        rtList.addItemListener(this);

        // Create buttons for adding/removing items from lists
        Button b;
        add(b = new Button(">"), 1, 0, 1, 1, 0, 1.0);
        b.addActionListener(this);
        add(b = new Button(">>"), 1, 1, 1, 1, 0, 1.0);
        b.addActionListener(this);
        add(b = new Button("<"), 1, 2, 1, 1, 0, 1.0);
        b.addActionListener(this);
        add(b = new Button("<<"), 1, 3, 1, 1, 0, 1.0);
        b.addActionListener(this);
        add(b = new Button("!"), 1, 4, 1, 1, 0, 1.0);
        b.addActionListener(this);

        for (int i=0; i<ITEMS; i++) {
            ltList.add("item "+i);
        }
        pack();
        show();
```

```
    }

    void add(Component comp,
            int x, int y, int w, int h, double weightx, double weighty) {
        GridBagLayout gbl = (GridBagLayout)getLayout();
        GridBagConstraints c = new GridBagConstraints();

        c.fill = GridBagConstraints.BOTH;
        c.gridx = x;
        c.gridy = y;
        c.gridwidth = w;
        c.gridheight = h;
        c.weightx = weightx;
        c.weighty = weighty;
        add(comp);
        gbl.setConstraints(comp, c);
    }

    void reverseSelections(List l) {
        for (int i=0; i<l.getItemCount(); i++) {
            if (l.isIndexSelected(i)) {
                l.deselect(i);
            } else {
                l.select(i);
            }
        }
    }

    void deselectAll(List l) {
        for (int i=0; i<l.getItemCount(); i++) {
            l.deselect(i);
        }
    }

    void replaceItem(List l, String item) {
        for (int i=0; i<l.getItemCount(); i++) {
            if (l.getItem(i).equals(item)) {
                l.replaceItem(item + "*", i);
            }
        }
    }

    void move(List l1, List l2, boolean all) {
        if (all) {
            for (int i=0; i<l1.getItemCount(); i++) {
                l2.add(l1.getItem(i));
            }
            l1.removeAll();
        } else {
            String[] items = l1.getSelectedItems();
            int[] itemIndexes = l1.getSelectedIndexes();

            deselectAll(l2);
            for (int i=0; i<items.length; i++) {
                l2.add(items[i]);          // add it
                l2.select(l2.getItemCount()-1);// and select it
                if (i == 0) {
                    l2.makeVisible(l2.getItemCount()-1);
                }
            }
        }
```

A
B
C
D
E
F
G
H
I
J
K
L
M
N
O
P
Q
R
S
T
U
V
W
X
Y
Z

```
                    for (int i=itemIndexes.length-1; i>=0; i--) {
                        ll.remove(itemIndexes[i]);
                    }
                }
            }

            public void actionPerformed(ActionEvent evt) {
                String arg = evt.getActionCommand();
                if (">".equals(arg)) {
                    move(ltList, rtList, false);
                } else if (">>".equals(arg)) {
                    move(ltList, rtList, true);
                } else if ("<".equals(arg)) {
                    move(rtList, ltList, false);
                } else if ("<<".equals(arg)) {
                    move(rtList, ltList, true);
                } else if ("!".equals(arg)) {
                    if (ltList.getSelectedItems().length > 0) {
                        reverseSelections(ltList);
                    } else if (rtList.getSelectedItems().length > 0) {
                        reverseSelections(rtList);
                    }
                } else {
                    Object target = evt.getSource();
                    if (target == rtList || target == ltList) {
                        replaceItem((List)target, arg);
                    }
                }
            }

            public void itemStateChanged(ItemEvent evt) {
                List target = (List)evt.getSource();
                if (target == ltList) {
                    deselectAll(rtList);
                } else if (target == rtList) {
                    deselectAll(ltList);
                }
            }

            public static void main(String[] args) {
                new Main();
            }
        }
```

add()

PURPOSE	Adds an item to this list.
SYNTAX	`public void add(String item)` `public synchronized void add(String item, int index)`
DESCRIPTION	This method adds the item `item` to this list. `index` specifies the index in this list at which to add `item`. If `index` is not specified or is −1 or greater than the

number of items in this list, item is added to the end of this list. If index is 0, the item becomes the first item in this list.

The set of selected items does not change.

This method is the same as addItem().

PARAMETERS

index   The zero-based index at which to add the item. If −1, add to the end of the list.

item   A non-null string to be added to this list.

SEE ALSO   addItem(), remove().

EXAMPLE   See the class example.

addActionListener()

PURPOSE   Adds a listener to receive action events fired by this list.

SYNTAX   `public synchronized void addActionListener(ActionListener listener)`

DESCRIPTION   An action event is fired when the mouse is double-clicked on an item in this list. See ActionEvent for more details. After this method is called, the action listener listener will receive action events fired by this list. If listener is null, this method does nothing.

PARAMETERS

listener   The possibly null action listener to add.

SEE ALSO   java.awt.event.ActionEvent, java.awt.event.ActionListener, removeActionListener().

EXAMPLE   See the List() example and the class example.

addItem()

PURPOSE   Adds an item to this list.

SYNTAX   `public void addItem(String item)`
`public synchronized void addItem(String item, int index)`

DESCRIPTION   This method adds the item item to this list. index specifies the index in this list at which to add item. If index is not specified or is −1 or greater than the number of items in this list, item is added to the end of this list. If index is 0, the item becomes the first item in this list.

The set of selected items does not change.

This method is the same as `add()`.

PARAMETERS

index   The `zero-based` index at which to add the item; if -1, add to the end of the list.

item   A non-`null` string to be added to this list.

SEE ALSO   `add()`, `remove()`.

EXAMPLE   In addition to the following example, see a similar usage of `add()` in the class example.

```
import java.awt.*;

class Main {
    final static int ITEMS = 10;
    static public void main(String[] args) {
        Frame f = new Frame("addItem Example");
        List l = new List(ITEMS, false);

        for (int i = 0; i < ITEMS; i++) {
            l.addItem("item "+i, 0);  // always insert at beginning
        }
        f.add(l, BorderLayout.CENTER);
        f.pack();
        f.show();
    }
}
```

addItemListener()

PURPOSE   Adds a listener to receive item events fired by this list.

SYNTAX   `public synchronized void addItemListener(ItemListener listener)`

DESCRIPTION   An item event is fired when an item in this list is selected or deselected. See `ItemEvent` and the class description for more details. After this method is called, the item listener `listener` will receive item events fired by this list. If `listener` is `null`, this method does nothing.

PARAMETERS

listener   The possibly `null` item listener to add.

SEE ALSO   `ItemSelectable`, `java.awt.event.ItemEvent`, `java.awt.event.ItemListener`, `removeItemListener()`.

EXAMPLE   See the class example.

addNotify()

PURPOSE	Creates this list's peer.
SYNTAX	`public void addNotify()`
DESCRIPTION	This method calls the `Toolkit.createList()` method to create this list's peer. This method should never be called directly. It is normally called by the component's container.
OVERRIDES	`Component.addNotify()`.
SEE ALSO	`Container, Toolkit`.
EXAMPLE	See `Component.setVisible()`.

allowsMultipleSelections()   *DEPRECATED*

PURPOSE	Replaced by `isMultipleMode()`.
SYNTAX	`public boolean allowsMultipleSelections()`
RETURNS	`true` if this list is in multiple-selection mode; `false` otherwise.
DEPRECATION	Replace the usage of this deprecated method, as in

```
    if (list.allowsMultipleSelections()) ...
```
with
```
    if (list.isMultipleMode()) ...
```

clear()   *DEPRECATED*

PURPOSE	Replaced by `removeAll()`.
SYNTAX	`public synchronized void clear()`
DEPRECATION	Replace the usage of this deprecated method, as in

```
    list.clear();
```
with
```
    list.removeAll();
```

countItems()   *DEPRECATED*

PURPOSE	Replaced by `getItemCount()`.
SYNTAX	`public int countItems()`
RETURNS	The number of items in this list. The result is always $>= 0$.
DEPRECATION	Replace the usage of this deprecated method, as in

```
        int num = list.countItems();
with
        int num = list.getItemCount();
```

delItem( )

PURPOSE	Deletes an item from this list.
SYNTAX	`public synchronized void delItem(int index)`
DESCRIPTION	This method deletes the item at index `index` from this list. It does not affect the selected state of the other items in this list.
	This method is the same as the form of `remove()` that accepts an index.
PARAMETERS	
`index`	The zero-based index of the item in this list.
EXCEPTIONS	
`ArrayIndexOutOfBoundsException`	
	If `index` is less than 0 or greater than `getItemCount()-1`.
SEE ALSO	`java.lang.ArrayIndexOutOfBoundsException`, `remove()`, `removeAll()`.
EXAMPLE	See the class example.

delItems( )   *DEPRECATED*

PURPOSE	Replaced by multiple invocations of `remove()`.
SYNTAX	`public synchronized void delItems(int start, int end)`
PARAMETERS	
`end`	The `zero-based` index of the last item in the range.
`start`	The `zero-based` index of the first item in the range.
DEPRECATION	Replace the usage of this deprecated method, as in

```
        list.delItems(start, end);
with
        for(int i=end; i >= start; i--) {
            list.remove(i);
        }
```

SEE ALSO	`removeAll()`.

deselect()

PURPOSE	Deselects an item in this list.
SYNTAX	`public synchronized void deselect(int index)`
DESCRIPTION	This method deselects the item specified at index `index`. The call is ignored if the item is not selected. The other selections are not affected.
PARAMETERS	
`index`	The `zero-based` index of the item in this list.
SEE ALSO	`select()`, `getSelectedItem()`, `isIndexSelected()`.
EXAMPLE	See the class example.

getItem()

PURPOSE	Retrieves an item from this list.
SYNTAX	`public String getItem(int index)`
DESCRIPTION	This method retrieves the item at index `index`.
PARAMETERS	
`index`	The `zero-based` index of the item in this list.
RETURNS	The non-`null` string item.
EXCEPTIONS	
`ArrayIndexOutOfBoundsException`	If `index` is less than 0 or greater than `getItemCount()-1`.
SEE ALSO	`getItemCount()`.
EXAMPLE	See the class example.

getItemCount()

PURPOSE	Retrieves the number of items in this list.
SYNTAX	`public int getItemCount()`
RETURNS	The number of items in this list. The result is always >= 0.
SEE ALSO	`getItem()`, `getItems()`.
EXAMPLE	See the class example.

A
B
C
D
E
F
G
H
I
J
K
L
M
N
O
P
Q
R
S
T
U
V
W
X
Y
Z

getItems()

PURPOSE   Retrieves the items in this list.

SYNTAX   `public synchronized String[] getItems()`

RETURNS   A new array whose elements are the items in this list in the order they appear in this list.

SEE ALSO   `getItem()`, `getItemCount()`.

EXAMPLE   This example prints the list's items when the Print button is pressed. See Figure 244.

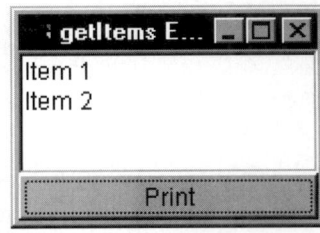

FIGURE 244: `List.getItems()`.

```java
import java.awt.*;
import java.awt.event.*;

class Main extends Frame implements ActionListener {
    List list = new List();
    Main() {
        super("getItems Example");

        list.addItem("Item 1");
        list.addItem("Item 2");
        add(list, BorderLayout.CENTER);
        Button b;
        add(b=new Button("Print"), BorderLayout.SOUTH);
        b.addActionListener(this);

        setSize(200, 200);
        show();
    }

    public void actionPerformed(ActionEvent evt) {
        String[] items = list.getItems();
        for (int i = 0; i<items.length; i++) {
            System.out.println(items[i]);
        }
    }

    static public void main(String[] args) {
        new Main();
    }
}
```

getMinimumSize()

PURPOSE   Calculates the minimum dimensions of this list.

SYNTAX   `public Dimension getMinimumSize()`
                   `public Dimension getMinimumSize(int rows)`

DESCRIPTION   This method calculates the minimum dimensions needed for this list given that the specified number of rows must be visible. If rows is less than or equal to 0 or is not specified, the value of getRows() is used.

If this list's peer does not exist, the result of Component.getSize() is returned. On most platforms, the preferred and minimum dimensions for this list are the same.

PARAMETERS

  rows   The number of rows.

RETURNS   The non-null minimum dimensions of this list.

OVERRIDES   Component.getMinimumSize().

SEE ALSO   getPreferredSize().

EXAMPLE   See LayoutManager.minimumLayoutSize().

getPreferredSize()

PURPOSE   Calculates the preferred dimensions needed for this list.

SYNTAX   public Dimension getPreferredSize()
                public Dimension getPreferredSize(int rows)

DESCRIPTION   This method calculates the preferred dimensions needed for this list given that the specified number of rows must be visible. If rows is less than or equal to 0 or is not specified, the value of getRows() is used.

If this list's peer does not exist, the result of Component.getSize() is returned. On most platforms, the preferred and minimum dimensions for this list are the same.

PARAMETERS

  rows   The number of rows.

RETURNS   The non-null preferred dimensions of this list.

OVERRIDES   Component.getPreferredSize().

EXAMPLE   See LayoutManager.preferredLayoutSize().

getRows()

PURPOSE   Retrieves the number of rows in this list.

SYNTAX   public int getRows()

A
B
C
D
E
F
G
H
I
J
K
L
M
N
O
P
Q
R
S
T
U
V
W
X
Y
Z

DESCRIPTION	The number of rows is specified when this list is created; it never changes, even if the dimensions of this list change. See the `List()` constructor for more details about rows.
RETURNS	The number of rows.
SEE ALSO	`List()`.
EXAMPLE	See `removeAll()`.

getSelectedIndex()

PURPOSE	Retrieves the index of the selected item.
SYNTAX	`public synchronized int getSelectedIndex()`
RETURNS	The zero-based index of the selected item or −1 if no item is selected. If this list is in multiple-selection mode, −1 is always returned.
SEE ALSO	`deselect()`, `getSelectedItem()`, `select()`.
EXAMPLE	See the class example.

getSelectedIndexes()

PURPOSE	Retrieves the indices of the selected items.
SYNTAX	`public synchronized int[] getSelectedIndexes()`
RETURNS	A non-`null` array containing the list of indices. The return array is never `null`, but it may have length 0, which indicates that no items were selected.
SEE ALSO	`getSelectedIndex()`, `getSelectedItem()`.
EXAMPLE	See the class example.

getSelectedItem()

PURPOSE	Retrieves the selected item.
SYNTAX	`public synchronized String getSelectedItem()`
RETURNS	The selected item; `null` if no items are selected. If this list is in multiple-selection mode, `null` is always returned.
SEE ALSO	`getSelectedIndex()`, `getSelectedIndexes()`.

EXAMPLE   This example creates a frame containing a list. As you click any item in the list, the currently selected item is printed. See Figure 245.

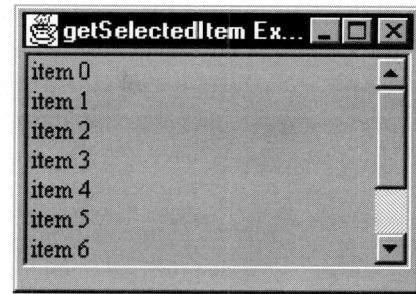

FIGURE 245: List.`getSelectedItem()`.

```java
import java.awt.*;
import java.awt.event.*;

class Main extends Frame
    implements ItemListener {
    static final int ITEMS = 10;
    static List l = new List(ITEMS, false);

    Main() {
        super("getSelectedItem Example");

        for (int i = 0; i < ITEMS; i++) {
            l.addItem("item "+i);
        }
        add(l, BorderLayout.CENTER);
        l.addItemListener(this);
        pack();
        show();
    }

    public void itemStateChanged(ItemEvent evt) {
        // Use quick way to print selected item
        System.out.println(l.getSelectedItem());

        // Use another way to print
        Object[] selected = l.getSelectedObjects();
        for (int i = 0; i < selected.length; i++) {
            System.out.println(selected[i]);
        }
    }

    static public void main(String[] args) {
        new Main();
    }
}
```

getSelectedItems( )

PURPOSE   Retrieves the selected items in this list.

SYNTAX   `public synchronized String[] getSelectedItems()`

RETURNS   A non-`null` array containing the names of the selected items on this list.

SEE ALSO   `getSelectedIndexes()`, `getSelectedItem()`.

EXAMPLE   See the class example.

getSelectedObjects( )

PURPOSE　　　Retrieves this list's currently selected items.

SYNTAX　　　`public synchronized Object[] getSelectedObjects()`

RETURNS　　　An array of strings containing this list's currently selected items. The return array is never `null`, but it may have length 0, which indicates that no items were selected.

SEE ALSO　　　`getSelectedIndex()`, `getSelectedIndexes()`, `getSelectedItem()`, `getSelectedItems()`, `ItemSelectable`.

EXAMPLE　　　See `getSelectedItem()`.

getVisibleIndex( )

PURPOSE　　　Retrieves the index of the item that was last made visible.

SYNTAX　　　`public int getVisibleIndex()`

DESCRIPTION　The item that was last made visible is the item passed to the most recent call to `makeVisible()`.

RETURNS　　　The zero-based index of the item that was last made visible with the `makeVisible()` method. If `makeVisible()` has not yet been called, 0 is returned.

SEE ALSO　　　`makeVisible()`.

isItemSelected( )

PURPOSE　　　Determines whether an item in this list is selected.

SYNTAX　　　`public boolean isItemSelected(int index)`

DESCRIPTION　This method determines whether the item at index `index` on this list is selected.

RETURNS　　　`true` if the item at index `index` is selected; `false` otherwise.

PARAMETERS
　`index`　　　The zero-based index of the item.

SEE ALSO　　　`deselect()`, `select()`.

EXAMPLE　　　See the class example.

isMultipleMode()

PURPOSE	Retrieves the selection mode of this list.
SYNTAX	`public boolean isMultipleMode()`
RETURNS	`true` if this list is in multiple-selection mode; `false` otherwise.
SEE ALSO	`setMultipleMode()`.
EXAMPLE	See `setMultipleMode()`.

isSelected()   *DEPRECATED*

PURPOSE	Replaced by `isIndexSelected()`.
SYNTAX	`public boolean isSelected(int index)`
PARAMETERS	
`index`	The zero-based index of the item.
RETURNS	`true` if the item at index `index` is selected; `false` otherwise.
DEPRECATION	Replace the usage of this deprecated method, as in

```
if (list.isSelected(index)) ...
```
with
```
if (list.isIndexSelected(index)) ...
```

List()

PURPOSE	Constructs a new list component.
SYNTAX	`public List()`
	`public List(int nrows)`
	`public List(int nrows, boolean multipleSelections)`
DESCRIPTION	The three forms of this constructor create a new list component tall enough to display `nrows` visible rows. If `nrows` is not specified, it defaults to 4. The number of rows can be retrieved at any time with `getRows()`. However, this value never changes, even if the dimensions of the list change. If `multiple-Selections` is `true`, the list is set in multiple-selection mode; otherwise, the list is set in single-selection mode. If `multipleSelections` is not specified, it defaults to `false`. The width of the list component is set to a platform-dependent value.

PARAMETERS

`multipleSelections`

Specifies the selection mode of the list.

nrows   The number of rows in the list is defined to be the number of items that can be visible at one time, where the first visible item is completely visible and the last visible item is at least partially visible. (Note that in implementations that allow both the first and last visible items to be partially visible, it's possible for more than nrows items to be visible.) In implementations in which a horizontal scrollbar automatically appears if needed, the number of visible items may be fewer than nrows when the scrollbar is present.

EXAMPLE   This example creates a list component that has two items. See Figure 246. The program prints out the current item whenever an item in the list is double-clicked.

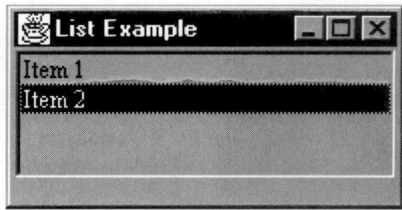

FIGURE 246: Simple List.

```
import java.awt.*;
import java.awt.event.*;

class Main extends Frame implements ActionListener {
    Main() {
        super("List Example");
        List list = new List();

        list.addItem("Item 1");
        list.addItem("Item 2");
        add(list, BorderLayout.CENTER);
        list.addActionListener(this);

        setSize(200, 200);
        show();
    }

    public void actionPerformed(ActionEvent evt) {
        System.out.println(evt.getActionCommand());
    }

    static public void main(String[] args) {
        new Main();
    }
}
```

makeVisible()

PURPOSE   Scrolls this list so that an item is visible.

SYNTAX   `public synchronized void makeVisible(int index)`

DESCRIPTION   This method scrolls this list so that the item at index `index` is visible.

PARAMETERS

index   The zero-based index of the item.

SEE ALSO   getVisibleIndex().

EXAMPLE   This example creates a list component with ten items and makes sure that the last item in the list is visible. See Figure 247.

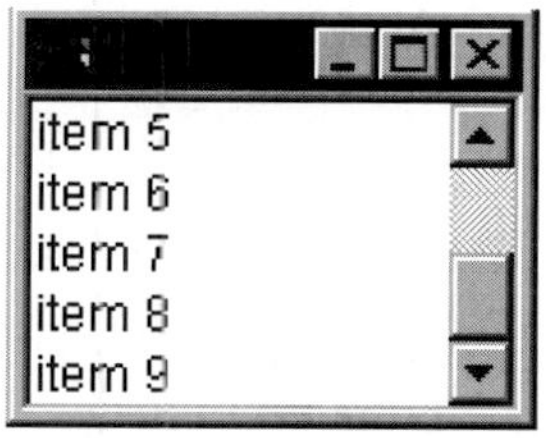

FIGURE 247: List.makeVisible().

```
import java.awt.*;

class Main extends Frame {
    static final int ITEMS = 10;
    static List l = new List(ITEMS/2, true);

    static public void main(String[] args) {
        Main f = new Main();

        for (int i = 0; i < ITEMS; i++) {
            l.addItem("item "+i);
        }
        f.add(l, BorderLayout.CENTER);
        f.pack();
        f.show();
        l.makeVisible(ITEMS-1);
    }
}
```

minimumSize()   *DEPRECATED*

PURPOSE   Replaced by getMinimumSize().

SYNTAX   public Dimension minimumSize()
                public Dimension minimumSize(int rows)

PARAMETERS

rows   The number of rows.

RETURNS   The non-null minimum dimensions of this list.

OVERRIDES   Component.minimumSize().

DEPRECATION   Replace the deprecated usage of this method, as in
                Dimension dim1 = list.minimumSize();
                Dimension dim2 = list.minimumSize(rows);
                with
                Dimension dim1 = list.getMinimumSize();
                Dimension dim2 = list.getMinimumSize(rows);

paramString()

PURPOSE	Generates a string representing this list's state.
SYNTAX	`protected String paramString()`
DESCRIPTION	A subclass of this class should override this method and return a concatenation of its state with the results of `super.paramString()`. This method is called by the `toString()` method and is typically used for debugging.
RETURNS	A non-`null` string representing this list's state.
OVERRIDES	`Component.paramString()`.
SEE ALSO	`Object.toString()`.
EXAMPLE	See `Component.paramString()`.

preferredSize() *DEPRECATED*

PURPOSE	Replaced by `getPreferredSize()`.
SYNTAX	`public Dimension preferredSize()` `public Dimension preferredSize(int rows)`
PARAMETERS rows	The number of rows.
RETURNS	The non-`null` preferred dimensions of this list.
OVERRIDES	`Component.preferredSize()`.

DEPRECATION	Replace the deprecated usage of this method, as in
	`Dimension dim1 = list.preferredSize();`
	`Dimension dim2 = list.preferredSize(rows);`
	with
	`Dimension dim1 = list.getPreferredSize();`
	`Dimension dim2 = list.getPreferredSize(rows);`

processActionEvent()

PURPOSE	Processes an action event enabled for this list.
SYNTAX	`protected void processActionEvent(ActionEvent evt)`
DESCRIPTION	An action event is fired when the mouse is double-clicked on an item in this list. See `ActionEvent` for more details. This method processes action events for this list by calling any registered `ActionListener`. It is invoked only if action events have been enabled for this list. This can happen either when an

action listener is added to this list or when action events are explicitly enabled via the use of `Component.enableEvents()`.

Typically, a program controls how action events for a list are processed by adding or removing action listeners. It overrides `processActionEvent()` only if it needs to do processing in addition to that performed by the registered listeners.

When a subclass does override `processActionEvent()`, it should call `super.processActionEvent()` to perform the processing intended by its base class (such as dispatching the listeners).

PARAMETERS

`evt`   The event to be processed.

SEE ALSO   `addActionListener()`, `Component.enableEvents()`,
            `java.awt.event.ActionEvent`, `java.awt.event.ActionListener`,
            `processEvent()`, `removeActionListener()`.

EXAMPLE   See the `AWTEventMulticaster` class example.

processEvent()

PURPOSE   Processes an event enabled for this list.

SYNTAX   `protected void processEvent(AWTEvent evt)`

DESCRIPTION This method extends `Component.processEvent()` by adding support for `ActionEvent` and `ItemEvent`.

PARAMETERS

`evt`   The event to be processed.

OVERRIDES   `Component.processEvent()`.

SEE ALSO   `AWTEvent`, `processActionEvent()`, `processItemEvent()`.

EXAMPLE   See the `AWTEventMulticaster` class example.

processItemEvent()

PURPOSE   Processes an item event enabled for this list.

SYNTAX   `protected void processItemEvent(ItemEvent evt)`

DESCRIPTION An item event is fired when an item in this list is selected/deselected. See `ItemEvent` and the class description for more details. This method processes item events for this list by calling any registered `ItemListener`. It is invoked only if item events have been enabled for this list. This can happen either when an item listener is added to this list or if item events are enabled explicitly via `Component.enableEvents()`.

Typically, a program controls how item events for a list are processed by adding or removing item listeners. It overrides `processItemEvent()` only if it needs to do processing in addition to that performed by the registered listeners.

When a subclass does override `processItemEvent()`, it should call `super.processItemEvent()` to perform the processing intended by its base class (such as dispatching the listeners).

PARAMETERS

`evt` The event to be processed.

SEE ALSO `addItemListener()`, `Component.enableEvents()`, `java.awt.event.ItemEvent`, `ItemSelectable`, `java.awt.event.ItemListener`, `processEvent()`, `removeItemListener()`.

EXAMPLE See `AWTEventMulticaster.itemStateChanged()`.

replaceItem( )

PURPOSE Replaces an item in this list.

SYNTAX `public synchronized void replaceItem(String newItem, int index)`

DESCRIPTION This method replaces the item at the index `index` with `newItem`.

PARAMETERS

`index` The zero-based index of the item.
`newItem` The non-`null` new item.

SEE ALSO `addItem()`.

EXAMPLE See the class example.

remove( )

PURPOSE Deletes an item from this list.

SYNTAX `public synchronized void remove(int index)`
`public synchronized void remove(String item)`

DESCRIPTION The first form of this method deletes the item at index `index` from this list. The second form deletes the first occurrence (from index 0) of the item `item` in this list. This method does not affect the selected state of the other items in this list.

The form of this method that accepts an index is the same as `delItem()`.

PARAMETERS

index   The zero-based index of the item in this list.

item   The item to remove.

EXCEPTIONS

`ArrayIndexOutOfBoundsException`
      If `index` is less than 0 or greater than `getItemCount()-1`.

`IllegalArgumentException`
      If `item` is not in this list.

SEE ALSO   `delItem()`, `java.lang.ArrayIndexOutOfBoundsException`, `java.lang.IllegalArgumentException`, `removeAll()`.

EXAMPLE   See the class example.

removeActionListener()

PURPOSE   Removes a listener from receiving action events from this list.

SYNTAX   `public synchronized void removeActionListener(ActionListener listener)`

DESCRIPTION   An action event is fired when the mouse is double-clicked on an item in this list. See `ActionEvent` for more details. After this method is called, the action listener `listener` will no longer receive action events from this list. If `listener` is `null`, this method does nothing.

PARAMETERS

listener   The possibly `null` action listener to remove.

SEE ALSO   `addActionListener()`, `java.awt.event.ActionEvent`, `java.awt.event.ActionListener`.

EXAMPLE   See `MenuItem.disableEvents()`.

removeAll()

PURPOSE   Removes all items from this list.

SYNTAX   `public synchronized void removeAll()`

DESCRIPTION   The effect of calling `removeAll()` is the same as calling `remove()` for every item in this list.

SEE ALSO   `remove()`.

EXAMPLE   This example creates
a list component that
has ten items. Press-
ing the Remove All
button removes all of
the items in the list.
See Figure 248.

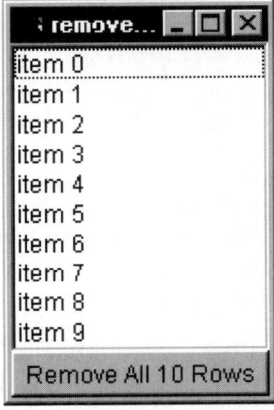 

FIGURE 248: List.removeAll().

```java
import java.awt.*;
import java.awt.event.*;

class Main extends Frame implements ActionListener {
    List l = new List(10,
        false);
    Button b;

    Main() {
        super("removeAll Example");

        for (int i = 0; i < 10; i++) {
            l.addItem("item "+i);
        }

    b = new Button("Remove All " + l.getRows() + " Rows");
        add(l, BorderLayout.CENTER);
        add(b, BorderLayout.SOUTH);
        b.addActionListener(this);
        pack();
        show();
    }

    static public void main(String[] args) {
        new Main();
    }

    public void actionPerformed(ActionEvent evt) {
        l.removeAll();

        // disable button and remove listener
        b.setEnabled(false);
    }
}
```

A
B
C
D
E
F
G
H
I
J
K
L
M
N
O
P
Q
R
S
T
U
V
W
X
Y
Z

removeItemListener()

PURPOSE | Removes an item listener from receiving item events from this list.

SYNTAX
```
public synchronized void removeItemListener(ItemListener
    listener)
```

DESCRIPTION | An item event is fired when an item in this list is selected/deselected. See `ItemEvent` and the class description for more details. After this method is called, the item listener `listener` will no longer receive item events from this list. If `listener` is `null`, this method does nothing.

PARAMETERS
listener | The possibly `null` item listener to remove.

SEE ALSO | `addItemListener()`, `ItemSelectable`, `java.awt.event.ItemEvent`, `java.awt.event.ItemListener`.

EXAMPLE | See `removeActionListener()` in `MenuItem.disableEvents()`.

removeNotify()

PURPOSE | Destroys this list's peer.

SYNTAX
```
public void removeNotify()
```

DESCRIPTION | This method should never be called directly. It is normally called by the component's container.

OVERRIDES | `Component.removeNotify()`.

SEE ALSO | `Component`.

EXAMPLE | See `Component.setVisible()`.

select()

PURPOSE | Selects an item in this list.

SYNTAX
```
public synchronized void select(int index)
```

DESCRIPTION | This method selects the item at the index `index`. The call is ignored if the item is already selected.

PARAMETERS
index | The zero-based index of the item.

EXCEPTIONS

ArrayIndexOutOfBoundsException

If index is less than 0 or greater than getItemCount()-1.

SEE ALSO deselect(), getSelectedItem(), isIndexSelected(), java.lang.ArrayIndexOutOfBoundsException.

EXAMPLE This example creates a list component that has every other item selected. See Figure 249.

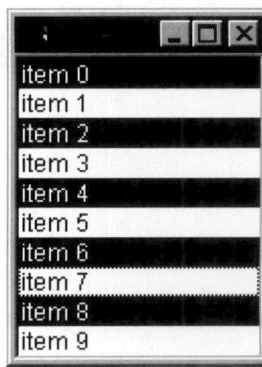

```
import java.awt.*;

class Main {
    static final int ITEMS = 10;
    static public void main(String[] args) {
        Frame f = new Frame();
        List l = new List(ITEMS, true);

        for (int i = 0; i < ITEMS; i++) {
            l.addItem("item "+i);
            if (i % 2 == 0) {
                l.select(i);
            }
        }
        f.add(l, BorderLayout.CENTER);
        f.pack();
        f.show();
    }
}
```

FIGURE 249:
List.select().

setMultipleMode( )

PURPOSE Sets this list's selection mode.

SYNTAX public synchronized void setMultipleMode(boolean on)

DESCRIPTION If on is true, this method sets this list in multi-selection mode; otherwise, it sets this list in single-selection mode.

PARAMETERS

on Specifies the new selection mode of the list.

SEE ALSO isMultipleMode().

EXAMPLE   This example creates a frame containing a list and a checkbox control. The checkbox control is used to toggle the multiple-selection model of the list control. See Figure 250.

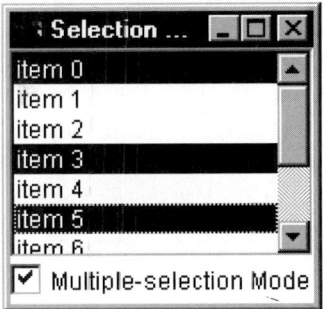

FIGURE 250:   **Turning Multiple Mode On and Off in** List.

```java
import java.awt.*;
import java.awt.event.*;

class Main extends Frame implements ItemListener {
    static final int ITEMS = 10;
    static List l = new List(ITEMS, false);
    static Checkbox b =
        new Checkbox("Multiple-selection Mode",
        null, false);

    Main() {
        super("Selection Mode Example");

        for (int i = 0; i < ITEMS; i++) {
            l.addItem("item "+i);
        }
        add(l, BorderLayout.CENTER);
        add(b, BorderLayout.SOUTH);

        b.addItemListener(this);
        pack();
        show();
    }

    public void itemStateChanged(ItemEvent evt) {
        l.setMultipleMode(evt.getStateChange() == ItemEvent.SELECTED);
        System.out.println("multiple mode: " + l.isMultipleMode());
    }

    static public void main(String[] args) {
        new Main();
    }
}
```

setMultipleSelections( )   *DEPRECATED*

PURPOSE   Replaced by `setMultipleMode()`.

SYNTAX   `public synchronized void setMultipleSelections(boolean on)`

PARAMETERS

on   Specifies the new selection mode of this list.

DEPRECATION   Replace the usage of this deprecated method, as in
               `setMultipleSelections(on);`
               with
               `setMultipleMode(on);`

A
B
C
D
E
F
G
H
I
J
K
M
N
O
P
Q
R
S
T
U
V
W
X
Y
Z

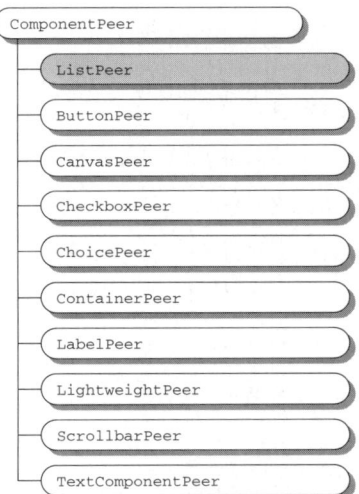

Syntax
```
public interface ListPeer extends ComponentPeer
```

Description
The list component (see the List class) in the AWT uses the platform's native implementation of a list. So that the AWT list behaves the same on all platforms, the list is assigned a *peer,* whose task is to translate the behavior of the platform's native list to the behavior of the AWT list.

AWT programmers normally do not directly use peer classes and interfaces. Instead, they deal with AWT components in the java.awt package. These in turn automatically manage their peers. Only someone who is porting the AWT to another platform should be concerned with the peer classes and interfaces. Consequently, most peer documentation refers to java.awt counterparts.

See Component and Toolkit for additional information about component peers.

MEMBER SUMMARY	

Peer Methods

add()	Adds an item to the list.
delItems()	Deletes a range of items from the list.
deselect()	Deselects an item in the list.
getMinimumSize()	Calculates the minimum dimensions of the list.
getPreferredSize()	Calculates the preferred dimensions of the list.
getSelectedIndexes()	Retrieves the indexes of the selected items.
makeVisible()	Scrolls the list so that an item is visible.
removeAll()	Removes all items from the list.
select()	Selects an item in the list.
setMultipleMode()	Sets the selection mode of the list.

Deprecated Methods

addItem()	Replaced by add().
clear()	Replaced by removeAll().
minimumSize()	Replaced by getMinimumSize().
preferredSize()	Replaced by getPreferredSize().
setMultipleSelections()	Replaced by setMultipleMode().

See Also

java.awt.Component, java.awt.List, java.awt.Toolkit.

add()

PURPOSE	Adds an item to the list.
SYNTAX	void add(String item, int index)
PARAMETERS	
item	The item to be added.
index	The position in the list at which to add the item.
SEE ALSO	java.awt.List.add().

addItem()   *DEPRECATED*

PURPOSE	Replaced by add().
SYNTAX	void addItem(String item, int index)

A
B
C
D
E
F
G
H
I
J
K
L
M
N
O
P
Q
R
S
T
U
V
W
X
Y
Z

PARAMETERS

`item` The item to be added.

`index` The position in the list at which to add the item.

DEPRECATION Replace the usage of this deprecated method, as in
  `peer.addItem(item, index);`
with
  `peer.add(item, index);`

clear( ) *DEPRECATED*

PURPOSE Replaced by `removeAll()`.

SYNTAX `void clear().`

DEPRECATION Replace the usage of this deprecated method, as in
  `peer.clear();`
with
  `peer.removeAll();`

delItems( )

PURPOSE Deletes a range of items from the list.

SYNTAX `void delItems(int start, int end)`

PARAMETERS

`end` The 0-based index of the last item in the range.

`start` The 0-based index of the first item in the range.

SEE ALSO `java.awt.List.delItems().`

deselect( )

PURPOSE Deselects an item in the list.

SYNTAX `void deselect(int index)`

PARAMETERS

`index` The 0-based index of the item to deselect.

SEE ALSO `java.awt.List.deselect().`

getMinimumSize( )

PURPOSE	Calculates the minimum dimensions of the list.
SYNTAX	`Dimension getMinimumSize(int rows)`
PARAMETERS	
rows	The number of rows the list must accommodate.
RETURNS	The minimum dimensions of the list.
SEE ALSO	`java.awt.List.getMinimumSize()`.

getPreferredSize( )

PURPOSE	Calculates the preferred dimensions of the list.
SYNTAX	`Dimension getPreferredSize(int rows)`
PARAMETERS	
rows	The number of rows the list must accommodate.
RETURNS	The preferred dimensions of the list.
SEE ALSO	`java.awt.List.getPreferredSize()`.

getSelectedIndexes( )

PURPOSE	Retrieves the indices of the selected items.
SYNTAX	`int[] getSelectedIndexes()`
RETURNS	An array containing the list of indices.
SEE ALSO	`java.awt.List.getSelectedIndexes()`.

makeVisible( )

PURPOSE	Scrolls the list so that an item is visible.
SYNTAX	`void makeVisible(int index)`
PARAMETERS	
index	The 0-based index of the item to make visible.
SEE ALSO	`java.awt.List.makeVisible()`.

A
B
C
D
E
F
G
H
I
J
K
L
M
N
O
P
Q
R
S
T
U
V
W
X
Y
Z

minimumSize( )   *DEPRECATED*

PURPOSE	Replaced by `getMinimumSize()`.
SYNTAX	`Dimension minimumSize(int rows)`
PARAMETERS	
rows	The number of rows the list must accommodate.
RETURNS	The minimum dimensions of the list.
DEPRECATION	Replace the usage of this deprecated method, as in

```
  Dimension min = peer.minimumSize();
```
with
```
  Dimension min = peer.getMinimumSize();
```

preferredSize( )   *DEPRECATED*

PURPOSE	Replaced by `getPreferredSize()`.
SYNTAX	`Dimension preferredSize(int rows)`
PARAMETERS	
rows	The number of rows the list must accommodate.
RETURNS	The preferred dimensions of the list.
DEPRECATION	Replace the usage of this deprecated method, as in

```
  Dimension pref = peer.minimumSize();
```
with
```
  Dimension pref = peer.getMinimumSize();
```

removeAll( )

PURPOSE	Removes all items from the list.
SYNTAX	`void removeAll().`
SEE ALSO	`java.awt.List.removeAll().`

select()

PURPOSE	Selects an item in the list.
SYNTAX	`void select(int index)`
PARAMETERS	
`index`	The index of the item to select.
SEE ALSO	`java.awt.List.select()`.

setMultipleMode()

PURPOSE	Sets the selection mode of the list.
SYNTAX	`void setMultipleMode(boolean on)`
PARAMETERS	
`on`	`true` means set the list control in multiple-selection mode; `false` means set the list in single-selection mode.
SEE ALSO	`java.awt.List.setMultipleSelections()`.

setMultipleSelections()   *DEPRECATED*

PURPOSE	Replaced by `setMultipleMode()`.
SYNTAX	`void setMultipleSelections(boolean on)`
PARAMETERS	
`on`	`true` means set the list control in multiple-selection mode; `false` means set the list in single-selection mode.

DEPRECATION	Replace the usage of this deprecated method, as in
	`peer.setMultipleSelections(on);`
	with
	`peer.setMultipleMode(on);`

MediaTracker

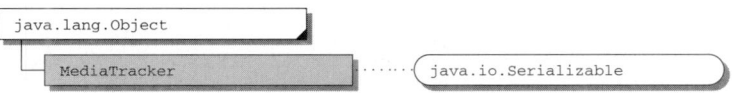

```
java.lang.Object
        MediaTracker  ·········  java.io.Serializable
```

Syntax

`public class MediaTracker implements Serializable`

Description

The imaging routines in the AWT are designed to allow images to be used before they're completely loaded or generated. However, in some cases, you may want or need to wait until all of the pixels of an image are available before rendering the image. For example, an application may wish to display an image for the user to view, while in the background it loads another image. Once the other image is loaded, the application replaces the currently displayed image.

The media tracker is used to manage the loading of images. It makes it convenient to determine when all of the pixels have been received or if an error occurred.

The media tracker also makes it convenient to track the loading status of a set of images. It does this by allowing you to choose an arbitrary integer called the *id* and then associating all of the images in the set with the id. By using the id, you can have the entire set of images treated as one image. For example, you can start the loading of all of the images in the set, or you can check if any image in the set has encountered an error, or you can wait until all of the images have been loaded and then determine if every image loaded successfully.

Media tracker ids are often used with an animation frame, which consists of many images that need to be loaded or generated. Typically, all of the images must be complete; otherwise, none of the images can be used. That is, if any one of the images in the set encounters an error during its construction, then the whole set should be considered invalid.

MEMBER SUMMARY	
Constructor	
MediaTracker()	Constructs a MediaTracker object.
Status Flag Constants	
ABORTED	Specifies that the image loading process was aborted.
COMPLETE	Specifies that the image loading process was completed successfully.
ERRORED	Specifies that the image loading process encountered an error.
LOADING	Specifies that the image loading process is in progress.

MEMBER SUMMARY	
Status Methods	
checkAll()	Determines if all images have been loaded.
checkID()	Determines if all images tagged with an id have been loaded.
getErrorsAny()	Retrieves a list of all images that have encountered an error.
getErrorsID()	Retrieves a list of all images tagged with an id that have encountered an error.
isErrorAny()	Determines if any image encountered an error during loading.
isErrorID()	Determines if any image tagged with an id encountered an error during loading.
statusAll()	Determines the combined status of all images.
statusID()	Determines the combined status of all images tagged with ids.
Image Methods	
addImage()	Adds a scaled image to the list of images being tracked.
imageUpdate()	Should not be used.
removeImage()	Removes an image from the list of images being tracked.
waitForAll()	Waits for all images to be loaded.
waitForID()	Waits for all images tagged with an id to be loaded.

A
B
C
D
E
F
G
H
I
J
K
L
M
N
O

See Also

java.io.Serializable.

Example

This example implements a slide show program. See Figure 251. The program is invoked with a list of files that contain images. The images are displayed in the order in which they appear in the list. They also are loaded in the same order; that is, an image does not begin loading until the previous image has been completely loaded.

The program provides two buttons—Next and Previous—for moving through the slides. The Next button displays the next image in the list. However, it is enabled only if the next image has been completely loaded.

A thread is used to successively load each

FIGURE 251: MediaTracker.

P
Q
R
S
T
U
V
W
X
Y
Z

image in order. So while the user views an image, the program is busily loading the next image. If an error occurs in the loading of an image, the image appears as a red rectangle. After all of the images have been loaded, the program prints status information about each image.

To implement the enabling and disabling of the two buttons, the program uses `statusID()` instead of `checkID()`. This is because `checkID()` returns `true` if an id has not been used (i.e., no image has been added using it), whereas `statusID()` returns 0 if the id has not been used. Using `statusID()` makes it easy to disable the buttons for the id that precede the first image and follow the last image. It might have been clearer simply to test for (`curImage-1 < 0`) or (`curImage+1 > images.length`), but we wanted to demonstrate the difference between `statusID()` and `checkID()`.

```java
import java.awt.*;
import java.awt.image.*;
import java.awt.event.*;

class Main extends Frame implements Runnable, ActionListener {
    MediaTracker tracker;
    Image[] images;
    ImageCanvas icv = new ImageCanvas();
    Button btnNext = new Button("Next");
    Button btnPrevious = new Button("Previous");

    Main(String[] files) {
        super("MediaTracker Example");

        tracker = new MediaTracker(icv);
        images = new Image[files.length];
        for (int i=0; i<images.length; i++) {
            images[i] = getToolkit().getImage(files[i]);
            tracker.addImage(images[i], i);
        }

        // First image is progressively rendered.
        if (images.length > 0) {
            icv.setImage(images[0]);
        }

        add(icv, BorderLayout.CENTER);
        add(btnPrevious, BorderLayout.NORTH);
        add(btnNext, BorderLayout.SOUTH);
        btnPrevious.addActionListener(this);
        btnNext.addActionListener(this);

        setSize(460, 250);
        show();
        (new Thread(this)).start();

        // Print overall status information.
        try {
            // We don't use waitForAll() because it forces
            // all images to start loading; we want to load
            // images one at a time.
            // tracker.waitForAll();
            while (!tracker.checkAll()) {
                Thread.sleep(1000);
            }
        } catch (Exception e) {
            e.printStackTrace();
            System.exit(1);
```

```
        }
        if (tracker.isErrorAny()) {
            System.out.println("Not all images have been successfully loaded.");
            Object[] list = tracker.getErrorsAny();
            for (int i=0; i<list.length; i++) {
                System.out.println(list[i]);
            }
        } else {
            System.out.println("All images have been successfully loaded");
        }
        for (int i=0; i<images.length; i++) {
            int s = tracker.statusID(i, false);

            System.out.print(files[i] + ": ");
            if ((s & MediaTracker.ABORTED) != 0) System.out.print("ABORTED ");
            if ((s & MediaTracker.COMPLETE) != 0) System.out.print("COMPLETE ");
            if ((s & MediaTracker.ERRORED) != 0) System.out.print("ERRORED ");
            if ((s & MediaTracker.LOADING) != 0) System.out.print("LOADING ");
            System.out.println();
        }
    }

    int curImage;
    final int DONE = (MediaTracker.ABORTED | MediaTracker.ERRORED
                    | MediaTracker.COMPLETE);
    public void paint(Graphics g) {
        if (tracker.isErrorID(curImage)) {
            icv.setImage(null);
        } else {
            icv.setImage(images[curImage]);
        }
        btnNext.setEnabled((tracker.statusID(curImage+1, false)&DONE) != 0);
        btnPrevious.setEnabled(
            (tracker.statusID(curImage-1, false)&DONE) != 0);

        /* See example description for explanation:
        btnNext.setEnabled(tracker.checkID(curImage+1));
        btnPrevious.setEnabled(tracker.checkID(curImage-1));
        */
    }

    public void actionPerformed(ActionEvent evt) {
        String arg = evt.getActionCommand();
        if ("Next".equals(arg)) {
            if (curImage < images.length-1) {
                ++curImage;
                repaint();
            }
        } else if ("Previous".equals(arg)) {
            if (curImage > 0) {
                --curImage;
                repaint();
            }
        }
    }

    public void run() {
        for (int i=0; i<images.length; i++) {
            //tracker.checkID(i);//, true);
            try {
```

A
B
C
D
E
F
G
H
I
J
K
L
M
N
O
P
Q
R
S
T
U
V
W
X
Y
Z

```
                        tracker.waitForID(i);
                } catch (Exception e) {
                    e.printStackTrace();
                }
                repaint();
            }
        }

        static public void main(String[] args) {
            new Main(args);
        }
    }

    class ImageCanvas extends Canvas {
        Image image;
        boolean clear;

        public void setImage(Image image) {
            this.image = image;
            clear = true;
            repaint();
        }

        public void update(Graphics g) {
            paint(g);
        }

        public void paint(Graphics g) {
            if (image == null) {
                g.setColor(Color.red);
                g.fillRect(0, 0, getSize().width, getSize().height);
            } else {
                if (clear) {
                    g.clearRect(0, 0, getSize().width, getSize().height);
                    clear = false;
                }
                int w = image.getWidth(this);
                int h = image.getHeight(this);
                if (w >= 0 && h >= 0) {
                    g.drawImage(image, (getSize().width-w)/2,
                        (getSize().height-h)/2, this);
                }
            }
        }
    }
```

ABORTED

PURPOSE   Specifies that the image loading process was aborted.

SYNTAX   `public static final int ABORTED`

DESCRIPTION   This field is a status flag that specifies that the image loading process was aborted. Its value is 2.

SEE ALSO   `statusAll()`, `statusID()`.

EXAMPLE   See the class example.

addImage()

PURPOSE	Adds a scaled image to the list of images being tracked.
SYNTAX	`public void addImage(Image image, int id)` `public synchronized void addImage(Image image, int id, int w, int h)`
DESCRIPTION	This method associates an image with the media tracker id `id`. Several images can be associated with `id`. The image will eventually be rendered at the indicated size.
PARAMETERS	
h	The height in pixels at which the image will be rendered.
id	The identifier used to later track this image.
image	The non-`null` image to be tracked.
w	The width in pixels at which the image will be rendered.
EXAMPLE	See the class example.

checkAll()

PURPOSE	Determines if all images have been loaded.
SYNTAX	`public boolean checkAll()` `public boolean checkAll(boolean load)`
DESCRIPTION	This method returns `true` if all of the images have been loaded. An image is defined to be loaded if either the image successfully loaded or it encountered an error. In other words, this method returns `true` if none of the images will receive more pixels. The method `isErrorAny()` can be used to determine if an error occurred during the loading of at least one image in the media tracker. If `load` is `true` and not all of the images have started loading, the loading process is started for all images. If `load` is not specified, it defaults to `false`.
PARAMETERS	
load	If `true`, the loading process is started for all images.
RETURNS	`true` if all images are loaded.
SEE ALSO	`checkID()`, `isErrorAny()`, `statusAll()`.
EXAMPLE	See the class example.

checkID()

PURPOSE	Determines if all images tagged with an id have been loaded.
SYNTAX	`public boolean checkID(int id)`
	`public boolean checkID(int id, boolean load)`

DESCRIPTION

This method returns `true` if all of the images tagged with `id` have been loaded. An image is defined to be loaded if either it successfully loaded or it encountered an error. In other words, this method returns `true` if no image tagged with `id` will receive more pixels. The method `isErrorID()` can be used to determine if an error occurred during the loading of at least one of the images tagged with `id`.

If load is `true` and the images tagged with `id` have not started loading, the loading process is started for these images. If `load` is not specified, it defaults to `false`.

`checkID()` calls `Component.checkImage()` on the images to obtain their status in order to construct the result.

If no images are associated with `id`, this method returns `true`.

PARAMETERS

`id`	The media tracker id.
`load`	If `true`, the loading process is started for all images tagged with `id`.
`verify`	If `true`, call `Component.checkImage()` on the tagged images when generating the status; if `false`, `Component.checkImage()` is not called.

RETURNS	`true` if all images tagged with `id` are loaded.
SEE ALSO	`checkID()`, `isErrorID()`, `statusID()`.

COMPLETE

PURPOSE	Specifies that the image loading process was completed successfully.
SYNTAX	`public static final int COMPLETE`

DESCRIPTION

This field is a status flag that specifies that the image loading process was completed successfully. Its value is 8.

SEE ALSO	`statusAll()`, `statusID()`.
EXAMPLE	See the class example.

A
B
C
D
E
F
G
H
I
J
K
L
M
N
O
P
Q
R
S
T
U
V
W
X
Y
Z

ERRORED

PURPOSE	Specifies that the image loading process encountered an error.
SYNTAX	`public static final int ERRORED`
DESCRIPTION	This field is a status flag that specifies that the image loading process encountered an error. Its value is 4.
SEE ALSO	`statusAll()`, `statusID()`.
EXAMPLE	See the class example.

getErrorsAny()

PURPOSE	Retrieves a list of all images that have encountered an error.
SYNTAX	`public synchronized Object[] getErrorsAny()`
DESCRIPTION	This method returns a list of all images that have encountered errors so far.
RETURNS	`null` if there are no errors or an array of all images that have encountered errors.
SEE ALSO	`getErrorsID()`, `isErrorAny()`.
EXAMPLE	See the class example.

getErrorsID()

PURPOSE	Retrieves a list of all images tagged with an id that have encountered an error.
SYNTAX	`public synchronized Object[] getErrorsID(int id)`
DESCRIPTION	This method returns a list of images tagged with `id` that have encountered errors so far.
PARAMETERS	
id	The media tracker id.
RETURNS	`null` if there are no errors or an array of all images that have encountered errors.
SEE ALSO	`isErrorID()`, `isErrorAny()`.
EXAMPLE	See the class example.

A
B
C
D
E
F
G
H
I
J
K
L
M
N
O
P
Q
R
S
T
U
V
W
X
Y
Z

imageUpdate()

PURPOSE	This method should not be used.
SYNTAX	`public boolean imageUpdate(Image img, int infoflags, int x, int y, int w, int h)`
DESCRIPTION	The `MediaTracker` class implements this method as part of the `ImageObserver` interface. It should not be used.
PARAMETERS	
h	Depends on the status bits enabled in `infoflags`.
img	The non-`null` image being updated.
infoflags	A set of status bits.
w	Depends on the status bits enabled in `infoflags`.
x	Depends on the status bits enabled in `infoflags`.
y	Depends on the status bits enabled in `infoflags`.
RETURNS	`true` if further calls to the `imageUpdate()` are needed.

isErrorAny()

PURPOSE	Determines if any images encountered an error during loading.
SYNTAX	`public synchronized boolean isErrorAny()`
RETURNS	`true` if any images encountered an error during loading; `false` otherwise.
SEE ALSO	`getErrorsAny()`, `isErrorID()`.
EXAMPLE	See the class example.

isErrorID()

PURPOSE	Determines if any images tagged with an id encountered an error during loading.
SYNTAX	`public synchronized boolean isErrorID(int id)`
PARAMETERS	
id	The media tracker id.
RETURNS	`true` if any of the images tagged with `id` encountered an error during loading; `false` otherwise.
SEE ALSO	`getErrorsID()`, `isErrorAny()`.
EXAMPLE	See the class example.

LOADING

PURPOSE   Specifies that the image loading process is in progress.

SYNTAX   `public static final int LOADING`

DESCRIPTION   This field is a status flag that specifies that the image loading process is in progress. Its value is 1.

SEE ALSO   `statusAll()`, `statusID()`.

EXAMPLE   See the class example.

MediaTracker()

PURPOSE   Constructs a `MediaTracker` object.

SYNTAX   `public MediaTracker(Component comp)`

DESCRIPTION   Constructs a new `MediaTracker` object for the component `comp`. The media tracker will register `comp` with the image producers of the images it maintains (see `ImageProducer`) and will process the `imageUpdate()` notifications from the image producers; these notifications are not passed on to `comp`. However, even if the media tracker has registered `comp`, `comp` is free to register itself with the same image producer if it also desires update notifications.

The `comp` object is used only in a call to `comp.prepareImage()` to start the loading of the image pixels.

PARAMETERS
comp   The non-`null` component on which the images will eventually be drawn.

EXAMPLE   See the class example.

removeImage()

PURPOSE   Removes an image from the list of images being tracked.

SYNTAX   `public synchronized void removeImage(Image image)`
`public synchronized void removeImage(Image image, int id)`
`public synchronized void removeImage(Image image, int id, int w,`
`    int h)`

DESCRIPTION   This method removes an image from the list of images being tracked. If only `image` is supplied, all instances of `image` are removed from the list. If the tracking id `id` is supplied, only instances of the image with `id` are removed. If width `w` and height `h` are specified, only instances of the image with `id` and the

A
B
C
D
E
F
G
H
I
J
K
L
M
N
O
P
Q
R
S
T
U
V
W
X
Y
Z

specified width and height are removed. Images with id but a different width and height are not removed.

PARAMETERS	
h	The height in pixels of the image to be removed from the tracking list.
id	The media tracking identifier of the images.
image	The non-null image to be removed from the tracking list.
w	The width in pixels of the image to be removed from the tracking list.

SEE ALSO   addImage().

statusAll( )

PURPOSE   Determines the combined status of all images.

SYNTAX   `public int statusAll(boolean load)`

DESCRIPTION   This method determines the status of all images in the media tracker and combines them into one status. For example, if some image is still in the process of being loaded, this method returns a status with the LOADING flag set. The status for an image that has not started loading is 0.

If load is true and the images have not started loading, the loading process is started for these images.

PARAMETERS

load   If true, the loading process is started for all images.

RETURNS   The bitwise "or" of the status of all images.

SEE ALSO   ABORTED, COMPLETE, ERRORED, LOADING, statusID().

EXAMPLE   See the class example.

statusID( )

PURPOSE   Determines the combined status of all images tagged with an id.

SYNTAX   `public int statusID(int id, boolean load)`

DESCRIPTION   This method determines the status of all images tagged with id and combines them into one status. For example, if one of the images tagged with id is still in the process of being loaded, this method returns a status with the LOADING flag set. The status for an image that has not started loading is 0.

If load is true and the images tagged with id have not started loading, the loading process is started for these images.

statusID() calls Component.checkImage() on the images to obtain their statuses in order to construct the result.

PARAMETERS

id   The media tracker id.

load   If true, the loading process is started for all images tagged with id.

RETURNS   The bitwise "or" of the status of all images tagged with id.

SEE ALSO   ABORTED, checkID(), COMPLETE, ERRORED, LOADING, statusAll().

EXAMPLE   See the class example.

waitForAll()

PURPOSE   Waits for all images to be loaded.

SYNTAX   public void waitForAll() throws InterruptedException
            public synchronized boolean waitForAll(long ms) throws
                InterruptedException

DESCRIPTION This method returns only when all of the images have been loaded or when ms milliseconds have expired. If ms is 0 or not specified, this method blocks until all of the images have been loaded.

An image is defined to be loaded if either it successfully loaded or it encountered an error. In other words, this method returns true if no image will receive more pixels. The method isErrorAny() can be used to determine if an error occurred during the loading of at least one image in the media tracker.

This method starts the loading process for any images that have not been loaded. If ms is not specified, this method does not return until all images have been loaded.

PARAMETERS

ms   The non-negative length of time in milliseconds to wait for the loading to complete.

RETURNS   true if all images were successfully loaded.

EXCEPTIONS

InterruptedException
            If another thread interrupted this thread.

SEE ALSO   isErrorAny(), waitForID().

EXAMPLE   See the class example.

waitForID()

PURPOSE	Waits for all images tagged with an id to be loaded.

SYNTAX

```
public void waitForID(int id) throws InterruptedException
public synchronized boolean waitForID(int id, long ms) throws
    InterruptedException
```

DESCRIPTION

This method returns only when all of the images tagged with id have been loaded or when ms milliseconds have expired. If ms is 0 or not specified, this method blocks until the images identified have been loaded.

An image is defined to be loaded if either it successfully loaded or it encountered an error. In other words, this method returns true if no image will receive more pixels. The method isErrorID() can be used to determine if an error occurred during the loading of at least one image in the media tracker.

This method starts the loading process for any images tagged with id that have not been loaded.

PARAMETERS

id   The media tracker id.

ms   The length of time in milliseconds to wait for the loading to complete.

RETURNS

true if all images tagged with id were successfully loaded.

EXCEPTIONS

InterruptedException
         If another thread interrupted this thread.

SEE ALSO   isErrorID(), waitForAll().

EXAMPLE   See the class example.

MemoryImageSource

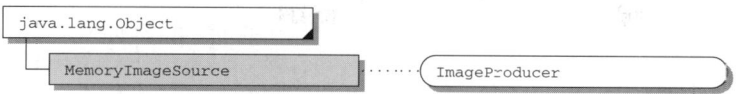

```
java.lang.Object
     MemoryImageSource          ImageProducer
```

Syntax

public class MemoryImageSource implements ImageProducer

Description

The MemoryImageSource class is used to create an image producer that delivers pixels from a buffer in memory. The pixel buffer can be a set of 24-bit RGB values or a set of 8-bit values and a color map. This class is most often used when an image is generated in memory using an algorithm and then needs to be converted into an image.

For a description of the image consumer and image producer framework, see the Image-Consumer interface.

Single-frame and Multiframe Modes

The MemoryImageSource class is also capable of creating a *multiframe* image. A multiframe *image* is an image whose set of pixels can change over time. An example of a multiframe image is an animated GIF. To create a multiframe image with an memory image source, you first set the memory image source in multiframe (see setAnimated()). Once one set of pixels (a frame) has been created, you next call newPixels() to deliver the current frame to the image consumers. Then you can start creating the next frame.

MEMBER SUMMARY	
Constructor	
MemoryImageSource()	Constructs a new MemoryImageSource instance.
Image Producer Methods	
addConsumer()	Registers an image consumer with this image producer.
isConsumer()	Determines if an image consumer is registered with this image producer.
removeConsumer()	Removes a registered image consumer from this image producer.
requestTopDownLeftRightResend()	Request by an image consumer to retransmit pixels in top-down, left-right order.
startProduction()	Triggers the delivery of image data to an image consumer.

Continued

MEMBER SUMMARY	
Animation Methods	
`newPixels()`	Sends pixels to image consumers.
`setAnimated()`	Sets this memory image source to multiframe or single-frame mode.
`setFullBufferUpdates()`	Sets whether this memory image source will update using complete pixel buffers.

Example

This example generates the Mandelbrot set in a pixel buffer and uses the `MemoryImageSource` image producer to create an image pixel buffer. A 16-color index color model is used to represent the pixel values. See Figure 252.

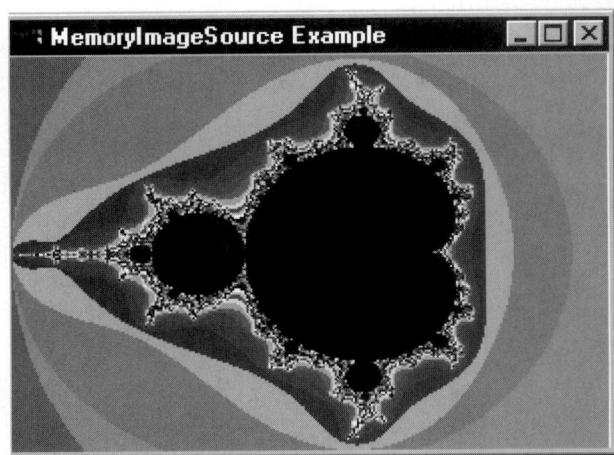

FIGURE 252: MemoryImageSource.

```
import java.awt.*;
import java.awt.image.*;
import java.net.*;
import java.util.*;

class Main extends Frame {
    Main() {
        super("MemoryImageSource Example");
        try {
            add(new MandelbrotCanvas(), BorderLayout.CENTER);
        } catch (Exception e) {
            e.printStackTrace();
        }
        setSize(300, 200);
        show();
    }

    static public void main(String[] args) {
        new Main();
    }
}

class MandelbrotCanvas extends Component {
    Image image;

    public void paint(Graphics g) {
        if (image == null ) {
            image = getToolkit().createImage(
                new MemoryImageSource(300, 200,
```

```
                generateColorModel(), generatePixels(300, 200), 0, 300));
        }
        g.drawImage(image, 0, 0, this);
    }

    IndexColorModel generateColorModel() {
        byte[] r = new byte[16];
        byte[] g = new byte[16];
        byte[] b = new byte[16];

        r[0] = 0; g[0] = 0; b[0] = 0;
        r[1] = 0; g[1] = 0; b[1] = (byte)192;
        r[2] = 0; g[2] = 0; b[2] = (byte)255;
        r[3] = 0; g[3] = (byte)192; b[3] = 0;
        r[4] = 0; g[4] = (byte)255; b[4] = 0;
        r[5] = 0; g[5] = (byte)192; b[5] = (byte)192;
        r[6] = 0; g[6] = (byte)255; b[6] = (byte)255;
        r[7] = (byte)192; g[7] = 0; b[7] = 0;
        r[8] = (byte)255; g[8] = 0; b[8] = 0;
        r[9] = (byte)192; g[9] = 0; b[9] = (byte)192;
        r[10] = (byte)255; g[10] = 0; b[10] = (byte)255;
        r[11] = (byte)192; g[11] = (byte)192; b[11] = 0;
        r[12] = (byte)255; g[12] = (byte)255; b[12] = 0;
        r[13] = (byte)80; g[13] = (byte)80; b[13] = (byte)80;
        r[14] = (byte)192; g[14] = (byte)192; b[14] = (byte)192;
        r[15] = (byte)255; g[15] = (byte)255; b[15] = (byte)255;

        return new IndexColorModel(4, 16, r, g, b);
    }

    final float xmin = -2.0f;
    final float xmax = 1.2f;
    final float ymin = -1.2f;
    final float ymax = 1.2f;
    byte[] generatePixels(int w, int h) {
        byte[] pixels = new byte[w * h];
        int pIx = 0;
        float[] p = new float[w];
        float q = ymin;
        float dp = (xmax-xmin)/w;
        float dq = (ymax-ymin)/h;

        p[0] = xmin;
        for (int i=1; i<w; i++) {
            p[i] = p[i-1] + dp;
        }

        for (int r=0; r<h; r++) {
            for (int c=0; c<w; c++) {
                int color = 1;
                float x = 0.0f;
                float y = 0.0f;
                float xsqr = 0.0f;
                float ysqr = 0.0f;
                do {
                    xsqr = x*x;
                    ysqr = y*y;
                    y = 2*x*y + q;
                    x = xsqr - ysqr + p[c];
                    color++;
```

A
B
C
D
E
F
G
H
I
J
K
L
M
N
O
P
Q
R
S
T
U
V
W
X
Y
Z

```
                    } while (color < 512 && xsqr + ysqr < 4);
                    pixels[pIx++] = (byte)(color % 16);
                }
                q += dq;
            }
            return pixels;
        }
    }
```

A
B
C
D
E
F
G
H
I
J
K
L
M
N
O
P
Q
R
S
T
U
V
W
X
Y
Z

addConsumer()

PURPOSE   Registers an image consumer with this image producer.

SYNTAX   `public synchronized void addConsumer(ImageConsumer ic)`

DESCRIPTION   This method registers the image consumer `ic` to receive pixels from this image producer. If `ic` is already one of its consumers, this method does nothing.

See `ImageProducer.addConsumer()` for details on how an image consumer should use this method.

PARAMETERS
`ic`   The non-`null` image consumer to register.

SEE ALSO   `ImageConsumer`.

EXAMPLE   See `ImageProducer.addConsumer()`.

isConsumer()

PURPOSE   Determines if an image consumer is registered with this image producer.

SYNTAX   `public synchronized boolean isConsumer(ImageConsumer ic)`

DESCRIPTION   See `ImageProducer.isConsumer()` for details on how an image consumer should use this method.

PARAMETERS
`ic`   The possibly `null` image consumer to check if registered.

RETURNS   `true` if `ic` has been registered; `false` otherwise.

SEE ALSO   `ImageConsumer`.

EXAMPLE   See `ImageProducer.isConsumer()`.

MemoryImageSource()

PURPOSE   Constructs a new `MemoryImageSource` instance.

SYNTAX

```
public MemoryImageSource(int width, int height, int[] pixels, int
    offset, int scansize)
public MemoryImageSource(int width, int height, int[] pixels, int
    offset, int scansize, Hashtable props)
public MemoryImageSource(int width, int height, ColorModel cm,
    byte[] pixels, int offset, int scansize)
public MemoryImageSource(int width, int height, ColorModel cm,
    int[] pixels, int offset, int scansize)
public MemoryImageSource(int width, int height, ColorModel cm,
    byte[] pixels, int offset, int scansize, Hashtable props)
public MemoryImageSource(int w, int h, ColorModel cm, int[]
    pixels, int offset, int scansize, Hashtable props)
```

DESCRIPTION

This constructor constructs a memory image source (image producer) that delivers pixels from a memory buffer. The memory image source is in single-frame mode by default.

`width` and `height` specify the width and height of the image.

`pixels` contains the pixel values of the image. The first pixel value is located at `pixels[offset]` and each row of pixel values in `pix` occupies `scansize` elements. In summary, the pixel (x, y) (the top-left corner pixel of the image) is stored in the pix array at `[x + y * scansize + offset]`.

`cm` specifies the color model in which the pixel values in `pixels` are encoded. If `cm` is not specified, the default color model is used (see the `ColorModel` class).

`props` is a hash table of image properties (see `ImageConsumer`) that the new image producer should deliver to the image consumer. If `props` is not specified or is `null`, an empty hash table is delivered to the image consumer.

PARAMETERS

cm   The non-`null` color model.

height   The height of the image in pixels.

offset   The index of the first pixel value in `pixels`.

pixels   The buffer of pixel values.

props   The possibly `null` hash table of image properties.

scansize   The width to use when extracting pixels from the `pixels` array.

width   The width of the image in pixels.

SEE ALSO   `ColorModel.getRGBdefault()`.

EXAMPLE   See the class example.

A
B
C
D
E
F
G
H
I
J
K
L
M
N
O
P
Q
R
S
T
U
V
W
X
Y
Z

newPixels()

PURPOSE	Sends new pixels to image consumers.

SYNTAX
```
public void newPixels()
public synchronized void newPixels(byte[] pixels, ColorModel cm,
    int offset, int scanSize)
public synchronized void newPixels(int[] pixels, ColorModel cm,
    int offset, int scanSize)
public synchronized void newPixels(int x, int y, int width, int
    height)
public synchronized void newPixels(int x, int y, int width, int
    height, boolean frameNotify)
```

DESCRIPTION

This method sends a new set of pixels to its image consumers. It is effective only if this memory image source is in multiframe (animated) mode; otherwise, it is ignored.

The first three forms of this method send pixels from the complete image. When an array of pixels `pixels` is supplied, this method first updates this memory image source's pixels, color model, offset, and scansize using the arguments specified before sending the complete image.

The last two forms of this method send pixels from a rectangle within the memory image source. `frameNotify` specifies whether to send a SINGLE-FRAMEDONE notification with the pixels. If `frameNotify` is unspecified, it defaults to `true`.

PARAMETERS

`cm`	The non-`null` color model.
`frameNotify`	If `true`, sends consumers a SINGLEFRAMEDONE notification; if `false`, does not send SINGLEFRAMEDONE notification to consumers.
`height`	The height of the rectangle of pixels to send.
`offset`	The index of the first pixel value in `pixels`.
`pixels`	The buffer of pixel values.
`scansize`	The width to use when extracting pixels from the `pixels` array.
`width`	The width of the rectangle of pixels to send.
`x`	The x-coordinate of the northwest corner of the rectangle of pixels to send.
`y`	The y-coordinate of the northwest corner of the rectangle of pixels to send.

SEE ALSO	`addConsumer()`, `setAnimated()`, `setFullBufferUpdates()`.
EXAMPLE	See `setAnimated()`.

removeConsumer()

PURPOSE	Removes a registered image consumer from this image producer.

SYNTAX   `public synchronized void removeConsumer(ImageConsumer ic)`

DESCRIPTION   See `ImageProducer.removeConsumer()` for details on how an image consumer should use this method.

PARAMETERS

   ic   The non-null image consumer to be removed.

EXAMPLE   See `ImageProducer.removeConsumer()`.

requestTopDownLeftRightResend( )

PURPOSE   Requests by an image consumer to retransmit pixels in top-down, left-right order.

SYNTAX   `public void requestTopDownLeftRightResend(ImageConsumer ic)`

DESCRIPTION   See `ImageProducer.requestTopDownLeftRightResend()` for details on how an image consumer should use this method. The implementation of this method for `MemoryImageSource` does nothing because a single-frame image is already in top-down, left-right format, and top-down, left-right format is not relevant for a multiframe image.

PARAMETERS

   ic   The non-null image consumer requesting the retransmission.

SEE ALSO   `ImageConsumer`.

EXAMPLE   See `ImageProducer.requestTopDownLeftRightResend()`.

setAnimated( )

PURPOSE   Sets this memory image source to multiframe or single-frame mode.

SYNTAX   `public synchronized void setAnimated(boolean animated)`

DESCRIPTION   If this method is used, it must be called immediately after the `MemoryImage-Source` instance is created to ensure that all image consumers receive the correct data. If an image consumer is added after this flag has been set, the image consumer may see only a snapshot of the data.

If the memory image source is being set to single-frame mode (`animated` is `false`), `STATICIMAGEDONE` is sent to all existing consumers and the list of consumers is cleared.

A
B
C
D
E
F
G
H
I
J
K
L
M
N
O
P
Q
R
S
T
U
V
W
X
Y
Z

PARAMETERS

animated   If `true`, sets image to multiframe mode; if `false`, sets image to single-frame mode.

SEE ALSO   `setFullBufferUpdates()`.

EXAMPLE   This example demonstrates how to use the memory image source to create an animated image. The program first reads in an image and then uses a pixel grabber to extract the pixels.

The Animator class is a thread that selectively copies portions of the image's pixels into a blank pixel buffer. Each

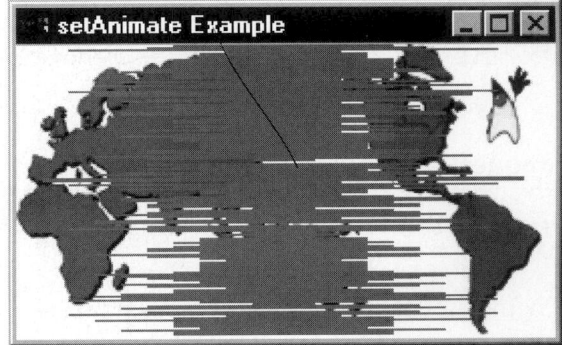

FIGURE 253: Animator.

time some pixels are copied into the pixel buffer, the thread notifies the image consumers. The resulting effect is that the image appears in a progressive fashion instead of all at once. See Figure 253.

```java
import java.awt.*;
import java.awt.event.*;
import java.awt.image.*;

class Main extends Frame {
    Image image;
    Main(String filename) {
        super("setAnimate Example");
        image = new Animator().getImage(getToolkit().getImage(filename));

        // Set the initial frame size and show the image.
        setSize(300, 390);
        show();
    }

    public void paint(Graphics g) {
        update(g);
    }
    public void update(Graphics g) {
        g.drawImage(image, getInsets().left, getInsets().top, this);
    }

    public static void main(String[] args) {
        if (args.length == 1) {
            new Main(args[0]);
        } else {
            System.err.println("Usage: java Main <image file>");
        }
    }
}
```

```
        }

class Animator extends Thread {
    PixelGrabber pg;
    MemoryImageSource mis;
    byte[] oldPixels;
    byte[] newPixels;

    Animator() {
    }
    Image getImage(Image image) {
        pg = new PixelGrabber(image, 0, 0, -1, -1, false);
        try {
            pg.grabPixels();
        } catch (Exception e) {
            e.printStackTrace();
        }

        // We only handle 8-bit images.
        if (!(pg.getPixels() instanceof byte[])) {
            return null;
        }

        oldPixels = (byte[])pg.getPixels();

        // Start the animation.
        start();

        newPixels = new byte[oldPixels.length];
        mis = new MemoryImageSource(pg.getWidth(), pg.getHeight(),
            pg.getColorModel(), newPixels, 0, pg.getWidth());
        mis.setAnimated(true);
        mis.setFullBufferUpdates(true);
        return Toolkit.getDefaultToolkit().createImage(mis);
    }

    int random(int r) {
        return (int)Math.floor(Math.random()*r);
    }

    public void run() {
        int w = pg.getWidth();
        int h = pg.getHeight();
        int[] x = new int[h];
        int inc = w/20;
        boolean done = false;

        try {
            while (!done) {
                done = true;

                // Modify buffer.
                for (int i=0; i<h; i++) {
                    if (x[i] < w/2 && random(3) == 0) {
                        // From the left.
                        int count = Math.min(inc, w-inc);
                        System.arraycopy(oldPixels, i*w+x[i],
                            newPixels, i*w+x[i], count);

                        // From the right.
```

A
B
C
D
E
F
G
H
I
J
K
L
M
N
O
P
Q
R
S
T
U
V
W
X
Y
Z

```
                                    count = Math.min(inc, w-inc);
                                    System.arraycopy(oldPixels, (i+1)*w-x[i]-count,
                                        newPixels, (i+1)*w-x[i]-count, count);
                                    x[i] += inc;
                                }
                                if (x[i] < w/2) {
                                    done = false;
                                }
                            }

                            // Send the new pixels to the consumers.
                            mis.newPixels(0, 0, pg.getWidth(), pg.getHeight());
                            Thread.sleep(33);
                        }
                    } catch (Exception e) {
                        e.printStackTrace();
                    }
                }
            }
```

setFullBufferUpdates()

PURPOSE   Sets whether this memory image source will update using complete pixel buff-
                ers.

SYNTAX   `public synchronized void setFullBufferUpdates(boolean full)`

DESCRIPTION   This method is effective only if this memory image source is in multiframe
                mode; otherwise, this method does nothing.

                If this method is used, it should be called immediately after the `MemoryImage-`
                `Source` instance has been created to ensure that all image consumers receive
                the correct pixel delivery hints.

PARAMETERS
`full`   If `true`, complete pixel buffers will be sent during updates; if `false`, only
                updated pixels will be sent.

SEE ALSO   `newPixels()`, `setAnimated()`.

EXAMPLE   See `setAnimated()`.

startProduction()

PURPOSE   Triggers the delivery of image data to an image consumer.

SYNTAX   `public void startProduction(ImageConsumer ic)`

DESCRIPTION   See `ImageProducer.startProduction()` for details on how an image con-
                sumer should use this method.

PARAMETERS

    `ic`   The non-`null` image consumer ready to receive pixels.

SEE ALSO   `ImageConsumer`.

EXAMPLE   See `ImageProducer.startProduction()`.

A
B
C
D
E
F
G
H
I
J
K
L
M
N
O
P
Q
R
S
T
U
V
W
X
Y
Z

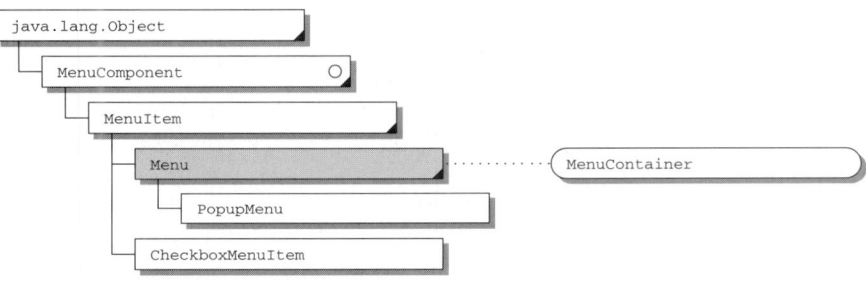

Syntax

`public class Menu extends MenuItem implements MenuContainer`

Description

A *menu* is an object that is inserted into a menu bar. See also `MenuBar`. Menus contain menu items. Figure 254 shows a menu bar with two menus: File and Edit. The File menu is active; it contains two menu items: New and Open... .

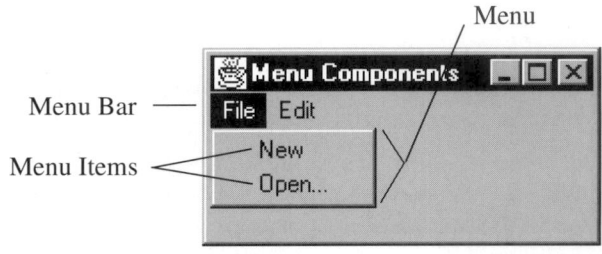

FIGURE 254: The Three Kinds of Menu Components.

The Label Property

A menu has a *label*, which is used when inserted into a menu bar. The menu bar normally displays only the menu's label. When the user clicks the menu's label, the menu appears.

The Tear-off Property

Some platforms support the menu *tear-off* property. If this property is supported and enabled, the user can make a user interface gesture to clone the menu as a top-level window. When a menu is torn off, both the original menu on the menu bar and the torn-off menu can be used to select menu items. The torn-off menu can be deleted by the user when it is no longer needed.

Cascading Menus

A cascading menu is created by adding a menu within another menu. There is no limit to the level of nesting of menus within another menu (see the `add()` example). When a menu displays its menu items, it typically shows menus differently that it does terminal menu items. For example, on the Windows platform, menus have an arrow beside them. The visual indication for menu items that are menus is platform-dependent.

Keyboard Shortcuts

The user can select an enabled menu item within a menu by either using mouse actions or by pressing the menu item's keyboard shortcut. Keyboard shortcuts for menu items inside cascading menus work in the same way they do for those inside noncascading menus. See `MenuItem` for details on keyboard shortcuts.

Events

When a menu item within a menu is selected, the menu item fires an action event (see `MenuItem`). The AWT does not require the programmer to enable action events for each menu item in a menu by adding action listeners to each menu item. Instead, it allows action listeners to be added to a menu. If a selected menu item does not have action events enabled but its parent menu does, the action event is passed up to the menu. Consequently, although a menu does not actually generate any events, it can be used to forward events fired by its menu items. In this way, a program needs only to enable action events for a menu and not individually for each menu item. When such an event is passed up, the event source of the event is the menu and not the menu item that was selected.

Note that such forwarding of action events is done only for one level of the menu containment hierarchy. More specifically, action events fired by a cascaded menu's menu items are not passed up to the cascaded menu's parent menu. Consequently, to handle action events fired by a cascaded menu's menu items, you need to add action listeners to the cascaded menu or to the cascaded menu's menu items. See the `add()` example.

MEMBER SUMMARY	
Constructor	
`Menu()`	Constructs a new `Menu` instance.
Menu Item Methods	
`add()`	Appends a menu item to this menu.
`addSeparator()`	Appends a menu item separator to this menu.
`insert()`	Inserts a menu item to this menu at a specified position.
`insertSeparator()`	Inserts a menu item separator to this menu at a specified position.
`getItem()`	Retrieves a menu item from this menu.
`getItemCount()`	Retrieves the number of menu items in this menu.
`remove()`	Removes a menu item from this menu.
`removeAll()`	Removes all menu items from this menu.
	Continued

A
B
C
D
E
F
G
H
I
J
K
L
M
N
O
P
Q
R
S
T
U
V
W
X
Y
Z

MEMBER SUMMARY

Property Method
isTearOff()   Determines if this menu is a tear-off menu.

Peer Methods
addNotify()   Creates this menu's peer hierarchy.
removeNotify()   Destroys this menu's peer hierarchy.

Debugging Method
paramString()   Generates a string representing this menu's state.

Deprecated Method
countItems()   Replaced by getItemCount().

See Also

java.awt.event.ActionEvent, java.awt.event.ActionListener, MenuBar, MenuComponent, MenuContainer, MenuItem.

Example

This example implements a menu whose menu items are always changing. (For a simpler example using a menu, see the Menu constructor example.) See Figure 255. It creates a Command menu that maintains a fixed list of commands. Each time a command is executed, it gets added to the top of the menu. If a command already appears in the menu, it is moved to the top of the menu. The menu can hold only ten commands, so if the menu is full, the menu item at the bottom of the list is first removed before a new command is added.

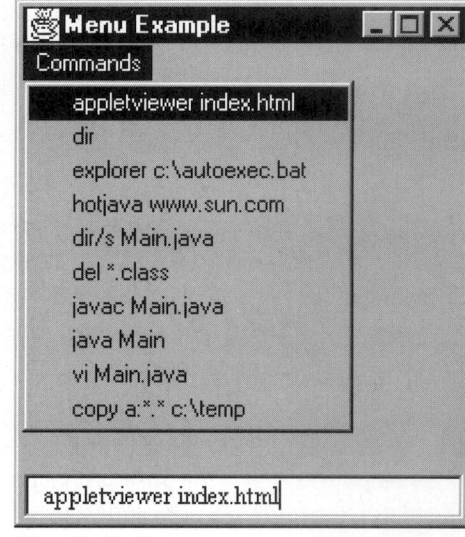

FIGURE 255: **Dynamically Updated Menu.**

```java
import java.awt.*;
import java.awt.event.*;
import java.util.*;

class Main extends Frame implements
ActionListener {
    Vector commands = new Vector();
    Menu m = new Menu("Commands");

    Main() {
        super("Menu Example");
        MenuBar mb = new MenuBar();
```

```
        // Add menu to menu bar.
        mb.add(m);

        // Set the menu bar on the frame.
        setMenuBar(mb);
        TextField tf = new TextField();
        add(tf, BorderLayout.SOUTH);
        tf.addActionListener(this);

        setSize(100, 100);
        show();
    }

    void updateMenu(Menu m) {
        // First remove all the menu items.
        m.removeAll();

        // Then add them back in.
        for (int i=0; i<commands.size(); i++) {
            m.add((String)commands.elementAt(i));
        }
    }

    public void addCommand(String cmd) {
        for (int i=0; i<m.getItemCount(); i++) {
            MenuItem mi = (MenuItem)m.getItem(i);
            if (mi.getLabel().equals(cmd)) {
                // Move command to top of list.
                commands.removeElementAt(i);
                commands.insertElementAt(cmd, 0);
                updateMenu(m);
                return;
            }
        }
        if (m.getItemCount() >= 10) {
            // Remove last command from list.
            commands.removeElementAt(commands.size()-1);
        }
        commands.insertElementAt(cmd, 0);
        updateMenu(m);
    }

    // Action handler for text field
    public void actionPerformed(ActionEvent evt) {
        String what = evt.getActionCommand();
        if (!what.equals("")) {
            addCommand(what);
            ((TextField)evt.getSource()).setText("");
        }
    }

    static public void main(String[] args) {
        new Main();
    }
}
```

add()

PURPOSE   Appends a menu item to this menu.

SYNTAX

```
public synchronized MenuItem add(MenuItem menuItem)
public void add(String label)
```

DESCRIPTION   This method adds the menu item menuItem to the end of this menu. If the string label is specified instead of a menu item, a menu item with the label label is automatically created and added to the menu. If label is "-", a separator is added to the menu. If the menu item already has a parent, it is first removed from its parent before being added to this menu.

Since Menu is a subclass of MenuItem, menuItem can be a Menu, in which case it would create a cascading menu off of this menu.

PARAMETERS

label   The non-null string specifying the label of the menu item.

menuItem   The non-null menu item.

RETURNS   The first form of add() returns the menu item added (menuItem).

SEE ALSO   addSeparator(), insert(), remove().

EXAMPLE   This example creates a couple of cascading menus (menus with submenus). See Figure 256. An action listener is added to each of the menus because action events do not propagate more than one ancestor level.

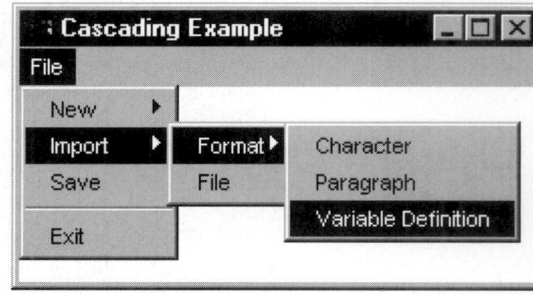

FIGURE 256:   **Cascading Menus.**

```
import java.awt.*;
import java.awt.event.*;

class Main extends Frame implements ActionListener {
    Main() {
        super("Cascading Example");
        MenuBar mb = new MenuBar();
        Menu m = new Menu("File");
        Menu newMenu = new Menu("New");
        MenuItem mi = newMenu.add(
            new MenuItem("Directory", new MenuShortcut(KeyEvent.VK_D)));
        mi.setActionCommand("Directory");
        mi = newMenu.add(
            new MenuItem("File", new MenuShortcut(KeyEvent.VK_F)));
        mi.setActionCommand("File");
        m.add(newMenu);
```

```
            Menu imp = new Menu("Import");
            Menu format = new Menu("Format");
            format.add("Character");
            format.add("Paragraph");
            format.add("Variable Definition");
            imp.add(format);
            imp.add("File");

            m.add(imp);
            m.add("Save");
            m.addSeparator();
            m.add("Exit");

            mb.add(m);

            // Add action listener for main menu and submenus
            m.addActionListener(this);
            newMenu.addActionListener(this);
            imp.addActionListener(this);
            format.addActionListener(this);

            // Set the menu bar on the frame.
            setMenuBar(mb);

            setSize(100, 100);
            show();
    }

    public void actionPerformed(ActionEvent evt) {
        System.out.println(evt.getActionCommand());
    }

    static public void main(String[] args) {
        new Main();
    }
}
```

addNotify()

PURPOSE	Creates this menu's peer hierarchy.
SYNTAX	`public void addNotify()`
DESCRIPTION	This method creates the menu's peer hierarchy if it does not yet exist. The menu's peer is created by calling the `Toolkit.createMenu()` method. This method should never be called directly. It is normally called by the menu component's container.
OVERRIDES	`MenuItem.addNotify()`.
SEE ALSO	`Toolkit`.
EXAMPLE	The usage of `addNotify()` is similar to `Component.addNotify()`. See the class example of `MenuContainer` for the usage of `Component.addNotify()`.

A
B
C
D
E
F
G
H
I
J
K
L

M

N
O
P
Q
R
S
T
U
V
W
X
Y
Z

addSeparator( )

PURPOSE   Appends a menu item separator to the menu.

SYNTAX   `public void addSeparator()`

DESCRIPTION   This method creates a menu item with the label "-" and adds it to the end of the menu.

SEE ALSO   `add()`, `insertSeparator()`.

EXAMPLE   This example creates a menu with three menu items, one enabled and two disabled. A separator is added after the first two menu items. See Figure 257.

FIGURE 257:
`Menu.addSeparator()`.

```
import java.awt.*;

class Main extends Frame {
    Main() {
        super("addSeparator Example");
        MenuBar mb = new MenuBar();
        Menu m = new Menu("File");
        MenuItem mi = m.add(new MenuItem("New"));
        mi.setEnabled(false);
        m.add("Open...");
        m.addSeparator();
        m.add("Exit");
        mb.add(m);

        // Set the menu bar on the frame.
        setMenuBar(mb);

        setSize(100, 100);
        show();
    }
    static public void main(String[] args) {
        new Main();
    }
}
```

countItems( )   *DEPRECATED*

PURPOSE   Replaced by `getItemCount()`.

SYNTAX   `public int countItems()`

RETURNS   The number of menu items in the menu.

DEPRECATION   Replace the usage of this deprecated method, as in
                `  int count = menu.countItems();`
                with
                `  int count = menu.getItemCount();`

getItem( )

PURPOSE	Retrieves a menu item from this menu.
SYNTAX	`public MenuItem getItem(int pos)`
DESCRIPTION	This method retrieves the menu item at index pos in this menu.
RETURNS	The menu item at the index pos.
PARAMETERS	
pos	The zero-based index of the menu item in this menu.
EXCEPTIONS	
`ArrayIndexOutOfBoundsException`	
	If pos is greater than `getItemCount()-1`.
SEE ALSO	`getItemCount()`. `java.lang.ArrayIndexOutOfBoundsException`.
EXAMPLE	See the class example.

getItemCount( )

PURPOSE	Retrieves the number of menu items in this menu.
SYNTAX	`public int getItemCount()`
DESCRIPTION	This method retrieves the number of menu items in this menu, including any menu item separators.
RETURNS	The number of menu items in this menu.
EXAMPLE	See the class example.

insert( )

PURPOSE	Inserts a menu item to this menu at a specified position.
SYNTAX	`public synchronized void insert(MenuItem menuItem, int pos)` `public void insert(String label, pos)`
DESCRIPTION	This method adds the menu item menuItem to this menu at position pos. All menu items at position pos or greater prior to the addition are shifted up one position in the menu. If the string label is specified instead of a menu item, a menu item with the label label is automatically created and added to the menu. If label is "-", a separator is added to the menu. If the menu item already has a parent, it is first removed from its parent before being added to the menu.

PARAMETERS

label	The non-null string specifying the label of the menu item.
menuItem	The non-null menu item.
pos	The zero-based index in this menu to insert the menu item.

EXCEPTIONS

IllegalArgumentException
>   If pos is negative.

SEE ALSO   add(), insertSeparator(), java.lang.IllegalArgumentException, remove().

EXAMPLE   This example accepts words from a text field and adds each word as a menu item to the top of the menu. Each set of words is separated by a separator. See Figure 258.

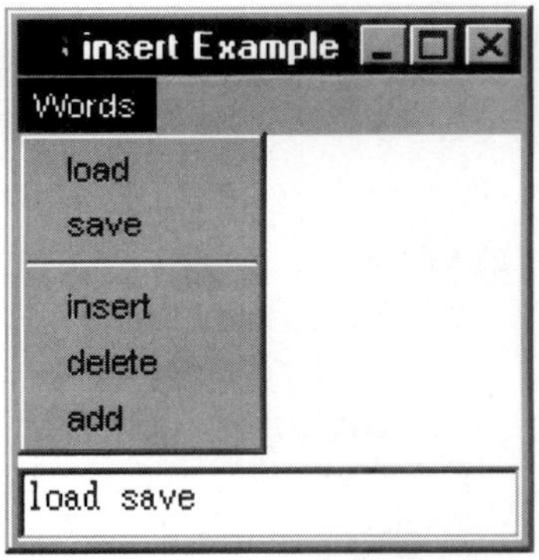

FIGURE 258: Menu.insert().

```java
import java.awt.*;
import java.awt.event.*;
import java.util.StringTokenizer;

class Main extends Frame implements ActionListener
{
    Menu m = new Menu("Words");
    boolean first = true;

    Main() {
        super("insert Example");
        MenuBar mb = new MenuBar();

        // Add menu to menu bar.
        mb.add(m);

        // Set the menu bar on the frame.
        setMenuBar(mb);
        TextField tf = new TextField();
        add(tf, BorderLayout.SOUTH);
        tf.addActionListener(this);

        setSize(100, 100);
        show();
    }

    void addWords(String sentence) {
        StringTokenizer parser = new StringTokenizer(sentence);
        int i;
        for (i = 0; parser.hasMoreTokens(); i++) {
            m.insert((String)parser.nextElement(), i);
        }
        if (!first) {
            m.insertSeparator(i);
        } else {
            first = false;
        }
    }
```

A
B
C
D
E
F
G
H
I
J
K
L
M
N
O
P
Q
R
S
T
U
V
W
X
Y
Z

```
    // Action handler for text field
    public void actionPerformed(ActionEvent evt) {
        String what = evt.getActionCommand();
        if (!what.equals("")) {
            addWords(what);
            ((TextField)evt.getSource()).setText("");
        }
    }

    static public void main(String[] args) {
        new Main();
    }
}
```

insertSeparator()

PURPOSE   Inserts a menu item separator to the menu at a specified position.

SYNTAX   `public void insertSeparator(int pos)`

DESCRIPTION   This method creates a menu item with the label "–" and adds it to this menu at
               position pos. All menu items at position pos or greater prior to the addition are
               shifted up one position in the menu.

PARAMETERS
pos   The zero-based index in this menu to insert the menu item.

EXCEPTIONS
IllegalArgumentException
               If pos is negative.

SEE ALSO   `addSeparator()`, `insert()`.

EXAMPLE   See `insert()`.

isTearOff()

PURPOSE   Determines if the menu is a tear-off menu.

SYNTAX   `public boolean isTearOff()`

DESCRIPTION   If a menu is a tear-off menu, the user can make a user interface gesture to clone
               the menu as a top-level window. See the class description for more information
               about tear-off menus.

RETURNS   `true` if the menu is a tear-off menu; `false` otherwise.

A
B
C
D
E
F
G
H
I
J
K
L
M
N
O
P
Q
R
S
T
U
V
W
X
Y
Z

Menu()

PURPOSE   Constructs a new Menu instance.

SYNTAX   ```
              public Menu()
              public Menu(String label)
              public Menu(String label, boolean tearOff)
              ```

DESCRIPTION   This constructor creates a new menu with the label label. If no label is speci-
              fied, it defaults to an empty label (""). If tearOff is true, then the menu can
              be torn off. If tearOff is not specified, it defaults to false. See the class
              description for details on tear-off menus. If an AWT implementation does not
              support tear-off menus, tearOff is ignored.

PARAMETERS
  label       The non-null string specifying the menu's label.
  tearOff     Specifies whether the menu can be torn off.

EXAMPLE       This example creates a menu bar that has a
              single menu, which has a single menu item.
              It demonstrates how to process action
              events fired by the menu item within the
              menu. See Figure 259.

FIGURE 259:   Menu.Menu().

```java
import java.awt.*;
import java.awt.event.*;

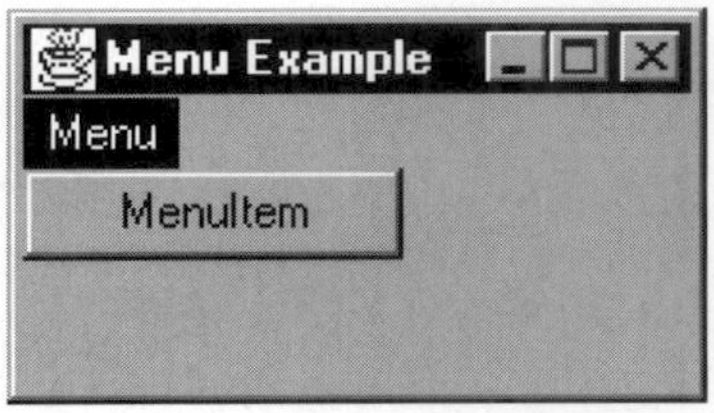

public class Main extends Frame implements ActionListener {
    Menu m = new Menu("Menu");

    Main() {
        super("Menu Example");
        MenuBar mb = new MenuBar();

        // Add item to menu.
        m.add("MenuItem");

        // Add listener for menu
        m.addActionListener(this);

        // Add menu to menu bar
        mb.add(m);

        // Set menu bar on frame.
        setMenuBar(mb);

        setSize(100, 100);
        show();
    }

    // Action handler for menu
    public void actionPerformed(ActionEvent evt) {
        System.out.println(evt.getActionCommand());
```
```

```
    }

    static public void main(String[] args) {
        new Main();
    }
}
```

paramString()

PURPOSE	Generates a string representation of this menu's state.
SYNTAX	`public String paramString()`
DESCRIPTION	The returned string includes an indication of whether the menu is a tear-off menu or a Help menu, plus that menu's menu item string representation. This method is called by the `toString()` method and is typically used for debugging.
RETURNS	A non-`null` string representing the menu item's state.
OVERRIDES	`MenuItem.paramString()`.
SEE ALSO	`MenuComponent.toString()`, `java.lang.Object.toString()`.
EXAMPLE	See `Component.paramString()`.

remove()

PURPOSE	Removes a menu item from this menu.
SYNTAX	`public synchronized void remove(int pos)` `public synchronized void remove(MenuComponent menuItem)`
DESCRIPTION	This method removes the menu item `menuitem` from this menu. If `menuItem` is not in the menu, this method call is ignored. If `pos` is specified instead of `menuItem`, then the menu item at index `pos` is removed.
PARAMETERS	
menuItem	The non-`null` menu item in the menu.
pos	The zero-based index of the menu item in the menu.
SEE ALSO	`add()`, `addSeparator()`, `insert()`, `insertSeparator()`, `removeAll()`.

removeAll()

EXAMPLE   This example creates a menu that has five items. Pressing the Rotate button brings the top menu item to the bottom. See Figure 260.

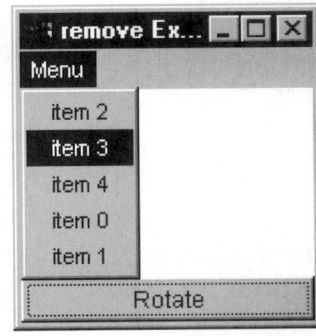

FIGURE 260:   **Rotating Menu Items.**

```java
import java.awt.*;
import java.awt.event.*;

class Main extends Frame implements ActionListener{
    Menu m = new Menu("Menu");
    Main() {
        super("remove Example");
        MenuBar mb = new MenuBar();

        // Add 5 menu items
        for (int i = 0; i < 5; i++) {
            m.add("item " + i);
        }

        // Add increment button.
        Button b;
        add(b = new Button("Rotate"), BorderLayout.SOUTH);
        b.addActionListener(this);

        // Set the menu bar on the frame.
        mb.add(m);
        setMenuBar(mb);
        setSize(100, 100);
        show();
    }

    // Action handler for button
    public void actionPerformed(ActionEvent evt) {
        MenuItem top = m.getItem(0);
        m.remove(0);
        m.add(top);
    }

    static public void main(String[] args) {
        new Main();
    }
}
```

removeAll()

PURPOSE   Removes all menu items from this menu.

SYNTAX   `public synchronized void removeAll()`

SEE ALSO   `remove()`.

EXAMPLE   See the class example.

removeNotify()

PURPOSE	Destroys this menu's peer hierarchy.
SYNTAX	`public void removeNotify()`
DESCRIPTION	This method should never be called directly. It is normally called by the component's container.
OVERRIDES	`MenuComponent.removeNotify()`.
EXAMPLE	The usage of `removeNotify()` is like that of `Component.removeNotify()`. See `Component.setVisible()` for a usage example of `Component.removeNotify()`.

A
B
C
D
E
F
G
H
I
J
K
L
M
N
O
P
Q
R
S
T
U
V
W
X
Y
Z

MenuBar

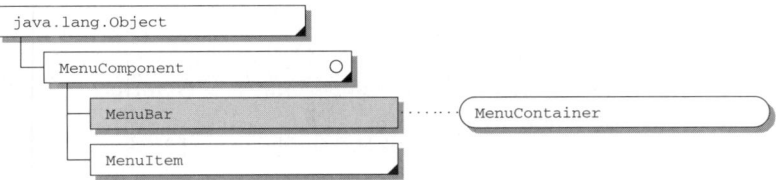

Syntax
`public class MenuBar extends MenuComponent implements MenuContainer`

Description

The *menu bar* is a strip across the top of a frame. If the frame has a title bar, the menu bar is located directly under the title bar. On some platforms, the menu bar appears at the top of the screen. The menu bar contains menus. Normally, only the menu labels are displayed. If the user clicks a menu label, the menu associated with the label appears.

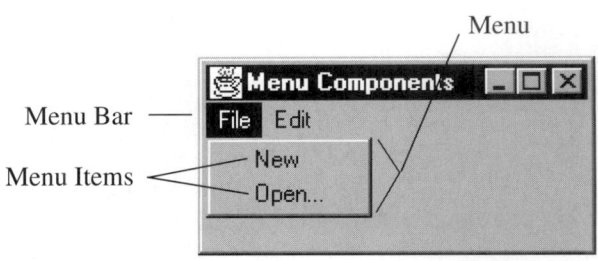

FIGURE 261: **The Three Kinds of Menu Components.**

Figure 261 shows a frame with both a title bar and a menu bar. The menu bar contains two menus: File and Edit. The File menu is being displayed; it contains two menu items: New and Open....

The list of menus in a menu bar can be modified at any time, regardless of whether the menu bar is installed. However, a menu can be inserted in only one menu bar at a time.

The only valid parent for a menu bar is a `Frame` instance.

The Help Menu
There is a special menu designated the Help menu. The only thing special about the Help menu is that on some platforms, it appears at the right edge of the menu bar.

Keyboard Shortcut
The user can access menu items contained within a menu in the menu bar by entering the menu item's *keyboard shortcut*. See the `MenuItem`'s class description for details. The menu bar class contains methods for finding and deleting menu short cuts within its hierarchy, as well as a method for enumerating all shortcuts.

Events

A menu bar does not fire any events.[1]

MEMBER SUMMARY	
Constructor	
MenuBar()	Constructs a new MenuBar instance.
Menu Methods	
add()	Adds a menu to this menu bar.
getMenu()	Retrieves a menu on this menu bar.
getMenuCount()	Retrieves the number of menus on this menu bar.
remove()	Removes a menu from this menu bar.
Help Menu Methods	
getHelpMenu()	Retrieves this menu bar's Help menu.
setHelpMenu()	Replaces this menu bar's Help menu.
Keyboard Shortcut Methods	
deleteShortcut()	Deletes a keyboard shortcut from menu items in this menu bar.
getShortcutMenuItem()	Retrieves the menu item in this menu bar that has the specified keyboard shortcut.
shortcuts()	Lists the keyboard shortcuts of menu items in this menu bar.
Peer Methods	
addNotify()	Creates this menu bar's peer.
removeNotify()	Destroys this menu bar's peer.
Deprecated Method	
countMenus()	Replaced by getMenuCount().

See Also

Frame.getMenuBar(), Frame.setMenuBar(), Menu, MenuComponent, MenuContainer, MenuItem, MenuShortcut.

---

1. In the deprecated Java 1.0 event model (Event), events fired by menu items contained in the menu bar can be passed up to the menu bar. These events are automatically passed on to the menu bar's frame. You can handle these events by overriding the frame's handleEvent() method.

Example

This example creates a menu bar with three menus. See Figure 262. To keep it short, only the File menu contains two menu items: New and Open... . This example also shows how to catch action events fired by menu items. For details on these events, see the `MenuItem` class.

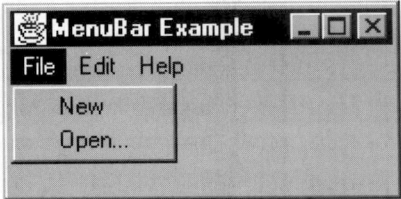

FIGURE 262:   MenuBar.

```java
import java.awt.*;
import java.awt.event.*;

class Main extends Frame implements ActionListener {
    Main() {
        super("MenuBar Example");
        MenuBar mb = new MenuBar();
        Menu m = new Menu("File");

        m.add("New");
        m.add("Open...");
        m.addActionListener(this);
        mb.add(m);

        // To keep it short, these menus don't have menu items.
        mb.add(new Menu("Edit"));
        mb.setHelpMenu(new Menu("Help"));

        // Set the menu bar on the frame.
        setMenuBar(mb);

        setSize(200, 100);
        show();
    }

    public void actionPerformed(ActionEvent evt) {
        String what = evt.getActionCommand();
        if ("New".equals(what)) {
            // do new
            System.out.println("action performed on New");
        } else if ("Open...".equals(what)) {
            // do open
            System.out.println("action performed on Open ...");
        }
    }

    static public void main(String[] args) {
        new Main();
    }
}
```

add()

PURPOSE Adds a menu to this menu bar.

SYNTAX `public synchronized Menu add(Menu menu)`

DESCRIPTION This method adds a menu to the end of the menu bar. If the menu already has a parent, it is first removed from its parent before being added to the menu bar. This means that the same menu cannot be inserted into more than one menu bar.

There is currently no way to insert a menu in the middle of a menu bar. To work around this, you need to remove all of the menus and reinsert them, placing the new menu in the desired spot.

PARAMETERS

menu The non-`null` menu to be added to the menu bar.

SEE ALSO Menu.

EXAMPLE This example creates a frame that has a checkbox. Only when the checkbox is checked does the Edit menu appear on the menu bar. See Figure 263. Figure 264 shows the Edit menu present.

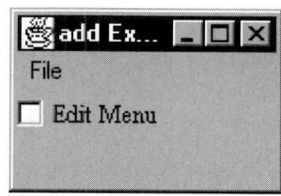

FIGURE 263: Before MenuBar.add().

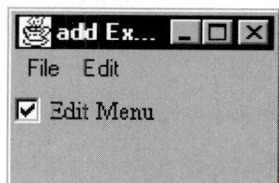

FIGURE 264: After MenuBar.add().

```java
import java.awt.*;
import java.awt.event.*;

class Main extends Frame implements ItemListener {
    Menu editMenu = new Menu("Edit");
    Checkbox editMenuCheckbox =
        new Checkbox("Edit Menu");

    Main() {
        super("add Example");
        MenuBar mb = new MenuBar();

        mb.add(new Menu("File"));
        setMenuBar(mb);

        add(editMenuCheckbox, BorderLayout.NORTH);
        editMenuCheckbox.addItemListener(this);

        setSize(100, 100);
        show();
    }

    static public void main(String[] args) {
        Main m = new Main();
    }

    // Item handler for checkbox
    public void itemStateChanged(ItemEvent evt) {
        if (evt.getStateChange() == ItemEvent.SELECTED) {
            getMenuBar().add(editMenu);
```

```
        } else {
            getMenuBar().remove(editMenu);
        }
    }
}
```

A
B
C
D
E
F
G
H
I
J
K
L
M
N
O
P
Q
R
S
T
U
V
W
X
Y
Z

addNotify()

PURPOSE	Creates this menu bar's peer hierarchy.
SYNTAX	`public void addNotify()`
DESCRIPTION	This method creates the menu bar's peer hierarchy, if it does not exist. The menu bar's peer is created by calling the `Toolkit.createMenuBar()` method. This method should never be called directly. It is normally called by the menu component's parent.
SEE ALSO	`Component, Toolkit`.

countMenus() *DEPRECATED*

PURPOSE	Replaced by `getMenuCount()`.
SYNTAX	`public int countMenus()`
RETURNS	The number of menus on the menu bar.

DEPRECATION	Replace the usage of this deprecated method, as in
	`int count = menubar.countMenus();`
	with
	`int count = menubar.getMenuCount();`

deleteShortcut()

PURPOSE	Deletes a keyboard shortcut from menu items in this menu bar.
SYNTAX	`public void deleteShortcut(MenuShortcut shortcut)`
DESCRIPTION	See the class description of `MenuItem` for details on keyboard shortcuts. This method deletes the keyboard shortcut `shortcut` from all menu items in menus on this menu bar. Menu items with other keyboard shortcuts are not affected. *Note*: In Java 1.1.2, `deleteShortcut()` deletes all shortcuts from all menus in this menu bar, not just `shortcut`. This is a bug.
PARAMETERS	
shortcut	The keyboard shortcut to delete.

SEE ALSO   getShortcutMenuItem(), MenuItem.deleteShortCut(),
MenuItem.getShortcut(), MenuItem.setShortcut(), MenuShortcut
shortcuts().

EXAMPLE   This example creates a menu bar that has a
menu, which has three menu items, each
containing a menu shortcut. See Figure
265. Using the checkboxes and text field at
the bottom of the frame, you can find or
delete menu shortcuts.

Note: Due to a bug in Java 1.1.2, checking
Delete deletes all shortcuts, regardless of
what is entered in the text field.

**FIGURE 265:   Menu Shortcuts in
a Menu Bar.**

```
import java.awt.*;
import java.awt.event.*;
import java.util.Enumeration;

class Main extends Frame implements ActionListener, ItemListener {
    MenuBar mb = new MenuBar();
    boolean delsc = false;

    Main() {
        super("deleteShortcut Example");
        Menu m = new Menu("File");
        MenuItem mi;

        mi = new MenuItem("New", new MenuShortcut(KeyEvent.VK_N));
        mi.setActionCommand("New");  // required for shortcut
        m.add(mi);

        mi = new MenuItem("Open...", new MenuShortcut(KeyEvent.VK_O));
        mi.setActionCommand("Open"); // required for shortcut
        m.add(mi);

        m.add("-");

        m.add(mi = new MenuItem("Exit", new MenuShortcut(KeyEvent.VK_E)));
        mi.setActionCommand("Exit"); // required for shortcut
        mb.add(m);

        // Add listener for menu (and its menu items)
        m.addActionListener(this);

        // Set the menu bar on the frame.
        setMenuBar(mb);

        // Add controls for viewing and deleting shortcuts
        Panel p = new Panel(new GridLayout(1, 0));
        CheckboxGroup cg = new CheckboxGroup();
        Checkbox del = new Checkbox("Delete", false, cg);
        Checkbox find = new Checkbox("Find", true, cg);
        del.addItemListener(this);
        find.addItemListener(this);
```

A
B
C
D
E
F
G
H
I
J
K
L
M
N
O
P
Q
R
S
T
U
V
W
X
Y
Z

```
                TextField tf = new TextField("");
                p.add(del);
                p.add(find);
                p.add(tf);
                tf.addActionListener(this);

                add(new TextArea("Text area"), BorderLayout.CENTER);
                add(p, BorderLayout.SOUTH);

                setSize(100, 100);
                show();
        }

        void printShortcuts(String msg, MenuBar mb) {
            System.out.print(msg);
            for (Enumeration sc = mb.shortcuts();
                 sc.hasMoreElements();
                 ) {
                System.out.print(sc.nextElement() + " ");
            }
            System.out.println("");
        }

        public void actionPerformed(ActionEvent evt) {
            if (evt.getSource() instanceof MenuItem) {
                System.out.println(evt.getActionCommand());
            } else if (evt.getSource() instanceof TextField) {
                String sc = evt.getActionCommand();
                MenuShortcut target = new MenuShortcut(sc.charAt(0));
                if (delsc) {
                    printShortcuts("Before delete: ", mb);
                    mb.deleteShortcut(target);
                    printShortcuts("After delete: ", mb);
                } else {
                    System.out.println(mb.getShortcutMenuItem(target));
                }
            }
        }

        public void itemStateChanged(ItemEvent evt) {
            delsc = (evt.getItem().equals("Delete"));
        }

        static public void main(String[] args) {
            new Main();
        }
    }
```

A
B
C
D
E
F
G
H
I
J
K
L
M
N
O
P
Q
R
S
T
U
V
W
X
Y
Z

getHelpMenu()

PURPOSE	Retrieves this menu bar's Help menu.
SYNTAX	`public Menu getHelpMenu()`
DESCRIPTION	A menu bar can have a special menu designated the Help menu. The only thing special about the Help menu is that on some platforms, it appears at the right edge of the menu bar.
RETURNS	This menu bar's Help menu. A return value of `null` means a Help menu has not been set.
SEE ALSO	`setHelpMenu()`.
EXAMPLE	This method removes the Help menu from the menu bar.

```
void removeHelpMenu(MenuBar menubar) {
    Menu hm = menubar.getHelpMenu();
    if (hm != null) {
        menubar.remove(hm);
    }
}
```

getMenu()

PURPOSE	Retrieves a menu on this menu bar.
SYNTAX	`public Menu getMenu(int pos)`
PARAMETERS	
pos	The zero-based index of the menu on the menu bar.
RETURNS	The non-`null` menu at the zero-based index `pos`.
EXCEPTIONS	
`ArrayIndexOutOfBoundsException`	If `pos` is beyond the size of this menu.
SEE ALSO	`addMenu()`, `getHelpMenu()`.
EXAMPLE	This method prints the labels of all of the menus on a menu bar.

```
void printMenuLabels(MenuBar menubar) {
    for (int i=0; i<menubar.getMenuCount(); i++) {
        System.out.println(menubar.getMenu(i).getLabel());
    }
}
```

A
B
C
D
E
F
G
H
I
J
K
L
M
N
O
P
Q
R
S
T
U
V
W
X
Y
Z

getMenuCount()

PURPOSE   Retrieves the number of menus on this menu bar.

SYNTAX   `public int getMenuCount()`

DESCRIPTION   This method retrieves the number of menus on this menu bar, including the Help menu.

RETURNS   The number of menus on this menu bar.

EXAMPLE   This example enables or disables all menu items in all of the menus in the menu bar. See Figures 266 and 267.

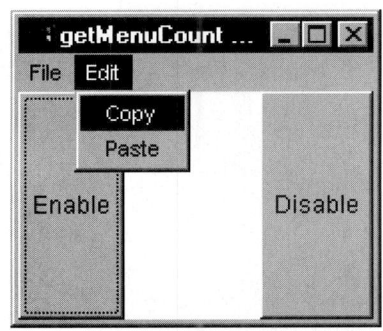

FIGURE 266:   **Enabled Menu Items.**

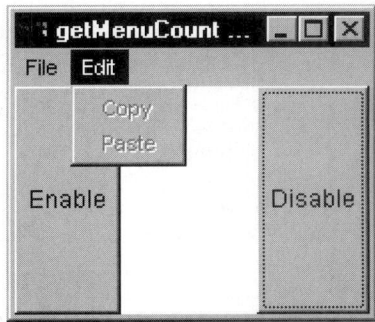

FIGURE 267:   **Disabled Menu Items.**

```java
import java.awt.*;
import java.awt.event.*;

class Main extends Frame implements ActionListener {

    Main(String title) {
        super(title);
        MenuBar mb = new MenuBar();
        Menu menu = new Menu("File");

        menu.add("New");
        menu.add("Open...");
        mb.add(menu);

        menu = new Menu("Edit");
        menu.add("Copy");
        menu.add("Paste");
        mb.add(menu);

        setMenuBar(mb);

        Button b;
        add(b=new Button("Enable"), BorderLayout.WEST);
```

```
        b.addActionListener(this);
        add(b=new Button("Disable"), BorderLayout.EAST);
        b.addActionListener(this);

        setSize(100, 100);
        show();
    }

    static public void main(String[] args) {
        Main m = new Main("getMenuCount Example");
    }

    void enableMenuItems(boolean enable) {
        for (int i=0; i<getMenuBar().getMenuCount(); i++) {
            Menu menu = getMenuBar().getMenu(i);
            for (int j=0; j<menu.getItemCount(); j++) {
                MenuItem menuitem = menu.getItem(j);
                menuitem.setEnabled(enable);
            }
        }
    }

    // Button action listener
    public void actionPerformed(ActionEvent evt) {
        String what = evt.getActionCommand();
        boolean enable = "Enable".equals(what);

        if (enable || "Disable".equals(what)) {
            enableMenuItems(enable);
        }
    }
}
```

getShortcutMenuItem()

PURPOSE	Retrieves the menu item in this menu bar that has the specified shortcut.
SYNTAX	`public MenuItem getShortcutMenuItem(MenuShortcut shortcut)`
DESCRIPTION	See the class description of `MenuItem` for a description of keyboard shortcuts. This method finds the first menu item in the menus on this menu bar that has the keyboard shortcut `shortcut`.
PARAMETERS	
shortcut	The non-`null` shortcut for which to search.
RETURNS	A menu item that has keyboard shortcut `shortcut`; `null` if no menu item has that shortcut.
SEE ALSO	`deleteShortcut()`, `MenuShortcut`, `MenuItem.setShortcut()`, `shortcuts()`.
EXAMPLE	See `deleteMenuShortcut()`.

A
B
C
D
E
F
G
H
I
J
K
L
M
N
O
P
Q
R
S
T
U
V
W
X
Y
Z

MenuBar( )

PURPOSE   Constructs a new `MenuBar` instance.

SYNTAX   `public MenuBar()`

DESCRIPTION This constructor creates a new `MenuBar` instance, which must be installed in a frame before it can be used by the user. A frame is the only valid parent that a `MenuBar` can have. The `MenuBar` instance can be assigned to only one frame.

SEE ALSO   `Frame.setMenuBar()`.

EXAMPLE   This example creates a frame that has a menu bar with a single menu File. The File menu is set to use a large font but its menu items do not inherit the font usage. See Figure 268.

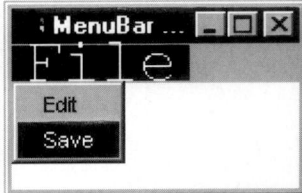

FIGURE 268: **MenuBar with Large Font Menu.**

```java
import java.awt.*;

class Main {
    static public void main(String[] args) {
        Frame f = new Frame("MenuBar Example");
        MenuBar menubar = new MenuBar();

        f.setMenuBar(menubar);
        Menu menu = new Menu("File");
        menu.setFont(new Font("Monospaced", Font.PLAIN, 32));
        menu.add("Edit");
        menu.add("Save");
        menubar.add(menu);
        f.setSize(100, 100);
        f.show();
    }
}
```

remove( )

PURPOSE   Removes a menu from this menu bar.

SYNTAX   `public synchronized void remove(int pos)`
            `public synchronized void remove(MenuComponent menu)`

DESCRIPTION This method removes a menu from this menu bar. The menu can be specified either by its index in the menu (pos) or by the menu component menu itself. All remaining menus that have indexes greater than the index of the removed menu are decreased by one. If the menu has a peer, the peer is destroyed.

PARAMETERS

menu   The non-null menu to be removed. If menu is not in this menu bar, this method does nothing.

pos   The zero-based index of the menu in the menu bar.

SEE ALSO   add().

EXAMPLE   See add().

removeNotify()

PURPOSE   Destroys this menu bar's peer.

SYNTAX   public void removeNotify()

DESCRIPTION   This method should never be called directly. It is normally called by the component's container.

OVERRIDES   MenuComponent.removeNotify().

SEE ALSO   MenuComponent.

EXAMPLE   See Component.setVisible().

setHelpMenu()

PURPOSE   Replaces this menu bar's Help menu.

SYNTAX   public synchronized void setHelpMenu(Menu menu)

DESCRIPTION   This method sets the menu menu to be this menu bar's Help menu. If a Help menu already exists, the current Help menu is removed from the menu bar and menu becomes the new Help menu.

PARAMETERS

menu   The non-null menu to be set.

EXAMPLE   This example creates a frame with a Help menu that contains three menu items. See Figure 269.

FIGURE 269:
MenuBar.setHelpMenu().

```
import java.awt.*;

class Main extends Frame {
    Main(String title) {
        super(title);
        MenuBar mb = new MenuBar();
```

```
                 Menu menu = new Menu("Help");

                 menu.add("Help Topics...");
                 menu.add("Search...");
                 menu.addSeparator();
                 menu.add("About...");
                 mb.setHelpMenu(menu);

                 // Set the menu bar on the frame.
                 setMenuBar(mb);
                 setSize(200, 200);
                 show();
             }

         static public void main(String[] args) {
             Main m = new Main("setHelpMenu Example");
         }
     }
}
```

A
B
C
D
E
F
G
H
I
J
K
L
M
N
O
P
Q
R
S
T
U
V
W
X
Y
Z

shortcuts()

PURPOSE	Lists the keyboard shortcuts associated with menu items in this menu bar.
SYNTAX	`public synchronized Enumeration shortcuts()`
RETURNS	A non-`null` enumeration of the keyboard shortcuts associated with all menu items in all menus on this menubar.
SEE ALSO	`deleteShortcut()`, `getShortcutMenuItem()`, `MenuItem.getShortcut()`, `MenuShortcut`.
EXAMPLE	See `deleteMenuShortcut()`.

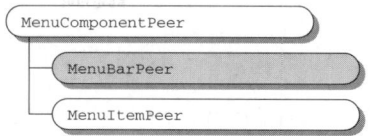

Syntax

`public interface MenuBarPeer extends MenuComponentPeer`

Description

The menu bar component (see the `MenuBar` class) in the AWT uses the platform's native implementation of a menu bar. So that the AWT menu bar behaves the same on all platforms, the menu bar is assigned a *peer,* whose task is to translate the behavior of the platform's native menu bar to the behavior of the AWT menu bar.

AWT programmers normally do not directly use peer classes and interfaces. Instead, they deal with AWT components in the `java.awt` package. These in turn automatically manage their peers. Only someone who is porting the AWT to another platform should be concerned with the peer classes and interfaces. Consequently, most peer documentation refers to `java.awt` counterparts.

Menu component peers serve the same role as component peers. See `Component` and `Toolkit` for additional information about component peers.

MEMBER SUMMARY	
Peer Methods	
`addHelpMenu()`	Replaces the Help menu.
`addMenu()`	Adds a menu to the menu bar.
`delMenu()`	Removes a menu from the menu bar.

See Also

`java.awt.Component`, `java.awt.MenuBar`, `java.awt.MenuComponent`, `java.awt.Toolkit`.

A
B
C
D
E
F
G
H
I
J
K
L
M
N
O
P
Q
R
S
T
U
V
W
X
Y
Z

addHelpMenu( )

PURPOSE	Replaces the Help menu.
SYNTAX	`void addHelpMenu(Menu menu)`
PARAMETERS	
`menu`	The non-null menu to be set.
SEE ALSO	`java.awt.MenuBar.setHelpMenu()`.

addMenu( )

PURPOSE	Adds a menu to the menu bar.
SYNTAX	`void addMenu(Menu menu)`
PARAMETERS	
`menu`	The non-null menu to be added to the menu bar.
SEE ALSO	`java.awt.MenuBar.add()`.

delMenu( )

PURPOSE	Removes a menu from the menu bar.
SYNTAX	`void delMenu(int pos)`
PARAMETERS	
`pos`	The zero-based index of the menu in the menu bar.
SEE ALSO	`java.awt.MenuBar.remove()`.

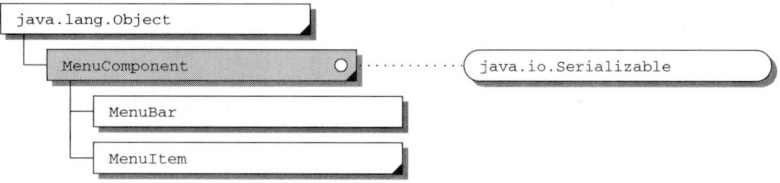

Syntax

`public abstract class MenuComponent implements Serializable`

Description

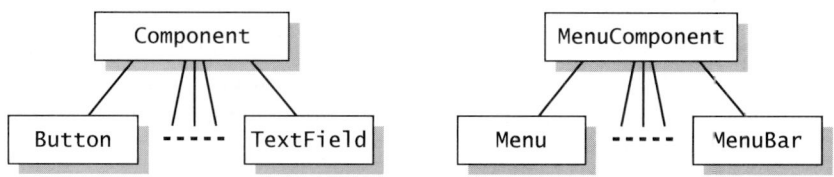

FIGURE 270:   Component and MenuComponent.

The MenuComponent class is similar to the Component class in that it is the superclass of all other AWT components. See Figure 270. Menu-related components do not extend from Component because menu components do not have most of the capabilities available to components. For example, you can't paint on menu components, control their layout (only their ordering), make them invisible, or change their colors. Moreover, no other events are fired by menu components, other than the action event fired by a menu item when it is selected.

This class serves as the superclass of all menu-related components. There are presently three kinds of menu components in the AWT package, as shown in Figure 271.

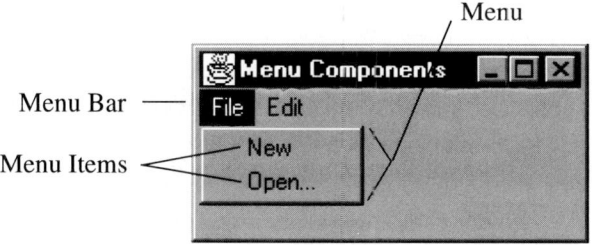

FIGURE 271:   The Three Kinds of Menu Components.

Events

Among menu components, only the menu item fires events. In particular, a menu item fires only action events. For convenience, action events not processed by menu items are forwarded to their parent (a menu). This allows action listeners to be added to the menu instead of to individual menu items. Menu bars do not fire any events.

Menu components participate in the AWT event flow in a similar way that `Component` objects do. The main difference between the two is that menu components can pass up their events to their menu component parents, while components do not pass up their events.[1] As described previously, selecting a menu item fires an action event, which may be passed up to its parent (a menu) if the parent is a menu component with action events enabled.

For a complete discussion on events, event handlers, and event flow, see the `AWTEvent` class.

The Name

Each instance of a menu component has a name associated with it. This is a string that is by default initialized to a unique identifier by its AWT class constructor. For example, the `MenuBar` class assigns a name of the form "menubar" concatenated with the value of a counter that it increments for each instance of `MenuBar` created (e.g., "menubar0"). The program can overwrite this default, by using `setName()`, to set it to a program-specific string.

A menu component's name is a placeholder for the program to record a locale-independent identifier for the component. Instead of using a possibly localized string, such as menu item's label, you would use the menu component's name for comparison when checking for a menu component's identity (see the `getName()` method, for example). Subclasses of `MenuItem` can also use the item's action command for similar purposes when dealing with the item's action events (see `MenuItem`).

In addition to obvious debugging uses, the menu component's name can be used, for example, by a GUI builder to allow the user to assign an identifier to each menu component instance the user creates.

MEMBER SUMMARY	
Font Methods	
`getFont()`	Retrieves this menu component's font.
`setFont()`	Sets this menu component's font.
Name Methods	
`getName()`	Retrieves this menu component's name.
`setName()`	Sets this menu component's name.
Parent Method	
`getParent()`	Retrieves this menu component's parent.

---

1. Components that use the deprecated event model (`Event`) still pass up their events to their parents.

MEMBER SUMMARY	
Event Methods	
dispatchEvent()	Dispatches an event to this menu component.
processEvent()	Processes an event enabled for this menu component.
Peer Method	
removeNotify()	Destroys this menu component's peer hierarchy.
Debugging Methods	
paramString()	Generates a string representation of this menu component's state.
toString()	Generates a string representation of this menu component's state.
Deprecated Methods	
getPeer()	Should not manipulate peers directly.
postEvent()	Replaced by dispatchEvent().

See Also
AWTEvent, java.io.Serializable, Menu, MenuItem.

Example
This example creates a frame that has the three kinds of menu components. See Figure 271.

```java
import java.awt.*;
class Main extends Frame {
    Main() {
        super("Menu Components");
        MenuBar mb = new MenuBar();
        Menu m = new Menu("File");

        // Add items to File menu
        m.add("New");
        m.add("Open...");

        // Add File and Edit menus to menubar
        mb.add(m);
        mb.add(new Menu("Edit"));

        // Set the menu bar on the frame.
        setMenuBar(mb);
        setSize(200, 100);
        show();
    }

    static public void main(String[] args) {
        new Main();
    }
}
```

A
B
C
D
E
F
G
H
I
J
K
L
M
N
O
P
Q
R
S
T
U
V
W
X
Y
Z

dispatchEvent()

PURPOSE   Dispatches an event to this menu component.

SYNTAX   `public final void dispatchEvent(AWTEvent evt)`

DESCRIPTION   This method dispatches the event `evt` to this menu component or its parent. If `evt` is one of the event types that have been enabled for this menu component, it is processed using `processEvent()`. If `evt`'s event type is not enabled for this menu component and `evt` is an action event, it is passed on to this menu component's parent if its parent has events enabled. For example, a menu item would pass up its action event to its parent (a menu).

PARAMETERS
evt   The non-null AWTEvent.

SEE ALSO   AWTEvent, processEvent().

EXAMPLE   This example creates a menu that has menu items that fire a user-defined type of event— SetFontEvent. When the menu item receives an action event to

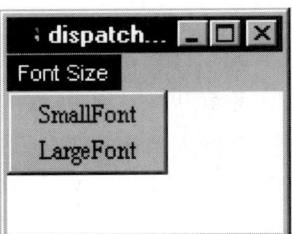

FIGURE 272:   **Supporting User-defined Event Types in Menu Component.**

change to font size, it fires a corresponding SetFontEvent to each of the menu items in the menu by calling dispatchEvent() on the menu items. See Figure 272.

The MainMenuItem class subclasses MenuItem and overrides processEvent() to handle the new type of event. Note that SetFontEvent is a subclass of ActionEvent and uses ActionEvent.ACTION_PERFORMED in order to allow the user-defined event type to be dispatched.

```
import java.awt.*;
import java.awt.event.*;

class Main extends Frame implements ActionListener {
    Menu menu = new Menu("Font Size");

    Main() {
        super("dispatchEvent Example");

        setLayout(new FlowLayout());
        MenuItem b;
        menu.add(b = new MainMenuItem("SmallFont"));
        b.addActionListener(this);
```

```
            menu.add(b = new MainMenuItem("LargeFont"));
            b.addActionListener(this);

            MenuBar mb = new MenuBar();
            mb.add(menu);
            setMenuBar(mb);

            setSize(200, 200);
            show();
        }

    public void actionPerformed(ActionEvent evt) {
        String arg = evt.getActionCommand();
        Font f = null;

        if ("SmallFont".equals(arg)) {
            f = new Font("Serif", Font.PLAIN, 12);
        } else if ("LargeFont".equals(arg)) {
            f = new Font("Serif", Font.PLAIN, 30);
        }
        if (f != null) {
            SetFontEvent fevt = new SetFontEvent(this, f);
            for (int i=0; i<menu.getItemCount(); i++) {
                MainMenuItem c = (MainMenuItem)menu.getItem(i);
                c.dispatchEvent(fevt);
            }
        }
    }

    public static void main(String[] args) {
        new Main();
    }
}

// Define new event for setting font of menu item
// Must be subclass of ActionEvent to get past dispatchEvent's filter

class SetFontEvent extends ActionEvent {
    Font font;
    public SetFontEvent(Object source, Font f) {
        // Must use ACTION_PERFORMED to get event pass
        // dispatchEvent's filter
        super(source, ActionEvent.ACTION_PERFORMED, null);
        font = f;
    }
    public Font getFont() {
        return font;
    }
}

class MainMenuItem extends MenuItem {
    MainMenuItem(String label) {
        super(label);
    }

    // Override to handle special new event (SetFontEvent)
    protected void processEvent(AWTEvent evt) {
        if (evt instanceof SetFontEvent) {
            // Change font as requested
            processSetFontEvent((SetFontEvent) evt);
```

A
B
C
D
E
F
G
H
I
J
K
L
M
N
O
P
Q
R
S
T
U
V
W
X
Y
Z

```
            } else {
                super.processEvent(evt);
            }
        }

        protected void processSetFontEvent(SetFontEvent evt) {
            // perform font change on this menu item
            setFont(evt.getFont());
        }
    }
```

getFont( )

PURPOSE   Retrieves this menu component's font.

SYNTAX   `public Font getFont()`

RETURNS   This menu component's font. The return value may be `null`, which means that
             neither the menu component nor any of its ancestors have been assigned a font.

SEE ALSO   `Font`, `setFont()`.

EXAMPLE   See `setFont()`.

getName( )

PURPOSE   Retrieves this menu component's name.

SYNTAX   `public String getName()`

DESCRIPTION A menu component's name is a placeholder for the program to record a locale-
             independent identifier for the component. See the class description for details.

RETURNS   This menu component's name.

SEE ALSO   `setName()`.

EXAMPLE   This example creates a menu of menu items
             with localized labels and locale-neutral names.
             See Figure 273. Because these are menu items,
             a similar effect could have been achieved
             using the menu items' action commands. See
             `MenuItem.setActionCommand()`.

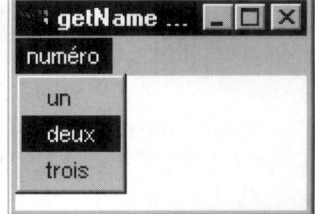

FIGURE 273:   Localized Menu.

```
import java.awt.*;
import java.awt.event.*;
import java.util.ResourceBundle;
import java.util.Locale;

public class Main extends Frame {
```

```
    Main() {
        super("getName Example");
    }

    void init(ActionListener l) {
        // Get localized labels for menu items
        ResourceBundle rb = ResourceBundle.getBundle("MyBundle", getLocale());
        String one = rb.getString("menuitemOne");
        String two = rb.getString("menuitemTwo");
        String three = rb.getString("menuitemThree");
        String heading = rb.getString("menuHeading");

        // Create checkboxes
        Menu menu = new Menu(heading);
        MenuItem m1 = new MenuItem(one);
        MenuItem m2 = new MenuItem(two);
        MenuItem m3 = new MenuItem(three);

        // Set internationalized identifiers for menu and menuitems
        menu.setName("number");
        m1.setName("one");
        m2.setName("two");
        m3.setName("three");

        // Add listener for menu and menu items
        menu.addActionListener(l);
        m1.addActionListener(l);
        m2.addActionListener(l);
        m3.addActionListener(l);

        // Add menu items to menu
        menu.add(m1);
        menu.add(m2);
        menu.add(m3);

        MenuBar mb = new MenuBar();
        mb.add(menu);
        setMenuBar(mb);

        setSize(100, 100);
        show();
    }

    static public void main(String[] args) {
        Main m = new Main();

        // Set locale of component
        m.setLocale(Locale.FRANCE);
        m.init(new ActionEventHandler());
    }
}

class ActionEventHandler implements ActionListener {
    public void actionPerformed(ActionEvent evt) {
        MenuComponent src = (MenuComponent)evt.getSource();
        String target = src.getName();
        int number = 0;

        if (target.equals("one")) {
            number = 1;
```

```
            } if (target.equals("two")) {
               number = 2;
            } if (target.equals("three")) {
               number = 3;
            }

            String label =  (src.getParent() instanceof MenuComponent ?
                               ((MenuComponent)(src.getParent())).getName() : "?");

            System.out.println(label + " = " + number);
         }
      }
```

getParent()

PURPOSE	Retrieves this menu component's parent.
SYNTAX	`public MenuContainer getParent()`
RETURNS	This menu component's parent. The return value may be `null`, which means that the menu component does not yet have a parent.
EXAMPLE	See `getName()`.

getPeer()   *DEPRECATED*

PURPOSE	Should not be manipulating peers directly.
SYNTAX	`public MenuComponentPeer getPeer()`
RETURNS	The menu component's peer. The return value may be `null`, which means that the menu component does not yet have a peer.

paramString()

PURPOSE	Generates a string representation of this menu component's state.
SYNTAX	`protected String paramString()`
DESCRIPTION	A menu component's state consists of its name. A subclass of this class should override this method and return a concatenation of its state with the results of `super.paramString()`. This method is called by the `toString()` method and is typically used for debugging.
RETURNS	A non-`null` string representing the menu component's state.
SEE ALSO	`toString()`.
EXAMPLE	`Component.paramString()`.

postEvent( )   *DEPRECATED*

PURPOSE   Replaced by `dispatchEvent()`.

SYNTAX   `public boolean postEvent(Event evt)`

PARAMETERS

`evt`   The non-`null` event to be posted.

RETURNS   `true` if the event was handled by some component; `false` otherwise.

DEPRECATION   Replace the usage of this deprecated method, as in
```
postEvent(evt);
```
with
```
dispatchEvent(awtEvt);
```

SEE ALSO   `AWTEvent`.

processEvent( )

PURPOSE   Processes an event enabled for this menu component.

SYNTAX   `protected void processEvent(AWTEvent evt)`

DESCRIPTION   This method is called (typically by `dispatchEvent()`) to deliver the event `evt` to this menu component. This method is invoked only if `evt` is an event type that has been enabled for this component. An event type is enabled automatically when a listener of that type is added to this menu component.

The default implementation of this method does nothing. A subclass of `Menu-Component` overrides this method to add support for event types that it wants to handle.

PARAMETERS

`evt`   The non-`null` event.

SEE ALSO   `dispatchEvent()`.

EXAMPLE   See `dispatchEvent()`.

removeNotify( )

PURPOSE   Destroys this menu component's peer hierarchy.

SYNTAX   `public void removeNotify()`

DESCRIPTION   This method destroys this menu component's peer hierarchy, if it exists. This method should never be called directly. It is normally called by the menu component's container.

SEE ALSO   Component.

EXAMPLE   See Component.setVisible().

setFont( )

PURPOSE   Sets this menu component's font.

SYNTAX   `public void setFont(Font font)`

PARAMETERS

font   The font to be set. The value may be null, in which case the default font is to be used.

SEE ALSO   Font, getFont().

EXAMPLE   This example creates a menu that has menu items. It allows you to change the font of the items on the menu. See Figure 274.

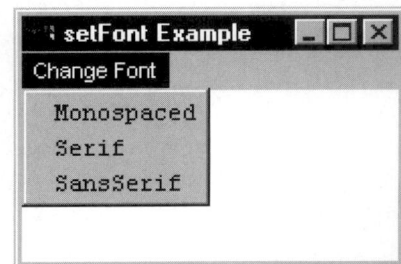

FIGURE 274:   **Changing a Menu Component's Font.**

```
import java.awt.*;
import java.awt.event.*;

class Main extends Frame implements ActionListener {
    Menu menu = new Menu("Change Font");

    Main() {
        super("setFont Example");

        menu.add(new MenuItem("Monospaced"));
        menu.add(new MenuItem("Serif"));
        menu.add(new MenuItem("SansSerif"));

        menu.addActionListener(this);

        MenuBar mb = new MenuBar();
        mb.add(menu);
        setMenuBar(mb);
        setSize(200, 200);
        show();
    }

    public void actionPerformed(ActionEvent evt) {
        System.out.println(evt);

        String arg = evt.getActionCommand();
        Font f = null;

        f = new Font(arg, Font.PLAIN, 12);
        if (f != null) {
            for (int i = 0; i <menu.getItemCount(); i++) {
                MenuItem src = menu.getItem(i);
```

```
                System.out.println("Changing font from: " + src.getFont());
                src.setFont(f);
            }
        }
    }

    public static void main(String[] args) {
        new Main();
    }
}
```

setName()

PURPOSE	Sets this menu component's name.
SYNTAX	`public void setName(String name)`
DESCRIPTION	This method sets the name of this component to name. See the class description for details.
PARAMETERS	
name	This menu component's new name.
SEE ALSO	`getName()`.
EXAMPLE	See `getName()`.

toString()

PURPOSE	Generates the string representation of this menu component's state.
SYNTAX	`public String toString()`
DESCRIPTION	The result string contains the menu component's class name and the results of calling `paramString()`. This method is typically used for debugging.
RETURNS	A non-`null` string representing the menu component's state.
OVERRIDES	`java.lang.Object.toString()`.
SEE ALSO	`paramString()`.
EXAMPLE	See `java.lang.Object.toString()`.

MenuComponentPeer

A
B
C
D
E
F
G
H
I
J
K
L
M
N
O
P
Q
R
S
T
U
V
W
X
Y
Z

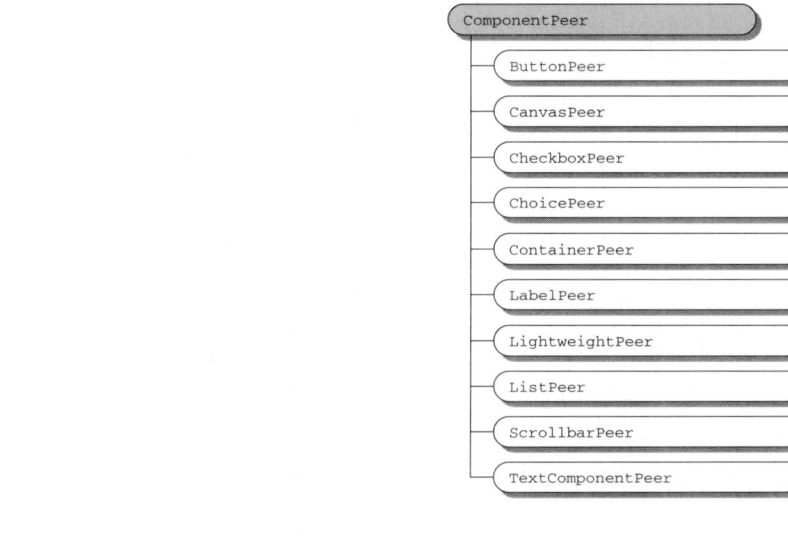

Syntax

```
public interface MenuComponentPeer
```

Description

The menu component (see the MenuComponent class) in the AWT uses the platform's native implementation of a menu component. So that the AWT menu component behaves the same on all platforms, the menu component is assigned a *peer*, whose task is to translate the behavior of the platform's native menu component to the behavior of the AWT menu component.

AWT programmers normally do not directly use peer classes and interfaces. Instead, they deal with AWT components in the java.awt package. These in turn automatically manage their peers. Only someone who is porting the AWT to another platform should be concerned with the peer classes and interfaces. Consequently, most peer documentation refers to java.awt counterparts.

Menu component peers serve the same role as component peers. See Component and Toolkit for additional information about component peers.

MEMBER SUMMARY	
Peer Method	
dispose()	Destroys the peer.

See Also

`java.awt.Component, java.awt.MenuComponent, java.awt.Toolkit.`

dispose()

PURPOSE   Destroys the peer.

SYNTAX   `void dispose()`

SEE ALSO   `java.awt.MenuComponent.removeNotify().`

```
MenuContainer ......... Component
          .......... Frame
          .......... Menu
          .......... MenuBar
```

Syntax

```
public interface MenuContainer
```

Description

This interface is implemented by classes that contain menu components. The AWT package has several menu component containers: `Menu`, `MenuBar`, `Frame` (a frame can have a menu bar), and `Component` (and its subclasses). A component can have popup menus and therefore is a menu container.

MEMBER SUMMARY	
Menu Container Methods	
getFont()	Retrieves this menu container's font.
remove()	Removes a menu component from this menu container.
Deprecated Method	
postEvent()	Replaced by `MenuComponent.dispatchEvent()`.

See Also

Component, Menu, MenuBar, Frame.

Example

This example implements a new type of menu container, `MenuFrame`, which accepts menus and displays them all in one frame. See Figure 275. Each menu label and menu item label is displayed one per line. When the user clicks a menu item, an action event is fired for that menu item.

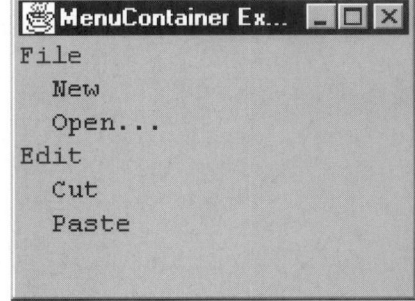

FIGURE 275: MenuFrame.

Note: In Java 1.1.2, a subclass outside the `java.awt` package cannot enable its self-defined action events. Therefore, the program calls `processEvent()` instead of `dispatchEvent()` to dispatch the event.

```java
import java.awt.*;
import java.awt.event.*;
import java.util.*;

public class Main implements ActionListener {
    Main () {
        MenuFrame mf = new MenuFrame();

        // Now create a few menus.
        Menu menu1 = new Menu("File");
        menu1.add("New");
        menu1.add("Open...");
        mf.add(menu1);

        Menu menu2 = new Menu("Edit");
        menu2.add("Cut");
        menu2.add("Paste");
        mf.add(menu2);

        // Add self as listener
        mf.addActionListener(this);

        // Display menu
        mf.setVisible(true);
    }

    // Action Listener for Menu Frame
    public void actionPerformed(ActionEvent evt) {
        System.out.println("action performed " + evt);
    }

    static public void main(String[] args) {
        new Main();
    }
}

class MenuFrame extends Frame implements MenuContainer {
    Font font = new Font("Monospaced", Font.PLAIN, 14);
    FontMetrics fontM;
    transient ActionListener actionListener;

    // Contains all the menu in this container.
    Vector menus = new Vector();

    // Contains all the menu items in this container.
    Vector menuItems = null;

    MenuFrame() {
        super("MenuContainer Example");
        this.menus = menus;
        fontM = getFontMetrics(font);

        setResizable(false);

        // Add listener for handling mouse clicks
```

```
            addMouseListener(new MouseEventHandler());

            // Enable mask for action events
            enableEvents(ActionEvent.ACTION_EVENT_MASK);
        }

        // Override show() to get MenuFrame size first
        public void setVisible(boolean show) {
            if (!show) {
                super.setVisible(false);
            }
            // Create the peers so that getInsets() returns correct value
            addNotify();

            Dimension dim = getPreferredSize();
            Insets insets = getInsets();
            setSize(insets.left+dim.width, insets.top+dim.height);
            super.show();   // calls Frame.show()
        }

        // Override to calculate size of frame based on menu items
        public Dimension getPreferredSize() {
            Vector labels = getLabels();
            int width = 0;

            for (int i=0; i<labels.size(); i++) {
                width = Math.max(width,
                             fontM.stringWidth((String)labels.elementAt(i)));
            }

            return new Dimension(width, labels.size() * fontM.getHeight());
        }

        public Font getFont() {
            return font;
        }

        // Generates a vector of labels.  The menu item labels are indented.
        Vector getLabels() {
            Vector result = new Vector();
            menuItems = new Vector();
            for (int i=0; i<menus.size(); i++) {
                Menu menu = (Menu)menus.elementAt(i);
                result.addElement(menu.getLabel());
                menuItems.addElement(null);

                for (int j=0; j<menu.getItemCount(); j++) {
                    result.addElement("  "+menu.getItem(j).getLabel());
                    menuItems.addElement(menu.getItem(j));
                }
            }
            return result;
        }

        // Paints the labels.
        public void paint(Graphics g) {
            Vector labels = getLabels();
            int y = fontM.getAscent();

            g.setFont(font);
```

```
        Insets insets = getInsets();
        for (int i=0; i<labels.size(); i++) {
            String label = (String)labels.elementAt(i);

            // Paint menu label blue
            if (label.charAt(0) != ' ') {
                g.setColor(Color.blue);
            }
            g.drawString(label, insets.left, insets.top+y);
            y += fontM.getHeight();
            g.setColor(Color.black);
        }
    }

    public void add(MenuComponent mcomp) {
        menus.addElement(mcomp);
        menuItems = null;          // invalidate old list
    }

    public void remove(MenuComponent mcomp) {
        menus.removeElement(mcomp);
        menuItems = null;          // invalidate old list
    }

    // ActionEvent methods
    public void addActionListener(ActionListener l) {
        actionListener = AWTEventMulticaster.add(actionListener, l);
    }

    protected void processEvent(AWTEvent evt) {
        if (evt instanceof ActionEvent) {
            processActionEvent((ActionEvent) evt);
        } else {
            super.processEvent(evt);
        }
    }

    protected void processActionEvent(ActionEvent evt) {
        if (actionListener != null) {
            actionListener.actionPerformed(evt);
        }
    }

    // Mouse Event Listener
    class MouseEventHandler extends MouseAdapter {
        // Determines which item was clicked on and fire an event for that item.
        public void mousePressed(MouseEvent evt) {
            Vector labels = getLabels();
            Insets insets = getInsets();
            int item = (evt.getY()-insets.top) / fontM.getHeight();

            // Don't generate events when the click it not on a label.
            if (item < labels.size()) {
                String label = ((String)labels.elementAt(item));

                //Don't generate event for menu labels.
                if (label.charAt(0) == ' ') {
                    ActionEvent action =
                        new ActionEvent(menuItems.elementAt(item),
                                        ActionEvent.ACTION_PERFORMED,
```

A
B
C
D
E
F
G
H
I
J
K
L
M
N
O
P
Q
R
S
T
U
V
W
X
Y
Z

```
                                              label.trim());
                      System.out.println("dispatched: " + action);
          //            dispatchEvent(action);
                      processEvent(action);
                  }
              }
          }
      }
  }
```

A
B
C
D
E
F
G
H
I
J
K
L
M
N
O
P
Q
R
S
T
U
V
W
X
Y
Z

getFont( )

PURPOSE	Retrieves this menu container's font.
SYNTAX	`Font getFont()`
RETURNS	The menu container's font. A result value of `null` means neither the menu container nor any of its ancestors have been assigned a font.
EXAMPLE	See the class example.

postEvent( ) *DEPRECATED*

PURPOSE	Replaced by `MenuComponent.dispatchEvent()`.
SYNTAX	`public boolean postEvent(Event evt)`
DESCRIPTION	This method posts the event `evt` to this menu container.
PARAMETERS	
evt	The non-`null` event to post.
RETURNS	`true` if the event was handled by some menu component or `Component` object; `false` otherwise.

DEPRECATION	Replace the usage of this deprecated method, as in
	  `postEvent(evt);`
	with
	  `dispatchEvent(awtEvt);`

SEE ALSO	`AWTEvent`.

remove()

PURPOSE   Removes a menu component from this menu container.

SYNTAX   void remove(MenuComponent mcomp)

PARAMETERS

mcomp   The non-null menu component to remove from this menu container.

EXAMPLE   See the class example.

A
B
C
D
E
F
G
H
I
J
K
L
M
N
O
P
Q
R
S
T
U
V
W
X
Y
Z

java.awt
MenuItem

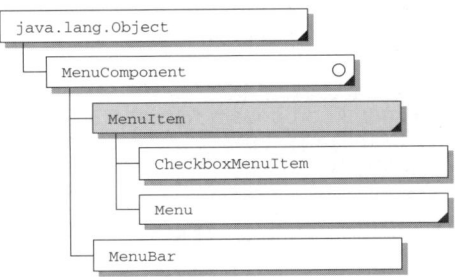

Syntax
`public class MenuItem extends MenuComponent`

Description

A *menu item* is a menu component that must exist in a menu. A menu item is typically used to invoke commands in the applications. Menu items are similar to buttons in function and use, except that they take up less screen space. The trade-off is that they are not as convenient to activate as buttons.

Figure 276 shows the three menu components in the AWT package. The displayed File menu contains two menu items: New and Open... .

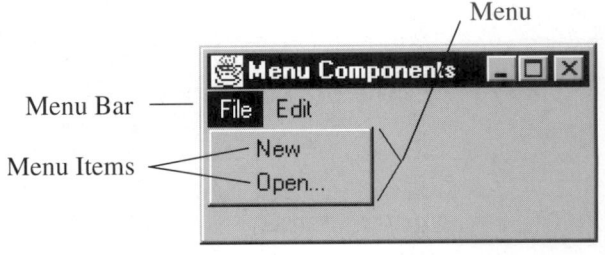

FIGURE 276:   The Three Kinds of Menu Components.

The Enabled Property

A menu item can be either enabled or disabled. When enabled, it can be selected by the user, and when selected, it will fire an action event. A disabled menu item cannot be selected and so cannot fire events. Enabled menu items look different from disabled menu items so that both can be visually distinguished.

Figure 277 shows a menu that has two enabled menu items (Open... and Exit) and one disabled menu item (New).

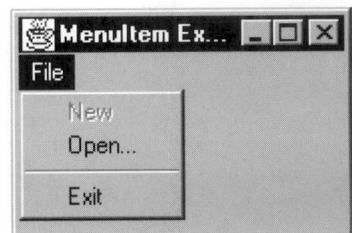

FIGURE 277:   MenuItem.

The Label Property and the Separator

The label of a menu item can be any string. There is one particular label, "-", which is treated specially. This label causes the menu item to become a separator. Separators are used to visually separate groups of menu items. This is useful if the menu has many menu items.

Separators are always disabled and never fire events. Figure 277 shows a menu with a separator between the Open... and Exit menu items.

Keyboard Shortcut

The user can select an enabled menu item either by using mouse actions or by pressing the menu item's *keyboard shortcut*. A keyboard shortcut is a sequence of key strokes that can be associated with a menu item. The keyboard shortcut can be installed, deleted, and changed at anytime. A menu item that has a keyboard shortcut typically displays its shortcut beside the menu item's label. How the shortcut is displayed is platform-dependent.

Note: In Java 1.1.2, you must use `setActionCommand()` on a menu item in order for its shortcut to work. Otherwise, the action event it fires as a result of a shortcut contains a `null` action command.

Events

An action event is fired when an enabled menu item is selected. See the `ActionEvent` class for details. The action event contains an *action command* indicating the command issued by this menu item. By default, the action command is the label of the menu item, unless it is set using `setActionCommand()`.

If the action event type is not enabled for the menu item itself, the action event fired by selecting a menu item is passed up to its container (a menu) The event source of such an event is the menu item's container, *not* the menu item itself. For example, suppose the menu item *A* is in the menu *X* and *A* does not have action events enabled. Selecting *A* causes an action event to be passed up to *X* if *X* has action events enabled. The event source of the resulting action event will be *X*, not *A*. If the menu item's parent is not a menu component or does not have action events enabled, the action event is not passed up. Notice that this algorithm passes action events up only one level. A cascading menu therefore cannot depend on its parent menu to handle the action events of its menu items. It must take care of adding action listeners for its own menu items. See `Menu` for details.

Note that a menu bar does not fire any events and therefore does not have any events enabled. Action events from a menu bar's menus are not passed up to the menu bar.

A
B
C
D
E
F
G
H
I
J
K
L
M
N
O
P
Q
R
S
T
U
V
W
X
Y
Z

MEMBER SUMMARY	

Constructor

MenuItem()   Constructs a new MenuItem instance.

Enable Methods

isEnabled()   Determines if this menu item is enabled.

setEnabled()   Enables and disables this component.

Label Methods

getLabel()   Retrieves this menu item's label.

setLabel()   Sets this menu item's label.

Keyboard Shortcut Methods

deleteShortcut()   Deletes this menu item's keyboard shortcut.

getShortcut()   Retrieves this menu item's keyboard shortcut.

setShortcut()   Sets this menu item's keyboard shortcut.

Event Methods

addActionListener()   Adds a listener to receive action events from this menu item.

enableEvents()   Enables event types for this menu item.

disableEvents()   Disables event types for this men item.

getActionCommand()   Retrieves the command name of action events fired by this menu item.

processActionEvent()   Processes an action event enabled for this menu item.

processEvent()   Processes an event enabled for this menu item.

removeActionListener()   Removes a listener from receiving action events from this menu item.

setActionCommand()   Sets the command name of action events fired by this menu item.

Peer Method

addNotify()   Creates this menu item's peer.

Debugging Method

paramString()   Generates a string representing this menu item's state.

Deprecated Methods

disable()   Replaced by setEnabled().

enable()   Replaced by setEnabled().

See Also

java.awt.event.ActionEvent, java.awt.event.ActionListener, MenuComponent.

Example

This example creates a menu that has two menu items—one enabled and one disabled. The menu is installed in a menu bar, which in turn is installed in a frame. This example also shows you how to handle action events fired by menu items. See Figure 277.

```java
import java.awt.*;
import java.awt.event.*;

class Main extends Frame implements ActionListener {
    Main() {
        super("MenuItem Example");
        MenuBar mb = new MenuBar();
        Menu m = new Menu("File");
        MenuItem mi;

        mi = new MenuItem("New");
        mi.setEnabled(false);
        m.add(mi);
        m.add("Open...");
        m.add("-");
        m.add("Exit");
        mb.add(m);
        m.addActionListener(this);

        // Set the menu bar on the frame.
        setMenuBar(mb);

        setSize(100, 100);
        show();
    }

    // Action handler for menu
    public void actionPerformed(ActionEvent evt) {
        String what = evt.getActionCommand();
        if ("New".equals(what)) {
            // do new
            System.out.println("doing new");
        } else if ("Open...".equals(what)) {
            // do open
            System.out.println("doing open");
        }
    }

    static public void main(String[] args) {
        new Main();
    }
}
```

A
B
C
D
E
F
G
H
I
J
K
L
M
N
O
P
Q
R
S
T
U
V
W
X
Y
Z

addActionListener()

PURPOSE   Adds a listener to receive action events fired by this menu item.

SYNTAX
```java
public synchronized void addActionListener(ActionListener
    listener)
```

DESCRIPTION	An action event is fired when this menu item is selected. See `ActionEvent` and the class description for more details. After this method is called, the action listener `listener` will receive action events fired by this menu item. If `listener` is `null`, this method does nothing.
PARAMETERS	
`listener`	The possibly `null` action listener to add.
SEE ALSO	`java.awt.event.ActionEvent`, `java.awt.event.ActionListener`, `removeActionListener()`.
EXAMPLE	See the class example.

addNotify()

PURPOSE	Creates this menu item's peer.
SYNTAX	`public void addNotify()`
DESCRIPTION	This method creates this menu items peer if it does not exist. The peer is created by calling the `Toolkit.createMenuItem()` method. This method should never be called directly. It is normally called by the menu component's parent.
SEE ALSO	`MenuComponent.removeNotify()`.
EXAMPLE	The usage of `addNotify()` is similar to that of `Component.addNotify()`. See the class example of `MenuContainer` for a usage of `Component.addNotify()`.

deleteShortcut()

PURPOSE	Deletes this menu item's keyboard shortcut.
SYNTAX	`public void deleteShortcut()`
DESCRIPTION	The user can select an enabled menu item either by using mouse actions or by pressing the menu item's keyboard shortcut. See the class description for details on keyboard shortcuts.
SEE ALSO	`getShortcut()`, `setShortcut()`.
EXAMPLE	See `setShortcut()`.

A
B
C
D
E
F
G
H
I
J
K
L
M
N
O
P
Q
R
S
T
U
V
W
X
Y
Z

disable( ) *DEPRECATED*

PURPOSE	Replaced by setEnabled( ).
SYNTAX	`public void synchronized disable()`
DEPRECATION	Replace the usage of this deprecated method, as in

```
menuitem.disable();
```
with
```
menuitem.setEnabled(false);
```

disableEvents( )

PURPOSE   Disables event types for this menu item.

SYNTAX   `protected final void disableEvents(long eventTypes)`

DESCRIPTION   An event type is enabled when a listener for that type is added to this menu item or when enableEvents( ) is invoked on this menu item with the event type's mask. This method disables the event types specified by the mask eventTypes. It is used by subclasses of MenuItem to undo the effects of enableEvents( ). If a menu item has listeners corresponding to the event type, events will always be delivered to its processEvent( ) method, independent of the effects of enableEvents( ) or disableEvents( ).

PARAMETERS
eventTypes   The event mask specifying the event types to disable. Event mask values are defined in AWTEvent.

SEE ALSO   AWTEvent, enableEvents( ), processEvent( ).

EXAMPLE   This example defines a subclass of Menu-Item—OnOffMenuItem—that allows action events fired from it to be switched on and off. The subclass does not support multiple listeners. When the checkbox is selected, the New menu item fires action events as normal. When the checkbox is deselected, the New menu item does not fire any action events. See Figure 278.

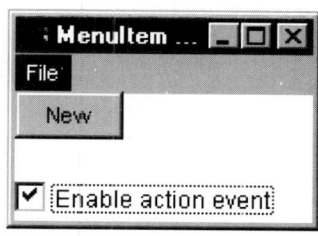

FIGURE 278: Disable and Enable events in a MenuItem.

```
import java.awt.*;
import java.awt.event.*;
import java.util.TooManyListenersException;

class Main extends Frame implements ActionListener, ItemListener {
    OnOffMenuItem mi;
```

```
                Main() {
                    super("MenuItem Example");
                    MenuBar mb = new MenuBar();
                    Menu m = new Menu("File");

                    mi = new OnOffMenuItem("New");
A                   m.add(mi);

B                   try {
                        mi.addMyActionListener(this);
C                   } catch (TooManyListenersException e) {
                        e.printStackTrace();
D                       System.exit(1);
                    }
E
                    mb.add(m);
F
                    // Set the menu bar on the frame.
G                   setMenuBar(mb);

H                   Checkbox cb = new Checkbox("Enable action event", true);
                    cb.addItemListener(this);
I                   add(cb, BorderLayout.SOUTH);

J                   setSize(100, 100);
                    show();
K               }

L               // Action handler for menu item
                public void actionPerformed(ActionEvent evt) {
M                   System.out.println(evt.getActionCommand());
                }
N
                // Item handler for checkbox
O               public void itemStateChanged(ItemEvent evt) {
                    if (evt.getStateChange() == ItemEvent.SELECTED) {
P                       mi.on();
                    } else {
Q                       mi.off();
                    }
R               }

                static public void main(String[] args) {
S                   new Main();
                }
T           }

U           class OnOffMenuItem extends MenuItem {
V               ActionListener myListener;

W               OnOffMenuItem(String label) {
                    super(label);
X               }

Y               void on() {
                    enableEvents(AWTEvent.ACTION_EVENT_MASK);
Z                   addActionListener(myListener);
                }

                void off() {
```

```
            disableEvents(AWTEvent.ACTION_EVENT_MASK);
            removeActionListener(myListener);
        }

    public synchronized void addMyActionListener(ActionListener l)
            throws TooManyListenersException {
            if (myListener != null) {
                throw new TooManyListenersException("OnOffMenuItem");
            }
            myListener = l;
            addActionListener(l);
        }
    }
```

enable()   *DEPRECATED*

PURPOSE   Replaced by setEnabled().

SYNTAX   public synchronized void enable()
               public void enable(boolean on)

PARAMETERS

on   If true, the menu item is enabled; otherwise, the menu item is disabled.

DEPRECATION   Replace the usage of this deprecated method, as in
                 menuitem.enable();
                 menuitem.enable(false);

               with
                 menuitem.setEnabled(true);
                 menuitem.setEnabled(false);

enableEvents()

PURPOSE   Enables event types for this menu item.

SYNTAX   protected final void enableEvents(long eventTypes)

DESCRIPTION   An event type is enabled when a listener for that type is added to this menu
               item. This method is used by subclasses of MenuItem to always deliver events
               of the specified type to its processEvent() method, regardless of whether it
               has any listeners. This method enables the event types specified by the mask
               eventTypes.

PARAMETERS

eventTypes   The event mask specifying the event types to enable. Event mask values are
               defined in AWTEvent.

               Note: In Java 1.1.2, only ActionEvent can be enabled. Enabling other event
               types has no effect.

SEE ALSO `AWTEvent, disableEvents(), processEvent()`.

EXAMPLE See `disableEvents()`.

getActionCommand()

PURPOSE Retrieves the command name of action events fired by this menu item.

SYNTAX `public String getActionCommand()`

DESCRIPTION An action event is fired when this menu item is selected. That action event contains an *action command* indicating the command issued by this menu item. By default, the action command is the label of the menu item. The command action can be modified using `setActionCommand()`.

RETURNS The possibly `null` command name of action events fired by this menu item. If no command name was set, the menu item's label is returned.

SEE ALSO `getLabel(), setActionCommand()`.

EXAMPLE See `setActionCommand()`.

getLabel()

PURPOSE Retrieves this menu item's label.

SYNTAX `public String getLabel()`

RETURNS This menu item's label. The return value may be `null`.

EXAMPLE This example prints all of the menu item labels in a menu:

```
void printLabels(Menu m) {
    for (int i=0; i<m.getItemCount(); i++) {
        System.out.println(m.getItem(i).getLabel());
    }
}
```

getShortcut()

PURPOSE Retrieves this menu item's keyboard shortcut.

SYNTAX `public MenuShortcut getShortcut()`

DESCRIPTION This menu item's keyboard shortcut is set by its constructor and can be changed at anytime using `setShortcut()` and `deleteShortcut()`.

RETURNS This menu item's keyboard shortcut. The return value may be `null`, which means this menu item has no keyboard shortcut.

SEE ALSO　deleteShortcut(), MenuShortcut, setShortcut().

EXAMPLE　See setShortcut().

isEnabled()

PURPOSE　Determines the menu item's enabled state.

SYNTAX　public boolean isEnabled()

RETURNS　true if the menu item is enabled; false otherwise.

SEE ALSO　setEnabled().

EXAMPLE　This example prints all enabled states of all of the menu items in a menu:

```
void printLabels(Menu m) {
    for (int i=0; i<m.getItemCount(); i++) {
        System.out.println(m.getItem(i).getLabel() + ": "
            + (m.getItem(i).isEnabled() ? "enabled" : "disabled"));
    }
}
```

MenuItem()

PURPOSE　Creates a new MenuItem instance.

SYNTAX
```
public MenuItem()
public MenuItem(String label)
public MenuItem(String label, MenuShortCut shortcut)
```

DESCRIPTION　This constructor creates a new MenuItem instance that has the label label. If no label is specified, an empty label ("") is used. If label is "-", the menu item becomes a separator. You can associate a keyboard shortcut with this menu item by supplying shortcut. If no shortcut is supplied, the menu item has no keyboard shortcut.

The menu item is enabled by default.

PARAMETERS
label　The non-null string specifying the menu item's label.

shortcut　This menu item's keyboard shortcut.

Note: In Java 1.1.2, you must invoke setActionCommand() in order for shortcut to fire the correct ActionEvent.

SEE ALSO　getShortcut().

EXAMPLE　See the class example.

paramString( )

PURPOSE	Generates a string representation of the menu item's state.
SYNTAX	`public String paramString()`
DESCRIPTION	The string includes the menu item's label and enabled state. This method is called by the `toString()` method and is typically used for debugging.
RETURNS	A non-`null` string representing the menu item's state.
OVERRIDES	`MenuComponent.paramString()`.
SEE ALSO	`MenuComponent.toString()`, `java.lang.Object.toString()`.
EXAMPLE	See `Component.paramString()`.

processActionEvent( )

PURPOSE	Processes an action event enabled for this menu item.
SYNTAX	`protected void processActionEvent(ActionEvent evt)`
DESCRIPTION	An action event is fired when this menu item is selected. See `ActionEvent` and the class description for more details. This method processes action events for this menu item by calling any registered `ActionListener`. This method is invoked only if action events have been enabled for this menu item. This can happen either when an action listener is added to this component or when action events are explicitly enabled via the use of `enableEvents()`.
	Typically, a program controls how action events for a menu item are processed by adding or removing action listeners. It overrides `processActionEvent()` only if it needs to do processing in addition to that performed by the registered listeners.
	When a subclass does override `processActionEvent()`, it should call `super.processActionEvent()` to perform the processing intended by its base class (such as dispatching the listeners).
PARAMETERS	
evt	The event to be processed.
SEE ALSO	`java.awt.event.ActionEvent`, `java.awt.event.ActionListener`, `processEvent()`.
EXAMPLE	This example is a variation of the one for `MenuComponent.dispatch-Event()`. It overrides `processActionEvent()` to support `SetFontEvent` (a subclass of `ActionEvent`). See Figure 279. The rest of the example is the same as that for `dispatchEvent()`; only `MainMenuItem` has changed.
	Note: In Java 1.1.2, the menu is not properly resized.

FIGURE 279: **Adding Support for a User-defined Event Type for MenuItem.**

```
class MainMenuItem extends MenuItem {
    MainMenuItem(String label) {
        super(label);
    }

    // Override to handle special new event (SetFontEvent)
    protected void processActionEvent(ActionEvent evt) {
        if (evt instanceof SetFontEvent) {
            // Change font as requested
            processSetFontEvent((SetFontEvent) evt);
        } else {
            super.processActionEvent(evt);
        }
    }

    protected void processSetFontEvent(SetFontEvent evt) {
        // perform font change on this menu item
        setFont(evt.getFont());
    }
}
```

processEvent()

PURPOSE   Processes an event enabled for this menu item.

SYNTAX   `protected void processEvent(AWTEvent evt)`

DESCRIPTION   Menu items currently only support action events. This method can be overridden by subclasses to handle new types of event, in which case the subclasses should call `super.processEvent()` to ensure that action events are handled properly.

PARAMETERS

evt   The event to be processed.

OVERRIDES   `MenuComponent.processEvent()`.

SEE ALSO   `AWTEvent`, `processActionEvent()`.

EXAMPLE   See `MenuComponent.dispatchEvent()`.

removeActionListener()

PURPOSE   Removes a listener from receiving action events from this menu item.

SYNTAX   `public synchronized void removeActionListener(ActionListener listener)`

DESCRIPTION   An action event is fired when this menu item is selected. See `ActionEvent` and the class description for more details. After this method is called, the action listener `listener` will no longer receive action events from this menu item. If `listener` is `null`, this method does nothing.

PARAMETERS

`listener`   The possibly `null` action listener to remove.

SEE ALSO   `addActionListener()`, `java.awt.event.ActionEvent`, `java.awt.event.ActionListener`.

EXAMPLE   See `disableEvents()`.

setActionCommand()

PURPOSE   Sets the command name of action events fired by this menu item.

SYNTAX   `public void setActionCommand(String command)`

DESCRIPTION   An action event is fired when this menu item is selected. That action event contains an *action command* indicating the command issued by this menu item. By default, the action command is the label of the menu item. This method sets the action command of this menu item to be `command`. It does not change the label of this menu item.

PARAMETERS

`command`   The command name of the action events fired by this menu item.

SEE ALSO   `getActionCommand()`, `getLabel()`.

EXAMPLE This example creates a menu that contains menu items whose labels can be localized. The menu item's action command is used to store a nonlocalized string for identifying the menu item. See Figure 280.

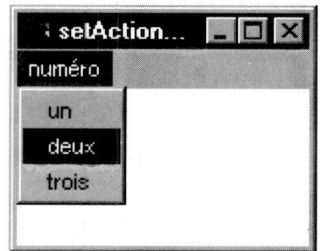

FIGURE 280: MenuItem Localization Using Action Commands.

```java
import java.awt.*;
import java.awt.event.*;
import java.util.ResourceBundle;
import java.util.Locale;

public class Main extends Frame {
    Main() {
        super("setActionCommand Example");
    }

    void init(ActionListener l) {
        // Get localized labels for menu items
        ResourceBundle rb = ResourceBundle.getBundle("MyBundle", getLocale());
        String one = rb.getString("menuitemOne");
        String two = rb.getString("menuitemTwo");
        String three = rb.getString("menuitemThree");
        String heading = rb.getString("menuHeading");

        // Create checkboxes
        Menu menu = new Menu(heading);
        MenuItem m1 = new MenuItem(one);
        MenuItem m2 = new MenuItem(two);
        MenuItem m3 = new MenuItem(three);

        // Set internationalized identifiers for menu and menuitems
        menu.setName("number");
        m1.setActionCommand("one");
        m2.setActionCommand("two");
        m3.setActionCommand("three");

        // Add listener for menu and menu items
        menu.addActionListener(l);
        m1.addActionListener(l);
        m2.addActionListener(l);
        m3.addActionListener(l);

        // Add menu items to menu
        menu.add(m1);
        menu.add(m2);
        menu.add(m3);

        MenuBar mb = new MenuBar();
        mb.add(menu);
        setMenuBar(mb);

        setSize(100, 100);
        show();
    }

    static public void main(String[] args) {
        Main m = new Main();
```

```
                    // Set locale of component
                    m.setLocale(Locale.FRANCE);
                    m.init(new ActionEventHandler());
                }
            }

class  ActionEventHandler implements ActionListener {
    public void actionPerformed(ActionEvent evt) {
        String target = evt.getActionCommand();
        int number = 0;

        if (target.equals("one")) {
            number = 1;
        } if (target.equals("two")) {
            number = 2;
        } if (target.equals("three")) {
            number = 3;
        }
        System.out.println("number = " + number);
    }
}
```

setEnabled()

PURPOSE Enables or disables the menu item.

SYNTAX `public synchronized void setEnabled(boolean on)`

DESCRIPTION This method enables or disables this menu item. See the class description for details on a menu item's enabled property. This method call is ignored if the enabled property of the menu item is not changed.

PARAMETERS

on If `true`, this menu item is enabled; otherwise, this menu item is disabled.

SEE ALSO `isEnabled()`.

EXAMPLE This example creates a frame that has two buttons. One button disables all menu items in the menu bar, and the other enables them. See Figure 281.

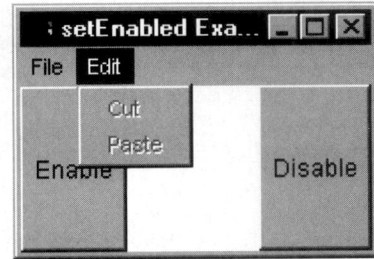

FIGURE 281: **Enabling and Disabling MenuItems.**

```
import java.awt.*;
import java.awt.event.*;

class Main extends Frame
    implements ActionListener {
    Main() {
        super("setEnabled Example");
        MenuBar mb = new MenuBar();
        Menu m = new Menu("File");

        m.add("New");
```

```
        m.add("Open...");
        mb.add(m);
        m = new Menu("Edit");
        m.add("Cut");
        m.add("Paste");
        mb.add(m);

        // Add the two enable/disable buttons.
        Button b;
        add(b = new Button("Enable"), BorderLayout.WEST);
        b.addActionListener(this);
        add(b = new Button("Disable"), BorderLayout.EAST);
        b.addActionListener(this);

        // Set the menu bar on the frame.
        setMenuBar(mb);
        setSize(100, 100);
        show();
    }

    // Action handler for buttons
    public void actionPerformed(ActionEvent evt) {
        String what = evt.getActionCommand();
        boolean enable = "Enable".equals(what);

        if (enable || "Disable".equals(what)) {
            for (int i=0; i<getMenuBar().getMenuCount(); i++) {
                Menu m = getMenuBar().getMenu(i);

                for (int j=0; j<getMenuBar().getMenu(i).getItemCount(); j++) {
                    m.getItem(j).setEnabled(enable);
                }
            }
        }
    }

    static public void main(String[] args) {
        new Main();
    }
}
```

setLabel()

PURPOSE   Sets the menu item's label.

SYNTAX   `public synchronized void setLabel(String label)`

DESCRIPTION   This method sets the label of this menu item to be the string `label`.

PARAMETERS

`label`   The non-`null` string specifying the menu item's new label.

A
B
C
D
E
F
G
H
I
J
K
L
M
N
O
P
Q
R
S
T
U
V
W
X
Y
Z

EXAMPLE   This example creates a menu that has one
menu item and two buttons: One and Two.
Clicking a button sets the label of the menu
item to the label of the button. See Figure 282.

FIGURE 282:
MenuItem.setLabel().

```java
import java.awt.*;
import java.awt.event.*;

class Main extends Frame implements ActionListener{
    MenuItem mi = new MenuItem("One");

    Main() {
        super("setLabel Example");
        MenuBar mb = new MenuBar();
        Menu m = new Menu("Menu");

        // Add menu item.
        m.add(mi);

        // Add the two buttons.
        Button b;
        add(b = new Button("One"), BorderLayout.WEST);
        b.addActionListener(this);
        add(b = new Button("Two"), BorderLayout.EAST);
        b.addActionListener(this);

        // Set the menu bar on the frame.
        mb.add(m);
        setMenuBar(mb);
        setSize(100, 100);
        show();
    }

    // Action handler for buttons
    public void actionPerformed(ActionEvent evt) {
        mi.setLabel(evt.getActionCommand());
    }

    static public void main(String[] args) {
        new Main();
    }
}
```

setShortcut( )

PURPOSE   Sets this menu item's keyboard shortcut.

SYNTAX   `public void setShortcut(MenuShortcut shortcut)`

DESCRIPTION   See the class description for details on keyboard shortcuts.

Note: In Java 1.1.2, setting a non-`null` shortcut does not update the visual
indication that this menu item has a shortcut.

PARAMETERS

shortcut   This menu item's keyboard shortcut. It may be null, which means this menu item has no keyboard shortcut.

SEE ALSO   deleteShortcut(), getShortcut().

EXAMPLE   This example creates a menu that has one menu item, which has a menu shortcut. A row of buttons controls the addition and deletion of the shortcut, as well as prints out the shortcut. See Figure 283.

FIGURE 283:
Menu Item Shortcuts.

```java
import java.awt.*;
import java.awt.event.*;
import java.util.Enumeration;

class Main extends Frame implements ActionListener
{
    MenuBar mb = new MenuBar();
    MenuShortcut shortcut = new MenuShortcut(KeyEvent.VK_S);
    MenuItem mi;
    Button view = new Button("Show");
    Button delete = new Button("Delete");
    Button add = new Button("Add");
    boolean delsc = false;

    Main() {
        super("deleteShortcut Example");
        Menu m = new Menu("File");

        mi = new MenuItem("Save", shortcut);
        mi.setActionCommand("Save");  // required for shortcut
        m.add(mi);

        // Add listener for menu (and its menu items)
        m.addActionListener(this);

        // Set the menu bar on the frame.
        mb.add(m);
        setMenuBar(mb);

        // Add controls for viewing, deleting, adding shortcuts
        Panel p = new Panel(new GridLayout(1, 0));
        add.setEnabled(false);
        p.add(view);
        p.add(delete);
        p.add(add);

        delete.addActionListener(this);
        view.addActionListener(this);
        add.addActionListener(this);

        add(new TextArea("Text area"), BorderLayout.CENTER);
        add(p, BorderLayout.SOUTH);

        setSize(100, 100);
```

```
            show();
        }

        public void actionPerformed(ActionEvent evt) {
            if (evt.getSource() instanceof MenuItem) {
                System.out.println(evt.getActionCommand());
            } else if (evt.getSource() instanceof Button) {
                String sc = evt.getActionCommand();
                if (sc.equals("Show")) {
                    System.out.println(mi.getShortcut());
                } else if (sc.equals("Delete")) {
                    mi.deleteShortcut();
                    delete.setEnabled(false);
                    add.setEnabled(true);
                } else if (sc.equals("Add")) {
                    mi.setShortcut(shortcut);
                    add.setEnabled(false);
                    delete.setEnabled(true);
                }
            }
        }

        static public void main(String[] args) {
            new Main();
        }
    }
```

A
B
C
D
E
F
G
H
I
J
K
L
M
N
O
P
Q
R
S
T
U
V
W
X
Y
Z

MenuItemPeer

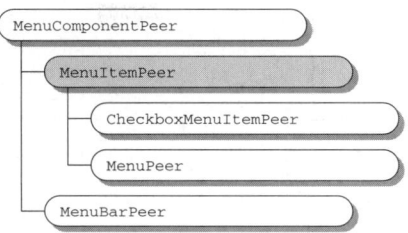

Syntax

```
public interface MenuItemPeer extends MenuComponentPeer
```

Description

The menu item (see the `MenuItem` class) in the AWT uses the platform's native implementation of a menu item. So that the AWT menu item behaves the same on all platforms, the menu item is assigned a *peer*, whose task is to translate the behavior of the platform's native menu item to the behavior of the AWT menu item.

AWT programmers normally do not directly use peer classes and interfaces. Instead, they deal with AWT components in the `java.awt` package. These in turn automatically manage their peers. Only someone who is porting the AWT to another platform should be concerned with the peer classes and interfaces. Consequently, most peer documentation refers to `java.awt` counterparts.

Menu component peers play the same role as component peers. See `Component` and `Toolkit` for additional information about component peers.

MEMBER SUMMARY	
Peer Methods	
setEnabled()	Enables or disables the menu item.
setLabel()	Sets the menu item's label.
Deprecated Methods	
disable()	Replaced by setEnabled().
enable()	Replaced by setEnabled().

See Also

java.awt.Component, java.awt.MenuComponent, java.awt.MenuItem,
java.awt.Toolkit.

disable()　　　　　　　　　　　　　　　　　　　　　　*DEPRECATED*

PURPOSE	Replaced by setEnabled().
SYNTAX	void disable()
DEPRECATION	Replace the usage of this deprecated method, as in

    peer.disable();

with

    peer.setEnabled(false);

enable()　　　　　　　　　　　　　　　　　　　　　　*DEPRECATED*

PURPOSE	Replaced by setEnabled().
SYNTAX	void enable()
DEPRECATION	Replace the usage of this deprecated method, as in

    peer.enable();

with

    peer.setEnabled(true);

setEnabled()

PURPOSE	Enables or disables the menu item.
SYNTAX	void setEnabled(boolean cond)
PARAMETERS	
cond	If true, this menu item is enabled; otherwise, it is disabled.
SEE ALSO	java.awt.MenuItem.setEnabled().

setLabel()

PURPOSE	Sets the menu item's label.
SYNTAX	void setLabel(String label)
PARAMETERS	
label	The string specifying the menu item's label.
SEE ALSO	MenuItem.setLabel().

A
B
C
D
E
F
G
H
I
J
K
L
M
N
O
P
Q
R
S
T
U
V
W
X
Y
Z

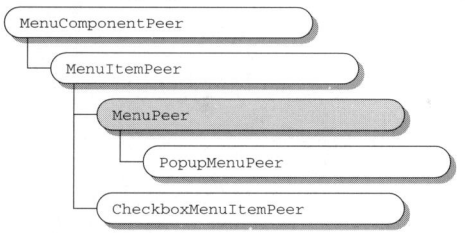

Syntax

`public interface MenuPeer extends MenuItemPeer`

Description

The menu (see the Menu class) in the AWT uses the platform's native implementation of a menu. So that the AWT menu behaves the same on all platforms, the menu is assigned a *peer,* whose task is to translate the behavior of the platform's native menu to the behavior of the AWT menu.

AWT programmers normally do not directly use peer classes and interfaces. Instead, they deal with AWT components in the java.awt package. These in turn automatically manage their peers. Only someone who is porting the AWT to another platform should be concerned with the peer classes and interfaces. Consequently, most peer documentation refers to java.awt counterparts.

Menu component peers play the same role as component peers. See Component and Toolkit for additional information about component peers.

MEMBER SUMMARY	
Peer Methods	
addItem()	Adds a menu item to the menu.
addSeparator()	Adds a menu item separator to the menu.
delItem()	Removes a menu item from the menu.

See Also

java.awt.Component, java.awt.Menu, java.awt.Toolkit.

addItem()

PURPOSE	Adds a menu item to the menu.
SYNTAX	`void addItem(MenuItem menuItem)`
PARAMETERS	
`menuItem`	The non-null menu item.
SEE ALSO	`java.awt.Menu.add()`.

addSeparator()

PURPOSE	Adds a menu item separator to the menu.
SYNTAX	`void addSeparator()`
SEE ALSO	`java.awt.Menu.addSeparator()`.

delItem()

PURPOSE	Removes a menu item from the menu.
SYNTAX	`void delItem(int pos)`
PARAMETERS	
`pos`	The zero-based index of the menu item in the menu.
SEE ALSO	`java.awt.Menu.remove()`.

MenuShortcut

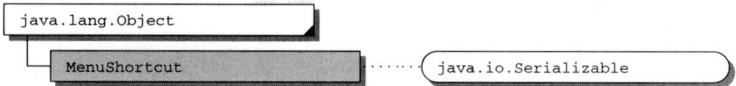

```
java.lang.Object
    MenuShortcut ............ java.io.Serializable
```

Syntax

```
public class MenuShortcut implements Serializable
```

Description

The user can select an enabled menu item either by using mouse actions or by pressing the menu item's *menu shortcut* (or *keyboard shortcut*). A menu shortcut is a sequence of key strokes that can be associated with a menu item. The shortcut can be installed, deleted, and changed at any time. A menu item that has a menu shortcut typically displays its shortcut beside the menu item's label. How the shortcut is displayed is platform-dependent.

Note: In Java 1.1.2, you must use `setActionCommand()` on a menu item in order for its shortcut to work. Otherwise, the action event it fires contains a `null` action command.

Key Sequence

When you create a shortcut, you specify a *virtual key code* (see `KeyEvent`). When the key corresponding to that key code and a modifier key determined by `Toolkit.getMenuShortcutKeyMask()` are pressed simultaneously, the corresponding menu item is selected. By default, the menu shortcut modifier key is Control (Ctrl). You can specify that a shortcut use the Shift key modifier as well, so that to select the menu item, you need to press the key corresponding to the key code simultaneously with the modifier key and the Shift key.

MEMBER SUMMARY	
Constructor	
`MenuShortcut()`	Constructs a new `MenuShortcut` instance.
Comparison Method	
`equals()`	Determines if two menu shortcuts are the same.
Key Methods	
`getKey()`	Retrieves this menu shortcut's virtual key code.
`usesShiftModifier()`	Determines whether this menu shortcut must be invoked with the Shift key.
Debugging Methods	
`paramString()`	Generates a string representation of this menu shortcut.
`toString()`	Generates a localized string representation of this menu shortcut.

See Also

`java.awt.event.KeyEvent`, `java.io.Serializable`, `MenuItem`,
`Toolkit.getMenuShortcutKeyMask()`.

A
B
C
D
E

Example

This example creates a menu with two menu items, each
having a menu shortcut. When the menu item is selected,
the action event handler prints out the action command of
the event, as well as information on the shortcut of the
menu item that fired the event. See Figure 284.

F

```
import java.awt.*;
import java.awt.event.*;
```

FIGURE 284: MenuShortcut.

G
H
I
J
K
L

M

```
class Main extends Frame implements ActionListener {
    Main() {
        super("MenuShortcut Example");
        Menu m = new Menu("File");

        // Create menu items with shortcuts
        MenuItem mi =
            new MenuItem("Edit", new MenuShortcut(KeyEvent.VK_E));
        mi.setActionCommand("Edit");  // required for shortcut
        mi.addActionListener(this);
        m.add(mi);

        mi = new MenuItem("Save", new MenuShortcut(KeyEvent.VK_S));
        mi.setActionCommand("Save");  // required for shortcut
        m.add(mi);
        mi.addActionListener(this);

        // Set the menu bar on the frame.
        MenuBar mb = new MenuBar();
        mb.add(m);
        setMenuBar(mb);

        setSize(100, 100);
        show();
    }

    public void actionPerformed(ActionEvent evt) {
        if (evt.getSource() instanceof MenuItem) {
            MenuItem mi = (MenuItem)evt.getSource();
            System.out.println("Source = " + mi.toString());
            MenuShortcut ms = mi.getShortcut();
            if (ms != null) {
                System.out.println("\tKey = " + ms.getKey());
                System.out.println("\tShift = " + ms.usesShiftModifier());
            }
        }
        System.out.println("Action Command = " + evt.getActionCommand());
    }

    static public void main(String[] args) {
        new Main();
```

N
O
P
Q
R
S
T
U
V
W
X
Y
Z

```
      }
   }
```

equals()

PURPOSE	Determines if two menu shortcuts are the same.
SYNTAX	`public boolean equals(MenuShortcut shortcut)`
DESCRIPTION	Two menu shortcuts are equal only if both use the same key and both use the Shift key in the same way (either both use or both don't use the Shift key).
PARAMETERS	
shortcut	The possibly `null` menu shortcut with which to compare.
RETURNS	`true` if this menu shortcut is equal to `shortcut`.
OVERRIDES	`java.lang.Object.equals()`.
EXAMPLE	See `java.lang.Object.equals()`.

getKey()

PURPOSE	Retrieves this menu shortcut's virtual key code.
SYNTAX	`public int getKey()`
DESCRIPTION	This is the key code with which this menu shortcut was created.
RETURNS	The key code of this menu shortcut.
SEE ALSO	`java.awt.event.KeyEvent`.
EXAMPLE	See the class example.

MenuShortcut()

PURPOSE	Constructs a new `MenuShortcut` instance.
SYNTAX	`public MenuShortcut(int keyCode)` `public MenuShortcut(int keyCode, boolean useShift)`
DESCRIPTION	This constructor creates a new instance of `MenuShortcut` for the key code `keyCode`. If `useShift` is `true`, then when typing in the shortcut the user must press the menu shortcut modifier key (by default Control) and the Shift key along with the key corresponding to `keyCode`. If `useShift` is `false` or

unspecified, only the menu shortcut modifier key must be pressed with the key when the shortcut is typed.

PARAMETERS

keyCode   The virtual key code for this menu shortcut (e.g., KeyEvent.VK_A ...).

useShift   If `true`, the Shift key must be pressed; if `false`, the Shift key must not be pressed.

SEE ALSO   getKey(), usesShiftModifier(), Toolkit.getMenuShortcutKeyMask().

EXAMPLE   This example creates a menu that has two menu items, each with a shortcut. One shortcut uses the Shift modifier; the other does not. See Figure 285.

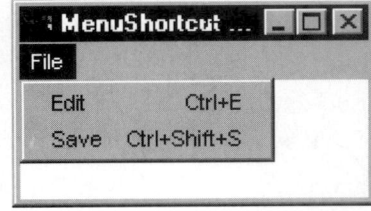

FIGURE 285: MenuShortcut().

```java
import java.awt.*;
import java.awt.event.*;

class Main extends Frame
    implements ActionListener {
    Main() {
        super("MenuShortcut Example");
        Menu m = new Menu("File");

        // Create menu items with shortcuts
        MenuItem mi =
            new MenuItem("Edit", new MenuShortcut(KeyEvent.VK_E));
        mi.setActionCommand("Edit");  // required for shortcut
        m.add(mi);
        mi = new MenuItem("Save",
                    new MenuShortcut(KeyEvent.VK_S, true)); // Shift
        mi.setActionCommand("Save");  // required for shortcut
        m.add(mi);

        // Add listener for menu (and its menu items)
        m.addActionListener(this);

        // Set the menu bar on the frame.
        MenuBar mb = new MenuBar();
        mb.add(m);
        setMenuBar(mb);

        setSize(100, 100);
        show();
    }

    public void actionPerformed(ActionEvent evt) {
        System.out.println(evt.getActionCommand());
    }

    static public void main(String[] args) {
        new Main();
    }
}
```

paramString()

PURPOSE	Generates a string representation of this menu shortcut.
SYNTAX	`protected String paramString()`
DESCRIPTION	The string representation consists of the menu shortcut's key code and an indication of whether the Shift key is used. A subclass of this class should override this method and return a concatenation of its state with the results of `super.paramString()`. This method is typically used for debugging.
RETURNS	The non-`null` string representation of this menu shortcut.
SEE ALSO	`toString()`.
EXAMPLE	See the `AWTEvent` class example.

toString()

PURPOSE	Generates a localized string representation of this menu shortcut.
SYNTAX	`public String toString()`
DESCRIPTION	The localized string representation consists of the menu shortcut's key code and whether the Shift key is required.
RETURNS	A non-`null` localized string of this menu shortcut.
OVERRIDES	`java.lang.Object.toString()`.
SEE ALSO	`paramString()`.
EXAMPLE	See the class example.

usesShiftModifier()

PURPOSE	Determines whether this menu shortcut must be invoked with the Shift key.
SYNTAX	`public boolean usesShiftModifier()`
RETURNS	`true` if the Shift key must be used; `false` if the Shift key must not be used.
SEE ALSO	`MenuShortcut()`.
EXAMPLE	See the class example.

A
B
C
D
E
F
G
H
I
J
K
L
M
N
O
P
Q
R
S
T
U
V
W
X
Y
Z

MethodDescriptor

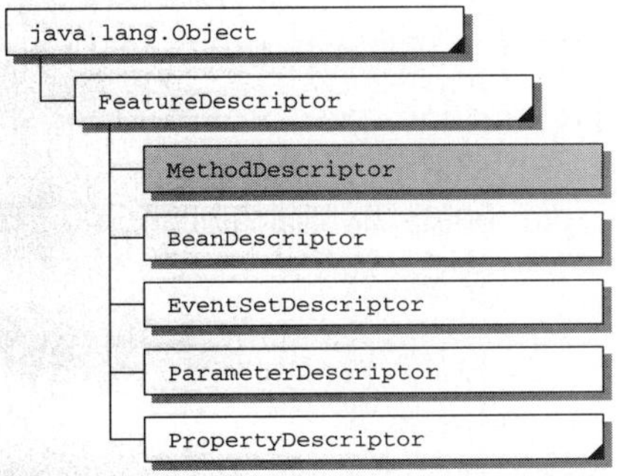

A B C D E F G H I J K L M N O P Q R S T U V W X Y Z

Syntax

`public class MethodDescriptor extends FeatureDescriptor`

Description

A *method descriptor* contains additional information about a public method in a bean, such as the method's localized name and whether it is meant for experts. There is one method descriptor for each public method. A bean's method descriptors can be retrieved through the introspector by calling `Introspector.getBeanInfo().getMethodDescriptors()`.

Method descriptors are also used by event set descriptors (see `EventSetDescriptor`) to represent the methods that support an event.

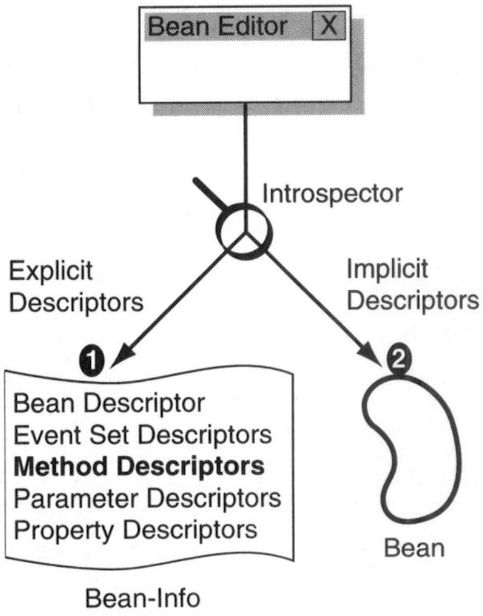

FIGURE 286: Method Descriptor.

For Bean Editors Only

The information contained in a method descriptor is meant for programs such as bean editors (programs that help connect together beans into an application); it is not used by the bean itself. These and other descriptors essentially help a bean editor to construct a meaningful user interface for editing the bean. When the bean is actually running in an application, the method descriptors are never used.

Implicit and Explicit Method Descriptors

When retrieving the method descriptors, the introspector first looks in the bean's bean-info (see `BeanInfo`) for any method descriptors that the bean has explicitly supplied. These are called *explicit* method descriptors. If none is found, the introspector must use introspection on the bean to discover all of the bean's methods and then create *implicit* method descriptors for the method. Implicit method descriptors are given default values for some of the method descriptor attributes. See Figure 286. Table 20 shows the attributes of a method descriptor and the default values for implicit method descriptors.

Attribute	Contents	Implicit Default Value
Method	The method's `Method` object.	The method's `Method` object.
Parameter descriptors	The method's parameter descriptors.	The method's parameter descriptors.
Name	The method's nonlocalized name.	The method's name.
Display name	The method's localized name.	The method's name.
Short description	A localized description of the method.	The method's name.
Expert	`true` if the method is considered for use by experts only.	`false`.
Hidden	`true` if the method is meant to be used by a tool; `false` if is meant to be used by a person.	`false`.

TABLE 20　Method Descriptor Attributes.

MEMBER SUMMARY	
Constructor	
`MethodDescriptor()`	Constructs a new `MethodDescriptor` instance.
Method Descriptor Method	
`getMethod()`	Retrieves the method descriptor's `Method` object.
Parameter Descriptor Method	
`getParameterDescriptors()`	Retrieves the method descriptor's parameter descriptors.

See Also

`java.lang.reflect.Method`, `ParameterDescriptor`.

Example

This example demonstrates how to construct method and parameter descriptors. A bean is created with two methods: one hidden and one expert. The expert method is given a short description and includes a parameter descriptor for its single parameter. The parameter descriptor expert attribute is set to `true` and is given a short description.

Bean.java

```java
public class Bean {
    public void useAtYourOwnRisk(int dangerousParameter) {
    }

    public void forToolsOnly() {
    }
}
```

BeanBeanInfo.java

```java
import java.beans.*;
import java.lang.reflect.*;

public class BeanBeanInfo extends SimpleBeanInfo {
    public MethodDescriptor[] getMethodDescriptors() {
        MethodDescriptor md[] = new MethodDescriptor[2];

        try {
            md[0] = new MethodDescriptor(getMethod(Bean.class, "forToolsOnly"));
            md[0].setHidden(true);

            ParameterDescriptor[] pd = new ParameterDescriptor[1];
            pd[0] = new ParameterDescriptor();
            pd[0].setShortDescription("Never ever set to 34121493839!!!");
            pd[0].setName("dangerousParameter");
            pd[0].setExpert(true);

            md[1] = new MethodDescriptor(getMethod(Bean.class,
                "useAtYourOwnRisk"), pd);
            md[1].setShortDescription(
                "ONLY use when Jupiter is aligned with Mars");
            md[1].setExpert(true);

            return md;
        } catch (IntrospectionException e) {
            e.printStackTrace();
        }
        return null;
    }

    Method getMethod(Class cls, String methodName)
        throws IntrospectionException {
        Method methods[] = cls.getMethods();

        for (int i=0; i<methods.length; i++) {
            if (methods[i].getName().equals(methodName)) {
                return methods[i];
            }
        }
        throw new IntrospectionException("No method \"" + methodName);
    }
}
```

getMethod()

PURPOSE Retrieves the method descriptor's `Method` object.

SYNTAX `public Method getMethod()`

DESCRIPTION A method descriptor contains one `Method` object and some attributes for that method. This method returns the `Method` object.

RETURNS The non-`null` `Method` object.

EXAMPLE See the `Introspector` class example.

getParameterDescriptors()

PURPOSE Retrieves the method descriptor's parameter descriptors.

SYNTAX `public ParameterDescriptor[] getParameterDescriptors()`

DESCRIPTION A method descriptor can optionally specify a set of parameter descriptors for any of its parameters (see `ParameterDescriptor`). The parameter descriptors must be supplied to the method descriptor constructor. This method returns any specified parameter descriptors. If none have been specified, then `null` is returned.

RETURNS A possibly `null` array containing the method's parameter descriptors.

EXAMPLE See the `Introspector` class example.

MethodDescriptor()

PURPOSE Constructs a new `MethodDescriptor` instance.

SYNTAX `public MethodDescriptor(Method method)`
`public MethodDescriptor(Method method, ParameterDescriptor`
`    parameterDescriptors[])`

DESCRIPTION Method descriptors are either implicitly created by the introspector or are explicitly created by a bean. See the class description for more information.

This constructor creates a method descriptor for the method `method`. `parameterDescriptors` specifies the method's parameter descriptors. If `parameterDescriptors` is not specified, it defaults to `null`.

When a method descriptor is created, two attributes are initialized:
- `Method` object
- Parameter descriptors

A
B
C
D
E
F
G
H
I
J
K
L
M
N
O
P
Q
R
S
T
U
V
W
X
Y
Z

MethodDescriptor()

All other attributes are given default values, which can be changed by methods in the `FeatureDescriptor` class. The default values for a method descriptor are shown in Table 20.

PARAMETERS

`method`   A non-`null` `Method` object.

`parameterDescriptors`

A possibly `null` array of the method's parameter descriptors.

EXAMPLE   See the class example.

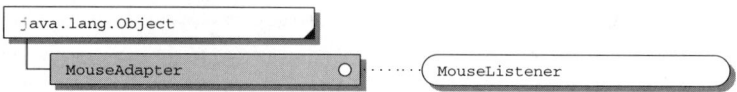

```
java.lang.Object
    MouseAdapter        O ········ MouseListener
```

Syntax

```
public abstract class MouseAdapter implements MouseListener
```

Description

The mouse adapter is a mouse listener in which all callback methods are empty implementations. The purpose of the mouse adapter is to make it more convenient for an object to listen for mouse events. In particular, by using the mouse adapter, you can implement only those callback methods in which you are interested. Without the mouse adapter, you are required to implement all callback methods, even if the method is empty.

To use a mouse adapter, you create a subclass of MouseAdapter and override the desired callback methods. You then create an instance of the mouse adapter subclass and call the component's addMouseListener() method with it. The mouse adapter subclass is typically an inner class.

MEMBER SUMMARY	
Mouse Event Callback Methods	
mouseClicked()	Called when the user clicks the source component.
mouseEntered()	Called when the cursor enters the source component's exposed bounds.
mouseExited()	Called when the cursor exits the source component's exposed bounds.
mousePressed()	Called when the user presses a mouse button in the source component.
mouseReleased()	Called when the user releases a mouse button in the source component.

See Also

java.awt.Component.addMouseListener(), MouseEvent, MouseListener.

Example

This example demonstrates how to display a short description of a component in a status bar when the mouse moves over the component. The example creates a new type of button that can hold a string containing a short description of the button. The frame creates a number of these buttons and then

FIGURE 287:   `MouseAdapter`.

listens for MOUSE_ENTERED and MOUSE_EXITED events from them. When a MOUSE_ENTERED event is received, the frame prints the button's description in its status bar; when a MOUSE_EXITED is received, the frame clears its status bar.   See Figure 287.

```
import java.awt.*;
import java.awt.event.*;

class Main extends Frame {
    Label statusbar = new Label("Ready");

    Main() {
        super("MouseAdapter Example");
        MainButton b;
        MouseEventHandler mhandler = new MouseEventHandler();
        Panel toolbar = new Panel(new FlowLayout());

        // Create the buttons.
        b = new MainButton("Create", "Create a new document.");
        b.addMouseListener(mhandler);
        toolbar.add(b);
        b = new MainButton("Open", "Open an existing document.");
        b.addMouseListener(mhandler);
        toolbar.add(b);
        b = new MainButton("Save", "Save the current document.");
        b.addMouseListener(mhandler);
        toolbar.add(b);
        b = new MainButton("Close", "Close the current document.");
        b.addMouseListener(mhandler);
        toolbar.add(b);

        add(toolbar, BorderLayout.CENTER);
        add(statusbar, BorderLayout.SOUTH);

        pack();
        show();
    }

    class MouseEventHandler extends MouseAdapter {
        public void mouseEntered(MouseEvent evt) {
            statusbar.setText(
                ((MainButton)evt.getSource()).getDescription());
        }
        public void mouseExited(MouseEvent evt) {
            statusbar.setText(null);
        }
    }
}
```

```
public static void main(String args[]) {
    new Main();
}
}

// The main purpose of this button subclass is simply to hold
// a description string.
class MainButton extends Button {
    String desc;

    MainButton(String label, String desc) {
        super(label);
        this.desc = desc;
    }

    String getDescription() {
        return desc;
    }
}
```

mouseClicked()

PURPOSE   Called when the user clicks the source component.

SYNTAX   `public void mouseClicked(MouseEvent evt)`

DESCRIPTION   This method is called after the `mousePressed()` and `mouseReleased()` methods are called in the case in which the mouse coordinates of both events are the same (or very close together). See `MouseEvent.MOUSE_CLICKED` for more details about mouse clicked events.

This method by default has an empty implementation.

PARAMETERS

evt   The non-null mouse event.

EXAMPLE   See the `MouseEvent` class example.

mouseEntered()

PURPOSE   Called when the cursor enters the source component's exposed bounds.

SYNTAX   `public void mouseEntered(MouseEvent evt)`

DESCRIPTION   This method, by default, has an empty implementation. It should be overridden to handle `MouseEvent.MOUSE_ENTERED` events. For details, see `Mouse-Event.MOUSE_ENTERED`.

PARAMETERS

evt   The non-null mouse event.

EXAMPLE   See the `MouseEvent` class example.

A
B
C
D
E
F
G
H
I
J
K
L
M
N
O
P
Q
R
S
T
U
V
W
X
Y
Z

mouseExited()

PURPOSE   Called when the cursor exits the source component's exposed bounds.

SYNTAX   `public void mouseExited(MouseEvent evt)`

DESCRIPTION   This method is called when the cursor is no longer on the source component's exposed bounds. For more details about mouse exited events, see `Mouse-Event.MOUSE_EXITED`.

This method, by default, has an empty implementation.

PARAMETERS
`evt`   The non-null mouse event.

EXAMPLE   See the `MouseEvent` class example.

mousePressed()

PURPOSE   Called when the user presses a mouse button in the source component.

SYNTAX   `public void mousePressed(MouseEvent evt)`

DESCRIPTION   This method is called when a mouse button is pressed. For more details about mouse pressed events, see `MouseEvent.MOUSE_PRESSED`.

This method, by default, has an empty implementation.

PARAMETERS
`evt`   The non-null mouse event.

EXAMPLE   This example implements a simple game. The component is infested with bugs, and your task is to smack them. When a bug is smacked, it turns into a beautiful flower. Unfortunately, the flowers can shield other bugs from being smacked. See Figure 288.

The mouse clicks are handled by a mouse event handler. Since only the mouse pressed event is needed, the program uses the mouse adapter to avoid writing empty implementation for the other mouse events.

FIGURE 288:   Bugs.

The bugs are controlled by a single thread. The thread works in two phases. In the first phase, it waits a random amount of time and then creates a bug. In the second phase, it makes the bug move until the bug moves off the field.

The example uses an off-screen image (bbuf) to implement double-buffering in order to eliminate flickering. The off-screen image is first cleared. Then all of the characters are painted at their current locations. The completed off-screen image is then painted on the screen.

```java
import java.awt.*;
import java.awt.event.*;

public class Main extends Frame {
    InfestedComponent bugs = new InfestedComponent();

    Main() {
        super("mousePressed Example");

        // Layout component.
        add(bugs, BorderLayout.CENTER);
        pack();
        show();
    }

    public static void main(String args[]) {
        new Main();
    }
}

class InfestedComponent extends Canvas implements Runnable {
    // Bug and field dimensions.  The flower is the same size
    // as a bug.
    int bugSize = 30;
    int fieldSize = 200;

    // true iff a bug is visible and running across the field.
    boolean bugRunning;

    // This field specifies which of the four bug images to use.
    int curImage = 0;

    // This field holds the increments that are applied to the
    // bug's (x, y) location to make it move across the field.
    Point bugDir;

    // Rectangles used the the hit detection code.
    Rectangle bugRect = new Rectangle(fieldSize, 0, bugSize, bugSize);
    Rectangle fieldRect = new Rectangle(0, 0, 200, 200);
    Rectangle[] flowers = new Rectangle[100];

    // Number of flowers on the field.
    int flowerCount;

    // Fields used for double-buffering.
    Image bbuf;
    Graphics bbufG;

    // Color of the field.
    Color bgColor = new Color(204, 255, 204);
```

A
B
C
D
E
F
G
H
I
J
K
L
M
N
O
P
Q
R
S
T
U
V
W
X
Y
Z

```
        Image bugImages[] = new Image[4];
        Image flowerImage;

        InfestedComponent() {
            // Load images.
            flowerImage = getToolkit().getImage("flower.gif");
            for (int i=0; i<4; i++) {
                bugImages[i] = getToolkit().getImage("bug"+i+".gif");
            }

            // Listen for mouse events.
            addMouseListener(new MouseEventHandler());

            // Start thread.
            (new Thread(this)).start();

            setSize(fieldSize, fieldSize);
        }

        public void paint(Graphics g) {
            update(g);
        }

        public void update(Graphics g) {
            // Create the double-buffer if necessary.
            if (bbuf == null) {
                bbuf = createImage(fieldSize, fieldSize);
                bbufG = bbuf.getGraphics();
            }

            // Clear the field.
            bbufG.setColor(bgColor);
            bbufG.fillRect(0, 0, fieldSize, fieldSize);

            // Paint the bug.
            if (bugRunning) {
                bbufG.setColor(Color.black);
                bbufG.drawImage(bugImages[curImage], bugRect.x, bugRect.y, this);
            }

            // Paint flowers.
            bbufG.setColor(Color.yellow);
            for (int i=0; i<flowerCount; i++) {
                bbufG.drawImage(flowerImage, flowers[i].x, flowers[i].y, this);
            }

            // Paint double-buffer on screen.
            g.drawImage(bbuf, 0, 0, this);
        }

        class MouseEventHandler extends MouseAdapter {
            public void mousePressed(MouseEvent evt) {
                int x = evt.getX();
                int y = evt.getY();

                // Check if bug is hit.
                if (bugRect.contains(x, y)) {
                    // First check that it's not on a flower.
                    for (int i=0; i<flowerCount; i++) {
```

```
                    if (flowers[i].contains(x, y)) {
                        return;
                    }
                }

                // Bug is hit now turn it into a flower.
                flowers[flowerCount++] = new Rectangle(bugRect);     A
                bugRunning = false;
                repaint();                                           B
            }
        }                                                            C
    }
                                                                     D
// Convenient integer random number generator.
int rand(int r) {                                                    E
    return (int)Math.floor(Math.random() * r);
}                                                                    F

public void run() {                                                  G
    int steps = 15;
    int delay = 60;                                                  H

    while (true) {                                                   I
        try {
            // Wait a little while before the next bug.             J
            Thread.sleep(rand(5000));
                                                                     K
            // Create a bug.
            bugRect.x = rand(fieldSize-bugSize);                     L
            bugRect.y = rand(fieldSize-bugSize);
                                                                     M
            // Pick a direction.
            curImage = rand(4);                                      N
            switch (curImage) {
              case 0:     // from north                              O
                bugRect.y = 0;
                bugDir = new Point(0, steps);                        P
                break;
              case 1:     // from west                               Q
                bugRect.x = 0;
                bugDir = new Point(steps, 0);                        R
                break;
              case 2:     // from south                              S
                bugRect.y = fieldSize;
                bugDir = new Point(0, -steps);                       T
                break;
              case 3:     // from east                               U
                bugRect.x = fieldSize;
                bugDir = new Point(-steps, 0);                       V
                break;
            }                                                        W

            // Start the bug running.                                X
            bugRunning = true;
                                                                     Y
            while (bugRunning) {
                // Move the bug.                                     Z
                bugRect.x += bugDir.x;
                bugRect.y += bugDir.y;
```

```
                           // Is the bug still on the field?
                           if (!fieldRect.intersects(bugRect)) {
                               bugRunning = false;
                           }
                           repaint();
                           Thread.sleep(delay);
                       }
                   } catch (Exception e) {
                       e.printStackTrace();
                   }
               }
           }
       }
```

mouseReleased()

PURPOSE   Called when the user releases a mouse button in the source component.

SYNTAX   `public void mouseReleased(MouseEvent evt)`

DESCRIPTION   This method is called when a mouse button is released. For more details about mouse released events, see `MouseEvent.MOUSE_RELEASED`.

This method, by default, has an empty implementation.

PARAMETERS

evt   The non-`null` mouse event.

EXAMPLE   See the `MouseEvent` class example.

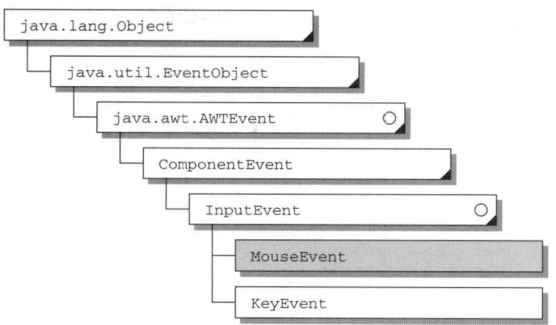

Syntax

```
public class MouseEvent extends InputEvent
```

Description

Mouse events are fired by a component (see Component) when the user interacts with the component using the mouse. For example, when the cursor enters the component bounds, a MOUSE_ENTERED event is fired and when the user clicks a mouse button, a MOUSE_PRESSED event is fired. For more general information about events, see AWTEvent.

Listening for Mouse Events

To listen for mouse events from a component, the listener must implement the Mouse-Listener interface. After that, the listener must be registered with the component. It becomes registered by calling the component's addMouseListener() method.

An alternative, and possibly more convenient, way of receiving mouse events is to use a mouse adapter. See MouseAdapter for more details.

Unlike with most events, mouse events are delivered to a component's listeners before the operation takes place. This gives the listeners an opportunity to consume the event. See InputEvent.consume() for more details.

Mouse Event Flow

Figure 289 shows how mouse events typically flow through the system. First, the event is fired by a component peer in response to the user's interacting with the mouse. This event is posted on the event queue (see EventQueue). When the event makes its way to the front of the queue, it is given to the component via its dispatchEvent() method. The main purpose of this method is to forward the event directly back to the component peer if the mouse event type is not enabled or if there are no mouse listeners. Otherwise, dispatchEvent() calls processEvent(), which in turn calls different methods depending on the event type. Since this is a mouse event, processMouseEvent() is called. The main purpose of this method is to notify the mouse event listeners. Finally, if the event has not been consumed (see InputEvent), it is forwarded back to the originating component peer.

A component can override processMouseEvent() to process mouse events before they are delivered to its listeners. The overridden method should call super.processMouse-Event() to ensure that events are dispatched to the component's listeners.

A
B
C
D
E
F
G
H
I
J
K
L
M
N
O
P
Q
R
S
T
U
V
W
X
Y
Z

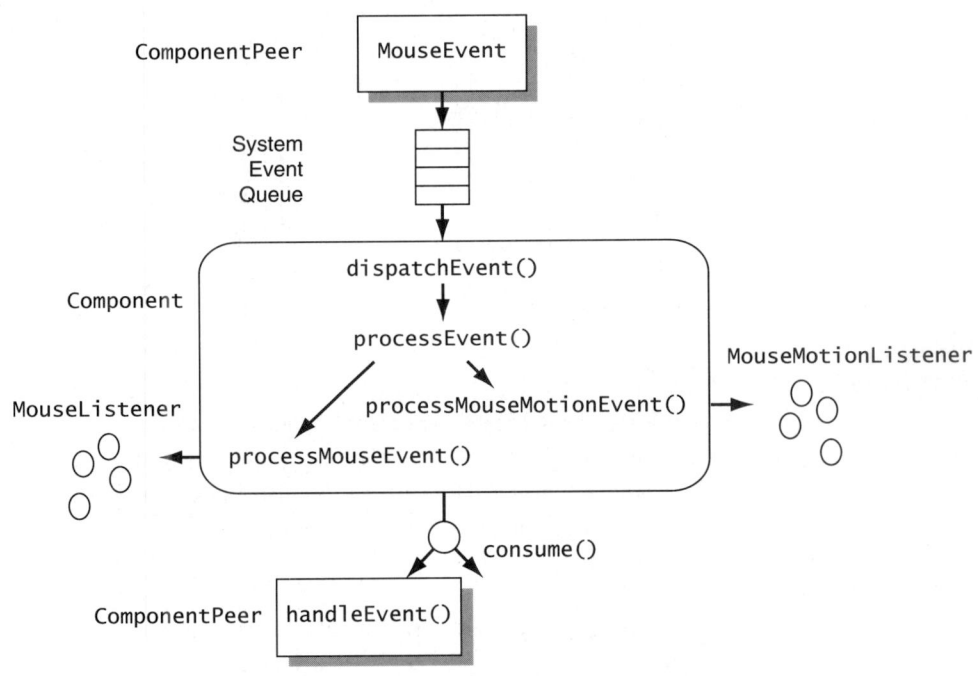

FIGURE 289:   Mouse Event Flow.

Simulating Mouse Events

Mouse events are normally created by the AWT system when the user interacts with the mouse. However, it is possible for any object to create key events in the same way. For example, a program designed to test a scrollbar can create various mouse events and deliver them to the scrollbar. The scrollbar will treat a mouse event exactly as if it came from the AWT system.

A created mouse event can be delivered to a component in one of two ways. Either by posting the event to the event queue (as in Figure 289) or by calling the component's dispatchEvent() method directly.

Mouse Buttons and Modifier Keys

The AWT system supports a three-button mouse—Button1, Button2, and Button3—and four modifier keys—Alt, Control, Meta, and Shift. The mapping between the four modifier keys and the actual keys on the keyboard is platform-dependent. Support for platforms that support fewer than three mouse buttons (e.g., the Macintosh mouse has only one button) involves using modifier keys to simulate extra mouse buttons. For example, when a mouse event is fired when the Meta modifier key pressed, it is considered to be from Button3. The modifier keys used to simulate a three-button mouse are shown in Table 21.

Modifier Keys	Mouse Button
No modifiers	Button1
Alt	Button2
Meta	Button3

TABLE 21:   Using Modifier Keys to Simulate a Three-button Mouse.

Mouse buttons are treated like modifier keys rather than like keys, as in key events. Therefore, to detect which mouse button has been pressed, you must apply one of the button masks to the modifier key state. Sometimes, more than one button may appear in the modifier key state. For example, if the user presses Button3 along with the Alt modifier key, both Button2 and Button3 will appear in the modifier key state. The best way to determine which mouse button was pressed is to apply the masks in descending order: BUTTON3_MASK, BUTTON2_MASK, and then BUTTON1_MASK.

When the mouse really has two or three buttons, pressing Button2 or Button3 will fire a mouse event with the appropriate modifier key set, regardless of whether the modifier key was really pressed. For example, pressing Button3 on a three-button mouse will fire a mouse event whose modifier key state contains BUTTON3_MASK and META_MASK.

The exact behavior of the modifier keys is not well-defined at this point (Java 1.1.2), so it may be platform-dependent. It is best not to build a user interface that uses Alt- or Meta-modified mouse gestures. Shift- and Control-modified mouse gestures are fine.

Because a mouse button is treated like a modifier key, you cannot determine which button was pressed when another was already down. In this case, you must remember the button that was previously pressed. By the same token, it is difficult to determine which button was released when more than one was down, especially if the state of the Alt or Meta modifier keys changed in the meantime.

For now, it is better to define simple behavior when a mouse button is pressed while another one is still down. For example, you could ignore the second mouse button event or perhaps interpret it as canceling the first.

A
B
C
D
E
F
G
H
I
J
K
L
M
N
O
P
Q
R
S
T
U
V
W
X
Y
Z

Coordinates

Mouse coordinates are relative to the component (called the *source component*) that fired the mouse event. Mouse coordinates are *bounds-relative*, which means that mouse location (0, 0) coincides with the (0, 0) point of the component's bounds.

The Click Count

The click count indicates the number of quick, consecutive clicks of a mouse button. It is typically used to detect double- and triple-click gestures. For example, a click count property value of 2 indicates a double-click. The click count is valid only for three mouse events: MOUSE_CLICKED, MOUSE_PRESSED, and MOUSE_RELEASED. For these, the click count is at least 1. For all other mouse events, the click count is 0.

The Popup Trigger Property

On some platforms, a certain type of mousing gesture can cause a popup menu to appear. For example, in Windows 95 this is done by clicking the right mouse button. On other platforms, it may be done by holding down a set of modifier clicks while clicking the mouse. So that programmers need not have to write platform-dependent AWT code, the AWT system determines when the user makes the special gesture and then informs the code via a specially marked mouse event. In particular, MOUSE_PRESSED and MOUSE_RELEASED events have a popup trigger property that indicates whether the user has made the gesture to show a popup menu.

Guaranteed Event Sequences

The AWT system provides certain guarantees to the ordering of mouse events. For example, a MOUSE_ENTERED event to a component is guaranteed to precede a MOUSE_EXIT event. Also, every MOUSE_ENTERED event is guaranteed to be eventually followed by a MOUSE_EXIT event (unless the process is destroyed).

These guaranteed sequences simplify the process of programming components. For example, suppose you want to build a component that turns red whenever the cursor is over the component. All that the component needs to do is turn itself red when it receives a MOUSE_ENTERED event and restore its original color when it receives a MOUSE_EXIT event. It does not need to handle the cases in which either it might receive a MOUSE_EXIT event before the MOUSE_ENTERED event or it might miss the MOUSE_EXIT event.

The set of guaranteed sequences has not been fully specified as of Java 1.1.2. Some of the known guarantees are described in the mouse event descriptions.

MEMBER SUMMARY	

Constructor

MouseEvent()	Constructs a MouseEvent instance.

Coordinate Methods

getPoint()	Retrieves the mouse event's location.
getX()	Retrieves the mouse event's x-coordinate.
getY()	Retrieves the mouse event's y-coordinate.
translatePoint()	Translates the mouse event's coordinates.

Property Methods

getClickCount()	Retrieves the mouse event's click count.
isPopupTrigger()	Retrieves the mouse event's popup trigger property.

Mouse Event Ids Constants

MOUSE_CLICKED	Event id indicating that a mouse button was pressed and released.
MOUSE_DRAGGED	Event id indicating that the mouse moved while a mouse button was pressed.
MOUSE_ENTERED	Event id indicating that the cursor entered a component's exposed bounds.
MOUSE_EXITED	Event id indicating that the cursor exited a component's exposed bounds.
MOUSE_FIRST	Constant specifying the first id in the range of mouse event ids.
MOUSE_LAST	Constant specifying the last id in the range of mouse event ids.
MOUSE_MOVED	Event id indicating that the mouse moved while in a component's exposed bounds.
MOUSE_PRESSED	Event id indicating that a mouse button was pressed.
MOUSE_RELEASED	Event id indicating that a mouse button was released.

Debugging Method

paramString()	Generates a string representing the mouse event's state.

See Also

java.awt.AWTEvent, InputEvent, MouseAdapter, MouseListener, MouseMotionAdapter, MouseMotionListener.

A
B
C
D
E
F
G
H
I
J
K
L
M
N
O
P
Q
R
S
T
U
V
W
X
Y
Z

Example

This example demonstrates how to get mouse events from a component that fires them. The example creates a frame that listens for mouse events on itself. In response to a mouse event, the specifics of the event are printed.

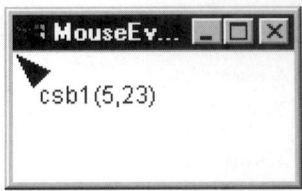

When the frame fires a MOUSE_PRESSED event, an arrow is drawn at the coordinates of the event. Also drawn are the mouse coordinates, and the identities of the pressed mouse button and any modifier keys.

FIGURE 290: MouseEvent.

Figure 290 shows that mouse button one (b1) was pressed at coordinate (5, 23). The Control and Shift modifier keys were down at the time the first mouse button was pressed. Notice that the northwest corner of the frame's drawable area is not (0, 0). This is because the frame has nonzero insets and mouse coordinates are always relative to a component's bounds. See Container for more information about insets.

```java
import java.awt.*;
import java.awt.event.*;

class Main extends Frame implements MouseListener {
    // The point where the mouse button was pressed.
    Point curPoint;

    // The current button.
    String curButton;

    Main() {
        super("MouseEvent Example");

        addMouseListener(this);
        setSize(150, 150);
        show();
    }

    // Paint an arrow and the coordinates.
    public void paint(Graphics g) {
        if (curPoint != null) {
            FontMetrics fm = g.getFontMetrics();
            Insets insets = getInsets();

            // Build the arrow.
            Polygon arrow = new Polygon();
            arrow.addPoint(curPoint.x, curPoint.y);
            arrow.addPoint(curPoint.x+9, curPoint.y+18);
            arrow.addPoint(curPoint.x+18, curPoint.y+9);

            g.fillPolygon(arrow);
            g.drawString(curButton+"("+curPoint.x+","+curPoint.y+")",
                curPoint.x+12, curPoint.y+14+fm.getAscent());
        }
    }

    public void mouseClicked(MouseEvent evt) {
        print("MOUSE_CLICKED", evt);
    }
```

A
B
C
D
E
F
G
H
I
J
K
L
M
N
O
P
Q
R
S
T
U
V
W
X
Y
Z

```
public void mouseEntered(MouseEvent evt) {
    print("MOUSE_ENTERED", evt);
}
public void mouseExited(MouseEvent evt) {
    print("MOUSE_EXITED", evt);
}
public void mousePressed(MouseEvent evt) {
    curPoint = evt.getPoint();
    curButton = getCurButton(evt);
    print("MOUSE_PRESSED", evt);
    repaint();
}
public void mouseReleased(MouseEvent evt) {
    print("MOUSE_RELEASED", evt);
}

// Returns a string representing the mouse button that was pressed.
String getCurButton(MouseEvent evt) {
    String result = "";
    int m = evt.getModifiers();

    if ((m & InputEvent.CTRL_MASK) != 0) {
        result += "c";
    }
    if ((m & InputEvent.SHIFT_MASK) != 0) {
        result += "s";
    }
    if ((m & InputEvent.BUTTON3_MASK) != 0) {
        result += "b3";
    } else if ((m & InputEvent.BUTTON2_MASK) != 0) {
        result += "b2";
    } else if ((m & InputEvent.BUTTON1_MASK) != 0) {
        result += "b1";
    }
    return result;
}

// Prints out the details of the mouse event.
void print(String eventName, MouseEvent evt) {
    String[] modNames = {"alt", "ctl", "meta", "shift", "b1", "b2", "b3"};
    int[] modMasks = {InputEvent.ALT_MASK,
        InputEvent.CTRL_MASK, InputEvent.META_MASK,
        InputEvent.SHIFT_MASK, InputEvent.BUTTON1_MASK,
        InputEvent.BUTTON2_MASK, InputEvent.BUTTON3_MASK};
    int m = evt.getModifiers();

    System.out.print(eventName + " (");
    for (int i=0; i<modMasks.length; i++) {
        if ((m & modMasks[i]) != 0) {
            System.out.print(modNames[i]+",");
        }
    }
    System.out.print(") ");
    System.out.print(" point="+evt.getX()+","+evt.getY());
    System.out.print(" clickCount="+evt.getClickCount());
    if (evt.isPopupTrigger()) {
        System.out.print(" isPopupTrigger");
    }
    System.out.println();
}
```

A
B
C
D
E
F
G
H
I
J
K
L
M
N
O
P
Q
R
S
T
U
V
W
X
Y
Z

```
        public static void main(String args[]) {
            new Main();
        }
    }
```

getClickCount()

PURPOSE	Retrieves the mouse event's click count.
SYNTAX	`public int getClickCount()`
DESCRIPTION	The click count indicates the number of quick, consecutive clicks of a mouse button. It is typically used to detect double- and triple-click gestures. For example, a click count property value of 2 indicates a double-click. The click count is valid only for three mouse events: `MOUSE_CLICKED`, `MOUSE_PRESSED`, and `MOUSE_RELEASED`. For these, the click count is at least 1. For all other mouse events, the click count is 0.
SEE ALSO	`MOUSE_CLICKED`, `MOUSE_PRESSED`, `MOUSE_RELEASED`.
EXAMPLE	See the class example.

getPoint()

PURPOSE	Retrieves the mouse event's location.
SYNTAX	`public Point getPoint()`
DESCRIPTION	The returned point is the location of the cursor relative to the source component's bounds when the mouse button was pressed. See the class description for more details about mouse event coordinates.
RETURNS	A non-`null` point indicating the mouse event's location.
EXAMPLE	See the class example.

getX()

PURPOSE	Retrieves the mouse event's *x*-coordinate.
SYNTAX	`public int getX()`
DESCRIPTION	For more details about the mouse coordinates, see the class description.
RETURNS	The mouse event's *x*-coordinate.
EXAMPLE	See the class example.

getY()

PURPOSE	Retrieves the mouse event's *y*-coordinate.
SYNTAX	`public int getY()`
DESCRIPTION	For more details about the mouse coordinates, see the class description.
RETURNS	The mouse event's *y*-coordinate.
EXAMPLE	See the class example.

isPopupTrigger()

PURPOSE	Retrieves the mouse event's popup trigger property.
SYNTAX	`public boolean isPopupTrigger()`
DESCRIPTION	If the popup menu trigger property for a mouse event is `true`, it indicates that the user made a mousing gesture to show a popup menu. The popup menu trigger property can be `true` only for `MOUSE_PRESSED` and `MOUSE_RELEASED` mouse events. See the class description for more details about the popup menu trigger. See `PopupMenu` for information about showing popup menus.
RETURNS	`true` if the event was a popup menu trigger; `false` otherwise.
SEE ALSO	`MOUSE_PRESSED, MOUSE_RELEASED, java.awt.PopupMenu.`
EXAMPLE	See the `java.awt.PopupMenu` class example.

MOUSE_CLICKED

PURPOSE	Event id indicating that a mouse button was pressed and released.
SYNTAX	`public static final int MOUSE_CLICKED`
DESCRIPTION	A mouse event with this id (value 500) is fired following a `MOUSE_PRESSED/` `MOUSE_RELEASED` event pair in which the mouse coordinates of both events are the same (or very close together). This event is most often used to listen for multiclicking mouse gestures. See `getClickCount()` for more details. The click count is always 1 or greater.
SEE ALSO	`MOUSE_PRESSED, MOUSE_RELEASED.`
EXAMPLE	See the class example.

A
B
C
D
E
F
G
H
I
J
K
L
M
N
O
P
Q
R
S
T
U
V
W
X
Y
Z

A
B
C
D
E
F
G
H
I
J
K
L
M
N
O
P
Q
R
S
T
U
V
W
X
Y
Z

MOUSE_DRAGGED

PURPOSE Event id indicating that the mouse moved while a mouse button was pressed.

SYNTAX `public static final int MOUSE_DRAGGED`

DESCRIPTION A mouse event with this id (value 506) is fired when the mouse is moved while a mouse button is down. A component fires this event only if the mouse button was pressed while the cursor was inside the component. So, for example, if the mouse button was pressed outside the component and dragged into the component, the component will not fire a MOUSE_DRAGGED event.

Unlike with the MOUSE_MOVED event, a component continues to fire this event until the mouse button is released, regardless of where the cursor is located. This means that the mouse coordinates may be outside the source component's bounds. This event is most often used for drag-and-drop operations.

The click count is always 0, and the popup menu trigger is always `false`.

SEE ALSO MOUSE_MOVED.

EXAMPLE See the class example.

MOUSE_ENTERED

PURPOSE Event id indicating that the cursor entered a component's exposed bounds.

SYNTAX `public static final int MOUSE_ENTERED`

DESCRIPTION A mouse event with this id (value 504) is fired whenever the cursor moves from a point not on the source component's exposed bounds to a point that is on the component's exposed bounds. One exception to this rule is when a popup menu is showing.

MOUSE_ENTERED and MOUSE_EXITED events are always fired in pairs, MOUSE_ENTERED being first. Therefore a component will never fire two MOUSE_ENTERED or two MOUSE_EXITED events in a row.

The event's coordinates is the point where the system first detected that the cursor was on the source component's exposed bounds. Therefore the closeness of the coordinates to the component's edge depends on how fast the cursor entered the bounds.

The click count is always 0.

SEE ALSO MOUSE_EXITED.

EXAMPLE See the class example.

MOUSE_EXITED

PURPOSE   Event id indicating that the cursor exited a component's exposed bounds.

SYNTAX   `public static final int MOUSE_EXITED`

DESCRIPTION   A mouse event with this id (value 505) is fired when the cursor is no longer on the source component's exposed bounds. One exception to this rule is when a popup menu is showing.

MOUSE_ENTERED and MOUSE_EXITED events are always fired in pairs, MOUSE_ENTERED being first. Therefore a component will never fire two MOUSE_ENTERED or two MOUSE_EXITED events in a row.

The event's coordinates is the point where the system first detected that the cursor was no longer on the source component's exposed bounds. Therefore the closeness of the coordinates to the component's bounds depends on how fast the cursor left the bounds.

The click count is always 0.

SEE ALSO   MOUSE_ENTERED.

EXAMPLE   See the class example.

MOUSE_FIRST

PURPOSE   Constant specifying the first id in the range of mouse event ids.

SYNTAX   `public static final int MOUSE_FIRST`

DESCRIPTION   All item event ids must be greater than or equal to MOUSE_FIRST (value 500).

SEE ALSO   MOUSE_LAST.

EXAMPLE   See `java.awt.Component.processEvent()`.

MOUSE_LAST

PURPOSE   Constant specifying the last id in the range of mouse event ids.

SYNTAX   `public static final int MOUSE_LAST`

DESCRIPTION   All item event ids must be less than or equal to MOUSE_LAST (value 506).

SEE ALSO   MOUSE_FIRST.

EXAMPLE   See `java.awt.Component.processEvent()`.

A
B
C
D
E
F
G
H
I
J
K
L
M
N
O
P
Q
R
S
T
U
V
W
X
Y
Z

MOUSE_MOVED

PURPOSE	Event id indicating that the mouse moved while in a component's exposed bounds.
SYNTAX	`public static final int MOUSE_MOVED`
DESCRIPTION	A mouse event with this id (value 503) is fired every time the mouse moves to a new point on the source component's exposed bounds.
	Note that mouse events may not be fired while the cursor is in the insets area of the component. This behavior is platform-dependent.
	The click count is always 0.
SEE ALSO	`MOUSE_DRAGGED`.
EXAMPLE	See the class example.

MOUSE_PRESSED

PURPOSE	Event id indicating that a mouse button was pressed.
SYNTAX	`public static final int MOUSE_PRESSED`
DESCRIPTION	A mouse event with this id (value 501) is fired when a mouse button is pressed. The AWT system guarantees that a `MOUSE_RELEASED` event will be fired for each `MOUSE_PRESSED` event fired, even if the mouse was released outside the component.
	The event's modifiers contain the state of the modifier keys at the time the mouse button was pressed. The modifier keys can be used to identify which mouse button was pressed. However, just testing the state of the modifier keys does not work in the case in which more than one button is down at time. See the class description for more details.
	The click count is always 1 or greater.
SEE ALSO	`MOUSE_CLICKED`, `MOUSE_RELEASED`.
EXAMPLE	See the class example.

MOUSE_RELEASED

PURPOSE	Event id indicating that a mouse button was released.
SYNTAX	`public static final int MOUSE_RELEASED`

DESCRIPTION	A mouse event with this id (value 502) is fired when a mouse button is released. The AWT system guarantees that a MOUSE_RELEASED event will be fired for each MOUSE_PRESSED event fired, even if the mouse was released outside the component.

The event's modifiers contains the state of the modifier keys at the time the mouse button was released. However, the state of the modifiers keys cannot reliably be used to determine which mouse button was released. For example, the Meta modifier key may or may not be set when the user releases Button3; whether it is depends on if the user is holding down the Meta key. See the class description for more details about the modifier keys.

The click count is always the same as that for the most recent MOUSE_PRESSED event.

The click count is always 1 or greater.

SEE ALSO	MOUSE_CLICKED, MOUSE_PRESSED.
EXAMPLE	See the class example.

MouseEvent()

PURPOSE	Constructs a MouseEvent instance.
SYNTAX	public MouseEvent(Component source, int id, long when, int modifiers,int x, int y, int clickCount, boolean popupTrigger)
DESCRIPTION	This constructor creates a mouse event with source as the component that fires this event. See the class description for more information on click counts, modifier keys, and popup triggers.

After the mouse event is created, the source object can distribute the event to its listeners by calling the mouse event-related methods in AWTEventMulticaster. If the event was not created by source, the creator can deliver the event to the source component either by posting the event to the event queue (see EventQueue.postEvent()) or by calling the source component's Component.dispatchEvent() method directly.

PARAMETERS
clickCount	The non-negative click count of this event.
id	One of the mouse event ids.
modifiers	The current state of the modifier keys.
popupTrigger	true if this event should cause a popup menu to appear.
source	The non-null component that is firing this mouse event.
when	The timestamp for this event. See System.currentTimeMillis().
x	The event's *x*-coordinate relative to the source's bounds.

A
B
C
D
E
F
G
H
I
J
K
L
M
N
O
P
Q
R
S
T
U
V
W
X
Y
Z

y	The event's *y*-coordinate relative to the source's bounds.
SEE ALSO	`getClickCount()`, `getPoint()`, `getX()`, `getY()`, `InputEvent.getModifiers()`, `InputEvent.getWhen()`, `isPopupTrigger()`, `java.awt.AWTEvent.getID()`, `java.awt.Component.dispatchEvent()`, `java.lang.System.currentTimeMills()`, `java.util.EventObject.getSource()`.

paramString()

PURPOSE	Generates a string representing the mouse event's state.
SYNTAX	`public String paramString()`
DESCRIPTION	The returned string contains the name of the mouse event, its coordinate, the key modifiers, and the click count. A subclass of this class should override this method and return a concatenation of its state with the results of `super.paramString()`. This method is called by the `AWTEvent.toString()` method and is typically used for debugging.
RETURNS	A non-`null` string representing the mouse event's state.
OVERRIDES	`java.awt.AWTEvent.paramString()`.
SEE ALSO	`java.awt.AWTEvent.toString()`, `java.lang.Object.toString()`.
EXAMPLE	See the `java.awt.AWTEvent` class example.

translatePoint()

PURPOSE	Translates the mouse event's coordinates.
SYNTAX	`public synchronized void translatePoint(int x, int y)`
DESCRIPTION	This method modifies the coordinates in the mouse event. In particular, x is added to the event's *x*-coordinate and y is added to the event's *y*-coordinate. For more details about mouse coordinates, see the class description.
PARAMETERS	
x	An integer value that is added to the event's *x*-coordinate.
y	An integer value that is added to the event's *y*-coordinate.
EXAMPLE	See the `MouseMotionListener` class example.

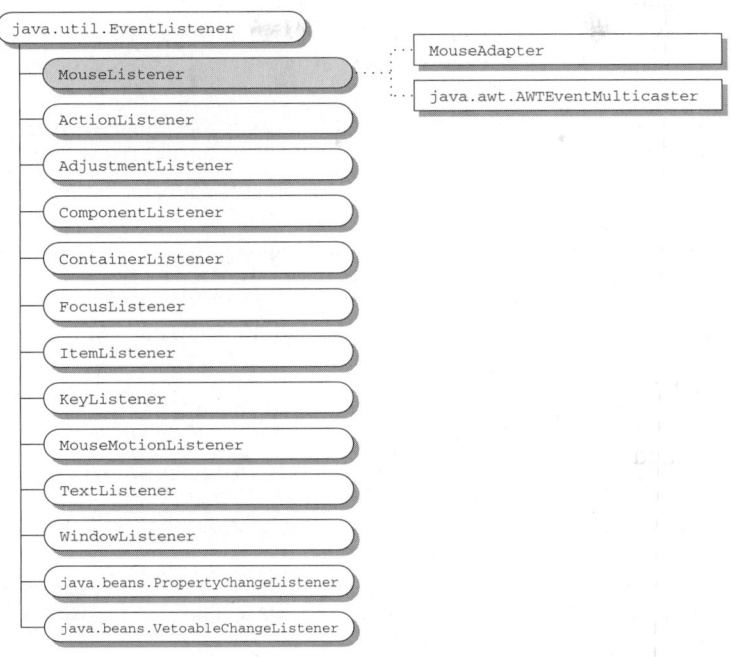

Syntax
```
public interface MouseListener extends EventListener
```

Description
When an object (listener) wishes to receive mouse events from a component (the source component), two things must be done:

1. The listener must implement the `MouseListener` interface and all of the methods it requires.
2. The listener must be registered with the source component by making a call to the source component's `addMouseListener()` method

For information about mouse events, see `MouseEvent`.

MEMBER SUMMARY	
Mouse Event Callback Methods	
mouseClicked()	Called when a mouse button is pressed and released.
mouseEntered()	Called when the cursor enters the source component's exposed bounds.
mouseExited()	Called when the cursor exits the source component's exposed bounds.
mousePressed()	Called when the user presses a mouse button in the source component.
mouseReleased()	Called when the user releases a mouse button in the source component.

See Also

`java.awt.Component.addMouseListener()`, `java.util.EventListener`, `MouseAdapter`, `MouseEvent`, `MouseMotionListener`.

Example

This example implements a lightweight component button. The button is arrow-shaped with transparent pixels around the arrow. It overrides the `contains()` method, so the transparent pixels are also transparent to mouse events.

Since the arrow button fires action events, it needs to provide the listener methods that are necessary to support action event listeners.

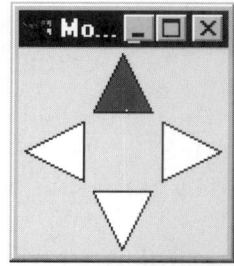

FIGURE 291: Arrow Buttons.

Note: In Java 1.1.2, clicking an arrow button turns it blue. Dragging outside of the button's outline should return it to red. However, the button doesn't return to red until the cursor is dragged outside of the whole window.

```
import java.awt.*;
import java.awt.event.*;

public class Main extends Frame {
    Main() {
        super("MouseListener Example");
        Component c;

        setBackground(Color.yellow);

        // Layout components.
        GridBagLayout gbl = new GridBagLayout();
        setLayout(gbl);

        add(c = new ArrowButton(ArrowButton.NORTH));
```

A
B
C
D
E
F
G
H
I
J
K
L
M
N
O
P
Q
R
S
T
U
V
W
X
Y
Z

```
        setConstraints(gbl, c, 1, 0);
        add(c = new ArrowButton(ArrowButton.WEST));
        setConstraints(gbl, c, 0, 1);
        add(c = new ArrowButton(ArrowButton.SOUTH));
        setConstraints(gbl, c, 1, 2);
        add(c = new ArrowButton(ArrowButton.EAST));
        setConstraints(gbl, c, 2, 1);

        pack();
        show();
    }

    // Setup the gridbag constraints for a component.
    void setConstraints(GridBagLayout gbl, Component comp, int x, int y) {
        GridBagConstraints cbc = new GridBagConstraints();

        cbc.gridx = x;
        cbc.gridy = y;
        cbc.insets = new Insets(2, 2, 2, 2);
        gbl.setConstraints(comp, cbc);
    }

    public static void main(String args[]) {
        new Main();
    }
}

class ArrowButton extends Component implements MouseListener {
    static final int NORTH = 0;
    static final int WEST = 1;
    static final int SOUTH = 2;
    static final int EAST = 3;

    // ne, nw, sw, se
    int[][] corners = {{1, 0}, {0, 0}, {0, 1}, {1, 1}};
    double[][] tips = {{.5, 0}, {0, .5}, {.5, 1}, {1, .5}};
    int width = 30;
    int height = 30;

    // The orientation of the button.  This value
    // is included in the action events this button fires.
    int orient;

    // If true and down is not true, the button should appear red.
    boolean highlight;

    // If true and highlight is true, the button should appear blue.
    boolean down;

    Polygon shape = new Polygon();

    ArrowButton(int o) {
        orient = o;

        // Prepare shape.
        int o1 = (o+1)%corners.length;
        int o2 = (o+2)%corners.length;
        int o3 = (o+3)%corners.length;
        int w = width-1;
        int h = height-1;
```

A
B
C
D
E
F
G
H
I
J
K
L
M
N
O
P
Q
R
S
T
U
V
W
X
Y
Z

```
                    shape.addPoint((int)(tips[o][0]*w), (int)(tips[o][1]*h));
                    shape.addPoint(corners[o2][0]*w, corners[o2][1]*h);
                    shape.addPoint(corners[o3][0]*w, corners[o3][1]*h);

                    // Listen for events.
                    addMouseListener(this);
                }

            public void paint(Graphics g) {
                if (highlight) {
                    if (down) {
                        g.setColor(Color.blue);
                    } else {
                        g.setColor(Color.red);
                    }
                } else {
                    g.setColor(Color.white);
                }
                g.fillPolygon(shape);
                g.setColor(Color.black);
                g.drawPolygon(shape);
            }

            // Mouse event handlers
            public void mouseClicked(MouseEvent evt) {
                // do nothing
            }
            public void mousePressed(MouseEvent evt) {
                down = true;
                repaint();
            }
            public void mouseReleased(MouseEvent evt) {
                if (down) {
                    // Fire an action event.
                    processActionEvent(
                        new ActionEvent(this, ActionEvent.ACTION_PERFORMED,
                            ""+orient));
                }
                down = false;
                repaint();
            }
            public void mouseEntered(MouseEvent evt) {
                highlight = true;
                repaint();
            }
            public void mouseExited(MouseEvent evt) {
                highlight = false;
                repaint();
            }

            // Returns true if the coordinate is inside the arrow.
            public boolean contains(int x, int y) {
                return shape.contains(x, y);
            }

            public Dimension getMinimumSize() {
                return new Dimension(width, height);
            }
            public Dimension getPreferredSize() {
```

```
            return new Dimension(width, height);
        }

        // Methods to support listeners of the action event.
        transient ActionListener actionListener;

        public synchronized void addActionListener(ActionListener l) {
            actionListener = AWTEventMulticaster.add(actionListener, l);
        }
        public synchronized void removeActionListener(ActionListener l) {
            actionListener = AWTEventMulticaster.remove(actionListener, l);
        }

        protected void processActionEvent(ActionEvent evt) {
            if (actionListener != null) {
                actionListener.actionPerformed(evt);
            }
        }
    }
}
```

mouseClicked()

PURPOSE   Called when a mouse button is pressed and released.

SYNTAX   `public void mouseClicked(MouseEvent evt)`

DESCRIPTION   This method is called after the `mousePressed()` and `mouseReleased()` methods are called and the mouse coordinates of both events are the same (or very close together). See `MouseEvent.MOUSE_CLICKED` for more details about mouse clicked events.

PARAMETERS
evt   The non-null mouse event.

EXAMPLE   See the class example.

mouseEntered()

PURPOSE   Called when the cursor enters the source component's exposed bounds.

SYNTAX   `public void mouseEntered(MouseEvent evt)`

DESCRIPTION   This method is called whenever the cursor moves from a point not on the source component's exposed bounds to a point that is on the component's exposed bounds. See `MouseEvent.MOUSE_ENTERED` for more details about mouse entered events.

PARAMETERS
evt   The non-null mouse event.

EXAMPLE   See the class example.

A
B
C
D
E
F
G
H
I
J
K
L
M
N
O
P
Q
R
S
T
U
V
W
X
Y
Z

mouseExited()

PURPOSE	Called when the cursor exits the source component's exposed bounds.
SYNTAX	`public void mouseExited(MouseEvent evt)`
DESCRIPTION	This method is called when the cursor is no longer on the source component's exposed bounds. See `MouseEvent.MOUSE_EXITED` for details about mouse exited events.
PARAMETERS	
`evt`	The non-`null` mouse event.
EXAMPLE	See the class example.

mousePressed()

PURPOSE	Called when the user presses a mouse button in the source component.
SYNTAX	`public void mousePressed(MouseEvent evt)`
DESCRIPTION	This method is called when a mouse button is pressed. See `MouseEvent.MOUSE_PRESSED` for more details about mouse pressed events.
PARAMETERS	
`evt`	The non-`null` mouse event.
EXAMPLE	See the class example.

mouseReleased()

PURPOSE	Called when the user releases a mouse button in the source component.
SYNTAX	`public void mouseReleased(MouseEvent evt)`
DESCRIPTION	This method is called when a mouse button is released. See `MouseEvent.MOUSE_RELEASED` for more details about mouse released events.
PARAMETERS	
`evt`	The non-`null` mouse event.
EXAMPLE	See the class example.

MouseMotionAdapter

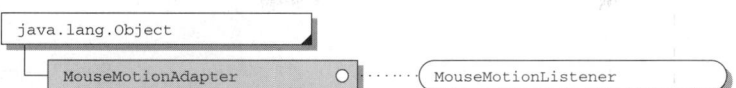

Syntax
`public abstract class MouseMotionAdapter implements MouseMotionListener`

Description
The mouse motion adapter is a mouse motion listener in which all callback methods are empty implementations. The purpose of the mouse motion adapter is to make it more convenient for an object to listen for mouse motion events. In particular, by using the mouse motion adapter, you can implement only those callback methods in which you are interested. Without the mouse motion adapter, you must implement all callback methods, even if the method is empty.

To use a mouse motion adapter, you create a subclass of `MouseMotionAdapter` and override the desired callback methods. You then create an instance of the mouse motion adapter subclass and call the component's `addMouseMotionListener()` method with it. The mouse motion adapter subclass is typically an inner class.

MEMBER SUMMARY	
Mouse Motion Event Callback Methods	
`mouseDragged()`	Called when the user drags the mouse on the source component.
`mouseMoved()`	Called when the user moves the mouse over the source component.

See Also
`java.awt.Component.addMouseMotionListener()`, `MouseEvent`, `MouseMotionListener`.

Example
This example implements a simple "stamping" program. The user can select an image (called the *stamp*) from a palette of images and then copy it anywhere on the stamp canvas. See Figure 292.

When the stamp canvas receives a mouse motion event, it displays the current stamp at mouse coordinates. When it receives a mouse pressed event, it records the stamp at the current location. When it receives a mouse exit event, it hides the stamp.

The stamps are simple components that paint the stamp image. They are displayed in a flow layout. The frame listens for mouse pressed events from the stamp components and uses them to get the stamp in the stamp canvas.

The stamp canvas uses an off-screen image (bbuf) to implement double-buffering in order to eliminate flickering. The off-screen image is first cleared and then all of the stamps are painted at their current locations. The complete off-screen image is then painted on the screen.

Possible additions to this program would be to highlight the current stamp and to allow the user to delete and move around painted stamps.

FIGURE 292:   A Stamping Program.

A
B
C
D
E
F
G
H
I
J
K
L
M
N
O
P
Q
R
S
T
U
V
W
X
Y
Z

```java
import java.awt.*;
import java.awt.event.*;
import java.util.*;

public class Main extends Frame {
    StampCanvas StampCanvas = new StampCanvas();
    Button startButton = new Button("Start");
    Panel palette = new Panel(new FlowLayout());

    Main() {
        super("MouseMotionAdapter Example");

        // Initialize palette with stamps.
        Stamp s;
        palette.add(s = new Stamp(getToolkit().getImage("duke.gif")));
        s.addMouseListener(new MouseEventHandler());
        palette.add(s = new Stamp(getToolkit().getImage("bird.gif")));
        s.addMouseListener(new MouseEventHandler());
        palette.add(s = new Stamp(getToolkit().getImage("house.gif")));
        s.addMouseListener(new MouseEventHandler());

        // Layout components
        add(palette, BorderLayout.SOUTH);
        add(StampCanvas, BorderLayout.CENTER);
        setSize(300, 300);
        show();
    }

    class MouseEventHandler extends MouseAdapter {
        public void mousePressed(MouseEvent evt) {
            Stamp stamp = (Stamp)evt.getSource();

            StampCanvas.setStamp(stamp.image);
        }
```

```
    }

    public static void main(String args[]) {
        new Main();
    }
}

class Stamp extends Component {
    int width, height;
    Image image;

    Stamp(Image image) {
        MediaTracker tracker = new MediaTracker(this);

        this.image = image;
        try {
            tracker.addImage(image, 0);
            tracker.waitForAll();
        } catch (Exception e) {
            e.printStackTrace();
        }
        width = image.getWidth(null);
        height = image.getHeight(null);
    }

    public void paint(Graphics g) {
        g.drawImage(image,
            (getSize().width-width)/2, (getSize().height-height)/2, this);
    }

    public Dimension getPreferredSize() {
        return new Dimension(width, height);
    }
}

class StampCanvas extends Canvas {
    // Vector of all stamped images.
    Vector stamps = new Vector();

    // Vector of all locations of the stamped images.
    Vector stampPts = new Vector();

    // The current stamp. If null, no stamp is set.
    Image curStamp;

    // The current location of the stamp's origin.
    // If null, don't display the stamp.
    Point curPoint;

    // Double buffer variables
    Image bbuf;
    Graphics bbufG;

    StampCanvas() {
        // Listen for events.
        addMouseListener(new MouseEventHandler());
        addMouseMotionListener(new MouseMotionEventHandler());
    }

    void setStamp(Image stamp) {
```

```
            curStamp = stamp;
        }

        public void paint(Graphics g) {
            update(g);
        }

        public void update(Graphics g) {
            int width = getSize().width;
            int height = getSize().height;

            // Create the double buffer if necessary.
            // Also make it bigger if necessary.
            if (bbuf == null
                    || bbuf.getWidth(null) < width
                    || bbuf.getHeight(null) < height) {
                bbuf = createImage(width, height);
                if (bbufG != null) {
                    bbufG.dispose();
                }
                bbufG = bbuf.getGraphics();
            }

            // Clear the background.
            bbufG.setColor(Color.lightGray);
            bbufG.fillRect(0, 0, width, height);

            // Paint all the stamps.
            for (int i=0; i<stamps.size(); i++) {
                Image stamp = (Image)stamps.elementAt(i);
                Point pt = (Point)stampPts.elementAt(i);

                bbufG.drawImage(stamp, pt.x, pt.y, this);
            }

            // Paint the current stamp.
            if (curStamp != null && curPoint != null) {
                bbufG.drawImage(curStamp, curPoint.x, curPoint.y, this);
            }

            // Draw the off-screen image to the display.
            g.drawImage(bbuf, 0, 0, this);
        }

        // Handler for mouse move events.
        class MouseMotionEventHandler extends MouseMotionAdapter {
            public void mouseMoved(MouseEvent evt) {
                if (curStamp != null) {
                    int x = evt.getX()-curStamp.getWidth(null)/2;
                    int y = evt.getY()-curStamp.getHeight(null)/2;

                    // Keep the image with the bounds of the canvas.
                    x = Math.max(0, Math.min(
                        x, getSize().width-curStamp.getWidth(null)));
                    y = Math.max(0, Math.min(
                        y, getSize().height-curStamp.getHeight(null)));

                    curPoint = new Point(x, y);
                    repaint();
                }
```

```
        }
    }

    // Handler for mouse pressed and exit events.
    class MouseEventHandler extends MouseAdapter {
        public void mousePressed(MouseEvent evt) {
            // Save the stamp.
            if (curStamp != null) {
                stamps.addElement(curStamp);
                stampPts.addElement(new Point(curPoint.x, curPoint.y));
                repaint();
            }
        }
        public void mouseExited(MouseEvent evt) {
            curPoint = null;
            repaint();
        }
    }
}
```

mouseDragged()

PURPOSE	Called when the user drags the mouse on the source component.
SYNTAX	`public void mouseDragged(MouseEvent evt)`
DESCRIPTION	This method, by default, has an empty implementation. It should be overridden to handle `MouseEvent.MOUSE_DRAGGED` events. See the `MouseEvent.MOUSE_DRAGGED` event for details.
PARAMETERS	
`evt`	The non-`null` mouse motion event.
EXAMPLE	See the `MouseMotionListener` class example.

mouseMoved()

PURPOSE	Called when the user moves the mouse over the source component.
SYNTAX	`public void mouseMoved(MouseEvent evt)`
DESCRIPTION	This method, by default, has an empty implementation. It should be overridden to handle `MouseEvent.MOUSE_MOVED` events. See the `MouseEvent.MOUSE_MOVED` event for details.
PARAMETERS	
`evt`	The non-`null` mouse motion event.
EXAMPLE	See the class example.

MouseMotionListener

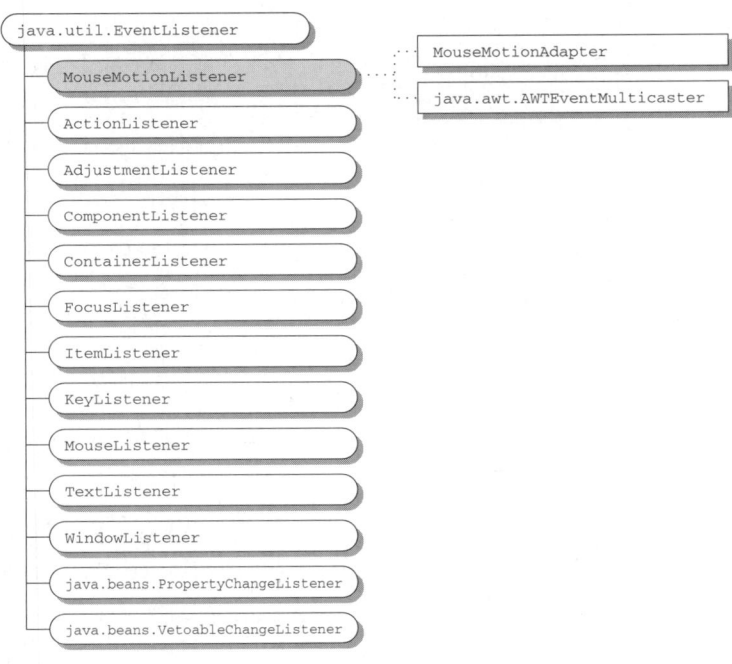

Syntax

```
public interface MouseMotionListener extends EventListener
```

Description

When an object (listener) wishes to receive mouse motion events from a component (the source component), two things must be done:

1. The listener must implement the MouseMotionListener interface and all of the methods it requires.
2. The listener must be registered with the source component. It becomes registered by making a call to the source component's addMouseMotionListener() method.

For information about mouse motion events, see MouseEvent.

MEMBER SUMMARY	
Mouse Motion Event Callback Methods	
mouseDragged()	Called when the user drags the mouse on the source component.
mouseMoved()	Called when the user moves the mouse over the source component.

See Also

java.awt.Container.getInsets(), java.util.EventListener, MouseEvent, MouseMotionAdapter.

Example

This example demonstrates how to use mouse motion events to drag a square around a frame's inset area. The frame's insets are used to constrain the square so that it cannot be outside the frame's inset area. See Figure 293.

Notice the addNotify() call. This is done to create the peers so that the getInsets() call will return valid results. See Container.getInsets() for more details.

The example also changes the cursor when the cursor is over the box.

FIGURE 293: MouseMotionListener.

```java
import java.awt.*;
import java.awt.event.*;

class Main extends Frame implements MouseMotionListener {
    Rectangle box = new Rectangle(0, 0, 30, 30);
    int curCursor = DEFAULT_CURSOR;

    Main() {
        super("MouseMotionListener Example");

        addMouseListener(new MouseEventHandler());
        addMouseMotionListener(this);
        setSize(200, 200);
        addNotify();
        box.x = getInsets().left;
        box.y = getInsets().top;
        show();
    }

    public void paint(Graphics g) {
        g.setColor(Color.red);
        g.fillRect(box.x, box.y, box.width, box.height);
    }

    public void mouseDragged(MouseEvent evt) {
        if (downPt != null) {
            Insets insets = getInsets();

            // Keep the box inside the frame inset area.
            box.x = Math.max(insets.left, Math.min(evt.getX()-downPt.x,
                getSize().width-box.width-insets.right));
            box.y = Math.max(insets.top, Math.min(evt.getY()-downPt.y,
                getSize().height-box.height-insets.bottom));
            repaint();
        }
    }
```

1155

A
B
C
D
E
F
G
H
I
J
K
L
M
N
O
P
Q
R
S
T
U
V
W
X
Y
Z

```java
    }

    public void mouseMoved(MouseEvent evt) {
        int oldCursor = curCursor;

        if (box.contains(evt.getX(), evt.getY())) {
            curCursor = Cursor.HAND_CURSOR;
        } else {
            curCursor = Cursor.DEFAULT_CURSOR;
        }
        if (oldCursor != curCursor) {
            setCursor(Cursor.getPredefinedCursor(curCursor));
        }
    }

    // Point where the mouse button was pressed relative to the box's origin.
    Point downPt;
    class MouseEventHandler extends MouseAdapter {
        public void mousePressed(MouseEvent evt) {
            if (curCursor == Cursor.HAND_CURSOR) {
                evt.translatePoint(-box.x, -box.y);
                downPt = evt.getPoint();
            }
        }
        public void mouseReleased(MouseEvent evt) {
            downPt = null;
        }
    }

    public static void main(String args[]) {
        new Main();
    }
}
```

mouseDragged()

PURPOSE   Called when the user drags the mouse on the source component.

SYNTAX   `public void mouseDragged(MouseEvent evt)`

DESCRIPTION   This method is called when the mouse is moved while a mouse button is held down. See `MouseEvent.MOUSE_DRAGGED` for more details about mouse dragged events.

PARAMETERS

    `evt`   The non-`null` mouse motion event.

EXAMPLE   See the class example.

mouseMoved()

PURPOSE	Called when the user moves the mouse over the source component.
SYNTAX	`public void mouseMoved(MouseEvent evt)`
DESCRIPTION	This method is called every time the mouse moves to a new point on the source component's exposed bounds. See `MouseEvent.MOUSE_MOVED` for details about mouse moved events.
PARAMETERS	
evt	The non-`null` mouse motion event.
EXAMPLE	See the class example.

A
B
C
D
E
F
G
H
I
J
K
L
M
N
O
P
Q
R
S
T
U
V
W
X
Y
Z

PaintEvent

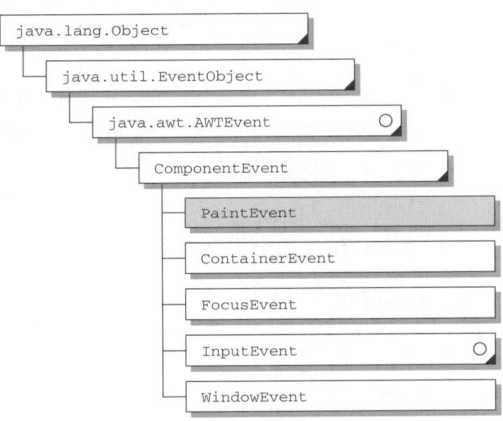

```
java.lang.Object
    java.util.EventObject
        java.awt.AWTEvent        ○
            ComponentEvent
                PaintEvent
                ContainerEvent
                FocusEvent
                InputEvent        ○
                WindowEvent
```

Syntax
```
public class PaintEvent extends ComponentEvent
```

Description
This class is used internally by the AWT system to manage the updating of component display areas. The AWT system does not provide any listener methods for paint events. Consequently, this class does not have any examples.

The event is fired by peer components and translated by a component into `Component.paint()` and `Component.update()` method calls. See `Component` for more details.

The Update Area
The *update area* is an area on the source component that needs to repainted. For example, if a component is partially occluded by a window and the window is removed, the component's update area is the newly revealed area.

MEMBER SUMMARY	
Constructor	
PaintEvent()	Constructs a PaintEvent instance.
Update Rectangle Methods	
getUpdateRect()	Retrieves the paint event's update area.
setUpdateRect()	Sets the paint event's update area.

MEMBER SUMMARY	
Paint Event Id Constants	
PAINT	Event id indicating that the update area has been filled and needs to be repainted.
PAINT_FIRST	Constant specifying the first id in the range of paint event ids.
PAINT_LAST	Constant specifying the last id in the range of paint event ids.
UPDATE	Event id indicating that the update area needs to be repainted.
Debugging Method	
paramString()	Generates a string representing the paint event's state.

See Also

java.awt.Component.paint(), java.awt.Component.update().

getUpdateRect()

PURPOSE   Retrieves the paint event's update area.

SYNTAX   public Rectangle getUpdateRect()

DESCRIPTION This method retrieves the rectangle representing the area that needs to be repainted in response to this event.

PAINT

PURPOSE   Event id indicating that the update area has been filled and needs to be repainted.

SYNTAX   public static final int PAINT

DESCRIPTION A paint event with this id (value 800) is fired when an area of the source component needs to be repainted. A PAINT event differs from an UPDATE event in that for a PAINT event, the AWT system automatically fills the update area with the background color, whereas it does not for an UPDATE event.

SEE ALSO   UPDATE.

A
B
C
D
E
F
G
H
I
J
K
L
M
N
O
P
Q
R
S
T
U
V
W
X
Y
Z

A
B
C
D
E
F
G
H
I
J
K
L
M
N
O

Q
R
S
T
U
V
W
X
Y
Z

PAINT_FIRST

PURPOSE	Constant specifying the first id in the range of paint event ids.
SYNTAX	`public static final int PAINT_FIRST`
DESCRIPTION	All paint event ids must be greater than or equal to PAINT_FIRST (value 800).
SEE ALSO	PAINT_LAST.
EXAMPLE	See `java.awt.Component.processEvent()`.

PAINT_LAST

PURPOSE	Constant specifying the last id in the range of paint event ids.
SYNTAX	`public static final int PAINT_LAST`
DESCRIPTION	All paint event ids must be less than or equal to PAINT_LAST (value 801).
SEE ALSO	PAINT_FIRST.
EXAMPLE	See `java.awt.Component.processEvent()`.

PaintEvent()

PURPOSE	Constructs a `PaintEvent` instance.
SYNTAX	`public PaintEvent(Component source, int id, Rectangle updateRect)`
DESCRIPTION	This constructor creates a paint event with `source` as the component that fires this event. Paint events are normally fired by the AWT system to notify components of areas that need to be repainted. You should not need to deal with paint events directly. To handle repaints, see `Component.paint()` and `Component.update()`.
PARAMETERS	
source	The non-`null` component that is firing this paint event.
id	One of the paint event ids.
updateRect	The non-`null` update area.
SEE ALSO	`getUpdateRect()`, `java.awt.AWTEvent.getID()`, `java.util.EventObject.getSource()`.

paramString()

PURPOSE	Generates a string representing the paint event's state.
SYNTAX	`public String paramString()`
DESCRIPTION	The returned string contains the name of the paint event and the bounds of the update area. A subclass of this class should override this method and return a concatenation of its state with the results of `super.paramString()`. This method is called by the `AWTEvent.toString()` method and is typically used for debugging.
RETURNS	A non-`null` string representing the paint event's state.
OVERRIDES	`java.awt.AWTEvent.paramString()`.
SEE ALSO	`java.awt.AWTEvent.toString()`, `java.lang.Object.toString()`.
EXAMPLE	See the `java.awt.AWTEvent` class example.

setUpdateRect()

PURPOSE	Sets the paint event's update area.
SYNTAX	`public void setUpdateRect(Rectangle updateRect)`
PARAMETERS	
updateRect	The non-`null` rectangle update area.
SEE ALSO	`getUpdateRect()`.

UPDATE

PURPOSE	Event id indicating that the update area needs to be repainted.
SYNTAX	`public static final int UPDATE`
DESCRIPTION	A paint event with this id (value 801) is fired when an area of the source component needs to be repainted. A PAINT event differs from an UPDATE event in that for a PAINT event, the AWT system automatically fills the update area with the background color, whereas it does not for an UPDATE event.
SEE ALSO	PAINT.

A
B
C
D
E
F
G
H
I
J
K
L
M
N
O
P
Q
R
S
T
U
V
W
X
Y
Z

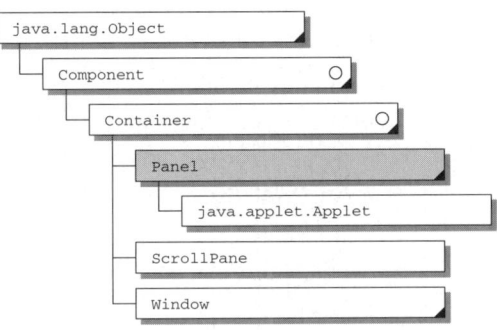

Syntax

`public class Panel extends Container`

Description

A *panel* is a component and a component container. Since a panel is itself a component, panels can be freely nested. Panels are typically used in the layout of components in a user interface. For example, suppose a user interface has two columns of buttons: one on the left and one on the right. In between the two columns is a display area that expands as the user expands the window. This layout would be implemented with three panels: a border layout panel (see `BorderLayout`) with two nested grid layout panels (see `GridLayout`).

A panel has no border or title; hence, its insets are always (0, 0, 0, 0). See the `Container` class for more information about insets and layout managers.

Events

The panel fires the same events as a component. See the `Component` class for details.

Panels and Lightweight Containers

With the introduction of lightweight components and containers (see `Component`), there is really no need to subclass the panel container. In fact, since a panel has a native peer and a lightweight container does not, it is much more efficient to use a lightweight container. If you are presently using a panel, you should consider changing it to a lightweight container.

In theory, changing your class from a panel to a lightweight container simply involves changing the extends from `Panel` to `Container`. However, there are a few problems with the current release that forces you to make a few more modifications before your class will work exactly the same. For details, see the `Container` class description on lightweights.

MEMBER SUMMARY	
Constructor	
Panel()	Constructs a new Panel instance.
Peer Method	
addNotify()	Creates this panel's peer hierarchy.

Example

This example creates four panels: "one," "two," "three," and "four." These four panels are in turn embedded in another panel with a card layout manager. Each panel contains from one to four labels. Four buttons are provided on the left side of the frame to control which of the four panels are displayed. See Figure 294.

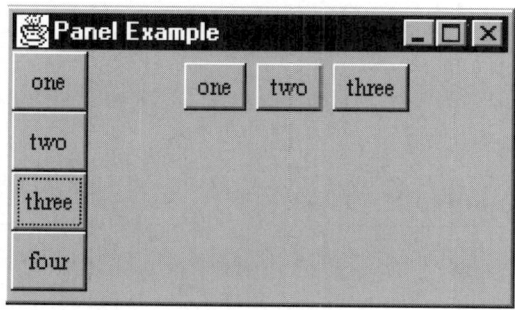

FIGURE 294:   Panel.

```java
import java.awt.*;
import java.awt.event.*;

class Main extends Frame implements ActionListener {
    CardLayout cardLayout = new CardLayout();
    Panel cardPanel = new Panel(cardLayout);
    String[] names = {"one", "two", "three", "four"};

    Main() {
        super("Panel Example");
        Panel p = new Panel(new GridLayout(0, 1));
        Button b;

        // Put column of buttons on the left
        for (int i=0; i<names.length; i++) {
            p.add(b = new Button(names[i]));
            b.addActionListener(this);
        }
        add(p, BorderLayout.WEST);

        // Place card panel in center
        for (int i=0; i<names.length; i++) {
            addPanel(cardPanel, i+1);
        }
        add(cardPanel, BorderLayout.CENTER);
        setSize(300, 150);
        show();
    }

    // Creates a panel with 'count' labels
    void addPanel(Panel parent, int count) {
        Panel p = new Panel();
```

```
                  Label 1;
                  for (int i=0; i<count; i++) {
                      l = new Label(names[i], Label.CENTER);
                      l.setBackground(Color.yellow);
                      p.add(l);
                  }
                  parent.add(names[count-1], p);
              }

          // Action handler for buttons
          public void actionPerformed(ActionEvent evt) {
              cardLayout.show(cardPanel, evt.getActionCommand());
          }

          static public void main(String[] args) {
              new Main();
          }
      }
```

addNotify()

PURPOSE	Creates this panel's peer hierarchy.
SYNTAX	`public void addNotify()`
DESCRIPTION	This method creates this panel's peer hierarchy, if necessary. The panel's peer is created by calling the `Toolkit.createPanel()` method. This method should never be called directly. It is normally called by the panel's parent.
OVERRIDES	`Container.addNotify()`.
SEE ALSO	`Component`, `Toolkit`.
EXAMPLE	See `Component.setVisible()`.

Panel()

PURPOSE	Constructs a new `Panel` instance.
SYNTAX	`public Panel()` `public Panel(LayoutManager layout)`
DESCRIPTION	This constructor creates a new visible `Panel` instance using the specified layout manager layout. If `layout` is not specified, the default layout manager is `FlowLayout`. All panels created with no layout share this same `FlowLayout` instance.
PARAMETERS	
layout	The possibly `null` layout manager to use for the newly created panel.
EXAMPLE	See the class example.

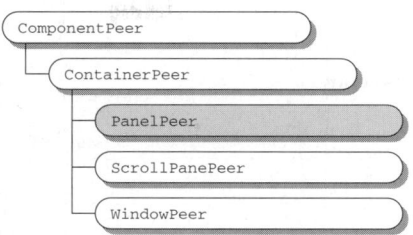

Syntax

`public interface PanelPeer extends ContainerPeer`

Description

The panel component (see the `Panel` class) in the AWT uses the platform's native implementation of a panel. So that the AWT panel behaves the same on all platforms, the panel is assigned a *peer*, whose task is to translate the behavior of the platform's native panel to the behavior of the AWT panel.

   AWT programmers normally do not directly use peer classes and interfaces. Instead, they deal with AWT components in the `java.awt` package. These in turn automatically manage their peers. Only someone who is porting the AWT to another platform should be concerned with the peer classes and interfaces. Consequently, most peer documentation refers to `java.awt` counterparts.

   See `Component` and `Toolkit` for additional information about component peers.

See Also

`java.awt.Component`, `java.awt.Panel`, `java.awt.Toolkit`.

ParameterDescriptor

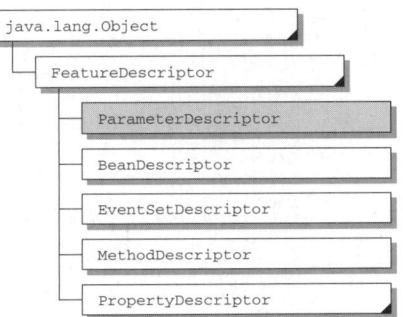

Syntax

```
public class ParameterDescriptor extends FeatureDescriptor
```

Description

A *parameter descriptor* contains information about a method parameter, such as its localized name and whether it is meant only for experts. A parameter descriptor does not presently have any other attributes beyond those in a feature descriptor (see `FeatureDescriptor`). See Figure 295.

See Also

`FeatureDescriptor`.

Example

See the `MethodDescriptor` class example.

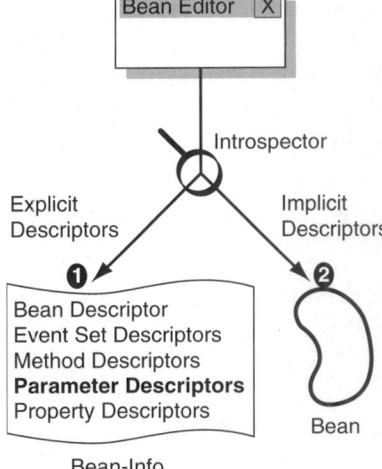

FIGURE 295: **Parameter Descriptor.**

PixelGrabber

java.lang.Object

PixelGrabber ············ ImageConsumer

Syntax

```
public class PixelGrabber implements ImageConsumer
```

Description

The PixelGrabber class is used to retrieve the pixels in an image or from an image producer. The retrieved pixel values are colors either in the default color model (see Color-Model.getRGBdefault()) or in the original color model of the source image.

MEMBER SUMMARY	
Constructor	
PixelGrabber()	Constructs a new PixelGrabber instance.
Pixel Retrieval Methods	
abortGrabbing()	Aborts retrieval of the pixels.
grabPixels()	Starts retrieval of the pixels and blocks waiting for the pixels.
startGrabbing()	Starts retrieval of the pixels.
Retrieval Information Methods	
getColorModel()	Retrieves the color model being used to accumulate the pixels.
getHeight()	Retrieves the height of the pixel buffer.
getPixels()	Retrieves the pixel buffer.
getStatus()	Determines the current state of the pixels.
getWidth()	Retrieves the width of the pixel buffer.
Image Consumer Method Called by the Image Producer	
imageComplete()	Called to deliver completion status.
setColorModel()	Called to deliver the color model for the source image.
setDimensions()	Called to deliver the dimensions of the source image.
setHints()	Called to specify how the pixels will be delivered.
setPixels()	Called to deliver pixels.
setProperties()	Called to deliver the properties for the source image.
Deprecated Method	
status()	Replaced by getStatus().

Example

This example displays an image and retrieves the pixel values of the image. See Figure 296. The program displays the color components of the pixel that is directly under the cursor. If you click the pixel, the program colors all identical pixels in the image red. The program also displays the number of times that pixel value appears in the image.

FIGURE 296: PixelGrabber.

The frame creates a label on the top and an ImageCanvas object in the center. The Image-Canvas object is created with an image and a label. It displays the image and watches the cursor. Using the supplied label, the `ImageCanvas` object displays the color components of the pixel that is directly under the cursor.

```java
import java.awt.*;
import java.awt.image.*;
import java.awt.event.*;

class Main extends Frame {
    Main(String filename) {
        super("PixelGrabber Example");
        Label label = new Label();

        add(label, BorderLayout.NORTH);
        add(new ImageCanvas(getToolkit().getImage(filename), label),
            BorderLayout.CENTER);
        setSize(300, 300);
        show();
    }

    static public void main(String[] args) {
        if (args.length == 1) {
            new Main(args[0]);
        } else {
            System.err.println("usage: java Main <image file>");
        }
    }
}

class ImageCanvas extends Component {
    Image image;
    Label label;
    int[] pixels;
    boolean paintTargetPixels;
    int targetPixelValue;

    ImageCanvas(Image image, Label label) {
        this.image = image;
        this.label = label;

        // Add listeners for canvas
        addMouseMotionListener(new MouseMotionEventHandler());
```

```
        addMouseListener(new MouseEventHandler());
    }

    void paintPixels(Graphics g, int w, int h) {
        int count = 0;
        g.setColor(Color.red);
        for (int x=0; x<w; x++) {
            for (int y=0; y<h; y++) {
                int p = pixels[y * w + x];
                if (p == targetPixelValue) {
                    g.fillRect(x, y, 1, 1);
                    count++;
                }
            }
        }
        label.setText("count: " + count);
    }

    public void update(Graphics g) {
        paint(g);
    }
    public void paint(Graphics g) {
        if (image != null) {
            g.drawImage(image, 0, 0, this);

            int w = image.getWidth(this);
            int h = image.getHeight(this);
            if (w < 0 || h < 0) return;
            if (paintTargetPixels) {
                paintPixels(g, w, h);
            }

            if (pixels == null) {
                // Create a pixel grabber and retrieve the pixels.
                pixels = new int[w * h];
                try {
                    PixelGrabber pg = new PixelGrabber(
                        image, 0, 0, w, h, pixels, 0, w);
                    pg.grabPixels();

                    // Check for errors.
                    if ((pg.status() & ImageObserver.ABORT) != 0) {
                        System.err.println("Error while fetching image");
                        System.exit(1);
                    }
                } catch (Exception e) {
                    e.printStackTrace();
                    System.exit(1);
                }
            }
        }
    }

    class MouseMotionEventHandler extends MouseMotionAdapter {
        public void mouseMoved(MouseEvent evt) {
            int x = evt.getX(), y = evt.getY();

            if (pixels == null ||
                x >= image.getWidth(ImageCanvas.this) ||
                y >= image.getHeight(ImageCanvas.this)) {
```

A
B
C
D
E
F
G
H
I
J
K
L
M
N
O
P
Q
R
S
T
U
V
W
X
Y
Z

```
                            label.setText("");
                            return;
                        }
                        ColorModel cm = ColorModel.getRGBdefault();
                        int p = pixels[y * image.getWidth(ImageCanvas.this) + x];

                        // The pixel value is translated into a color using
                        // the default color model.
                        label.setText(x + "," + y + ":      " + cm.getRed(p) + " "
                                    + cm.getGreen(p) + " " + cm.getBlue(p)
                                    + "   a("+cm.getAlpha(p) + ")");
                    }
                }

                class MouseEventHandler extends MouseAdapter {
                    public void mousePressed(MouseEvent evt) {
                        int x = evt.getX(), y = evt.getY();
                        if (pixels == null ||
                            x >= image.getWidth(ImageCanvas.this) ||
                            y >= image.getHeight(ImageCanvas.this)) {
                            return;
                        }
                        targetPixelValue = pixels[y * image.getWidth(ImageCanvas.this) + x];
                        paintTargetPixels = true;
                        repaint();
                    }

                    public void mouseReleased(MouseEvent evt) {
                        paintTargetPixels = false;
                        repaint();
                    }
                }
            }
        }
```

abortGrabbing()

PURPOSE   Aborts retrieval of the pixels.

SYNTAX   `public synchronized void abortGrabbing()`

DESCRIPTION   This method aborts the retrieval of the pixels by this pixel grabber by calling `imageComplete()` with IMAGEABORTED.

SEE ALSO   `getStatus()`, `imageComplete()`, `startGrabbing()`.

getColorModel()

PURPOSE   Retrieves the color model being used to accumulate the pixels.

SYNTAX   `public synchronized ColorModel getColorModel()`

DESCRIPTION   If this pixel grabber was constructed with an explicit pixel buffer or if it was created with `forceRGB` set to `true`, this method always returns the default RGB color model. If it was created with `forceRGB` set to `false`, the color model being used is that of the source image (i.e., the color model passed to `setPixels()`). If a different color model is passed to `setPixels()` at any time, the default RGB color model is used. The color model returned may be `null` if the color model has not been determined.

RETURNS   The color model currently being used for accumulating the pixels; `null` if not yet determined.

SEE ALSO   `ColorModel`, `ColorModel.getRGBDefault()`, `PixelGrabber()`, `setPixels()`.

EXAMPLE   See `MemoryImageSource.setAnimate()`.

getHeight()

PURPOSE   Retrieves the height of the pixel buffer.

SYNTAX   `public synchronized int getHeight()`

DESCRIPTION   If this pixel grabber was constructed with a non-negative height, this method returns that height. If it was created with a negative height, the height of the pixel buffer is determined by the height of the source image when the dimensions of the image are delivered (see `setDimensions()`). If the dimensions are not yet available, this method returns -1.

RETURNS   The final height of the pixel buffer; -1 if not yet determined.

SEE ALSO   `PixelGrabber()`, `setDimensions()`, `setPixels()`.

EXAMPLE   See `MemoryImageSource.setAnimate()`.

getPixels()

PURPOSE   Retrieves the pixel buffer.

SYNTAX   `public synchronized Object getPixels()`

DESCRIPTION   If this pixel grabber was constructed with an explicit pixel buffer, this method always returns that pixel buffer. Otherwise, it returns the pixel buffer dynamically allocated for this pixel grabber. The color model being used affects the type of the buffer used (whether `byte` array or `int` array). Moreover, because the color model can be changed at any time due to calls to `setPixels()` (see

A
B
C
D
E
F
G
H
I
J
K
L
M
N
O
P
Q
R
S
T
U
V
W
X
Y
Z

getColorModel()), the object returned by this method may change over time until the pixel grabbing has completed.

RETURNS   The pixel buffer containing the pixels grabbed; null if the size and format of the pixel buffer has not yet been determined. The value returned is either a byte array or an int array, depending on the color model being used to accumulate the pixels.

SEE ALSO   PixelGrabber(), setPixels().

EXAMPLE   See MemoryImageSource.setAnimate().

getStatus()

PURPOSE   Determines the current state of the pixels.

SYNTAX   public synchronized int getStatus()

DESCRIPTION   The result value indicates the current state of the pixels. The result value is a bitwise "or" of flags in the ImageObserver interface. See the ImageObserver class for details on available status bits.

SEE ALSO   ImageObserver.

EXAMPLE   See the class example.

getWidth()

PURPOSE   Retrieves the width of the pixel buffer.

SYNTAX   public synchronized int getWidth()

DESCRIPTION   If this pixel grabber was constructed with a non-negative width, this method returns that width. If it was created with a negative width, the width of the pixel buffer is determined by the width of the source image when the dimensions of the image are delivered (see setDimensions()). If the dimensions are not yet available, this method returns −1.

RETURNS   The final width of the pixel buffer; −1 if not yet determined.

SEE ALSO   PixelGrabber(), setDimensions(), setPixels().

EXAMPLE   See MemoryImageSource.setAnimate().

grabPixels( )

PURPOSE	Starts retrieval of the pixels and blocks waiting for the pixels.

SYNTAX	`public synchronized boolean grabPixels() throws`
	    `InterruptedException`
	`public synchronized boolean grabPixels(long ms) throws`
	    `InterruptedException`

DESCRIPTION   This method causes the image or image producer to start delivering pixels to the pixel grabber. This method returns when all of the images in the desired rectangle (as specified in the constructor) are retrieved. If `ms` is specified and is greater than `0`, this method returns either when all of the pixels are retrieved or when `ms` milliseconds have elapsed.

     If this method returns `false`, the pixels were not successfully retrieved. The cause can be determined using the `getStatus()` method.

     This method can be called more than once and will return immediately if either all of the pixels have been retrieved or if there has been an error. Typically, this method is called more than once if a time-out has been specified.

PARAMETERS

  `ms`   The number of milliseconds to wait for the image pixels. This value must be greater than `0`.

RETURNS   `true` if the pixels were successfully retrieved; `false` otherwise.

EXCEPTIONS

  `InterruptedException`

     If another thread interrupted this thread before `ms` milliseconds has expired or before all of the pixels were retrieved.

SEE ALSO   `getStatus()`, `java.lang.InterruptedException`, `startGrabbing()`.

EXAMPLE   See the class example.

imageComplete( )

PURPOSE	Called by the image producer to deliver completion status to the pixel grabber.
SYNTAX	`public synchronized void imageComplete(int status)`

DESCRIPTION   The `PixelGrabber` class implements this method as part of the `ImageConsumer` interface. It should not be used.

PARAMETERS

  `status`   A combination of the status bits as defined in the `ImageConsumer` class.

SEE ALSO   `ImageConsumer.imageComplete()`.

EXAMPLE   See `ImageConsumer`.

PixelGrabber()

PURPOSE   Constructs a new `PixelGrabber` instance.

SYNTAX
```
public PixelGrabber(Image img, int x, int y, int w, int h, int[]
    pix, int off, int scansize)
public PixelGrabber(ImageProducer ip, int x, int y, int w, int h,
    int[] pix, int off, int scansize)
public PixelGrabber(Image img, int x, int y, int w, int h, boolean
    forceRGB)
```

DESCRIPTION   This constructor constructs a new `PixelGrabber` instance to retrieve the pixels in the rectangle defined by (x, y, w, h). If the image `img` is specified, the pixels are retrieved from `img`. If the image producer `ip` is specified, the pixels are retrieved from `ip`.

The first two forms of the constructor provide for the pixel values to be stored in the `pix` integer array in the default color model. The pixel value for pixel (i, j), where (i, j) is inside the rectangle (x, y, w, h), is stored in the array at `pix[(j - y) * scansize + (i - x) + off]`. The pixels are accumulated using the default RGB color model.

The third form of the constructor provides for a buffer to be allocated for the pixel grabber to store the pixels. If `forceRGB` is `true`, the pixels are accumulated using the default RGB color model. If `forceRGB` is `false`, the pixels are accumulated using the color model of the source image (i.e., the color model passed to `setPixels()`). If different color models are passed to different calls to `setPixels()`, the default RGB color model is used.

The action of retrieving the pixels is not started until the `grabPixels()` method is called.

PARAMETERS

`forceRGB`   If `true`, accumulate the pixels using the default RGB color model; if `false`, use the color model of the source image.

`h`   The height of the rectangle of pixels to retrieve. If negative, the height will be determined by the height of the source image.

`img`   The non-`null` image.

`ip`   The non-`null` image producer.

`off`   The offset into the array at which to store the first retrieved pixel.

`scansize`   The width of one row of pixels in `pix` (not necessarily the same as w).

`w`   The width of the rectangle of pixels to retrieve. If negative, the width will be determined by the height of the source image.

`x`   The *x*-coordinate of the upper-left corner of the rectangle.

`y`   The *y*-coordinate of the upper-left corner of the rectangle.

`pix`   The non-`null` array of integers to hold the retrieved pixels.

SEE ALSO   `ColorModel.getRGBdefault()`, `setDimensions()`, `setPixels()`.

EXAMPLE   See the class example.

setColorModel()

PURPOSE   Called by the image producer to deliver the color model for the source image.

SYNTAX   `public void setColorModel(ColorModel model)`

DESCRIPTION   The `PixelGrabber` class implements this method as part of the `ImageConsumer` interface. It should not be called directly.

PARAMETERS
`model`   A non-`null` color model.

SEE ALSO   `ImageConsumer.setColorModel()`.

EXAMPLE   See `ImageConsumer`.

setDimensions()

PURPOSE   Called by the image producer to deliver the dimensions of the source image.

SYNTAX   `public void setDimensions(int width, int height)`

DESCRIPTION   The `PixelGrabber` class implements this method as part of the `ImageConsumer` interface. It should not be called directly.

PARAMETERS
`height`   The height of the image in pixels.
`width`   The width of the image in pixels.

SEE ALSO   `ImageConsumer.setDimensions()`.

EXAMPLE   See `ImageConsumer`.

setHints()

PURPOSE   Called by the image producer to specify how the pixels will be delivered.

SYNTAX   `public void setHints(int hints)`

DESCRIPTION   The `PixelGrabber` class implements this method as part of the `ImageConsumer` interface. It should not be called directly.

PARAMETERS
`hints`   A set of bits that specify how pixels will be delivered.

SEE ALSO	`ImageConsumer.setHints()`.
EXAMPLE	See `ImageConsumer`.

setPixels( )

PURPOSE	Called by the image producer to deliver pixels to the image consumer.

SYNTAX	`public void setPixels(int x, int y, int w, int h, ColorModel`
	    `model, byte pixels[], int offset, int scansize)`
	`public void setPixels(int x, int y, int w, int h, ColorModel`
	    `model, int pixels[], int offset, int scansize)`

DESCRIPTION	The `PixelGrabber` class implements this method as part of the `ImageConsumer` interface. It should not be called directly.

PARAMETERS

h	The height of the rectangle in which the pixels are destined.
model	The non-`null` color model used to translate the pixel values.
offset	The index of the first pixel in the pixel array.
pixels	The non-`null` array of pixel values.
scansize	The width to use when extracting pixels from `pixels`.
w	The width of the rectangle in which the pixels are destined.
x	The x-coordinate of the rectangle in which the pixels are destined.
y	The y-coordinate of the rectangle in which the pixels are destined.

SEE ALSO	`ImageConsumer.setPixels()`
EXAMPLE	See `ImageConsumer`.

setProperties( )

PURPOSE	Called by the image producer to deliver the properties for the source image.
SYNTAX	`public void setProperties(Hashtable props)`
DESCRIPTION	The `PixelGrabber` class implements this method as part of the `ImageConsumer` interface. It should not be called directly.

PARAMETERS

props	A non-`null` hash table of properties.

SEE ALSO	`ImageConsumer.setProperties()`.
EXAMPLE	See `ImageConsumer`.

startGrabbing()

PURPOSE	Starts retrieval of the pixels.
SYNTAX	`public synchronized void startGrabbing()`
DESCRIPTION	This method causes the image or image producer to start delivering pixels to the pixel grabber. Unlike `grabPixels()`, it returns immediately. This method can be called more than once and will return immediately if either all of the pixels have been retrieved or there has been an error. `getStatus()` can be called subsequently to check on the status of the retrieval.
SEE ALSO	`getStatus()`, `grabPixels()`, `abortGrabbing()`.

status()   *DEPRECATED*

PURPOSE	Replaced by `getStatus()`.
SYNTAX	`public synchronized int status()`
DEPRECATION	Replace the usage of this deprecated method, as in

```
int status = grabber.status();
```
with
```
int status = grabber.getStatus();
```

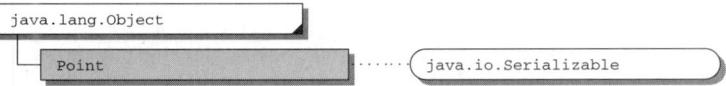

Syntax

`public class Point implements Serializable`

Description

A *point* represents a location on a 2D plane. The coordinates of the point are integers, so only integral locations can be represented. A point is typically used in conjunction with AWT painting operations and with layout managers. In the AWT coordinate system, the *y*-coordinates increase downward rather than upward, as in classical analytical geometry.

In general, when returning a `Point` instance in a method call, either return a copy if you need to retain the instance or discard the instance after returning it. If you pass a point instance in a method call and wish to continue using the instance, note whether the method will retain the instance or will copy the values.

MEMBER SUMMARY	
Constructor	
`Point()`	Constructs a new `Point` instance.
Point Methods	
`getLocation()`	Retrieves a copy of this point.
`setLocation()`	Moves this point to a new location.
`translate()`	Adds an offset to this point.
Fields	
`x`	Contains this point's *x*-coordinate.
`y`	Contains this point's *y*-coordinate.
Object Override Methods	
`equals()`	Determines whether an object is equal to this point.
`hashCode()`	Calculates the hash code for this point.
`toString()`	Generates a string representation of this point.
Deprecated Method	
`move()`	Moves this point to a new location.

Sidebar index: A B C D E F G H I J K L M N O P Q R S T U V W X Y Z

See Also

`java.io.Serializable`.

Example

This example creates a "mine field" of hidden random points. If you move the cursor over a point, it turns red. See Figure 297.

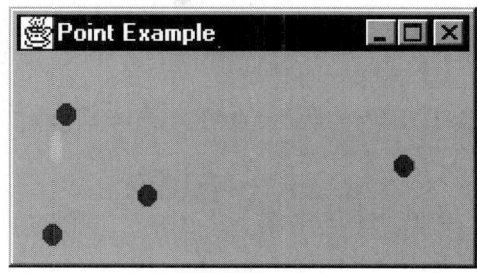

FIGURE 297: Point.

```java
import java.awt.*;
import java.awt.event.*;

class Main extends Frame {
    int dotSize = 10;
    Point[] pts = new Point[100];

    Main() {
        super("Point Example");
        for (int i=0; i<pts.length; i++) {
            pts[i] = new Point();
        }
        setForeground(Color.red);

        // Add mouse motion listener for frame
        addMouseMotionListener(new MouseMotionHandler());
        setSize(200, 200);
        show();
    }

    // Returns a random integer in the range [0..r-1].
    int random(int r) {
        r = Math.max(r, 0);
        return (int)(Math.floor(Math.random()*r));
    }

    public void paint(Graphics g) {
        Insets insets = getInsets();
        int w = getSize().width-insets.left-insets.right;
        int h = getSize().height-insets.top-insets.bottom;

        for (int i=0; i<pts.length; i++) {
            pts[i].setLocation(random(w-dotSize), random(h-dotSize));
        }
    }

    public void update(Graphics g) {
        for (int i=0; i<pts.length; i++) {
            if (pts[i].x < 0) {
                g.fillOval(-pts[i].x, -pts[i].y, dotSize, dotSize);
            }
        }
    }

    // Mouse motion handler for movement within frame
    class MouseMotionHandler extends MouseMotionAdapter {
        public void mouseMoved(MouseEvent evt) {
            int x = evt.getX();
```

A
B
C
D
E
F
G
H
I
J
K
L
M
N
O

Q
R
S
T
U
V
W
X
Y
Z

```
                    int y = evt.getY();
                    Point p = new Point(x-dotSize/2, y-dotSize/2);

                    for (int i=0; i<pts.length; i++) {
                        if (p.equals(pts[i])) {
                            pts[i].x = -pts[i].x;
                            pts[i].y = -pts[i].y;
                            repaint();
                            break;
                        }
                    }
                }
            }

        static public void main(String[] args) {
            new Main();
        }
    }
```

A
B
C
D
E
F
G
H
I
J
K
L
M
N
O

Q
R
S
T
U
V
W
X
Y
Z

equals()

PURPOSE	Determines whether an object is equal to this point.
SYNTAX	`public boolean equals(Object object)`
DESCRIPTION	Two points are equal if both their *x*- and *y*-coordinates are equal.
PARAMETERS	
`object`	The point to which to compare.
RETURNS	`true` if `object` is an instance of `Point` and is equal to this point; `false` otherwise.
OVERRIDES	`java.lang.Object.equals()`.
EXAMPLE	See the class example.

getLocation()

PURPOSE	Retrieves a copy of this point.
SYNTAX	`public Point getLocation()`
RETURNS	A new non-`null` point containing this point's coordinates.
SEE ALSO	`setLocation()`.
EXAMPLE	This example moves a point vertically.

```
    void moveVertical(Point pt, int deltaY) {
        Point orig = pt.getLocation();
        pt.setLocation(orig.x, orig.y+deltaY);
    }
```

hashCode()

PURPOSE	Calculates the hash code for this point.
SYNTAX	`public int hashCode()`
DESCRIPTION	This point's hash code is an integer that is calculated from the point's *x*- and *y*-coordinates. If `equals(p1, p2)` is true, then `p1` and `p2` will have the same hash code. Otherwise, `p1` and `p2` will very likely have different hash codes.
RETURNS	The point's hash code.
OVERRIDES	`java.lang.Object.hashCode()`.
SEE ALSO	`equals()`.
EXAMPLE	This method uses a hash table to associate a point with an integer count.

```
Hashtable ht = new Hashtable();
void inc(Point p) {
    int i = 0;
    Integer integer = (Integer)ht.get(p);
    if (integer != null) {
        i = integer.intValue();
    }
    ht.put(p, new Integer(i+1));
}
```

move()   *DEPRECATED*

PURPOSE	Replaced by `setLocation()`.
SYNTAX	`public void move(int x, int y)`
PARAMETERS	
x	The new *x*-coordinate.
y	The new *y*-coordinate.
DEPRECATION	Replace the usage of this deprecated method, as in

   `point.move(x, y);`

with

   `point.setLocation(x, y);`.

Point()

PURPOSE	Constructs a new `Point` instance.
SYNTAX	`public Point()`
	`public Point(Point src)`
	`public Point(int x, int y)`

DESCRIPTION	This constructor creates a new `Point` object and initializes it using either the coordinates x and y or the coordinates from the point src. If no coordinates are specified, they default to 0, 0.
PARAMETERS	
src	The point whose *x*- and *y*-coordinates to use for constructing the new point.
x	The *x*-coordinate.
y	The *y*-coordinate.
EXAMPLE	See the class example.

setLocation( )

PURPOSE	Moves this point to a new location.
SYNTAX	`public void setLocation(int x, int y)` `public void setLocation(Point pt)`
DESCRIPTION	This method changes the *x*- and *y*-coordinates of this point to be x and y or the coordinates indicated by the point pt.
PARAMETERS	
pt	The non-`null` point of the new location.
x	The new *x*-coordinate.
y	The new *y*-coordinate.
SEE ALSO	`getLocation()`
EXAMPLE	See the class example.

toString( )

PURPOSE	Generates the string representation of this point.
SYNTAX	`public String toString()`
DESCRIPTION	This method generates this point's string representation, which consists of the point's coordinates. This method is typically used for debugging output.
RETURNS	A non-`null` string containing the coordinates of the point.
OVERRIDES	`java.lang.Object.toString()`.
EXAMPLE	These statements print identical string representations of the point.

```
Point p = new Point(10, 20);
System.out.println("p = " + p.toString());
System.out.println("p = " + p);
```

translate()

PURPOSE	Adds an offset to this point.
SYNTAX	`public void translate(int x, int y)`
DESCRIPTION	This method adds x to the point's *x*-coordinate and adds y to the point's *y*-coordinate.
PARAMETERS	
x	The offset to add to the point's *x*-coordinate.
y	The offset to add to the point's *y*-coordinate.
EXAMPLE	This example paints a red square with a shadow at point p:

```
public void paintShadowRect(Graphics g, Point p) {
    p.translate(5, 5);
    g.setColor(Color.gray);
    g.fillRect(p.x, p.y, 100, 100);
    p.translate(-5, -5);
    g.setColor(Color.red);
    g.fillRect(p.x, p.y, 100, 100);
}
```

x

PURPOSE	Contains this point's *x*-coordinate.
SYNTAX	`public int x`
EXAMPLE	See the class example.

y

PURPOSE	Contains this point's *y*-coordinate.
SYNTAX	`public int y`
EXAMPLE	See the class example.

A
B
C
D
E
F
G
H
I
J
K
L
M
N
O
P
Q
R
S
T
U
V
W
X
Y
Z

1183

Polygon

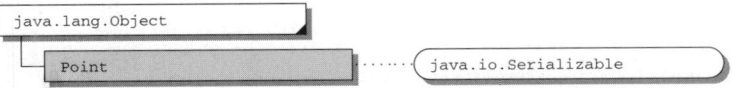

Syntax

```
public class Polygon implements Serializable
```

Description

A polygon is a data structure that maintains a list of points. This class is primarily used in conjunction with `Graphics.drawPolygon()` and `Graphics.fillPolygon()`. The polygon maintains a *bounding box*, which is the smallest rectangle that includes all of the points in the polygon. See `getBounds()` for more details.

MEMBER SUMMARY	
Constructor	
Polygon()	Constructs a new Polygon instance.
Fields	
bounds	Contains this polygon's bounding rectangle.
npoints	Contains the number of points in this polygon.
xpoints	Array containing the x-coordinates of this polygon's points.
ypoints	Array containing the y-coordinates of this polygon's points.
Point Methods	
addPoint()	Adds a point to this polygon.
contains()	Determines if a point is inside this polygon.
translate()	Adds an offset to all points in this polygon.
Bounding Box Method	
getBounds()	Calculates this polygon's bounding box.
Deprecated Methods	
getBoundingBox()	Replaced by getBounds().
inside()	Replaced by contains().

See Also

java.io.Serializable, Point.

Example

This example generates a random polygon and allows you to flip it or shift it. See Figure 298. There are four buttons that modify the polygon. The New button creates a new random polygon based on the current size of the canvas. The Flip Ver button flips the polygon around the *x*-axis. The Flip Hor button flips the polygon around the *y*-axis. The Shift button moves the polygon down and to the right 5 pixels.

Also, a label at the top indicates whether the position pointed to by the cursor is considered to be inside or outside the polygon.

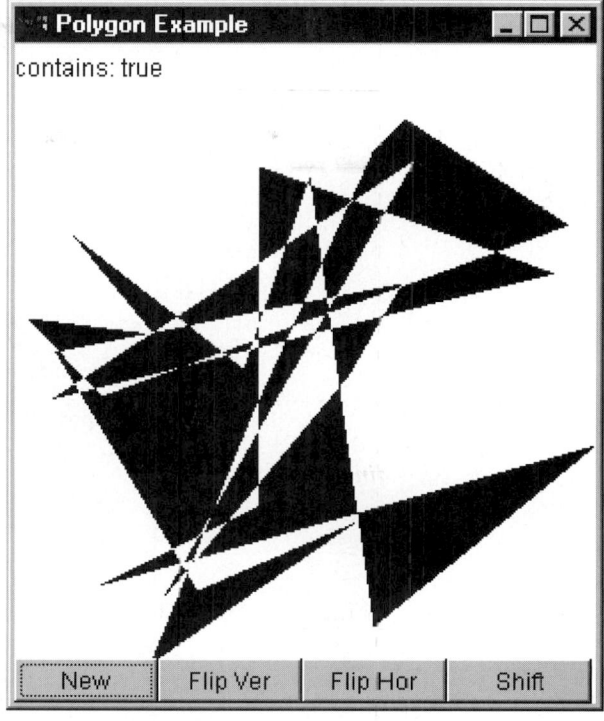

FIGURE 298: Polygon.

```
import java.awt.*;
import java.awt.event.*;

public class Main
    extends Frame
    implements
        ActionListener {
Label l = new Label();
MainCanvas cv =
    new MainCanvas(l);

Main() {
    super("Polygon Example");
    Panel p = new Panel(new GridLayout(1, 0));

    Button b;
    p.add(b = new Button("New"));
    b.addActionListener(this);
    p.add(b = new Button("Flip Ver"));
    b.addActionListener(this);
    p.add(b = new Button("Flip Hor"));
    b.addActionListener(this);
    p.add(b = new Button("Shift"));
    b.addActionListener(this);

    add(p, BorderLayout.SOUTH);

    cv.setSize(300, 300);
    add(cv, BorderLayout.CENTER);
    add(l, BorderLayout.NORTH);
    pack();
    show();
}
```

A
B
C
D
E
F
G
H
I
J
K
L
M
N
O
P
Q
R
S
T
U
V
W
X
Y
Z

```
                    // Action handler for buttons
                    public void actionPerformed(ActionEvent evt) {
                        String what = evt.getActionCommand();
                        if ("New".equals(what)) {
                            cv.polygon = null;
                        } else if (cv.polygon != null) {
                            if ("Shift".equals(what)) {
                                cv.polygon.translate(5, 5);
                            } else {
                                boolean ver =  "Flip Ver".equals(what);
                                Rectangle r = cv.polygon.getBounds();

                                r.add(0, 0);
                                for (int i=0; i<cv.polygon.npoints; i++) {
                                    if (ver) {
                                        cv.polygon.ypoints[i] = r.height - cv.polygon.ypoints[i];
                                    } else {
                                        cv.polygon.xpoints[i] = r.width - cv.polygon.xpoints[i];
                                    }
                                }
                            }
                        }
                        cv.repaint();
                    }

                    static public void main(String[] args) {
                        new Main();
                    }
                }

            class MainCanvas extends Canvas {
                Label label;
                Polygon polygon;

                MainCanvas(Label label) {
                    this.label = label;
                    addMouseMotionListener(new MouseMotionHandler());
                }

                // Returns a random number in the range [0..r-1].
                int random(int r) {
                    return (int)(Math.floor(Math.random()*r));
                }

                public void paint(Graphics g) {
                    int w = getSize().width;
                    int h = getSize().height;

                    if (polygon == null) {
                        polygon = new Polygon();
                        for (int i=0; i<25; i++) {
                            // Points need to be one pixel from the
                            // right and bottom edges otherwise the polygon
                            // will extend outside the canvas bounds.
                            polygon.addPoint(random(w-1), random(h-1));
                        }
                    }
                    g.fillPolygon(polygon);
                }
```

```
// Mouse motion handler for canvas
class MouseMotionHandler extends MouseMotionAdapter {
    public void mouseMoved(MouseEvent evt) {
        if (polygon != null) {
            label.setText("contains: " +
                polygon.contains(evt.getX(), evt.getY()));
        }
    }
}
```

A
B
C
D
E
F
G
H
I
J
K
L
M
N
O

Q
R
S
T
U
V
W
X
Y
Z

addPoint()

PURPOSE	Adds a point to this polygon.
SYNTAX	`public void addPoint(int x, int y)`
DESCRIPTION	This method adds the point (x, y) to the polygon. After this method, the point will be included in the polygon's bounding box.
	If you call `getBounds()` and retain a handle to the rectangle instance, the values in the rectangle instance will be automatically updated after calling `addPoint()`.
PARAMETERS	
x	The x-coordinate of the new point.
y	The y-coordinate of the new point.
SEE ALSO	`getBounds()`.
EXAMPLE	See the class example.

bounds

PURPOSE	Contains this polygon's bounding box.
SYNTAX	`protected Rectangle bounds`
DESCRIPTION	The bounding box is described in the class description. If the bounding box has not been calculated yet, this field is `null`. The bounding box is calculated when `contains()` or `getBounds()` is called.

A
B
C
D
E
F
G
H
I
J
K
L
M
N
O
P
Q
R
S
T
U
V
W
X
Y
Z

contains()

PURPOSE	Determines if a point is inside this polygon.
SYNTAX	`public boolean contains(int x, int y)` `public boolean contains(Point pt)`
DESCRIPTION	This method determines if point (x, y) or `pt` is inside the polygon. It uses an even-odd insideness rule (otherwise known as an alternating rule).
PARAMETERS	
pt	The non-`null` point whose coordinates are to be tested.
x	The *x*-coordinate of the point to be tested.
y	The *y*-coordinate of the point to be tested.
RETURNS	`true` if the point is inside the polygon; `false` otherwise.
EXAMPLE	See the class example.

getBoundingBox()   *DEPRECATED*

PURPOSE	Replaced by `getBounds()`.
SYNTAX	`public Rectangle getBoundingBox()`
RETURNS	A non-`null` rectangle defining the bounds of the polygon. Do not modify the rectangle.

DEPRECATION	Replace the usage of this deprecated method, as in
	`    Rectangle box = polygon.getBoundingBox();`
	with
	`    Rectangle box = polygon.getBounds();`

getBounds()

PURPOSE	Calculates this polygon's bounding box.
SYNTAX	`public Rectangle getBounds()`
DESCRIPTION	The bounding box is defined to be the smallest rectangle that includes all of the points in the polygon. The values in the returned rectangle are updated automatically as points are added to the polygon.
	If either `getBounds()` or `contains()` has been called, do not directly modify any of the fields npoints, xpoints, or ypoints. Modifying these after the bounding box has been calculated will invalidate the bounding box. However, there's no way to recalculate the bounding box, except to create a new polygon instance.

RETURNS	A non-null rectangle defining the bounds of the polygon. Do not modify the rectangle.
SEE ALSO	bounds.
EXAMPLE	See the class example.

inside() *DEPRECATED*

PURPOSE	Replaced by contains().
SYNTAX	public boolean inside(int x, int y)
PARAMETERS	
x	The x-coordinate of the point to be tested.
y	The y-coordinate of the point to be tested.
RETURNS	true if the point is inside the polygon; false otherwise.
DEPRECATION	Replace the usage of this deprecated method, as in

```
 if (polygon.inside(x, y)) ...
```
with
```
 if (polygon.contains(x,y)) ...
 if (polygon.contains(new Point(x, y))) ...
```

npoints

PURPOSE	Contains the number of points in this polygon.
SYNTAX	public int npoints
DESCRIPTION	Do not modify this field if either getBounds() or contains() has been called. See getBounds() for details.
SEE ALSO	getBounds().
EXAMPLE	See the class example.

Polygon()

PURPOSE	Constructs a new Polygon instance.
SYNTAX	public Polygon() public Polygon(int[] xpoint, int[] ypoints, int npoints)
DESCRIPTION	The two forms of this constructor create a new Polygon instance with npoints points. The point coordinates are specified in the arrays xpoints and

A
B
C
D
E
F
G
H
I
J
K
L
M
N
O
P
Q
R
S
T
U
V
W
X
Y
Z

A
B
C
D
E
F
G
H
I
J
K
L
M
N
O
P
Q
R
S
T
U
V
W
X
Y
Z

ypoints. The *x*- and *y*-coordinates of point i are, respectively, xpoints[i] and ypoints[i]. If no parameters are specified, the polygon is created with no points.

PARAMETERS

npoints   The number of supplied points in xpoints and ypoints.
xpoints   The non-null array of *x*-coordinates.
ypoints   The non-null array of *y*-coordinates.

EXAMPLE   See the class example.

translate()

PURPOSE   Adds an offset to all points in this polygon.

SYNTAX   `public void translate(int x, int y)`

DESCRIPTION   For each point in this polygon, this method adds x to the point's *x*-coordinate and adds y to the point's *y*-coordinate.

PARAMETERS

x   The offset to add to the *x*-coordinate of the points in this polygon.
y   The offset to add to the *y*-coordinate of the points in this polygon.

SEE ALSO   `Point.translate()`.

EXAMPLE   See the class example.

xpoints

PURPOSE   Array containing the *x*-coordinates of this polygon's points.

SYNTAX   `public int[] xpoints`

DESCRIPTION   Do not modify this field if either getBounds() or contains() has been called. See getBounds() for details.

SEE ALSO   `getBounds()`.

EXAMPLE   See the class example.

ypoints

PURPOSE	Array containing the *y*-coordinates of this polygon's points.
SYNTAX	`public int[] ypoints`
DESCRIPTION	Do not modify this field if either `getBounds()` or `contains()` has been called. See `getBounds()` for details.
SEE ALSO	`getBounds()`.
EXAMPLE	See the class example.

A
B
C
D
E
F
G
H
I
J
K
L
M
N
O

Q
R
S
T
U
V
W
X
Y
Z

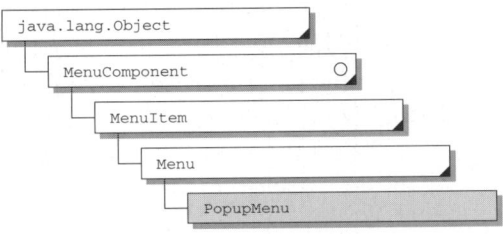

Syntax

`public class PopupMenu extends Menu`

Description

A *popup menu* is a menu that "pops up" near a component as a result of the user's making a *popup menu gesture*. Most often, a popup menu is created with menu items specific to the current object and is typically displayed at the cursor position where the popup menu gesture was made. For example, displaying a popup menu on an HTML hyperlink in an HTML editor could show operations such as change color and change URL. Similarly, displaying a popup menu on a file folder could show operations on the file folder, such as open, move, and delete. Figure 299 shows a popup menu on a file.

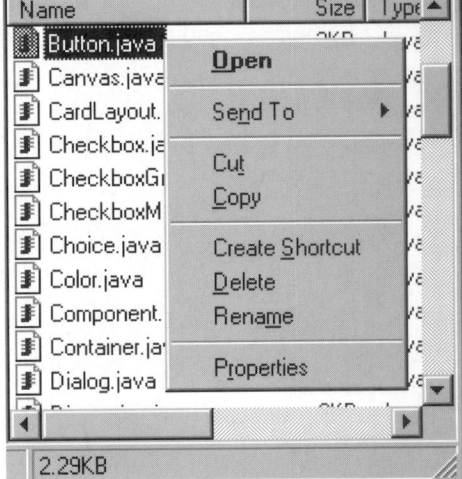

FIGURE 299: Popup Menu for a File.

The Parent and Origin

Before a popup menu can be displayed, it must have a *parent*. The parent can be any component. Although the popup menu must be a child of some component, it can actually be displayed on any descendant of the popup menu's parent. The code that displays the popup menu controls where to locate it. By convention, the popup menu's top-left corner is displayed at the cursor position.

The Popup Trigger

The popup menu gesture is platform-dependent. To prevent people from having to write platform-specific code to detect the popup menu gesture, the AWT takes care of watching for the gesture and notifying the application when it occurs.

More specifically, the AWT assumes that popup menus are triggered by some kind of mousing gesture. So when it detects the mouse event that should display the popup, it tags it with a property called the *popup menu trigger* (see `MouseEvent.isPopupTrigger()`). If this property is `true`, it means the user made the popup menu gesture and that the popup menu is to be displayed.

You must do the following to make a popup menu work for a component:

1. Use `Component.add()` to add the popup to the component.
2. Write code to detect when the popup trigger occurs and to display the popup menu.

Step 2 can be done either by overriding the component's `processMouseEvent()` or by adding a listener for the mouse events that are typically used for popup triggers. Although the popup trigger is platform-dependent, it is usually associated with either the mouse released or the mouse pressed event.

If either step is omitted, the component's popup menu will not be displayed.

Popups and AWT Components

In Java 1.1.2, support for popup menus is not consistent across AWT components. The class example creates various components and adds popup menus for each. For example, `TextArea` is an AWT component that has a popup menu already defined for editing its contents. If you attempt to add a popup menu to a text area, the menu will not override the one defined by the system. It will just be ignored.

Keyboard Shortcuts

If a menu item in a popup menu has a keyboard shortcut, the shortcut is ignored. To have the desired effect of a shortcut for a popup menu item, make a copy of the menu item with the shortcut and add it to a menu in the menu bar.

Events

A popup menu fires the same events that a menu fires and follows the same rules used by a menu in dealing with menu items that fire events. See the `Menu` class for details.

MEMBER SUMMARY	
Constructor	
`PopupMenu()`	Constructs a new `PopupMenu` instance.
Show Method	
`show()`	Displays this popup menu.
Peer Method	
`addNotify()`	Creates this popup menu's peer.

See Also

```
Component.add(), Component.remove(),
java.awt.event.MouseEvent.isPopupTrigger().
```

Example

This example creates various AWT components and adds to each a popup menu. Use the popup trigger to attempt to bring up the popup menu for each component and see how each behaves. See Figure 300.

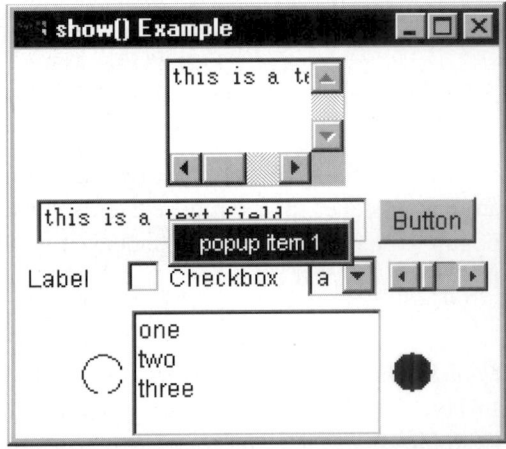

FIGURE 300: **PopupMenu** for various AWT Components.

```java
import java.awt.*;
import java.awt.event.*;

class Main extends Frame {
    Component[] comp =
        new Component[11];
    PopupMenu[] popup =
        new PopupMenu[11];

    Main() {
        super("show() Example");
        setLayout(new FlowLayout());

        // Create various types of components
        comp[0] = new TextArea("this is a text area", 3, 10);
        comp[1] = new TextField("this is a text field");
        comp[2] = new Button("Button");
        comp[3] = new Label("Label");
        comp[4] = new Checkbox("Checkbox");
        Choice c = new Choice();
        c.addItem("a");
        c.addItem("b");
        c.addItem("c");
        comp[5] = c;
        comp[6] = new Scrollbar(Scrollbar.HORIZONTAL);
        Canvas canvas = new MyCanvas();
        canvas.setSize(20, 20);
        comp[7] = canvas;
        List l = new List();
        comp[8] = l;
        l.addItem("one");
        l.addItem("two");
        l.addItem("three");
        Component lw = new MyComponent();
        comp[9] = lw;
        comp[10] = this;

        MouseListener ml = new MouseEventHandler();

        // Add listener and popup menus to components
        for (int i = 0; i <= 10; i++) {
            comp[i].addMouseListener(ml);
            popup[i] = new PopupMenu("popup" + i);
            popup[i].add("popup item "+i);
```

```
        comp[i].add(popup[i]);
        if (i != 10)
            add(comp[i]);
    }

    setSize(150, 150);
    show();
}

// Native component
class MyCanvas extends Canvas {
    public void paint(Graphics g) {
        g.drawOval(0, 0, getSize().width, getSize().height);
    }
}

// Lightweight component
class MyComponent extends Component {
    public Dimension getPreferredSize() {
        return new Dimension(20, 20);
    }
    public void paint(Graphics g) {
        g.fillOval(0, 0, getSize().width, getSize().height);
    }
}


// Override mouseReleased() and mousePressed() to
// catch popup menu trigger.
class MouseEventHandler extends MouseAdapter {
    int findComponent(Component c) {
        for (int i = 0; i <= 10; i++) {
            if (c.equals(comp[i])) {
                return i;
            }
        }
        return -1;
    }
    public void mouseReleased(MouseEvent evt) {
        if (evt.isPopupTrigger()) {
            int i = findComponent((Component)evt.getSource());
            if (i > 0) {
                popup[i].show(comp[i], evt.getX(), evt.getY());
            } else {
                System.out.println("no popup");
            }
        }
    }
    public void mousePressed(MouseEvent evt) {
        if (evt.isPopupTrigger()) {
            int i = findComponent((Component)evt.getSource());
            if (i > 0) {
                popup[i].show(comp[i], evt.getX(), evt.getY());
            } else {
                System.out.println("no popup");
            }
        }
    }
}
```

A
B
C
D
E
F
G
H
I
J
K
L
M
N
O
P
Q
R
S
T
U
V
W
X
Y
Z

```
        public static void main(String args[]) {
            new Main();
        }
    }
```

addNotify()

PURPOSE	Creates this popup menu's peer.
SYNTAX	`public synchronized void addNotify()`
DESCRIPTION	This method creates the peer for this popup menu if it does not yet exist. The peer is created by a call to `Toolkit.createPopupMenu()`. The `addNotify()` method should never be called directly. It is normally called by the parent.
OVERRIDES	`Component.addNotify()`.
SEE ALSO	`Component, Toolkit`.
EXAMPLE	See `Component.addNotify()`.

PopupMenu()

PURPOSE	Constructs a new `PopupMenu` instance.
SYNTAX	`public PopupMenu()` `public PopupMenu(String label)`
DESCRIPTION	This constructor creates a new popup menu instance. If `label` is not specified, it defaults to "".
PARAMETERS	
`label`	A non-`null` string specifying the popup menu's label.
EXAMPLE	See the class example.

show()

PURPOSE	Displays this popup menu.
SYNTAX	`public void show(Component origin, int x, int y)`
DESCRIPTION	This method displays this popup menu at the coordinates x, y relative to the bounds of the component `origin`. The `origin` parameter must be in the component hierarchy of this popup menu's parent. Furthermore, the parent of this

popup menu must be visible and showing on the screen. Otherwise, a runtime exception is thrown.

PARAMETERS

origin   The non-null component that defines the coordinate space.

x   The *x*-coordinate position to display the popup menu.

y   The *y*-coordinate position to display the popup menu.

EXCEPTIONS

IllegalArgumentException

If this popup menu's parent is not an ancestor of origin.

RuntimeException

If this popup menu's parent is not showing.

SEE ALSO   Component.isShowing(), java.lang.IllegalArgumentException, java.lang.RuntimeException.

EXAMPLE   This example creates a frame that has a popup menu that is shown relative to a child component (a Button). See Figure 301.

One of the menu items in the popup has a shortcut, but it is always ignored.

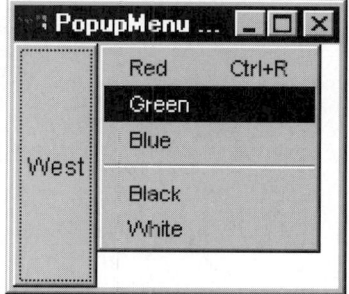

FIGURE 301:   **Showing a Popup Menu in a Child Component.**

```
import java.awt.*;
import java.awt.event.*;

class Main extends Frame
    implements ActionListener {
    PopupMenu pm = new PopupMenu("Colors");

    Button button = new Button("West");

    Main() {
        super("PopupMenu Example");

        // You can add shortcut but it is ignored for popups
        pm.add(new MenuItem("Red", new MenuShortcut(KeyEvent.VK_R)));
        pm.add("Green");
        pm.add("Blue");
        pm.add("-");
        pm.add("Black");
        pm.add("White");
        add(pm);

        add(button, BorderLayout.WEST);

        // Enable mouse events and listen for action events.
        pm.addActionListener(this);
        enableEvents(AWTEvent.MOUSE_EVENT_MASK|AWTEvent.KEY_EVENT_MASK);

        setSize(150, 150);
        show();
    }
```

A
B
C
D
E
F
G
H
I
J
K
L
M
N
O
P
Q
R
S
T
U
V
W
X
Y
Z

```
public void actionPerformed(ActionEvent evt) {
    System.out.println(evt.getActionCommand());
}

protected void processMouseEvent(MouseEvent evt) {
    if (evt.isPopupTrigger()) {
        // Illustrates that you can make popup show up in
        // subcomponents, using any coordinates
        pm.show(button, button.getSize().width, 0);
    }
    super.processMouseEvent(evt);
}

public static void main(String args[]) {
    new Main();
}
}
```

PopupMenuPeer

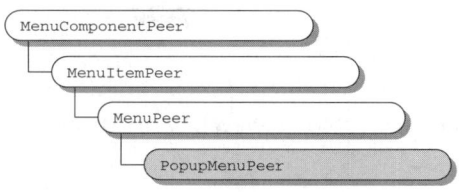

Syntax

`public interface PopupMenuPeer extends MenuPeer`

Description

The popup menu component (see the `PopupMenu` class) in the AWT uses the platform's native implementation of a popup menu. So that the AWT popup menu behaves the same on all platforms, the popup menu is assigned a *peer,* whose task is to translate the behavior of the platform's native popup menu to the behavior of the AWT popup menu.

AWT programmers normally do not directly use peer classes and interfaces. Instead, they deal with AWT components in the `java.awt` package. These in turn automatically manage their peers. Only someone who is porting the AWT to another platform should be concerned with the peer classes and interfaces. Consequently, most peer documentation refers to `java.awt` counterparts.

Menu component peers serve the same role as component peers. See `Component` and `Toolkit` for additional information about component peers.

MEMBER SUMMARY	
Peer Method	
show()	Displays the popup menu.

See Also

`java.awt.Component`, `java.awt.PopupMenu`, `java.awt.Toolkit`.

show()

PURPOSE	Displays the popup menu.
SYNTAX	`void show(Event evt)`
DESCRIPTION	This method displays the popup menu at the coordinates specified in the event `evt` relative to the coordinate system of the source component specified in the event.
SEE ALSO	`java.awt.PopupMenu.show()`.

A
B
C
D
E
F
G
H
I
J
K
L
M
N
O
P
Q
R
S
T
U
V
W
X
Y
Z

PrintGraphics

Syntax

`public interface PrintGraphics`

Description

Generating a printed page is very similar to painting on the screen. In particular, you need to create a special graphics context for the printer rather than for the screen. See Figure 302. Use the `PrintJob.getGraphics()` method to create such a print graphics context. After obtaining a print graphics context, you can use all of the normal drawing operations in the `Graphics` class on the print graphics context. For example, to draw a line on the page, you would use `Graphics.drawLine()`.

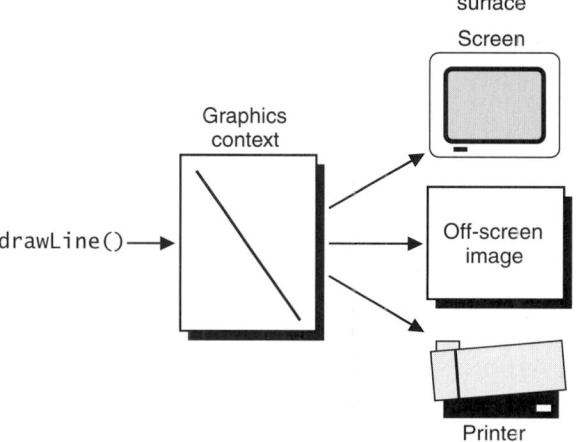

FIGURE 302:   **Graphics Context Drawing Surfaces.**

The coordinate system for a print graphics context is identical to the coordinate system of the screen; that is, the y-coordinate at the top of the page is 0 and increases from top to bottom. See Figure 303.

You can obtain the printable dimensions of the print graphics object by calling `PrintJob.getPageDimension()`.

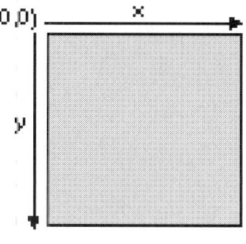

FIGURE 303:
`PrintGraphics`
Coordinates.

MEMBER SUMMARYY	
Print Job Method	
getPrintJob()	Retrieves the print job associated with this print graphics context.

A
B
C
D

See Also
Graphics, PrintJob.

E
F

Example
See the PrintJob class example.

G
H
I

getPrintJob()

J
K

PURPOSE	Retrieves the print job associated with this print graphics context.
SYNTAX	public PrintJob getPrintJob()
DESCRIPTION	This method returns the print job object from which this printer graphics context was created. This method can be useful when a painting method wants to behave differently if the graphics context is actually a printer graphics object.
RETURNS	A non-null PrintJob object.
SEE ALSO	PrintJob
EXAMPLE	See the PrintJob class example.

L
M
N
O
P
Q
R
S
T
U
V
W
X
Y
Z

```
java.lang.Object

        PrintJob
```

Syntax

`public abstract class PrintJob`

Description

This class is used to print to the system's printer. Generating a printed page is very similar to painting on the screen. For example, to draw a line on the page, you would use `Graphics.drawLine()`. The coordinate system for a printed page is identical to the coordinate system of the screen; that is, the *y*-coordinate at the top of the page is 0 and increases from top to bottom. See `PrintGraphics`.

All of the drawing operations that you can perform on the screen can be performed on a printed page.

Steps to Print

1. To start a print job, you must call `Toolkit.getPrintJob()` to get a print job instance. Calling this method causes a platform-dependent modal printer options dialog to appear. The user must select the options and click either Cancel to cancel the print job or OK to continue with the print job.
2. With the print job instance, you must call `getGraphics()` to obtain a graphics context on which you can paint. Anything painted on this graphics context will appear on a printed page. When the page is completed, `dispose()` must be called on the graphics context.
3. To print more pages, you call `getGraphics()` for each page. After each page is completed, the graphics context must be disposed of.
4. Finally, once all of the pages have been generated, the print job's `end()` method must be called to cause the pages to be printed.

Limitations and Bugs

The print job class will be enhanced in future versions. However, here are some of its present limitations:

- There is no way to abort a print job once it has been created. Once the user has decided to go ahead with the print job and the program starts to generate pages, the program cannot decide to abort the job.

- There is no way for a program to select printer options. For example, the program cannot choose to print in portrait mode or landscape mode. Which mode to use must be indicated by the user in the printer options dialog. If the user chooses incorrectly, the pages will be printed incorrectly.

- The method to determine the page dimensions, `getPageDimension()`, may return incorrect results. This is a bug. The workaround is to use the screen resolution (see `Toolkit.getScreenResolution()`) to determine the page dimensions. In other words, multiply the screen resolution by 8.5 to get the page's pixel width and by 11 to get the page's pixel height. However, not all of this area is printable; the page typically has a margin in which it cannot print. At present, there is no way to determine the size of this margin, so the user must guess. Also, the guessed number may not work for all printers.

- After the user selects the printer options from the printer options dialog, the set of selected options are not available to the program. In particular, the `props` parameter to `Toolkit.getPrintJob()` is ignored.

- Images that contain transparent pixels are not painted correctly. The transparent pixels are painted with a color from the image's color map. The pixels behind the transparent pixels cannot show through.

- A true preview of the print job on the screen before printing it is not possible to attain. At present, the best you can do is render it on the screen using the screen resolution and screen font metrics and hope that the printer resolution and font metrics are similar.

MEMBER SUMMARY	
Graphics Method	
`getGraphics()`	Creates a graphics context for painting on a printed page.
Page Properties	
`getPageDimension()`	Retrieves the dimensions of the page in pixels.
`getPageResolution()`	Retrieves the resolution of the printed page in pixels per inch.
`lastPageFirst()`	Determines if pages should be printed backwards.
End Job Method	
`end()`	Completes the print job.
Garbage Collector Method	
`finalize()`	Completes the print job.

See Also

`Component.print()`, `Component.printAll()`, `Graphics`, `PrintGraphics`, `Toolkit.getPrintJob()`.

Example

This rather long example implements a fully functional program that will print a text file in landscape mode with two pages per sheet of paper. See Figure 305. For a simple example, see `getGraphics()`.

With the program, you can set a font size and preview the results on the screen. However, due to restrictions of the printer methods, what appears on the screen may not be identical to what appears on paper. This could happen if the font metrics for the desired font size supported by the screen and those supported by the printer do not match.

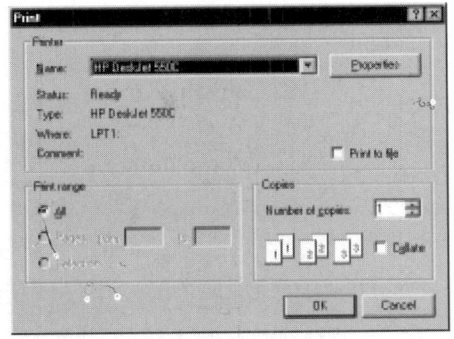

FIGURE 304: **Printer Control Dialog.**

The previewer maintains a vector of lines that have been broken to fit in the page. The methods that render the page always check the supplied graphics context for any changes to the page dimensions or font metrics. If there are any changes, it recomputes the vector of broken lines.

To indicate broken lines, the program displays a *continuation character* (depicted as an arc) at the end of the line. The program remembers to display the continuation character

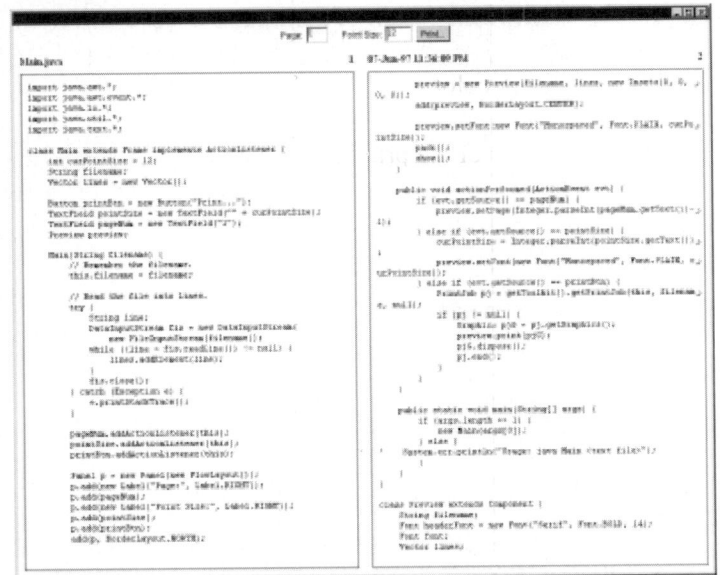

FIGURE 305: **Sample PrintJob Output.**

by appending a + at the end of lines that have been broken. When the program prints the line, it print the continuation symbol instead of the +.

Note: In Java 1.1.2, the `getPageDimension()` method returns incorrect results. The workaround is to determine a page size by applying the screen resolution on an 8.5-×-11-inch sheet of paper. However, most printers cannot print in all of this area. At present, there is no way to determine the exact size of the printable area, so we simply guess and reduce the area's width and height by three-fourths of an inch.

```
import java.awt.*;
import java.awt.event.*;
import java.io.*;
import java.util.*;
import java.text.*;

class Main extends Frame implements ActionListener {
    int curPointSize = 12;
    String filename;
    Vector lines = new Vector();

    Button printBtn = new Button("Print...");
    TextField pointSize = new TextField("" + curPointSize);
    TextField pageNum = new TextField("1");
    Preview preview;

    Main(String filename) {
        super("PrintJob Example");
        // Remember the filename.
        this.filename = filename;

        // Read the file into lines.
        try {
            String line;
            BufferedReader fis = new BufferedReader(
                new InputStreamReader(new FileInputStream(filename)));
            while ((line = fis.readLine()) != null) {
                lines.addElement(line);
            }
            fis.close();
        } catch (Exception e) {
            e.printStackTrace();
        }

        // Listen for events.
        pageNum.addActionListener(this);
        pointSize.addActionListener(this);
        printBtn.addActionListener(this);

        // Layout and show components.

        Panel p = new Panel(new FlowLayout());
        p.add(new Label("Page:", Label.RIGHT));
        p.add(pageNum);
        p.add(new Label("Point Size:", Label.RIGHT));
        p.add(pointSize);
        p.add(printBtn);
        add(p, BorderLayout.NORTH);

        // Create and prepare the preview component.
        preview = new Preview(filename, lines);
        add(preview, BorderLayout.CENTER);
        preview.setFont(new Font("Monospaced", Font.PLAIN, curPointSize));

        pack();
        show();
    }

    public void actionPerformed(ActionEvent evt) {
        if (evt.getSource() == pageNum) {
```

```
                // Set the page.
                preview.setPage(Integer.parseInt(pageNum.getText())-1);
            } else if (evt.getSource() == pointSize) {
                // Set the point size.
                curPointSize = Integer.parseInt(pointSize.getText());
                preview.setFont(new Font("Monospaced", Font.PLAIN, curPointSize));
            } else if (evt.getSource() == printBtn) {
                // Print the file.
                Properties props = new Properties();
                PrintJob pj = getToolkit().getPrintJob(this, filename, props);

                if (pj != null) {
                    // Print out any properties.
                    for (Enumeration e = props.propertyNames() ;
                            e.hasMoreElements() ;) {
                        System.out.println(e.nextElement());
                    }

                    Graphics pjG = pj.getGraphics();
                    int pages = preview.getPageCount(pjG);

                    // Always print even number of pages.
                    if (pages % 2 == 1) {
                        pages++;
                    }
                    for (int i=0; i<pages; i += 2) {
                        if (pjG == null) {
                            pjG = pj.getGraphics();
                        }
                        if (pj.lastPageFirst()) {
                            preview.print(pjG, pages-i-2);
                        } else {
                            preview.print(pjG, i);
                        }
                        pjG.dispose();
                        pjG = null;
                    }
                    pj.end();
                }
            }
        }
    }

    public static void main(String[] args) {
        if (args.length == 1) {
            new Main(args[0]);
        } else {
            System.err.println("Usage: java Main <text file>");
        }
    }
}

class Preview extends Component {
    int page;
    String filename;
    Font headerFont = new Font("Serif", Font.BOLD, 14);
    Font font;
    Vector lines;

    Preview(String filename, Vector lines) {
        this.filename = filename;
```

A
B
C
D
E
F
G
H
I
J
K
L
M
N
O
P
Q
R
S
T
U
V
W
X
Y
Z

```
                        this.lines = lines;
                    }

                    // Sets the font and repaints the display.
                    public void setFont(Font f) {
                        font = f;
                        repaint();
                    }

                    // p is 0-based.
                    void setPage(int p) {
                        page = p;
                        repaint();
                    }

                    // Returns the page count relative to the metrics in g.
                    int getPageCount(Graphics g) {
                        prepareLayoutValues(g);
                        return (brokenLines.size()-1) / linesPerPage + 1;
                    }

                    // Prints the page p and p+1.
                    // p is 0-based.
                    public void print(Graphics g, int p) {
                        page = p;
                        paint(g);
                    }

                    public void paint(Graphics g) {
                        prepareLayoutValues(g);

                        g.setFont(headerFont);
                        FontMetrics fm = g.getFontMetrics();

                        // Draw the filename.
                        g.drawString(filename, boxRect.x, fm.getHeight()/2+fm.getAscent());

                        // Draw the date and page number.
                        g.drawString(
                            DateFormat.getDateTimeInstance().format(new Date()),
                            boxRect.x + pageRect.width, fm.getHeight()/2+fm.getAscent());


                        for (int p=0; p<2; p++) {
                            if (page + p >= (brokenLines.size()-1) / linesPerPage + 1) {
                                break;
                            }

                            // Draw page number.
                            String s = "" + (page + p + 1);
                            g.setFont(headerFont);
                            fm = g.getFontMetrics();
                            g.drawString(s,
                                boxRect.x + p*pageRect.width + boxRect.width -
                                  fm.stringWidth(s),
                                fm.getHeight()/2+fm.getAscent());

                            g.drawRect(boxRect.x + p*pageRect.width,
                                boxRect.y, boxRect.width-1, boxRect.height-1);
```

A
B
C
D
E
F
G
H
I
J
K
L
M
N
O
P
Q
R
S
T
U
V
W
X
Y
Z

```
            // Find the starting line on the current page.
            int l = Math.min(brokenLines.size(), (page+p) * linesPerPage);

            g.setFont(font);
            fm = g.getFontMetrics();
            int x = listingRect.x + p*pageRect.width;
            int y = listingRect.y + fm.getAscent();
            for (int i=0; i<linesPerPage && l+i < brokenLines.size(); i++) {
                s = (String)brokenLines.elementAt(l + i);

                if (s.length() > charsPerLine) {
                    int charWidth = fm.charWidth('M');
                    s = s.substring(0, charsPerLine);

                    // Draw the continuation symbol.
                    g.drawArc(
                        listingRect.x+charsPerLine*charWidth + p*pageRect.width,
                        y-fm.getAscent()+fm.getHeight()/2,
                        charWidth, fm.getHeight()/2,
                        45, -180);
                }
                g.drawString(s, x, y);
                y += fm.getHeight();
            }
        }
    }
}

// External margin in which the printer cannot print.
int pageMargin;

// Internal margin between boxes and text.
int margin = 10;
Insets margins = new Insets(10, 10, 10, 10);;

// Bounds which includes the header, box, and listing.
Rectangle pageRect;

// The bounds of the box.
Rectangle boxRect;

// The bounds of the listing.  This rectangle strictly contains
// the text and not the continuation character.
Rectangle listingRect;

// Number of characters per line.
int charsPerLine;

// Number of lines per page.
int linesPerPage;

// The lines after they have been broken so they fit within charsPerLine.
Vector brokenLines;

// This method calculates and sets up all the fields above
// based on the metrics in g.
void prepareLayoutValues(Graphics g) {
    Dimension pageSize;
    int res;
```

A
B
C
D
E
F
G
H
I
J
K
L
M
N
O
P
Q
R
S
T
U
V
W
X
Y
Z

```
                    if (g instanceof PrintGraphics) {
                        PrintJob pj = ((PrintGraphics)g).getPrintJob();
                        res = pj.getPageResolution();
                        pageSize = pj.getPageDimension();

                        // getPageDimension() does not return the correct result.
                        // The following is a workaround.
                        res = getToolkit().getScreenResolution();
                        pageSize = new Dimension((int)(8.5 * res), 11 * res);
                    } else {
                        res = getToolkit().getScreenResolution();
                        pageSize = new Dimension((int)(8.5 * res), 11 * res);
                    }
                    pageMargin = (int)(.75 * res);
                    pageSize = new Dimension(pageSize.height-pageMargin,
                        pageSize.width-pageMargin);

                    // Reserve space for the header.
                    FontMetrics fm = g.getFontMetrics(headerFont);

                    pageRect = new Rectangle(0, 0, pageSize.width/2, pageSize.height);
                    boxRect = inset(pageRect, margin, 2*fm.getHeight(), margin, 0);
                    listingRect = inset(boxRect, margin, margin, margin, margin);

                    // Set up listing font.
                    fm = g.getFontMetrics(font);

                    int lpp = listingRect.height/fm.getHeight();
                    int cpp = listingRect.width/fm.charWidth('M');

                    // The metrics have changed so recompute the broken lines.
                    if (lpp != linesPerPage || cpp != charsPerLine) {
                        brokenLines = new Vector();
                        for (int i=0; i<lines.size(); i++) {
                            String s = (String)lines.elementAt(i);

                            while (s.length() > cpp) {
                                brokenLines.addElement(s.substring(0, cpp)+"+");
                                s = s.substring(cpp);
                            }
                            brokenLines.addElement(s);
                        }

                        linesPerPage = lpp;
                        charsPerLine = cpp;
                    }
                }

        Rectangle inset(Rectangle r, int left, int top, int right, int bottom) {
            Rectangle s = new Rectangle(r);
            s.x += left;
            s.y += top;
            s.width -= left+right;
            s.height -= top+bottom;
            return s;
        }
    }
```

A
B
C
D
E
F
G
H
I
J
K
L
M
N
O
P
Q
R
S
T
U
V
W
X
Y
Z

end()

PURPOSE	Completes the print job.
SYNTAX	`public abstract void end()`
DESCRIPTION	On some systems, the printer may not start printing pages until this method is called. After this method is called, this object can no longer be used.
	At present, there is no way to abort a print job once the print job object has been created.
EXAMPLE	See the class example.

finalize()

PURPOSE	Completes the print job.
SYNTAX	`public void finalize()`
DESCRIPTION	This method is not typically called directly. Use `end()` instead. This method is normally called by the garbage collector when there are no more references to this print job object. When this method is called, any remaining pages that have not yet printed will be printed.
SEE ALSO	`end()`.

getGraphics()

PURPOSE	Creates a graphics context for painting on a printed page.
SYNTAX	`public abstract Graphics getGraphics()`
DESCRIPTION	Anything that is drawn on the returned graphics context will appear on the printed page. To determine the printable area on the graphics context, use `getPageDimension()`. When a page is completed, `Graphics.dispose()` should be called in order for the page to be printed.
	Whenever a new page is needed, this method must be called again to obtain a new graphics context. In fact, it is not necessary to dispose of a graphics context before creating a new one. This allows pages to be generated concurrently. The pages are ordered by when the graphics contexts are created, not by when `dispose()` is called. For example, if `getGraphics()` is called twice and the second graphics context is disposed of before the first, the page associated with the first graphics context will still be printed first (when it is disposed of).

A
B
C
D
E
F
G
H
I
J
K
L
M
N
O
P
Q
R
S
T
U
V
W
X
Y
Z

Note: In Java 1.1.2, creating multiple graphics contexts does not work on all platforms. At present, it is safer to dispose of one graphics context before creating another.

RETURNS   A non-`null` graphics context that is a subclass of `PrintGraphics`.

SEE ALSO   `PrintGraphics`.

EXAMPLE   This example demonstrates the steps needed to print an image and string centered on a sheet of paper. See Figure 306.

It is necessary to wait until all of the pixels in the image have been loaded before printing can occur. This program uses the media tracker class to force all of the pixels to be loaded. Since the media tracker requires a component to do its work, a simple component, called `ImageReader`, is defined for the media tracker.

FIGURE 306: **Printing an Image and a String.**

Note: In Java 1.1.2, the `getPageDimension()` method returns incorrect results. The workaround is to determine a page size by applying the screen resolution on an 8.5-×-11-inch sheet of paper. However, most printers cannot print in all of this area. At present, there is no means to determine the exact size of the printable area, so we simply guess and reduce the area's width and height by three-fourths of an inch.

```
import java.awt.*;
import java.util.*;

class Main {
    public static void main(String[] args) {
        if (args.length != 1) {
            System.err.println("Usage: java Main <image file>");
            System.exit(1);
        }

        // Get the image.
        Image image = new ImageReader(args[0]).image;

        // Get the print job object.
        PrintJob pj =
            Toolkit.getDefaultToolkit().getPrintJob(null, "Title", null);

        if (pj == null) {
            System.err.println("The print request was cancelled.");
            System.exit(1);
        }

        // Get the pixel dimensions of the page.
        Dimension d = pj.getPageDimension();
```

```
        // The above is currently not working in Java 1.1.2.
        // The following is a workaround. Given the screen resolution,
        // determine pixel size of 8.5x11 inch sheet of paper.
        int res = Toolkit.getDefaultToolkit().getScreenResolution();
        d = new Dimension((int)(res * 8.5), (int)(res * 11));

        // Reduce the dimension of the page due to margins around
        // the page.
        d.width -= (int)(res * .75/*in*/);
        d.height -= (int)(res * .75/*in*/);

        // Get graphics context for first page.
        Graphics g = pj.getGraphics();

        // Paint the image.
        g.drawImage(image, (d.width-image.getWidth(null))/2,
            d.height/2-image.getHeight(null), null);

        // Set up the string and font.
        String msg = "\u5496\u5561?";
        g.setFont(new Font("Serif", Font.PLAIN, 48));
        FontMetrics fm = g.getFontMetrics();

        // Draw the string in the center.
        g.drawString(msg, (d.width-fm.stringWidth(msg))/2,
            d.height/2+fm.getAscent());

        g.dispose();

        // Start printing.
        pj.end();

        System.exit(0);
    }
}

class ImageReader extends Component {
    Image image;
    ImageReader(String filename) {
        image = getToolkit().getImage(filename);
        MediaTracker tracker = new MediaTracker(this);
        try {
            tracker.addImage(image, 0);
            tracker.waitForAll(0);
        } catch (Exception e) {
            e.printStackTrace();
        }
    }
}
```

A
B
C
D
E
F
G
H
I
J
K
L
M
N
O

Q
R
S
T
U
V
W
X
Y
Z

getPageDimension()

PURPOSE	Retrieves the dimensions of the page in pixels.
SYNTAX	`public abstract Dimension getPageDimension()`
DESCRIPTION	This method retrieves the printable dimension of a page in pixels. Any painting done in this area will appear on the page; any painting outside this area might not appear on the page.
	The dimensions returned are always in portrait mode, regardless of what orientation the user chose.
	Note: In Java 1.1.2, this method returns incorrect results. See the class description for more details on how to work around this bug.
RETURNS	The non-`null` pixel dimensions of a page.
EXAMPLE	See the class example.

getPageResolution()

PURPOSE	Retrieves the resolution of the printed page in pixels per inch.
SYNTAX	`public abstract int getPageResolution()`
DESCRIPTION	This value is used to determine the exact pixel dimensions of the printed page. For example, for a 3-×-5-inch sheet of paper, the pixel width would be 3*`resolution` and the pixel height would be 5*`resolution`.
RETURNS	The non-negative resolution of the printed page in pixels per inch.
EXAMPLE	See the class example.

lastPageFirst()

PURPOSE	Determines if pages should be printed backwards.
SYNTAX	`public abstract boolean lastPageFirst()`
DESCRIPTION	When a printer prints paper such that new pages are stacked face up on top of old pages, the pages need to be printed backwards. Otherwise, the stack of pages will be in the wrong order. For such printers, this method returns `true`.
	Note: In Java 1.1.2, this method might not return the correct results.
RETURNS	`true` if the last page will appear on top of a printed stack; `false` otherwise.
EXAMPLE	See the class example.

PropertyChangeEvent

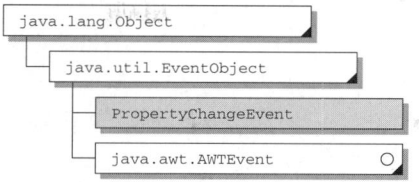

Syntax

```
public class PropertyChangeEvent extends EventObject
```

Description

A property change event is fired by a bean when one of its *bound* or *constrained* properties is changed.

Bound Properties

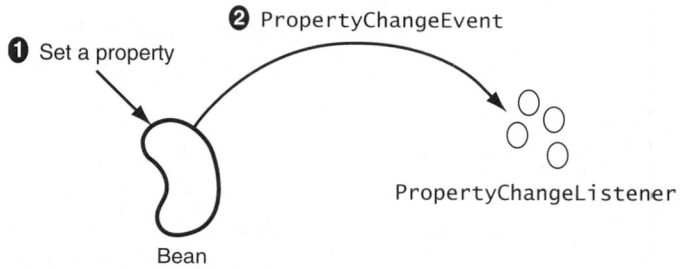

FIGURE 307: **Bound Property Event Flow.**

A *bound* property is any bean property that, when modified, fires a property change event to notify any property change listeners (see `PropertyChangeListener`) of the change. See Figure 307. Property change listeners cannot listen for changes to a particular bound property in a bean; they will receive property change events when *any* bound property in the bean is modified. However, the property change event sometimes contains information about which property was modified.

A
B
C
D
E
F
G
H
I
J
K
L
M
N
O
P
Q
R
S
T
U
V
W
X
Y
Z

Constrained Properties

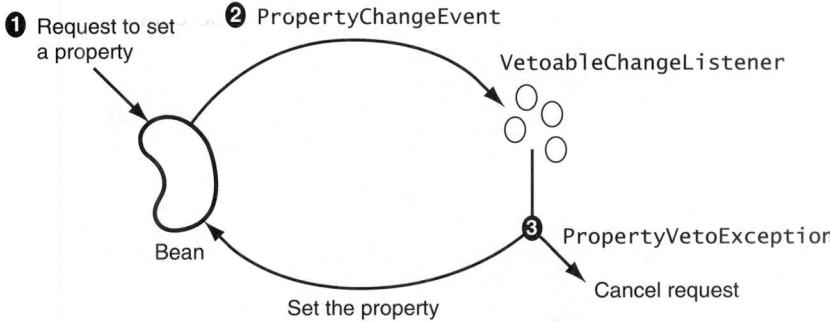

FIGURE 308: Constrained Property Event Flow.

A *constrained* property is similar to a bound property, except that *just before* the property value is actually modified, the bean fires a property change event to notify vetoable change listeners of the requested change. Any *vetoable change listener* can *veto* the requested change, thereby canceling the change. If no listener vetoes the change, the property value is changed (see `VetoableChangeListener` for more details). At this point, if the property is also bound, a property change event is fired to the property change listeners. See Figure 308.

Note that although there are two kinds of listeners—property change listeners and vetoable change listeners—both use `PropertyChangeEvent` to notify their listeners.

Listening for Property Change Events

Any bean with a bound property must provide both an `addPropertyChangeListener()` and a `removePropertyChangeListener()` method so that objects can listen for these events. See `PropertyChangeListener` and `PropertyChangeSupport` for more details. The event is delivered to the listeners by a call to each listener's `propertyChange()` method.

Any bean with a constrained property must provide both an `addVetoableChangeListener()` and a `removeVetoableChangeListener()` method so that objects can listen for these events. See `VetoableChangeListener` and `VetoableChangeSupport` for more details. The event is delivered to listeners by a call to each listener's `vetoableChange()` method.

Property Name

A property change event includes the name of the property that changed. The property name can be `null`, which means that many properties have changed and that the listener should retrieve all relevant values from the bean. See the following "Multichange Event" section for more details.

Old and New Values

The event includes the old and new values of the changed property. The values have the type `Object`, so if the value is actually a primitive type, it must be contained in a wrapper. For example, a `boolean` needs to be wrapped in a `Boolean` object.

Before a property change event is fired, a check should be made to ensure that the new value is different from the old value. The recommended way to check this is to first compare references and then use the `Object.equals()` method.

Multichange Event

In most cases, one property change event is fired for each bound or constrained property that changes. However, when many properties have been changed at one time, a bean may reduce the number of fired events by firing only one event. In this case, the property name, the old value, and the new value of the event must all be `null`.

Care must be taken when using this feature of property change events. Since the listeners have no way of knowing which properties changed, they must get every bean property value in which they are interested. This flurry of "gets" may result in more overhead than the savings in fired events.

Propagation Id

The propagation id property of a property change event is reserved for future use. Its only requirement is that if a listener receives a property change event and then proceeds to forward the same event or a derived version, the propagation ids of both events must be the same.

MEMBER SUMMARY	
Constructor	
PropertyChangeEvent()	Constructs a new `PropertyChangeEvent` instance.
Value Methods	
getNewValue()	Retrieves the changed property's new value.
getOldValue()	Retrieves the changed property's old value.
Name Method	
getPropertyName()	Retrieves the name of the changed property.
Propagation Id Methods	
getPropagationId()	Reserved for future use.
setPropagationId()	Reserved for future use.

See Also

PropertyChangeListener, PropertyChangeSupport, VetoableChangeListener.

Example

This example demonstrates both an object that fires property change events (because a bound property changed) and one that listens for these events.

This example implements an invisible bean that has one bound property: "price." When the bean is created, it creates a thread that occasionally changes its price. When the price changes, the bean fires a property change event to its listeners. The bean uses Property-ChangeSupport to implement the property change event listeners list.

The Main object creates the bean and then listens for property change events. Whenever an event occurs, Main prints out the price difference.

```java
import java.awt.*;
import java.beans.*;

class Main implements PropertyChangeListener {
    Main() {
        Bean bean = null;

        try {
            // Create the bean.
            bean = (Bean)Beans.instantiate(Main.class.getClassLoader(), "Bean");
        } catch (Exception e) {
            e.printStackTrace();
        }
        bean.addPropertyChangeListener(this);
    }

    public void propertyChange(PropertyChangeEvent evt) {
        float p1 = ((Float)evt.getOldValue()).floatValue();
        float p2 = ((Float)evt.getNewValue()).floatValue();

        // Only show two digits after decimal point.
        float diff = Math.round((p2-p1)*100)/100.0f;

        System.out.print(evt.getPropertyName());
        if (p2 > p1) {
            System.out.println(" increase by " + diff);
        } else {
            System.out.println(" decrease by " + -diff);
        }
    }

    public static void main(String args[]) {
        new Main();
    }
}

public class Bean implements Runnable {
    float price = 1.49f;

    // Constructor
    public Bean() {
        (new Thread(this)).start();
    }

    // The price is a bound property.
    public float getPrice() {
```

```
        return price;
    }

    public void setPrice(float newPrice) {
        float oldPrice = price;

        price = newPrice;                                            A
        pceListeners.firePropertyChange("price",
            new Float(oldPrice), new Float(newPrice));               B

    }                                                                C

    // Create the listener list.                                     D
    PropertyChangeSupport pceListeners =
        new PropertyChangeSupport(this);                             E

    // The listener list wrapper methods.                            F
    public synchronized void addPropertyChangeListener(
                            PropertyChangeListener l) {
        pceListeners.addPropertyChangeListener(l);                   G

    }                                                                H
    // removePropertyChangeListener() method omitted...
                                                                     I
    public void run() {
        try {                                                        J
            while (true) {
                // Change price up or down by .50.                   K
                setPrice(Math.max(1.0f, price + .5f - (float)Math.random()));
                                                                     L
                // Sleep for a random amount of time.
                Thread.sleep(Math.round(Math.random() * 5000));      M
            }
        } catch (Exception e) {                                      N
            e.printStackTrace();
        }                                                            O
    }
}
```

Q

R

S

T

U

V

Output

```
price decrease by 0.35
price increase by 0.01
price increase by 0.38
price increase by 0.37
price decrease by 0.18
price decrease by 0.38
price increase by 0.48
```

getNewValue()

W

X

Y

Z

PURPOSE	Retrieves the changed property's new value.
SYNTAX	`public Object getNewValue()`
DESCRIPTION	If the new value and the event's property name are `null`, this event is a multi-change event. See the class description for more details.

RETURNS	The changed property's possibly `null` new value.
EXAMPLE	See the class example.

getOldValue()

PURPOSE	Retrieves the changed property's old value.
SYNTAX	`public Object getOldValue()`
DESCRIPTION	If the old value and the event's property name are `null`, this event is a multi-change event. See the class description for more details.
RETURNS	The changed property's possibly `null` old value.
EXAMPLE	See the class example.

getPropagationId()

PURPOSE	The propagation property is reserved for future use.
SYNTAX	`public Object getPropagationId()`
DESCRIPTION	This property's only requirement is that if a listener receives a property change event and then proceeds to forward the same event or a derived version, the propagation ids of both events must be the same.
RETURNS	The event's propagation id.

getPropertyName()

PURPOSE	Retrieves the name of the changed property.
SYNTAX	`public String getPropertyName()`
DESCRIPTION	If the property name is `null`, this event is a multichange event. See the class description for more details.
RETURNS	The possibly `null` name of the changed property. May be `null` if multiple properties have changed.
EXAMPLE	See the class example.

PropertyChangeEvent()

PURPOSE   Constructs a new `PropertyChangeEvent` instance.

SYNTAX   ```
public PropertyChangeEvent(Object source, String propertyName,
    Object oldValue, Object newValue)
```

DESCRIPTION     This constructor creates a property change event with `source` as the object that fires the event. The `propertyName` parameter may be `null`, which indicates that this is a multichange event. In that case, then `oldValue` and `newValue` must also be `null`. See the class description for more details.

PARAMETERS

newValue        The possibly `null` new value of the changed property.

oldValue        The possibly `null` old value of the changed property.

propertyName

                The possibly `null` name of the changed property

source          The non-`null` object that is firing this property change event.

EXAMPLE     This example fragment demonstrates what typically happens before and after a property change event is created. The values should be checked for equality by first comparing references and then using the `Object.equals()` method. If the values are equal, the event is not fired.

After the event is created, it should be distributed to all listeners.

A bean does not typically have to create property change events. The functionality of maintaining a listener list, creating a property change event, and distributing that event to the listeners is provided by `PropertyChangeSupport`. See `PropertyChangeSupport` for more details.

```
public void firePropertyChange(Object source,
        String propertyName,
        Object oldValue, Object newValue) {

    // Check if the values are different before firing an event.
    if (oldValue != null && oldValue.equals(newValue)) {
        return;
    }

    PropertyChangeEvent evt = new PropertyChangeEvent(
        source, propertyName, oldValue, newValue);

    // Now distribute the event to all its listeners...
}
```
```

A
B
C
D
E
F
G
H
I
J
K
L
M
N
O
P
Q
R
S
T
U
V
W
X
Y
Z

setPropagationId()

PURPOSE   The propagation property is reserved for future use.

SYNTAX   `public void setPropagationId(Object propagationId)`

DESCRIPTION   This property's only requirement is that if a listener receives a property change event and then proceeds to forward the same event or a derived version, the propagation ids of both events must be the same.

PARAMETERS

  `propagationId`
                 The event's propagation id.

PropertyChangeListener

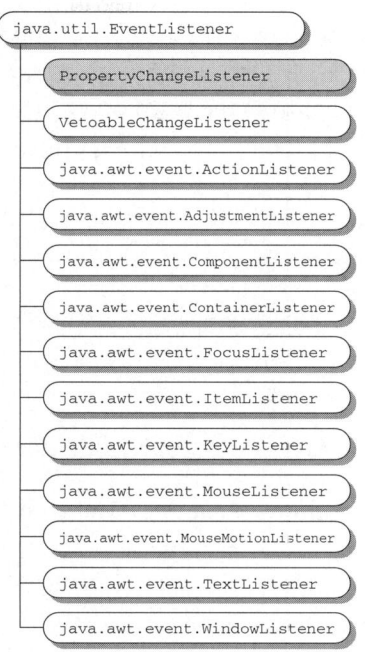

Syntax

```
public interface PropertyChangeListener extends EventListener
```

Description

When a bound property in a bean is changed, the bean will fire a property change event to notify listeners of the change. See Figure 309. See PropertyChangeEvent for more details. To listen for these events, you must define an object that implements the method in this interface and then register the object as a listener by calling the bean's addPropertyChangeListener() method.

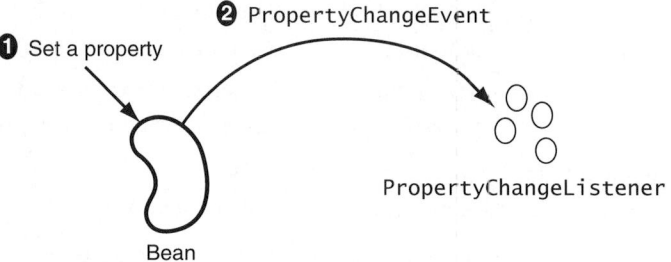

FIGURE 309: Bound Property Event Flow.

Extra Events

When a listener is removed from a bean's listener list, it should be prepared to receive a few more property change events. Whether a listener will receive the extra events depends on how the bean distributes events. In particular, a bean has the option of using a copy of the listener list while delivering events. If the listener is removed while an event is being delivered, it is removed from the main list but not from the copy. Since the listener is still in the copied list, it may receive the event.

MEMBER SUMMARY

Event Callback Method
propertyChange()   Called when a bean's bound property has changed.

See Also

Bean, java.util.EventListener, PropertyChangeEvent.

Example

See the PropertyChangeEvent class example.

propertyChange()

PURPOSE	Called when a bean's bound property has changed.
SYNTAX	void propertyChange(PropertyChangeEvent evt)
DESCRIPTION	This method is called when the source bean fires a property change event after a bound property is changed. See PropertyChangeEvent for details.
	This method may be called a few more times even after the listener is removed from the bean's listener list. See the class description for details.
PARAMETERS	
evt	A non-null property change event.
EXAMPLE	See the PropertyChangeEvent class example.

PropertyChangeSupport

```
java.lang.Object
    PropertyChangeSupport ......... java.io.Serializable
```

Syntax

`public class PropertyChangeSupport implements Serializable`

Description

Any bean that has bound properties must be able to deliver property change events (see PropertyChangeEvent). This involves maintaining a list of property change event listeners and delivering events to these listeners. This class can be used by a bean to maintain the listener list and to deliver the events.

There are two ways a bean can use this class. First, it can have the bean extend this class. This is not typical, since it prevents the bean from inheriting other useful classes, such as Component. The second, and typical way, is for the bean to create an instance of this class and provide wrapper methods for addPropertyChangeListener() and removePropertyChangeListener(). These bean methods should simply call the methods in this class that have the same name.

MEMBER SUMMARY	
Constructor	
PropertyChangeSupport()	Constructs a new PropertyChangeSupport instance.
Listener Methods	
addPropertyChangeListener()	Adds a listener for receiving property change events.
removePropertyChangeListener()	Stops a listener from receiving property change events.
Event Method	
firePropertyChange()	Delivers a property change event to the listeners.

See Also

java.awt.Component, java.io.Serializable, PropertyChangeEvent, PropertyChangeListener.

Example

This example implements a simple bean that maintains a price that is a floating-point value. When the price changes, the property change event listeners (if any) are notified of the change.

Figure 310 shows the property sheet of the Beanbox when this example bean is selected. Notice the price field.

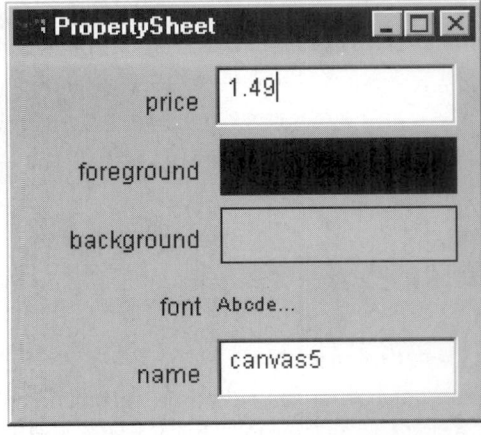

FIGURE 310: PropertyChangeSupport.

```java
import java.awt.*;
import java.beans.*;

public class Bean extends Canvas {
    float price = 1.49f;

    // Constructor
    public Bean() {
        // A couple of calls to make the bean visible.
        setBackground(Color.pink);
        setSize(50, 50);
    }

    // The price is a bound property.
    public float getPrice() {
        return price;
    }

    public void setPrice(float newPrice) {
        float oldPrice = price;

        price = newPrice;
        pceListeners.firePropertyChange("price",
            new Float(oldPrice), new Float(newPrice));
    }

    // Create the listener list.
    PropertyChangeSupport pceListeners =
        new PropertyChangeSupport(this);

    // The listener list wrapper methods.
    public synchronized void addPropertyChangeListener(
                            PropertyChangeListener l) {
        pceListeners.addPropertyChangeListener(l);
    }

    public synchronized void removePropertyChangeListener(
                            PropertyChangeListener l) {
        pceListeners.removePropertyChangeListener(l);
    }
}
/*
    manifest.txt file:
        Name: Bean.class
        Java-Bean: True
    jar command:
        jar cfm bean.jar manifest.txt Bean.class
*/
```

addPropertyChangeListener()

PURPOSE   Adds a listener for receiving property change events.

SYNTAX

```
public synchronized void
    addPropertyChangeListener(PropertyChangeListener listener)
```

DESCRIPTION   This method adds `listener` to the listener list. The method does not check if `listener` has already been added, so a listener can be added to the list more than once.

PARAMETERS

`listener`   A non-`null` property change event listener.

SEE ALSO   `removePropertyChangeListener()`.

EXAMPLE   See the class example.

firePropertyChange()

PURPOSE   Delivers a property change event to the listeners.

SYNTAX

```
public void firePropertyChange(String propertyName, Object
    oldValue, Object newValue)
```

DESCRIPTION   This method creates a new property change event and delivers it to all listeners. Listeners should not throw any exceptions. An exception that is thrown is consider a programming error.

This method first checks if `oldValue` and `newValue` are equal. If they are, the method call is ignored. The two values are equal if

```
oldValue != null && oldValue.equals(newValue).
```

If `oldValue` is not equal to `newValue`, a new property change event is created with the values `propertyName`, `oldValue`, and `newValue`. The event's source is the one that was used when creating this class. This new event is delivered to each of the listeners.

The parameter `propertyName` can be `null`, which indicates that this is a multichange event (see `PropertyChangeEvent` for details). In this case, `oldValue` and `newValue` will also be `null`.

PARAMETERS

`newValue`   The possibly `null` new value of the property.
`oldValue`   The possibly `null` old value of the property.
`propertyName` A possibly `null` property name.

EXAMPLE   See the class example.

PropertyChangeSupport()

PURPOSE   Constructs a new PropertyChangeSupport instance.

SYNTAX   `public PropertyChangeSupport(Object source)`

DESCRIPTION   This method creates a new property change support object and records source as the object that will be firing property change events. The source object will always be included in every new property change event that is fired by firePropertyChange(). The source object cannot be changed.

PARAMETERS
source   The non-null bean that will be generating property change events.

SEE ALSO   firePropertyChange().

EXAMPLE   See the class example.

removePropertyChangeListener()

PURPOSE   Stops a listener from receiving property change events.

SYNTAX   `public synchronized void`
                    `removePropertyChangeListener(PropertyChangeListener listener)`

DESCRIPTION   This method removes listener from the listener list.

                 The removed listener should be prepared to receive a few more property change events. See PropertyChangeListener for more details.

PARAMETERS
listener   A non-null property change event listener.

SEE ALSO   addPropertyChangeListener().

EXAMPLE   See the class example.

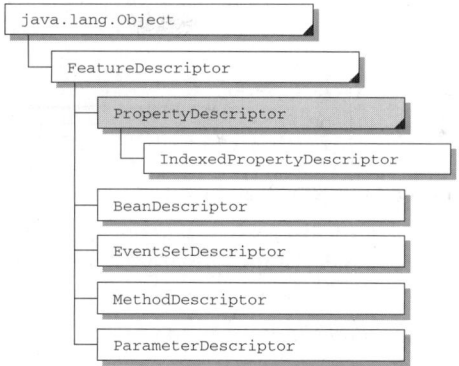

Syntax

```
public class PropertyDescriptor extends FeatureDescriptor
```

Description

A *property descriptor* contains information about a bean property, such as its localized name and whether it is bound. There is one property descriptor for each property. A bean's property descriptors can be retrieved through the introspector by calling `Introspector.getBeanInfo().getProperty-Descriptors()`.

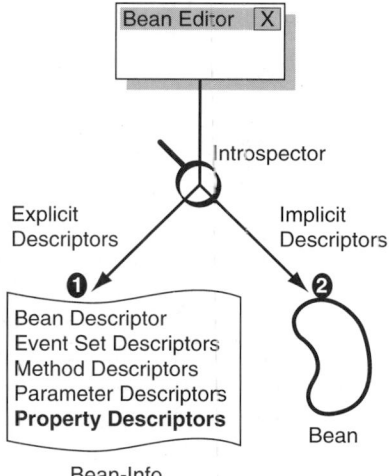

FIGURE 311:   Property Descriptor.

For Bean Editors Only

The information contained in a property descriptor is meant for programs such as bean editors (programs that help connect together beans into an application). It is not used by the bean itself. These and other descriptors essentially help a bean editor to construct a meaningful user interface for editing the bean. When the bean is actually running in an application, the property descriptors are never used.

Implicit and Explicit Property Descriptors

When retrieving the property descriptors, the introspector first looks in the bean's bean-info (see `BeanInfo`) for any property descriptors that the bean has explicitly supplied. These are called *explicit* property descriptors. If none are found, the introspector must use introspection on the bean to discover all the bean's properties and then create *implicit* property descriptors for the properties. See Figure 311. Implicit property descriptors are given default values for some of the property descriptor attributes. Table 22 shows the attributes of a property descriptor and the default values for implicit property descriptors.

Attribute	Contents	Default Value
Bound	`true` if the property is bound.	`false`.[a]
Constrained	`true` if the property is constrained.	`false`.[b]
Property type	The `Class` object of the property type.	The `Class` object of the property type.
Read method	The `Method` object of the property's read accessor method.	The `Method` object of the property's read accessor method.
Write method	The `Method` object of the property's write accessor method.	The `Method` object of the property's write accessor method.
Property editor class	The `Class` object of the property's property editor.	`null`.
Name	The property's nonlocalized name.	The property's nonlocalized name.
Display name	The property's localized name.	The property's nonlocalized name.
Short description	A localized description of the property.	The property's nonlocalized name.
Expert	`true` if the property is considered for use by experts only.	`false`.
Hidden	`true` if the property is meant to be used by a tool; `false` if meant to be used by a person.	`false`.

TABLE 22: Property Descriptor Attributes.

　　a. If the introspector discovers that the bean fires the property change event (see `PropertyChangeEvent`), then the bound attribute for implicit property descriptors is set to `true`.

　　b. If the introspector discovers that the property's indexed or nonindexed write accessor methods throws `PropertyVetoException` (see `PropertyVetoException`), then the constrained attribute for the property will be `true`.

A
B
C
D
E
F
G
H
I
J
K
L
M
N
O
Q
R
S
T
U
V
W
X
Y
Z

Accessor Method Signature Conventions

The bean specification defines conventions for the signatures of property read and write accessor methods. These conventions serve two purposes.

1. They makes the bean's API easier for a programmer to read. That is, it's easy to see which methods are accessor methods and which are not.
2. They enable the introspector to discover a bean's properties and create implicit property descriptors. In other words, the introspector looks at the entire list of a bean's public methods. When a method is found that matches the accessor method signature convention, the introspector assumes that it must be an accessor method. From the signature of the accessor method, it can deduce the name and type of the property.

For example, if the name of a property is *PropertyName* and its type is *PropertyType*, the convention of a read accessor method signature is

```
public PropertyType getCapPropertyName()
```

where *CapPropertyName* is the property name, with the first character capitalized. The convention of a write accessor method signature is

```
public void setCapPropertyName(PropertyType)
```

If *PropertyType* is `boolean`, then the read method can be replaced or complemented by a read accessor with the signature

```
public PropertyType isCapPropertyName()
```

For example, if the property name is "roasted" and the property type is `boolean`, then the set of accessor methods is

```
public boolean isRoasted()
public boolean getRoasted()
public void setRoasted(boolean r)
```

When the read method is not explicitly specified and both "is" and "get" methods are available, the "is" read method is used. If only a read accessor method is found, the property is assumed to be read-only. If only a write accessor method is found, the property is assumed to be write-only.

MEMBER SUMMARY	
Constructor	
PropertyDescriptor()	Constructs a `PropertyDescriptor` instance.
Bound Property Methods	
isBound()	Determines if this property is bound.
setBound()	Specifies whether the property is bound.
	Continued

MEMBER SUMMARY	
Constrained Property Methods	
isConstrained()	Determines if this property is constrained.
setConstrained()	Specifies whether the property is constrained.
Property Type Method	
getPropertyType()	Retrieves the property's type.
Property Accessor Methods	
getReadMethod()	Retrieves the property's read accessor method.
getWriteMethod()	Retrieves the property's write accessor method.
Property Editor Class Methods	
getPropertyEditorClass()	Retrieves the property's property editor class.
setPropertyEditorClass()	Sets a property editor for the property.

See Also

BeanInfo.getPropertyDescriptors(), java.lang.Class, PropertyEditor.

Example

This example implements a bean that has a single property: "price." The bean displays the current value of price in a label. See Figure 312.. The price property is both bound and constrained, so the bean will fire both vetoable and regular property change events when the price is changed.

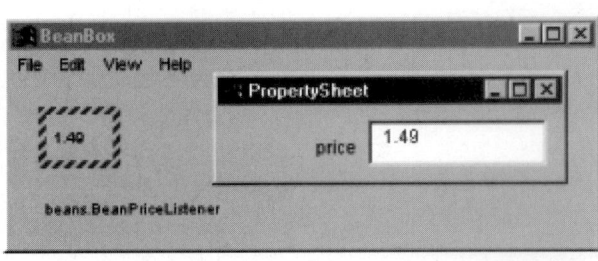

FIGURE 312: **"price" Property Sheet.**

This example also includes a listener, BeanPriceListener, for that bean. The listener listens for both vetoable property change events and regular property change events. The listener is setup to veto change prices increases that exceed 50 cents.

To run this example, you need to hook up the listener to the bean. First, in the Beanbox, select the bean and then select Edit->Events->vetoableChange->vetoableChange. Next, click the bean listener and select Edit->Events->propertyChange->propertyChange. Finally, click the bean listener again. The bean listener is now registered for both events.

For other examples, see any of the examples in the PropertyEditorSupport and IndexedPropertyDescriptor classes.

Note: The Beanbox in the BDK 1.0apr97 requires that the bean and bean listener be in a named package. When they are in an unnamed package, the Beanbox will not hook up the bean listener to the bean.

classexample/Bean.java

```
package classexample;

import java.awt.*;
import java.beans.*;

public class Bean extends Panel {
    float price = 1.49f;
    Label l = new Label(""+price);

    public Bean() {
        add(l);
    }

    // The price is a bound and constrained property.
    public float getPrice() {
        return price;
    }

    public void setPrice(float newPrice) {
        float oldPrice = price;

        try {
            vceListeners.fireVetoableChange("price",
                new Float(oldPrice), new Float(newPrice));

            // No vetos so update the price
            price = newPrice;

            pceListeners.firePropertyChange("price",
                new Float(oldPrice), new Float(newPrice));
        } catch (PropertyVetoException e) {
            // Don't change the price
        }
        l.setText(""+price);
    }

    // Create the vetoable property change listener list.
    VetoableChangeSupport vceListeners =
        new VetoableChangeSupport(this);

    // The listener list wrapper methods.
    public synchronized void addVetoableChangeListener(
                        VetoableChangeListener l) {
        vceListeners.addVetoableChangeListener(l);
    }
    public synchronized void removeVetoableChangeListener(
                        VetoableChangeListener l) {
        vceListeners.removeVetoableChangeListener(l);
    }

    // Create the property change listener list.
    PropertyChangeSupport pceListeners =
        new PropertyChangeSupport(this);
```

A
B
C
D
E
F
G
H
I
J
K
L
M
N
O
Q
R
S
T
U
V
W
X
Y
Z

```
        // The listener list wrapper methods.
        public synchronized void addPropertyChangeListener(
                              PropertyChangeListener l) {
            pceListeners.addPropertyChangeListener(l);
        }
        public synchronized void removePropertyChangeListener(
                              PropertyChangeListener l) {
            pceListeners.removePropertyChangeListener(l);
        }
    }
    /*
        manifest.txt:
            Name: classexample/Bean.class
            Java-Bean: True

            Name: classexample/BeanPriceListener.class
            Java-Bean: True
        jar command (Solaris):
            jar cfm bean.jar manifest.txt classexample/*.class
        jar command (Windows):
            jar cfm bean.jar manifest.txt classexample\*.class
    */
```

classexample/BeanBeanInfo.java

```
    package classexample;

    import java.beans.*;

    public class BeanBeanInfo extends SimpleBeanInfo {
        public PropertyDescriptor[] getPropertyDescriptors() {
            PropertyDescriptor pd[] = new PropertyDescriptor[1];

            try {
                pd[0] = new PropertyDescriptor("price", Bean.class);
                pd[0].setBound(true);
                pd[0].setConstrained(true);
                return pd;
            } catch (Exception e) {
                e.printStackTrace();
                return null;
            }
        }
    }
```

classexample/BeanPriceListener.java

```
    package classexample;

    import java.awt.*;
    import java.beans.*;
    import java.util.*;

    public class BeanPriceListener implements PropertyChangeListener, Veto-
    ableChangeListener {
        Vector priceChangeLog = new Vector();

        // If the price difference is too high, veto it.
        public void vetoableChange(PropertyChangeEvent evt)
            throws PropertyVetoException {
            float oldPrice = ((Float)evt.getOldValue()).floatValue();
```

```
        float newPrice = ((Float)evt.getNewValue()).floatValue();

        if (newPrice - oldPrice > .5f) {
            throw(new PropertyVetoException("Too Much!", evt));
        }
    }
}

    // Save the new price.
    public void propertyChange(PropertyChangeEvent evt) {
        priceChangeLog.addElement(evt.getNewValue());
    }
}
```

getPropertyEditorClass()

PURPOSE   Retrieves the property's property editor class.

SYNTAX   `public Class getPropertyEditorClass()`

DESCRIPTION   This method is typically called by a bean
               editor when it needs to determine property
               editors for the bean's properties. The
               returned `Class` object, when instantiated,
               will yield an object of type `PropertyEdi-`
               `tor`. See `PropertyEditor` for more
               details.

               If the returned value is `null`, the bean edi-
               tor will determine the type of the property
               and then ask the property editor manager if
               it has a property editor for that type. See
               `PropertyEditorManager` for more
               details.

               The property editor class for a property
               descriptor can be set only by a call to `set-`
               `PropertyEditorClass()`.

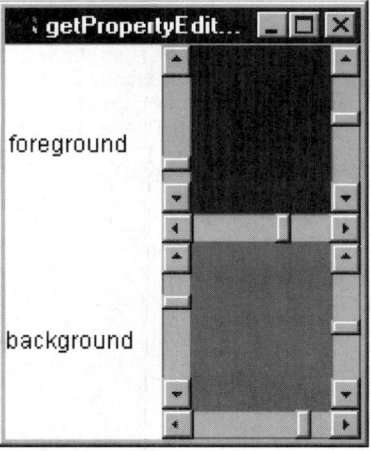

FIGURE 313: Displaying Custom
Property Editors.

RETURNS   A possibly `null` `Class` object for a property editor.

SEE ALSO   `setPropertyEditorClass()`.

EXAMPLE   This example implements a program that uses the filename of a class file con-
               taining a bean to discover if bean has any custom property editors. If it does,
               the program creates instances of them and displays them. Figure 313 shows the
               example when run on the bean in the `PropertyEditorSupport.getCus-`
               `tomEditor()` example.

This example uses the `FileClassLoader` class to load the bean from a file. The source code for this class is in the `Introspector` class example.

A gridbag layout is used to lay out the custom property editors and their labels.

Main.java

```java
import java.awt.*;
import java.beans.*;
import java.io.*;
import java.lang.reflect.*;
import java.util.*;
import java.net.*;

class Main {
    public static void main(String[] args) {
        if (args.length != 1) {
            System.err.println("Usage: java Main <name of bean class file>");
            System.exit(1);
        }

        try {
            // Load the bean class and get the property descriptors.
            // (See the Introspector class example for FileClassLoader
            // source code.)
            Class beanClass = FileClassLoader.load(args[0]);
            BeanInfo beanInfo = Introspector.getBeanInfo(beanClass);
            PropertyDescriptor pds[] = beanInfo.getPropertyDescriptors();
            Frame frame = null;

            for (int i=0; i<pds.length; i++) {
                PropertyEditor peditor = null;
                Class peClass = pds[i].getPropertyEditorClass();

                if (peClass != null) {
                    try {
                        // Instatiate the custom editor
                        peditor = (PropertyEditor)peClass.newInstance();
                    } catch (Exception e) {
                    }
                }
                if (peditor != null && peditor.supportsCustomEditor()) {
                    try {
                        // Instantiate the bean.
                        Object bean = beanClass.newInstance();
                        Method getter = pds[i].getReadMethod();
                        Object arguments[] = { };
                        peditor.setValue(getter.invoke(bean, arguments));

                        // Create a frame for the custom editor.
                        if (frame == null) {
                            frame = new Frame("getPropertyEditorClass Example");
                            frame.setLayout(new GridBagLayout());
                        }
                        addComp(frame, pds[i].getName(),
                            peditor.getCustomEditor());
                    } catch (InvocationTargetException e) {
                        e.printStackTrace();
                    } catch (InstantiationException e) {
                        e.printStackTrace();
                    } catch (IllegalAccessException e) {
```

```
                    e.printStackTrace();
            }
        }
    }
    if (frame != null) {
        frame.pack();
        frame.show();
    }
} catch (IntrospectionException e) {
    e.printStackTrace();
}
}

static void addComp(Container cont, String label, Component comp) {
    GridBagLayout gbl = (GridBagLayout)cont.getLayout();
    GridBagConstraints c = new GridBagConstraints();

    // Add label.
    Label l= new Label(label);
    cont.add(l);
    gbl.setConstraints(comp, c);

    // Add component.
    cont.add(comp);
    c = new GridBagConstraints();
    c.gridwidth = GridBagConstraints.REMAINDER;
    gbl.setConstraints(comp, c);
    }
}
```

getPropertyType()

PURPOSE   Retrieves the property's type.

SYNTAX   `public Class getPropertyType()`

DESCRIPTION   The property's type is represented by a `Class` object of that type. For example, if the type is a `String` or an `int`, then this method returns `java.lang.String.class` or `int.class`, respectively.

If the property is an indexed property (see `IndexedPropertyDescriptor`) with no nonindexed accessor methods, this method returns `null`.

The property's type is determined in the constructor. See the property descriptor constructor for more details on how this is done.

RETURNS   The possibly `null` `Class` object of the property's type.

EXAMPLE   See the `Introspector` class example.

getReadMethod()

PURPOSE Retrieves the property's read accessor method.

SYNTAX   `public Method getReadMethod()`

DESCRIPTION The property's read accessor method is used to read the property value. It is typically called by the bean editor as the user edits the property value through a property editor (see `PropertyEditor`). The read accessor method does not take any arguments. It returns an object of the same type as that returned by `getPropertyType()`.

       The property's read accessor method is determined by the constructor. The method may have been specified in a bean-info or discovered through introspection. See the constructor for more details.

       If the property does not have a public read accessor method, this method returns `null`.

RETURNS The possibly `null` read accessor method.

SEE ALSO `java.lang.reflect.Method`, `getPropertyType()`, `getWriteMethod()`, `IndexedPropertyDescriptor`.

EXAMPLE This example demonstrates how to invoke the property's read accessor method. The program loads a bean and its bean-info, if present. It then instantiates the bean. Finally, it iterates over the bean's list of properties and prints out the initial value of each one.

       Component beans are treated specially. This is because the property values for a component are not accurate until the component's peer is created. For the peer to be created, the component is inserted into a frame and `addNotify()` is called on the frame.

       The creation of the frame causes various internal AWT threads to be created that prevent the program from exiting at the end of the `main()` method. To exit, the program explicitly calls `System.exit()`.

       This example uses the `FileClassLoader` class to load the bean from a file. The source code for `FileClassLoader` is in the `Introspector` class example.

Main.java
```
import java.awt.*;
import java.beans.*;
import java.io.*;
import java.lang.reflect.*;
import java.util.*;
import java.net.*;

class Main {
    public static void main(String[] args) {
        if (args.length != 1) {
```

```java
            System.err.println("Usage: java Main <name of bean class file>");
            System.exit(1);
        }

        try {
            // Load the bean and get the bean-info.
            // (See the Introspector class example for
            // FileClassLoader source code.)
            Class beanClass = FileClassLoader.load(args[0]);
            BeanInfo beanInfo = Introspector.getBeanInfo(beanClass);

            // Instantiate the bean.
            Object bean = beanClass.newInstance();

            // Components are treated specially.
            if (Beans.isInstanceOf(bean, Component.class)) {
                Frame frame = new Frame();
                frame.add((Component)bean);
                frame.addNotify();
            }

            // Now print each property and its value.
            PropertyDescriptor pds[] = beanInfo.getPropertyDescriptors();
            for (int i=0; i<pds.length; i++) {
                Method reader = pds[i].getReadMethod();
                Object[] arguments = {};

                // Invoke the read accessor method.
                Object value = reader.invoke(bean, arguments);

                // Print the results.
                print(pds[i].getName(), 15);
                System.out.println(value);
            }
        } catch (IntrospectionException e) {
            e.printStackTrace();
        } catch (IllegalAccessException e) {
            e.printStackTrace();
        } catch (InvocationTargetException e) {
            e.printStackTrace();
        } catch (InstantiationException e) {
            e.printStackTrace();
        }

        System.exit(0);
    }

    // Prints s and pads the string with Math.max(1, width-s.length()) spaces.
    static void print(String s, int width) {
        System.out.print(s);
        for (int i=0; i<Math.max(1, (width-s.length())); i++) {
            System.out.print(" ");
        }
    }
}
```

A
B
C
D
E
F
G
H
I
J
K
L
M
N
O
P
Q
R
S
T
U
V
W
X
Y
Z

Output   Here is the output of the program when run on the `OurButton` demo bean that
comes with BDK 1.0apr97:

```
enabled         true
preferredSize   java.awt.Dimension[width=44,height=23]
foreground      java.awt.Color[r=0,g=0,b=0]
label           press
visible         true
background      java.awt.Color[r=192,g=192,b=192]
fontSize        12
font            java.awt.Font[family=Dialog,name=Dialog,style=plain,size=12]
name            canvas0
largeFont       false
debug           false
minimumSize     java.awt.Dimension[width=44,height=23]
```

getWriteMethod()

PURPOSE   Retrieves the property's write accessor method.

SYNTAX   `public Method getWriteMethod()`

DESCRIPTION   The property's write accessor method is used to modify the property value. It
is typically called by the bean editor as the user edits the property value
through a property editor (see `PropertyEditor`). The write accessor method
takes one argument and does not return any. The argument must be the same
type as that of the argument returned by `getPropertyType()`.

The property's write accessor method is determined by the constructor. The
method may have been specified in a bean-info or discovered through introspection. See the constructor for more details.

If the property does not have a public write accessor method, this method
returns `null`.

RETURNS   The possibly `null` write accessor method.

SEE ALSO   `java.lang.reflect.Method`, `getPropertyType()`, `getReadMethod()`,
`IndexedPropertyDescriptor`.

EXAMPLE   This example implements a program that loads a bean, instantiates it, finds all
properties of the type `Color`, randomizes those colors, and finally serializes
the bean:

Main.java
```java
import java.awt.*;
import java.beans.*;
import java.io.*;
import java.lang.reflect.*;
import java.util.*;
import java.net.*;
```

```
class Main {
    public static void main(String[] args) {
        if (args.length != 2) {
            System.err.println(
                "Usage: java Main <bean class file> <output file>.ser");
            System.exit(1);
        }
        if (!args[1].endsWith(".ser")) {
            System.err.println("Output file must end with .ser");
            System.exit(1);
        }

        try {
            // Load the bean and get the bean-info.
            // (See the Introspector class example for
            // FileClassLoader source code.)
            Class beanClass = FileClassLoader.load(args[0]);
            BeanInfo beanInfo = Introspector.getBeanInfo(beanClass);

            // Instantiate the bean.
            Object bean = beanClass.newInstance();

            // Find all color properties.
            PropertyDescriptor pds[] = beanInfo.getPropertyDescriptors();
            for (int i=0; i<pds.length; i++) {
                if (pds[i].getPropertyType() == Color.class) {
                    // Create a random color.
                    Color color = new Color(Color.HSBtoRGB(
                        (float)Math.random(), (float)Math.random(),
                        (float)Math.random()));

                    // Get the write method.
                    Method writer = pds[i].getWriteMethod();

                    // Invoke the write accessor method.
                    Object[] arguments = {color};
                    writer.invoke(bean, arguments);

                    // Print the results.
                    System.out.println(pds[i].getName() + ":    " + color);
                }
            }

            // Serialize the bean.
            java.io.FileOutputStream fos =
                new java.io.FileOutputStream(args[1]);
            java.io.ObjectOutput os =
                new java.io.ObjectOutputStream(fos);
            os.writeObject(bean);
            os.close();
        } catch (IOException e) {
            e.printStackTrace();
        } catch (IntrospectionException e) {
            e.printStackTrace();
        } catch (IllegalAccessException e) {
            e.printStackTrace();
        } catch (InvocationTargetException e) {
            e.printStackTrace();
        } catch (InstantiationException e) {
            e.printStackTrace();
```

A
B
C
D
E
F
G
H
I
J
K
L
M
N
O
P
Q
R
S
T
U
V
W
X
Y
Z

A
B
C
D
E
F
G
H
I
J
K
L
M

```
                    }

                    System.exit(0);
                }
            }
        /*
            command to run example:
                java Main Bean.class random-color-bean.ser
            manifext.txt:
                Name: random-color-bean.ser
                Java-Bean: True
            jar command:
                jar cfm bean.jar manifest.txt *.ser
        */
```

Bean.java

```
    import java.awt.*;

    public class Bean extends Canvas {
        public Bean() {
            setSize(100, 50);
        }

        public void paint(Graphics g) {
            g.fillOval(0, 0, getSize().width, getSize().height);
        }
    }
```

N
O
P
Q
R
S
T
U
V
W
X
Y
Z

isBound()

PURPOSE   Determines if this property is bound.

SYNTAX   `public boolean isBound()`

DESCRIPTION   A bean property is *bound* if it fires a property change event at the time that the property value changes (as opposed to a *constrained* property, which fires a property change event when the property value is *about to* change). See `PropertyChangeEvent` for more details.

This method is typically called by a bean container to determine which of the bean's properties are bound. A bean container cannot determine by introspection which properties are bound. If a bean wants to inform the bean container which properties are bound, it must create a property descriptor for each bound property, call `setBound(true)` on them, and publish the property descriptors in the bean's bean-info descriptor (see `BeanInfo`).

RETURNS   `true` if this is a bound property.

SEE ALSO   `setBound()`.

EXAMPLE   See the `Introspector` class example.

isConstrained()

PURPOSE   Determines if this property is constrained.

SYNTAX   `public boolean isConstrained()`

DESCRIPTION   A bean property is *constrained* if it fires a vetoable property change event when the property value is *about to* change (as opposed to a *bound* property, which fires a property change event at the time that the property value is changed). See `PropertyChangeEvent` and `VetoableChangeSupport` for more details.

This method is typically called by a bean container to determine which of the bean's properties are constrained. A bean container can determine by introspection which properties are constrained. In addition, a bean can inform the bean container of additional properties that are constrained. It does this by creating a property descriptor for each and then calling `setConstrained(true)` on them. The bean can then publish these explicitly created property descriptors in the bean's bean-info descriptor (see `BeanInfo`).

RETURNS   `true` if this is a constrained property.

SEE ALSO   `setConstrained()`.

EXAMPLE   See the `Introspector` class example.

PropertyDescriptor()

PURPOSE   Constructs a `PropertyDescriptor` instance.

SYNTAX   `public PropertyDescriptor(String propertyName, Class beanClass)`
       `throws IntrospectionException`
`public PropertyDescriptor(String propertyName, Class beanClass,`
       `String readerName, String writerName) throws`
       `IntrospectionException`
`public PropertyDescriptor(String propertyName, Method reader,`
       `Method writer) throws IntrospectionException`

DESCRIPTION   Property descriptors are either implicitly created by the introspector or explicitly created by a bean. See the class description for more information.

When a property descriptor is created, five attributes are initialized:
- Property name
- `Class` object of the bean
- Read accessor method
- Write accessor method
- Property type

All other attributes are given default values that can be changed by methods in this class and in the `FeatureDescriptor` class. The default values for a property descriptor are shown in Table 22.

The property type is not specified. Rather, it is determined by using reflection to examine the read and write methods. Basically, the type returned by the read method becomes the property type.

If `reader` and `writer` are specified, a check is made to ensure that the methods have the appropriate signatures. The signatures are discussed in the class description.

If `readerName` and `writerName` are specified, reflection is used to look for methods with these names. (Although they don't have to use the "is/get/set" naming conventions, it is highly recommended that they do.) The method can be in either the bean or one of its ancestors. Once these methods are found, they are subject to the signature compatibility check as discussed in the class description.

If the accessor methods are not specified, they are discovered using reflection and the following rules:

- The first letter of the property name is capitalized. For example, "roasted" becomes "Roasted." For purposes here, the capitalized property name is CapPropertyName.
- Reflection is used to look for a method named set*CapPropertyName* that has the appropriate signature. The method can be in either the bean class or one of its ancestors. If one is found, it becomes the write method and the parameter type becomes the property type; otherwise, `IntrospectionException` is thrown.
- If the property type is `boolean`, reflection is used to look for a method named is*CapPropertyName* that has the appropriate signature. The method can be in either the bean class or one of its ancestors. For example, if "roasted" is the property name, then `isRoasted()` is the read method. If a method is found, it becomes the read method.
- Otherwise, reflection is used to look for a method named get*CapPropertyName* that has the appropriate signature. The method can be in either the bean class or one of its ancestors. If one is found, it becomes the read method; otherwise, `IntrospectionException` is thrown.

PARAMETERS

`beanClass`	The bean's `Class` object.
`propertyName`	The non-`null` nonlocalized name of the property.
`reader`	The possibly `null` `Method` object of the property's read accessor method.
`readerName`	The possibly `null` name of the property's read accessor method.
`writer`	The possibly `null` `Method` object of the property's write accessor method.
`writerName`	The possibly `null` name of the property's write accessor method.

EXCEPTIONS

IntrospectionException

If the signatures of the read and write methods are incompatible. For example, the type returned by `reader` does not match what is accepted by `writer`.

EXAMPLE This example demonstrates how to use the three different forms of the constructor. The bean has three integer parameters: `property1`, `property2`, and `property3`. The bean-info class, `BeanBeanInfo`, creates three property descriptors, one for each of the three properties, using the three different constructors.

Bean.java

```
public class Bean {
    int property1;
    int property2;
    int property3;

    public int getProperty1() {
        return property1;
    }
    public void setProperty1(int v) {
        property1 = v;
    }

    public int getProperty2() {
        return property2;
    }
    public void setProperty2(int v) {
        property2 = v;
    }

    public int getProperty3() {
        return property3;
    }
    public void setProperty3(int v) {
        property3 = v;
    }
}
/*
    manifest.txt:
        Name: Bean.class
        Java-Bean: True
    jar command:
        jar cfm bean.jar manifest.txt *.class
*/
```

BeanBeanInfo.java

```
import java.beans.*;
import java.lang.reflect.*;

public class BeanBeanInfo extends SimpleBeanInfo {
    public PropertyDescriptor[] getPropertyDescriptors() {
        PropertyDescriptor pd[] = new PropertyDescriptor[3];

        try {
            // The getter and setter methods are derived from the property name.
```

```
                    pd[0] = new PropertyDescriptor("property1", Bean.class);

                    // The names of the getter and setter methods are supplied.
                    pd[1] = new PropertyDescriptor("property2", Bean.class,
                        "getProperty2", "setProperty2");

                // The Method objects of the getter and setter methods are supplied.
                Class[] getArgs = {};

                    // The getter method must not take any parameters.
                    Method getter = Bean.class.getMethod("getProperty3", getArgs);

                    // The setter must take one parameter and it must have the
                    // same type as returned by the getter method.
                    Class[] setArgs = {getter.getReturnType()};
                    Method setter = Bean.class.getMethod("setProperty3", setArgs);
                    pd[2] = new PropertyDescriptor("property3", getter, setter);

                    return pd;
            } catch (NoSuchMethodException e) {
                    e.printStackTrace();
            } catch (IntrospectionException e) {
                    e.printStackTrace();
            }
            return null;
        }
    }
```

setBound()

PURPOSE   Specifies whether the property is bound.

SYNTAX   `public void setBound(boolean bound)`

DESCRIPTION   A bean property is *bound* if it fires a property change event at the time that the property value changes (as opposed to a *constrained* property, which fires a property change event when the property value is *about to* change). See `PropertyChangeEvent` for more details.

A bean container cannot determine by introspection which properties are bound. If a bean wants to inform the bean container which properties are bound, it must create a property descriptor for each bound property, call `setBound(true)` on them, and publish the property descriptors in the bean's bean-info descriptor (see `BeanInfo`).

PARAMETERS

bound   `true` if this is a bound property; `false` otherwise.

SEE ALSO   `getBound()`.

EXAMPLE   See the class example.

setConstrained()

PURPOSE	Specifies whether the property is constrained.
SYNTAX	`public void setConstrained(boolean constrained)`

DESCRIPTION A bean property is *constrained* if it fires a vetoable property change event when the property value is about to change (as opposed to a *bound* property, which fires a property change event at the time that the property value is changed). See `PropertyChangeEvent` and `VetoableChangeSupport` for more details.

A bean container can determine by introspection which properties are constrained. In addition, a bean can inform the bean container of additional properties that are constrained. It does this by creating a property descriptor for each and then calling `setConstrained(true)` on them. The bean can then publish these explicitly created property descriptors in the bean's bean-info descriptor (see `BeanInfo`).

PARAMETERS

`constrained` `true` if this is a constrained property; `false` otherwise.

SEE ALSO `getConstrained()`.

EXAMPLE See the class example.

setPropertyEditorClass()

PURPOSE	Sets a property editor for the property.
SYNTAX	`public void setPropertyEditorClass(Class propertyEditorClass)`

DESCRIPTION A property editor is essentially a user interface for editing a bean property. A bean editor provides property editors for many common property types. However, if the property type is not one of these types, you must supply your own property editor. See `PropertyEditor` for complete details on building property editors.

This method is typically called in a bean-info while a property descriptor is being set up. This method associates a property editor with the property.

PARAMETERS

`propertyEditorClass`

The non-`null` property editor class.

EXAMPLE See the class example or any of the examples in the `PropertyEditorSupport` and `IndexedPropertyDescriptor` classes.

A
B
C
D
E
F
G
H
I
J
K
L
M
N
O
P
Q
R
S
T
U
V
W
X
Y
Z

Syntax
```
public interface PropertyEditor
```

Description

A *property editor* is essentially a user interface for editing a bean property. The property must have both a read and write accessor method. Different property types require different property editors. For example, in the case of a string property, the string property editor might provide a text field for editing the string. In the case of a color, the color property editor might provide knobs for controlling each of the color's components. Figure 314 shows a few of the property editors provided by the Beanbox. Shown are the property editors for the types double, int, String, and boolean.

FIGURE 314: **Property Editors Provided by the Beanbox.**

Property editors are objects that are created and used by a bean editor. They must implement the PropertyEditor interface and must have a public null constructor.

The Value

A property editor maintains a copy of the bean's property value. However, if the property type is primitive, this value must be contained in the corresponding wrapper object. For example, if the primitive type is boolean, the returned object will be a Boolean object.

This value must be updated (via a call to setValue()) whenever the user modifies the value. For more details about how this is done, see the event flow discussion that follows.

One important note about this value is that when the user makes a modification, a new object must be created to hold the new value. In other words, the current value object should not be changed. This is because, for efficiency, the bean editor uses a quick reference comparison to determine if a property value has changed. So, if the original value is modified rather than copied and modified, the bean editor incorrectly assumes that the value has not changed, since the references have not changed. (Efficiency is important because whenever one property value changes, the bean editor must check every other property value in case they also changed.)

Note: In the case of indexed properties (see `IndexedPropertyDescriptor`), it may be very inefficient to clone a large array when only one element has changed. The bean specification does not yet address this issue.

Locating Property Editors

When a bean editor edits a bean, it not only needs to determine the properties in the bean. It also needs to find a property editor for each property to allow the user to edit it. There are two places a bean editor can find a property editor for a property:

1. In the bean-info. The bean may have explicitly defined a property editor for the property. If so, it would appear in the bean-info. See `BeanInfo` for more details.
2. In the property editor manager registry. If no property editor is defined for that property in the bean-info, the bean editor then determines the property's type and asks the property editor manager if it has a property editor for that type. See `PropertyEditorManager` for more details.

If neither place yields a property editor, then the property cannot be edited.

Default Property Editors

The property editor manager provides property editors for a few types. The following types have default property editors:

```
boolean
byte
short
int
long
float
double
java.lang.String
java.awt.Font
```

If the property type is not one of these types, you must supply your own property editor.

Three Kinds of Property Editors

In most cases, it is convenient to think of a property editor as an AWT component designed for editing a bean property. However, the truth is that the `PropertyEditor` class is not a component. Rather, it contains information from which a bean editor can construct a component to edit the property. For example, suppose you have an "align" property that can have one of three possible integer values with the names LEFT, CENTER, and RIGHT. When the bean editor encounters the align property, it can see that the property is of type `int`. However, it has no way of knowing that only three values are allowed and what the names of the these values are. This information is provided by a property editor. With this information, a bean editor can construct a component that lets the user choose one of those values, typically using a choice component.

A
B
C
D
E
F
G
H
I
J
K
L
M
N
O
PO
Q
R
S
T
U
V
W
X
Y
Z

In short, the true purpose of a property editor is to help a bean editor construct a component for editing a property. There are several ways by which it can do this, but in general, a property editor falls into one of three kinds:

1. Property editors that convert property types to and from strings
2. Property editors that have tags
3. Property editors that support a custom editor

Each kind of property editor is described later in this item.

There is no flag that identifies with what kind of property editor a bean editor is dealing. Instead, the bean editor first checks to see if the property editor supports a custom editor (by calling supportsCustomEditor() described shortly). If it doesn't, the bean editor checks to see if the property editor has tags (by calling getTags()). If not, the bean editor assumes that the property editor is the type that converts property types to and from strings.

Property Editors That Convert Property Types To and From Strings

This kind of property editor takes the property value and converts it to a human-readable string. It also must be able to reconvert a string into a valid property value. For example, suppose the property is an integer IP address and you want the user to edit in *dotted string notation*, which has the form "byte.byte.byte.byte." The property editor would have to provide methods for converting a 32-bit IP address to and from dotted string notation. More specifically, it needs to implement the getAsText() and setAsText() methods.

Property Editors That Have Tags

Some properties have values that can be from only a small set of values. The set of four compass points is such a property. For such properties, a property editor can supply a set of *tags* by overriding getTags() and returning the tags. A tag is the name of one of the values. For example, in the case of the compass points, there would be four tags: "north," "south," "east," and "west."

When a bean editor detects this kind of property editor, it retrieves the set of tags and presents them to the user. Most bean editors typically use a Choice component to display the tags.

Unless the property is a string, the property editor must also implement getAsText() and setAsText() to convert the tags to the native property type. For example, if the compass property were actually an integer, then getAsText() and setAsText() would have to convert the tags to and from integer values.

Property Editors That Support Custom Editors

When a property cannot be represented as a single string or as a set of tags, it is necessary to provide a *custom editor*. A custom editor is a true AWT component. For example, a font is made up of at least three parts: the font family, the font style, and the font size. Such a property would be better edited with a special component rather than as a string. Figure 315 shows the Beanbox's two custom editors: color and font custom.

The bean editor is responsible for disposing of the custom editor. It does not inform the custom editor when it is about to be disposed of. This means that if the custom editor wants to "batch" the changes so that the bean property is not updated immediately, the custom editor must provide a button to allow the user to save the changes.

Unfortunately, at present, the custom editor is not informed before it is disposed of.

Note: The Beanbox in BDK 1.0apr97 requires that property editors that support custom editors have a paintable area (see the following discussion). This may not be required in other bean editors.

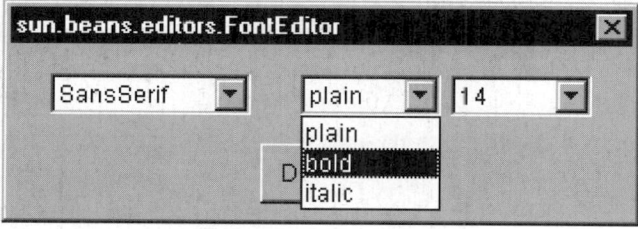

(a) Font Property Editor

The Paintable Area

The paintable area of a property editor is some visible area on the bean editor. It is used in conjunction with a custom editor and allows a bean to give some visual representation of the property value. For example, for a color property, the actual color could be painted in the paintable area. Fig-

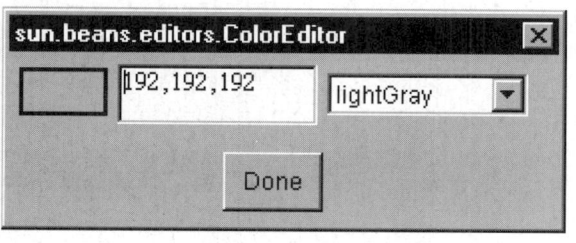

(b) Color Property Editor

FIGURE 315:   Custom Editors Provided by the Beanbox.

ure 315 shows the paintable areas for the Beanbox's color and font property editors.

The size and location of the paintable area is determined by the bean editor and cannot be controlled by the property editor.

Note: The Beanbox in BDK 1.0apr97 requires that property editors that have a paintable area also support a custom editor (see previously). This may not be required in other bean editors.

Data and Event Flow

While a bean editor is editing a bean, all of the property values in the bean are kept in sync with the property values in the property editors. Here's how it's done:

1. Just after the bean editor creates the property editor, it retrieves the property value from the bean (by invoking the read accessor method) and passes it to the property editor via a call to `setValue()`. If the property type is a primitive type, the bean editor wraps the value in the appropriate wrapper object before calling `setValue()`.
2. The bean editor registers itself with the new property editor so as to receive property change events.
3. If the property editor does not support a custom editor, the bean editor calls its `getAs-`

Text() method to retrieve a string representation of the current value. Otherwise, if the property editor does support a custom editor, the bean editor calls its getCustomEditor() method and displays the custom editor. The custom editor is responsible for initializing itself from the property editor.

4. If the user changes the property value in the property editor, the bean editor calls the property editor's setAsText() method, using the new value. The property editor then converts the new string to an object of the property type and calls setValue(). If the property value is changed through a custom editor, the custom editor must also call setValue() with the new value.

5. The setValue() method saves the new value in a private field and then fires a multichange property change event to the bean editor.

6. The bean editor receives the property change event, determines which property editor fired it, and then retrieves the new property value by calling the property editor's getValue() method.

7. The bean editor uses the new value to update the bean's property by calling the bean property's write accessor method. If the property editor supports a custom editor, the bean editor will call the property editor's paintValue() method to update the paintable area.

8. Since a change to one property can affect another property, the bean editor must retrieve all property values from the bean (by calling all of the read accessor methods) and check for changes. The bean editor maintains a list of all previous property values from the bean, so it can compare the values from this list with the retrieved property values (it simply does a reference comparison to determine if two values are the same). For each value that has changed, it calls the setValue() method for the appropriate property editor with the new value.

Note: If a property in the bean changed, the property editor showing its value is not immediately updated. However, that property editor will be updated as soon as the user uses any property editor to make a change.

MEMBER SUMMARY	
Value Methods	
getValue()	Retrieves the current property value.
setValue()	Sets a new value for the property.
String Conversion Methods	
getAsText()	Generates a string representation of the property value.
setAsText()	Converts a string representation of a property value to an object of the property type.
Tag Method	
getTags()	Retrieves the property editor's tag list, if any.

MEMBER SUMMARY	
Paint Methods	
isPaintable()	Determines if the property editor can paint a representation of the property.
paintValue()	Called to paint a representation of the property value.
Custom Editor Methods	
getCustomEditor()	Retrieves the property editor's custom editor, if any.
supportsCustomEditor()	Determines whether the property editor supports a custom editor.
Listener Methods	
addPropertyChangeListener()	Adds a listener for receiving property change events.
removePropertyChangeListener()	Stops a listener from receiving property change events.
Java Initialization String Method	
getJavaInitializationString()	Generates a fragment of Java source code for creating an instance of the property value.

See Also

PropertyEditorSupport.

Example

This example demonstrates a simple property editor that uses tags. The example has a property called "flavor." Although the property is a string, it can hold only a string that is from a fixed set of strings. A property editor, FlavorEditor, is defined for the flavor property. Since the property is a string, only the get-

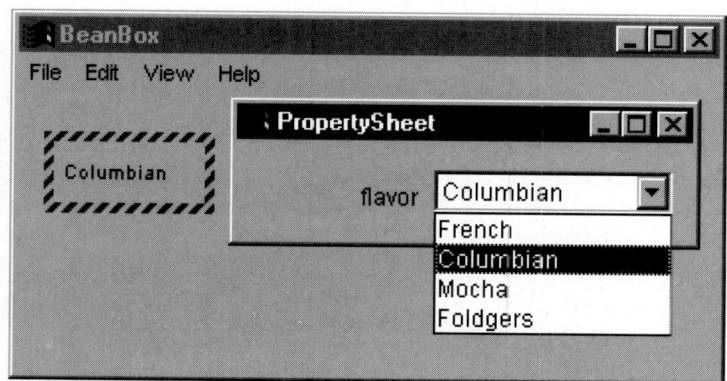

FIGURE 316: FlavorEditor.

Tags() method needs to be overridden in order to return the list of flavors. See Figure 316. (For an example of where the property is an int, see the PropertyEditorSupport.setAsText() example.)

A bean-info is necessary to associate `FlavorEditor` with the bean's "flavor" property. The bean-info must be defined in a class, with the bean's name appended with "`BeanInfo`," in this case, is `BeanBeanInfo`.

Bean.java

```java
import java.awt.*;
import java.beans.*;

public class Bean extends Panel {
    public static String[] flavors =
        {"French", "Columbian", "Mocha", "Foldgers"};
    String curFlavor = flavors[0];

    // Use a label to display the current flavor.
    Label l = new Label(curFlavor);

    public Bean() {
        add(l);
    }
    public String getFlavor() {
        return curFlavor;
    }
    public void setFlavor(String f) {
        l.setText(curFlavor = f);
    }
}
/*
    manifest.txt:
        Name: Bean.class
        Java-Bean: True
    jar command:
        jar cfm bean.jar manifest.txt Bean.class FlavorEditor.class BeanBean-
Info.class
*/
```

FlavorEditor.java

```java
import java.beans.*;

public class FlavorEditor extends PropertyEditorSupport {
    public String[] getTags() {
        return Bean.flavors;
    }
}
```

BeanBeanInfo.java

```java
import java.beans.*;

public class BeanBeanInfo extends SimpleBeanInfo {
    public PropertyDescriptor[] getPropertyDescriptors() {
        PropertyDescriptor pd[] = new PropertyDescriptor[1];

        try {
            pd[0] = new PropertyDescriptor("flavor", Bean.class);
            pd[0].setPropertyEditorClass(FlavorEditor.class);
            pd[0].setBound(true);
            return pd;
        } catch (Exception e) {
```

```
        e.printStackTrace();
        return null;
      }
    }
  }
```

addPropertyChangeListener()

PURPOSE   Adds a listener for receiving property change events.

SYNTAX   `void addPropertyChangeListener(PropertyChangeListener listener)`

DESCRIPTION   This method should add `listener` to the listener list. After calling this method, the property editor should notify `listener` of any changes to the property by way of property change events. The property name, old value, and new value fields of the events will all be set to `null`.

This method is typically called by a bean editor so that it can be notified when the user changes the value in the property editor.

PARAMETERS
`listener`   A non-`null` property change event listener.

SEE ALSO   `removePropertyChangeListener()`.

EXAMPLE   See the `PropertyChangeEvent` class example as an example of how to use `PropertyChangeSupport` to implement this method.

getAsText()

PURPOSE   Generates a string representation of the property value.

SYNTAX   `String getAsText()`

DESCRIPTION   If the property editor does not have a custom editor and the bean property is not a string, it is necessary to provide methods to convert the property type to and from a string. This method converts the property type to a string in a form that `setAsText()` can reconvert to the property type.

This method typically retrieves the property value to convert by calling `getValue()`.

If a custom editor is available or if the property is a string, the property editor does not need to do string conversions, so this method should simply return `null`.

RETURNS   The possibly `null` string representing the property value.

SEE ALSO   `getValue()`, `setAsText()`.

EXAMPLE   See the `PropertyEditorSupport` class example, `PropertyEditorSup-`
`port.getCustomEditor()`, and `PropertyEditorSupport.getAsText()`.

getCustomEditor()

PURPOSE   Retrieves the property editor's custom editor, if any.

SYNTAX   `Component getCustomEditor()`

DESCRIPTION   When a property cannot be represented as a single string or as a set of tags, it is necessary to provide a *custom editor*. A custom editor is a component specially designed for editing the property. It must not be a window, since the bean editor needs to insert it into an existing container. In the case of the Beanbox, the custom editor is inserted into a frame by clicking a Done button.

A property editor should implement this method to return the custom editor. If no custom editor is available, `null` should be returned.

The custom editor is typically created when this method is called. It should provide a means for reporting changes to the property editor as the user interacts with the custom editor. The simplest way is for the custom editor to save a reference to the property editor and call the property editor's `setValue()` or `setAsText()` methods when appropriate. Another way is for the custom editor to fire property change events whenever the value changes. The custom editor will then have to provide the property change listener methods so that the property editor can register for events. See `PropertyChangeSupport` for more details on how to do this.

RETURNS   A possibly `null` component for editing the property.

SEE ALSO   `supportsCustomEditor()`.

EXAMPLE   See `PropertyEditorSupport.getCustomEditor()`.

getJavaInitializationString()

PURPOSE   Generates a fragment of Java source code for creating an instance of the property value.

SYNTAX   `String getJavaInitializationString()`

DESCRIPTION   This method should take the current value (as returned by `getValue()`) and generate a fragment of Java source code that, when compiled (within a compilation unit), will yield the current value in the property's type. The fragment may create an object; in this case, it must include the new keyword and fully qualified object type.

This method is used by some bean editors to generate initialization Java source code. When compiled and run, this code will initialize the properties of a bean.

RETURNS   A non-`null` fragment of Java source code.

EXAMPLE   If the property type is `float`:

```
public String getJavaInitializationString() {
    return "" + getValue() + "f";
}
```

If the property type is `Font`:

```
public String getJavaInitializationString() {
    Font f = (Font)getValue();
    return "new java.awt.Font(\"" + f.getFamily() - "\", " +
        f.getStyle() + ", " + f.getSize() + ")";
}
```

getTags()

PURPOSE   Retrieves the property editor's tag list, if any.

SYNTAX   `String[] getTags()`

DESCRIPTION   If the property editor uses tags, the implementation of this method should return a non-`null` array of tags. See the class description for more information about tags,

If the type of the property is not a string, then `getAsText()` and `setAsText()` must be implemented to return and accept any of the tags. See the method descriptions for details.

RETURNS   A possibly `null` array of tags.

SEE ALSO   `getAsText()`, `setAsText()`.

EXAMPLE   See `PropertyEditorSupport.getTags()`.

getValue()

PURPOSE   Retrieves the current property value.

SYNTAX   `Object getValue()`

DESCRIPTION   This method should simply return the most recent value passed in by `set-Value()`. It is typically called by the bean editor immediately after it receives a property change event from some property editor in order to determine if the property has changed. This method can be called by `getAsText()` when it needs to create a string representation of the property value.

A
B
C
D
E
F
G
H
I
J
K
L
M
N
O
P
Q
R
S
T
U
V
W
X
Y
Z

If the property type is a primitive type, this method will return the property value contained in the corresponding wrapper object. For example, if the primitive type is `boolean`, the returned object will be a `Boolean` object. This method does not have to create the wrapper object, since the wrapper object will already have been created before `setValue()` is called.

The returned value should be treated as immutable and should not be modified.

RETURNS   The possibly `null` current property value.

SEE ALSO   `getAsText()`, `setValue()`.

EXAMPLE   See `PropertyEditorSupport.getAsText()`.

A
B
C
D
E
F
G

isPaintable()

H
I
J
K
L
M
N
O
P
Q
R
S
T
U
V
W
X
Y
Z

PURPOSE   Determines if the property editor can paint a representation of the property.

SYNTAX   `boolean isPaintable()`

DESCRIPTION If the property editor can paint a representation of the property, the implementation of this method should return `true`. For example, if the property is a color, this method could paint the color. Or if the property is an image, this method could paint a scaled version of the image.

This method is typically called by the bean editor. If this method returns `true`, the bean editor will also call the property editor's `paintValue()` method whenever the property value must be painted.

Note: The Beanbox in the BDK 1.0apr97 ignores this method unless `supportsCustomEditor()` also returns `true`. This may not be required in other bean editors.

RETURNS   `true` if the property editor can paint a representation of the property; `false` otherwise.

EXAMPLE   See `PropertyEditorSupport.getCustomEditor()`.

paintValue()

PURPOSE   Called to paint a representation of the property value.

SYNTAX   `void paintValue(Graphics g, Rectangle box)`

DESCRIPTION If `isPaintable()` is `true`, this method will be called by the bean editor to allow the property editor to paint a representation of the property value within the box. For example, if the property is a color, this method could paint the color in the box. Or if the property is an image, this method could paint a scaled version of the image in the box. This method is called each time the property editor fires a property change event.

The size and location of box is determined by the bean editor and cannot by specified by the property editor.

If this method might paint outside the box rectangle, it must set the clipping rectangle on g. The box instance is a new instance, so it can be modified without affecting the bean editor's state.

Note: When the Beanbox in BDK 1.0apr97 is used, the width and height of box are 2 pixels too wide and 2 pixels too high. Subtract 2 from both the width and height to get the true dimensions.

PARAMETERS

box   A new non-`null` `Rectangle` specifying the area in g in which to paint.

g   A new non-`null` graphics context on which to paint.

SEE ALSO   `java.awt.Graphics`, `java.awt.Rectangle`.

EXAMPLE   See `PropertyEditorSupport.getCustomEditor()`.

removePropertyChangeListener()

PURPOSE   Stops a listener from receiving property change events.

SYNTAX   `void removePropertyChangeListener(PropertyChangeListener`
                          `listener)`

DESCRIPTION   This method should remove `listener` from the listener list. If `listener` is not in the listener list, the method call should be ignored.

The implementation of this method does not have to stop delivery of events immediately. That is, after this method is called, the listener may receive a few more property change events. See `PropertyChangeListener` for more details.

PARAMETERS

listener   A non-`null` property change event listener.

SEE ALSO   `addPropertyChangeListener()`.

EXAMPLE   See the `PropertyChangeEvent` class example for an example of how to use `PropertyChangeSupport` to implement this method.

setAsText()

PURPOSE	Converts a string representation of a property value to an object of the property type.
SYNTAX	`void setAsText(String text) throws IllegalArgumentException`
DESCRIPTION	If the property editor does not have a custom editor and the bean property is not a string, methods must be provided to convert the property type to and from a string. The `getAsText()` method converts the property type to a string. This method must be able to reconvert the string to the property type.

If the property type is a primitive type, the new value must be wrapped in the appropriate wrapper object. For example, if the property type is `boolean`, then the new value must be wrapped in a `Boolean` object.

If `text` is successfully converted to a valid property value, this method must call `setValue()` with the new value. (Note that the value passed to `set-Value()` must be a new instance of the property type; this method must not modify the current property value.) `setValue()` will notify the bean editor that the value has changed.

PARAMETERS

text   The non-`null` string representation of the property value.

EXCEPTIONS

`IllegalArgumentException`
                If `text` cannot be converted to a valid property value.

SEE ALSO   `getAsText()`, `java.lang.IllegalArgumentException`, `setValue()`.

EXAMPLE   See `PropertyEditorSupport.setAsText()`.

setValue()

PURPOSE	Sets a new value for the property.
SYNTAX	`void setValue(Object value)`
DESCRIPTION	This method is called by the bean editor to initialize the property editor just after it is created. It is also called whenever the user changes the value of the property. For example, if the property is the label of a button, this method will be called each time the user changes the button's label.

If the value has indeed changed, the caller should create a completely new instance of the value before calling `setValue()`. That is,
    `getValue() != value`.

See the class description for more details. The new value should be stored in a private field in the property editor. The bean editor will later retrieve the new value (via a call to getValue()) and then directly update the property value in the bean.

This method may also be called by setAsText() when a string representation of the property value is converted to an object of the property type.

If the property type is a primitive type, the new value must be wrapped in the appropriate wrapper object. For example, if the property type is boolean, then the new value must be wrapped in a Boolean object.

This method must also fire a property change event to any property change event listeners. The property change event should be a multichange event (see PropertyChangeEvent), so the property name, old value, and new value should all be null.

PARAMETERS

value   The possibly null new property value.

SEE ALSO   getValue(), setAsText().

EXAMPLE   See the PropertyEditorSupport class example, PropertyEditorSupport.getCustomEditor(), and PropertyEditorSupport.setAsText().

supportsCustomEditor()

PURPOSE   Determines whether the property editor supports a custom editor.

SYNTAX   boolean supportsCustomEditor()

DESCRIPTION   A property editor should implement this method to return true if a custom editor is available; false otherwise.

Note: The Beanbox in the BDK 1.0apr97 ignores this method unless isPaintable() also returns true. This may not be required in other bean editors.

RETURNS   true if the property editor supports a custom editor.

SEE ALSO   getCustomEditor().

EXAMPLE   See PropertyEditorSupport.getCustomEditor().

A
B
C
D
E
F
G
H
I
J
K
L
M
N
O
P
Q
R
S
T
U
V
W
X
Y
Z

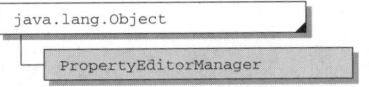

```
java.lang.Object
    PropertyEditorManager
```

Syntax

`public class PropertyEditorManager`

Description

The `PropertyEditorManager` is used to locate a property editor (see `PropertyEditor`) for a particular type. For example, if the type is `int.class`, the property editor manager will try to locate a property editor suitable for editing integer values.

The property editor manager supplies property editors for the following types:

```
boolean
byte
short
int
long
float
double,
java.lang.String
java.awt.Color
java.awt.Font
```

You may override your own property editor for any of these types, or you may provide new property editors for new types.

The Search Path

When the property editor manager does not have a registered property editor for a type, it tries to find one. Where it looks is determined by the *search path*. The search path is an array of package names; the way in which these package names are used is described in the next section.

The property editor manager's default search path is `sun.beans.editors`.

Locating a Property Editor

When no association between a requested type and a property editor exists, the property editor manager tries to find one. It first takes the package-qualified class name and appends the string "Editor". It then tries to instantiate a class with that name. For example, if the type is `java.awt.Image`, it tries to instantiate a class named `java.awt.ImageEditor`.

If no class with that name is found, it removes the package name from the class name. For example, `java.awt.ImageEditor` becomes `ImageEditor`. It then prefixes each of the package names in the search path with the class name (separated by ".") and then tries to instantiate that class. For example, if the search path contained `sun.first` and `sun.second`, the property editor manager tries to instantiate `sun.first.ImageEditor`. If that fails, it tries `sun.second.ImageEditor`.

MEMBER SUMMARY

Find Method
`findEditor()`	Locates a property editor for a type.

Registration Method
`registerEditor()`	Associates a property editor with a type.

Search Path Methods
`getEditorSearchPath()`	Retrieves the property manager's search path.
`setEditorSearchPath()`	Sets the property manager's search path.

See Also
`PropertyEditor`.

Example

This example implements a bean that, when loaded (it doesn't even need to be instantiated), replaces the property editor manager's default color editor. This means that after this bean is loaded, all beans that have the type `Color` will use the replacement color editor.

The color editor is in the package "editors," so the "editors" package name needs to be inserted in the property editor manager's search path. Next, the current color editor entry in the property editor manager is cleared. Then the next time the bean editor looks for a color property editor, it will find the replacement version, since the package name is placed in the search path before its own.

The bean also implements a dummy property of the type `Image`. Since there is no default image property editor, the property editor manager tries to find one and will locate the one in the editors package.

Bean.java
```
import java.awt.*;
import java.beans.*;

public class Bean extends Component {
    public Bean() {
    }

    // Some dummy methods.
    public Image getImage() {
        // Need to return a non-null image, otherwise
        // property editor is not created.
        return createImage(1, 1);
```

```
        }
        public void setImage(Image image) {
        }

        static {
            String[] searchPath = PropertyEditorManager.getEditorSearchPath();
            String[] newPath = new String[searchPath.length + 1];

            newPath[0] = "editors";
            for (int i=0; i<searchPath.length; i++) {
                newPath[i+1] = searchPath[i];
            }
            PropertyEditorManager.setEditorSearchPath(newPath);

            // Clear out current entry.
            PropertyEditorManager.registerEditor(Color.class, null);

            // Rather than set search path, the bean could instead explicitly
            // register the property editor, like so:
            //PropertyEditorManager.registerEditor(Color.class,
            //    editors.ColorEditor.class);

            // Just checking to see if the search path worked.
            PropertyEditor pe = null;
            try {
                pe = PropertyEditorManager.findEditor(Color.class);
                if (pe == null) {
                    System.err.println("Could not find the color editor");
                }

                String s = pe.getClass().getName();
                if (!s.equals("editors.ColorEditor")) {
                    System.err.println("Wrong color editor found");
                }
            } catch (Exception e) {
                e.printStackTrace();
            }
        }
    }
    /*
        manifest.txt:
            Name: Bean.class
            Java-Bean: True
        jar command:
            jar cfm bean.jar manifest.txt *.class editors/*.class
    */
```

ColorEditor.java

```
    package editors;

    import java.awt.*;
    import java.awt.event.*;
    import java.beans.*;
    import java.util.*;

    public class ColorEditor extends PropertyEditorSupport {
        public boolean isPaintable() {
            return true;
```

```
    }

    public void paintValue(Graphics g, Rectangle box) {
        g.setColor((Color)getValue());
        g.fillRect(box.x, box.y, box.width, box.height);
        g.setColor(Color.black);
        // There's a bug in the bean box where box width and height are too
        // big by 4 pixels.
        g.drawRect(box.x, box.y, box.width-5, box.height-5);
    }

    public boolean supportsCustomEditor() {
        return true;
    }

    public java.awt.Component getCustomEditor() {
        return new ColorCustomEditor(this, (Color)getValue());
    }
}
```

A
B
C
D
E
F
G
H
I
J
K
L
M
N
O

Q
R
S
T
U
V
W
X
Y
Z

findEditor()

PURPOSE   Locates a property editor for a type.

SYNTAX   `public static PropertyEditor findEditor(Class targetType)`

DESCRIPTION   The property editor manager first checks to see if a property editor has been registered for `targetType`. If one has not, it tries to locate the property editor. See the class description for details on how this is done. If no property editor is found, `null` is returned.

PARAMETERS

`targetType`   A non-`null` `Class` object.

RETURNS   A possibly `null` property editor for `targetType`.

EXAMPLE   See the class example.

getEditorSearchPath()

PURPOSE   Retrieves the property manager's search path.

SYNTAX   `public static String[] getEditorSearchPath()`

DESCRIPTION   This method returns the property editor manager's search path, which is used to find a property editor when a property editor has not been explicitly registered for a type. See the class description for details on how the search path is used.

The search path initially contains a single element: `sun.beans.editors`.

RETURNS	A non-null array of package names.
SEE ALSO	setEditorSearchPath().
EXAMPLE	See the class example.

registerEditor()

PURPOSE	Associates a property editor with a type.
SYNTAX	public static void registerEditor(Class targetType, Class editorClass)
DESCRIPTION	This method explicitly associates a type targetType with a property editor editorClass. If a property editor was already associated with targetType, it will be overridden with editorClass. If editorClass is null, this method will remove any association of a property editor with targetType. In this case, when a property editor is needed for targetType, the property editor manager needs to search for one (see the class description for more details).
	Changing associations using this method affects all beans in the bean environment. For example, setting a new property editor for int (i.e., Integer.TYPE) means any bean property with type int will use the new property editor.

PARAMETERS

editorClass	The possibly null Class object of the property editor.
targetType	The non-null Class object of the type.

EXAMPLE	See the class example.

setEditorSearchPath()

PURPOSE	Sets the property manager's search path.
SYNTAX	public static void setEditorSearchPath(String path[])
DESCRIPTION	This method sets the property editor manager's search path, which is used to find a property editor when a property editor has not been explicitly registered for a type. See the class description for details on how the search path is used.
	When setting a new search path, you should include the elements of the current search path in the new search path. The old search path can be retrieved by calling getEditorSearchPath().

PARAMETERS

path	A possibly null array of package names.

SEE ALSO	getEditorSearchPath().
EXAMPLE	See the class example.

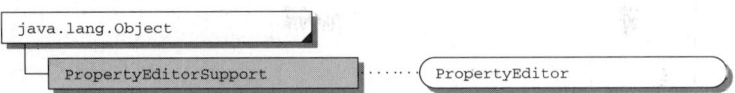

```
java.lang.Object
      PropertyEditorSupport    ........  PropertyEditor
```

Syntax
`public class PropertyEditorSupport implements PropertyEditor`

Description

A *property editor* is essentially a user interface for editing a bean property. When a bean editor edits a bean, it needs to create a property editor for each of the bean's properties. A bean editor provides a default property editor for a number of types, but if a property type is not one of these, then you must provide a property editor for that property type. This class provides a convenient superclass for building a property editor. See `PropertyEditor` for complete information on property editors and how to build them.

MEMBER SUMMARY	
Constructor	
PropertyEditorSupport()	Constructs a new PropertyEditorSupport instance.
Value Methods	
getValue()	Retrieves the current property value.
setValue()	Sets a new value for the property.
Text Methods	
getAsText()	Generates a string representation of the property value.
setAsText()	Converts a string representation of a property value to an object of the property type.
Tag Method	
getTags()	Retrieves the property editor's tag list, if any.
Custom Editor Methods	
getCustomEditor()	Retrieves the property editor's custom editor, if any.
supportsCustomEditor()	Determines whether the property editor supports a custom editor.
	Continued

MEMBER SUMMARY

Paint Methods

isPaintable()	Determines if the property editor can paint a representation of the property.
paintValue()	Called to paint a representation of the property value.

Listener Methods

addPropertyChangeListener()	Adds a listener for receiving property change events.
firePropertyChange()	Delivers a property change event to the listeners.
removePropertyChangeListener()	Removes a listener from receiving property change events.

Initialization String Method

getJavaInitializationString()	Generates a fragment of Java source code for creating an instance of the property value.

See Also

PropertyChangeEvent, PropertyChangeListener, PropertyEditor.

Example

FIGURE 317:　Locale-sensitive Date Bean and Editor.

This example implements a date bean that can display a date in any locale. (For simpler examples of property editors, see the method examples in this class.)

The date bean has three properties: date, locale, and date format style. The date property is represented by a `Date` object and basically contains the day, month, and year. The locale property contains one of the available locales. The style property is an attribute of the date formatter and specifies how long the string representation of the date should be (see `java.text.DateFormat` for more details). See Figure 317.

The `DateEditor` demonstrates a property editor that converts a property type, `Date`, to and from a string. Both `LocaleEditor` and `StyleEditor` demonstrate property editors that use tags.

A bean-info is necessary to associate the three property editors with the bean's property. The bean-info must be defined in a class with the bean's name appended with "`BeanInfo`," in this case, `BeanBeanInfo`.

Bean.java
```
import java.awt.*;
import java.beans.*;
import java.text.*;
import java.util.*;

public class Bean extends Panel {
    public Date date = new Date();
    public Locale locale = Locale.getDefault();
    public int style = DateFormat.MEDIUM;

    // Use a label to display the current flavor.
    Label l = new Label(toString());

    public Bean() {
        add(l);
    }

    // Date accessor methods.
    public Date getDate() {
        return date;
    }
    public void setDate(Date date) {
        this.date = date;
        l.setText(toString());
    }

    // Format Style accessor methods.
    public int getStyle() {
        return style;
    }
    public void setStyle(int style) {
        this.style = style;
        l.setText(toString());
    }

    // Locale accessor methods.
    public Locale getLocale() {
        return locale;
    }
    public void setLocale(Locale locale) {
        this.locale = locale;
        l.setText(toString());
```

```
        }

        // Converts the date into a string using the current locale and style.
        public String toString() {
            return DateFormat.getDateInstance(style, locale).format(date);
        }
    }
    /*
        manifest.txt:
            Name: Bean.class
            Java-Bean: True
        jar command:
            jar cfm bean.jar manifest.txt *.class
    */
```

BeanBeanInfo.java

```
    import java.beans.*;

    public class BeanBeanInfo extends SimpleBeanInfo {
        public PropertyDescriptor[] getPropertyDescriptors() {
            PropertyDescriptor pd[] = new PropertyDescriptor[3];

            try {
                pd[0] = new PropertyDescriptor("date", Bean.class);
                pd[0].setPropertyEditorClass(DateEditor.class);
                pd[1] = new PropertyDescriptor("style", Bean.class);
                pd[1].setPropertyEditorClass(StyleEditor.class);
                pd[2] = new PropertyDescriptor("locale", Bean.class);
                pd[2].setPropertyEditorClass(LocaleEditor.class);
                return pd;
            } catch (Exception e) {
                e.printStackTrace();
                return null;
            }
        }
    }
```

DateEditor.java

```
    import java.beans.*;
    import java.text.*;
    import java.util.*;

    // This property editor allows the user to edit the date
    // in the default locale, using the SHORT format.

    public class DateEditor extends PropertyEditorSupport {
        public String getAsText() {
            return DateFormat.getDateInstance(
                DateFormat.SHORT, Locale.getDefault()).format(((Date)getValue()));
        }

        public void setAsText(String text) throws IllegalArgumentException {
            try {
                setValue(DateFormat.getDateInstance(
                    DateFormat.SHORT, Locale.getDefault()).parse(text));
                return;
            } catch (Exception e) {
                // It doesn't matter what the exception is.
```

```
        }
        throw new IllegalArgumentException(text);
    }
}
```

LocaleEditor.java

```java
import java.beans.*;
import java.text.*;
import java.util.*;

public class LocaleEditor extends PropertyEditorSupport {
    Locale[] locales = DateFormat.getAvailableLocales();
    String[] localeNames = new String[locales.length];

    public LocaleEditor() {
        super();
        for (int i=0; i<locales.length; i++) {
            localeNames[i] = locales[i].getDisplayName();
        }
    }

    public String[] getTags() {
        return localeNames;
    }

    public String getAsText() {
        return ((Locale)getValue()).getDisplayName();
    }

    public void setAsText(String text) throws IllegalArgumentException {
        for (int i=0; i<locales.length; i++) {
            if (text.equals(localeNames[i])) {
                setValue(locales[i]);
                return;
            }
        }
        throw new IllegalArgumentException(text);
    }
}
```

StyleEditor.java

```java
import java.beans.*;
import java.text.*;

public class StyleEditor extends PropertyEditorSupport {
    int[] styleValues =
        {DateFormat.SHORT, DateFormat.MEDIUM,
         DateFormat.LONG, DateFormat.FULL};
    String[] styleNames =
        {"SHORT", "MEDIUM", "LONG", "FULL"};

    public String[] getTags() {
        return styleNames;
    }

    public String getAsText() {
        int s = ((Integer)getValue()).intValue();
```

```
                for (int i=0; i<styleNames.length; i++) {
                    if (s == styleValues[i]) {
                        return styleNames[i    ];
                    }
                }
                // This should not occur
                return null;
            }

            public void setAsText(String text) throws IllegalArgumentException {
                for (int i=0; i<styleNames.length; i++) {
                    if (text.equals(styleNames[i])) {
                        setValue(new Integer(styleValues[i]));
                        return;
                    }
                }
                throw new IllegalArgumentException(text);
            }
        }
```

addPropertyChangeListener()

PURPOSE   Adds a listener for receiving property change events.

SYNTAX

```
public synchronized void
    addPropertyChangeListener(PropertyChangeListener listener)
```

DESCRIPTION   This method adds `listener` to the listener list. The method does not check if `listener` has already been added, so a listener can be added to the list more than once.

Unless you need to distribute events in a way different from this implementation, it is not necessary to override this method. However, if this method is overridden, then two other methods must also be overridden: `removePropertyChangeListener()` and `firePropertyChange()`.

This method is typically called by a bean editor so that it can be notified when the user changes the value in the property editor.

PARAMETERS

listener   A non-`null` property change event listener.

SEE ALSO   `removePropertyChangeListener()`, `firePropertyChange()`.

EXAMPLE   See the `PropertyChangeEvent` class example.

firePropertyChange()

PURPOSE   Delivers a property change event to the listeners.

SYNTAX   `public void firePropertyChange()`

DESCRIPTION   This method creates a new property change event and delivers it to all listeners. The source of the event is this object. All of the other properties of the event—property name, old value, new value—are `null`.

Listeners should not throw exceptions. Exceptions thrown are considered programming errors.

SEE ALSO   `PropertyChangeEvent.`

EXAMPLE   See `setValue()`.

getAsText()

PURPOSE   Generates a string representation of the property value.

SYNTAX   `public String getAsText()`

DESCRIPTION   If the property type is a string, this method returns the property value; otherwise, it returns `null`. If the property editor does not have a custom editor and the bean property is not a string, this method should be overridden to generate a string representation of the current property value. The string representation must be in a form that can be reconverted to the property value by `setAsText()`.

This method should retrieve the property value to convert by calling `getValue()`.

RETURNS   The possibly-`null` string representing the property value.

SEE ALSO   `getValue(), setAsText().`

EXAMPLE   This example bean has a property called "align," which is an integer in a fixed range of integers. The range is small, so the property is made a tagged property. A property editor, `AlignEditor`, is defined and returns the alignment names as tags. Since the alignment is an integer and

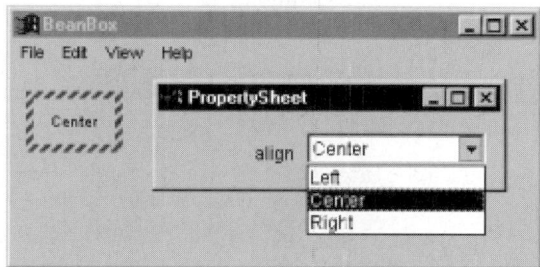

FIGURE 318: "Align" Property Editor.

not a string, `AlignEditor` needs to convert integer values to strings and vice versa. It does this by overriding `getAsText()` and `setAsText()`. See Figure 318.

A bean-info is necessary to associate `AlignEditor` with the bean's align property. It must be defined in a class with the bean's name appended with "Bean-Info," in this case, `BeanBeanInfo`.

Bean.java

```
import java.awt.*;
import java.beans.*;

public class Bean extends Panel {
    public static final int LEFT = 0;
    public static final int CENTER = 1;
    public static final int RIGHT = 2;

    public static String[] alignNames =
        {"Left", "Center", "Right"};

    int curAlign = CENTER;

    // Use a label to display the current flavor.
    Label l = new Label(alignNames[curAlign], CENTER);

    public Bean() {
        add(l);
    }
    public int getAlign() {
        return curAlign;
    }
    public void setAlign(int a) {
        l.setText(alignNames[curAlign = a]);
        l.setAlignment(a);
    }
}
/*
    manifest.txt:
        Name: Bean.class
        Java-Bean: True
    jar command:
        jar cfm bean.jar manifest.txt Bean.class AlignEditor.class BeanBean-
Info.class
*/
```

AlignEditor.java

```
import java.beans.*;

public class AlignEditor extends PropertyEditorSupport {
    public String[] getTags() {
        return Bean.alignNames;
    }

    public String getAsText() {
        return Bean.alignNames[((Integer)getValue()).intValue()];
    }

    public void setAsText(String text) throws IllegalArgumentException {
        for (int i=0; i<Bean.alignNames.length; i++) {
            if (Bean.alignNames[i].equals(text)) {
                setValue(new Integer(i));
                return;
```

```
                }
            }
            throw new IllegalArgumentException(text);
        }
    }
```

BeanBeanInfo.java
```
    import java.beans.*;

    public class BeanBeanInfo extends SimpleBeanInfo {
        public PropertyDescriptor[] getPropertyDescriptors() {
            PropertyDescriptor pd[] = new PropertyDescriptor[1];

            try {
                pd[0] = new PropertyDescriptor("align", Bean.class);
                pd[0].setPropertyEditorClass(AlignEditor.class);
                return pd;
            } catch (Exception e) {
                e.printStackTrace();
                return null;
            }
        }
    }
```

getCustomEditor()

PURPOSE   Retrieves the property editor's custom editor, if any.

SYNTAX   `public Component getCustomEditor()`

DESCRIPTION   When a property cannot be represented as a single string or as a set of tags, a *custom editor* must be provided. A custom editor is a component specially designed for editing the property. It must not be a window, since the bean editor needs to insert it into an existing container. In the case of the Beanbox, the custom editor is inserted into a frame by clicking a Done button.

This method by default returns `null`. If a custom editor is available, a property editor should override this method and return the custom editor.

The custom editor is typically created when this method is called. It should provide a means for reporting changes to the property editor as the user interacts with the custom editor. The simplest way to do this is for the custom editor to save a reference to the property editor and call the property editor's `set-Value()` or `setAsText()` methods when appropriate. Another way is for the custom editor to fire property change events whenever the value changes. The custom editor would then have to provide the property change listener methods so that the property editor can register for events. See `PropertyChangeSupport` for more details on how to do this.

RETURNS   `null`. Override to return the custom editor.

A

B

C

D

E

F

G

H

I

J

K

L

M

N

O

P

Q

R

S

T

U

V

W

X

Y

Z

SEE ALSO   supportsCustomEditor().

EXAMPLE   This example implements a `Color` property editor different from the one provided by the Beanbox. This color editor has three scrollbars for adjusting the hue, saturation, and brightness of the color. See Figure 319.

A bean-info is necessary to associate the `ColorEditor` class with the bean's two color properties: foreground and background. The bean-info must be defined in a class with the bean's name appended with "BeanInfo," in this case, `BeanBeanInfo`.

Bean.java
```java
import java.awt.*;
import java.beans.*;

public class Bean
    extends Component {
    public Bean() {
        setSize(100, 50);
    }

    // Paint the background color
    // on the left and the fore-
    // ground color on the right.
    public void paint(Graphics g)
    {
        g.clearRect(0, 0,
            getSize().width/2,
            getSize().height);
        g.fillRect(
            getSize().width/2, 0, getSize().width/2, getSize().height);
    }
}
/*
    manifest.txt:
        Name: Bean.class
        Java-Bean: True
    jar command:
        jar cfm bean.jar manifest.txt *.class
*/
```

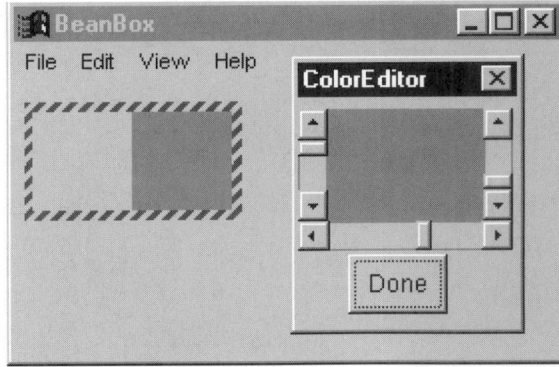

FIGURE 319:   Custom Color Property Editor.

ColorEditor.java
```java
import java.awt.*;
import java.awt.event.*;
import java.beans.*;
import java.util.*;

public class ColorEditor extends PropertyEditorSupport {
    public boolean isPaintable() {
        return true;
    }

    public void paintValue(Graphics g, Rectangle box) {
        g.setColor((Color)getValue());
        g.fillRect(box.x, box.y, box.width, box.height);
        g.setColor(Color.black);
```

```
        // There's a bug in the bean box where box width and height are too
        // big by 4 pixels.
        g.drawRect(box.x, box.y, box.width-5, box.height-5);
    }

    public boolean supportsCustomEditor() {
        return true;
    }

    public java.awt.Component getCustomEditor() {
        return new ColorCustomEditor(this, (Color)getValue());
    }
}
```

ColorCustomEditor.java

```
    import java.awt.*;
    import java.awt.event.*;
    import java.beans.*;

    public class ColorCustomEditor extends Panel implements AdjustmentListener {
        Color curColor;
        PropertyEditor pe;
        Scrollbar hSbar = new Scrollbar(Scrollbar.VERTICAL, 500, 1, 0, 1000);
        Scrollbar sSbar = new Scrollbar(Scrollbar.HORIZONTAL, 500, 1, 0, 1000);
        Scrollbar bSbar = new Scrollbar(Scrollbar.VERTICAL, 500, 1, 0, 1000);

        public ColorCustomEditor(PropertyEditor pe, Color c) {
            if (c == null) {
                c = Color.gray;
            }
            float[] hsbvals =
                Color.RGBtoHSB(c.getRed(), c.getGreen(), c.getBlue(), null);

            this.pe = pe;
            curColor = c;
            setLayout(new BorderLayout());

            hSbar.addAdjustmentListener(this);
            sSbar.addAdjustmentListener(this);
            bSbar.addAdjustmentListener(this);
            hSbar.setValue((int)Math.round(hsbvals[0]*1000));
            sSbar.setValue((int)Math.round(hsbvals[1]*1000));
            bSbar.setValue((int)Math.round(hsbvals[2]*1000));
            add(hSbar, BorderLayout.WEST);
            add(sSbar, BorderLayout.SOUTH);
            add(bSbar, BorderLayout.EAST);
        }

        public Dimension getPreferredSize() {
            return new Dimension(100, 100);
        }

        public void paint(Graphics g) {
            g.setColor(curColor);
            g.fillRect(0, 0, getSize().width, getSize().height);
        }

        public void adjustmentValueChanged(AdjustmentEvent evt) {
```

A
B
C
D
E
F
G
H
I
J
K
L
M
N
O
P
Q
R
S
T
U
V
W
X
Y
Z

```
                curColor = Color.getHSBColor(
                    hSbar.getValue()/1000.0f,
                    sSbar.getValue()/1000.0f,
                    bSbar.getValue()/1000.0f);
                pe.setValue(curColor);
                repaint();
            }
        }
```

A
B
C
D

getJavaInitializationString()

PURPOSE   Generates a fragment of Java source code for creating an instance of the property value.

SYNTAX   `public String getJavaInitializationString()`

DESCRIPTION   This method should take the current value as returned by `getValue()` and generate a fragment of Java source code that, when compiled (within a compilation unit), will yield the current value in the property's type. The fragment may create an object. In this case, it must include the new keyword and the fully qualified object type.

RETURNS   A non-`null` fragment of Java source code.

EXAMPLE   If the property type is a `float`:
```
public String getJavaInitializationString() {
    return "" + getValue() + "f";
}
```
If the property type is a `font`:
```
public String getJavaInitializationString() {
    Font f = (Font)getValue();
    return "new java.awt.Font(\"" + f.getFamily() + "\", " +
        f.getStyle() + ", " + f.getSize() + ")";
}
```

getTags()

PURPOSE   Retrieves the property editor's tag list, if any.

SYNTAX   `public String[] getTags()`

DESCRIPTION   If the property editor is one that uses tags, this method should be overridden to return a non-`null` array of tags. See the class description for more information about tags,

If the type of the property is not `String`, then `getAsText()` and `setAsText()` must be overridden to return and accept any of the tags. See the method descriptions for details.

RETURNS	A possibly `null` array of tags.
SEE ALSO	`getAsText()`, `setAsText()`.
EXAMPLE	See the `PropertyEditor` example.

getValue()

PURPOSE	Retrieves the current property value.
SYNTAX	`public Object getValue()`
DESCRIPTION	By default, this method returns the most recent value passed in by `set-Value()`. There is typically no need to override this method. The returned value should be treated as immutable and should not be modified.
	This method is typically called by the bean editor immediately after it receives a property change event from some property editor in order to determine if the property has changed. This method can be called by `getAsText()` when it needs to create a string representation of the property value.
	If the property type is a primitive type, this method will return the property value contained in the corresponding wrapper object. For example, if the primitive type is `boolean`, the returned object will be a `Boolean` object. This method does not have to create the wrapper object, since the wrapper object will already have been created before `setValue()` is called.
RETURNS	The possibly `null` current property value.
SEE ALSO	`getAsText()`, `setValue()`.
EXAMPLE	See `getCustomEditor()`.

isPaintable()

PURPOSE	Determines if the property editor can paint a representation of the property.
SYNTAX	`public boolean isPaintable()`
DESCRIPTION	This method returns `false` by default. If this property editor can paint a representation of the property, this method should be overridden to return `true`. For example, if the property is a color, this method could paint the color. Or if the property is an image, it could paint a scaled version of the image.
	This method is typically called by the bean editor. If it returns `true`, the bean editor will also call this property editor's `paintValue()` method whenever the property value must be painted.

Note: The Beanbox in BDK 1.0apr97 ignores this method unless `supports-CustomEditor()` also returns `true`.

RETURNS   `true` if the property editor can paint a representation of the property; `false` otherwise.

EXAMPLE   See `getCustomEditor()`.

paintValue()

PURPOSE   Called to paint a representation of the property value.

SYNTAX   `public void paintValue(Graphics g, Rectangle box)`

DESCRIPTION If `isPaintable()` is true, this method will be called by the bean editor to allow the property editor to paint a representation of the property value within the box. For example, if the property is a color, this method could paint the color in the box. Or if the property is an image, this method could paint a scaled version of the image in the box. By default, this method does nothing. It is called each time the property editor fires a property change event.

The size and location of box is determined by the bean editor and cannot by specified by the property editor.

If this method might paint outside the rectangle specified by box, it must set the clipping rectangle on g,

Note: When the Beanbox in BDK 1.0apr97 is used, the width and height of box are 2 pixels too wide and 2 pixels too high. Subtract 2 from both the width and height to get the true dimensions.

PARAMETERS
box   A non-`null` `Rectangle` within the graphics object on which to paint.
g   A non-`null` graphics context on which to paint.

SEE ALSO   `java.awt.Graphics`, `java.awt.Rectangle`.

EXAMPLE   See `getCustomEditor()`.

PropertyEditorSupport()

PURPOSE   Constructs a new `PropertyEditorSupport` instance.

SYNTAX   `protected PropertyEditorSupport()`
             `protected PropertyEditorSupport(Object source)`

DESCRIPTION   This constructor is typically called by a bean editor while it is creating property editors for each of the bean's properties. If this constructor is overridden by a subclass, the subclass must call the super().

The source object will be included in any property change events that this property editor support object fires. If source is not specified, it defaults to the new property editor support object itself.

PARAMETERS
source   The non-null object that will be generating property change events.

removePropertyChangeListener()

PURPOSE   Stops a listener from receiving property change events.

SYNTAX   public synchronized void
              removePropertyChangeListener(PropertyChangeListener listener)

DESCRIPTION   This method removes listener from the listener list. If listener is not in the listener list, the method call is ignored.

The removed listener should be prepared to receive a few more property change events. See PropertyChangeListener for more details.

Unless you need to distribute events in a way different from this implementation, it is not necessary to override this method. However, if this method is overridden, then two other methods must also be overridden: addPropertyChangeListener() and firePropertyChange().

PARAMETERS
listener   A non-null property change event listener.

SEE ALSO   addPropertyChangeListener(), firePropertyChange().

EXAMPLE   See the PropertyChangeEvent class example.

setAsText()

PURPOSE   Converts a string representation of a property value into an object of the property type.

SYNTAX   public void setAsText(String text) throws
              IllegalArgumentException

DESCRIPTION   This method, by default, calls setValue() with text. If the property editor does not have a custom editor and the bean property is not a string, this method should be overridden to convert text to a value in the property type.

A
B
C
D
E
F
G
H
I
J
K
L
M
N
O
P
Q
R
S
T
U
V
W
X
Y
Z

A

B

C

D

E

F

G

H

I

J

K

L

M

N

O

P

Q

R

S

T

U

V

W

X

Y

Z

If the property type is a primitive type, the new value must be wrapped in the appropriate wrapper object. For example, if the property type is `boolean`, then the new value must be wrapped in a `Boolean` object.

If `text` is successfully converted into a valid property value, this method must call `setValue()` with the new value. (Note that the value passed to `set-Value()` must be a new instance of the property type; this method must not modify the current property value.) `setValue()` will notify the bean editor that the value has changed.

PARAMETERS

 `text`   The non-`null` string representation of the property value.

EXCEPTIONS

 `IllegalArgumentException`

    If `text` cannot be converted to a valid property value.

SEE ALSO   `getAsText()`, `java.lang.IllegalArgumentException`, `setValue()`.

EXAMPLE

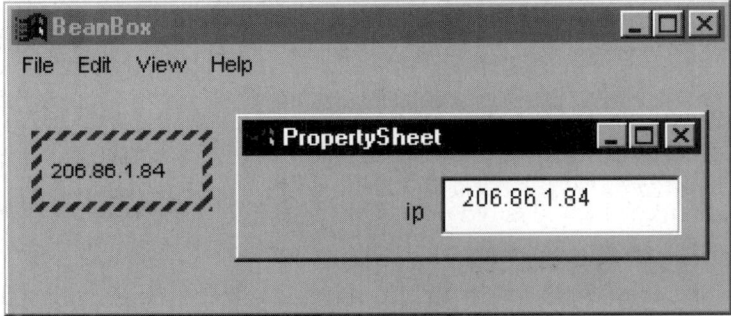

FIGURE 320: IPEditor.

This example bean has a property called "ip," which has the type Ip (TCP/IP address). The bean makes the ip property editable by providing a property editor called `IpEditor`. The `IpEditor` converts the Ip type to and from the *dotted string notation*, which has the form "byte.byte.byte.byte." It overrides the `setAsText()` method, which parses such strings and, if the string is valid, calls the `setValue()` method. See Figure 320.

There is no need to override the `getAsText()` method, since, by default, the `getAsText()` method calls the property value's `toString()` method. Calling the Ip object's `toString()` method yields the desired string.

A bean-info is necessary to associate `IpEditor` with the bean's ip property. The bean-info must be defined in a class with the bean's name appended with "BeanInfo," in this case, `BeanBeanInfo`.

Bean.java

```java
import java.awt.*;
import java.beans.*;

public class Bean extends Panel {
    Ip curIp = new Ip(0x7f000001);     // 127.0.0.1

    // Use a label to display the current flavor.
    Label l = new Label(curIp.toString());

    public Bean() {
        add(l);
    }
    public Ip getIp() {
        return curIp;
    }
    public void setIp(Ip ip) {
        curIp = ip;
        l.setText(ip.toString());
    }
}
/*
    manifest.txt:
        Name: Bean.class
        Java-Bean: True
    jar command:
        jar cfm bean.jar manifest.txt Bean*.class Ip*.class
*/
```

BeanBeanInfo.java

```java
import java.beans.*;

public class BeanBeanInfo extends SimpleBeanInfo {
    public PropertyDescriptor[] getPropertyDescriptors() {
        PropertyDescriptor pd[] = new PropertyDescriptor[1];

        try {
            pd[0] = new PropertyDescriptor("ip", Bean.class);
            pd[0].setPropertyEditorClass(IpEditor.class);
            return pd;
        } catch (Exception e) {
            e.printStackTrace();
            return null;
        }
    }
}
```

Ip.java

```java
public class Ip {
    int ipaddr;

    Ip(int ipaddr) {
        this.ipaddr = ipaddr;
    }
    public String toString() {
        int v = ipaddr;
        String result = "";
```

A
B
C
D
E
F
G
H
I
J
K
L
M
N
O

Q
R
S
T
U
V
W
X
Y
Z

```
                for (int i=0; i<4; i++) {
                    if (i > 0) {
                        result += ".";
                    }
                    result += (v>>((3-i)*8))&0xff;
                }
                return result;
            }
        }
```

IpEditor.java

```
        import java.beans.*;
        import java.util.*;

        public class IpEditor extends PropertyEditorSupport {
            // Make sure the string is in the form of an ip address.
            public void setAsText(String text) throws IllegalArgumentException {
                // Break text up into strings separated by dots.
                StringTokenizer st = new StringTokenizer(text, ".");
                int result = 0;

                try {
                    for (int i=0; i<4; i++) {
                        int t = Integer.parseInt(st.nextToken());

                        if (t < 0 || t > 255) {
                            throw new IllegalArgumentException(text);
                        }
                        result |= (t<<(3-i)*8);
                    }
                    setValue(new Ip(result));
                } catch (Exception e) {
                    // It doesn't matter what the exception is.
                }
                throw new IllegalArgumentException(text);
            }
        }
```

setValue()

PURPOSE   Sets a new value for the property.

SYNTAX   `public void setValue(Object value)`

DESCRIPTION   By default, this method saves `value` in a private field and fires a property change event to any listeners. There is typically no need to override this method.

This method is called by the Beanbox to initialize the property editor just after the editor is created. It is also called whenever the user changes the value of the property. For example, if the property is the label of a button, this method will be called each time the user changes the button's label.

If the value has indeed changed, the caller should create a completely new instance of the value before calling setValue(); that is,

getValue() != value.

See the PropertyEditor class description for more details. The new value should be stored in a private field in the property editor. The bean editor will later retrieve the new value (via a call to getValue()) and then directly update the property value in the bean.

This method may also be called by setAsText() when a string representation of the property value is converted into an object of the property type.

If the property type is a primitive type, the new value must be wrapped in the appropriate wrapper object. For example, if the property type is boolean, then the new value must be wrapped in a Boolean object.

This method must also fire a property change event to any property change event listeners. The event should be a multichange event (see Property-ChangeEvent), so the property name, old value, and new value should all be null.

PARAMETERS

value   The possibly null new property value.

SEE ALSO   getValue(), setAsText().

EXAMPLE   See the class example, getCustomEditor(), and setAsText().

supportsCustomEditor()

PURPOSE   Determines whether the property editor supports a custom editor.

SYNTAX   public boolean supportsCustomEditor()

DESCRIPTION   This method returns false by default. If the property editor supports a custom editor, it should override this method and have it return true.

Note: The Beanbox in BDK 1.0apr97 ignores this method unless isPaint-able() also returns true.

RETURNS   false. Override if a custom editor is supported.

SEE ALSO   getCustomEditor().

EXAMPLE   See getCustomEditor().

A
B
C
D
E
F
G
H
I
J
K
L
M
N
O
P
Q
R
S
T
U
V
W
X
Y
Z

PropertyVetoException

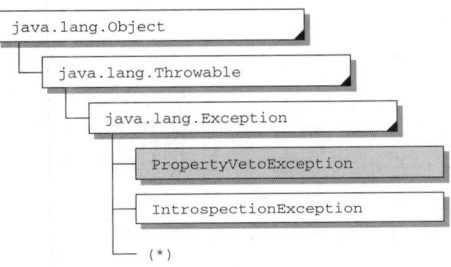

```
java.lang.Object
    java.lang.Throwable
        java.lang.Exception
            PropertyVetoException
            IntrospectionException
            (*)
```

(*) 27 classes from other packages not shown; see java.lang.Exception for complete listing.

Syntax

`public class PropertyVetoException extends Exception`

Description

When a constrained property is about to be changed, a bean must fire a vetoable property change event to all vetoable change listeners (see `VetoableChangeListener`). When a vetoable change listener receives the change property event, it can decide to *veto* the change request, thereby canceling the change. It does this by throwing `PropertyVetoException`. See Figure 321. For more details on this process, see `VetoableChangeListener` and `VetoableChangeSupport`.

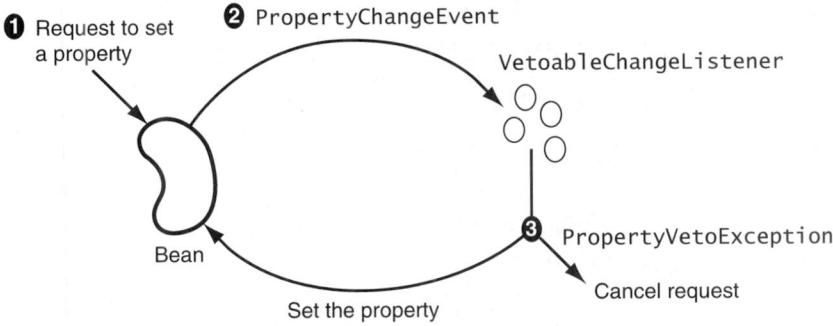

FIGURE 321: Constrained Property Event Flow.

MEMBER SUMMARY	
Constructor	
PropertyVetoException()	Constructs a PropertyVetoException instance.
Get Event Method	
getPropertyChangeEvent()	Retrieves the exception's property change event.

See Also

PropertyChangeEvent, VetoableChangeListener, VetoableChangeSupport.

Example

See the VetoableChangeListener class example.

getPropertyChangeEvent()

PURPOSE	Retrieves the exception's property change event.
SYNTAX	public PropertyChangeEvent getPropertyChangeEvent()
RETURNS	The exception's possibly null property change event.
EXAMPLE	See the VetoableChangeListener example.

PropertyVetoException()

PURPOSE	Constructs a PropertyVetoException instance.
SYNTAX	public PropertyVetoException(String msg, PropertyChangeEvent evt)
DESCRIPTION	The evt parameter should be the property change event that is being vetoed.
PARAMETERS	
evt	The possibly null property change event that was vetoed.
msg	A possibly null string describing the reason for the veto.
EXAMPLE	See the VetoableChangeListener class example.

A
B
C
D
E
F
G
H
I
J
K
L
M
N
O
P
Q
R
S
T
U
V
W
X
Y
Z

java.awt
Rectangle

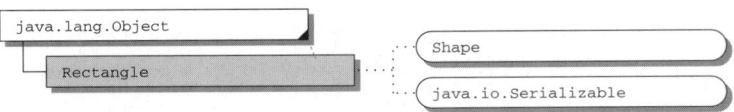

Syntax

`public class Rectangle implements Shape, Serializable`

Description

A rectangle represents a rectangular area on a 2D plane. A rectangle is defined by four values: *x*, *y*, *width*, and *height*. *x* and *y* define the top-left corner of the rectangle; *width* and *height* define the size of the rectangle. Rectangles are typically used in the layout of components and in graphics operations.

When using the methods in this class, note whether a new rectangle is returned. Some methods modify the current instance, while others return a new instance. In general, when having a rectangle instance returned in a method call, either have a copy returned, if you need to retain the instance, or have the instance discarded after it is returned. If you have passed a rectangle instance in a method call and wish to continue using the instance, note whether the method will either retain the instance or copy the values.

MEMBER SUMMARY	
Constructor	
`Rectangle()`	Creates a new `Rectangle` instance.
Rectangle Tests	
`equals()`	Determines if an object is equal to this rectangle.
`contains()`	Determines if a point lies inside this rectangle.
`intersects()`	Determines if a rectangle intersects with this rectangle.
`isEmpty()`	Determines if this rectangle has any area.
Rectangle Operations	
`add()`	Enlarges this rectangle.
`getBounds()`	Retrieves a new instance of this rectangle's bounds.
`getLocation()`	Retrieves the coordinates of this rectangle's top-left corner.
`getSize()`	Retrieves the width and height of this rectangle.
`grow()`	Shifts all four edges of this rectangle.
`intersection()`	Calculates the intersection of a rectangle with this rectangle.
`setBounds()`	Modifies this rectangle's bounds.
`setLocation()`	Moves this rectangle to a new location.

MEMBER SUMMARY	
setSize()	Modifies this rectangle's size.
translate()	Moves this rectangle by a relative distance.
union()	Calculates the union of a rectangle with this rectangle.
Fields	
height	Holds the rectangle's height.
width	Holds the rectangle's width.
x	Holds the rectangle's x-coordinate.
y	Holds the rectangle's y-coordinate.
Hash Code Method	
hashCode()	Calculates the hash code for this rectangle.
Debugging Method	
toString()	Generates a string representation of this rectangle.
Deprecated Methods	
inside()	Replaced by contains().
move()	Replaced by setLocation().
reshape()	Replaced by setBounds().
resize()	Replaced by setSize().

See Also

java.io.Serializable, Shape.

Example

This example demonstrates how to implement drag-and-drop within a frame. The program creates three coins and three slots in the three primary colors. The coins can be dragged over a slot and dropped on it. A coin changes color only if it's over the same-colored slot. If the coin is dropped on the proper slot, the coin disappears. See Figure 322.

The double-buffering technique is used to eliminate flicker during the dragging of the coins.

```
import java.awt.*;
import java.awt.event.*;

class Main extends Frame {
    Main() {
        super("Rectangle Example");
```

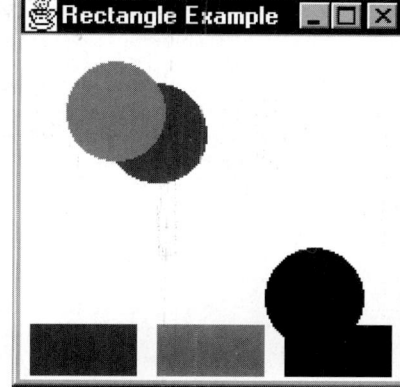

FIGURE 322: Rectangle.

```
                add(new ImageCanvas(), BorderLayout.CENTER);
                setSize(200, 200);
                show();
            }

            public static void main(String[] args) {
                new Main();
            }
        }

        class ImageCanvas extends Component {
            int numCoins = 3;
            Rectangle[] coins = new Rectangle[numCoins];
            Rectangle[] slots = new Rectangle[numCoins];
            Color[] colors = {Color.red, Color.green, Color.blue};
            Image bbuf;
            Graphics bbufG;

            ImageCanvas() {
                for (int i=0; i<numCoins; i++) {
                    coins[i] = new Rectangle(rand(50), rand(50), 50, 50);
                    slots[i] = new Rectangle();
                }
                addMouseListener(new MouseEventHandler());
                addMouseMotionListener(new MouseMotionEventHandler());
            }

            int rand(int r) {
                return (int)Math.floor(Math.random()*r);
            }

            public void paint(Graphics g) {
                update(g);
            }

            public void update(Graphics g) {
                int w = getSize().width;
                int h = getSize().height;

                if (bbuf == null
                    || w > bbuf.getWidth(null)
                    || h > bbuf.getHeight(null)) {
                    bbuf = createImage(w, h);
                    bbufG = bbuf.getGraphics();
                }

                bbufG.setColor(Color.white);
                bbufG.fillRect(0, 0, getSize().width, getSize().height);

                // paint slots
                for (int i=0; i<numCoins; i++) {
                    slots[i].setBounds(i*w/3, h-30, w/3, 30);
                    slots[i].grow(-5, -2);
                    bbufG.setColor(colors[i]);
                    bbufG.fillRect(slots[i].x, slots[i].y,
                        slots[i].width, slots[i].height);
                }

                // paint coins
                for (int i=0; i<numCoins; i++) {
```

```
        if (!coins[i].isEmpty()) {
            if (dragging == i && coins[i].intersects(slots[i])) {
                bbufG.setColor(Color.black);
            } else {
                bbufG.setColor(colors[i]);
            }
            bbufG.fillOval(coins[i].x, coins[i].y,
                coins[i].width, coins[i].height);
        }
    }
    g.drawImage(bbuf, 0, 0, this);
}

int dragging = -1;
Point offset;

// Handles mouse presses and releases
class MouseEventHandler extends MouseAdapter {
    public synchronized void mousePressed(MouseEvent evt) {
        int x = evt.getX(), y = evt.getY();
        for (int i=coins.length-1; i>=0; i--) {
            if (!coins[i].isEmpty() && coins[i].contains(x, y)) {
                dragging = i;
                offset = new Point(coins[i].x-x, coins[i].y-y);
                return;
            }
        }
    }
    public synchronized void mouseReleased(MouseEvent evt) {
        if (dragging >= 0) {
            if (coins[dragging].intersects(slots[dragging])) {
                coins[dragging].width = 0;    // make it empty
                dragging = -1;
            }
            repaint();
        }
    }
}

// Handles mouse drags
class MouseMotionEventHandler extends MouseMotionAdapter {
    public synchronized void mouseDragged(MouseEvent evt) {
        int x = evt.getX(), y = evt.getY();
        if (dragging >= 0) {
            coins[dragging].setLocation(x, y);
            coins[dragging].translate(offset.x, offset.y);
            repaint();
        }
    }
}
}
```

A
B
C
D
E
F
G
H
I
J
K
L
M
N
O
P
Q
R
S
T
U
V
W
X
Y
Z

A
B
C
D
E
F
G
H
I
J
K
L
M
N
O
P
Q
R
S
T
U
V
W
X
Y
Z

add()

PURPOSE	Enlarges this rectangle.
SYNTAX	`public void add(int x, int y)`
	`public void add(Point point)`
	`public void add(Rectangle rectangle)`

DESCRIPTION   This method enlarges this rectangle, if necessary, to include another point or rectangle. If x and y are specified, they define a point; the rectangle's bounds are modified to be just large enough to include the point. If `point` is specified, the rectangle's bounds are modified to be just large enough to include the point. If `rectangle` is specified, the rectangle's bounds are modified to be just large enough to include all of the points in the rectangle.

The following invariants for `add()` hold:

- After `r.add(x, y)`, `r.contains(x, y)` is `true`.
- After `r.add(point)`, `r.contains(point.x, point.y)` is `true`.
- After `r.add(rectangle)`, `r.contains(r.union(rectangle))` is `true`.

PARAMETERS

`point`	The non-`null` point to include.
`rectangle`	The non-`null` rectangle to include.
`x`	The *x*-coordinate of the point to include.
`y`	The *y*-coordinate of the point to include.

SEE ALSO   `contains()`.

EXAMPLE   This example takes points defined by clicking the mouse and adds them to a rectangle:

```
Rectangle rect = new Rectangle();

public void mousePressed(MouseEvent evt) {
    int x = evt.getX(), y = evt.getY();
    rect.add(x, y);
    downX = x;
    downY = y;
}
```

contains()

PURPOSE	Determines if a point lies inside this rectangle.
SYNTAX	`public boolean contains(int x, int y)`
	`public boolean contains(Point pt)`

DESCRIPTION   A point is inside a rectangle if the following condition is `true`:
`pt.x >= x && pt.y >= y && (pt.x-x) < width && (pt.y-y) < height`

The point can be specified either by its *x*- and *y*- coordinates or by a `Point` instance `pt`.

PARAMETERS

`pt`   The point to check.

`x`   The point's *x*-coordinate.

`y`   The point's *y*-coordinate.

RETURNS   `true` if the point is inside the rectangle; `false` otherwise.

EXAMPLE   This example defines a `mousePressed()` method that responds only if the user clicks inside the rectangle `rect`.

```
Rectangle rect = new Rectangle();

public void mousePressed(MouseEvent evt) {
    int x = evt.getX(), y = evt.getY();
    if (rect.contains(x, y)) {
        // (x, y) are inside the rectangle; perform some task
    }
}
```

equals( )

PURPOSE   Determines if an object is equal to this rectangle.

SYNTAX   `public boolean equals(Object object)`

DESCRIPTION   Two rectangles are equal if their *x*- and *y*-coordinates, width, and height are identical.

PARAMETERS

`object`   The object to check for equality. This can be `null`.

RETURNS   `true` if `object` is a rectangle and is equal to this rectangle; `false` otherwise.

OVERRIDES   `java.lang.Object.equals()`.

EXAMPLE   This example defines a method that searches through an array of rectangles looking for one that exactly matches a particular rectangle. If a match exists, the method returns the index of the rectangle; otherwise, it returns −1.

```
Rectangle[] rects = new Rectangle[100];

int findEqual(Rectangle r) {
    for (int i=0; i<rects.length; i++) {
        if (r.equals(rects[i]);
        return i;
    }
    return -1;
}
```

A
B
C
D
E
F
G
H
I
J
K
L
M
N
O
P
Q
R
S
T
U
V
W
X
Y
Z

getBounds()

PURPOSE	Retrieves a new instance of this rectangle.
SYNTAX	`public Rectangle getBounds()`
RETURNS	A new instance of this rectangle.
SEE ALSO	`setBounds()`.
EXAMPLE	

```
Rectangle rect = new Rectangle(0, 10, 50, 100);
Rectangle bounds = rect.getBounds(); // new rectangle (0, 10, 50, 100);
```

getLocation()

PURPOSE	Retrieves the coordinates of this rectangle's top-left corner.
SYNTAX	`public Point getLocation()`
RETURNS	A new non-`null` point of this rectangle's top-left corner.
SEE ALSO	`setLocation()`.
EXAMPLE	

```
Rectangle rect = new Rectangle(0, 10, 50, 100);
Point corner = rect.getLocation(); // (0, 10)
```

getSize()

PURPOSE	Retrieves the width and height of this rectangle.
SYNTAX	`public Dimension getSize()`
RETURNS	A non-`null` `Dimension` object created using this rectangle's width and height.
SEE ALSO	`setSize()`.
EXAMPLE	

```
Rectangle rect = new Rectangle(0, 10, 50, 100);
Dimension dim = rect.getSize(); // 50 x 100
```

grow()

PURPOSE	Shifts all four edges of this rectangle.
SYNTAX	`public void grow(int hor, int ver)`

DESCRIPTION   This method modifies this rectangle such that its left edge is shifted left by hor and its width is increased by 2 * hor. Also, its top edge is shifted up by ver and its height is increased by 2 * ver.

hor or ver can be negative. If either value is negative, the rectangle will shrink instead.

PARAMETERS

hor   The amount to shift the rectangle's left and right edges.

ver   The amount to shift the rectangle's top and bottom edges.

EXAMPLE   This example defines a keyPressed() method, whereby if 'g' is pressed, the rectangle increases in width and height by 2 pixels each and if 's' is pressed, the rectangle decreases in width and height by 2 pixels each.

```
public void keyPressed(MouseEvent evt) {
    char key = evt.getKeyChar();
    if (key == 'g') {
        rect.grow(1, 1);        // enlarge
    } else if (key == 's') {
        rect.grow(-1, -1);      // shrink
    }
}
```

hashCode()

PURPOSE   Calculates the hash code for this rectangle.

SYNTAX   public int hashCode()

DESCRIPTION   A rectangle's hash code is an integer calculated from the rectangle's bounds. If equals(r1, r2) is true, then r1 and r2 will have the same hash codes; otherwise, r1 and r2 will likely have different hash codes.

OVERRIDES   java.lang.Object.hashCode().

RETURNS   This rectangle's hash code.

EXAMPLE   See equals() and java.lang.Object.hashCode().

height

PURPOSE   This field holds this rectangle's height.

SYNTAX   public int height

DESCRIPTION   To change the height of this rectangle, use setSize().

SEE ALSO   getSize(), setSize(), width.

EXAMPLE   This example paints a rectangle on the screen:

```
Rectangle rect = new Rectangle();

public void paint(Graphics g) {
    g.fillRect(rect.x, rect.y, rect.width, rect.height);
}
```

inside()   *DEPRECATED*

PURPOSE   Replaced by `contains()`.

SYNTAX   `public boolean inside(int x, int y)`

PARAMETERS
x   The point's *x*-coordinate.
y   The point's *y*-coordinate.

RETURNS   `true` if the point is inside the rectangle; `false` otherwise.

DEPRECATION   Replace the usage of this deprecated method, as in
```
    if (rect.inside(x, y)) ...
```
with
```
    if (rect.contains(x, y)) ...
```

intersection()

PURPOSE   Calculates the intersection of a rectangle with this rectangle.

SYNTAX   `public Rectangle intersection(Rectangle rectangle)`

DESCRIPTION   The intersection of two rectangles is defined to be the set of all points that lie in both rectangles.

PARAMETERS
rectangle   The non-`null` rectangle with which to intersect.

RETURNS   A new non-`null` `Rectangle` instance that is the intersection of this rectangle and `rectangle`.

EXAMPLE   This example paints two rectangles and then paints their intersection red:

```
Rectangle r1 = new Rectangle();
Rectangle r2 = new Rectangle();

public void paint(Graphics g) {
    g.fillRect(r1.x, r1.y, r1.width, r1.height);
    g.fillRect(r2.x, r2.y, r2.width, r2.height);
    g.setColor(Color.red);
    Rectangle r = r1.intersection(r2);
```

```
    g.fillRect(r.x, r.y, r.width, r.height);
}
```

intersects( )

PURPOSE   Determines if a rectangle intersects with this rectangle.

SYNTAX   `public boolean intersects(Rectangle rectangle)`

DESCRIPTION   The intersection of two rectangles is defined to be the set of all points that lie in both rectangles. Two rectangles intersect if the intersection is not empty.

PARAMETERS
rectangle   The non-`null` rectangle to intersect with this rectangle.

RETURNS   `true` if this rectangle intersects `rectangle`; `false` otherwise.

EXAMPLE   See the class example.

isEmpty( )

PURPOSE   Determines if this rectangle has any area.

SYNTAX   `public boolean isEmpty()`

DESCRIPTION   A rectangle is empty or has no area if either of its width or height is less than or equal to 0.

RETURNS   `true` if the rectangle is empty; `false` otherwise.

EXAMPLE   See the class example.

move( )   *DEPRECATED*

PURPOSE   Replaced by `setLocation()`.

SYNTAX   `public void move(int x, int y)`

PARAMETERS
x   The rectangle's new *x*-coordinate.
y   The rectangle's new *y*-coordinate.

DEPRECATION   Replace the usage of this deprecated method, as in
```
  rect.move(x, y);
```
with
```
  rect.setLocation(x, y);
```

Rectangle()

PURPOSE	Constructs a new `Rectangle` instance.

SYNTAX

```
public Rectangle()
public Rectangle(int width, int height)
public Rectangle(int x, int y, int width, int height)
public Rectangle(Point point)
public Rectangle(Dimension dimension)
public Rectangle(Point point, Dimension dimension)
public Rectangle(Rectangle rect)
```

DESCRIPTION   This constructor creates a new `Rectangle` instance that has the specified bounds. Various ways are available to initialize the rectangle's bounds. If no parameters are specified, `x`, `y`, `width`, and `height` all default to `0`. If only `width` and `height` are specified, `x` and `y` default to `0`. If only a point is specified, the rectangle's top-left corner is at `point`, but `width` and `height` default to `0`. If only a dimension is specified, `x` and `y` default to `0` and `width` and `height` are taken from `dimension`. If both a point and a dimension are specified, the rectangle's top-left corner is at `point` and `width` and `height` are taken from `dimension`. If a rectangle `rect` is specified, the bounds from `rect` are used.

PARAMETERS

dimension	The non-`null` dimension specifying the new rectangle's size.
height	The height of the rectangle.
point	The non-`null` point specifying the new rectangle's top-left corner.
rect	The rectangle specifying the bounds to use.
width	The width of the rectangle.
x	The new rectangle's *x*-coordinate.
y	The new rectangle's *y*-coordinate.

EXAMPLE   This example creates a hundred rectangles and lays them out in a 10-×-10 grid:

```
Rectangle[] rects = new Rectangle[100];

for (int x=0; x<10; x++) {
    for (int y=0; y<10; y++) {
        rects[i] = new Rectangle(x*10, y*10, 10, 10);
    }
}
```

reshape()   *DEPRECATED*

PURPOSE	Replaced by `setBounds()`.

SYNTAX   `public void reshape(int x, int y, int width, int height)`

PARAMETERS

height	The rectangle's new height.
width	The rectangle's new width.
x	The rectangle's new *x*-coordinate.
y	The rectangle's new *y*-coordinate.

DEPRECATION Replace the usage of this deprecated method, as in

```
rect.reshape(x, y, width, height);
```

with

```
rect.setBounds(x, y, width, height);
```

resize()   *DEPRECATED*

PURPOSE Replaced by `setSize()`.

SYNTAX `public void resize(int width, int height)`

PARAMETERS

height	The rectangle's new height.
width	The rectangle's new width.

DEPRECATION Replace the usage of this deprecated method, as in

```
rect.resize(width, height);
```

with

```
rect.setSize(width, height);
```

setBounds()

PURPOSE Modifies this rectangle's bounds.

SYNTAX `public void setBounds(int x, int y, int width, int height)`
`public void setBounds(Rectangle rect)`

DESCRIPTION This method modifies the rectangle's top-left corner to be at x and y and its size to be width and height. If rect is specified instead, rect's bounds are used for this rectangle.

PARAMETERS

height	The rectangle's new height.
rect	The non-`null` rectangle specifying the new bounds.
width	The rectangle's new width.
x	The rectangle's new *x*-coordinate.
y	The rectangle's new *y*-coordinate.

SEE ALSO `getBounds()`.

A
B
C
D
E
F
G
H
I
J
K
L
M
N
O
P
Q
R
S
T
U
V
W
X
Y
Z

A
B
C
D
E
F
G
H
I
J
K
L
M
N
O
P
Q
R
S
T
U
V
W
X
Y
Z

EXAMPLE This example defines two methods for handling mouse events that together allow the user to stretch a rectangle. The mousePressed() method sets the top-left corner of the rectangle, and the mouseDragged() method adjusts the dimensions of the rectangle.

```java
Rectangle rect = new Rectangle();
int downX, downY;

public void mousePressed(MouseEvent evt) {
    downX = evt.getX();
    downY = evt.getY();
}

public void mouseDragged(MouseEvent evt) {
    rect.setBounds(downX, downY, evt.getX()-downX, evt.getY()-downY);
}
```

setLocation()

PURPOSE Moves this rectangle to a new location.

SYNTAX
```java
public void setLocation(int x, int y)
public void setLocation(Point pt)
```

DESCRIPTION The method sets the top-left corner of this rectangle to be at the new specified location. The new location can be specified by using either a Point instance or x- and y- coordinates.

PARAMETERS
pt The non-null point specifying the new coordinates.
x The rectangle's new x-coordinate.
y The rectangle's new y-coordinate.

SEE ALSO getLocation(), translate().

EXAMPLE This example defines a mouseDragged() method that drags around a rectangle:

```java
Rectangle rect = new Rectangle();

public void mouseDragged(MouseEvent evt) {
    rect.setLocation(evt.getX(), evt.getY());
    repaint();
}
```

setSize()

PURPOSE	Modifies this rectangle's size.
SYNTAX	`public void setSize(int width, int height)` `public void setSize(Dimension dim)`
DESCRIPTION	This method modifies the rectangle's size to be `width` and `height` or the dimensions specified by `dim`.
PARAMETERS	
dim	The non-`null` dimension specifying the new size.
height	The rectangle's new height.
width	The rectangle's new width.
SEE ALSO	`getSize()`.
EXAMPLE	This example defines a `mouseDragged()` method that allows you to resize a rectangle:

```java
Rectangle rect = new Rectangle();

public void mouseDragged(MouseEvent evt) {
    int x = evt.getX(), y = evt.getY();
    rect.setSize(x-rect.x, y-rect.y);
}
```

toString()

PURPOSE	Generates a string representation of this rectangle.
SYNTAX	`public String toString()`
DESCRIPTION	This method generates this rectangle's string representation, which consists of the rectangle's bounds. This method is typically used for debugging.
RETURNS	A non-`null` string representing the rectangle's state.
OVERRIDES	`java.lang.Object.toString()`.
EXAMPLE	See `java.lang.Object.toString()`.

translate()

PURPOSE	Moves this rectangle by a relative distance.
SYNTAX	`public void translate(int dx, int dy)`

A
B
C
D
E
F
G
H
I
J
K
L
M
N
O
P
Q
R
S
T
U
V
W
X
Y
Z

DESCRIPTION	This method modifies this rectangle so that its *x*-coordinate is shifted by dx and its *y*-coordinate is shifted by dy. In particular, the rectangle's new *x*-coordinate is x + dx and the rectangle's new *y*-coordinate is y + dy.
PARAMETERS	
dx	The amount by which to shift the rectangle's *x*-coordinate.
dy	The amount by which to shift the rectangle's *y*-coordinate.
SEE ALSO	setLocation().
EXAMPLE	This example creates a thread that moves a rectangle toward the southeast, one pixel at a time, every 30 ms:

```
Rectangle rect = new Rectangle(;

public void run() {
    for (int i=0; i<100; i++) {
        rect.translate(1, 1);
        repaint();
        try {
            Thread.sleep(30);
        } catch (Exception e) {
            e.printStackTrace();
        }
    }
}
```

union( )

PURPOSE	Calculates the union of a rectangle with this rectangle.
SYNTAX	public Rectangle union(Rectangle rectangle)
DESCRIPTION	The union of two rectangles is defined to be the smallest rectangle that includes all points in both rectangles.
PARAMETERS	
rectangle	The non-null rectangle with which to perform the union.
RETURNS	A new non-null rectangle instance that is the union of this rectangle and rectangle.
EXAMPLE	This example paints two rectangles and then paints a box around them:

```
Rectangle r1 = new Rectangle();
Rectangle r2 = new Rectangle();

public void paint(Graphics g) {
    g.fillRect(r1.x, r1.y, r1.width, r1.height);
    g.fillRect(r2.x, r2.y, r2.width, r2.height);
    g.setColor(Color.red);
    Rectangle r = r1.union(r2);
    g.drawRect(r.x, r.y, r.width, r.height);
}
```

width

PURPOSE   This field holds this rectangle's width.

SYNTAX   `public int width`

DESCRIPTION   To change the width of this rectangle, use `setSize()`.

SEE ALSO   `getSize()`, `height`, `setSize()`.

EXAMPLE   This example paints a rectangle on the screen:

```
Rectangle rect = new Rectangle();

public void paint(Graphics g) {
    g.fillRect(rect.x, rect.y, rect.width, rect.height);
}
```

x

PURPOSE   This field holds this rectangle's x-coordinate.

SYNTAX   `public int x`

DESCRIPTION   To change the x-coordinate of this rectangle, use `setLocation()`.

SEE ALSO   `getLocation()`, `setLocation()`, `y`.

EXAMPLE   This example paints a rectangle on the screen:

```
Rectangle rect = new Rectangle();

public void paint(Graphics g) {
    g.fillRect(rect.x, rect.y, rect.width, rect.height);
}
```

y

PURPOSE   This field holds this rectangle's y-coordinate.

SYNTAX   `public int y`

DESCRIPTION   To change the y-coordinate of this rectangle, use `setLocation()`.

SEE ALSO   `getLocation()`, `setLocation()`, `x`.

EXAMPLE   This example paints a rectangle on the screen:

```
Rectangle rect = new Rectangle();

public void paint(Graphics g) {
    g.fillRect(rect.x, rect.y, rect.width, rect.height);
}
```

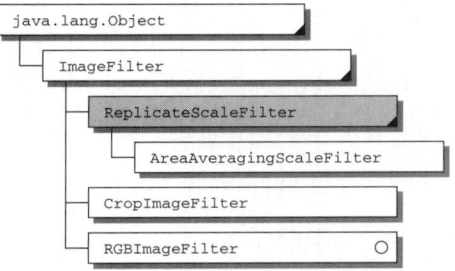

A
B
C
D
E
F
G
H
I
J
K
L
M
N
O
P
Q
R
S
T
U
V
W
X
Y
Z

Syntax

`public class ReplicateScaleFilter extends ImageFilter`

Description

The *replicate scale filter* is an image filter that scales images using a simple pixel replication algorithm. When a dimension of an image is scaled down, pixels are omitted. For a higher-quality scaling image filter, see `AreaAveragingScaleFilter`.

This image filter is meant to be used in conjunction with a `FilteredImageSource` object, which assumes the responsibility for delivering an image to this image filter to scale. See `ImageFilter` for more information about the image filtering architecture.

MEMBER SUMMARY	
Constructor	
ReplicateScaleFilter()	Constructs a ReplicateScaleFilter instance.
Image Consumer Methods Called by the Image Producer	
setDimensions()	Called to deliver the dimensions of the source image.
setPixels()	Called to deliver pixels to this image filter.
setProperties()	Called to deliver the properties for the source image.
Protected Fields	
destHeight	Holds the height of the scaled image in pixels.
destWidth	Holds the width of the scaled image in pixels.
outpixbuf	Holds a row of pixel values.
srccols[]	Holds an array of special values used by the replication algorithm.
srcHeight	Holds the height of the original image in pixels.
srcrows[]	Holds an array of special values used by the replication algorithm.
srcWidth	Holds the width of the original image in pixels.

See Also
FilteredImageSource.

Example
See the AreaAveragingScaleFilter class example.

destHeight

PURPOSE	Holds the height of the scaled image in pixels.
SYNTAX	`protected int destHeight`
DESCRIPTION	This value of this field is the same as the height value supplied to the constructor.
SEE ALSO	ReplicateScaleFilter().

destWidth

PURPOSE	Holds the width of the scaled image in pixels.
SYNTAX	`protected int destWidth`
DESCRIPTION	This value of this field is the same as the width value supplied to the constructor.
SEE ALSO	ReplicateScaleFilter().

outpixbuf

PURPOSE	Holds a row of pixel values.
SYNTAX	`protected Object outpixbuf`
DESCRIPTION	This field contains either an array of bytes or an array of pixels, depending on which setPixels() method is used. It is used by the image filter to store a row of scaled pixels.

ReplicateScaleFilter()

PURPOSE	Constructs a ReplicateScaleFilter instance.
SYNTAX	`public ReplicateScaleFilter(int width, int height)`

DESCRIPTION	This method creates a replicate scale filter that scales an image to `width` and `height`. This image filter is meant to be used in conjunction with a `FilteredImageSource` object, which assumes the responsibility for delivering an image to this image filter to scale.
	If `width` is negative, it defaults to the width of the incoming image. Likewise for `height`.
PARAMETERS	
`height`	The new height of the image in pixels. If < 0, defaults to the height of the incoming image.
`width`	The new width of the image in pixels. If < 0, defaults to the width of the incoming image.
SEE ALSO	`FilteredImageSource`.
EXAMPLE	See the `AreaAveragingScaleFilter` class example.

setDimensions()

PURPOSE	Called by the image producer to deliver the dimensions of the source image.
SYNTAX	`public void setDimensions(int w, int h)`
DESCRIPTION	Although this method is public, it is not meant to be called. This method is part of the image filtering process and is called by an image producer. For more information on image filters, see `ImageFilter`.
PARAMETERS	
`height`	The height of the image in pixels.
`width`	The width of the image in pixels.
OVERRIDES	`ImageFilter.setDimensions()`.
SEE ALSO	`ImageConsumer.setDimensions()`.
EXAMPLE	See `ImageConsumer`.

setPixels()

PURPOSE	Called by the image producer to deliver pixels to this image filter.
SYNTAX	`public void setPixels(int x, int y, int w, int h, ColorModel` `    model, byte pixels[], int off, int scansize)`
DESCRIPTION	Although this method is public, it is not meant to be called. This method is part of the image filtering process and is called by an image producer. For more information on image filters, see `ImageFilter`.

PARAMETERS

h	The height of the rectangle in which the pixels are destined.
model	The non-null color model used to translate the pixel values.
off	The index of the first pixel in the pixel array.
pixels	The non-null array of pixel values.
scansize	The width to use when extracting pixels from the pixel array.
w	The width of the rectangle in which the pixels are destined.
x	The *x*-coordinate of the rectangle in which the pixels are destined.
y	The *y*-coordinate of the rectangle in which the pixels are destined.

OVERRIDES   ImageFilter.setPixels().

SEE ALSO   ImageConsumer.setPixels().

EXAMPLE   See ImageConsumer.

setProperties()

PURPOSE   Called by the image producer to deliver the properties for the source image.

SYNTAX   public void setProperties(Hashtable props)

DESCRIPTION   Although this method is public, it is not meant to be called. This method is part of the image filtering process and is called by an image producer. For more information on image filters, see ImageFilter.

PARAMETERS

props	A non-null hash table of image properties.

OVERRIDES   ImageFilter.setProperties().

SEE ALSO   ImageConsumer.setProperties().

EXAMPLE   See ImageConsumer.setProperties().

srccols[]

PURPOSE   Holds an array of special values used by the replication algorithm.

SYNTAX   protected int srccols[]

DESCRIPTION   This field is not typically used by subclasses, since the values are specific to the replicate scale filter replication algorithm.

srcHeight

PURPOSE	Holds the height of the original image in pixels.
SYNTAX	`protected int srcHeight`
DESCRIPTION	This field is initialized when the image producer calls `setDimensions()`.
SEE ALSO	`setDimensions()`.

srcrows[]

PURPOSE	Holds an array of special values used by the replication algorithm.
SYNTAX	`protected int srcrows[]`
DESCRIPTION	This field is not typically used by subclasses, since the values are specific to the replicate scale filter replication algorithm.

srcWidth

PURPOSE	Holds the width of the original image in pixels.
SYNTAX	`protected int srcWidth`
DESCRIPTION	This field is initialized when the image producer calls `setDimensions()`.
SEE ALSO	`setDimensions()`.

A
B
C
D
E
F
G
H
I
J
K
L
M
N
O
P
Q
R
S
T
U
V
W
X
Y
Z

RGBImageFilter

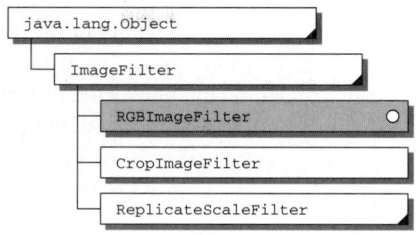

Syntax
```
public abstract class RGBImageFilter extends ImageFilter
```

Description

The RGBImageFilter class is used to modify the pixel values in an image. This can be done by either modifying the colors in the color table of the image (if the image uses an index color model) or modifying each pixel in the image. The former is much more efficient if color changes don't depend on the location of pixels. An example of this is a filter that simply brightens all colors. The latter method is necessary if the color changes depend on the location of the pixels. An example of this is a filter that gradually darkens pixels toward one edge of the image.

This class is an abstract class and is meant to be subclassed. Only the filterRGB() method needs to be overridden. This method is responsible for converting pixel values. filterRGB() receives the coordinates of the pixel so that it can convert the color based on the location of the pixel. By default, all pixels in the image are filtered through filterRGB(). It is also possible just to filter the colors in the color table by setting the field canFilterIndexColorModel to true. When this happens, all of the colors in the color table are passed through filterRGB() and a new color model is created. This new color model is then used for the pixels that flow through the filter.

MEMBER SUMMARY
Image Consumer Methods Called by the Image Producer
setColorModel()   Called to deliver the color model of the source image.
setPixels()   Called to deliver pixels to the image filter.

Continued

MEMBER SUMMARY	
Fields	
`canFilterIndexColorModel`	Indicates whether color filtering is applied to the color table.
`newmodel`	Holds the converted color model.
`origmodel`	Holds the color model passed to the `setColorModel()` method.
Color Model Substitution	
`substituteColorModel()`	Replaces the color model of the source image.
Filter Methods	
`filterIndexColorModel()`	Filters the colors in the color table.
`filterRGB()`	Override to filter each pixel value.
`filterRGBPixels()`	Override to filter a batch of pixel values.

Example

This example implements a gradient filter using the `RGBImageFilter` class. See Figure 323. The example displays an image in a canvas, which in turn is embedded in a frame. The image is brightened at the top-left corner and is gradually darkened toward the bottom-right corner. Since the transformation of a pixel value depends on its location, `canFilterIndexColorModel` must be `false`.

FIGURE 323:   Gradient Filter using `RGBImageFilter`.

```
import java.awt.*;
import java.awt.image.*;
import java.util.*;

class Main extends Frame {
    Main(String filename) {
        super("RGBFilter Example");
        add(new ImageCanvas(getToolkit().getImage(filename)),
            BorderLayout.CENTER);

        setSize(50, 100);
        show();
    }

    static public void main(String[] args) {
        if (args.length == 1) {
            new Main(args[0]);
        } else {
            System.err.println("usage: java Main <image file>");
        }
    }
}
```

```
class ImageCanvas extends Component {
    Image gradientImage;

    ImageCanvas(Image image) {
        GradientFilter imgf = new GradientFilter();
        ImageProducer ip = image.getSource();
        ip = new FilteredImageSource(ip, imgf);
        gradientImage = getToolkit().createImage(ip);
        repaint();
    }

    public void paint(Graphics g) {
        g.drawImage(gradientImage, 0, 0, this);
    }
}

class GradientFilter extends RGBImageFilter {
    float[] hsb = new float[3];
    int width, height;

    public void setDimensions(int w, int h) {
        super.setDimensions(w, h);
        width = w;
        height = h;
    }

    public int filterRGB(int x, int y, int rgb) {
        Color c = new Color(rgb);
        Color.RGBtoHSB(c.getRed(), c.getGreen(), c.getBlue(), hsb);
        hsb[2] += .5f - (float)x / width;
        hsb[2] += .5f - (float)y / height;
        hsb[2] = Math.max(0.0f, Math.min(1.0f, hsb[2]));
        return Color.HSBtoRGB(hsb[0], hsb[1], hsb[2]);
    }
}
```

canFilterIndexColorModel

PURPOSE   Indicates whether color filtering is applied to the color table.

SYNTAX   `protected boolean canFilterIndexColorModel`

DESCRIPTION   The subclass of this filter should set this `boolean` value to indicate whether to
               color filter just the color table or every pixel. If `canFilterIndexColorModel`
               is set to `true` and if the image's color model is indeed an index color model,
               then all of the colors in the color model are transformed using the `filter-`
               `RGB()` method and the pixel values flowing through the filter are not modified.

               If the color filtering does not depend on the position of the pixel values in the
               image, then for the most efficient implementation, this field should be set to
               `true`.

A
B
C
D
E
F
G
H
I
J
K
L
M
N
O
P
Q
R
S
T
U
V
W
X
Y
Z

SEE ALSO   `filterRGB()`, `IndexColorModel`, `substituteColorModel()`.

EXAMPLE   This example implements a brightness filter. An image is painted in a canvas, which is in turn embedded in a frame. See Figure 324. The image is passed through a brightness filter, which brightens or darkens all of the entries in the image's color map. Typing a + brightens the image by 10%, and typing a – darkens the image by 10%.

FIGURE 324:   Brightness Filter using RGBImageFilter.

```java
import java.awt.*;
import java.awt.image.*;
import java.awt.event.*;
import java.util.*;

class Main extends Frame {
    Main(String filename) {
        super("canFilterIndexColorModel Example");
        add(new ImageCanvas(getToolkit().getImage(filename)),
            BorderLayout.CENTER);

        setSize(50, 100);
        show();
    }

    static public void main(String[] args) {
        if (args.length == 1) {
            new Main(args[0]);
        } else {
            System.err.println("usage: java Main <image file>");
        }
    }
}

class ImageCanvas extends Component {
    Image brightImage;
    Image image;
    BrightnessFilter imgf = new BrightnessFilter();

    ImageCanvas(Image image) {
        this.image = image;
        processImage();
        addKeyListener(new KeyEventHandler());
    }

    public void paint(Graphics g) {
        g.drawImage(brightImage, 0, 0, this);
    }

    void processImage() {
        ImageProducer ip = image.getSource();

        ip = new FilteredImageSource(ip, imgf);
        brightImage = getToolkit().createImage(ip);
        repaint();
    }
```

```
        class KeyEventHandler extends KeyAdapter {
            public void keyTyped(KeyEvent evt) {
                char key = evt.getKeyChar();
                if (key == '+') {
                    imgf.addBrightness(.1f);
                } else if (key == '-') {
                    imgf.addBrightness(-.1f);
                }
                processImage();
            }
        }
    }

    class BrightnessFilter extends RGBImageFilter {
        float bDelta;
        float[] hsb = new float[3];
        int width, height;

        BrightnessFilter() {
            canFilterIndexColorModel = true;
        }

        public void setDimensions(int w, int h) {
            super.setDimensions(w, h);
            width = w;
            height = h;
        }

        public void addBrightness(float f) {
            bDelta += f;
        }

        public int filterRGB(int x, int y, int rgb) {
            // x and y are both -1
            Color c = new Color(rgb);
            Color.RGBtoHSB(c.getRed(), c.getGreen(), c.getBlue(), hsb);
            hsb[2] = Math.max(0.0f, Math.min(1.0f, hsb[2] + bDelta));
            return Color.HSBtoRGB(hsb[0], hsb[1], hsb[2]);
        }
    }
```

filterIndexColorModel()

PURPOSE   Filters the colors in the color table.

SYNTAX   `public IndexColorModel filterIndexColorModel(IndexColorModel icm)`

DESCRIPTION   This method filters an index color model instance by running each entry in its color tables through the `filterRGB()` function that `RGBImageFilter` subclasses must implement. This method uses coordinates of –1 to indicate that a color table entry, rather than a pixel value taken from the image, is being filtered.

PARAMETERS

icm   The index color model instance to be filtered.

RETURNS   A new index color model representing the filtered colors.

EXAMPLE   This example implements a filter that allows you to specify a color in the color table and highlight those pixels in an image that use that color. The example changes the highlighted pixels to red. See Figure 325.

The frame contains a canvas, which displays the image. At the bottom of the frame is a text field in which you can type an index of a color in the color table.

FIGURE 325:   **Color Highlighting Using** `RGBImageFilter`.

```java
import java.awt.*;
import java.awt.image.*;
import java.awt.event.*;
import java.net.*;
import java.util.*;

class Main extends Frame implements ActionListener {
    ImageCanvas icv;
    TextField textField = new TextField();

    Main(String filename) {
        super("filterIndexColorModel Example");
        try {
            add(icv = new ImageCanvas(getToolkit().getImage(filename)),
                BorderLayout.CENTER);
            add(textField, BorderLayout.SOUTH);
            textField.addActionListener(this);
        } catch (Exception e) {
            e.printStackTrace();
        }
        setSize(50, 100);
        show();
    }

    public void actionPerformed(ActionEvent evt) {
        icv.seeColor(Integer.parseInt(textField.getText()));
        textField.setText("");
    }

    static public void main(String[] args) {
        if (args.length == 1) {
            new Main(args[0]);
        } else {
            System.err.println("usage: java Main <image file>");
        }
    }
}
```

```
class ImageCanvas extends Component {
    Image seeColorImage;
    Image image;
    SeeColorFilter imgf = new SeeColorFilter();

    ImageCanvas(Image image) {
        this.image = image;
        processImage();
    }

    void seeColor(int colorIndex) {
        imgf.seeColor(colorIndex);
        processImage();
    }

    public void paint(Graphics g) {
        g.drawImage(seeColorImage, 0, 0, this);
    }

    void processImage() {
        ImageProducer ip = image.getSource();

        ip = new FilteredImageSource(ip, imgf);
        seeColorImage = getToolkit().createImage(ip);
        repaint();
    }
}

class SeeColorFilter extends RGBImageFilter {
    int colorIndex = -1;

    SeeColorFilter() {
        canFilterIndexColorModel = true;
    }

    void seeColor(int colorIndex) {
        this.colorIndex = colorIndex;
    }

    public IndexColorModel filterIndexColorModel(IndexColorModel icm) {
        int mapsize = icm.getMapSize();
        byte r[] = new byte[mapsize];
        byte g[] = new byte[mapsize];
        byte b[] = new byte[mapsize];

        icm.getReds(r);
        icm.getGreens(g);
        icm.getBlues(b);
        if (colorIndex >= 0) {
            r[colorIndex] = (byte)255;
            g[colorIndex] = 0;
            b[colorIndex] = 0;
        }
        return new IndexColorModel(icm.getPixelSize(), mapsize,
                                   r, g, b, icm.getTransparentPixel());
    }

    public int filterRGB(int x, int y, int rgb) {
        return rgb;
    }
}
```

A
B
C
D
E
F
G
H
I
J
K
L
M
N
O
P
Q
R
S
T
U
V
W
X
Y
Z

filterRGB( )

PURPOSE	Override to filter each pixel value.
SYNTAX	`public abstract int filterRGB(int x, int y, int rgb)`
DESCRIPTION	The `rgb` parameter is a pixel value encoded in the default color model (see `ColorModel.getRGBdefault ()`). `x` and `y` are the coordinates of the pixel value in the image.
	Subclasses must specify a method to convert a single input pixel in the default RGB `ColorModel` to a single output pixel.
PARAMETERS	
`rgb`	The pixel value encoded in the default color model.
`x`	The *x*-coordinate of the pixel value's location in the image; −1 if the color table is being filtered.
`y`	The *y*-coordinate of the pixel value's location in the image; −1 if the color table is being filtered.
SEE ALSO	`ColorModel.getRGBdefault()`, `filterRGBPixels()`.
EXAMPLE	See the class example.

filterRGBPixels( )

PURPOSE	Override to filter a batch of pixel values.
SYNTAX	`public void filterRGBPixels(int x, int y, int w, int h, int[]` `      pixels, int offset, int scansize)`
DESCRIPTION	The pixel values in `pixels` are encoded in the default color model (see `ColorModel.getRGBdefault`). All pixels flowing through this filter pass through this method. By default, this method simply takes each pixel value in the `pixels` array and calls the `filterRGB()` method. It then stores the result back into the same location in the `pixels` array.
	This method can be overridden to avoid calling `filterRGB()` for each pixel, thereby making for a more efficient implementation.
PARAMETERS	
`h`	The height of the rectangle in which the pixels are destined.
`model`	The non-`null` color model used to translate the pixel values.
`offset`	The index of the first pixel in the pixel array `pixels`.
`pixels`	The non-`null` array of pixel values encoded in the default color model.
`scansize`	The width to use when extracting pixels from the pixel array `pixels`.
`w`	The width of the rectangle in which the pixels are destined.
`x`	The *x*-coordinate of the rectangle in which the pixels are destined.
`y`	The *y*-coordinate of the rectangle in which the pixels are destined.

SEE ALSO   `ColorModel.getRGBdefault()`, `filterRGB()`.

EXAMPLE   This example is identical to the class example, except that the `filterRGB-Pixels()` method, instead of the `filterRGB()` method, is overridden. Note that the `filterRGB()` method is defined even though it is not used; this is done to make the class nonabstract. See Figure 326.

FIGURE 326:   Gradient Filter II Using `RGBImageFilter`.

```java
import java.awt.*;
import java.awt.image.*;
import java.net.*;
import java.util.*;

class Main extends Frame {
    Main(String filename) {
        super("filterRGBPixels Example");
        try {
            add(new ImageCanvas(getToolkit().getImage(filename)),
                BorderLayout.CENTER);
        } catch (Exception e) {
            e.printStackTrace();
        }
        setSize(50, 100);
        show();
    }

    static public void main(String[] args) {
        if (args.length == 1) {
            new Main(args[0]);
        } else {
            System.err.println("usage: java Main <image file>");
        }
    }
}

class ImageCanvas extends Component {
    Image gradientImage;

    ImageCanvas(Image image) {
        GradientFilter imgf = new GradientFilter();
        ImageProducer ip = image.getSource();
        ip = new FilteredImageSource(ip, imgf);
        gradientImage = getToolkit().createImage(ip);
        repaint();
    }

    public void paint(Graphics g) {
        g.drawImage(gradientImage, 0, 0, this);
    }
}

class GradientFilter extends RGBImageFilter {
    float[] hsb = new float[3];
    int width, height;
```

```
public void setDimensions(int w, int h) {
    super.setDimensions(w, h);
    width = w;
    height = h;
}

public void filterRGBPixels(int x, int y, int w, int h,
                            int pixels[], int offset, int scansize) {
    int i = offset;
    for (int cy = 0; cy < h; cy++) {
        for (int cx = 0; cx < w; cx++) {
            Color c = new Color(pixels[i]);

            Color.RGBtoHSB(c.getRed(), c.getGreen(), c.getBlue(), hsb);
            hsb[2] += .5f - (float)x / width;
            hsb[2] += .5f - (float)y / height;
            hsb[2] = Math.max(0.0f, Math.min(1.0f, hsb[2]));
            pixels[i] = Color.HSBtoRGB(hsb[0], hsb[1], hsb[2]);
            i++;
        }
        i += scansize - w;
    }
    consumer.setPixels(x, y, w, h, ColorModel.getRGBdefault(),
                       pixels, offset, scansize);
}

// Never called.
public int filterRGB(int x, int y, int rgb) {
    return 0;
}
}
```

newmodel

PURPOSE	This field holds the converted color model.
SYNTAX	`protected ColorModel newmodel`
DESCRIPTION	If `canFilterIndexColorModel` is `true` and the color model of the source image is an index color model, this field holds the converted color model.
SEE ALSO	`origmodel`.

origmodel

PURPOSE	This field holds the color model passed to the `setColorModel()` method.
SYNTAX	`protected ColorModel origmodel`

DESCRIPTION   If `canFilterIndexColorModel` is `true` and the color model of the source image is an index color model, this field holds the original color model. If this field is not `null`, then the `setPixels()` method checks whether the color model it gets is the same as `origmodel`. If the field is `null`, then `newmodel` is substituted and the pixels are not modified.

SEE ALSO   `newmodel`.

setColorModel( )

PURPOSE   Called by the image producer to deliver the color model of the source image.

SYNTAX   `public void setColorModel(ColorModel model)`

DESCRIPTION   This method is called by the image producer to deliver the color model of the source image to the image filter. Therefore it must not be called directly. Instead, it can be overridden if necessary to introduce behavior different from the default implementation. The default implementation checks the `canFilterIndexColorModel` field to see if it should set a new color model by calling `filterIndexColorModel()`. If `canFilterIndexColorModel` is `true` and `model` is an index color model, a new color model is created and enabled by calling `substituteColorModel()`. Otherwise, the image filter passes the default color model to the image consumer.

PARAMETERS
 `model`   The non-`null` color model of the source image.

OVERRIDES   `ImageFilter.setColorModel()`.

SEE ALSO   `canFilterIndexColorModel`, `ColorModel.getRGBdefault()`, `filterIndexColorModel()`, `substituteColorModel()`.

EXAMPLE   See `ImageConsumer.setColorModel()`.

setPixels( )

PURPOSE   Called by the image producer to deliver pixels to the image filter.

SYNTAX   `public void setPixels(int x, int y, int w, int h, ColorModel`
`    model, byte[] pixels, int offset, int scansize)`
`public void setPixels(int x, int y, int w, int h, ColorModel`
`    model, int[] pixels, int offset, int scansize)`

DESCRIPTION   This method is called by the image producer to deliver pixels to the image filter. Therefore it must not be called directly. Instead, it can be overridden if necessary to introduce behavior different from the default `RGBImageFilter`

A
B
C
D
E
F
G
H
I
J
K
L
M
N
O
P
Q
R
S
T
U
V
W
X
Y
Z

implementation. The default implementation creates a temporary buffer, translates the pixel values in `pixels` to the default color model, saves the pixels in the temporary buffer, and then calls `filterRGBPixels()` with the temporary buffer of pixel values.

PARAMETERS

`h`	The height of the rectangle in which the pixels are destined.
`model`	The non-`null` color model used to translate the pixel values.
`offset`	The index of the first pixel in the pixel array `pixels`.
`pixels`	The non-`null` array of pixel values.
`scansize`	The width to use when extracting pixels from the pixel array `pixels`.
`w`	The width of the rectangle in which the pixels are destined.
`x`	The *x*-coordinate of the rectangle in which the pixels are destined.
`y`	The *y*-coordinate of the rectangle in which the pixels are destined.

OVERRIDES   `ImageFilter.setPixels()`.

SEE ALSO   `ColorModel.getRGBdefault()`, `filterRGBPixels()`,
            `ImageConsumer.setPixels()`.

EXAMPLE   See `ImageConsumer.setPixels()`.

substituteColorModel()

PURPOSE   Replaces the color model of the source image.

SYNTAX   `public void substituteColorModel(ColorModel oldcm, ColorModel newcm)`

DESCRIPTION As pixels flow through this filter via the `setPixels()` method, a check is made to see if the pixels have been encoded with the `oldcm` color model. If so, the pixels are not converted. They are simply forwarded to the image consumer with `newcm` as the color model.

PARAMETERS

`newcm`	The non-`null` color model to replace `oldcm` on the fly.
`oldcm`	The color model to be replaced by `newcm`. May be `null`.

SEE ALSO   `setPixels()`.

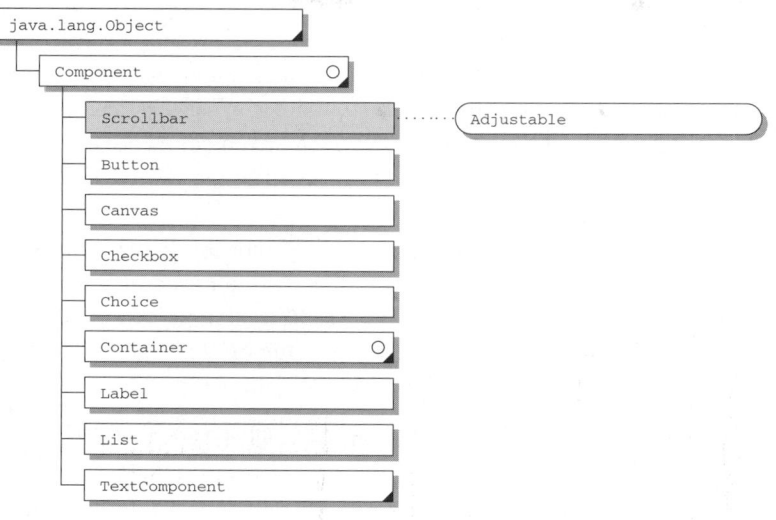

Syntax

`public class Scrollbar extends Component implements Adjustable`

Description

The `Scrollbar` component is used to specify a particular integer value in a range of values. A scrollbar has an orientation that can be either vertical or horizontal. The orientation is specified as the scrollbar is created and can be changed at any time. Figure 327 shows a horizontal scrollbar with labels on all of its parts.

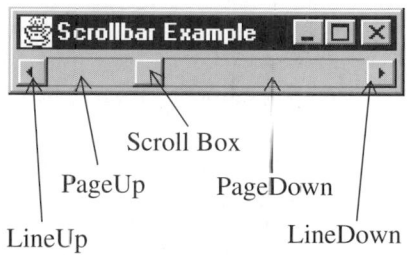

FIGURE 327:   Parts of a Horizontal Scrollbar.

The Adjustable Value and Its Range

The scrollbar has an *adjustable value,* which controls the location of the scrollbar's scroll box. A scrollbar also has an *adjustable value range,* which is defined by two integer values: the minimum and the maximum. The range can be any integer value, positive or negative. However, the maximum value must be greater than or equal to the minimum value. The range can be modified at any time.

The adjustable value must be within the adjustable range. The actual location of the scroll box within the scrollbar matches the relative position of the adjustable value within the scrollbar range. The adjustable value can be changed at any time, and the scroll box will move accordingly. When the user moves the scroll box, the adjustable value is automatically updated and an adjustment event is fired.

Proportional Indicator (Visible Amount)

If the scrollbar is used to pan around a large image, it is useful to have an indication of what fraction of the entire image is visible. The size of the scroll box in relation to the size of the entire scrollbar is typically used to indicate the size of the visible area in proportion to the entire image. For example, if the scroll box is about half the size of the scrollbar, then about half of the image is visible. The scrollbar's "visible amount" property controls the size of the scroll box (note that not all platforms support variable-sized scroll boxes). It also controls the actual maximum of the scrollbar's value, which is the difference between the scrollbar's maximum and its visible amount.

Note that the adjustable value can never exceed the scrollbar's maximum minus the size of the scroll box. For example, if you create a scrollbar with a range of 0 to 100 and a scrollbar visible amount of 10 (scroll box is size 10), the scrollbar's value can be at most 90. To allow the scrollbar with a scroll box size of 10 to return a value of 100, you must create the scrollbar with a range of 0 to 110. The following rule is always followed:

```
minimum <= adjustable value <= maximum-visible
```

Block and Unit Increments

The scrollbar *unit* and *block* increments control the amounts by which the adjustable value is changed when the Line Up, Line Down, Page Up, or Page Down key is pressed. If applying the increment modifies the adjustable value outside the scrollbar range, the adjustable value is set to either the maximum or minimum value. The scrollbar unit and block increments can be changed at any time.

Events

A scrollbar fires adjustment events when its scroll box is dragged, when the Line Up, Line Down, Page Up, or Page Down key is pressed, or when the ends of the scrollbar are clicked. The scrollbar generally does not fire an event if the adjustable value does not change; the exception is when the scroll box is dragged. So if the scroll box is at the bottom of the scrollbar, pressing the Line Down or Page Down key does not fire an event.

See the `AdjustmentEvent` class for details on adjustment events. In addition to the adjustment event, a scrollbar fires all of the events fired by the `Component` class. See the `Component` class for details. See the `AWTEvent` class for general information on events and how to filter or handle them.

MEMBER SUMMARY

Constructor

Scrollbar()	Constructs a new Scrollbar instance.

Orientation Constant Fields and Methods

getOrientation()	Retrieves this scrollbar's orientation.
HORIZONTAL	The orientation constant specifying a horizontal scrollbar.
setOrientation()	Sets this scrollbar's orientation.
VERTICAL	The orientation constant specifying a vertical scrollbar.

Scrollbar Values Methods

getMaximum()	Retrieves this scrollbar's maximum value.
getMinimum()	Retrieves this scrollbar's minimum value.
getValue()	Retrieves this scrollbar's adjustable value.
getVisibleAmount()	Retrieves this scrollbar's visible value.
setMaximum()	Sets this scrollbar's maximum value.
setMinimum()	Sets this scrollbar's minimum value.
setValue()	Sets this scrollbar's adjustable value.
setValues()	Sets various scrollbar values.
setVisibleAmount()	Sets this scrollbar's visible value.

Unit and Block Increment Methods

getBlockIncrement()	Retrieves this scrollbar's block increment value.
getUnitIncrement()	Retrieves this scrollbar's unit increment value.
setBlockIncrement()	Sets this scrollbar's block increment.
setUnitIncrement()	Sets the scrollbar's unit increment.

Event Methods

addAdjustmentListener()	Adds a listener to receive this scrollbar's adjustment events.
processEvent()	Processes an event enabled for this scrollbar.
processAdjustmentEvent()	Processes an adjustment event enabled for this scrollbar.
removeAdjustmentListener()	Removes a listener from receiving this scrollbar's adjustment events.

Peer Method

addNotify()	Create the scrollbar's peer.

Debugging Method

paramString()	Generates a string representing the scrollbar's state.

Deprecated Method

getLineIncrement()	Replaced by getUnitIncrement().
getPageIncrement()	Replaced by getBlockIncrement().
getVisible()	Replaced by getVisibleAmount().
setLineIncrement()	Replaced by setUnitIncrement().
setPageIncrement()	Replaced by setBlockIncrement().

A
B
C
D
E
F
G
H
I
J
K
L
M
N
O
P
Q
R
S
T
U
V
W
X
Y
Z

See Also

```
Adjustable, java.awt.event.AdjustmentEvent,
java.awt.event.AdjustmentListener, ScrollPane.
```

Example

This example creates a canvas that paints a very large grid and two scrollbars to pan around the grid. See Figure 328. The maximum values of the scrollbars are set to the pixel size of the grid so that the value of the scrollbar can be used to determine the location of the visible area. For simplicity, the `paint()` method always paints the entire grid such that the top-left corner is at (0, 0). Also, the `Graphics.translate()` method is used to adjust the graphics context's origin so that the correct part of the grid will be visible. A more efficient implementation would paint only the visible portion of the grid.

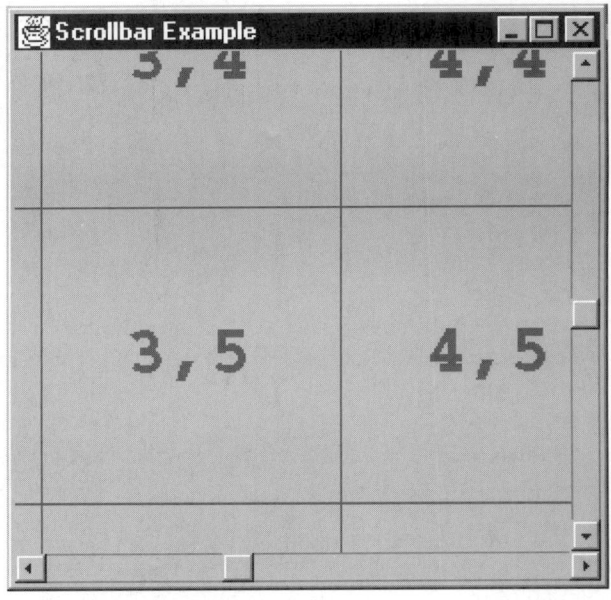

FIGURE 328: Scrollbar.

Note: The `ScrollPane` component should be used for viewing large components. This example is for demonstration purposes only.

See also the `Color` class example for a use of `Scrollbar`.

```java
import java.awt.*;
import java.awt.event.*;

class Main extends Frame implements AdjustmentListener {
    Scrollbar sbVer = new Scrollbar(Scrollbar.VERTICAL);
    Scrollbar sbHor = new Scrollbar(Scrollbar.HORIZONTAL);
    MainCanvas cv = new MainCanvas(sbVer, sbHor);

    Main() {
        super("Scrollbar Example");
        add(cv, BorderLayout.CENTER);
        add(sbVer, BorderLayout.EAST);
        add(sbHor, BorderLayout.SOUTH);

        // Add adjustment listener for scrollbars
        sbVer.addAdjustmentListener(this);
        sbHor.addAdjustmentListener(this);

        setSize(200, 200);
        show();
```

```
        }

    public void adjustmentValueChanged(AdjustmentEvent evt) {
        Scrollbar sb = (Scrollbar)evt.getSource();
        System.out.println(((sb.getOrientation() == Scrollbar.VERTICAL) ?
                            "ver" : "hor")
                     + " li=" + sb.getUnitIncrement()
                     + " pi=" + sb.getBlockIncrement()
                     + " max=" + sb.getMaximum()
                     + " vis=" + sb.getVisibleAmount());
        cv.sbChanged();
    }

    static public void main(String[] args) {
        new Main();
    }
}

// Creates a very large square grid.
// Each grid cell is labelled to help with navigation.
class MainCanvas extends Component {
    int gridSize = 1500;
    int gridCells = 10;
    int cellSize = gridSize/gridCells;
    int originX, originY;
    Scrollbar sbVer;
    Scrollbar sbHor;

    MainCanvas(Scrollbar sbVer, Scrollbar sbHor) {
        this.sbVer = sbVer;
        this.sbHor = sbHor;
        setFont(new Font("Courier", Font.BOLD, 36));
    }

    public void sbChanged() {
        originY = -sbVer.getValue();
        originX = -sbHor.getValue();
        repaint();
    }

    // If the size of the component changes, we need to update
    // the scrollbar values.
    public void doLayout() {
        super.doLayout();
        int w = getSize().width;
        int h = getSize().height;

        sbVer.setValues(sbVer.getValue(), h, sbVer.getMinimum(), gridSize);
        sbVer.setBlockIncrement(Math.min(cellSize, h));
        sbVer.setUnitIncrement(Math.min(cellSize, h/5));
        sbHor.setValues(sbHor.getValue(), w, sbHor.getMinimum(), gridSize);
        sbHor.setBlockIncrement(Math.min(cellSize, w));
        sbHor.setUnitIncrement(Math.min(cellSize, w/5));

        // This ensures that if the grid is larger than the viewable
        // area, you will never see space around the grid.
        originX = -Math.max(0, Math.min(gridSize-w, sbHor.getValue()));
        originY = -Math.max(0, Math.min(gridSize-h, sbVer.getValue()));
    }
```

A
B
C
D
E
F
G
H
I
J
K
L
M
N
O
P
Q
R
S
T
U
V
W
X
Y
Z

```
public void paint(Graphics g) {
    FontMetrics fm = g.getFontMetrics();

    // Using translate() simplifies the painting code
    // since it doesn't have to worry about origin changes.
    g.translate(originX, originY);
    g.setColor(Color.red);
    for (int i=0; i<gridCells; i++) {
        int c = i * cellSize;
        g.drawLine(c, 0, c, gridSize);
        g.drawLine(0, c, gridSize, c);
    }
    g.drawRect(0, 0, gridSize-1, gridSize-1);
    for (int i=0; i<gridCells; i++) {
        for (int j=0; j<gridCells; j++) {
            String str = "" + i + "," + j;
            int x = i * cellSize;
            int y = j * cellSize;

            g.drawString(str, x+(cellSize-fm.stringWidth(str))/2,
                y+(cellSize-fm.getHeight())/2+fm.getAscent());
        }
    }
}
```

addAdjustmentListener()

PURPOSE   Adds a listener for receiving this scrollbar's adjustment events.

SYNTAX   ```
              public synchronized void
                  addAdjustmentListener(AdjustmentListener listener)
              ```

DESCRIPTION   Adjustment events are fired when the scrollbar's value is changed. See
              AdjustmentEvent for more details. After this method is called, the adjust-
              ment listener `listener` will receive adjustment events fired by this scrollbar.
              If `listener` is `null`, this method does nothing.

PARAMETERS
  listener    The possibly `null` adjustment listener to add.

SEE ALSO      java.awt.event.AdjustmentEvent,
              java.awt.event.AdjustmentListener, removeAdjustmentListener().

EXAMPLE       See the class example.
              ```

addNotify()

PURPOSE   Creates this scrollbar's peer.

SYNTAX   `public void addNotify()`

DESCRIPTION   This method creates the peer if it does not exist. The peer is created by calling the `Toolkit.createScrollbar()` method. This method should never be called directly. It is normally called by the parent.

OVERRIDES   `Component.addNotify()`.

SEE ALSO   `Component`, `Toolkit`.

getBlockIncrement()

PURPOSE   Retrieves this scrollbar's block increment value.

SYNTAX   `public int getBlockIncrement()`

DESCRIPTION   The scrollbar's block increment value controls the amount by which the adjustable value is changed when the Page Up or Page Down key is pressed. If applying the increment modifies the adjustable value outside the scrollbar range, the adjustable value is set to either the maximum or minimum value. The scrollbar's block increment value can be changed at any time using `set-BlockIncrement()`.

RETURNS   The scrollbar's block increment value.

SEE ALSO   `getUnitIncrement()`, `setBlockIncrement()`.

EXAMPLE   See the class example.

getLineIncrement()   *DEPRECATED*

PURPOSE   Replaced by `getUnitIncrement()`.

SYNTAX   `public int getLineIncrement()`

RETURNS   The scrollbar's line increment value.

DEPRECATION   Replace the usage of this deprecated method, as in
```
  int increment = scrollbar.getLineIncrement();
```
with
```
  int increment = scrollbar.getUnitIncrement();
```

getMaximum()

PURPOSE	Retrieves this scrollbar's maximum value.
SYNTAX	`public int getMaximum()`
DESCRIPTION	The maximum value (along with the visible amount) determines how large the scrollbar's value can be. See the class description for more information about the scrollbar's maximum value.
RETURNS	This scrollbar's maximum value.
SEE ALSO	`getMinimum()`, `getValue()`, `getVisibleAmount()`, `setMaximum()`.
EXAMPLE	See the class example.

getMinimum()

PURPOSE	Retrieves this scrollbar's minimum value.
SYNTAX	`public int getMinimum()`
DESCRIPTION	The minimum value determines how small the scrollbar's value can be. See the class description for more information about the scrollbar's minimum value.
RETURNS	This scrollbar's minimum value.
SEE ALSO	`getMaximum()`, `getValue()`, `getVisibleAmount()`, `setMinimum()`.
EXAMPLE	See the class example.

getOrientation()

PURPOSE	Retrieves this scrollbar's orientation.
SYNTAX	`public int getOrientation()`
DESCRIPTION	A scrollbar has an orientation that can be either vertical or horizontal. The orientation is specified as the scrollbar is created and can be changed using `setOrientation()`.
RETURNS	The scrollbar's orientation. This value can be either VERTICAL or HORIZONTAL.
SEE ALSO	`setOrientation()`.
EXAMPLE	See the class example.

getPageIncrement()   *DEPRECATED*

PURPOSE   Replaced by `getBlockIncrement()`.

SYNTAX   `public int getPageIncrement()`

RETURNS   The scrollbar's page increment value.

DEPRECATION Replace the usage of this deprecated method, as in
```
int increment = scrollbar.getPageIncrement();
```
with
```
int increment = scrollbar.getBlockIncrement();
```

getUnitIncrement()

PURPOSE   Retrieves this scrollbar's unit increment value.

SYNTAX   `public int getUnitIncrement()`

DESCRIPTION The scrollbar's unit increment value controls the amount by which the adjustable value is changed when the Line Up or Line Down key is pressed. If applying the increment modifies the adjustable value outside the scrollbar range, the adjustable value is set to either the maximum or minimum value. The scrollbar's unit increment value can be changed at any time by using `setUnitIncrement()`.

RETURNS   The scrollbar's unit increment value.

SEE ALSO   `getBlockIncrement()`, `setUnitIncrement()`.

EXAMPLE   See the class example.

getValue()

PURPOSE   Retrieves this scrollbar's adjustable value.

SYNTAX   `public int getValue()`

DESCRIPTION See the class description for more information about the scrollbar's adjustable value.

RETURNS   This scrollbar's adjustable value.

SEE ALSO   `getMaximum()`, `getMinimum()`, `getVisibleAmount()`, `setValue()`.

EXAMPLE   See the class example.

A
B
C
D
E
F
G
H
I
J
K
L
M
N
O
P
Q
R

T
U
V
W
X
Y
Z

getVisible()   *DEPRECATED*

PURPOSE	Replaced by `getVisibleAmount()`.
SYNTAX	`public int getVisible()`
RETURNS	The scrollbar's visible value.
DEPRECATION	Replace the usage of this deprecated method, as in

```
  int vis = scrollbar.getVisible();
```
with
```
  int vis = scrollbar.getVisibleAmount();
```

getVisibleAmount()

PURPOSE	Retrieves the scrollbar's visible amount.
SYNTAX	`public int getVisible()`
DESCRIPTION	The scrollbar's visible amount controls the size of the scroll box. It is typically used to indicate how much of the document is visible. For example, if only one-third of the document is visible, the scrollbar's visible amount should be set to `(getMaximum()-getMinimum())/3` so that the size of the scroll box will be one third the size of the whole scrollbar.
RETURNS	The scrollbar's visible value.
SEE ALSO	`getMaximum()`, `getMinimum()`, `getValue()`, `setVisibleAmount()`.
EXAMPLE	See the class example.

HORIZONTAL

PURPOSE	The orientation constant specifying a horizontal scrollbar.
SYNTAX	`public static final int HORIZONTAL`
EXAMPLE	See the class example.

paramString()

PURPOSE	Generates a string representing the scrollbar's state.
SYNTAX	`protected String paramString()`

DESCRIPTION | A subclass of this class should override this method and return a concatenation of its state with the results of `super.paramString()`. This method is called by the `toString()` method and is typically used for debugging.

RETURNS | A non-`null` string representing the scrollbar's state.

OVERRIDES | `Component.paramString()`.

SEE ALSO | `java.lang.Object.toString()`.

EXAMPLE | See `Component.paramString()`.

processAdjustmentEvent()

PURPOSE | Processes an adjustment event enabled for this scrollbar.

SYNTAX | `protected void processAdjustmentEvent(AdjustmentEvent evt)`

DESCRIPTION | Adjustment events are fired when this scrollbar's value changes. See the class description and `AdjustmentEvent` for more details. This method processes adjustment events for this scrollbar by calling any registered `AdjustmentListener`. This method is invoked only if adjustment events have been enabled for this scrollbar. This can happen either when an adjustment listener is added to this scrollbar or when `Component.enableEvents()` is called to enable adjustment events.

Typically, a scrollbar controls how its adjustment events are processed by adding or removing adjustment listeners. It overrides `processAdjustmentEvent()` only if it needs to do processing in addition to that performed by the registered listeners.

When a subclass does override `processAdjustmentEvent()`, it should call `super.processAdjustmentEvent()` to perform the processing intended by its base class (such as dispatching the listeners).

PARAMETERS

evt | The non-`null` adjustment event.

SEE ALSO | `addAdjustmentListener()`, `Component.enableEvents()`, `Component.disableEvents()`, `java.awt.event.AdjustmentEvent`, `java.awt.event.AdjustmentListener`, `processEvent()`, `removeAdjustmentListener()`.

EXAMPLE | See `AWTEventMulticaster.adjustmentValueChanged()`.

A
B
C
D
E
F
G
H
I
J
K
L
M
N
O
P
Q
R
S
T
U
V
W
X
Y
Z

processEvent()

PURPOSE	Processes an event enabled for this scrollbar.
SYNTAX	`protected void processEvent(AWTEvent evt)`
DEPRECATION	This method extends `Component.processEvent()` by adding support for `AdjustmentEvent`. This method can be overridden to handle new types of events for this scrollbar. When a subclass does override `processEvent()`, it should call `super.processEvent()` to perform the processing intended by its base class (such as dispatching the listeners for different event types).
PARAMETERS	
evt	The non-null event to be processed.
OVERRIDES	`Component.processEvent()`.
SEE ALSO	`AWTEvent`, `processAdjustmentEvent()`.
EXAMPLE	See the `Component` class example.

removeAdjustmentListener()

PURPOSE	Removes a listener from receiving this scrollbar's adjustment events.
SYNTAX	`public synchronized void removeFocusListener(AdjustmentListener listener)`
DESCRIPTION	Adjustment events are fired when this scrollbar's value is changed. See `AdjustmentEvent` for more details. After this method is called, the adjustment listener `listener` will no longer receive adjustment events from this scrollbar. If `listener` is `null`, this method does nothing.
PARAMETERS	
listener	The possibly `null` adjustment listener to remove.
SEE ALSO	`addAdjustmentListener()`, `java.awt.event.AdjustmentEvent`, `java.awt.event.AdjustmentListener`.
EXAMPLE	See `removeActionListener()` in `MenuItem.disableEvents()`.

Scrollbar()

PURPOSE	Constructs a new `Scrollbar` instance.
SYNTAX	`public Scrollbar()` `public Scrollbar(int orientation)`

```
public Scrollbar(int orientation, int value, int visible, int
    minimum, int maximum)
```

DESCRIPTION This constructor creates a new Scrollbar instance that has the orientation orientation and initial values and range. If orientation is not specified, it defaults to VERTICAL. If value and minimum are not specified, they default to 0. If visible is not specified, it defaults to 10. If maximum is not specified, it defaults to 100. The line increment defaults to 1, and the page increment defaults to 10. The supplied values are adjusted if necessary to satisfy the following constraint:

```
minimum <= value <= maximum
```

The constraint is achieved with the following rules. If maximum < minimum, maximum is set to minimum. If value > maximum, value is set to maximum; if value < minimum, value is set to minimum. If the visible amount is larger than the range between maximum and minimum, the visible amount is set to this range and the scroll box is made as large as the scrollbar, thereby preventing the scrollbar from generating any events.

PARAMETERS

maximum   The scrollbar's maximum value.
minimum   The scrollbar's minimum value.
orientation   The scrollbar's orientation. Must be one of HORIZONTAL or VERTICAL.
value   The scrollbar's initial value.
visible   The scrollbar's visible amount.

EXCEPTIONS

IllegalArgumentException
              If orientation is not valid.

EXAMPLE This example creates a horizontal scrollbar and prints out all events fired by the scrollbar. See Figure 329.

FIGURE 329: Scrollbar().

```
import java.awt.*;
import java.awt.event.*;

public class Main extends Frame implements AdjustmentListener {
    Main() {
        super("Scrollbar Example");
        Scrollbar sb = new Scrollbar(Scrollbar.HORIZONTAL, 0, 50, 0, 100);

        sb.addAdjustmentListener(this);
        add(sb, BorderLayout.SOUTH);
        pack();
        show();
    }

    public void adjustmentValueChanged(AdjustmentEvent evt) {
```

```
                System.out.println(evt);
        }

        static public void main(String[] args) {
            new Main();
        }
    }
```

A

B

C

setBlockIncrement( )

PURPOSE	Sets this scrollbar's block increment.
SYNTAX	`public synchronized void setBlockIncrement(int increment)`
DESCRIPTION	This method sets the scrollbar's block increment value to be `increment`. The scrollbar's block increment value controls the amount by which the adjustable value is changed when the Page Up or Page Down key is pressed. If applying the increment modifies the adjustable value outside the scrollbar range, the adjustable value is set to either the maximum or minimum value.
PARAMETERS	
`increment`	The non-negative block increment.
SEE ALSO	`getBlockIncrement()`, `setUnitIncrement()`.
EXAMPLE	See the class example.

setLineIncrement( )   *DEPRECATED*

PURPOSE	Replaced by `setUnitIncrement()`.
SYNTAX	`public void setLineIncrement(int increment)`
PARAMETERS	
`increment`	The non-negative line increment.

DEPRECATION	Replace the usage of this deprecated method, as in
	  `scrollbar.setLineIncrement(increment);`
	with
	  `scrollbar.setUnitIncrement(increment);`

setMaximum( )

PURPOSE	Sets this scrollbar's maximum value.
SYNTAX	`public synchronized void setMaximum(int max)`

DESCRIPTION   This method sets the maximum value possible for this scrollbar to be max. The scrollbar's adjustable value may be adjusted if its current value is greater than max. The scrollbar's maximum may be adjusted (to be 1 greater than the minimum) if it is less than the scrollbar's minimum value.

PARAMETERS
max   The scrollbar's new maximum value.

SEE ALSO   getMinimum(), setMaximumValue(), setVisibleAmount(), setValue().

EXAMPLE   See setMinimum().

setMinimum()

PURPOSE   Sets this scrollbar's minimum value.

SYNTAX   public synchronized void setMinimum(int min)

DESCRIPTION   This method sets the minimum value possible for this scrollbar to be min. The scrollbar's value may be adjusted if its current value is less than min. The scrollbar's maximum may be adjusted (to be 1 greater than min) if it is less than min.

PARAMETERS
min   The scrollbar's new minimum value.

SEE ALSO   getMinimum(), setMaximumValue(), setVisibleAmount(), setValue().

EXAMPLE   This example creates a set of buttons for controlling the visibility amount, orientation, maximum, and minimum of a scrollbar. See Figure 330.

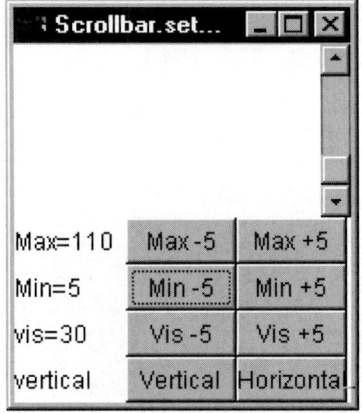
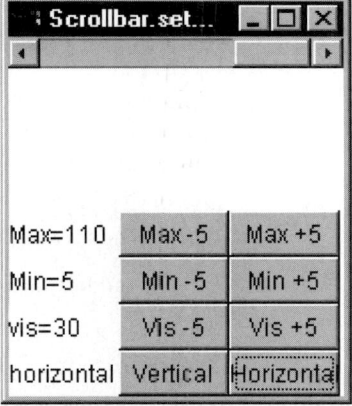

FIGURE 330:   Changing a Scrollbar's properties.

```
import java.awt.*;
import java.awt.event.*;

class Main extends Frame implements ActionListener, AdjustmentListener {
    Scrollbar scrollbar = new Scrollbar(Scrollbar.VERTICAL, 0, 10, 10, 100);
    Label max, min, vis, posn;

    Main() {
        super("Scrollbar.setMinimum");
        Panel p = new Panel(new GridLayout(4, 0));

        max = new Label("Max=" + scrollbar.getMaximum());
        p.add(max);

        Button b = new Button("Max -5");
        p.add(b);
        b.addActionListener(this);
        b = new Button("Max +5");
        p.add(b);
        b.addActionListener(this);

        min = new Label("Min=" + scrollbar.getMinimum());
        p.add(min);
        b = new Button("Min -5");
        p.add(b);
        b.addActionListener(this);
        b = new Button("Min +5");
        p.add(b);
        b.addActionListener(this);

        vis = new Label("Vis=" + scrollbar.getVisibleAmount());
        p.add(vis);
        b = new Button("Vis -5");
        p.add(b);
        b.addActionListener(this);
        b = new Button("Vis +5");
        p.add(b);
        b.addActionListener(this);

        posn = new Label("vertical");
        p.add(posn);
        b = new Button("Vertical");
        p.add(b);
        b.addActionListener(this);
        b = new Button("Horizontal");
        p.add(b);
        b.addActionListener(this);

        add(p, BorderLayout.SOUTH);
        add(scrollbar, BorderLayout.EAST);

        scrollbar.addAdjustmentListener(this);
        pack();
        show();
    }

    public void actionPerformed(ActionEvent evt) {
        String cmd = evt.getActionCommand();
        if (cmd.equals("Max -5")) {
```

```
                scrollbar.setMaximum(scrollbar.getMaximum()-5);
                max.setText("Max=" + scrollbar.getMaximum());
        } else if (cmd.equals("Max +5")) {
                scrollbar.setMaximum(scrollbar.getMaximum()+5);
                max.setText("Max=" + scrollbar.getMaximum());
        } else  if (cmd.equals("Min -5")) {
                scrollbar.setMinimum(scrollbar.getMinimum()-5);
                min.setText("Min=" + scrollbar.getMinimum());
        } else if (cmd.equals("Min +5")) {
                scrollbar.setMinimum(scrollbar.getMinimum()+5);
                min.setText("Min=" + scrollbar.getMinimum());
        } else  if (cmd.equals("Vis -5")) {
                scrollbar.setVisibleAmount(scrollbar.getVisibleAmount()-5);
                vis.setText("vis=" + scrollbar.getVisibleAmount());
        } else if (cmd.equals("Vis +5")) {
                scrollbar.setVisibleAmount(scrollbar.getVisibleAmount()+5);
                vis.setText("vis=" + scrollbar.getVisibleAmount());
        } else  if (cmd.equals("Horizontal")) {
                if (scrollbar.getOrientation() != Scrollbar.HORIZONTAL) {
                    scrollbar.setOrientation(Scrollbar.HORIZONTAL);
                    posn.setText("horizontal");
                    remove(scrollbar);
                    add(scrollbar, BorderLayout.NORTH);
                    validate();
                }
        } else if (cmd.equals("Vertical")) {
                if (scrollbar.getOrientation() != Scrollbar.VERTICAL) {
                    scrollbar.setOrientation(Scrollbar.VERTICAL);
                    posn.setText("vertical");
                    remove(scrollbar);
                    add(scrollbar, BorderLayout.EAST);
                    validate();
                }
        }
    }

    public void adjustmentValueChanged(AdjustmentEvent evt) {
        System.out.println("value = " + scrollbar.getValue() +
                        " visible = " + scrollbar.getVisibleAmount() +
                        " min = " + scrollbar.getMinimum() +
                        " max = " + scrollbar.getMaximum());
    }

    public static void main(String[] args) {
        new Main();
    }
}
```

setOrientation()

PURPOSE   Sets this scrollbar's orientation.

SYNTAX   `public synchronized void setOrientation(int orientation)`

DESCRIPTION   A scrollbar has an orientation that can be either vertical or horizontal. This
method sets this scrollbar's orientation to be orientation. If the scrollbar

already has this orientation, this method does nothing. Otherwise, the scroll-bar's peer is re-created with the new orientation.

PARAMETERS

orientation The scrollbar's orientation, which can be either VERTICAL or HORIZONTAL.

EXCEPTIONS

IllegalArgumentException

If orientation is neither VERTICAL nor HORIZONTAL.

SEE ALSO   getOrientation().

EXAMPLE   See setMinimum().

setPageIncrement( )   *DEPRECATED*

PURPOSE   Replaced by setBlockIncrement().

SYNTAX   public void setPageIncrement(int increment)

PARAMETERS

increment   The non-negative page increment.

DEPRECATION   Replace the usage of this deprecated method, as in
               scrollbar.setPageIncrement(increment);
               with
               scrollbar.setBlockIncrement(increment);

setUnitIncrement( )

PURPOSE   Sets the scrollbar's line increment.

SYNTAX   public synchronized void setUnitIncrement(int increment)

DESCRIPTION   This method sets the scrollbar's unit increment value to increment. The scrollbar's unit increment value controls the amount by which the adjustable value is changed when the Line Up or Line Down key is pressed. If applying the increment modifies the adjustable value outside the scrollbar range, the adjustable value is set to either the maximum or minimum value.

PARAMETERS

increment   The non-negative unit increment.

SEE ALSO   getUnitIncrement(), setBlockIncrement().

EXAMPLE   See the class example.

setValue( )

PURPOSE	Sets this scrollbar's value.
SYNTAX	`public synchronized void setValue(int value)`
DESCRIPTION	This method updates the position of the scrollbar's scroll box to be `value`. `value` is adjusted if necessary to be greater than or equal to the scrollbar's minimum value and less than or equal to the scrollbar's maximum value. Calling `setValue()` does not fire an `AdjustmentEvent`.
PARAMETERS	
value	The scrollbar's new value.
SEE ALSO	`getValue()`.
EXAMPLE	See the `Color` class example.

setValues( )

PURPOSE	Sets various scrollbar values.
SYNTAX	`public synchronized void setValues(int value, int visible, int minimum, int maximum)`
DESCRIPTION	The supplied values are adjusted if necessary to satisfy the following constraint:

$$minimum <= value <= maximum-visible.$$

The constraint is achieved with the following rules. If `maximum < minimum`, `maximum` is set to `minimum`. If `value > maximum-visible`, `value` is set to `maximum-visible`; if `value < minimum`, `value` is set to `minimum`. If the visible amount is larger than the range between the maximum and the minimum, it is set to the range and the scroll box is made as large as the scrollbar, thereby preventing the scrollbar from generating any events.

PARAMETERS	
maximum	The scrollbar's maximum value.
minimum	The scrollbar's minimum value.
value	The scrollbar's value.
visible	The scrollbar's visible area.
SEE ALSO	`setMaximum()`, `setMinimum()`, `setValue()`, `setVisibleAmount()`.
EXAMPLE	See the class example.

A
B
C
D
E
F
G
H
I
J
K
L
M
N
O
P
Q
R
S
T
U
V
W
X
Y
Z

A
B
C
D
E
F
G
H
I
J
K
L
M
N
O
P
Q
R
S
T
U
V
W
X
Y
Z

setVisibleAmount( )

PURPOSE	Sets this scrollbar's visible amount.
SYNTAX	`public synchronized void setVisible(int vis)`
DESCRIPTION	See the class description for details on a scrollbar's visible amount. This method sets this scrollbar's visible amount to the maximum of 1 and `vis`.
PARAMETERS	
`vis`	The scrollbar's new visible amount.
SEE ALSO	`getMaximum()`, `getMinimum()`, `getValue()`, `getVisibleAmount()`.
EXAMPLE	See `setOrientation()`.

VERTICAL

PURPOSE	The orientation constant specifying a vertical scrollbar.
SYNTAX	`public static final int VERTICAL`
EXAMPLE	See the class example.

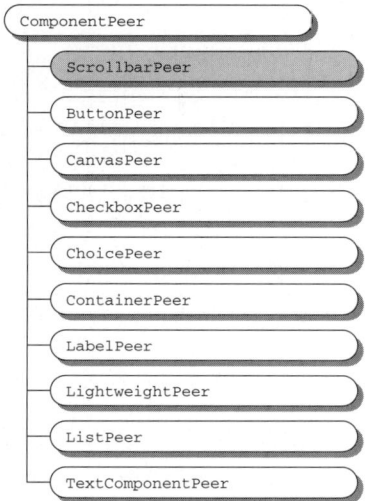

ComponentPeer
ScrollbarPeer
ButtonPeer
CanvasPeer
CheckboxPeer
ChoicePeer
ContainerPeer
LabelPeer
LightweightPeer
ListPeer
TextComponentPeer

Syntax

`public interface ScrollbarPeer extends ComponentPeer`

Description

The scrollbar (see `Scrollbar` class) in the AWT uses the platform's native implementation of a scrollbar. So that the AWT scrollbar behaves the same on all platforms, the scrollbar is assigned a *peer*, whose task is to translate the behavior of the platform's native scrollbar to the behavior of the AWT scrollbar.

AWT programmers normally do not directly use peer classes and interfaces. Instead, they deal with AWT components in the `java.awt` package. These in turn automatically manage their peers. Only someone who is porting the AWT to another platform should be concerned with the peer classes and interfaces. Consequently, most peer documentation refers to `java.awt` counterparts.

See `Component` and `Toolkit` for additional information about component peers.

MEMBER SUMMARY	
Peer Methods	
`setLineIncrement()`	Sets the scrollbar's unit increment.
`setPageIncrement()`	Sets the scrollbar's block increment.
`setValues()`	Sets various scrollbar values.

See Also

`java.awt.Component, java.awt.Scrollbar, java.awt.Toolkit.`

setLineIncrement()

PURPOSE	Sets the scrollbar's unit increment.
SYNTAX	`void setLineIncrement(int increment)`
PARAMETERS	
`increment`	The non-negative unit increment.
SEE ALSO	`java.awt.Scrollbar.setUnitIncrement().`

setPageIncrement()

PURPOSE	Sets the scrollbar's block increment.
SYNTAX	`void setPageIncrement(int increment)`
PARAMETERS	
`increment`	The non-negative block increment.
SEE ALSO	`java.awt.Scrollbar.setBlockIncrement().`

setValues()

PURPOSE	Sets various scrollbar values.
SYNTAX	`void setValues(int value, int visible, int minimum, int maximum)`
PARAMETERS	
`maximum`	The scrollbar's maximum value.
`minimum`	The scrollbar's minimum value.
`value`	The scrollbar's value.
`visible`	The scrollbar's visible size.
SEE ALSO	`java.awt.Scrollbar.setValues().`

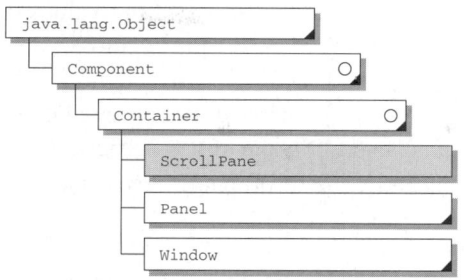

Syntax

```
public class ScrollPane extends Container
```

Description

A *scroll pane* is a container that contains a single child component and displays it through the *viewport* (see Figure 331). The dimensions of the viewport can be smaller than the child component. In this case, not all of the child component is visible. The scroll pane contains a horizontal scrollbar and a vertical scrollbar that the user can use to view different parts of the child component.

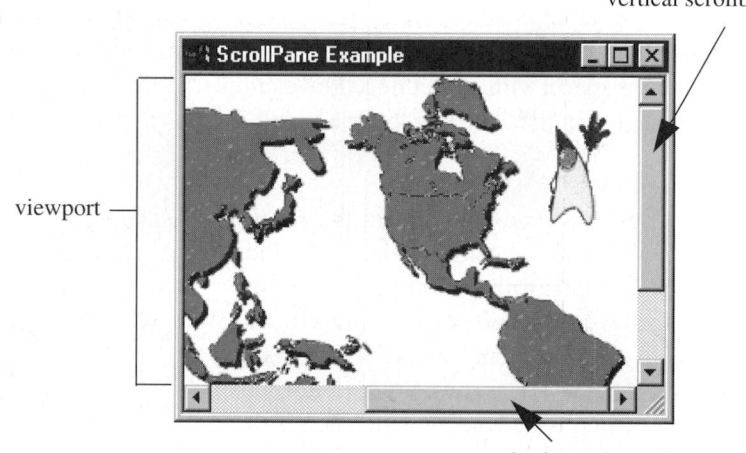

FIGURE 331: Parts of a ScrollPane.

The main purpose of the scroll pane is to simplify the work needed to implement a scrollable component. Using a scroll pane, you need only insert the component into the scroll pane; much of the work involved in scrolling the component is handled by the scroll pane. However, the child component may need a couple of small changes in order to behave properly. These changes are discussed in the following sections.

A
B
C
D
E
F
G
H
I
J
K
L
M
N
O
P
Q
R
S
T
U
V
W
X
Y
Z

Viewport

You can view different parts of the child component by moving the scroll pane's viewport. The viewport can be moved in one of three ways: by setting values on the scrollbars (through the `Adjustable` interface), by calling `setScrollPosition()`, or by the user's interacting with the scrollbars.

The dimensions of the viewport, which can be retrieved by calling `getViewportSize()`, do not include the scroll pane's scrollbars or other borders. The viewport bounds are exactly the scroll pane bounds, reduced by the scroll pane's insets (see `Container.getInsets()`).

Preparing the Child Component

To behave properly in a scroll pane, a child component must do two things. First, it must implement `getPreferredSize()` and return the dimensions needed to fully display itself. For example, if the child displays a 100-x-100 image, it should return new `Dimension(100, 100)`. This information is used by the scroll pane to control the scrollbars.

Second, the child must handle the case in which its bounds are larger than its preferred size. To do its work, the scroll pane modifies the child's bounds as the viewport bounds change. The child's bounds are never made smaller than its preferred size, but if the viewport is larger than the child's preferred size, the scroll pane stretches the child's bounds to fill the viewport. The child must therefore paint its contents somewhere in this larger space and then fill the extra space with something. For example, if the child is showing an image, it could paint the image in the center of the space and fill the extra space with a gray color.

Scroll Position

The viewport has a property called the *scroll position*, which is a position relative to the child. For example, if the scroll position is (0, 0), the northwest corner of the child will be visible. On the other hand, if the scroll position is (1, 1), the left-most column and top-most row of pixels will be hidden. The scroll position values are bounded. In particular, the *x*-coordinate is

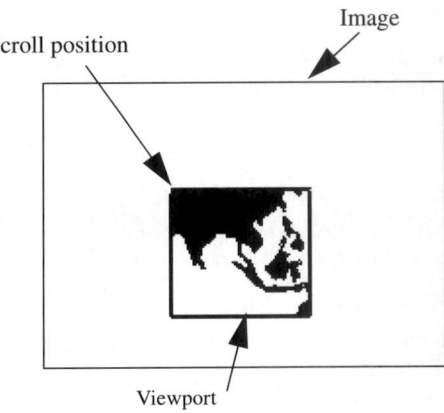

FIGURE 332:   **Scroll Position.**

```
x = Math.max(0,
    child.getPreferredSize().width-
        getViewportSize().width);
y = Math.max(0,
    child.getPreferredSize().height-
        getViewportSize().height);
```

This means that if the child is fully visible, the scroll position will not change from (0, 0).

When the viewport is smaller than the child's preferred size, the scroll pane implements the ability to see different parts of the child by modify the child's location. (See `Component.getLocation()`.) In particular, the location of the child is exactly

```
childLocation = (0-scrollPositionX, 0-scrollPositionY).
```

The Scrollbars

The scroll pane has a horizontal and vertical scrollbar whose values make up the scroll position. In particular, the scroll position's x-coordinate is the identical to the horizontal scrollbar's adjustment value. Likewise for the scroll position's y-coordinate. The scroll pane's scroll position can be updated by modifying the scrollbar's adjustment values.

The scroll pane scrollbars fire adjustment events (see `AdjustmentEvent`) whenever the scroll position changes. Unlike all other components, which fire events only when the user interacts with them, the scroll pane scrollbars fire events if the program changes the scroll position. However, the adjustment type is always `AdjustmentEvent.TRACK` no matter how the scrollbars are used. See `AdjustmentEvent` for more information on adjustment events.

Since the scroll pane itself does not generate any events, if you want to know when the scroll position changes, you need to listen for adjustment events on both scrollbars. The scrollbars always exist and can fire events even if they are not visible.

Scrollbar Display Policies

There are three ways in which the scrollbars can be made to appear in the scroll pane. These three scrollbar display policies must be specified at the time the scroll pane is created and cannot be changed later. See Table 23.

SCROLLBARS_ALWAYS	The scrollbars are always displayed.
SCROLLBARS_AS_NEEDED	The scrollbars appear only when needed.
SCROLLBARS_NEVER	The scrollbars are never displayed.

TABLE 23: ScrollPane Display Policies.

MEMBER SUMMARY	
Constructor	
ScrollPane()	Constructs a new ScrollPane instance.
Component Method	
addImpl()	Adds a component to this scroll pane.
Viewport Methods	
getScrollPosition()	Retrieves the viewport's scroll position.
getViewportSize()	Retrieves the dimensions of this scroll pane's viewport.
setScrollPosition()	Moves the viewport's scroll position.
	Continued

MEMBER SUMMARY	
Scrollbar Methods	
getHAdjustable()	Retrieves this scroll pane's horizontal scrollbar.
getHScrollbarHeight()	Retrieves the height of this scroll pane's horizontal scrollbar.
getVAdjustable()	Retrieves this scroll pane's vertical scrollbar.
getVScrollbarWidth()	Retrieves the width of this scroll pane's vertical scrollbar.
Scrollbar Display Policy Method and Constants	
getScrollbarDisplayPolicy()	Retrieves this scroll pane's scrollbar display policy.
SCROLLBARS_ALWAYS	The scrollbar display policy specifying that scrollbars are always displayed.
SCROLLBARS_AS_NEEDED	The scrollbar display policy specifying that scrollbars are displayed as needed.
SCROLLBARS_NEVER	The scrollbar display policy specifying that scrollbars are never displayed.
Layout Methods	
doLayout()	Invokes this scroll pane's layout manager.
setLayout()	This method does nothing.
Print Method	
printComponents()	Prints this scroll pane and its child.
Peer Method	
addNotify()	Creates this scroll pane's peer.
Debugging Method	
paramString()	Generates a string representation of this scroll pane's state.
Deprecated	
layout()	Replaced by doLayout().

See Also
Adjustable, java.awt.event.AdjustableEvent, Scrollbar.

Example
A scroll pane provides scrollbars for the user to view different parts of the child component. This example demonstrates how you can implement another way to move the scroll pane's viewport: by "grabbing." The grabbing gesture is made by clicking the child component and

dragging. For example, when you drag left, the child component moves left (which means that the viewport moves right). See Figure 333.

The program retrieves the scroll pane's scrollbars and increases their unit increment to 2.

Notice that in the image component `mouseDragged()` method, the scroll pane is retrieved by calling `getParent()` twice. This is because when a lightweight component is added to a scroll pane, the component is not added to the scroll pane. What actually happens is that a new panel is created and the component is added to the panel. The panel is then added to the scroll pane. It might be more prudent to pass the scroll pane reference to the child to avoid any problems if this changes in the future.

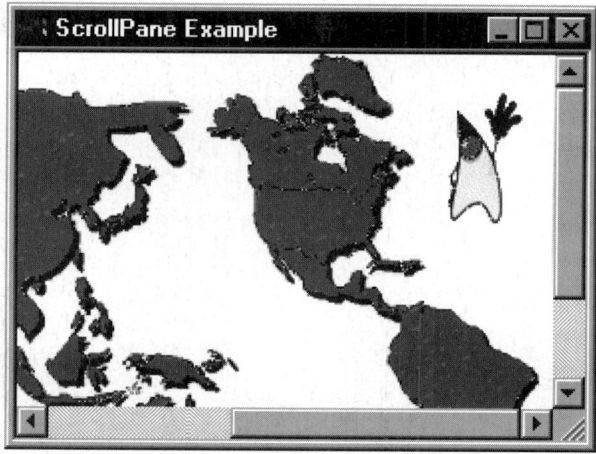

FIGURE 333: `ScrollPane`.

```java
import java.awt.*;
import java.awt.event.*;

class Main extends Frame {
    Main(String filename) {
        super("ScrollPane Example");
        Image image;
        ScrollPane sp = new ScrollPane();

        // Increase the scrollbar unit increments to 2.
        sp.getHAdjustable().setUnitIncrement(2);
        sp.getVAdjustable().setUnitIncrement(2);

        // Add the canvas to the scrollpane.
        sp.add(new ImageComponent(getToolkit().getImage(filename)));

        // Add the scrollpane to the frame and show.
        add(sp, BorderLayout.CENTER);
        setSize(200, 150);
        show();
    }

    public static void main(String args[]) {
        if (args.length != 1) {
            System.err.println("Usage: java Main <image-file>");
            System.exit(1);
        }
        new Main(args[0]);
    }
}

class ImageComponent extends Component {
```

```
    Image image;

    ImageComponent(Image image) {
        this.image = image;
        setBackground(Color.lightGray);

        // Set the cursor to be a hand cursor.
        setCursor(Cursor.getPredefinedCursor(Cursor.HAND_CURSOR));

        // Use the media tracker to retrieve the dimensions
        // of the image since we need them immediately.
        try {
            MediaTracker tracker = new MediaTracker(this);

            tracker.addImage(image, 0);
            tracker.waitForAll(0);
        } catch (Exception e) {
            e.printStackTrace();
        }

        // Listen for mouse events.
        addMouseListener(new MouseEventHandler());
        addMouseMotionListener(new MouseMotionEventHandler());
    }

    public Dimension getPreferredSize() {
        return new Dimension(image.getWidth(null), image.getHeight(null));
    }

    public void paint(Graphics g) {
        int iw = image.getWidth(this);
        int ih = image.getHeight(this);

        // Only if the dimensions are available do we draw the image.
        if (iw >= 0 && ih >= 0) {
            g.setColor(getBackground());
            g.clearRect(0, 0, size().width, size().height);

            // Draw the image centered.
            g.drawImage(image, (getSize().width-iw)/2,
                (getSize().height-ih)/2, this);
        }
    }

    Point downPt;
    class MouseEventHandler extends MouseAdapter {
        public void mousePressed(MouseEvent evt) {
            // Record the location of the down click.
            downPt = evt.getPoint();
        }
    }

    class MouseMotionEventHandler extends MouseMotionAdapter {
        public void mouseDragged(MouseEvent evt) {
            ScrollPane sp = (ScrollPane)(getParent().getParent());
            Point pt = sp.getScrollPosition();
            Dimension sz = sp.getViewportSize();

            // Calculate new position of viewport.
            pt.translate(downPt.x-evt.getX(), downPt.y-evt.getY());
```

```
            // Ensure that the new position is in the valid range.
            pt.x = Math.max(0, Math.min(getSize().width-sz.width, pt.x));
            pt.y = Math.max(0, Math.min(getSize().height-sz.height, pt.y));

            // Update the position of the viewport.
            sp.setScrollPosition(pt);
        }
    }
}
```

addImpl()

PURPOSE   Adds a component to this scroll pane.

SYNTAX   `protected final void addImpl(Component comp, Object constraints, int pos)`

DESCRIPTION   This method is called whenever `Container.add()` is called; it adds a child component to the scroll pane. The scroll pane can contain only one child component at a time. If the scroll pane already contains a component, that component is removed before `comp` is added.

               If `comp` is a lightweight component, a new panel (see `Panel`) is created and `comp` is added to the panel. The panel is then added to the scroll pane. This is important to note if `comp` wants to use `getParent()` to retrieve a handle to the scroll pane. In this case, a lightweight component must call `getParent()` twice.

PARAMETERS
`comp`   The non-`null` component to be added to the scroll pane.
`constraints`   This parameter is ignored.
`pos`   The value of this parameter is irrelevant, except that it must be `<= 0`.

EXCEPTIONS
`IllegalArgumentException`
                If `pos` is `> 0`.

OVERRIDES   `Container.addImpl()`.

SEE ALSO   `Container.add()`.

EXAMPLE   See the class example.

addNotify()

PURPOSE   Creates this scroll pane's peer.

SYNTAX   `public void addNotify()`

DESCRIPTION	This method creates the peer if it does not exist. The peer is created by a call to `Toolkit.createScrollpane()`. The `addNotify()` method should never be called directly. It is normally called by the scroll pane's parent.
OVERRIDES	`Container.addNotify()`.
EXAMPLE	See `Component.setVisible()`.

doLayout()

PURPOSE	Invokes this scroll pane's layout manager.
SYNTAX	`public void doLayout()`
DESCRIPTION	Ensures that the child component is at its preferred size. This method also updates the viewport location (see the class description) and scrollbar values, if necessary.
	This method is not normally called. It is called by the system whenever the size of the scroll pane changes. However, it can be overridden to detect changes in the viewport dimensions. The override must call `super.doLayout()`.
OVERRIDES	`Container.doLayout()`.
SEE ALSO	`Component.validate()`.
EXAMPLE	See `getViewportSize()`.

getHAdjustable()

PURPOSE	Retrieves this scroll pane's horizontal scrollbar.
SYNTAX	`public Adjustable getHAdjustable()`
DESCRIPTION	This method returns an adjustable object that represents this scroll pane's horizontal scrollbar. See the `Adjustable` interface for more information about how to manipulate the scrollbar. However, three `Adjustable` methods—`setMinimum()`, `setMaximum()`, and `setVisibleAmount()`—must not be called; if any is called, it throws an `AWTError` exception.
RETURNS	A non-`null` adjustable object representing the horizontal scrollbar.
SEE ALSO	`getVAdjustable()`.

A
B
C
D
E
F
G
H
I
J
K
L
M
N
O
P
Q
R
S
T
U
V
W
X
Y
Z

EXAMPLE   This example demonstrates how to change the scroll position of the viewport by modifying the scroll pane's scrollbars. (setScrollPosition(), however, is a more convenient method.) The program creates one hundred buttons. Clicking a button causes the viewport to shift such that the button is displayed in the top-left corner of the viewport. See Figure 334.

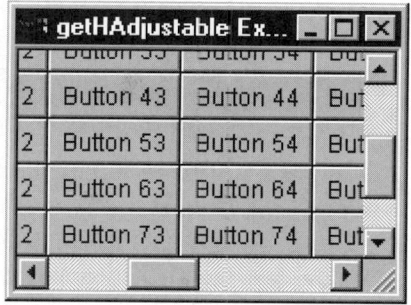

FIGURE 334:   Changing the Viewport's Scroll Position.

```java
import java.awt.*;
import java.awt.event.*;

class Main extends Frame implements ActionListener {
    ScrollPane sp = new ScrollPane();

    Main() {
        super("getHAdjustable Example");
        Panel p = new Panel(new GridLayout(10, 0));

        // Create a hundred buttons and add them to the panel.
        for (int i=0; i<100; i++) {
            Button b = new Button("Button "+i);

            b.addActionListener(this);
            p.add(b);
        }

        // Layout and show components.
        sp.add(p);
        add(sp, BorderLayout.CENTER);
        setSize(200, 150);
        show();
    }

    public void actionPerformed(ActionEvent evt) {
        Rectangle r = ((Component)evt.getSource()).getBounds();
        Adjustable hadj = sp.getHAdjustable();
        Adjustable vadj = sp.getVAdjustable();

        hadj.setValue(r.x);
        vadj.setValue(r.y);
    }

    public static void main(String args[]) {
        new Main();
    }
}
```

A
B
C
D
E
F
G
H
I
J
K
L
M
N
O
P
Q
R

T
U
V
W
X
Y
Z

getHScrollbarHeight()

PURPOSE	Retrieves the height of this scroll pane's horizontal scrollbar.
SYNTAX	`public int getHScrollbarHeight()`
DESCRIPTION	This method returns the height of this scroll pane's horizontal scrollbar. This number is typically used in size calculations that involve the scroll pane's viewport. The returned value is independent of whether the scrollbar is currently being displayed.
	If the scroll pane's peer is not created, this method returns 0.
RETURNS	The non-negative pixel height of the horizontal scrollbar.
SEE ALSO	`getVScrollbarWidth()`.
EXAMPLE	See `getViewportSize()`.

getScrollbarDisplayPolicy()

PURPOSE	Retrieves this scroll pane's scrollbar display policy.
SYNTAX	`public int getScrollbarDisplayPolicy()`
DESCRIPTION	See the class description for more information about scrollbar display policies.
RETURNS	One of SCROLLBARS_ALWAYS, SCROLLBARS_AS_NEEDED, or SCROLLBARS_NEVER.
EXAMPLE	See SCROLLBARS_ALWAYS.

getScrollPosition()

PURPOSE	Retrieves the viewport's scroll position.
SYNTAX	`public Point getScrollPosition()`
DESCRIPTION	The scroll position is the location of the viewport relative to the child. It can have values in this range:

```
x = Math.max(0,
        child.getPreferredSize().width-getViewportSize().width);
y = Math.max(0,
        child.getPreferredSize().height-getViewportSize().height);
```

	See the class description for more details.
RETURNS	A non-`null` point containing the viewport's scroll position.
EXAMPLE	See the class example.

getVAdjustable()

PURPOSE   Retrieves this scroll pane's vertical scrollbar.

SYNTAX   `public Adjustable getVAdjustable()`

DESCRIPTION   This method returns an adjustable object that represents the scroll pane's vertical scrollbar. See the `Adjustable` interface for more information on how to manipulate the scrollbar. However, three `Adjustable` methods—`setMinimum()`, `setMaximum()`, and `setVisibleAmount()`—must not be called; if any is called, it throws an `AWTError` exception.

RETURNS   A non-`null` adjustable object representing the vertical scrollbar.

SEE ALSO   `getHAdjustable()`.

EXAMPLE   See `getHAdjustable()`.

getViewportSize()

PURPOSE   Retrieves the dimensions of this scroll pane's viewport.

SYNTAX   `public Dimension getViewportSize()`

DESCRIPTION   The viewport dimensions do not include the scroll pane's scrollbars or other borders. The viewport bounds are exactly the scroll pane bounds, reduced by the scroll pane's insets (see `Container.getInsets()`).

FIGURE 335:   **ScrollPane's Viewport.**

RETURNS   A non-`null` `Dimension` object containing the dimensions of the viewport.

EXAMPLE   This example demonstrates how to resize a frame so that the child component within a scroll pane is completely visible. It does this by first comparing the size of the viewport with the size of the child and then enlarging the frame by the difference in size. See Figure 335.

```
import java.awt.*;
import java.awt.event.*;

class Main extends Frame implements ActionListener {
    ScrollPane sp = new ScrollPane();
    Button fullviewBtn = new Button("FullView");
    Circle circle = new Circle();
```

A
B
C
D
E
F
G
H
I
J
K
L
M
N
O
P
Q
R
S
T
U
V
W
X
Y
Z

```
Main() {
    super("getViewportSize Example");

    fullviewBtn.addActionListener(this);
    // Layout and show the components.
    sp.add(circle);
    add(sp, BorderLayout.CENTER);
    add(fullviewBtn, BorderLayout.NORTH);
    setSize(200, 150);
    show();
}

public void actionPerformed(ActionEvent evt) {
    Dimension d = sp.getViewportSize();
    Dimension cd = circle.getSize();
    int dW = cd.width - d.width;
    int dH = cd.height - d.height;

    // Take into account the width of the scrollbar if necessary.
    dW -= (dH > 0) ? sp.getVScrollbarWidth() : 0;
    dH -= (dW > 0) ? sp.getHScrollbarHeight() : 0;

    setSize(getSize().width + dW, getSize().height + dH);
    validate();
    fullviewBtn.enable(false);
}

public void doLayout() {
    super.doLayout();

    Dimension d = sp.getViewportSize();
    fullviewBtn.enable(
        d.width < circle.getPreferredSize().width
        || d.height < circle.getPreferredSize().height);
}

public static void main(String args[]) {
    new Main();
}
}

class Circle extends Component {
    Dimension size = new Dimension(200, 200);

    public Dimension getPreferredSize() {
        return size;
    }

    public void paint(Graphics g) {
        g.setColor(Color.lightGray);
        g.fillRect(0, 0, getSize().width, getSize().height);

        // Center the painted circle.
        g.setColor(Color.red);
        g.fillOval((getSize().width-size.width)/2,
            (getSize().height-size.height)/2, size.width-1, size.height-1);
    }
}
```

getVScrollbarWidth()

PURPOSE   Retrieves the width of this scroll pane's vertical scrollbar.

SYNTAX   `public int getVScrollbarWidth()`

DESCRIPTION   This method returns the width of this scroll pane's vertical scrollbar. This number is typically used in size calculations that involve the scroll pane's viewport. The returned value is independent of whether the scrollbar is currently being displayed.

              If the scroll pane's peer is not created, this method returns 0.

RETURNS   The non-negative pixel width of a vertical scrollbar.

SEE ALSO   `getHScrollbarHeight()`.

EXAMPLE   See `getViewportSize()`.

layout()   *DEPRECATED*

PURPOSE   Replaced by `doLayout()`.

SYNTAX   `public void layout()`

OVERRIDES   `Container.layout()`.

DEPRECATION   See `Container.layout()`.

paramString()

PURPOSE   Generates a string representation of this scroll pane's state.

SYNTAX   `public String paramString()`

DESCRIPTION   A subclass of this class should override this method and return a concatenation of its state with the results of `super.paramString()`. This method is called by `toString()` and is typically used for debugging.

OVERRIDES   `Container.paramString()`.

SEE ALSO   `java.lang.Object.toString()`.

EXAMPLE   See `Component.paramString()`.

printComponents()

PURPOSE   Prints this scroll pane and its child.

SYNTAX	`public void printComponents(Graphics g)`
DESCRIPTION	This methods prints the scroll pane and its child on g. The g parameter is typically a `PrintGraphics` object.
PARAMETERS	
g	A non-`null` graphics context.
OVERRIDES	`Container.printComponents()`.
SEE ALSO	`Component.print()`, `Component.printAll()`.
EXAMPLE	See `Component.printAll()`.

SCROLLBARS_ALWAYS

PURPOSE	The scrollbar display policy specifying that scrollbars are always displayed.
SYNTAX	`public static final int SCROLLBARS_ALWAYS`
SEE ALSO	`SCROLLBARS_AS_NEEDED`, `SCROLLBARS_NEVER`.
EXAMPLE	This example demonstrates the three different scrollbar display policies. A choice object is used to select between the policies. Since you cannot change the scrollbar display policy on an existing scroll pane, a new scroll pane must be created whenever the policy is changed. The current scroll pane in the frame is then replaced by the new scroll pane. Figure 336 shows the scroll pane when SCROLLBARS_NEVER and SCROLLBARS_NEEDED are used.

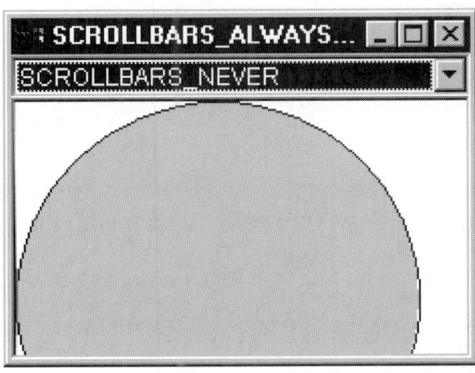 

FIGURE 336:   Examples of Scrollbar Display Policies.

```
import java.awt.*;
import java.awt.event.*;

class Main extends Frame implements ItemListener {
    Choice policyCh = new Choice();

    ScrollPane sp = new ScrollPane(ScrollPane.SCROLLBARS_ALWAYS);
```

```
        CircleComponent circle = new CircleComponent();

        Main() {
            super("SCROLLBARS_ALWAYS Example");

            // Initialize policy choice.
            policyCh.addItem("SCROLLBARS_ALWAYS");
            policyCh.addItem("SCROLLBARS_AS_NEEDED");
            policyCh.addItem("SCROLLBARS_NEVER");
            policyCh.select(0);
            policyCh.addItemListener(this);

            // Layout and show components.
            sp.add(circle);
            add(sp, BorderLayout.CENTER);
            add(policyCh, BorderLayout.NORTH);

            setSize(200, 150);
            show();
        }

        public void itemStateChanged(ItemEvent evt) {
            int p = sp.getScrollbarDisplayPolicy();

            if ("SCROLLBARS_ALWAYS".equals(evt.getItem())) {
                p = ScrollPane.SCROLLBARS_ALWAYS;
            } else if ("SCROLLBARS_AS_NEEDED".equals(evt.getItem())) {
                p = ScrollPane.SCROLLBARS_AS_NEEDED;
            } else if ("SCROLLBARS_NEVER".equals(evt.getItem())) {
                p = ScrollPane.SCROLLBARS_NEVER;
            }
            if (sp.getScrollbarDisplayPolicy() != p) {
                // Create a new scrollpane with the new display policy.
                remove(sp);
                sp = new ScrollPane(p);
                sp.add(circle);
                add(sp, BorderLayout.CENTER);
                validate();

            System.out.println(sp.getHAdjustable());
            System.out.println(sp.getVAdjustable());
            }
        }

        public static void main(String args[]) {
            new Main();
        }
    }

class CircleComponent extends Canvas {
    public Dimension getPreferredSize() {
        return new Dimension(200, 200);
    }

    public void paint(Graphics g) {
        g.setColor(Color.lightGray);
        g.fillOval(0, 0, 200, 200);
        g.setColor(Color.black);
        g.drawOval(0, 0, 200, 200);
    }
}
```

A
B
C
D
E
F
G
H
I
J
K
L
M
N
O
P
Q
R
S
T
U
V
W
X
Y
Z

A
B
C
D
E
F
G
H
I
J
K
L
M
N
O
P
Q
R
S
T
U
V
W
X
Y
Z

SCROLLBARS_AS_NEEDED

PURPOSE The scrollbar display policy specifying that scrollbars are displayed as needed.

SYNTAX `public static final int SCROLLBARS_AS_NEEDED`

DESCRIPTION Under this scrollbar display policy, the horizontal scrollbar appears only when the child's preferred width is wider than the viewport's width. The vertical scrollbar appears only when the child's preferred height is higher than the viewport's height.

SEE ALSO SCROLLBARS_ALWAYS, SCROLLBARS_NEVER.

EXAMPLE See SCROLLBARS_ALWAYS.

SCROLLBARS_NEVER

PURPOSE The scrollbar display policy specifying that scrollbars are never displayed.

SYNTAX `public static final int SCROLLBARS_NEVER`

DESCRIPTION Under this scrollbar display policy, the scrollbars are never displayed. However, the scrollbars do exist and can be retrieved using `getHAdjustable()` or `getVAdjustable()`.

SEE ALSO `getHAdjustable()`, `getVAdjustable()`, SCROLLBARS_ALWAYS, SCROLLBARS_AS_NEEDED.

EXAMPLE See SCROLLBARS_ALWAYS.

ScrollPane()

PURPOSE Constructs a new `ScrollPane` instance.

SYNTAX `public ScrollPane()`
`public ScrollPane(int sbPolicy)`

DESCRIPTION This constructor creates a new scroll pane that has a scrollbar display policy of sbPolicy. If sbPolicy is not specified, the constructor defaults to SCROLLBARS_AS_NEEDED. The dimensions of the new scroll pane are 100-x-100 pixels.

PARAMETERS
sbPolicy Must be one of the scrollbar display policies.

SEE ALSO SCROLLBARS_ALWAYS, SCROLLBARS_AS_NEEDED, SCROLLBARS_NEVER.

EXAMPLE See the class example.

setLayout()

PURPOSE	This method does nothing.
SYNTAX	`public final void setLayout(LayoutManager mgr)`
DESCRIPTION	The scroll pane has a built-in layout manager and should not be changed. This method is overridden and declared final so that any attempt to override this method or set the layout manager will be ignored.
PARAMETERS	
`mgr`	This parameter is ignored.
OVERRIDES	`Container.setLayout()`.

setScrollPosition()

PURPOSE	Moves the viewport's scroll position.
SYNTAX	`public void setScrollPosition(int x, int y)` `public void setScrollPosition(Point pt)`
DESCRIPTION	This method moves the viewport's scroll position to the location `pt`. If `pt` is not specified, the new scroll position is (`x`, `y`). If the scroll position is not in the range:

```
x = Math.max(0,
        child.getPreferredSize().width-getViewportSize().width);
y = Math.max(0,
        child.getPreferredSize().height-getViewportSize().height);
```

it is silently moved within this range. For example, if the coordinate is negative, it becomes 0. See the class description for more information about the scroll position.

A call to this method is only valid if the scroll pane contains a child otherwise `NullPointerException` is thrown.

PARAMETERS	
`pt`	A non-`null` point container the scroll position.
`x`	The *x*-coordinate of the scroll position.
`y`	The *y*-coordinate of the scroll position.
EXAMPLE	See the class example.

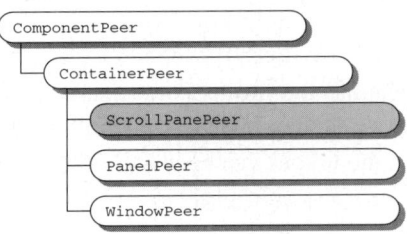

Syntax

```
public interface ScrollPanePeer extends ContainerPeer
```

Description

The scroll pane (see the ScrollPane class) in the AWT uses the platform's native implementation of a scroll pane. So that the AWT scroll pane behaves the same on all platforms, the scroll pane is assigned a *peer*, whose task is to translate the behavior of the platform's native scroll pane to the behavior of the AWT scroll pane.

AWT programmers normally do not directly use peer classes and interfaces. Instead, they deal with AWT components in the java.awt package. These in turn automatically manage their peers. Only someone who is porting the AWT to another platform should be concerned with the peer classes and interfaces. Consequently, most peer documentation refers to java.awt counterparts.

See Component and Toolkit for additional information about component peers.

MEMBER SUMMARY	
Peer Methods	
childResized()	Notifies the peer that the child component has been resized.
getHScrollbarHeight()	Retrieves the height of the scroll pane's horizontal scrollbar.
getVScrollbarWidth()	Retrieves the width of the scroll pane's vertical scrollbar.
setScrollPosition()	Sets the scroll pane's coordinates.
setUnitIncrement()	Sets the scroll pane's unit increment.
setValue()	Sets this scroll pane's value.

See Also

java.awt.Component, java.awt.ScrollPane, java.awt.Toolkit.

Sidebar: A B C D E F G H I J K L M N O P Q R T U V W X Y Z

childResized()

PURPOSE   Notifies the peer that the child component has been resized.

SYNTAX   `void childResized(int w, int h)`

PARAMETERS

  h   The height of the scroll pane's child component.

  w   The width of the scroll pane's child component.

SEE ALSO   `java.awt.ScrollPane.doLayout()`.

getHScrollbarHeight()

PURPOSE   Retrieves the height of the scroll pane's horizontal scroll bar.

SYNTAX   `int getHScrollbarHeight()`

RETURNS   The height of the scroll pane's horizontal scroll bar.

SEE ALSO   `java.awt.ScrollPane.getHScrollbarHeight()`.

getVScrollbarWidth()

PURPOSE   Retrieves the width of the scroll pane's vertical scroll bar.

SYNTAX   `int getVScrollbarWidth()`

RETURNS   The width of the scroll pane's vertical scroll bar.

SEE ALSO   `java.awt.ScrollPane.getVScrollbarWidth()`.

setScrollPosition()

PURPOSE   Scrolls to a position within the child component in the scroll pane.

SYNTAX   `void setScrollPosition(int x, int y)`

PARAMETERS

  x   The x-coordinate to which to scroll.

  y   The y-coordinate to which to scroll.

SEE ALSO   `java.awt.ScrollPane.setScrollPosition()`.

setUnitIncrement()

PURPOSE	Sets the scroll pane's unit increment.
SYNTAX	`void setUnitIncrement(Adjustable adj, int increment)`
PARAMETERS	
`adj`	The adjustable (scroll pane) to increment.
`increment`	The non-negative unit increment.
SEE ALSO	`java.awt.Adjustable, java.awt.ScrollPane.setUnitIncrement().`

setValue()

PURPOSE	Sets the value of an adjustable in this scroll pane.
SYNTAX	`void setValue(Adjustable adj, int value)`
PARAMETERS	
`adj`	The adjustable whose value to set.
`value`	The adjustable's new value.
SEE ALSO	`java.awt.Adjustable, java.awt.ScrollPane.setValue().`

A
B
C
D
E
F
G
H
I
J
K
L
M
N
O
P
Q
R
S
T
U
V
W
X
Y
Z

Shape ·········· Polygon

·········· Rectangle

Syntax
`public interface Shape`

Description
The Shape interface is used to represent a geometric shape, such as a circle or a rectang e, on a 2D plane. Currently, the only supported shape in the AWT is `Rectangle`. This interface is subject to change in future releases and should not be used directly.

MEMBER SUMMARY	
Shape Method	
getBounds()	Retrieves the bounding rectangle of this shape.

See Also
`Rectangle`.

Example
This example defines two new shapes: a square and a circle. It creates three instances of different shapes (square, rectangle, and circle) and then prints out their bounds.

```java
import java.awt.*;

class Square extends Rectangle {
    public Square(int x, int y, int length) {
        super(x, y, length, length);
    }
}

class Circle implements Shape {
    int x, y, radius;

    // circle centered at x, y, with radius 'radius'
    public Circle(int x, int y, int radius) {
        this.x = x;
        this.y = y;
        this.radius = radius;
    }
```

```
            public Rectangle getBounds() {
                // (x, y) is center of circle; offset x and y by circle's radius
                return new Rectangle(x-radius, y-radius, radius*2, radius*2);
            }
        }

        class Main {
            public static void main(String[] args) {
                Shape s1 = new Square(15, 20, 50);
                Shape s2 = new Rectangle(65, 20, 25, 30);
                Shape s3 = new Circle(115, 20, 10);

                System.out.println("square: " + s1.getBounds());
                System.out.println("rectangle: " + s2.getBounds());
                System.out.println("circle: " + s3.getBounds());
            }
        }
```

A
B
C
D
E
F
G
H
I
J
K
L
M
N
O
P
Q
R
S
T
U
V
W
X
Y
Z

getBounds()

PURPOSE	Retrieves the bounding rectangle of this shape.
SYNTAX	`public Rectangle getBounds()`
RETURNS	The non-`null` bounding rectangle of this shape.
SEE ALSO	`Rectangle.getBounds()`.
EXAMPLE	See the class example.

SimpleBeanInfo

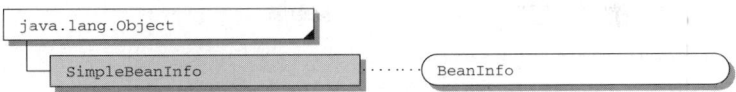

Syntax

```
public class SimpleBeanInfo implements BeanInfo
```

Description

When a bean editor loads a bean, it asks the introspector (see Introspector) to construct a set of feature descriptors (see FeatureDescriptor) that contain information used by a bean editor to create an interface for editing the bean. By default, the introspector uses a process called *introspection* to discover the feature descriptors for a bean. This process basically involves detecting signature patterns in the bean's public methods (see Introspector for more details). However, some feature descriptors created by introspection may not have the desired values (since there are some things that the introspector cannot determine). In this case, the bean must provide explicit feature descriptors for the introspector. These explicit feature descriptors are packaged in an object called a *bean-info*.

This class provides a convenient superclass for building a bean-info. It provides simple defaults for all of the bean-info methods. See BeanInfo for complete information on bean-infos and how to build them.

MEMBER SUMMARY	
Descriptor Methods	
getBeanDescriptor()	Retrieves the bean-info's bean descriptor.
getEventSetDescriptors()	Retrieves the bean-info's event set descriptors.
getMethodDescriptors()	Retrieves the bean-info's method descriptors.
getPropertyDescriptors()	Retrieves the bean-info's property descriptors.
Additional Info Method	
getAdditionalBeanInfo()	Retrieves a set of additional bean-info objects.
Default Index Methods	
getDefaultEventIndex()	Retrieves the index of the bean-info's default event set.
getDefaultPropertyIndex()	Retrieves the index of the bean-info's default property.
Image Methods	
getIcon()	Retrieves the bean-info's icon.
loadImage()	Loads an image relative to the bean-info.

See Also

BeanDescriptor, BeanInfo, EventSetDescriptor, IndexedPropertyDescriptor,
MethodDescriptor, PropertyDescriptor.

Example

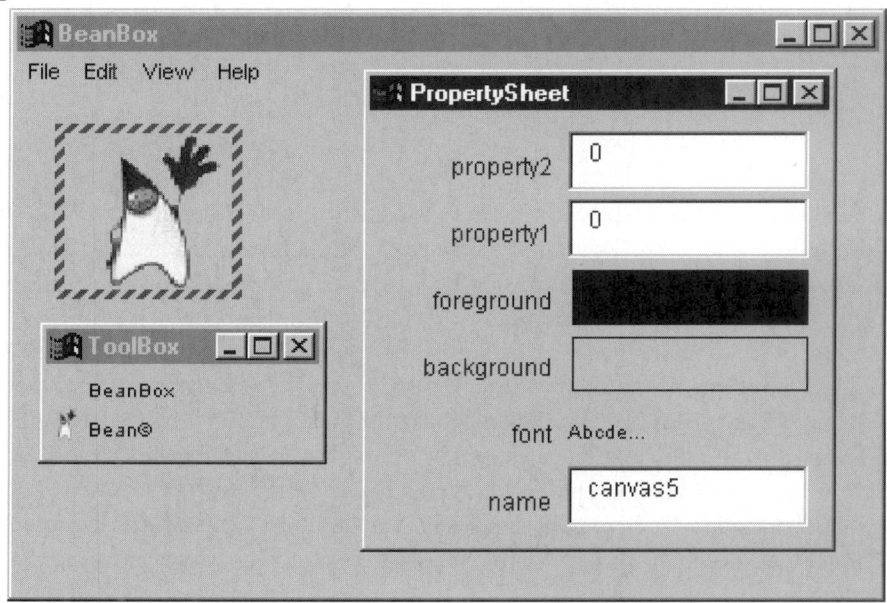

FIGURE 337: `SimpleBeanInfo`.

This example is a simple demonstration of how to provide implementations for all of the methods in a bean-info. The bean loads and displays an image. The image is scaled to fit exactly in the bounds of the bean. The bean also has number of dummy methods used to demonstrate various methods in the bean-info. See Figure 337.

The image used by the bean is bundled in the same jar file as the bean. The bean must use `Class.getResource()` to find and load it.

The bean-info defines feature descriptors for each of the four categories (bean descriptor, event set descriptor, method descriptor and property descriptor). Two property descriptors are defined so that one of them can be set to be the default. Also, two event set descriptors are defined so that one of them can be set to be the default.

The bean-info also contains images for each of the icon types (`Bean-Info.ICON_COLOR16x16`, `BeanInfo.ICON_COLOR32x32`, `BeanInfo.ICON_MONO16x16`, `BeanInfo.ICON_MONO32x32`).

Bean.java

```java
import java.awt.*;
import java.awt.image.*;
import java.io.*;
import java.net.*;

public class Bean extends Canvas {
    Image image;

    public Bean() {
        try {
            URL url = getClass().getResource("duke.gif");
            Toolkit tk = Toolkit.getDefaultToolkit();
            image = tk.createImage((ImageProducer)url.getContent());
        } catch (IOException e) {
            e.printStackTrace();
        }
    }

    public void paint(Graphics g) {
        if (image != null) {
            g.drawImage(image, 0, 0, size().width, size().height, this);
        }
    }

    public void method() {
    }

    public int getProperty1() {
        return 0;
    }
    public void setProperty1(int s) {
    }
    public int getProperty2() {
        return 0;
    }
    public void setProperty2(int s) {
    }

    public void addJumpListener(JumpListener evt) {
    }
    public void removeJumpListener(JumpListener evt) {
    }
}
/*
    manifest.txt:
        Name: Bean.class
        Java-Bean: True
    jar command:
        jar cfm bean.jar manifest.txt *.class *.gif
*/
```

BeanBeanInfo.java

```java
import java.beans.*;

public class BeanBeanInfo extends SimpleBeanInfo {
    public BeanInfo[] getAdditionalBeanInfo() {
        try {
            BeanInfo[] bi = new BeanInfo[1];
```

```
                    bi[0] = Introspector.getBeanInfo(Bean.class.getSuperclass());
                    return bi;
                } catch (IntrospectionException e) {
                    e.printStackTrace();
                }
                return null;
            }

            public BeanDescriptor getBeanDescriptor() {
                BeanDescriptor bd = new BeanDescriptor(Bean.class);

                bd.setDisplayName("Bean\u00a9");       // Copyright symbol
                return bd;
            }

            public MethodDescriptor[] getMethodDescriptors() {
                try {
                    MethodDescriptor md[] = new MethodDescriptor[1];

                    md[0] = new MethodDescriptor(Bean.class.getMethod("method", null));
                    return md;
                } catch (NoSuchMethodException e) {
                    e.printStackTrace();
                }
                return null;
            }

            public int getDefaultPropertyIndex() {
                return 1;
            }
            public PropertyDescriptor[] getPropertyDescriptors() {
                try {
                    PropertyDescriptor pd[] = new PropertyDescriptor[2];

                    // The getter and setter methods are derived from the property name.
                    pd[0] = new PropertyDescriptor("property1", Bean.class);
                    pd[1] = new PropertyDescriptor("property2", Bean.class);

                    return pd;
                } catch (IntrospectionException e) {
                    e.printStackTrace();
                }
                return null;
            }

            public int getDefaultEventIndex() {
                return 1;
            }
            public EventSetDescriptor[] getEventSetDescriptors() {
                try {
                    EventSetDescriptor[] esd = new EventSetDescriptor[2];

                    esd[0] = new EventSetDescriptor(Bean.class,
                            "event1", JumpListener.class, "beanJumped");

                    esd[1] = new EventSetDescriptor(Bean.class,
                            "event2", JumpListener.class, "beanJumped");

                    return esd;
```

```
        } catch (IntrospectionException e) {
            e.printStackTrace();
        }
        return null;
    }

    public java.awt.Image getIcon(int iconKind) {
        switch (iconKind) {
          case ICON_COLOR_16x16:
            return loadImage("duke-color-16x16.gif");
          case ICON_COLOR_32x32:
            return loadImage("duke-color-32x32.gif");
          case ICON_MONO_16x16:
            return loadImage("duke-mono-16x16.gif");
          case ICON_MONO_32x32:
            return loadImage("duke-mono-32x32.gif");
          default:
            return null;
        }
    }
}
```

JumpListener.java
```
import java.awt.*;

public class JumpListener {
    public void beanJumped(AWTEvent evt) {
    }
}
```

getAdditionalBeanInfo()

PURPOSE   Retrieves a set of additional bean-info objects.

SYNTAX   `public BeanInfo[] getAdditionalBeanInfo()`

DESCRIPTION A bean may provide bean-info objects in addition to its own. This gives a bean editor more information for editing the bean. In practice, the additional bean-info objects are typically of the bean's superclasses. For example, if a bean extends from Component, it may include the component's bean-info in the list of additional bean-info objects. In this way, the user will be able to edit not only the bean's features (properties, methods, and so on) but also the features of component.

This method returns null. If additional bean-info objects are available, this method should be overridden to return them in an array. If there are any conflicts between the bean-info objects in the returned array, the bean-info object with the highest index takes precedence (for example, one property descriptor says a property is bound, while the other says it is not). However, the descriptors in this bean-info object take precedence over the bean-info objects in the returned array.

RETURNS   A possibly `null` array of bean-info objects. The length of the array indicates the number of bean-info objects.

EXAMPLE   See the class example.

getBeanDescriptor()

PURPOSE   Retrieves the bean-info's bean descriptor.

SYNTAX   `public BeanDescriptor getBeanDescriptor()`

DESCRIPTION   This method returns `null`. If an explicit bean descriptor is available, this method should be overridden to return it.

This method is typically called by the introspector (see `Introspector`). When it returns `null`, the introspector determines the bean descriptor through introspection.

RETURNS   A possibly `null` bean descriptor.

SEE ALSO   `BeanDescriptor`.

EXAMPLE   See the `BeanDescriptor` class example.

getDefaultEventIndex()

PURPOSE   Retrieves the index of the bean-info's default event set.

SYNTAX   `public int getDefaultEventIndex()`

DESCRIPTION   This method returns −1, which informs the caller that a default event set does not exist. If a default event set does exist, this method should be overridden to return the index of the event set descriptor (for the default event set) within the array returned by `getEventSetDescriptors()`.

If `getEventSetDescriptors()` returns `null`, this method must return −1.

RETURNS   The index of the default event set in the `getEventSetDescriptors()` array; −1 if no event set exists.

SEE ALSO   `getEventSetDescriptors()`, `EventSetDescriptor`.

EXAMPLE   See the class example.

getDefaultPropertyIndex()

PURPOSE	Retrieves the index of the bean-info's default property.
SYNTAX	`public int getDefaultPropertyIndex()`
DESCRIPTION	This method returns −1, which informs the caller that no default property exists. If a default property does exist, this method should be overridden to return the index of the property descriptor (for the default property) within the array returned by `getPropertyDescriptors()`. If `getPropertyDescriptors()` returns `null`, this method must return −1.
RETURNS	The index of default property in the `getPropertyDescriptors()` array; −1 if no default property exists.
SEE ALSO	`getPropertyDescriptors, PropertyDescriptor`.
EXAMPLE	See the class example.

getEventSetDescriptors()

PURPOSE	Retrieves the bean-info's event set descriptors.
SYNTAX	`public EventSetDescriptor[] getEventSetDescriptors()`
DESCRIPTION	This method returns `null`, which informs the caller that no explicit event set descriptors are available. If the bean-info has any explicit event set descriptors, this method should be overridden to return them in an array. This method is typically called by the introspector (see `Introspector`). When it returns `null`, the introspector determines the bean's event sets through introspection.
RETURNS	A possibly `null` array of event set descriptors. The length of the array indicates the number of event set descriptors.
SEE ALSO	`EventSetDescriptor`.
EXAMPLE	See the `EventSetDescriptor` class example.

getIcon()

PURPOSE	Retrieves the bean-info's icon.
SYNTAX	`public java.awt.Image getIcon(int iconKind)`
DESCRIPTION	This method always returns `null`, which informs the caller that no icons are available.

You should override this method to return an image that a bean editor can use to represent the bean. The method should return `null` if the requested icon type is not available. If the requested icon type is a color image but is not available, the method can return a monochrome image in the requested size.

The background pixels of the returned image should be transparent.

PARAMETERS

iconKind   The desired icon type. Must be one of `BeanInfo.ICON_COLOR_16x16`, `Bean-Info.ICON_COLOR_32x32`, `BeanInfo.ICON_MONO_16x16`, or `Bean-Info.ICON_MONO_32x32`.

SEE ALSO   `java.awt.Image`.

EXAMPLE   See the class example.

getMethodDescriptors()

PURPOSE   Retrieves the bean-info's method descriptors.

SYNTAX   `public MethodDescriptor[] getMethodDescriptors()`

DESCRIPTION   This method returns `null`, which informs the caller that no explicit method descriptors are available. If the bean-info has any explicit method descriptors, this method should be overridden to return them in an array.

This method is typically called by the introspector (see `Introspector`). When it returns `null`, the introspector determines the bean's methods through introspection.

RETURNS   A possibly `null` array of method descriptors. The length of the array indicates the number of method descriptors.

SEE ALSO   `MethodDescriptor`.

EXAMPLE   See the `MethodDescriptor` class example.

getPropertyDescriptors()

PURPOSE   Retrieves the bean-info's property descriptors.

SYNTAX   `public PropertyDescriptor[] getPropertyDescriptors()`

DESCRIPTION   This method returns `null`, which informs the caller that no explicit property descriptors are available. If the bean-info has any explicit property descriptors, this method should be overridden to return them in an array.

Any indexed property descriptors should also be included in the returned array. The caller can determine which property descriptors are indexed property descriptors by using the `instanceof` operator.

This method is typically called by the introspector (see `Introspector`). When it returns `null`, the introspector determines the bean's properties through introspection.

RETURNS   A possibly `null` array of property descriptors. The length of the array indicates the number of property descriptors.

SEE ALSO   `PropertyDescriptor`.

EXAMPLE   See the `PropertyDescriptor` class example.

loadImage()

PURPOSE   Loads an image relative to the bean-info.

SYNTAX   `public java.awt.Image loadImage(String resourceName)`

DESCRIPTION   This method is used to load an image that has a location relative to the bean-info class file. For example, if the bean-info class file is in directory D and the image is located in `D/images/image.gif`, then `resourceName` should be `images/image.gif`. This method is used most often when the image is contained in the same jar file as the bean-info (and bean).

PARAMETERS

  `resourceName`The non-`null` relative pathname of an image.

RETURNS   A possibly `null` image object containing an icon.

EXAMPLE   See the class example.

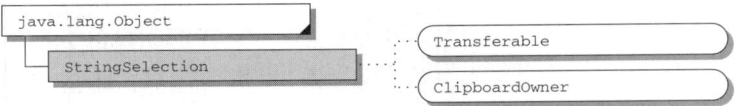

Syntax

`public class StringSelection implements Transferable, ClipboardOwner`

Description

The most common data type that appears on the clipboard is the *string*. However, strings cannot be placed on the clipboard directly, since a clipboard can hold only transferable objects (see `Transferable`). A string must first be placed inside a transferable object before it can be placed on the clipboard.

This class makes it convenient to place strings on the clipboard. It implements a transferable object called a *string selection* that holds strings. You need only to create a string selection containing the desired string and place the string selection on the clipboard using `Clipboard.setContents()`. Other applications can then retrieve the string selection from the clipboard using `Clipboard.getContents()`. See `Clipboard` for more details.

Data Flavors

When an application stores some data on the clipboard, it also must include with the data all of the data flavors that are supported. See the `DataFlavor` class for a detailed discussion on data flavors.

A string selection supports two data flavors: string and plain text. When an application specifies string flavor, the string is returned as a `String` object. When an application specifies plain text flavor, a string reader (see `StringReader`) is returned that contains the string. With either data flavor, the resulting strings are identical.

These two data flavors are provided, by default, in the `DataFlavor` class. The name of the string flavor is `DataFlavor.stringFlavor`. The name of the plain text flavor is `DataFlavor.plainTextFlavor`.

MEMBER SUMMARY	
Constructor	
`StringSelection()`	Constructs a new `StringSelection` instance.
Data Method	
`getTransferData()`	Retrieves the string contained in the string selection.

A
B
C
D
E
F
G
H
I
J
K
L
M
N
O
P
Q
R
S
T
U
V
W
X
Y
Z

MEMBER SUMMARY	
Data Flavor Methods	
getTransferDataFlavors()	Returns an array of supported data flavors.
isDataFlavorSupported()	Determines if this string selection supports a data flavor.
Clipboard Method	
lostOwnership()	Called when this string selection loses ownership of the clipboard.

See Also

Clipboard, DataFlavor, java.io.StringReader, Transferable.

Example

This example creates a list of text items. Selecting an item causes a string selection to be created for that item and to be set on the system clipboard. This makes the text item available to be copied by any other application on the desktop. See Figure 338.

For an example that demonstrates how to retrieve the string stored in a string selection, see the getTransferData() example.

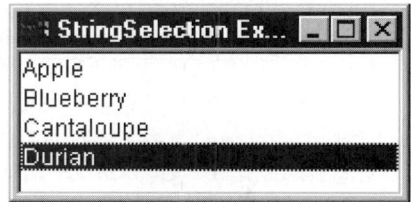

FIGURE 338: Putting a String on the System Clipboard.

```java
import java.awt.*;
import java.awt.datatransfer.*;
import java.awt.event.*;

class Main extends Frame implements ItemListener {
    List l = new List();

    Main() {
        super("StringSelection Example");

        // Initialize list.
        l.addItem("Apple");
        l.addItem("Blueberry");
        l.addItem("Cantaloupe");
        l.addItem("Durian");
        add(l, BorderLayout.CENTER);

        // Listen for item events.
        l.addItemListener(this);

        setSize(100, 150);
        show();
    }
```

```
        public void itemStateChanged(ItemEvent evt) {
            // Retrieve item index.
            int item = ((Integer)evt.getItem()).intValue();

            // Retrieve handle to clipboard.
            Clipboard clipboard = getToolkit().getSystemClipboard();

            // Create the string selection.
            StringSelection ss = new StringSelection(l.getItem(item));

            // Set contents of clipboard with string selection.
            clipboard.setContents(ss, null);
        }
        public static void main(String[] args) {
            new Main();
        }
    }
```

getTransferData()

PURPOSE   Retrieves the string contained in the string selection.

SYNTAX   public synchronized Object getTransferData(DataFlavor flavor)
                 throws UnsupportedFlavorException, IOException

DESCRIPTION The string selection supports two data flavors: DataFlavor.stringFlavor
             and DataFlavor.plainTextFlavor.

             If the requested data flavor is DataFlavor.stringFlavor, this method
             returns a non-null String object. If the requested data flavor is DataFla-
             vor.plainTextFlavor, this method returns a StringReader from which the
             string can be read.

             Note: In Java 1.1.2, the representation class of DataFlavor.plainTextFla-
             vor is java.io.InputStream; it should be java.io.StringReader.

PARAMETERS
  flavor   The non-null requested data flavor.

RETURNS   A non-null data flavor.

EXCEPTIONS
  IOException If the data is no longer available.
  UnsupportedFlavorException
             If flavor is neither DataFlavor.stringFlavor nor DataFlavor.plain-
             TextFlavor.

SEE ALSO   DataFlavor, java.lang.String, java.io.StringReader.

EXAMPLE   This example assumes that a string selection is on the clipboard and shows how to print its contents:

```java
import java.awt.*;
import java.awt.datatransfer.*;
import java.io.*;

class Main {
    // getTransferData Example
    public static void main(String[] args) {
        int numRead;
        char buffer[] = new char[1024];
        PrintWriter out = new PrintWriter(System.out);

        // Retrieve handle to clipboard and contents
        Clipboard clipboard =
            Toolkit.getDefaultToolkit().getSystemClipboard();
        Transferable t = clipboard.getContents(null);

        if (t == null) {
            // Clipboard is empty.
            return;
        }

        try {
            // Retrieve as string flavor.
            String s = (String)t.getTransferData(
                DataFlavor.stringFlavor);
            System.out.println("Clipboard Contents = "+s);

            // Retrieve as plain text flavor.
            StringReader r = (StringReader)t.getTransferData(
                DataFlavor.plainTextFlavor);
            while ((numRead = r.read(buffer, 0, buffer.length)) >= 0) {
                out.write(buffer, 0, numRead);
            }
        } catch (IOException e) {
        } catch (UnsupportedFlavorException e) {
        }
    }
}
```

A
B
C
D
E
F
G
H
I
J
K
L
M
N
O
P
Q
R
S
T
U
V
W
X
Y
Z

getTransferDataFlavors()

PURPOSE   Returns an array of supported data flavors.

SYNTAX   `public synchronized DataFlavor[] getTransferDataFlavors()`

DESCRIPTION   The string selection supports two data flavors: `DataFlavor.stringFlavor` and `DataFlavor.plainTextFlavor`. This method returns a two-element array containing these flavors.

RETURNS   A non-`null` array of the two supported data flavors.

SEE ALSO   `DataFlavor`.

EXAMPLE   This example prints the data flavors supported by the current content of the
system clipboard. If the content is a string selection, the output is shown as follows:

```
import java.awt.*;
import java.awt.datatransfer.*;
import java.io.*;

class Main {
    // getTransferDataFlavors Example
    public static void main(String[] args) {
        // Retrieve reference to clipboard and contents
        Clipboard clipboard =
            Toolkit.getDefaultToolkit().getSystemClipboard();
        Transferable t = clipboard.getContents(null);

        if (t == null) {
            // Clipboard is empty.
            return;
        }

        DataFlavor flavors[] = t.getTransferDataFlavors();
        for (int i=0; i<flavors.length; i++) {
            System.out.println(flavors[i].getHumanPresentableName());
            System.out.println("  "+flavors[i].getRepresentationClass());
            System.out.println("  "+flavors[i].getMimeType());
        }
    }
}
```

OUTPUT   This output would appear if the system clipboard contained a string selection.
Note that this output has been doctored to show correct results. In Java 1.1.2, the
text `class java.io.StringReader` actually comes out as `null`. There is a
bug where the representation class is `null`.

```
Unicode String
  class java.lang.String
  application/x-java-serialized-object
Plain Text
  class java.io.StringReader
  text/plain; charset=unicode
```

isDataFlavorSupported()

PURPOSE   Determines if this string selection supports a data flavor.

SYNTAX   `public boolean isDataFlavorSupported(DataFlavor flavor)`

DESCRIPTION   The string selection supports two data flavors: `DataFlavor.stringFlavor`
and `DataFlavor.plainTextFlavor`.

PARAMETERS

flavor   The non-null requested data flavor.

RETURNS   true if flavor is supported by this string selection; false otherwise.

SEE ALSO   DataFlavor.

EXAMPLE   This code fragment shows how to check for the two flavors that a string selec-
              tion supports:

```
// Retrieve handle to clipboard and contents
Clipboard clipboard =
    Toolkit.getDefaultToolkit().getSystemClipboard();
Transferable t = clipboard.getContents(null);

if (t == null) {
    // Clipboard is empty.
    return;
}

if (t.isDataFlavorSupported(DataFlavor.stringFlavor)) {
    System.out.println("yes");
}

if (t.isDataFlavorSupported(DataFlavor.plainTextFlavor)) {
    System.out.println("yes");
}
```

lostOwnership()

PURPOSE   Called when this string selection loses ownership of the clipboard.

SYNTAX   public void lostOwnership(Clipboard clipboard, Transferable
                  contents)

DESCRIPTION   This method is called by the AWT system when this string selection is no
              longer in clipboard. The contents parameter should be equal (have the
              same reference as) to this string selection object.

              This method, as defined in StringSelection, does nothing. For this method
              to do something useful, it must be overridden by a subclass.

PARAMETERS

clipboard   The non-null handle to a clipboard.
contents   The non-null old contents of the clipboard.

EXAMPLE   See ClipboardOwner.lostOwnership().

StringSelection()

PURPOSE   Constructs a new StringSelection instance.

SYNTAX   public StringSelection(String str)

DESCRIPTION   This method creates a transferable object containing str. The string can be retrieved using Transferable.getTransferData() in either string format (see DataFlavor.stringFlavor) or in plain text format (see DataFlavor.plainTextFlavor).

If str is null, it is first modified to be the empty string "".

PARAMETERS
str   A possibly null string.

SEE ALSO   DataFlavor, Transferable.getTransferData().

EXAMPLE   See the class example.

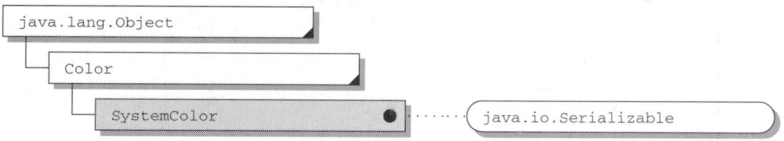

A
B
C
D
E
F
G
H
I
J
K
L
M
N
O
P
Q
R

T
U
V
W
X
Y
Z

Syntax

`public final class SystemColor extends Color implements Serializable`

Description

The SystemColor class contains most of the colors that are used by the platform to paint native components. For example, the background color of a button and the color of its text are retrieved from this class. The availability of these colors enables you to create components that blend with the native components. Figure 339 contains a map of the colors defined by this class.

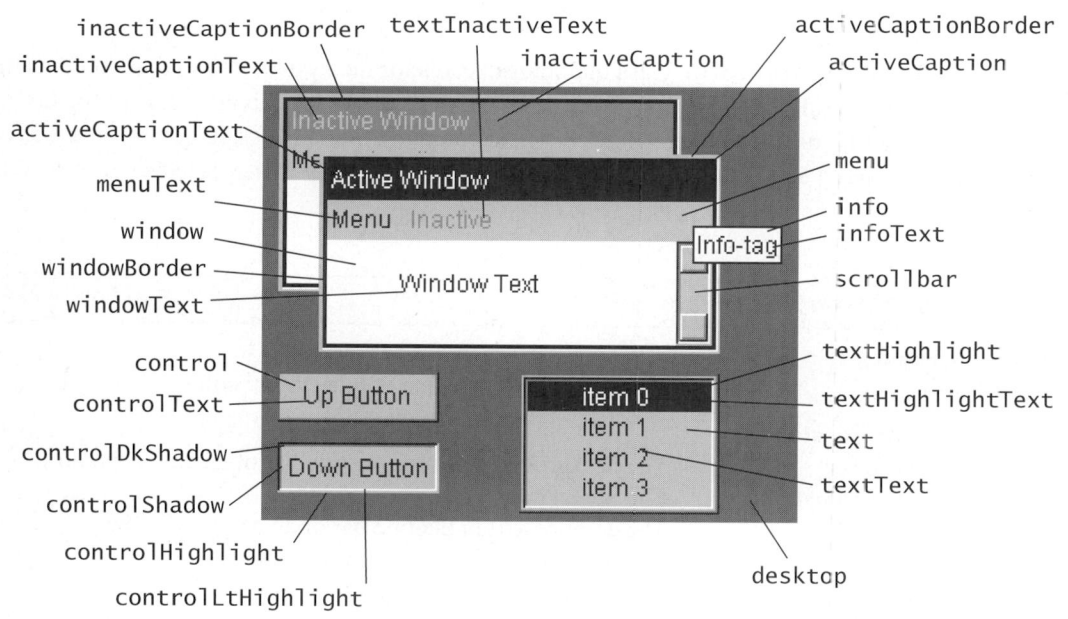

FIGURE 339:   Map of System Colors.

On some platforms, the system-wide colors of these windowing system parts is dynamically configurable by the user. For example, the user can choose the background color of his desktop, the background color of menu bars, and so on. When such changes are allowed, the colors in this class are updated to reflect those changes. *Note*: In Java 1.1.2, this is not yet working; the Java program must be restarted in order to see the new system colors.

Info-tags

An *info-tag* is a small window that displays a short description of an object. Info-tags are typically displayed near the cursor when you roll over the object. For example, if you roll over a Cancel button, the info-tag might say, "Stops the printing process." In Windows, info-tags are called Tooltips; on a Macintosh, they are called Balloon Help.

Note: Info-tag is not an official name for these little windows. Since JavaSoft has not yet named them, we picked a name in order to talk about them.

Component Colors

When painting a component outline, you need four colors to achieve a 3D look. The four colors are (in the order of brightest first) the `controlLtHighlight`, `controlHighlight`, `controlShadow`, and `controlDkShadow`. The background of the component should be painted in the `control` color. See the `control` example for a typical way in which these colors are used.

System Color Cache

For efficiency, the `SystemColor` class maintains a cache of the system colors that contains the colors' RGB values. The `SystemColor` entries in this cache use the private fields of the `Color` class in a slightly different way. Hence, when comparing a `SystemColor` with a `Color` instance that is not a `SystemColor`, you should check for equality using `getRGB()`, instead of `equals()`.

MEMBER SUMMARY	
RGB Method	
getRGB()	Retrieves the RGB value of this system color.
System Color Constants	
activeCaption	The background color for the title bar of an active window.
activeCaptionBorder	The border color of an active window.
activeCaptionText	The color of text in the title bar of an active window.
control	The background color of a component.
controlDkShadow	The darkest color of a 3D component's outline.
controlHighlight	The second brightest color of a 3D component's outline.
controlLtHighlight	The brightest color of a 3D component's outline.
controlShadow	The second darkest color of a 3D component's outline.
controlText	The color of text in a component's label.

MEMBER SUMMARY

`desktop`	The background color of the platform's window system desktop.
`inactiveCaption`	The background color for the title bar of an inactive window.
`inactiveCaptionBorder`	The border color of an inactive window.
`inactiveCaptionText`	The color of text in the title bar of an inactive window.
`info`	The background color of an info-tag.
`infoText`	The color of text in an info-tag.
`menu`	The background color of a menu component.
`menuText`	The color of text in a menu component.
`scrollbar`	The background color of a scrollbar.
`text`	The background color of text components.
`textHighlight`	The background color of highlighted text.
`textHighlightText`	The color of highlighted text.
`textInactiveText`	The color of inactive text.
`textText`	The color of text in a text component.
`window`	The background color of a window.
`windowBorder`	The border color of a window.
`windowText`	The color of text in a window.

Debugging Method

`toString()`	Generates a string representing this system color.

Constants Used for System Color Cache[a]

`ACTIVE_CAPTION`	Index of the background color of active captions in window borders.
`ACTIVE_CAPTION_BORDER`	Index of the border color of active captions in window borders.
`ACTIVE_CAPTION_TEXT`	Index of the text color of active captions in window borders.
`CONTROL`	Index of the background color of control objects.
`CONTROL_DK_SHADOW`	Index of the dark shadow color of control objects.
`CONTROL_HIGHLIGHT`	Index of the color of highlighted control objects.
`CONTROL_LT_HIGHLIGHT`	Index of the color for lightly highlighted control objects.
`CONTROL_SHADOW`	Index of the shadow color of control objects.
`CONTROL_TEXT`	Index of the color for the text of a control.
`DESKTOP`	Index of the background color of the desktop.
`INACTIVE_CAPTION`	Index of the background color of inactive captions in window borders
`INACTIVE_CAPTION_BORDER`	Index of the border color of inactive captions in window borders.
`INACTIVE_CAPTION_TEXT`	Index of the text color of inactive captions in window borders.
`INFO`	Index of the background color of help components.
`INFO_TEXT`	Index of the text color of help components.

Continued

A
B
C
D
E
F
G
H
I
J
K
L
M
N
O
P
Q
R
S
T
U
V
W
X
Y
Z

MEMBER SUMMARY

Constants Used for System Color Cache *(Continued)*

MENU	Index of the background color of menus.
MENU_TEXT	Index of the text color of menus.
NUM_COLORS	The number of system colors.
SCROLLBAR	Index of the background color of scrollbars.
TEXT	Index of the background color of text components.
TEXT_HIGHTLIGHT	Index of the background color of highlighted text components.
TEXT_HIGHLIGHT_TEXT	Index of the text color of highlighted text components.
TEXT_INACTIVE_TEXT	Index of the text color of inactive text components.
TEXT_TEXT	Index of the text color of text components.
WINDOW	Index of the background color of windows.
WINDOW_BORDER	Index of the border color of windows.
WINDOW_TEXT	Index of the text color of windows.

---

a. See the method description of `toString()` for the numeric values of these constants. These constants are not described elsewhere in this book because they are not intended to be used directly. Use the System `Color` constants instead.

See Also

`Color, java.io.Serializable.`

Example

This example implements various "fake" components that use the system colors. The left side of the display shows the fake components. On the right side is a set of a checkbox buttons, one for each system color. When you select a checkbox button for a system color, those parts of the fake components that use that system color will start to blink. See Figure 340.

The fake desktop container contains all of the fake components. It implements double-buffering in order to eliminate the flashing that would otherwise occur as all of the fake components are updated.

This example uses many different source files to implement the various fake components. Showing all of the files here would be make the listing too long and unwieldy, so instead, we scattered the fake component source files among the various system color descriptions. Only the `Main.java` source file is shown here. The fake component source files are located in the following system color field descriptions:

- `FakeTitleBar.java` is located in `activeCaption`
- `FakeWindow.java` is located in `activeCaptionBorder`
- `FakeMenuBar.java` is located in `menu`
- `FakeList.java` is located in `text`
- `FakeButton.java` is located in `control`
- `FakeScrollbar.java` is located in `scrollbar`

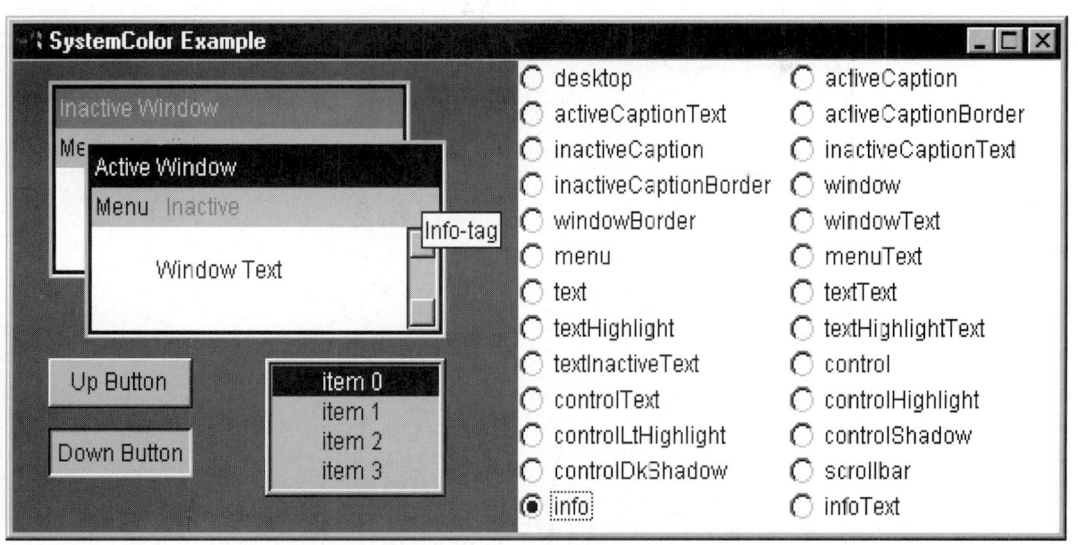

FIGURE 340:   **Component System Colors.**

```java
import java.awt.*;
import java.awt.event.*;

class Main extends Frame implements Runnable {
    FakeDesktop desktop = new FakeDesktop();

    Main() {
        super("SystemColor Example");

        // Set up first window.
        FakeWindow w = new FakeWindow(
            SystemColor.WINDOW, SystemColor.WINDOW_TEXT, true);
        w.setBounds(40, 40, 200, 100);
        desktop.add(w);

        // Set up second window.
        w = new FakeWindow(
            SystemColor.WINDOW, SystemColor.WINDOW_TEXT, false);
        w.setBounds(20, 10, 200, 100);
        desktop.add(w);

        // Set up first button.
        FakeButton b = new FakeButton(true);
        b.setBounds(20, 150, 80, 25);
        desktop.add(b);

        // Set up second button.
        b = new FakeButton(false);
        b.setBounds(20, 185, 80, 25);
        desktop.add(b);

        // Set up list.
        FakeList l = new FakeList();
```

A
B
C
D
E
F
G
H
I
J
K
L
M
N
O
P
Q
R
S
T
U
V
W
X
Y
Z

```
        l.setBounds(140, 150, 100, 70);
        desktop.add(l);

        // Set up the desktop.
        add(desktop, BorderLayout.CENTER);

        // Set up control panel.
        add(new ControlPanel(this), BorderLayout.EAST);
        setSize(590, 260);

        // Show the whole thing.
        show();

        // Start the blinking thread.
        (new Thread(this)).start();
    }

    static Color[] colors = {
        SystemColor.desktop, SystemColor.activeCaption,
        SystemColor.activeCaptionText, SystemColor.activeCaptionBorder,
        SystemColor.inactiveCaption, SystemColor.inactiveCaptionText,
        SystemColor.inactiveCaptionBorder, SystemColor.window,
        SystemColor.windowBorder, SystemColor.windowText,
        SystemColor.menu, SystemColor.menuText,
        SystemColor.text, SystemColor.textText,
        SystemColor.textHighlight, SystemColor.textHighlightText,
        SystemColor.textInactiveText, SystemColor.control,
        SystemColor.controlText, SystemColor.controlHighlight,
        SystemColor.controlLtHighlight, SystemColor.controlShadow,
        SystemColor.controlDkShadow, SystemColor.scrollbar,
        SystemColor.info, SystemColor.infoText,
    };

    int curColor;
    void setCurColor(int c) {
        curColor = c;
    }

    public void run() {
        Color[] savedColors = (Color[])colors.clone();
        boolean on = false;
        int c = curColor;

        while (true) {
            // curColor changed so restore it before
            // blinking new color.
            if (c != curColor) {
                colors[c] = savedColors[c];
                c = curColor;
            }

            try {
                if (on) {
                    colors[c] = savedColors[c];
                } else {
                    colors[c] = Color.red;
                }
                on = !on;
                repaintAll(desktop);
                Thread.sleep(500);
```

```
            } catch (Exception e) {
            }
        }
    }

    public void update(Graphics g) {
        super.paint(g);
    }

    public void repaintAll(Component c) {
        if (c instanceof Container) {
            Container cont = (Container)c;
            Component[] children = cont.getComponents();

            for (int i=0; i<children.length; i++) {
                repaintAll(children[i]);
            }
        }
        c.repaint();
    }

    public static void main(String[] args) {
        new Main();
    }
}

class FakeDesktop extends Container {
    FakeDesktop() {
        setLayout(null);

        // Listen for events.
        addMouseListener(new MouseEventHandler());
        addMouseMotionListener(new MouseMotionEventHandler());
    }

    public void paint(Graphics g) {
        update(g);
    }

    Image bbuf;
    Graphics bbufG;
    public void update(Graphics g) {
        FontMetrics fm = g.getFontMetrics();
        int w = getSize().width;
        int h = getSize().height;

        if (bbuf == null
                || bbuf.getWidth(null) < w
                || bbuf.getHeight(null) < h) {
            bbuf = createImage(w, h);
            bbufG = bbuf.getGraphics();
        }
        bbufG.setColor(Main.colors[SystemColor.DESKTOP]);
        bbufG.fillRect(0, 0, w, h);

        bbufG.clipRect(0, 0, w, h);
        // Paint all of the lightweight's children.
        super.paint(bbufG);

        // Paint Info-tag.
```

A

B

C

D

E

F

G

H

I

J

K

L

M

N

O

P

Q

R

S

T

U

V

W

X

Y

Z

```
        if (mousePt != null) {
            w = fm.stringWidth("Info-tag")+4;
            h = fm.getHeight()+4;

            // Paint Info-tag background color.
            bbufG.setColor(Main.colors[SystemColor.INFO]);
            bbufG.fillRect(mousePt.x, mousePt.y, w, h);

            // Paint Info-tag text.
            bbufG.setColor(Main.colors[SystemColor.INFO_TEXT]);
            bbufG.drawString("Info-tag",
                mousePt.x+2, mousePt.y+2+fm.getAscent());
            bbufG.drawRect(mousePt.x, mousePt.y, w-1, h-1);
        }

        g.drawImage(bbuf, 0, 0, this);
    }

    // If non-null, holds current location of mouse
    Point mousePt;

    class MouseEventHandler extends MouseAdapter {
        public void mouseExited(MouseEvent evt) {
            mousePt = null;
            repaint();
        }
    }
    class MouseMotionEventHandler extends MouseMotionAdapter {
        public void mouseMoved(MouseEvent evt) {
            mousePt = evt.getPoint();
            repaint();
        }
    }
}

class ControlPanel extends Panel implements ItemListener {
    CheckboxGroup cbg = new CheckboxGroup();
    Main frame;

    ControlPanel(Main f) {
        frame = f;
        setLayout(new GridLayout(0, 2));

        for (int i=0; i<SystemColor.NUM_COLORS; i++) {
            Checkbox cb = new Checkbox(colorNames[i], i==0, cbg);

            cb.setName(""+i);
            cb.addItemListener(this);
            add(cb);
        }

    }

    public void itemStateChanged(ItemEvent evt) {
        frame.setCurColor(
            Integer.parseInt(cbg.getSelectedCheckbox().getName()));
    }

    static String[] colorNames = {
        "desktop", "activeCaption",
```

```
        "activeCaptionText", "activeCaptionBorder",
        "inactiveCaption", "inactiveCaptionText",
        "inactiveCaptionBorder", "window",
        "windowBorder", "windowText",
        "menu", "menuText",
        "text", "textText",
        "textHighlight", "textHighlightText",
        "textInactiveText", "control",
        "controlText", "controlHighlight",
        "controlLtHighlight", "controlShadow",
        "controlDkShadow", "scrollbar",
        "info", "infoText",
    };
}
```

activeCaption

PURPOSE   The background color for the title bar of an active window.

SYNTAX   `public final static SystemColor activeCaption`

DESCRIPTION   If a component has an area that the user can grab with the mouse in order to
               drag the component (e.g., a title bar), this color is typically used to color the
               area when the window is active.

               The default value for `activeCaption` is
               `0xFF00008 // activeCaption = new Color(0,0,128);`

EXAMPLE   This class implements a fake title bar for a window. It uses the various caption
               system colors to paint the different parts of the title bar. See the class example
               to see how this class is used.

```
import java.awt.*;

class FakeTitleBar extends Component {
    boolean active;

    FakeTitleBar(boolean active) {
        this.active = active;
    }

    public Dimension getPreferredSize() {
        return new Dimension(Math.max(1, getSize().width), 20);
    }

    public void paint(Graphics g) {
        FontMetrics fm = g.getFontMetrics();
        int w = getSize().width;
        int h = getSize().height;

        if (active) {
            // Paint caption background.
            g.setColor(Main.colors[SystemColor.ACTIVE_CAPTION]);
```

```
                g.fillRect(0, 0, w, h);

                // Paint window title.
                g.setColor(Main.colors[SystemColor.ACTIVE_CAPTION_TEXT]);
                g.drawString("Active Window",
                    (h-fm.getHeight())/2,
                    (h-fm.getHeight())/2+fm.getAscent());
            } else {
                // Paint caption background.
                g.setColor(Main.colors[SystemColor.INACTIVE_CAPTION]);
                g.fillRect(0, 0, w, h);

                // Paint window title.
                g.setColor(Main.colors[SystemColor.INACTIVE_CAPTION_TEXT]);
                g.drawString("Inactive Window",
                    (h-fm.getHeight())/2,
                    (h-fm.getHeight())/2+fm.getAscent());
            }
        }
    }
```

activeCaptionBorder

PURPOSE   The border color of an active window.

SYNTAX   `public final static SystemColor activeCaptionBorder`

DESCRIPTION   The border of a window consists of pixels along the perimeter of the window. A window may have two borders: an active border, which changes color depending on whether the window is active, and a regular window border, which does not change color. `activeCaptionBorder` is the color of the active border when the window is active.

The default value for `activeCaptionBorder` is
`0xFFC0C0C0 // activeCaptionBorder = Color.lightGray;`

EXAMPLE   This class implements a fake window. It uses the various window border and background system colors to paint the different parts of the window. The window also uses a fake title bar and fake menu bar. See the class example to see how this class is used.

```
import java.awt.*;

class FakeWindow extends Container {
    int bgColor;
    int textColor;
    boolean active;

    FakeScrollbar scrollbar = new FakeScrollbar();
    FakeWindowHeader header;

    FakeWindow(int bgColor, int textColor, boolean active) {
        this.bgColor = bgColor;
```

```
            this.textColor = textColor;
            this.active = active;

            setLayout(new BorderLayout());
            add(scrollbar, BorderLayout.EAST);
            header = new FakeWindowHeader(active);
            add(header, BorderLayout.NORTH);
        }

    public Insets getInsets() {
        return new Insets(4, 4, 4, 4);
    }

    public void paint(Graphics g) {
        FontMetrics fm = g.getFontMetrics();
        int w = getSize().width;
        int h = getSize().height;

        // Paint window background color.
        g.setColor(Main.colors[bgColor]);
        g.fillRect(0, 0, w, h);

        if (active) {
            // Paint active window border.
            g.setColor(Main.colors[SystemColor.ACTIVE_CAPTION_BORDER]);
        } else {
            // Paint inactive window border.
            g.setColor(Main.colors[SystemColor.INACTIVE_CAPTION_BORDER]);
        }
        g.drawRect(0, 0, w-1, h-1);
        g.drawRect(1, 1, w-2, h-2);

        // Paint window border.
        g.setColor(Main.colors[SystemColor.WINDOW_BORDER]);
        g.drawRect(2, 2, w-5, h-5);
        g.drawRect(3, 3, w-7, h-7);

        // Paint text color
        g.setColor(Main.colors[textColor]);
        g.drawString("Window Text", 40, 70);

        // Needed to paint lightweight container's children.
        super.paint(g);
    }
}

class FakeWindowHeader extends Container {
    FakeWindowHeader(boolean active) {
        setLayout(new GridLayout(0, 1));

        add(new FakeTitleBar(active));
        add(new FakeMenuBar());
    }
}
```

A
B
C
D
E
F
G
H
I
J
K
L
M
N
O
P
Q
R

T
U
V
W
X
Y
Z

activeCaptionText

PURPOSE   The color of text in the title bar of an active window.

SYNTAX   `public final static SystemColor activeCaptionText`

DESCRIPTION   If a component has an area that the user can grab with the mouse in order to
              drag the component (e.g., a title bar), this color is used to paint any text that
              appears in that area when the window is active.

              The default value for `activeCaptionText` is
              `0xFFFFFFFF // activeCaptionText = Color.white;`

EXAMPLE   See `activeCaption`.

control

PURPOSE   The background color of a component.

SYNTAX   `public final static SystemColor control`

DESCRIPTION   This color is used to paint the background of a component. The outline of the
              component is painted with four other system colors. See the class description
              for details.

              The default value for `control` is
              `0xFFC0C0C0 // control = Color.lightGray;`

EXAMPLE   This class implements a fake button. It uses the various component system col-
              ors to paint the different parts of the button. See the class example to see how
              this class is used.

```
import java.awt.*;
import java.awt.event.*;

class FakeButton extends Component {
    boolean up;

    FakeButton(boolean up) {
        this.up = up;

        // Listen for mouse clicks.
        addMouseListener(new MouseEventHandler());
    }

    public void paint(Graphics g) {
        FontMetrics fm = g.getFontMetrics();
        int w = getSize().width;
        int h = getSize().height;
        String label = up ? "Up Button" : "Down Button";

        // Paint control background.
        g.setColor(Main.colors[SystemColor.CONTROL]);
```

```
        g.fillRect(0, 0, w, h);

        // Paint 3D outline.
        draw3DOutline(g, up, w, h);

        // Adjust the position of the text.
        //
        int adjust = up ? -1 : 0;

        // Paint component text.
        g.setColor(Main.colors[SystemColor.CONTROL_TEXT]);
        g.drawString(label, adjust+(w-fm.stringWidth(label))/2,
            adjust+(h-fm.getHeight())/2 + fm.getAscent());

    }

    // Paint a 3D outline using the system colors.
    public void draw3DOutline(Graphics g, boolean up, int w, int h) {
        Color c1 = Main.colors[SystemColor.CONTROL_LT_HIGHLIGHT];
        Color c2 = Main.colors[SystemColor.CONTROL_HIGHLIGHT];
        Color c3 = Main.colors[SystemColor.CONTROL_SHADOW];
        Color c4 = Main.colors[SystemColor.CONTROL_DK_SHADOW];

        if (!up) {
            c1 = Main.colors[SystemColor.CONTROL_DK_SHADOW];
            c2 = Main.colors[SystemColor.CONTROL_SHADOW];
            c3 = Main.colors[SystemColor.CONTROL_LT_HIGHLIGHT];
            c4 = Main.colors[SystemColor.CONTROL_HIGHLIGHT];
        }

        // Paint outer left and top edge.
        g.setColor(c1);
        g.drawLine(0, 0, w-1, 0);
        g.drawLine(0, 0, 0, h-1);

        // Paint inner left and top edge.
        g.setColor(c2);
        g.drawLine(1, 1, w-2, 1);
        g.drawLine(1, 1, 1, h-2);

        // Paint inner shadow right and bottom edge.
        g.setColor(c3);
        g.drawLine(w-2, h-2, w-2, 1);
        g.drawLine(w-2, h-2, 1, h-2);

        // Paint outter shadow right and bottom edge.
        g.setColor(c4);
        g.drawLine(w-1, h-1, w-1, 0);
        g.drawLine(w-1, h-1, 0, h-1);
    }

    class MouseEventHandler extends MouseAdapter {
        public void mousePressed(MouseEvent evt) {
            up = !up;
            repaint();
        }
    }
}
```

A
B
C
D
E
F
G
H
I
J
K
L
M
N
O
P
Q
R
S
T
U
V
W
X
Y
Z

controlDkShadow

PURPOSE   The darkest color of a 3D component's outline.

SYNTAX   `public final static SystemColor controlDkShadow`

DESCRIPTION   This is one of the four colors used to paint a component's outline. See the class description for more information.

The default value for `controlDkShadow` is
`0xFF000000 // controlDkShadow = Color.black;`

EXAMPLE   See `control`.

controlHighlight

PURPOSE   The second brightest color of a 3D component's outline.

SYNTAX   `public final static SystemColor controlHighlight`

DESCRIPTION   This is one of the four colors used to paint a component's outline. See the class description for more information.

The default value for `controlHighlight` is
`0xFFFFFFFF // controlHighlight = Color.white;`

EXAMPLE   See `control`.

controlLtHighlight

PURPOSE   The brightest color of a 3D component's outline.

SYNTAX   `public final static SystemColor controlLtHighlight`

DESCRIPTION   This is one of the four colors used to paint a component's outline. See the class description for more information.

The default value for `controlLtHighlight` is
`0xFFE0E0E0 // controlLtHighlight = new Color(224,224,224);`

EXAMPLE   See `control`.

controlShadow

PURPOSE   The second darkest color of a 3D component's outline.

SYNTAX   `public final static SystemColor controlShadow`

DESCRIPTION	This is one of the four colors used to paint a component's outline. See the class description for more information.
	The default value for `controlShadow` is
	`0xFF808080 // controlShadow = Color.gray;`
EXAMPLE	See `control`.

controlText

PURPOSE	The color of text in a component's label.
SYNTAX	`public final static SystemColor controlText`
DESCRIPTION	When a component is enabled, this color is used to paint the label. When a component is disabled, the color of the text should be `textInactiveText`.
	The default value for `controlText` is
	`0xFF000000 // controlText = Color.black;`
EXAMPLE	See `control`.

desktop

PURPOSE	The background color of the window system desktop.
SYNTAX	`public final static SystemColor desktop`
DESCRIPTION	This color is typically used by a top-level window when it wants to make it appear that the desktop is "showing through" parts of the window. However, some platforms allow the background to be painted with an image, and in this case, the desktop color will not be accurate.
	The default value of `desktop` is
	`0xFF005C5C // desktop = new Color(0,92,92);`
EXAMPLE	See the class example

getRGB()

PURPOSE	Retrieves the RGB value of this system color.
SYNTAX	`public int getRGB()`
DESCRIPTION	This method is used to compare for equality this system color with a `Color` instance that is not a `SystemColor` instance.
RETURNS	The 24-bit RGB representation of this system color.

A
B
C
D
E
F
G
H
I
J
K
L
M
N
O
P
Q
R
S
T
U
V
W
X
Y
Z

OVERRIDES	`Color.getRGB()`.
EXAMPLE	See the `Color` class example.

A

inactiveCaption

B

PURPOSE	The background color for the title bar of an inactive window.
SYNTAX	`public final static SystemColor inactiveCaption`

C

D

E

DESCRIPTION	If a component has an area that the user can grab with the mouse in order to drag the component (e.g., a title bar), this color is typically used to color the area when the window is inactive.

F

G

The default value for `inactiveCaption` is
```
0xFF808080 // inactiveCaption = Color.gray;
```

H

EXAMPLE	See `activeCaption`.

I

J

inactiveCaptionBorder

K

PURPOSE	The border color of an inactive window.
SYNTAX	`public final static SystemColor inactiveCaptionBorder`

L

M

N

DESCRIPTION	The border of a window consists of pixels along the perimeter of the window. A window may have two borders: an active border, which changes color depending whether the window is active, and a regular window border, which does not change color. `inactiveCaptionBorder` is the color of the active border when the window is inactive.

O

P

Q

The default value for `inactiveCaptionBorder` is
```
0xFFC0C0C0 // inactiveCaptionBorder = Color.lightGray;
```

R

S

EXAMPLE	See `activeCaptionBorder`.

T

inactiveCaptionText

U

V

PURPOSE	The color of text in the title bar of an inactive window.
SYNTAX	`public final static SystemColor inactiveCaptionText`

W

X

Y

DESCRIPTION	If a component has an area that the user can grab with the mouse in order to drag the component (e.g., a title bar), this color is used to paint any text that appears in that area when the window is inactive.

Z

The default color for `inactiveCaptionText` is
```
0xFFC0C0C0 // inactiveCaptionText = Color.lightGray;
```

EXAMPLE	See `activeCaption`.

info

PURPOSE	The background color of an info-tag.
SYNTAX	`public final static SystemColor info`
DESCRIPTION	An info-tag is a small window that displays a short description of a visible object. It is typically displayed near the cursor when you roll over the object. This is the background color of info-tag windows.

The default value for `info` is
```
0xFFE0E000 // info = new Color(224,224,0);
```

EXAMPLE	See `activeCaptionBorder`.

infoText

PURPOSE	The color of text in an info-tag.
SYNTAX	`public final static SystemColor infoText`
DESCRIPTION	An info-tag is a small window that displays a short description of a visible object. It is typically displayed near the cursor when you roll over the object. This is the color of the text in info-tag windows.

The default value for `infoText` is
```
0xFF000000 // infoText = Color.black;
```

EXAMPLE	See `activeCaptionBorder`.

menu

PURPOSE	The background color of a menu component.
SYNTAX	`public final static SystemColor menu`
DESCRIPTION	This is the background color of menu components such as menu bars (see MenuBar), popup menus (see PopupMenu), and menu items (see MenuItem).

The default value for `menu` is
```
0xFFC0C0C0 // menu = Color.lightGray;
```

EXAMPLE	This class implements a fake menu bar. It uses the various menu system colors to paint the different parts of the menubar. See the class example to see how this class is used.

```
import java.awt.*;
import java.awt.event.*;

class FakeMenuBar extends Component {
```

```
public void paint(Graphics g) {
    FontMetrics fm = g.getFontMetrics();
    int w = getSize().width;
    int h = getSize().height;

    // Paint menu background.
    g.setColor(Main.colors[SystemColor.MENU]);
    g.fillRect(0, 0, w, h);

    // Paint menu text.
    int x = (h-fm.getHeight())/2;
    g.setColor(Main.colors[SystemColor.MENU_TEXT]);
    g.drawString("Menu", x, (h-fm.getHeight())/2+fm.getAscent());

    x += fm.stringWidth("Menu      ");
    g.setColor(Main.colors[SystemColor.TEXT_INACTIVE_TEXT]);
    g.drawString("Inactive", x, (h-fm.getHeight())/2+fm.getAscent());
    }
}
```

menuText

PURPOSE   The color of text in a menu component.

SYNTAX   `public final static SystemColor menuText`

DESCRIPTION   This color should be used for painting the text in menu components such as menu bars (see `MenuBar`), popup menus (see `PopupMenu`), and menu items (see `MenuItem`).

The default value for `menuText` is
    `0xFF000000 // menuText = Color.black;`

EXAMPLE   See `menu`.

scrollbar

PURPOSE   The background color of a scrollbar.

SYNTAX   `public final static SystemColor scrollbar`

DESCRIPTION   This color is used to paint the background of adjustable objects such as scroll-bars (see `Scrollbar`) and sliders.

The default value for `scrollbar` is
    `0xFFE0E0E0 // scrollbar = new Color(224,224,224);`

EXAMPLE   This class implements a fake scrollbar. It uses the various scrollbar and component system colors to paint the different parts of the scrollbar. See the class example to see how this class is used.

```
import java.awt.*;
import java.awt.event.*;

class FakeScrollbar extends Component {
    public void paint(Graphics g) {
        int w = getSize().width;
        int h = getSize().height;

        g.setColor(Main.colors[SystemColor.SCROLLBAR]);
        g.fillRect(0, 0, w, h);

        draw3DOutline(g, false, 0, 0, w, h);
        draw3DOutline(g, true, 2, 2, w-4, w-4);
        draw3DOutline(g, true, 2, h-w+2, w-4, w-4);
    }

    public Dimension getPreferredSize() {
        return new Dimension(18, Math.max(1, getSize().height));
    }

    // Paint a 3D outline using the system colors.
    public void draw3DOutline(Graphics g, boolean up,
            int x, int y, int w, int h) {
        Color c1 = Main.colors[SystemColor.CONTROL_LT_HIGHLIGHT];
        Color c2 = Main.colors[SystemColor.CONTROL_HIGHLIGHT];
        Color c3 = Main.colors[SystemColor.CONTROL_SHADOW];
        Color c4 = Main.colors[SystemColor.CONTROL_DK_SHADOW];

        if (!up) {
            c1 = Main.colors[SystemColor.CONTROL_DK_SHADOW];
            c2 = Main.colors[SystemColor.CONTROL_SHADOW];
            c3 = Main.colors[SystemColor.CONTROL_LT_HIGHLIGHT];
            c4 = Main.colors[SystemColor.CONTROL_HIGHLIGHT];
        }

        // Paint outer left and top edge.
        g.setColor(c1);
        g.drawLine(x, y, x+w-1, y);
        g.drawLine(x, y, x, y+h-1);

        // Paint inner left and top edge.
        g.setColor(c2);
        g.drawLine(x+1, y+1, x+w-2, y+1);
        g.drawLine(x+1, y+1, x+1, y+h-2);

        // Paint inner shadow right and bottom edge.
        g.setColor(c3);
        g.drawLine(x+w-2, y+h-2, x+w-2, y+1);
        g.drawLine(x+w-2, y+h-2, x+1, y+h-2);

        // Paint outer shadow right and bottom edge.
        g.setColor(c4);
        g.drawLine(x+w-1, y+h-1, x+w-1, y);
        g.drawLine(x+w-1, y+h-1, x, y+h-1);
    }
}
```

A
B
C
D
E
F
G
H
I
J
K
L
M
N
O
P
Q
R
S
T
U
V
W
X
Y
Z

text

PURPOSE The background color of text components.

SYNTAX `public final static SystemColor text`

DESCRIPTION This color should be used for painting the background of components that have selectable text, such as a text field (see `TextField`) and a list (see `List`).

The default value for `text` is
```
0xFFC0C0C0 // text = Color.lightGray;
```

EXAMPLE This class implements a fake list. It uses the various text and component system colors to paint the list border and items in the list. See the class example to see how this class is used.

```java
import java.awt.*;
import java.awt.event.*;

class FakeList extends Component {
    FontMetrics fm;
    int curItem;

    FakeList() {
        // Listen for mouse clicks.
        addMouseListener(new MouseEventHandler());
    }

    public void paint(Graphics g) {
        int w = getSize().width;
        int h = getSize().height;

        if (fm == null) {
            fm = g.getFontMetrics();
        }

        // Paint control background.
        g.setColor(Main.colors[SystemColor.CONTROL]);
        g.fillRect(0, 0, w, h);

        // Paint 3D outline.
        draw3DOutline(g, true, 0, 0, w, h);
        draw3DOutline(g, false, 2, 2, w-4, h-4);

        // Don't paint over the borders.
        g.setClip(4, 4, w-8, h-8);

        for (int i=0; i<=h/fm.getHeight(); i++) {
            String item = "item "+i;

            if (i == curItem) {
                // Paint the select item background.
                g.setColor(Main.colors[SystemColor.TEXT_HIGHLIGHT]);
                g.fillRect(0, 4+i*fm.getHeight(), w, fm.getHeight());

                g.setColor(Main.colors[SystemColor.TEXT_HIGHLIGHT_TEXT]);
            } else {
                // Paint the select item background.
```

A
B
C
D
E
F
G
H
I
J
K
L
M
N
O
P
Q
R
S
T
U
V
W
X
Y
Z

```
        g.setColor(Main.colors[SystemColor.TEXT]);
        g.fillRect(0, 4+i*fm.getHeight(), w, fm.getHeight());

        g.setColor(Main.colors[SystemColor.TEXT_TEXT]);
      }

      // Paint item label.
      // The 4 is to adjust for the border.
      g.drawString(item, 4+(h-fm.getHeight())/2,
        4+i*fm.getHeight() + fm.getAscent());
    }
  }

  // Paint a 3D outline using the system colors.
  public void draw3DOutline(Graphics g, boolean up,
      int x, int y, int w, int h) {
    Color c1 = Main.colors[SystemColor.CONTROL_LT_HIGHLIGHT];
    Color c2 = Main.colors[SystemColor.CONTROL_HIGHLIGHT];
    Color c3 = Main.colors[SystemColor.CONTROL_SHADOW];
    Color c4 = Main.colors[SystemColor.CONTROL_DK_SHADOW];

    if (!up) {
      c1 = Main.colors[SystemColor.CONTROL_DK_SHADOW];
      c2 = Main.colors[SystemColor.CONTROL_SHADOW];
      c3 = Main.colors[SystemColor.CONTROL_LT_HIGHLIGHT];
      c4 = Main.colors[SystemColor.CONTROL_HIGHLIGHT];
    }

    // Paint outer left and top edge.
    g.setColor(c1);
    g.drawLine(x, y, x+w-1, y);
    g.drawLine(x, y, x, y+h-1);

    // Paint inner left and top edge.
    g.setColor(c2);
    g.drawLine(x+1, y+1, x+w-2, y+1);
    g.drawLine(x+1, y+1, x+1, y+h-2);

    // Paint inner shadow right and bottom edge.
    g.setColor(c3);
    g.drawLine(x+w-2, y+h-2, x+w-2, y+1);
    g.drawLine(x+w-2, y+h-2, x+1, y+h-2);

    // Paint outer shadow right and bottom edge.
    g.setColor(c4);
    g.drawLine(x+w-1, y+h-1, x+w-1, y);
    g.drawLine(x+w-1, y+h-1, x, y+h-1);
  }

  class MouseEventHandler extends MouseAdapter {
    public void mousePressed(MouseEvent evt) {
      if (fm != null) {
        // The 4 is to adjust for the border pixels.
        curItem = (evt.getY()-4)/fm.getHeight();
        repaint();
      }
    }
  }
}
```

A
B
C
D
E
F
G
H
I
J
K
L
M
N
O
P
Q
R
S
T
U
V
W
X
Y
Z

A
B
C
D
E
F
G
H
I
J
K
L
M
N
O
P
Q
R
S
T
U
V
W
X
Y
Z

textHighlight

PURPOSE The background color of highlighted text.

SYNTAX   `public final static SystemColor textHighlight`

DESCRIPTION This color should be used for painting the background of selected text in components that have selectable text, such as a text field (see `TextField`) or a list (see `List`).

      The default value for `textHighlight` is
      `0xFF000080 // textHighlight = new Color(0,0,128);`

EXAMPLE See `text`.

textHighlightText

PURPOSE The color of highlighted text.

SYNTAX   `public final static SystemColor textHighlightText`

DESCRIPTION This color should be used for painting selected text in components that have selectable text, such as a text field (see `TextField`) or a list (see `List`).

      The default value for `textHighlightText` is
      `0xFFFFFFFF // textHighlightText = Color.white;`

EXAMPLE See `text`.

textInactiveText

PURPOSE The color of inactive text.

SYNTAX   `public final static SystemColor textInactiveText`

DESCRIPTION When a component or item is disabled so that it cannot be activated or selected, the color of the text should be painted in this color. In the case of a component, the background color should be `control`; for an item, the background color should be `text`.

      The default value for `textInactiveText` is
      `0xFF808080 // textInactiveText = Color.gray;`

EXAMPLE See `menu`.

textText

PURPOSE	The color of text in a text component.
SYNTAX	`public final static SystemColor textText`
DESCRIPTION	This color should be used for painting the text in components that have selectable text, such as a text field (see `TextField`) and a list (see `List`).

The default value for `textText` is
```
0xFF000000 // textText = Color.black;
```

EXAMPLE	See `text`.

toString()

PURPOSE	Generates the string representation of this system color.
SYNTAX	`public String toString()`
DESCRIPTION	The string representation of a system color consists of the color's class name and its index position in the system color cache. Table 24 shows the index positions of the system color values in the system color cache. This method is typically used for debugging purposes.

0	DESKTOP	14	TEXT_HIGHTLIGHT
1	ACTIVE_CAPTION	15	TEXT_HIGHLIGHT_TEXT
2	ACTIVE_CAPTION_TEXT	16	TEXT_INACTIVE_TEXT
3	ACTIVE_CAPTION_BORDER	17	CONTROL
4	INACTIVE_CAPTION	18	CONTROL_TEXT
5	INACTIVE_CAPTION_TEXT	19	CONTROL_HIGHLIGHT
6	INACTIVE_CAPTION_BORDER	20	CONTROL_LT_HIGHLIGHT
7	WINDOW	21	CONTROL_SHADOW
8	WINDOW_BORDER	22	CONTROL_DK_SHADOW
9	WINDOW_TEXT	23	SCROLLBAR
10	MENU	24	INFO
11	MENU_TEXT	25	INFO_TEXT
12	TEXT	14	TEXT_HIGHTLIGHT
13	TEXT_TEXT		

TABLE 24: Index Positions of System Colors Values in the System Color Cache.

RETURNS	The non-`null` string representation of this system color.
OVERRIDES	`Color.toString()`.
EXAMPLE	See `java.lang.Object.toString()`.

A
B
C
D
E
F
G
H
I
J
K
L
M
N
O
P
Q
R
S
T
U
V
W
X
Y
Z

window

PURPOSE   The background color of a window.

SYNTAX   `public final static SystemColor window`

DESCRIPTION   Unless a window's background color has been explicitly set using `Compo-`
               `nent.setBackground()`, the window's background should be painted in this
               color.

               The default value for `window` is
               `0xFFFFFFFF // window = Color.white;`

EXAMPLE   See `activeCaptionBorder`.

windowBorder

PURPOSE   The border color of a window.

SYNTAX   `public final static SystemColor windowBorder`

DESCRIPTION   The border of a window consists of pixels along the perimeter of the window.
               A window may have two borders: an active border, which changes color
               depending whether the window is active, and a regular window border, which
               does not change color. `windowBorder` is the color of the regular window bor-
               der.

               The default value for `windowBorder` is
               `0xFF000000 // windowBorder = Color.black;`

EXAMPLE   See `activeCaptionBorder`.

windowText

PURPOSE   The color of text in a window.

SYNTAX   `public final static SystemColor windowText`

DESCRIPTION   Unless the foreground color of a window has been explicitly set using `Compo-`
               `nent.setForeground()`, text painted in a window should be painted in this
               color.

               The default value for `windowText` is
               `0xFF000000 // windowText = Color.black;`

EXAMPLE   See `activeCaptionBorder`.

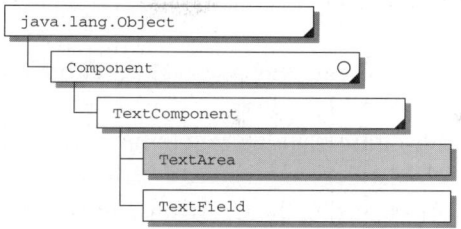

Syntax

```
public class TextArea extends TextComponent
```

Description

The *text area* is a text component that displays editable text. The text area is similar to the text field component, except that the text area can display multiple lines and has vertical and horizontal scrollbars.

The text area component is typically used for entering text messages or comments to a program and for displaying text output from a program.

Figure 341 shows an example of text area.

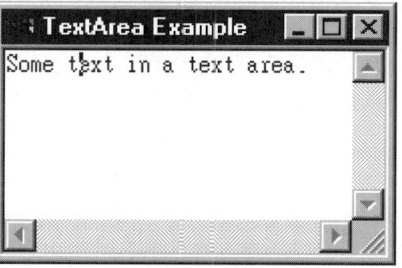

FIGURE 341: TextArea.

Preferred Number of Rows and Columns and Preferred Size

A text area can be created with a preferred number of rows and columns that determines the preferred size of the component. The preferred size is based on the average size of a character, which is a platform-dependent value. The preferred number of rows and columns can be changed at any time using `setRows()` and `setColumns()`. Calling these methods causes the text area's preferred size to be recalculated.

The preferred number of rows and columns in a text area does not limit the number of characters or lines that can be entered. Also, resizing the text area does not change its preferred number of rows or columns. A text area can be resized to be larger or smaller than its preferred number of rows and columns.

Scrollbars and Line-wrapping

A text area can be created with either a horizontal scrollbar, a vertical scrollbar, or both.

If the horizontal scrollbar is absent, the text area is set in line-wrapping mode. This means that any line that is longer than the width of the text area is automatically broken into multiple lines, each line wide enough to fit within the text area's width. However, the line breaks are not permanent; if the text area was made wide enough, these lines would be displayed unbroken again. Line breaking is strictly a visual effect and does not affect the update methods in any way. That is, although the number of visual lines may have increased, the number of true lines in the text area has not changed. In fact, it is not possible for a program to tell whether a line is broken.

If the horizontal scrollbar is present, long lines are never broken. You can use the horizontal scrollbar to see different parts of a long line.

The presence of a vertical scrollbar allows you to move up and down a long document by using the scrollbar. However, regardless of whether a vertical scrollbar is present, you can still move up and down the text area by using the UpArrow and DownArrow keys.

Note: In Java 1.1, there is no way to obtain a handle on the text area's scrollbars.

Newlines

The text of a text area can consists of multiple lines. Each line is separated by a single newline character (\n). This is true for all platforms, even when the platform may internally use other representations for newlines (such as \n\r).

Events

A text area fires the events fired by a text component. See `TextComponent` for details.

MEMBER SUMMARY

Constructor

`TextArea()`	Constructs a new `TextArea` instance.

Scrollbar Method and Constants

`getScrollbarVisibility()`	Retrieves which scrollbars are displayed for this text area.
`SCROLLBARS_BOTH`	Display both vertical and horizontal scrollbars.
`SCROLLBARS_HORIZONTAL_ONLY`	Display only the horizontal scrollbar.
`SCROLLBARS_VERTICAL_ONLY`	Display only the vertical scrollbar.
`SCROLLBARS_NONE`	Display no scrollbar.

Row and Column Methods

`getColumns()`	Retrieves the preferred number of columns in this text area.
`getRows()`	Retrieves the preferred number of rows in this text area.
`setColumns()`	Sets the number of columns in this text area.
`setRows()`	Sets the number of rows in this text area.

Layout Methods

`getMinimumSize()`	Calculates the minimum dimensions of this text area.
`getPreferredSize()`	Calculates the preferred dimensions of this text area.

MEMBER SUMMARY

Text Update Methods

append()	Appends a string to this text area.
insert()	Inserts a string in this text area.
replaceRange()	Replaces a range of characters in this text area with another range of characters.

Peer Method

addNotify()	Creates the text area's peer.

Debugging Method

paramString()	Generates a string representing the text area's state.

Deprecated Methods

appendText()	Replaced by append().
insertText()	Replaced by insert().
minimumSize()	Replaced by getMinimumSize().
preferredSize()	Replaced by getPreferredSize().
replaceText()	Replaced by replaceRange().

Example

This example creates a text area and displays it in a frame. See Figure 341 for a screen shot of the example.

```
import java.awt.*;
class Main extends Frame {
    TextArea ta = new TextArea(1, 1);

    Main() {
        super("TextArea Example");
        add(ta, BorderLayout.CENTER);
        pack();
        show();
    }

    static public void main(String[] args) {
        new Main();
    }
}
```

A
B
C
D
E
F
G
H
I
J
K
L
M
N
O
P
Q
R
S
U
V
W
X
Y
Z

A
B
C
D
E
F
G
H
I
J
K
L
M
N
O
P
Q
R
S
T
U
V
W
X
Y
Z

addNotify()

PURPOSE   Creates this text area's peer.

SYNTAX   `public void addNotify()`

DESCRIPTION   This method creates the text area's peer if it does not yet exist. The text area's peer is created by calling the `Toolkit.createTextArea()` method. This method should never be called directly. It is normally called by the text area's parent.

OVERRIDES   `Component.addNotify()`.

SEE ALSO   `Component`, `Toolkit`.

EXAMPLE   `Component.show()`.

append()

PURPOSE   Appends a string to this text area.

SYNTAX   `public synchronized void append(String text)`

DESCRIPTION   This method appends the string `text` to the end of the text area.

PARAMETERS
  text   The non-`null` string to be appended.

SEE ALSO   `insert()`, `replaceRange()`.

EXAMPLE   This example creates a frame containing a text area and a text field. The text typed in the text field is appended to the text area when you press Return. See Figure 342.

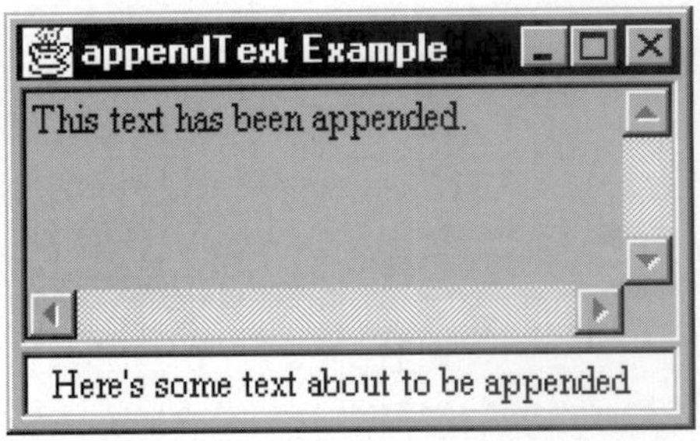

FIGURE 342: Appending Text to a TextArea.

```
import java.awt.*;
import java.awt.event.*;

class Main extends Frame implements ActionListener {
    TextField tf = new TextField();
    TextArea ta = new TextArea();

    Main() {
        super("append Example");
        ta.setEditable(false);
        add(ta, BorderLayout.CENTER);
        add(tf, BorderLayout.SOUTH);

        // Add listener for text field
```

```
        tf.addActionListener(this);

        pack();
        show();
    }

    public void actionPerformed(ActionEvent evt) {
        ta.append(tf.getText() + "\n");
        tf.setText("");
    }

    static public void main(String[] args) {
        new Main();
    }
}
```

A
B
C
D
E
F
G

appendText( )

H
I
J
K
L
M
N
O
P
Q
R
S

PURPOSE	Replaced by append().
SYNTAX	`public void appendText(String text)`
PARAMETERS	
text	The non-null string to be appended.
DEPRECATION	Replace the usage of this deprecated method, as in

```
    textarea.appendText(text);
```
with
```
    textarea.append(text);
```

getColumns( )

PURPOSE	Retrieves the preferred number of columns in this text area.
SYNTAX	`public int getColumns()`
DESCRIPTION	The preferred number of columns determines the text area's preferred width. See the class description for details.
RETURNS	The preferred number of columns in this text area.
SEE ALSO	getRows(), getPreferredSize(), setColumns(), TextArea().

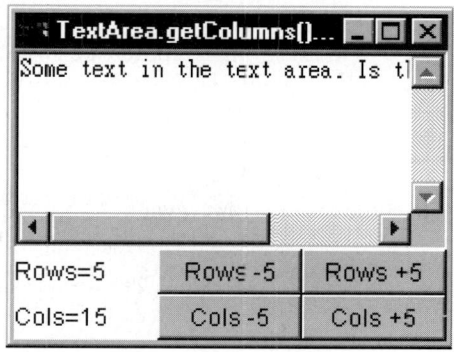

FIGURE 343: Rows and Columns of a TextArea.

U
V
W
X
Y
Z

EXAMPLE   This example creates a text area whose rows and columns are controlled by some buttons at the bottom of the frame. See Figure 343.

```
import java.awt.*;
import java.awt.event.*;

class Main extends Frame implements ActionListener {
    TextArea ta = new TextArea();
    Label rows, cols;

    Main() {
        super("TextArea.getColumns() Example");
        Panel p = new Panel(new GridLayout(2, 0));

        rows = new Label("Rows=" + ta.getRows());
        p.add(rows);

        Button b = new Button("Rows -5");
        p.add(b);
        b.addActionListener(this);
        b = new Button("Rows +5");
        p.add(b);
        b.addActionListener(this);

        cols = new Label("Cols=" + ta.getColumns());
        p.add(cols);
        b = new Button("Cols -5");
        p.add(b);
        b.addActionListener(this);
        b = new Button("Cols +5");
        p.add(b);
        b.addActionListener(this);

        add(p, BorderLayout.SOUTH);
        add(ta, BorderLayout.CENTER);

        pack();
        show();
    }

    public void actionPerformed(ActionEvent evt) {
        String cmd = evt.getActionCommand();
        if (cmd.equals("Rows -5")) {
            ta.setRows(ta.getRows()-5);
            rows.setText("Rows=" + ta.getRows());
        } else if (cmd.equals("Rows +5")) {
            ta.setRows(ta.getRows()+5);
            rows.setText("Rows=" + ta.getRows());
        } else  if (cmd.equals("Cols -5")) {
            ta.setColumns(ta.getColumns()-5);
            cols.setText("Cols=" + ta.getColumns());
        } else if (cmd.equals("Cols +5")) {
            ta.setColumns(ta.getColumns()+5);
            cols.setText("Cols=" + ta.getColumns());
        }
    }

    public static void main(String[] args) {
        new Main();
    }
}
```

getMinimumSize()

PURPOSE Calculates the minimum dimensions of this text area.

SYNTAX `public Dimension getMinimumSize()`
`public Dimension getMinimumSize(int rows, int cols)`

DESCRIPTION The minimum dimensions of a text area are based on the dimensions needed to display the specified number of rows and columns of characters. The size of a character depends on the text area's current font. If the text area's font has variable-width characters, then the width is based on the average size of a character and the result is an approximation. The average width of a character is a platform-dependent value. If `rows` and `cols` are not specified, they default to the current preferred number of rows and columns.

If the text area's peer is not yet created, the resulting dimensions are (0, 0). On most platforms, the minimum and preferred dimensions are the same.

PARAMETERS
`cols` A non-negative integer specifying the width in characters.
`rows` A non-negative integer specifying the height in character lines.

RETURNS A new non-null `Dimension` instance containing the minimum dimensions of the text area.

OVERRIDES `Component.getMinimumSize()`.

SEE ALSO `getColumns()`, `getPreferredSize()`, `getRows()`.

EXAMPLE See the `LayoutManager` class example.

getPreferredSize()

PURPOSE Calculates the preferred dimensions of this text area.

SYNTAX `public Dimension getPreferredSize()`
`public Dimension getPreferredSize(int rows, int cols)`

DESCRIPTION The preferred dimensions of a text area are based on the dimensions needed to display the specified number of rows and columns of characters. The size of a character depends on the text area's current font. If the text area's font has variable-width characters, the width is based on the average size of a character and the result is an approximation. The average width of a character is a platform-dependent value. If `rows` and `cols` are not specified, they default to the current preferred number of rows and columns.

If the text area's peer is not yet created, the resulting dimensions are (0, 0). On most platforms, the minimum and preferred dimensions are the same.

A
B
C
D
E
F
G
H
I
J
K
L
M
N
O
P
Q
R
S
T
U
V
W
X
Y
Z

PARAMETERS

cols   A non-negative integer specifying the width in characters.

rows   A non-negative integer specifying the height in character lines.

RETURNS   A new non-null `Dimension` instance containing the preferred dimensions of the text area.

OVERRIDES   `Component.getPreferredSize()`.

SEE ALSO   `getColumns()`, `getMinimumSize()`, `getRows()`.

EXAMPLE   See the `LayoutManager` class example.

getRows( )

PURPOSE   Retrieves the number of rows in this text area.

SYNTAX   `public int getRows()`

DESCRIPTION   The preferred number of rows determines the text area's preferred height. See the class description for details.

RETURNS   The preferred number of rows in this text area.

SEE ALSO   `getColumns()`, `getPreferredSize()`, `setRows()`, `TextArea()`.

EXAMPLE   See `getColumns()`.

getScrollbarVisibility( )

PURPOSE   Retrieves which scrollbars are displayed for this text area.

SYNTAX   `public int getScrollbarVisibility()`

DESCRIPTION   This method returns a constant specifying which scrollbars are being displayed for this text area. This value is identical to the one used to create the text area. One of `SCROLLBARS_BOTH`, `SCROLLBARS_NONE`, `SCROLLBARS_HORIZONTAL_ONLY`, or `SCROLLBARS_VERTICAL_ONLY`.

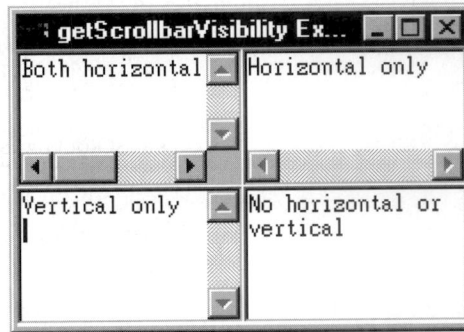

FIGURE 344:   Scrollbars in a `TextArea`.

SEE ALSO   `SCROLLBARS_BOTH`, `SCROLLBARS_NONE`, `SCROLLBARS_HORIZONTAL_ONLY`, `SCROLLBARS_VERTICAL_ONLY`.

EXAMPLE   This example creates a frame that has four text areas. The text areas are distinguished by the types of scrollbars they have. Modifying the text in a text area causes a message to be displayed indicating the text area in which the change occurred. See Figure 344.

```java
import java.awt.*;
import java.awt.event.*;

class Main extends Frame implements TextListener {
    Main () {
        super("getScrollbarVisibility Example");
        Panel p =
            new Panel(new GridLayout(2, 2));
        TextArea both = new TextArea("Both horizontal and vertical",
                            10, 10, TextArea.SCROLLBARS_BOTH);
        TextArea hor = new TextArea("Horizontal only",
                            10, 10, TextArea.SCROLLBARS_HORIZONTAL_ONLY);
        TextArea ver = new TextArea("Vertical only",
                            10, 10, TextArea.SCROLLBARS_VERTICAL_ONLY);
        TextArea none = new TextArea("No horizontal or vertical",
                            10, 10, TextArea.SCROLLBARS_NONE);

        p.add(both);
        p.add(hor);
        p.add(ver);
        p.add(none);
        both.addTextListener(this);
        hor.addTextListener(this);
        ver.addTextListener(this);
        none.addTextListener(this);

        add(p);
        pack();
        show();
    }

    public void textValueChanged(TextEvent evt) {
        TextArea src = (TextArea)evt.getSource();
        switch (src.getScrollbarVisibility()) {
        case TextArea.SCROLLBARS_BOTH:
            System.out.println("both");
            break;
        case TextArea.SCROLLBARS_HORIZONTAL_ONLY:
            System.out.println("horizontal only");
            break;
        case TextArea.SCROLLBARS_VERTICAL_ONLY:
            System.out.println("vertical only");
            break;
        case TextArea.SCROLLBARS_NONE:
            System.out.println("none");
            break;
        }
    }

    static public void main(String[] args) {
        new Main();
    }
}
```

A
B
C
D
E
F
G
H
I
J
K
L
M
N
O
P
Q
R
S
T
U
V
W
X
Y
Z

A
B
C
D
E
F
G
H
I
J
K
L
M
N
O
P
Q
R
S

U
V
W
X
Y
Z

insert( )

PURPOSE   Inserts a string in this text area.

SYNTAX   `public synchronized void insert(String text, int pos)`

DESCRIPTION   This method inserts the string `text` at index `pos` of this text area.

PARAMETERS

pos   The zero-based index at which to insert the text.

text   The non-`null` text to be inserted.

SEE ALSO   `append()`, `replaceRange()`.

EXAMPLE   This example creates a frame containing a text area and a choice. The choice contains a number of words that can be inserted into the text area when selected. See Figure 345.

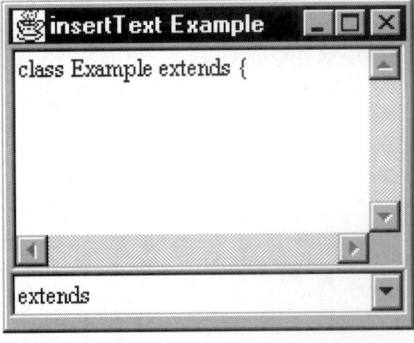

FIGURE 345:   Inserting Text into a TextArea.

```java
import java.awt.*;
import java.awt.event.*;

class Main extends Frame implements ItemListener {
    String[] keywords =
        {"class", "extends", "import", "interface", "synchronized"};
    TextArea ta = new TextArea();
    Choice c = new Choice();

    Main() {
        super("insert Example");
        for (int i=0; i<keywords.length; i++) {
            c.addItem(keywords[i]);
        }
        add(ta, BorderLayout.CENTER);
        add(c, BorderLayout.SOUTH);

        // Add listener for choice
        c.addItemListener(this);

        pack();
        show();
    }

    public void itemStateChanged(ItemEvent evt) {
        ta.insert((String)evt.getItem(),ta.getSelectionEnd());
        ta.requestFocus();
    }

    static public void main(String[] args) {
        new Main();
    }
}
```

insertText() *DEPRECATED*

PURPOSE   Replaced by `insert()`.

SYNTAX   `public void insertText(String text, int pos)`

PARAMETERS

pos   The zero-based index at which to insert the text.

text   The non-`null` text to be inserted.

DEPRECATION   Replace the usage of this deprecated method, as in

```
textarea.insertText(text, pos);
```

with

```
textarea.insert(text, pos);
```

minimumSize() *DEPRECATED*

PURPOSE   Replaced by `getMinimumSize()`.

SYNTAX   `public Dimension minimumSize()`
            `public Dimension minimumSize(int rows, int cols)`

PARAMETERS

cols   A non-negative integer specifying the width in characters.

rows   A non-negative integer specifying the height in character lines.

RETURNS   A new non-`null` `Dimension` instance containing the minimum dimensions of the text area.

OVERRIDES   `Component.minimumSize()`.

DEPRECATION   Replace the usage of this deprecated method, as in

```
Dimension dim = textarea.minimumSize();
Dimension dim2 = textarea.minimumSize(rows, cols);
```

with

```
Dimension dim = textarea.getMinimimSize();
Dimension dim2 = textarea.getMinimumSize(rows, cols);
```

paramString()

PURPOSE   Generates the string representing this text area's state.

SYNTAX   `protected String paramString()`

DESCRIPTION   The string representation of a text area consists of the string representation of `TextComponent`, plus the text area's preferred number of rows and columns, and which scrollbars are displayed. A subclass of this class should override this method and return a concatenation of its state with the results of super.paramString(). This method is called by the toString() method and is typically used for debugging.

RETURNS   A non-null string representing the text area's state.

OVERRIDES   TextComponent.paramString().

SEE ALSO   Component.toString(), java.lang.Object.toString().

EXAMPLE   See Component.paramString().

preferredSize( ) _____ _DEPRECATED_

PURPOSE   Replaced by getPreferredSize().

SYNTAX
```
public Dimension preferredSize()
public Dimension preferredSize(int rows, int cols)
```

PARAMETERS
cols   A non-negative integer specifying the width in characters.
rows   A non-negative integer specifying the height in character lines.

RETURNS   A new non-null Dimension instance containing the preferred dimensions of the text area.

OVERRIDES   Component.preferredSize().

DEPRECATION   Replace the usage of this deprecated method, as in
```
Dimension dim = textarea.preferredSize();
Dimension dim2 = textarea.preferredSize(rows, cols);
```
with
```
Dimension dim = textarea.getPreferredSize();
Dimension dim2 = textarea.getPreferredSize(rows, cols);
```


replaceRange( )

PURPOSE   Replaces a range of characters in this text area with another string.

SYNTAX
```
public synchronized void replaceRange(String str, int startPos,
    int endPos)
```

DESCRIPTION   This method replaces the text between startPos and endPos with str in this text area. The length of the range is endPos - startPos.

PARAMETERS
endPos   The zero-based end position of the range. The character at end is not included in the range.
startPos   The zero-based index of the first character in the range.
str   The non-null replacement string.

SEE ALSO   append(), insert().

EXAMPLE   This example demonstrates searching and
replacing text by creating a
text area and two text
fields. See Figure 346. In
one text field, you specify a
search string and in the
other, you specify a
replacement string. When
you press Return while in
either text field, the first
occurrence of the search
string after the caret in the
text area is replaced by the
replacement string.

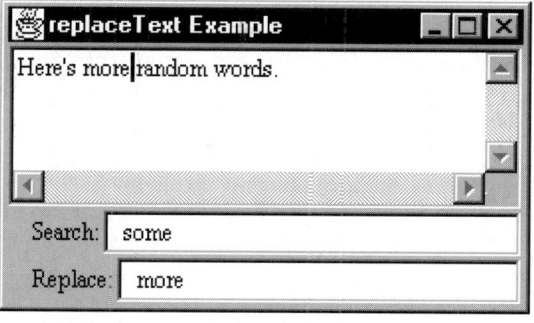

FIGURE 346: Search and Replace in a TextArea.

```java
import java.awt.*;
import java.awt.event.*;

class Main extends Frame implements ActionListener {
    TextField tfSearch = new TextField();
    TextField tfReplace = new TextField();
    TextArea ta = new TextArea(10, 40);

    Main() {
        super("replaceRange Example");
        Panel southPanel = new Panel(new GridLayout(2, 1));
        Panel p = new Panel(new BorderLayout());

        p.add(new Label("Search:"), BorderLayout.WEST);
        p.add(tfSearch, BorderLayout.CENTER);

        southPanel.add(p);

        p = new Panel(new BorderLayout());
        p.add(new Label("Replace:"), BorderLayout.WEST);
        p.add(tfReplace, BorderLayout.CENTER);
        southPanel.add(p);

        add(ta, BorderLayout.CENTER);
        add(southPanel, BorderLayout.SOUTH);

        // Add listeners for search and replace text fields
        tfReplace.addActionListener(this);
        tfSearch.addActionListener(this);

        pack();
        show();
    }

    public void actionPerformed(ActionEvent evt) {
```

```
                    String str = tfSearch.getText();
                    int s = ta.getText().indexOf(str, ta.getSelectionStart());

                    if (s < 0 && ta.getSelectionStart() > 0) {
                        // Let's try from the beginning.
                        s = ta.getText().indexOf(str, 0);
                    }
                    if (s >= 0) {
                        String strRep = tfReplace.getText();
                        ta.replaceRange(strRep, s, s + str.length());
                        ta.select(s + strRep.length(), s + strRep.length());
                        ta.requestFocus();
                    }
                }

                static public void main(String[] args) {
                    new Main();
                }
            }
        }
```

A
B
C
D
E
F
G
H
I

replaceText()   *DEPRECATED*

J
K
L
M
N
O
P
Q
R
S
T
U
V
W
X
Y
Z

PURPOSE	Replaced by `replaceRange()`.
SYNTAX	`public void replaceText(String str, int startPos, int endPos)`
PARAMETERS	
endPos	The zero-based end position of the range. The character at end is not included in the range.
startPos	The o-based index of the first character in the range.
str	The non-`null` replacement string.

DEPRECATION	Replace the usage of this deprecated method, as in
	`textarea.replaceText(str, startPos, endPos);`
	with
	`textarea.replaceRange(str, startPos, endPos);`

SCROLLBARS_BOTH

PURPOSE	Display both vertical and horizontal scrollbars.
SYNTAX	`public static final int SCROLLBARS_BOTH`
DESCRIPTION	This constant indicates that the text area is to have both horizontal and vertical scrollbars. See the class description for details on a text area's scrollbars. It is used as a parameter to the `TextArea()` constructor. Its value is 0.
SEE ALSO	`getScrollbarVisibility()`, `SCROLLBARS_HORIZONTAL_ONLY`, `SCROLLBARS_NONE`, `SCROLLBARS_VERTICAL_ONLY`, `TextArea()`.
EXAMPLE	See `TextArea()`.

SCROLLBARS_HORIZONTAL_ONLY

PURPOSE	Display only the horizontal scrollbar.
SYNTAX	`public static final int SCROLLBARS_HORIZONTAL_ONLY`
DESCRIPTION	This constant indicates that the text area is to have only a horizontal scrollbar. See the class description for details on a text area's scrollbars. It is used as a parameter to the `TextArea()` constructor. Its value is 2.
SEE ALSO	`getScrollbarVisibility()`, `SCROLLBARS_BOTH`, `SCROLLBARS_NONE`, `SCROLLBARS_VERTICAL_ONLY`, `TextArea()`.
EXAMPLE	See `TextArea()`.

SCROLLBARS_NONE

PURPOSE	Display neither horizontal nor vertical scrollbars.
SYNTAX	`public static final int SCROLLBARS_NONE`
DESCRIPTION	This constant indicates that the text area is to have no scrollbars. See the class description for details on a text area's scrollbars. It is used as a parameter to the `TextArea()` constructor. Its value is 3.
SEE ALSO	`getScrollbarVisibility()`, `SCROLLBARS_BOTH`, `SCROLLBARS_HORIZONTAL_ONLY`, `SCROLLBARS_VERTICAL_ONLY`, `TextArea()`.
EXAMPLE	See `TextArea()`.

SCROLLBARS_VERTICAL_ONLY

PURPOSE	Display only the vertical scrollbar.
SYNTAX	`public static final int SCROLLBARS_VERTICAL_ONLY`
DESCRIPTION	This constant indicates that the text area is to have only the vertical scrollbar. See the class description for details on a text area's scrollbars. It is used as a parameter to the `TextArea()` constructor. Its value is 1.
SEE ALSO	`getScrollbarVisibility()`, `SCROLLBARS_BOTH`, `SCROLLBARS_HORIZONTAL_ONLY`, `SCROLLBARS_NONE`, `TextArea()`.
EXAMPLE	See `TextArea()`.

A
B
C
D
E
F
G
H
I
J
K
L
M
N
O
P
Q
R
S
U
V
W
X
Y
Z

setColumns()

PURPOSE	Sets the number of columns in this text area.
SYNTAX	`public void setColumns(int cols)`
DESCRIPTION	The preferred number of columns determines the text area's preferred width and does not limit the number of columns that can be entered in the text area. See the class description for details.
PARAMETERS	
`cols`	The number of columns.
EXCEPTIONS	
`IllegalArgumentException`	If `cols` < 0.
SEE ALSO	`getColumns()`, `TextArea()`.
EXAMPLE	See `getColumns()`.

setRows()

PURPOSE	Sets the number of rows in this text area.
SYNTAX	`public void setRows(int rows)`
DESCRIPTION	The preferred number of rows determines the text area's preferred height and does not limit the number of rows that can be entered in the text area. See the class description for details.
PARAMETERS	
`rows`	The number of rows.
EXCEPTIONS	
`IllegalArgumentException`	If `rows` < 0.
SEE ALSO	`getRows()`, `TextArea()`.
EXAMPLE	See `getColumns()`.

A
B
C
D
E
F
G
H
I
J
K
L
M
N
O
P
Q
R
S
T
U
V
W
X
Y
Z

TextArea( )

PURPOSE   Creates a new TextArea instance.

SYNTAX
```
public TextArea()
public TextArea(String text)
public TextArea(int rows, int cols)
public TextArea(String text, int rows, int cols)
public TextArea(String text, int rows, int cols, int scrollbarVis)
```

DESCRIPTION   This constructor creates a new editable TextArea initialized by using the string text. If text is not specified, it defaults to "".

rows and cols specify the preferred number of rows and columns of the text area. See the class description for details. If rows and cols are not specified, the defaults are chosen by the platform.

scrollbarVis specifies which scrollbars to display with the text area. If scrollbarVis is not specified, it defaults to SCROLLBARS_BOTH. See the class description for details on a text area's scrollbars.

PARAMETERS
cols   A non-negative integer specifying the preferred width in characters.

rows   A non-negative integer specifying the preferred height in character lines.

scrollbarVisSpecifies which scrollbars to display, one of SCROLLBARS_BOTH, SCROLLBARS_HORIZONTAL_ONLY, SCROLLBARS_VERTICAL_ONLY, or SCROLLBARS_NONE.

text   The string specifying the initial text for the text component. May be null.

SEE ALSO   getRows( ), getColumns( ), getScrollbarVisibility( ).

EXAMPLE   This example creates four text areas, each with a different scrollbar visibility setting. Resize the window and see how the formatting differs for each text area depending on which scrollbars it has. See Figure 347.

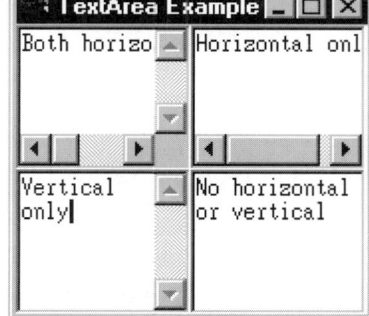

FIGURE 347: TextArea and its Scrollbars.

```
import java.awt.*;

class Main extends Frame {
    Main () {
        super("TextArea Example");
        Panel p =
            new Panel(new GridLayout(2, 2));
        TextArea both = new TextArea("Both horizontal and vertical",
                            10, 10, TextArea.SCROLLBARS_BOTH);
        TextArea hor = new TextArea("Horizontal only",
                            10, 10, TextArea.SCROLLBARS_HORIZONTAL_ONLY);
```

A
B
C
D
E
F
G
H
I
J
K
L
M
N
O
P
Q
R
S
T
U
V
W
X
Y
Z

TextArea()

```
            TextArea ver = new TextArea("Vertical only",
                            10, 10, TextArea.SCROLLBARS_VERTICAL_ONLY);
            TextArea none = new TextArea("No horizontal or vertical",
                            10, 10, TextArea.SCROLLBARS_NONE);

            p.add(both);
            p.add(hor);
            p.add(ver);
            p.add(none);

            add(p);
            pack();
            show();
        }

        static public void main(String[] args) {
            new Main();
        }
    }
```

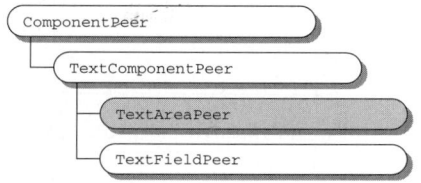

Syntax

```
public interface TextAreaPeer extends TextComponentPeer
```

Description

The text area component (see the TextArea class) in the AWT uses the platform's native implementation of a text area. So that the AWT text area behaves the same on all platforms, the text area is assigned a *peer,* whose task is to translate the behavior of the platform's native text area to the behavior of the AWT text area.

AWT programmers normally do not directly use peer classes and interfaces. Instead, they deal with AWT components in the java.awt package. These in turn automatically manage their peers. Only someone who is porting the AWT to another platform should be concerned with the peer classes and interfaces. Consequently, most peer documentation refers to java.awt counterparts.

See Component and Toolkit for additional information about component peers.

MEMBER SUMMARY	
Peer Methods	
getMinimumSize()	Calculates the minimum dimensions of the text area.
getPreferredSize()	Calculates the preferred dimensions of the text area.
insert()	Inserts some text in the text area.
replaceRange()	Replaces a range of characters in the text area with another range of characters.
Deprecated Methods	
insertText()	Replaced by insert().
minimumSize()	Replaced by getMinimumSize().
preferredSize()	Replaced by getPreferredSize().
replaceText()	Replaced by replaceRange().

A
B
C
D
E
F
G
H
I
J
K
L
M
N
O
P
Q
R
S
T
U
V
W
X
Y
Z

See Also

java.awt.Component, java.awt.TextArea, java.awt.Toolkit.

getMinimumSize( )

PURPOSE	Calculates the minimum dimensions of the text area.
SYNTAX	Dimension getMinimumSize(int rows, int cols)
PARAMETERS	
cols	A non-negative integer specifying the width in characters.
rows	A non-negative integer specifying the height in character lines.
RETURNS	The non-null minimum dimensions for the text area.
SEE ALSO	java.awt.TextArea.getMinimumSize().

getPreferredSize( )

PURPOSE	Calculates the preferred dimensions of the text area.
SYNTAX	Dimension getPreferredSize(int rows, int cols)
PARAMETERS	
cols	A non-negative integer specifying the width in characters.
rows	A non-negative integer specifying the height in character lines.
RETURNS	The non-null preferred dimensions for the text area.
SEE ALSO	java.awt.TextArea.getPreferredSize().

insert( )

PURPOSE	Inserts some text in the text area.
SYNTAX	void insert(String text, int pos)
PARAMETERS	
pos	The zero-based position at which to insert the text.
text	The non-null text to be inserted.
SEE ALSO	java.awt.TextArea.insert().

insertText( )   *DEPRECATED*

PURPOSE   Replaced by `insert()`.

SYNTAX   `void insertText(String text, int pos)`

PARAMETERS
 `pos`   The zero-based position at which to insert the text.
 `text`   The non-`null` text to be inserted.

DEPRECATION   Replace the usage of this deprecated method, as in
               `peer.insertText(text, pos);`
               with
               `peer.insert(text, pos);`

minimumSize( )   *DEPRECATED*

PURPOSE   Replaced by `getMinimumSize()`.

SYNTAX   `Dimension minimumSize(int rows, int cols)`

PARAMETERS
 `cols`   A non-negative integer specifying the width in characters.
 `rows`   A non-negative integer specifying the height in character lines.

RETURNS   The non-`null` minimum dimensions for the text area.

DEPRECATION   Replace the usage of this deprecated method, as in
               `Dimension min = peer.minimumSize(rows, cols);`
               with
               `Dimension min = peer.getMinimumSize(rows, cols);`

preferredSize( )   *DEPRECATED*

PURPOSE   Replaced by `getPreferredSize()`.

SYNTAX   `Dimension preferredSize(int rows, int cols)`

PARAMETERS
 `cols`   A non-negative integer specifying the width in characters.
 `rows`   A non-negative integer specifying the height in character lines.

RETURNS   The non-`null` preferred dimensions for the text area.

DEPRECATION   Replace the usage of this deprecated method, as in
               `Dimension min = peer.preferredSize(rows, cols);`
               with
               `Dimension min = peer.getPreferredSize(rows, cols);`

A
B
C
D
E
F
G
H
I
J
K
L
M
N
O
P
Q
R
S
T
U
V
W
X
Y
Z

A
B
C
D
E
F
G
H
I
J
K
L
M
N
O
P
Q
R
S

U
V
W
X
Y
Z

replaceRange()

PURPOSE   Replaces a range of characters in the text area with another range of characters.

SYNTAX   `void replaceRange(String str, int start, int end)`

PARAMETERS
  end   The zero-based exclusive end position.
  start   The zero-based inclusive start position.
  str   The non-null replacement string.

SEE ALSO   `java.awt.TextArea.replaceRange()`.

replaceText()   *DEPRECATED*

PURPOSE   Replaced by `replaceRange()`.

SYNTAX   `void replaceText(String str, int start, int end)`

PARAMETERS
  end   The zero-based exclusive end position.
  start   The zero-based inclusive start position.
  str   The non-null replacement string.

DEPRECATION   Replace the usage of this deprecated method, as in
  `peer.replaceText(str, start, end);`
with
  `peer.replaceRange(str, start, end);`

TextComponent

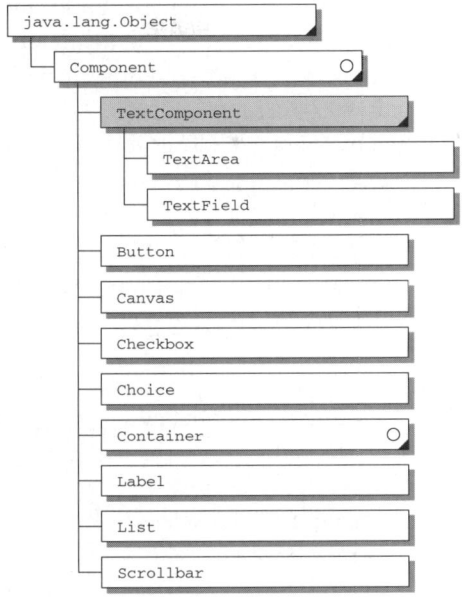

```
java.lang.Object
    Component                    ○
        TextComponent
            TextArea
            TextField
        Button
        Canvas
        Checkbox
        Choice
        Container                ○
        Label
        List
        Scrollbar
```

Syntax
`public class TextComponent extends Component`

Description

The text component is a component that displays edit-able text. The text can be modified by either the user or a program. There are two text components in the AWT package: the text field and the text area. Both are subclasses of `TextComponent`. The `TextComponent` class itself is not instantiated. Its main purpose is to encapsulate the functionality that is common between the text field and text area components. Figure 348 shows a frame containing a text area and text field.

FIGURE 348: TextArea and TextField.

The Editable Property

A text component has an editable property that controls whether the user can edit the text in the text component. The editable property affects only edits by the user; edits by a program are still allowed. On some platforms, the text component has some distinguishing visual feature to indicate its editable state.

A
B
C
D
E
F
G
H
I
J
K
L
M
N
O
P
Q
R
S
T
U
V
W
X
Y
Z

Text Component Positions

Text component positions refer to a character in the text. A position is zero-based, meaning the position of the first character in the text is 0 and the position of the last character is the length of the text minus 1. A newline entered by the user to the text component is treated as a single character (\n) regardless of the newline's representation in its native platform (which, for example, would be \r\n on Windows).

Two positions specify a range of characters. The start position refers to the first character in the range. The end position also refers to a character in the text, but that character is not included in the range; the text before the character at the end position is included in the range. Therefore, when the start and end positions are the same, the range is empty. Moreover, to select the last characters in the text, you should set the end position to the length of the text. (end - start) is the number of characters in the range.

The Selection and Caret

A *selection* is a range of text in the text component. Both the user and a program can set and change the selection. There is only one selection per text component. The appearance and exact behavior of the selection is platform-dependent, but on most systems, only one selection is allowed in the entire system. Typically, the active selection is in the text component that is receiving keyboard input. Although the selections in other text components are not active, a program can still operate on the selection, modifying the range or

FIGURE 349:   The Selection.

the text in the range. Figure 349 shows the selection on the text "word" in the text area component.

A selection can become empty. It still has a position in the text component, but it does not contain any text. In fact, both the start and end positions are equal. When the active selection is empty, it becomes the "caret." The caret indicates where in the text component characters will appear as the user types, marking the text component's *text insertion point*. The caret moves forward with each character typed. As with the active selection, there is only one caret in the entire system.

Figure 350 shows the caret between the words "these words." On most platforms, when the user types a character at the active selection, the text in the selection is deleted, the active selection is turned into a caret, and then the character is inserted.

FIGURE 350:   The Caret.

Events

A text component not only generates basic component events (focus, key, mouse, mouse motion, and component), but also fires a text event when the text of the text component changes. See the `Tex-tEvent` and `Component` classes for details.

　　If the text component is not editable, key events are still fired, but they are not inserted into the text component.

MEMBER SUMMARY

Text Methods

`getText()`	Retrieves the text in this text component.
`setText()`	Replaces the text of this text component.

Selection Methods

`getSelectedText()`	Retrieves the selected text in this text component.
`getSelectionEnd()`	Retrieves the end position of this text component's selection.
`getSelectionStart()`	Retrieves the start position of this text component's selection.
`select()`	Sets the selection in this text component.
`selectAll()`	Selects all of the text in this text component.
`setSelectionEnd()`	Retrieves the end position of this text component's selection.
`setSelectionStart()`	Retrieves the start position of this text component's selection.

Editable Methods

`isEditable()`	Retrieves this text component's current editable state.
`setEditable()`	Sets this text component's editable state.

Caret Methods

`getCaretPosition()`	Retrieves this text component's text insertion point.
`setCaretPosition()`	Sets this text component's text insertion point.

Event Methods

`addTextListener()`	Adds a listener to receive this text component's text events.
`processEvent()`	Processes an event enabled for this text component.
`processTextEvent()`	Processes a text event enabled for this text component.
`removeTextListener()`	Removes a listener from receiving this text component's text events.

Peer Method

`removeNotify()`	Destroys this text component's peer.

Debugging Method

`paramString()`	Generates a string representation of this text component's state.

A
B
C
D
E
F
G
H
I
J
K
L
M
N
O
P
Q
R
S

U
V
W
X
Y
Z

See Also

java.awt.event.TextEvent, java.awt.event.TextListener, TextArea, TextField.

Example

This example creates a frame containing both kinds of text components: a text field and a text area. See Figure 348 for a screen shot of the example.

```
import java.awt.*;
class Main {

    static public void main(String[] args) {
        Frame f = new Frame("TextComponent Example");
        f.add(new TextField(), BorderLayout.SOUTH);
        f.add(new TextArea(), BorderLayout.CENTER);
        f.pack();
        f.show();
    }
}
```

addTextListener( )

PURPOSE	Adds a listener for receiving this text component's text events.
SYNTAX	public synchronized void addTextListener(TextListener listener)
DESCRIPTION	Text events are fired when the component's text is changed. See TextEvent for more details. After this method is called, the text listener listener will receive text events fired by this text component. If listener is null, this method does nothing.
PARAMETERS	
listener	The possibly null text listener to add.
SEE ALSO	java.awt.event.TextEvent, java.awt.event.TextListener, removeTextListener().

EXAMPLE   This example creates a frame containing two text areas. Changes made in one text area are automatically made in the other text listener via the use of a text listener. See Figure 351.

FIGURE 351: **Echoing TextAreas.**

```
import java.awt.*;
import java.awt.event.*;

class Main extends Frame implements TextListener {
    TextArea ta1 = new TextArea(null, 10, 40);
    TextArea ta2 = new TextArea(null, 10, 40);

    Main() {
        super("addTextListener Example");
        setLayout(new GridLayout(1, 2));
        add(ta1);
        add(ta2);

        // Add text listener for text areas
        ta1.addTextListener(this);
        ta2.addTextListener(this);

        pack();
        show();
    }

    public void textValueChanged(TextEvent evt) {
        TextComponent src = (TextComponent)evt.getSource();
        if (src == ta1) {
            ta2.setText(ta1.getText());
        } else {
            ta1.setText(ta2.getText());
        }
    }

    static public void main(String[] args) {
        new Main();
    }
}
```

getCaretPosition()

PURPOSE	Retrieves this text component's text insert point.
SYNTAX	`public int getCaretPosition()`
DESCRIPTION	The caret position indicates where characters will be inserted as the user types. See the class description for details on caret.
RETURNS	The zero-based index of the caret's position. Text will be inserted just before the character referred to by the index.
SEE ALSO	`setCaretPosition()`.

A
B
C
D
E
F
G
H
I
J
K
L
M
N
O
P
Q
R
S

U
V
W
X
Y
Z

EXAMPLE   This example creates a text area for entering text and a label at the bottom for displaying the current caret position. Repositioning the caret using the mouse also updates the label. See Figure 352.

```java
import java.awt.*;
import java.awt.event.*;
```

FIGURE 352:   **TextComponent's Caret Position.**

```java
class Main extends Frame {
    TextArea ta =
        new TextArea(null, 10, 40);
    Label caret = new Label("caret=0");

    Main() {
        super("getCaretPosition Example");

        add(ta, BorderLayout.CENTER);
        add(caret, BorderLayout.SOUTH);

        // Add listeners for text area
        ta.addKeyListener(new KeyEventHandler());
        ta.addMouseListener(new MouseEventHandler());

        pack();
        show();
    }

    class KeyEventHandler extends KeyAdapter {
        public void keyTyped(KeyEvent evt) {
            caret.setText("caret="+ta.getCaretPosition());
        }
    }
    class MouseEventHandler extends MouseAdapter {
        public void mouseClicked(MouseEvent evt) {
            caret.setText("caret="+ta.getCaretPosition());
        }
    }

    static public void main(String[] args) {
        new Main();
    }
}
```

getSelectedText( )

PURPOSE   Retrieves the selected text in this text component.

SYNTAX   `public synchronized String getSelectedText()`

DESCRIPTION   This method retrieves the selected text in this text component. Each text component has a selection that may be empty.

RETURNS   A non-`null` string containing the text in the selection. The length of the result value may be 0.

SEE ALSO   `select()`.

EXAMPLE   This example creates a frame containing both kinds of text components—the text field and the text area—and a Print button. See Figure 353. Clicking the Print button causes the current selection of both text components to be printed on standard output.

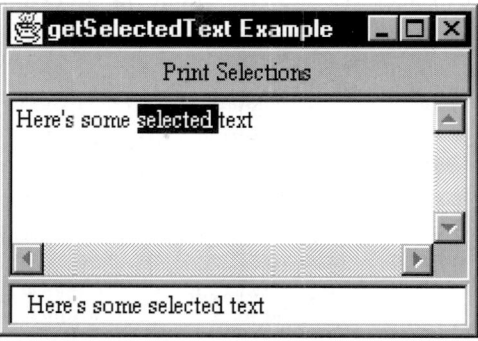

FIGURE 353:   **Retrieving the Selected Text from a `TextComponent`.**

```
import java.awt.*;
import java.awt.event.*;

class Main extends Frame implements ActionListener {
    TextField tf = new TextField();
    TextArea ta = new TextArea();

    Main() {
        super("getSelectedText Example");
        Button b = new Button("Print Selections");

        add(b, BorderLayout.NORTH);
        add(ta, BorderLayout.CENTER);
        add(tf, BorderLayout.SOUTH);

        // Add listener for button
        b.addActionListener(this);

        pack();
        show();
    }

    // Action listener for button
    public void actionPerformed(ActionEvent evt) {
        System.out.println("------ text area -------");
        System.out.println(ta.getSelectedText());
        System.out.println("------ text field ------");
        System.out.println(tf.getSelectedText());
    }

    static public void main(String[] args) {
        new Main();
    }
}
```

A
B
C
D
E
F
G
H
I
J
K
L
M
N
O
P
Q
R
S
U
V
W
X
Y
Z

1433

getSelectionEnd( )

PURPOSE   Retrieves the end position of this text component's selection.

SYNTAX   `public synchronized int getSelectionEnd()`

DESCRIPTION   The selection end position can
be in the range 0 to the length
of text in the text component.
The selection's start position
must be less than or equal to
the selection's end position.

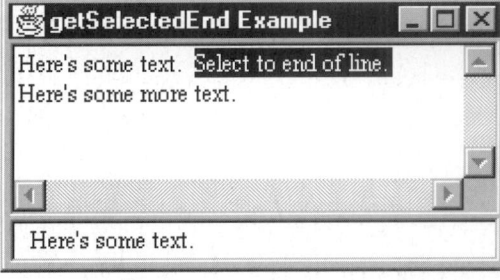

RETURNS   The zero-based index of the
selection's end position. Note
that the character referred to
by the index is not in the
selection.

**FIGURE 354:   Selecting to the End-of-line in a
`TextComponent`.**

SEE ALSO   `getSelectionStart()`, `setSelectionEnd()`.

EXAMPLE   This example creates a frame containing both kinds of text components—the
text field and the text area. See Figure 354. Typing Ctrl-E in one of these components will extend the selection to the end-of-line, not including the newline
character.

```
import java.awt.*;
import java.awt.event.*;

class Main extends Frame {
    TextField tf = new TextField();
    TextArea ta = new TextArea();

    Main() {
        super("getSelectedEnd Example");
        add(ta, BorderLayout.CENTER);
        add(tf, BorderLayout.SOUTH);

        // Add listeners for textfield and textarea
        KeyEventHandler listener = new KeyEventHandler();
        ta.addKeyListener(listener);
        tf.addKeyListener(listener);

        pack();
        show();
    }

    class KeyEventHandler extends KeyAdapter {
        public void keyPressed(KeyEvent evt) {
            if (evt.isControlDown() && evt.getKeyCode() == KeyEvent.VK_E) {
                TextComponent tc = (TextComponent)evt.getSource();
                String str = tc.getText();
                int e = str.indexOf('\n', tc.getSelectionEnd());
```

```
                    tc.setSelectionEnd(e < 0 ? str.length() : e);
            }
        }
    }

    static public void main(String[] args) {
        new Main();
    }
}
```

getSelectionStart()

PURPOSE   Retrieves the start position of this text component's selection.

SYNTAX   `public synchronized int getSelectionStart()`

DESCRIPTION   The selection start posi-
               tion can be in the range
               0 to the length of text in
               the text component.
               The selection's end
               position must be greater
               than or equal to the
               selection's start posi-
               tion.

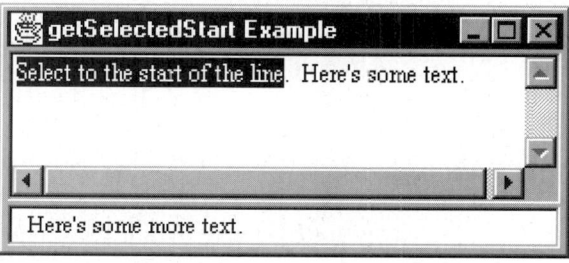

FIGURE 355:   Selecting to the Beginning of the Line in
a `TextComponent`.

RETURNS   The zero-based index
               of the selection's start
               position.

SEE ALSO   `getSelectionEnd()`, `setSelectionStart()`.

EXAMPLE   This example creates a frame containing both kinds of text components—the
               text field and the text area. See Figure 355. Typing Ctrl-A in one of these com-
               ponents will extend the selection to the start-of-line.

```
import java.awt.*;
import java.awt.event.*;

class Main extends Frame {
    TextField tf = new TextField();
    TextArea ta = new TextArea();

    Main() {
        super("getSelectedStart Example");
        add(ta, BorderLayout.CENTER);
        add(tf, BorderLayout.SOUTH);

        // Add listeners for textfield and textarea
        KeyEventHandler listener = new KeyEventHandler();
        ta.addKeyListener(listener);
```

```
                    tf.addKeyListener(listener);

                    pack();
                    show();
                }

                class KeyEventHandler extends KeyAdapter {
                    public void keyPressed(KeyEvent evt) {
                        if (evt.isControlDown() &&  evt.getKeyCode() == KeyEvent.VK_A) {
                            TextComponent tc = (TextComponent)evt.getSource();
                            String str = tc.getText();
                            int s = str.lastIndexOf('\n', tc.getSelectionStart()-1) + 1;

                            tc.setSelectionStart(s);
                        }
                    }
                }

                static public void main(String[] args) {
                    new Main();
                }
            }
```

getText( )

PURPOSE   Retrieves the text in this text component.

SYNTAX   `public synchronized String getText()`

RETURNS   A non-`null` string containing the entire text in the text component.

SEE ALSO   `setText()`.

EXAMPLE   See `setText()`.

isEditable( )

PURPOSE   Retrieves this text component's current editable state.

SYNTAX   `public boolean isEditable()`

RETURNS   `true` if the text component is editable; `false` otherwise.

SEE ALSO   `setEditable()`.

EXAMPLE   This example creates a frame containing a text area and a text field. Typing Ctrl-T toggles the editable state of the text component. See Figure 356.

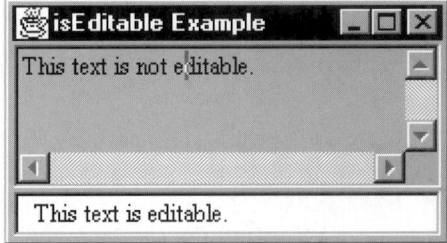

FIGURE 356:   **Editable and Noneditable TextComponents.**

```
import java.awt.*;
import java.awt.event.*;

class Main extends Frame {
    TextField tf = new TextField();
    TextArea ta = new TextArea();
    Label status = new Label ("Editable");

    Main() {
        super("isEditable Example");
        add(status, BorderLayout.NORTH);
        add(ta, BorderLayout.CENTER);
        add(tf, BorderLayout.SOUTH);

        // Add listeners for textfield and textarea
        KeyEventHandler listener = new KeyEventHandler();
        ta.addKeyListener(listener);
        tf.addKeyListener(listener);

        pack();
        show();
    }

    class KeyEventHandler extends KeyAdapter {
        public void keyPressed(KeyEvent evt) {
            if (evt.isControlDown() && evt.getKeyCode() == KeyEvent.VK_T) {
                TextComponent tc = (TextComponent)evt.getSource();
                tc.setEditable(!tc.isEditable());
                if (tc.isEditable()) {
                    status.setText("Editable");
                } else {
                    status.setText("Not Editable");
                }
            }
        }
    }

    static public void main(String[] args) {
        new Main();
    }
}
```

A
B
C
D
E
F
G
H
I
J
K
L
M
N
O
P
Q
R
S
U
V
W
X
Y
Z

paramString()

PURPOSE	Generates a string representation of this text component's state.
SYNTAX	`protected String paramString()`
DESCRIPTION	The string representation of a text component consists of the string representation of a `Component`, plus information stating whether it is editable and the text selected. A subclass of this class should override this method and return a concatenation of its state with the results of `super.paramString()`. This method is called by the `toString()` method and is typically used for debugging.

A
B
C
D
E
F
G
H
I
J
K
L
M
N
O
P
Q
R
S
U
V
W
X
Y
Z

RETURNS	A non-`null` string representing the text component's state.
OVERRIDES	`Component.paramString()`.
SEE ALSO	`Component.toString()`, `java.lang.Object.toString()`.
EXAMPLE	See `Component.paramString()`.

processEvent()

PURPOSE	Processes an event enabled for this text component.
SYNTAX	`protected void processEvent(AWTEvent evt)`
DEPRECATION	This method extends `Component.processEvent()` by adding support for `TextEvent`. This method can be overridden to handle new types of events for this text component. When a subclass overrides `processEvent()`, it should call `super.processEvent()` to perform the processing intended by its base class (such as dispatching events to the listeners).
PARAMETERS	
evt	The event to be processed.
OVERRIDES	`Component.processEvent()`.
SEE ALSO	`AWTEvent`, `processTextEvent()`.
EXAMPLE	See the `Component` class example.

processTextEvent()

PURPOSE	Processes a text event enabled for this text component.
SYNTAX	`protected void processTextEvent(TextEvent evt)`
DESCRIPTION	Text events are fired when this text component's text changes. See the class description and `TextEvent` for more details. This method processes text events for this text component by notifying the registered `TextListener`. This method is invoked only if text events have been enabled for this text component. This can happen either when a text listener is added to this text component or when `Component.enableEvents()` is called to enable text events.
	Typically, a text component controls how its text events are processed by adding or removing text listeners. It overrides `processTextEvent()` only if it needs to do processing in addition to that performed by the registered listeners.

When a subclass does override `processTextEvent()`, it should call `super.processTextEvent()` to perform the processing intended by its base class (such as dispatching events to the listeners).

PARAMETERS

`evt`   The non-`null` text event.

SEE ALSO   `addTextListener()`, `Component.enableEvents()`, `Component.disableEvents()`, `java.awt.event.TextEvent`, `java.awt.event.TextListener`, `processEvent()`, `removeTextListener()`.

EXAMPLE   See `AWTEventMulticaster.textValueChanged()`.

removeNotify()

PURPOSE   Destroys this text component's peer.

SYNTAX   `public void removeNotify()`

DESCRIPTION   This method should never be called directly. It is normally called by the component's container.

OVERRIDES   `Component.removeNotify()`.

SEE ALSO   `Component`.

EXAMPLE   See `Component.setVisible()`.

removeTextListener()

PURPOSE   Removes a listener from receiving this text component's text events.

SYNTAX   `public void removeTextListener(TextListener listener)`

DESCRIPTION   Text events are fired when this text component's text is changed. See `TextEvent` for more details. After this method is called, the text listener `listener` will no longer receive text events from this text component. If `listener` is `null`, this method does nothing.

PARAMETERS

`listener`   The possibly `null` text listener to remove.

SEE ALSO   `addTextListener()`, `java.awt.event.TextEvent`, `java.awt.event.TextListener`.

EXAMPLE   See `removeActionListener()` in `MenuItem.disableEvents()`.

select( )

PURPOSE	Sets the selection in this text component.
SYNTAX	`public synchronized void select(int selStart, int selEnd)`
DESCRIPTION	This method selects the text located between the positions `selStart` and `selEnd`, inclusive. If a position is negative, the position is set to 0. If a position is greater than the length of text in the text component, the position is set to the length. If `selEnd` < `selStart`, `selEnd` is set to `selStart`.

PARAMETERS

`selEnd`	The zero-based end position of the text range.
`selStart`	The zero-based start position of the text range.

SEE ALSO   `setSelectionEnd()`, `setSelectionStart()`.

EXAMPLE   This example creates a text area and a text field in a frame. See Figure 357. Pressing Return while in the text field causes a search for the string in the text field.

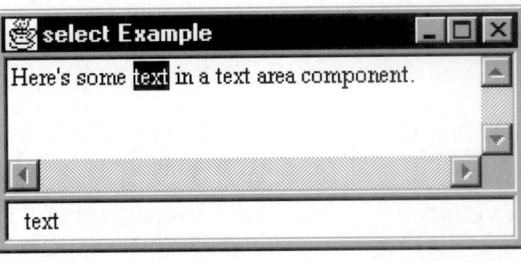

FIGURE 357: **Selecting Text in a `TextComponent`.**

```
import java.awt.*;
import java.awt.event.*;

class Main extends Frame implements ActionListener {
    TextField tf = new TextField();
    TextArea ta = new TextArea(10, 40);

    Main() {
        super("select Example");
        add(ta, BorderLayout.CENTER);
        add(tf, BorderLayout.SOUTH);

        // Add listener for text field
        tf.addActionListener(this);

        pack();
        show();
    }

    public void actionPerformed(ActionEvent evt) {
        String str = tf.getText();
        int s = ta.getText().indexOf(str, ta.getSelectionStart());

        if (s < 0 && ta.getSelectionStart() > 0) {
            // Let's try from the beginning.
            s = ta.getText().indexOf(str, 0);
        }
```

```
        if (s >= 0) {
            ta.select(s, s + str.length());
            ta.requestFocus();
        }
    }

    static public void main(String[] args) {
        new Main();
    }
}
```

selectAll()

PURPOSE   Selects the text in this text component.

SYNTAX   `public synchronized void selectAll()`

DESCRIPTION   This method selects the entire text in the text component.

SEE ALSO   select(),
               setSelectionEnd(),
               setSelectionStart().

EXAMPLE   This example creates a frame containing a menu bar and a text area. The menu bar contains an Edit menu with the item Select All, which causes the text area to request the focus and select all of its text. See Figure 358.

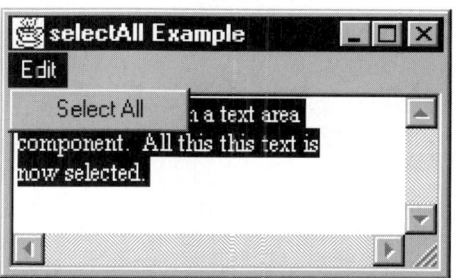

FIGURE 358:   Selecting All of the Text in a TextComponent.

```
import java.awt.*;
import java.awt.event.*;

class Main extends Frame implements ActionListener {
    TextArea ta = new TextArea();

    Main() {
        super("selectAll Example");
        MenuBar mb = new MenuBar();
        Menu menu = new Menu("Edit");

        menu.add("Select All");

        mb.add(menu);
        setMenuBar(mb);
        add(ta, BorderLayout.CENTER);

        // Add listener for Edit menu
        menu.addActionListener(this);
```

A
B
C
D
E
F
G
H
I
J
K
L
M
N
O
P
Q
R
S

U
V
W
X
Y
Z

1441

```
            pack();
            show();
        }

        public void actionPerformed(ActionEvent evt) {
            if ("Select All".equals(evt.getActionCommand())) {
                ta.selectAll();
                ta.requestFocus();
            }
        }

        static public void main(String[] args) {
            new Main();
        }
    }
```

setCaretPosition( )

PURPOSE   Sets this text component's text insertion point.

SYNTAX   `public void setCaretPosition(int caret)`

DESCRIPTION   The caret position indicates where characters will be inserted as the user types. See the class description for details.

PARAMETERS

caret   The zero-based index of the caret's position. Text will be inserted just before the character referred to by the index.

SEE ALSO   `getCaretPosition()`.

EXAMPLE   This example creates a text field. When you press the Enter key, the caret is moved to the beginning of the text field. See Figure 359.

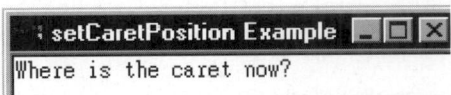

FIGURE 359: Setting a TextComponent's Caret.

```
import java.awt.*;
import java.awt.event.*;

class Main extends Frame {
    TextField tf = new TextField();

    Main() {
        super("setCaretPosition Example");
        add(tf);

        // Add key listener for text field
        tf.addKeyListener(new KeyEventHandler());

        pack();
        show();
    }
```

```
class KeyEventHandler extends KeyAdapter {
    public void keyPressed(KeyEvent evt) {
        if (evt.getKeyCode() == KeyEvent.VK_ENTER) {
            tf.setCaretPosition(0);
        }
    }
}

static public void main(String[] args) {
    new Main();
}
}
```

setEditable()

PURPOSE   Sets this text component's editable state.

SYNTAX   `public synchronized void setEditable(boolean editable)`

PARAMETERS

editable   If `true`, the text component becomes editable; otherwise, it becomes uneditable.

SEE ALSO   `isEditable()`.

EXAMPLE   This example creates a frame containing a text area and a checkbox. The checkbox sets the editable state of the text area. See Figure 360.

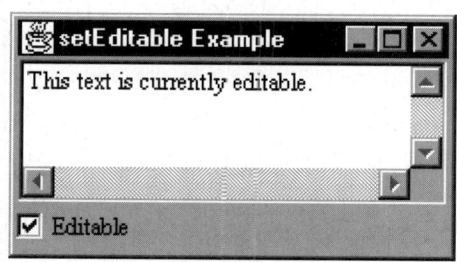

FIGURE 360:   Editable **TextComponent**.

```
import java.awt.*;
import java.awt.event.*;

class Main extends Frame
    implements ItemListener {
    TextArea ta = new TextArea();
    Checkbox cb =
        new Checkbox("Editable", null, true);

    Main() {
        super("setEditable Example");
        add(ta, BorderLayout.CENTER);
        add(cb, BorderLayout.SOUTH);

        // Add listener for checkbox
        cb.addItemListener(this);

        pack();
        show();
    }
```

```
public void itemStateChanged(ItemEvent evt) {
    ta.setEditable(cb.getState());
}

static public void main(String[] args) {
    new Main();
}
}
```

A
B
C
D

setSelectionEnd()

PURPOSE   Sets the end position of this text component's selection.

SYNTAX   `public synchronized void setSelectionEnd(int posn)`

DESCRIPTION   The end position of a text component's selection can be in the range 0 to the length of text in the text component. The selection's start position must be less than or equal to the selection's end position. This method sets the selection's end position to be `posn` and selects the text between `getSelectionStart()` and `posn`.

PARAMETERS
posn   The noninclusive, zero-based index of the end position of this text component's selection. Note that the character referred to by the index is not in the selection.

SEE ALSO   `getSelectionEnd()`, `select()`, `selectAll()`, `setSelectionStart()`.

EXAMPLE   See `getSelectionEnd()`.

setSelectionStart()

PURPOSE   Sets the start position of this text component's selection.

SYNTAX   `public synchronized void setSelectionStart(int start)`

DESCRIPTION   The start position of a text component's selection can be in the range 0 to the length of text in the text component. The selection's end position must be greater than or equal to the selection's start position. This method sets the selection's start position to be `start` and selects the text between `start` and `getSelectionEnd()`.

PARAMETERS
start   The zero-based index of the start position of this text component's selection.

SEE ALSO   `getSelectionStart()`, `select()`, `selectAll()`, `setSelectionEnd()`.

EXAMPLE   See `getSelectionStart()`.

setText()

PURPOSE   Replaces the text of this text component.

SYNTAX   `public synchronized void setText(String text)`

DESCRIPTION   This method replaces the entire text of the text component with the string
              `text`.

PARAMETERS
 `text`   A string containing the text. A value of `null` is the same as "".

SEE ALSO   `getText()`.

EXAMPLE   This example creates
              a frame containing two
              text areas. Typing Ctrl-
              T swaps the text in the
              components. See Fig-
              ure 361.

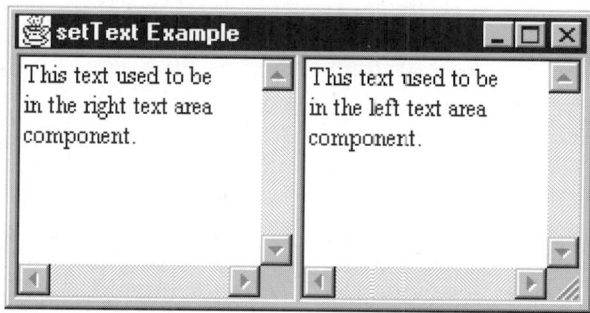

FIGURE 361:   Swapping Text.

```
import java.awt.*;
import java.awt.event.*;

class Main extends Frame {
    TextArea ta1 = new TextArea(null, 10, 40);
    TextArea ta2 = new TextArea(null, 10, 40);

    Main() {
        super("setText Example");
        setLayout(new GridLayout(1, 2));
        add(ta1);
        add(ta2);

        // Add key listener for text areas
        KeyEventHandler listener = new KeyEventHandler();
        ta1.addKeyListener(listener);
        ta2.addKeyListener(listener);

        pack();
        show();
    }

    class KeyEventHandler extends KeyAdapter {
        public void keyPressed(KeyEvent evt) {
            if (evt.isControlDown() && evt.getKeyCode() == KeyEvent.VK_T) {
                String str = ta1.getText();

                ta1.setText(ta2.getText());
                ta2.setText(str);
            }
        }
    }
```

A
B
C
D
E
F
G
H
I
J
K
L
M
N
O
P
Q
R
S

U
V
W
X
Y
Z

```
        }

    static public void main(String[] args) {
        new Main();
    }
}
```

A

B

C

D

E

F

G

H

I

J

K

L

M

N

O

P

Q

R

S

U

V

W

X

Y

Z

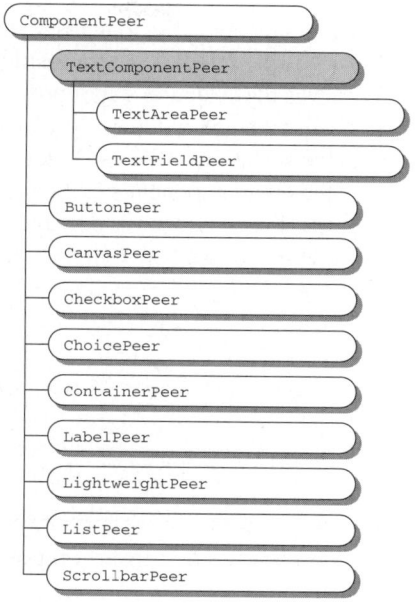

Syntax

```
public interface TextComponentPeer extends ComponentPeer
```

Description

The text component (see the TextComponent class) in the AWT uses the platform's native implementation of a text component. So that the AWT text component behaves the same on all platforms, the text component is assigned a *peer*, whose task is to translate the behavior of the platform's native text component to the behavior of the AWT text component.

AWT programmers normally do not directly use peer classes and interfaces. Instead, they deal with AWT components in the java.awt package. These in turn automatically manage their peers. Only someone who is porting the AWT to another platform should be concerned with the peer classes and interfaces. Consequently, most peer documentation refers to java.awt counterparts.

See Component and Toolkit for additional information about component peers.

```
┌─────────────────────────────────────────────────────────────────────────┐
│  MEMBER SUMMARY                                                          │
├─────────────────────────────────────────────────────────────────────────┤
│  Peer Methods                                                           │
│  getCaretPosition()    Retrieves the text component's text insertion point. │
│  getSelectionEnd()     Retrieves the selection's end position.          │
│  getSelectionStart()   Retrieves the selection's start position.        │
│  getText()             Retrieves the text in the text component.        │
│  select()              Sets the selection in the text component.        │
│  setCaretPosition()    Sets the text component's text insertion point.  │
│  setEditable()         Sets the text component's editable state.        │
│  setText()             Sets the text of the text component.             │
└─────────────────────────────────────────────────────────────────────────┘
```

See Also

java.awt.Component, java.awt.TextComponent, java.awt.Toolkit.

getCaretPosition()

PURPOSE   Retrieves this text component's text insertion point.

SYNTAX   `public int getCaretPosition()`

RETURNS   The 0-based index of the caret's position. Text will be inserted just before the character referred to by the index.

SEE ALSO   java.awt.TextComponent.getCaretPosition().

getSelectionEnd()

PURPOSE   Retrieves the selection's end position.

SYNTAX   `int getSelectionEnd()`

RETURNS   The 0-based index of the selection's end position.

SEE ALSO   java.awt.TextComponent.getSelectionEnd().

getSelectionStart()

PURPOSE   Retrieves the selection's start position.

SYNTAX   `int getSelectionStart()`

RETURNS   The 0-based index of the selection's start position.

SEE ALSO   java.awt.TextComponent.getSelectionStart().

getText( )

PURPOSE	Retrieves the text in the text component.
SYNTAX	`String getText()`
RETURNS	A non-`null` string containing the entire text in the text component.
SEE ALSO	`java.awt.TextComponent.getText()`.

select( )

PURPOSE	Sets the selection in the text component.
SYNTAX	`void select(int selStart, int selEnd)`
PARAMETERS	
`selEnd`	The 0-based end position of the text range.
`selStart`	The 0-based start position of the text range.
SEE ALSO	`java.awt.TextComponent.select()`.

setCaretPosition( )

PURPOSE	Sets the text component's text insertion point.
SYNTAX	`public void setCaretPosition(int caret)`
PARAMETERS	
`caret`	The 0-based index of the caret's position. Text will be inserted just before the character referred to by the index.
SEE ALSO	`java.awt.TextComponent.setCaretPosition()`.

setEditable( )

PURPOSE	Sets the text component's editable state.
SYNTAX	`void setEditable(boolean editable)`
PARAMETERS	
`editable`	If `true`, the text component becomes editable; otherwise, it becomes uneditable.
SEE ALSO	`java.awt.TextComponent.setEditable()`.

A
B
C
D
E
F
G
H
I
J
K
L
M
N
O
P
Q
R
S

U
V
W
X
Y
Z

setText()

PURPOSE	Sets the text of the text component.
SYNTAX	`void setText(String text)`
PARAMETERS	
text	A string containing the text. A value of `null` is the same as `""`.
SEE ALSO	`java.awt.TextComponent.setText()`.

A
B
C
D
E
F
G
H
I
J
K
L
M
N
O
P
Q
R
S
T
U
V
W
X
Y
Z

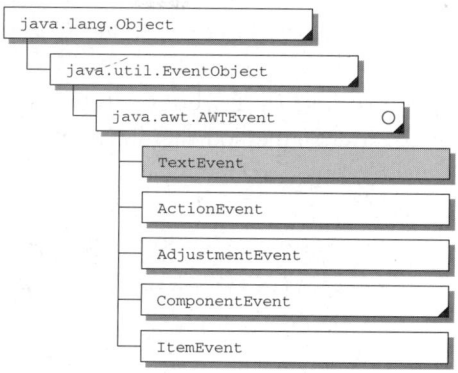

Syntax

```
public class TextEvent extends AWTEvent
```

Description

Text events are fired by text components (see TextComponent) whenever the contents of the text component changes. The AWT has two text components that fire text events: TextArea and TextField. For more general information about events, see AWTEvent.

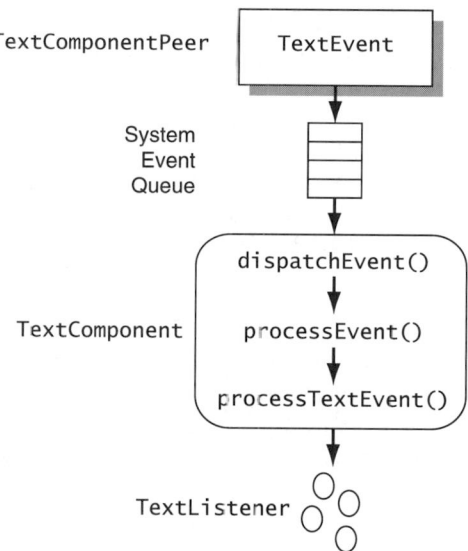

FIGURE 362: Text Event Flow.

Listening for Text Events

To listen for text events from a component, the listener must implement the TextListener interface. After that, the listener must be registered with the object. It becomes registered by calling the object's addTextListener() method. As with most events, text events are delivered to its listeners after the operation has taken place.

Text Event Flow

Figure 362 shows how text events typically flow through the system. First, the event is fired by a text component peer. This event is posted on the event queue (see EventQueue). When the event makes its way to the front of the queue, it is given to the component via its dispatchEvent() method. The main purpose of this method is to discard the event if the text event type is not enabled or if there are no text event listeners. Otherwise, dispatchEvent() calls processEvent(), which in turn calls different methods depending on the event type. Since this is an text event, processTextEvent() is called. The main purpose of this method is to notify the text event listeners.

A component can override processTextEvent() to process text events before they are delivered to its listeners. The overridden method should call super.processTextEvent() to ensure that events are dispatched to the component's listeners.

MEMBER SUMMARY	
Constructor	
TextEvent()	Constructs a TextEvent instance.
Text Event Id Constants	
TEXT_FIRST	Constant specifying the first id in the range of text event ids.
TEXT_LAST	Constant specifying the last id in the range of text event ids.
TEXT_VALUE_CHANGED	Event id indicating that a text event occurred.
Debugging Method	
paramString()	Generates a string representing the text event's state.

See Also

jav.awt.AWTEvent, java.awt.AWTEventMulticaster.textValueChanged(),
java.awt.Component.dispatchEvent(), java.awt.TextArea, java.awt.TextField,
TextListener.

Example

This example demonstrates how to get text events from a component that fires them. The example creates a text area and listens for text events from the text area. In response to a text event, the specifics of the event are printed. See Figure 363.

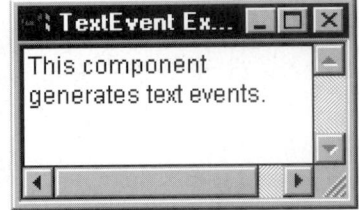

FIGURE 363: TextEvent.

```
import java.awt.*;
import java.awt.event.*;

class Main extends Frame implements TextListener {
    Main() {
        super("TextEvent Example");
        TextArea ta = new TextArea();
```

```
        // Listen for text events.
        ta.addTextListener(this);

        add(BorderLayout.CENTER, ta);
        pack();
        show();
    }

    public void textValueChanged(TextEvent evt) {
        System.out.println(evt);
    }

    public static void main(String args[]) {
        new Main();
    }
}
```

paramString()

PURPOSE	Generates a string representing the text event's state.
SYNTAX	`public String paramString()`
DESCRIPTION	The returned string contains the name of the text event. A subclass of this class should override this method and return a concatenation of its state with the results of `super.paramString()`. This method is called by the `AWTEvent.toString()` method and is typically used for debugging.
RETURNS	A non-`null` string representing the text event's state.
OVERRIDES	`java.awt.AWTEvent.paramString()`.
SEE ALSO	`java.awt.AWTEvent.toString()`, `java.lang.Object.toString()`.
EXAMPLE	See the `java.awt.AWTEvent` class example.

TEXT_FIRST

PURPOSE	Constant specifying the first id in the range of text event ids.
SYNTAX	`public static final int TEXT_FIRST`
DESCRIPTION	All text event ids must be greater than or equal to TEXT_FIRST (value 900).
SEE ALSO	TEXT_LAST.
EXAMPLE	See `java.awt.Component.processEvent()`.

A
B
C
D
E
F
G
H
I
J
K
L
M
N
O
P
Q
R
S
T
U
V
W
X
Y
Z

TEXT_LAST

PURPOSE	Constant specifying the last id in the range of text event ids.
SYNTAX	`public static final int TEXT_LAST`
DESCRIPTION	All text event ids must be less than or equal to TEXT_LAST (value 900).
SEE ALSO	TEXT_FIRST.
EXAMPLE	See `java.awt.Component.processEvent()`.

TEXT_VALUE_CHANGED

PURPOSE	Event id indicating that a text event occurred.
SYNTAX	`public static final int TEXT_VALUE_CHANGED`
DESCRIPTION	Text events are fired by text components (see `TextComponent`) whenever the contents of the text component change. All text events fired by the components `TextArea` and `TextField` have this id (value 900).
SEE ALSO	TextEvent().
EXAMPLE	See the `java.awt.Component` class example.

TextEvent()

PURPOSE	Constructs a `TextEvent` instance.
SYNTAX	`public TextEvent(Object source, int id)`
DESCRIPTION	This constructor creates a new text event with `source` as the object that fires this event. At present, there is only one text event id, so `id` must be set to TEXT_VALUE_CHANGED.

The source object should implement the various methods that support text event listeners: `addTextListener()`, `removeTextListener()`, `processEvent()`, and `processTextEvent()`. For an example of a component implementing these methods, see the `KeyEvent` constructor example. After the text event is created, the source object can distribute the text event by calling `AWTEventMulticaster.textValueChanged()`. If the event is not created by `source`, the creator can deliver the event to the source component either by posting the event to the event queue (see `EventQueue.postEvent()`) or by calling the source component's `Component.dispatchEvent()` method directly.

PARAMETERS

source	The non-null text component that is firing this text event.
id	Must be TEXT_VALUE_CHANGED.

SEE ALSO   `java.awt.AWTEvent.getID()`, `java.util.EventObject.getSource()`, `java.awt.AWTEventMulticaster.textValueChanged()`, `java.awt.Component.dispatchEvent()`, `TEXT_VALUE_CHANGED`.

EXAMPLE   See the `java.awt.Component` class example.

A
B
C
D
E
F
G
H
I
J
K
L
M
N
O
P
Q
R
S
T
U
V
W
X
Y
Z

TextField

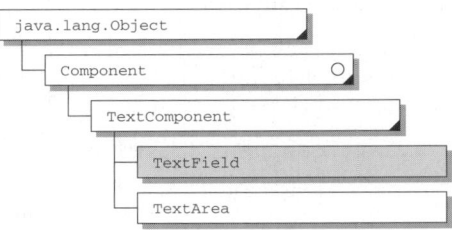

```
java.lang.Object
    Component              O
        TextComponent
            TextField
            TextArea
```

Syntax
```
public class TextField extends TextComponent
```

Description
A *text field* is a text component that displays editable text. The text field is similar to the text area component, except that the text field holds only a single line of text.

A text field is typically used to obtain textual input from the user. Figure 364 shows a text area and a text field.

FIGURE 364: `TextField.`

The Echo Property
The text field can be set in a mode in which all characters typed into the text field are displayed as a different character called the *echo character*. The text field still maintains the original characters, but it disguises them as the echo character. The disguises can be removed by setting the echo character to 0.

Preferred Number of Columns and Preferred Size
A text field can be created with a preferred number of columns used to calculate its preferred width. The width calculation is based on the average size of a character, and the result is an approximation. The average width of a character is a platform-dependent value. The preferred number of columns can be changed at any time using `setColumns()`. When this happens, the preferred size is changed as well.

The number of columns in a text field does not limit the number of characters that can be entered. The text field automatically scrolls to the right as additional characters are appended beyond its component size (regardless of the number of columns). The contents of the text field can be scrolled and viewed using the left and right arrow keys.

A text field can be resized to be larger or smaller than its preferred number of columns.

Events

A text field not only generates the events fired by a text component, but also fires an action event when the Return key is pressed. The action command associated with the action event is the text field's contents. See `ActionEvent` for details.

MEMBER SUMMARY	
Constructor	
TextField()	Constructs a new `TextField` instance.
Echo Character Methods	
echoCharIsSet()	Determines if this text field's echo character has been set.
getEchoChar()	Retrieves this text field's echo character.
setEchoChar()	Sets this text field's echo character.
Layout Methods	
getColumns()	Retrieves the number of columns in this text field.
getMinimumSize()	Calculates the minimum dimensions of this text field.
getPreferredSize()	Calculates the preferred dimensions of this text field.
setColumns()	Sets the number of columns in this text field.
Event Methods	
addActionListener()	Adds a listener to receive action events from this text field.
processActionEvent()	Processes an action event enabled for this text field.
processEvent()	Processes an event enabled for this text field.
removeActionListener()	Removes a listener from receiving action events from this text field.
Peer Method	
addNotify()	Creates this text field's peer.
Debugging Method	
paramString()	Generates a string representation of this text field's state.
Deprecated Methods	
minimumSize()	Replaced by `getMinimumSize()`.
preferredSize()	Replaced by `getPreferredSize()`.
setEchoCharacter()	Replaced by `setEchoChar()`.

A
B
C
D
E
F
G
H
I
J
K
L
M
N
O
P
Q
R
S
U
V
W
X
Y
Z

See Also

TextArea.

Example

This simple example creates a frame that has a text field. When you press Return while in the text field, it prints the contents of the text field. See Figure 364 for a screen shot of the example.

```java
import java.awt.*;
import java.awt.event.*;

public class Main extends Frame implements ActionListener {
    TextField tf = new TextField("TextField");

    Main() {
        super("TextField Example");
        add(tf, BorderLayout.CENTER);

        // Add listener for text field
        tf.addActionListener(this);
        pack();
        show();
    }

    public void actionPerformed(ActionEvent evt) {
        System.out.println(tf.getText());
    }

    static public void main(String[] args) {
        new Main();
    }
}
```

addActionListener()

PURPOSE	Adds a listener for receiving this text component's action events.
SYNTAX	`public synchronized void addActionListener(ActionListener listener)`
DESCRIPTION	Action events are fired when the Return key is pressed. See `ActionEvent` for more details. After this method is called, the action listener `listener` will receive action events fired by this text component. If `listener` is `null`, this method does nothing.
PARAMETERS	
`listener`	The possibly `null` text listener to add.
SEE ALSO	`java.awt.event.ActionEvent`, `java.awt.event.ActionListener`, `remove.ActionListener()`.
EXAMPLE	See the class example.

addNotify()

PURPOSE   Creates the text field's peer.

SYNTAX   `public void addNotify()`

DESCRIPTION   This method creates the text field's peer if it does not exist. The text field's peer is created by calling the `Toolkit.createTextArea()` method. This method should never be called directly. It is normally called by the text field's parent.

OVERRIDES   `Component.addNotify()`.

SEE ALSO   `Component, Toolkit`.

EXAMPLE   See `Component.setVisible()`.

echoCharIsSet()

PURPOSE   Determines if the text field's echo character has been set.

SYNTAX   `public boolean echoCharIsSet()`

RETURNS   `true` if the text field's echo character has been set; `false` otherwise.

SEE ALSO   `getEchoChar(), setEchoChar()`.

EXAMPLE   This example creates a text field. Typing Ctrl-A toggles whether or not an echo character is set for the text field. See Figure 365.

FIGURE 365:
Echoing `TextField` Contents.

```java
import java.awt.*;
import java.awt.event.*;

class Main extends Frame {
    TextField tf = new TextField(40);

    Main() {
        super("echoCharIsSet Example");
        add(tf, BorderLayout.NORTH);

        tf.addKeyListener(new KeyEventHandler());

        pack();
        show();
    }

    class KeyEventHandler extends KeyAdapter {
        public void keyPressed(KeyEvent evt) {
            int key = evt.getKeyCode();
            if (evt.isControlDown() && key == KeyEvent.VK_A) {
                if (tf.echoCharIsSet()) {
                    key = 0;
```

```
                            } else {
                                key = '*';
                            }
                            tf.setEchoChar((char)key);
                        }
                    }
A                   }

B           static public void main(String[] args) {
                new Main();
C           }
        }
D

E

F       getColumns()
G
        PURPOSE       Retrieves the preferred number of columns in this text field.
H
        SYNTAX        public int getColumns()
I
        DESCRIPTION   The preferred number of columns determines the text field's preferred width.
J                     See the class description for details.

K       RETURNS       The number of columns used in this text field.

L       SEE ALSO      setColumns().
```

EXAMPLE This example creates an automati-
cally expanding
text field. See Fig-
ure 366. The text
field's number of

FIGURE 366:   An Automatically Expanding `TextField`.

columns is doubled when the number of characters entered equals the number
of columns.

```
import java.awt.*;
import java.awt.event.*;

class Main extends Frame implements TextListener {
    TextField tf = new TextField(10);

    Main() {
        super("getColumns Example");
        add(tf, BorderLayout.NORTH);

        // Add text listener fof text field
        tf.addTextListener(this);

        pack();
        show();
    }
```

```
    public void textValueChanged(TextEvent e) {
        int cols = tf.getColumns();
        if (tf.getText().length() == cols) {
            tf.setColumns(cols+cols); // double
            pack();  // adjust Frame to accommodate new size
        }
    }

    static public void main(String[] args) {
        new Main();
    }
}
```

getEchoChar()

PURPOSE	Retrieves this text field's echo character.
SYNTAX	`public char getEchoChar()`
DESCRIPTION	This method retrieves the text field's echo character. The result is not meaningful unless `echoCharIsSet()` returns `true`.
RETURNS	The text field's echo character.
SEE ALSO	`echoCharIsSet()`, `setEchoChar()`.
EXAMPLE	See `setEchoCharacter()`.

getMinimumSize()

PURPOSE	Calculates the minimum dimensions of this text field.
SYNTAX	`public Dimension getMinimumSize()` `public Dimension getMinimumSize(int cols)`
DESCRIPTION	The minimum dimensions of a text field are based on the dimensions needed for displaying one row of `cols` characters. The size of a character depends on the text field's current font. If the text field's font has variable-width characters, then `cols` is based on the average size of a character and the result is an approximation. The average width of a character is a platform-dependent value. If `cols` is not specified, it defaults to the current preferred number of columns.
	If the text field's peer is not yet created, the resulting dimensions are (0, 0). On most platforms, the minimum and preferred dimensions are the same.
PARAMETERS	
cols	A non-negative integer specifying the width in characters.

RETURNS	A new non-`null` `Dimension` instance containing the minimum dimensions of the text field.
OVERRIDES	`Component.getMinimumSize()`.
EXAMPLE	See the `LayoutManager` class example.

getPreferredSize( )

PURPOSE	Calculates the preferred dimensions of this text field.
SYNTAX	`public Dimension getPreferredSize()` `public Dimension getPreferredSize(int cols)`
DESCRIPTION	The preferred dimensions of a text field are based on the dimensions needed for displaying one row of `cols` characters. The size of a character depends on the text field's current font. If the text field's font has variable-width characters, then `cols` is based on the average size of a character and the result is an approximation. The average width of a character is a platform-dependent value. If `cols` is not specified, it defaults to the current preferred number of columns.

If the text field's peer is not yet created, the resulting dimensions are (0, 0). On most platforms, the minimum and preferred dimensions are the same. |
PARAMETERS	
`cols`	A non-negative integer specifying the width in characters.
RETURNS	A new non-`null` `Dimension` instance containing the preferred dimensions of the text field.
OVERRIDES	`Component.getPreferredSize()`.
EXAMPLE	See the `LayoutManager` class example.

minimumSize( ) *DEPRECATED*

PURPOSE	Replaced by `getMinimumSize()`.
SYNTAX	`public Dimension minimumSize()` `public Dimension minimumSize(int cols)`
PARAMETERS	
`cols`	A non-negative integer specifying the width in characters.
RETURNS	A new non-`null` `Dimension` instance containing the minimum dimensions of the text field.

OVERRIDES   `Component.minimumSize()`.

DEPRECATION   Replace the usage of this deprecated method, as in
```
Dimension dim = textfield.minimumSize();
Dimension dim2 = textfield.minimumSize(cols);
```
with
```
Dimension dim = textfield.getMinimumSize();
Dimension dim2 = textfield.getMinimumSize(cols);
```

paramString()

PURPOSE   Generates a string representation of this text field's state.

SYNTAX   `protected String paramString()`

DESCRIPTION   The string representation of a text field consists of the string representation of TextComponent and the echo character of this text field. A subclass of this class should override this method and return a concatenation of its state with the results of `super.paramString()`. This method is called by the `toString()` method and is typically used for debugging.

A non-`null` string representing the text field's state.

OVERRIDES   `TextComponent.paramString()`.

SEE ALSO   `Component.paramString()`, `Component.toString()`, `java.lang.Object.toString()`.

preferredSize()   *DEPRECATED*

PURPOSE   Replaced by `getPreferredSize()`.

SYNTAX   `public Dimension preferredSize()`
`public Dimension preferredSize(int cols)`

PARAMETERS
cols   A non-negative integer specifying the width in characters.

RETURNS   A new non-`null` `Dimension` instance containing the preferred dimensions of the text field.

OVERRIDES   `Component.preferredSize()`.

DEPRECATION   Replace the usage of this deprecated method, as in
```
Dimension dim = textfield.preferredSize();
Dimension dim2 = textfield.preferredSize(cols);
```
with
```
Dimension dim = textfield.getPreferredSize();
Dimension dim2 = textfield.getPreferredSize(cols);
```

A
B
C
D
E
F
G
H
I
J
K
L
M
N
O
P
Q
R
S
T
U
V
W
X
Y
Z

processActionEvent()

PURPOSE	Processes an action event enabled for this text component.
SYNTAX	`protected void processActionEvent(ActionEvent evt)`

DESCRIPTION   Action events are fired when the user presses Return while in this text field. See the class description and `ActionEvent` for more details. This method processes action events for this text field by notifying registered `ActionListener`. This method is invoked only if action events have been enabled for this text field. This can happen either when an action listener is added to this text field or when `Component.enableEvents()` is called to enable action events.

Typically, a text field controls how its action events are processed by adding or removing action listeners. It overrides `processActionEvent()` only if it needs to do processing in addition to that performed by the registered listeners.

When a subclass does override `processActionEvent()`, it should call `super.processActionEvent()` to perform the processing intended by its base class (such as dispatching the listeners).

PARAMETERS

evt   The non-`null` action event.

SEE ALSO   `addActionListener()`, `Component.enableEvents()`,
`Component.disableEvents()`, `java.awt.event.ActionEvent`,
`java.awt.event.ActionListener`, `processEvent()`,
`removeActionListener()`.

EXAMPLE   See `AWTEventMulticaster.actionPerformed()`.

processEvent()

PURPOSE	Processes an event enabled for this text component.
SYNTAX	`protected void processEvent(AWTEvent evt)`

DESCRIPTION   This method extends `TextComponent.processEvent()` by adding support for `ActionEvent`. It can be overridden to handle new types of events for this text field. When a subclass does override `processEvent()`, it should call `super.processEvent()` to perform the processing intended by its base class (such as dispatching events to the listeners).

PARAMETERS

evt   The event to be processed.

OVERRIDES   `TextComponent.processEvent()`.

SEE ALSO   `AWTEvent`, `processActionEvent()`.

EXAMPLE   See the `Component` class example.

removeActionListener()

PURPOSE	Removes a listener from receiving this text field's action events.
SYNTAX	`public synchronized void removeActionListener(ActionListener` `listener)`
DESCRIPTION	Action events are fired when the user presses the Return key while in this text field. See `ActionEvent` and the class description for more details. After this method is called, the action listener `listener` will no longer receive action events from this text field. If `listener` is `null`, this method does nothing.
PARAMETERS	
`listener`	The possibly `null` action listener to remove.
SEE ALSO	`addActionListener()`, `java.awt.event.ActionEvent`, `java.awt.event.ActionListener`.
EXAMPLE	See `MenuItem.disableEvent()`.

setColumns()

PURPOSE	Sets the number of columns in this text field.
SYNTAX	`public void setColumns(int cols)`
DESCRIPTION	The preferred number of columns determines the text field's preferred width and does not limit the number of characters that can be entered in the text field. See the class description for details.
PARAMETERS	
`cols`	The number of columns.
EXCEPTIONS	
`IllegalArgumentException`	If `cols < 0`.
SEE ALSO	`getColumns()`.
EXAMPLE	See `getColumns()`.

setEchoChar()

PURPOSE	Sets the text field's echo character.
SYNTAX	`public void setEchoChar(char ch)`

A
B
C
D
E
F
G
H
I
J
K
L
M
N
O
P
Q
R
S
T
U
V
W
X
Y
Z

DESCRIPTION   This method sets the echo character of this text field to be the character ch. ch can be any character and can be changed at any time. The value 0 is used to clear the echo character. After the echo character is set to 0, the characters in the text field will be visible and echoCharIsSet() will return false.

PARAMETERS

ch   The echo character. A value of 0 clears the echo character.

SEE ALSO   echoCharIsSet(), getEchoChar().

EXAMPLE   This example creates two text fields. See Figure 367. In one text field, you specify an echo character. In the other, the echo character is used. If you enter the same echo character twice in a row, the echo character is cleared.

FIGURE 367:   **Changing the Echo Character of a TextField.**

```java
import java.awt.*;
import java.awt.event.*;

class Main extends Frame {
    TextField tf = new TextField();
    TextField tfEcho = new TextField();

    Main() {
        super("setEchoChar Example");
        Panel p = new Panel();

        p.setLayout(new BorderLayout());
        p.add(new Label("Echo Character:"), BorderLayout.WEST);
        p.add(tfEcho, BorderLayout.CENTER);

        // Add listener for echo char text field
        tfEcho.addKeyListener(new KeyEventHandler());

        add(p, BorderLayout.SOUTH);
        add(tf, BorderLayout.NORTH);

        pack();
        show();
    }

    class KeyEventHandler extends KeyAdapter {
        public void keyPressed(KeyEvent evt) {
            char key = evt.getKeyChar();
            if (key == tf.getEchoChar()) {    // clear the echo char
                key = 0;
                tfEcho.setText("");
            } else {
                tfEcho.setText(String.valueOf(key));
            }
            tf.setEchoChar(key);
            tf.requestFocus();
        }
```

```
        }

    static public void main(String[] args) {
        new Main();
    }
}
```

setEchoCharacter( )   *DEPRECATED*

PURPOSE   Replaced by `setEchoChar()`.

SYNTAX   `public void setEchoCharacter(char ch)`

PARAMETERS

ch   The echo character. A value of 0 clears the echo character.

DEPRECATION   Replace the usage of this deprecated method, as in
```
textfield.setEchoCharacter(ch);
```
with
```
textfield.setEchoChar(ch);
```

TextField( )

PURPOSE   Creates a new `TextField` instance.

SYNTAX
```
public TextField()
public TextField(int cols)
public TextField(String text)
public TextField(String text, int cols)
```

DESCRIPTION   This constructor creates a new `TextField` instance. If `text` is not specified or is `null`, it defaults to "". `cols` specifies the preferred number of columns for the text field. See the class description for details. If `cols` is not specified, the default is chosen by the platform (usually wide enough to hold `text` if `text` has been specified). If both `cols` and `text` are specified, `cols` determines the preferred number of columns. If `text` does not fit within the width specified by `cols`, its tail is not displayed and can be viewed using the right arrow key.

               The echo character is initially not set.

PARAMETERS

cols   A non-negative integer specifying the initial width in characters. See the class description for details.

text   The string specifying the initial text for the text component. May be `null`.

SEE ALSO   `setColumns()`.

EXAMPLE   See the class example.

A
B
C
D
E
F
G
H
I
J
K
L
M
N
O
P
Q
R
S
T
U
V
W
X
Y
Z

TextFieldPeer

Syntax
```
public interface TextFieldPeer extends TextComponentPeer
```

Description
The text field component (see the `TextField` class) in the AWT uses the platform's native implementation of a text field. So that the AWT text field behaves the same on all platforms, the text field is assigned a *peer*, whose task is to translate the behavior of the platform's native text field to the behavior of the AWT text field.

AWT programmers normally do not directly use peer classes and interfaces. Instead, they deal with AWT components in the `java.awt` package. These in turn automatically manage their peers. Only someone who is porting the AWT to another platform should be concerned with the peer classes and interfaces. Consequently, most peer documentation refers to `java.awt` counterparts.

See `Component` and `Toolkit` for additional information about component peers.

MEMBER SUMMARY	
Peer Methods	
getMinimumSize()	Calculates the minimum dimensions of the text field.
getPreferredSize()	Calculates the preferred dimensions of the text field.
setEchoChar()	Sets the text field's echo character.
Deprecated Methods	
minimumSize()	Replaced by getMinimumSize().
preferredSize()	Replaced by getPreferredSize().
setEchoCharacter()	Replaced by setEchoChar().

See Also
java.awt.Component, java.awt.TextField, java.awt.Toolkit.

getMinimumSize()

PURPOSE	Calculates the minimum dimensions of the text field.
SYNTAX	`Dimension getMinimumSize(int cols)`
PARAMETERS	
`cols`	A non-negative integer specifying the width in characters.
RETURNS	The non-`null` minimum dimensions for the text field.
SEE ALSO	`java.awt.TextField.getMinimumSize()`.

getPreferredSize()

PURPOSE	Calculates the preferred dimensions of the text field.
SYNTAX	`Dimension preferredSize(int cols)`
PARAMETERS	
`cols`	A non-negative integer specifying the width in characters.
RETURNS	The non-`null` preferred dimensions for the text field.
SEE ALSO	`java.awt.TextField.getPreferredSize()`.

minimumSize()   *DEPRECATED*

PURPOSE	Replaced by `getMinimumSize()`.
SYNTAX	`Dimension minimumSize(int cols)`
PARAMETERS	
`cols`	A non-negative integer specifying the width in characters.
RETURNS	The non-`null` minimum dimensions for the text field.
DEPRECATION	Replace the usage of this deprecated method, as in

```
Dimension min = peer.minimumSize(cols);
```
with
```
Dimension min = peer.getMinimumSize(cols);.
```

A
B
C
D
E
F
G
H
I
J
K
L
M
N
O
P
Q
R
S
T
U
V
W
X
Y
Z

preferredSize( )

DEPRECATED

PURPOSE	Calculates the preferred dimensions of the text field.
SYNTAX	`Dimension preferredSize(int cols)`
PARAMETERS	
`cols`	A non-negative integer specifying the width in characters.
RETURNS	The non-`null` preferred dimensions for the text field.
DEPRECATION	Replace the usage of this deprecated method, as in

```
Dimension pref = peer.preferredSize(cols);
```
with
```
Dimension pref = peer.getPreferredSize(cols);.
```

setEchoChar( )

PURPOSE	Sets the text field's echo character.
SYNTAX	`void setEchoChar(char c)`
PARAMETERS	
`c`	The echo character. A value of 0 clears the echo character.
SEE ALSO	`java.awt.TextField.setEchoChar()`.

setEchoCharacter( )

DEPRECATED

PURPOSE	Replaced by `setEchoChar()`.
SYNTAX	`void setEchoCharacter(char c)`
PARAMETERS	
`c`	The echo character. A value of 0 clears the echo character.
DEPRECATION	Replace the usage of this deprecated method, as in

```
peer.setEchoCharacter(c);
```
with
```
peer.setEchoChar(c);
```

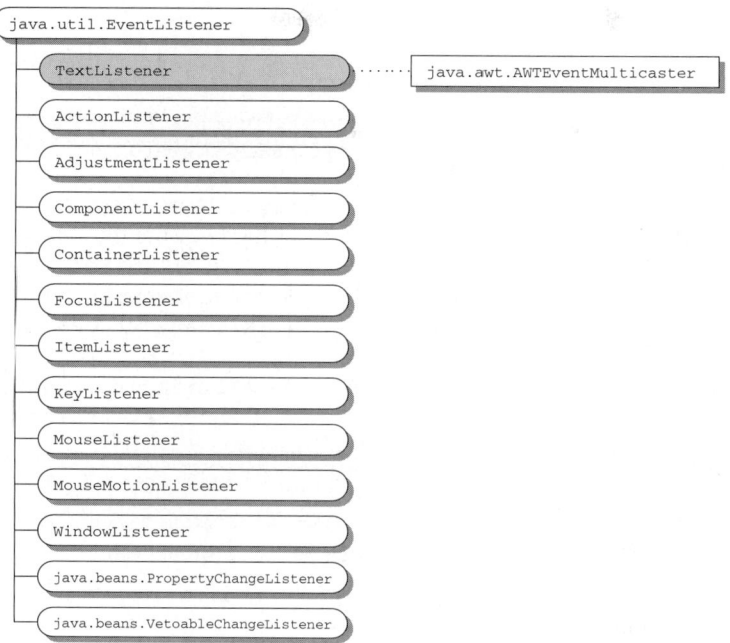

java.util.EventListener
- TextListener .... java.awt.AWTEventMulticaster
- ActionListener
- AdjustmentListener
- ComponentListener
- ContainerListener
- FocusListener
- ItemListener
- KeyListener
- MouseListener
- MouseMotionListener
- WindowListener
- java.beans.PropertyChangeListener
- java.beans.VetoableChangeListener

A
B
C
D
E
F
G
H
I
J
K
L
M
N
O
P
Q
R
S
T
U
V
W
X
Y
Z

Syntax

```
public interface TextListener extends EventListener
```

Description

When an object (listener) wishes to receive text events from an object that fires them (the source object), two things must be done:

1. The listener must implement the `TextListener` interface and the `textValueChanged()` method it requires.
2. The listener must be registered with the source object by making a call to the source object's `addTextListener()` method.

For information about text events, see `TextEvent`.

In the AWT, the `TextArea` and `TextField` components fire text events.

MEMBER SUMMARY
Text Event Callback Method
`textValueChanged()`   Called when the contents of a text component changes.

See Also
`java.awt.TextArea`, `java.awt.TextComponent`, `java.awt.TextField`,
`java.util.EventListener`, `TextEvent`.

Example

This example implements a simple text editor. For a simple example demonstrating text change events, see Figure 368.

The editor watches for any changes to the text area. When a change is made, the Save button is enabled. Also, the frame removes itself from the text area's listener list, since it is no longer interested in any more text change events.

When the user clicks the Save button, the file is saved and the Save button is disabled. Also, the frame adds itself back onto the text area's listener list, since it is now interested in any changes to the text area.

For a simpler example, see `TextEvent`.

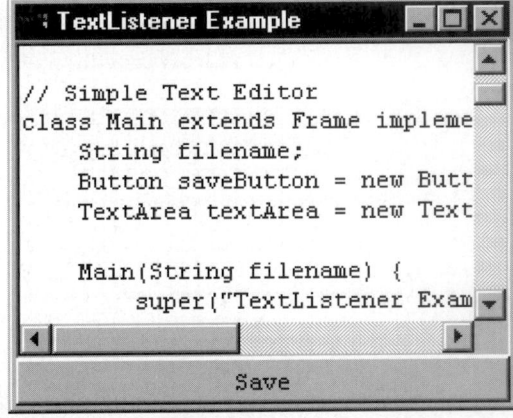

FIGURE 368:   Simple Editor.

```java
import java.awt.*;
import java.awt.event.*;
import java.io.*;

class Main extends Frame implements TextListener, ActionListener {
    String filename;
    Button saveButton = new Button("Save");
    TextArea textArea = new TextArea();

    Main(String filename) {
        super("TextListener Example");
        this.filename = filename;

        try {
            char[] buffer = new char[1024];
            int count = 0;
            FileReader rd = new FileReader(filename);

            // Read in the contents of the file
            // and append them to the text area.
            while ((count = rd.read(buffer, 0, 1024)) != -1) {
                textArea.append(new String(buffer, 0, count));
            }
            rd.close();
        } catch (Exception e) {
            System.err.println("Could not open: " + filename);
            System.exit(1);
        }
```

```
        // Listen for events.
        textArea.addTextListener(this);
        saveButton.addActionListener(this);
        saveButton.setEnabled(false);

        // Layout components.
        add(textArea, BorderLayout.CENTER);
        add(saveButton, BorderLayout.SOUTH);
        setFont(new Font("Monospaced", Font.PLAIN, 12));
        pack();
        show();
    }

    // Handler for text events.
    public void textValueChanged(TextEvent evt) {
        // No need to listen for more text change events
        // so remove from listener list.
        textArea.removeTextListener(this);

        saveButton.setEnabled(true);
    }

    // Handler for action events.
    public void actionPerformed(ActionEvent evt) {
        // Listen for text change events again.
        textArea.addTextListener(this);

        saveButton.setEnabled(false);

        // Now save the changes back to the file.
        try {
            FileWriter wr = new FileWriter(filename);
            String contents = textArea.getText();

            wr.write(contents, 0, contents.length());
            wr.close();
        } catch (Exception e) {
            System.err.println("Could not save: " + filename);
        }
    }

    public static void main(String args[]) {
        if (args.length != 1) {
            System.err.println("Usage: java Main <filename>");
            System.exit(1);
        }

        new Main(args[0]);
    }
}
```

A
B
C
D
E
F
G
H
I
J
K
L
M
N
O
P
Q
R
S
T
U
V
W
X
Y
Z

textValueChanged()

PURPOSE	Called when the contents of a text component changes.
SYNTAX	`public void textValueChanged(TextEvent evt)`
DESCRIPTION	This method is called whenever the contents of the source text component changes.
PARAMETERS	
evt	The non-`null` text event.
SEE ALSO	`java.awt.TextComponent`, `TextEvent`.
EXAMPLE	See the class example.

A
B
C
D
E
F
G
H
I
J
K
L
M
N
O
P
Q
R
S

U
V
W
X
Y
Z

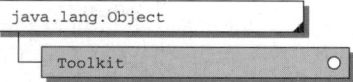

Syntax

public abstract class Toolkit

Description

This class is used to create platform-specific peers and to perform other global functions, such as retrieving the screen resolution, creating a print job object for printing, and reading AWT-specific properties.

Creating Peers

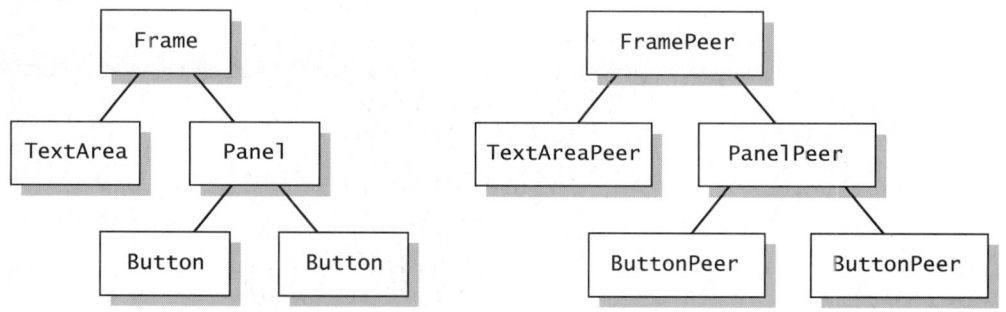

FIGURE 369:   A Component Hierarchy and Its Corresponding Peer Class Hierarchy.

A component, such as a button, in the AWT uses the platform's native implementation of a button. For example, on Solaris, the AWT button uses the Motif button widget, while in Windows 95, the AWT button uses the button control. So that the AWT button component behaves the same on all platforms, the button is assigned a *peer* (see Component), whose task is to translate the behavior of the platform's native button to the behavior of the AWT button.

Each platform has its own complete set of peers to match each of the AWT components. The purpose of the abstract class Toolkit is to deliver the correct set of peers that are appropriate for the current platform. For example, when an AWT button object needs a button peer, it calls getDefaultToolkit() to retrieve an instance of this class and then uses that instance to create a button peer.

There is only one instance of the Toolkit class in existence at any time. That instance is created with the first call to getDefaultToolkit(). Each platform has an implementation of this class. The awt.toolkit system property is used to determine the instance of the toolkit to create. The `awt.toolkit` system property names the class to create (the class must, of course, be a subclass of `Toolkit`).

Most of the peer creation methods in this class are not typically used directly by AWT programmers, since they are indirectly available through other classes.

A
B
C
D
E
F
G
H
I
J
K
L
M
N
O
P
Q
R
S
T
U
V
W
X
Y
Z

MEMBER SUMMARY	
Initialization Method	
`getDefaultToolkit()`	Retrieves the `Toolkit` instance to use when creating component peers.
Peer Methods	
`createButton()`	Creates a button peer.
`createCanvas()`	Creates a canvas peer.
`createCheckbox()`	Creates a checkbox peer.
`createCheckboxMenuItem()`	Creates a checkbox menu item peer.
`createChoice()`	Creates a choice peer.
`createComponent()`	Creates a lightweight peer for a component or a container.
`createDialog()`	Creates a dialog peer.
`createFileDialog()`	Creates a file dialog peer.
`createFrame()`	Creates a frame peer.
`createLabel()`	Creates a label peer.
`createList()`	Creates a list peer.
`createMenu()`	Creates a menu peer.
`createMenuBar()`	Creates a menu bar peer.
`createMenuItem()`	Creates a menu item peer.
`createPanel()`	Creates a panel peer.
`createPopupMenu()`	Creates a popup menu peer.
`createScrollbar()`	Creates a scrollbar peer.
`createScrollPane()`	Creates a scrollpane peer.
`createTextArea()`	Creates a text area peer.
`createTextField()`	Creates a text field peer.
`createWindow()`	Creates a window peer.
Color Methods	
`getColorModel()`	Retrieves the color model for the screen.
`loadSystemColors()`	Loads current system colors into an array.
Event Methods	
`getMenuShortcutKeyMask()`	Retrieves the event modifier mask used for menu shortcuts.
`getSystemEventQueue()`	Retrieves the event queue for this application or applet.
`getSystemEventQueueImpl()`	Retrieves the event queue for this application or applet.

MEMBER SUMMARY	
Font Methods	
getFontList()	Retrieves a list of the names of all available AWT fonts.
getFontPeer()	Creates the font peer for a font.
getFontMetrics()	Retrieves the font metrics for a font.
Image Methods	
checkImage()	Retrieves the construction status of an image.
createImage()	Creates an image using image data supplied by an image producer.
getImage()	Retrieves an image from a file or URL.
prepareImage()	Triggers the loading of image data for an image.
Print Method	
getPrintJob()	Creates a new PrintJob instance.
Screen Methods	
getScreenResolution()	Retrieves the resolution of the screen.
getScreenSize()	Retrieves the size of the screen.
sync()	Flushes any pending operations on active graphics contexts.
System-wide Methods	
beep()	Emits an audio "beep."
getNativeContainer()	Retrieves the native container of a component.
getProperty()	Retrieves a property from the awt.properties list.
getSystemClipboard()	Retrieves the system clipboard.

Example

This example creates a frame and centers it on the screen. See Figure 370. The frame also displays the screen resolution and an estimate of the size of the screen based on the screen size and resolution.

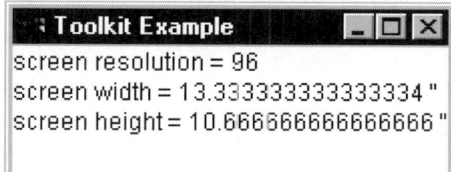

FIGURE 370:   Centering a Frame on the Screen.

```
import java.awt.*;

class Main extends Frame {
    Main() {
        super("Toolkit Example");
        Dimension d;
        d = Toolkit.getDefaultToolkit().getScreenSize();

        setSize(225, 100);
        setLocation((d.width-getBounds().width)/2,
                    (d.height-getBounds().height)/2);
        show();
```

```
        }

    public void paint(Graphics g) {
        FontMetrics fm = g.getFontMetrics();
        int resol = Toolkit.getDefaultToolkit().getScreenResolution();
        Dimension d = Toolkit.getDefaultToolkit().getScreenSize();
        Insets insets = getInsets();
        int x = insets.left;
        int y = insets.top + fm.getAscent();

        g.drawString("screen resolution = "+resol, x, y);
        y += fm.getHeight();
        g.drawString("screen width = "
            + ((double)d.width/resol) + " \"", x, y);
        y += fm.getHeight();
        g.drawString("screen height = "
            + ((double)d.height/resol) + " \"", x, y);
    }

    public static void main(String[] args) {
        new Main();
    }
}
```

A
B
C
D
E
F
G
H
I
J
K

beep()

PURPOSE	Emits an audio "beep."
SYNTAX	`public abstract void beep()`
EXAMPLE	This example creates a button that, when pushed, emits an audio "beep." See Figure 371.

FIGURE 371:   **Beeping Button.**

L
M
N
O
P
Q
R
S
T
U
V
W
X
Y
Z

```
import java.awt.*;
import java.awt.event.*;

class Main extends Frame implements ActionListener {
    Main() {
        super("Toolkit.beep() Example");

        Button b = new Button("Beep");
        add(b, BorderLayout.CENTER);
        b.addActionListener(this);

        pack();
        show();
    }

    public void actionPerformed(ActionEvent evt) {
        Toolkit.getDefaultToolkit().beep();
    }

    public static void main(String[] args) {
        new Main();
    }
}
```

checkImage( )

PURPOSE	Retrieves the construction status of an image.
SYNTAX	`public abstract int checkImage(Image image, int width, int height, ImageObserver obs)`
DESCRIPTION	See `Component.checkImage()` for a complete description of this method.
PARAMETERS	
`height`	If >= 0, specifies the height of the scaled version of the image to check.
`image`	The non-`null` image to check.
`obs`	If non-`null`, specifies the image observer to be notified whenever the status changes.
`width`	If >= 0, specifies the width of the scaled version of the image to check.
RETURNS	The combination of status bits as defined by the `ImageObserver` interface.
SEE ALSO	`Component.checkImage()`.
EXAMPLE	See `Component.checkImage()`.

createButton( )

PURPOSE	Creates a button peer.
SYNTAX	`protected abstract ButtonPeer createButton(Button target)`
DESCRIPTION	This method is called by `Button.addNotify()` as the peers for a component hierarchy are created. For a complete description of the behavior of the button peer, see the `Button` class.
PARAMETERS	
`target`	The non-`null` AWT button requiring a button peer.
RETURNS	A button peer for the AWT button target.
SEE ALSO	`Button`.

createCanvas( )

PURPOSE	Creates a canvas peer.
SYNTAX	`protected abstract CanvasPeer createCanvas(Canvas target)`
DESCRIPTION	This method is called by `Canvas.addNotify()` as the peers for a component hierarchy are created. For a complete description of the behavior of the canvas peer, see the `Canvas` class.

A
B
C
D
E
F
G
H
I
J
K
L
M
N
O
P
Q
R
S
U
V
W
X
Y
Z

PARAMETERS

target   The non-null AWT canvas requiring a canvas peer.

RETURNS   A canvas peer for the AWT canvas target.

SEE ALSO   Canvas.

createCheckbox( )

PURPOSE   Creates a checkbox peer.

SYNTAX   `protected abstract CheckboxPeer createCheckbox(Checkbox target)`

DESCRIPTION   This method is called by `Checkbox.addNotify()` as the peers for a component hierarchy are created. For a complete description of the behavior of the checkbox peer, see the `Checkbox` class.

PARAMETERS

target   The non-null AWT checkbox requiring a checkbox peer.

RETURNS   A checkbox peer for the AWT checkbox target.

SEE ALSO   Checkbox.

createCheckboxMenuItem( )

PURPOSE   Creates a checkbox menu item peer.

SYNTAX   `protected abstract CheckboxMenuItemPeer`
                 `createCheckboxMenuItem(CheckboxMenuItem target)`

DESCRIPTION   This method is called by `CheckboxMenuItem.addNotify()` as the peers for a component hierarchy are created. For a complete description of the behavior of the checkbox menu item peer, see the `CheckboxMenuItem` class.

PARAMETERS

target   The non-null AWT checkbox menu item requiring a checkbox menu item peer.

RETURNS   A checkbox menu item peer for the AWT checkbox menu item target.

SEE ALSO   CheckboxMenuItem.

createChoice( )

PURPOSE   Creates a choice peer.

SYNTAX	`protected abstract ChoicePeer createChoice(Choice target)`
DESCRIPTION	This method is called by `Choice.addNotify()` as the peers for a component hierarchy are created. For a complete description of the behavior of the choice peer, see the `Choice` class.
PARAMETERS	
target	The non-`null` AWT choice requiring a choice peer.
RETURNS	A choice peer for the AWT choice target.
SEE ALSO	`Choice`.

createComponent()

PURPOSE	Creates a peer for a lightweight component.
SYNTAX	`protected abstract LightweightPeer createComponent(Component target)`
DESCRIPTION	This method is called by `Component.addNotify()` as the peers for a component hierarchy are created. A lightweight component is a component that does not have a corresponding peer in the window system. Instead, it has a peer represented entirely in Java. For a complete description of the behavior of lightweight components, see the `Component` class.
PARAMETERS	
target	The non-`null` AWT component or container requiring a peer.
RETURNS	A lightweight peer for the AWT component.
SEE ALSO	`Component`.

createDialog()

PURPOSE	Creates a dialog peer.
SYNTAX	`protected abstract DialogPeer createDialog(Dialog target)`
DESCRIPTION	This method is called by `Dialog.addNotify()` as the peers for a component hierarchy are created. For a complete description of the behavior of the dialog peer, see the `Dialog` class.
PARAMETERS	
target	The non-`null` AWT dialog requiring a dialog peer.
RETURNS	A dialog peer for the AWT dialog target.
SEE ALSO	`Dialog`.

A
B
C
D
E
F
G
H
I
J
K
L
M
N
O
P
Q
R
S
T
U
V
W
X
Y
Z

createFileDialog()

PURPOSE	Creates a file dialog peer.
SYNTAX	`protected abstract FileDialogPeer createFileDialog(FileDialog target)`
DESCRIPTION	This method is called by `FileDialog.addNotify()` as the peers for a component hierarchy are created. For a complete description of the behavior of the file dialog peer, see the `FileDialog` class.
PARAMETERS	
`target`	The non-`null` AWT file dialog requiring a file dialog peer.
RETURNS	A file dialog peer for the AWT file dialog target.
SEE ALSO	`FileDialog`.

createFrame()

PURPOSE	Creates a frame peer.
SYNTAX	`protected abstract FramePeer createFrame(Frame target)`
DESCRIPTION	This method is called by `Frame.addNotify()` as the peers for a component hierarchy are created. For a complete description of the behavior of the frame peer, see the `Frame` class.
PARAMETERS	
`target`	The non-`null` AWT frame requiring a frame peer.
RETURNS	A frame peer for the AWT frame target.
SEE ALSO	`Frame`.

createImage()

PURPOSE	Creates an image.

SYNTAX	`public abstract Image createImage(ImageProducer producer)`
	`public abstract Image createImage(byte[] imageData)`
	`public abstract Image createImage(byte[] imageData, int offset, int count)`

DESCRIPTION	The first form of this method creates an image based on the image data generated by the image producer `producer`. When the method returns, it does not contain any image information. The production of image information must be triggered by calling either `prepareImage()` or `Graphics.drawImage()`.

A
B
C
D
E
F
G
H
I
J
K
L
M
N
O
P
Q
R
S
T
U
V
W
X
Y
Z

Since the image is not loaded before this method returns, the image may become invalid later (when an error is eventually encountered). See the Image class description for more information about the asynchronous loading of image data.

The second and third forms of this method create an image using count number of bytes stored in an array imageData, starting at index offset. If offset and count are not specified, the entire byte array is used. The data in image-Data must be in a format supported by the toolkit. The currently supported formats include GIF and JPEG.

PARAMETERS

count	The number of bytes to use.
imageData	The byte array containing the image.
offset	The index in imageData at which to start getting the image data.
producer	The non-null image producer.

RETURNS   A reference to a new image. null may be returned if the producer is not valid.

SEE ALSO   Image, java.awt.image.ImageProducer.

EXAMPLE   See Component.createImage().

createLabel()

PURPOSE   Creates a label peer.

SYNTAX   protected abstract LabelPeer createLabel(Label target)

DESCRIPTION   This method is called by Label.addNotify() as the peers for a component hierarchy are created. For a complete description of the behavior of the label peer, see the Label class.

PARAMETERS

target   The non-null AWT label requiring a label peer.

RETURNS   A label peer for the AWT label target.

SEE ALSO   Label.

createList()

PURPOSE   Creates a list peer.

SYNTAX   protected abstract ListPeer createList(List target)

DESCRIPTION   This method is called by `List.addNotify()` as the peers for a component hierarchy are created. For a complete description of the behavior of the list peer, see the `List` class.

PARAMETERS

target   The non-null AWT list requiring a list peer.

RETURNS   A list peer for the AWT list target.

SEE ALSO   `List`.

createMenu( )

PURPOSE   Creates a menu peer.

SYNTAX   `protected abstract MenuPeer createMenu(Menu target)`

DESCRIPTION   This method is called by `Menu.addNotify()` as the peers for a component hierarchy are created. For a complete description of the behavior of the menu peer, see the `Menu` class.

PARAMETERS

target   The non-null AWT menu requiring a menu peer.

RETURNS   A menu peer for the AWT menu target.

SEE ALSO   `Menu`.

createMenuBar( )

PURPOSE   Creates a menu bar peer.

SYNTAX   `protected abstract MenuBarPeer createMenuBar(MenuBar target)`

DESCRIPTION   This method is called by `MenuBar.addNotify()` as the peers for a component hierarchy are created. For a complete description of the behavior of the menu bar peer, see the `MenuBar` class.

PARAMETERS

target   The non-null AWT menu bar requiring a menu bar peer.

RETURNS   A menu bar peer for the AWT menu bar target.

SEE ALSO   `MenuBar`.

createMenuItem()

PURPOSE	Creates a menu item peer.
SYNTAX	`protected abstract MenuItemPeer createMenuItem(MenuItem target)`
DESCRIPTION	This method is called by `MenuItem.addNotify()` as the peers for a component hierarchy are created. For a complete description of the behavior of the menu item peer, see the `MenuItem` class.
PARAMETERS	
target	The non-`null` AWT menu item requiring a menu item peer.
RETURNS	A menu item peer for the AWT menu item target.
SEE ALSO	`MenuItem`.

createPanel()

PURPOSE	Creates a panel peer.
SYNTAX	`protected abstract PanelPeer createPanel(Panel target)`
DESCRIPTION	This method is called by `Panel.addNotify()` as the peers for a component hierarchy are created. For a complete description of the behavior of the panel peer, see the `Panel` class.
PARAMETERS	
target	The non-`null` AWT panel requiring a panel peer.
RETURNS	A panel peer for the AWT panel target.
SEE ALSO	`Panel`.

createPopupMenu()

PURPOSE	Creates a popup menu peer.
SYNTAX	`protected abstract PopupMenuPeer createPopupMenu(PopupMenu target)`
DESCRIPTION	This method is called by `PopupMenu.addNotify()` as the peers for a component hierarchy are created. For a complete description of the behavior of the popup menu peer, see the `PopupMenu` class.
PARAMETERS	
target	The non-`null` AWT popup menu requiring a popup menu peer.
RETURNS	A popup menu peer for the AWT popup menu target.
SEE ALSO	`PopupMenu`.

A
B
C
D
E
F
G
H
I
J
K
L
M
N
O
P
Q
R
S

U
V
W
X
Y
Z

A
B
C
D
E
F
G
H
I
J
K
L
M
N
O
P
Q
R
S

U
V
W
X
Y
Z

createScrollbar()

PURPOSE	Creates a scrollbar peer.
SYNTAX	`protected abstract ScrollbarPeer createScrollbar(Scrollbar target)`
DESCRIPTION	This method is called by `Scrollbar.addNotify()` as the peers for a component hierarchy are created. For a complete description of the behavior of the scrollbar peer, see the `Scrollbar` class.
PARAMETERS	
`target`	The non-`null` AWT scrollbar requiring a scrollbar peer.
RETURNS	A scrollbar peer for the AWT scrollbar target.
SEE ALSO	`Scrollbar`.

createScrollPane()

PURPOSE	Creates a scrollpane peer.
SYNTAX	`protected abstract ScrollPanePeer createScrollpane(ScrollPane target)`
DESCRIPTION	This method is called by `ScrollPane.addNotify()` as the peers for a component hierarchy are created. For a complete description of the behavior of the scroll pane peer, see the `ScrollPane` class.
PARAMETERS	
`target`	The non-`null` AWT scroll pane requiring a scroll pane peer.
RETURNS	A scroll pane peer for the AWT scroll pane target.
SEE ALSO	`ScrollPane`.

createTextArea()

PURPOSE	Creates a text area peer.
SYNTAX	`protected abstract TextAreaPeer createTextArea(TextArea target)`
DESCRIPTION	This method is called by `TextArea.addNotify()` as the peers for a component hierarchy are created. For a complete description of the behavior of the text area peer, see the `TextArea` class.
PARAMETERS	
`target`	The non-`null` AWT text area requiring a text area peer.

1486

RETURNS   A text area peer for the AWT text area target.

SEE ALSO   TextArea.

createTextField( )

PURPOSE   Creates a text field peer.

SYNTAX   `protected abstract TextFieldPeer createTextField(TextField`
               `    target)`

DESCRIPTION   This method is called by `TextField.addNotify()` as the peers for a compo-
               nent hierarchy are created. For a complete description of the behavior of the
               text field peer, see the `TextField` class.

PARAMETERS
  target   The non-`null` AWT text field requiring a text field peer.

RETURNS   A text field peer for the AWT text field target.

SEE ALSO   TextField.

createWindow( )

PURPOSE   Creates a window peer.

SYNTAX   `protected abstract WindowPeer createWindow(Window target)`

DESCRIPTION   This is called by `Window.addNotify()` as the peers for a component hierar-
               chy are created. For a complete description of the behavior of the window peer,
               see the `Window` class.

PARAMETERS
  target   The non-`null` AWT window requiring a window peer.

RETURNS   A window peer for the AWT window target.

SEE ALSO   Window.

getColorModel( )

PURPOSE   Retrieves the color model for the screen.

SYNTAX   `public abstract ColorModel getColorModel()`

RETURNS   The non-`null` color model of the screen.

SEE ALSO   ColorModel.

EXAMPLE   See `ColorModel` for an example that displays the colors in the screen's color
               table.

A
B
C
D
E
F
G
H
I
J
K
L
M
N
O
P
Q
R
S
T
U
V
W
X
Y
Z

getDefaultToolkit( )

PURPOSE	Retrieves the `Toolkit` instance to use when creating component peers.
SYNTAX	`public static synchronized Toolkit getDefaultToolkit()`
DESCRIPTION	The first time this method is called, `getDefaultToolkit()` reads the `awt.toolkit` system property to determine which version of the `Toolkit` to create. The toolkit instance is created only once and cannot be replaced.
RETURNS	The non-`null` toolkit instance.
EXCEPTIONS	
`AWTError`	If the toolkit could not be created.
EXAMPLE	See the class example.

getFontList( )

PURPOSE	Retrieves a list of the names of all available AWT fonts.
SYNTAX	`public abstract String[] getFontList()`
DESCRIPTION	See `Font`'s class description for list of currently supported fonts. The returned list should not be modified.
RETURNS	A non-`null` list of all available AWT font names.
SEE ALSO	`Font`.
EXAMPLE	See the `Font` class.

getFontMetrics( )

PURPOSE	Retrieves the font metrics for a font.
SYNTAX	`public abstract FontMetrics getFontMetrics(Font font)`
DESCRIPTION	This method retrieves the font metrics for the font `font`.
PARAMETERS	
`font`	The non-`null` font.
RETURNS	The non-`null` font metrics for `font`.
SEE ALSO	`FontMetrics`, `Graphics.getFontMetrics()`.

A
B
C
D
E
F
G
H
I
J
K
L
M
N
O
P
Q
R
S
T
U
V
W
X
Y
Z

getFontPeer()

PURPOSE   Creates the font peer for a font.

SYNTAX   `protected abstract FontPeer getFontPeer(String fontName, int style)`

DESCRIPTION   This method creates the font peer for the font with the logical font name `font-Name` and the font style `style`.

PARAMETERS

`fontName`   The non-`null` logical font name (e.g., "Serif" or "Monospaced").

`style`   Bits specifying the font's style. It is a mask constructed using `Font.ITALIC`, `Font.PLAIN`, and `Font.BOLD`.

RETURNS   The non-`null` font peer for the specified font.

SEE ALSO   `FontMetrics`, `Graphics.getFontMetrics()`.

getImage()

PURPOSE   Creates an image from a file or URL.

SYNTAX   `public abstract Image getImage(String filename)`
`public abstract Image getImage(URL url)`

DESCRIPTION   The two forms of this method return a reference to an `Image` object. The pixels contained in the file `filename` or at the URL `url` are not immediately loaded into the image. To start the loading of the pixel data, call `Component.prepareImage()` or `Graphics.drawImage()`. Since the image is not loaded before this method returns, the image may become invalid later (when an error is eventually encountered). See the `Image` class description for more information about the asynchronous loading of image data.

PARAMETERS

`filename`   The non-`null` string specifying the file that contains the image.

`url`   The non-`null` URL specifying the location of the image.

RETURNS   A reference to the image that will eventually contain the pixel data. `null` is returned if `filename` or `url` is invalid.

SEE ALSO   `Image`, `java.net.URL`.

A
B
C
D
E
F
G
H
I
J
K
L
M
N
O
P
Q
R
S
T
U
V
W
X
Y
Z

EXAMPLE   This example demonstrates how
               a URL can be derived from a
               pathname and then be used to
               load an image. See Figure 372.
               The program creates a frame and
               a canvas in which to display the
               image. The image is scaled to
               the size of the canvas.

FIGURE 372:   **Loading an Image Using a URL.**

```java
import java.awt.*;
import java.net.*;

class Main extends Frame {
    Main(String filename) {
        super("getImage Example");
        try {
            // Retrieve the image.
            URL url = new URL("file:///" + System.getProperty("user.dir")
                + "/" + filename);
            Image urlImage = getToolkit().getImage(url);

            add(new ImageCanvas(urlImage), BorderLayout.CENTER);
        } catch (Exception e) {
            e.printStackTrace();
        }
        setSize(50, 100);
        show();
    }

    static public void main(String[] args) {
        if (args.length == 1) {
            new Main(args[0]);
        } else {
            System.err.println("usage: java Main <image file>");
        }
    }
}

class ImageCanvas extends Component {
    Image image;

    ImageCanvas(Image image) {
        this.image = image;
    }

    public void paint(Graphics g) {
        update(g);
    }

    public void update(Graphics g) {
        g.drawImage(image, 0, 0, getSize().width, getSize().height, this);
    }
}
```

getMenuShortcutKeyMask()

PURPOSE   Retrieves the event modifier mask to use for menu shortcuts.

SYNTAX   `public int getMenuShortcutKeyMask()`

DESCRIPTION   This method defines the event modifier mask to use for menu shortcuts. The default value returned is `InputEvent.CTRL_MASK`. A toolkit should override this method if it uses another modifier for menu shortcuts.

RETURNS   The event modifier mask for menu shortcuts.

SEE ALSO   `AWTEvent, java.awt.event.InputEvent, MenuShortcut.`

getNativeContainer()

PURPOSE   Retrieves the native container of a component.

SYNTAX   `protected static Container getNativeContainer(Component`
                      `component)`

DESCRIPTION   The immediate container of a component may not be a native component. The container might have a lightweight peer instead. This method allows a program to find the first container of the component `component` that has a native peer traversing up its container hierarchy.

PARAMETERS
  `component`   The component whose native container to obtain.

RETURNS   The native container that contains `component`.

SEE ALSO   `Container.`

getPrintJob()

PURPOSE   Creates a new `PrintJob` instance.

SYNTAX   `public abstract PrintJob getPrintJob(Frame frame, String title,`
                      `Properties props)`

DESCRIPTION   This method creates and returns a new `PrintJob` instance. Calling this method causes a modal dialog to appear. The dialog displays the printer options from which the user can choose. Until the user dismisses the dialog, this method does not return.

The `frame` parameter is ignored.

The `title` parameter is printed on any header pages that the printer prints.

A B C D E F G H I J K L M N O P Q R S T U V W X Y Z

If `props` is not `null`, it will be filled with the various printer options that the user has chosen. *Note*: In Java 1.1.2, the `props` parameter is ignored.

PARAMETERS

`frame`	The possibly `null` frame from which the print job was initiated.
`props`	The possibly `null` properties associated with the print job.
`title`	The possibly `null` title of the print job.

RETURNS   A possibly `null` `PrintJob` instance.

SEE ALSO   `PrintJob`.

EXAMPLE   See the `PrintJob` class example.

getProperty()

PURPOSE   Retrieves a property from the `awt.properties` list.

SYNTAX   `public static String getProperty(String key, String defaultValue)`

DESCRIPTION   Visible strings used by the AWT are stored in the `awt.properties` property list in the `lib` subdirectory in which Java is installed (i.e., in the file `$JAVA-HOME/lib/awt.properties`). This method retrieves the value associated with the property key. If key is not found in `awt.properties`, default-Value is returned.

PARAMETERS

`defaultValue`	The default value to return if key is not in the `awt.properties` list.
`key`	The name of the property to retrieve.

RETURNS   The value associated with key in the `awt.properties` set; `defaultValue` if key is not found.

SEE ALSO   `java.lang.System.getProperty()`, `java.util.Properties`.

EXAMPLE   This example displays the textual representation of a function key.

```
void PrintFunctionKey(int fkey) {
    switch(fkey) {
    case VK_F1:
        System.out.Print(Toolkit.getProperty("AWT.f1", "F1"));
        break;
    case VK_F2:
        System.out.Print(Toolkit.getProperty("AWT.f2", "F2"));
        break;
    ...
    }
}
```

A
B
C
D
E
F
G
H
I
J
K
L
M
N
O
P
Q
R
S
T
U
V
W
X
Y
Z

getScreenResolution()

PURPOSE	Retrieves the resolution of the screen.
SYNTAX	`public abstract int getScreenResolution()`
DESCRIPTION	Dividing the screen size by the screen resolution should yield the physical size of the screen.
RETURNS	The resolution of the screen in dots-per-inch.
EXAMPLE	See the class example.

getScreenSize()

PURPOSE	Retrieves the size of the screen.
SYNTAX	`public abstract Dimension getScreenSize()`
RETURNS	The non-`null` dimensions of the screen in pixels.
EXAMPLE	See the class example.

getSystemClipboard()

PURPOSE	Retrieves the system clipboard.
SYNTAX	`public abstract Clipboard getSystemClipboard()`
DESCRIPTION	The system clipboard allows data to be transferred between Java programs and native programs.
RETURNS	The system clipboard.
SEE ALSO	`java.awt.datatransfer.Clipboard`.
EXAMPLE	See the `Clipboard` class example.

getSystemEventQueue()

PURPOSE	Retrieves the event queue of this application or applet.
SYNTAX	`public final EventQueue getSystemEventQueue()`
DESCRIPTION	Using the system event queue, you can add events to the queue to be processed later. (Contrast this with `Component.dispatchEvent()`, which dispatches the event synchronously at invocation time.)

Depending on the toolkit implementation, applets running on the same virtual machine may not necessarily share the same system event queue. The system event queue can be obtained only if allowed to do so by the security manager in place.

RETURNS   The non-`null` event queue for this application or applet.

EXCEPTIONS

    `SecurityException`

                If not allowed to access the application or applet's system event queue.

SEE ALSO   `AWTEvent, EventQueue, getSystemEventQueueImpl(),`
                `java.lang.SecurityManager.checkAwtEventQueueAccess().`

EXAMPLE   See the `java.awt.peer.ActiveEvent` class example and the `AWTEvent` class example.

getSystemEventQueueImpl()

PURPOSE   Retrieves the event queue of this application or applet.

SYNTAX   `protected abstract EventQueue getSystemEventQueueImpl()`

DESCRIPTION   A toolkit provides an implementation for this method, which is used by `get-SystemEventQueue()`.

                Depending on the toolkit implementation, applets running on the same virtual machine may not necessarily share the same event queue.

RETURNS   The event queue for this application or applet.

SEE ALSO   `EventQueue, getSystemEventQueue().`

loadSystemColors()

PURPOSE   Retrieves the current system colors into an array.

SYNTAX   `protected void loadSystemColors(int[] systemColors)`

DESCRIPTION   This method loads the array `systemColors` with the system colors. Each entry in the array represents a particular system color (the background color for scrollbars, the background color for the menu text, and so on). Each value in the array is the RGB value of the color.

PARAMETERS

    `systemColors` A preallocated array to store the system color values. It must have at least `SystemColor.NUM_COLORS` elements.

SEE ALSO   `SystemColor.`

prepareImage( )

PURPOSE	Triggers the loading of image data for an image.
SYNTAX	`public abstract boolean prepareImage(Image image, int width, int` `height, ImageObserver observer)`
DESCRIPTION	This method starts the loading or production of image data associated with image `image` or a scaled version of `image`. If `width` and `height` are −1, no scaling of `image` is done. If `width` and `height` are non-negative, they specify that `image` should not only be loaded, but also scaled so that its width is `width` and its height is `height`.
	This method is typically used to preload image data for an image or a scaled version of an image so that `Graphics.drawImage()` can operate as quickly as possible.

PARAMETERS

`height`	−1 or the scaled height of the returned image.
`image`	The non-`null` image to load.
`observer`	The non-`null` image observer.
`width`	−1 or the scaled width of the returned image.
RETURNS	`true` if all of the image data for `image` is available; `false` otherwise.
SEE ALSO	`Component.checkImage()`.
EXAMPLE	See `Component.checkImage()`.

sync( )

PURPOSE	Flushes any pending operations on active graphics contexts.
SYNTAX	`public abstract void sync()`
DESCRIPTION	This method is useful on platforms that batch painting calls to a graphics context. It currently is not used.
SEE ALSO	`Graphics`.

A
B
C
D
E
F
G
H
I
J
K
L
M
N
O
P
Q
R
S
T
U
V
W
X
Y
Z

Transferable .... StringSelection

Syntax

```
public interface Transferable
```

Description

When an application wants to place data on a clipboard, it must first encapsulate the data in an object that implements the `Transferable` interface. Similarly, when an application retrieves the contents of a clipboard, it is given a transferable object that it must use to retrieve the encapsulated data.

A transferable object provides several features:

1. It can contain any type of data: an image, a string, a bean, and so on. Through the use of data flavors (see `DataFlavor`), it allows an application to determine exactly what is encapsulated by the transferable object.
2. It can support the delivery of the encapsulated data in different ways. For example, if the transferable object contains a JPEG image, it may support the delivery of the image as an `Image` object, as a byte stream, or as an array of pixels. An application decides how it wants the data delivered through the use of data flavors (see `DataFlavor`).
3. It does not necessarily have to contain the actual data, only a reference to that data. For example, an application may display a list of files containing images. When one of those image files is copied onto a clipboard, it does not have to provide the image pixels. When some other application finally requests the data, the application reads the pixels from the file and delivers them.

Note: Transferable objects will play a role in drag-and-drop when it becomes available in a future release.

Supported Data Flavors

A transferable object must be able to supply a list of all data flavors that it supports. This allows an application to go through the list of data flavors looking for a data flavor that it can use to retrieve the encapsulated data. Alternatively, an application can simply try to retrieve the data with a data flavor and see if the transferable object will grant or reject the request.

MEMBER SUMMARY	
Data Method	
`getTransferData()`	Retrieves the data encapsulated in this transferable object.
Data Flavor Methods	
`getTransferDataFlavors()`	Returns an array of data flavors that this transferable object supports.
`isDataFlavorSupported()`	Determines whether this object supports a particular data flavor.

See Also

`Clipboard, DataFlavor.`

Example

This example demonstrates how one could exchange images on a clipboard. Since the system clipboard does not support images, the example uses a private clipboard. The example creates an *image palette*—a frame containing a number of images (see the "Copy" frame in Figure 373). Clicking one of the images causes that image to be highlighted and placed on the private clipboard. The highlight is drawn only if the image is still in the clipboard; if the clipboard no longer contains the image, the highlight is removed.

The other frame (the "Paste" frame in Figure 373) can copy the highlighted image shown on the image palette. This is done by the user's choosing the Copy menu item from the Edit menu. The copied image is displayed in the frame's display area.

The Edit menu also contains a Clear Clipboard command, which simply sets an empty string in the clipboard. This is used to test that the current image in the image palette loses its highlight.

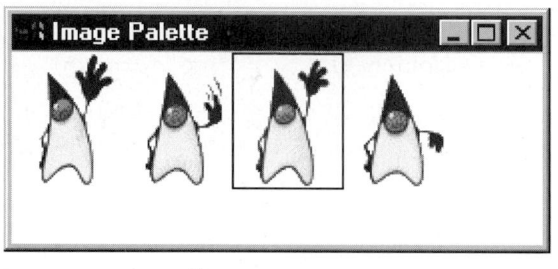

Copy

Paste

FIGURE 373: Copy and Paste Using `Transferable`.

```
            import java.awt.*;
            import java.awt.datatransfer.*;
            import java.awt.event.*;
            import java.io.*;

            class Main extends Frame implements ActionListener {
A               static Clipboard mainClipboard = new Clipboard("Main Clipboard");
                Image currentImage;
B
                Main() {
C                   super("Transferable Example");
                    MenuBar mb = new MenuBar();
D                   Menu m = new Menu("Edit");

E                   m.add("Paste");
                    m.add("Clear Clipboard");
F                   m.addActionListener(this);
                    mb.add(m);
G                   setMenuBar(mb);

H                   setSize(100, 150);
                    show();
I               }

J               public static void main(String[] args) {
                    new Main();
K
                    Frame f = new Frame("Image Palette");
L                   f.add(new ImagePalette(), BorderLayout.CENTER);
                    f.pack();
M                   f.show();
                }
N
                public void actionPerformed(ActionEvent evt) {
O                   if (evt.getActionCommand().equals("Paste")) {
                        // Get the image in the clipboard.
P                       Transferable t = mainClipboard.getContents(this);

Q                       try {
                            if (t != null) {
R                               currentImage = (Image)t.getTransferData(
                                    ImageSelection.imageFlavor);
S                               repaint();
                            }
                        } catch (IOException e) {
                        } catch (UnsupportedFlavorException e) {
                        }
U                   } else {
V                       // Clear Clipboard
                        mainClipboard.setContents(null, null);
W                   }
                    repaint();
X               }

Y               public void paint(Graphics g) {
                    if (currentImage != null) {
Z                       g.drawImage(currentImage, getInsets().left, getInsets().top, this);
                    }

                    // All containers must call super.paint() in case
```

```
            // it contains lightweight components.
            super.paint(g);
        }
    }

class ImagePalette extends Component implements ClipboardOwner {
    // If >= 0, points the currently selected image.
    int curImage = -1;

    // This field holds all the images.
    Image images[] = new Image[4];

    // This field holds the bounds for each image.
    Rectangle rects[] = new Rectangle[4];

    ImagePalette() {
        MediaTracker tracker = new MediaTracker(this);

        // Use a media tracker because we need to know the
        // dimensions of the images immediately.
        for (int i=0; i<images.length; i++) {
            images[i] = getToolkit().getImage("duke"+i+".gif");
            tracker.addImage(images[i], 0);
        }
        try {
            // Wait for images to load.
            tracker.waitForAll();
        } catch (Exception e) {
            e.printStackTrace();
        }

        // Determine the location of each image.
        int x = 0;
        int h = 0;
        for (int i=0; i<images.length; i++) {
            rects[i] = new Rectangle(x, 0,
                images[i].getWidth(null), images[i].getHeight(null));
            x += rects[i].width;
            h = Math.max(h, rects[i].height);
        }

        addMouseListener(new MouseEventHandler());
        setSize(x, h);
    }

    public void paint(Graphics g) {
        for (int i=0; i<images.length; i++) {
            g.drawImage(images[i], rects[i].x, rects[i].y, this);
            if (i == curImage) {
                // Draw border around current image.
                g.drawRect(rects[i].x, rects[i].y,
                    rects[i].width, rects[i].height);
            }
        }
    }

    class MouseEventHandler extends MouseAdapter {
        public void mousePressed(MouseEvent evt) {
            for (int i=0; i<rects.length; i++) {
                // Find out if an image has been clicked.
```

A
B
C
D
E
F
G
H
I
J
K
L
M
N
O
P
Q
R
S
T
U
V
W
X
Y
Z

```
                    if (rects[i].contains(evt.getX(), evt.getY())) {
                        // Place image into clipboard.
                        Main.mainClipboard.setContents(
                            new ImageSelection(images[i]), ImagePalette.this);

                        curImage = i;
                        repaint();
                        break;
                    }
                }
            }
        }

        public void lostOwnership(Clipboard clipboard, Transferable contents) {
            // Remove border around current image.
            curImage = -1;
            repaint();
        }
    }

    class ImageSelection implements Transferable {
        // Initialize supported flavors.
        public static DataFlavor imageFlavor;

        private Image data;

        public ImageSelection(Image data) {
            this.data = data;
        }

        public synchronized DataFlavor[] getTransferDataFlavors() {
            return flavors;
        }

        public boolean isDataFlavorSupported(DataFlavor flavor) {
            return flavor.equals(imageFlavor);
        }

        public synchronized Object getTransferData(DataFlavor flavor)
                        throws UnsupportedFlavorException, IOException {
            if (flavor.equals(imageFlavor)) {
                return (Object)data;
            } else {
                throw new UnsupportedFlavorException(flavor);
            }
        }

        static {
            try {
                imageFlavor = new DataFlavor(
                    Class.forName("java.awt.Image"), "Java Image");
                imageFlavor.setHumanPresentableName("A Java Image Object");
            } catch (Exception e) {
            }
        }

        DataFlavor flavors[] = {imageFlavor};
    }
```

A
B
C
D
E
F
G
H
I
J
K
L
M
N
O
P
Q
R
S
T
U
V
W
X
Y
Z

getTransferData()

PURPOSE	Retrieves the data encapsulated in this transferable object.

SYNTAX   `public Object getTransferData(DataFlavor flavor) throws`
              `UnsupportedFlavorException, IOException`

DESCRIPTION   This method retrieves the transferable object's encapsulated data in the data
              flavor `flavor`.

PARAMETERS
  `flavor`   The non-`null` data flavor.

RETURNS   A possibly `null` object in the data flavor `flavor`.

EXCEPTIONS

`UnsupportedFlavorException`
              If `flavor` is neither `DataFlavor.stringFlavor` nor `DataFlavor.plain-`
              `TextFlavor`.

`IOException` If the data is no longer available.

SEE ALSO   `DataFlavor.getRepresentationClass()`.

EXAMPLE   See the class example for a class that implements this method. The following
              example retrieves and prints the contents of the clipboard in the string data fla-
              vor. The `System.exit()` method calls are necessary in this code to terminate
              the program. This is because retrieving a reference to the system clipboard pre-
              vents the process from terminating.

```
import java.awt.*;
import java.awt.datatransfer.*;
import java.io.*;

class Main {
    public static void main(String[] args) {
        Clipboard clipboard =
            Toolkit.getDefaultToolkit().getSystemClipboard();
        Transferable t = clipboard.getContents(null);

        if (t == null) {
            System.out.println("The clipboard is empty");
            System.exit(0);
        }
        try {
            String s = (String)t.getTransferData(DataFlavor.stringFlavor);

            System.out.println("-----------------------");
            System.out.println(s);
            System.out.println("-----------------------");
        } catch (IOException e) {
            System.out.println(
                "The data is no longer available in the string flavor");
        } catch (UnsupportedFlavorException e) {
            System.out.println(
```

A
B
C
D
E
F
G
H
I
J
K
L
M
N
O
P
Q
R
S
T
U
V
W
X
Y
Z

```
                         "The data is not available in the string flavor");
            }

            System.exit(0);
        }
    }
```

getTransferDataFlavors()

PURPOSE   Returns an array of data flavors that this transferable object supports.

SYNTAX   `public DataFlavor[] getTransferDataFlavors()`

DESCRIPTION   The data flavors in the returned array should be ordered in such a way that the more descriptive data flavors come first. For example, suppose a transferable object contains some rich text and allows the text to be delivered in the same rich text format or converted to plain text. The rich text data flavor should come before the plain text data flavor.

RETURNS   A non-`null` array of data flavors.

EXAMPLE   See the class example.

isDataFlavorSupported()

PURPOSE   Determines whether this object supports a particular data flavor.

SYNTAX   `public boolean isDataFlavorSupported(DataFlavor flavor)`

DESCRIPTION   This method determines whether `flavor` is one of the supported data flavors. The transferable object should use `DataFlavor.equals()` to determine equality.

PARAMETERS
flavor   The non-`null` desired flavor for the data.

RETURNS   `true` if the data flavor is supported; `false` otherwise.

EXAMPLE   See the class example.

UnsupportedFlavorException

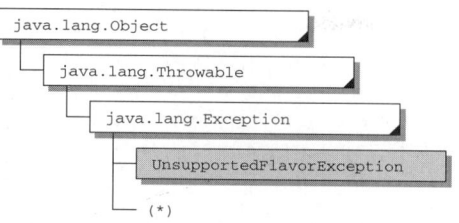

```
java.lang.Object
    java.lang.Throwable
        java.lang.Exception
            UnsupportedFlavorException
        (*)
```

(*) 28 classes from other packages not shown; see java.lang.Exception for complete listing.

A
B
C
D
E
F
G
H
I
J
K
L
M
N
O
P
Q
R
S
T
U
V
W
X
Y
Z

Syntax

public class UnsupportedFlavorException extends Exception

Description

This exception can be thrown when trying to retrieve data from a Transferable object. If the transferable object (see Transferable) cannot return the data in the desired flavor (see DataFlavor), the transferable object must throw this exception.

The Exception Message

The exception's message property contains the flavor's human presentable name (see DataFlavor.getHumanPresentableName()).

MEMBER SUMMARY	
Constructor	
UnsupportedFlavorException()	Constructs an UnsupportedFlavorException instance.

See Also

Clipboard, DataFlavor, Transferable.

Example

This example retrieves the clipboard contents as an illegal flavor called "chocolate." This causes Transferable.getTransferData() to throw the UnsupportedFlavorException.

For an example demonstrating how a transferable object throws this exception, see the Transferable class example.

```
import java.awt.*;
import java.awt.datatransfer.*;
import java.awt.event.*;
import java.io.*;

class Main extends Frame {
    // UnsupportedFlavorException Example
    public static void main(String[] args) {
        // Retrieve handle to clipboard and contents.
        Clipboard clipboard =
            Toolkit.getDefaultToolkit().getSystemClipboard();
        Transferable t = clipboard.getContents(null);

        if (t == null) {
            // The clipboard is empty
            System.exit(0);
        }
        try {
            t.getTransferData(new DataFlavor("chocolate", "chocolate"));
        } catch (UnsupportedFlavorException e) {
            System.out.println("This transferable object does not "
                +"support the "+e.getMessage() +" data flavor.");
        } catch (IOException e) {
            e.printStackTrace();
            System.out.println("The transferable data is "
                +"no longer available.");
        }
    }
}
```

UnsupportedFlavorException()

PURPOSE	Constructs an UnsupportedFlavorException instance.
SYNTAX	public UnsupportedFlavorException(DataFlavor flavor)
DESCRIPTION	This exception is generated by transferable objects when a request is made for an unsupported data flavor. The flavor parameter should be the one that was requested.
PARAMETERS	
flavor	The non-null unsupported data flavor.
EXAMPLE	See the Transferable class example.

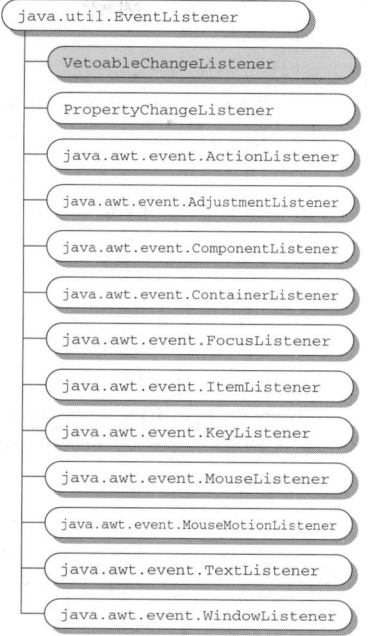

```
java.util.EventListener
    VetoableChangeListener
    PropertyChangeListener
    java.awt.event.ActionListener
    java.awt.event.AdjustmentListener
    java.awt.event.ComponentListener
    java.awt.event.ContainerListener
    java.awt.event.FocusListener
    java.awt.event.ItemListener
    java.awt.event.KeyListener
    java.awt.event.MouseListener
    java.awt.event.MouseMotionListener
    java.awt.event.TextListener
    java.awt.event.WindowListener
```

Syntax

`public interface VetoableChangeListener extends EventListener`

Description

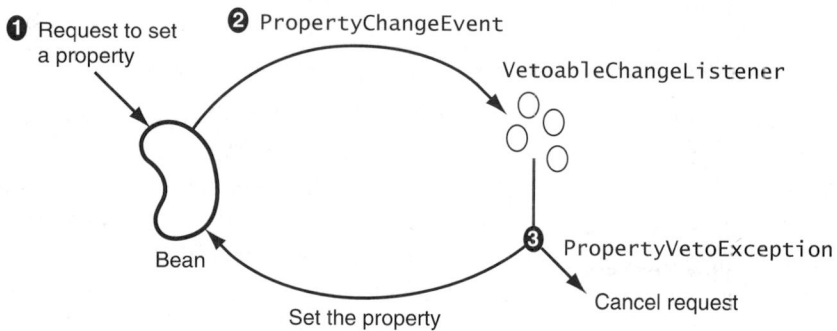

FIGURE 374: Constrained Property Event Flow.

When a constrained property in a bean (see Bean) is about to change, the bean will fire a property change event to notify listeners of the requested change. Any listener can *veto* the requested change, thereby cancelling the change. See Figure 374. To listen for these events, an object must define the method in this interface and then call the bean's `addVetoableChange-Listener()` method.

Vetoing Events

When a vetoable change listener receives the change property event, it can decide to *veto* the change request. It does this by throwing `PropertyVetoException`. Should this occur, the bean should not change the property value and should inform all vetoable change listeners that had received and not vetoed the event that the value was not changed. See Figure 374. See `VetoableChangeSupport.fireVetoableChange()` for more details about this process.

Extra Events

When a listener is removed from a bean's listener list, it should be prepared to receive a few more property change events. Whether it will receive the extra events depends on how the bean distributes events. In particular, a bean has the option of using a copy of the listener list while delivering events. If the listener is removed while an event is being delivered, it is removed from the main list but not from the copy. Since the listener is still in the copied list, it may receive the event.

MEMBER SUMMARY

Callback Method
`vetoableChange()`   Called whenever a bean's constrained property is about change.

See Also

`java.util.EventListener`, `PropertyChangeEvent`, `PropertyChangeListener`, `PropertyVetoException`, `VetoableChangeSupport`.

Example

This example demonstrates both an object that fires property change events (because a constrained property is about to change) and one that listens for those events.

This example implements an invisible bean that has one constrained property: "price." When the bean is created, it also creates a thread that constantly changes its price. When the price is about to change, the bean fires a property change event to notify its vetoable change listeners. The bean uses `VetoableChangeSupport` to implement the list of vetoable change listeners.

The `Main` object creates the bean and then listens for property change events. Whenever an event occurs, `Main` prints out the new price. However, if the new price exceeds $2.50, `Main` vetoes the change request.

Bean.java

```java
import java.awt.*;
import java.beans.*;

class Main implements VetoableChangeListener {
    Main() {
        Bean bean = null;

        try {
            // Create the bean.
            bean = (Bean)Beans.instantiate(Main.class.getClassLoader(), "Bean");
        } catch (Exception e) {
            e.printStackTrace();
        }
        bean.addVetoableChangeListener(this);
    }

    // Print the new price.  If too high, veto it.
    public void vetoableChange(PropertyChangeEvent evt)
        throws PropertyVetoException {
        float newPrice = ((Float)evt.getNewValue()).floatValue();

        System.out.print(evt.getPropertyName() + ": " + newPrice);

        // Don't let the price go up to more than $2.50
        if (newPrice > 2.50f) {
            System.out.println(" VETO");
            throw(new PropertyVetoException("Too Much!", evt));
        } else {
            System.out.println();
        }
    }

    public static void main(String args[]) {
        new Main();
    }
}

public class Bean implements Runnable {
    float price = 1.49f;

    // Constructor
    public Bean() {
        (new Thread(this)).start();
    }

    // The price is a constrained property.
    public float getPrice() {
        return price;
    }

    public void setPrice(float newPrice) {
        try {
            vceListeners.fireVetoableChange("price",
                new Float(price), new Float(newPrice));
            price = newPrice;
        } catch (PropertyVetoException e) {
            // Don't change the price
            PropertyChangeEvent pce = e.getPropertyChangeEvent();
            System.out.print("Some listener didn't like the new price "
```

A
B
C
D
E
F
G
H
I
J
K
L
M
N
O
P
Q
R
S
T
U
V
W
X
Y
Z

A
B
C
D
E
F
G
H
I
J
K
L
M
N
O
P
Q
R
S
T
U
V
W
X
Y
Z

```
                                    + ((Float)pce.getNewValue()).floatValue());
                    System.out.println(" - " + e.getMessage());
                }
            }

            // Create the listener list.
            VetoableChangeSupport vceListeners =
                new VetoableChangeSupport(this);

            // The listener list wrapper methods.
            public synchronized void addVetoableChangeListener(
                                        VetoableChangeListener l) {
                vceListeners.addVetoableChangeListener(l);
            }
            public synchronized void removeVetoableChangeListener(
                                        VetoableChangeListener l) {
                vceListeners.removeVetoableChangeListener(l);
            }

            public void run() {
                try {
                    while (true) {
                        // Change price up or down by .50.
                        setPrice(Math.max(1.0f, price + .5f - (float)Math.random()));

                        Thread.sleep(500);
                    }
                } catch (Exception e) {
                    e.printStackTrace();
                }
            }
        }
```

Output
```
    price: 2.1139786
    price: 1.9831498
    price: 2.2478595
    price: 2.6623638
    VETO price: 2.2478595
    Some listener didn't like the new price 2.6623638 - Too Much!
    price: 2.4985642
    price: 2.3612332
```

vetoableChange()

PURPOSE   Called whenever a bean's constrained property is about change.

SYNTAX   void vetoableChange(PropertyChangeEvent evt) throws
                 PropertyVetoException

DESCRIPTION This method is called when the source bean fires a property change event just
             before a constrained property is about to be changed. See PropertyChange-
             Event for details.

If the listener wants to veto the property change request, it should throw `PropertyVetoException`. See the class description for more details.

This method may be called a few more times even after the listener is removed from the bean's listener list. See the class description for details.

PARAMETERS

evt   A non-`null` property change event.

EXCEPTIONS

`PropertyVetoException`

If a change is being vetoed by a listener.

VetoableChangeSupport

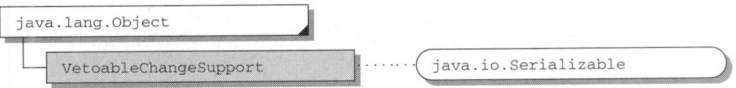

Syntax

```
public class VetoableChangeSupport implements Serializable
```

Description

Any bean that has constrained properties (see `Beans`) must be able to deliver vetoable property change events (see `PropertyChangeEvent`). This involves maintaining a list of vetoable change event listeners and delivering events to those listeners. This class can be used by a bean to maintain the listener list and to deliver the events.

There are two ways a bean can use this class. First, the bean can extend this class. This is not typical, however, since it prevents the bean from inheriting other useful classes such as `Component`. The second, and typical way, is for the bean to create an instance of this class and provide wrapper methods for `addVetoableChangeListener()` and `removeVetoableChangeListener()`. These bean methods should simply call the methods in this class that have the same names.

Extra Events

After a listener is removed from the listener list, the listener might still receive more vetoable property change events. This is due to the way `fireVetoableChange()` is implemented. In particular, it makes a copy of the listener list just before it delivers a new event. If a listener is removed while an event is being delivered, the listener is removed from the main listener list but not from the copy. Since the listener is still in the copied list, it may receive the event. The removed listener may also receive an extra vetoable property change event if the event was vetoed by some other listener.

Vetoed Events

As a bean is delivering a vetoable property change event to all of the vetoable change listeners, a listener may decide to veto the event. It does so by throwing `PropertyVetoException`. Should this occur, the bean should stop the delivery of the event to the remaining listeners. It should then inform all of the change listeners who had received and not vetoed the event that the value was not changed. See `fireVetoableChange()` for details on exactly how it implements this reversion process.

MEMBER SUMMARY	
Constructor	
VetoableChangeSupport()	Constructs a new VetoableChangeSupport instance.
Listener Methods	
addVetoableChangeListener()	Adds a listener for receiving vetoable property change events.
removeVetoableChangeListener()	Stops a listener from receiving vetoable property change events.
Event Method	
fireVetoableChange()	Delivers a vetoable property change event to the listeners.

See Also

java.io.Serializable, PropertyChangeSupport, VetoableChangeListener.

Example

See the VetoableChangeListener class example.

addVetoableChangeListener()

PURPOSE   Adds a listener for receiving vetoable property change events.

SYNTAX   public synchronized void
              addVetoableChangeListener(VetoableChangeListener listener)

DESCRIPTION   This method adds listener to the listener list. If listener is null, the
              method call is ignored. The method does not check if listener has already
              been added, so a listener can be added to the list more than once.

PARAMETERS
listener   A possibly null vetoable change event listener.

SEE ALSO   removeVetoableChangeListener().

EXAMPLE   See the VetoableChangeListener class example.

fireVetoableChange()

PURPOSE   Delivers a vetoable property change event to the listeners.

SYNTAX   `public void fireVetoableChange(String propertyName, Object oldValue, Object newValue) throws PropertyVetoException`

DESCRIPTION   The `oldValue` parameter is the current value of the constrained property. The `newValue` parameter is the requested new value of the constrained property.

This method creates a new property change event and delivers it to all listeners. If a listener throws `PropertyVetoException`, this method will stop delivering the event and then undo the changes. In particular, it creates another property change event in which its old value is `newValue` and the new value is `oldValue`. It then delivers this new event to the entire list of listeners. (A more efficient policy might be to deliver only to the listeners that received the vetoed event.) During this process, all `PropertyVetoExceptions` are ignored. After all listeners have been notified of the vetoed event, this method throws the vetoed event.

This method first checks if `oldValue` and `newValue` are equal. If they are, the method call is ignored. The two values are equal if

`oldValue != null && oldValue.equals(newValue).`

If they are not equal, a new property change event is created with the values `propertyName`, `oldValue`, and `newValue`. The event's source is the one that was used when this class was created. This new event is delivered to each listener.

The parameter `propertyName` can be `null`, which indicates that this is a multichange event (see `PropertyChangeEvent` for details). In this case, `oldValue` and `newValue` will also be `null`.

After a listener is removed from the listener list, it might still receive more vetoable property change events. See the class description for more details.

PARAMETERS

`newValue`   The possibly `null` requested new value of the property.

`oldValue`   The possibly `null` old value of the property.

`propertyName`A possibly `null` property name.

EXAMPLE   See the `VetoableChangeListener` class example.

removeVetoableChangeListener()

PURPOSE	Stops a listener from receiving vetoable property change events.
SYNTAX	`public synchronized void` `    removeVetoableChangeListener(VetoableChangeListener listener)`
DESCRIPTION	This method removes `listener` from the listener list. If `listener` is `null` or not in the listener list, the method call is ignored.
	The removed listener should be prepared to receive a few more vetoable property change events. See the class description for more details.
PARAMETERS	
`listener`	A possibly `null` vetoable change event listener.
SEE ALSO	`addVetoableChangeListener()`.
EXAMPLE	See the `VetoableChangeListener` class example.

VetoableChangeSupport()

PURPOSE	Constructs a new `VetoableChangeSupport` instance.
SYNTAX	`public VetoableChangeSupport(Object source)`
DESCRIPTION	This method creates a new vetoable change support object and records `source` as the object that will be firing vetoable property change events. The source object will always be included in every new event that is fired by `fireVetoableChange()`. The source object cannot be changed.
PARAMETERS	
`source`	The non-`null` bean that will be generating vetoable property change events.
SEE ALSO	`fireVetoableChange()`.
EXAMPLE	See the `VetoableChangeListener` class example.

A
B
C
D
E
F
G
H
I
J
K
L
M
N
O
P
Q
R
S
T
U
V
W
X
Y
Z

Visibility

Syntax

```
public interface Visibility
```

Description

This interface can be implemented by beans that can be run on servers that may or may not have a display or window system. For example, a timer bean could read its settings from a configuration file if a window system was unavailable. Otherwise, it would display a graphical user interface for setting the timing variables.

This interface is not meant for the typical bean. Hence, to avoid confusing bean users, the get*PropertyName* and set*PropertyName* method signature patterns are not used for the methods in this interface.

UseGUI Flag

A bean that implements this interface should maintain a useGUI flag, which determines whether the bean can display a graphical user interface (GUI). The methods in this interface query and set this flag. The flag should be initialized to false.

MEMBER SUMMARY	
GUI Methods	
avoidingGui()	Determines if the bean can display a GUI.
dontUseGui()	Instructs the bean not to display a GUI.
needsGui()	Determines if the bean must display a GUI.
okToUseGui()	Instructs the bean that it can display a GUI.

Example

This example implements a bean that can display a window containing a message if a GUI is available. If a GUI is not available, the bean prints to standard out. To run the bean with a GUI, invoke the command

```
java Main yes
```

To run the bean without a GUI, invoke the command

```
java Main no
```

Main.java
```java
import java.beans.*;

class Main {
    public static void main(String[] args) {
        Bean bean = null;

        if (args.length != 1) {
            System.out.println("Usage: java Main [yes|no]");
            System.exit(1);
        }

        // Should the bean use a gui?
        boolean useGui = args[0].equals("yes");

        Beans.setGuiAvailable(useGui);

        try {
            // Create the bean.
            bean = (Bean)Beans.instantiate(Main.class.getClassLoader(), "Bean");
        } catch (Exception e) {
            e.printStackTrace();
            System.err.println("Failed to create bean.");
            System.exit(1);
        }

        if (Beans.isGuiAvailable()) {
            bean.okToUseGui();
        } else {
            bean.dontUseGui();
        }
    }
}
```

Bean.java
```java
import java.beans.*;

public class Bean implements Runnable, Visibility {
    boolean dontUseGui = true;

    public Bean() {
        (new Thread(this)).start();
    }

    public boolean needsGui() {
        return false;
    }
    public void dontUseGui() {
        dontUseGui = true;
    }
    public void okToUseGui() {
        dontUseGui = false;
    }
    public boolean avoidingGui() {
        return dontUseGui;
```

```
                    }

                MessageFrame frame;
                public void run() {
                    while (true) {
                        try {
                            if (Math.random() > .9944) {
                                if (!avoidingGui() && (frame == null ||
                                    !frame.isShowing())) {
                                    frame = new MessageFrame("JACKPOT!!!");
                                } else {
                                    System.out.println("JACKPOT!!!");
                                }
                            }
                            Thread.sleep(100);
                        } catch (Exception e) {
                        }
                    }
                }
            }
```

MessageFrame.java

```
        import java.awt.*;
        import java.awt.event.*;

        public class MessageFrame extends Frame implements ActionListener {
            MessageFrame(String msg) {
                super("Message");

                // Create the components.
                Button b = new Button("OK");
                Label l = new Label(msg, Label.CENTER) {
                    // This adds some space around the text.
                    public Dimension getPreferredSize() {
                        Dimension d = super.getPreferredSize();
                        return new Dimension(d.width+40, d.height+40);
                    }
                };

                // Listen for events.
                b.addActionListener(this);
                addWindowListener(new WindowEventHandler());

                // Layout components.
                add(l, BorderLayout.NORTH);
                add(b, BorderLayout.SOUTH);

                pack();
                show();
            }

            public void actionPerformed(ActionEvent evt) {
                dispose();
            }

            class WindowEventHandler extends WindowAdapter {
                public void windowClosing(WindowEvent evt) {
                    dispose();
                }
            }
        }
```

avoidingGui()

PURPOSE	Determines if the bean can display a GUI.
SYNTAX	`boolean avoidingGui()`
RETURNS	`true` if the bean cannot display a GUI; `false` otherwise.
EXAMPLE	See the class example.

dontUseGui()

PURPOSE	Instructs the bean not to display a GUI.
SYNTAX	`void dontUseGui()`
DESCRIPTION	This method sets the `useGUI` flag to `false`. When the flag is `false`, the bean cannot create a GUI.
EXAMPLE	See the class example.

needsGui()

PURPOSE	Determines if the bean must display a GUI.
SYNTAX	`boolean needsGui()`
DESCRIPTION	This method should be implemented to return `true` if the bean must display a GUI. If the bean does not have a GUI or does not have to display a GUI, this method should return `false`.
RETURNS	`true` if the bean must display a GUI; `false` otherwise.
EXAMPLE	See the class example.

okToUseGui()

PURPOSE	Instructs the bean that it can display a GUI.
SYNTAX	`void okToUseGui()`
DESCRIPTION	This method sets the `useGui` flag to `true`. When the flag is `true`, the bean is allowed to create and present a GUI if it wants to.
EXAMPLE	See the class example.

A
B
C
D
E
F
G
H
I
J
K
L
M
N
O
P
Q
R
S
T
U
W
X
Y
Z

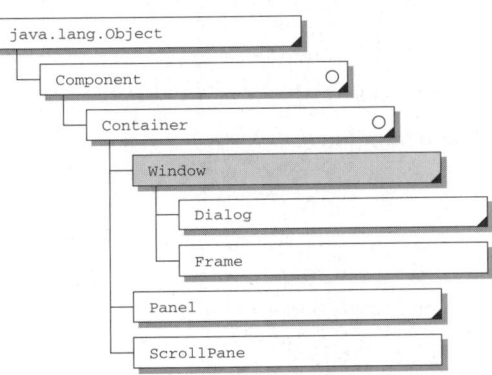

Syntax

`public class Window extends Container`

Description

A *window* is a top-level window that has no title, menu bar, or border. It could be used to implement a popup window.

The Warning Message Property

The warning message is a string that is displayed in a nonsecure window; it is not displayed in secure windows. A nonsecure window is a window that has a security manager installed and for which calling `SecurityManager.checkTopLevelWinow()` yields `false`. The warning message is displayed somewhere in the window and cannot be hidden or disguised by the application. This prevents an application from disguising a window to look like a critical window, such as a login window, in order to steal information. Figure 375 shows a nonsecure window on the Windows platform.

FIGURE 375:   A Non-secure Window.

The default warning message string is retrieved from the `awt.appletWarning` system property. See the `Properties` class for more details about system properties.

Coordinates, Sizes, and Insets

The insets for a window are normally (0, 0, 0, 0) because a window has no title, menu bar, or border. However, if the window has a warning message that is displayed, the insets can be non-zero.

The Peer Hierarchy

The peers for most AWT components require that both the component's parent and its peer exist. The window component (and its subclasses) is the exception. The window's peer can be created even if it does not have a parent. This means that the other components need to have a window at the root of their ancestor chain before their peers can be created.

The Toolkit Property

A *toolkit* is a factory that creates AWT components such as buttons, scrollbars, and windows. The default toolkit that AWT uses supplies components that use the platform's native windowing toolkit. For example, when running an AWT application on Windows 95, the default toolkit creates wrappers around Windows controls, while on Motif, the default toolkit creates wrappers around Motif widgets.

Events

A window fires all of the events fired by the `Container` class. It also fires window events. A window event occurs when the window is closed/opened or iconified/deiconified or when it gains/loses focus. See `WindowEvent` for more details. See `AWTEvent` for details on events and how to filter and handle them.

A B C D E F G H I J K L M N O P Q R S T U V **W** X Y Z

MEMBER SUMMARY

Constructor

`Window()`	Constructs a new `Window` instance.

Event Methods

`addWindowListener()`	Adds a listener for receiving events fired by this window.
`processEvent()`	Processes an event enabled for this window.
`processWindowEvent()`	Processes a window event enabled for this window.
`removeWindowListener()`	Removes a listener from receiving events fired by this window.

Focus Method

`getFocusOwner()`	Retrieves the component in this window that has the focus.

Property Methods

`getLocale()`	Retrieves this window's locale.
`getToolkit()`	Retrieves this window's toolkit.
`getWarningString()`	Retrieves this window's warning message.

Continued

MEMBER SUMMARY

Visibility Methods

show()	Makes this window visible.
toBack()	Moves this window behind all other windows.
toFront()	Moves this window in front of all other windows.

Peer Methods

addNotify()	Creates this window's peer hierarchy.
dispose()	Destroys this window's peer hierarchy.

Layout Method

pack()	Resizes this window to its preferred size.

Example

This example displays characters represented by a range of Unicode values on a mouse-sensitive canvas. Rolling the mouse over a character displays the character's Unicode value on the status bar above the canvas.

You can display a different range of Unicode values by entering a 32-bit hexadecimal number in the text field that is supplied and then pressing Return. Otherwise, the next block of unicode characters will be displayed (the size of a block is the number of visible rows of characters).

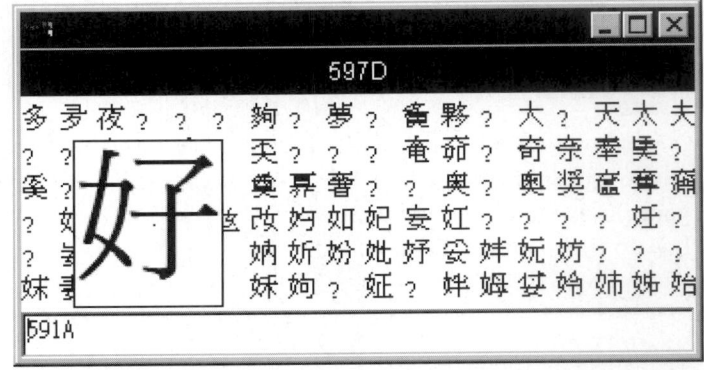

FIGURE 376:   **Window for Rendering Unicode Characters.**

When you click a character, the character is displayed in a popup window. The popup window is visible only while the mouse is pressed. See Figure 376.

Note: In Java 1.1.2, the window must listen for mouse up events in order to dispose of itself. This is because the component that received the mouse pressed event does not receive the mouse up event because of the newly created popup window. This will be fixed in a later release.

```java
import java.awt.*;
import java.awt.event.*;

class Main extends Frame implements ActionListener {
    TextField inputTf = new TextField();
    Label statusBar = new Label("", Label.CENTER);
```

```
    CharDisplay charDisplay = new CharDisplay(statusBar);

    Main() {
        // Set up listeners.
        inputTf.addActionListener(this);

        // Initialize status bar.
        statusBar.setForeground(Color.white);
        statusBar.setBackground(Color.black);

        // Layout components.
        add(statusBar, BorderLayout.NORTH);
        add(charDisplay, BorderLayout.CENTER);
        add(inputTf, BorderLayout.SOUTH);
        setSize(400, 400);
        show();
    }

    char oldCode = (char)-1;
    public void actionPerformed(ActionEvent evt) {
        // Change starting code.
        char code = (char)Integer.parseInt(inputTf.getText(), 16);

        if (code == oldCode) {
            code = charDisplay.nextPage();
        } else {
            charDisplay.setStartCode(code);
        }
        inputTf.setText(Integer.toHexString(code).toUpperCase());
        oldCode = code;
    }

    public static void main(String[] args) {
        new Main();
    }
}

class CharDisplay extends Canvas {
    char startCode;
    Label statusBar;
    int charW;
    int charH;
    int charsPerLine = 32;

    Font font = new Font("Monospaced", Font.PLAIN, 14);
    FontMetrics fontM;

    CharDisplay(Label statusBar) {
        this.statusBar = statusBar;

        // Set up font information.
        setFont(font);
        fontM = getFontMetrics(font);
        charW = fontM.getMaxAdvance();
        charH = fontM.getHeight();

        // Listen for mouse events.
        addMouseListener(new MouseEventHandler());
        addMouseMotionListener(new MouseMotionEventHandler());
    }
```

A
B
C
D
E
F
G
H
I
J
K
L
M
N
O
P
Q
R
S
T
U
V
W
X
Y
Z

```
              // Sets the starting code.
              void setStartCode(char startCode) {
                  this.startCode = startCode;
                  repaint();
              }

              char nextPage() {
                  startCode += charsPerLine * size().height/charH;
                  repaint();
                  return startCode;
              }

              public void paint(Graphics g) {
                  int s = startCode;
                  int y = 0;
                  int lines = size().height/fontM.getHeight();
                  char[] buf = new char[1];
                  Rectangle clip = g.getClipBounds();

                  // The following could also be used to retrieve the clipping area.
                  // Rectangle clip = g.getClip();

                  // Grow the clipping area to include surrounding characters.
                  if (clip != null) {
                      clip.x -= charW;
                      clip.width += 2 * charW;
                      clip.y -= charH;
                      clip.height += 2 * charH;
                  }

                  for (int i=0; i<lines; i++) {
                      // Fill one line with character.
                      for (int j=0; j<charsPerLine; j++) {
                          buf[0] = (char)s++;
                          // Don't paint the character if not in the clipping area.
                          if (clip == null || clip.contains(j*charW, y)) {
                              g.drawChars(buf, 0, 1, j*charW, y+fontM.getAscent());
                          }
                      }
                      y += charH;
                  }
              }

              class MouseEventHandler extends MouseAdapter {
                  Window window;

                  public void mousePressed(MouseEvent evt) {
                      char code = (char)(evt.getX()/charW
                          + evt.getY()/charH * charsPerLine
                          + startCode);

                      Component c = CharDisplay.this;
                      while (!(c instanceof Frame)) {
                          c = c.getParent();
                      }

                      // Display the window
                      Point pt = getLocationOnScreen();
                      pt.translate(evt.getX(), evt.getY());
```

A
B
C
D
E
F
G
H
I
J
K
L
M
N
O
P
Q
R
S
T
U
V
W
X
Y
Z

```
                window = new LargeChar(code, (Frame)c, pt);
        }
        public void mouseReleased(MouseEvent evt) {
            window.dispose();
        }
    }

    class MouseMotionEventHandler extends MouseMotionAdapter {
        public void mouseMoved(MouseEvent evt) {
            int code = evt.getX()/charW
                + evt.getY()/charH * charsPerLine
                + startCode;

            statusBar.setText(Integer.toHexString(code).toUpperCase());
        }
    }
}

class LargeChar extends Window {
    FontMetrics fontM;
    char ch;

    LargeChar(char ch, Frame frame, Point pt) {
        super(frame);
        this.ch = ch;

        Font font = new Font("Monospaced", Font.BOLD, 72);
        fontM = getFontMetrics(font);
        setFont(font);

        // Listen for mouse events.
        addMouseListener(new MouseEventHandler());

        // Set bounds and show.
        setSize(fontM.charWidth(ch)+2, fontM.getHeight()+2);
        setLocation(pt.x-size().width/2, pt.y-size().height/2);
        show();
    }

    public void paint(Graphics g) {
        g.drawString(""+ch, 1, fontM.getAscent()+1);
        g.drawRect(0, 0, size().width-1, size().height-1);
    }

    class MouseEventHandler extends MouseAdapter {
        public void mouseReleased(MouseEvent evt) {
            dispose();
        }
    }
}
```

A

B

C

D

E

F

G

H

I

J

K

L

M

N

O

P

Q

R

S

T

U

V

W

X

Y

Z

A
B
C
D
E
F
G
H
I
J
K
L
M
N
O
P
Q
R
S
T
U
V
W
X
Y
Z

addNotify()

PURPOSE	Creates this window's peer hierarchy.
SYNTAX	`public void addNotify()`
DESCRIPTION	This method creates this window's peer hierarchy, if necessary. The window's peer is created by calling the `Toolkit.createWindow()` method. This method should be called before the window's minimum or preferred size is calculated. The methods `pack()` and `show()` automatically call `addNotify()`.
OVERRIDES	`Container.addNotify()`.
SEE ALSO	`Component.addNotify()`.
EXAMPLE	See `Component.setVisible()`.

addWindowListener()

PURPOSE	Adds a listener to receive window events fired by this window.
SYNTAX	`public synchronized void addWindowListener(WindowListener listener)`
DESCRIPTION	See `WindowEvent` and the class description for more details on window events. After this method is called, the window listener `listener` will receive window events fired by this window. If `listener` is `null`, this method does nothing.
PARAMETERS	
`listener`	The possibly `null` window listener to add.
SEE ALSO	`java.awt.event.WindowEvent`, `java.awt.event.WindowListener`, `removeWindowListener()`.
EXAMPLE	See the `WindowEvent` class example.

dispose()

PURPOSE	Destroys this window's peer hierarchy.
SYNTAX	`public void dispose()`
DESCRIPTION	This window's peer hierarchy is destroyed, if it exists, thereby freeing any resources used by the peers. The state of the window hierarchy is left intact and can be reused. The peer hierarchy can be restored by calling `addNotify()`.
EXAMPLE	See the class example.

getFocusOwner()

PURPOSE   Retrieves the component in this window that has the focus.

SYNTAX   `public Component getFocusOwner()`

DESCRIPTION   If this window is active, then one of the components within this window has the focus.

RETURNS   The component with the focus; `null` if no component in this window has the focus.

SEE ALSO   `Component.requestFocus()`, `Component.transferFocus()`, `java.awt.event.FocusEvent`.

EXAMPLE   This example creates a window that has various buttons and text fields. Use the Tab or Shift-Tab keys to change the focus among components. The program prints, every 5 sec, the component that has the focus. If the window is not selected, `null` is printed as the focus owner. See Figure 377.

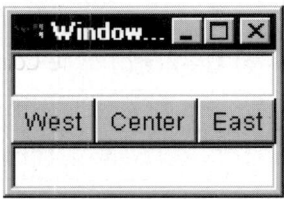

FIGURE 377:   Determining the Focus Owner.

```java
import java.awt.*;

class Main extends Frame implements Runnable {
    Main() {
        super ("Window.getFocusOwner() Example");

        add(new TextField(), BorderLayout.NORTH);
        add(new Button("West"), BorderLayout.WEST);
        add(new Button("Center"), BorderLayout.CENTER);
        add(new Button("East"), BorderLayout.EAST);
        add(new TextField(), BorderLayout.SOUTH);

        pack();
        show();

        (new Thread(this)).start();
    }

    public void run() {
        while (true) {
            try {
                System.out.println("focus owner = " + getFocusOwner());
                Thread.sleep(5000);
            } catch (InterruptedException e) {
            }
        }
    }

    static public void main(String[] args) {
        new Main();
    }
}
```

A
B
C
D
E
F
G
H
I
J
K
L
M
N
O
P
Q
R
S
T
U
V
W
X
Y
Z

getLocale()

PURPOSE	Retrieves this window's locale.
SYNTAX	`public Locale getLocale()`
RETURNS	This window's locale if it has been set; otherwise, the Java runtime's default locale.
OVERRIDES	`Component.getLocale()`.
SEE ALSO	`Component.setLocale()`, `java.util.Locale.getDefault()`.
EXAMPLE	See `Component.getName()`.

getToolkit()

PURPOSE	Retrieves this window's toolkit.
SYNTAX	`public Toolkit getToolkit()`
DESCRIPTION	This method calls `Toolkit.getDefaultToolkit()` and returns the result. If a window implements its own toolkit, it should override this method to return its own toolkit.
RETURNS	This window's toolkit.
OVERRIDES	`Component.getToolkit()`.
SEE ALSO	`Toolkit.getDefaultToolkit()`.
EXAMPLE	See `Toolkit`.

getWarningString()

PURPOSE	Retrieves this window's warning message.
SYNTAX	`public final String getWarningString()`
RETURNS	The warning message. A return value of `null` means the window is a secure window.

FIGURE 378: `Window.getWarningString()`.

EXAMPLE	This example implements an applet that creates a window.

With most browsers, the security manager forces a warning message to be displayed on any external window that an applet creates. In this example, the external window simply displays the warning message in its center. See Figure 378. Notice that the window's insets are used to calculate the center of the window's paintable area. The insets of a window are normally all zero, since a window does not have any window decorations such as a title or border. The only exception is when the window displays a warning message.

```java
import java.awt.*;
import java.awt.event.*;
import java.applet.*;
public class Main extends Applet {
    MyWindow w;

    public void init() {
        // Find the applet's frame.
        Component f = getParent();
        while (f != null && !(f instanceof Frame)) {
            f = f.getParent();
        }

        w = new MyWindow((Frame)f);
        w.setBounds(0, 0, 200, 200);
        w.show();
    }

    public void start() {
        w.show();
    }

    public void stop() {
        w.setVisible(false);
    }

    public void destroy() {
        if (w != null) {
            w.dispose();
            w = null;
        }
    }
}

class MyWindow extends Window {
    MyWindow(Frame frame) {
        super(frame);
        this.addMouseListener(new MouseEventHandler());
    }

    public void paint(Graphics g) {
        FontMetrics fm = g.getFontMetrics();
        String s = getWarningString();
        int w = getSize().width - getInsets().left - getInsets().right;
        int h = getSize().height - getInsets().top - getInsets().bottom;

        if (s != null) {
            g.drawString(s, (w-fm.stringWidth(s))/2,
                (h-fm.getHeight())/2 + fm.getAscent());
        }
    }
```

A
B
C
D
E
F
G
H
I
J
K
L
M
N
O
P
Q
R
S
T
U
V
W
X
Y
Z

```
class MouseEventHandler extends MouseAdapter {
    public void mousePressed(MouseEvent evt) {
        setVisible(false);
    }
}
```

Input   Here is the HTML necessary to start the applet:

```
<applet code=Main width=100 height=100>
</applet>
```

pack()

PURPOSE   Resizes this window to its preferred size.

SYNTAX   `public void pack()`

DESCRIPTION   This method resizes this window to its preferred size. It calls the `addNotify()` method before the window's preferred size is calculated. This is important to note because the preferred size of some components is valid only if the component's peer exists.

SEE ALSO   `Container.getPreferredSize()`.

EXAMPLE   See show().

postEvent()   *DEPRECATED*

PURPOSE   Replaced by `Component.dispatchEvent()`.

SYNTAX   `public boolean postEvent(Event evt)`

PARAMETERS
`evt`   The non-`null` event.

RETURNS   `false` if the event should be passed up to the component's parent; `true` otherwise.

OVERRIDES   `Component.postEvent()`.

DEPRECATION   See `Component.postEvent()` for how to replace deprecated usage of this method.

processEvent()

PURPOSE	Processes an event enabled for this window.
SYNTAX	`protected void processEvent(AWTEvent evt)`
	This method extends `Container.processEvent()` by adding support for `WindowEvent`. When a subclass overrides `processEvent()`, it should call `super.processEvent()` to perform the processing intended by its base class (such as dispatching the types of events to its listeners).
PARAMETERS*	
evt	The event to be processed.
OVERRIDES	`Container.processEvent()`.
SEE ALSO	`AWTEvent, processWindowEvent()`.
EXAMPLE	See the `Component` class example.

processWindowEvent()

PURPOSE	Processes a window event enabled for this window.
SYNTAX	`protected void processWindowEvent(IWindowEvent evt)`
DESCRIPTION	See `WindowEvent` and the class description for more details on window events. This method processes window events for this window by calling any registered `WindowListener`. This method is invoked only if window events have been enabled for this window. This can happen either when a window listener is added to this window or if window events are enabled explicitly via `Component.enableEvents()`.
	Typically, a program controls how window events for a choice are processed by adding or removing window listeners. It overrides `processWindowEvent()` only if it needs to do processing in addition to that performed by the registered listeners.
	When a subclass does override `processWindowEvent()`, it should call `super.processWindowEvent()` to perform the processing intended by its base class (such as dispatching its listeners).
PARAMETERS	
evt	The non-`null` window event to be processed.
OVERRIDES	`Container.processEvent()`.
SEE ALSO	`java.awt.event.WindowEvent, java.awt.event.WindowListener, processEvent()`.
EXAMPLE	See `AWTEventMulticaster.windowActivated()`.

A
B
C
D
E
F
G
H
I
J
K
L
M
N
O
P
Q
R
S
T
U
V
W
X
Y
Z

A
B
C
D
E
F
G
H
I
J
K
L
M
N
O
P
Q
R
S
T
U
V
W
X
Y
Z

removeWindowListener()

PURPOSE Removes a listener from receiving window events from this window.

SYNTAX `public synchronized void removeWindowListener(WindowListener`
`listener)`

DESCRIPTION See `WindowEvent` and the class description for more details on window events. After this method is called, the window listener `listener` will no longer receive window events from this window. If `listener` is `null`, this method does nothing.

PARAMETERS

listener The possibly `null` window listener to remove.

SEE ALSO `addWindowListener()`, `java.awt.event.WindowEvent`,
`java.awt.event.WindowListener`.

EXAMPLE See `removeActionListener()` in `MenuItem.disableEvents()`.

show()

PURPOSE Makes this window visible.

SYNTAX `public void show()`

DESCRIPTION This method calls the `addNotify()` method, validates the window's layout, and then makes the window visible. The window does not necessarily appear in front of all other windows; the exact behavior is platform-dependent. To force the window to be displayed in front of all other windows, call the `toFront()` method. If the window is already visible, the window is brought to the front.

OVERRIDES `Component.show()`.

SEE ALSO `Component.setVisible()`.

EXAMPLE This example creates a window that has a button that, when pressed, hides the window. The window reappears within 5 sec. See Figure 379.

FIGURE 379:
Window Visibility.

```
import java.awt.*;
import java.awt.event.*;

class MainWindow extends Window implements Runnable, ActionListener {
    MainWindow(Frame parent) {
        super(parent);
        Button b = new Button("Hide");
        b.addActionListener(this);
        add(b, BorderLayout.CENTER);
        setSize(100, 50);
```

```
        show();
        (new Thread(this)).start();
    }

    // Hides window when button is pressed
    public void actionPerformed(ActionEvent evt) {
        setVisible(false);
    }

    public void run() {
        while (true) {
            try {
                show();
                Thread.sleep(5000);
            } catch (InterruptedException e) {};
        }
    }
}

class Main {
    static public void main(String[] args) {
        new MainWindow(new Frame());
    }
}
```

toBack()

PURPOSE   Moves the window behind all other windows.

SYNTAX   `public void toBack()`

DESCRIPTION   The window is moved behind all windows in the system, regardless of whether they are AWT windows. The position of the window with respect to other windows is not necessarily maintained; the exact behavior is platform-dependent. For example, if the window was behind some windows, hidden, and then is shown again, it may not reappear behind the same windows.

SEE ALSO   `toFront()`.

EXAMPLE   See `toFront()`.

toFront()

PURPOSE   Moves the window in front of all other windows.

SYNTAX   `public void toFront()`

DESCRIPTION   The window is moved in front of all other windows in the system, regardless of whether they are AWT windows.

EXAMPLE   This example creates a window that has a button that sends the window to the back. The window returns to the front within 5 sec. See Figure 380.

FIGURE 380:
Window.toFront().

```java
import java.awt.*;
import java.awt.event.*;

class MainWindow extends Window implements Runnable,
ActionListener {
    MainWindow(Frame parent) {
        super(parent);
        Button b = new Button("Back");
        b.addActionListener(this);
        add(b, BorderLayout.CENTER);
        setSize(100, 50);
        show();
        (new Thread(this)).start();
    }

    // Hides window when button is pressed
    public void actionPerformed(ActionEvent evt) {
        toBack();
    }

    public void run() {
        while (true) {
            try {
                toFront();
                Thread.sleep(5000);
            } catch (InterruptedException e) {};
        }
    }
}

class Main {
    static public void main(String[] args) {
        new MainWindow(new Frame());
    }
}
```

Window()

PURPOSE   Constructs a new `Window` instance.

SYNTAX   `public Window(Frame parent)`

DESCRIPTION   This constructor creates a new invisible, modeless `Window` instance that has the parent `parent`. The new window has a border layout manager.

PARAMETERS

parent   The non-`null` owner of the window.

EXCEPTIONS

`IllegalArgumentException`

> If parent is null.

SEE ALSO

`BorderLayout`, `java.lang.IllegalArgumentException`, `show()`.

EXAMPLE

This example demonstrates how to create a popup window. Clicking the frame creates a window at the point of the click. Releasing the mouse button disposes of the window. See Figure 381. Notice that a mouse listener must be installed for the popup window in addition to the mouse listener for the main frame. This is because sometimes two consecutive mouse downs will create two popups, the first of which can only be disposed by its own mouse listener.

FIGURE 381:   A Popup Window.

```java
import java.awt.*;
import java.awt.event.*;

class Main extends Frame {
    PopupWindow pm = null;
    Main() {
        super("Window Example");

        // Install listener
        this.addMouseListener(new MouseEventHandler());

        setSize(100, 100);
        show();
    }

    class MouseEventHandler extends MouseAdapter {
        public void mousePressed(MouseEvent evt) {
            Rectangle r = getBounds();
            int x = evt.getX();
            int y = evt.getY();

            // Create popup at position of mouse
            pm = new PopupWindow(Main.this);
            pm.setBounds(r.x + x, r.y + y, 100, 50);
            pm.show();
        }

        public void mouseReleased(MouseEvent evt) {
            if (pm != null) {
                // get rid of peer
                pm.dispose();
```

```
                              pm = null;
                      }
              }
      }

      static public void main(String[] args) {
          new Main();
      }
}

class PopupWindow extends Window {
    PopupWindow(Frame f) {
        super(f);
        setBackground(Color.yellow);

        // Listener to remove popup when mouse button released.
        // Need listener within popup menu because popup menu is modal.
        this.addMouseListener(new MouseEventHandler());
    }

    public void paint(Graphics g) {
        FontMetrics fm = g.getFontMetrics();
        String s = "Popup Window";

        g.drawString(s, (getSize().width-fm.stringWidth(s))/2,
                    (getSize().height-fm.getHeight())/2 + fm.getAscent());
    }

    class MouseEventHandler extends MouseAdapter {
        public void mouseReleased(MouseEvent evt) {
            // get rid of peer
            dispose();
        }
    }
}
```

A
B
C
D
E
F
G
H
I
J
K
L
M
N
O
P
Q
R
S
T
U
V
W
X
Y
Z

WindowAdapter

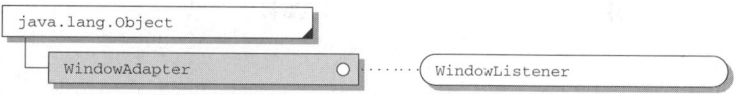

```
java.lang.Object
    WindowAdapter          ○·······  WindowListener
```

Syntax

```
public abstract class WindowAdapter implements WindowListener
```

Description

The *window adapter* is a window listener in which all callback methods are empty implementations. The window adapter makes it more convenient for an object to listen for window events. In particular, by using the window adapter, you can implement only those callback methods in which you are interested. Without the window adapter, you must implement all callback methods, even if the method is empty.

To use a window adapter, you create a subclass of WindowAdapter and override the desired callback methods. You then create an instance of the window adapter subclass and use it to call the window's addWindowListener() method. The window adapter subclass is typically an inner class.

MEMBER SUMMARY	
Window Event Callback Methods	
windowActivated()	Called after a window is activated.
windowClosed()	Called after a window is closed.
windowClosing()	Called when a window is about to close.
windowDeactivated()	Called after a window is deactivated.
windowDeiconified()	Called after a window is deiconified.
windowIconified()	Called after a window is iconified.
windowOpened()	Called after a window has been shown for the first time.

See Also

java.awt.AWTEventMulticaster, java.awt.Window.addWindowListener(), java.util.EventListener, WindowEvent, WindowListener.

Example

See the java.awt.Dialog class example.

windowActivated()

PURPOSE   Called after a window is activated.

SYNTAX   `public void windowActivated(WindowEvent evt)`

DESCRIPTION   This method is called after a window is activated. A window can be activated by the user or by calling `Component.requestFocus()` on the window. At present, there is no method call for determining a window's current, activated state. If this information is needed, you must override `windowActivated()` and `windowDeactivated()` and maintain the state yourself.

This method, by default, has an empty implementation.

PARAMETERS

evt   The non-null window event.

EXAMPLE   See the `WindowEvent` class example.

windowClosed()

PURPOSE   Called after a window is closed.

SYNTAX   `public void windowClosed(WindowEvent e)`

DESCRIPTION   This method is called after `Window.dispose()` has been called on the window. After a window's `dispose()` method is called, the window is considered closed. This is the only way to close a window. When a window is closed, it is simply hidden and its peer are destroyed. This means that it is possible to call `show()` on the window again.

This method is not called when the user requests that the window be closed (using a platform-specific gesture); rather, `windowClosing()` is called. It is the application that must call `Window.dispose()` on the window in order for the window to be closed and the `windowClosed()` method to be called.

This method, by default, has an empty implementation.

PARAMETERS

evt   The non-null window event.

EXAMPLE   See the `WindowEvent` class example.

windowClosing()

PURPOSE   Called when a window is about to close.

SYNTAX   `public void windowClosing(WindowEvent e)`

DESCRIPTION   This method is called when the user has requested that the window be closed (see `windowClosed()` for more details about closed windows). The application must call the window's `dispose()` method in order for the close operation to be completed. If `dispose()` is not called, the user's close request is ignored.

                     If the window is closed by calling `dispose()`, this method is not called; only the `windowClosed()` method is called.

                     The main purpose of this method is to let the application check if any data needs to be saved and then ask the user whether to save the data.

                     This method, by default, has an empty implementation.

PARAMETERS

evt   The non-`null` window event.

EXAMPLE   See the `WindowEvent` class example.

windowDeactivated()

PURPOSE   Called after a window is deactivated.

SYNTAX   `public void windowDeactivated(WindowEvent e)`

DESCRIPTION   This method is called after a window is deactivated. A window is deactivated when the user moves the focus to another window or if `Component.request-Focus()` is called on another window. At present, there is no method call for determining a window's current, activated state. If this information is needed, you must override `windowActivated()` and `windowDeactivated()` and maintain the state yourself.

                     This method, by default, has an empty implementation.

PARAMETERS

evt   The non-`null` window event.

EXAMPLE   See the `WindowEvent` class example.

windowDeiconified()

PURPOSE   Called after a window is deiconified.

SYNTAX   `public void windowDeiconified(WindowEvent e)`

DESCRIPTION   This method is called after a window has been deiconified. At present, there is no method call that can deiconify a window; only the user can do this. Also, there is no method call for determining a window's current, iconified state. If

A
B
C
D
E
F
G
H
I
J
K
L
M
N
O
P
Q
R
S
T
U
V
W
X
Y
Z

this information is needed, you must override `windowIconified()` and `win-dowDeiconified()` and maintain the state yourself.

This method, by default, has an empty implementation.

PARAMETERS

   `evt`   The non-`null` window event.

EXAMPLE   See the `WindowEvent` class example.

windowIconified()

PURPOSE   Called after a window is iconified.

SYNTAX   `public void windowIconified(WindowEvent e)`

DESCRIPTION This method is called after a window is iconified. At present, there is no method call that can iconify a window; only the user can do this. Also, there is no method call for determining a window's current, iconified state. If this information is needed, you must override `windowIconified()` and `window-Deiconified()` and maintain the state yourself.

This method, by default, has an empty implementation.

PARAMETERS

   `evt`   The non-`null` window event.

EXAMPLE   See the `WindowEvent` class example.

windowOpened()

PURPOSE   Called after a window has been shown for the first time.

SYNTAX   `public void windowOpened(WindowEvent e)`

DESCRIPTION This method is called after a window is shown for the first time. When this event is processed, calling `Component.isShowing()` on the source component returns `true`.

This method, by default, has an empty implementation.

PARAMETERS

   `evt`   The non-`null` window event.

EXAMPLE   See the `WindowEvent` class example.

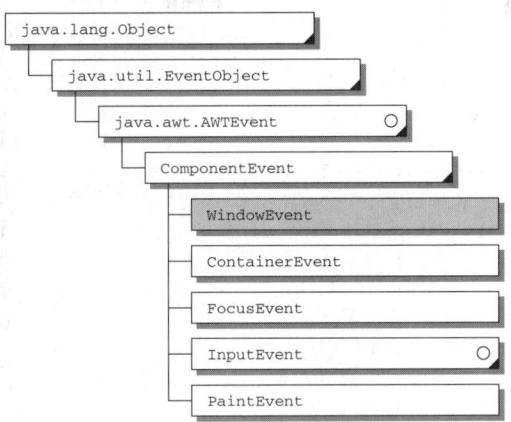

```
java.lang.Object

    java.util.EventObject

        java.awt.AWTEvent          ○

            ComponentEvent

                WindowEvent

                ContainerEvent

                FocusEvent

                InputEvent         ○

                PaintEvent
```

Syntax
```
public class WindowEvent extends ComponentEvent
```

Description
Window events are fired by a window (see Window) whenever the window is opened/closed, activated/deactivated, or iconified/deiconified. For more general information about events, see AWTEvent.

Listening for Window Events
To listen for window events from a window, the listener must implement the WindowListener interface. Next, it must be registered with the window. It becomes registered by calling the window's addWindowListener() method.

An alternative, and possibly more convenient, way of receiving window events is to use a window adapter. See WindowAdapter for more details.

As with most events, window events are delivered to the window's listeners after the operation has taken place.

The Iconified Property
A window is *iconified* if the window has been reduced to a small icon on the system's desktop. At present, there is no method call for determining a window's current, iconified state. If this information is needed, you must listen for all changes to a window's iconified state and manually maintain the state.

The Activated Property

A window is *activated* if it or some child component it contains has the focus. At present, there is no method call for determining a window's current, activated state. If this information is needed, you must listen for all changes to a window's activated state and manually maintain the state.

Window Event Flow

Figure 382 shows how window events typically flow through the system. First, the event is fired by a component peer in response to some user gesture. This event is posted on the event queue (see Event-Queue). When the event makes its way to the front of the queue, it is given to the component via its dispatchEvent() method. The main purpose of this method is to discard the event if there are no window event listeners. Otherwise, dispatch-Event() calls processEvent(), which in turn calls different methods depending on the event type. Since this is a window event, processWindow-Event() is called. The main purpose of this method is to notify the window listeners of the event.

A component can override processWindow-Event() to process window events before they are delivered to the component's listeners. The overridden method should call super.processWindow-Event() to ensure that events are dispatched to the component's listeners.

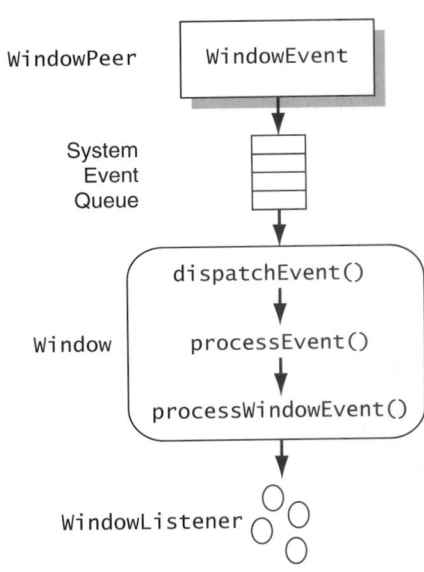

FIGURE 382:   Window Event Flow.

MEMBER SUMMARY	
Constructor	
WindowEvent()	Constructs a new WindowEvent instance.
Window Method	
getWindow()	Retrieves the window that fired this event.
Window Event Id Constants	
WINDOW_ACTIVATED	Event id indicating that a window was activated.
WINDOW_CLOSED	Event id indicating that a window was closed.
WINDOW_CLOSING	Event id indicating that a window is about to close.
WINDOW_DEACTIVATED	Event id indicating that a window was deactivated.
WINDOW_DEICONIFIED	Event id indicating that a window was deiconified.

MEMBER SUMMARY	
WINDOW_FIRST	Constant specifying the first id in the range of window event ids.
WINDOW_ICONIFIED	Event id indicating that a window was iconified.
WINDOW_LAST	Constant specifying the last id in the range of window event ids.
WINDOW_OPENED	Event id indicating that a window has been shown for the first time.
Debugging Method	
paramString()	Generates a string representing the window event's state.

See Also

java.awt.AWTEvent, java.awt.Component.dispatchEvent(),
java.awt.Component.processEvent(), java.awt.Window, WindowAdapter,
WindowListener.

Example

This example implements a *frame manager* that can control and display the current property state of all AWT frames. The left frame in Figure 383 shows all existing AWT frames, of which there are four. The left part of the item is the title of the frame, while the right

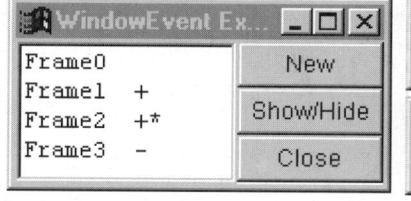
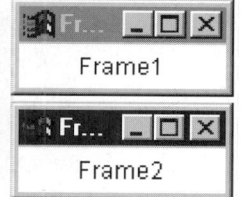

FIGURE 383: Frame Manager.

part of the item shows the frame's current property state. The + indicates that the frame is deiconified; the - indicates that it is iconified; and the * indicates that it is activated. The absence of a symbol indicates the frame is hidden.

The two frames on the right represent two visible AWT frames. Frame0 is hidden and Frame3 is iconified, so they do not appear on the screen.

Clicking the New button on the frame manager creates a new hidden frame. Clicking the Show/Hide button shows the selected frame (if the frame is hidden) or hides the selected frame (if the frame is showing). Double-clicking an item in the list does the same thing. Clicking the Close button disposes of the selected frame.

Although the AWT can inform you when the iconified or activated states of a frame changes, it does not allow you to query these states on a frame. Consequently, this example creates a subclass of the frame that listens to window events on the frame. In this way, the frame can maintain an accurate picture of its current state that can then be used by the frame manager.

Notice that `MyFrame` also listens to the component events that are fired whenever the frame becomes hidden or shown. `MyFrame` uses these events to inform the frame manager to update its display.

```java
import java.awt.*;
import java.awt.event.*;
import java.util.*;

class Main extends Frame implements ActionListener {
    FrameManager frameManager = new FrameManager();

    Main() {
        super("WindowEvent Example");
        Button b;
        Panel p = new Panel(new GridLayout(0, 1));

        // Populate the control panel.
        p.add(b = new Button("New"));
        b.addActionListener(this);
        p.add(b = new Button("Show/Hide"));
        b.addActionListener(this);
        p.add(b = new Button("Close"));
        b.addActionListener(this);

        add(p, BorderLayout.EAST);
        add(frameManager, BorderLayout.CENTER);
        frameManager.addActionListener(this);

        setSize(200, 100);
        show();
    }

    // Button actions.
    public void actionPerformed(ActionEvent evt) {
        if (evt.getActionCommand().equals("New")) {
            new MyFrame(frameManager);
            return;
        }

        MyFrame f = frameManager.getFrame();
        if (f == null) {
            return;
        }
        if (evt.getActionCommand().equals("Show/Hide")
                || evt.getSource() == frameManager) {
            if (f.isShowing()) {
                f.setVisible(false);
            } else {
                f.show();
            }
            frameManager.update(f);
        } else if (evt.getActionCommand().equals("Close")) {
            frameManager.close(f);
            f.dispose();
        }
    }

    public static void main(String args[]) {
        new Main();
```

```
        }
}

class MyFrame extends Frame implements WindowListener {
    FrameManager frameManager;
    static int count;      // for naming the frames.
    boolean iconified;
    boolean activated;

    MyFrame(FrameManager wl) {
        super("Frame"+(count++));
        frameManager = wl;

        // Add this frame to the window list.
        frameManager.add(this);

        // Listen for events.
        addWindowListener(this);
        addComponentListener(new ComponentEventHandler());

        add(new Label(getTitle(), Label.CENTER), BorderLayout.CENTER);
        setSize(100, 50);
    }

    // Window Events
    public void windowOpened(WindowEvent evt) {
        System.out.println("WINDOW_OPENED");
    }
    public void windowClosing(WindowEvent evt) {
        dispose();
    }
    public void windowClosed(WindowEvent evt) {
        frameManager.close((MyFrame)evt.getSource());
    }
    public void windowIconified(WindowEvent evt) {
        iconified = true;
        frameManager.update(this);
    }
    public void windowDeiconified(WindowEvent evt) {
        iconified = false;
        frameManager.update(this);
    }
    public void windowActivated(WindowEvent evt) {
        activated = true;
        frameManager.update(this);
    }
    public void windowDeactivated(WindowEvent evt) {
        activated = false;
        frameManager.update(this);
    }

    // Component Events
    class ComponentEventHandler extends ComponentAdapter {
        public void componentShown(ComponentEvent evt) {
            frameManager.update((MyFrame)evt.getSource());
        }
        public void componentHidden(ComponentEvent evt) {
            frameManager.update((MyFrame)evt.getSource());
        }
    }
}
```

```
        }

class FrameManager extends List {
    // This holds a list of frames.  The order of the frames
    // in this vector corresponds to the order of the frames
    // in the list component.
    Vector frames = new Vector();

    FrameManager() {
        setFont(new Font("Monospaced", Font.PLAIN, 12));
    }

    // Returns the currently selected frame or null if there
    // is no selected item.
    MyFrame getFrame() {
        int ix = getSelectedIndex();

        if (ix >= 0) {
            return (MyFrame)frames.elementAt(ix);
        }
        return null;
    }

    void add(MyFrame f) {
        add(f.getTitle());
        frames.addElement(f);
        update(f);
    }

    void close(MyFrame f) {
        int ix = frames.indexOf(f);

        if (ix >= 0) {
            frames.removeElementAt(ix);
            remove(ix);
        }
    }

    void update(MyFrame f) {
        int ix = frames.indexOf(f);

        if (ix >= 0) {
            String s = f.getTitle() + "   ";

            if (f.isShowing()) {
                if (f.iconified) {
                    s += '-';
                } else {
                    s += '+';
                }
                if (f.activated) {
                    s += '*';
                } else {
                    s += ' ';
                }
            }
            replaceItem(s, ix);
        }
    }
}
```

getWindow()

PURPOSE	Retrieves the window that fired this event.
SYNTAX	`public Window getWindow()`
DESCRIPTION	This method returns the component that fired the component event. This is the same object returned by `EventObject.getSource()`.
RETURNS	The non-`null` window that fired this event.
SEE ALSO	`java.awt.Window`, `java.util.EventObject.getSource()`.
EXAMPLE	See the class example.

paramString()

PURPOSE	Generates a string representing the window event's state.
SYNTAX	`public String paramString()`
DESCRIPTION	The returned string contains the name of the window event. A subclass of this class should override this method and return a concatenation of the window event's state with the results of `super.paramString()`. This method is called by the `AWTEvent.toString()` method and is typically used for debugging.
RETURNS	A non-`null` string representing the window event's state.
OVERRIDES	`java.awt.AWTEvent.paramString()`.
SEE ALSO	`java.awt.AWTEvent.toString()`, `java.lang.Object.toString()`.
EXAMPLE	See the `java.awt.AWTEvent` class example.

WINDOW_ACTIVATED

PURPOSE	Event id indicating that a window was activated.
SYNTAX	`public static final int WINDOW_ACTIVATED`
DESCRIPTION	An event with this id (value 205) is fired by a window when it is activated. A window can be activated by the user or by calling `Component.requestFocus()` on the window. At present, there is no method call for determining a window's current, activated state. If this information is needed, you must listen for `WINDOW_ACTIVATED` and `WINDOW_DEACTIVATED` events and maintain the state yourself.
SEE ALSO	`java.awt.Component.requestFocus()`, `WINDOW_DEACTIVATED`.
EXAMPLE	See the class example.

A
B
C
D
E
F
G
H
I
J
K
L
M
N
O
P
Q
R
S
T
U
V
W
X
Y
Z

WINDOW_CLOSED

PURPOSE   Event id indicating that a window was closed.

SYNTAX   `public static final int WINDOW_CLOSED`

DESCRIPTION   An event with this id (value 202) is fired by a window after `Window.dispose()` has been called on the window. After a window's `dispose()` method is called, the window is considered closed. This is the only way to close a window. When a window is closed, it is simply hidden and its peers are destroyed. This means that it is possible to call `show()` on the window again.

This event is not fired when the user requests that the window be closed (using a platform-specific gesture); rather, a `WINDOW_CLOSING` event is fired. It is the application that must call `Window.dispose()` on the window in order for the window to be closed and the `WINDOW_CLOSED` event to be fired.

SEE ALSO   `WINDOW_CLOSING`.

EXAMPLE   See the class example.

WINDOW_CLOSING

PURPOSE   Event id indicating that a window is about to close.

SYNTAX   `public static final int WINDOW_CLOSING`

DESCRIPTION   An event with this id (value 201) is fired by a window when the user has requested that the window be closed (see `WINDOW_CLOSED` for more details about closed windows). The application must call the window's `dispose()` method in order for the close operation to be completed. If `dispose()` is not called, the user's close request is ignored.

If the window is closed by calling `dispose()`, this event is not fired; only the `WINDOW_CLOSED` event is fired.

The main purpose for the `WINDOW_CLOSING` event is to let the application check if any data needs to be saved and then ask the user whether to save the data.

SEE ALSO   `java.awt.Window.dispose()`, `WINDOW_CLOSED`.

EXAMPLE   See the class example.

A
B
C
D
E
F
G
H
I
J
K
L
M
N
O
P
Q
R
S
T
U
V
W
X
Y
Z

WINDOW_DEACTIVATED

PURPOSE   Event id indicating that a window was deactivated.

SYNTAX   `public static final int WINDOW_DEACTIVATED`

DESCRIPTION   An event with this id (value 206) is fired by a window when it is deactivated. A window is deactivated when the user moves the focus to another window or if `Component.requestFocus()` is called on another window. At present, there is no method call for determining a window's current, activated state. If this information is needed, you must listen for `WINDOW_ACTIVATED` and `WINDOW_DEACTIVATED` events and maintain the state yourself.

SEE ALSO   `java.awt.Component.requestFocus()`, `WINDOW_ACTIVATED`.

EXAMPLE   See the class example.

WINDOW_DEICONIFIED

PURPOSE   Event id indicating that a window was deiconified.

SYNTAX   `public static final int WINDOW_DEICONIFIED`

DESCRIPTION   An event with this id (value 204) is fired by a window when it is deiconified. At present, there is no method call that will deiconify a window; only a user can do this. Also, there is no method call for determining a window's current, iconified state. If this information is needed, you must listen for `WINDOW_ICONIFIED` and `WINDOW_DEICONIFIED` events and maintain the state yourself.

SEE ALSO   `WINDOW_ICONIFIED`.

EXAMPLE   See the class example.

WINDOW_FIRST

PURPOSE   Constant specifying the first id in the range of window event ids.

SYNTAX   `public static final int WINDOW_FIRST`

DESCRIPTION   All window event ids must be greater than or equal to `WINDOW_FIRST` (value 200).

SEE ALSO   `WINDOW_LAST`.

EXAMPLE   See `java.awt.Component.processEvent()`.

A
B
C
D
E
F
G
H
I
J
K
L
M
N
O
P
Q
R
S
T
U
V
W
X
Y
Z

WINDOW_ICONIFIED

PURPOSE	Event id indicating that a window was iconified.
SYNTAX	`public static final int WINDOW_ICONIFIED`
DESCRIPTION	An event with this id (value 203) is fired by a window when it is iconified. At present, there is no method call that will iconify a window; only a user can do this. Also, there is no method call for determining a window's current, iconified state. If this information is needed, you must listen for `WINDOW_ICONIFIED` and `WINDOW_DEICONIFIED` events and maintain the state yourself.
SEE ALSO	`WINDOW_DEICONIFIED`.
EXAMPLE	See the class example.

WINDOW_LAST

PURPOSE	Constant specifying the last id in the range of window event ids.
SYNTAX	`public static final int WINDOW_LAST`
DESCRIPTION	All window event ids must be less than or equal to `WINDOW_LAST` (value 206).
SEE ALSO	`WINDOW_FIRST`.
EXAMPLE	See `java.awt.Component.processEvent()`.

WINDOW_OPENED

PURPOSE	Event id indicating that a window has been shown for the first time.
SYNTAX	`public static final int WINDOW_OPENED`
DESCRIPTION	An event with this id (value 200) is fired by a window when it is shown for the first time. When this event is processed, calling `Component.isShowing()` on the source component returns `true`.
EXAMPLE	See the class example.

WindowEvent()

PURPOSE	Constructs a `WindowEvent` instance.
SYNTAX	`public WindowEvent(Window source, int id)`

A
B
C
D
E
F
G
H
I
J
K
L
M
N
O
P
Q
R
S
T
U
V
W
X
Y
Z

DESCRIPTION   This constructor creates a new window event instance with `source` as the window that fires this event.

After the window event is created, the source window can distribute the event to its listeners by calling the window event-related methods in `AWTEventMulticaster`. If the event is not created by `source`, the creator can deliver the event to the source component either by posting the event to the event queue (see `EventQueue.postEvent()`) or by calling the source component's `Component.dispatchEvent()` method directly.

PARAMETERS

source   The non-`null` window that is firing this window event.

id   One of the window event ids.

SEE ALSO   `java.awt.AWTEvent.getID()`, `java.util.EventObject.getSource()`.

A
B
C
D
E
F
G
H
I
J
K
L
M
N
O
P
Q
R
S
T
U
V
W
X
Y
Z

A
B
C
D
E
F
G
H
I
J
K
L
M
N
O
P
Q
R
S
T
U
V
W
X
Y
Z

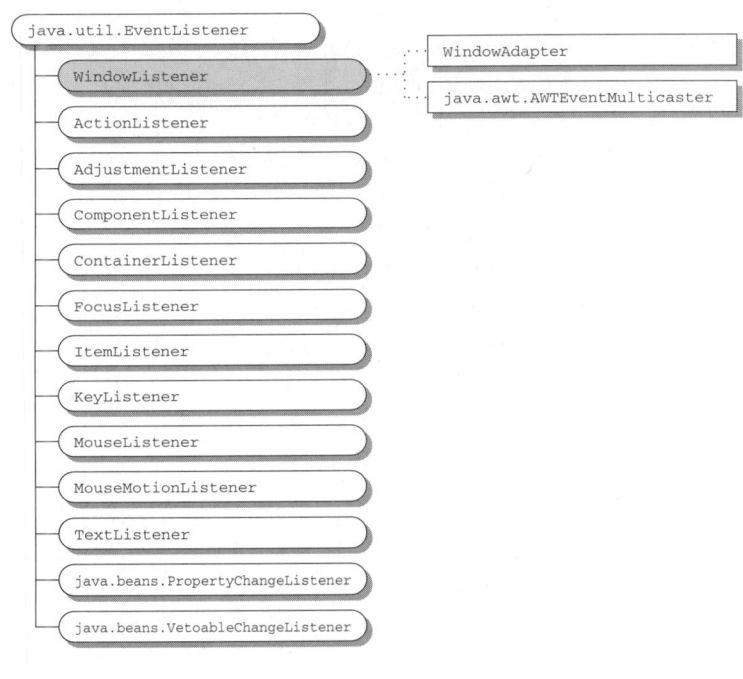

Syntax

```
public interface WindowListener extends EventListener
```

Description

When an object (listener) wishes to receive window events from a window (the source window), two things must be done:

1. The listener must implement the WindowListener interface and all of the interface's required methods.
2. The listener must be registered with the source window. It becomes registered by making a call to the source window's addWindowListener().

For information about window events, see WindowEvent. For more information about windows, see Window.

MEMBER SUMMARY	
Window Event Callback Methods	
windowActivated()	Called after a window is activated.
windowClosed()	Called after a window is closed.
windowClosing()	Called when a window is about to be closed.
windowDeactivated()	Called after a window is deactivated.
windowDeiconified()	Called after a window is deiconified.
windowIconified()	Called after a window is iconified.
windowOpened()	Called after a window has been shown for the first time.

See Also

java.awt.Window.addWindowListener(), java.util.EventListener, WindowAdapter, WindowEvent.

Example

See the WindowEvent class example.

windowActivated()

PURPOSE   Called after a window is activated.

SYNTAX   public void windowActivated(WindowEvent evt)

DESCRIPTION   This method is called after a window is activated. A window can be activated by the user or by calling Component.requestFocus() on the window. At present, there is no method call for determining a window's current, activated state. If this information is needed, you must implement windowActivated() and windowDeactivated() to maintain the state.

PARAMETERS
evt   The non-null window event.

EXAMPLE   See the WindowEvent class example.

windowClosed()

PURPOSE   Called after a window is closed.

SYNTAX   public void windowClosed(WindowEvent evt)

A
B
C
D
E
F
G
H
I
J
K
L
M
N
O
P
Q
R
S
T
U
V
W
X
Y
Z

<table>
<tr><td>DESCRIPTION</td><td>This method is called after `Window.dispose()` has been called on the window. After a window's `dispose()` method has been called, the window is considered closed. This is the only way to close a window. When a window is closed, it is simply hidden and its peers are destroyed. This means that it is possible to call `show()` on the window again.</td></tr>
</table>

This method is not called when the user requests that the window be closed (using a platform-specific gesture); rather, `windowClosing()` is called. It is the application that must call `Window.dispose()` on the window in order for the window to be closed and the `windowClosed()` method to be called.

PARAMETERS

evt　　　　The non-`null` window event.

EXAMPLE　　See the `WindowEvent` class example.

windowClosing()

PURPOSE　　Called when a window is about to be closed.

SYNTAX　　`public void windowClosing(WindowEvent evt)`

DESCRIPTION　This method is called when the user has requested that the window be closed (see `windowClosed()` for more details about closed windows). The application must call the window's `dispose()` method in order for the close operation to be completed. If `dispose()` is not called, the user's close request is ignored.

If the window is closed by calling `dispose()`, this method is not called; only the `windowClose()` method is called.

The main purpose of this method is to let the application check if any data needs to be saved and then ask the user whether to save the data.

PARAMETERS

evt　　　　The non-`null` window event.

EXAMPLE　　See the `WindowEvent` class example.

windowDeactivated()

PURPOSE　　Called after a window is deactivated.

SYNTAX　　`public void windowDeactivated(WindowEvent evt)`

DESCRIPTION　This method is called after a window is deactivated. A window is deactivated when the user moves the focus to another window or `Component.request-`

Focus() is called on another window. At present, there is no method call for determining a window's current, activated state. If this information is needed, you must implement windowActivated() and windowDeactivate() to maintain the state.

PARAMETERS

evt   The non-null window event.

EXAMPLE   See the WindowEvent class example.

windowDeiconified()

PURPOSE   Called after a window is deiconified.

SYNTAX   public void windowDeiconified(WindowEvent evt)

DESCRIPTION This method is called after a window has been deiconified. At present, there is no method call that will deiconify a window; only a user can do this. Also, there is no method call for determining a window's current, iconified state. If this information is needed, you must implement windowIconified() and windowDeiconified() to maintain the state.

PARAMETERS

evt   The non-null window event.

EXAMPLE   See the WindowEvent class example.

windowIconified()

PURPOSE   Called after a window is iconified.

SYNTAX   public void windowIconified(WindowEvent evt)

DESCRIPTION This method is called after a window is iconified. At present, there is no method call that will iconify a window; only a user can do this. Also, there is no method call for determining a window's current, iconified state. If this information is needed, you must implement windowIconified() and windowDeiconified() to maintain the state.

PARAMETERS

evt   The non-null window event.

EXAMPLE   See the WindowEvent class example.

A
B
C
D
E
F
G
H
I
J
K
L
M
N
O
P
Q
R
S
T
U
V
W
X
Y
Z

windowOpened()

PURPOSE   Called after a window has been shown for the first time.

SYNTAX   `public void windowOpened(WindowEvent evt)`

DESCRIPTION   This method is called after a window is shown for the first time. When this event is processed, calling `Component.isShowing()` on the source component returns `true`.

PARAMETERS
evt   The non-`null` window event.

EXAMPLE   See the `WindowEvent` class example.

WindowPeer

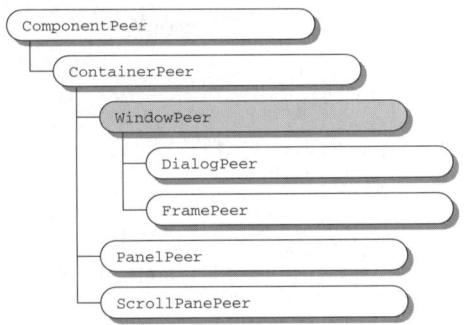

Syntax

```
public interface WindowPeer extends ContainerPeer
```

Description

The window component (see the Window class) in the AWT uses the platform's native implementation of a window. So that the AWT window behaves the same on all platforms, the window is assigned a *peer*, whose task is to translate the behavior of the platform's native window to the behavior of the AWT window.

AWT programmers normally do not directly use peer classes and interfaces. Instead, they deal with AWT components in the java.awt package. These in turn automatically manage their peers. Only someone who is porting the AWT to another platform should be concerned with the peer classes and interfaces. Consequently, most peer documentation refers to java.awt counterparts.

See Component and Toolkit for additional information about component peers.

MEMBER SUMMARY	
Peer Methods	
toBack()	Moves the window behind all other windows.
toFront()	Moves the window in front of all other windows.

See Also

java.awt.Component, java.awt.Toolkit, java.awt.Window.

toBack()

PURPOSE	Moves the window behind all other windows.
SYNTAX	`void toBack()`
SEE ALSO	`java.awt.Window.toBack()`.

toFront()

PURPOSE	Moves the window in front of all other windows.
SYNTAX	`void toFront()`
SEE ALSO	`java.awt.Window.toFront()`.

A
B
C
D
E
F
G
H
I
J
K
L
M
N
O
P
Q
R
S
T
U
V
W
X
Y
Z

Index

retrieving,
  Choice.getItem(); 257
  Choice.getItemCount(); 257
  Choice.getSelectedIndex(); 257
  Choice.getSelectedItem(); 258
  Choice.getSelectedObjects(); 258
selecting,
  Choice.select(); 263
  ChoicePeer.select(); 267
ChoicePeer; 265
  add(); 266
  addItem(), replaced by add(); 266
  remove(); 267
  select(); 267
choices,
  components,
    checkbox group vs, CheckboxGroup; 233
    Choice; 251
  event types fired by, *Table*, AWTEvent; 115
  peers,
    ChoicePeer; 265
    creating, Choice. addNotify(); 255
    Toolkit.createChoice(); 1480
  state, Choice.paramString(); 259
  term definition, Choice; 251
circles,
  filled, Graphics.fillOval(); 717
  outline, Graphics.drawOval(); 704
Class objects,
  data flavor use, DataFlavor; 500
clear(),
  List, replaced by removeAll(); 991
  ListPeer, replaced by removeAll(); 1012
clearRect(),
  Graphics; 689
clickCount,
  Event, replaced by
    MouseEvent.getClickCount(); 552
clipboard,
  callback method,
    ClipboardOwner.lostOwnership(); 277
    StringSelection.lostOwnership(); 1379
  Clipboard; 268
  contents,
    Clipboard.getContents(); 271
    Clipboard.setContents(); 275
    field, Clipboard.contents; 271
  converting strings for, StringSelection; 1374
  data flavor use, DataFlavor; 500

encapsulating data for, Transferable; 1496
name,
  Clipboard.getName(); 274
  term definition, Clipboard; 268
owner,
  ClipboardOwner; 276
  field, Clipboard.owner; 275
  term definition, Clipboard; 268
retrieving, Toolkit.getSystemClipboard(); 1493
system, term definition, Clipboard; 268
term definition, Clipboard; 268
Clipboard; 268
  Clipboard(); 271
  contents; 271
  getContents(); 271
  getName(); 274
  owner; 275
  setContents(); 275
Clipboard(),
  Clipboard; 271
ClipboardOwner; 276
  lostOwnership(); 277
clipping area,
  retrieving,
    Graphics.getClip(); 724
    Graphics.getClipBounds(); 725
  setting, Graphics.setClip(); 728
  shrinking, Graphics.clipRect(); 690
  term definition, Graphics; 687
clipRect(),
  Graphics; 690
clone(),
  GridBagConstraints; 743
  ImageFilter; 827
  Insets; 884
cloning,
  gridbag, GridBagConstraints.clone(); 743
  image filters, ImageFilter.clone(); 827
  insets, Insets.clone(); 884
code base URL,
  applet,
    Applet; 75
    Applet.getCodeBase(); 84
    AppletStub.getCodeBase(); 99
collection,
  gridbag as collection of components,
    GridBagConstraints; 738

D

E

S

T

U

W

X